Art and Philosophy

ART AND PHILOSOPHY

Readings in Aesthetics

W. E. KENNICK
Amherst College

ST MARTIN'S PRESS · NEW YORK

To A. H. K.

Preface

IN JAMES JOYCE's *A Portrait of the Artist as a Young Man*, Stephen Dedalus asks, "If a man hacking in fury at a block of wood make there an image of a cow, is that image a work of art?" Such questions frequently and naturally arise; in them lies the origin of aesthetics as a philosophical discipline. It is but a step from Stephen's question to the larger question, "What is art?" around which much of aesthetics has centered. It is tempting to suppose that both Stephen's question and the larger one to which it leads can be answered either by a scrutiny of art itself or by looking up the definition of "art" in a dictionary. But neither of these methods will resolve the issue; otherwise the question would not so persistently arise.

Philosophical questions are typically conceptual in nature. As Stephen Dedalus' question illustrates, they tend to arise where the applicability of a familiar but important concept is in doubt: in Dedalus' case, the concept of art; elsewhere in aesthetics, the concepts of beauty and goodness, truth and fiction, expression and emotion, form and content, and a host of others. Such questions are to be settled—if they can be settled—only by argument. One gives *reasons* for saying that the image hacked in fury out of a block of wood is, or is not, a work of art; and on the persuasiveness of these reasons the resolution of the issue depends.

The pedagogical consequence of this is that philosophy, including aesthetics, can be learned only by active engagement in reasoning, or, to use a current idiom, by "doing philosophy." Philosophy is obviously not a body of established doctrine, of proved theorems or confirmed hypotheses. To teach it as if it were chemistry or history is inappropriate and foreign to its nature.

Aesthetics may be taught in a variety of ways. The historical approach consists of a chronological survey of what has been said about the nature of art, beauty, aesthetic experience, etc. by thinkers of the past. The result is rarely more than information: Plato said this and Hegel said that. The importance of such information is not to be underestimated, but the person who has it is not a philosopher, and to impart it is not to teach him what it is to be one.

The comparative approach is akin to the historical. It presents conflicting answers to each of the questions of aesthetics. The advantage to this method is that it makes the student aware of the diversity of answers given by intelligent and sophisticated thinkers to the same question. But the usual result, when it is not mere confusion, is again information about who said what and why and how his views differ from someone else's. The importance of this sort of information is also not to be underrated, but unless the student becomes actively engaged in reasoning through the conflicts presented to him, he will learn little philosophy.

A third approach is the systematic, the presentation of a reasoned set of answers to the questions of aesthetics. That this can be an effective way of teaching philosophy cannot be denied. Its disadvantages are that it tends to be doctrinaire, too little concerned with opposing points of view, and that it presents the problems of philosophy in one, frequently dreary, style. In teaching philosophy there is much to be said for acquainting the student with more than one style of philosophizing.

The problems approach, for which this book is designed, aims to give the student a clear view of some important problems in aesthetics and to engage his mind in thinking them through. The best means to this end is good example. Although several considerations have perforce determined the selection of the material for this book, the most prominent has been the desire to secure the best, liveliest, and most interesting essays available, to give the student something worth working with. No attempt has been made to represent all important views on any given problem.

With the exception of selections from Hanslick's *The Beautiful in Music* (1854) and two ancient philosophers in Appendices A and B, the material collected here is modern. The *terminus a quo* is the date of Santayana's *The Sense of Beauty,* 1896. Within modern aesthetics two general strains of thought are discernible. One is close in style and method to the "classical" philosophical tradition; the other is characterized by its use of more recent analytic or "linguistic" techniques. Both strains are represented in this book: the former by philosophers such as Croce, Maritain, and Santayana; the latter by philosophers such as Bouwsma, Stevenson, and Ziff. No effort has been made to give equal space to both strains for the simple reason that the differences between them are not that important. If the emphasis falls on one, however, it is the analytic.

The selections have been grouped somewhat arbitrarily under seven headings. Some essays might fit as well under other headings, but these I judged to be more pertinent to the problems with which I have associated them. There are, however, cross references to other essays throughout the book.

Each main section is prefaced with a brief introduction. Lengthy introductions to unfamiliar material are rarely helpful: before the student has become engaged with the problems, the introduction is meaningless; afterwards, it is forgotten. A frequently followed practice is therefore reversed and there is appended a brief essay to each main section. The aim of these essays, which are largely interrogative, is not to set the student straight about aesthetics or to give him "the answers." It is rather to raise provocative questions about the collected materials which, hopefully, will generate in the student's mind a friction productive of thought, and to indicate lines along which further discussion and investigation might profitably be pursued. Many of my questions have to do with the nature of aesthetics itself—with the kinds of questions it consists of and with the logical status of answers to them.

Many claims have been made for aesthetics: that it will improve art by enlightening artists, that it will clarify criticism or raise its standards and put it on a sound foundation, that it will lead to a fuller and deeper appreciation of art, and so on. I am skeptical of all such claims; I have found no evidence to support any of them. Why, then, study aesthetics? The best answer I know is that given by George Leigh Mallory when asked why he troubled to climb Mt. Everest: "Because it is there." The problems of aesthetics are inherently intriguing; the pursuit of them intellectually worthwhile apart from inflated claims about the practical worth of their solution.

I am indebted to many persons who have helped me with this book, but especially to Mrs. O. Stachura and Mrs. A. M. Hiron of London who typed the bulk of the manuscript; to the librarians of Bennington College, Williams College, and University College, London, who kindly put the full use of their facilities at my disposal; and to the publishers, editors, and authors who have graciously permitted me to reprint material owned by them.

Work on this book was largely completed during a sabbatical leave of absence, 1961-62, made possible by a special grant from the President of Amherst College, Dr. Calvin H. Plimpton.

W.E.K.

Abbreviations Used in the Bibliographies

J.A.A.C.: The Journal of Aesthetics and Art Criticism
J. Phil.: The Journal of Philosophy
P.A.S.: Proceedings of the Aristotelian Society
P.B.A.: Proceedings of the British Academy
Phil. Quart.: Philosophical Quarterly
Phil. and Phen.: The Journal of Philosophy and Phenomenological Research
Phil. Rev.: The Philosophical Review
Phil. Studs.: Philosophical Studies
Rev. Met.: The Review of Metaphysics

Contents

Preface   *v*

I THE NATURE OF ART

Introduction   *3*
LEO TOLSTOY   *What Is Art?*   *7*
BENEDETTO CROCE   *Art as Intuition*   *19*
CLIVE BELL   *The Aesthetic Hypothesis*   *33*
DEWITT H. PARKER   *The Nature of Art*   *47*
JACQUES MARITAIN   *Art as a Virtue of the Practical Intellect*   *62*
SUSANNE K. LANGER   *Expressiveness*   *78*
Definition and Theory in Aesthetics   *86*
Suggestions for Additional Reading   *93*

II THE WORK OF ART AND THE AESTHETIC OBJECT

Introduction   *97*
R. G. COLLINGWOOD   *The Work of Art as an Imaginary Object*   *99*
STEPHEN C. PEPPER   *The Aesthetic Work of Art*   *108*
RENÉ WELLEK AND AUSTIN WARREN   *The Analysis of the Literary Work of Art*   *126*
Works of Art and Aesthetic Objects   *142*
Suggestions for Additional Reading   *149*

III THE ARTS

Introduction   *153*
ISABEL C. HUNGERLAND   *Language and Poetry*   *155*
EDUARD HANSLICK   *The Beautiful in Music*   *190*

FRANK ANDERSON TRAPP   *On the Nature of Painting*   *214*
SIR HERBERT READ   *The Art of Sculpture*   *226*
BRUNO ZEVI   *Architecture as Space*   *239*
Aesthetics and the Arts   *248*
Suggestions for Additional Reading   *255*

IV EXPRESSION, CREATIVITY, TRUTH, AND FORM

Introduction   *259*
O. K. BOUWSMA   *The Expression Theory of Art*   *261*
VINCENT TOMAS   *Creativity in Art*   *283*
MARGARET MACDONALD   *The Language of Fiction*   *295*
JOHN HOSPERS   *Implied Truths in Literature*   *309*
ARNOLD ISENBERG   *The Problem of Belief*   *324*
MORRIS WEITZ   *The Form-Content Distinction*   *339*
FRANK SIBLEY   *Aesthetic Concepts*   *351*
Expression, Creativity, Truth, and Form   *374*
Suggestions for Additional Reading   *384*

V PROBLEMS OF INTERPRETATION

Introduction   *389*
ERWIN PANOFSKY   *Iconography and Iconology*   *391*
HENRY DAVID AIKEN   *The Aesthetic Relevance of Artists'*
    Intentions   *403*
ERNST KRIS AND ABRAHAM KAPLAN   *Esthetic Ambiguity*   *413*
ISABEL C. HUNGERLAND   *Symbols in Poetry*   *425*
MAX BLACK   *Metaphor*   *449*
CHARLES L. STEVENSON   *Interpretation and Evaluation in*
    Aesthetics   *466*
Interpreting Works of Art   *498*
Suggestions for Additional Reading   *509*

VI BEAUTY AND THE AESTHETIC EXPERIENCE

Introduction 513
GEORGE SANTAYANA   *The Nature of Beauty* 515
T. E. JESSOP   *The Definition of Beauty* 524
EDWARD BULLOUGH   *"Psychical Distance" as a Factor in Art and an Aesthetic Principle* 534
J. O. URMSON   *What Makes a Situation Aesthetic?* 552
Beauty and the Aesthetic Experience — 565
Suggestions for Additional Reading 572

VII ART CRITICISM

Introduction 577
STUART HAMPSHIRE   *Logic and Appreciation* 579
HELEN KNIGHT   *The Use of "Good" in Aesthetic Judgments* 586
MARGARET MACDONALD   *Some Distinctive Features of Arguments Used in Criticism of the Arts* 597
PAUL ZIFF   *Reasons in Art Criticism* 605
Art Criticism 623
Suggestions for Additional Reading 630

Appendix A: PLATO, *Republic X* 635
Appendix B: ARISTOTLE, *Poetics* 649
Appendix C: SIGMUND FREUD, *Creative Writers and Day-Dreaming* 667

I

The Nature
of Art

Introduction

A PRINCIPAL QUESTION of aesthetics is "What is art?" Despite its apparent simplicity, the question is unclear, but it is usually taken as a request for a definition of art. Although there are many kinds of definition,[1] the most prominent—often commended by logicians as the ideal of all definition—is a statement of the characteristics common and peculiar to a number of things, by virtue of which we properly apply the same term to them; for example, "A hexapod is an animal having six feet."[2] But because "art" refers to certain human activities as well as to the products of them, "What is art?", as a request for this sort of definition, may mean one of two things: (1) What distinguishes the fine arts as practices from other activities? (2) What distinguishes works of art from other objects?

It was not until the eighteenth century that the fine arts were thought of as distinct from the crafts, sciences, and other human enterprises. An aesthetic, or theory of fine art, thus had no place in ancient and medieval thought. The Greek *techne* and the Latin *ars*, both of which are often rendered as "art," were applied to all skilled activities, including many we would call crafts or sciences. Plato and Aristotle considered *mimesis* or "imitation" to be common to some poetry, music, painting, sculpture, and the dance,[3] but this was also, as they saw it, common to sophistry and the imitation of bird calls. And as late as the Renaissance, the study of poetry, as a part of rhetoric, was included in the "trivium," with grammar and logic; the study of music belonged to the "quadrivium," with arithmetic, geometry, and astronomy. Painting, sculpture, and architecture were classed with such manual crafts as carpentry and shoemaking.

By the sixteenth century painting, sculpture, and architecture had gained enough cultural prestige to be separated from the crafts and referred to by a separate name. They were called *Arti del disegno* by Vasari. But as late as 1690 Charles Perrault, in his *Le Cabinet des Beaux Arts*, included optics and mechanics among the eight "fine arts."

The modern system of fine arts was first clearly delineated by the Abbé

Batteux in his *Les Beaux Arts Réduits à un Même Principe* (1746). He argued that the fine arts—music, poetry, painting, sculpture, and the dance—differ from the mechanical arts in having pleasure as their end; eloquence and architecture are both pleasant and useful. Despite the superficiality of the basis of Batteux' distinction, his system was given general currency by Diderot and the other authors of the great *Encyclopédie* of 1751.[4] It was also adopted by such German philosophers as A. G. Baumgarten, who coined the term "aesthetics," Moses Mendelssohn, and Immanuel Kant; aesthetics as a philosophical discipline was born.[5]

Prior to the eighteenth century it would no more have occurred to anyone to seek a common denominator in poetry, painting, music, sculpture and architecture as similar activities than it would occur to us to look for one in square roots, oceans, and parliaments. But once things are classified together and referred to by the same name, we tend to suppose that there must be a single basis of classification and reference.

The authors of all of the selections to be found in this section appear to be looking for the defining feature of art. Leo Tolstoy argues that art is a means of communication singular in its capacity to transmit the feelings of one man to others; other modes of communication transmit thoughts. According to Benedetto Croce, the communicative function of art is incidental; essentially, art is the expression of a nonintellectual intuition, a spiritual activity which culminates in a nonconceptual insight that is identical with its expression. Restricting himself to the "visual arts,"[6] Clive Bell finds nonrepresentational "significant form" to be their defining property. Looking for a single quality common to all art strikes DeWitt Parker as simple-minded; art is a "complex fact," and he therefore posits a complex three-sided definition, based on imaginative satisfaction, social significance, and harmony. Jacques Maritain, like Croce, finds the distinguishing feature of art in a certain mode of mental activity. Unlike Croce, however, he holds that the essential activity is intellectual: the practical intellect, when guided by "creative intuition" and the urge to make something beautiful, produces art as opposed to nonartistic artifacts. Susanne Langer, like Tolstoy, sees art as essentially communicative or expressive. But, in contrast to Tolstoy, she holds that a work of art's capacity to transmit feelings is incidental; what is essential is that it be a symbol expressive of what the artist knows about human sentience.

Notes

1. For a thorough discussion of these definitions, see Richard Robinson, *Definition*, Oxford, The Clarendon Press, 1950.
2. Although this tells us what all, and only, hexapods have in common, it

does not rule out the possibility that all, and only, hexapods may have *other* features in common; if they do, however, the statement that they do is not a definition of "hexapod."

3. See Appendices A and B of this book.

4. The second edition of the *Encyclopedia* (1781) contained an article on aesthetics which gave the following definition: "Aesthetics . . . a new term invented to designate a science formulated only a few years ago. It is the philosophy of the fine arts."

5. For a more detailed history of the development of our concept of fine art, see P. O. Kristeller, "The Modern System of the Arts: A Study in the History of Aesthetics," *Journal of the History of Ideas,* XII (1951), 496-527, and XIII (1952), 17-46.

6. For Bell's views on literature, see his "The 'Difference' of Literature," *New Republic,* XXXIII (1922), 18-19.

LEO TOLSTOY

What Is Art?

"WHAT IS ART?" What a question! Art is architecture, sculpture, painting, music, and poetry in all its forms, usually replies the ordinary man, the art amateur or even the artist himself, imagining the matter about which he is talking to be perfectly clear and uniformly understood by everybody. But in architecture, one inquires further, are there not simple buildings which are not objects of art, and buildings with artistic pretensions which are unsuccessful and ugly and therefore not to be considered works of art? Wherein lies the characteristic sign of a work of art?

It is the same in sculpture, in music, and in poetry. Art in all its forms is bounded on one side by the practically useful, and on the other by unsuccessful attempts at art. How is art to be marked off from each of these? The ordinary educated man of our circle, and even the artist who has not occupied himself specially with aesthetics, will not hesitate at this question either. He thinks the solution was found long ago, and is well known to everyone.

"Art is activity that produces beauty," says such a man.

If art consists in that,—then is a ballet or an operetta art? you inquire.

"Yes," says the ordinary man, though with some hesitation, "a good ballet or a graceful operetta is also art, in so far as it manifests beauty. . . ."

What then is this conception of beauty, so stubbornly held to by people of our circle and day as furnishing a definition of art?

In its subjective aspect, we call beauty that which supplies us with a particular kind of pleasure.

In its objective aspect, we call beauty something absolutely perfect, and we acknowledge it to be so only because we receive from the manifestation of this absolute perfection a certain kind of pleasure: so that this

From *What is Art? and Essays on Art* by Leo Tolstoy, translated by Aylmer Maude, World's Classics Series, 1930 and reprinted by permission of Oxford University Press, London.

objective definition is nothing but the subjective conception differently expressed. In reality both conceptions of beauty amount to one and the same thing, namely, the reception by us of a certain kind of pleasure; that is to say, we call "beauty" that which pleases us without evoking in us desire. . . .

In order to define any human activity, it is necessary to understand its sense and importance; and in order to do this it is primarily necessary to examine that activity in itself, in its dependence on its causes and in connexion with its effects, and not merely in relation to the pleasure we can get from it.

If we say that the aim of any activity is merely our pleasure and define it solely by that pleasure, our definition will evidently be a false one. But this is precisely what has occurred in the efforts to define art. Now if we consider the food question it will not occur to any one to affirm that the importance of food consists in the pleasure we receive when eating it. Everybody understands that the satisfaction of our taste cannot serve as a basis for our definition of the merits of food, and that we have therefore no right to presuppose that dinners with cayenne pepper, Limburg cheese, alcohol, and so on, to which we are accustomed, and which please us, form the very best human food.

In the same way beauty, or that which pleases us, can in no sense serve as a basis for the definition of art; nor can a series of objects which afford us pleasure serve as the model of what art should be.

To see the aim and purpose of art in the pleasure we get from it, is like assuming (as is done by people of the lowest moral development, for instance by savages) that the purpose and aim of food is the pleasure derived when consuming it.

Just as people who conceive the aim and purpose of food to be pleasure cannot recognize the real meaning of eating, so people who consider the aim of art to be pleasure cannot realize its true meaning and purpose, because they attribute to an activity the meaning of which lies in its connexion with the other phenomena of life, the false and exceptional aim of pleasure. People come to understand that the meaning of eating lies in the nourishment of the body, only when they cease to consider that the object of that activity is pleasure. And it is the same with regard to art. People will come to understand the meaning of art only when they cease to consider that the aim of that activity is beauty, that is to say, pleasure. The acknowledgement of beauty (that is, of a certain kind of pleasure received from art) as being the aim of art, not only fails to assist us in finding a definition of what art is, but on the contrary by transferring the question into a region quite foreign to art (into metaphysical, psychological, physiological, and even historical, discussions as to why such a production pleases one person and such another displeases or pleases some one else), it renders such definition impossible. And since discussions as to why one man likes pears and another prefers meat do not help towards finding a definition of what is essential in nourishment, so the solution of questions of taste in art (to which the discussions on art involuntarily come) not only does not help to make clear in what this particular human activity which we call art really consists, but renders such elucidation quite impossible until we rid ourselves of a conception which justifies every kind of art at the cost of confusing the whole matter. . . .

In order to define art correctly it is necessary first of all to cease to consider it as a means to pleasure, and to consider it as one of the conditions of human life. Viewing it in this way we cannot fail to observe that art is one of the means of intercourse between man and man.

Every work of art causes the receiver to enter into a certain kind of relationship both with him who produced or is producing the art, and with all those who, simultaneously, previously, or subsequently, receive the same artistic impression.

Speech transmitting the thoughts and experiences of men serves as a means of union among them, and art serves a similar purpose. The peculiarity of this latter means of intercourse, distinguishing it from intercourse by means of words, consists in this, that whereas by words a man transmits his thoughts to another, by art he transmits his feelings.

The activity of art is based on the fact that a man receiving through his sense of hearing or sight another man's expression of feeling, is capable of experiencing the emotion which moved the man who expressed it. To take the simplest example: one man laughs, and another who hears becomes merry, or a man weeps, and another who hears feels sorrow. A man is excited or irritated, and another man seeing him is brought to a similar state of mind. By his movements or by the sounds of his voice a man expresses courage and determination or sadness and calmness, and this state of mind passes on to others. A man suffers, manifesting his suffering by groans and spasms, and this suffering transmits itself to other people; a man expresses his feelings of admiration, devotion, fear, respect, or love, to certain objects, persons, or phenomena, and others are infected by the same feelings of admiration, devotion, fear, respect, or love, to the same objects, persons, or phenomena.

And it is on this capacity of man to receive another man's expression of feeling and to experience those feelings himself, that the activity of art is based.

If a man infects another or others directly, immediately, by his appearance or by the sounds he gives vent to at the very time he experiences the feeling; if he causes another man to yawn when he himself cannot help yawning, or to laugh or cry when he himself is obliged to laugh or cry, or to suffer when he himself is suffering—that does not amount to art.

Art begins when one person with the object of joining another or others to himself in one and the same feeling, expresses that feeling by certain external indications. To take the simplest example: a boy having experienced, let us say, fear on encountering a wolf, relates that encounter, and in order to evoke in others the feeling he has experienced, describes himself, his condition before the encounter, the surroundings, the wood, his own lightheartedness, and then the wolf's appearance, its movements, the distance between himself and the wolf, and so forth. All this, if only the boy when telling the story again experiences the feelings he had lived through, and infects the hearers and compels them to feel what he has experienced—is art. Even if the boy had not seen the wolf but had frequently been afraid of one, and if wishing to evoke in others the fear he had felt, he invented an encounter with a wolf and recounted it so as to make his hearers share the feelings he experienced when he feared the wolf, that would also be art. And just in the same way it is art if a man, having experienced either the fear of suffering or the attraction of enjoyment (whether in reality or in imagination), expresses these feelings on canvas or in marble so that others are infected by them. And it is also art if a man feels, or imagines to himself, feelings of delight, gladness, sorrow, despair, courage, or despondency, and the transition from one to another of these feelings, and expresses them by sounds so that the hearers are infected by them and experience them as they were experienced by the composer.

The feelings with which the artist infects others may be most various—very strong or very weak, very important or very insignificant, very bad or very good: feelings of love of one's country, self-devotion and submission to fate or to God expressed in a drama, raptures of lovers described in a novel, feelings of voluptuousness expressed in a picture, courage expressed in a triumphal march, merriment evoked by a dance, humour evoked by a funny story, the feeling of quietness transmitted by an evening landscape or by a lullaby, or the feeling of admiration evoked by a beautiful arabesque—it is all art.

If only the spectators or auditors are infected by the feelings which the author has felt, it is art.

To evoke in oneself a feeling one has once experienced and having evoked it in oneself then by means of movements, lines, colours, sounds, or forms expressed in words, so to transmit that feeling that others experience the same feeling—this is the activity of art.

Art is a human activity consisting in this, that one man consciously by means of certain external signs, hands on to others feelings he has lived through, and that others are infected by these feelings and also experience them.

Art is not, as the metaphysicians say, the manifestation of some mysterious Idea of beauty or God; it is not, as the aesthetic physiologists say, a game in which man lets off his excess of stored-up energy; it is not the expression of man's emotions by external signs; it is not the production of pleasing objects; and, above all, it is not pleasure; but it is a means of union among men joining them together in the same feelings, and indispensable for the life and progress towards well-being of individuals and of humanity.

As every man, thanks to man's capacity to express thoughts by words, may know all that has been done for him in the realms of thought by all humanity before his day, and can in the present, thanks to his capacity to understand the thoughts of others, become a sharer in their activity and also himself hand on to his contemporaries and descendants the thoughts he has assimilated from others as well as those that have arisen in himself; so, thanks to man's capacity to be infected with the feelings of others by means of art, all that is being lived through by his contemporaries is accessible to him, as well as the feelings experienced by men thousands of years ago, and he has also the possibility of transmitting his own feelings to others.

If people lacked the capacity to receive the thoughts conceived by men who preceded them and to pass on to others their own thoughts, men would be like wild beasts, or like Kasper Hauser.[1]

And if men lacked this other capacity of being infected by art, people might be almost more savage still, and above all more separated from, and more hostile to, one another.

And therefore the activity of art is a most important one, as important as the activity of speech itself and as generally diffused.

As speech does not act on us only in sermons, orations, or books, but in all those remarks by which we interchange thoughts and experiences with one another, so also art in the wide sense of the word permeates our whole life, but it is only to some of its manifestations that we apply the term in the limited sense of the word.

We are accustomed to understand art to be only what we hear and see in theatres, concerts, and exhibitions; together with buildings, statues, poems, and novels. . . . But all this is but the smallest part of the art by which we communicate with one another in life. All human life is filled with works of art of every kind—from cradle-song, jest, mimicry, the ornamentation of houses, dress, and utensils, to church services, buildings, monuments, and triumphal processions. It is all artistic activity. So that by art, in the limited sense of the word, we do not mean all human activity transmitting feelings but only that part which we for some reason select from it and to which we attach special importance.

This special importance has always been given by men to that part of this activity which transmits feelings flowing from their religious perception, and this small part they have specifically called art, attaching to it the full meaning of the word.

That was how men of old—Socrates, Plato, and Aristotle—looked on art. Thus did the Hebrew prophets and the ancient Christians regard art. Thus it was, and still is, understood by the Mohammedans, and thus it is still understood by religious folk among our own peasantry.

Some teachers of mankind—such as Plato in his *Republic,* and people like the primitive Christians, the strict Mohammedans, and the Buddhists —have gone so far as to repudiate all art.

People viewing art in this way (in contradiction to the prevalent view of to-day which regards any art as good if only it affords pleasure) held and hold that art (as contrasted with speech, which need not be listened to) is so highly dangerous in its power to infect people against their wills, that mankind will lose far less by banishing all art than by tolerating each and every art.

Evidently such people were wrong in repudiating all art, for they denied what cannot be denied—one of the indispensable means of communication without which mankind could not exist. But not less wrong are the people of civilized European society of our class and day in favouring any art if it but serves beauty, that is, gives people pleasure.

Formerly people feared lest among works of art there might chance to be some causing corruption, and they prohibited art altogether. Now they only fear lest they should be deprived of any enjoyment art can afford, and they patronize any art. And I think the last error is much grosser than the first and that its consequences are far more harmful. . . .

There is one indubitable sign distinguishing real art from its counterfeit—namely, the infectiousness of art. If a man without exercising effort and without altering his standpoint, on reading, hearing, or seeing another man's work experiences a mental condition which unites him with that man and with others who are also affected by that work, then the object evoking that condition is a work of art. And however poetic, realistic, striking, or interesting, a work may be, it is not a work of art if it does not evoke that feeling (quite distinct from all other feelings) of joy and of spiritual union with another (the author) and with others (those who are also infected by it).

It is true that this indication is an *internal* one and that there are people who, having forgotten what the action of real art is, expect something else from art (in our society the great majority are in this state), and that therefore such people may mistake for this aesthetic feeling the feeling of diversion and a certain excitement which they receive from counterfeits of art. But though it is impossible to undeceive these people, just as it may be impossible to convince a man suffering from colour-blindness that green is not red, yet for all that, this indication remains perfectly definite to those whose feeling for art is neither perverted nor atrophied, and it clearly distinguishes the feeling produced by art from all other feelings.

The chief peculiarity of this feeling is that the recipient of a truly artistic impression is so united to the artist that he feels as if the work were his own and not some one else's—as if what it expresses were just what he had long been wishing to express. A real work of art destroys in the consciousness of the recipient the separation between himself and the artist, and not that alone, but also between himself and all whose minds receive this work of art. In this freeing of our personality from its separation and isolation, in this uniting of it with others, lies the chief characteristic and the great attractive force of art.

If a man is infected by the author's condition of soul, if he feels this emotion and this union with others, then the object which has effected this is art; but if there be no such infection, if there be not this union with the author and with others who are moved by the same work—then it is not art. And not only is infection a sure sign of art, but the degree of infectiousness is also the sole measure of excellence in art.

The stronger the infection the better is the art, as art, speaking of it now apart from its subject-matter—that is, not considering the value of the feelings it transmits.

And the degree of the infectiousness of art depends on three conditions:-

(1) On the greater or lesser individuality of the feeling transmitted; (2) on the greater or lesser clearness with which the feeling is transmitted; (3) on the sincerity of the artist, that is, on the greater or lesser force with which the artist himself feels the emotion he transmits.

The more individual the feeling transmitted the more strongly does it act on the recipient; the more individual the state of soul into which he is transferred the more pleasure does the recipient obtain and therefore the more readily and strongly does he join in it.

Clearness of expression assists infection because the recipient who mingles in consciousness with the author is the better satisfied the more clearly that feeling is transmitted which, as it seems to him, he has long known and felt and for which he has only now found expression.

But most of all is the degree of infectiousness of art increased by the degree of sincerity in the artist. As soon as the spectator, hearer, or reader, feels that the artist is infected by his own production and writes, sings, or plays, for himself, and not merely to act on others, this mental condition of the artist infects the recipient; and, on the contrary, as soon as the spectator, reader, or hearer, feels that the author is not writing, singing, or playing, for his own satisfaction—does not himself feel what he wishes to express, but is doing it for him, the recipient—resistance immediately springs up, and the most individual and the newest feelings and the cleverest technique not only fail to produce any infection but actually repel.

I have mentioned three conditions of contagion in art, but they may all be summed up into one, the last, sincerity; that is, that the artist should be impelled by an inner need to express his feeling. That condition includes the first; for if the artist is sincere he will express the feeling as he experienced it. And as each man is different from every one else, his feeling will be individual for every one else; and the more individual it is— the more the artist has drawn it from the depths of his nature—the more sympathetic and sincere will it be. And this same sincerity will impel the artist to find clear expression for the feeling which he wishes to transmit.

Therefore this third condition—sincerity—is the most important of the three. It is always complied with in peasant art, and this explains why such art always acts so powerfully; but it is a condition almost entirely absent from our upper-class art, which is continually produced by artists actuated by personal aims of covetousness or vanity.

Such are the three conditions which divide art from its counterfeits, and which also decide the quality of every work of art considered apart from its subject-matter.

The absence of any one of these conditions excludes a work from the category of art and relegates it to that of art's counterfeits. If the work does not transmit the artist's peculiarity of feeling and is therefore not individual, if it is unintelligibly expressed, or if it has not proceeded from the author's inner need for expression—it is not a work of art. If all these conditions are present even in the smallest degree, then the work even if a weak one is yet a work of art.

The presence in various degrees of these three conditions: individuality, clearness, and sincerity, decides the merit of a work of art as art, apart from subject-matter. All works of art take order of merit according to the degree in which they fulfil the first, the second, and the third, of these conditions. In one the individuality of the feeling transmitted may predominate; in another, clearness of expression; in a third, sincerity; while a fourth may have sincerity and individuality and be deficient in clearness; a fifth, individuality and clearness, but less sincerity; and so forth, in all possible degrees and combinations.

Thus is art divided from what is not art, and thus is the quality of art, as art, decided, independently of its subject-matter, that is to say, apart from whether the feelings it transmits are good or bad.

But how are we to define good and bad art with reference to its content or subject-matter? . . .

Art like speech is a means of communication and therefore of progress, that is, of the movement of humanity forward towards perfection. Speech renders accessible to men of the latest generations all the knowledge discovered by the experience and reflection both of preceding generations and of the best and foremost men of their own times; art renders accessible to men of the latest generations all the feelings experienced by their predecessors and also those felt by their best and foremost contemporaries. And as the evolution of knowledge proceeds by truer and more necessary knowledge dislodging and replacing what was mistaken and unnecessary, so the evolution of feeling proceeds by means of art—feelings less kind and less necessary for the well-being of mankind being replaced by others kinder and more needful for that end. That is the purpose of art. And speaking now of the feelings which are its subject-matter, the more art fulfills that purpose the better the art, and the less it fulfills it the worse the art.

The appraisement of feelings (that is, the recognition of one or other set of feelings as more or less good, more or less necessary for the well-being of mankind) is affected by the religious perception of the age.

In every period of history and in every human society there exists an understanding of the meaning of life, which represents the highest level to which men of that society have attained—an understanding indicating the highest good at which that society aims. This understanding is the religious perception of the given time and society. And this religious perception is always clearly expressed by a few advanced men and more or less vividly perceived by members of the society generally. Such a religious perception and its corresponding expression always exists in every society. If it appears to us that there is no religious perception in our society, this is not because there really is none, but only because we do not wish to see it. And we often wish not to see it because it exposes the fact that our life is inconsistent with that religious perception.

Religious perception in a society is like the direction of a flowing river. If the river flows at all it must have a direction. If a society lives, there must be a religious perception indicating the direction in which, more or less consciously, all its members tend.

And so there always has been, and is, a religious perception in every society. And it is by the standard of this religious perception that the feelings transmitted by art have always been appraised. It has always been only on the basis of this religious perception of their age, that men have chosen from amid the endlessly varied spheres of art that art which transmitted feelings making religious perception operative in actual life. And such art has always been highly valued and encouraged, while art transmitting feelings outlived, flowing from the antiquated religious perceptions of a former age, has always been condemned and despised. All the rest of art transmitting those most diverse feelings by means of which people commune with one another was not condemned and was tolerated if only it did not transmit feelings contrary to religious perception. Thus for instance among the Greeks, art transmitting feelings of beauty, strength, and courage (Hesiod, Homer, Phidias) was chosen, approved, and encouraged, while art transmitting feelings of rude sensuality, despondency, and effeminacy, was condemned and despised. Among the Jews, art transmitting feelings of devotion and submission to the God of the Hebrews and to His will (the epic of Genesis, the prophets, the Psalms) was chosen and encouraged, while art transmitting feelings of idolatry (the Golden Calf) was condemned and despised. All the rest of art—stories, songs, dances, ornamentation of houses, of utensils, and of clothes—which was not contrary to religious perception, was neither distinguished nor discussed. Thus as regards its subject-matter has art always and everywhere been appraised and thus it should be appraised, for this attitude towards art proceeds from the fundamental characteristics of human nature, and those characteristics do not change.

I know that according to an opinion current in our times religion is a superstition humanity has outgrown, and it is therefore assumed that no such thing exists as a religious perception common to us all by which art in our time can be appraised. I know that this is the opinion current in the pseudo-cultured circles of today. People who do not acknowledge Christianity in its true meaning because it undermines their social privileges, and who therefore invent all kinds of philosophic and aesthetic theories to hide from themselves the meaninglessness and wrongfulness of their lives, cannot think otherwise. These people intentionally, or sometimes unintentionally, confuse the notion of a religious cult with the notion of religious perception, and think that by denying the cult they get rid of the perception. But even the very attacks on religion and the attempts to establish an idea of life contrary to the religious perception of our times, most clearly demonstrate the existence of a religious perception condemning the lives that are not in harmony with it.

If humanity progresses, that is, moves forward, there must inevitably be a guide to the direction of that movement. And religions have always furnished that guide. All history shows that the progress of humanity is accomplished no otherwise than under the guidance of religion. But if the race cannot progress without the guidance of religion—and progress is always going on, and consequently goes on also in our own times,—then there must be a religion of our times. So that whether it pleases or displeases the so-called cultured people of to-day, they must admit the existence of religion—not of a religious cult, Catholic, Protestant, or another, but of religious perception—which even in our times is the guide always present where there is any progress. And if a religious perception exists amongst us, then the feelings dealt with by our art should be appraised on the basis of that religious perception; and as has been the case always and everywhere, art transmitting feelings flowing from the religious perception of our time should be chosen from amid all the indifferent art, should be acknowledged, highly valued, and encouraged, while art running counter to that perception should be condemned and despised, and all the remaining, indifferent, art should neither be distinguished nor encouraged.

The religious perception of our time in its widest and most practical application is the consciousness that our well-being, both material and spiritual, individual and collective, temporal and eternal, lies in the growth of brotherhood among men—in their loving harmony with one another. This perception is not only expressed by Christ and all the best men of past ages, it is not only repeated in most varied forms and from most diverse sides by the best men of our times, but it already serves as a clue to all the complex labour of humanity, consisting as this labour does on the one hand in the destruction of physical and moral obstacles to the union of men, and on the other hand in establishing the principles common to all men which can and should unite them in one universal brotherhood. And it is on the basis of this perception that we should appraise all the phenomena of our life and among the rest our art also: choosing from all its realms and highly prizing and encouraging whatever transmits feelings flowing from this religious perception, rejecting whatever is contrary to it, and not attributing to the rest an importance that does not properly belong to it. . . .

The essence of the Christian perception consists in the recognition by every man of his sonship to God and of the consequent union of men with God and with one another, as is said in the Gospel (John xvii. 21).[2] Therefore the subject-matter of Christian art is of a kind that feeling can unite men with God and with one another.

The expression *unite men with God and with one another* may seem obscure to people accustomed to the misuse of these words that is so customary, but the words have a perfectly clear meaning nevertheless. They indicate that the Christian union of man (in contradiction to the partial, exclusive, union of only certain men) is that which unites all without exception.

Art, all art, has this characteristic, that it unites people. Every art causes those to whom the artist's feeling is transmitted to unite in soul with the artist and also with all who receive the same impression. But non-Christian art while uniting some people, makes that very union a cause of separation between these united people and others; so that union of this kind is often a source not merely of division but even of enmity towards others. Such is all patriotic art, with its anthems, poems, and monuments; such is all Church art, that is, the art of certain cults, with their images, statues, processions, and other local ceremonies. Such art is belated and non-Christian, uniting the people of one cult only to separate them yet more sharply from the members of other cults, and even to place them in relations of hostility to one another. Christian art is such only as tends to unite all without exception, either by evoking in them the perception that each man and all men stand in a like relation towards God and towards their neighbour, or by evoking in them identical feelings, which may even be the very simplest, provided that they are not repugnant to Christianity and are natural to every one without exception. . . .

Whatever the work may be and however it may have been extolled, we have first to ask whether this work is one of real art, or a counterfeit. Having acknowledged, on the basis of the indication of its infectiousness even to a small class of people, that a certain production belongs to the realm of art, it is necessary on this basis to decide the next question, Does this work belong to the category of bad exclusive art opposed to religious perception, or of Christian art uniting people? And having acknowledged a work to belong to real Christian art, we must then, according to whether it transmits feelings flowing from love of God and man, or merely the simple feelings uniting all men, assign it a place in the ranks of religious art, or in those of universal art.

Only on the basis of such verification shall we find it possible to select from the whole mass of what in our society claims to be art, those works which form real, important, necessary, spiritual food, and to separate them from all the harmful and useless art and from the counterfeits of art which surround us. Only on the basis of such verification shall we be able to rid ourselves of the pernicious results of harmful art and avail ourselves of that beneficent action which is the purpose of true and good art, and which is indispensable for the spiritual life of man and of humanity.

Notes

1. "The foundling of Nuremberg," found in the market-place of that town on 23rd May, 1828, apparently some sixteen years old. He spoke little and was almost totally ignorant even of common objects. He subsequently explained that he had been brought up in confinement underground and visited by only one man, whom he saw but seldom.

2. "That they may all be one; even as thou, Father, are in me, and I am in Thee, that they also may be in us."

BENEDETTO CROCE

Art as Intuition

Intuition and Expression

KNOWLEDGE HAS TWO FORMS: it is either *intuitive* knowledge or *logical* knowledge; knowledge obtained through the *imagination* or knowledge obtained through the *intellect;* knowledge of the *individual* or knowledge of the *universal;* of *individual things* or of the *relations* between them: it is, in fact, productive either of *images* or of *concepts.*

In ordinary life, constant appeal is made to intuitive knowledge. It is said that we cannot give definitions of certain truths; that they are not demonstrable by syllogisms; that they must be learnt intuitively. The politician finds fault with the abstract reasoner, who possesses no lively intuition of actual conditions; the educational theorist insists upon the necessity of developing the intuitive faculty in the pupil before everything else; the critic in judging a work of art makes it a point of honour to set aside theory and abstractions, and to judge it by direct intuition; the practical man professes to live rather by intuition than by reason.

But this simple acknowledgement granted to intuitive knowledge in ordinary life, does not correspond to an equal and adequate acknowledgement in the field of theory and of philosophy. There exists a very ancient science of intellectual knowledge, admitted by all without discussion, namely, Logic; but a science of intuitive knowledge is timidly and with difficulty asserted by but a few. Logical knowledge has appropriated the lion's share; and if she does not slay and devour her companion outright, yet yields her but grudgingly the humble place of maid-servant or door-keeper—What can intuitive knowledge be without the light of intellectual knowledge? It is a servant without a master; and though a master find a servant useful, the master is a necessity to the servant, since he enables him to gain his livelihood. Intuition is blind; intellect lends her eyes.

Now, the first point to be firmly fixed in the mind is that intuitive knowledge has no need of a master, nor to lean upon any one; she does

From *Aesthetic* by Benedetto Croce, 2nd ed., 1922, translated by Douglas Ainslie, and reprinted by permission of Farrar, Straus & Co. and Macmillan & Company Ltd, London. Published 1953 by the Noonday Press.

not need to borrow the eyes of others, for she has excellent eyes of her own. Doubtless it is possible to find concepts mingled with intuitions. But in many other intuitions there is no trace of such a mixture, which proves that it is not necessary. The impression of a moonlight scene by a painter; the outline of a country drawn by a cartographer; a musical motive, tender or energetic; the words of a sighing lyric, or those with which we ask, command and lament in ordinary life, may well all be intuitive facts without a shadow of intellectual relation. But, think what one may of these instances, and admitting further the contention that the greater part of the intuitions of civilized man are impregnated with concepts, there yet remains to be observed something more important and more conclusive. Those concepts which are found mingled and fused with the intuitions are no longer concepts, in so far as they are really mingled and fused, for they have lost all independence and autonomy. They have been concepts, but have now become simply elements of intuition. The philosophical maxims placed in the mouth of a personage of tragedy or of comedy, perform there the function, not of concepts, but of characteristics of such personage; in the same way as the red in a painted face does not there represent the red colour of the physicists, but is a characteristic element of the portrait. The whole is that which determines the quality of the parts. A work of art may be full of philosophical concepts; it may contain them in greater abundance and they may there be even more profound than in a philosophical dissertation, which in its turn may be rich to overflowing with descriptions and intuitions. But notwithstanding all these concepts the total effect of the work of art is an intuition; and notwithstanding all those intuitions, the total effect of the philosophical dissertation is a concept. The *Promessi Sposi* contains copious ethical observations and distinctions, but does not for that reason lose as a whole its character of simple story or intuition. In like manner the anecdotes and satirical effusions to be found in the works of a philosopher like Schopenhauer do not deprive those works of their character of intellectual treatises. The difference between a scientific work and a work of art, that is, between an intellectual fact and an intuitive fact, lies in the difference of the total effect aimed at by their respective authors. This it is that determines and rules over the several parts of each, not these parts separated and considered abstractly in themselves.

But to admit the independence of intuition as regards concept does not suffice to give a true and precise idea of intuition. Another error arises among those who recognize this, or who at any rate do not explicitly make intuition dependent upon the intellect, to obscure and confuse the real nature of intuition. By intuition is frequently understood *perception,* or the knowledge of actual reality, the apprehension of something as *real.*

Certainly perception is intuition: the perceptions of the room in which I am writing, of the ink-bottle and paper that are before me, of the pen I am using, of the objects that I touch and make use of as instruments of my person, which, if it write, therefore exists;—these are all intuitions. But the image that is now passing through my brain of me writing in another room, in another town, with different paper, pen and ink, is also an intuition. This means that the distinction between reality and non-reality is extraneous, secondary, to the true nature of intuition. If we imagine a human mind having intuitions for the first time, it would seem that it could have intuitions of actual reality only, that is to say, that it could have perceptions of nothing but the real. But since knowledge of reality is based upon the distinction between real images and unreal images, and since this distinction does not at the first moment exist, these intuitions would in truth not be intuitions either of the real or of the unreal, not perceptions, but pure intuitions. Where all is real, nothing is real. The child, with its difficulty of distinguishing true from false, history from fable, which are all one to childhood, can furnish us with a sort of very vague and only remotely approximate idea of this ingenuous state. Intuition is the undifferentiated unity of the perception of the real and of the simple image of the possible. In our intuitions we do not oppose ourselves as empirical beings to external reality, but we simply objectify our impressions, whatever they be.

Those, therefore, who look upon intuition as sensation formed and arranged simply according to the categories of space and time, would seem to approximate more nearly to the truth. Space and time (they say) are the forms of intuition; to have an intuition is to place it in space and in temporal sequence. Intuitive activity would then consist in this double and concurrent function of spatiality and temporality. But for these two categories must be repeated what was said of intellectual distinctions, when found mingled with intuitions. We have intuitions without space and without time: the colour of a sky, the colour of a feeling, a cry of pain and an effort of will, objectified in consciousness: these are intuitions which we possess, and with their making space and time have nothing to do. In some intuitions, spatiality may be found without temporality, in others, *vice versa;* and even when both are found, they are perceived by later reflexion: they can be fused with the intuition in like manner with all its other elements; that is, they are in it *materialiter* and not *formaliter*, as ingredients and not as arrangement. Who, without an act of reflexion which for a moment breaks in upon his contemplation, can think of space while looking at a drawing or a view? Who is conscious of temporal sequence while listening to a story or a piece of music without breaking into it with a similar act of reflexion? What intuition reveals in a work of art is not space and time, but *character, individual physiognomy*. The view here maintained is confirmed in several quarters of modern philosophy. Space and time, far from being simple and primitive functions, are nowadays conceived as intellectual constructions of great complexity. And further, even in some of those who do not altogether deny to space and time the quality of formative principles, categories and functions, one observes an effort to unite them and to regard them in a different manner from that in which these categories are generally conceived. Some limit intuition to the sole category of spatiality, maintaining that even time can only be intuited in terms of space. Others abandon the three dimensions of space as not philosophically necessary, and conceive the function of spatiality as void of all particular spatial determination. But what could such a spatial function be, a simple arrangement that should arrange even time? It represents, surely, all that criticism and refutation have left standing—the bare demand for the affirmation of some intuitive activity in general. And is not this activity truly determined, when one single function is attributed to it, not spatializing it nor temporalizing, but characterizing? Or rather, when it is conceived as itself a category or function which gives us knowledge of things in their concreteness and individuality?

Having thus freed intuitive knowledge from any suggestion of intellectualism and from every later and external addition, we must now explain it and determine its limits from another side and defend it from a different kind of invasion and confusion. On the hither side of the lower limit is sensation, formless matter, which the spirit can never apprehend in itself as simple matter. This it can only possess with form and in form, but postulates the notion of it as a mere limit. Matter, in its abstraction, is mechanism, passivity; it is what the spirit of man suffers, but does not produce. Without it no human knowledge or activity is possible; but mere matter produces animality, whatever is brutal and impulsive in man, not the spiritual dominion, which is humanity. How often we strive to understand clearly what is passing within us! We do catch a glimpse of something, but this does not appear to the mind as objectified and formed. It is in such moments as these that we best perceive the profound difference between matter and form. These are not two acts of ours, opposed to one another; but the one is outside us and assaults and sweeps us off our feet, while the other inside us tends to absorb and identify itself with that which is outside. Matter, clothed and conquered by form, produces concrete form. It is the matter, the content, which differentiates one of our intuitions from another: the form is constant: it is spiritual activity, while matter is changeable. Without matter spiritual activity would not forsake its abstractedness to become concrete and real activity, this or that spiritual content, this or that definite intuition.

It is a curious fact, characteristic of our times, that this very form, this very activity of the spirit, which is essentially ourselves, is so often ignored or denied. Some confound the spiritual activity of man with a metaphorical and mythological activity of what is called nature, which is mechanism and has no resemblance to human activity, save when we imagine, with Aesop, that *"arbores loquuntur non tantum ferae."*[1] Some affirm that they have never observed in themselves this "miraculous" activity, as though there were no difference, or only one of quantity, between sweating and thinking, feeling cold and the energy of the will.

Others, certainly with greater reason, would unify activity and mechanism in a more general concept, though they are specifically distinct. Let us, however, refrain for a moment from examining if such a final unification be possible, and in what sense, but admitting that the attempt may be made, it is clear that to unify two concepts in a third implies to begin with the admission of a difference between the two first. Here it is this difference that concerns us and we set it in relief.

Intuition has sometimes been confused with simple sensation. But since this confusion ends by being offensive to common sense, it has more frequently been attenuated or concealed with a phraseology apparently designed at once to confuse and to distinguish them. Thus, it has been asserted that intuition is sensation, but not so much simple sensation as *association* of sensations. Here a double meaning is concealed in the word "association." Association is understood, either as memory, mnemonic association, conscious recollection, and in that case the claim to unite in memory elements which are not intuited, distinguished, possessed in some way by the spirit and produced by consciousness, seems inconceivable: or it is understood as association of unconscious elements, in which case we remain in the world of sensation and of nature. But if with certain associationists we speak of an association which is neither memory nor flux of sensations, but a *productive* association (formative, constructive, distinguishing) ; then our contention is admitted and only its name is denied to it. For productive association is no longer association in the sense of the sensationalists, but *synthesis,* that is to say, spiritual activity. Synthesis may be called association; but with the concept of productivity is already posited the distinction between passivity and activity, between sensation and intuition.

Other psychologists are disposed to distinguish from sensation something which is sensation no longer, but is not yet intellectual concept: the *representation* or *image*. What is the difference between their representation or image and our intuitive knowledge? Everything and nothing: for "representation" is a very equivocal word. If by representation be understood something cut off and standing out from the psychic basis of the sensations, then representation is intuition. If, on the other hand, it be conceived as complex sensation we are back once more in crude sensation, which does not vary in quality according to its richness or poverty, or according to whether the organism in which it appears is rudimentary or highly developed and full of traces of past sensations. Nor is the ambiguity remedied by defining representation as a psychic product of secondary degree in relation to sensation, defined as occupying the first place. What does secondary degree mean here? Does it mean a qualitative, formal difference? If so, representation is an elaboration of sensation and therefore intuition. Or does it mean greater complexity and complication, a quantitative, material difference? In that case intuition is once more confused with simple sensation.

And yet there is a sure method of distinguishing true intuition, true representation, from that which is inferior to it: the spiritual fact from the mechanical, passive, natural fact. Every true intuition or representation is also *expression*. That which does not objectify itself in expression is not intuition or representation, but sensation and mere natural fact. The spirit only intuits in making, forming, expressing. He who separates intuition from expression never succeeds in reuniting them.

Intuitive activity *possesses intuitions to the extent that it expresses them.* Should this proposition sound paradoxical, that is partly because, as a general rule, a too restricted meaning is given to the word "expression." It is generally restricted to what are called verbal expressions alone. But there exist also non-verbal expressions, such as those of line, colour and sound, and to all of these must be extended our affirmation, which embraces therefore every sort of manifestation of the man, as orator, musician, painter, or anything else. But be it pictorial, or verbal, or musical, or in whatever other form it appear, to no intuition can expression in one of its forms be wanting; it is, in fact, an inseparable part of intuition. How can we really possess an intuition of a geometrical figure, unless we possess so accurate an image of it as to be able to trace it immediately upon paper or on the blackboard? How can we really have an intuition of the contour of a region, for example of the island of Sicily, if we are not able to draw it as it is in all its meanderings? Every one can experience the internal illumination which follows upon his success in formulating to himself his impressions and feelings, but only so far as he is able to formulate them. Feelings or impressions, then, pass by means of words from the obscure region of the soul into the clarity of the contemplative spirit. It is impossible to distinguish intuition from expression in this cognitive process. The one appears with the other at the same instant, because they are not two, but one.

The principal reason which makes our view appear paradoxical as we maintain it, is the illusion or prejudice that we possess a more complete intuition of reality than we really do. One often hears people say that they have many great thoughts in their minds, but that they are not able to express them. But if they really had them, they would have coined them into just so many beautiful, sounding words, and thus have expressed them. If these thoughts seem to vanish or to become few and meagre in the act of expressing them, the reason is that they did not exist or really were few and meagre. People think that all of us ordinary men imagine and intuit countries, figures and scenes like painters, and bodies like sculptors; save that painters and sculptors know how to paint and carve such images, while we bear them unexpressed in our souls. They believe that any one could have imagined a Madonna of Raphael; but that Raphael was Raphael owing to his technical ability in putting the Madonna upon canvas. Nothing can be more false than this view. The world which as a rule we intuit is a small thing. It consists of little expressions, which gradually become greater and wider with the increasing spiritual concentration of certain moments. They are the words we say to ourselves, our silent judgments: "Here is a man, here is a horse, this is heavy, this is sharp, this pleases me," etc. It is a medley of light and colour, with no greater pictorial value than could be expressed by a haphazard splash of colours, from among which one could barely make out a few special, distinctive traits. This and nothing else is what we possess in our ordinary life; this is the basis of our ordinary action. It is the index of a book. The labels tied to things (it has been said) take the place of the things themselves. This index and these labels (themselves expressions) suffice for small needs and small actions. From time to time we pass from the index to the book, from the label to the thing, or from the slight to the greater intuitions, and from these to the greatest and most lofty. This passage is sometimes far from easy. It has been observed by those who have best studied the psychology of artists that when, after having given a rapid glance at any one, they attempt to obtain a real intuition of him, in order, for example, to paint his portrait, then this ordinary vision, that seemed so precise, so lively, reveals itself as little better than nothing. What remains is found to be at the most some superficial trait, which would not even suffice for a caricature. The person to be painted stands before the artist like a world to discover. Michael Angelo said, "One paints, not with the hands, but with the brain." Leonardo shocked the prior of the Convent of the Graces by standing for days together gazing at the "Last Supper," without touching it with the brush. He remarked of this attitude: "The minds of men of lofty genius are most active in invention when they are doing the least external work." The painter is a painter, because he sees what others only feel or catch a glimpse of, but do not see. We think we see a smile, but in reality we have only a vague impression of it, we do not perceive all the characteristic traits of which it is the sum, as the painter discovers them after he has worked upon them and is thus able to fix them on the canvas. We do not intuitively possess more even of our intimate friend, who is with us every day and at all hours, than at most certain traits of physiognomy which enable us to distinguish him from others. The illusion is less easy as regards musical expression; because it would seem strange to every one to say that the composer had added or attached notes to a motive which was already in the mind of him who is not the composer; as if Beethoven's Ninth Symphony were not his own intuition and his intuition the Ninth Symphony. Now, just as one who is deluded as to the amount of his material wealth is confuted by arithmetic, which states its exact amount, so he who nourishes delusions as to the wealth of his own thoughts and images is brought back to reality, when he is obliged to cross the *Pons Asinorum* of expression. Let us say to the former, count; to the latter, speak; or, here is a pencil, draw, express yourself.

Each of us, as a matter of fact, has in him a little of the poet, of the sculptor, of the musician, of the painter, of the prose writer: but how little, as compared with those who bear those names, just because they possess the most universal dispositions and energies of human nature in so lofty a degree! How little too does a painter possess of the intuitions of a poet! And how little does one painter possess those of another painter! Nevertheless, that little is all our actual patrimony of intuitions or representations. Beyond these are only impressions, sensations, feelings, impulses, emotions, or whatever else one may term what still falls short of the spirit and is not assimilated by man; something postulated for the convenience of exposition, while actually non-existent, since to exist also is a fact of the spirit.

We may thus add this to the various verbal descriptions of intuition, noted at the beginning: intuitive knowledge is expressive knowledge. Independent and autonomous in respect to intellectual function; indifferent to later empirical discriminations, to reality and to unreality, to formations and apperceptions of space and time, which are also later: intuition or representation is distinguished as *form* from what is felt and suffered, from the flux or wave of sensation, or from psychic matter; and this form, this taking possession, is expression. To intuit is to express; and nothing else (nothing more, but nothing less) than *to express*.

Intuition and Art

Before proceeding further, it may be well to draw certain consequences from what has been established and to add some explanations.

We have frankly identified intuitive or expressive knowledge with the aesthetic or artistic fact, taking works of art as examples of intuitive knowledge and attributing to them the characteristics of intuition, and *vice versa*. But our identification is combated by a view held even by many philosophers, who consider art to be an intuition of an altogether special sort. "Let us admit," (they say) "that art is intuition; but intuition is not always art: artistic intuition is a distinct species differing from intuition in general by something *more*."

But no one has ever been able to indicate of what this something more consists. It has sometimes been thought that art is not a simple intuition, but an intuition of an intuition, in the same way as the concept of science has been defined, not as the ordinary concept, but as the concept of a concept. Thus man would attain to art by objectifying, not his sensations, as happens with ordinary intuition, but intuition itself. But this process of raising to a second power does not exist; and the comparison of it with the ordinary and scientific concept does not prove what is intended, for the good reason that it is not true that the scientific concept is the concept of a concept. If this comparison proves anything, it proves just the opposite. The ordinary concept, if it be really a concept and not a simple representation, is a perfect concept, however poor and limited. Science substitutes concepts for representations; for those concepts that are poor and limited it substitutes others, larger and more comprehensive; it is ever discovering new relations. But its method does not differ from that by which is formed the smallest universal in the brain of the humblest of men. What is generally called *par excellence* art, collects intuitions that are wider and more complex than those which we generally experience, but these intuitions are always of sensations and impressions.

Art is expression of impressions, not expression of expression.

For the same reason, it cannot be asserted that the intuition, which is generally called artistic, differs from ordinary intuition as intensive intuition. This would be the case if it were to operate differently on the same matter. But since the artistic function is extended to wider fields, yet does not differ in method from ordinary intuition, the difference between them is not intensive but extensive. The intuition of the simplest popular love-song, which says the same thing, or very nearly, as any declaration of love that issues at every moment from the lips of thousands of ordinary men, may be intensively perfect in its poor simplicity, although it be extensively so much more limited than the complex intuition of a love-song by Leopardi.

The whole difference, then, is quantitative, and as such is indifferent to philosophy, *scientia qualitatum*. Certain men have a greater aptitude, a more frequent inclination fully to express certain complex states of the soul. These men are known in ordinary language as artists. Some very complicated and difficult expressions are not often achieved, and these are called works of art. The limits of the expression-intuitions that are called art, as opposed to those that are vulgarly called non-art, are empirical and impossible to define. If an epigram be art, why not a simple word? If a story, why not the news-jottings of the journalist? If a landscape, why not a topographical sketch? The teacher of philosophy in Moliere's comedy was right: "whenever we speak, we create prose." But there will always be scholars like Monsieur Jourdain, astonished at having spoken prose for forty years without knowing it, who will have difficulty in persuading themselves that when they call their servant John to bring their slippers, they have spoken nothing less than—prose.

We must hold firmly to our identification, because among the principal reasons which have prevented Aesthetic, the science of art, from revealing the true nature of art, its real roots in human nature, has been its separation from the general spiritual life, the having made of it a sort of special function or aristocratic club. No one is astonished when he learns from physiology that every cell is an organism and every organism a cell or synthesis of cells. No one is astonished at finding in a lofty mountain the same chemical elements that compose a small stone fragment. There is not one physiology of small animals and one of large animals; nor is there a special chemical theory of stones as distinct from mountains. In the same way, there is not a science of lesser intuition as distinct from a science of greater intuition, nor one of ordinary intuition as distinct from artistic intuition. There is but one Aesthetic, the science of intuitive or expressive knowledge, which is the aesthetic or artistic fact. And this Aesthetic is the true analogue of Logic, which includes, as facts of the same nature, the formation of the smallest and most ordinary concept and the most complicated scientific and philosophical system.

Nor can we admit that the word *genius* or artistic genius, as distinct from the non-genius of the ordinary man, possesses more than a quantitative signification. Great artists are said to reveal us to ourselves. But how could this be possible, unless there were identity of nature between their imagination and ours, and unless the difference were only one of quantity? It were better to change *poeta nascitur* into *homo nascitur poeta:* some men are born great poets, some small. The cult of the genius with all its attendant superstitions has arisen from this quantitative difference having been taken as a difference of quality. It has been forgotten that genius is not something that has fallen from heaven, but humanity itself. The man of genius who poses or is represented as remote from humanity finds his punishment in becoming or appearing somewhat ridiculous. Examples of this are the *genius* of the romantic period and the *superman* of our time.

But it is well to note here, that those who claim unconsciousness as the chief quality of an artistic genius, hurl him from an eminence far above humanity to a position far below it. Intuitive or artistic genius, like every form of human activity, is always conscious; otherwise it would be blind mechanism. The only thing that can be wanting to artistic genius is the *reflective* consciousness, the superadded consciousness of the historian or critic, which is not essential to it.

The relation between matter and form, or between *content* and *form,* as is generally said, is one of the most disputed questions in Aesthetic. Does the aesthetic fact consist of content alone, or of form alone, or of both together? This question has taken on various meanings, which we shall mention, each in its place. But when these words are taken as signifying what we have above defined, and matter is understood as emotionality not aesthetically elaborated, or impressions, and form as intellectual activity and expression, then our view cannot be in doubt. We must, that is to say, reject both the thesis that makes the aesthetic fact to consist of the content alone (that is, the simple impressions) , and the thesis which makes it to consist of a junction between form and content, that is, of impressions plus expressions. In the aesthetic fact, expressive activity is not added to the fact of the impressions, but these latter are formed and elaborated by it. The impressions reappear as it were in expression, like water put into a filter, which reappears the same and yet different on the other side. The aesthetic fact, therefore, is form, and nothing but form.

From this was inferred not that the content is something superfluous (it is, on the contrary, the necessary point of departure for the expressive fact); but that *there is no passage* from the qualities of the content to those of the form. It has sometimes been thought that the content, in order to be aesthetic, that is to say, transformable into form, should possess some determined or determinable qualities. But were that so, then form and content, expression and impression, would be the same thing. It is true that the content is that which is convertible into form, but it has no determinable qualities until this transformation takes place. We know nothing about it. It does not become aesthetic content before, but only after it has been actually transformed. The aesthetic content has also been defined as the *interesting*. That is not an untrue statement; it is merely void of meaning. Interesting to what? To the expressive activity? Certainly the expressive activity would not have raised the content to the dignity of form, had it not been interested in it. Being interested is precisely the raising of the content to the dignity of form. But the word "interesting" has also been employed in another and an illegitimate sense, which we shall explain further on.

The proposition that art is *imitation of nature* has also several meanings. Sometimes truths have been expressed or at least shadowed forth in these words, sometimes errors have been promulgated. More frequently, no definite thought has been expressed at all. One of the scientifically legitimate meanings occurs when "imitation" is understood as representation or intuition of nature, a form of knowledge. And when the phrase is used with this intention, and in order to emphasize the spiritual character of the process, another proposition becomes legitimate also: namely, that art is the *idealization* or *idealizing* imitation of nature. But if by imitation of nature be understood that art gives mechanical reproductions, more or less perfect duplicates of natural objects, in the presence of which is renewed the same tumult of impressions as that caused by natural objects, then the proposition is evidently false. The coloured waxen effigies that imitate the life, before which we stand astonished in the museums where such things are shown, do not give aesthetic intuitions. Illusion and hallucination have nothing to do with the calm domain of artistic intuition. But on the other hand if an artist paint the interior of a wax-work museum, or if an actor give a burlesque portrait of a man-statue on the stage, we have work of the spirit and artistic intuition. Finally, if photography have in it anything artistic, it will be to the extent that it transmits the intuition of the photographer, his point of view, the pose and grouping which he has striven to attain. And if photography be not quite an art, that is precisely because the element of nature in it remains more or less unconquered and ineradicable. Do we ever, indeed, feel complete satisfaction before even the best of photographs? Would not an artist vary and touch up much or little, remove or add something to all of them?

The statements repeated so often, that art is not knowledge, that it does not tell the truth, that it does not belong to the world of theory, but to the world of feeling, and so forth, arise from the failure to realize exactly the theoretic character of simple intuition. This simple intuition is quite distinct from intellectual knowledge, as it is distinct from perception of the real; and the statements quoted above arise from the belief that only intellectual cognition is knowledge. We have seen that intuition is knowledge, free from concepts and more simple than the so-called perception of the real. Therefore art is knowledge, form; it does not belong to the world of feeling or to psychic matter. The reason why so many aestheticians have so often insisted that art is *appearance (Schein)*, is precisely that they have felt the necessity of distinguishing it from the more complex fact of perception, by maintaining its pure intuitiveness. And if for the same reason it has been claimed that art is *feeling* the reason is the same. For if the concept as content of art, and historical reality as such, be excluded from the sphere of art, there remains no other content than reality apprehended in all its ingenuousness and immediacy in the vital impulse, in its *feeling*, that is to say again, pure intuition.

The theory of the *aesthetic senses* has also arisen from the failure to establish, or from having lost to view, the character of expression as distinct from impression, of form as distinct from matter.

This theory can be reduced to the error just indicated of wishing to find a passage from the qualities of the content to those of the form. To ask, in fact, what the aesthetic senses are, implies asking what sensible impressions are able to enter into aesthetic expressions, and which must of necessity do so. To this we must at once reply, that all impressions can enter into aesthetic expressions or formations, but that none are bound to do so of necessity. Dante raised to the dignity of form not only the "sweet colour of the oriental sapphire" (visual impressions) , but also tactual or thermic impressions, such as the "dense air" and the "fresh rivulets" which "parch the more" the throat of the thirsty. The belief that a picture yields only visual impressions is a curious illusion. The bloom on a cheek, the warmth of a youthful body, the sweetness and freshness of a fruit, the edge of a sharp knife, are not these, too, impressions obtainable from a picture? Are they visual? What would a picture mean to an imaginary man, lacking all or many of his senses, who should in an instant acquire the organ of sight alone? The picture we are looking at and believe we see only with our eyes would seem to his eyes to be little more than an artist's paint-smeared palette.

Some who hold firmly to the aesthetic character of certain groups of impressions (for example, the visual and auditive) , and exclude others, are nevertheless ready to admit that if visual and auditive impressions enter *directly* into the aesthetic fact, those of the other senses also enter into it, but only as *associated*. But this distinction is altogether arbitrary. Aesthetic expression is synthesis, in which it is impossible to distinguish direct and indirect. All impressions are placed by it on a level, in so far as they are aestheticized. A man who absorbs the subject of a picture or poem does not have it before him as a series of impressions, some of which have prerogatives and precedence over others. He knows nothing as to what has happened prior to having absorbed it, just as, on the other hand, distinctions made after reflexion have nothing whatever to do with art as such.

The theory of the aesthetic senses has also been presented in another way; as an attempt to establish what physiological organs are necessary for the aesthetic fact. The physiological organ or apparatus is nothing but a group of cells, constituted and disposed in a particular manner; that is to say, it is merely physical and natural fact or concept. But expression does not know physiological facts. Expression has its point of departure in the impressions, and the physiological path by which these have found their way to the mind is to it altogether indifferent. One way or another comes to the same thing: it suffices that they should be impressions.

It is true that the want of given organs, that is, of certain groups of cells, prevents the formation of certain impressions (when these are not otherwise obtained through a kind of organic compensation). The man born blind cannot intuit and express light. But the impressions are not conditioned solely by the organ, but also by the stimuli which operate upon the organ. One who has never had the impression of the sea will never be able to express it, in the same way as one who has never had the impression of the life of high society or of the political arena will never express either. This, however, does not prove the dependence of the expressive function on the stimulus or on the organ. It merely repeats what we know already: expression presupposes impression, and particular expressions particular impressions. For the rest, every impression excludes other impressions during the moment in which it dominates; and so does every expression.

Another corollary of the conception of expression as activity is the *indivisibility* of the work of art. Every expression is a single expression. Activity is a fusion of the impression in an organic whole. A desire to express this has always prompted the affirmation that the work of art should have *unity*, or, what amounts to the same thing, *unity in variety*. Expression is a synthesis of the various, or multiple, in the one.

The fact that we divide a work of art into parts, a poem into scenes, episodes, similes, sentences, or a picture into single figures and objects, background, foreground, etc., may seem opposed to this affirmation. But such division annihilates the work, as dividing the organism into heart, brain, nerves, muscles, and so on, turns the living being into a corpse. It is true that there exist organisms in which division gives rise to other living beings, but in such a case we must conclude, maintaining the analogy between the organism and the work of art, that in the latter case too there are numerous germs of life each ready to grow, in a moment, into a single complete expression.

It may be said that expression sometimes arises from other expressions.

There are simple and there are *compound* expressions. One must surely admit some difference between the *eureka,* with which Archimedes expressed all his joy at his discovery, and the expressive act (indeed all the five acts) of a regular tragedy.—Not in the least: expression always arises directly from impressions. He who conceives a tragedy puts into a crucible a great quantity, so to say, of impressions: expressions themselves, conceived on other occasions, are fused together with the new in a single mass, in the same way as we can cast into a melting furnace formless pieces of bronze and choicest statuettes. Those choicest statuettes must be melted just like the pieces of bronze, before there can be a new statue. The old expressions must descend again to the level of impressions, in order to be synthetized in a new single expression.

By elaborating his impressions, man *frees* himself from them. By objectifying them, he removes them from him and makes himself their superior. The liberating and purifying function of art is another aspect and another formula of its character as activity. Activity is the deliverer, just because it drives away passivity.

This also explains why it is usual to attribute to artists both the maximum of sensibility or *passion,* and the maximum of insensibility or Olympian *serenity.* The two characters are compatible, for they do not refer to the same object. The sensibility or passion relates to the rich material which the artist absorbs into his psychic organism; the insensibility or serenity to the form with which he subdues and dominates the tumult of the sensations and passions.

Note

1. "trees speak, not only beasts."

CLIVE BELL

The Aesthetic Hypothesis

I T IS IMPROBABLE that more nonsense has been written about aesthetics than about anything else: the literature of the subject is not large enough for that. It is certain, however, that about no subject with which I am acquainted has so little been said that is at all to the purpose. The explanation is discoverable. He who would elaborate a plausible theory of aesthetics must possess two qualities—artistic sensibility and a turn for clear thinking. Without sensibility a man can have no aesthetic experience, and, obviously, theories not based on broad and deep aesthetic experience are worthless. Only those for whom art is a constant source of passionate emotion can possess the data from which profitable theories may be deduced; but to deduce profitable theories even from accurate data involves a certain amount of brain-work, and, unfortunately, robust intellects and delicate sensibilities are not inseparable. As often as not, the hardest thinkers have had no aesthetic experience whatever. I have a friend blessed with an intellect as keen as a drill, who, though he takes an interest in aesthetics, has never during a life of almost forty years been guilty of an aesthetic emotion. So, having no faculty for distinguishing a work of art from a handsaw, he is apt to rear up a pyramid of irrefragable argument on the hypothesis that a handsaw is a work of art. This defect robs his perspicuous and subtle reasoning of much of its value; for it has ever been a maxim that faultless logic can win but little credit for conclusions that are based on premises notoriously false. Every cloud, however, has its silver lining, and this insensibility, though unlucky in that it makes my friend incapable of choosing a sound basis for his argument, mercifully blinds him to the absurdity of his conclusions while leaving him in full enjoyment of his masterly dialectic. People who set out from the hypothesis that Sir Edwin Landseer was the finest painter that ever lived will find no uneasiness about an aesthetic which proves that Giotto

First published in 1914 and reprinted from the Capricorn edition of *Art* by Clive Bell by permission of G. P. Putnam's Sons and Chatto and Windus Ltd, London.

was the worst. So, my friend, when he arrives very logically at the conclusion that a work of art should be small or round or smooth, or that to appreciate fully a picture you should pace smartly before it or set it spinning like a top, cannot guess why I ask him whether he has lately been to Cambridge, a place he sometimes visits.

On the other hand, people who respond immediately and surely to works of art, though, in my judgment, more enviable than men of massive intellect but slight sensibility, are often quite as incapable of talking sense about aesthetics. Their heads are not always very clear. They possess the data on which any system must be based, but, generally, they want the power that draws correct inferences from true data. Having received aesthetic emotions from works of art, they are in a position to seek out the quality common to all that have moved them, but, in fact, they do nothing of the sort. I do not blame them. Why should they bother to examine their feelings when for them to feel is enough? Why should they stop to think when they are not very good at thinking? Why should they hunt for a common quality in all objects that move them in a particular way when they can linger over the many delicious and peculiar charms of each as it comes? So, if they write criticism and call it aesthetics, if they imagine they are talking about Art when they are talking about particular works of art or even about the technique of painting, if loving particular works they find tedious the consideration of art in general, perhaps they have chosen the better part. If they are not curious about the nature of their emotion, nor about the quality common to all objects that provoke it, they have my sympathy, and, as what they say is often charming and suggestive, my admiration too. Only let no one suppose that what they write and talk is aesthetics: it is criticism, or just "shop."

The starting-point for all systems of aesthetics must be the personal experience of a peculiar emotion. The objects that provoke this emotion we call works of art. All sensitive people agree that there is a peculiar emotion provoked by works of art. I do not mean, of course, that all works provoke the same emotion. On the contrary, every work produces a different emotion. But all these emotions are recognisably the same in kind; so far, at any rate, the best opinion is on my side. That there is a particular kind of emotion provoked by works of visual art, and that this emotion is provoked by every kind of visual art, by pictures, sculptures, buildings, pots, carvings, textiles, etc., etc., is not disputed, I think, by anyone capable of feeling it. This emotion is called the aesthetic emotion; and if we can discover some quality common and peculiar to all the objects that provoke it, we shall have solved what I take to be the central problem of aesthetics. We shall have discovered the essential quality in a work of art, the quality that distinguishes works of art from all other classes of objects.

For either all works of visual art have some common quality, or when we speak of "works of art" we gibber. Everyone speaks of "art," making a mental classification by which he distinguishes the class "works of art" from all other classes. What is the justification of this classification? What is the quality common and peculiar to all members of this class? Whatever it be, no doubt it is often found in company with other qualities; but they are adventitious—it is essential. There must be some one quality without which a work of art cannot exist; possessing which in the least degree, no work is altogether worthless. What is this quality? What quality is shared by all objects that provoke our aesthetic emotions? What quality is common to St. Sophia and the windows at Chartres, Mexican sculpture, a Persian bowl, Chinese carpets, Giotto's frescoes at Padua, and the masterpieces of Poussin, Piero della Francesca, and Cézanne? Only one answer seems possible—significant form. In each, lines and colours combined in a particular way, certain forms and relations of forms, stir our aesthetic emotions. These relations and combinations of lines and colours, these aesthetically moving forms, I shall call "Significant Form"; and "Significant Form" is the one quality common to all works of visual art.

At this point it may be objected that I am making aesthetics a purely subjective business, since my only data are personal experiences of a particular emotion. It will be said that the objects that provoke this emotion vary with each individual, and that therefore a system of aesthetics can have no objective validity. It must be replied that any system of aesthetics which pretends to be based on some objective truth is so palpably ridiculous as not to be worth discussing. We have no other means of recognising a work of art than our feeling for it. The objects that provoke aesthetic emotion vary with each individual. Aesthetic judgments are, as the saying goes, matters of taste; and about tastes, as everyone is proud to admit, there is no disputing. A good critic may be able to make me see in a picture that had left me cold things that I had overlooked, till at last, receiving the aesthetic emotion, I recognise it as a work of art. To be continually pointing out those parts, the sum, or rather the combination, of which unite to produce significant form, is the function of criticism. But it is useless for a critic to tell me that something is a work of art; he must make me feel it for myself. This he can do only by making me see; he must get at my emotions through my eyes. Unless he can make me see something that moves me, he cannot force my emotions. I have no right to consider anything a work of art to which I cannot react emotionally, and I have no right to look for the essential quality in anything that I have not *felt* to be a work of art. The critic can affect my aesthetic theories only by affecting my aesthetic experience. All systems of aesthetics must be based on personal experience—that is to say, they must be subjective.

Yet, though all aesthetic theories must be based on aesthetic judgments, and ultimately all aesthetic judgments must be matters of personal taste, it would be rash to assert that no theory of aesthetics can have general validity. For, though A, B, C, D are the works that move me, and A, D, E, F the works that move you, it may well be that *x* is the only quality believed by either of us to be common to all the works in his list. We may all agree about aesthetics, and yet differ about particular works of art. We may differ as to the presence or absence of the quality *x*. My immediate object will be to show that significant form is the only quality common and peculiar to all the works of visual art that move me; and I will ask those whose aesthetic experience does not tally with mine to see whether this quality is not also, in their judgment, common to all works that move them, and whether they can discover any other quality of which the same can be said.

Also at this point a query arises, irrelevant indeed, but hardly to be suppressed: "Why are we so profoundly moved by forms related in a particular way?" The question is extremely interesting, but irrelevant to aesthetics. In pure aesthetics we have only to consider our emotion and its object: for the purposes of aesthetics we have no right, neither is there any necessity, to pry behind the object into the state of mind of him who made it. Later, I shall attempt to answer the question; for by so doing I may be able to develop my theory of the relation of art to life. I shall not, however, be under the delusion that I am rounding off my theory of aesthetics. For a discussion of aesthetics, it need be agreed only that forms arranged and combined according to certain unknown and mysterious laws do move us in a particular way, and that it is the business of an artist so to combine and arrange them that they shall move us. These moving combinations and arrangements I have called, for the sake of convenience and for a reason that will appear later, "Significant Form."

A third interruption has to be met.

"Are you forgetting about colour?" someone inquires. Certainly not; my term "significant form" included combinations of lines and of colours. The distinction between form and colour is an unreal one; you cannot conceive a colourless line or a colourless space; neither can you conceive a formless relation of colours. In a black and white drawing the spaces are all white and all are bounded by black lines; in most oil paintings the spaces are multi-coloured and so are the boundaries; you cannot imagine a boundary line without any content, or a content without a boundary line. Therefore, when I speak of significant form, I mean a combination of lines and colours (counting white and black as colours) that moves me aesthetically.

Some people may be surprised at my not having called this "beauty." Of course, to those who define beauty as "combinations of lines and colours that provoke aesthetic emotion," I willingly concede the right of substituting their word for mine. But most of us, however strict we may be, are apt to apply the epithet "beautiful" to objects that do not provoke that peculiar emotion produced by works of art. Everyone, I suspect, has called a butterfly or a flower beautiful. Does anyone feel the same kind of emotion for a butterfly or a flower that he feels for a cathedral or a picture? Surely, it is not what I call an aesthetic emotion that most of us feel, generally, for natural beauty. I shall suggest, later, that some people may, occasionally, see in nature what we see in art, and feel for her an aesthetic emotion; but I am satisfied that, as a rule, most people feel a very different kind of emotion for birds and flowers and the wings of butterflies from that which they feel for pictures, pots, temples and statues. Why these beautiful things do not move us as works of art move is another, and not an aesthetic question. For our immediate purpose we have to discover only what quality is common to objects that do move us as works of art. In the last part of this chapter, when I try to answer the question—"Why are we so profoundly moved by some combinations of lines and colours?" I shall hope to offer an acceptable explanation of why we are less profoundly moved by others.

Since we call a quality that does not raise the characteristic aesthetic emotion "Beauty," it would be misleading to call by the same name the quality that does. To make "beauty" the object of the aesthetic emotion, we must give to the word an over-strict and unfamiliar definition. Everyone sometimes uses "beauty" in an unaesthetic sense; most people habitually do. To everyone, except perhaps here and there an occasional aesthete, the commonest sense of the word is unaesthetic. Of its grosser abuse, patent in our chatter about "beautiful huntin'" and "beautiful shootin'," I need not take account; it would be open to the precious to reply that they never do so abuse it. Besides, here there is no danger of confusion between the aesthetic and the non-aesthetic use; but when we speak of a beautiful woman there is. When an ordinary man speaks of a beautiful woman he certainly does not mean only that she moves him aesthetically; but when an artist calls a withered old hag beautiful he may sometimes mean what he means when he calls a battered torso beautiful. The ordinary man, if he be also a man of taste, will call the battered torso beautiful, but he will not call a withered hag beautiful because, in the matter of women, it is not to the aesthetic quality that the hag may possess, but to some other quality that he assigns the epithet. Indeed, most of us never dream of going for aesthetic emotions to human beings, from whom we ask something very different. This "something," when we find it in a young woman, we are apt to call "beauty." We live in a nice age. With the man-in-the-street "beautiful" is more often than not synonymous with "desirable"; the word does not necessarily connote any aesthetic reaction whatever, and I am tempted to believe that in the minds of many the sexual flavour of the word is stronger than the aesthetic. I have noticed a consistency in those to whom the most beautiful thing in the world is a beautiful woman, and the next most beautiful thing a picture of one. The confusion between aesthetic and sensual beauty is not in their case so great as might be supposed. Perhaps there is none; for perhaps they have never had an aesthetic emotion to confuse with their other emotions. The art that they call "beautiful" is generally closely related to the women. A beautiful picture is a photograph of a pretty girl; beautiful music, the music that provokes emotions similar to those provoked by young ladies in musical farces; and beautiful poetry, the poetry that recalls the same emotions felt, twenty years earlier, for the rector's daughter. Clearly the word "beauty" is used to connote the objects of quite distinguishable emotions, and that is a reason for not employing a term which would land me inevitably in confusions and misunderstandings with my readers.

On the other hand, with those who judge it more exact to call these combinations and arrangements of form that provoke our aesthetic emotions, not "significant form," but "significant relations of form," and then try to make the best of two worlds, the aesthetic and the metaphysical, by calling these relations "rhythm," I have no quarrel whatever. Having made it clear that by "significant form" I mean arrangements and combinations that move us in a particular way, I willingly join hands with those who prefer to give a different name to the same thing.

The hypothesis that significant form is the essential quality in a work of art has at least one merit denied to many more famous and more striking—it does help to explain things. We are all familiar with pictures that interest us and excite our admiration, but do not move us as works of art. To this class belongs what I call "Descriptive Painting"—that is, painting in which forms are used not as objects of emotion, but as means of suggesting emotion or conveying information. Portraits of psychological and historical value, topographical works, pictures that tell stories and suggest situations, illustrations of all sorts, belong to this class. That we all recognize the distinction is clear, for who has not said that such and such a drawing was excellent as illustration, but as a work of art worthless? Of course many descriptive pictures possess, amongst other qualities, formal significance, and are therefore works of art: but many more do not. They interest us; they may move us too in a hundred different ways, but they do not move us aesthetically. According to my hypothesis they are not works of art. They leave untouched our aesthetic emotions because it is not their forms but the ideas or information suggested or conveyed by their forms that affect us.

Few pictures are better known or liked than Frith's "Paddington Station"; certainly I should be the last to grudge it its popularity. Many a weary forty minutes have I whiled away disentangling its fascinating incidents and forging for each an imaginary past and an improbable future. But certain though it is that Frith's masterpiece, or engravings of it, have provided thousands with half-hours of curious and fanciful pleasure, it is not less certain that no one has experienced before it one half-second of aesthetic rapture—and this although the picture contains several pretty passages of colour, and is by no means badly painted. "Paddington Station" is not a work of art; it is an interesting and amusing document. In it line and colour are used to recount anecdotes, suggest ideas, and indicate the manners and customs of an age: they are not used to provoke aesthetic emotion. Forms and the relations of forms were for Frith not objects of emotion, but means of suggesting emotion and conveying ideas.

The ideas and information conveyed by "Paddington Station" are so amusing and so well presented that the picture has considerable value and is well worth preserving. But, with the perfection of photographic processes and of the cinematograph, pictures of this sort are becoming otiose. Who doubts that one of those *Daily Mirror* photographers in collaboration with a *Daily Mail* reporter can tell us far more about "London day by day" than any Royal Academician? For an account of manners and fashions we shall go, in future, to photographs, supported by a little bright journalism, rather than to descriptive painting. Had the imperial academicians of Nero, instead of manufacturing incredibly loathsome imitations of the antique, recorded in fresco and mosaic the manners and fashions of their day, their stuff, though artistic rubbish, would now be an historical gold-mine. If only they had been Friths instead of being Alma Tademas! But photography has made impossible any such transmutation of modern rubbish. Therefore it must be confessed that pictures in the Frith tradition are grown superfluous; they merely waste the hours of able men who might be more profitably employed in works of a wider beneficence. Still, they are not unpleasant, which is more than can be said for that kind of descriptive painting of which "The Doctor" is the most flagrant example. Of course "The Doctor" is not a work of art. In it form is not used as an object of emotion, but as a means of suggesting emotions. This alone suffices to make it nugatory; it is worse than nugatory because the emotion it suggests is false. What it suggests is not pity and admiration but a sense of complacency in our own pitifulness and generosity. It is sentimental. Art is above morals, or, rather, all art is moral because, as I hope to show presently, works of art are immediate means to good. Once we have judged a thing a work of art, we have judged it ethically of the first importance and put it beyond the reach of the moralist. But descriptive pictures which are not works of art, and, therefore, are not necessarily means to good states of mind, are proper subjects of the ethical philosopher's attention. Not being a work of art, "The Doctor" has none of the immense ethical value possessed by all objects that provoke aesthetic ecstasy; and the state of mind to which it is a means, as illustration, appears to me undesirable.

The works of those enterprising young men, the Italian Futurists, are notable examples of descriptive painting. Like the Royal Academicians, they use form, not to provoke aesthetic emotions, but to convey information and ideas. Indeed, the published theories of the Futurists prove that their pictures ought to have nothing whatever to do with art. Their social and political theories are respectable, but I would suggest to young Italian painters that it is possible to become a Futurist in thought and action and yet remain an artist, if one has the luck to be born one. To associate art with politics is always a mistake. Futurist pictures are descriptive because they aim at presenting in line and colour the chaos of the mind at a particular moment; their forms are not intended to promote aesthetic emotion but to convey information. These forms, by the way, whatever may be the nature of the ideas they suggest, are themselves anything but revolutionary. In such Futurist pictures as I have seen—perhaps I should except some by Severini—the drawing, whenever it becomes representative as it frequently does, is found to be in that soft and common convention brought into fashion by Besnard some thirty years ago, and much affected by Beaux-Art students ever since. As works of art, the Futurist pictures are negligible; but they are not to be judged as works of art. A good Futurist picture would succeed as a good piece of psychology succeeds; it would reveal, through line and colour, the complexities of an interesting state of mind. If Futurist pictures seem to fail, we must seek an explanation, not in a lack of artistic qualities that they were never intended to possess, but rather in the minds the states of which they are intended to reveal.

Most people who care much about art find that of the work that moves them most the greater part is what scholars call "Primitive." Of course there are bad primitives. For instance, I remember going, full of enthusiasm, to see one of the earliest Romanesque churches in Poitiers (Notre-Dame-La-Grande), and finding it as ill-proportioned, over-decorated, coarse, fat and heavy as any better class building by one of those highly civilised architects who flourished a thousand years earlier or eight hundred later. But such exceptions are rare. As a rule primitive art is good—and here again my hypothesis is helpful—for, as a rule, it is also free from descriptive qualities. In primitive art you will find no accurate representation; you will find only significant form. Yet no other art moves us so profoundly. Whether we consider Sumerian sculpture or pre-dynastic Egyptian art, or archaic Greek, or the Wei and T'ang masterpieces, or those early Japanese works of which I had the luck to see a few superb examples (especially two wooden Bodhisattvas) at the Shepherd's Bush Exhibition in 1910, or whether, coming nearer home, we consider the primitive Byzantine art of the sixth century and its primitive developments amongst the Western barbarians, or, turning far afield, we consider that mysterious and majestic art that flourished in Central and South America before the coming of the white men, in every case we observe three common characteristics—absence of representation, absence of technical swagger, sublimely impressive form. Nor is it hard to discover the connection between these three. Formal significance loses itself in preoccupation with exact representation and ostentatious cunning.

Naturally, it is said that if there is little representation and less saltimbancery in primitive art, that is because the primitives were unable to catch a likeness or cut intellectual capers. The contention is beside the point. There is truth in it, no doubt, though, were I a critic whose reputation depended on a power of impressing the public with a semblance of knowledge, I should be more cautious about urging it than such people generally are. For to suppose that the Byzantine masters wanted skill, or could not have created an illusion had they wished to do so, seems to imply ignorance of the amazingly dexterous realism of the notoriously bad works of that age. Very often, I fear, the misrepresentation of the primitives must be attributed to what the critics call, "wilful distortion." Be that as it may, the point is that, either from want of skill or want of will, primitives neither create illusions, nor make display of extravagant accomplishment, but concentrate their energies on the one thing needful —the creation of form. Thus they have created the finest works of art that we possess.

Let no one imagine that representation is bad in itself; a realistic form may be as significant, in its place as part of the design, as an abstract. But if a representative form has value, it is as form, not as representation. The representative element in a work of art may or may not be harmful; always it is irrelevant. For, to appreciate a work of art we need bring with us nothing from life, no knowledge of its ideas and affairs, no familiarity with its emotions. Art transports us from the world of man's activity to a world of aesthetic exultation. For a moment we are shut off from human interests; our anticipations and memories are arrested; we are lifted above the stream of life. The pure mathematician rapt in his studies knows a state of mind which I take to be similar, if not identical. He feels an emotion for his speculations which arises from no perceived relation between them and the lives of men, but springs, inhuman or super-human, from the heart of an abstract science. I wonder, sometimes, whether the appreciators of art and of mathematical solutions are not even more closely allied. Before we feel an aesthetic emotion for a combination of forms, do we not perceive intellectually the rightness and necessity of the combination? If we do, it would explain the fact that passing rapidly through a room we recognise a picture to be good, although we cannot say that it has provoked much emotion. We seem to have recognized intellectually the rightness of its forms without staying to fix our attention, and collect, as it were, their emotional significance. If this were so, it would be permissible to inquire whether it was the forms themselves or our perception of their rightness and necessity that caused aesthetic emotion. But I do not think I need linger to discuss the matter here. I have been inquiring why certain combinations of forms move us; I should not have travelled by other roads had I enquired, instead, why certain combinations are perceived to be right and necessary, and why our perception of their rightness and necessity is moving. What I have to say is this: the rapt philosopher, and he who contemplates a work of art, inhabit a world with an intense and peculiar significance of its own; that significance is unrelated to the significance of life. In this world the emotions of life find no place. It is a world with emotions of its own.

To appreciate a work of art we need bring with us nothing but a sense of form and colour and a knowledge of three-dimensional space. That bit of knowledge, I admit, is essential to the appreciation of many great works, since many of the most moving forms ever created are in three dimensions. To see a cube or a rhomboid as a flat pattern is to lower its significance, and a sense of three-dimensional space is essential to the full appreciation of most architectural forms. Pictures which would be insignificant if we saw them as flat patterns are profoundly moving because, in fact, we see them as related planes. If the representation of three-dimensional space is to be called "representation," then I agree that there is one kind of representation which is not irrelevant. Also, I agree that along with our feeling for line and colour we must bring with us our knowledge of space if we are to make the most of every kind of form. Nevertheless, there are significant designs to an appreciation of which this knowledge is not necessary; so, though it is not irrelevant to the appreciation of some works of art it is not essential to the appreciation of all. What we must say is that the representation of three-dimensional space is neither irrelevant nor essential to all art, and that every other sort of representation is irrelevant.

That there is an irrelevant representative or descriptive element in many great works of art is not in the least surprising. Why it is not surprising I shall try to show elsewhere. Representation is not of necessity baneful, and highly realistic forms may be extremely significant. Very often, however, representation is a sign of weakness in an artist. A painter too feeble to create forms that provoke more than a little aesthetic emotion will try to eke that little out by suggesting the emotions of life. To evoke the emotions of life he must use representation. Thus a man will paint an execution, and, fearing to miss with his first barrel of significant form, will try to hit with his second by raising an emotion of fear or pity. But if in the artist an inclination to play upon the emotions of life is often the sign of a flickering inspiration, in the spectator a tendency to seek, behind form, the emotions of life is a sign of defective sensibility always. It means that his aesthetic emotions are weak or, at any rate, imperfect. Before a work of art people who feel little or no emotion for pure form find themselves at a loss. They are deaf men at a concert. They know that they are in the presence of something great, but they lack the power of apprehending it. They know that they ought to feel for it a tremendous emotion, but it happens that the particular kind of emotion it can raise is one that they can feel hardly or not at all. And so they read into the forms of the work those facts and ideas for which they are capable of feeling emotion, and feel for them the emotions that they can feel—the ordinary emotions of life. When confronted by a picture, instinctively they refer back its forms to the world from which they came. They treat created form as though it were imitated form, a picture as though it were a photograph. Instead of going out on the stream of art into a new world of aesthetic experience, they turn a sharp corner and come straight home to the world of human interests. For them the significance of a work of art depends on what they bring to it; no new thing is added to their lives, only the old material is stirred. A good work of visual art carries a person who is capable of appreciating it out of life into ecstasy; to use art as a means to the emotions of life is to use a telescope for reading the news. You will notice that people who cannot feel pure aesthetic emotions remember pictures by their subjects; whereas people who can, as often as not, have no idea what the subject of a picture is. They have never noticed the representative element, and so when they discuss pictures they talk about the shapes of forms and the relations and quantities of colours. Often they can tell by the quality of a single line whether or not a man is a good artist. They are concerned only with lines and colours, their relations and quantities and qualities; but from these they win an emotion more profound and far more sublime than any that can be given by the description of facts and ideas.

This last sentence has a very confident ring—over-confident, some may think. Perhaps I shall be able to justify it, and make my meaning clearer too, if I give an account of my own feelings about music. I am not really musical. I do not understand music well. I find musical form exceedingly difficult to apprehend, and I am sure that the profounder subtleties of harmony and rhythm more often than not escape me. The form of a musical composition must be simple indeed if I am to grasp it honestly. My opinion about music is not worth having. Yet, sometimes, at a concert, though my appreciation of the music is limited and humble, it is pure. Sometimes, though I have a poor understanding, I have a clean palate. Consequently, when I am feeling bright and clear and intent, at the beginning of a concert, for instance, when something that I can grasp is being played, I get from music that pure aesthetic emotion that I get from visual art. It is less intense, and the rapture is evanescent; I understand music too ill for music to transport me far into the world of pure aesthetic ecstasy. But at moments I do appreciate music as pure musical form, as sounds combined according to the laws of a mysterious necessity, as pure art with a tremendous significance of its own and no relation whatever to the significance of life; and in those moments I lose myself in that infinitely sublime state of mind to which pure visual form transports me. How inferior is my normal state of mind at a concert. Tired or perplexed, I let slip my sense of form, my aesthetic emotion collapses, and I begin weaving into the harmonies, that I cannot grasp, the ideas of life. Incapable of feeling the austere emotions of art, I begin to read into the musical forms human emotions of terror and mystery, love and hate, and spend the minutes, pleasantly enough, in a world of turbid and inferior feeling. At such times, were the grossest pieces of onomatopoeic representation—the song of a bird, the galloping of horses, the cries of children, or the laughing of demons—to be introduced into the symphony, I should not be offended. Very likely I should be pleased; they would afford new points of departure for new trains of romantic feeling or heroic thought. I know very well what has happened. I have been using art as a means to the emotions of life and reading into it the ideas of life. I have been cutting blocks with a razor. I have tumbled from the superb peaks of aesthetic exaltation to the snug foothills of warm humanity. It is a jolly country. No one need be ashamed of enjoying himself there. Only no one who has ever been on the heights can help feeling a little crestfallen in the cosy valleys. And let no one imagine, because he had made merry in the warm tilth and quaint nooks of romance, that he can even guess at the austere and thrilling raptures of those who have climbed the cold, white peaks of art.

About music most people are as willing to be humble as I am. If they cannot grasp musical form and win from it a pure aesthetic emotion, they confess that they understand music imperfectly or not at all. They recognise quite clearly that there is a difference between the feeling of the musician for pure music and that of the cheerful concert-goer for what music suggests. The latter enjoys his own emotions, as he has every right to do, and recognises their inferiority. Unfortunately, people are apt to be less modest about their powers of appreciating visual art. Everyone is inclined to believe that out of pictures, at any rate, he can get all that there is to be got; everyone is ready to cry "humbug" and "imposter" at those who say that more can be had. The good faith of people who feel pure aesthetic emotions is called in question by those who have never felt anything of the sort. It is the prevalance of the representative element, I suppose, that makes the man in the street so sure that he knows a good picture when he sees one. For I have noticed that in matters of architecture, pottery, textiles, etc., ignorance and ineptitude are more willing to defer to the opinions of those who have been blest with peculiar sensibility. It is a pity that cultivated and intelligent men and women cannot be induced to believe that a great gift of aesthetic appreciation is at least as rare in visual as in musical art. A comparison of my own experience in both has enabled me to discriminate very clearly between pure and impure appreciation. Is it too much to ask that others should be as honest about their feelings for pictures as I have been about mine for music? For I am certain that most of those who visit galleries do feel very much what I feel at concerts. They have their moments of pure ecstasy; but the moments are short and unsure. Soon they fall back into the world of human interests and feel emotions, good no doubt, but inferior. I do not dream of saying that what they get from art is bad or nugatory; I say that they do not get the best that art can give. I do not say that they cannot understand art; rather I say that they cannot understand the state of mind of those who understand it best. I do not say that art means nothing or little to them; I say they miss its full significance. I do not suggest for one moment that their appreciation of art is a thing to be ashamed of; the majority of the charming and intelligent people with whom I am acquainted appreciate visual art impurely; and, by the way, the appreciation of almost all great writers has been impure. But provided that there be some fraction of pure aesthetic emotion, even a mixed and minor appreciation of art is, I am sure, one of the most valuable things in the world—so valuable, indeed, that in my giddier moments I have been tempted to believe that art might prove the world's salvation.

Yet, though the echoes and shadows of art enrich the life of the plains, her spirit dwells on the mountains. To him who woos, but woos impurely, she returns enriched what is brought. Like the sun, she warms the good seed in good soil and causes it to bring forth good fruit. But only to the perfect lover does she give a new strange gift—a gift beyond all price. Imperfect lovers bring to art and take away the ideas and emotions of their own age and civilisation. In twelfth-century Europe a man might have been greatly moved by a Romanesque church and found nothing in a T'ang picture. To a man of a later age, Greek sculpture meant much and Mexican nothing, for only to the former could he bring a crowd of associated ideas to be the objects of familiar emotions. But the perfect lover, he who can feel the profound significance of form, is raised above the accidents of time and place. To him the problems of archaeology, history, and hagiography are impertinent. If the forms of a work are significant its provenance is irrelevant. Before the grandeur of those Sumerian figures in the Louvre he is carried on the same flood of emotion to the same aesthetic ecstasy as, more than four thousand years ago, the Chaldean lover was carried. It is the mark of great art that its appeal is universal and eternal.[1] Significant form stands charged with the power to provoke aesthetic emotion in anyone capable of feeling it. The ideas of men go buzz and die like gnats; men change their institutions and their customs as they change their coats; only great art remains stable and unobscure. Great art remains stable and unobscure because the feelings that it awakens are independent of time and place, because its kingdom is not of this world. To those who have and hold a sense of the significance of form what does it matter whether the forms that move them were created in Paris the day before yesterday or in Babylon fifty centuries ago? The forms of art are inexhaustible; but all lead by the same road of aesthetic emotion to the same world of aesthetic ecstasy.

Note

1. Mr. Roger Fry permits me to make use of an interesting story that will illustrate my view. When Mr. Okakura, the Government editor of *The Temple Treasures of Japan*, first came to Europe, he found no difficulty in appreciating the pictures of those who from want of will or want of skill did not create illusions but concentrated their energies on the creation of form. He understood immediately the Byzantine masters and the French and Italian Primitives. In the

Renaissance painters, on the other hand, with their descriptive preoccupations, their literary and anecdotic interests, he could see nothing but vulgarity and muddle. The universal and essential quality of art, significant form, was missing, or rather had dwindled to a shallow stream, overlaid and hidden beneath weeds, so the universal response, aesthetic emotion, was not evoked. It was not till he came on to Henri-Matisse that he again found himself in the familiar world of pure art. Similarly, sensitive Europeans who respond immediately to the significant forms of great Oriental art, are left cold by the trivial pieces of anecdote and social criticism so lovingly cherished by Chinese dilettanti. It would be easy to multiply instances did not decency forbid the labouring of so obvious a truth.

DEWITT H. PARKER

The Nature of Art

THE ASSUMPTION underlying every philosophy of art is the existence of some common nature present in all the arts, despite their differences in form and content; something the same in painting and sculpture; in poetry and drama; in music and architecture. Every single work of art, it is admitted, has a unique flavor, a *je ne sais quoi* which makes it incomparable with every other work; nevertheless, there is some mark or set of marks which, if it applies to any work of art, applies to all works of art, and to nothing else—a common denominator, so to say, which constitutes the definition of art, and serves to separate, though not to isolate, the field of art from other fields of human culture. Consistent with this assumption is the experience that the study of one art throws light upon the study of the other arts—painting upon sculpture; music upon poetry and painting, and so on; expressed by the familiar habit of characterizing one art in terms of another art, as when we speak of architecture as frozen music; poetry as a picture; the poetry of architecture; the music of color and line; and the like.

The philosophy of art has however many things against it. The very possibility of a definition of art may be challenged, on at least two grounds. In the first place, it may be claimed that there is no significant nature common to all the arts which could serve as a basis for a definition. One may try to show that only confusion has resulted from the interpretation of one art in terms of another art; and to what a long history of fruitless controversy and darkening of counsel could one point as evidence with regard, for example, to Horace's famous phrase—*ut pictura poesis;* poetry like a picture. Each art, one might hold, since it makes use of a peculiar medium—color, tone, or what else—is subject to laws uniquely characteristic of it, and follows no others. Even such terms as "painting" are likely to be more misleading than useful; for water color is a different sort of thing from oil; and mural painting, from easel pic-

Reprinted from the *Revue Internationale de Philosophie,* July 1939.

tures; and there is all the difference in the world, say, between a Byzantine mosaic and a Renaissance nude. Or what have ceramics in common with music; a skyscraper with Michaelangelo's "Day and Night"? And while there may be some convenience in using a term like literature to include both the novels of Sinclair Lewis and Baudelaire's *Fleurs du Mal*, let anyone beware of judging either by the standards of the other! It is equally convenient in the general delivery room of a postoffice to put all letters the names of whose addresses begin with B in one box, and those whose names begin with P in another box; but it does not follow that the owners of the letters in one box are more significantly like each other than they are like the owners of letters in the other box. Thus might one oppose a radical pluralism regarding the arts to the monism maintained by the philosophers.

The second ground for scepticism regarding the possibility of a definition of art is the difficulty of finding, not some nature common to all the arts, which was the first difficulty, but some criterion by means of which the sphere of art can be definitely separated from other human activities. It is interesting to recall that the Greeks never sharply distinguished the aesthetic arts from the other arts and crafts, using a single word, *techne,* for all; and that, for them, beauty and the good, which may be present in any experience, were identical. And until the beginning of the eighteenth century, expert opinion—barring certain prophetic exceptions—was against any absolute separation of art from other elements of culture, leaning in general to the view that beauty is a kind of truth, distinguishable from the truth of science or philosophy in no essential particular. When finally as a result of the reflexions of such men as Dubos, Vico, Kant, and Schiller there was promise of a genuine philosophy of art, the view that art has a unique nature and function came, not long after, in the middle of the last century, to be associated with the so-called theory of art for art's sake—a theory which, because it tended completely to isolate art from life, brought the whole philosophy of art into disrepute. Aside from its philosophic basis, the theory of art for art's sake was largely a reaction of sensitive minds against what seemed at the time to be the brutalities of industrialism and democracy. A vivid expression of this attitude is given by Th. Gauthier in the introduction to his poems: "My world is bounded by my window pane," he says, "I write poetry because I have nothing to do; and I have nothing to do in order that I may write poetry." In other words, art is a realm entirely separated from the interests of real life—a refuge for detached and gifted souls from sordid political and economic struggles.

It was thus the unhappy fate of the philosophy of art to become entangled with the point of view of the dwellers in the ivory tower. And it was inevitable that there should appear a counter-movement of ideas going to the opposite extreme, seeking not only to bring art back into connection with life, but to prove against the philosophers that art has no peculiar nature or function. The psychological motivation behind this attitude is interesting to notice; for it was the exact opposite of the motive that lay behind the theory of art for art's sake. For whereas that was expressive of a horrified retreat from life, this was expressive of an intense love of life, and a constant preoccupation with its larger social problems. While for the aesthetes the life of their own time was hateful; for the defenders of this counter point of view there was loveliness and fascination in all that was novel and characteristic of the present as compared with the past.[1] The railway carriage seemed to them an aesthetically more effective thing than the horse-drawn carriage; the steamboat than the sailboat; the factory than the shop; the open forum of democratic discussion than the stuffy cabinet of kings. Beauty, it was felt, is no privilege of art; but a pervasive property of our common experience. The doctrine of the aesthetes that art is a more perfect thing than life was reversed: in comparison with the zestful richness of life, art seemed a poor affair, winning for itself significance only through its connection with life itself.

In our own day we find the same two opposing attitudes towards art. The one is well represented by such a statement as this from *Art* by Clive Bell: ". . . to appreciate a work of art we need bring with us nothing from life, no knowledge of its ideas and affairs, no familiarity with its emotions." To represent the counter point of view I would quote from a young writer on aesthetics as follows: "Anything in the world which satisfies any desire may be regarded as beautiful . . . anyone who uses intelligence and skill to fill a need is an artist; and every work of man which ministers to want is a work of art."[2] And the same motive is at work as in the last century, protesting against the effort to find some distinctive sphere for art and beauty, namely, the wish to think well of life in its current form—to proclaim the beauty of its democratic texture and the glory of its mechanisms; only instead of steamboats and steam engines we hear of motor cars and airplanes. Or the motive may be associated with that of the reformer, namely, to wish to transform life into a new and presumably better form, that of socialism. This motive is well expressed by a distinguished veteran in philosophic analysis, who has recently turned his attention from the troubled ground of social theory to the quieter pastures of art, as follows: "The hostility to association of fine art with normal processes of living is a pathetic, even tragic commentary on life as it is ordinarily lived. Only because that life is usually so stunted, aborted, slack, or heavy laden, is the idea entertained that there is some inherent antagonism between the process of normal living, and creation and enjoyment of works of aesthetic art."[3] Sometimes the doctrine that there is some feature distinctive of art as compared with an airplane, or some quality peculiar to beauty as compared with ordinary satisfactory experience is deemed to be a superstition symptomatic of an aristocratic or bourgeois ideology that should long ago have atrophied in the body-politic. And in this also history is repeating itself.

To find the motivation of a point of view is not to refute it; and no theory is ever held for long by serious men, or recurs again and again in the history of thought without some evidence in its favor. The student of aesthetic theories who watches the rhythmic appearance of opposing ideas learns to look for the facts covered by each, and to draw the moral that none was wrong, but only inadequate. And while it is impossible to frame a satisfactory theory by mere eclectic synthesis of opinions, it remains true that the aesthetician who neglects the history of his subject runs the risk of proclaiming as new ideas that are centuries old, or of overlooking some aspect of a subject-matter so complex and subtle that no one mind is able to see around and into all of it. There are two deductions from the study of ideas regarding art that leap to the eyes with especial force. The first is the impossibility of finding some simple formula that will serve as a definition of art. All the so popular brief definitions of art—"significant form," "expression," "intuition," "objectified pleasure,"—are fallacious, either because, while true of art, they are also true of much that is not art, and hence fail to differentiate art from other things; or else because they neglect some essential aspect of art. Art is itself so complex a fact that a satisfactory definition of it must also be complex, that is to say, must involve many characteristics. As the mathematicians would say, the characteristics must be not only necessary but sufficient. They must penetrate deep enough into the roots of art to meet the challenge of the pluralists and show that there is, after all, a significant sameness in all the arts,—despite their differences in technique and media,—connecting the fine with the applied arts, so far as the latter are beautiful, and the realistic with the fanciful and the idyllic. The other deduction is that however sharply art is differentiated from life, its deep connection with life must be revealed in any definition. This is the enduring truth underlying all criticism of the ivory tower. With these lessons from history in mind, I shall now briefly explain how I think a good account of art may be framed.

I begin with a truism, that a work of art has value; or, in other words, that it is a source of satisfaction. For a work of art is not a given thing, like a star or a tree, but a thing made by man, and for his pleasure. And I wish further to premise that all value, as satisfaction, arises through the appeasement of what in a general way may be called desire. Desire in the broad sense in which I am using that term is at once the motivation of all experience, its inward drive, and the source of its value. And the truth underlying the opposition to every type of theory of art for art's sake is the fact that the substance of the aesthetic experience is the same as the substance of all experience, a satisfaction that is the result of the appeasement of identical desires. Almost any desire that urges man on in life reappears in his art. There are no peculiar elementary aesthetic interests or emotions. What is different is the mode by which desire is appeased. For while, in ordinary experience, desire is occupied with real objects and is satisfied through a course of action leading to a goal that involves interaction with the real environment physical or social, in the case of art, desire is directed upon immanent or fictitious objects, and is appeased, not through a course of action leading to a distant goal, but in present, given experience. This mode of satisfying desire I call satisfaction in the imagination. Such a use of the term imagination has been criticized on the ground that aesthetic appreciation is not always concerned with images or fictions, but in the case of music, or the color and line patterns of a picture, with sensory material. But such criticism betrays ignorance of the long use of the term in exactly the sense in which I am employing it in the history of critical writing. For example, in the *Spectator* Addison writes of the Pleasures of the Imagination, in which he includes the pleasures of a country landscape. But while it is true that in the aesthetic experience, sensory material is as important as imaginal, it is also true that all material there has the status of the image; that is to say, it has the same freedom from reference to the physical world of action that is possessed by images, as in a dream.

I can explain what I mean by imagination through a comparison between the experience to be derived from a still life picture and the experience which is had from the set-up from which it is painted. Let us suppose that the set-up contains a cup. Then the sensory material of our experience in each case with regard to the item of the cup is much the same—there is color and there is shape. And whatever satisfaction so dear to the connoisseur may be gained from the shape as shape and the color as color, will also be much the same. Moreover, the interpretation of this sensory material is the same in both cases: it is interpreted through the idea or meaning, cup. But observe now the differences between the two experiences. For while the interests that center on the real cup, such as filling it and drinking out of it, may be satisfied by a series of actions and interactions with it, these same interests cannot be so satisfied with regard to the picture of the cup. Yet they can be satisfied in a way, but only by the idea or appearance of the cup, as if the cup were seen in a dream. We can still *imagine* ourselves touching it and filling it and drinking out of it; to us it may be *as if* we were actually doing all these things with it; and so imagining we may provide a satisfaction of a sort to the same habits or interests that would be satisfied if we were actually to handle it and drink from it. If we could give to a dream of a cup all the sensuous fullness and vividness characteristic of perception, then the aesthetic satisfaction which we could get out of the dream would be the same as that which we get out of the still life picture. In both cases the satisfaction would be a satisfaction in a given sensuous shape and in the immediacy of an idea or meaning, rather than a satisfaction in a course of action upon a real thing which this shape and this meaning might suggest. And that is what Kant meant when he said that aesthetic satisfaction is disinterested—a satisfaction in mere representation of objects, independent of anything that we can get out of the existence of the objects.

In imagination, ideas or meanings are as important as sensuous shapes. The denial of this is the grand error of our contemporary aesthetes. I have already quoted from the famous passage of Clive Bell in which this denial is expressed. Let me cite the whole of it. "The representative element in a work of art may or may not be helpful; always it is irrelevant. For to appreciate a work of art, we need bring with us nothing from life, no knowledge of its ideas and affairs, no familiarity with its emotions." But could we say of any poetry, of such lines as these for example,

> O western wind, when wilt thou blow
> That the small rain down can rain?
>
> Christ, that my love were in my arms
> And I in my bed again.

that to appreciate their beauty we need bring with us nothing from life, no knowledge of its ideas and affairs, no familiarity with its emotions? It is true, of course, that without beauty of sensuous form there is no poetry; but it is equally true that without ideas, poetry is nothing but a sweet trivial jingle. One may object that Clive Bell was writing of painting, not of poetry; but it is no less false to the whole tradition and intent of painting to claim that the representative element, which is the element of meaning, is irrelevant. Significant indeed was the movement of modern art away from conventional and literal representation; but there is a valid middle ground, which all important painters have occupied, between the extremes of prosaic copying, and no representation at all. Universally significant for painting is the presence of object-meanings derived from nature and human life: the figure, the landscape, even the inner life as revealed through the face; the precise way in which such meanings are conveyed is unimportant, varying all the way from the schematism of early Christian art to the realism of a Masaccio; but the meanings as meanings have as legitimate a place in the art as rhythm, mass, space, light, and shade, and color. No one can fairly compare an abstraction of Braque with a painting by Renoir and fail to appreciate the rich value that is added by meaning; the former offers to the imagination an elemental satisfaction through the factors enumerated (Roger Fry's list); the latter, all of this, and a world besides. Music is the only art that can satisfy the hunger of the imagination through sensuous shape alone.

The necessity for the inclusion of meaning in imagination is proved by the case of architecture: As in a poem, there is a union of the sensuous beauty of formal pattern with underlying meaning, so in architecture there is a union of formal with functional layers of beauty. To eliminate either is arbitrarily to distort the simple facts of both creation and appreciation. The same truth holds for every work of the industrial and applied arts. The sole alternative to the recognition of the part that functional ideas play in the beauty of these things is to exclude them from the house of art altogether; but to do so with regard to, say pottery and basketry, would be as arbitrary as to deny beauty to Chartres or La Miniatura.[4] The industrial arts have always proved to be stumbling blocks to aesthetic theory. It is said that the field of art is mere appearance, unreality, illusion: well, what is more real than a building or a pot? Or it is said that beauty has nothing to do with utility: well, is it not obvious that fitness of form to function plays a part in the beauty of pots, baskets, houses, and the like? The only way to solve the difficulty is to recognize that the practical meaning, as a pure meaning, does enter into the aesthetic experience of such things. It is of course true that the aesthetic value of a building is not the same as its practical value: one does not have to live in it or own it in order to appreciate its beauty. Or one does not have to wear a shoe in order to know that it is beautiful; "window shopping"—a good example of imaginative satisfaction—proves that this is so. Not that wearing the shoe or living in the house is a hindrance to appreciation; they may, on the contrary, be helps; but the value that arises from use is not the same as the aesthetic value. The aesthetic value is a transfer of the practical value to the plane of imagination. The beauty of the shoe is in the way the shoe looks, not in the way it feels; but it must look as if it would feel good. So the beauty of the house is not the living well in it; but the way it looks as if one could live well in it. It is in the memory or anticipation of its service—twin phases of imagination —that its beauty resides. The use is in action; the beauty in the pure meaning. The recognition that the practical meaning, as a pure meaning, may enter into the beauty of an object thus solves the paradox of the industrial arts, and reconciles the contention of those who insist on the connection of art with life, with the disinterestedness of beauty proclaimed by the aesthetes and the philosophers.

Our first item in the definition of art is then the provision of satisfaction in the imagination, imagination being defined in a rich sense, inclusive of sensuous patterns and meanings, in the way indicated. But like other single-idea definitions, this criterion while necessary is not sufficient; for it does not serve to exclude from art things that we know do not belong there. It does not exclude the dream at night, the day-dream, and many kinds of play. The simplest of all examples of satisfaction through the imagination is perhaps the day-dream. If a politician seeking office by election allows himself to day-dream the ceremony whereby he is proclaimed the winner, it is clear that he is getting satisfaction, not by a real course of action that leads him in fact to his goal, but through a purely fictitious occurrence which he conjures up in his own mind, for himself. But, be it noted, the motivating desire is the same in both cases, as I have insisted; the difference lying in the method by means of which the desire is satisfied. In the case of the dream at night—certainly when the dream is what we call a pleasant dream—there is again satisfaction of desire, but obviously not by means of a course of action leading to a goal—for the dreamer, fast asleep, acts not at all—but by means of images created by the desire itself. The same formula of satisfaction through the imagination holds for the phantasy play of the child. The lonely child that creates for itself a dream-companion, and carries on an animated conversation with it; the little girl playing, as we say, with a doll, but actually with an imaginary baby, are both satisfying an interest or habit through an ideal, substitute object; like the dreamer and the artist, they are creating a world out of fancies to meet their desires. It is correct therefore to speak of art as a dream—a waking dream—in both there is the same creativeness; the same absorption in immediacy; and yet it is clear that mere dreaming is not art.

The second criterion that I would propose in order that we may come closer to the distinctive nature of art, is that art is social. By this I mean, first negatively, that the satisfactions of art do not depend upon factors peculiar to an individual, but rather, positively, upon types of objects that may be present in the experience of anyone. The satisfaction that is taken in a keepsake—a lock of hair, a faded rose—illustrates a satisfaction that depends upon the special "conditioning" of the individual; so likewise does the satisfaction taken by the victor in a conquest—impossible obviously for the vanquished. It is equally impossible for me to share your satisfaction in your dreams, because both the sources of satisfaction and the dream images which are the objects of the satisfaction, are private. But in the case of art, the satisfaction does not depend upon the peculiar circumstances and conditioning of the individual, but upon patterns of sense and meanings that are potentially universal. You cannot dream the dream that I dream, but you can see the same pattern of color or hear the same harmonies and melodies that I hear; and you can understand the same meanings that I understand, when we both read a poem or look at a picture. I do not mean to deny, of course, the evident differences that exist among the experiences of the same work of art in the case of different individuals. When I read

> Son of man
> You cannot say or guess, for you know only
> A heap of broken images, where the sun beats

the associations aroused by each key word in my mind and in yours will differ; yet there will be a core of meaning that will be the same; and this sameness will grow greater and approximate the meaning of the poet, as we study the poem more carefully. Sometimes no definite meaning, but only a mood will be communicated, as when we read Gertrude Stein's *Portrait of Picasso,* a mood that the writer may mistake for the essence of the object—but that does not matter.

But when I say that art is social I mean even more than this. I mean not only that there are common factors in our enjoyment of it, but that our enjoyment depends partly upon knowing that this is so. We may enjoy a work of art in loneliness, but afterwards we want to talk about it to our friends, and make sure that they enjoyed it too. I would even venture to assert that if some despot were to decree that no one should from this day forth speak or write or in any other way communicate with his fellows about books, pictures, plays, music, there would be an end to aesthetic creation and enjoyment. Art could not survive in a world of utter privacy and silence. The communicability of the value of art is, as Kant insisted, an essential fact about it. A work of art cannot be beautiful just for me, because its beauty, that is to say, its value, depends upon the possibility of sharing it.

Not only our pleasures, but also our standards with regard to art are social. In all aesthetic appreciation we can distinguish two phases, a primary phase of direct pleasure in what is offered us, and a secondary phase that arises through the fact that the work of art meets the standards which we bring to bear upon it. Without the direct appeal, the work of art is ineffective; but unless, besides, it measures up to our expectations, we are disappointed and disturbed. We come to every work of art with a fairly definite idea of what a work of art of that kind should be like; our approach is not naive, but critical and sophisticated. A good picture, a good play, a good musical composition, must be so and so; or so and so. In this respect, to be sure, art is not peculiar; for we bring to every type of experience a preconceived idea of excellence. Every smoker has his own idea of what makes a good smoke. For one, it is a briar pipe, with a certain brand of tobacco; for another, it is a fine Havana cigar; for a third, a Lucky Strike; for a fourth, a Camel. What is peculiar about art in comparison with say, smoking, is that we claim for our standards social validity. If you like Camels, while I like Luckies; well, it is all right with me; we will agree to disagree, and that's the end of it; but if you don't like John Marin, I shall feel that there is something wrong with you, and I may call you a Philistine, and tell you that you are sadly in need of aesthetic education. And what you think of James Joyce is not a matter of indifference to me. If you give me provocation, I shall dispute with you about it until midnight. And unlike our standards of smoking, our standards for art are formed not merely on a basis of personal experience and comparison, but like our standards of manners and morals, on a basis of tradition and education. An aesthetic value is not a given thing, to take or to leave, but something to be educated into. What a long way we are from the mere dream! A work of art is part of the history and culture of a people; a dream is a transitory and trivial happening in an isolated brain. It would be an indignity to mention such commonplaces, were they not so flagrantly contradicted by certain "authorities."

Moreover, art is social not only for the appreciator, but also for the artist. A really fatal misunderstanding about this matter has arisen in certain quarters, in connection with the definition of art as "expression." That art is expression or self-expression, no one would deny. It is a free creation of an imaginary world through which the artist finds surcease for his desires and a solution for his problems. But art is not self-expression the way a baby's cry or a bird's song is; it is not even what Wordsworth called poetry, a spontaneous overflow of powerful feelings. No genuine artist is content merely to give form to his feelings, burning desire clean in creation, and out of its flame warming his heart with a merely private joy. On the contrary, he is building something for his group from whom he demands sympathy and understanding. He is not trying to please the group; that is the last thing he wishes to do; rather he is insisting that his group find pleasure in what pleases him. The idea that art is mere expression is valid only for the work of amateurs and dilettantes. Such people are, in fact, just expressing themselves for the sake of expression; amusing, pleasing themselves. They do not care whether anyone likes what they do or not; that is no part of their purpose. The improviser does not need an audience; the amateur painter will not show his work except perhaps and grudgingly to his wife or intimate friend. How different is the artist! He stands for something in a group and insists that what he creates shall be known and valued as he values it.

A final implication of the social character of art is the necessity that imagination shall be embodied in some physical thing by means of which it may be reproduced in many minds and at many moments. So close in fact is the connection between imagination and physical embodiment that common sense hardly knows how to distinguish between them. The unphilosophical mind means by the "Mona Lisa," a canvas that hangs on a wall in the Louvre; by the "Venus de Milo" a sculptured block of marble set up in another room of the palace; and by a poem something he can find written on a certain page of a certain book. He is like the Pagan who believes that God can be found in a certain temple or even in a certain piece of wood in a shrine. If you remind him that the same poem can be found in many books; the same statue in many blocks of marble, of which the one in the Louvre was probably not the original; or ask how a landscape can hang on a wall, or Venus who dwells on Olympus can live in a museum; and enquire how it happens that the same music may be heard in Budapest that he is hearing in New York, he would probably be as much puzzled as the Pagan nurtured in a creed outworn would be if you were to ask him how God can inhabit so many shrines and temples at once. The solution of the problem is, of course, as follows: just as the theologian distinguishes between God, whom no man hath seen at any time, and the temple, shrine or icon, where God may be supposed to "appear"; so we can distinguish between the *aesthetic object* or experience —a sensuous form, together with meanings underlying the form, which exists only in the imagination, and what I would call the *aesthetic instrument,* which is the vehicle for the imagination, and a part of the physical world. The "Mona Lisa" as a pattern of color and shape, and a system of meanings that may enter the same into the minds of thousands, is what I am calling the aesthetic object; while the painted canvas that one can dust and carry about and steal and recover is the aesthetic instrument; the *Waste Land,* as a system of words and meanings that you and I and the generations after may hear and, with sufficient pains, understand, is an aesthetic object, while any printed page upon which the poem is written is an aesthetic instrument; the "Venus de Milo," a gracious form beheld and adored by countless worshippers, is an aesthetic object, but the blocks of marble in which this form is incarnate are aesthetic instruments. But while it is important that this distinction be made and its validity recognized, one must not go the lengths of a Croce in affirming that the instrument has nothing to do with art. For the appreciator, the instrument is essential, because it makes the aesthetic experience communicable; and preserves it for future generations. Without the instrument it would be a mere dream, unknowable and ephemeral. Imagination and physical embodiment are two aspects of a single fact.

The physical aspect of a work of art is of supreme importance to the artist, also. It was said of Raphael that he painted with his mind, not with his hands; but however much truth this paradox contains, like all paradoxes, it conceals an equal amount of falsehood. For every painter knows that unless he has vision in his fingers he cannot have it in his mind. His long effort to conquer the physical medium of his art is essential to the growth of his imagination. Michelangelo's conception of the form as lying sleeping in the marble was, as Bosanquet remarked, a truer account of the facts regarding sculpture than ever Vasari's was regarding painting. And what of the relation of the violinist to his instrument or the dancer's to hers—her own body? Does not the instrument enter into the very meaning of their art for them? There are, it is true, certain arts where it almost seems as if the creative, as distinguished from the merely receptive phase of the art, has acquired independence of the instrument, even as Aristotle thought that intellect could free itself of the body and so become immortal: poetry, where the use of pen and paper, or perhaps today the typewriter, appears so irrelevant; the poet sometimes composing his verses entirely in his head, as Goethe composed his *Wanderers Nachtlied* during a walk; the music of the composer, as contrasted with the music of the performer, which may be born complete in the head of a Mozart; for which reason every Platonizing philosopher has felt that these two arts were superior to such arts as painting, sculpture, and dancing, where the relation of the artist to his instrument seems to be essential, and where the activity of the artist, since it involves manual skill no less than imagination places him among the handicraftsmen. And following out this relationship between imagination and instrument, we might go on to distinguish between these same arts of poetry and music, on the one hand, where the preservation and communication of imagination depend indeed upon a physical instrument—the score of a sonata or the page of a book of poetry—yet may be multiplied a millionfold; and the beauty of a building or a dance, on the other hand, that are tied once and for all to unique materials of stone and steel, or of flesh and bones, and die with them; then, such intermediate arts as painting and sculpture, where reproduction is possible, but always imperfect. But interesting as these distinctions are, they are not important; the important matter is the fact that the full meaning of art includes its social and historical significance, which would be impossible without the material aesthetic instrument.

We come finally to the last of the marks by means of which I am seeking to define and distinguish art. There are a number of words, more or less synonymous, which have been used to designate what I have in mind —*harmony, form, pattern, design.* This is an absolutely universal characteristic of all works of art, of every kind. But while design is a necessary mark of art, it is not sufficient, for it is not a distinguishing mark. There are other things besides works of art that possess design. The human body possesses its design; so does any machine, an airplane or motor car. Yet while this is true, it deserves to be pointed out that there are certain differences between the form of the human body and the machine, on the one hand, and the form of a work of art, on the other hand. In order to make this clear, I wish to distinguish between two types of design in aesthetic objects, which I shall call intrinsic form and extrinsic or representational form, respectively. By representational form, I mean structure that is determined by the meanings that underlie the sensuous surface. I can make this clear by asking whether even the most radical post-impressionist would be willing to have the part of a statue that represents a head attached to the part that represents the ankle; or in a picture whether he would be willing to have the shapes that represent the sky below those that represent the earth, and the tree tops touching the ground, with the trunks in the air. Whether, not in a fairy story, but in a novel, he would be willing to have the men look like women, the babes talk and the grown-ups babble; or whether in a line of verse, for example,

Shall I compare thee to a summer's day?

it would be just as well to write,

I shall compare thee to a summer's day.

In all such cases it is plain that part of the pattern of the work is determined by connexions between meanings, reproduced from nature and human life and thought. In other words, we demand of a work of art that represents nature or human life and thought, an analogous pattern of its parts. Now so far as this type of form in works of art is concerned, it is obviously closely similar to the form found in machines and the organism.

Just as the purpose to represent a human body requires that such and such parts of a statue represent such and such portions of the human body, and with a certain comparable arrangement; so the embodied purposes of the organism itself demand the parts and organs necessary for the carrying out of this purpose. But notice that there is a difference. For whereas in the case of the human body or the machine, the various parts are meaningless and functionless, except with relation to an environment in which they operate—a foot in relation to the ground; an eye in relation to things to be seen; a mouth in relation to food; the wheel of an automobile in relation to a road; the seat in relation to passengers; on the other hand, in the case of a work of art, there is no relation of parts to an environment, but only of parts to parts within a whole. The foot of the statue rests, not on the ground, but on a pedestal; and while its eyes may be said to see, there is nothing for them to see, and if its mouth may be said to speak, there is no one to listen to what is said. Spencer defined life as a continual adjustment of inner relations to outer relations; and he might have defined a machine in much the same way. In a work of art, however, there are internal relations only; a part refers to other parts, within the whole, in accordance with the idea that is expressed there, but does not refer to anything outside itself. It is a microcosm, a self-sufficient little world of embodied, interrelated meanings, in need of nothing to give it life and significance, save only the mind of the spectator.

One might hope to make out a better case for the uniqueness of aesthetic form in regard to what I have been calling intrinsic form. This type of form is significant in complete independence of meanings. Absolute music is the best example, for there all form is intrinsic form. The rhythmic and harmonic structure of music is effective and intelligible wholly by itself; we understand why certain harmonies are present or certain dissonances resolved without any reference to the objects and events in nature or human life. In the same way we understand why in a picture a certain color demands its contrasting and complementary color, or a certain line its balancing line, independent of what the color is the color of, or the line the line of. In a poem, we know that a word of certain length and sound texture is demanded, independent of its meaning, because of the necessities of rime and rhythm. And even in a statue, where it might seem as if every part had to be just what it is because of the laws of anatomy, there are relations of harmony and balance of line and mass that cannot be understood in *that* way, but are intelligible in their own way. I do not mean to imply that intrinsic and extrinsic form are as separate in any work of art as might appear from my discussion; for, on the contrary, there must be a fine adaptation of one to the other, for beauty. Yet I would insist that they are two very different types of form, springing from different roots; the one type following the objective laws of nature, and so creating in every work of art some semblance of truth; the other based on those subjective principles of human nature upon which depend all value or satisfaction. Elsewhere[5] I have tried to formulate these laws; but I have no room to go into the matter here. What is of immediate concern to us is the possibility of defining art in terms of intrinsic form. That intrinsic form is a universal factor in works of art, and for that reason belongs among the indispensable elements in any definition, can I think be proved. But that it is no exclusive characteristic, and cannot therefore function as a sufficient criterion, can also be shown. For all the activities of man, so far as they are valuable, display it. His walk is rhythmic, when he enjoys it; his body is beautiful to him when harmonious and well-balanced; even his life as a whole is happy when it possesses intrinsic form. It is true, I think, that intrinsic form is most perfect in works of art; because imagination is of all spheres the most plastic to desire, and because the technique of expression of the imagination in the medium of the arts, being vastly simpler than the technique of business or politics, has achieved a perfection there unmatched anywhere, except perhaps in mathematics. For this reason art will always seem to be the superlative example of form, even though, as has been shown, it be not the sole example.

In conclusion, let me summarize the chief points I have been making in regard to the definition of art. I have tried to show that there is no single and sufficient criterion by means of which art may be defined. There are single characteristics which apply to all works of art; but none which applies exclusively to art. The definition of art must therefore be in terms of a complex of characteristics. Failure to recognize this has been the fault of all the well-known definitions. The definition which I have proposed contains three parts: the provision of satisfaction through the imagination, social significance, and harmony. I am claiming that nothing except works of art possesses all three of these marks. By imagination is meant the whole realm of given experience, inclusive of sensations and meanings as well as of images, so far as it is under the control of desire, and capable of being viewed in independence of action and reality. By the social significance of art I have meant the fact that the satisfaction which art provides does not depend upon factors peculiar to the individual, but upon patterns of sensations and meanings which may become parts of the experience of many minds, and the further fact that an important element of aesthetic satisfaction comes from knowledge that other minds are having or may have a like satisfaction. We saw, in addition, that the possibility of the social significance of art depends upon the fashioning of relatively permanent physical objects, called by us *aesthetic instruments,* which function as stimuli of the aesthetic experience for many minds and vehicles for its transmission to future generations. It is a peculiarity of the imagination of the artist that, despite its freedom, it seeks a local habitation, and a deathless name, in these instruments, and in creating them, the artist acts as both dreamer and artisan. What we call a work of art is on the one hand a thing; on the other hand, an experience.

If we are asked to express the nature of this experience in a single sentence, we may venture to say that it is the satisfaction of desire through a harmonious and socially significant imaginative object which, because it is superlatively harmonious and of more than personal significance, becomes the symbol of all order and all goodness.

Notes

1. The best example is the work of J. M. Guyau.
2. Van Meter Ames, *Introduction to Beauty*, p. xi.
3. John Dewey, *Art as Experience*.
4. Work by Frank Lloyd Wright.
5. *The Analysis of Art*, Yale University Press.

JACQUES MARITAIN

Art as a Virtue of the Practical Intellect

The Practical Intellect

BEFORE SEWING ONE MUST CUT. A philosopher who is in search of the nature of things is obliged to begin with sharp distinctions. These distinctions may seem brutal. They simply deal with certain essences taken in themselves: and how could we bring out otherwise the intelligibility of things from the confused flux of existence? To isolate an essence does not imply any disregard for the complexity and continuity in the real. It is indispensable in order to analyze this complexity and continuity in a correct manner—and finally to become aware of their very richness and meaning.

In this chapter I shall limit myself to the consideration of art—art in its most basic and primordial form, or in its fundamental nature, which is, in one sense, contradistinguished to poetry. For it is in the useful arts that we may discover the most obvious and typical characteristics of art in so far as it is art, and its most universal significance as a root activity of the human race. In prehistoric ages, it seems that the search for beauty and adornment was contemporary with the search for contriving tools and weapons, and that the painting and carving activity of the primitive man was not always, nor even from the very beginning, directed toward magical purposes.[1] The fact remains, nevertheless, that the "pleasure of imitation" and the poetic impulse were but one with the effort to satisfy some need of human life—even if it was the need for adornment and ornamentation, in which beauty is, no doubt, instinctively sought for but not for its own sake (the intended aim being to make woman more attractive or man more formidable, or the human dwelling place more stamped with the mark of man and of his vision). With regard to the natural develop-

From *Creative Intuition in Art and Poetry* by Jacques Maritain and reprinted by permission of the Bollingen Foundation and Wm. Collins Sons. Copyright by the Trustees of the National Gallery of Art, Washington, 1953.

ment of its potentialities, art does not begin with freedom and beauty for beauty's sake. It begins with making instruments for human life, canoes, vases, arrows, necklaces, or wall paintings destined to subject, through magical or nonmagical signs, the human environment to the mastery of man. Art must never forget its origins. Man is *homo faber* and *homo poeta* together. But in the historical evolution of mankind the *homo faber* carries on his shoulders the *homo poeta*. Thus I shall point, first of all, to the art of the craftsman; and, secondarily, compare the universe of this art of the craftsman with the universe of the art of those for whom, since the Renaissance and its demi-gods, we reserve the name of artists.

2. Aristotle has shown—this is an example of an acquisition definitely made by philosophy (at least, if philosophers were aware of their own treasures) —that the absolutely first and primordial division to be recognized with respect to the activity of the intellect is the division between the speculative or theoretical intellect and the practical intellect. This does not mean a distinction between two separate powers but a distinction between two basically different ways in which the same power of the soul—the intellect or reason—exercises its activity.

The speculative intellect knows only for the sake of knowledge. It longs to see, and only to see. Truth, or the grasping of that which is, is its only goal, and its only life.

The practical intellect knows for the sake of action. From the very start its object is not Being to be grasped, but human activity to be guided and human tasks to be achieved. It is immersed in creativity. To mold intellectually that which will be brought into being, to judge about ends and means, and to direct or even command our powers of execution —these are its very life.

Such a distinction does not deal with accidental circumstances. It is an essential distinction. For the entire dynamism of the intellect and its typical approach to its object depend on this very object, and they are basically different when the object is merely knowledge and when the object is action.

3. We see this more clearly if we take into account two fundamental points: first, the part played by the *appetite;* and second, the nature of *truth*—either when it comes to the activity of the speculative intellect or when it comes to the activity of the practical intellect. The difference between these two kinds of intellectual activity is so deep that neither the vital relation between the intellect and the appetite nor even what truth consists of are the same in the two cases in question.

In the case of the speculative intellect, the appetite—that is to say, the will, but not in the sense of a mere power of decision, rather in the larger sense of man's energy of desire and love, intent on some existential good —the appetite intervenes only to bring the intellect to the exercise of its own power, say, to embark on and pursue a mathematical problem or an anthropological inquiry. But once the intellect is at work, the appetite has nothing to do with this work, which depends only, as far as normal knowledge through concepts is concerned, on the weapons of reason.

On the other hand, in the case of the practical intellect, the appetite plays an essential part in the very work of knowledge. In one way or another, and to quite various degrees (for practicality admits of a vast scale of varying degrees), reason, then, operates in conjunction with the will. For the intellect taken in itself tends uniquely to grasp Being; and it is only as permeated, in one way or another, by the movement of the appetite toward its own ends that the intellect concerns itself, not with Being to be grasped, but with action to be brought about.

As a result, truth, in speculative knowledge, is the adequation or conformity of the intellect with Being, with what things are. But in practical knowledge how could this be so? In practical or creative knowledge there is no previously existing thing with which the intellect can make itself consonant. The thing does not yet exist, it is to be brought into being. It is not with being, it is with the straight tendential dynamism of the human subject with regard to this thing not yet existing, but to be created, that the intellect must make itself consonant. In other words, truth, in practical knowledge, is the adequation or conformity of the intellect with the straight appetite, with the appetite as straightly tending to the ends with respect to which the thing that man is about to create will exist. This statement, basic in Thomist philosophy, applies to the various fields of practical knowledge in the most diversified ways, and in an analogous, not univocal manner. But it holds true for the whole realm of practical knowledge.

The Virtue of Art

4. Now there is a second essential division to be taken into consideration, this time in practical knowledge itself. The activity of the practical intellect divides into human actions to be done (within the universe of man's destiny) and works to be made (by man, but within the universe of things, outside the universe of man's destiny); in other words, it divides into moral activity and artistic activity.

Morality is concerned with what the Schoolmen called *agibilia*, or what pertains to doing: that is, the very use of human free will, on which depends the fact of a man's being good or bad. Art is concerned with what the Schoolmen called *factibilia*, or what pertains to making: that is, the making of a work, on which depends the fact of this very work's being good or bad.

Thus prudence, the moral virtue par excellence (I mean old *prudentia* in its genuine sense, practical wisdom at the highest degree of practicality, the virtue through which the Bold make an infallible decision, not our bourgeois and timorous prudence) —prudence is the straight intellectual determination of actions to be done. Art, on the contrary, is the straight intellectual determination of works to be made.[2]

Art resides in the soul and is a certain perfection of the soul. It is what Aristotle called an ἕξις, in Latin a *habitus,* an inner quality or stable and deep-rooted disposition that raises the human subject and his natural powers to a higher degree of vital formation and energy—or that makes him possessed of a particular strength of his own: when a *habitus,* a "state of possession"[3] or master quality, an inner demon if you prefer—has developed in us, it becomes our most treasured good, our most unbending strength, because it is an ennoblement in the very kingdom of human nature and human dignity.

Art is a virtue—not a moral virtue (it is contradistinguished to moral virtues). Art is a virtue in the larger and more philosophical sense the ancients gave to this word: a *habitus* or "state of possession," an inner strength developed in man, which perfects him with regard to his ways of acting, and makes him—to the extent to which he uses it—undeviating in a given activity. The virtuous man is not infallible, because often, while acting, he does not use his virtue; but virtue, in itself, is never wrong. The man who possesses the virtue of art is not infallible in his work, because often, while acting, he does not use his virtue. But the virtue of art is, of itself, never wrong.

Art is a virtue of the practical intellect—that particular virtue of the practical intellect which deals with the creation of objects to be made.

We see, then, how essential is the relationship between art and reason. Art is intellectual by essence, as the odor of the rose pertains to the rose, or spark to fire. Art, or the proper virtue of working reason, is—in the realm of making—an intrinsic perfection of the intellect. Not in Phidias and Praxiteles only, but in the village carpenter and blacksmith as well, the Doctors of the Middle Ages acknowledged an intrinsic development of reason, a nobility of the intellect. The virtue of the craftsman was not, in their eyes, strength of muscle or nimbleness of fingers. It was a virtue of the intellect, and endowed the humblest artisan with a certain perfection of the spirit.[4]

5. But, in contradistinction to prudence, which is also a perfection of the practical intellect, art is concerned with the good of the work, not with the good of man. The ancients took pleasure in laying stress on this difference, in their thoroughgoing comparison of art and prudence. If only he contrives a good piece of woodwork or jewelwork, the fact of a craftsman's being spiteful or debauched is immaterial, just as it is immaterial for a geometer to be a jealous or wicked man, if only his demonstrations provide us with geometrical truth. As Thomas Aquinas put it, art, in this respect, resembles the virtues of the speculative intellect: it causes man to act in a right way, not with regard to the use of man's own free will, and to the rightness of the human will, but with regard to the rightness of a particular operating power. The good that art pursues is

not the good of the human will but the good of the very artifact. Thus, art does not require, as a necessary precondition, that the will or the appetite should be undeviating with respect to its own nature and its own —human or moral—ends and dynamism, or in the line of human destiny. Oscar Wilde was but a good Thomist when he wrote: "The fact of a man being a poisoner is nothing against his prose."

Here we are confronted with a problem which is beyond the subject of this book, but about which it is perhaps not irrelevant to say a few words, parenthetically. As I observed at the beginning, the prime obligation of philosophy is to bring out and circumscribe the nature or essence of the given thing, taken in itself, which it considers: for instance the nature or essence of art taken in itself or in its own basic and constitutive requirements. Yet the trouble is that in actual existence we do not deal with essences taken in themselves, but with essences embodied in concrete reality. Art in itself pertains to a sphere separate from, and independent from, the sphere of morality. It breaks into human life and human affairs like a moon prince or a mermaid into a custom office or a congregation; it will always make trouble and arouse suspicion. But art exists in a human being—the artist. As a result, though the fact of a man's being a poisoner is nothing against his prose, the fact of a man's being a drug addict can be, in the long run, something harmful to his prose. Baudelaire himself has warned us against the exclusive passion for art, which progressively destroys the human subject and finally—through an indirect repercussion, owing to material or subjective causality—destroys art itself. For once a man is through, his art is through also.

But things are still more complicated, because of the fact that the artist is aware of this kind of impact of his own moral life on his art, and therefore is tempted, when he totally yields to his cherished demon, to develop, for the sake of his art, a peculiar morality and peculiar moral standards of his own, directed to the good of the work, not of his soul. Then he will endeavour to taste all the fruits and silts of the earth, and will make curiosity or recklessness in any new moral experiment or vampiric singularity his supreme moral virtue, in order to feed his art. And the undertaking will finally prove to be a miscalculation, for in this adventure he will warp in a more subtle manner—and in a manner more closely connected with the sphere of creativity—that general temperament of thought and sensibility, and that general relationship of the sense and the intellect to reality, which are the human ambiance of the activity of art.

Yet he can still remain an artist—even a great artist, however injured in some respects: the fact is that his very being has been offered in self-sacrifice to the all-devouring glory of art; well, to the glory of the world also, and to our own delights, and to the spiritual welfare of mankind. For St. Teresa of Avila said that without poetry life would not be tolerable—even for contemplatives. We do not have to judge him. God will work it out with him, somehow or other.

Useful Arts and Fine Arts

6. It is a basic maxim in Aristotelian philosophy that the practical intellect works always, in one way or another, in conjunction with the will, and that, in practical knowledge, truth is the conformity of the intellect with the straight appetite. This statement applies to art and prudence in totally different manners. In the case of prudence, it is in so far as the appetite tends to the ends of human life that it plays an indispensable part in practical knowledge; and truth is conformity with the straight will or appetite in so far as the appetite has been made straight by moral virtues.

But in the case of art, the will plays its part in so far as it tends to the work: and the fact of the will's or appetite's being straight means that it tends to the good of the work as it is to be brought into existence by means of the rules discovered by the intellect; so that the judgment of the artist about each of the movements his fingers have to make is true when it is in conformity with the appetite straightly tending to the production of the work through the appropriate rules born out of the intellect. Thus, in the last analysis, the main part is played by the intellect, and art is much more intellectual than prudence.

Let us think (purposely using an oversimplified imagery) of the first boat invented by men, on a day when neither the word nor the idea of boat yet existed. Nothing was present except a will to satisfy a certain need—the need of crossing a river or an arm of the sea. This need to be satisfied—this was the only rule or ruler for the operation of the inventor's intellect. When, by using certain bits of knowledge previously acquired (men had seen trunks of trees floating on the water), and by putting them together into a newborn idea, the intellect contrived a first appropriate means, its judgment was true because it was in conformity with the first rule.

The first contrived raft was probably something quite defective and clumsy. It had to be improved. Now the intellect had to heed two rules: the first and primary rule (the need, grasped by the intellect, the satisfying of which was wanted by the appetite), a rule in conformity with which the first raft had been contrived; and a second rule, the newborn rule of making which the intellect had just discovered in the very process of creating the first raft. The second raft was thus contrived in conformity with these two rules; and at the same time a third newborn rule of making, dealing with the improvement brought about in the making of the second raft, was discovered—and kept in memory. And so the process continued, both by the intellect heeding previously discovered rules, and discovering newborn rules. We have the same story with the invention and progressive improvement of the airplane, the cyclotron, the calculating machine, etc.

I hope I shall be pardoned the excessive simplicity of the example I have just used. It helps us to bring out some truths which are also quite simple indeed, but basic for our purpose. The first one is that even in the useful arts, the rules are not ready-made recipes, taught by professors in schools and museums, but vital ways of operating discovered by the creative eyes of the intellect in its very labour of invention. Once discovered, they tend, it is true, to become recipes; but then they become obstacles as well as aids to the life of art.[5]

Another basic truth is that whatever the more and more refined and more and more ingenious rules discovered by the craftsman may be, his primary obligation remains to obey the primary rule—the need to be satisfied, toward which, from the very start, his will basically tends.

Finally, to sum up, let us say that in the useful arts, what the will or appetite demands is the satisfying of a particular need; and the straightness of the appetite means that it tends to the satisfying of this particular need by means of the rules discovered by the intellect, the first of which is this very need as grasped by intelligence.

7. Now what about those arts which are designated (I shall say later on why I distrust the expression) as the fine arts? Here I would say that in the fine arts what the will or appetite demands is the release of the pure creativity of the spirit, in its longing for beauty—for that enigmatic beauty whose love affairs and quarrels with poetry will occupy us in a further chapter.

And the straightness of the appetite means that it tends to this aim as to be achieved by means of the rules discovered by the intellect, the first of which is the creative intuition from which the whole work originates. Creativity, or the power of engendering, does not belong only to material organisms, it is a mark and privilege of life in spiritual things also. "To be fertile, so as to manifest that which one possesses within oneself," John of St. Thomas wrote, "is a great perfection, and it essentially belongs to the intellectual nature."[6] The intellect in us strives to engender. It is anxious to produce, not only the inner word, the concept, which remains inside us, but a work at once material and spiritual, like ourselves, and into which something of our soul overflows. Through a natural superabundance the intellect tends to express and utter *outward,* it tends to sing, to manifest itself in a work. This natural desire, because it goes beyond the boundaries of the intellect, can be implemented only through the movement of the will and the appetitive powers, which make the intellect go out of itself—in accordance with its own natural aspiration—and which determine thereby the operative practicality of intelligence, in its most primordial and general impulse.

This creativity of the spirit is the first ontological root of the artistic activity. And in fine arts it is pure, cleared of all adventitious elements.

And the pure creativity of spiritual intelligence tends to achieve something in which spiritual intelligence finds its own delight, that is, to produce an object in beauty. Left to the freedom of its spiritual nature, the intellect strives to engender in beauty.[7]

Such is, in its longing for beauty, that pure creativity of the spirit, to the release of which the appetite basically tends, together with the intellect, in the vital dynamism of fine arts.

Here we do not have a demand for the satisfying of a particular need in human life. We are beyond the realm of the useful. The need is not extraneous to the intellect, it is one with the intellect. We have a demand for the participation, through the object created, in something which is itself spiritual in nature. For beauty, which is of no use, is radiant with intelligence and is as transcendental and infinite as the universe of the intellect. Thus the very end—transcendent end—intended pertains to the realm of the intellect, or its exultation and joy, not to the world of utility, and the intellectuality of art is in the fine arts (though more bound there with the sensitive and emotional powers) at a much higher degree than in the arts of the craftsman. The need of the intellect to manifest externally what is grasped within itself, in creative intuition, and to manifest it in beauty, is simply the essential thing in the fine arts.

From this point of view we may perceive how short of the mark inevitably fall all the explanations and theories of art offered by psychological or sociological, materialist, empiricist, logical-empiricist, or pragmatist positivism, or by those who, as Allen Tate[8] puts it, explain to us "how the *stimuli* of poems elicit *responses* in such a way as to *organize our impulses* toward action," and who tell us that "poetry is a kind of applied psychology," or else (this is logical positivism) that it is "only *amiable insanity*," because "it 'designates' but it does not denote anything *real*."

8. Let us come now to that with which the creative judgment, if it is true, comes into accordance, namely the rules—or the straight appetite tending toward beauty to be participated in by a work produced according to the appropriate rules.

This very notion of rule, in the fine arts, is transfigured, through the impact of beauty on the activity of art.

First, the rules, in fine arts, are subjected to a law of perpetual renewal infinitely more exacting than in useful arts. They must be perpetually newborn rules, not only with respect to a given object—boat, vase, or calculating machine—to be improved, but with respect to beauty to be participated in; and beauty is infinite. Outside any particular style or lineage of masterworks, there is always an infinity of other ways to achieve participation in beauty. No form of art, however perfect, can encompass beauty within its limits. The artist is faced with an immense and desert sea,

. . . sans mâts, sans mâts, ni fertiles îlots,

and the mirror he holds up to it is no bigger than his own heart. He is bound to go hunting a new analogate, a new typically different participation in beauty; and this new participation in beauty will involve and require new ways of making—either a new adaptation of the fundamental and perennial rules, or the use of rules not hitherto employed, which are simply new, and which at first disconcert people. It seems relevant, moreover, to lay stress at this point on the spiritual universality of what I just called the fundamental and perennial rules of art—or, better, the eternal laws of art. These eternal laws of art are not to be found at the level of the particular rules of making, say, the famous Golden Number. They exist only at the supremely universal level of philosophy, and of that wisdom (more lived than conceptualized) which is concealed in the roots of the virtue of art. They are in the artist the spiritual, and general, foundations of his intellectual virtue, prior to any particular, technical manifestation of this virtue. And it is through an infinite diversity in application that they are exemplified by the great works of any epoch and any style.

In the second place, the work to be made, in the case of the fine arts, is an end in itself, and an end totally singular, absolutely unique. Then, every time and for every single work, there is for the artist a new and unique way to strive after the end, and to impose on matter the form of the mind. As a result, the rules of making—which, as concern art in general, are fixed and determined, as opposed to the rules used by prudence —come in the fine arts to share in the infinite suppleness and adaptability of the rules used by prudence, because they deal every time with the utter singularity of a new case, which is, in actual fact, unprecedented. It is, then, with prudential rules not fixed beforehand but determined according to the contingency of singular cases, it is with the virtues proper to prudence—perspicacity, circumspection, precaution, industry, boldness, shrewdness, and guile—that the craftsmanship of the artist succeeds in engendering in beauty.

In the third place, and also because the work to be made is an end in itself and a certain singular and original, totally unique participation in beauty, reason alone is not enough for the artist to form and conceive this work within himself as an infallible creative judgment. For, as Aristotle put it, "as everyone is, so does the end appear to him." Everyone judges of his own ends, when they engage his own self, in accordance with what he himself actually is. And since the final transcendent end is beauty —not a particular need to be satisfied, but beauty to be seduced—such a spiritual and transcendental, self-sufficient, absolute, all-exacting end demands that the very self and subjectivity of the artist should be committed to it. As a result, in order for the artist to form and conceive his work within himself in an infallible creative judgment, it is necessary that his subjective dynamism, his will and appetite straightly tend to beauty. At this point the statement that the truth of the practical intellect consists in conformity with the straight appetite takes on a new meaning.

And we see that the fine arts, though they are more fully intellectual than the useful arts, imply, however, a much greater and more essential part played by the appetite, and require that the love for beauty should make the intellect co-natured with beauty. Because, in the last analysis, in art as in contemplation, intellectuality at its peak goes beyond concepts and discursive reason, and is achieved through a congeniality or connaturality with the subject, which love alone can bring about. To produce in beauty the artist must be in love with beauty. Such undeviating love is a supra-artistic rule—a precondition, not sufficient as to the ways of making, yet necessary as to the vital animation of art—which is presupposed by all the rules of art.

9. The most significant point remains to be made. In speaking of the useful arts, we have observed that however important and necessary the secondary, more and more refined rules discovered by the craftsman may be, his primary obligation is to the primary rule, which is, in his case, the satisfying of a certain need, toward which, from the very start, his will basically tends. A splendid house with no doorway is not a good piece of architecture.

Now what is this primary rule in the case of the fine arts? I have said that in this case the appetite, together with the intellect, basically tends to the release of the pure creativity in the spirit, in its longing for beauty. Consequently, the primary rule is the vital actuation or determination through which this free creativity of the spirit expresses itself first and foremost—and to which, therefore, the mind and the hand of the artist must first of all be loyal.

Thus for the apprentice as a painter or as a composer the primary rule is to follow purely the pleasure of his eyes or ears in the colors or sounds he will be responsible for; to respect this pleasure, and pay total attention to it; at every instant to produce nothing but what the senses are fully pleased with. For the creativity of the spirit, in its longing for beauty, passes through the senses, and is first vigilant in them, in a fragile way. Moreover, as soon as a tyro begins to discover, or to be taught, a particular rule of making, he happens more often than not to lose these fragile, inchoate awakenings of art, because he lacks the inner strength to master the particular rule in question, which then becomes a recipe and mars, along with his fidelity to his pleasure, the primary rule of art.

But with all that the threshold of art has not yet been crossed. It is crossed when the making of a work passes under the regime, no longer of the pleasure of intelligence-permeated senses, but of the creative intuition, which is born in the deepest depths of the Intellect. For the really genuine vital actuation through which the free creativity of the spirit expresses itself first and foremost is this creative or poetic intuition, to which the entire work to be engendered in beauty, in its perfect singularity as a kind of unique cosmos, is appendent. I shall have to discuss creative intuition in a subsequent chapter; I am only mentioning it now.

What I should like to stress is the fact that in creative intuition we have the primary rule to which, in the case of the fine arts, the whole fidelity, obedience, and heedfulness of the artist must be committed. I also should like to stress the fact that between this primary, primordial, primitive rule and all the other rules of making, however indispensable they may be, there exists an essential difference, so to speak infinite, as between heaven and earth. All other rules are of the earth, they deal with particular ways of operation in the making of the work. But this primary rule is a heavenly rule, because it deals with the very conception, in the bosom of the spirit, of the work to be engendered in beauty. If creative intuition is lacking, a work can be perfectly made, and it is nothing; the artist has nothing to say. If creative intuition is present, and passes, to some extent, into the work, the work exists and speaks to us, even if it is imperfectly made and proceeds from a man

> *c'ha l'habito de l'arte e man che trema,*
> —who has the habit of art and a hand which shakes.

At the summit of artistic activity, and for the one who has long traveled along the road of the rules, finally there is no longer any road. For the sons of God are under no law. Just as finally the unique law of the perfect soul, according to the saying of St. Augustine (not literally of him, but it does not matter), is *"ama et fac quod vis"*—love and do what you want—so the unique rule of the perfect artist is finally: "Cling to your creative intuition, and do what you want." "This kind of excellence . . . we recognize in a person in whom we are aware of a rare presence, a pure creative force, or an untrammeled spirit."[9]

Transcendence of the Fine Arts

10. The division between the useful arts and the fine arts must not be understood in too absolute a manner.[10] In the humblest work of the craftsman, if art is there, there is a concern for beauty, through a kind of indirect repercussion that the requirements of the creativity of the spirit exercise upon the production of an object to serve human needs. Furthermore, especially in works produced by our industrial age, in the various kinds of machines, or machinelike objects, contrived by the art of engineering or by our modern engineering-minded arts, the mere search for the pure technical exigencies of the utility, the solidity, and the good functioning of the thing made, without any search for beauty, naturally results in a beauty of its own. Our modern steamships, constructed only with a view to speed and utility, do not need the ornamentation of ancient galleys to provide a joy of the eyes and the mind by their perfect shape. I do not think that Brooklyn Bridge was built with any intention

of beauty; and it was able to stir the deepest emotions of Hart Crane, and is bound forever to his lines. The chaos of bridges and skyways, desolated chimneys, gloomy factories, queer industrial masts and spars, infernal and stinking machinery which surrounds New York is one of the most moving —and beautiful—spectacles in the world.

All that is true. But for all that I consider the theories of Le Corbusier to be faulty dogmatism, and any system of aesthetics which gets clear of beauty for the sake of mechanical adjustment to be puritanism of forms and spurious austerity. For the kind of beauty I just described exists indeed: but as an accidental occurrence, a quite peculiar case in the whole universe of art, and I even wonder whether the delight we find in it does not flatter, perhaps, some perverse instinct of our too civilized eyes. In actual fact, nature does not follow the teachings of Le Corbusier. Flowers, insects, and birds are not constructed with a view to the mere necessities of living; they display an amazing extravagance of ornament and luxury. And the beauty of the baroque also exists. And finally the same concern for beauty which was present in the craftsman, the same repercussion of the requirements of the creativity of the spirit, surreptitiously creeps into the very construction of machines and the very art of engineering. The beauty of the lines of an automobile is not indifferent to the engineers who draw its blueprint. And I doubt whether the engineers who built the George Washington Bridge or the Delaware Memorial Bridge were mere puritans of utility.

As to the great artists who take pleasure in describing themselves as mere engineers in the manufacturing of an artifact of words or sounds, as Paul Valery did, and as Stravinsky does, I think that they purposely do not tell the truth, at least completely. In reality the spiritual content of a creative intuition, with the poetic or melodic sense it conveys, animates their artifact, despite their grudge against inspiration. And they are well aware of the vital value of this God-given element. But because it is scanty in them, or arises only from some secret stir in the working reason of a touchy Muse, they make good this very aridity, and manage to sidetrack us, by magnifying it, so as to glory in what they falsely describe as a total lack—lack of a quality that Plato has supposedly invented, and which is nothing, they say, for real art. For all that, Stravinsky is not a narcissist but a genuine creator, "a ferocious intellect which has fallen in love with the song of the daughters of man."[11]

11. Now the essential thing I should like to point out in our present comparison between useful arts and fine arts is contained in this twofold assertion: First, the fine arts, because of their immediate relation to beauty and to the pure creativity of the spirit—are free—with the very freedom of the spirit. They belong, therefore, in actual fact, to the world of liberal arts: a truth which the ancients did not recognize with respect to most of the fine arts, because any manual labor bore in their eyes the stamp of the servile condition. And this spiritual freedom of the fine arts

causes them to dwell in a place which admits of no common, univocal measure with the useful arts. Everything said about art in general is to be transfigured when applied to them. They are virtues of the practical intellect; but, as we shall see in our further chapters, the intellect or reason which plays the principal and royal part in them is not conceptual, discursive, logical reason, nor even working reason. It is intuitive reason, in the obscure and high regions which are near the center of the soul, and in which the intellect exercises its activity at the single root of the soul's powers and conjointly with them. Thus it is that the fine arts are transcendent with regard to the useful arts.

Yet—this is my second point—the fine arts, from the very fact that they belong in the generic nature of art, participate in the law of the useful arts. Thus the conceptual, discursive, logical reason, or better (since we are in the practical order), the working reason, plays an essential and necessary—though secondary—part in the fine arts. This part, which relates to the particular ways of the making of an object, and of the realization of a creative intuition in matter, is an instrumental part: not only secondary, but merely instrumental. As soon as it gets the upper hand, the work is but a corpse of a work of art—a product of academicism. But when the resourcefulness of discursive reason, and the rules involved—which I called a moment ago the secondary rules—are used as instruments of a master *habitus,* and as the fingers, so to speak, of creative intuition, they compose the indispensable arsenal of prudence, shrewdness, and cleverness of the life of art. Degas pointed at all that when he said: "A painting is a thing which requires as much cunning, rascality, and viciousness as the perpetration of a crime."[12] To make fun of the rules, in proclaiming the liberty of art, is just an excuse provided by foolishness to mediocrity. "It is clear," Baudelaire wrote, "that systems of rhetoric and prosodies are not forms of tyranny arbitrarily devised, but a collection of rules required by the very organization of the spiritual being; never have prosodies and systems of rhetoric prevented originality from manifesting itself distinctly. The opposite would be far more true, that they have been a help to the blossoming forth of originality."[13] And Coleridge's sentence is still more to the point: "As it must not, so genius cannot, be lawless: for it is even this that constitutes it genius—the power of acting creatively under laws of its own origination."[14]

12. Two final remarks must be made. I have tried to bring out, and to lay stress upon, the pure essentials of art in its very nature, as operative virtue of the practical intellect. But obviously no virtue of the intellect can live in isolation. Since art is a virtue of the intellect, it demands to communicate with the entire universe of the intellect. Hence it is that the normal climate of art is intelligence and knowledge: its normal soil, the civilized heritage of a consistent and integrated system of beliefs and values; its normal horizon, the infinity of human experience enlightened by the passionate insights of anguish or the intellectual virtues of a con-

templative mind. The worshiping of ignorance and rudeness is for an artist but a sign of inner weakness. Yet, the fact remains that all the treasures of the earth are profitable to art only if it is strong enough to master them and make them a *means* for its own operation, an aliment for its own spark. And not all poets have the strength of a Dante.

On the other hand, the intellect is reflective by nature; so, no virtue of the intellect, even practical virtues, can genuinely develop in its own particular sphere without a more or less simultaneous development of reflectivity. Now what is the name of reflective intelligence in the domain of art? Its name is critical reason. Baudelaire wrote in this connection: "It would be quite a new departure in the history of the arts for a critic" (Baudelaire meant a critic who is born with *only* the gifts of a critic—which is, in my opinion, a nonsensical assumption) "to turn poet, a reversal of all psychological laws, a monstrosity; on the contrary, every great poet becomes naturally, inevitably, a critic. I am sorry for poets who are guided by instinct alone; I consider them incomplete. In the spiritual life of great poets a crisis infallibly arises, in which they want to reason out their art, to discover the obscure laws by virtue of which they have produced, and to derive from such a scrutiny a set of precepts whose divine aim is infallibility in poetic production. It would be a prodigy for a critic to turn poet and it is impossible for a poet not to contain a critic within himself."[15] These views are, I think, simply true as regards the poet. As regards the critic, they must be qualified, as we shall have an opportunity to see in a further chapter.

To conclude, let us observe that if it is true that art is a creative virtue of the intellect, which tends to engender in beauty, and that it catches hold, in the created world, of the secret workings of nature in order to produce its own work—a new creature—the consequence is that art continues in its own way the labor of divine creation. It is therefore true to say with Dante that our human art is, as it were, the grandchild of God—

Si che vostr' arte a Dio quasi e nipote.

Notes

1. Cf. G. H. Luquet, *L'Art et la Religion des Hommes fossiles* (Paris: Masson, 1926). The author insists in an illuminating manner on the genuinely aesthetic and poetic sense which permeated the art of the primitive man. But his vocabulary is sometimes confused, and he leaves blurred, in my opinion, the fact that this art, while being instinctively interested in beauty, was always and primarily, at the same time, subservient to the needs of human life. (I do not say limited to utilitarian aims in the too strict sense of this word in our civilized language. The truth of the matter is, I think, that the art of the primitive man was undifferentiated—more disinterested than our useful arts, and more subservient

to human needs than our fine arts. We may safely assume, moreover, that this destination of satisfying the needs of human life was prevalent in the *conscious-ness* of the primitive artist.)

2. As a rule the thing to be made, or the work to be done, refers to the realm of knowledge for the sake of action, not of knowledge for the sake of knowledge. That is why it is said in a general way that art belongs to the sphere of the practical intellect. Yet there are certain categories of works and, consequently, certain categories of arts which do not belong to this sphere, but to the speculative one; there are speculative arts, such as Logic is for instance. (Cf. *Sum. theol.* II-II, 47, 2, ad 3.) Such arts perfect the speculative Intellect, by the practical Intellect: but the kind of knowledge involved is still akin to the practical in its *mode,* and it constitutes an *art* only because it implies the *making of a work*—this time a work wholly within the mind, and whose sole object is the achievement of knowledge, a work which consists for instance in shaping an idea or a definition, in setting our concepts in order, in framing a proposition or a reasoning. The fact remains, therefore, that wherever we find *art* we find some productive operation to be contrived, some work to be made. Cf. *Art and Scholasticism* (New York: Scribner, 1930) , Chapter II.

Given the abstractive and discursive nature of man's intellect, the part of the making, the manufacture of the tools of science, is (unfortunately) essential and necessary, and immense, in the immanent operations of knowledge and the inner life of the mind. But when all this is not vivified by intuition and actual knowledge, we are tempted to see in it, as Faust did, only "Skeletons of animals and bones of the dead."

3. "State of possession" renders *habitus* (ἕξις) better, it seems to me, than the expression "state of capacity" used by W. D. Ross in his translation.

4. Cf. *Art and Scholasticism,* p. 20.—In the Scholastic vocabulary "art" is synonymous with "practical science," in the sense that it is a kind of science which is practical in its very essence or its very way of knowing, and practical from the very start—science of the work to be made.

Practical science in this genuine sense is entirely different from applied science, that is, from a science which is theoretical in essence—and then particularized or applied (by art or practical science) in order to achieve a practical result.

A greater or less amount of theoretical science (the science of anatomy, for instance) is indeed involved in art (in medicine for instance) as *presupposed* by it, and *applied* by it. But it would be a fundamental error to mistake practical science for applied theoretical science. Medicine is not applied science of anatomy, it applies in its own way and in its own light the science of anatomy.

Sayings like 'L'art c'est la science faite chair" (Jean Cocteau, "Le Secret professionel," in *Le Rappel à l'Ordre,* Paris: Stock, 1930) or "L'art ce n'est que la science humanisée" (Gino Serverini, *Du Cubisme au Classicisme,* Paris: Povolozky, 1921) are therefore inaccurate if they relate to theoretical science as embodied in the work. Mathematics may be considered a basic *pre-required* discipline for the painter, yet painting is not humanized mathematics. Painting applies mathematics—it is not applied mathematics.

But such sayings take on fully true meaning if they relate to that knowledge which is implied in the very essence of fine arts, namely to poetic knowledge (See Chapter IV, §§6 and 7, and Chapter V, §9) . We must thus admit, if we get rid of our "scienticist" modern prejudices, the existence of a poetic science which differs *toto coelo* from theoretical sciences, and which is however a real knowledge, attained through creative intuition. Its object is neither the essential structure of the object known nor the laws of phenomena; it is real nevertheless —the existential aspects and relations of things grasped through emotion and connaturality. Thus the painter has a real knowledge or "science" of "Nature," or the world of visible matter—a knowledge or "science" which has nothing to do either with mathematics or with physics, the theoretical science of nature (though the art of painting in its ways and means of execution has to apply certain mathematical and certain physical, especially optical, laws).

5. Be it noted, furthermore, that the truth of the creative judgment does not consist in judging of the work in conformity with the rules (theoretically known); it consists in judging of the work in conformity with the appetite straightly tending to the production of this work through the appropriate rules. So art—*recta ratio factibilium*—is a virtue of working reason. But an element of knowledge through connaturality, a certain "instinct" developed in reason, is already involved in the basic notion of the truth of the artistic judgment, since this truth is conformity with *the appetite* intent on the use of the appropriate rules.

6. *Cursus theol.*, t. IV, disp. 12, a. 6, §21.

7. The phrase "engendering in beauty" is Platonic in origin. Cf. *Symposium*, 206.

8. *On the Limits of Poetry* (New York: The Swallow Press and William Morrow, 1948) pp. 9, 15.

9. George Rowley, *Principles of Chinese Painting*, p. 80.

10. Even, as we shall see further, the stock phrases "useful arts" and "fine arts," which I am using now to conform to the accepted vocabulary, are not, in my opinion, philosophically well grounded. I would prefer to say "subservient arts" and "free" or "self-sufficient arts."

11. "The Freedom of Song," in my *Art and Poetry*, (New York: Philosophical Library, 1943), p. 72.

12. Quoted by Etienne Charles in *Renaissance de l'Art français*, April, 1918.— Cf. *Artists on Art*, p. 308.

13. "L'Oeuvre et la vie d'Eugène Delacroix," in *L'Art romantique* (Paris: Calmann-Lévy, 1885), p. 13.

14. *Lectures and Notes on Shakespeare and Other Dramatists* (New York: Harper, 1853), p. 54.

15. "Richard Wagner et Tannhauser," in *op. cit.*, p. 229.

SUSANNE K. LANGER

Expressiveness

WHEN WE TALK about "Art" with a capital "A"—that is, about any or all of the arts: painting, sculpture, architecture, the potter's and goldsmith's and other designers' arts, music, dance, poetry, and prose fiction, drama and film—it is a constant temptation to say things about "Art" in this general sense that are true only in one special domain, or to assume that what holds for one art must hold for another. For instance, the fact that music is made for performance, for presentation to the ear, and is simply not the same thing when it is given only to the tonal imagination of a reader silently perusing the score, has made some aestheticians pass straight to the conclusion that literature, too, must be physically heard to be fully experienced, because words are originally spoken, not written; an obvious parallel, but a careless and, I think, invalid one. It is dangerous to set up principles by analogy, and generalize from a single consideration.

But it is natural, and safe enough, to ask analogous questions: "What is the function of sound in music? What is the function of sound in poetry? What is the function of sound in prose composition? What is the function of sound in drama?" The answers may be quite heterogeneous; and that is itself an important fact, a guide to something more than a simple and sweeping theory. Such findings guide us to exact relations and abstract, variously exemplified basic principles.

At present, however, we are dealing with principles that have proven to be the same in all the arts, when each kind of art—plastic, musical, balletic, poetic, and each major mode, such as literary and dramatic writing, or painting, sculpturing, building plastic shapes—has been studied in its own terms. Such candid study is more rewarding than the usual passionate declaration that all the arts are alike, only their materials differ, their principles are all the same, their techniques all analagous, etc. This

"Expressiveness" from *Problems of Art*, pp. 13-26, by Susanne K. Langer (Copyright © 1957 Susanne K. Langer) is used by permission of Charles Scribner's Sons and Routledge & Kegan Paul Ltd.

is not only unsafe, but untrue. It is in pursuing the differences among them that one arrives, finally, at a point where no more differences appear; then one has found, not postulated, their unity. At that deep level there is only one concept exemplified in all the different arts, and that is the concept of Art.

The principles that obtain wholly and fundamentally in every kind of art are few, but decisive; they determine what is art, and what is not. Expressiveness, in one definite and appropriate sense, is the same in all art works of any kind. What is created is not the same in any two distinct arts—this is, in fact, what makes them distinct—but the principle of creation is the same. And "living form" means the same in all of them.

A work of art is an expressive form created for our perception through sense or imagination, and what is expressed is human feeling. The word "feeling" must be taken here in its broadest sense, meaning *everything that can be felt,* from physical sensation, pain and comfort, excitement and repose, to the most complex emotions, intellectual tensions, or the steady feeling-tones of a conscious human life. In stating what a work of art is, I have just used the words "form," "expressive," and "created"; these are key words. One at a time, they will keep us engaged.

Let us first consider what is meant, in this context, by a *form*. The word has many meanings, all equally legitimate for various purposes; even in connection with art it has several. It may, for instance—and often does—denote the familiar, characteristic structures known as the sonnet form, the sestina, or the ballad form in poetry, the sonata form, the madrigal, or the symphony in music, the contredance or the classical ballet in choreography, and so on. This is not what I mean; or rather, it is only a very small part of what I mean. There is another sense in which artists speak of "form" when they say, for instance, "form follows function," or declare that the one quality shared by all good works of art is "significant form," or entitle a book *The Problem of Form in Painting and Sculpture,* or *The Life of Forms in Art,* or *Search for Form.* They are using "form" in a wider sense, which on the one hand is close to the commonest, popular meaning, namely just the *shape* of a thing, and on the other hand to the quite unpopular meaning it has in science and philosophy, where it designates something more abstract; "form" in its most abstract sense means structure, articulation, a whole resulting from the relation of mutually dependent factors, or more precisely, the way that whole is put together.

The abstract sense, which is sometimes called "logical form," is involved in the notion of expression, at least the kind of expression that characterizes art. That is why artists, when they speak of achieving "form," use the word with something of an abstract connotation, even when they are talking about a visible and tangible art object in which that form is embodied.

The more recondite concept of form is derived, of course, from the naive one, that is, material shape. Perhaps the easiest way to grasp the idea of "logical form" is to trace its derivation.

Let us consider the most obvious sort of form, the shape of an object, say a lampshade. In any department store you will find a wide choice of lampshades, mostly monstrosities, and what is monstrous is usually their shape. You select the least offensive one, maybe even a good one, but realize that the color, say violet, will not fit into your room; so you look about for another shade of the same shape but a different color, perhaps green. In recognizing this same shape in another object, possibly of another material as well as another color, you have quite naturally and easily abstracted the concept of this shape from your actual impression of the first lampshade. Presently it may occur to you that this shade is too big for your lamp; you ask whether they have *this same shade* (meaning another one of this shape) in a smaller size. The clerk understands you.

But what is *the same* in the big violet shade and the little green one? Nothing but the interrelations among their respective various dimensions. They are not "the same" even in their spatial properties, for none of their actual measures are alike; but their shapes are congruent. Their respective spatial factors are put together in the same way, so they exemplify the same form.

It is really astounding what complicated abstractions we make in our ordinary dealing with forms—that is to say, through what twists and transformations we recognize the same logical form. Consider the similarity of your two hands. Put one on the table, palm down, superimpose the other, palm down, as you may have superimposed cut-out geometrical shapes in school—they are not alike at all. But their shapes are *exact opposites*. Their respective shapes fit the same description, provided that the description is modified by a principle of application whereby the measures are read one way for one hand and the other way for the other—like a timetable in which the list of stations is marked: "Eastbound, read down; Westbound, read up."

As the two hands exemplify the same form with a principle of reversal understood, so the list of stations describes two ways of moving, indicated by the advice to "read down" for one and "read up" for the other. We can all abstract the common element in these two respective trips, which is called the *route*. With a return ticket we may return only by the same route. The same principle relates a mold to the form of the thing that is cast in it, and establishes their formal correspondence, or common logical form.

So far we have considered only objects—lampshades, hands, or regions of the earth—as having forms. These have fixed shapes; their parts remain in fairly stable relations to each other. But there are also substances that have no definite shapes, such as gases, mist, and water, which take the shape of any bounded space that contains them. The interesting thing about such amorphous fluids is that when they are put into violent motion they do exhibit visible forms, not bounded by any container. Think of the momentary efflorescence of a bursting rocket, the mushroom cloud of an atomic bomb, the funnel of water or dust screwing upward in a whirlwind. The instant the motion stops, or even slows beyond a certain degree, those shapes collapse and the apparent "thing" disappears. They are not shapes of things at all, but forms of motions, or dynamic forms.

Some dynamic forms, however, have more permanent manifestations, because the stuff that moves and makes them visible is constantly replenished. A waterfall seems to hang from the cliff, waving streamers of foam. Actually, of course, nothing stays there in mid-air; the water is always passing; but there is more and more water taking the same paths, so we have a lasting shape made and maintained by its passage—a permanent dynamic form. A quiet river, too, has dynamic form; if it stopped flowing it would either go dry or become a lake. Some twenty-five hundred years ago, Heracleitos was struck by the fact that you cannot step twice into the same river at the same place—at least, if the river means the water, not its dynamic form, the flow.

When a river ceases to flow because the water is deflected or dried up, there remains the river bed, sometimes cut deeply in solid stone. That bed is shaped by the flow, and records as graven lines the currents that have ceased to exist. Its shape is static, but it *expresses* the dynamic form of the river. Again, we have two congruent forms, like a cast and its mold, but this time the congruence is more remarkable because it holds between a dynamic form and a static one. That relation is important; we shall be dealing with it again when we come to consider the meaning of "living form" in art.

The congruence of two given perceptible forms is not always evident upon simple inspection. The common *logical* form they both exhibit may become apparent only when you know the principle whereby to relate them, as you compare the shapes of your hands not by direct correspondence, but by correspondence of opposite parts. Where the two exemplifications of the single logical form are unlike in most other respects one needs a rule for matching up the relevant factors of one with the relevant factors of the other; that is to say, a *rule of translation,* whereby one instance of the logical form is shown to correspond formally to the other.

The logical form itself is not another thing, but an abstract concept, or better an *abstractable* concept. We usually don't abstract it deliberately, but only use it, as we use our vocal chords in speech without first learning all about their operation and then applying our knowledge. Most people perceive intuitively the similarity of their two hands without thinking of them as conversely related; they can guess at the shape of a hollow inside a wooden shoe from the shape of a human foot, without any abstract study of topology. But the first time they see a map in the Mercator projection—with parallel lines of longitude, not meeting at the poles—they find it hard to believe that this corresponds logically to the circular map they used in school, where the meridians bulged apart toward the equator and met at both poles. The visible shapes of the continents are different on the two maps, and it takes abstract thinking to match up the two representations of the same earth. If, however, they have grown up with both maps, they will probably see the geographical relationships either way with equal ease, because these relationships are not *copied* by either map, but *expressed,* and expressed equally well by both; for the two maps are different *projections* of the same logical form, which the spherical earth exhibits in still another—that is, a spherical—projection.

An expressive form is any perceptible or imaginable whole that exhibits relationships of parts, or points, or even qualities or aspects within the whole, so that it may be taken to represent some other whole whose elements have analogous relations. The reason for using such a form as a symbol is usually that the thing it represents is not perceivable or readily imaginable. We cannot see the earth as an object. We let a map or a little globe express the relationships of places on the earth, and think about the earth by means of it. The understanding of one thing through another seems to be a deeply intuitive process in the human brain; it is so natural that we often have difficulty in distinguishing the symbolic expressive form from what it conveys. The symbol seems to be the thing itself, or contain it, or be contained in it. A child interested in a globe will not say: "This means the earth," but, "Look, this is the earth." A similar identification of symbol and meaning underlies the widespread conception of holy names, of the physical efficacy of rites, and many other primitive but culturally persistent phenomena. It has a bearing on our perception of artistic import; that is why I mention it here.

The most astounding and developed symbolic device humanity has evolved is language. By means of language we can conceive the intangible, incorporeal things we call our *ideas,* and the equally inostensible elements of our perceptual world that we call *facts.* It is by virtue of language that we can think, remember, imagine, and finally conceive a universe of facts. We can describe things and represent their relations, express rules of their interactions, speculate and predict and carry on a long symbolizing process known as reasoning. And above all, we can communicate, by producing a serried array of audible or visible words, in a pattern commonly known, and readily understood to reflect our multifarious concepts and precepts and their interconnections. The use of language is *discourse;* and the pattern of discourse is known as *discursive form.* It is a highly versatile, amazingly powerful pattern. It has impressed itself on our tacit thinking, so that we call all systematic reflection "discursive thought." It has made, far more than most people know, the very frame of our sensory experience—the frame of objective facts in which we carry on the practical business of life.

Yet even the discursive pattern has its limits of usefulness. An expressive form can express any complex of conceptions that, via some rule of projection, appears congruent with it, that is, appears to be of that form.

Whatever there is in experience that will not take the impress—directly or indirectly—of discursive form, is not discursively communicable or, in the strictest sense, logically thinkable. It is unspeakable, ineffable; according to practically all serious philosophical theories today, it is unknowable.

Yet there is a great deal of experience that is knowable, not only as immediate, formless, meaningless impact, but as one aspect of the intricate web of life, yet defies discursive formulation, and therefore verbal expression: that is what we sometimes call the *subjective aspect* of experience, the direct feeling of it—what it is like to be walking and moving, to be drowsy, slowing down, or to be sociable, or to feel self-sufficient but alone; what it feels like to pursue an elusive thought or to have a big idea. All such directly felt experiences usually have no names—they are named, if at all, for the outward conditions that normally accompany their occurrence. Only the most striking ones have names like "anger," "hate," "love," "fear," and are collectively called "emotion." But we feel many things that never develop into any designable emotion. The ways we are moved are as various as the lights in a forest; and they may intersect, sometimes without cancelling each other, take shape and dissolve, conflict, explode into passion, or be transfigured. All these inseparable elements of subjective reality compose what we call the "inward life" of human beings. The usual factoring of that life-stream into mental, emotional, and sensory units is an arbitrary scheme of simplification that makes scientific treatment possible to a considerable extent; but we may already be close to the limit of its usefulness, that is, close to the point where its simplicity becomes an obstacle to further questioning and discovery instead of the revealing, ever-suitable logical projection it was expected to be.

Whatever resists projection into the discursive form of language is, indeed, hard to hold in conception, and perhaps impossible to communicate, in the proper and strict sense of the word "communicate." But fortunately our logical intuition, or form-perception, is really much more powerful than we commonly believe, and our knowledge—genuine knowledge, understanding—is considerably wider than our discourse. Even in the use of language, if we want to name something that is too new to have a name (e.g. a newly invented gadget or a newly discovered creature), or want to express a relationship for which there is no verb or other connective word, we resort to metaphor; we mention it or describe it as something else, something analogous. The principle of metaphor is simply the principle of saying one thing and meaning another, and expecting to be understood to mean the other. A metaphor is not language, it is an idea expressed by language, an idea that in its turn functions as a symbol to express something. It is not discursive and therefore does not really make a statement of the idea it conveys; but it formulates a new conception for our direct imaginative grasp.

Sometimes our comprehension of a total experience is mediated by a metaphorical symbol because the experience is new, and language has words and phrases only for familiar notions. Then an extension of language will gradually follow the wordless insight, and discursive expression will supersede the non-discursive pristine symbol. This is, I think, the normal advance of human thought and language in the whole realm of knowledge where discourse is possible at all.

But the symbolic presentation of subjective reality for contemplation is not only tentatively beyond the reach of language—that is, not merely beyond the words we have, it is impossible in the essential frame of language. That is why those semanticists who recognize only discourse as a symbolic form must regard the whole life of feeling as formless, chaotic, capable only of symptomatic expression, typified in exclamations like "Ah!" "Ouch!" "My sainted aunt!" They usually do believe that art is an expression of feeling, but that "expression" in art is of this sort, indicating that the speaker has an emotion, a pain, or other personal experience, perhaps also giving us a clue to the general kind of experience it is—pleasant or unpleasant, violent or mild—but not setting that piece of inward life objectively before us so we may understand its intricacy, its rhythms and shifts of total appearance. The differences in feeling-tones or other elements of subjective experience are regarded as differences in quality, which must be felt to be appreciated. Furthermore, since we have no intellectual access to pure subjectivity, the only way to study it is to study the symptoms of the person who is having subjective experiences. This leads to physiological psychology—a very important and interesting field. But it tells us nothing about the phenomena of subjective life, and sometimes simplifies the problem by saying they don't exist.

Now, I believe the expression of feeling in a work of art—the function that makes the work an expressive form—is not symptomatic at all. An artist working on a tragedy need not be in personal despair or violent upheaval; nobody, indeed, could work in such a state of mind. His mind would be occupied with the causes of his emotional upset. Self-expression does not require composition and lucidity; a screaming baby gives his feeling far more release than any musician, but we don't go into a concert hall to hear a baby scream; in fact, if that baby is brought in we are likely to go out. We don't want self-expression.

A work of art presents feeling (in the broad sense I mentioned before, as everything that can be felt) for our contemplation, making it visible or audible or in some way perceivable through a symbol, not inferable from a symptom. Artistic form is congruent with the dynamic forms of our direct sensuous, mental, and emotional life; works of art are projections of "felt life," as Henry James called it, into spatial, temporal, and poetic structures. They are images of feeling, that formulate it for our cognition. What is artistically good is whatever articulates and presents feeling to our understanding.

Artistic forms are more complex than any other symbolic forms we know. They are, indeed, not abstractable from the works that exhibit them. We may abstract a shape from an object that has this shape, by disregarding color, weight and texture, even size; but to the total effect that is an artistic form, the color matters, the thickness of line matters, and the appearance of texture and weight. A given triangle is the same in any position, but to an artistic form its location, balance, and surroundings are not indifferent. Form, in the sense in which artists speak of "significant form" or "expressive form," is not an abstracted structure, but an apparition; and the vital processes of sense and emotion that a good work of art expresses seem to the beholder to be directly contained in it, not symbolized but really presented. The congruence is so striking that symbol and meaning appear as one reality. Actually, as one psychologist who is also a musician has written, "Music sounds as feelings feel." And likewise, in good painting, sculpture, or building, balanced shapes and colors, lines and masses look as emotions, vital tensions and their resolutions feel.

An artist, then, expresses feeling, but not in the way a politician blows off steam or a baby laughs and cries. He formulates that elusive aspect of reality that is commonly taken to be amorphous and chaotic; that is, he objectifies the subjective realm. What he expresses, is, therefore, not his own actual feelings, but what he knows about human feeling. Once he is in possession of a rich symbolism, that knowledge may actually exceed his entire personal experience. A work of art expresses a conception of life, emotion, inward reality. But it is neither a confessional nor a frozen tantrum; it is a developed metaphor, a non-discursive symbol that articulates what is verbally ineffable—the logic of consciousness itself.

Definition and Theory in Aesthetics

WHEN A MAN asks himself "What is art?" and propounds the sort of theory represented by the foregoing selections, what is he doing? We shall consider three possible answers to this question:

1. He is giving a definition of art in the form of a statement about the properties something must have if it is properly to be called a work of art;

2. he is offering an empirical theory about the nature of art in the form of a statement about what all works of art have distinctively in common;

3. he is making a linguistic recommendation, urging a reform in how we use such expressions as "art" and "work of art."

1. *Definition.* In the eleventh book of his *Confessions*, St. Augustine asks, "What is time?" and he says, "If I am not asked, I know; if I am asked, I know not." Do we not face a similar problem in the case of art? As long as we are not asked, we know perfectly well what art is. We recognize it when we see it: we know, for example, that Botticelli's "Primavera" is a work of art and that a tree or a shoelace is not. And we know what the expressions "art" and "work of art" mean, for we can apply them correctly. There are times, to be sure, when we are not certain whether something is a work of art. Are the political cartoons of Herblock or the marches of Sousa works of art? If we are in doubt, it is probably because "art" and "work of art," like most general expressions, are vague in application and admit of "borderline cases." But the fact that we are occasionally in doubt whether a term is applicable does not necessarily imply that we do not know what it means.

The aesthetic theorist who wants to know what art is does not want to be shown examples of art, nor does he want to know how the word "art" is used, to what it is applied. He too knows what art is in *this* way. What, then, is he after?

According to Clive Bell, the aesthetic theorist is looking for the quality that "distinguishes works of art from all other classes of objects." "For," he adds, "either all works of visual art have some common quality, or when we speak of 'works of art' we gibber. . . . There must be some one quality without which a work of art cannot exist."[1] DeWitt Parker agrees: every work of art is unique and hence incomparable with every other work; nevertheless, there must be "a common denominator, so to say, which constitutes the definition of art, and serves to separate . . . the field of art from other fields of human culture."

The claim that there *must* be a property common and peculiar to the things to which we apply the same name and by virtue of which we apply it to them, has been made by philosophers from Socrates up to the present. It alone appears to account for our being able to learn the application of such general words as "cat," "chair," and "hexapod," as opposed to that of such proper names as "Napoleon" and "Socrates." For after having had a number of things pointed out to him, each of which is identified by the same word, how could one then go on to apply that word to other things except by recognizing some distinctive feature in them?

Despite its initial plausibility, this claim is vulnerable and leads to paradoxical results in the practice of those very philosophers who make it. For if general words are applied to things by virtue of their having some distinctive property, those who know how to apply them must already know that property. Yet philosophers who hold this view spend time *searching* for that property and think that finding it would be a *discovery*. Furthermore, they disagree with one another as to what that property is, although they can equally well apply the word whose meaning it is supposed to be.[2]

If we look at how general words are actually applied, we note that we call things by the same name for a variety of reasons: (1) sometimes because they share a distinctive property; (2) sometimes because they resemble one another in different ways without a single property common to all to mark the boundaries of correct use;[3] (3) sometimes because they are analogous to one another as are the top of a mountain, the top of a class, and the top of a list; (4) sometimes because a word is used paronymously, as when we speak of a healthy man, healthy exercise, and a healthy complexion.[4] The history of the development of its meaning shows that "art" has come to be applied to very different things principally for the second and third reasons. This explains why there is no ready definition of art analogous to the definition of a hexapod. It also explains why we know what art is when we are not asked, and do not know what it is—cannot give a simple definition of it—when we are asked.[5]

This does not mean, as some philosophers have urged, that art *cannot* be defined. It is obviously possible to give a complex disjunctive definition of art, *i.e.* such as "A work of art is anything that has this set of properties *or* that set *or*. . . ." And of course it is possible to give non-descriptive definitions, which do not pretend to tell us how "art" is applied; for example, legal definitions for customs and tariff purposes.

If we take statements such as "Art is significant form" *as* dictionary definitions of art, it is not hard to see that they are inadequate. A dictionary definition purports to tell us what an expression means. But "art" obviously does not mean significant form, or intuition, or a certain virtue of the practical intellect, any more than "hexapod" means a four-sided polygon. This fact can hardly have eluded the aesthetic theorists in question; hence, it is unlikely that, despite what they sometimes say, they are trying to give a correct definition of art. If this is so, then it would be a mistake to try to support or refute their theories by noting how "art" is actually applied.[6]

2. *Empirical Theories.* If we do not apply the word "art" to things *because* they share some distinctive feature, it may still be the case that what we call works of art, for whatever reason, do share such a feature. We do not call a certain substance "water" *because* it is composed of two parts of hydrogen to one of oxygen, yet it is a distinctive property of water that it is so composed—a fact that was proven experimentally. It is therefore possible that when aesthetic theorists ask "What is art?" they are asking if there is, as a matter of empirical fact, some feature that works of art and only works of art share, and, if so, what it is.

It is tempting to think of aesthetic theories in this way, but a closer look at how they are stated and defended finds it implausible that they are intended to be empirical theories about the nature of art.

If a theory is to be *empirical,* it must be possible for there to be an observable state of affairs which would count against the truth of the theory. But what would, or could, count against such a theory as "Art is significant form"? If someone should say that an Ingres portrait, on the ground that it is no more than an excellent likeness of the sitter, is a work of art that lacks significant form, what would Bell's reply be? "If an Ingres portrait lacks significant form, it is not a work of art."[7] But if an aesthetician's reply to any challenge to his theory takes this form, then there is no possible way in which his theory can be refuted: it is logically, not merely physically, impossible to find evidence against it. If it is impossible to refute a theory by producing contrary evidence, if we cannot even imagine a work of art which, if it did exist, would serve to refute it, then it is also impossible to confirm such a theory by producing evidence for it. One could produce only *instances* of it, which is something else.[8]

Another difficulty confronts us if we try to take aesthetic theories as empirical. The predicates of these theories are such that it is almost impossible to tell if something is rightly describable by them, save by the fact that it is a work of art. Can we really tell if something does or does not have significant form, does or does not express an intuition, is or is not a certain product of the practical intellect, except by the fact that it is a work of art? The meaning of "art" is much clearer to us than the meaning of any of these predicates.

To the extent, however, that we can tell whether something has significant form or expresses an intuition, etc., *independent of its being a work of art,* we notice something curious: either there are works of art that do not have significant form, are not expressions of intuitions, etc.; or there are things that are not works of art that do have significant form, are expressions of intuitions, etc. Hence, either these theories are false empirical theories about the distinctive nature of art, or they are not empirical theories at all. Since their falsity as empirical theories can hardly have eluded their authors, we must suppose that they were not intended to be empirical theories and that it is inappropriate to criticize them as if they were.

It is instructive in this connection to compare any of the theories represented in this section with Freud's theory of art.[9] Freud's theory may seem at first sight to be on all fours with Croce's or Bell's—indeed, it bears some interesting resemblances to DeWitt Parker's; but it was intended to be an integral part of a complex psychological hypothesis, subject to clinical confirmation. If one were to find a work of art that did not provide a substitute gratification of unfulfilled wishes, Freud's theory would, to that extent, be shown to be inadequate.

3. *Linguistic Recommendations.* If aesthetic theories are neither definitions of art nor empirical hypotheses, what are they? A suggestion made by several philosophers is that statements such as "Art is significant form" express linguistic recommendations. A linguistic recommendation is an invitation to use words in a new way, to *mean by them* something different from what they customarily *mean.* As such, it is neither true nor false. If someone says "Let us mean by 'work of art' anything that has significant form," we can accept or reject his invitation, but we cannot refute him. Moreover, if he has already chosen to mean by "art" significant form, then, *as he uses the words,* "Art is significant form" is as necessarily true as "A hexapod has six feet."

Aesthetic theories, to be sure, are not explicitly phrased as linguistic recommendations. On the contrary, they are phrased in a manner typical of dictionary definitions or empirical hypotheses; which is why they are likely to be mistaken for them. Hence, if they are linguistic recommendations, they are implicit ones.

Moreover, they are not arbitrary in the way that "Art is a six-footed animal" would be arbitrary. To be persuasive, they must be couched in terms applicable to some, usually outstanding, works of art. And that is why insight can be gained into the nature of some works of art from these theories.

But why should anyone wish to use words in a new way or invite us to modify our normal linguistic behavior? Is our language not satisfactory as it stands?

In his essay "The Aesthetic Relevance of Artists' Intentions,"[10] Professor Aiken says that we call something a work of art primarily because we think that, if approached and handled in certain ways, it will give pleasure or satisfaction. If a picture or a poem can be admired or appreciated for its own sake, we are apt to call it a work of art; if not, we resist the temptation so to classify it. "The point is that 'work of art' is an expression of commendation. . . . A work of art is something which is admirable, which is worthy of admiration, and which, perhaps, ought to be admired."[11]

The fact that expressions such as "art" and "work of art" are used to praise and commend things as well as to classify and describe them lends a point to efforts to redefine them. Our linguistic behavior is continuous with our behavior generally: what we call something, how we classify or describe it, often reflects, and determines, our attitudes and reactions to it. Thus one way to urge a reform in people's behavior toward something is to urge a reform in what they call it. Is abortion murder? If you can convince people so to classify it, you can get them to adopt attitudes toward it different from those they might otherwise have.

Clive Bell, for example, wrote *Art* in 1913 when the taste of his contemporaries was restricted largely to what is called "academic" painting, painting in which subject matter is of prime importance. Bell had seen paintings of Cézanne, Matisse, and other post-Impressionists, and he noted that subject matter was not of prime importance in them, that their value did not rest on realism or sentimental associations but on what he called "significant form": lines, colors, patterns, and harmonies that are exciting in themselves. He found also that he could look at other paintings, those by the Venetian masters, for example, and at vases, carpets, and sculptures in much the same way as he looked at the pictures of Matisse, and with the same reward. But when he turned to the pictures of the academicians, the thrill disappeared. He announced his discovery by saying "Art *is* significant form." What he had discovered, however, was not the essence or distinctive trait of art, as he supposed, but a new way of looking at works of visual art; one which, if generally adopted, would lead people to describe academic pictures as "not art," or "not *really* art," and the pictures of Cézanne and Matisse as "real art."

Tolstoy's theory, to take a very different case, had a similar job to do. He was not mainly interested in the formal values or beauty of art, but rather in its power to convey emotions, particularly sentiments of brotherhood. When he wrote *What is Art?*, his consuming interests were religious. He wanted to break down the barriers that divide men and bring them together in the bonds of what he understood as Christian love. Everything was to be subordinated to this end, including art. Hence, if a folksong tends to "infect" people with feelings of fellowship more than a Beethoven symphony does, only the folksong is "real art."

Not all aesthetic theories can be supposed to have this sort of reform as their object. Jacques Maritain and Susanne Langer seem to be quite satisfied with the taste of their time; accepting the theory of either would entail no significant change in one's critical sensibilities. They do not invite us to classify as art things we should not normally so classify, or to refuse to classify as art things we should normally so classify. The linguistic reforms they urge involve a readjustment of our attitudes towards art as a whole: they ask us to look at it differently, to think of it as of a kind with things with which it would ordinarily be contrasted.

Mrs. Langer, for example, asks us to look upon works of art as symbols which express the artist's insights into the nature of our emotional life in a way analogous to that in which a scientific theory expresses the insights of a Newton or Einstein into the workings of the physical world. But feelings are ineffable, indescribable by language.[12] Any scientific investigation of them is thus bound to tell us very little of their nature, however adequately it may describe their conditions. But art succeeds where science fails. Hence, we must regard works of art—at least all *good* works of art —with the same admiration and respect appropriate to sound scientific theories, as expressions of an important sort of *knowledge*.

Assuming that theories about the nature of art do express linguistic recommendations, what changes in our verbal behavior are urged by Croce, Maritain, and Parker? And why? What difference would accepting any of these theories make in our responses to art?

We have found reasons for supposing that, despite what aestheticians sometimes say about their own work, their theories about the nature of art are neither definitions nor empirical hypotheses. We have suggested that they might be linguistic recommendations. This suggestion has the virtue of accounting for certain features of aesthetic theories that would otherwise be mysterious, but it is not irresistible. If aesthetic theories are not definitions, or empirical hypotheses, or linguistic recommendations, what are they? We cannot accept all of them. Either we must ignore them all, which would solve nothing and would still leave the problem of what sophisticated and intelligent men are doing when they propound a theory of art; or we must either accept one and reject the rest, or reject them all. But what reasons can we give for rejecting any theory of art? Since our reasons must be relevant to the theory, whatever reasons we give will show how we understand the theory, what sort of theory we take it to be; and that is precisely the issue we have here been concerned with.

Notes

1. But why does Bell restrict his argument to works of *visual* art? The phrase "works of art" covers more than works of visual art, as the use of the qualifying adjective "visual" attests. Hence, to be consistent, Bell should say, "Either *all* works of art have some common quality, or when we speak of 'works of art' we gibber."

2. For a fuller development of this line of criticism, see Morris Lazerowitz,

The Structure of Metaphysics, London, Routledge and Kegan Paul, 1955, Ch. III, esp. pp. 90-96.

3. Ludwig Wittgenstein refers to such resemblances as "family resemblances." See his *Philosophical Investigations,* trans. by G. E. M. Anscombe, Oxford, Basil Blackwell, 1953, p. 32e.

4. On this point, see J. L. Austin, "The Meaning of a Word," *Philosophical Papers,* ed. by J. O. Urmson and G. J. Warnock, Oxford, The Clarendon Press, 1961, 23-43, esp. 37-43.

5. Recommended exercise: Take a number of actual or imaginary cases of things you would *not* call "art" and note the reasons you would offer in each case for not doing so.

6. Philosophers sometimes draw a distinction between the definition of a term and an analysis of its meaning. An analysis is either a statement of logical equivalence, *e.g.* "A hexapod is an animal having six feet" (or "Something is a hexapod if and only if it is an animal having six feet"), or a necessary implication, *e.g.* "A cat is an animal" (or "If something is a cat, then it is an animal"). (Other forms of statement are called "analyses" in philosophy, but this kind of analysis is the only one that can plausibly be supposed to fit such statements as "Art is intuition.") An equivalence gives us a complete analysis of the meaning of an expression; a necessary implication, a partial analysis. The difference between a definition and an analysis is simply the difference between "The word 'hexapod' means an animal having six feet" and "A hexapod is an animal having six feet." Both definition and analysis give the meaning of an expression; for, all I know when I know that a hexapod is an animal having six feet is the meaning of the word "hexapod." What makes an analysis correct or incorrect, then, is a verbal fact, a fact about the meaning of an expression. If "hexapod" means an animal having six feet, then "A hexapod is an animal having six feet," being equivalent to "An animal having six feet is an animal having six feet," is necessarily true and is a correct analysis of the meaning of "hexapod."

Since "art" does not mean significant form, intuition, etc., statements such as "Art is significant form" are no more correct analyses of the meaning of "art" than they are correct definitions.

7. For precisely this sort of reply, see Bell's discussion of Frith's *Paddington Station* and Sir Luke Fildes's *The Doctor.* Note also what Maritain says in reply to Valéry and Stravinsky: "I think that they purposely do not tell the truth. . . ." Why does Maritain suppose that Valéry and Stravinsky are lying, except that they say things about themselves that are apparently incompatible with his theory?

8. The fact that the interior angles of a given triangle equal 180 degrees is not *evidence for* the truth of the proposition of geometry that the interior angles of all triangles equal 180 degrees; it is simply an instance of the truth of that proposition.

9. Freud's paper "Creative Writers and Day-Dreaming" appears in Appendix C of this book. This paper does not contain a full statement of Freud's theory, but it is indicative of the sort of writing on art that Freud did and it contains some of his characteristic ideas. For an excellent account of Freud's whole theory, see Richard Sterba, "The Problem of Art in Freud's Writings," *The Psychoanalytic Quarterly,* IX (1940), 256-268.

10. Reprinted in Section V of this book.

11. Strictly speaking this is incorrect. It brings out only one side of our use of such expressions as "art" and "work of art," their honorific or commendatory use. Thus, one might say of a painting, "That's not art; that's just scribbling" or ". . .just a display of technical virtuosity." But "art" and "work of art" are also used for such neutral purposes as identifying and classifying. We would not

accuse the director of an art museum of having made a *classificatory* mistake in hanging the painting we refer to pejoratively as childish scribbling.

12. For the criticism of this claim, see W. E. Kennick, "Art and the Ineffable," *Journal of Philosophy,* LVIII (1961), 309-320.

Suggestions for Additional Reading

Commentaries on, and criticisms of, theories presented in this section:

H. W. Garrod, *Tolstoy's Theory of Art* (Oxford, 1935); I. Knox, "Tolstoy's Esthetic Definition of Art," *J. Phil.,* XXVII (1930), 65-70; Theodore Redpath, *Tolstoy* (London, 1958); B. Bosanquet, "Croce's Aesthetic," *P.B.A.,* 9 (1919-20), 261-288; E. F. Carritt, "Croce and His Aesthetic," *Mind,* LXII (1953), 452-465; John Hospers, "The Croce-Collingwood Theory of Art," *Philosophy,* XXXI (1956), 291-308; Bernard Mayo, "Art, Language, and Philosophy in Croce," *Phil. Quart.,* 5 (1955), 245-260; G. N. G. Orsini, *Benedetto Croce: Philosopher of Art and Literary Critic* (Carbondale, Ill., 1961); C. J. Ducasse, *The Philosophy of Art* (New York, 1929), Chs. 2-4; Morris Weitz, *Philosophy of the Arts* (Cambridge, 1950), Chs. 1, 2; Paul Welsh, "Discursive and Presentational Symbols," *Mind,* LXIV (1955), 181-199.

Other theories of the nature of art:

T. E. Hulme, "Bergson's Theory of Art," *Speculations* (London, 1924), 143-169; Roger Fry, "An Essay in Aesthetics," *Vision and Design* (London, 1920; New York, 1956), 16-38; John Dewey, *Art as Experience* (New York, 1934); Ernst Cassirer, *An Essay on Man* (New Haven, 1944), Ch. 9; I. A. Richards, *Principles of Literary Criticism* (London, 1925); C. J. Ducasse, *The Philosophy of Art,* Ch. 8; Charles W. Morris, "Science, Art and Technology," Kenyon Review, I (1939), 409-423; Paul Weiss, *The World of Art* (Carbondale, Ill., 1961).

On the problem of defining the nature of art:

W. B. Gallie, "Art as an Essentially Contested Concept," *Phil. Quart.,* 6 (1956), 97-114, "Essentially Contested Concepts," *P.A.S.,* LVI (1955-56), 167-198; W. E. Kennick, "Does Traditional Aesthetics Rest on a Mistake?," *Mind,* LXVII (1958), 317-334; Beryl Lake, "A Study of the Irrefutability of Two Aesthetic Theories," *Aesthetics and Language,* W. Elton ed. (Oxford, 1954); Morris Weitz, "The Role of Theory in Aesthetics," *J.A.A.C.,* XV (1956), 27-35, reprinted in *Problems in Aesthetics* (New York, 1959) along with a reply by Erich Kahler, "What is Art?"; Paul Ziff, "The Task of Defining a Work of Art," *Phil. Rev.,* LXII (1953), 58-78.

II

The Work of Art and
The Aesthetic Object

Introduction

WHAT SORT OF ENTITY is a work of art? Is it, like a stone, a material object? Or, like a shadow or a reflection on water, something non-material but physical? Or is it an imaginary object like the Cheshire Cat? Or, like an angel, a spiritual being? Or is it a mental entity, something that exists only in the mind? Or is it something different from any of these?

Many philosophers have held that, whatever else it might be, no work of art is physical or material. They do not deny that there are in museums objects composed of canvas and pigment or of stone that people *call* works of art, but they contend that it is a mistake to *identify* these objects with the works of art that we appreciate, criticize, and value. Only an "unphilosophical mind," says DeWitt Parker, thinks that the "Mona Lisa" is a canvas that hangs on a wall in the Louvre, that the "Venus de Milo" is a carved block of marble set up in another room of that palace, or that a poem is a set of ink marks on paper.

This doctrine is of relatively recent origin, a product of nineteenth-century post-Kantian Idealism. As a metaphysical thesis, Idealism is the denial of the independent existence of matter and the affirmation that all reality is mental or spiritual in nature, that "the world," as Josiah Royce put it, "is such stuff as ideas are made of." But the doctrine is not merely a corollary of Idealism. It has been argued for independently by such philosophers as Parker and Pepper, who are not Idealists. Their aim is to isolate and describe the object of aesthetic appreciation and criticism so as to illuminate the nature of these activities.

We tend to think of things as being of certain very general kinds—physical, material, imaginary, spiritual, etc.—partly by reference to the ways in which they are, or might be, apprehended. Think of the reasons why we assign the following to different "ontological" categories: a stone, the number three, a dream, and the rainbow. The sort of entity a work of art is, therefore, appears to be determined in part by how, *as a work of art,* it is apprehended. This in turn cannot but have profound consequences for appreciation and criticism, for the very possibility of shared appreciation and objective criticism depends upon a work of art being open to inspection by different observers. (If works of art were "private" in the way dreams are, criticism and appreciation would be either impossible or very different from what they now are.) Herein lies the importance for aesthetics of the problem at issue.

Collingwood, who was influenced by the Idealist Croce, holds that works of art are imaginary objects; Stephen C. Pepper, that they consist of perceptions. Both offer a general answer to the question, "What sort of entity is a work of art?" Wellek and Warren do not. They are interested solely in what a poem is, but the arguments by which they arrive at the conclusion that a poem is a system or structure of norms have interesting implications for art generally.[1]

Note

1. For further material bearing on the problem of this section, see, in addition to Parker's essay and the selection from Croce in Section I, the selections of Sections VI and VII.

R. G. COLLINGWOOD

The Work of Art as an
Imaginary Object

IF THE MAKING of a tune is an instance of imaginative creation, a tune is an imaginary thing. And the same applies to a poem or a painting or any other work of art. This seems paradoxical; we are apt to think that a tune is not an imaginary thing but a real thing, a real collection of noises; that a painting is a real piece of canvas covered with real colours; and so on. I hope to show, if the reader will have patience, that there is no paradox here; that both these propositions express what we do as a matter of fact say about works of art; and that they do not contradict one another, because they are concerned with different things.

When, speaking of a work of art (tune, picture, etc.), we mean by art a specific craft, intended as a stimulus for producing specific emotional effects in an audience, we certainly mean to designate by the term "work of art" something that we should call real. The artist as magician or purveyor of amusement is necessarily a craftsman making real things, and making them out of some material according to some plan. His works are as real as the works of an engineer, and for the same reason.

But it does not at all follow that the same is true of an artist proper. His business is not to produce an emotional effect in an audience, but, for example, to make a tune. This tune is already complete and perfect when it exists merely as a tune in his head, that is, an imaginary tune. Next, he may arrange for the tune to be played before an audience. Now there comes into existence a real tune, a collection of noises. But which of these two things is the work of art? Which of them is the music? The answer is implied in what we have already said: the music, the work of art, is not the collection of noises, it is the tune in the composer's head. The noises made by the performers, and heard by the audience, are not

From *The Principles of Art* by R. G. Collingwood, 1938 and reprinted by permission of Clarendon Press, Oxford.

the music at all; they are only means by which the audience, if they listen intelligently (not otherwise) can reconstruct for themselves the imaginary tune that existed in the composer's head.

This is not a paradox. It is not something contrary to what we ordinarily believe and express in our ordinary speech. We all know perfectly well, and remind each other often enough, that a person who hears the noises the instruments make is not thereby possessing himself of the music. Perhaps no one can do that unless he does hear the noises; but there is something else which he must do as well. Our ordinary word for this other thing is listening; and the listening which we have to do when we hear the noises made by musicians is in a way rather like the thinking we have to do when we hear the noises made, for example, by a person lecturing on a scientific subject. We hear the sound of his voice; but what he is doing is not simply to make noises, but to develop a scientific thesis. The noises are meant to assist us in achieving what he assumes to be our purpose in coming to hear his lecture, that is, thinking this same scientific thesis for ourselves. The lecture, therefore, is not a collection of noises made by the lecturer with his organs of speech; it is a collection of scientific thoughts related to those noises in such a way that a person who not only hears but thinks as well becomes able to think these thoughts for himself. We may call this the communication of thought by means of speech, if we like; but if we do, we must think of communication not as an "imparting" of thought by the speaker to the hearer, the speaker somehow planting his thought in the hearer's receptive mind, but as a "reproduction" of the speaker's thought by the hearer, by virtue of his own active thinking.

The parallel with listening to music is not complete. The two cases are similar at one point, dissimilar at another. They are dissimilar in that a concert and a scientific lecture are different things, and what we are trying to "get out of" the concert is a thing of a different kind from the scientific thoughts we are trying to "get out of" the lecture. But they are similar in this: that just as what we get out of the lecture is something other than the noises we hear proceeding from the lecturer's mouth, so what we get out of the concert is something other than the noises made by the performers. In each case, what we get out of it is something which we have to reconstruct in our own minds, and by our own efforts; something which remains forever inaccessible to a person who cannot or will not make efforts of the right kind, however completely he hears the sounds that fill the room in which he is sitting.

This, I repeat, is something we all know perfectly well. And because we all know it, we need not trouble to examine or criticize the ideas of aestheticians (if there are any left to-day—they were common enough at one time) who say that what we get out of listening to music, or looking at paintings, or the like, is some peculiar kind of sensual pleasure. When we do these things, we certainly may, in so far as we are using our senses, enjoy sensual pleasures. It would be odd if we did not. A colour, or a shape, or an instrumental timbre may give us an exquisite pleasure of a purely sensual kind. It may even be true (though this is not so certain) that no one would become a lover of music unless he were more suscep-tible than other people to the sensual pleasure of sound. But even if a special susceptibility to this pleasure may at first lead some people to-wards music, they must, in proportion as they are more susceptible, take the more pains to prevent that susceptibility from interfering with their power of listening. For any concentration on the pleasantness of the noises themselves concentrates the mind on hearing, and makes it hard or impossible to listen. There is a kind of person who goes to concerts mainly for the sensual pleasure he gets from the sheer sounds; his pres-ence may be good for the box-office, but it is as bad for music as the presence of a person who went to a scientific lecture for the sensual pleas-ure he got out of the tones of the lecturer's voice would be for science. And this, again, everybody knows.

It is unnecessary to go through the form of applying what has been said about music to the other arts. We must try instead to make in a positive shape the point that has been put negatively. Music does not consist of heard noises, paintings do not consist of seen colours, and so forth. Of what, then, do these things consist? Not, clearly, of a "form," understood as a pattern or a system of relations between the various noises we hear or the various colours we see. Such "forms" are nothing but the perceived structures of bodily "works of art," that is to say, "works of art" falsely so called; and these formalistic theories of art, popular though they have been and are, have no relevance to art proper and will not be further considered in this book. The distinction between form and matter, on which they are based, is a distinction belonging to the philosophy of craft, and not applicable to the philosophy of art.

The work of art proper is something not seen or heard, but something imagined. But what is it that we imagine? We have suggested that in mu-sic the work of art proper is an imagined tune. Let us begin by develop-ing this idea.

Everybody must have noticed a certain discrepancy between what we actually see when looking at a picture or statue or play and what we see imaginatively; what we actually see when listening to music or speech and what we imaginatively hear. To take an obvious example: in watching a puppet-play we could (as we say) swear that we have seen the expression on the puppets' faces change with their changing gestures and the puppet-man's changing words and tones of voice. Knowing that they are only puppets, we know that their facial expression cannot change; but that makes no difference; we continue to see imaginatively the expressions which we know that we do not see actually. The same thing happens in the case of masked actors like those of the Greek stage.

In listening to the pianoforte, again, we know from evidence of the

same kind that we must be hearing every note begin with a *sforzando,*
and fade away for the whole length of time that it continues to sound.
But our imagination enables us to read into this experience something
quite different. As we seem to see the puppets' features move, so we seem
to hear a pianist producing a *sostenuto* tone, almost like that of a horn;
and in fact the notes of the horn and the pianoforte are easily mistaken
one for the other. Still stranger, when we hear a violin and pianoforte
playing together in the key, say, of G, the violin's F sharp is actually
played a great deal sharper than the pianoforte's. Such a discrepancy
would sound intolerably out of tune except to a person whose imagination was trained to focus itself on the key of G, and silently corrected
every note of the equally tempered pinaoforte to suit it. The corrections
which imagination must thus carry out, in order that we should be able
to listen to an entire orchestra, beggar description. When we listen to a
speaker or singer, imagination is constantly supplying articulate sounds
which actually our ears do not catch. In looking at a drawing in pen or
pencil, we take a series of roughly parallel lines for the tint of a shadow.
And so on.

Conversely, in all these cases imagination works negatively. We dis-
imagine, if I may use the word, a great deal which we actually see and
hear. The street noises at a concert, the noises made by our breathing and
shuffling neighbours, and even some of the noises made by the performers,
are thus shut out of the picture unless by their loudness or in some other
way they are too obtrusive to be ignored. At the theatre, we are strangely
able to ignore the silhouettes of the people sitting in front of us, and a
good many things that happen on the stage. Looking at a picture, we do
not notice the shadows that fall on it or, unless it is excessive, the light
reflected from its varnish.

All this is commonplace. And the conclusion has already been stated
by Shakespeare's Theseus: "the best in this kind ['works of art,' as things
actually perceived by the senses] are but shadows, and the worst are no
worse if imagination amend them." The music to which we listen is not
heard sound, but that sound as amended in various ways by the listener's
imagination, and so with the other arts.

But this does not go nearly far enough. Reflection will show that the
imagination with which we listen to music is something more, and more
complex, than any inward ear; the imagination with which we look at
paintings is something more than "the mind's eye." Let us consider this
in the case of painting.

The change which came over painting at the close of the nineteenth
century was nothing short of revolutionary. Every one in the course of
that century had supposed that painting was "a visual art"; that the
painter was primarily a person who used his eyes, and used his hands
only to record what the use of his eyes had revealed to him. Then came
Cézanne, and began to paint like a blind man. His stilllife studies, which

enshrine the essence of his genius, are like groups of things that have been groped over with the hands; he uses colour not to reproduce what he sees in looking at them but to express almost in a kind of algebraic notation what in this groping he has felt. So with his interiors; the spectator finds himself bumping about those rooms, circumnavigating with caution those menacingly angular tables, coming up to the persons that so massively occupy those chairs and fending himself off them with his hands. It is the same when Cézanne takes us into the open air. His landscapes have lost almost every trace of visuality. Trees never looked like that; that is how they feel to a man who encounters them with his eyes shut, blundering against them blindly. A bridge is no longer a pattern of colour, as it is for Cotman; or a patch of colour so distorted as to arouse in the spectator the combined emotions of antiquarianism and vertigo, as it is for Mr. Frank Brangwyn; it is a perplexing mixture of projections and recessions, over and round which we find ourselves feeling our way as one can imagine an infant feeling its way, when it has barely begun to crawl, among the nursery furniture. And over the landscape broods the obsession of Mont Saint-Victoire, never looked at, but always felt, as a child feels the table over the back of its head.

Of course Cézanne was right. Painting can never be a visual art. A man paints with his hands, not with his eyes. The Impressionist doctrine that what one paints is light[1] was a pedantry which failed to destroy the painters it enslaved only because they remained painters in defiance of the doctrine: men of their hands, men who did their work with fingers and wrist and arm, and even (as they walked about the studio) with their legs and toes. What one paints is what can be painted; no one can do more; and what can be painted must stand in some relation to the muscular activity of painting it. Cézanne's practice reminds one of Kant's theory that the painter's only use for his colours is to make shapes visible. But it is really quite different. Kant thought of the painter's shapes as two-dimensional shapes visibly traced on the canvas; Cézanne's shapes are never two-dimensional, and they are never traced on the canvas; they are solids, and we get at them through the canvas. In this new kind of painting the "plane of the picture" disappears; it melts into nothing, as we go through it.[2]

Vernon Blake, who understood all this very well from the angle of the practising artist, and could explain himself in words like the Irishman he was, told draughtsmen that the plane of the picture was a mere superstition. Hold your pencil vertical to the paper, said he; don't stroke the paper, dig into it; think of it as if it were the surface of a slab of clay in which you were going to cut a relief, and of your pencil as a knife. Then you will find that you can draw something which is not a mere pattern on paper, but a solid thing lying inside or behind the paper.

In Mr. Berenson's hands the revolution became retrospective. He found that the great Italian painters yielded altogether new results when approached in this manner. He taught his pupils (and every one who takes any interest in Renaissance painting nowadays is Mr. Berenson's pupil) to look in paintings for what he called "tactile values"; to think of their muscles as they stood before a picture, and notice what happened in their fingers and elbows. He showed that Masaccio and Raphael, to take only two outstanding instances, were painting as Cézanne painted, not at all as Monet or Sisley painted; not squirting light on a canvas, but exploring with arms and legs a world of solid things where Masaccio stalks giant-like on the ground and Raphael floats through serene air.

In order to understand the theoretical significance of these facts, we must look back at the ordinary theory of painting current in the nineteenth century. This was based on the conception of a "work of art," with its implication that the artist is a kind of craftsman producing things of this or that kind, each with the characteristics proper to its kind, according to the difference between one kind of craft and another. The musician makes sounds; the sculptor makes solid shapes in stone or metal; the painter makes patterns of paint on canvas. What there is in these works depends, of course, on what kind of works they are; and what the spectator finds in them depends on what there is in them. The spectator in looking at a picture is simply seeing flat patterns of colour, and he can get nothing out of the picture except what can be contained in such patterns.

The forgotten truth about painting which was rediscovered by what may be called the Cézanne-Berenson approach to it was that the spectator's experience on looking at a picture is not a specifically visual experience at all. What he experiences does not consist of what he sees. It does not even consist of this as modified, supplemented, and expurgated by the work of the visual imagination. It does not belong to sight alone, it belongs also (and on some occasions even more essentially) to touch. We must be a little more accurate, however. When Mr. Berenson speaks of tactile values, he is not thinking of things like the texture of fur and cloth, the cool roughness of bark, the smoothness or grittiness of a stone, and other qualities which things exhibit to our sensitive finger-tips. As his own statements abundantly show, he is thinking, or thinking in the main, of distance and space and mass: not of touch sensations, but of motor sensations such as we experience by using our muscles and moving our limbs. But these are not actual motor sensations, they are imaginary motor sensations. In order to enjoy them when looking at a Masaccio we need not walk straight through the picture, or even stride about the gallery; what we are doing is to imagine ourselves as moving in these ways. In short: what we get from looking at a picture is not merely the experience of seeing, or even partly seeing and partly imagining, certain visible objects; it is also, and in Mr. Berenson's opinion more importantly, the imaginary experience of certain complicated muscular movements.

Persons especially interested in painting may have thought all this, when Mr. Berenson began saying it, something strange and new; but in the case of other arts the parallels were very familiar. It was well known that in listening to music we not only hear the noises of which the "music," that is to say the sequences and combinations of audible sounds, actually consists; we also enjoy imaginary experiences which do not belong to the region of sound at all, notably visual and motor experiences. Everybody knew, too, that poetry has the power of bringing before us not only the sounds which constitute the audible fabric of the "poem," but other sounds, and sights, and tactile and motor experiences, and at times even scents, all of which we possess, when we listen to poetry, in imagination.

This suggests that what we get out of a work of art is always divisible into two parts. (1) There is a specialized sensuous experience, an experience of seeing or hearing as the case may be. (2) There is also a non-specialized imaginative experience, involving not only elements homogeneous, after their imaginary fashion, with those which make up the specialized sensuous experience, but others heterogeneous with them. So remote is this imaginative experience from the specialism of its sensuous basis, that we may go so far as to call it an imaginative experience of total activity.

At this point the premature theorist lifts up his voice again. "See," he exclaims, "how completely we have turned the tables on the old-fashioned theory that what we get out of art is nothing but the sensual pleasure of sight or hearing! The enjoyment of art is no merely sensuous experience, it is an imaginative experience. A person who listens to music, instead of merely hearing it, is not only experiencing noises, pleasant though these may be. He is imaginatively experiencing all manner of visions and motions; the sea, the wind, the stars; the falling of the rain-drops, the rushing of the wind, the storm, the flow of the brook;[3] the dance, the embrace, and the battle. A person who looks at pictures, instead of merely seeing patterns of colour, is moving in imagination among buildings and landscapes and human forms. What follows? Plainly this: the value of any given work of art to a person properly qualified to appreciate its value is not the delightfulness of the sensuous elements in which as a work of art it actually consists, but the delightfulness of the imaginative experience which those sensuous elements wake in him. Works of art are only means to an end; the end is this total imaginative experience which they enable us to enjoy."

This attempt to rehabilitate the technical theory depends on distinguishing what we find in the work of art, its actual sensuous qualities, as put there by the artist, from something else which we do not strictly find in it, but rather import into it from our own stores of experience and powers of imagination. The first is conceived as objective, really belonging to the work of art: the second as subjective, belonging not to it but to activities which go on in us when we contemplate it. The peculiar value of this contemplation, then, is conceived as lying not in the first thing but in the second. Any one having the use of his senses could see all the colours and shapes that a picture contains, and hear all the sounds which together make up a symphony; but he would not on that account be enjoying an aesthetic experience. To do that he must use his imagination, and so proceed from the first part of the experience, which is given in sensation, to the second part, which is imaginatively constructed.

This seems to be the position of the "realistic" philosophers who maintain that what they call "beauty" is "subjective." The peculiar value which belongs to an experience such as that of listening to music or looking at pictures arises, they think, not from our getting out of these things what is really in them, or "apprehending their objective nature," but from our being stimulated by contact with them to certain free activities of our own. It is in these activities that the value really resides; and although (to use Professor Alexander's word) we may "impute" it to the music or the picture, it actually belongs not to them but to us.[4]

But we cannot rest in this position. The distinction between what we find and what we bring is altogether too naive. Let us look at it from the point of view of the artist. He presents us with a picture. According to the doctrine just expounded, he has actually put into this picture certain colours which, by merely opening our eyes and looking at it, we shall find there. Is this all he did in painting the picture? Certainly not. When he painted it, he was in possession of an experience quite other than that of seeing the colours he was putting on the canvas; an imaginary experience of total activity more or less like that which we construct for ourselves when we look at the picture. If he knew how to paint, and if we know how to look at a painting, the resemblance between this imaginary experience of his and the imaginary experience which we get from looking at his work is at least as close as that between the colours he saw in the picture and those we see; perhaps closer. But if he paints his picture in such a way that we, when we look at it using our imagination, find ourselves enjoying an imaginary experience of total activity like that which he enjoyed when painting it, there is not much sense in saying that we bring this experience with us to the picture and do not find it there. The artist, if we told him that, would laugh at us and assure us that what we believed ourselves to have read into the picture was just what he put there.

No doubt there is a sense in which we bring it with us. Our finding of it is not something that merely happens to us, it is something we do, and do because we are the right kind of people to do it. The imaginary experience which we get from the picture is not merely the kind of experience the picture is capable of arousing, it is the kind of experience we are capable of having. But this applies equally to the colours. He has not put into the picture certain colours which we passively find there. He has painted, and seen certain colours come into existence as he paints. If we, looking at his picture afterwards, see the same colours, that is because our own powers of colour-vision are like his. Apart from the activity of our senses we should see no colours at all.

Thus the two parts of the experience are not contrasted in the way in which we fancied them to be. There is no justification for saying that the sensuous part of it is something we find and the imaginary part something we bring, or that the sensuous part is objectively "there" in the "work of art," the imaginary part subjective, a mode of consciousness as distinct from the quality of a thing. Certainly we find the colours there in the painting; but we find them only because we are actively using our eyes, and have eyes of such a kind as to see what the painter wanted us to see, which a colour-blind person could not have done. We bring our powers of vision with us, and find what they reveal. Similarly, we bring our imaginative powers with us, and find what they reveal: namely, an imaginary experience of total activity which we find in the picture because the painter had put it there.

Notes

1. Anticipated by Uvedale Price as long ago as 1801: "I can imagine a man of the future, who may be born without the sense of feeling, being able to see nothing but light variously modified" (*Dialogue on the distinct characters of the Picturesque and Beautiful*).

2. The "disappearance" of the picture-plane is the reason why, in modern artists who have learnt to accept Cézanne's principles and to carry their consequences a stage further than he carried them himself, perspective (to the great scandal of the man in the street, who clings to the picture-plane as unconsciously and as convulsively as a drowning man to a spar) has disappeared too. The man in the street thinks that this has happened because these modern fellows can't draw; which is like thinking that the young men of the Royal Air Force career about in the sky because they can't walk.

3. Ernest Newman, "Programme Music," in *Musical Studies* (1905), p. 109.

4. So Alexander, *Beauty and Other Forms of Value* (1933), pp. 25-6; Carritt, *What is Beauty?* (1932), ch. iv. I am not forgetting that Professor Alexander has a chapter (*op. cit.* ch. x) on "The Objectivity of Beauty."

STEPHEN COBURN PEPPER

The Aesthetic Work of Art

THE MAIN CONCERN of aesthetic criticism is with works of art. Objects of nature—shells, ferns, mosses, trees, insects, animals, snowflakes, rock formations, mountains, water, clouds, the sun, and the moon—come in for aesthetic approval and delight, and the aesthetic perception of them is essentially the same as that for works of art, but not being objects of human construction they have not so urgently called for human criticism. Also, beyond natural objects there is a large field of experience generally regarded as aesthetic in character which we scarcely even subject to critical judgment and usually think it rather pointless to try to criticize. I refer to dreams, reveries, objectless moods and emotions, floating images, personal thoughts, and personal activities like walking and leaping, and many types of social activity like companionship, conversation, games, business competition, intellectual argument, mutual cooperation, or the mere exhilaration of being in a crowd. All these probably fall within the aesthetic field, yet they rarely raise serious controversies of aesthetic judgment. Perhaps they should, but in fact they rarely do. The great controversies of aesthetic judgment rotate about works of art. The practical field of aesthetic criticism is thus smaller than the total aesthetic field. It is the field of works of art.

The instinct of writers on criticism to seek the justification of aesthetic criticism among the properties of the total aesthetic field is sound. But these men have tended to leap too far too soon. There has been a strange neglect of the nature of the work of art. . . .

What are the general characteristics of an aesthetic work of art? It is a very peculiar sort of object. In order to keep our description clear, I shall begin with just one kind of work of art, the simplest kind to describe, the one employed in the lectures, namely a picture, and then I will proceed to other kinds gathering up the various characteristics of the aesthetic work of art in general as we go along. I begin then with a description of what a picture is as a work of art. We shall take this as a sort of normal description and then later show how this norm is added to or modified in terms of other kinds of works of art. Finally we shall gather all the material together for a total rounded description. We shall find that quite a number of muddles connected with aesthetic criticism solve themselves as a result of this analysis.

To be specific, let us take as our picture the El Greco "Toledo." Now what is the aesthetic object here which is the focus of aesthetic judgment and criticism? There is the physical canvas and pigment, which El Greco worked upon, which has passed through various hands, and which now hangs on a wall of the New York Metropolitan Art Museum. There is next the subject who comes in and looks at it—you or me. Lastly there is the perception of the picture that comes to the subject whenever he looks at it. Now let us make the diagram of these three factors:

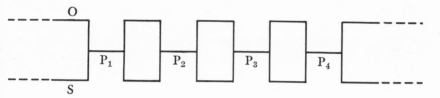

$O =$ the physical object

$S =$ the subject

$P =$ a perception of O

O represents the continuity of the physical object: in our present example, the canvas and pigment of El Greco's picture. That physical picture continues right along on the wall whether perceived or not. It is represented by the continuous upper line that periodically drops into perception and out of it. When not perceived it is just O, but when perceived it is P_1, P_2, P_3, P_4, four successive perceptions into which it enters. Time is conceived as moving from left to right. Since the physical object continues in and out of perceptions, we may call it a physical continuant.

S in the diagram represents the subject such as you or me. The subject also is a continuant and exists during periods when it is not perceiving things. The subject, so far as we identify it with our physical body, is much like the physical continuant. It has mass and electrical and chemical properties, but besides these the subject has other continuous characteristics which we lump together in the term "mind." The subject has feelings, memories, thoughts, and so on, which continue when he is not perceiving. The continuity of the subject is accordingly represented in our diagram by the continuous lower line which comes up every now and then to the perception of the picture. Without committing ourselves as to whether the subject is mainly mind or body, or even upon the final validity of this distinction, we may safely for the purposes of this analysis call the subject a psychophysical continuant. In some sense, you or I or any critic continues to exist before, through, and after our perceptions of a picture.

Now, a perception occurs only when a subject and an object get into some sort of touch with each other. This contact in perception between S and O we represent by P, and the successive P_1, P_2, P_3, P_4 represent different perceptions of the same object by the same subject.

Though the diagram represents the perception as a complete merging of subject and object, that is never literally the case. Both are very complex and only parts of each actually get in touch with each other directly or indirectly in any given perception. The physical picture has many properties that do not enter into any perception of it, and the subject (you or me) has large portions of his personality that are not touched in the perception of the picture. But not to complicate a sufficiently complicated situation even at its simplest, the diagram merely represents that in some sense in perception a physical object does get in touch with a subject like you or me, and that reciprocally you or I do get in touch with a physical object. We see the picture, and what we see is the result of ourselves and the physical picture somehow getting together. So, the diagram represents the two continuants as coming together in perception.

El Greco's physical picture O, then, hangs in a room of the museum. You or I enter the room and see it for the first time, P_1. We go out and come back and see it again, P_2, and a third time, P_3, and a fourth, P_4. The intervals between perception may be minutes, days, or years. But we go on as psychophysical continuants and the picture goes on as a physical continuant through the interims.

The repeatedly perceived picture, however, it should be noticed, is not a continuant. The perceived picture consists of a succession of intermittent perceptions—at least so far as we gather from any ordinary direct evidence concerning the situation. And what is particularly striking about this situation is that it is the *perceived picture,* not the continuous physical picture nor the continuous self who looks at it, that is the object appreciated and, if so be, critically judged. The central aesthetic object turns out to be an intermittent object made up of fugitive successive perceptions.

There are two important things to notice at once about this perceived aesthetic object—El Greco's "Toledo," for instance, as something seen. First, the features of this object—the colors and lines and volumes and movements in pictorial space and the representations of hills, buildings and clouds—are contributed to the perception from the *two* continuants. That is what makes it legitimate to merge the two continuants in the diagram wherever a perception is indicated. The shapes, for instance, are determined partly, as we learn from physics, by the distribution of pigments on the canvas and the configurations of reflected light from these pigments, but partly also, as we learn from physiology and psychology, by the structure of eye and nervous system and the activities of memory, association, feeling and the like which come out of ourselves.

Just how much is contributed by the physical continuant and how much by the perceiving self in an act of perception like this is one of the much discussed problems in modern psychology and philosophy. There are a number of reputable theories of perception, some placing most of the contributions to perception in the physical continuant and leaving to the perceiving self little besides a selective activity. For such a view, the colors and the sensuous shapes and perhaps even the representations of hills and houses all lie in the physical picture, and the mind merely selects what it sees in any single act of perception. It rarely sees all that is there, and may distort some features, but it makes no positive contributions to the perception. An opposite theory places nearly all of the contributions to perception in the mind of the continuant self. For this view, the colors and the sensuous shapes and the representations are all in the perceiver's mind, and the only contribution from the physical object is a stimulation of the sensory apparatus of the nervous system. All the rest is done in the mind of the perceiving self. Between these two extreme views various proportionings of the contributions are possible. But all views agree that in perception there are contributions from both the structure of the physical object and of the perceiving self, even if only a push-button stimulation from the object, or only a selective activity from the subject.

It follows that the object of aesthetic appreciation and the object of a critic's judgment in any such perception is necessarily a fugitive and intermittent object. This object occurs only when a self is actually in perceptive contact with a physical object, and lasts only as long as that contact lasts. Clear as this fact appears upon reflection, it is rarely fully taken in by writers on criticism and appreciation. The preponderant tendency is to identify the aesthetic object either with some conception of a physical continuant, or with some completely mental activity.

Since the aesthetic object in the appreciation and judgment of a work of art is always a perceived object, it is clear that here at least such identifications as those just mentioned cannot be made. For the one characteristic that makes a perception a perception and not an image or dream is that some contribution enters into the situation from both sides. How to proportion these contributions in detail need not concern us at this stage. The important thing is to see that in the normal act of critical aesthetic judgment we are dealing with perceptions, and that perceptions in their very nature are fugitive and depend on some degree of temporary cooperation between a physical object and a self. It will be best if we assume for the present that there is a rather large contribution from both sides.

So far, then, we have discovered that the object of critical aesthetic judgment is perceptions which are the fugitive and intermittent results of contributions from two continuants. The next thing we discover is that the successive perceptions (P_1, P_2, P_3, P_4), which a single subject has of a single physical object, carry a cumulative effect. The first time we look at the El Greco, for instance, we may notice principally the threatening clouds and the hills; the next time the dynamic movement of the forms; the next time details here and there that we had not noticed like the little figures down in the stream; the next time subtle repetitions of shapes; and so on. All of these perceptions are ordinarily regarded as relevant to the aesthetic object, and in giving a critical judgment of it are considered features to be taken account of. There are, moreover, certain psychological mechanisms that make it possible to carry over the results of one perception to considerable degree into the next, so that successive perceptions tend to become enriched by those that have gone before. This action is sometimes called "funding." A late perception in a series thus carries to considerable degree the results of previous perceptions as its constituents.

The cumulative effect is thus of two sorts. In part, it consists in finding more and more in the object, adding detail to detail out of the physical object through the successive perceptions. So far as this effect goes, each new perception might be quite different from its predecessor, since it brings out something quite new in the object. The only unity in the perceptive series so viewed would be the fact that the perceptions were all stimulated by the same physical continuant. The unity of the successive perceptions of a single object is, however, clearly much greater than that. This is achieved by the second sort of cumulative effect which we called funding. Through funding previous perceptions are carried over into later ones by means of memory and recognition, so that a later perception in some degree summarizes all its predecessors.

The object of aesthetic judgment and of appreciation in a work of art, then, is not this, that, or the other perception as it comes, but rather the total series, P_1-P_2-P_3-P_4, which we shall call the *perceptive series*. This is literally the aesthetic work of art. Different aesthetic philosophies differ in their ways of handling and interpreting this series. But in some sense or other it is clear that this perceptive series is the aesthetic object in the critical judgment and appreciation of works of art. The actual aesthetic object for the practical critic or everyday spectator is not a physical object, nor an idea, nor even a single act of perception, but the intermittent cumulative succession of perceptions which we call the perceptive series.

The peculiarities of aesthetic judgment, and the uncertainty on the part of many critics as to just what it is they are judging, all derive from the peculiarity of this practical object of aesthetic criticism and appreciation, for it is not a continuous object but an intermittent object, and it is not a succession of identically repeated perceptions but is a succession of perceptions with a cumulative growth at least up to a point.

Light begins to dawn on the problem of criticism when the situation is fully realized in this sense, and fully accepted. There is a strong tendency among critics and writers on aesthetics to try to reduce the aesthetic object to one of the continuants which make it up, or else to try to break it down into the atomic perceptions or transitory states that are cumulatively collected into its totality. These attempts to simplify the problem miss it at the start. We shall have many qualifications and amplifications to make of this primary analysis of a work of art. But the original facts from which any constructive thought about aesthetic criticism must clearly start are those which we have just elicited and have represented in our diagram. We may summarize them as follows:

A. In practical criticism, a critic is dealing with perceptions.

B. The content of these perceptions is partly a contribution from a continuous physical object, partly a contribution from a continuous psychophysical subject.

C. The aesthetic work of art and object of criticism is not a continuant, but an intermittent series of perceptions with a cumulative effect, namely, the perceptive series.

The analysis so far has been frankly preliminary and tentative. The illustration held in mind was of only one kind of work of art, a painting; and we took into consideration only one perceiver. We must now spread our analysis over the great variety of works of art that there are, and over the great variety of subjects perceiving them. We must consider variations in the physical continuants and in the psychophysical continuants. And first we ask, what variations are there in the physical continuants?

We shall pass under review the principal kinds of works of art. These kinds are associated with what are called "arts." All sorts of theoretical classifications of the arts can be made, but the classification that holds in practice, and so may be called the actual classification (the common division into painting, sculpture, architecture, music, literature, drama, and dance), is based on the nature of the physical continuants and on the limits of human capacities in dealing with them. It is physical materials together with the techniques for handling them that separate the aesthetic arts from one another.

If we may make a distinction between the ground for division and the reason for it, we may say that the *ground* for the actual divisions among the arts lies in the diverse materials out of which physical works of art are made, but that the *reason* lies in the limited technical capacities of men. Physical materials demand special techniques to handle them. It ordinarily takes all of a man's time to master one major technique. Few men become expert at more than one. For that reason the men training in one technique inevitably gather together in schools, and tend to continue together ever after, for, in a sense, the schooling never ceases. The divisions among the arts are thus divisions among men who from the limitations of human powers have had to become specialists in creative techniques, which techniques in turn depend upon the physical materials of the work of art.

Accordingly, in comparing the characteristic features of works from the various arts, we may expect to find a good many striking differences. But, at the same time, we shall discover some surprising hidden similarities. For we shall find that prominent features of works of art in one art were present but overlooked in the works of another art. By these comparisons we can thus gain a much more complete understanding of what a work of art as an object of critical and appreciative judgment is.

So far we have been dealing only with a painting. A painting, however, presents the simplest problem for the kind of analysis we have been doing. (Do not think this means that pictures are easier to criticize than other works of art. If anything, the contrary. I only mean that the analysis of the main factors involved in a work of art is most easily brought out in the case of a picture.) For in a picture we are concerned with only one physical object, and with only one surface of that object, and with that total surface open to vision whenever the picture is an object of appreciation. Moreover, the medium of light that reflects to the eye the patterns of pigments on the canvas is so transparent as to be easily overlooked and nearly negligible. The perceiver seems to be in direct touch with the controlling physical continuant, so that the merging of this physical continuant literally with the subject in perception (as shown in the diagram) closely describes the appearance of the situation.

Now, when we turn to sculpture, the situation is immediately complicated by the relevant use of the three dimensions. A statue in the round has a multiplicity of aspects or points of view, where a picture has but one.

There is still ordinarily just one statue standing as the work of art, say Michelangelo's "Moses." There is only one original "Moses." But a single adequate view of the "Moses" means walking all around it and synthesizing the perceptions of each aspect into a connecting circuit of aspects. The perceptual judgment involved in building up this aesthetic object thus requires a synthesis of juxtaposed aspects which is not involved in the appreciation of a picture. In the appreciation of a statue, one complete grasp of it, so to speak, requires a synthesis of a succession of perceptual aspects. A picture has only one aspect. Every aspect of a statue, of course, carries its own perceptive series. We thus learn the distinction between a perceptive series and a perceptual grasp, which is a summation and synthesis of the perceptive series of all the relevant aspects of the physical continuant. We see that a picture is a special case in which the perceptual grasp is telescoped into a single aspect. Most works of art have many aspects and demand the extension of the perceptive series, which we described in terms of one aspect only, to every aspect of the perceptual grasp. We may imagine a methodical subject who looks at a statue several times and each time makes a complete circuit of its aspects. With each circuit we then complete one perceptual grasp. But with each circuit he is also building up his perceptive series for each aspect. The total result would then have to be symbolized somewhat like the following, supposing that we considered four aspects: P^A, being a perception of aspect A, P^B of aspect B, P^C of aspect C, and P^D of D. And G will stand for a perceptual grasp as a result of a circuit of the aspects.

$$G_1 (P^A{}_1 + P^B{}_1 + P^C{}_1 + P^D{}_1) + G_2 (P^A{}_2 + P^B{}_2 + P^C{}_2 + P^D{}_2) + G_3 (P^A{}_3 + P^B{}_3 + P^C{}_3 + P^D{}_3) + G_4 (P^A{}_4 + P^B{}_4 + P^C{}_4 + P^D{}_4)$$

It is clear that this is just a complication of our original perceptive series to take care of a variety of aspects when, as usually, these occur. An aesthetic work of art in sculpture is made up of perceptions in intermittent cumulative series just as in painting, but the organization of these perceptions is more complex due to the presence of diverse aspects.

Of course, actually an appreciative critic does not build up his aesthetic statue in the methodical way diagrammed but in a much more haphazard (or rather sensitively controlled) manner. A man does not always take in every aspect of a statue each time he looks at it. He builds up his perceptual grasp of it simultaneously with his enrichment of the different aspects, and usually some aspects are intrinsically richer than others and require much more funding.

In architecture even more than in sculpture we see the importance of the perceptual grasp. For a building is not only three dimensional but has an inside relevant to aesthetic perception as well as an outside. Moreover, the aspects of a building are not all visual. There are many tactile and kinaesthetic aspects having to do with the texture of materials which are intended to be felt, walked upon, sat upon, and the like, and there are spaces to be walked through, and to, and from. Some of these, we notice, sculpture also often has. It should not, however, be assumed that differences of sensory material in perception involve differences of aspect, as if tactile sensations could not merge with visual. Besides, the further one goes in building up the perceptive materials of a work of art the harder it becomes to decide whether we are repeating perceptions of a single aspect or getting a new perceptive aspect and the more arbitrary the distinction seems. The essential thing is to be well aware of the different sorts of perceptive materials in a work of art to see that we miss none. But in a broad way, the distinction between an intensive appreciation of one aspect through a perceptive series and an organization of a number of aspects through a perceptual grasp is a useful one.

Turning from the visual arts to music we come upon a number of new features that still further add to our understanding of the nature of a work of art. In music the physical continuant is the musical score. And this is a set of symbols on paper.

The audible structure perceived by the senses is sounds produced by musical instruments or the human voice. Musical instruments are, of course, also physical continuants as well as the performers who convert the symbols of the score into the patterns of sounds perceived; but the perceived patterns of sounds are preserved not in the instruments but in the score. The instruments and those who perform upon them are in the nature of a medium between the physical continuant and the perceiving subject. And in this instance the medium is alone what is prominent in direct perception, while the score which determines the structure of the perception is pushed out of sight of the perceiver and is in the nature of a remote control. Literally one does not perceive the score in musical appreciation; one perceives the sound patterns controlled by the score. Yet the sound patterns literally perceived have no permanence apart from the score as a physical continuant. The score in practical criticism is as essential to a rich cumulative aesthetic judgment of a work of music as the canvas and pigments of a painting or the marble and bronze of a statue. Clearly the patterns symbolized in the score do pass over into the auditory perception as a definite contribution from the physical continuant. What strikes us in the physical setup for music is the very important function a medium may have on the physical side of the perceptive situation. Actually in every perception except a purely tactile one a medium is involved, and the physical continuant is more or less remote from the subject. Every visual work of art, for instance, depends upon the medium of light. In music the controlling continuant is simply more remote than usual, and its contribution to perception more indirect. The contribution from the score, however, is definitely contained in the auditory perception, just as much as if it were directly given off the mediating instruments—as in gramophone records it actually is. The remoteness of the physical continuant in music, or wherever it occurs, does not, therefore, make any serious modification in our original analysis.

It does, however, frequently result in a splitting of the judgment in an aesthetic work of art. There will be a judgment on the continuant and a judgment on the medium. So, critics will make certain judgments of a composer's composition and other judgments on the performer's interpretation. We tend to take it for granted that the judgment of the composition is really of the score or physical continuant with an assumption of perfect performance, and that the judgment of the performer's interpretation is about the medium. However, when the medium is human as the performer of a musical instrument is, the judgment about the medium may become very important, even exceeding in interest that of the continuant. Scores may then be written mainly as instruments to exhibit the performers. Then the situation becomes almost reversed, the score becoming practically a medium for a voice or a technique, and the voice or technique in the body of the performer becoming the physical continuant. This rivalry for the center of judgment is always possible where the medium is human, and it is one of the problems of criticism to distribute the judgments properly for any particular work of art, and also to consider the degree of aesthetic justification for that particular distribution. It is fairly safe to say that the greater the aesthetic value of the composition or score in its own right the greater the aesthetic necessity for a performer to regard himself as only a medium to convert the symbols of the score into the perceptual materials they signify. There are no scores, however, that do not admit of some freedom of interpretation on the part of the performer, so that the nature of a performance calls for criticism as well as the composition. Whenever a work of art passes through the medium of a human interpreter it is safe to say that a two-fold judgment is always required, one on the contribution from the continuant, and one on that from the interpreter. Both belong intrinsically to such an aesthetic work of art, for the work must be interpreted in some way to become perceptible. From this observation we discover that a single work of art may have several valid alternative interpretations, all belonging equally to it. The complete judgment of the total work would thus have to consider all the valid interpretations.

Once we get this idea, we realize that in some degree any kind of work of art may have alternative interpretations. In a painting, for instance, lines may now be taken as representative symbols, and now as abstract plastic elements. The painting may be perceived exclusively as a representation, or exclusively as a plastic structure. These two interpretations can indeed be combined in one that includes both. But also identical lines may function now as depth cues with one set of forms in the picture, and now with another set of forms as a surface arabesque, and these latter two interpretations are contrary to each other and cannot be combined in a single clear perception, any more than two musical interpretations can—though each may carry the funded memory of the other in its outskirts.

So, we learn that in the perceptive structure of a work of art there may be intrinsic ambiguities, alternative representations. According to some views, the greater the quantity of these ambiguities the richer the work, and the greater its aesthetic value. Here, accordingly, is one respect in which an aesthetic object differs markedly from a scientific object since the latter is expected to be unequivocal. And here again we receive a warning against trying to impose scientific and practical criteria of objectivity upon the aesthetic object. The criteria of objectivity in the two fields are quite different.

But besides bringing out the possible remoteness of control of a physical continuant, and the possibility of alternative interpretations relevant to a physical continuant, a musical score reveals another peculiarity of many works of art. For a musical score is what may be called a multiple physical continuant. There are hundreds of scores of any well-known piece of music. Whereas there is only one genuine El Greco "Toledo," there are thousands of scores of Beethoven's Fifth Symphony, and any one of them as genuine a physical continuant as another. We need not dilate upon this feature because it is so obvious. It conduces greatly, incidentally, to the preservation of a work of art. A multiple continuant is much harder to destroy than a single continuant, though one be made of paper and the other of stone.

And again once we get the idea of a work of art being a multiple continuant on its physical side, we see that many kinds of works of art are so constituted. There are often several genuine copies of a bronze statue. Prints, such as wood-blocks, lithographs, etchings, have multiple continuants. Most ceramics and textiles have multiple continuants.

While we are on this topic we should note the assistance that can be given in building up our perceptive structure of a work of art by reproductions of various sorts. There is, for instance, a good reproduction of El Greco's "Toledo." The reproduction is a multiple continuant with a great deal of merit on its own. But this merit is all derived from its approximation to the genuine El Greco. Many people who speak of the "Toledo" have never seen anything but the reproduction. And to a certain approximation they have actually perceptive material relevant to the original picture. Perhaps we should admit the conception of approximate multiple continuants, such as reproductions of all kinds (including gramophone records and the like in music, and translations in literature), and note that these may add perceptive material that is literally incorporated into the aesthetic structure of the genuine work of art. They are in a shadowy way part of the physical continuant of the work of art.

One more feature comes to us with a degree of novelty out of an examination of the functioning of the musical work of art, and that is the nature of its perceptual grasp. A musical composition resembles a statue or a building in requiring a perceptual grasp. But the temporal perceptual grasp of a piece of music is different from the spatial perceptual grasp of a visual object. A statue may be walked around in either direction. The various exterior and interior aspects of a building may be gathered from many routes. But the diverse auditory perceptions that go to make up one hearing or perceptual grasp of a musical composition are meant to be passed through by one route only. A musical composition is, of course, a multitude of diverse perceptions, for the duration of a single present perception cannot exceed a few moments. When we are hearing the second phrase of a piece of music, the first phrase has passed into memory and is no longer directly heard. The total hearing of a musical composition is a succession of such auditory perceptions overlapping one another. These are synthesized in the perceptual grasp of the whole piece. And in a piece of music this synthesis is intended to be made in one direction only, passing from the beginning to the end. A section of a piece of music may be taken out and quoted, but, for just criticism and appreciation, it must be felt in its place in the total sequence as so far from the beginning with such and such musical material to follow. The direction and route of the perceptual grasp are rigidly fixed in music.

Once we observe this demand strongly working in music, we may look back and see it also working less prominently in the visual arts. Aspects must be seen in their place in the total space organization, too, and within limits are intended to be approached in certain ways. A building is generally constructed with definite approaches, and visual climaxes are composed in view of these approaches. But a spatial work of art is not subject to the single rigorous order of time, in the way a temporal work of art is. In short, there is a freedom of routes for a perceptual grasp in most visual works of art, but only one route in a temporal work of art.

When we turn to works of literature we meet some new surprises. Here the strictly sensuous perceptual factor seems to drop out altogether. The physical continuant is the printed book or poem. This like the musical score is a set of symbols, and like the musical score there are hundreds of copies of the book all of them equally good substitutes for one another. A book is a multiple continuant. Moreover a work of literature like a piece of music is a temporal work of art and demands a perceptual grasp along one route only. One reading of a book or poem is like one hearing of a piece of music.

But, different from music, a book or poem is ordinarily read directly off the printed page by the person appreciating it. The physical continuant is not a remote control of the aesthetic work of art in literature, but the direct stimulus. It is, most amazingly, the intervening physical stimuli of perception, such as the sounds of music, that are wanting. In the ordinary experience of reading a book a sensuous content is almost totally lacking and in its place are images and meanings all aroused entirely within the mind of the reader, as we say. Strictly speaking there is practically no perception at all. In terms of our original analysis of the diagram, this is amazing.

It might be said that the act of reading a book or poem to oneself is a telescoped art in which a literal perception of a narrator's or a bard's voice is understood. That is, it could be argued that the prototype or norm of reading and appreciating a literary work of art is reading it aloud, so that the sounds and rhythms of the words are perceptually heard just as in music. It could be pointed out that even music can be read off the score by a highly trained musician and heard and appreciated in his mind, without the actual intervening perception of the audible tones produced on musical instruments. But a musician never (or, at least, very rarely) regards this sort of appreciation as an adequate substitute for the actually perceived sounds. He reads music from the score only when it is inconvenient to produce it on an instrument, and he likes to verify his mental appreciation with an actual perceptual one.

To a certain degree this may be said to be true of poetry where the sounds of the words and their rhythms count heavily in the appreciation of the aesthetic work of art. We are often told that we should read a poem aloud if we want to appreciate it fully. We probably always should. But actually we rarely do. We feel so sure of the reliability of our images of the sounds and rhythms that we regard the sensations of them unnecessary. When it comes to prose, however, in reading novels and essays where much less weight is ordinarily thrown upon the sounds of the words, then it seems rather ridiculous to ask us to read aloud. Certainly these works are rarely, if ever, written with this expectation. We must, I think, accept the situation that at least for a large proportion of literature an actual perception of the sounds of the words is not expected but only an adequate image of them. A work of literature is not, it would seem, exactly analogous to a piece of music. No rich sensuous perception is regularly expected between the symbols of a page and the experienced aesthetic content. The pages of a book are as a rule not a remote control as in music, but the direct control of the aesthetic work of art. In this respect the physical continuant in literature resembles that of a visual work of art. It is, in fact, a visual stimulus. But it differs from a picture or statue in being almost entirely symbolic, and in this respect resembles, as we said, a musical score.

An important qualification of our original analysis is obviously called for to take care of the non-perceptual character of the typical literary work of art. There is a tendency to carry the qualification to an extreme, however. Because no perceptual material of any great importance appears in the silent reading of a book or poem, it is tempting to place the literary work of art entirely within the subject, and to deny that there is any relevant physical contribution whatever. The physical book is just a lot of symbols, it is said, black marks on a page. These do not literally enter into the immediate content of the appreciated poem or novel, which is entirely produced out of the mental activities of the subject. The subject, it is tempting to say, contributes everything to the aesthetic work of art, and the physical printed book nothing. But this is clearly false, since were it not for the printed book there would be no more communicable form in literature than in idle revery.

We have here a type of experience that has received no name. For it is not strictly imagining or thinking since these experiences are supposed to go on without external control. And the term perception is usually regarded as involving sensory material, which, as we have shown, is very nearly lacking from this sort of experience. This sort of experience is that of externally controlled imagery and thought. I propose to call it "unsensory perception."

And as with the other observations we have made with different sorts of works of art so here once we notice the fact of perceptual control of other than sensory material, we are aware that in varying degrees this goes on in every work of art. Every sort of work of art wakes and controls images, thoughts, and, while we are about it, emotions and memories as well. There is no set limit to the material which may enter into a perception. In fact, if there were only sensory material in a perception we should find that the experience was merely sensation, a mere aggregate of sensations. It is the seepage of meanings and memories into the sensation aggregate that coagulates the whole into what is properly called a perception. El Greco's "Toledo" is full of meanings and recognitions and so is Beethoven's Fifth Symphony. But ordinarily in perception there is a firm relevant core of sensation in which these meanings inhere. In literature this relevant sensory core is omitted. The whole perception is essentially unsensory.

Literature serves also to bring out another feature, and one, moreover, which our original diagram did not at all represent. That is the cultural contribution. Every work of art contains a cultural contribution, and it is often very hard to discern just how great this is. But in a work of literature it is easy to see that at least all that it owes to language is a cultural contribution. A language exists in some sense outside the physical continuant and outside the subject. The meanings of words—all that is connoted by the term "usage"—are not derived from the purely personal reactions of the subject and are certainly not contained in the physical ink stimuli on a page. The subject and the stimuli are the channels through which the cultural contribution finds its way into the aesthetic work of art, but these channels are not the source of the contribution. This point is not brought out in our original simple analysis and must be recognized.

Culture means a system of social relationships; and cultural objects are the instruments that mediate these relationships. Some writers on art tend to absorb all of art into culture and to treat works of art as if they were nothing but cultural objects. For them criticism resolves itself into an analysis of the social relationships exhibited in art, descriptions of schools and styles of art tracing the sources and development of these, examinations of the influence of religion, economic, political, and other institutions upon art, comparisons of cultural institutions to mark general cultural traits that run through a period and characterize the whole art of a period. Art is thus regarded as a cultural institution, and works of art as expressions of the culture of a period. Any single work of art is an item in this cultural expression.

In this way of treating a work of art its aesthetic value, the sort of thing we have been describing in these lectures, tends to be either neglected or to be equated with the degree in which the work expresses or influences its culture. This cultural factor in aesthetic criticism has been repeatedly recognized in the lectures, particularly in the formistic account. But from our point of view, and on the basis of our previous analyses, the proposal to absorb all aesthetic questions in cultural questions is clearly an attempt to reduce a work of art to one of its factors only.

There is also a contrary danger of neglecting the cultural factor and trying to reduce it to physical and psychophysical terms. With one's attention on the perception of a single work of art, it is easy to forget the cultural factor, since this enters into the perception not directly but always through the channels of the physical continuant and the subject continuant. A cultural institution is also in a sense a continuant which makes its contribution to the aesthetic work of art, but it is not clearly discernible until we are forced to consider the influence of other men upon any one man's perceptions. Language forces this consideration upon us, since verbal symbols could not control a man's meanings except through the social compulsion of usage. And once we have noticed the nature and the extent of the cultural contribution in one kind of work of art, we become aware of it in all others. Whatever acts like language in a work of art is a cultural contribution. We accordingly add culture as a third continuant that makes its contribution to the work of art.

Of the chief kinds of works of art there now remains only that of the theater. The group of theater arts have the common trait of being performed on a stage. In the drama the physical continuant is the written play, which controls the characters on the stage; and the actors and the scenery and lighting are the direct stimuli for the perceived aesthetic object. A drama, accordingly, closely resembles a piece of music. It has a remote control and the patterns of the physical continuant are transmitted to the perceiving subject through performers. In the drama, however, the performing actors are generally expected to contribute more by themselves to the perceived object than the performers of music. The *visual* characterization is almost entirely in their hands.

In the dance, however, we come again upon something new. Here the physical continuant in the ordinary sense as a source of constant control practically disappears. This is almost as surprising as the disappearance of a sensory medium in literature. In the dance there is a good strong sensory medium in the form of our visual sensation of the dancers' bodies. But there is no physical continuant of any importance like the written play in the drama or the score in music. We do not think of choreographic arts as things to study for criticism—as yet, at least. And a choreographer is more like a play director or orchestral conductor than like a dramatist or composer. The continuance of a dance depends upon the life of the dancer, or the holding together of a dance troupe—or on the transmission of a tradition from group to group and from generation to generation. That is why the dance is strongest in those localities where there is a strong tradition of the dance. In short, a cultural continuant takes the place of a physical continuant.

The peculiarity of the dance, then, is that, lacking an ordinary physical continuant, this is replaced by a cultural continuant, the patterns of which are transmitted to perception through the medium of the dancers. The cultural continuant thus acts as a remote control upon the perceptual structure, just like a written play or a musical score except that its locus of existence is not on physical paper but in men's memories.

Before books were written, literature, of course, also relied upon a cultural continuant in the memories of bards. The dance serves to remind us that the cultural factor may on occasion serve as a controlling continuant in place of the physical continuant. To some degree it probably functions in this way in all works of art. Wherever the perceptions of a work of art are directly controlled by tradition, there we have evidence of the action of a cultural continuant.

We have now passed in review various important types of works of art, and noticed the variations they produce upon our original simple analysis. This amounts to a more careful description of the nature of the physical continuant and its effects upon the aesthetic perception.

It remains to ask what effects upon this perception come to light when we consider the contributions of a variety of subjects. Our answer here may be quite brief because already in answering the first question we have been forced to trespass upon the second. For we have already been forced to notice the contribution of a culture, and a culture presupposes a multiplicity of subjects. Within these subjects as a group and in the texture of their mutual relations and activities, a culture has its life and its existential locus.

When we are led to consider the question of the effects of many subjects upon the aesthetic work of art, we discover that our interest shifts from trying to find how much variety is produced to trying to find how much uniformity can be asserted to exist in the object of all these subjects' perceptions. The presence of a multiplicity of subjects before a work of art suggests the possibility of a great relativity of perception. If a hundred different subjects look at El Greco's "Toledo" will there not be a hundred different subjective contributions to the perceived object, and so a hundred different perceptions, and so again a hundred different aesthetic objects? Is El Greco's "Toledo" in any legitimate sense a single aesthetic work of art to so many subjects, or is it not as numerous as the subjects that see it? We are faced again with the question of the objectivity of the work of art. How much stability, constancy, invariancy, has it, if any? We have been assuming in this essay that it has much. Moreover our analysis so far must have assured us that an extreme aesthetic relativism cannot be maintained. For the physical continuant at any rate is nearly or quite changeless. Its contribution to the aesthetic object is practically constant whatever variety the subjects' contributions may produce.

But there are also two other pervasive factors making for a considerable degree of uniformity and these are on the subjects' side. They are the biological and the cultural factors. Men are all of one species, and apart from color blindness, tone deafness, and similar physiological and psychological effects can be counted on to perceive about the same thing. Where the defects exist we have means for detecting them and for judging how much men so constituted lack of the full perception of a work of art. Likewise, so far as men partake of a common culture, we can count on a constancy in the subjects' contribution.

Furthermore, it must not be forgotten that the aesthetic work of art is not realized in any casual perception but is a perceptive series and involves a perceptual grasp. Normally constituted men brought up in the same culture may approach a work of art from quite different aspects and obtain quite different initial perceptions, but as they enlarge their perceptive series and build up the total perceptive structure of the work of art, this total structure is bound to become more and more nearly identical for the various men.

Due to similar biological constitution, and a common culture when participated in, and the funding of the earlier perceptions with the later in the perceptive series, there is altogether what may be called a convergence effect towards a pretty high degree of identity in the total perceptive series of different subjects—that is, in the aesthetic work of art. The aesthetic work of art is, in fact, the common object of these subjects. It is that which the constancy of the physical continuant, the common biological constitution of the subjects, a culture common to these subjects, and the fully rounded experience which we call the total perceptive series of these subjects brings into being. All of these factors, it should be noticed, came out of our preceding analysis. We are simply putting them together and noticing the result, and the result is something with quite an impressive objectivity and constancy.

The aesthetic work of art actually involves a multiplicity of subjects, just as it involves a multiplicity of perceptions. What we have called the convergence effect here among subjects corresponds to the funding effect among perceptions. Just as the aesthetic work of art is no single perception but the result of the total perceptive series, so the aesthetic work of art is not the perception of any one subject but a convergence effect among the perceptions of many subjects, which cancels out individual idiosyncracies. The aesthetic work of art is thus not a private object. It intrinsically involves, in the way we have shown, other subjects. Or to put it another way, we find upon complete analysis that the subject continuant of a work of art is always a multiple continuant.

Now let us gather together the traits of a work of art which we have successively discovered in the course of our analysis. A work of art involves (1) a physical continuant and (2) a subject continuant. These make contributions to perceptions, and give rise to (3) a perceptive series with a funding effect. This intermittent perceptive series is the aesthetic work of art in its barest form. Generally, however, a work of art has numerous aspects (each with its own perceptive series) which become organized through (4) a perceptual grasp. Also, the physical continuant is rarely in direct contact with the subject and exerts a (5) remote control over perception through a (6) medium. When the medium is human performers and interpreters of the remote controlling physical continuant as in music and drama, a twofold judgment is required, one on the physical continuant proper, and one on the interpretation. Several equally valid interpretations may thus be intrinsic to a work of art, and in general (7) intrinsic ambiguities are characteristic of most works of art. Many works of art have (8) multiple physical continuants. Some lack a sensory medium and are built up from (9) "unsensory perceptions," from which we note that all works of art have more or less material that is not sensory. All works of art participate in (10) cultural continuants. In some works of art there is no physical continuant and a cultural continuant takes its place. (11) The subject continuant is always a multiple continuant. There is finally (12) a convergence effect in every work of art functioning through (a) the constant physical continuant, (b) the biological uniformity of the human subjects, (c) a common culture, and (d) the funding effect in the perceptive series, all of which tend towards a considerable objectivity and stability in the perceptive structure of the aesthetic work of art.

This is the object of aesthetic criticism. The field of such objects is the field of aesthetic criticism.

RENÉ WELLEK and AUSTIN WARREN

The Analysis of the
Literary Work of Art

THE NATURAL AND SENSIBLE starting point for work in literary scholarship is the interpretation and analysis of the works of literature themselves. After all, only the works themselves justify all our interest in the
life of an author, in his social environment and the whole process of literature. But, curiously enough, literary history has been so preoccupied
with the setting of a work of literature that its attempts at an analysis of
the works themselves have been slight in comparison with the enormous
efforts expended on the study of environment. Some reasons for this over-
emphasis on the conditioning circumstances rather than on the works
themselves are not far to seek. Modern literary history arose in close connection with the Romantic movement, which could subvert the critical
system of Neo-Classicism only with the relativist argument that different
times required different standards. Thus the emphasis shifted from the
literature itself to its historical background, which was used to justify the
new values ascribed to old literature. In the nineteenth century, explanation by causes became the great watchword, largely in an endeavor to
emulate the methods of the natural sciences. Besides, the breakdown of
the old "poetics," which occurred with the shift of interest to the individual "taste" of the reader, strengthened the conviction that art, being
fundamentally irrational, should be left to "appreciation." Sir Sidney Lee,
in his inaugural lecture, merely summed up the theory of most academic
literary scholarship when he said: "In literary history we seek the external circumstances—political, social, economic—in which literature is produced."[1] The result of a lack of clarity on questions of poetics has been
the astonishing helplessness of most scholars when confronted with the
task of actually analyzing and evaluating a work of art.

In recent years a healthy reaction has taken place which recognizes that the study of literature should, first and foremost, concentrate on the actual works of art themselves. The old methods of classical rhetoric, poetics, or metrics are and must be reviewed and restated in modern terms. New methods based on a survey of the wider range of forms in modern literature are being introduced. In France the method of *explication de textes,* in Germany the formal analyses based on parallels with the history of fine arts, cultivated by Oskar Walzel,[2] and especially the brilliant movement of the Russian formalists and their Czech and Polish followers[3] have brought new stimuli to the study of the literary work, which we are only beginning to see properly and to analyze adequately. In England some of the followers of I. A. Richards have paid close attention to the text of poetry[4] and also in this country a group of critics have made a study of the work of art the center of their interest. Several studies of the drama[5] which stress its difference from life and combat the confusion between dramatic and empirical reality point in the same direction. Similarly, many studies of the novel[6] are not content to consider it merely in terms of its relations to the social structure but try to analyze its artistic methods—its points of view, its narrative technique.

The Russian Formalists most vigorously objected to the old dichotomy of "content versus form," which cuts a work of art into two halves: a crude content and a superimposed, purely external form.[7] Clearly, the aesthetic effect of a work of art does not reside in what is commonly called its content. There are few works of art which are not ridiculous or meaningless in synopsis (which can be justified only as a pedagogical device).[8] But a distinction between form as the factor aesthetically active and a content aesthetically indifferent meets with insuperable difficulties. At first sight the boundary line may seem fairly definite. If we understand by content the ideas and emotions conveyed in a work of literature, the form would include all linguistic elements by which contents are expressed. But if we examine this distinction more closely, we see that content implies some elements of form: e.g. the events told in a novel are parts of the content, while the way in which they are arranged into a "plot" is part of the form. Dissociated from this way of arrangement they have no artistic effect whatsoever. The common remedy proposed and widely used by the Germans, i.e. the introduction of the term "inner form," which originally dates back to Plotinus and Shaftesbury, is merely complicating matters, as the boundary line between inner and outer form remains completely obscure. It must simply be admitted that the manner in which events are arranged in a plot is part of the form. Things become even more disastrous for the traditional concepts when we realize that even in the language, commonly considered part of the form, it is necessary to distinguish between words in themselves, aesthetically indifferent, and the manner in which individual words make up units of sound and meaning, aesthetically effective. It would be better to rechristen all the aesthetically indifferent elements "materials," while the manner in which they acquire aesthetic efficacy may be styled "structure." This distinction is by no means a simple renaming of the old pair, content and form. It cuts right across the old boundary lines. "Materials" include elements formerly considered part of the content, and parts formerly considered formal. "Structure" is a concept including both content and form so far as they are organized for aesthetic purposes. The work of art is, then, considered as a whole system of signs, or structure of signs, serving a specific aesthetic purpose.

How, more concretely, can we envisage an analysis of this structure? What is meant by this totality, and how can it be analyzed? What is meant by saying that an analysis is wrong or mistaken? This raises an extremely difficult epistemological question, that of the "mode of existence" or the "ontological situs" of a literary work of art (which, for brevity's sake, we shall call a "poem" in what follows). What is the "real" poem; where should we look for it; how does it exist? A correct answer to these questions must solve several critical problems and open a way to the proper analysis of a work of literature.

To the question what and where is a poem, or rather a literary work of art in general, several traditional answers have been given which must be criticized and eliminated before we can attempt an answer of our own. One of the most common and oldest answers is the view that a poem is an "artifact," an object of the same nature as a piece of sculpture or a painting. Thus the work of art is considered identical with the black lines of ink on white paper or parchment or, if we think of a Babylonian poem, with the grooves in the brick. Obviously this answer is quite unsatisfactory. There is, first of all, the huge oral "literature." There are poems or stories which have never been fixed in writing and still continue to exist. Thus the lines in black ink are merely a method of recording a poem which must be conceived as existing elsewhere. If we destroy the writing or even all copies of a printed book we still may not destroy the poem, as it might be preserved in oral tradition or in the memory of a man like Macaulay, who boasted of knowing *Paradise Lost* and *Pilgrim's Progress* by heart. On the other hand, if we destroy a painting or a piece of sculpture or a building, we destroy it completely, though we may preserve descriptions or records in another medium and might even try to reconstruct what has been lost. But we shall always create a different work of art (however similar), while the mere destruction of the copy of a book or even of all its copies may not touch the work of art at all.

That the writing on the paper is not the "real" poem can be demonstrated also by another argument. The printed page contains a great many elements which are extraneous to the poem: the size of the type, the sort of type used (roman, italic), the size of the page, and many other factors. If we should take seriously the view that a poem is an artifact, we would have to come to the conclusion that every single copy is a different work of art. There would be no *a priori* reason why copies in different editions should be copies of the same book. Besides, not every printing is considered by us, the readers, a correct printing of a poem. The very fact that we are able to correct printers' errors in a text which we might not have read before or, in some rare cases, restore the genuine meaning of the text shows that we do not consider the printed lines as the genuine poem. Thus we have shown that the poem (or any literary work of art) can exist outside its printed version and that the printed artifact contains many elements which we all must consider as not included in the genuine poem.

Still, this negative conclusion should not blind us to the enormous practical importance, since the invention of writing and printing, of our methods of recording poetry. There is no doubt that much literature has been lost and thus completely destroyed because its written records have disappeared and the theoretically possible means of oral tradition have failed or have been interrupted. Writing and especially printing have made possible the continuity of literary tradition and must have done much to increase the unity and integrity of works of art. Besides, at least in certain periods of the history of poetry, the graphic picture has become a part of some finished works of art.

In Chinese poetry, as Ernest Fenellosa has shown, the pictorial ideograms form a part of the total meaning of the poems. But also in the Western tradition there are the graphic poems of the *Greek Anthology*, the "Altar" or the "Church-floor" of George Herbert, and similar poems of the Metaphysicals which can be paralleled on the Continent in Spanish Gongorism, Italian Marinism, in German Baroque poetry, and elsewhere. Also modern poetry in America (e.e. cummings), in Germany (Arno Holz), in France (Apollinaire), and elsewhere has used graphic devices like unusual line arrangements or even beginnings at the bottom of the page, different colors of printing, etc.[9] In the novel *Tristram Shandy*, Sterne used, as far back as the eighteenth century, blank and marbled pages. All such devices are integral parts of these particular works of art. Though we know that a majority of poetry is independent of them, they cannot and should not be ignored in those cases.

Besides, the role of print in poetry is by no means confined to such comparatively rare extravaganzas; the line-ends of verses, the grouping into stanzas, the paragraphs of prose passages, eye-rhymes or puns which are comprehensible only through spelling, and many similar devices must be considered integral factors of literary works of art. A purely oral theory tends to exclude all considerations of such devices, but they cannot be ignored in any complete analysis of many literary works of art. Their existence merely proves that print has become very important for the practice of poetry in modern times, that poetry is written for the eye as well as for the ear. Though the use of graphic devices is not indispensable, they are far more frequent in literature than in music, where the printed score is in a position similar to the printed page in poetry. In music such uses are rare, though by no means non-existent. There are many curious optical devices (colors, etc.) in Italian madrigal scores of the sixteenth century. The supposedly "pure" composer Handel wrote a chorus speaking of the Red Sea flood where the "water stood like a wall," and the notes on the printed page of music form firm rows of evenly spaced dots suggesting a phalanx or wall.[10]

We have started with a theory which probably has not many serious adherents today. The second answer to our question puts the essence of a literary work of art into the sequence of sounds uttered by a speaker or reader of poetry. This is a widely accepted solution favored especially by reciters. But the answer is equally unsatisfactory. Every reading aloud or reciting of a poem is merely a performance of the poem and not the poem itself. It is on exactly the same level as the performance of a piece of music by a musician. There is—to follow the line of our previous argument—a huge written literature which may never be sounded at all. To deny this, we have to subscribe to some such absurd theory as that of some behaviorists that all silent reading is accompanied by movements of the vocal chords. Actually, all experience shows that, unless we are almost illiterate or are struggling with the reading of a foreign language or want to articulate the sound whisperingly on purpose, we usually read "globally," that is, we grasp printed words as wholes without breaking them up into sequences of phonemes and thus do not pronounce them even silently. In reading quickly we have no time even to articulate the sounds with our vocal chords. To assume besides that a poem exists in the reading aloud leads to the absurd consequence that a poem is non-existent when it is not sounded and that it is recreated afresh by every reading. Moreover, we could not show how a work like Homer's *Iliad,* or Tolstoy's *War and Peace,* exists as a unity, as it can never be read aloud all in one sitting.

But most importantly, every reading of a poem is more than the genuine poem: each performance contains elements which are extraneous to the poem and individual idiosyncrasies of pronunciation, pitch, tempo, and distribution of stress—elements which are either determined by the personality of the speaker or are symptoms and means of his interpretation of the poem. Moreover, the reading of a poem not only adds individual elements but always represents only a selection of factors implicit in the text of a poem: the pitch of the voice, the speed in which a passage is read, the distribution and intensity of the stresses, these may be either right or wrong, and even when right, may still represent only one version of reading a poem. We must acknowledge the possibility of several readings of a poem: readings which we either consider wrong readings, if we feel them to be distortions of the true meaning of the poem, or readings which we have to consider as correct and admissible, but still may not consider ideal.

The reading of the poem is not the poem itself, for we can correct the performance mentally. Even if we hear a recitation which we acknowledge to be excellent or perfect, we cannot preclude the possibility that somebody else, or even the same reciter at another time, may give a very different rendering which would bring out other elements of the poem equally well. The analogy to a musical performance is again helpful: the performance of a symphony even by a Toscanini is not the symphony itself, for it is inevitably colored by the individuality of the performers and adds concrete details of tempo, rubato, timbre, etc., which may be changed in a next performance, though it would be impossible to deny that the same symphony has been performed for the second time. Thus we have shown that the poem can exist outside its sounded performance, and that the sounded performance contains many elements which we must consider as not included in the poem.

Still, in some literary works of art (especially in lyrical poetry) the vocal side of poetry may be an important factor of the general structure. Attention can be drawn to it by various means like meter, patterns of vowel or consonant sequences, alliteration, assonance, rhyme, etc. This fact explains—or rather helps to explain—the inadequacy of much translating of lyrical poetry, since these potential sound-patterns cannot be transferred into another linguistic system, though a skillful translator may approximate their general effect in his own language. There is, however, an enormous literature which is relatively independent of sound-patterns, as can be shown by the historical effects of many works in even pedestrian translations. Sound may be an important factor in the structure of a poem, but the answer that a poem is a sequence of sounds is as unsatisfactory as the solution which puts faith in the print on the page.

The third, very common answer to our question says that a poem is the experience of the reader. A poem, it is argued, is nothing outside the mental processes of individual readers and is thus identical with the mental state or process which we experience in reading or listening to a poem. Again, this "psychological" solution seems unsatisfactory. It is true, of course, that a poem can be known only through individual experiences, but it is not identical with such an individual experience. Every individual experience of a poem contains something idiosyncratic and purely individual. It is colored by our mood and our individual preparation. The education, the personality of every reader, the general cultural climate of a time, the religious or philosophical or purely technical preconceptions of every reader will add something instantaneous and extraneous to every reading of a poem. Two readings at different times by the same individual may vary considerably either because he has matured mentally or because he is weakened by momentary circumstances such as fatigue, worry, or distraction. Every experience of a poem thus both leaves out something or adds something individual. The experience will never be commensurate with the poem: even a good reader will discover new details in poems which he had not experienced during previous readings, and it is needless to point out how distorted or shallow may be the reading of a less trained or untrained reader.

The view that the mental experience of a reader is the poem itself leads to the absurd conclusion that a poem is non-existent unless experienced and that it is recreated in every experience. There thus would not be one *Divine Comedy* but as many Divine Comedies as there are and were and will be readers. We end in complete skepticism and anarchy and arrive at the vicious maxim of *De gustibus non est disputandum*. If we should take this view seriously, it would be impossible to explain why one experience of a poem by one reader should be better than the experience of any other reader and why it is possible to correct the interpretation of another reader. It would mean the definite end of all teaching of literature which aims at enhancing the understanding and appreciation of a text. The writings of I.A. Richards, especially his book on *Practical Criticism,* have shown how much can be done in analyzing the individual idiosyncrasies of readers and how much a good teacher can achieve in rectifying false approaches. Curiously enough, Richards, who constantly criticizes the experiences of his pupils, holds to an extreme psychological theory which is in flat contradiction to his excellent critical practice. The idea that poetry is supposed to order our impulses and the conclusion that the value of poetry is in some sort of psychical therapy lead him finally to the admission that this goal may be accomplished by a bad as well as a good poem, by a carpet, a pot, a gesture as well as by a sonata.[11] Thus the supposed pattern in our mind is not definitely related to the poem which caused it.

The psychology of the reader, however interesting in itself or useful for pedagogical purposes, will always remain outside the object of literary study—the concrete work of art—and is unable to deal with the question of the structure and value of the work of art. Psychological theories must be theories of effect and may lead in extreme cases to such criteria of the value of poetry as that proposed by A. E. Housman in a lecture, *The Name and Nature of Poetry* (1933), where he tells us, one hopes with his tongue in his cheek, that good poetry can be recognized by the thrill down our spine. This is on the same level as eighteenth-century theories which measured the quality of a tragedy by the amount of tears shed by the audience or the movie scout's conception of the quality of a comedy on the basis of the number of laughs he has counted in the audience. Thus anarchy, skepticism, a complete confusion of values is the result of every psychological theory, as it must be unrelated either to the structure or the quality of a poem.

The psychological theory is only very slightly improved by I. A. Richards when he defines a poem as the "experience of the right kind of reader."[12] Obviously the whole problem is shifted to the conception of the *right* reader—and the meaning of that adjective. But even assuming an ideal condition of mood in a reader of the finest background and the best training, the definition remains unsatisfactory, as it is open to all the criticism we have made of the psychological method. It puts the essence of the poem into a momentary experience which even the right kind of reader could not repeat unchanged. It will always fall short of the full meaning of a poem at any given instance and will always add inevitable personal elements to the reading.

A fourth answer has been suggested to obviate this difficulty. The poem, we hear, is the experience of the author. Only in parenthesis, we may dismiss the view that the poem is the experience of the author at any time of his life after the creation of his work, when he rereads it. He then has obviously become simply a reader of his work and is liable to errors and misrepresentations of his own work almost as much as any other reader. Many instances of glaring misinterpretations by an author of his own work could be collected: the old anecdote about Browning professing not to understand his own poem has probably its element of truth. It happens to all of us that we misinterpret or do not fully understand what we have written some time ago. Thus the suggested answer must refer to the experience of the author during the time of the creation. By "experience of the author" we might mean, however, two different things: the conscious experience, the intentions which the author wanted to embody in his work, or the total conscious and unconscious experience during the prolonged time of creation. The view that the genuine poem is to be found in the intentions of an author is widespread even though it is not always explicitly stated. It justifies much historical research and is at the bottom of many arguments in favor of specific interpretations. However, for most works of art we have no evidence to reconstruct the intentions of the author except the finished work itself. Even if we are in possession of contemporary evidence in the form of an explicit profession of intentions, such a profession need not be binding on a modern observer. "Intentions" of the author are always "rationalizations," commentaries which certainly must be taken into account but also must be criticized in the light of the finished work of art. The "intentions" of an author may go far beyond the finished work of art: they may be merely pronouncements of plans and ideals, while the performance may be either far below or far aside the mark. If we could have interviewed Shakespeare he probably would have expressed his intentions in writing *Hamlet* in a way which we should find most unsatisfactory. We would still quite rightly insist on finding meanings in *Hamlet* (and not merely inventing them) which were probably far from clearly formulated in Shakespeare's conscious mind.

Artists may be strongly influenced by a contemporary critical situation and by contemporary critical formulae while giving expression to their intentions, but the critical formulae themselves might be quite inadequate to characterize their actual artistic achievement. The Baroque age is an obvious case in point, since a surprisingly new artistic practice found little expression either in the pronouncements of the artists or the comments of the critics. A sculptor such as Bernini could lecture to the Paris Academy expounding the view that his own practice was in strict conformity to that of the ancients and Daniel Adam Pöppelmann, the architect of that highly rococo building in Dresden called the Zwinger, wrote a whole pamphlet in order to demonstrate the strict agreement of his creation with the purest principles of Vitruvius. The metaphysical poets had only a few quite inadequate critical formulae (like "strong lines") which scarcely touch the actual novelty of their practice: and medieval artists frequently had purely religious or didactic "intentions" which do not even begin to give expression to the artistic principles of their practice. Divergence between conscious intention and actual performance is a common phenomenon in the history of literature. Zola sincerely believed in his scientific theory of the experimental novel, but actually produced highly melodramatic and symbolic novels. Gogol thought of himself as a social reformer, as a "geographer" of Russia, while, in practice, he produced novels and stories full of fantastic and grotesque creatures of his imagination. It is simply impossible to rely on the study of the intentions of an author, as they might not even represent a reliable commentary on his work, and at their best are not more than such a commentary. There can be no objections against the study of "intention," if we mean by it merely the study of the integral work of art directed towards the total meaning.[13] But this use of the term "intention" is different and somewhat misleading.

But also the alternative suggestion—that the genuine poem is in the total experience, conscious and unconscious, during the time of the creation—is very unsatisfactory. In practice, this conclusion has the serious disadvantage of putting the problem into a completely inaccessible and purely hypothetical x which we have no means of reconstructing or even of exploring. Beyond this insurmountable practical difficulty, the solution is also unsatisfactory because it puts the existence of the poem into a subjective experience which already is a thing of the past. The experiences of the author during creation ceased precisely when the poem had begun to exist. If this conception were right, we should never be able to come into direct contact with the work of art itself, but have constantly to make the assumption that our experiences in reading the poem are in some way identical with the long-past experiences of the author. E. M. Tillyard in his book on *Milton* has tried to use the idea that *Paradise Lost* is about the state of the author when he wrote it, and could not, in a long and frequently irrelevant exchange of arguments with C. S. Lewis, acknowledge that *Paradise Lost* is, first of all, about Satan and Adam and Eve and hundreds and thousands of different ideas, representations, and concepts, rather than about Milton's state of mind during creation.[14] That the whole content of the poem was once in contact with the conscious and unconscious mind of Milton is perfectly true; but this state of mind is inaccessible and might have been filled, in those particular moments, with millions of experiences of which we cannot find a trace in the poem itself. Taken literally, this whole solution must lead to absurd speculations about the exact duration of the state of mind of the creator and its exact content, which might include a toothache at the moment of creation.[15] The whole psychological approach through states of mind, whether of the reader or the listener, the speaker or the author, raises more problems than it can possibly solve.

A better way is obviously in the direction of defining the work of art in terms of social and collective experience. There are two possibilities of solution, which, however, still fall short of solving our problem satisfactorily. We may say that the work of art is the sum of all past and possible experiences of the poem: a solution which leaves us with an infinity of irrelevant individual experiences, bad and false readings, and perversions. In short, it merely gives us the answer that the poem is in the state of mind of its reader, multiplied by infinity. Another answer solves the question by stating that the genuine poem is the experience common to all the experiences of the poem.[16] But this answer would obviously reduce the work of art to the common denominator of all these experiences. This denominator must be the *lowest* common denominator, the most shallow, most superficial and trivial experience. This solution, besides its practical difficulties, would completely impoverish the total meaning of a work of art.

An answer to our question in terms of individual or social psychology cannot be found. A poem, we have to conclude, is not an individual experience or a sum of experiences, but only a potential cause of experiences. Definition in terms of states of mind fails because it cannot account for the normative character of the genuine poem, for the simple fact that it might be experienced correctly or incorrectly. In every individual experience only a small part can be considered as adequate to the true poem. Thus, the real poem must be conceived as a structure of norms, realized only partially in the actual experience of its many readers. Every single experience (reading, reciting, and so forth) is only an attempt —more or less successful and complete—to grasp this set of norms or standards.

The term "norms" as used here should not, of course, be confused with norms which are either classical or romantic, ethical or political. The norms we have in mind are implicit norms which have to be extracted from every individual experience of a work of art and together make up the genuine work of art as a whole. It is true that if we compare works of art among themselves, similarities or differences between these norms will be ascertained, and from the similarities themselves it ought to be possible to proceed to a classification of works of art according to the type of norms they embody. We may finally arrive at theories of genres and ultimately at theories of literature in general. To deny this as it has been denied by those who, with some justification, stress the uniqueness of every work of art, seems to push the conception of individuality so far that every work of art would become completely isolated from tradition and thus finally both incommunicable and incomprehensible. Assuming that we have to start with the analysis of an individual work of art, we still can scarcely deny that there must be some links, some similarities, some common elements or factors which would approximate two or more given works of art and thus would open the door to a transition from the analysis of one individual work of art to a type such as Greek tragedy and hence to tragedy in general, to literature in general, and finally to some all-inclusive structure common to all arts.

But this is a further problem. We, however, have still to decide where and how these norms exist. A closer analysis of a work of art will show that it is best to think of it as not merely one system of norms but rather of a system which is made of several strata, each implying its own subordinate group. The Polish philosopher, Roman Ingarden, in an ingenious highly technical analysis of the literary work of art,[17] has employed the methods of Husserl's "Phenomenology" to arrive at such distinctions of strata. We need not follow him in every detail to see that his general distinctions are sound and useful: there is, first, the sound-stratum which is not, of course, to be confused with the actual sounding of the words, as our preceding argument must have shown. Still, this pattern is indispensable, as only on the basis of sounds can the second stratum arise: the units of meaning. Every single word will have its meaning, will combine into units in the context, into syntagmas and sentence patterns. Out of this syntactic structure arises a third stratum, that of the objects represented, the "world" of a novelist, the characters, the setting. Ingarden adds two other strata which may not have to be distinguished as separable. The stratum of the "world" is seen from a particular viewpoint, which is not necessarily stated but implied. An event presented in literature can be, for example, presented as "seen" or as "heard": even the same event, for example, the banging of a door; a character can be seen in its "inner" or "outer" characteristic traits. And finally, Ingarden speaks of a stratum of "metaphysical qualities" (the sublime, the tragic, the terrible, the holy) of which art can give us contemplation. This stratum is not indispensable, and may be missing in some works of literature. Possibly the two last strata can be included in the "world," in the realm of represented objects. But they also suggest very real problems in the analysis of literature. The "point of view" has, at least in the novel, received considerable attention since Henry James and since Lubbock's more systematic exposition of the Jamesian theory and practice. The stratum of "metaphysical qualities" allows Ingarden to reintroduce questions of the "philosophical meaning" of works of art without the risk of the usual intellectualist errors.

It is useful to illustrate the conception by the parallel which can be drawn from linguistics. Linguists such as the Geneva School and the Prague Linguistic Circle carefully distinguish between *langue* and *parole*,[18] the system of language and the individual speech-act; and this distinction corresponds to that between the individual experience of the poem and the poem as such. The system of language is a collection of conventions and norms whose workings and relations we can observe and describe as having a fundamental coherence and identity in spite of very different, imperfect, or incomplete pronouncements of individual speakers. In this respect at least, a literary work of art is in exactly the same position as a system of language. We as individuals shall never realize it completely, for we shall never use our own language completely and perfectly. The very same situation is actually exhibited in every single act of cognition. We shall never know an object in all its qualities, but still we can scarcely deny the identity of objects even though we may see them from different perspectives. We always grasp some "structure of determination" in the object which makes the act of cognition not an act of arbitrary invention or subjective distinction but the recognition of some norms imposed on us by reality. Similarly, the structure of a work of art has the character of a "duty which I have to realize." I shall always realize it imperfectly, but in spite of some incompleteness, a certain "structure of determination" remains, just as in any other object of knowledge.[19]

Modern linguists have analyzed the potential sounds as phonemes; they can also analyze morphemes and syntagmas. The sentence, for instance, can be described not merely as an *ad hoc* utterance but as a syntactic pattern. Outside of phonemics, modern functional linguistics is still comparatively undeveloped; but the problems, though difficult, are not insoluble or completely new: they are rather restatements of the morphological and syntactical questions as they were discussed in older grammars. The analysis of a literary work of art encounters parallel problems in units of meaning and their specific organization for aesthetic purposes. Such problems as those of poetic semantics, diction, and imagery are reintroduced in a new and more careful statement. Units of meaning, sentences, and sentence structures refer to objects, construct imaginative realities such as landscapes, interiors, characters, actions, or ideas. These also can be analyzed in a way which does not confuse them with empirical reality and does not ignore the fact that they inhere in linguistic structures. A character in a novel grows only out of the units of meaning, is made of the sentences either pronounced by the figure or pronounced about it. It has an indeterminate structure in comparison with a biological person who has his coherent past. These distinctions of strata have the advantage of superseding the traditional, misleading distinction between content and form. The content will reappear in close contact with the linguistic substratum, in which it is implied and on which it is dependent.

But this conception of the literary work of art as a stratified system of norms still leaves undetermined the actual mode of existence of this system. To deal with this matter properly we should have to settle such controversies as those of nominalism versus realism, mentalism versus behaviorism—in short, all the chief problems of epistemology. For our purposes, however, it will be sufficient to avoid two opposites, extreme Platonism and extreme nominalism. There is no need to hypostatize or "reify" this system of norms, to make it a sort of archetypal idea presiding over a timeless realm of essences. The literary work of art has not the same ontological status as the idea of a triangle, or of a number, or a quality like "redness." Unlike such "subsistences," the literary work of art is, first of all, created at a certain point in time, and, secondly, is subject to change and even to complete destruction. In this respect it rather resembles the system of language, though the exact moment of creation or death is probably much less clearly definable in the case of language than in that of the literary work of art, usually an individual creation. On the other hand, one should recognize that an extreme nominalism which rejects the concept of a "system of language" and thus of a work of art in our sense, or admits it only as a useful fiction or a "scientific description," misses the whole problem and the point at issue. The narrow assumptions of behaviorism define anything to be "mystical" or "metaphysical" which does not conform to a very limited conception of empirical reality. Yet to call a phoneme a "fiction," or the system of language merely a "scientific description of speech-acts," is to ignore the problem of truth. We recognize norms and deviations from norms and do not merely devise some purely verbal descriptions. The whole behaviorist point of view is, in this respect, based on a bad theory of abstraction. Numbers or norms are what they are, whether we construct them or not. Certainly I perform the counting, I perform the reading; but number presentation or recognition of a norm is not the same as the number or the norm itself. The pronouncement of the sound h is not the phoneme h. We recognize a structure of norms within reality and do not simply invent verbal constructs. The objection that we have access to these norms only through individual acts of cognition, and that we cannot get out of these acts or beyond them, is only apparently impressive. It is the objection which has been made to Kant's criticism of our cognition, and it can be refuted with the Kantian arguments.

It is true we are ourselves liable to misunderstandings and lack of comprehension of these norms, but this does not mean that the critic assumes a superhuman role of criticizing our comprehension from the outside or that he pretends to grasp the perfect whole of the system of norms in some act of intellectual intuition. Rather, we criticize a part of our knowledge in the light of the higher standard set by another part. We are not supposed to put ourselves into the position of a man who, in order to test his vision, tries to look at his own eyes, but into the position of a man who compares the objects he sees clearly with those he sees only dimly, makes then generalizations as to the kinds of objects which fall into the two classes, and explains the difference by some theory of vision which takes account of distance, light, and so forth.

Analogously, we can distinguish between right and wrong readings of a poem, or between a recognition or a distortion of the norms implicit in a work of art, by acts of comparison, by a study of different false or incomplete realizations. We can study the actual workings, relations, and combinations of these norms, just as the phoneme can be studied. The literary work of art is neither an empirical fact, in the sense of being a state of mind of any given individual or of any group of individuals, nor is it an ideal changeless object such as a triangle. The work of art may become an object of experience; it is, we admit, accessible only through individual experience, but it is not identical with any experience. It differs from ideal objects such as numbers precisely because it is only accessible through the empirical part of its structure, the sound-system, while a triangle or a number can be intuited directly. It also differs from ideal objects in one important respect. It has something which can be called "life." It arises at a certain point of time, changes in the course of history, and may perish. A work of art is "timeless" only in the sense that, if preserved, it has some fundamental structure of identity since its creation, but it is "historical" too. It has a development which can be described. This development is nothing but the series of concretizations of a given work of art in the course of history which we may, to a certain extent, reconstruct from the reports of critics and readers about their experiences and judgments and the effect of a given work of art on other works. Our consciousness of earlier concretizations (readings, criticisms, misinterpretations) will affect our own experience: earlier readings may educate us to a deeper understanding or may cause a violent reaction against the prevalent interpretations of the past. All this shows the importance of the history of criticism or, in linguistics, of historical grammar, and leads to difficult questions about the nature and limits of individuality. How far can a work of art be said to be changed and still remain identical? The *Iliad* still "exists"; that is, it can become again and again effective and is thus different from a historical phenomenon like the battle of Waterloo which is definitely past, though its course may be reconstructed and its effects may be felt even today. In what sense can we, however, speak of an identity between the *Iliad* as the contemporary Greeks heard or read it and the *Iliad* we now read? Even assuming that we know the identical text, our actual experience must be different. We cannot contrast its language with the everyday language of Greece, and cannot therefore feel the deviations from colloquial language on which much of the poetic effect must depend. We are unable to understand many verbal ambiguities which are an essential part of every poet's meaning. Obviously it requires in addition some imaginative effort, which can have only very partial success, to think ourselves back into the Greek belief in gods, or the Greek scale of moral values. Still, it could scarcely be denied that there is a substantial identity of "structure" which has remained the same throughout the ages. This structure, however, is dynamic: it changes throughout the process of history while passing through the minds of its readers, critics, and fellow artists. Thus the system of norms is growing and changing and will remain, in some sense, always incompletely and imperfectly realized. But this dynamic conception does not mean mere subjectivism and relativism. All the different points of view are by no means equally right. It will always be possible to determine which point of view grasps the subject most thoroughly and deeply. A hierarchy of viewpoints, a criticism of the grasp of norms, is implied in the concept of the adequacy of interpretation. All relativism is ultimately defeated by the recognition that "the Absolute is in the relative, though not finally and fully in it."[20]

The work of art, then, appears as an object of knowledge *sui generis* which has a special ontological status. It is neither real (like a statue) nor mental (like the experience of light or pain) nor ideal (like a triangle). It is a system of norms of ideal concepts which are intersubjective. They must be assumed to exist in collective ideology, changing with it, accessible only through individual mental experiences based on the sound-structure of its sentences.

We have not discussed the question of artistic values. But the preceding examination should have shown that there is no structure outside norms and values. We cannot comprehend and analyze any work of art without reference to values. The very fact that I recognize a certain structure as a "work of art" implies a judgment of value. The error of pure phenomenolgy is in the assumption that such a dissociation is possible, that values are superimposed on structure, "inhere" on or in structures. This error of analysis vitiates the penetrating book of Roman Ingarden, who tries to analyze the work of art without reference to values. The root of the matter lies, of course, in the phenomenologist's assumption of an eternal, non-temporal order of "essences" to which the empirical individualizations are added only later. By assuming an absolute scale of values we necessarily lose contact with the relativity of individual judgments. A frozen Absolute faces a valueless flux of individual judgments.

The unsound thesis of absolutism and the equally unsound antithesis of relativism must be superseded and harmonized in a new synthesis which makes the scale of values itself dynamic, but does not surrender it as such. "Perspectivism," as we have termed such a conception,[21] does not mean an anarchy of values, a glorification of individual caprice, but a process of getting to know the object from different points of view which may be defined and criticized in their turn. Structure, sign, and value form three aspects of the very same problem and cannot be artificially isolated.

Notes

1. Sir Sidney Lee, *The Place of English Literature in the Modern University*, London, 1931 (reprinted in *Elizabethan and Other Essays*, London, 1929, p. 7).
2. E.g., Oskar Walzel, *Wechselseitige Erhellung der Künste*, Berlin, 1917; *Gehalt und Gestalt im Kunstwerk des Dichters*, Potsdam, 1923; *Das Wortkunstwerk*, Leipzig, 1926.

3. For studies of the Russian movement, cf. Manfred Kridl in *American Bookman* (1944), pp. 19-30; Nina Gourfinkel in *Le Monde Slave*, VI (1929), pp. 234-63; and V. Zhirmunsky, in *Zeitschrift für slavische Philologie*, I, (1925), pp. 117-52.

4. Cf. esp. William Empson, *Seven Types of Ambiguity*, London, 1930; F. R. Leavis, *New Bearings in English Poetry*, London, 1932; Geoffrey Tillotson, *On the Poetry of Pope*, 1938.

5. L. C. Knights, *How many Children had Lady Macbeth?*, London, 1933, pp. 15-54 (reprinted in *Explorations*, London, 1946, pp. 15-54), states the case against the confusion of drama and life well. The writings of E. E. Stoll, L. L. Schucking, and others have particularly emphasized the role of convention and the distance from life in drama.

6. The writings of Joseph Warren Beach and Percy Lubbock's *The Craft of Fiction*, London, 1921, are outstanding. In Russia, Viktor Shklovsky's *O Teoriyi prozy*, (*The Theory of Prose*), 1925, and many writings by V. V. Vinogradov and B. M. Eikhenbaum apply the Formalist approach to the novel.

7. Jan Mukařovský, Introduction to *Máchův Máj* (*Mácha's May*), Prague, 1928, pp. iv-vi.

8. Cf. "The actual story of a novel eludes the epitomist as completely as character. . . . only as precipitates from the memory are plot or character tangible; yet only in solution have either any emotive valency." (C. H. Rickword, "A Note on Fiction," *Toward Standards of Criticism* (Ed. F. R. Leavis), London, 1935, p. 33).

9. Ernest Fenollosa, *The Chinese Written Character as a Medium for Poetry*, New York, 1936; Margaret Church, "The First English Pattern Poems," PMLA, LXI (1946), pp. 636-50.

10. Cf. Alfred Einstein, "Augenmusik im Madrigal," *Zeitschrift der internationalen Musikgesellschaft*, XIV (1912), pp. 8–21.

11. I. A. Richards, *Principles of Literary Criticism*, London, 1924, pp. 125, 248. Cf. *Practical Criticism*, London, 1929, p. 349.

12. Richards, *Principles*, pp. 225-27.

13. As Spingarn says, "The Poet's aim must be judged at the moment of creative art, that is to say, by the art of the poem itself." ("The New Criticism," *Criticism and America*, New York, 1924, pp. 24-5.)

14. E. M. Tillyard and C. S. Lewis, *The Personal Heresy: A Controversy*, London, 1934; Tillyard's *Milton*, London, 1930, p. 237.

15. In his *Biographie de l'oeuvre littéraire*, Paris, 1925, Pierre Audiat has argued that the work of art "represents a period in the life of the writer," and has consequently become involved in just such impossible and quite unnecessary dilemmas.

16. Jan Mukařovský, "L'art comme fait sémiologique," paper read before the International Congress of Philosophy, Prague, September, 1934.

17. Roman Ingarden, *Das literarische Kunstwerk*, Halle, 1931.

18. Esp. in De Saussure's *Cours de Linguistique Générale*, Paris, 1916.

19. Cf. E. Husserl's *Méditations Cartésiennes*, Paris, 1931, pp. 38-9.

20. Cf. Ernst Troeltsch's "Historigraphy," in Hastings' *Encyclopaedia of Religion and Ethics*, Edinburgh, 1913, Vol. VI, p. 722.

21. This term is used, though differently, by Ortega y Gasset.

Works of Art and Aesthetic Objects

Works of Art as Imaginary Objects. "If the making of a tune is an instance of imaginative creation," says Collingwood, "a tune is an imaginary thing." And the same, he holds, applies to any other work of art. "Music does not consist of heard noises, paintings do not consist of seen colours, and so forth. . . .[1] The work of art proper is not something seen or heard, but something imagined."

At first sight this argument seems to be a non-sequitur, for the imaginative and the imaginary are not related in the way Collingwood suggests. The imaginative is that which shows imagination, is inventive or unusual. The imaginary, on the other hand, we contrast with the real—Mr. Pickwick, the imaginary person, with Mr. Dickens, the real person; imaginary tunes, such as those played by Orpheus, with real tunes, such as those by Mozart and Brahms. The imaginary, in short, is the merely imagined, that which exists only in imagination or fancy. Thus, as the terms are normally used, the fact that something is a product of imaginative creation does not imply that it is imaginary.

By an "imaginary" tune, however, Collingwood means simply a tune as it exists in someone's head, in contrast to a "real" tune, one that is played or sung. And so with "imaginative": the "imaginative" creation of music consists in making up tunes in one's head, as opposed to setting them down on paper or singing them. According to Collingwood's peculiar use of the terms, therefore, his argument reduces to a tautology. It is like saying, "If making a shoe is an instance of manufacture, then (assuming that all shoes are made) a shoe is something manufactured."

But Collingwood clearly intends to say more than this. Artistic creation consists *solely* in "imagining" a tune, a poem, or a picture; hence, works of art are "imaginary," exist *solely* in someone's head. "Real" tunes and pictures, *i.e.* played sounds and painted canvases, are not products of artistic creation but of craft; they only *appear* to be works of art, which is why we are deceived into thinking that music consists of heard noises, paintings of seen colors.

Although Collingwood says that this view is not paradoxical, it has several paradoxical consequences:

(1) A "real" tune or picture not only *is* not, but *cannot* be, a work of art. Is this not contrary to what we ordinarily believe and say?

(2) A "real" tune or picture only appears to be a work of art; we mistakenly suppose that it is one. But what kind of mistake is this? If it is an empirical mistake, it must be one to which observable data would be relevant to correct. But are any observable data relevant to the correction of this mistake? What data? Further, if this is an empirical mistake, then it must at least be *possible* for a "real" picture to be a work of art. If I can mistakenly suppose that a tower is round when in fact it is square, it must be *possible* for the tower to *be* round rather than square. But on Collingwood's view it is impossible for a "real" picture to be a work of art.

On the other hand, if the mistake is verbal, like saying that a square is a rhombus because one does not know what "rhombus" means, then it must be one that can be corrected by showing that the word in question is inapplicable. But is the expression "work of art" inapplicable to painted pictures? Is saying "That painted picture is a work of art" paradoxical in the same way as saying "That square is a rhombus"? Is it not paradoxical to say "No painted picture can be a work of art"?

(3) If Milton had merely made up poems in his head and had never written them down or spoken them, if Raphael had merely imagined pictures or composed them in his head—things he could do without knowing even how to hold a brush—would Milton have been a poet, Raphael a painter? It is not clear what Collingwood's answer to these questions would be. If he says "Yes," then a man can be a painter even if he never paints a picture or causes one to be painted. But if he says "No; Milton would not have been a *poet* or Raphael a *painter*, but both of them would still have been *artists*," then a man can be an artist without being a poet, or a painter, or a composer, etc. This is like saying that something can be an animal without being any kind or species of animal.

The second part of Collingwood's argument is just as perplexing. People who intelligently look at pictures, listen to music, and so on, are, he says, like people who listen with understanding to a lecture on science. If they just hear sounds, they do not grasp what the lecturer says any more than a dog that can also hear sounds but lacks imagination. To understand a work of art, we must (1) reconstruct in imagination the work that existed in the artist's head, and (2) use our imagination in other ways, *e.g.* to ignore the difference between two tones, ignore the heads of people sitting in front of us at a play, imagine ourselves moving about in a picture, etc.

Can someone tell, however, whether you have listened intelligently to a piece of music, or have understood it, by ascertaining whether you have reconstructed in imagination the tune that existed in the composer's head? Is this what intelligent listening and understanding consist of? Or is that discovered through what you have to say about the piece of music? Your humming a tune in such a way that the composer would recognize it would test your ability to reconstruct what he had in his head, but would it have anything to do with your intelligence as a listener?

Suppose that the tune the composer made up in his head is not the one he wrote—he was distracted and set down something different. To listen intelligently when it is played, must I imagine precisely what the composer had in his head? If this were possible, could it count as listening intelligently to the tune played?

To make up a tune, or to reconstruct one in imagination, is simply to make up, or to reconstruct, a series of notes or tones. Yet the music itself, on Collingwood's theory, does not reside in a series of notes or tones, but somehow behind it. Hence, reconstruction brings one no closer to the music than hearing it. The theory requires that the tune that is played be the *same* one the composer made up, which in turn must be the *same* one the listener reconstructs. That is, there can be only a numerical difference between them, like the difference between two copies of the same book; if they differ significantly in any other way, we are faced with the puzzle posed in the preceding paragraph. But if the tune that is played is the same as the others, why can we not dispense with the others and simply listen intelligently to the tune that is played?

A note struck on the piano begins with a *sforzando* and fades away, but we hear a *sostenuto* tone. Does our hearing the tone as *sostenuto* require an exercise of imagination, as Collingwood supposes? There is a difference between a tone sounding *sostenuto* and our imagining it as *sostenuto;* indeed, if we merely imagined it as *sostenuto* we would not hear it as *sostenuto,* any more than if we merely imagined two lines as converging we would see them as converging. So with the difference between the piano's G and the violin's F-sharp, the street noises at the concert hall, and so on. Do we not simply *ignore* them? Must we also imagine that they are not there?

Consider the other examples Collingwood offers. Does the appreciation of art require imagination in the ways he suggests? And even if it does, does this imply that a work of art is an imaginary object? Or need terms be redefined to make it one?

Works of Art as Funded Perceptions. How can my appreciation of a painting grow if what I see is the same every time I look at it? And how can critical judgments of the same painting, honestly based on what the critics see, run counter to one another, if *what* the critics see is the same? Because, says Pepper, what one appreciates and criticizes is not a painting, an object composed of pigment and canvas, but a *perceived picture* which consists of "a succession of intermittent perceptions." Thus appreciation can grow through the "funding" of a "perceptive series," and critical disagreement would naturally arise when the "perceptive series" of critics differ.

Despite its apparent plausibility, doesn't Pepper's theory create more problems than it solves? Two of these he tries to meet: how to extend the theory to cover arts other than painting, and how to avoid fruitlessly multiplying entities by turning every perception into a separate aesthetic object. But even if these problems are soluble, isn't Pepper's theory, like Collingwood's, paradoxical?

One consequence of Pepper's theory is that critical *disagreement* is impossible. Critics voicing apparently contrary judgments of the same work of art are not really rendering contrary judgments, because they are not, and *can never* be, talking about the same thing. Critic A is speaking about one perceptive series, critic B about another. To be sure, Pepper allows for what he calls a "convergence effect"—that is, for A's perceptive series to approximate B's. But how can we tell whether A's series does approximate B's? Only if they say the same things about them; otherwise we must suppose that the series differ. Yet if the series differ, they are not criticizing the same thing and hence cannot disagree. But if it is impossible for two critics to *disagree,* is it not also impossible for them to agree? (What could agreement be if disagreement is impossible?) If it is possible for them to disagree, must there not be something wrong with Pepper's theory?

What I see in a picture on one occasion may differ from what I see in it on another. What you see in it may differ from what I see in it. Does this mean, as Pepper supposes it does, that the *object* I see on one occasion is different from that which I see on another, or that you and I are seeing different things?

When do we say that there is a difference between what you and I see? (1) When the objects we see are different—you are watching a football game and see a player make a forward pass while I am looking at my watch and see its dial and hands; (2) when the object we are looking at is the same, *e.g.* El Greco's "View of Toledo," but the features of it you notice are different from those I notice. In either case we might say that our *perceptions* differ. But does the word "perception" here refer to some entity in addition to the percipients and the things they are looking at? Or is to have a perception of the "View of Toledo" simply to *see* it?

Pepper speaks of perceptions as if they were ghostly photographs of objects, or images in the distorting mirror of the mind. Hence, the perceived picture, which one would suppose to be the picture that is perceived, *i.e.* the "View of Toledo" that hangs in the Metropolitan Museum, turns out to be composed of perceptions rather than of canvas and pigment. This is clearly paradoxical. But how does this paradox arise? Are we driven to it, as Pepper suggests we are, by certain *facts* about perception? Or is it rather a product of an implicit redefinition of terms?

Pepper calls our attention to the important fact that, as objects of appreciation and criticism, works of art are "perceptual" objects: the features open to aesthetic appreciation and to which we can refer to support our criticisms are those discernible by inspection, *i.e.* by looking, listening, reading, etc. But does this support the conclusion that, as aesthetic objects, works of art are intangible, that they are *merely* perceptual and hence in a class with mirages, hallucinations, and after-images?[2]

Poems as Structures of Norms. "What is the 'real poem'?" ask Wellek and Warren; "where should we look for it; how does it exist?" They consider seven answers to this question. The first six they reject; the seventh is their own.

The second to sixth answers have the following form: "A poem is identical with . . . of the poem." Apart from Wellek's and Warren's criticisms of these answers, can any such thesis be logically satisfactory, whatever words may be used to fill the blank?

Consider the third thesis: a poem is identical with the experience of the reader of the poem. Reader of what? Of the poem. What is the poem? The experience of the reader of the poem. Hence, a poem is identical with the experience of the reader of the experience of the reader of . . . ? It is as if a phonograph needle had stuck and we keep hearing the same phrase repeated. (But in this case we can't move the needle over and continue with the music.) The same holds for the other theses: a poem is identical with the sequence of sounds uttered by a reader or speaker of the poem; with the experience of the author of the poem; with the sum of all past and possible experiences of the poem; and with the experience common to all experiences of the poem.

But this same difficulty would seem to face Wellek's and Warren's own thesis: "The real poem must be conceived as a structure of norms, realized only partially in the actual experience of its many readers." The thesis seems to be unproblematic until the question arises *of* what these norms are the norms. (One cannot have norms or standards of nothing.) They are the norms of reading the poem, for there must be norms or standards by reference to which we can distinguish between correct and incorrect readings. But if this is so, does not the thesis become, "A poem is identical with the structure of norms for reading the poem correctly"? And does this in turn not become "A poem is identical with the structure of norms for reading the structure of norms for reading the structure of norms . . ."?

If all of these answers are logically unsatisfactory, are we forced to accept the first thesis? That thesis creates the difficulty to begin with: if a poem is not identical with ink marks on paper, where is it and what is it?[3] We can say where Vermeer's "View of Delft" is; it is in The Hague. But where is Keats's "Ode to the Nightingale"? We cannot say that it is in this book, for it is also in that one. And how can the same thing be in two places at once?

Works of Art as Tokens and as Types. There is a possible way out of this predicament. Consider the following sentence: "The cat is on the mat." How many words does it contain? Six, or only five? That depends on whether we count "the" once or twice. The same word, we say, occurs twice in the sentence. The occurrences of a word are called tokens; the word is called a type. There are thus two tokens of the same type in the sentence given. This same relation holds between the copies of a poem, the performances of a symphony, and so forth. They are tokens of the same type.

The token-type distinction can be applied to all the arts. Many paintings exist only in "the original," but we can imagine there being many copies of it. We can also, for certain purposes, consider a picture and reproductions of it tokens of the same type. If my acquaintance with Michelangelo's "Last Judgment" is entirely through photographs, am I in no position to say anything about it?[4]

The relation between the performances of a symphony or play, however, is not strictly analogous to that between *word*-tokens. Performances of a symphony may have different aesthetic or artistic merits, whereas word-tokens of the same type, except from a typographer's or bibliophile's point of view, do not vary analogously. One performance or production of *Hamlet* may be artistically superior to another. This is why we think of acting, conducting, playing a musical instrument, and dancing as arts —*performing* arts—in addition to painting, writing, composing, etc. Different impressions of the same etching may also vary in aesthetic merit, which is often why collectors prefer one impression to another. Where such differences are of interest and importance, a token may be regarded as an aesthetic object in its own right.

That the printed texts (tokens) of a poem are physical—ink-marks on paper—does not imply that a poem is. Nor does this in turn imply that paintings and statues are not material. The token-type distinction is not the same as, or analogous to, that between the physical and the nonphysical, the material and the immaterial. Token-expressions, *e.g.* "that statue" in "Move that statue to the left," refer to material objects and physical events. This does not mean that type-expressions, *e.g.* "this symphony" in "This symphony has only three movements," refer to objects of knowledge *sui generis* which have a special ontological status. A poem, as opposed to its printed texts, is no more an object separate and distinct from all texts, recitations, and so forth, than is the dime as a monetary unit from all minted coins. If poems come into being they can also pass away, as the lost tragedies of Aeschylus show, when all copies of them have disappeared and they are no longer remembered.[5]

Works of Art as Aesthetic Objects. Whether we accept or reject such arguments as those of Collingwood, Pepper, and Wellek and Warren— and remember, the objections raised above do not show that their conclusions are false—they nevertheless call our attention to a distinction of some importance: that between a work of art *as* a physical or material object and *as* an object of aesthetic appreciation and criticism. As a material object, Manet's "Les Hirondelles" measures $25\frac{3}{4}$ by $31\frac{7}{8}$ inches, is about $\frac{3}{4}$ of an inch thick, weighs so many pounds, and hangs on a wall in Zurich; as an aesthetic object, it contains an interesting use of black, shows two women seated on the grass, and has an open and subtly unified composition.[6] As a physical event, a performance of *The Cherry Orchard* takes place in a certain theater, lasts so many hours,[7] and is visible and audible. As an aesthetic object, it is beautiful, intelligent, perceptive, amusing.

Statements about a work of art as an aesthetic object are relevant to appreciation and criticism; they can be used to guide appreciation and to support criticism. But are statements about a work of art as a physical object ever relevant to appreciation or criticism?[8]

Notes

1. Note that for Pepper music *does* consist of heard noises, paintings of seen colors, and so forth.

2. For additional arguments in support of an affirmative answer to this question, see Monroe C. Beardsley, *Aesthetics, Problems in the Philosophy of Criticism*, New York, Harcourt, Brace & Co., 1958, Ch. 1.

3. There is an uncomfortable similarity between "Where is a poem?" and the old conundrum, "Where does your lap go when you stand up, your fist when you open your hand?"

4. The token-type distinction can be drawn at several levels. We may, for example, introduce the expression "sub-type" to refer to different editions of a poem, each of which may exist in many copies, or different productions of a play, each of which may run for many performances. The different copies or performances (tokens) of a given edition or production (sub-type) of a poem or play (type) are copies or performances of the same edition or production of the same poem or play.

5. The expressions "a (the) poem" and "a (the) statue" are not logically analogous. "The poem," except where it is an ellipsis for "the text (manuscript, copy) of the poem," is a type-expression. "The statue" is both a token-expression ("The statue is in the Louvre") and a type-expression ("Only three casts of the statue were made").

6. It has been held by some philosophers (*e.g.* M. C. Beardsley, *ibid.*) that the distinction in question is ontological, *i.e.* one between separate and distinct objects. For what we say about a painting as a physical object may contradict what we say about it as an aesthetic object. "Les Hirondelles," for example, shows two women seated on the grass about a mile from a village in the distance. This implies that it has considerable depth. But it is also flat, being only $3/4$ of an inch thick. Hence, "It has considerable depth" cannot refer to the same thing as "It is flat"; any more than "He is only five feet tall" and "He is six feet tall" can be true of the same man at the same time.

Paul Ziff in his "Art and the 'Object of Art,'" *Mind*, LX (1951), 466-80, has argued that statements such as those about "Les Hirondelles" are not contradictory. They appear to conflict but do not do so, for they have different uses in different situations and for different purposes: *"There are two descriptions, not two objects."* Well, *are* such statements contradictory? *Are* there two objects or only two descriptions? How can we tell?

7. "The recorded production of the first movement of Beethoven's D Minor Symphony (No. 9) by Toscanini lasts about thirteen minutes; that by Furt-

wängler about seventeen minutes. If we ask, How long is the first movement of Beethoven's D Minor Symphony? we get contradictory but true answers." (Beardsley, *op. cit.,* p. 56.) But how can the answers be both contradictory and true? Isn't the answer to "How long is the first movement of Beethoven's D Minor Symphony?" "So many *bars,*" not "So many minutes"? A recorded *production* lasts so many minutes. Is there any contradiction in saying that one recorded production lasts longer than another?

8. For further discussion of this issue, see Paul Ziff, "Reasons in Art Criticism," Section VII below.

Suggestions for Additional Reading

Additional views of the nature of the aesthetic object:

Virgil C. Aldrich, *Philosophy of Art* (Englewood Cliffs, N.J., 1963), Chs. 1-2; Monroe C. Beardsley, *Aesthetics* (New York, 1958), Ch. 1; Etienne Gilson, *Painting and Reality* (New York, 1958), Ch. 1; E. H. Gombrich, *Art and Illusion* (New York, 1960); Joseph Margolis, "Mode of Existence of a Work of Art," *Rev. Met.,* 12 (1958), 26-34; Jean-Paul Sartre, *The Psychology of Imagination* (New York, 1948); Donald W. Sherburne, *A Whiteheadian Aesthetic* (New Haven, 1961), Ch. 6; Paul Weiss, *The World of Art* (Carbondale, Ill., 1961), Ch. 10.

Criticisms of some views of the nature of the aesthetic object:

W. B. Gallie, "The Function of Philosophical Aesthetics," *Mind,* LVII (1948), 302-321, reprinted in *Aesthetics and Language,* W. Elton, ed. (Oxford, 1954); Donald F. Henze, "Is the Work of Art a Construct?," *J. Phil.,* LII (1955), 433-439, and "The Work of Art," *ibid.,* LIV (1957), 429-442; Beryl Lake, "A Study of the Irrefutability of Two Aesthetic Theories," *Aesthetics and Language,* 100-113; Margaret Macdonald, "Art and Imagination," *P.A.S.,* LIII (1952-53), 205-266; Richard Rudner, "The Ontological Status of the Aesthetic Object," *Phil. and Phen.,* X (1950), 380-388; Charles L. Stevenson, "On 'What is a Poem?,' " *Phil. Rev.,* LXIV (1957), 329-362; Paul Ziff, "Art and the 'Object of Art,' " *Mind,* LX (1951), 466-480, reprinted in *Aesthetics and Language.*

Also relevant to the problem:

Joseph Margolis, "The Identity of a Work of Art," *Mind,* LXVII (1959), 34-50; R. Meager, "The Uniqueness of a Work of Art," *P.A.S.,* LIX (1959), 49-70.

III

The Arts

Introduction

A MONG THE MOST INFLUENTIAL theories of art produced by the ancient Greeks and Romans are Plato's on music and poetry,[1] Aristotle's theory of poetry,[2] which established poetics as a special branch of philosophy, Horace's *Ars Poetica*, Aristoxenus' *Harmonics*, and Vitruvius' *De Architectura*.

The two arts most extensively treated were poetry and music. These writers approached poetry from both the poet's and the reader's point of view. The Pythagorean discovery of the numerical proportions underlying the intervals, however, led to a treatment of music along mathematical lines, bringing about an alliance between musical theory and the mathematical sciences which lasted until the Renaissance. In the Middle Ages, for example, musical theory was part of the *Quadrivium* along with arithmetic, geometry, and astronomy. Until the eighteenth century, in fact, treatises on the several arts represented distinct branches of writing.

Again, until the eighteenth century, such treatises were also concerned largely with technical matters. They were works addressed primarily to practitioners in the arts, not to laymen or amateurs. But the seventeenth and eighteenth centuries saw the rise of a demand for treatises, both theoretical and critical, on the arts, written by and for laymen, and an alliance between these writings and philosophy. This demand has steadily increased.

The most prominent theory of literature in recent years has been the Emotive Theory, according to which imaginative literature is distinguished from other types of discourse by the prevalence in it of "emotive meaning." Mrs. Hungerland challenges this theory: poetry, or literature in general, she argues, is not marked off from other kinds of writing either by a specific kind of meaning, or by a special feature or function of language.

The aesthetics of music has also been concerned with meaning. Many writers hold that a musical composition represents feelings and emotions in the way a picture represents a person or a place. Eduard Hanslick challenges this view: music, he holds, is simply "sound and motion" and its beauties may not otherwise be rationalized.

Painting, sculpture, and architecture are not thought to be distinguished from the other arts by the kind of meaning they possess, but by the type of sensibility to which they appeal. Painting, according to Trapp, has primarily a two-dimensional appeal; it is something to be looked at from a relatively fixed point of view. On the other hand, sculpture, according to Read, is not something to be looked at so much as something to be touched and handled. And for Zevi, a building is not just a large piece of sculpture; architecture appeals to us by virtue of its enclosed or internal space.

Notes

1. The Greek word *mousike* was applied to poetry and the dance as well as to what we should call music. For one of Plato's most important passages on poetry, see Appendix A of this book.
2. Most of this work appears in Appendix B of this book.

ISABEL C. HUNGERLAND

Language and Poetry

I

THAT POETRY IS DISCOURSE and that it differs in some ways from the discourse of science is a proposition which few, if any, would dispute. The difficulty, of course, lies in attempting to say just what these differences are. An old and persistent tradition in philosophy, taking somewhat different forms in different periods, offers a clear-cut dichtomy to deal with the problem. On the one side, we find intellect, reason, cognition; on the other, feeling, emotion, attitude. The division is further sharpened by putting on the cognitive side discourse which can be true or false and, on the side of emotion, discourse which cannot be true or false or which makes at best pseudo-statements. For a time, linguistic meaning resided exclusively with cognition. Hɪw, some philosophers asked, could a sentence be meaningful unless it were verifiable? "Life is a tale told by an idiot" is hardly the kind of sentence that reports facts, describes things—it cannot be either true or false; it is, accordingly, meaningless. (The philosophers in question did not, of course, deny that poetry has human and rhetorical significance, but they failed to find meaning "in the strict linguistic sense" in much of poetic discourse.) Unfortunately, many of those who rebelled at this highhanded appropriation of meaning tried to get it back into the field of poetry by using the same stratagem of capture. Poetry *is* meaningful discourse because it does give us truth—of course, of a kind different from and higher than the truth of science. Literature is a kind of knowledge or cognition. So ran the argument.

In recent years, the dichotomy has appeared in a new and strange guise. Meaning resides on both sides: on the side of cognition, as descriptive meaning; on the side of feeling and attitude, as emotive meaning. ("Evocative" and "expressive" are also employed to characterize poetic meaning.) But truth, no longer inseparable from meaning, remains with cognition. It will pay us to take a closer critical look at this situation. Although

First published in the *University of California Publications in Philosophy*, Vol. 33 (1958).

this version of the dichotomy has, on the whole, been abandoned, its influence lingers on in subtle ways. . . .

The descriptive-emotive classification has resulted not so much from a careful study of the myriad forms and functions of language as from psychological speculations about what happens in us when we use language. Thus, the meaning of words is taken as what tends to happen in us when we read or hear them. Some words and sentences dispose us to be cognitive; others, emotive. (From the viewpoint of the speaker, the use of some words, or complexes of words, is ordinarily caused by cognition; others by emotions.) In case anyone should think the distinction too sharp, it is pointed out that most ordinary words and sentences, having both kinds of effects, have both kinds of meaning.[1]

This account does not throw much light either on discourse in general or on discourse of various sorts. An article by a physicist, explaining to the public something of the workings of the hydrogen bomb, might tend to produce rather strong responses of fear and dread in readers. (Presumably, the use of language by the writer would not be caused by states of dread and fear.) The following lines from a poem appear to contain much the same sort of word and sentence form that we find people using to report facts, describe scenes and events.

> And there's a barrel that I didn't fill
> Beside it, and there may be two or three
> Apples I didn't pick upon some bough.[2]

Not many readers would feel strongly moved by reading these lines, either in or out of context. (They are taken from a poem which is generally rated high by literary critics.) Now if, in applying the descriptive-emotive dichotomy, it turns out that emotive meanings can predominate in scientific articles, and descriptive meanings in poetry, surely our instrument of analysis is faulty.

It could be replied to this line of criticism that what is needed to make the classification more workable is merely the following qualification. The effects or causes (cognitive or emotive) of language must, to qualify as meanings, be directly connected with our learning of the conventional rules of language. Thus, a word or sentence will have emotive meaning, as distinguished from just an emotive effect, if our disposition to be affected emotionally by it results from our learning its common linguistic uses. In an explanatory article by a physicist, the words are not of the sort conventionally employed to vent feelings or arouse attitudes. Therefore, we need not attribute emotive meaning to the language, even though it does dispose most readers to feel strongly.

The interesting thing about this kind of emendation is that it refers us back to the forms and functions of language. The point which I wish to stress here is that this is where we should begin. I do not, be it understood, wish to say that remarks about thinking, believing, feeling, about aims, needs, attitudes, are out of place in a philosophical (as distinct from a psychological) account of language. Using language is a form of human behavior, or, as some prefer to say, a "form of life." It can never be adequately discussed by philosophers without reference to ways of acting and living. But it should not be forgotten that using language is a very special form of behavior, of life. No matter how closely meshed it may be with extralinguistic behavior, it is still distinct, requiring its own set of explanatory concepts. . . .

When the dichotomy is, by the qualification noted above, referred back to language, it is still beset by difficulties. Let us start by noticing a matter, very minor in itself, but connected with more important issues: the inappropriateness of the epithets "descriptive" and "emotive." Theories of science and narratives of historical events must be labeled "descriptive," along with listings of qualities and characteristics of a single person or place. Cookbooks, instructions for playing games, sermons, political speeches, and most of philosophy must all be called "emotive."

To turn to more important issues, the dichotomy appears to be in part an attempt to put on one side of the fence those sentences which we use to make assertions and which we call "statements." Statements are, of course, true or false, depending on what happens to be the case—for example, "The door is closed," spoken in appropriate circumstances. Other sentences, equally meaningful, are not employed to make statements and cannot be said to be true or false—for example, "Close the door, please." Now this distinction is both legitimate and important for an understanding of language. It does not, however, serve even to get all the discourse of science neatly and simply on the side of truth or falsity. Some logicians have thought that theories, laws, generalizations, and certain sorts of *if-then* sentences cannot be true or false, or at least not in the same sense in which statements that report particular events or ascribe characteristics to particular things can be true or false. Fortunately, it is not necessary for my purpose to decide on the proper interpretation of laws, theories, rules, and so forth. It is enough to note the fact that the division between statements and nonstatements will not yield a sharp segregation of the discourse of science from other kinds of discourse. We can, however, by noting certain logical relations between singular statements and generalizations, laws, and theories, form of scientific discourse a family of linguistic expressions. But even this family kind of grouping will not, without difficulty, serve to separate science from poetry. Looking over the boundary line, we find poetic discourse consisting in expressions which, as far as their make-up and form are concerned, are indistinguishable from members of the scientific grouping.

These striking similarities between supposedly segregated families of expressions have proved a source of embarrassment to philosophers. Attempts to deal with the problem of scientific discourse versus literature or fiction have been, I think, singularly unilluminating. Some philosophers have expounded the view that although writers of fiction are not writing about objects in the ordinary world, they are writing about objects in an extraordinary world. The dog in my yard, the neighbor across the street, *exist;* centaurs, Ophelia, Mr. Pickwick, *subsist.* Somewhat more satisfactory than this verbal solution is the following account. Poets and writers of fiction in general do use sentences that are indistinguishable from sentences that we commonly use, truly or falsely, to describe, report, or characterize things and events. But these sentences are pseudostatements, because the writer is only *pretending* to describe, report, characterize—he is not really doing so. The writer is a kind of linguistic actor, going through the gestures convincingly, but not really doing what he seems to be doing.

The advocates of both the less and the more plausible of these views have been misled in part by the ambiguity of "fiction." In its narrow sense, "fiction" is opposed to "fact," "fictitious" characters to "real" ones. In its wide sense, "fiction" is roughly synonymous with "literature." Now statements, and indeed true statements, are by no means absent from literature. When Dylan Thomas writes a poem about what he did, thought, and felt on his thirtieth birthday, it is quite possible that much of what he says is true. If so, presumably Thomas, when he wrote the poem, knew this and was not just pretending to make statements. Surely, the more sensible thing to say is that the poet, when he is writing a poem, is not necessarily pretending to do anything. He is really writing a poem, and when he does so, he may or may not make statements, and these statements may or may not be true. . . .

The discussion has now led to the point at which the question "How is one to go about the job of distinguishing poetic discourse from other kinds of discourse?" arises with some insistence. I have rejected the descriptive-emotive dichotomy as being an effective instrument for the task. How should one go about finding a better one?

There are certain traditional ways of treating an inadequate dichotomy. A trichotomy is often substituted. For example, action, with its corresponding kind of linguistic meaning, might supplement the cognition and emotion of the descriptive-emotive division. Or, one of the two divided kinds might be reduced to the other. Thus, descriptive meaning could be alleged to derive from an all-inclusive, basic expressive meaning, or vice versa. Finally, in situations where neat divisions are hard to make, some philosophers resort to mysticism, turning their backs on all attempts to distinguish, classify, sort out, and segregate.

None of these traditional modes of philosophic behavior seems to me advisable in the present situation. But I have no unusual scheme of classification to offer. What I am going to suggest is not so much the adoption of a scheme of classifying as an approach to schemes of classifying language.

First and foremost, I suggest that we give up the notion that the logical ideals of classification and division, as set forth in the textbooks, should be attained. I am not denying that these ideals have their legitimacy in certain fields and for certain purposes. I am saying that when our problem is to understand the place of poetry within the whole field of discourse, these logical ideals are misleading. For example, the textbooks tell us that, so far as possible, the things within a given field should be divided, at any one step, on the basis of a single characteristic. The concept of meaning is of extreme, if not basic, importance in relation to language. Here, then, appears to the philosopher with the logical ideal in mind, the single *fundamentum divisionis* needed. What more clear and simple than to divide the genus language into two or three or more basic coördinate species of meaning? There is a grave error in this approach. The error lies in the assumption that because, verbally, our basis of division is single, there is a single common characteristic of all linguistic expressions, namely their having a meaning, analogous to characteristics like having height, or color, or a backbone. Now while there are different heights and colors and different kinds of backbones, there are not basically different ways of *having* height or color or a backbone. In the case of language, there are many different ways of *having* meaning, or being meaningful. A word has meaning in a way different from that in which a sentence has meaning. Also, some words are names for objects, some are used to characterize objects, and some neither name, characterize, nor in any manner apply to objects—examples are "and," "if," and "or." Sentences, too, are meaningful in many different ways: "How lovely!" "Please close the window." "It is cold in here." Corresponding to the various ways of having meaning, or being meaningful, are ways of not having meaning, or being meaningless. Language can be abused or misused. It is abused when some accepted rule is violated—under certain conditions and in certain contexts, I wish to add. . . . Attempting to divide logically the field of meaning is rather like attempting to divide logically the field of manners. In neither case is there a single characteristic, analogous to that of having height, color, or a backbone. Not having a backbone is not violating any rule of community behavior. Nor is there, as a substitute for a single common characteristic, a single supreme rule, either for meaning or for manners. . . .

Another of those ideals which can be misleading for our purposes is that of dividing a field into mutually exclusive classes. The zoologist does not ignore or explain away the Australian platypus, even though the creature confounds some of his basic divisions. We should remember that language has had an evolution, that it was not invented for classifiers, and hence we should be prepared to acknowledge forms and functions that cut across otherwise tidy groupings. We should also remember that evolution has not ended.

Lastly, the logical ideal of an exhaustive division or classification sometimes leads to extending a given distinction far beyond the area in which it is useful. For example, the descriptive-emotive dichotomy does throw light on propaganda techniques and, in general, on the difference between emotion-packed and neutral words and phrases. But, as a division of the whole field of language, the distinction is inadequate.

What I propose to do, then, is to examine the relevance for poetry of several distinctions already lying at hand. None of them cuts through, in any final way, all discourse, and none of them makes a completely clean cut. I might have made a different selection, and there is a somewhat different reason for each of my choices. I chose the first kind of distinction because its importance for poetry has been neglected, and the last because the concepts involved, though recognized as important, have not been sufficiently analyzed by literary critics. A study of the whole set will, I believe, support in detailed ways the two interrelated points I wish to make in this chapter: first, that the descriptive-emotive dichotomy or any analogous substitute for it is an inadequate instrument for analyzing poetic discourse; and, second, that poetry cannot be characterized in terms of any kind of linguistic meaning or device peculiar to it.

II

Consider the following excerpts from four poems:

> If there be rags enough, he will know her name
> And be well pleased remembering it, for in the old days,
> Though she had young men's praise and old men's blame,
> Among the poor both old and young gave her praise.
> (From "Her Praise," Yeats[3])

> She walks in beauty, like the night
> Of cloudless climes and starry skies,
> And all that's best of dark and bright
> Meet in her aspect and her eyes;
> (From "She Walks in Beauty," Byron)

> She lived unknown and few could know
> When Lucy ceased to be;
> But she is in her grave, and, oh,
> The difference to me!
> (From "She Dwelt Among the Untrodden Ways," Wordsworth)

> Let us roll all our strength and all
> Our sweetness up into one ball,
> And tear our pleasures with rough strife
> *Through the iron gates of life.*
> (From "To His Coy Mistress," Marvell)

Each of these excerpts is from a poem which predominantly or in part is concerned with praise of a woman. Any adequate analysis of the poems would have to take account of the different situation indicated in each, the references which delimit the subject matter, the dramatic development, the diction, the pattern of sound and rhythm, and other aspects. For my present purposes it will be enough to show that in the quoted lines—with the whole poem understood as context—certain differences in tone depend, in part, on the different kinds of sentences employed.

The concept of tone has been widely and effectively used by literary critics for more than two decades with little or no analysis, beyond this: tone, in written discourse, is analogous to tone of voice in spoken discourse; "tone" applies, not to what is said, but to the way or manner of saying it; adverbs like "calmly," "excitedly," "formally," "informally," indicate qualities of tone. I shall, for the present, employ the concept as the critics do, postponing an analysis of it till later in the chapter.

The tone of Yeats's lines is more restrained than that of Byron's lines. There is an urgency in Marvell's language and an abrupt increase in intensity in the lines by Wordsworth. These differences in tonal effect appear to depend partly on the kind of sentence employed by each poet. Yeats employs a subjunctive hypothetical and a statement of evidence for it. Such sentences thus related belong in the family of expressions characteristic of scientific discourse. Byron's sentences contain in their predicates and subjects words of commendation: "beauty," "best." Wordsworth changes from a statement to an exclamation, and Marvell employs a polite form of the imperative. Notice, for example, the flat effect if one substitutes in Wordsworth's lines ". . . and, all/Is different for me" for ". . . and, oh,/The difference to me!" The substitution brings, of course, some changes in information conveyed and in sound and rhythm, but these changes are very slight.

Now, I am not suggesting that we forthwith exchange the descriptive-emotive dichotomy for the trichotomy of declarative, imperative, and exclamatory sentences. I want merely, starting with certain common-place grammatical features of the poet's medium, to see what kinds of groupings are indicated.

Perhaps the first thing that strikes one about the distinctions in question is that they mark out different modes of being significant units of discourse. "Close the door" is no less meaningful than "The door is closed," though it cannot be verified, cannot be true or false, since it is not an assertion-form sentence. Further, there seems to be no reason to make the meaningfulness of sentences other than the declarative somehow derivative from the meaningfulness of the latter. As we learn to use language, we learn, at the same time, how and when to report, describe, exclaim, commend, and command. There is no privileged primary form or function here. The notion that there is arises from regarding scientific discourse as the paradigm of language in general.

A second look at the distinctions will find them, legitimate as they are, blurring and shifting. The reasons for this are worth noting. In the first place, grammatical form alone will not give us satisfactory groupings. For example, the class of declarative sentences will include statements, definitions, and appraisals or commendations. In these different groups the declarative form has different linguistic functions. We must, then, supplement our basis of classification by taking linguistic function as a joint, or, in some cases, alternative principle. But language can function in several ways at once, and functions are not as easy to distinguish as are grammatical forms. The resultant groupings will be of the nature of overlapping families, rather than of homogeneous, clear-cut classes. This means neither that the groupings are completely arbitrary, nor that they are without some arbitrary element. Let us look, now, at the phenomena in question.

A declarative sentence, by the simple device of the exclamation point, or its oral equivalent in tone of voice, may have both an assertive and an exclamatory function: for example, "He was asleep!" Analogous considerations hold for imperatives, "Close the door!" being both an imperative and an exclamation. Furthermore, the characteristic exclamatory sentence "How happy I am!" might be analyzed into a combination of a statement and an interjection. The American slang idiom "I'm happy, and how!" suggests this. In brief, neither the exclamatory form nor the exclamatory function yields a homogeneous and clear-cut class.

Within the class of imperative sentences, unless we arbitrarily confine the group to the stark imperative form, we must admit as family relatives the politer forms, such as "Let us. . . ." But then we seem to have opened the door to a whole flock of expressions with allied request functions, but very different grammatical form, for example, "Would that you. . . ." And entreaties, couched in the subjunctive, shade into interrogatives: "Would you mind . . . ?" Here, however blurred at the edges the division may be, there is need for an additional grouping, that of interrogatory expressions.

This new group has a curious feature, often neglected by philosophers of language. It has been supposed that a question is a kind of request-blank for a statement and thus derives its significance from the significance of the statement. But one can proffer blanks for sentences that are not statements, for example: "Is this a morally good action?" "Ought I to do this?" Questions, then, are not on a par with the other groupings considered. They range over these groupings in the sense that appropriate answers to questions may be statements, appraisals, imperatives, or even, perhaps, exclamations. This fact alone shows the futility of trying to split the field of meaning into something like coördinate species. Furthermore, rhetorical questions and expressions like "Is it not so?" "Nicht war?" and "N'est-ce-pas?" appear to be indirect ways of making and emphasizing assertions.

By far the most puzzling group, however, for philosophers searching for mutually exclusive classes of meanings, is that of appraisive sentences, those which contain "good," "bad," or other less general terms of commendation. On some occasions when we employ terms of praise or dispraise we seem to be doing little more than uttering an interjection, "Good!" "Beautiful!" "Horrible!" But on other occasions "This is good" appears to be renderable as a factual report—as either "I like it" or "Most people like it." On still other occasions the translation of "This is a good . . ." into "This . . . has characteristics of *a, b, c*" has plausibility. Finally, "good" is applied to things like actions, and there are times when "This is a good action" might be rendered by "You ought to do this," which, in turn might be taken as a less stark way of saying, "Do this." Thus, appraisive sentences, depending on the occasion and context of their use, show resemblances to exclamations, statements, and imperatives. A notorious characteristic of the philosophic temperament is the tendency to seize upon one feature of a complex phenomenon and label it "the essence." It is not, then, surprising that a large part of the philosophic arguments of the past twenty years on the so-called "theory of value" has centered around the question "Are sentences with 'good' or 'bad' as predicates disguised (or quasi-) statements, or exclamations, or imperatives?" Each of the theories resulting from the selection of one of the alternatives has some plausibility, because of the resemblances just noted. If, however, we look at the core of our appraising activities, none of the theories will do. When we make serious aesthetic or moral appraisals, we are not merely venting our feelings. Nor are we just reporting our own satisfactions or those of other people, nor, in a curiously veiled fashion, describing things. Appraisals make a claim that things are worth liking, and cannot therefore be reduced to expressions which make no claim. . . .

The descriptive-emotive dichotomy, it should now be clear, does not make a useful cut through language. For example, in trying to classify the excerpts from four poems on this basis, we seem at first to get Yeats on one side, with descriptive meaning, and the other three, lumped together across the divide, with emotive meaning. On the other hand, since Yeats's "description" would ordinarily arouse some feelings in the reader, Yeats's lines apparently have both kinds of meaning. Also, since the other excerpts contain what the theory calls "descriptive words," they cannot be purely emotive in meaning. We end, then, with the unenlightening conclusion that all four excerpts have both kinds of meaning. This does not help us to understand certain tonal differences between one excerpt and the others.

Finally, the absurdity of attempting to define poetic discourse in terms of the predominance of some special kind of meaning should be apparent. I have been concerned with one such attempt, namely that represented by the descriptive-emotive classification and its near relatives. But there are others. For example, Charles Morris has suggested, apparently on the basis of a passage from Whitman's "Song of Myself," that poetic discourse

is characterized by the predominance of appraisive meanings.⁴ Now, no
one could deny that in the well-known lines the poet appraises, very
highly, the scent of his armpits and various other aspects of his physical
person. But a poet is not bound by his profession to utter mainly appraisive or any other kind of language. His profession binds him to utter,
but not to utter any special kind of word or sentence. In brief, there is no
such thing as a poetic language, either as a diction or as a mode of sentential meanings. The nearest approach to this occurs when a tradition in
poetry has so cut itself off from the ordinary spoken language as to have
a diction and grammar confined almost exclusively to itself. Whether or
not the separation is always a deathbed phenomenon I leave for the historians of literature to decide.

I wish to conclude this discussion of modes of meaning by considering
the role, in poetry, of a class of words that belong to the province of the
logician. I have in mind such words as "and," "either . . . or," "if . . .
then," the so-called "logical" or "syntactical" words used to connect
phrases, clauses, or sentences. These words neither name, describe, nor
apply to objects. Their function is to order, in various ways, other units
of discourse. It has often been assumed that the function of such syntactical words is irrelevant to poetry. This assumption is wrong. The more
discerning critics are aware of the relevance of syntactical form to tone,
though they do not pursue this matter as diligently as they track down
images or disclose ambiguities. Certain of the comments of Brooks, Purser,
and Warren on the tone of Hardy's poem "Neutral Tones," the first verse
of which follows, will suffice to indicate the kind of relationship which
syntactical structure of the kind in question may have to tone.

> We stood by a pond that winter day,
> And the sun was white, as though chidden of God,
> And a few leaves lay on the starving sod;
>   —They had fallen from an ash, and were gray.⁵

These critics write:

> The sentence structure, too, is such that the loose groping movement
> of the mind trying to repicture a scene is perceived by the reader; for the
> whole sentence . . . is constructed by the accumulation of detail . . . strung
> together by *and's* and then followed by a dash and an afterthought. The
> structure of the sentence by its very logical crudity implies that groping
> movement, the mind trying to recollect something that has already been
> mentioned. That is, the tone here is conversational and meditative.⁶

There is a vein for study here not yet fully exploited by the critics.

III

The next set of distinctions which I want to examine and develop for their relevance to poetry lies conveniently at hand. That language conveys more than it states, that words connote and that sentences suggest more than they mean are commonplaces both of literary criticism and of applied logic. Both literary critics and writers of textbooks in practical logic have well and amply illustrated these distinctions in their respective fields. It is not, then, my intention merely to point to these important but obvious discriminations, or to add to the already ample body of illustrations. Rather, these discriminations need to be scrutinized somewhat more carefully than they have been, and for the following reasons. The relations indicated by "suggest," "convey," and "imply" (in one of its nontechnical senses), and like words, are many and diverse. Some of the concepts involved apply to words, some only to sentences. In some cases, rules of language are at issue, in others, empirical generalizations. For certain purposes it is permissible to lump together the phenomena in question under a single heading in contrast to the somewhat limited sense of "meaning" employed by philosophers and logicians. But there are a number of confusions, both in literary and in linguistic theory, which can be traced back to confusing one form of the general suggestive power of language with another. There are also mistakes arising from a confusion of one or all kinds of suggestion with meaning. Again, an inadequate analysis of the kinds of suggestion is at fault. I shall confine myself in this section to pointing out how a "middlebrow" and a highbrow doctrine of literary criticism and the theory of emotive meaning derive from mistaken notions about the suggestive power of words.

It will be convenient to look first at the variety of effects that are commonly grouped under the heading *the suggestive power of words*. Words, of course, are constituents of sentences, but one can consider them in isolation from this or that sentence. When one does so, the kind of example of verbal suggestion that often comes to mind is found in games, both parlor and psychological, of word association. Thus, presented with the word "apple" and asked to associate freely, a theologian might say "Eve," a gardener "fertilizer," a man with an apple allergy, "doctor," and any number of men in an erotic mood, "breast." What is exhibited here is the familiar process whereby we associate one thing with another on the basis of their similarity, spatiotemporal contiguity, or causal connection. It will pay us, however, to study this familiar phenomenon more closely.

We are apt to call the associations which result in this sort of verbal suggestiveness "personal." The reason for applying the epithet here is obvious enough. We believe that the subject's training, background, individual career, and dominant interests, along with his momentary mood, determine his associations under the conditions of the word-association game. This is why the game can be used to detect the guilt of the criminal or to reveal the complexes of the neurotic. However, we should remember in this connection that "personal" association is not necessarily opposed to "communal" association. My associations in any word-game situation are my own, but many of them may not be at all idiosyncratic. My linkages may reflect a good deal of common experience of one sort or another, as the preceding examples make plain. I wish, in a moment, to contrast personal word association, which may or may not be idiosyncratic, with word connotation, which must be based on shared experience. But first, let us notice a trait exhibited in all associations, whether idiosyncratic or communal.

Associations do not work between two single objects, the one presented or somehow called to mind, the other suggested. What the present draws along from the past is a network, a configuration, of associations. One object suggests, by means of association, a whole experienced context of which it was part. When erotic associations work, it is the whole world of love that is drawn along. Similarly, the theological and gardening connections of our example link the story of Genesis and the causal processes of plant growth to an apple. Since the point I am making is well evidenced by psychological experiment, I shall not labor it further. It has been necessary to mention it only because it is occasionally lost sight of in writings on literature.

The question "What does this word suggest?" (or "What are the suggestions of this word?") can have reference either to some form of word-association game or to the quite different matter of verbal connotation. (Logicians have employed "connotation" in the sense of the *definiens* of a given *definiendum*. Plainly, I am not employing the word in its logical sense, but rather in its literary sense.) In drawing a line between what for short I shall call "word association" and connotation, I do not intend to make out a completely hard and fast boundary. Most of the differences I shall list admit of degree. Also, the personal associations of a poet may, through obvious social processes, lead to the change of a word's connotation. But the differences as well as their importance are clear in examples like the following. Suppose that a professor of English literature who is exploring the effectiveness of "father" in the context of the last stanza of Dylan Thomas' "Do Not Go Gentle into That Good Night" asks for the connotations of the word. If a student should reply, "Dry martinis and golf—my father always drinks the one and plays the other," the answer is clearly inappropriate, a good enough answer to another question, but not to this one. What are the differences at issue here?

First, as I have already indicated, the associations that give connotation to a word must be communal, the result of shared experience. Just how communal or how large the community or how the community is selected are matters determined in the situation in which questions about connotation arise. The community might include all English-speaking people (for example, "father"); but for some words, it might be limited to those English-speaking people who have a high degree of literacy and are familiar with a certain range of literature (for example, "incarnadine.") Furthermore, the associations which give this or that connotation to a word may be the result of a variety of social circumstances. Thus, the connotations of "father" which go in the direction of *the man who guides, protects, rears with love and justice* reflect widespread social notions of the characteristics that fathers *ought* to have. Certainly no one thinks that all fathers, or even most fathers, do have these characteristics. The same, of course, could be said of the corresponding connotations of "mother." In contrast, a scientific theory, the Freudian, has resulted in giving "father," for a fairly large community, an altogether different line of connotation—*the man against whom a son rebels, of whom he is jealous, the first man with whom a daughter falls in love,* and so on.

Before considering the next distinctive feature of connotation, I wish to call attention to a point applicable to both word association and connotation. As is clear in the example of "father," the connotation of a word in the context of a poem is not to be confused with its connotations when considered apart from this or that sentence or phrase. "Father," in relative isolation, has, we have seen, two opposed lines of connotation. A poet may use one line, suppressing the other, or exploit both, depending on the kind of poem he is writing. Analogously, the associations that a word may have in a word-game situation are to be distinguished from the associations it may have in a given literary context. Later in the section I shall return to and discuss further the difference between verbal suggestion within a literary work and verbal suggestion in other situations.

A convenient way of getting at other features of connotation is to notice how, in contrast to word association, it resembles formal definition. Neither giving the connotation of a word nor giving its associations is, of course, subject to the basic requirement of defining the meaning of the word, namely: that a linguistic expression be produced which can be substituted in a certain range of contexts for the word without change in meaning. However, just as an answer to the question "What is the meaning (definition) of 'father'?" can be right or wrong, so can an answer to the question "What is the connotation of 'father'?" But in a word-association game, *right* and *wrong* do not apply to the answers. One can lie or possibly deceive oneself, but there is no way of being objectively right or wrong about one's word associations.

Furthermore, in either defining or giving the connotation of a word like "father," characteristics are specified. In defining, we say that "father" means the same as "man who has at least one child" or "male parent"; in giving connotations, we say perhaps that "father" has the connotation of *a man who guides, protects* (etc.). The free associations of "father," however, are usually given by uttering another class name. The characteristics that link one thing with another are not made explicit, though sometimes they may be obvious, as in a child's "father"—"king" transition.

Finally, any kind of word, not just substantives, has a dictionary definition, and any kind of word can have a connotation. But word games are normally played with substantival words or phrases, not with words like "if," "the," "perhaps." Also, the substantives are usually class names referring to the familiar objects of everyday perception. This is so because the basic associations in the word game are extralinguistic. "Father" and "apple" call forth other nouns, because fathers and apples have been associated with the referents of these nouns. Any other nouns which had approximately the same reference would do as well in setting off the association. But "father," "dad," "papa," "pater," "the old man," have different connotations. Connotation is a matter, in part, of the associations of a word with other words. "Father" derives it connotations partly from its Biblical and other literary occurrences. The synonymous pair "brother" and "male sibling" afford a good example of sameness of meaning and difference in connotation. It is not, be it noted, that the second is a "pure" scientific word, devoid of connotation. The contexts of its employment have resulted in its entanglement, not with the Christian story, but with that of the clinic and the couch.

. . . The suggestive power of language, the power that links objects to contexts, is rightly regarded as the chief means by which literature depicts and evokes emotion. The topic of emotion and literature, unless carefully limited, is one of those that calls for book-length treatment. To forestall such expansion, I propose to confine myself to the briefest of answers to the following questions. What kind of thing is an emotion? What is the difference between depicting and evoking an emotion? Are the emotions evoked by literature different from real-life emotions?

Prominent contemporary trends in philosophy and psychology give similar, and relatively new, answers to the first question. Whether this is a case of philosophy catching up with psychology or vice versa or both, I do not know. At any rate, we hear today from both disciplines that an emotion like love, fear, or hate, is not an inner mental event or state. The concept of an emotion is much like that of an attitude. An emotion is a disposition or tendency to behave in certain ways in certain sorts of situations. Now, while the behavioral and dispositional account of emotions is an improvement on the older mentalistic one, it suffers from oversimplification. An emotion is a far more complicated thing than an attitude, for it has, as components, many short-term attitudes and much else besides. Let us consider a man in love, and assume that he is modern and has been brought up in a Western culture. What does his state, as we conceive it, include? Certainly, it includes a tendency to display courting behavior in certain situations. But if the man is in love, some of the behavior must have been displayed. In brief, the emotion cannot be characterized solely in terms of *if-then* propositions stating what a man would do under such and such conditions. To be in love is, in part, to have had some of these conditions realized and hence to have done some of these things. . . . Finally, the dispositions involved in being in love are extremely various in nature and are related in complex ways. As a consequence, to say that being in love is characterizable (in part) as a set of partially realized dispositions is to say very, very little. And to say that all these dispositions are behavioral ones is to say something that is false.

Let us take a brief look at the complexity of the romantic state. Some of the dispositions involved are passive ones. Prominent among these are the pronenesses to have a variety of feelings which include more than the erotic. These are the familiar pangs and thrills and the generalized feeling of vitality and well-being. Would we say that a man who displayed courting behavior, but reported that he had none of the well-known feelings, was in love? Another passive disposition is the proneness to be subject to alternating moods of elation and depression. Moods are partially realized tendencies to have certain feelings and to display certain behavior and to show certain looks and faces and to see our environment in certain ways. There are complex relations here—the relation between the surrounding circumstances and a whole mood; and within a mood, the relations between the thrill and the smile, the erotic feeling and the languishing look, and between these facial expressions and over-all behavior.

Again there is the tendency to idealize the beloved, and this is realized, not just in chivalrous behavior but in having certain sorts of daydreams and fantasies. There are, too, the changes in ordinary attitude toward friends and acquaintances and family, connected with the new guise the whole world wears.

Finally, there are characteristic situations in which love arises, and there are patterns characteristic of its career in various circumstances.

The particular form which love takes for any individual will, of course, depend on age, sex, personality structure, and social status, the character of the beloved, the circumstances of the romance, and so on. However, as one looks over the literature on and of love in the modern Western world, one may be as much struck with the constancy of certain forms and the similarities amid variations as with the differences of feeling and behaving and perceiving. Dante's behavior on first seeing Beatrice was unusual in showing an extreme degree of the usual—it was not eccentric. Women in love are in some ways different from, and in other ways much like, men in love. The generation of the 1950's, in the United States, has been brought up on "scientific approaches" to and courses on sex, courtship, selecting a mate, marriage. This conditioning, no doubt, has produced its effects. But love seems to remain, even for the scientifically reared, a wonderful, crazy, and painful state. All this is connected with the fact that we cannot notice differences in any field without also noting similarities, and vice versa, although it is possible, of course, for us to concentrate on or stress the one more than the other.

Enough has been said to make the point that an emotion is neither a single mental event nor a simple disposition to behave in certain ways. It is a complex of ways of behaving and perceiving, feeling and manifesting, which arises under certain conditions, and has a character and career determined, in part, by the nature of the actors and the setting of the action. In brief, to have an emotion is to live in a certain way for a certain period in a certain situation as a result of certain factors.

How, then, does a writer depict an emotion, like love, hate, or fear? (I use "depict" here to include both narration and dramatic forms of presenting character.) Plainly, by depicting characters living in a certain way in certain situations. But there are choices in selection here which should be noticed. The novelist, because of the great scope of techniques available to him, will serve as a good example. He may take the viewpoint of a behaviorist psychologist of the 1920's, and confine himself to dialogue and descriptions of behavior. Or he may describe the inner feelings, the dreams and fantasies, of his hero or heroine. He may stress what is typical or what is idiosyncratic. Environment and causal circumstances may be prominent or subordinate. In any case, the novelist's selection and concentration do not deny the existence of the components of emotion omitted or subordinated. They are there in the background, ready to be summoned by association, to form part of the suggested aura of the story. In Hemingway's "The Killers," Nick's feelings are never described, but the reader knows their nature. In fact, the whole point of the story depends on how the boy feels.

So much for the depiction of emotion in literature. But literature not only shows us characters loving, hating, fearing; it also moves us, and does this largely by its depiction of emotion. Emotions evoked by the depiction are usually, of course, different from those depicted. They are spectator emotions, not participator emotions. The remark that one does not necessarily feel jealous when reading *Othello* points to the distinction. It is legitimate enough, but needs qualification. A spectator sometimes "sympathizes" (in the root meaning of the word) with the participators in a human drama. We may fear *with* the hero or heroine—we may indeed share some of Othello's anguish and Desdemona's dread. This phenomenon is not at all peculiar to literature, for in real life also we usually feel with the persons who are close to us in one way or another. . . .

How do the emotions evoked by literature differ from real-life emotions? There are a number of answers here. Each has something to be said for it, but each, I shall maintain, errs in attempting to make an absolute distinction where none exists. Moreover, the plausibility of the various answers depends in part, I think, on adopting an over-simplified conception of emotions.

There is, first, the familiar notion that the emotions evoked by litera-ture are less intense than those evoked in real-life situations. In this view, emotions seem to be identified with feelings, bodily and other, which, of course, can be more or less intense. What the proponents of the view have in mind is apparently the well-known fact that seeing something happen usually evokes more intense feelings in us than merely reading about a happening, whether a real or fictional one. However, this limited generali-zation applies to journalistic reports as well as to literature, and it is pos-sible that in respect to literature there are more exceptions to the rule than in respect to newspaper accounts. More important, there seems to be little evidence that the difference between witnessing and reading about is correlated with a difference in resoluteness in action. Reading about, say, the victims of some disaster might or might not prompt one to give the same financial aid as would witnessing the event. Emotions, we have seen, include partially realized tendencies to action as well as feelings.

Another answer to our question tells us that the emotions evoked by literature are not real ones. This answer results from a misplacement of the adjective "real." The immediate objects of our emotions may be Lear or Falstaff, who are, of course, not real. But we may weep real tears for Lear and laugh real laughs at Falstaff. We neither fake feelings nor pre-tend the more complex emotions when literature moves us. The view that these emotions are unreal, however, points, I believe, to the following conditions. Ordinarily, the emotions evoked in reading literature cannot be very completely developed—only a few dispositions are realizable. We have pangs or thrills or chills; we weep or laugh or frown or show a face of horror. But either the fictional status of the characters, or, if they are real, their removal in space and time, prevents the development of pat-terns of action typical of the emotion. There is, then, much in our emo-tions in reading literature or seeing plays that is incipient merely, held in reserve or truncated. But incompleteness is not unreality in the sense of faked or pretended emotions. In real life, lovers soon separated by cir-cumstance may have a very incomplete experience of love—their emotion is not thereby made fake or false. To be sure, it is one thing to have some component dispositions of an emotion toward a real object blocked by circumstance, and quite another to have these dispositions blocked by a knowledge that the object is imaginary. (However, the fact alone that the object is imaginary obviously does not suffice to yield a special sort of emotion. A great many objects of real-life emotions have proved to be imaginary or revered and feared for imaginary qualities.) Does this un-deniable difference compel us to recognize two very different species of emotion? In dealing with the next view, I shall give reasons for answering the question in the negative.

A more plausible view than the ones just considered is that the usual conditions under which literature evokes emotions, by cutting us off from both personal involvement and practical action, produces a qualitative change in the emotions. They become "impersonal," "contemplative," in brief, "aesthetic." That some changes are generally produced in one or another of the various components of an emotion, I would not, of course, deny; I doubt only the truth of the two-species hypothesis. If it were true, then any literary work which mingles fact and fiction, situations close to the reader and situations distant, would evoke two sets of emotions in him, the one aesthetic, the other not. Did the intimate friends of Yeats who read Auden's memorial poem to him, have a species of emotion completely different from our emotions when we read it? Let us not forget that many literary works of high merit deal with real people and real situations. Furthermore, practical action of one sort or another may be prompted by reading a literary work. A fine memorial poem may make me reach for my check book to contribute to a memorial fund. Does this mean that the poem was not literature for me?

Moreover, when we turn to fictional literary works, is what the psychologists call "ego-involvement" completely absent, and are our practical actions unaffected? At this point, without apology, I shall indulge in some psychological speculations. I believe that, for almost all of us, the degree of ego-involvement in reading fiction is high, and that our practical lives are often as profoundly influenced by our reading as by the advice given and examples set us in ordinary living. The relationships and effects are subtle and indirect, but not non-existent. Those who believe in the doctrine of the aesthetic emotions are willing to admit that the emotions of the adolescent girl or boy reading love stories are neither impersonal nor contemplative nor cut off from practical life. But they are misled by the spectacle of middle-aged men and women reading, say, T. S. Eliot, with some attention to literary forms and techniques. If these readers have a need or taste for nonsavage irony and refined anguish and regret, there may be as much imaginative identification and resulting shaping of attitudes in their case as in that of the adolescents.

. . . The familiar notion that literature orders as well as arouses the emotions points to another, though not absolute, difference between real-life emotions and emotions evoked by literary works. The notion has reference both to emotions depicted and to those evoked. In depicting emotions, the writer, by means of the selecting, forming, and abstracting techniques of his craft, can present us with a simplified and clarified account of human predicaments. The relations between person and person, the lines of motivation, the shape of a dramatic action, the features of a passion may emerge, sharp and plain, without the clutter and confusion of detail that surround them in our everyday comprehension. I say that the writer's depiction *may* have these characteristics. There is no doubt that Shakespeare's depiction of one form of human jealousy in *Othello* does; I can think of many literary works that do not. Also, there is no reason why the same kind of clarified vision of men in action might not be granted to someone just viewing the real human scene. As for the emo-

tions evoked by an ordered depiction of a human plight, they seem, provided the order be grasped, correspondingly ordered. When, as spectator,
I am confused about what the emotions of the participators in any action
are, my own response is hesitating and wavering. When I am not confused, my responses can be said to be more "ordered" than in the other
case.

At this point I may be charged with having overlooked the prescriptive
or imperative function of philosophic remarks about the aesthetic emotions. The point of the two-species hypothesis of emotions, it might be argued, is not to describe how people do respond to works of art, but how
they *ought* to. And this *ought* is not of an arbitrary kind; it is bound up
with the concept of what it is to be a work of art, and what it is to have
an aesthetic attitude or experience. The covert prescription is, as it were,
a rule of the game in question, a part of permissible behavior in the context. The traditional philosophers, to be sure, confused the prescription
with a description, but the fact that they did affords no reason for continuing the confusion. To this kind of objection, my reply is that I am
here concerned with the descriptive aspects of the hypothesis of the aesthetic emotions. The descriptions of these purified emotions are surely
supposed to be true of somebody, at least of the "sensitive reader." Otherwise, the *ought* would be vacuous, the decorum a mere possibility, the
game imaginary. What I have been saying is that the traditional descriptions of the aesthetic emotions are not true, or at best are only half true,
of the sensitive and attentive reader.

It is time now to examine two doctrines of literary criticism in the light
of the distinctions developed in this section. There is, first, a middlebrow
doctrine, not advocated by any of the reputable critics of the day but
found frequently among students, for whom it has a certain convenience.
It is, I suspect, in derivation a simplified version of the old impressionistic
romantic tradition in criticism. It amounts to supposing that the suggestions and evocations of the language of a poem depend almost entirely on
the experience and personality of the reader, not at all on the poem, except so far as it is broken up into a list of words. The doctrine rests in
part on the correct notion that what is suggested by the language of a
poem is just as important as what is articulated or stated, if not more so.
But the other basis for the doctrine is the incorrect notion that words in
the context of phrase, sentence, or line will have for a reader the same
associations that they have for him out of context. The word game and
free association are wrongly taken as the models for the suggestive power
of language. Connotation is disregarded, and unlimited variability is attributed to suggestion by association.

My objection to the doctrine is not that one cannot "read" a poem as
an exercise in word association but that one need not, and should not.
For the attentive reader, reading a poem and not playing a word game,
"death" will have one main line of association and evocation when con-

nected with "dust" and "worms" in certain ways, and another when connected with "peace" and "sleep" in certain ways. To take a more complex
example, consider the context of "death" in the following poem by Yeats.

> *A Deep-Sworn Vow*
> Others because you did not keep
> That deep-sworn vow have been friends of mine;
> Yet always when I look death in the face,
> When I clamber to the heights of sleep,
> Or when I grow excited with wine,
> Suddenly I meet your face.[7]

That the connotation of words like "death" and "friends" are important here can be seen by substituting the synonyms or synonymous phrases
given by the dictionary: for "death," substitute "decease," "demise," "extinction," "passing" or "passing over"; for "friends," substitute "intimate
acquaintances," "comrades," "companions," or "allies." The differences in
direction of suggestion between Yeats's words and any of their synonyms
depend on certain facts about the English language. They depend on the
reader only in the platitudinous sense that if his knowledge of English is
poor, he will not be aware of the lines of suggestion. Since the middlebrow
doctrine ignores connotation altogether, I shall in what follows concentrate on word associations in context and the emotions depicted and
evoked thereby.

"Death" occurs in the poem after the statement of the consequences of
breaking a deep-sworn vow. Its immediate context in the whole complicated sentence of the poem is a subordinate clause which, in a semi-
metaphorical way, gives death a face, and states one condition of some
happening the nature of which is not yet revealed. Then, two alternative
conditions of the happening are given, the descriptions of which contain,
in this order, references to sleep and slight intoxication. In the final line,
the repetition of "face" (unexpected in the rhyme scheme) relates the
you of the poem to death. The fact that the order of the references, as
well as the immediate context of certain nouns in phrase and clause, suppresses some possible line of association and of evocation is as important
as the fact that other lines are developed. For example, what precedes
"death" and what follows it rule out evocation of both sentimental and
morbid attitudes and feelings. Neither golden harps nor worms are suggested. The clausal context of "sleep," along with the preceding and following clauses, suppresses suggestions of peace and quiet, and develops
suggestions in another direction. In sleep, a dream image may appear
after struggle or dream experience of effort, and this image (according to
some views) may yield an insight unavailable to us in our practical working life. In the fifth line, the suggestions of comic behavior which reference to slight intoxication often has, are ruled out by the first four lines.

The state of exhilaration and release from inhibition which is suggested evokes something quite different from the leer and the chuckle. Much more, of course, might be said about the network of suggestions, but this account will suffice to make my point. In a poem, associations are not "free" (controlled only by a reader's unconscious problems, mood, background, and so on), because a poem is not a word list—it is a structure of phrase, clause, sentence. It is part of the poet's craft to control the direction of suggestion and evocation in the composition of the various linguistic units employed.

It might be objected here that some attentive reader of Yeats's poem might find rather different lines of suggestion from those I have found. To this I would agree. In rejecting the view that any reading of a poem is acceptable, I am not embracing the view that only one reading is. . . .

The highbrow doctrine of criticism, which I wish to examine next, amounts to elevating verbal ambiguities in poetry into a universal criterion of excellence. The apparent plausibility of this performance rests on an ambiguous use of "ambiguity." The doctrine is concerned with kinds of ambiguity other than the verbal; for example, the so-called "multi-level" story. I shall, for the sake of brevity, confine myself to considering the simplest kind of ambiguity, that of words. The proponents of this literary theory tend to take verbal ambiguity as embracing not only the characteristic of having more than one dictionary meaning, but also that of having high suggestive power in the context of a poem. For example, Kaplan and Kris, in listing the various meanings of "shrunken" relevant to its occurrence in the third stanza of Eliot's "Sweeney Among the Nightingales," write:

> Confining ourselves to the ambiguities in just the word "shrunken" we may note the following. Most directly the reference is to the state of the tides. . . But shrunken is also withered and old, and especially in the case of the seas, dried up; there is a suggestion that we are present at the end of a world. To shrink is to contract, huddle, cower; hence we find an attitude of "fearful" expectancy appropriate to impending death. . . Again the shrunken sea is at its most vulnerable, smallest, and weakest, and indeed has already to some degree been awed and overpowered; the crashing waves have been hushed. And the vulnerability extends perhaps to the land on which the murderous action is to take place: the seas have withdrawn, leaving the land naked, exposed, forsaken.[8]

Here the authors include in the meaning of the ambiguous word "shrunken" all the lines of association which the word has in the context, as well as the emotions evoked by and those depicted in the poem. But, although old people are usually shrunken in various ways, "shrunken" does not mean the same as "old." Shrinking is often caused by drying up, but dried-up is not one of the meanings of "shrunken." Again, the image of dried-up seas may well suggest an end-of-the-world scene and evoke appropriate responses in the reader, but this whole complex of suggestion and evocation cannot be counted as one of the several meanings of "shrunken"—unless, of course, we wish to pack everything that words do into the concept of meaning.

If one starts this way with the ordinary meaning of "ambiguity" and then extends it, one can quite easily demonstrate that not only Eliot and Donne employ ambiguity as an artistic device, but also Wordsworth and any other admired poet. What has been demonstrated, of course, is only the commonplace that part of the poet's business is to manipulate the suggestive power of language. No one has ever doubted this, though a number of people have doubted that the Eliot- or Donne-like poem, which does employ verbal ambiguity as a central device, yields *the* model for poetic perfection. At this point, a certain resemblance appears between the middlebrow and highbrow doctrines we have just examined. Both neglect the fact that the poet is as much concerned with excluding certain meanings, suggestions, and evocations from his lines as in including certain others. To be sure, those who find the secret of poetic effect in ambiguity are aware that the mere presence of ambiguous words will not make a poem good. Kaplan and Kris, for example, tell us that the various meanings must work together in the poem, be integrated, and so on. But even this sort of qualification does not, I fear, yield the desired criterion. For surely, when a popular American poet tells us what it takes to make a house a home, he is employing ambiguities (nicely reinforced by alliteration) which in suggestion and evocation go well together.

We are now in a position to make a more comprehensive and hence fairer survey than we have thus far made of the doctrine of emotive meaning. The holders of the view rightly attempt to take account of the fact that not all words are descriptive or referential and that not all sentences are of the statement type. However, the mistake is made of trying to pack into the concept of meaning (whether of words or sentences) any fairly regular line of suggestion and evocation. Consider, for example, the notion of "dependent emotive meaning,"[9] formulated for the meaning of words. A word will have dependent emotive meaning, we are told, if it tends to arouse certain emotions because the referent of the word arouses these emotions. But this will lead to absurdity. "Father" will provide a good illustration. Suppose that Freud is correct about the prevalence of the Oedipus complex, at least in Western society. It would follow that the word "father," even in such contexts as "Johnny Smith's father is J. A. Smith," would tend to arouse in Western males certain attitudes and feelings. According to the emotive-descriptive doctrine, "father," under these circumstances, has "dependent emotive meaning." But here we have a very odd sense of "meaning" which has nothing to do with linguistic rules or conventions and which I cannot determine by any study of the workings of language. In fact, I could only determine whether or not the word has this odd kind of meaning by determining whether or not a highly speculative psychological hypothesis were true. Yet in the customary sense of "meaning" I know quite well what "father" means. If I am asked to explain its meaning, what techniques I employ will vary with the questioner's knowledge of English, but what I try to convey in every case is first that "father" is a class name applying to anyone who is male and a parent. To complete the account, two points should be added. "Father" is also employed to name one's male parent in a manner similar to the employment of a proper name. Moreover, in certain metaphorical contexts "father" has a laudatory meaning; that is, acceptable paraphrases would use words conventionally classed as laudatory. None of this "knowing the meaning of 'father' " requires me to have deep insight into the unconscious of the Western male. To be sure, widespread acquaintance with Freudian theory, as I said earlier, has contributed to a new line of connotation for "father." But I do not subscribe to the view that knowledge of Freudian theory, or even belief in it, generally causes the complexes and attitudes postulated in the theory.

Our example of "father," however, does show how easy it is to slide over the differences between the psychological causes and effects of employing linguistic expressions, on the one hand, and linguistic meanings, on the other. If "father" does, in some metaphorical contexts, have a laudatory meaning, this is connected with one line of connotation of the word. This line of connotation, we have seen, is determined in part by social approval of certain characteristics of some male parents. And connotation, in some ways, resembles meaning. One should note, too, that words for a long time neutral may become laudatory or derogatory in meaning because of group attitudes toward the things they refer to or are used to describe. "Statism" in the United States is a good example. Its shift in recent years from a neutral term to one synonymous with "too much government" has been recorded in American dictionaries. The shift appears to be partly due to Republican propaganda against the Democratic party. Again, a given word, at any time, may be employed neutrally in one context, appraisively in another. But the criterion for this difference is not some psychic circumstance in either speaker or hearer. The criterion is a linguistic one, namely: if a word is employed as laudatory, then it is redundant to conjoin it with "good" in that context and inconsistent to conjoin it with "bad.". . .

IV

Thus far, under the category of suggestion, I have considered the suggestive force of words, not sentences. To be sure, the suggestions which words make in the context of sentences has been treated, but this is not the same as the suggestive force of sentences, the basic units of significant speech. The suggestions which sentences have are indicated by everyday, nonlogical uses of "imply." Only sentences have implications—words do not. I shall briefly mark out one large family of such implications, mainly in order to distinguish it from another group which is of special importance to dramatic literature.

Logical implication, sometimes called "entailment," may be defined as follows: a sentence *p* entails a sentence *q* if and only if *p and not-q* is a contradiction. When this relation holds, we say that the meaning of *q* is "part of," or "contained in," the meaning of *p*. Clearly enough, many of our everyday uses of "imply" fall outside the domain of logical implication or entailment. Of these, there are no doubt a large variety, as yet insufficiently examined by philosophers of language. But for my purposes, it will suffice to lump a number of nonlogical implications together. Examples from the group I have in mind are the relation between "All my children are asleep" and "I have children" and the relation between "I know it" and "I believe it." (I assume here, of course, that each pair of sentences is uttered by the same person, on the same occasion, and so on.) There is no formal contradiction in saying "All my children are asleep and I have no children" or "I know it and I don't believe it," but the sentences are of a sort that has been happily called "logically odd."[10] Something in these cases has gone very wrong with the use of language, but the wrongness is not of the kind exhibited in contradiction. The examples exhibit two characteristics of the group from which they come, namely, that the implying relation, in a plain sense, holds between the sentences concerned, and that the relation is determined by certain conventions of language. To recognize a compound sentence as logically odd is to notice something about language rules concerning the constituent sentences. If a man should say "All my children are asleep" and then add, "By the way, I have no children," we would be inclined to say that he didn't know how to employ the sentences in question.

The relation which I wish to examine as especially important for literature is of another sort. It is not, in the way just illustrated, a relation between sentences, and the only kind of oddity involved in its definition would be psychological, not logical. My reasons for introducing it in this context are that "imply" is often used in referring to it, that it is exhibited in situations in which sentences are employed, and that, as a result, it is sometimes confused with relations definable in terms of logical oddity.

The relationship I have in mind is illustrated in certain inferences made by listeners about speakers. From the fact that Mr. Jones, in a situation which I know to be annoying to him, makes, in a strained tone of voice, a remark which has no reference to the situation, I may, for example, infer that Jones is annoyed, is trying to conceal it, and hence is pretending an interest in other matters. Sometimes our inferences of this sort are based on very general connections. For example, in general, when people make statements, we infer that they believe what they say, since the statement form is the conventional one for expressing and communicating belief. But people sometimes lie, and there are situations—storytelling, play-acting—in which we know that the speaker does not believe the statements he utters. There is no logical oddity about the sentence, "Mr. Jones said he loved his wife, but didn't believe it."

Before turning to the implication relation correlated with the group of inferences in question, it will be helpful to note the following points about them. These inferences are of the sort on which psychoanalysts concentrate in their professional capacity. However, the analyst is usually interested in states and conditions of the speaker which are obscure, that is, difficult to get at. Accordingly, he normally knows that he is making inferences and has some critical awareness of weight of evidence. But in daily life, our inferences are often of a telescoped, "intuitive," uncritical character. We seem to *see* that a man is angry, wants to humiliate his enemy, and so on, from what he says and how he says it in a certain situation. In many instances, our certainty is, indeed, justified, in that the states we infer are not "buried" in the unconscious, and the connections involved are fairly regular ones. It should be evident, now, that the inferences I am considering form a family of some diversity. For dealing with certain philosophical problems, it might be essential to divide and distinguish varieties. For the matters which concern me here, it will suffice to treat the group as a whole. In the next section, our inferences about the purpose of a speaker in saying something will receive attention.

Let us turn now from consideration of inference to consideration of implication. Whenever we are justified in inferring a sentence q from a sentence p, p (in one sense or another) implies q. It follows from this that the correlate of the inferences just considered can, of course, be exhibited as a relation between sentences. But the relation does *not hold between the sentence uttered* and *some other sentence* presupposed by or in some way implicit in it. When Jones says, "I love my wife" and we infer that he dislikes her, the implication in question does not hold between "I love my wife" and "I dislike my wife"; rather, it holds between a sentence describing the fact that Jones utters the sentence "I love my wife" in a certain way and in a certain situation (which includes Jones) and a sentence describing an attitude of dislike on the part of Jones toward his wife. In order to mark off this relationship from other implications, and to have a name that is appropriate to nonformal treatment, I propose to call it "conveying." I shall say, then, that the fact that someone says something under certain circumstances and in a certain way conveys various sorts of information about the speaker. Whether or not the conveying is deliberate on the part of the speaker does not concern me here.

It is plain that what speech conveys is of particular importance to dramatic literature. We learn about the motivations, purposes, momentary states, characters, and, hence, discern the outline of a play's action, largely by what dialogue conveys. Consider Othello's speech as he enters Desdemona's bedchamber in the final act of the play, especially "Put out the light, and then put out the light" and the following lines. The imperative presupposes that there is, in the scene, a light burning, and "light" has associations with life, which, in the context, are developed by Othello. Quite another matter is what the speech conveys about Othello's state, his intentions, his feelings for Desdemona, his character and personality.

V

In the preceding sections, I have been content merely to use the noun "use" in relation to language, leaving it to the context to make plain the relevant sense of this ambiguous word. That "use" is, in ordinary parlance, as ambiguous as "meaning," does not count against the philosophic position which takes the meaning of a linguistic expression to be its use. On the contrary, the position is strengthened by the parallel ambiguities of the two words. Moreover, there are good reasons for recommending that, in philosophizing, we speak of the use of a linguistic expression, instead of the meaning—for example, that we ask "What is the use of 'good,' what role does it play in discourse?" rather than "What is the meaning of 'good'?" One well-advertised reason is that this diction does not mislead us into looking for queer sorts of objects that might be the meaning of a word. A more important reason, I think, is that the new way of speaking directs our attention to features of discourse hitherto neglected, leads us to ask new questions that need asking. However, "use" will not be of much use to us, unless its various uses are, when occasion demands, made clear. For the task of analyzing poetry, it is important to distinguish between the meaning of the language (what is given in a paraphrase), the tone of the utterance, and the purpose or intent of the speaker. For example, if the purpose of the speaker in Browning's dramatic monologue "My Last Duchess" is not grasped, the whole point of the poem is missed. Yet the fictional speaker's intent is not stated by him, is no part of the paraphrasable meaning. The tone of the Duke's utterance also is not part of the meaning of his speech and is different from the purpose. One can say the same thing in different tones and for different purposes. The notion of use, however, is involved in all three cases. It will be well, then, to explicate some of the different senses of "use." (In what follows, I shall be concerned not only with what are called "different senses" of a word, but also with different applications of the same sense. However, since in the case of "use" there is a tendency to transfer features of one application to another, the distinction seems quibbling here, and I shall leave it at times to the context to make plain whether I am discussing different kinds of use or different senses of the word.)

Let us separate first two different senses of "use" that we discover when we look up words in a dictionary. We find usually a phrase which, as we ay, "defines the meaning" and a list of single words called "synonyms." Now, if we know how to operate linguistically with the phrase or synonym, then the dictionary has indicated to us how to operate linguistically with the unfamiliar word. That this indication is exceedingly rough and approximate is plain enough. A dictionary is an aid to, not a substitute for, reading and conversing and listening as a way of learning a language. Without going into all the features of a word's use (for example, grammatical classification) which a dictionary can only point to, not exhaust, I wish to call attention to the difference between specifying how a word is used by giving defining phrases, synonyms, and grammatical function, and the following sort of information. A dictionary not only defines words and lists the grammatical classes for each, but also tells us whether a word is colloquial, archaic, slang, obscene, and whether it is a technical term of law, medicine, mathematics, psychiatry, and so on. This information indicates to us how to use a word, not merely correctly, but appropriately. A man speaking in a language other than his native one might use formal words on an informal occasion, or slang expressions on a formal one, or sidewalk words when he wishes to make some scientific observation about sex. In this sort of situation, we understand what the man is saying—his mistake is neither grammatical nor definitional. We would be inclined to say, I think, that the man knows the meaning of the words in question, but is ignorant of the appropriate social context of their use. The tone of his utterance is wrong. A good deal of humor in literature, we might note here, depends on contrasts of tone—for example, the extreme formality of Jeeves's speech as contrasted with the informality of Bertie Wooster's in the P. G. Wodehouse stories.

Another ambiguity is found when we speak of the "use" of a word and the "use" of a sentence. Words are potential components of sentences. As linguistic expressions, they have a kind of incompleteness about them. Except where they function as elliptical expressions for sentences, words do not, in isolation, report, describe, appraise, question. It is by means of words in combination that something is said, that discourse takes place. This is why the dictum, *to know the meaning of a word is to know how to use it in sentences,* is a serviceable one. To know the meaning of a sentence, however, is to know the meaning of its component words (including, of course, words like "is") in the particular context and relationship in which they occur. Accordingly, while, as we shall see, we can sensibly say a good deal about various uses of sentences, these uses are not the same as, or even analogous to, the use of a word.

Thus far, the ambiguities considered are not apt to lead to serious confusions in the domain of our enquiry. The cluster of ambiguities I wish to examine next has led to misunderstandings of poetic discourse. The ambiguities here concern the uses of sentences, not words.

There are, first, differences in the use of sentences which relate to different kinds of language situations. The sentence "The night was dark

and stormy" may be part of an account of a journey I have taken; it may
be uttered when I am making up a bedtime story for a child, or repeating
what someone else has said, or reciting a poem, or showing someone who
is learning English how to say it. Only in the first instance is the declarative sentence used to assert something, to make a statement. It should be
noticed that there is not, and, indeed, could not be, different sentential
forms to correspond to the varieties of this kind of use. In order to pretend to make, or play at making, or show someone how to make an assertion I must employ the language form which conventionally has this
function. I depend upon the social and linguistic context to make clear
to my hearers how the sentence is used.

When, above, I spoke of forms which conventionally have a certain
function, I was referring to another kind of use of linguistic expressions,
"function" and "use" being in many contexts interchangeable. By convention, the declarative sentence form has a statement function, the imperative a request-command function. Since we learn such correspondences of
form and linguistic function while we are learning to talk, no one but an
adult just beginning to learn a language, or a philosopher, would ever
ask questions about them. A man learning English might well ask why
"The door is shut" is employed in one context and "Shut the door" in
another. The answer, of course, would be that in the one case a statement
is being made and the sentence must therefore have the proper form for a
statement, whereas in the second case a command is being given and the
imperative form is the right one. Here "proper" and "right" point to
rules or conventions. The English language might have developed in such
a way that "Shut the door" would be a statement form, or it might have
developed without formal devices to mark the differences in function.
Since neither of these possibilities was realized, there is little point, as we
saw earlier, in questioning the legitimacy of any form-function, or in trying to make one of them basic, the paradigm of significant discourse.

We are now in a position to take a look at the important concept of the
use, in the sense of the purpose, of an utterance. Clearly, the purpose of
the speaker is one of the things that can be conveyed (deliberately or not)
by the saying of something in certain circumstances. We have looked at
the relation of conveying in general. Let us see how, in this instance, confusion of concepts arises. Consider a mother saying to her child, "Your
father wants you to do this." Under ordinary circumstances, easily imagined, the mother utters the sentence in order to get the child to do what
is indicated. Her "purpose" or "intent," we say, is to effect a certain kind
of behavior in the child. We might also say that she is "using" the declarative sentence to induce the child to perform an action. It is at this point
that there begins a muddling of the three senses of "use" under discussion,
namely: the kind of language situation involved, the conventional linguistic function of the form of sentence uttered, and the aim or purpose
of the speaker in saying something. It is recognized, quite rightly, that in

order to understand what is going on linguistically, the whole situation, not just the sentence uttered, must be taken into account. But the philosophic question "Why (for what purpose) did the speaker employ the statement form?" to which the proper and truistic answer is, "Because she wanted to assert such and such and this form is the conventional one for doing so"—is confused with the unphilosophic question "Why (for what purpose) did the mother make the statement that . . .?"—to which the answer is not truistic, and is often difficult to ascertain. As a result of this muddling, some philosophers have supposed that "Your father wants you to do this" uttered in the situation in question can be paraphrased as "Do this," and hence is not a "real" statement but an imperative in disguise. Here we have a confused linguistic Pragmatism. The very inducing of the child to do something, in the case in question, cannot be explained unless it is assumed that the child understands the statement and accepts it as true. Furthermore, the effects on a hearer of a statement of facts which constitute *reasons* for doing something are ordinarily quite different in certain ways from the effects of a stark imperative. In both cases the same action may be performed, but in the latter case rebelliously, with determination not to do so again. Such differences in effect, familiar to all of us, cannot be explained on the theory that a declarative sentence in a certain context is "really" an imperative.

The linguistic Pragmatism just noted has confused linguistic function and life function. The first concerns what we want to do with language—make statements, appraise, command, question; the second concerns what we want to do by means of the language function exhibited. To be sure, language function hooks up with life function. If no one had ever wanted to communicate information or to make others perform actions, the declarative and the imperative forms would not have been invented. But it is at just the point of hookup that philosophical confusions arise, as we slide from considerations of language forms and rules to considerations of psychology, via the same words, "purpose," "function," "use," employed in a different way. . . .

How do we ascertain the purposes of our friends' talk? Plainly, no amount of knowledge of language alone can let us know the purposes which language may serve. What is required is knowledge of human beings and human situations. In any particular case, we ascertain purpose by an inference based on our fund of such knowledge. Furthermore, a single utterance may serve several purposes of the speaker. While some or one of a speaker's purposes may be easily known by either speaker or hearer, it may take years on an analyst's couch to ascertain others. For example, consider again the mother who says to her child, "Your father wants you to do this." Depending on the psychological make-up of the persons involved, their inter-relations, the kind of action indicated, and so on, the speaker might have any one of several of the following purposes: to make the child refrain from performing the action; to make the child perform the action quickly without fuss; to humiliate the child; to make the child hate his father; to make the child respect his father. It might be difficult for either the speaker or an onlooker to ascertain some of these purposes, easy to ascertain others. Whether or not the task is easy, in learning the purpose of a piece of discourse we learn something about the lives of the people involved. We are ascertaining the goals and directions of human behavior, including that very important kind of behavior, talking.

It is for this reason that the concept of the speaker's purpose is important in literary analysis, particularly in dramatic literature. Character and dramatic action are linked with purpose. In literature, as in life, sometimes purpose is easily determined, sometimes not. In Browning's "My Last Duchess" we "read off" the speaker's purpose so easily that we are tempted to confuse it with the meaning of his speech. However, a paraphrase of the Duke's speech along the lines of "The Count's daughter had better be obedient and subservient to my wishes, or she'll die as my last Duchess did" would miss the character of the Duke. That he is not the kind of man to utter a direct threat is part of the dramatic point of the poem. When the purpose of fictional speakers is more difficult to determine, its difference from the meaning of the utterance as well as its importance is plainer. In Act III, scene ii, of *Hamlet,* we understand without difficulty, though perhaps only with the help of scholars, the meaning of Hamlet's speeches to Ophelia. There is no puzzle about the Elizabethan vulgarities in his lines. But there is a puzzle, which cannot be settled by scholarship alone, about the purpose of Hamlet's rudeness. The Oedipus reading of the play gives one answer, and the alternative readings give others. The question is still open. It is a crucial one for any interpretation of the play.

VI

The last concept which I propose to examine in this chapter in its application to poetic discourse is that of tone. Thus far, I have used "tone" without much explication. I have pointed out that the tone of a piece of discourse is determined by what modes of meaning the author employs and by the character of his diction and grammatical constructions. I have also accepted the common usage of "tone" in assuming that tone varies in a number of ways. A man may speak seriously or humorously, or in both ways at once; he may talk (or write) excitedly or in a restrained fashion, pompously or humbly, formally or not, and in a practically unlimited variety of other ways. These examples of the application of "tone" indicate that the concept is a complicated one, in fact, probably a cluster of concepts rather than a single one. Important as the concept has been in

the literary criticism of the last three decades, it has received little more
elucidation than that given in the following account by I. A. Richards:

> . . .*the speaker has ordinarily an attitude to his listener*. He chooses or
> arranges his words differently as his audience varies, in automatic or
> deliberate *recognition of his relation to them*. The tone of his utterance
> reflects his awareness of this relation, his sense of how he stands towards
> those he is addressing.[11]

It is not clear from this passage whether Richards intends to identify
tone with the speaker's attitude toward his audience, or with manner of
speaking or writing. The speaker's or writer's manner, which is determined by the choice and arrangement of words, may *reflect* his attitude
toward the audience, but could not, of course, be identical with the attitude. Furthermore, Richards' concentration on attitude toward the audience appears to place unwarranted limitations on what a given manner of
speaking or writing may "reflect." The tone of a speaker would ordinarily
be said to vary according as, for example, he has respect for his audience
and his subject, none for his audience but respect for his subject, and
so on.

However, the important question here is not just what attitude, or how
many attitudes, diction and grammar may "reflect." Attitudes are psychological dispositions. We have already seen that the fact that certain linguistic expressions are employed in certain contexts will convey to the
listener (or reader) various sorts of information about the speaker. So far
as tone is identified (as it sometimes is) with certain of the speaker's attitudes, it belongs, along with purpose, under the heading of what language
conveys. Tone, thus understood, would be distinguished from purpose
only by the following features: the diction and grammar of a piece of discourse would be the main clues for our inferences about the states of the
speaker or writer; our inferences would be concerned with certain of his
attitudes. But, as Richards' account indicates, "tone" is also applied as
though the linguistic expressions themselves had certain tonal qualities.
We call pieces of discourse serious or humorous in tone, restrained, or excited, and we seem to be talking about the language, not the speaker,
about qualities of speech, not states or dispositions of people. Also, we
seem to be talking, not about inferred characteristics, but about something that we recognize, that we are aware of as we hear or read the
language.

Is this impression an illusion generated by metaphorical ways of talking about talk? For example, when we speak of discourse itself as "restrained," are we employing a figure which can be translated as "the
diction and construction of this piece of discourse are of the sort commonly used by people who have an attitude of restraint"? There is no
doubt that as far as inferences to states and conditions of the speaker are

concerned, this kind of translation is adequate. But one is left with an uneasy feeling. Is this all there is to it? Has not some part of our experience with language been left out of account? I believe that something has been left out and that it is important, for several reasons, to isolate the missing factor. Poets write about it and take it into account while composing. Thus, T. S. Eliot, in Part V of "Little Gidding," writes:

> And every phrase
> And sentence that is right (where every word
>   is at home,
> Taking its place to support the others,
> The word neither diffident nor ostentatious,
> An easy commerce of the old and the new,
> The common word exact without vulgarity,
> The formal word precise but not pedantic,
> The complete consort dancing together).[12]

To ignore what concerns the poet is to widen still further the breach in theory between the man whose main business is to write poetry and the man whose main business is to write about it. Also, the factor in question, when unmentioned and unlooked for, becomes an elusive and mysterious something to plague us, making us dissatisfied with almost all accounts of meaning and discourse in general. Let us try, then, to isolate the concept of tone as applicable directly to language itself.

A helpful analogy here is that of tone of voice. The tone of a man's voice is not a state or disposition either in him or in the listener. One may speak in an angry tone of voice without being angry or arousing anger in the listener. To say that the angry tone just *is* one of those aspects of the sound—a particular pitch or timbre, for example—which in our experience have been often displayed by people who are angry, is not an adequate account of the matter. It confuses the causal processes that make us have a certain kind of perception, with the character of the perception itself. When I hear an angry tone of voice, I may or may not infer that the speaker is angry and I may or may not make judgments about similarities. The point is that I hear the tone as angry, however I may have come to have this kind of experience.

The analogy, of course, has its limits, so let us return to the kind of linguistic example dealt with earlier.

"Excellent" and "swell" are both conventionally employed to accord a high estimate of worth, and thus have roughly the same meaning. But "This is an excellent poem" and "This is a swell poem" are tonally different. Again, discourse employing scientific words and discourse employing obscene words have different tonal quality, even though the words refer to the same sexual objects. There are tonal differences determined by the predominance of one kind of sentence in a piece of writing or by a change from one mode of meaning to the other.

As for the causal conditions of our apprehending tonal quality, these are twofold. There is, first, the kind of intralinguistic association which we noted in examining connotation. Virginia Woolf is writing about this kind of association when she tells us:

> Words, English words, are full of echoes, or memories, of associations— naturally. They have been out and about, on people's lips, in their houses, in the streets, in the fields, for so many centuries. . . . The splendid word "incarnadine," for example—who can use it without remembering also, "multitudinous seas"?[13]

Notice that it is the words "incarnadine" and "multitudinous seas" that have the echoes. "To make pink or flesh color or crimson" and "numerous waves" are silent in this respect.

In addition to familiarity with the verbal contexts of words, phrases, and sentences, one needs, to apprehend tone, knowledge of the attitudes of speakers or writers in employing them on certain occasions. These are causal conditions, as I have indicated, not the experience of language for which they are causal conditions. Tone is not, like connotation, a species of the suggestive power of language. Nor can it be defined in terms of inference to attitudes of the speaker, though these inferences no doubt regularly accompany our apprehension of tone.

The gestalt psychologists have long made us aware of the "expressive qualities" of various combinations of colors and sounds. I am, I suppose, talking about an analogous sort of thing in relation to language. But I do not want to embrace all the doctrines of gestalt theory; in particular, I do not want to accept the notion that our apprehension of expressive qualities is, typically, independent of learning processes and associations. In the beginning of studying a foreign language, our apprehension of tonal quality is almost entirely lacking. The language will acquire tonal quality for us only after we have considerable familiarity with oral and written contexts of expressions and with the ways of the people who speak and write it.

I. A. Richards and other critics of his general persuasion have made us aware of the importance of tone in poetry, of how it can make or break a poem. There is no need, then, for further illustrations of this point. But in order to illustrate the distinctions I have made, I conclude with a brief consideration of the tone of the following poem by Yeats, from which I have already quoted.

Her Praise

She is foremost of those that I would hear praised.
I have gone about the house, gone up and down
As a man does who has published a new book,
Or a young girl dressed out in her new gown,
And though I have turned the talk by hook and crook

Until her praise should be the uppermost theme,
A woman spoke of some new tale she had read,
A man confusedly in a half dream
As though some other name ran in his head.
She is foremost of those that I would hear praised.
I will talk no more of books or the long war
But walk by the dry thorn until I have found
Some beggar sheltering from the wind, and there
Manage the talk until her name come round.
If there be rags enough he will know her name
And be well pleased remembering it, for in the old days,
Though she had young men's praise and old men's blame,
Among the poor both old and young gave her praise.[14]

None of the words or linguistic constructions in the poem is extremely formal or traditionally poetic. These characteristics may be called the *basis* for a casual tone in a sense analogous to that in which a certain pitch, or timbre, may be called the basis for an angry quality of voice. Tone is not inferred from the basis, but things which have these characteristics are perceived or experienced as having a certain tonal quality. The tone, however, is not that of a homely or highly colloquial conversation, for the words and phrases on the whole have a certain dignity. We lose this quality if we make changes like the following: in the first line (prominent as first line and also as a repeated line) substitute "first" or "best" or "most important" for "foremost"; change the construction "that I would hear praised" to "whom I'd like to hear praised" or "that I want to have people praise." The syntax has some complication, but it is not an obstructing or difficult complication—it orders the thought clearly, giving a quality of directness to the language. Finally, there is a predominance of referential or descriptive words and statements, which serve to give a tone of relative restraint, though the appraisive aspects of the first line and the "I will" give emotional intensity.

The characteristics that are the basis for tone will at the same time "reflect" for us certain abilities of the speaker toward his audience and his subject. But there is more to what is conveyed about the speaker than a casual, direct, and serious attitude toward subject and listener. Attitudes, feelings, and emotions come in bundles. Also, what is, in sum, conveyed by a piece of discourse depends on more than diction and construction. What is selected for report or description and the circumstances of the utterance enter in, too. Considering all these factors along with the speaker's manner, what we surmise from the discourse is, I think, something like the following: that the speaker, though aware of the somewhat extravagant nature of his devotion, is not ashamed of it; that he is not addressing his listeners with the condescension of a man who feels his love to be evidence of some special sensitivity on his part; that he wishes to conceal nothing from them or himself.

Notes

1. The concept of emotive meanings seems to have been first carefully made out by Charles L. Stevenson in *Ethics and Language* (New Haven, Yale University Press, 1944). Stevenson's book was an important contribution to ethics, and, except for a few scattered remarks, it contains no attempt to apply the doctrine to poetry. But the earlier work of I. A. Richards, along with Stevenson's sharpening of the doctrine, fostered the approach that I am criticizing.

2. From "After Apple-Picking," by Robert Frost, in *Complete Poems of*. . . . (New York, Henry Holt and Company, 1949), pp. 88-89. Copyright 1930, 1949, by Henry Holt and Company, Inc. Copyright 1936, 1948, by Robert Frost. By permission of the publishers.

3. W. B. Yeats, from *The Wild Swans at Coole*, in *The Collected Poems of*. . . . (New York, The Macmillan Company, 1940), pp. 170-171. Copyright 1919, reprinted by permission of The Macmillan Company.

4. Charles Morris, *Signs, Language and Behavior* (New York, Prentice-Hall, Inc., 1946), p. 136.

5. Thomas Hardy, *Collected Poems of*. . . . (New York, The Macmillan Company, 1931), p. 9. Reprinted by permission of the publishers.

6. Cleanth Brooks, Jr., John Thibaut Purser, and Robert Penn Warren, *An Approach to Literature* (3rd ed.; New York, Appleton-Century-Crofts, Inc., 1952), p. 330. Copyright 1952.

7. Yeats, *op. cit.*, p. 176.

8. Abraham Kaplan and Ernst Kris, "Esthetic Ambiguity," *Philosophy and Phenomenological Research*, Vol. VIII (March, 1948), pp. 415-435. [Reprinted in Section V of this book, Ed.]

9. See Stevenson, *op. cit.*, p. 72.

10. See P. F. Strawson, *Introduction to Logical Theory* (London, Methuen and Co., Ltd., and New York, John Wiley and Sons, Inc., 1952), p. 175, and "On Referring," *Mind*, Vol. LIX (1950), pp. 320-344; see also P. H. Nowell-Smith, *Ethics* (London, Penguin Books, 1954), pp. 80-87. Strawson is concerned with a nonentailment relation between sentences and statements, a distinction which is clearly required in the case of sentences containing indexical words like "I," "my," "this," "I was born in California" being used to make a true statement when uttered by some people, but a false one when uttered by others. However, we often speak of sentences as being true or false, or of two sentences as being inconsistent, the conditions of utterances being assumed or taken for granted, and I have employed this language as suitable for my purposes. Nowell-Smith makes out a relation of "contextual implication" which, I think, confuses the two groups of relations I distinguish in this section.

11. I. A. Richards, *Practical Criticism* (New York, Harcourt, Brace and Company, 1929), p. 182. Richards' italics.

12. T. S. Eliot, *Four Quartets* (New York, Harcourt, Brace and Company, 1943), p. 38.

13. Virginia Woolf, *The Death of the Moth and Other Essays* (New York, Harcourt, Brace and Company, 1942), p. 203.

14. Yeats, *op. cit.*, pp. 170-171.

EDUARD HANSLICK

The Beautiful in Music

Does Music Represent Feelings?

THE PROPOSITION that the feelings are the subject which music has to represent is due partly to the theory according to which the ultimate aim of music is to excite feelings and partly to an amended form of this theory.

A philosophical disquisition into an art demands a clear definition of its subject matter. The diversity of the subject matter of the various arts and the fundamental difference in the mode of treatment are a natural sequence of the dissimilarity of the senses to which they severally appeal. Every art comprises a range of ideas which it expresses after its own fashion in sound, language, color, stone, etc. A work of art, therefore, endows a definite conception with a material form of beauty. This definite conception, its embodiment, and the union of both are the conditions of an aesthetic ideal with which a critical examination into every art is indissolubly connected.

The subject of a poem, a painting, or a statue may be expressed in words and reduced to ideas. We say, for instance, this picture represents a flower girl, this statue a gladiator, this poem one of Roland's exploits. Upon the more or less perfect embodiment of the particular subject in the artist's production depends our verdict respecting the beauty of the work of art.

The whole gamut of human feelings has with almost complete unanimity been proclaimed to be the subject of music, since the emotions were thought to be in antithesis to the definiteness of intellectual conceptions. This was supposed to be the feature by which the musical ideal is distinguished from the ideal of the other fine arts and poetry. According to this theory, therefore, sound and its ingenious combinations are but the material and the medium of expression by which the composer represents love, courage, piety, and delight. The innumerable varieties of emotion constitute the idea which, on being translated into sound, assumes

From Eduard Hanslick, *The Beautiful in Music,* translated by Gustav Cohen, edited by Morris Weitz, copyright © 1957, and reprinted by permission of the Liberal Arts Press Division of The Bobbs-Merrill Company, Inc.

the form of a musical composition. The beautiful melody and the skillful harmony as such do not charm us, but only what they imply: the whispering of love, or the clamor of ardent combatants.

In order to escape from such vague notions we must, first of all, sever from their habitual associations metaphors of the above description. The *whispering* may be expressed, true, but not the whispering of love; the *clamor* may be reproduced, undoubtedly, but not the clamor of ardent combatants. Music may reproduce phenomena such as whispering, storming, roaring, but the feelings of love or anger have only a subjective existence.

Definite feelings and emotions are unsusceptible of being embodied in music.

Our emotions have no isolated existence in the mind and cannot, therefore, be evoked by an art which is incapable of representing the remaining series of mental states. They are, on the contrary, dependent on physiological and pathological conditions, on notions and judgments—in fact, on all the processes of human reasoning which so many conceive as antithetical to the emotions.

What, then, transforms an indefinite feeling into a definite one—into the feeling of longing, hope, or love? Is it the mere degree of intensity, the fluctuating rate of inner emotion? Assuredly not. The latter may be the same in the case of dissimilar feelings or may, in the case of the same feeling, vary with the time and the person. Only by virtue of ideas and judgments—unconscious though we may be of them when our feelings run high—can an indefinite state of mind pass into a definite feeling. The feeling of hope is inseparable from the conception of a happier state which is to come, and which we compare with the actual state. The feeling of sadness involves the notion of a past state of happiness. These are perfectly definite ideas or conceptions, and in default of them—the apparatus of thought, as it were—no feeling can be called "hope" or "sadness," for through them alone can a feeling assume a definite character. On excluding these conceptions from consciousness, nothing remains but a vague sense of motion which at best could not rise above a general feeling of satisfaction or discomfort. The feeling of love cannot be conceived apart from the image of the beloved being, or apart from the desire and the longing for the possession of the object of our affections. It is not the kind of psychical activity but the intellectual substratum, the subject underlying it, which constitutes it love. Dynamically speaking, love may be gentle or impetuous, buoyant or depressed, and yet it remains love. This reflection alone ought to make it clear that music can express only those qualifying adjectives, and not the substantive, love, itself. A determinate feeling (a passion, an emotion) as such never exists without a definable meaning which can, of course, only be communicated through the medium of definite ideas. Now, since music as an "indefinite form of speech" is admittedly incapable of expressing definite ideas, is it not a psychologically unavoidable conclusion that it is likewise incapable of expressing definite emotions? For the definite character of an emotion rests entirely on the meaning involved in it.

How it is that music may, nevertheless, awaken feelings (though not necessarily so) such as sadness and joy we shall try to explain hereafter when we come to examine music from a subjective point of view. At this stage of our inquiry it is enough to determine whether music is capable of representing any definite emotion whatever. To this question only a negative answer can be given, the definiteness of an emotion being inseparably connected with concrete notions and conceptions, and to reduce these to a material form is altogether beyond the power of music. A certain class of ideas, however, is quite susceptible of being adequately expressed by means which unquestionably belong to the sphere of music proper. This class comprises all ideas which, consistently with the organ to which they appeal, are associated with audible changes of strength, motion, and ratio: the ideas of intensity waxing and diminishing; of motion hastening and lingering; of ingeniously complex and simple progression, etc. The aesthetic expression of music may be described by terms such as graceful, gentle, violent, vigorous, elegant, fresh—all these ideas being expressible by corresponding modifications of sound. We may, therefore, use those adjectives as directly describing musical phenomena without thinking of the ethical meanings attaching to them in a psychological sense, and which, from the habit of associating ideas, we readily ascribe to the effect of the music, or even mistake for purely musical properties.

The ideas which a composer expresses are mainly and primarily of a purely musical nature. His imagination conceives a definite and graceful melody aiming at nothing beyond itself. Every concrete phenomenon suggests the class to which it belongs or some still wider conception in which the latter is included, and by continuing this process the idea of the absolute is reached at last. This is true also of musical phenomena. This melodious adagio, for instance, softly dying away, suggests the ideas of gentleness and concord in the abstract. Our imaginative faculty, ever ready to establish relations between the conceptions of art and our sentiments, may construe these softly ebbing strains of music in a still lotfier sense, e.g., as the placid resignation of a mind at peace with itself; and they may rouse even a vague sense of everlasting rest.

The primary aim of poetry, sculpture, and painting is likewise to produce some concrete image. Only by way of inference can the picture of a flower girl call up the wider notion of maidenly content and modesty, the picture of a snow-covered churchyard the transitoriness of earthly existence. In like manner, but far more vaguely and capriciously, may the listener discover in a piece of music the idea of youthful contentedness or that of transitoriness. These abstract notions, however, are by no means the subject matter of the pictures or the musical compositions, and it is still more absurd to talk as if the feelings of "transitoriness" or of "youthful contentedness" could be expressed by them.

There are ideas which, though not occurring as feelings, are yet capable of being fully expressed by music; and conversely, there are feelings which affect our minds but which are so constituted as to defy their adequate expression by any ideas which music can represent.

What part of the feelings, then, can music represent, if not the subject involved in them?

Only their dynamic properties. It may reproduce the motion accompanying psychical action, according to its momentum: speed, slowness, strength, weakness, increasing and decreasing intensity. But motion is only one of the concomitants of feeling, not the feeling itself. It is a popular fallacy to suppose that the descriptive power of music is sufficiently qualified by saying that, although incapable of representing the subject of a feeling, it may represent the feeling itself—not the object of love, but the feeling of love. In reality, however, music can do neither. It cannot reproduce the feeling of love but only the element of motion; and this may occur in any other feeling just as well as in love, and in no case is it the distinctive feature. The term "love" is as abstract as "virtue" or "immorality," and it is quite superfluous to assure us that music is unable to express abstract notions. No art can do this, for it is a matter of course that only definite and concrete ideas (those that have assumed a living form, as it were) can be incorporated by an art. But no instrumental composition can describe the ideas of love, wrath, or fear, since there is no causal nexus between these ideas and certain combinations of sound. Which of the elements inherent in these ideas, then, does music turn to account so effectually? Only the element of motion—in the wider sense, of course, according to which the increasing and decreasing force of a single note or chord is "motion" also. This is the element which music has in common with our emotions and which, with creative power, it contrives to exhibit in an endless variety of forms and contrasts.

Though the idea of motion appears to us a most far-reaching and important one, it has hitherto been conspicuously disregarded in all inquiries into the nature and action of music.

Whatever else there is in music that apparently pictures states of feeling is symbolical.

Sounds, like colors, are originally associated in our minds with certain symbolical meanings which produce their effects independently of and antecedently to any design of art. Every color has a character of its own; it is not a mere cipher into which the artist blows the breath of life, but a force. Between it and certain states of mind, Nature herself has established a sympathetic connection. Are we not all acquainted with the unsophisticated meanings of colors, so dear to the popular imagination, which cultured minds have exalted into poetic refinement? Green is associated with a feeling of hope, blue with fidelity. Rosenkrantz recognizes "graceful dignity" in orange, "philistine politeness" in violet, etc. (*Psychologie*, 2nd ed., p. 102.)

In like manner, the first elements of music, such as the various keys, chords, and timbres, have severally a character of their own. There exists, in fact, a but-too-ready art of interpreting the meanings of musical elements. Schubert's symbolism of the keys in music forms a counterpart, as it were, to Goethe's interpretation of colors. Such elements (sounds, colors), however, when employed for the purposes of art, are subject to laws quite distinct from those upon which the effect of their isolated action depends. When looking at a historical painting we should never think of construing the red appearing in it as always meaning joy, or the white as always meaning innocence. Just as little in a symphony would the key of A flat major always awaken romantic feelings or the key of B minor always misanthropic ones, every triad a feeling of satisfaction and every diminished seventh a feeling of despair. Aesthetically speaking, such primordially distinctive traits are nonexistent when viewed in the light of those wider laws to which they are subordinate. The relation in question cannot for a moment be assumed to express or represent anything definite whatsoever. We called it "symbolical" because the subject is exhibited not directly but in a form essentially different from it. If yellow is the emblem of jealousy, the key of G major that of gaiety, the cypress that of mourning, such interpretations, and the definite character of our emotions, imply a psychophysiological relation. The color, the sound, or the plant as such are not related to our emotions, but only the meanings we ourselves attach to them. We cannot, therefore, speak of an isolated chord as representing a determinate feeling, and much less can we do so when it occurs in a connected piece of music.

Beyond the analogy of motion, and the symbolism of sounds, music possesses no means for fulfilling its alleged mission.

Seeing, then, how easy it is to deduce from the inherent nature of sound the inability of music to represent definite emotions, it seems almost incredible that our everyday experience should nevertheless have failed firmly to establish this fact. Let those who, when listening to some instrumental composition, imagine the strings to quiver with a profusion of feeling clearly show what feeling is the subject of the music. The experiment is indispensable. If, for instance, we were to listen to Beethoven's "Overture to Prometheus," an attentive and musical ear would successively discover more or less the following: the notes of the first bar, after a fall into the lower fourth, rise gently and in rapid succession, a movement repeated in the second bar. The third and fourth bars continue it in wider limits. The jet propelled by the fountain comes trickling down in drops, but rises once more, only to repeat in the following four bars the figure of the preceding four. The listener thus perceives that the first and second bars of the melody are symmetrical, that these two bars and the succeeding two are likewise so, and that the same is true of the wider arc of the first four bars and the corresponding arc of the following four. The bass which indicates the rhythm marks the beginning of each of the first three bars with one single beat, the fourth with two beats, while the same rotation is observed in the next four bars. The fourth bar, therefore, is different from the first three, and, this point of difference becoming symmetrical through being repeated in the following four bars, agreeably impresses the ear as an unexpected development within the former limits. The harmony of the theme exhibits the same correspondence of one large and two small arcs: the common chord of C of the first four bars corresponds to the chord of $\frac{6}{4}$ of the fifth and sixth, and to the chord of $\frac{6}{5}$ of the seventh and eighth bars. This systematic correspondence of melody, rhythm, and harmony results in a structure composed of parts at once symmetrical and dissimilar, into which further gradations of light and shade are introduced through the timbre peculiar to each instrument and the varying volume of sound. . . .

Any other subject than the one alluded to we absolutely fail to find in the theme, and still less could we state what feeling it represents or necessarily arouses in the listener. An analysis of this kind, it is true, reduces to a skeleton a body glowing with life; it destroys the beauty, but at the same time it destroys all false constructions.

No other theme of instrumental music will fare any better than the one which we have selected at random. A numerous class of music lovers think that it is a characteristic feature only of the older "classical" music to disregard the representation of feelings, and it is readily admitted that no feeling can be shown to form the subject of the forty-eight preludes and fugues of J. S. Bach's *Well-Tempered Clavichord*. However glaringly unscientific and arbitrary such a distinction may be—a distinction, by the way, which has its explanation in the fact that the older music affords still more unmistakable proof that it aims at nothing beyond itself, and that interpretations of the kind mentioned would, in this case, present more obstacles than attractions—this alone is enough to prove that music need not necessarily awaken feelings, or that it must necessarily be the object of music to represent them. The whole domain of florid counterpoint would then have to be ignored. But if large departments of art, which can be defended both on historical and aesthetic grounds, have to be passed over for the sake of a theory, it may be concluded that such a theory is false. Though a single leak will sink a ship, those who are not content with that are at liberty to knock out the whole bottom. Let them play the theme of a symphony by Mozart or Haydn, an adagio by Beethoven, a scherzo by Mendelssohn, one of Schumann's or Chopin's compositions for the piano, anything, in short, from the stock of our standard music; or again, the most popular themes from overtures of Auber, Donizetti, and Flotow. Who would be bold enough to point out a definite feeling as the subject of any of these themes? One will say "love."

He may be right. Another thinks it is "longing." Perhaps so. A third feels it to be "religious fervor." Who can contradict him? Now, how can we talk of a definite feeling being represented when nobody really knows what is represented? Probably all will agree about the beauty or beauties of the composition, whereas all will differ regarding its subject. To "represent" something is to exhibit it clearly, to set it before us distinctly. But how can we call that the subject represented by an art which is really its vaguest and most indefinite element, and which must, therefore, forever remain highly debatable ground?

We have intentionally selected examples from instrumental music, for only what is true of the latter is true also of music as such. If we wish to decide the question whether music possesses the character of definiteness, what its nature and properties are, and what its limits and tendencies, no other than instrumental music can be taken into consideration. What instrumental music is unable to achieve lies also beyond the pale of music proper, for it alone is pure and self-subsistent music. No matter whether we regard vocal music as superior to or more effective than instrumental music—an unscientific proceeding, by the way, which is generally the upshot of one-sided dilettantism—we cannot help admitting that the term "music," in its true meaning, must exclude compositions in which words are set to music. In vocal or operatic music it is impossible to draw so nice a distinction between the effect of the music and that of the words that an exact definition of the share which each has had in the production of the whole becomes practicable. An inquiry into the subject of music must leave out even composition with inscriptions, or so-called program music. Its union with poetry, though enhancing the power of the music, does not widen its limits.

Vocal music is an undecomposable compound, and it is impossible to gauge the relative importance of each of its constituents. In discussing the effects of poetry, nobody, surely, will cite the opera as an example. Now, it requires a greater effort, but no deeper insight, to follow the same line of thought when the fundamental principles of musical aesthetics are in question.

Vocal music colors, as it were, the poetic drawing. In the musical elements we were able to discover the most brilliant and delicate hues and an abundance of symbolic meanings. Though by their aid it might be possible to transform a second-rate poem into a passionate effusion of the soul, it is not the music but the words which determine the subject of a vocal composition. Not the coloring but the drawing renders the represented subject intelligible. We appeal to the listener's faculty of abstraction, and beg him to think, in a purely musical sense, of some dramatically effective melody apart from the context. A melody, for instance, which impresses us as highly dramatic and which is intended to represent the feeling of rage can express this state of mind in no other way than by quick and impetuous motion. Words expressing passionate love, though diametrically opposed in meaning, might, therefore, be suitably rendered by the same melody.

At a time when thousands (among whom there were men like Jean Jacques Rousseau) were moved to tears by the air from *Orpheus:*

> *J'ai perdu mon Eurydice,*
> *Rien n'égale mon malheur,*＊

Boyé, a contemporary of Gluck, observed that precisely the same melody would accord equally well, if not better, with words conveying exactly the reverse, thus:

> *J'ai trouvé mon Eurydice,*
> *Rien n'égale mon bonheur. . . .†*

What is true of isolated passages is true also in a wider application. There are many cases where an entirely new text has been employed for a complete musical work. If Meyerbeer's *Huguenots,* after changing the scene of action, the time, the characters, and the plot, were to be performed as "The Ghibellines of Pisa," though so clumsy an adaptation would undoubtedly produce a disagreeable impression, the purely musical part would in no way suffer. And yet the religious feeling and fanaticism which are entirely wanting in "The Ghibellines" are supposed to be the motive power in *The Huguenots.* Luther's hymn must not be cited as counter-evidence, as it is merely a quotation. From a musical point of view it is consistent with any profession of faith whatever. Has the reader ever heard the *allegro fugato* from the overture to *The Magic Flute* changed into a vocal quartet of quarreling Jewish peddlers? Mozart's music, though not altered in the smallest degree, fits the low text appallingly well, and the enjoyment we derive from the gravity of the music in the opera can be no heartier than our laugh at the farcical humor of the parody. We might quote numberless instances of the plastic character of every musical theme and every human emotion. . . .

The proposition which we are endeavoring to disprove has become, as it were, part and parcel of current musical aesthetics, so that all derivative and collateral theories enjoy the same reputation of invulnerability. To the latter belongs the theory that music is able to reproduce visual and auditory impressions of a nonmusical nature. Whenever the question of the representation of objects by musical means (*Tonmalerei*) is under debate we are, with an air of wisdom, assured over and over again that, though music is unable to portray phenomena which are foreign to its

---

＊ "I have lost my own Eurydice, / Nothing can compare with my unhappiness." Ed.

† "I have found my own Eurydice, / Nothing can compare with my happiness." Ed.

province, it nevertheless may picture the feelings which they excite. The very reverse is the case. Music can undertake to imitate objective phenomena only, and never the specific feeling they arouse. The falling of snow, the fluttering of birds, and the rising of the sun can be painted musically only by producing auditory impressions which are dynamically related to those phenomena. In point of strength, pitch, velocity, and rhythm, sounds present to the ear a figure bearing that degree of analogy to certain visual impressions which sensations of various kinds bear to one another. As there is, physiologically speaking, such a thing as a vicarious function (up to a certain point), so may sense impressions, aesthetically speaking, become vicarious also. There is a well-founded analogy between motion in space and motion in time; between the color, texture, and size of an object and the pitch, timbre, and strength of a tone; and it is for this reason quite practicable to paint an object musically. The pretension, however, to describe by musical means the "feeling" which the falling snow, the crowing cock, or a flash of lightning excites in us is simply ludicrous.

Although, as far as we remember, all musical theorists tacitly accept and base their arguments on the postulate that music has the power of representing definite emotions, yet their better judgment has kept them from openly avowing it. The conspicuous absence of definite ideas in music troubled their minds and induced them to lay down the somewhat modified principle that the object of music was to awaken and represent indefinite, not definite, emotions. Rationally understood, this can only mean that music ought to deal with the *motion* accompanying a feeling, regardless of its essential part, with what is felt; in other words, that its function is restricted to the reproduction of what we termed the dynamic element of an emotion, a function which we unhesitatingly conceded to music. But this property does not enable music to represent indefinite feelings, for to "represent" something "indefinite" is a contradiction in terms. Psychical motion, considered as motion apart from the state of mind it involves, can never become the object of an art, because without an answer to the query, What is moving, or what is being moved? an art has nothing tangible to work upon. That which is implied in the proposition—namely, that music is not intended to represent a definite feeling (which is undoubtedly true)—is only a negative aspect of the question. But what is the positive, the creative, factor in a musical composition? An indefinite feeling as such cannot supply a subject; to utilize it an art would, first of all, have to solve the problem: What *form* can be given to it? The function of art consists in *individualizing,* in evolving the definite out of the indefinite, the particular out of the general. The theory respecting "indefinite feelings" would reverse this process. It lands us in even greater difficulties than the theory that music represents something, though it is impossible to define what. This position is but a step removed from the clear recognition that music represents no feelings, either definite or indefinite. Yet where is the musician who would deprive his art of that domain which from time immemorial has been claimed as belonging to it? . . .

Having absolutely denied the possibility of representing emotions by musical means, we must be still more emphatic in refuting the fallacy which considers this the aesthetic touchstone of music.

The beautiful in music would not depend on the accurate representation of feelings even if such a representation were possible. Let us, for argument's sake, assume the possibility and examine it from a practical point of view.

It is manifestly out of the question to test this fallacy with instrumental music, as the latter could be shown to represent definite feelings only by arguing in a circle. We must, therefore, make the experiment with vocal music as being that music whose office it is to emphasize clearly defined states of mind.

Here the words determine the subject to be described; music may give it life and breath, and impart to it a more or less distinct individuality. This is done by utilizing as far as possible the characteristics peculiar to motion and the symbols associated with sounds. If greater attention is bestowed on the words than on the production of purely musical beauty, a high degree of individuality may be secured—nay, the delusion may even arise that the music alone expresses the emotion which, though susceptible of intensification, was already immutably contained in the words. Such a tendency is in its consequences on a par with the alleged practicability of representing a certain feeling as the subject of a given "piece of music." Suppose there did exist perfect congruity between the real and the assumed power of music, that it was possible to represent feelings by musical means, and that these feelings were the subject of musical compositions. If this assumption be granted, we should be logically compelled to call those compositions the best which perform the task in the most perfect manner. Yet do we not all know compositions of exquisite beauty without any definite subject? We need but instance Bach's preludes and fugues. On the other hand, there are vocal compositions which aim at the most accurate expression of certain emotions within the limits referred to, and in which the supreme goal is truthfulness in this descriptive process. On close examination we find that the rigor with which music is subordinated to words is generally in an inverse ratio to the independent beauty of the former; otherwise expressed, that rhetorico-dramatical precision and musical perfection go together but halfway, and then proceed in different directions.

The recitative affords a good illustration of this truth, since it is that form of music which best accommodates itself to rhetorical requirements down to the very accent of each individual word, never even attempting to be more than a faithful copy of rapidly changing states of mind. This, therefore, in strict accordance with the theory before us, should be the highest and most perfect music. But in the recitative, music degenerates into a mere shadow and relinquishes its individual sphere of action altogether. Is not this proof that the representing of definite states of mind is contrary to the nature of music, and that in their ultimate bearings they are antagonistic to one another? Let anyone play a long recitative, leaving out the words, and inquire into its musical merit and subject. Any kind of music claiming to be the sole factor in producing a given effect should be able to stand this test.

This is by no means true of the recitative alone; the most elevated and excellent forms of music equally bear out the assertion that the beautiful tends to disappear in proportion as the expression of some specific feeling is aimed at; for the former can expand only if untrammeled by alien factors, whereas the latter relegates music to a subservient place.

We will now ascend from the declamatory principle in the recitative to the dramatic principle in the opera. In Mozart's operas there is perfect congruity between the music and the words. Even the most intricate parts, the finales, are beautiful if judged as a whole, quite apart from the words, although certain portions in the middle might become somewhat obscure without them. To do justice in a like degree both to the musical and the dramatic requirements is rightly considered to be the ideal of the opera. But that for this reason there should be perpetual warfare between the principles of dramatic nicety and musical beauty, entailing never-ending concessions on both sides, has, to my knowledge, never been conclusively demonstrated. The principle involved in the opera is not undermined or weakened by the fact that all the parts are sung—our imagination being easily reconciled to an illusion of this kind—but it is the constraint imposed alike upon music and words that leads to continual acts of trespass or concession, and reduces the opera, as it were, to a constitutional government whose very existence depends upon an incessant struggle between two parties equally entitled to power. It is from this conflict, in which the composer allows now one principle and now the other to prevail, that all the imperfections of the opera arise, and from which, at the same time, all rules important for operatic works are deduced. The principles in which music and the drama are grounded, if pushed to their logical consequences, are mutually destructive; but they point in so similar a direction that they appear almost parallel.

The dance is a similar case in point, of which any ballet is a proof. The more the graceful rhythm of the figures is sacrificed in an attempt to speak by gesture and dumb show, and to convey definite thoughts and emotions, the closer is the approximation to the low rank of mere pantomime. The prominence given to the dramatic principle in the dance proportionately lessens its rhythmical and plastic beauty. The opera can never be quite on a level with recited drama or with purely instrumental music. A good opera composer will, therefore, constantly endeavor to combine and reconcile the two factors instead of automatically emphasizing now one and now the other. When in doubt, however, he will always allow the claim of music to prevail, the chief element in the opera not being dramatic but musical beauty. This is evident from the different attitudes of mind in which we listen to a play or an opera in which the same subject is treated. The neglect of the musical part will always be far more keenly felt. . . .

The connection of poetry with music and with the opera is a sort of morganatic union, and the more closely we examine this morganatic union of musical beauty and definite thoughts, the more skeptical do we become as regards its indissolubility.

How is it that in every song slight alterations may be introduced which, without in the least detracting from the accuracy of expression, immediately destroy the beauty of the theme? This would be impossible if the latter were inseparably connected with the former. Again, how is it that many a song, though adequately expressing the drift of the poem, is nevertheless quite intolerable? The theory that music is capable of expressing emotion furnishes us with no explanation. In what, then, consists the beautiful in music, if it does not consist in the emotional element?

An altogether different and independent element remains, which we shall presently examine more closely.

The Beautiful in Music

So far we have considered only the negative aspect of the question, and have sought to expose the fallacy that the beautiful in music depends upon the accurate expression of feelings.

We must now, by way of completing the exposition, bring to light also its positive aspect, and endeavor to determine the nature of the beautiful in music.

Its Nature Is Specifically Musical. By this we mean that the beautiful is not contingent upon nor in need of any subject introduced from without, but that it consists wholly of sounds artistically combined. The ingenious coordination of intrinsically pleasing sounds, their consonance and contrast, their flight and reapproach, their increasing and diminishing strength—this it is which, in free and unimpeded forms, presents itself to our mental vision.

The primordial element of music is euphony, and rhythm is its soul: rhythm in general, or the harmony of a symmetrical structure, and rhythm in particular, or the systematically reciprocal motion of its several parts within a given measure. The crude material which the composer has to fashion, the vast profusion of which it is impossible to estimate fully, is the entire scale of musical notes and their inherent adaptability to an endless variety of melodies, harmonies, and rhythms. Melody, unexhausted, nay, inexhaustible, is pre-eminently the source of musical beauty.

Harmony, with its countless modes of transforming, inverting, and intensifying, offers the material for constantly new developments; while rhythm, the main artery of the musical organism, is the regulator of both, and enhances the charms of the timbre in its rich variety.

To the question: What is to be expressed with all this material? the answer will be: Musical ideas. Now, a musical idea reproduced in its entirety is not only an object of intrinsic beauty but also an end in itself, and not a means for representing feelings and thoughts.

The essence of music is sound and motion.

The arabesque, a branch of the art of ornamentation, dimly betokens in what manner music may exhibit forms of beauty though no definite emotion be involved. We see a plexus of flourishes, now bending into graceful curves, now rising in bold sweeps; moving now toward, and now away from each other; correspondingly matched in small and large arcs; apparently incommensurable, yet duly proportioned throughout; with a duplicate or counterpart to every segment; in fine, a compound of oddments, and yet a perfect whole. Imagine now an arabesque, not still and motionless, but rising before our eyes in constantly changing forms. Behold the broad and delicate lines, how they pursue one another; how from a gentle curve they rise up into lofty heights, presently to descend again; how they widen and contract, surprising the eye with a marvelous alternation of quiescence and mobility. The image thus becomes nobler and more exalted. If, moreover, we conceive this living arabesque as the active emanation of inventive genius, the artistic fullness of whose imagination is incessantly glowing into the heart of these moving forms, the effect, we think, will be not unlike that of music.

When young, we have probably all been delighted with the ever-changing tints and forms of a kaleidoscope. Now, music is a kind of kaleidoscope, though its forms can be appreciated only by an infinitely higher ideation. It brings forth a profusion of beautiful tints and forms, now sharply contrasted and now almost imperceptibly graduated; all logically connected with each other, yet all novel in their effect; forming, as it were, a complete and self-subsistent whole, free from any alien admixture. The main difference consists in the fact that the musical kaleidoscope is the direct product of a creative mind, whereas the optic one is but a cleverly constructed mechanical toy. If, however, we stepped beyond the bounds of analogy, and in real earnest attempted to raise mere color to the rank of music by foisting on one art the means of another, we should be landed in the region of such puerile contrivances as the "color piano" or the "ocular organ," though these contrivances significantly prove both phenomena to have, morphologically, a common root.

If any sentimental lover of music thinks that analogies such as the one mentioned are degrading to the art, we reply that the only question is whether they are relevant or not. A subject is not degraded by being studied. If we wish to disregard the attributes of motion and successive formation, which render a comparison with the kaleidoscope particularly applicable, we may, forsooth, find a more dignified parallel for beautiful music in architecture, the human body, or a landscape, because all these possess original beauty of outline and color quite irrespective of the intellectual substratum, the soul.

The reason why people have failed to discover the beauties in which pure music abounds is, in great measure, to be found in the underrating by the older systems of aesthetics of the sensuous element and in its subordination to morality and feeling—in Hegel, to the "idea." Every art sets out from the sensuous and operates within its limits. The theory relating to the expression of feelings ignores this fact and, disdainfully pushing aside the act of hearing, it passes on immediately to the feelings. Music, they say, is food for the soul, and the organ of hearing is beneath their notice.

True, it is not for the organ of hearing as such, for the "labyrinth" or the "tympanum," that a Beethoven composes. But our imagination, which is so constituted as to be affected by auditory impressions (and in relation to which the term "organ" means something very different from a channel directed toward the world of physical phenomena), delights in the sounding forms and musical structures and, conscious of their sensuous nature, lives in the immediate and free contemplation of the beautiful.

It is extremley difficult to define this self-subsistent and specifically musical beauty. As music has no prototype in nature, and expresses no definite conceptions, we are compelled to speak of it either in dry, technical terms, or in the language of poetic fiction. Its kingdom is, indeed, "not of this world." All the fantastic descriptions, characterizations, and paraphrases are either metaphorical or false. What in any other art is still descriptive is in music already figurative. Of music it is impossible to form any but a musical conception, and it can be comprehended and enjoyed only in and for itself.

The "specifically musical" must not, however, be understood only in the sense of acoustic beauty or symmetry of parts—both of which elements it embraces as of secondary importance—and still less can we speak of "a display of sounds to tickle the ear," or use similar phraseology which is generally intended to emphasize the absence of an intellectual principle. But, by laying stress on musical beauty, we do not exclude the intellectual principle; on the contrary, we imply it as essential, for we would not apply the term "beautiful" to anything wanting in intellectual beauty; and in tracing the essential nature of beauty to a morphological source, we wish it to be understood that the intellectual element is most intimately concerned with these sonorific forms. The term "form" in musical language is peculiarly significant. The forms created by sound are not empty; not the envelope enclosing a vacuum, but a well, replete with the living creation of inventive genius. Music, then, as compared with the arabesque, is a picture, yet a picture the subject of which we cannot define in words, or include in any one category of thought. In music there is both meaning and logical sequence, but in a musical sense; it is a language we speak and understand, but which we are unable to translate. . . .

The logic in music, which produces in us a feeling of satisfaction, rests on certain elementary laws of nature which govern both the human organism and the phenomena of sound. It is, above all, the primordial law of "harmonic progression" which, like the curve lines in painting and sculpture, contains the germ of development in its main forms, and the (unfortunately almost unexplained) cause of the link which connects the various musical phenomena.

All musical elements are in some occult manner connected with each other by certain natural affinities, and since rhythm, melody, and harmony are under their invisible sway, the music created by man must conform to them—and combinations conflicting with them bearing the impress of caprice and ugliness. Though not demonstrable with scientific precision, these affinities are instinctively felt by every experienced ear, and the organic completeness and logic, or the absurdity and unnaturalness of a group of sounds, are intuitively known without the intervention of a definite conception as the standard of measure, the *tertium comparationis*.

From this negative rationalness, inherent in music and founded on laws of nature, springs the possibility of its becoming invested also with positive forms of beauty.

The act of composing is a mental working on material capable of receiving the forms which the mind intends to give. The musical material in the hands of creative genius is as plastic and pliable as it is profuse. Unlike the architect, who has to mold the coarse and unwieldy rock, the composer reckons with the ulterior effect of past sounds. More ethereal and subtle than the material of any other art, sound adapts itself with great facility to any idea the composer may have in his mind. Now, as the union of sounds (from the interdependence of which the beautiful in music flows) is not effected by mechanically stringing them together but by acts of a free imagination, the intellectual force and idiosyncrasy of the particular mind will give to every composition its individual character. A musical composition, as the creation of a thinking and feeling mind, may, therefore, itself possess intellectuality and pathos in a high degree. Every musical work ought to bear this stamp of intellectuality, but the music itself must furnish evidence of its existence. Our opinion regarding the seat of the intellectual and emotional elements of a musical composition stands in the same relation to the popular way of thinking as the idea of immanence does to that of transcendence. The object of every art is to clothe in some material form an idea which has originated in the artist's imagination. In music this idea is an acoustic one; it cannot be expressed in words and subsequently translated into sounds. The initial force of a composition is the invention of some definite theme, and not the desire to describe a given emotion by musical means. Thanks to that primitive and mysterious power whose mode of action will forever be hidden from us, a theme, a melody, flashes on the composer's mind. The origin of this first germ cannot be explained, but must simply be · accepted as a fact. When once it has taken root in the composer's imagination, it forthwith begins to grow and develop, the principal theme being the center round which the branches group themselves in all conceivable ways, though always unmistakably related to it. The beauty of an independent and simple theme appeals to our aesthetic feeling with that directness which tolerates no explanation except, perhaps, that of its inherent fitness and the harmony of parts, to the exclusion of any alien factor. It pleases for its own sake, like an arabesque, a column, or some spontaneous product of nature—a leaf or a flower. . . .

One musical thought is refined in and through itself and, for no further reason, another is vulgar; this final cadence is imposing, while by the alteration of but two notes it becomes commonplace. We are perfectly justified in calling a musical theme "grand, graceful, warm, hollow, vulgar"; but all these terms are exclusively suggestive of the musical character of the particular passage. To define the musical complexion of a given theme, we often speak in terms used to describe emotions, such as "proud, gloomy, tender, ardent, longing." But we may with equal justice select them from a different order of phenomena, and call a piece of music "sweet, fresh, cloudy, cold." To be descriptive of the character of a musical composition, our feelings must be regarded in the light of mere phenomena, just like any other phenomenon which happens to present certain analogies. Epithets such as we have mentioned may be used so long as we remain fully conscious of their figurative sense—nay, we may even be unable to avoid them; but let us never say, This piece of music "expresses" pride, etc.

A close examination of the musical definiteness of a theme convinces us, however—the inscrutability of the ultimate ontological causes notwithstanding—that there are various proximate causes with which the intellectual element in a composition is intimately associated. Every musical factor (such as an interval, the timbre, a chord, the rhythm, etc.) has a distinctive feature of its own and its individual mode of action. Though the composer's mind be a mystery, its product is quite within the grasp of our understanding.

A theme harmonized with the common chord sounds different if harmonized with the chord of the sixth; a melody progressing by an interval of the seventh produces an effect quite distinct from one progressing by an interval of the sixth. The rhythm, the volume of sound, or the timbre —each alters the specific character of a theme entirely; in fine, every single musical factor necessarily contributes to a certain passage assuming just *this* particular aspect, and affecting the listener in *this* particular way. What is it that makes Halévy's music appear fantastic, that of Auber graceful—what enables us immediately to recognize Mendelssohn or Spohr —all this may be traced to purely musical causes, without having recourse to the mysterious element of the feelings.

On the other hand, why the frequent chords of $\frac{6}{4}$ and the concise, diatonic themes of Mendelssohn, the chromatic and enharmonic music of Spohr, the short two-bar rhythm of Auber, etc., invariably produce this specific impression and none other—this enigma, it is true, neither psychology nor physiology can solve.

If, however, we inquire into the proximate cause—and that is, after all, what concerns us most in any art—we shall find that the thrilling effect of a theme is owing, not to the supposed extreme grief of the composer, but to the extreme intervals; not to the beating of his heart, but to the beating of the drums; not to the craving of his soul, but to the chromatic progression of the music. The link connecting the two we would by no means ignore; on the contrary, we shall presently subject it to a careful analysis. Meanwhile, we must remember that a scientific inquiry into the effect of a theme can deal only with such musical factors as have an enduring and objective existence, and not with the presumable state of mind in which the composer happened to be. The conclusion reached by arguing from the composer's state of mind directly to the effect of the music might, perchance, be correct; but the most important part of the syllogism, the middle term, i. e., the music itself, would thus be ignored.

A good composer, perhaps more by intuition than by rote, always has a *practical* knowledge of the character of every musical element; but in order to give a rationale of the various musical sensations and impressions we require a *theoretical* knowledge of those characters from the most intricate combinations down to the scarcely distinguishable gradations. The specific effect of a melody must not be taken as "a marvel mysterious and unaccountable" which we can only "feel" or "divine"; but it is the inevitable result of the musical factors united in this particular manner. A short or long rhythm, a diatonic or chromatic progression—each has its individual physiognomy and an effect of its own. An intelligent musician will, therefore, get a much clearer notion of the character of a composition which he has not heard himself by being told that it contains, for instance, too many diminished sevenths, or too many tremolos, than by the most poetic description of the emotional crises through which the listener passed.

To asecrtain the nature of each musical factor, its connection with a specific effect—its proximate, not its ultimate cause—and, finally, to explain these particular observations by more general laws, would be to establish that "philosophic foundation of music" to which so many writers aspire, though none has ever told us in what sense he understands this phrase. The psychical or physical effect of a chord, a rhythm, or an interval is not accounted for by saying that this is the expression of hope, that the expression of disappointment—as we should say this is red, that green —but only by placing specifically musical attributes in general aesthetic categories, and the latter under one supreme principle. After having explained the isolated action of each single element, it would be incumbent upon us to show in what manner they govern and modify one another in all their various combinations. Most music critics have ascribed the intellectual merit of a composition more particularly to the harmony and the contrapuntal accompaniment. The arguments, however, are both superficial and desultory. Melody, the alleged vehicle of sensuousness and emotion, was attributed to the inspiration of genius—the Italian school accordingly receiving a gracious word of praise; while harmony, the supposed vehicle of sterling thought in contradistinction to melody, was deemed to be simply the result of study and reflection. It is strange how long people were satisfied with so unscientific a view of the subject. Both propositions contain a grain of truth, but they are neither universally applicable nor are the two factors in question in reality ever so strictly isolated. The soul and the talent for musical construction are bound up in one inseparable whole. Melody and harmony issue simultaneously in one and the same armor from the composer's mind. Neither the principle of subordination nor that of contrast affects the nature of the relation of harmony to melody. Both may display now an equal force of independent development, and now an equally strong tendency to voluntary subordination—yet, in either case, supreme intellectual beauty may be attained. Is it, perchance, the (altogether absent) harmony in the principal themes of Beethoven's overture to *Coriolanus* or of Mendelssohn's overture to *The Hebrides* which gives them the character of profound thought? Is the intellectual merit of Rossini's theme "Oh, Matilda!" or of some Neapolitan song likely to be enhanced by substituting for the original meager harmony a *basso continuo* or some complicated succession of chords? The theme was conceived with *that* harmony, *that* rhythm, and *that* instrumentation. The intellectual merit lies in the union of all these factors; hence the mutilation of one entails that of the others. The prominence of the melody, the rhythm, or the harmony, as the case may be, improves the effect of the whole, and it is sheer pedantry to say that the excellence or the triviality is owing here to the presence of certain chords, and there to their absence. The camellia is destitute of odor, and the lily of color; the rose is rich in both odor and color; each is beautiful, and yet their respective attributes cannot be interchanged.

A "philosophic foundation of music" would first of all require us, then, to determine the definite conceptions which are invariably connected with each musical element and the nature of this connection. The double requirement of a strictly scientific framework and an extremely comprehensive casuistry renders it a most arduous though not an impossible task, unless, indeed, our ideal is that of a science of music in the sense in which chemistry and physiology are sciences!

The manner in which the creative act takes place in the mind of a composer of instrumental music gives us a very clear insight into the peculiar nature of musical beauty. A musical idea originates in the composer's imagination; he develops it—more and more crystals coalesce with it, until by imperceptible degrees the whole structure in its main features appears before him. Nothing then remains to be done but to examine the composition, to regulate its rhythm and modify it according to the canons of the art. The composer of instrumental music never thinks of representing a definite subject; otherwise he would be placed in a false position, rather outside than within the domain of music. His composition in such a case would be program music, unintelligible without the program. If this brings the name of Berlioz to mind, we do not thereby call into question or underrate his brilliant talent. In his steps followed Liszt, with his much weaker "Symphonic Poems."

As the same block of marble may be converted by one sculptor into the most exquisite forms, by another into a clumsy botch, so the musical scale, by different manipulation, becomes now an overture of Beethoven, and now one of Verdi. In what respect do they differ? Is it that one of them expresses more exalted feelings, or the same feelings more accurately? No, but simply because its musical structure is more beautiful. One piece of music is good, another bad, because one composer invents a theme full of life, another a commonplace one; because the former elaborates his music with ingenious originality, whereas with the latter it becomes, if anything, worse and worse; because the harmony in one case is varied and novel, whereas in the other it drags on miserably in its poverty; because in one the rhythm is like a pulse, full of strength and vitality, whereas in the other it is not unlike a tattoo. . . .

As the musical elements of a composition are the source of its beauty, so are they likewise the source of its laws and its construction. A great number of false and confused notions are entertained on this subject, but we will single out only one. We mean the commonly accepted theory of the sonata and the symphony, grounded on the assumption that feelings are expressible by musical means. In accordance with this theory, the task of the composer is to represent in the several parts of the sonata four states of mind, all differing among themselves, and yet related to one another. (How?) In order to account for the connection which undoubtedly exists between the various parts, and to explain the differences in their effect, it is naïvely taken for granted that a definite feeling underlies each of them. The construction put upon them sometimes fits, but more frequently it does not, and it never follows as a necessary consequence. It will always, however, be a matter of course that the four different parts are bound up in a harmonious whole, and that each should set off and heighten the effect of the others according to the aesthetic laws of music. . . .

It is often alleged that Beethoven, when making the rough sketch of a

composition, had before him certain incidents or states of mind. Whenever Beethoven (or any other composer) adopted this method, he did so
to smooth his task, to render the achievement of musical unity easier by
keeping in view the connecting links of certain objective phenomena. If
Berlioz, Liszt, and others fancied that a poem, a title, or an event yielded
them something more than that, they were laboring under a delusion. It
is the frame of mind bent on musical unity which gives to the four parts
of a sonata the character of an organically related whole, and not their
connection with an object which the composer may have in view. Where
the latter denied himself the luxury of these poetic leading strings and
followed purely musical inspiration, we shall find no other than a musical unity of parts. Aesthetically speaking, it is utterly indifferent whether
Beethoven really did associate all his works with certain ideas. We do not
know them, and as far as the composition is concerned, they do not exist.
It is the composition itself, apart from all comment, which has to be
judged; and as the lawyer completely ignores whatever is not in his brief,
so aesthetic criticism must disregard whatever lies outside the work of
art. If the several parts of a composition bear the stamp of unity, their
correlation must have its root in musical principles. . . .

Not long since, the fashion began to regard works of art in connection
with the ideas and events of the time which gave them birth. This connection is undeniable and probably exists also in music. Being a product
of the human mind, it must naturally bear some relation to the other
products of mind: to contemporaneous works of poetry and the fine arts;
to the state of society, literature, and the sciences of the period; and, finally, to the individual experiences and convictions of the author. To
observe and demonstrate the existence of this connection in the case of
certain composers and works is not only a justifiable proceeding but also
a true gain to knowledge. We should, nevertheless, always remember that
parallelisms between specific works of art and events of certain epochs
belong to the history of art rather than to the science of aesthetics.
Though methodological considerations may render it necessary to connect the history of art with the science of aesthetics, it is yet of the utmost
importance that the proper domain of each of these sciences be rigorously
guarded from encroachment by the other. The historian viewing a work
of art in all its bearings may discover in Spontini "the expression of
French imperialism," in Rossini "the political restoration"; but the student of aesthetics must restrict himself to the examination of the works
themselves, in order to determine what is beautiful in them and why it is
so. The aesthetic inquirer knows nothing (nor can he be expected to
know anything) about the personal circumstances or the political surroundings of the composer—he hears and believes nothing but what the
music itself contains. He will, therefore, without knowing the name or
the biography of the author, detect in Beethoven's symphonies impetu-
ousness and struggle, unsatisfied longing and defiance, all supported by a

consciousness of strength. But he could never glean from his works that the composer favoured republicanism, that he was a bachelor and deaf, or any of the numerous circumstances on which the art historian is wont to dilate; nor could such facts enhance the merit of the music. It may be very interesting and praiseworthy to compare the various schools of philosophy to which Bach, Mozart, and Haydn belonged, and to draw a parallel between them and the works of these composers. It is, however, a most arduous undertaking, and one which can but open the door to fallacies in proportion as it attempts to establish causal relations. The danger of exaggeration is exceedingly great once this principle is accepted. The slender influence of contemporariness may easily be construed as an inherent necessity, and the ever-untranslatable language of music be interpreted in the way which best fits the particular theory: all depends on the reasoning abilities; the same paradox which in the mouth of an accomplished dialectician appears a truism seems the greatest nonsense in the mouth of an unskilled speaker. . . .

Many schools of aesthetics think musical enjoyment is fully accounted for by the pleasure derived from mere regularity and symmetry, but these never were the sole attributes of beauty in the abstract, and much less so of beauty in music. The most insipid theme may be symmetrical. "Symmetry" connotes proportion only, and leaves unanswered the question: *What* is it that impresses us as being symmetrical? A systematic distribution of parts, both uninteresting and commonplace, often exists in the most pitiable compositions, but the musical sense wants symmetry combined with originality.

Oerstedt, to crown all, carried this Platonic doctrine so far as to cite the circle (for which he claims positive beauty) as a parallel case. Could he himself never have experienced the horror of a completely round composition?

From caution rather than from necessity we may add that the beautiful in music is totally independent of mathematics. Amateurs (among whom there are also some sentimental authors) have a singularly vague notion of the part played by mathematics in the composition of music. Not content with the fact that the vibrations of sound, the intervals, and the phenomena of consonance and dissonance rest on mathematical principles, they feel convinced that the beautiful in a composition may likewise be reduced to numbers. The study of harmony and counterpoint is looked upon as a kind of cabala, teaching the "calculus," as it were, of musical composition.

Mathematics, though furnishing an indispensable key to the study of the physical aspect of music, must not be overrated as regards its value in the finished composition. No mathematical calculation ever enters into a composition, be it the best or the worst. Creations of inventive genius are not arithmetical sums. Experiments with the monochord, the figures producible by sonorous vibrations, the mathematical ratios of musical intervals, etc., all lie outside the domain of aesthetics, which begins only where those elementary relations cease to be of importance. Mathematics merely controls the intellectual manipulation of the primary elements of music, and is secretly at work in the most simple relations. The musical thought, however, originates without the aid of mathematics. What Oerstedt means by inquiring whether the lifetime of several "mathematicians would suffice to calculate all the beauties in one symphony by Mozart" we, for our part, are at a loss to understand. What is to be, or can be, calculated? Is it the number of vibrations of each note as compared with the next, or the relative length of the divisions and subdivisions of the composition? That which raises a series of musical sounds into the region of music proper and above the range of physical experiment is something free from external constraint, a spiritualized and, therefore, incalculable something. Mathematics has as little and as much to do with musical compositions as such as with the generative processes of the other arts; for mathematics must, after all, guide also the hand of the painter and sculptor; it is the rhythmical principle of verse; it regulates the work of the architect and the figures of the dancer. Though in all accurate knowledge mathematics must have a place, we should never attribute to it a positive and creative power as some musicians, the conservatives in the science of aesthetics, would fain have us do. Mathematics and the excitation of feelings are in a similar position—they have a place in all arts, but in no art is there so much stress laid upon them as in music.

Between language and music parallels have also frequently been drawn and attempts made to lay down for the latter laws governing only the former. The relation between song and language is patent enough, whether we base it on the identity of physiological conditions or on the character which both have in common, namely that of expressing thoughts and feelings by means of the human voice. The analogy, indeed, is so obvious as to render further discussion unnecessary. We admit at once that wherever music is merely the subjective manifestation of a state of mind, the laws of speech are, in a measure, also applicable to singing. That under the influence of passion the pitch of the voice is raised, while the propitiating orator lowers it; that sentences of great force are spoken slowly, and unimportant ones quickly—these and kindred facts the composer of songs, and the musical dramatist especially, will ever bear in mind. People, however, did not rest satisfied with these limited analogies; but conceiving music proper to be a kind of speech (though more indefinite and subtle), they forthwith deduced its aesthetic laws from the properties of language. Every attribute and every effect of music was believed to have its analogy in speech. We ourselves are of the opinion that where the question turns on the nature of a specific art, the points in which it differs from cognate subjects are more important than the points of resemblance. An aesthetic inquiry, unswayed by such analogies as, though often tempting, do not affect the essence of music, must ever advance toward the point where speech and music irreconcilably part. Only from beyond this point may we hope to discover truly useful facts in respect to music. The fundamental difference consists in this: while sound in speech is but a sign, that is, a means for the purpose of expressing something which is quite distinct from its medium, sound in music is the end, that is, the ultimate and absolute object in view. The intrinsic beauty of the musical forms in the latter case, and the exclusive dominion of thought over sound as a mere medium of expression in the former, are so utterly distinct as to render the union of these two elements a logical impossibility.

Speech and music, therefore, have their centers of gravity at different points, around which the characteristics of each are grouped; and while all specific laws of music will center in its independent forms of beauty, all laws of speech will turn upon the correct use of sound as a medium of expressing ideas.

The most baneful and confused notions have sprung from the attempt to define music as a kind of speech, and we may observe their practical consequences every day. Composers of feeble genius, in particular, were only too ready to denounce as false and sensual the ideal of intrinsic musical beauty because it was beyond their reach, and to parade in its place the characteristic significance of music. Quite irrespective of Richard Wagner's operas, we often find in the most trivial instrumental compositions disconnected cadences, recitatives, etc., which interrupt the flow of the melody, and which, while startling the listener, affect to have some deep meaning, though in reality they display only a want of beauty. Modern pieces, in which the principal rhythm is constantly upset in order to bring into prominence certain mysterious appendages and a superabundance of glaring contrasts, are praised for striving to pass the "narrow limits" of music, and to elevate it to the rank of speech. Such praise has always appeared to us somewhat ambiguous. The limits of music are by no means narrow, but they are clearly defined. Music can never be "elevated to the rank of speech"—musically speaking, "lowered" would be a more appropriate term—for music, to be speech at all, would, of course, be a superlative degree of speech.

Our singers always forget this when in moments of intense emotion they ejaculate sentences as though they were speaking and think they thus attain the highest degree of musical expression. It does not always strike them that the transition from song to speech is always a descent, so that the highest pitch of normal speech sounds deeper than the low notes in singing, though both proceed from the same organ. As mischievous in their practical consequences (if not more so, because of the impossibility of disproving them by actual experiment) are those theories which try to impose on music the laws of development and construction peculiar to speech, as in former days Rameau and Rousseau, and in modern times the disciples of Richard Wagner, have endeavored to do. In this attempt the life of the music is destroyed, the innate beauty of form annihilated in pursuit of the phantom "meaning." One of the most important tasks of the aesthetics of music would, therefore, be that of demonstrating with inexorable logic the fundamental difference between music and language, and of never departing from the principle that, wherever the question is a specifically musical one, all parallelisms with language are wholly irrelevant.

FRANK ANDERSON TRAPP

On the Nature of Painting

IN CONTRAST to other visual arts, such as sculpture and architecture, the art of painting has solely and specifically visual meaning. It serves no utilitarian function, as architecture usually does, nor does it actually occupy three dimensional space, as both the other forms do. In its essential restriction to the occupation of a two-dimensional surface, painting can at most *imply* some measure of existence in the world of three-dimensional actuality. At the same time, painting enjoys certain advantages in being freed of the more rigid material limitations of its sister arts. It need not be accommodated to the fulfillment of practical needs or complex structural techniques. The extent of the world to which it may refer is immeasurably greater than that accessible to the sculptor. No architect could ever control his terrain, tame or agitate his skies, or, for that matter throw up the gravity-defying walls that a painter may conjure at will. The painter thus "creates" in a rather different sense from his fellows who pursue other modes of visual expression and invention. That his products cannot assume the tangibility of form potential in sculpture is compensated for in the other ranges of reference the painter enjoys, if he wishes. Though his object cannot be "useful" in the sense of an architectural structure, it can serve other purposes—and often painting does have a symbolic utility (a quality which architecture itself not infrequently incorporates). Certain broad discriminations can therefore be made among the visual arts—sufficiently well, at least, to begin discussion of the art of painting as a distinct aspect of man's imaginative life.

In the days when man still *found* his "architecture" in trees and caves, when his first intuitions of sculpture were yet stunted by crudeness of tools and craft, some of the world's most astounding paintings were made. In the caves at Altamira and Lascaux working by dim light, shamans, perhaps not even *homo sapiens* nor possessed of what we would recognize as the power of speech, conjured with unsurpassed skill, images of the animals that were their quarry. Their value doubtless lay in the very magic of their mimesis. Modern distinctions of "art" and "life," which now apply, could hardly have counted in the origin of these astounding beasts, whose makers sought to steal something of nature's own powers by simulating the appearance of its creatures.

The wonder is that these first great masters of the world's art were painters. If their tools were less intransigent than the sculptor's, the *abstraction* of their act was far greater in its further removal from the physical characteristics of the nature they wished to describe. They could not rely so directly on recollections of touch or relationships of mass and space. Granting the very contours of the rock seem chosen to receive the images painted on them, the painter had to translate his sense of the solid and moving body into the restricted means of essentially two dimensional color, shape, and line. The refinement and range of his conventions suggest that these were the products of an already old and developed tradition whose convincing synopses were readily legible to those the maker served—or ruled.

Theirs was an invention as portentous as the discovery of fire or the principle of the wheel; but it was different. Future scientists could build upon what their predecessors had learned, so that "progress" could be made. In painting, techniques could be improved and rules of craft inculcated. Traditions and conventions could be established. These could be learned. Yet in the end each painter who is also an artist must work out his own destiny within the limits of his own abilities as they are formed by the society that surrounds him.

Thus quite without willing it, these primordial painters faced the challenges that have confronted painters and their viewers ever since. In discussing their works one must take into account both intention and result and the changing interpretations which may be placed upon them. The artifact, ever the starting point, remains a product of the maker's materials as transformed by his techniques, which at once limit the range of forms and suggest their nature. For all their analogies with natural appearances, the artist's forms were necessarily transformations of fact, not literal imitations of it. This meant a process of selection and emphasis, the formulation of conventions, understandable to the creator and presumably to others as well by a kind of "willing suspension of disbelief." In short, there emerged the interplay of forces, both material and ideal, which have tantalized philosophers and critics for more than two thousand years.

Unfortunately the philosophers have too often proceeded from an at best meager acquaintance with actual works of art and, if anything, even less concern for understanding them in particular. The critics, on the other hand, have been characteristically subjective in their attention to the immediate, particular, and sometimes the ephemeral. While the insights introduced by the study of the history of art do not in themselves

provide full clarification, they do offer possibilities of discussion overlooked, even by many of the art historians themselves. For the problem
of delimiting the nature of painting is indistinguishably one with that of
establishing means of talking sensibly about it.

Even at the primary level of material description, definition is at times
difficult to reconcile with specific application. To observe that a "painting" is the product of one who paints says little aside from recalling the
gerundial nature of the word and pointing up the fact that some distinguishing trace of the creative act survives in the appearance of that product. The same may be said for a "drawing." A painting and a drawing
are not the same thing, even though a painting normally includes aspects
of technique that we commonly call drawing. The distinctions between
the two forms become at times difficult to assign and at best arbitrary.
Whether a lightly toned "drawing" in ink and wash is at the same time a
watercolor "painting" is a matter of marginal distinction. A Chinese landscape scroll executed in monochrome ink and wash on paper has traditionally been called a "painting." A Claude representation of the Roman
Campagna, also executed in ink and wash on paper, is usually called a
drawing. Such differences of usage, suggesting more habit than system,
seem unreliable in their authority.

Distinctions even between sculpture and painting are not always simple. Although it may be agreed that sculpture has a three-dimensional
actuality which painting lacks in its usual restriction to two-dimensional
surface, the margins of such a distinction are often blurred by exceptions. Many low reliefs appeal so minimally to our realizations of actual
three-dimensionality as to find much of their meaning within the contexts
normally reserved for painting. This is especially true in considering
polychromed sculptured reliefs which are in large measure the products
of painters, as well as of sculptors.

One must realize too that our present separation of the two arts is
abnormal within the range of historical practice. Much, if not most of the
world's sculpture was once polychrome, and often combined with painting without sense of distinction. In Northern Europe of the late Gothic
era, for example, altarpieces were frequently the collaborative product of
both painters and sculptors working in full innocence of the distinctions
that are sometimes made between their respective arts. So renowned a
painter as Roger van der Weyden was at least once employed to color
sculptures fashioned by another—and was, in fact, more highly paid than
the sculptor himself for his efforts. The isolating convention of the "picture plane" was an invention of the Italian Renaissance—and even the
Italian painters of the Renaissance sometimes ignored their own quaran-
tine of the so-called "picture space" from the world of actuality. So too
these men often worked interchangeably as sculptors, architects, or painters without a sense of the more specialized limitations sometimes placed

upon the activities of an artist. That Ghiberti seems to have aspired to the conditions of painting in his sculptured "Gates of Paradise" or that Michelangelo seems to have regarded his Sistine Chapel frescoes more as sculpture than as paintings may provide some critics with the pretext for puristic distinctions, but cannot diminish the greatness of their creative achievement.

Another obvious proposal is that a "painting" is made with paint. Gertrude Stein's cryptic aphorism, "Oil painting is *oil* painting," is not wholly frivolous. Tempera, gouache, water color, or encaustic are also accepted as readily recognized mediums of the painter's art. But what of pastel, which chemically resembles water color or gouache, though it is differently applied? When does a pastel "drawing" become a pastel "painting"? Is a monochrome study in oil paint on canvas a "drawing" or a "painting"? Distinctions of completeness, complexity, or "finish" are not necessarily helpful here. One may, of course, refer to such a work as a "sketch" or a "study." In doing so, however, he is avoiding certain basic issues if the nature of painting, and painting alone, is to be alluded to.

The fact is that distinctions according to medium also break down in so many instances that their utility is severely limited. A Byzantine mosaic may, after all, be profitably regarded as a form of painting even though it is made of bits of colored glass, not what we would normally consider "paint." Much the same may be said for stained glass windows, tapestries, or primitive pictures and decorations formed of bits of butterfly wings or varicolored feathers. That these are not "paintings" in the most limited material definition should not obscure the fact that they must be discussed in much the same way as paintings. They are not sculpture, architecture, literature, or music. Their appeal is primarily visual and two dimensional. They are hence *like* paintings, if not paintings in the narrowest sense of the word.

Many twentieth century artists have, in fact, made it their goal to test and extend the traditional limits of painting. If Burri's or Schwitters' *collages* are not to be considered as paintings, but as some other kind of painting-like object, well and good. But they are best understood within the context of modern painting and share so many common characteristics with abstractions made in the more conventional materials of painting that such a distinction seems valueless. Other artists such as the Spaniard, Millares, may at times actually puncture the picture surface and manipulate surface relief and textural contrast. Whether these are paintings, pictures of another kind, or some form of sculpture is a matter some, at least, would find impossible to decide and perhaps not worth the effort. Some may argue that they are not these or any other form of art; but the decision of this question will come not through the logic of categorical definitions, but through some more ponderous, unpredictable, but enduring process of historical selection and cultural assimilation.

If this last and most elusive category of *collages* and other "painting-like" objects suggests at least some analogies with more traditionally accepted forms of painting, the isolation of the characteristics they share with painting may provide some insights into the general nature of painting itself. Whether or not a *collage,* for example, has much actual three-dimensionality (and, after all, a van Gogh painting may sometimes have more "relief" than an Egyptian bas-relief sculpture), its appeal is mostly to the sense of sight within the established reference of its enframement. Even the textural elements, such as cloth, metal, or wood ultimately function in much the same way as paint, which may also have a variety of textures, with all that may imply of a direct sensuous appeal. That some of these efforts tempt also the sense of touch and seem at times more intended to invade the world of the spectator than to remain apart from actuality recalls historical attempts at *trompe l'oeil.* Pompeiian wall decorations or Baroque ceiling paintings defy restriction to the surface they are painted on. The still lifes of painters like Harnett show violins, shooting irons, quarry, and stamped envelopes painted so as to seem to project from the surface they are portrayed against. Yet in all these examples the artist has had to relate his elements to each other within the two-dimensional limits of the enframement. These factors of two-dimensional structure or "design" are common to all paintings, if not exclusive only to painting.

All painters must in some way take problems of design into account. Some (often referred to as "decorative") may stress these qualities of organization to the exclusion, or at least the minimization, of other possible emphases. A Mondrian "Composition" or a late Kandinsky "Painting" represent something close to ultimate reduction in their purposeful restriction to a vocabulary of line, shape and color, used without reference to representation. In the mid-twentieth century many others have continued to pursue this self-limiting tradition in the attempt to find in the formal elements alone an ultimate purity of statement. That some modest degree of space illusion or associative sensation may at times be inferred from their constructions is, it would seem, rather incidental. Their basic aim was to strip away what they had come to consider peripheral and usually distractive characteristics of painting and to return the art to a kind of primitive innocence of purpose and simplicity of means.

During the nineteenth and twentieth centuries the painters themselves, not the critics, have taken the lead in the search for clarity of understanding and the possibilities of verbal statement about the nature of painting. Although the theoretical observations of Rood, Helmholtz, and Chevreuil provided the scientific basis for modern attitudes towards color and color perception, it was Delacroix, the Impressionists, the Neo-Impressionists, and their successors who were to translate those clues into artistic relevance. It was the painters themselves who thereby provided the critics and public alike with the terms of subsequent discussion.

Modern attentiveness to the qualities of abstract form has led to an unprecedented precision and consistency of reference to matters of pictorial or design structure. Symmetry, for example, which once had a loose range of meanings, has come to refer to specific characteristics of form, namely, the usually bilateral correspondence of elements within a centrally divided composition. Any other mode of composition is therefore specifically describable as asymmetrical. The degree of deviation from the absolute norm thus becomes subject to intelligible discussion and a matter of characterization, not value judgment. So too have other elements of descriptive analysis been systematized—not with the aim of passing judgment on artistic merits, but as a guide to more accurate observation—hence to clearer communication.

Whether or not the critic may agree with either the aims or the results of this serious and considered effort, one must agree that the painters of the modern movement have not only made their own artistic contributions, but have illuminated and revitalized the critics' ways of looking at painting of the past—however different its outward forms may be from the contemporary. Thus Vermeer's "Self Portrait" is now seen, not only as a sovereign example of Baroque illusionism, but as a tight pictorial structure whose classic sense of order is in many ways startlingly similar to the neat constructions of his later countryman, Mondrian. Seen as "design," David's "Oath of the Horatii" may elicit from those who cannot now respond to the chilly Romanism of its political message a more direct stimulus in the stunning precision and force of its very forms and their relationship as abstract, pictorial elements. In ways such as these it is possible to see how the painter not only redefines the very nature of his art, but at the same time recasts both the role and the vocabulary of those who choose to discuss it.

While pictorial form may in itself carry some kind of meaning, it often serves the more complex function of clarifying and enhancing a painter's subject-matter. It is his means of transforming description into art. Most painting has involved the attempt to reconcile the contrasting demands of form and subject. It is in the resolution of these forces into a total unity that one finds the ultimate "content" of a picture. To the extent that representation is also present, it too must therefore be taken into account. A still life, a landscape, and a devotional painting may all display similar characteristics of formal order, yet have very dissimilar "content," largely by virtue of their differences of representation, and all that may imply about the attitudes of the painter and the public for whom he worked. To arrive at this level of understanding requires considerable knowledge, both of the physical character of the painting itself and of the culture, perhaps also of the artist who produced it.

Much, if not most of our knowledge of particular paintings has been conveyed to us with some measure of distortion. To view, say, the great bison from Altamira by the light of an electric torch is already to impose upon it alien conditions. To reproduce it, however faithfully in colored

ink upon a page or a sheet of paper framed upon a wall, is to wrench it
even further from its true physical context. To the extent that any painting possesses specific physical properties of size, placement, and material
character, any translation of these is in some degree a distortion.

Leonardo's "Last Supper," faded and mutilated by restoration even
within the painter's own lifetime, lives for most more as an idea than as a
material object. Few know it in its original site, where seeming to extend
from the very refectory that contains it, the frescoed scene finds even its
source of illusory illumination on the same side as the actual room itself.
Its perspective has been carefully constructed to take the vantage point of
the spectator into account, to put him and his world in a defined relationship to that superior world the painter reveals to him. How little of its
still vivid wonder survives in that nasty scrap of paper that bears its
diminished *ushabti?*

Even to remove a fourteenth-century Italian altarpiece from its original
setting to the harsh light of a modern museum interior or to place a
French Impressionist painting, stripped of its frame against the clinical,
unflattering glare of a white wall is to impose inimical conditions upon it.
To deprive the painting further of its actual size, and the material character—the "feel"—of its paint is not just to take it one step more from the
hand and eye of its maker, but to rob it of qualities essential to its very
nature. Yet we are accustomed to accept these translations and to imagine
our way back towards the original by means of analogous experiences
with other works of art. Just as the amateur of former days was prepared
to accept the literal copy or the engraving as a plausible substitute for
the original, the modern viewer accommodates his sensibilities to the
photographic reproduction in which much, if not all of the artist's handi-
work survives.

In a sense, the artist himself has intuitively accepted similar limitations
in his original translations of his experiences, perceptual or imaginary,
into the conventional limitations of his art. By a gradual, sometimes unconscious process, he has selected salient aspects of his experience which
lend themselves to restatement within the material conditions of his medium and his powers to manipulate them. The profound difference is, of
course, that the painter's goal is to attain a specific, fixed statement of his
aims. The spectator, beginning where the painter has left off, must enter
into a fluid and unconcluded relationship with the work of art in the
attempt to define it as an aesthetic fact by virtue of his own powers of
vision and imagination.

He must recognize, for example, the dramatic moment Leonardo depicted in his "Last Supper." He must appreciate the full purport of that
instant of tragic prescience (the Master's prophecy: "One of ye shall
betray me. . . .") to understand the quiver of response that animates the
straining disciples, and the resigned, yet reassuring calm of the dominat-
ing Christ. He must realize that in his choice of this instant of the drama,
Leonardo has both summarized and interpreted the drama of a whole

episode. The viewer, as well as the artist, needs knowledge and imagination.

The viewer, even the most intimate friend of the artist, cannot fully share the creator's own sense of his achievement. He can only infer intentions on the basis of his own experience of the results, amplified and refined by whatever measure of relevant information he can attain. That this implies some advantage in his more direct dependence on the objective evidence of the work itself is a factor not to be overlooked. But to balance objective observation with subjective assimilation is one of the most taxing feats of intellectual imagination. And the further the viewer is removed from the presence of the actual object of his speculation, the more the work has been transformed by time, or mutilation, the more alien the cultural context of the creation, the more fallible and tentative becomes the act of understanding.

To return to the Altamira "Bison," now known as an illustration in a book, a classroom slide, or as a neatly framed reproduction set in a modern domestic interior—all derived not from the original, but most likely from the pastel copy made by its discoverer, Abbé Breuil—what can be said about its nature? For all one may admire its technical virtuosity, what modern viewer can recapture the sense of primitive wonder it must once have inspired? No longer a ritual object, lacking even the fading Christian associations of Leonardo's "Last Supper," it has now become a source of aesthetic satisfaction, an anthropological document, or for some, simply a curio. One's delight in the vivid selectivity of its line, color, and shading are genuine enough responses to it. The lingering realization that this is as it were a noble quotation known through modern translation, and hence imperfectly, is itself to some extent a healthful qualification of the fragmentary, but persistent aesthetic call of its "significant form." The rest must be left to anthropological speculation or to poetic reverie. Who made this work (if not Abbé Breuil) and what were his intentions cannot be surely known.

Since much of the world's great art has been produced by now nameless artisans, it is often necessary to rely on a general knowledge of their culture in the search for contextual revelation. Those unacquainted with the "use" of ancient Egyptian tomb paintings and unprepared to interpret their conventions of representation and structure are likely to find them rather awkward and inept compared with more recent forms of illusionism, which correspond more directly with their own habits of perception. To "understand" the "Banquet Scene" from the Eighteenth Dynasty Tomb of Nakht at Thebes requires the rudiments of knowledge about the culture of the time, not just a titillation at the chaste beauty of its delicate lines and simple coloration. Indeed, one might go so far as to suggest that it is not until knowledge entices one to more careful scrutiny that he is enabled to refine his sense of the abstract qualities of style. In this sense systematic inquiry into extra-artistic factors may serve to enhance intuitive responses: not to confuse them, as it is sometimes asserted.

This more relativistic approach is not, of course, without its hazards. Some are too readily enticed into the search for a schematic reduction that avoids the ultimate problem of response to the particular object. This confusion leads also to the conundrum of cultural relativism, whose evasion of all value-judgment reduces aesthetic response to its lowest level. To do this is in the end to respect only those aspects of a work of art which may become common knowledge, and to ignore what is crucially distinctive: its individual meaning.

In some measure, the "Banquet Scene" from the Tomb of Nakht is, to be sure, "typical" of Egyptian painting in general. In a more specific sense it may be appropriately designated as "Eighteenth Dynasty," by virtue of its *style,* the persistent syntax of its forms, not just by its inscription alone. Yet finally, this cycle of murals is somehow different from other paintings of the same culture and historic period. For that matter, each scene differs from its neighbors and may be separately, perhaps unequally enjoyed. Whether the cycle be the product of a single artist or a closely knit "shop," subtle differences of quality and character of style may be observed, just as they may be seen among the Parthenon friezes or the superficially resemblant sculptures of a French Gothic façade. Whether or not his name is now known, the artist was at work and inevitably left his individual mark.

It is often the case, however, that not only the painter's name, but something of his life is known. One could hardly imagine a stronger contrast of critical situation than to oppose the example of the troglodytic *animalier* to that of Vincent van Gogh. Surely no painter in all history—not even Michelangelo or Delacroix—has left so complete a verbal document of his inner life. Seen in the context of his letters, "Vincent's" self-portraits reveal added meaning. A viewer ignorant of the tragic incident of the painter's severed ear could hardly understand the "Self Portrait" painted shortly thereafter, in which he unabashedly includes the bandages around his head as the badge of the very mutilation they hide from sight. Even the turn of the head in his later portrayals of himself thus takes on certain potentialities of meaning. Although the scars of that self-destructive act (premonitory of his eventual suicide) may be kept from view, once learned about, they cannot evade our consciousness. They become an interpretive condition of the painting.

Even van Gogh's genre scenes, or his still lifes and landscapes often require some measure of biographical knowledge. "The Potato Eaters" is a moral and religious document, as well as a description of oppressive impoverishment. "Gauguin's Armchair" is not just another still life study, but Vincent's pathetic testimonial to an impossible but cherished association with the other man—and, by extension, with all others, save his brother Theo alone. To learn that the "Starry Night" was inspired by a dream, a kind of religious hallucination, permits the viewer to return to the work with insights which complement its directly accessible levels of content.

If only as fragmentary clues, biographical information may thus provide what are often crucial insights. It is easy to associate Renoir's admiration for flesh "that takes the light" with his glowing female nudes. Cézanne's misogyny is perhaps almost as apparent in his anonymous, abstract bathers. What is more often missed in the common acceptance of Cézanne's "classic" attitude towards form (as defined by Roger Fry and others) is that there is another current in his artistic development, one quite contrasting and no less important. The painter's neurotic instability asserted itself not only in his youthful "romantic" poems and "expressionist" paintings, but continued to provoke those tensions that animate the most "classic" of his mature canvases and recur with renewed intensity in the late works, such as his "Bathers." And, indeed, those late views of Mount Saint Victoire rival, almost exceed, the restless, churning energy of van Gogh's "Starry Night."

Used out of context or to the exclusion of other aspects of vision and knowledge, biographical information may lead to distortion. It would be misleading to accept van Gogh's "Night Café at Arles" simply as "a place where one can ruin one's self, run mad, or commit a crime"—even though that is what the painter said he wished to represent. Though he tried, as he said, "to express the terrible passions of humanity by means of red and green," the viewer should see the method as well as the madness. He must take into account Vincent's periods of great lucidity and professional probity. He can thereby also recognize in the red and green van Gogh's careful study of the Impressionist palette and Gauguin's Symbolist theories of form and color, as well as his adulation of the Japanese printmaker's decorative simplifications. He must attempt to reconcile, as the man himself failed to do, except in his work, the human conditions of inner contradiction and the ineluctable privacy of each individual. He must learn to accept, to treasure mystery. Deprived of these and other relevant levels of meaning and association, the brooding intensity of the "Night Café" is warped into lurid melodrama.

The painter's attempts to explain his own works (an increasingly common practice in our age of annotation) may at times serve as much to corrupt as to clarify our knowledge of them. It would seem, for example, that much of the discussion of Cézanne's achievement has been unduly dominated by statements made by the artist himself, especially in his later years. He may, to be sure, have followed his own advice: "to represent nature by means of the cylinder, the sphere, and the cone." But it was *nature* he was painting, not a geometer's paradise. Nor should the significant but arbitrary relationship of the Cubists' paintings to Cézanne's obscure the profound differences between his own aims and accomplishments and theirs. If Cézanne was as he believed, the "primitive" of a great, new school, his paintings gain meaning when seen in that historical context. At the same time one cannot forget that he was a nineteenth, not a twentieth century painter.

Cézanne's words of admiration for the "classics," such as Poussin, have taken on an almost axiomatic authority for students of the master's art. Yet they sometimes overlook the fact that he copied engravings of El Greco and Sebastiano del Piombo canvases, however anti-classical their Mannerist forms may be. That reproductions of Rubens' compositions sometimes served as substitutes for live models also deserves attention. The measure of the importance of this kind of information is to be found in the paintings themselves. The painter's own surviving comments may be helpful as confirmations of the visual evidence. They cannot be used to contradict it. The words and the painting may find fruitful association, but they must never be confused.

Still more treacherous is the once common failure to distinguish between the painter and his art. The stern Victorians who regarded Rembrandt as an irresponsible libertine could hardly find the deeper meanings of his works. Yet to shut off all knowledge of the ways in which the painter's life itself was poured into his conceptions would be to reduce them to superb, but heartless craft. It is far from profitless to speculate about the man who could conceive—even more, who could paint—the "Supper at Emmaus."

The reaction against biographical confusion has been perhaps too extreme. While it is now fashionable to dismiss the nineteenth century fascination for Fra Filippo Lippi's philanderings or Andrea del Sarto's checkered career, these facts are not necessarily irrelevant. They should simply not be exaggerated at the expense of other insights. Fra Filippo's unclerical hedonism shows itself almost undisguised in his charming renditions of the Madonna and Child subject. His sense of feminine beauty and human affection speaks more of familial than of monastic experience. By contrast, Fra Angelico's austere and sexless forms bear out the evidence of accounts of his devout withdrawal from secular involvements. His simple, unfaltering faith illuminated his art. Far from irrelevant, legends of his piety help make his painting more fully accessible. They are a due part of its lustre.

Some of this narrative association has little direct application. Yet, here too, considered with discretion, it may apply. Andrea del Sarto's proud, beautiful Madonnas, said to have been sometimes painted from his wife as model, reflect something of the painter's worldly devotion. If it is unnecessary to know of his marital problems or his financial defaults to understand the artistic character of his works, it is not wholly without meaning that Andrea could adore physical beauty more than honesty or courage. The untroubled felicity of the paintings themselves is in no way diminished, maybe even somehow confirmed, by recognition of their maker's weak and shallow nature. To take psychological factors into account does not inevitably promote confusion of moral and aesthetic values.

Used as a tool of understanding, not as a pretext for moral judgment, David's patriotism, Carravaggio's violence, Leonardo's homosexuality, or Rubens' worldliness—even such biographical fragments as these—can lead to areas of understanding inaccessible to those who remain content with the conventional modes of historical and stylistic analysis. The relationship between the maker and his art is as subtle as it is profound. If the two may not be confused, neither can they be divorced. These insights too are a part of the nature of painting.

That the search for insight is often fallible and subjective should surprise no one. Our knowledge of the works and their contexts is at best imperfect. Each viewer's needs and talents differ as much as those of the painters themselves. While certain aspects of the art of painting may be defined with some measure of precision, the value of such definitions lies in the whole of their relationship. Each must determine for himself how to cope with these complexities. Some may choose to deny that a painting finds fulfillment only in the eye and mind of a beholder. But this too, it would seem, is an essential part of the nature of painting.

SIR HERBERT READ

The Art of Sculpture

The Discovery of Space

THE PECULIARITY OF SCULPTURE as an art is that it creates a three-dimensional object *in space*. Painting may strive to give, on a two-dimensional plane, the illusion of space, but it is space itself as a perceived quantity that becomes the particular concern of the sculptor. We may say that for the painter space is a luxury; for the sculptor it is a necessity.

A solid object is situated in space; it occupies or displaces a definite amount of space. It becomes an object for us by being differentiated from other objects and by being delimited from the space surrounding it. We have a sensation of the amount of space occupied by the object, which is the *quality* of volume, or *bulk*. If we refer to the *quantity* of matter the object contains, we speak of its *mass*.

We are not born with a notion of the object as a distinct entity, existing and moving in a spatial field; such a notion is built up during the first two years of life by processes of discrimination, association, and selection.[1] Out of the original chaotic experience of vastness (to use William James's phrase) the infant constructs real space, and this construction involves several subordinate processes that are gradually co-ordinated. As a beginning, separate objects have to be discriminated within the total field of vision. In itself this process involves several stages of development: the objects must be arranged in a definite order, and then their relative sizes must be perceived and assessed. At the same time, all the different sensations—of sight, touch, hearing, taste, and the rest—must "coalesce" in the same thing. In this process, one of the sensations usually will be "held to *be* the thing," while "the other sensations are taken for its more or less accidental *properties*, or modes of appearance."[2] We tend to see the bulk of a tree, for example, but to feel the bulk of a piece of furniture, a tool, or a book. The point to emphasize, for our present purposes, is that space perception is almost entirely acquired by education. We say "almost entirely" because the individual may be conditioned to his environment by certain hereditary biological processes; we are not born into a static or a mechanical world but are insinuated into a continuous process of organic evolution.[3]

When we consider the evolution of sculpture, it is important for us to realize that the kind of coherent space perception that man now possesses is a construction of the intelligence, and that even so, as William James pointed out, "touch-space is one world; sight-space is another world. The two worlds have no essential or intrinsic congruence, and only through the 'association of ideas' do we know what a seen object signifies in terms of touch." James mentions the case of a patient cured of congenital cataracts by surgical aid who said, "It might very well be *a horse*," when a ten-liter bottle was held up a foot from his face. All this goes to show, as James says, that "it needs a subtler sense for analogy than most people have, to discern the *same* spatial aspects and relations" in optical sensations "which previously known tactile and motor experiences have yielded."[4]

I shall suggest . . . that sculpture is primarily an art of "touch-space"— is and always should have been—whereas painting is primarily an art of "sight-space"; and that in both arts most of the confusion between theory and practice is due to the neglect of this distinction. There may be some ambiguity in the word *primarily*, but though a complexity, or rather a complicity, of sensations is always involved in the creation and appreciation of a work of art, one and only one of these sensations "touches off" the process. This is the sensation I call primary. I think we must set out from the same point as Berkeley, who, in his *Essay towards a New Theory of Vision*, held that the tangible "feel" of a thing and the "look" of it to the eye are "specifically distinct."[5] It is not necessary to draw Berkeley's metaphysical conclusions from these primitive facts; however, we must remember that the peculiarity of the artist is that he deals with primitive facts, with sensations in their state of innocence. He works on the basis of a direct feeling and not on the basis of concepts, which are secondary intellectual constructions.

There is, perhaps, a mental process of this secondary kind that the phrase "tactile imagination" describes; and Bernard Berenson used the phrase to indicate the particular contribution that Giotto made to the development of the art of painting: ". . . it was of the power to stimulate the tactile consciousness . . . that Giotto was supreme master. This is his everlasting claim to greatness." Berenson dismissed all paintings before Giotto as negligible because "none of these masters had the power to stimulate the tactile imagination, and, consequently, they never painted a figure which has artistic existence. Their works have value, if at all, as highly elaborate, very intelligible symbols, capable, indeed, of communicating something, but losing all higher value the moment the message is delivered."[6]

I cannot so lightly dismiss the pictorial art of the Byzantine period—Mr. Berenson's strictures would apply to its mosaics as well as to its paintings—nor medieval painting in general as represented in wall paintings, stained-glass paintings, and illuminated manuscripts. It has always seemed to me that the evaluation of art according to the number of dimensions it includes is a curiously materialistic procedure. A *"keener* sense of reality," which the introduction of tactile values into painting is supposed to give, is not necessarily an artistic achievement. The intention of the artist might be to give a keener sense of irreality or superreality; and that, indeed, was the intention of the medieval artist. To lend "a higher co-efficient of reality to the object represented," another of Mr. Berenson's phrases, is the aim that gradually corrupted the artistic consciousness and led the art of painting into the morasses of academicism and sentimentalism.[7]

For the sculptor, tactile values are not an illusion to be created on a two-dimensional plane: they constitute a reality to be conveyed directly, as existent mass. Sculpture is an art of *palpation*—an art that gives satisfaction in the touching and handling of objects. That, indeed, is the only way in which we can have direct sensation of the three-dimensional shape of an object. It is only as our hands move over an object and trace lines of direction that we get any physical sensation of the difference between a sphere and a square; touch is essential to the perception of subtler contrasts of shape and texture. A genuine sculptor is continually passing his hands over the work in progress, not to test its surface quality, though that may be one purpose, but simply to realize and assess the shape and volume of the object. Unfortunately visitors to a museum "are requested not to touch the exhibits"—unfortunately, because that request deprives them of one of the essential modes of appreciating sculpture, which is palpation, handling. Admittedly, there is much sculpture in our public galleries that would not yield any pleasure as a result of this approach. If we merely "look at" sculpture, even with our sophisticated vision, which is capable of reading into the visual image the conceptual knowledge we possess from previous experience of three-dimensional objects, still we get merely a two-dimensional impression of a three-dimensional object. We are recommended, in manuals of art appreciation, to walk round a piece of sculpture and to allow all the various points of view to coalesce in our imagination. This difficult feat, if successful, might conceivably give us a ghostlike version of the solid object. Sculpture, again, is often mounted on turntables to save us the trouble of circumambulation. We see an object twisting and twirling in our line of vision, and from that impression of shifting planes and lights we are supposed to derive a sensation of solidity!

We observed in the first chapter that, in the early stages of the evolution of the art of sculpture, sculptural objects were small and palpable, or if they were on a scale too large to be handled they were not to be detached from a background, a matrix. Prehistoric sculpture takes the form either of small amulets or of relief sculpture such as the *Venus* of Laussel. The two bison modeled out of clay at Tuc d'Audoubert, which are 24.4 and 25.2 inches long, are built up against a projecting rock and are hardly to be considered as detached monuments. A considerable number of prehistoric relief sculptures have been discovered—the great majority representing animals—but sculpture in the round is extremely rare.

If we turn to the sculpture of Egypt we find a similar predominance of relief sculpture, and even when the statues are in the round they are often supported by a background. There are two possible but not contradictory explanations of this characteristic. In Egypt carved sculpture is historically later than clay modelling, and it was the practice to give support to the early clay figures, not in the modern way by inserting an armature of wire, but by leaning the figure against a vertical strip or sheaf of bamboo. This device, it is argued, was copied by the sculptor in stone. A much more plausible explanation is provided, however, by a consideration of the function of sculpture in Egypt. It was never regarded as a separate and distinct art. From the beginning it was subordinate to architecture, and the nature of the architecture determined the nature and even the technique of the sculpture. A statue of Ateta, from Sakkara,[8] shows the typical architectural setting of a piece of Egyptian sculpture of the Old Kingdom, in a rectangular niche surrounded by designs and inscriptions in low relief. . . .

The intention behind Egyptian art is functional. The architecture is functional, and so is the subordinate sculpture. There is no room for the play of fantasy, as Worringer has pointed out. This being the situation, the Egyptian sculptor has no desire to isolate the human figure in space, to dissociate it from its niche or socket, for to do so would have served no rational purpose. Space *as such* was not felt by the Egyptians, who were complete strangers to what the Germans call *Raumgefühl*. Their satisfaction with relief sculpture derived from this lack. Relief sculpture is, in fact, the typical art of ancient Egypt, and as Worringer has said, "No stranger, more consistent two-dimensional art has ever existed, but it is just two-dimensional art and no more. We may think of Greek art—how much artistic thinking had to be employed by it before it discovered its ideal relief style, that wonderfully delicate play of balance between surface and depth which even in the most perfect productions still always reflects the hesitations of a never-to-be-overcome tension between surface and depth. The Egyptian relief is from the very first complete in its pure surface character. No unrest born of depth finds its way into it. It is entirely without tension and conflict. The third dimension, the dimension by which we are actually aware of depth, from which all that is more profound in the drama of artistic creation draws its inspiration, is not present at all as a resistant in the artistic consciousness of the Egyptian."[9]

From the point of view I am presenting, we can state that no complete plastic consciousness was possible in Egyptian sculpture, because the form was never isolated in space and was never handled as a three-dimensional object. The technique was one of incision, essentially linear, essentially graphic. Egyptian sculpture was made to be read, like the Egyptian pictorial script. It kept this limited character for three milleniums, into the Ptolemaic period. Only the relatively small bronze or wooden servant statues, votive tomb figures, and folk art in general offer any exception to this rigid limitation of plastic feeling.

In this connection, the German art historian, Alois Riegel, invented the term "space shyness," and certainly the Egyptians were shy of space. It plays no part in their architecture nor in any of their subordinate arts, and all their arts, as I have previously pointed out, were subordinate to architecture. There are, however, two senses in which we can speak of space shyness: space as a practical necessity, to which we can react on a merely sensational level, and space as a concept, to which we react emotionally and spiritually. Worringer, who defines space as metaphysical consciousness, argues that the Egyptians were not aware of space in this second sense and that they were neutral and indifferent to the very idea. Their space shyness, therefore, was a form of inarticulateness. They were like children who have not yet discovered that space exists, except as a relationship between groups of objects. The same, with some qualifications, is true of the Greeks. "According to Aristotle," observes a modern physicist, C. F. von Weizsäcker, "the world is finite in extent. In its center is the ball-shaped earth, its outer boundary is the sphere of the fixed stars. Outside that sphere there is no thing and hence no place, since every place is the place of some thing. The idea of space as such, existing even if it is not filled by something, was unknown to the Greeks—with the exception of the atomistic school."[10]

In accordance with this essentially practical and limited conception of space, we get the characteristic of Greek sculpture that has been called "the law of frontality," which is really no "law" at all but merely a limitation of sensibility. The development of Greek sculpture is often represented as an age-long struggle with this very problem. "The agile mind of the Greek," writes Dr. Richter, "determined to wrestle with these problems [of modeling and perspective]. Not content with what had been accomplished before him, he was eager to solve new problems, and so he started out on his adventure of representing a human body in all manner of postures, with bones and muscles correctly indicated, in proper relation and in right perspective, both in the round and in relief. To a pioneer in the field it was a formidable task. But with infinite patience the Greek artist accomplished it, and his solution of these problems was like the removal of shackles which had hampered the free development of art for generations. Thenceforward the road was clear. In a century or two we pass from the Apollo of Tenea to the Idolino, from the Nike of Delos to the Nike of Paionios, from the Spartan ancestor relief to the Hegeso stele."[11]

. . . for reasons that have little to do with any conception of space the Greek sculptor arrived at a completely realistic rendering of the human body image. Yet apart from this narcissistic form of projection, this re-creation of the self, Greek sculpture remained either bound to architecture, as in the Parthenon frieze, or anchored in some way to the earth. The Hegeso stele, mentioned by Dr. Richter, is a case in point. It represents the acme of the Greek sculptor's skill, but the figures, in all their grace and realism, remain prisoners within the architectural framework of the stele. This may be taken as a symbol of all Greek sculpture and indeed of all sculpture down to our own period. Even at the end of the nineteenth century, in 1893, we find the German sculptor, Adolf Hilde-brand, in his famous treatise on sculpture, exercising all his ingenuity to establish the two-dimensional unity of the relief as a standard for all the plastic arts. He calls it an unchangeable law of art, and he says further that "The thousandfold judgments and movements of our observation find in this mode of presentation their stability and clearness. It is an essential to all artistic form, be it in a landscape or in the portràyal of a head. In this way the visual content is universally arranged, bound together, and put in repose. Through all figurative art this idea is the same, the one guiding thought. It acts always as a general condition and requirement to which all else is subordinate, in which everything finds a place and a unity."[12]

What we may call the visual prejudice cannot go farther. It is true that Hildebrand is prepared to free relief from its dependence on architecture; but his real object is to eliminate all sense impressions save those given in visual contemplation from a fixed point of view. Such a result can be achieved only by ignoring the palpability of the sculptured object and by confining the senses within a pictorial framework. . . .

If the artist has succeeded by these means in giving us aesthetic satisfaction, what harm, we may ask, is done? For centuries the Western world has admired this kind of sculpture. Must we now be robbed of our simple pleasures? Of course not; as one kind of sculpture, giving a specific though a limited pleasure, the typical reliefs of the Renaissance are justified. The aesthetics of relief sculpture cannot be wholly identified with those of painting. There are problems of texture, of the conveyance of three-dimensional qualities by means of actual light and shade rather than by color and chiaroscuro, that distinguish a carved or modeled relief from a panel painting of the same period. Into his reliefs, such as the *Lamenta-tion* in the Victoria and Albert Museum, and the later panels on the pulpit in San Lorenzo, Donatello put all the expressive power of which a "painterly" art is capable, but the reliefs remain essentially painterly (*malerisch*) . As I hope to show . . . , there are other qualities that can be conveyed *only* by the art of sculpture, but by an art of sculpture completely emancipated from painterly prejudices.

The Realization of Mass

The distinction between sight-space and touch-space . . . , had the effect of disengaging, from the purely visual apprehension of reality, the quantity known as *volume* or bulk. If, in addition to touching an object, we lift it or try to lift it, we get a sensation of its *ponderability* or mass. We may have an intuition of ponderability without actually lifting the object, merely from our generalized knowledge of the relative weights of such materials as marble, clay, bronze, and lead.

Our knowledge of an object is complete only when we have exhausted all our sensational reactions to it. Taste and smell are normally excluded from the aesthetic field. Sound is so distinctive as a sensation that the aesthetics of music has its separate vocabulary, and we can only trace analogies between this art and other arts. But the other two sensations, sight and touch, are both actively engaged in our aesthetic experiences, and it is often very difficult in any given case to dissociate entirely our visual reactions from our tactile reactions. Even when one organ is not directly involved, as when we look at a surface, a whole series of associations based on the tactile knowledge of surfaces may be aroused. It is a false simplification to base the various arts on any one sensation, for what actually takes place, in any given experience, is a chain reaction or *Gestaltkreis* in which one sensation touches off and involves other sensations, either by memory association or by actual sensory motor connections. An art owes its particularity to the emphasis or preference given to any one organ of sensation. If sculpture has any such particularity, it is to be distinguished from painting as the plastic art that gives preference to tactile sensations as against visual sensations, and it is precisely when this preference is clearly stated that sculpture attains its highest and its unique aesthetic values. This peculiarity does not mean, of course, that we can discount our visual reactions to sculpture; nor does it mean that we refuse any aesthetic value to sculpture that is visually conceived. We are seeking the basic principles of this art, and these, I contend, involve tactile sensations.

Jean Piaget has shown, in one of his fascinating studies of the mental development of the child, how the child arrives at a quantification of qualities—how he passes from the conception of number and numerical relations such as the relation of parts to the whole (quantities that may be called "intensive" or logical) , to a conception of "extensive" quantities such as weight and physical volume. The conscious awareness of these sensations, like the awareness of space . . . , is not given at birth: it has to be acquired by a patient process of learning.[13] A child does not take long to learn that an object is solid or heavy or that it emits light or heat. Not merely the measurement of these quantities, however, but a comparative estimate of them is only slowly evolved. Our knowledge of the external world is due to a gradual sorting out and comparison of such quantitative estimates.

Consciousness is selective, and people can be divided into psychological types according to the predominance of any one sensation in the imagination. Thus there are visual types, and audile types. There is perhaps a normal type in whose mind the imagery due to the various sensations is evenly or appropriately mixed, but there can be no doubt that the acuteness of some one type of imagery determines whether an artist becomes a poet,[14] a musician, a painter, or a sculptor. Similarly, the strength of our reactions to one or another of these arts, our particular preference among the arts, is due to the relative acuteness in our selves of one type of imagination. We may expect, therefore, to find visual types who have no appreciation of the tactile values of sculpture; and . . . we may even find visual artists like Leonardo who conceive and execute sculpture with a predominantly visual equipment. It was Hildebrand's contention, in his treatise *The Problem of Form in Painting and Sculpture,* that the unity essential to a work of art can be achieved only in vision and that the sculptor strives to accommodate his three-dimensional forms to the visual ease of a two-dimensional surface. That is the heresy I wish to contest. . . . My intention is to show that sculpture owes its individuality as an art to unique plastic qualities, to the possession and exploitation of a special kind of sensibility. Its uniqueness consists in its realization of an integral mass in actual space. The sensibility required for this effort of realization has nothing in common with visual perception, i.e. with the visual impression of a three-dimensional form on a two-dimensional plane.

The specifically plastic sensibility, is, I believe, more complex than the specifically visual sensibility. It involves three factors: a sensation of the tactile quality of surfaces; a sensation of volume as denoted by plane surfaces; and a synthetic realization of the mass and ponderability of the object. . . .

A sensibility to surface quality is involved in other arts. Even the surface quality of a painting has considerable aesthetic significance, as we may realize if we compare the surface of a painting by Rembrandt with the surface of a painting by Vermeer. Surface is one of the elements of a painting's "facture." Even the surface quality of a sheet of paper used for a drawing or an engraving or even for writing, is of considerable aesthetic importance. Surface plays its part in all metal-work and ironwork, in jewelry and textiles, and is of supreme importance in the art of pottery. It would not be necessary to insist on the aesthetic significance of surface impressions in sculpture had there not grown up during and since the Renaissance a convention based on the ideals of the Hellenistic decadence. This convention systematically tended toward the denaturing of all materials and toward the choice of certain materials, like pure white marble, devoid of any surface irregularities and therefore not emphasizing the materiality of the sculptural mass. The problem is not one of smoothness: smoothness, polish, and a scintillating surface can be used for aesthetic effect, as in certain Renaissance bronzes. Pieces such as these exploit the smooth surface as a reflector of light. . . . In the typical academic statue of white marble, however, the surface is monotonous and dead. The object seems to be to produce the visual impression of a plane surface shaded like white paper. To secure the opposite effect—to call attention to mass—the modern sculptor tends either to use stones that are mottled or striated or to leave a rougher surface, even one showing the marks of his chisel or hammer. He has to a large extent abandoned the immaculate marbles of the pseudoclassical tradition and uses instead a wide variety of stone, wood, metal, or indeed any material that offers a surface aesthetically stimulating, especially to the tactile sensibility.

Still, important as they are, there is nothing specifically sculptural about such surface aesthetics, so let us pass to the more difficult problem of volume.

Rodin related, in his conversation with Paul Gsell, how he came to realize the importance of relief in sculpture. This subject was taught to him by a sculptor called Constant, and one day Constant was watching Rodin as he modeled in clay a capital decorated with foliage.

"Rodin," he said to the young student, "you are going about that in the wrong way. All your leaves seem flat. That is why they do not look real. Make some with the tips pointed at you, so that, in seeing them, one has the sensation of depth."

Rodin followed his advice and was amazed at the results he obtained.

"Always remember what I am about to tell you," Constant went on to say. "Henceforth, when you carve, never see the form in length, but always in thickness. Never consider a surface except as the extremity of a volume, as the point, more or less large, which it directs toward you. In that way you will acquire the *science* of modeling."

This principle, said Rodin, had quite astonishing results: "I applied it to the execution of figures. Instead of imagining the different parts of a body as surfaces more or less flat, I represented them as projections of interior volumes. I forced myself to express in each swelling of the torso or of the limbs the efflorescence of a muscle or of a bone which lay deep beneath the skin. And so the truth of my figures, instead of being merely superficial, seems to blossom from within to the outside, like life itself."[15]

Rodin's observation may seem simple, even naïve to those who are accustomed to the art of sculpture either as sculptors or as amateurs. Nevertheless for the average person brought up to approach every work of art with binocular vision, this kind of vision, from depth to surface or from surface to depth, requires a new effort, a re-education of the senses.

Even more difficult is the third aesthetic effort of apprehension involved in the art of sculpture, what I have called a synthetic realization of the mass and ponderability of the object. This sensation is comparatively easy to convey in the case of small objects. We feel the hard roundness of the pingpong ball and may even get an aesthetic satisfaction from that sensation. We react aesthetically to the feel of the handle of a stick and to many other solid objects that we habitually use. The Chinese and Japanese have developed a class of small objects carved out of such materials as jade, amber, and ivory, some of which are carried in the pocket and fondled from time to time. Some people treasure pebbles in this way, and a few pieces of modern sculpture have been produced with the intention that they be fondled.

This sensation of palpability, so evident in the small object, is felt by the sculptor toward his carving, *whatever its size*. It is one of the essential faculties engaged in the appreciation of sculpture. In his description of the mental process here involved . . . , Henry Moore has emphasized this sense of physical possession. The sculptor "gets the solid shape, as it were, inside his head—he thinks of it, whatever its size, as if he were holding it completely enclosed in the hollow of his hand. He mentally visualizes a complex form *from all round itself*; he knows while he looks at one side what the other side is like; he identifies himself with its center of gravity, its mass, its weight; he realizes its volume, as the space that the shape displaces in the air."[16]

Naturally any piece of sculpture has volume: it is a crude mass of some sort. But the aim of a sculptor like Bernini and indeed of the whole tradition of sculpture—until late in the nineteenth century Rodin began to reconsider the aesthetics of sculpture—was to create a pictorial illusion in which the ponderability of the material was etherealized, an effect that the sculptor's favorite material, white marble, usually made all too easy. The sculptor worked with and for the eye and never conceived his work as possessing any other unity than that of a visual image.

The mind, said Rodin, only with difficulty familiarizes itself with the notion of depth. It always tends to play over surfaces. Nevertheless, the sculptor's task is to see surfaces as thicknesses, to conceive form as volume. It may be asked, "Why be so dogmatic about the aims of the sculptor?" The aims of the artist in any material are the same: to produce a certain emotional reaction in the spectator. It is the unique privilege of art to convey a reaction that we may define variously as wonder, pleasure, enhanced vitality, and so on. This particular experience cannot be obtained by any other means than art. As between the various arts, however, one art may be more appropriate or more efficient than another for a desired effect: there are degrees of consciousness that can be expressed only by music, others only by poetry. No real confusion of means has ever existed between poetry and music or even between poetry and painting, though the relationship between these arts has been endlessly discussed. A very real confusion has always existed between the arts of sculpture and painting, however, a confusion due to the psychological fact that no clear separation is made in experience between the faculties of sight and touch. No clear separation *can* be made by people possessing both faculties in normal strength. Nevertheless, distinct reactions are experienced according to whether we give priority to touch (or imagined touch and haptic sensations generally) and prefer the palpable image. I know that we can get on quite well with a life of visual sensations, with perhaps a merely subcutaneous or subconscious life of tactile sensations. Still, that is not the point. Art is the sensuous apprehension or plastic cognition of the world: its purpose is to increase our sense of the wholeness of being, to develop our consciousness of reality. In that sense it becomes part of our conception of evolutionary purpose, and there is a spiritual as well as a physical joy in the experience of such a conquest. To confine sculpture to the field of visual sensation is to neglect the possibilities of the field of palpable sensation. It is a restriction of the range or scope of art, and it deprives the sculptor of a challenge that in the past has given rise to the greatest achievements. Michelangelo is not superior to Bernini in technical accomplishment or in any of those tricks that create what we call "the living image." He is greater because his work is informed by a generative power that we can identify with natural forces. Great works of art, said Rodin, "express, indeed, all that genius feels in the presence of Nature; they represent Nature with all the clearness, with all the magnificence which a human being can discover in her; but they also fling themselves against that immense Unknown which everywhere envelops our little world of the known. For, after all, we only feel and conceive those things which are patent to us and which impress our minds and our senses. But all the rest is plunged in infinite obscurity. Even a thousand things which should be clear to us are hidden because we are not organized to seize them."[17] The function of art, Rodin went on to say, is not only to tell us all that can be known but to make us aware that there is a limit to what is known. Great works of art bring us to the edge of this abyss, and they make us feel a little dizzy.

It is a question of gamut, of the possible range of sensational apprehension and expressive power. There is, in the full scale of plastic sensibility, a power attaching to ponderability and mass, to the gestated and palpable volume of a solid creation, that cannot be experienced in any other manner, by any other means. Sculpture declined as and when it lost the feeling for these qualities; it has revived in our time precisely because certain of our sculptors have recovered that feeling. The sculptor who was responsible for the recovery of the true tradition of the art was, as I have already said, Rodin; yet even Rodin was still seduced by dramatic effects that are predominantly visual in their appeal, by a surface play of light and shade that has no relevance to the mass beneath. He was, after all, a contemporary of the Impressionists. Hildebrand, who was a contemporary of Rodin and whose treatise on sculpture is so representative of the whole Renaissance tradition, had a clear conception of the process of artistic creation, but he was willing to sacrifice the palpable values of mass to the visual unity of a plane surface and was therefore logically driven to the absurd proposition that the ideal sculpture is relief sculpture. It was left to their successor, Aristide Maillol, to represent plastic form in its essential massiveness, to allow it to stand resolutely and assertively in space. A torso by Maillol is a palpable reality: we may apprehend it visually, but the eye is not pandered to, is not flattered. The forms are expressed from a vital depth, and our sensations, if we become aware of them, are sensations of thrust, of weight, or solid existence. The same sensations, as organic forces embodied in a nonfigurative or "abstract" form, are aroused by the sculpture of Jean Arp.

Notes

1. These processes have been observed in great detail by Jean Piaget. Cf. especially *La Construction du reel chez l'enfant* (Neuchatel and Paris, 1937; tr. Margaret Cook as *The Construction of Reality in the Child*, New York, 1954; as *The Child's Construction of Reality*, London, 1955).

2. William James, *Psychology*, (London and New York, 1892), p. 339. In general I am relying on James's treatment of this subject.

3. Piaget (N.Y. edn.), p. 218. Cf. p. 217: Hence, in the last analysis, it is the functioning of intelligence which explains the construction of space. Space is an organization of movements such as to impress upon the perceptions shapes that are increasingly coherent. The basis of these shapes derives from the very conditions of assimilation that entail the elaboration of groups. But it is the progressive equilibrium of this assimilation with the accommodation of the motor schemata to the diversity of objects which accounts for the formation of sequential structures. Space is therefore the produce of an interaction between the organism and the environment in which it is impossible to dissociate the organization of the universe perceived from that of the activity itself."

4. James, p. 349.

5. (Dublin, 1709); reprinted with *Alciphron*, (London, 1732), II; and in *Works*, ed. A. C. Fraser (rev. edn., Oxford, 1901), I, 93-210.

6. *The Italian Painters of the Renaissance*, (London and New York, 1952), pp. 40-41.

7. *Ibid.*, pp. 41, 42 respectively for the two phrases quoted.

8. Margaret Alice Murray, *Egyptian Sculpture*, (London, 1930), pp. 61-62 and pl. xi.

9. *Egyptian Art*, tr. and ed. Bernard Reckham (London, 1928), p. 25.

10. Cf. von Weizsäcker, *The History of Nature*, tr. Fred. D. Wieck, (Chicago and London, 1949), p. 65.

11. Gisela M. A. Richter, *The Sculpture and Sculptors of the Greeks*, (New Haven and London, 1930), p. 24.

12. *The Problem of Form in Painting and Sculpture*, tr. and rev. with the author's co-operation by Max Meyer and Robert Morris Green (2nd ed., New York, 1945), p. 83.

13. Jean Piaget and Barbel Inhelder, *Le Developpement des quantitiés chez l'enfant* (Neuchâtel and Paris, 1941).

14. The poet is a special case, perhaps, because there are "visual" as well as "musical" (audile) poets, and no doubt a good poet is fairly acute in all his senses.

15. *Art*, tr. Mrs. Romilly Feden. (Boston, 1912) pp. 63-65.

16. Henry Moore, "Notes on Sculpture," in Herbert Read, *Henry Moore: Sculpture and Drawings* (2nd edn., New York, 1946), p. xl.

17. *Art*, p. 181.

BRUNO ZEVI

Architecture as Space

Space—Protagonist of Architecture

A SATISFACTORY HISTORY of architecture has not yet been written, because we are still not accustomed to thinking in terms of *space*, and because historians of architecture have failed to apply a coherent method of studying buildings from a spatial point of view.

Everyone who has thought even casually about the subject knows that the specific property of architecture—the feature distinguishing it from all other forms of art—consists in its working with a three-dimensional vocabulary which includes man. Painting functions in two dimensions, even if it can suggest three or four. Sculpture works in three dimensions, but man remains apart, looking on from the outside. Architecture, however, is like a great hollowed-out sculpture which man enters and apprehends by moving about within it.

When you want a house built, the architect shows you a rendering of one of the exterior views and perhaps a perspective sketch of the living room. Then he submits plans, elevations and cross-sections; in other words, he represents the architectural volume by breaking it down into the vertical and horizontal planes which enclose and divide it: floors, roof, exterior and interior walls. Our illiteracy regarding space derives mainly from the use of these means of representation, which have been carried over into technical books on the history of architecture and into popular histories of art, where they are supplemented by photographs.

The plan of a building, being nothing more than an abstract projection on a horizontal plane of all its walls, has reality only on paper and is justified only by the necessity of measuring the distances between the various elements of the construction for the practical execution of the work. The façades and cross-sections of the exteriors and interiors serve to measure height. Architecture, however, does not consist in the sum of the width, length and height of the structural elements which enclose space, but in the void itself, the enclosed space in which man lives and moves. What we are doing, then, is to consider as a complete representation of architecture what is nothing more than a practical device used by the architect to put on paper specific measurements for the use of the builder. For the purpose of learning how to look at architecture, this would be more or less equivalent to a method which described a painting by giving the dimensions of its frame, calculating the areas covered by the various colors and then reproducing each color separately.

It is equally obvious that a poem is something more than just a sum of fine verses. To judge a poem, you must study it as a whole, and even if you then proceed to the analysis of each of its verses, you must do it with reference to the context. Anyone entering on the study of architecture must understand that even though a plan may have abstract beauty on paper, the four façades may seem well-balanced and the total volume well-proportioned, the building itself may turn out to be poor architecture. Internal space, that space which, as we shall see in the next chapter, cannot be completely represented in any form, which can be grasped and felt only through direct experience, is the protagonist of architecture. To grasp space, to know how to *see* it, is the key to the understanding of building. Until we have learned not only to understand space theoretically, but also to apply this understanding as a central factor in the criticism of architecture, our history, and thus our enjoyment, of architecture will remain haphazard. We shall continue to flounder in a critical language which describes buildings in terms proper only to painting and sculpture. At best we shall be praising space as abstractly imagined and not as concretely experienced. Studies and research will be limited to philological contributions, such as the study of social factors (function), constructional data (technics), volumetric or decorative characteristics (plastic and pictorial elements). These contributions are unquestionably highly useful, but they are ineffectual in communicating the value of architecture, if we omit its spatial essence. Our use of words like *rhythm, scale, balance, mass* will continue to be vague until we have succeeded in giving them meaning specific to the reality which defines architecture, and that is: space.

An enormous and certainly disproportionate number of pages devoted to architecture in textbooks on art deal with the sculptural, pictorial social and sometimes even the psychological history (through the study of artists' personalities) of buildings; not with their architectural reality or with their spatial essence. Of course, such material has its value. For example, anyone unacquainted with Italian who wishes to read the *Divine Comedy* will, obviously, find it useful to learn the meaning of its words and, by studying the syntax of Medieval Italian, learn the meaning of its sentences. It would be useful, as well, to learn the history and theology of the Middle Ages, the material and psychological vicissitudes in the life of Dante. But it would be absurd to forget, in the course of these preparatory labors, one's original motivation and final purpose, which is to relive the *Divine Comedy*. All archeological and philological study is useful only insofar as it prepares and enriches the ground for an integral history of architecture.

What, then, is architecture? And, perhaps equally important, what is non-architecture? Is it proper to identify architecture with a beautiful building and non-architecture with an ugly building? Is the distinction between architecture and non-architecture based on purely aesthetic criteria? And what is "space," which we are calling "the protagonist of architecture"? How many dimensions does it have?

These are the basic questions which present themselves in formulating a criticism of architecture. We shall try to answer them by beginning with the last, which is the most specific.

The façade and walls of a house, church or palace, no matter how beautiful they may be, are only the container, the box formed by the walls; *the content is the internal space.* In America, schools of industrial design teach the art and craft of designing packages, but none of them has ever thought of confusing the value of the box with the value of what it contains. In many cases, container and contained are mutually inter-dependent, as in a French Gothic cathedral or in the majority of genuinely modern buildings, but this cannot be taken as a rule, because it is not true of a vast number of buildings, notably those of the Baroque period. Frequently in the course of the history of architecture, we find buildings which show a clear discrepancy between container and con-tained, and even a hasty analysis will show that often, in fact too often, the box formed by the walls has been the object of more thought and labor than the architectural space itself. Now, then, how many dimen-sions does this building-container have? Can they be legitimately identi-fied with the dimensions of the space contained, which is architecture?

The discovery of *perspective* or graphic representation in three di-mensions—height, width, depth—led Renaissance artists of the fifteenth century to believe they had finally mastered the dimensions of archi-tecture and the means of reproducing them. The buildings illustrated in *pre*-Renaissance painting do, in fact, look flat and distorted. Giotto took great pains to put architectural backgrounds into his frescoes, but tech-nically his success was only relative. (He knew, of course, how to turn his limitation to good esthetic account, emphasizing flat chromatic design which would have been completely altered had he known and used three-dimensional representation.) At that time painters still worked in two dimensions, but the rigid frontality of the Byzantine was giving way to a more naturalistic style, at least in the figures. A greater ability to paint pictorial passages from light to dark made it possible to transfer to a flat surface the results of plastic experiments in sculpture. In Pisan archi-tecture the surfaces of cathedral façades were broken and given depth, as well as chromatic vibrancy, through the use of superimposed rows of colonnettes. Not before the discovery of perspective, however, was it possible to achieve an adequate representation of architectural interiors or exteriors. Once the laws of perspective had been elaborated, the problem appeared to be solved: architecture, it was said, has three dimensions; here is the method of drawing them, which anyone can use. From the time of Masaccio, Fra Angelico and Benozzo Gozzoli to Bramante and the Baroque masters on up to the nineteenth century, innumerable painters worked along with designers and architects to represent architecture in perspective.

When, in the last decade of the nineteenth century, the reproduction of photographs, and thus their mass distribution, became a simple process, photographers took the place of draftsmen, and a click of the shutter replaced those perspectives which enthusiastic students of architecture had been laboriously tracing ever since the Renaissance. But at that very moment, when everything seemed critically clear and technically perfect, the mind of man discovered that a *fourth* dimension existed in addition to the three dimensions of perspective. This was the Cubist revolution in the concept of space, which took place shortly before the First World War.

We shall not take more time in discussing the fourth dimension than is strictly necessary for our purpose. The Paris painter of the late 1900's reasoned more or less as follows: "I see and represent an object, for example a box or table. I see it from one point of view. But if I hold the box in my hands and turn it, or if I walk around the table, my point of view changes, and to represent the object from each new viewpoint I must draw a new perspective of it. The reality of the object, therefore, is not exhausted by its representation in the three dimensions of one perspective. To capture it completely, I must draw an infinite number of perspectives from the infinite points of view possible." This successive displacement *in time* of the angle of vision adds a new dimension to the three dimensions of tradition. Thus *time* was baptized the "fourth dimension." (The means used by Cubist painters to render the fourth dimension—superimposing the images of an object seen from various points of view, in order to project them all simultaneously on canvas—do not concern us here.)

The Cubists were not content with the plural representation of the exterior of an object. Their passion for discovery, for grasping the total reality of an object, led them to the following thought: in every physical structure there is not only an external form, there is also an internal organism; besides the skin, there are the muscles and the skeleton, the internal constitution. And so in their paintings they show simultaneously not only the external aspects of a box, for example, but also the box in plan, the box exploded, the box smashed.

The Cubist conquest of the fourth dimension is of immense historical importance quite apart from the esthetic evaluation that can be made for or against Cubist painting. You may prefer a Byzantine mosaic to a fresco of Mantegna without thereby denying the importance of perspective in the development of experiments in dimension. Similarly, it is possible to dislike the paintings of Picasso and still recognize the value of the fourth dimension. The fourth dimension has had a decided application to architecture, not so much for the translation of the pictorial language of the Cubists into architectural terms in the early stages of the modern French and German movements, as for the scientific support it has given to the critical distinction between real buildings and buildings on paper, between architecture and stage designing—a distinction which for a long time has been problematical.

The concept of the fourth dimension seemed to end, once and for all, the search for dimensions characteristic of architecture. To examine a statuette, we pick it up and turn it in our hands. We look at it from all angles. We walk around larger figures and groups to examine them from all sides, close-up and from a distance. In architecture, it was reasoned, there is the same element of time. In fact, this element is indispensable to architecture: from the first hut to the modern house, from the cave of primitive man to the church, school or office of today, no work of architecture can be experienced and understood without the fourth dimension, without the time needed for our walk of discovery within it. The problem again appeared to be solved.

However, a dimension common to all the arts obviously cannot be peculiar to any one of them, and therefore architectural space cannot be thought of entirely in terms of four dimensions. This new factor of *time* has, in fact, a meaning in architecture which is antithetical to its meaning in painting.

In painting, the fourth dimension is a quality *inherent* in the representation of an object, an element in its reality which a painter may choose to project on a flat surface without requiring physical participation on the part of the observer.

The same thing is true of sculpture: in sculpture the "movement" of a form, for example by Boccioni, is a quality *inherent* in the statue we are looking at, which we must relive visually and psychologically.

But in architecture we are dealing with a concrete phenomenon which is entirely different: here, *man moving about within the building*, studying it from successive points of views, himself creates, so to speak, the fourth dimension, giving the space an integrated reality.

Elaborate treatises have of course been written on the subject; our problem here is simply to give a clear explanation of an experience familiar to everyone. To be more precise, the fourth dimension is sufficient to define the architectural volume, that is, the box formed by the walls which enclose space. But the space itself—the essence of architecture —transcends the limits of the four dimensions.

How many dimensions, then, does space, this architectural "void," have? Five, ten, an infinite number perhaps. For our purpose it is enough to establish that architectural space cannot be defined in terms of the dimensions of painting and sculpture. The phenomenon of space becomes concrete reality only in architecture and therefore constitutes its specific character.

Having arrived at this point, the reader will understand that the question, "What is architecture?", has already been answered. To say, as is usual, that architecture is "beautiful building" and that non-architecture is "ugly building" does not explain anything, because "ugly" and "beautiful" are relative terms. It would be necessary, in any case, first to formulate an analytic definition of "What is a building?" which would mean starting once more from the beginning.

The most exact definition of architecture that can be given today is that which takes into account *interior space*. Beautiful architecture would then be architecture in which the interior space attracts us, elevates us and dominates us spiritually (as in the case of Chartres Cathedral); ugly architecture would be that in which the interior space disgusts and repels us (you might prefer to choose your own example). But the important thing is to establish that no work lacking interior space can be considered architecture.

If we admit this much—and to admit it seems to be a matter of common sense, not to say of logic—we must recognize that most histories of architecture are full of observations that have nothing to do with architecture in this specific meaning. They devote page after page to the façades of buildings which in effect are sculpture on a large scale, but have little to do with architecture in the *spatial* sense of the word. An obelisk, a fountain, a monument, a bridge, big as they may be—a portal, a triumphal arch—are all works of art which are discussed in histories of architecture although they are not properly architecture. Architectural backdrops or any sort of painted or drawn architecture are not true architecture any more than a play not yet put into dialogue, but only sketched in its broad outlines, can be regarded as a dramatic performance. In other words, the experience of space is not communicated until the actual mechanical expression has rendered material the poetic conception. Were we to take any history of architecture and severely prune it of everything not strictly concerned with architecture, it is certain that we should have to do away with at least eighty out of every hundred pages.

At this point, two serious misunderstandings may arise in the mind of the reader which would not only destroy the value of the preceding argument, but would even make the interpretation of architecture as space ridiculous. They are:

(1) that architectural space can be experienced only in the interior of a building, and therefore urban or city-planned space, for all practical purposes, does not exist or have any value;

(2) that space is not only the protagonist of architecture, but represent

the *whole* of architectural experience, and that consequently the interpretation of a building in terms of space is the *only* critical tool required in judging architecture.

These two possible misunderstandings must be cleared up immediately:

The experience of space, which we have indicated as characteristic of architecture, has its extension in the city, in the streets, squares, alleys and parks, in the playgrounds, and in the gardens, wherever man has defined or limited a *void* and so has created an enclosed space. If, in the interior of a building, space is defined by six planes (floor, ceiling and four walls), this does not mean that a void enclosed by five planes instead of six—as, for example, a (roofless) courtyard or public square—cannot be regarded with equal validity as space. It is doubtful whether the experience of space one has in riding in an automobile along a straight highway through miles of uninhabited flatland can be defined as an architectural experience in our present use of the term, but it is certain that all urban space wherever the view is screened off, whether by stone walls or rows of trees or embankments, presents the same features we find in architectural space.

Since every architectural volume, every structure of walls, constitutes a boundary, a pause in the continuity of space, it is clear that every building functions in the creation of two kinds of space: its internal space, completely defined by the building itself, and its external or urban space, defined by that building and the others around it. It is evident then that all those subjects which we have excluded as not being true architecture—bridges, obelisks, fountains, triumphal arches, groups of trees and, in particular, the façades of buildings—are brought into play in the creation of urban space. The specific esthetic value of these elements must remain a question of minor importance until we clear up our second misunderstanding. What interests us at the present point in our discussion is their function in determining an enclosed space. Just as four beautifully decorated walls do not in themselves create a beautiful environment, so a group of excellent houses can define a poor urban space, and *vice versa*.

The second possible misunderstanding would carry our argument to a *reductio ad absurdum* with conclusions totally foreign to our intention in prospoing a spatial interpretation of architecture. To maintain that internal space is the essence of architecture does not mean that the value of an architectural work rests *entirely* on its spatial values. Every building can be characterized by a plurality of values: economic, social, technical, functional, esthetic, spatial and decorative. Anyone is free to write economic, social, technical, or volumetric histories of architecture, in the same way that it is possible to write a cosmological, Thomistic or political analysis of the *Divine Comedy*.

The reality of a work of art, however, is in the *sum* of all these factors; and a valid history cannot omit any of them. Even if we neglect the economic, social and technical factors, it is clear that space in itself, although it is the principal element in architecture, is not enough to define it. While it is incontestable that beautiful decoration will never create beautiful space, it is also true that a satisfactory space, if it is not complemented by an adequate treatment of the walls which enclose it, is not sufficient to create an esthetic environment. It is common to see a beautiful room ruined by badly used colors, unsuitable furniture or poor lighting. Doubtless, these elements are of relatively little importance; they can easily be changed, whereas the space remains fixed. But an esthetic judgment of a building is based both on its specific architectural value and on the various secondary factors, which may be sculptural, as in applied or three-dimensional decoration, pictorial, as in the case of mosaics, frescoes and easel paintings or on other factors, such as furniture.

After a century of predominantly decorative, sculptural and a- or non-spatial architecture, the modern movement with the splendid intent of returning architecture to the expression proper to it, banished decoration from building, insisting on the thesis that volumetric and spatial values are the only values legitimate to architecture. (European Functionalism emphasized volumetric values in architecture; the Organic Movement was more concerned with those of space.)

If it is clear, then, that as architects we should not underscore the *decorative* rather than the *spatial* in architecture, then as critics and historians we should not advance our preferences or dislikes in the field of decorative or figurative means and expressions as the sole yardstick for our judgment of architecture of all periods. This is all the more true because decoration (not in the form of applied ornamentation, but in the new play of contrasting natural materials, in the new sense of color, and so on) is now, quite properly, coming back into architecture after twenty years of architectural nudism, glacial volumetrics, stylistic sterilization and the purging of decorative details, contrary to psychological and spiritual needs. "Freedom from decoration," as an architectural program, can be no more than a polemical, and therefore ephemeral, slogan.

At this point the uninitiated reader will, perhaps, feel confused. If decoration has some importance, if sculpture and painting, earlier thrown out, reappear in the field of architecture, what end has our discussion served? It has not been to invent esoteric theories about architecture, but simply to put order and system into current ideas intuitively felt by everyone. Certainly decoration, sculpture and painting enter into the study of buildings (no less than economic causes, social or functional values and technical considerations). Everything figures in architecture, as it does in every great human phenomenon of art, thought or practice. But how? Not without differentiation, as one might believe in asserting a generic and vacuous unity of all the arts. Decorating, sculpture and painting enter into the grammar of architecture in their proper places as adjectives, not as substantives.

The history of architecture is primarily the history of spatial conceptions. Judgment of architecture is fundamentally judgment of the internal space of buildings. If, because of its lack of interior space, a work cannot be judged on this basis, as in the case of the types of constructions mentioned above, the structure or building—be it the Arch of Titus, the Column of Trajan or a fountain by Bernini—falls outside the history of architecture and belongs properly, as a volumetric entity, to the history of urbanism; and, with respect to its intrinsic artistic value, to the history of sculpture. If judgment of its internal space proves negative, the structure falls into the category of non-architecture, even if its decorative elements can be treated as belonging to the history of truly fine sculpture. If judgment of its architectural space is positive, the building must be included in the history of architecture, even if the decoration is ineffectual; even if, that is to say, the building as a whole is not entirely satisfactory. When, finally, the judgment of the spatial conception of a building, of its volumetrics and of its decorative quality, proves positive, we are then in the presence of one of those rare, integral works of art in which all the figurative means combine in a superlative artistic creation.

In conclusion, even if the other arts contribute to architecture, it is *interior space*, the space which surrounds and includes us, which is the basis for our judgment of a building, which determines the "yea" or "nay" of esthetic pronouncement on architecture. All the rest is important or perhaps we should say *can* be important, but always in a subordinate relation to the spatial idea. Whenever critics and historians lose sight of this hierarchy, they create confusion and accentuate the present disorientation in architecture.

That space—void—should be the protagonist of architecture is after all natural. Architecture is not art alone, it is not merely a reflection of conceptions of life or a portrait of systems of living. Architecture is environment, the stage on which our lives unfold.

Aesthetics and the Arts

Literature. That poems, plays, and novels are discourse and that they differ from newspaper articles, treatises on science, and biographies is obvious. The difficulty lies in trying to say what the differences are. According to the Emotive Theory, literature is marked off from other kinds of discourse by the predominance of "emotive meaning" in it. Mrs. Hungerland makes a case against this theory on the grounds that since there are many different *ways* of having meaning, there is no single characteristic that can serve as a basis for dividing language into two kinds.

She draws an analogy between meaning and manners: having manners and having meaning consist in following or observing rules; not having manners and not having meaning, in violating rules. And just as one can be ill- or well-mannered in a variety of *ways,* so in a similar variety of ways a word or sentence can be meaningful.

Is this analogy apt? Can a word be meaningful, or meaningless, in different ways by virtue of its being employed, or not employed, according to different rules of usage?

It is not certain that words are used according to rules or that these are rules of meaning. What would such rules be? Presumably definitions; for example, " 'russet' means reddish brown." Suppose, however, that I mistakenly think that "russet" means greenish-yellow and use it accordingly. Does "russet" cease to have meaning or have meaning in a different way? *Ex hypothesi,* a rule of usage is being violated; but doesn't "russet" still mean reddish-brown regardless of how I use, or misuse, it?

One might want to say that *as* I use it, "russet" means greenish-yellow. Still, does it follow that as I use the word, it has meaning in one way and as it is normally used, it has meaning in another? If so, then isn't to have meaning in different *ways* simply to have different meanings? And does the fact that words have different meanings imply that having meaning is *not* a single characteristic like having color, any more than the fact that things have different colors implies that having color is not a single characteristic? What sort of question is this anyway: Is "meaningful" the name of a single characteristic? Would we—how?—know what the *right* answer to this question is?

The Emotive Theory holds that meaning is a function of effect or response; there are different kinds of meaning according as language has different kinds of effects on readers and hearers. If this is wrong, *how* is it wrong? It is not clear from Mrs. Hungerland's argument whether she takes the Emotive Theory, and hence also the considerations she adduces in refutation of it, to be about literature or about the meaning of "literature." Is the emotive theorist simply saying something false about literature, namely, that poems, plays, and novels affect us emotionally more than newspaper reports, biographies, and the like? Or is he mistaken about what the word "literature" means? But he must know that some newspaper reports and telegrams are more emotionally affecting than are many poems and novels, and that the word "literature" does not mean discourse in which emotive meaning is more predominant than any other kind. Moreover, there is no reason why an emotive theorist could not accept all of Mrs. Hungerland's remarks about certain literary works. What, then, are we to make of this disparity of views?

The same difficulty faces us in alternative theories of literature, two of which, because of their present prominence, may be mentioned briefly here.

Some literary works rely heavily for their effects on what Mrs. Hungerland calls the "suggestive powers of language"; this has led to the so-called "semantic" theory, that literature is discourse in which the suggestive powers are important as well as the meaning.[1] But, again, how are we to construe this theory? Does it say what "literature" means?

The "use theory" says that in literature language is being *used* in a special or distinctive way. But "use" is ambiguous. Of its several senses, as delineated by Mrs. Hungerland, only one will fit, *viz.* that in which we speak of language as being used by a speaker or writer to effect certain aims or purposes. Is there, however, a distinctive aim or purpose in writing that constitutes the unique feature of literature? Or do we identify a work of literature by ascertaining the aims of the writer? In practice this is often impossible, even when we know that a piece of writing *is* literature. What were the aims and purposes of Aeschylus, or Homer, or Shakespeare?

It is a curious feature of theories of literature, as it is of theories of art generally, that theorists can agree on which works are, and which are not, literature, and yet disagree in theory. Does this tell us anything about the nature of such theories? If so, what?

Music. "Does this piece of music have a meaning?" and "What does this piece of music mean?" are odd questions, like "Does this flower have a meaning?" and "What does this flower mean?" Their oddness stems partly from the fact that what is at issue is not literally *meaning* at all. A note, a chord, a theme, a sonata literally mean nothing in the sense in which a word means something.

In discussions of music, as in those of literature, meaning is often iden-tified with things only peripherally connected with it: associations, sug-gestions, emotional effects, etc. Hence, if by the "meaning" of music one means what a selection may suggest, the images or thoughts it may evoke, the feelings it may arouse, the feelings of the composer that it may con-vey, then the questions "Does music have meaning?" and "What does it mean?" are easily answered. Music "means" these things. The fact that a composer writes music of a certain sort, together with other relevant data, may let us infer things about him, including how he may have felt when he wrote the music. This too may be what his music "means." Pieces of music also are gay, sad, joyful, somber, serene, etc.; hence, a sad melody can be said to "mean" sadness, a joyful melody, joy, and so forth.[2]

The problem of meaning in music goes deeper than this, however; if this were all there were to it, there would be nothing to it. Those who claim that music has meaning often have in mind that it *represents* some-thing in the way a picture or map represents something. A piece of music is a picture of an emotion. This view Hanslick seeks to refute.

Hanslick argues that an emotion cannot be represented musically. He also agrees with Mrs. Hungerland that emotions are not simple sensations —as an itch is, for example. Love and hate are love and hate *of* someone or something, and usually for a reason; hope is hope *for* something; and so on. If music could represent love or hate or any other "definite" emo-tion, would it not be possible to answer *from the music* such queries as "Whose love?" "Love of whom or what?" "Sad about what?" "Why afraid?" etc.? But can this be done—unless we take musical elements and *give* them a meaning, like words, in which case are we any longer dealing with music? (Is an array of hieroglyphics a picture?)

A writer represents emotions, as Mrs. Hungerland says, "by depicting characters living in a certain way in certain situations." For example, an actor depicts an emotion such as jealousy by behaving as a jealous man characteristically would. This music alone cannot do. In painting, emo-tions can be represented only through persons with certain looks, perhaps performing certain acts.[3] This too is denied to music. An *adagio* may *sug-gest* ideas of gentleness or concord; it may *call up* the idea of youthful contentedness or of transitoriness. "These abstract notions, however, are by no means the subject matter of musical compositions; they are not what music is about, what it represents."

Why not say they *are* what music is about or represents? Because if a picture is a picture of something, a map a map of some area, we must in principle be able to settle the question *what* it is a picture or map *of.* So also with music. "The experiment is indispensable." Yet if one person says that a piece of music represents love, another that it represents hate, how can the disagreement be settled? If a piece of music can with equal validity be said to represent love and hate, can it be said to represent either? If one term is no more appropriate than another, is any term appropriate? Is a picture that is a picture of everything—a blank canvas, say —a picture of anything?

Morris Weitz interprets Hanslick to mean that "musical sounds are like certain general features of human experience and, in this dimension, can be said to represent something non-musical. . . . Music is a language of the dynamic properties of emotions and can be said to mean—*i.e.* to represent or denote—these properties."[4]

Hanslick does say that music has dynamic properties—momentum, speed, strength, increasing and decreasing intensity, etc.—in common with the inner or psychical motion of our lives. There is what he calls "an analogy of motion" between music and life. Music, therefore, by virtue of this analogy is *capable* of representing these dynamic properties of the life of feeling. But *does* it?

Music and the emotions are not alone in having dynamic properties. If anger rises and falls, so do the tides, the barometer, and the daily temperature. Has the rising and falling of music any more in common with emotions than with many other things? Can it be said to represent the dynamic properties of the emotions any more than of the others? What are the dynamic elements of music to be correlated with? Aren't the dynamic elements of music simply properties of the music?

What has Hanslick demonstrated, if anything? That music, as a matter of empirical fact, does not represent emotions? Or that the concept of representation is inapplicable to music? What, in short, is the logical status of Hanslick's claim that the beautiful in music "is specifically musical," that apart from a program, text, or libretto, music expresses nothing but "musical ideas"?

Painting. Trapp's claim that a painting "has solely and specifically visual meaning," that it is something to be looked at and appreciated for its own sake, raises several interesting questions.

The boundaries between painting and other artistic media are fluid and imprecise. Even to say that a painting is something painted is to say nothing exact. For what is paint, and what is it to paint? All sorts of substances are used in making pictures, and there are many techniques for applying them. Are distinctions according to media, therefore, practicable or of any use to us? Do we know (how?) or care (why?) what distinguishes a painting from drawing, collage, mosaic, tapestry, etc.? Trapp holds that these distinctions are relatively unimportant, that whether we classify a collage, a mosaic, or a picture made of feathers as a painting or not, it is at least a picture (though not necessarily a picture *of* anything) ; that is, an object whose appeal is primarily visual.

A painting, it is suggested, is something to be looked at in any one of a range of ways relevant to two-dimensional objects.[5] As a physical object, a painting is three-dimensional; is its third-dimension aesthetically relevant except as a possible condition of artistic effects?

Clearly the third dimension *in* a painting, *e.g.* depth and what Berenson calls "tactile values," is aesthetically important. But how is this dimension appreciated? Are tactile values and depth things to be *seen in* a painting, or are they illusions? According to some aestheticians,[6] looking at a picture is the same as having a visual illusion. A picture of objects in space or depth is an illusion of objects in space or of depth. But in an illusion, though A appears to be behind or far away from B, in fact it is not. In Van Eyck's Arnolfini portrait, is the circular mirror really behind the couple holding hands; or does it merely appear to be there, when really it is—where?—in front of or on a level with the couple? We cannot, of course, reach into the picture and feel around. But does it even seem as though we might? Is the claim that a picture, such as Van Eyck's portrait, is an illusion, or the claim that it is not, a psychological claim? A claim about the applicability of the concept of illusion? Or what?

The statement that a picture is something to be looked at two-dimensionally, so to speak, has been taken to mean that the picture is to be regarded as nothing but a visual design, something of which the "significant form" alone is to be appreciated. Some pictures are simply visual designs; they have no subject or subject matter. In others—often called "decorative" pictures—the importance of subject matter is minimal. Now *any* picture, as Clive Bell saw, can be looked at in either of these ways; does this mean that in every picture subject matter is artistically irrelevant? Is subject matter any more artistically irrelevant in many pictures than the meaning of the words is in much poetry?

To understand and appreciate the subject matter of a picture often requires considerable knowledge and experience.[7] The colored shapes an infant sees in a painting he may not recognize as images of men and women; the men and women some adults see in a painting are not recognized as Jesus, or Venus, or Charles II. Does this imply that what the knowledgeable person sees in a picture is not *really* there, that everything but the colored patches is "projected" into the picture? How do we tell—or can we tell?—when we have ceased to see what is in a picture and begun to project things into it?[8]

The problems we have elicited point to a connection between the questions "What is a painting?" and "What is relevant to the understanding or appreciation of a painting?" How are we to answer these questions or settle disputes about how they are to be answered?

Sculpture. Because most sculpture was designed simply to be seen, because much of it is inaccessible to touch, and because some of it is too large to be handled, Read's view that sculpture is essentially something to be touched and handled raises immediate difficulties. His response to these difficulties is twofold. First, he tends to disparage as "painterly" any sculpture designed merely to be seen, including "all sculpture down to our own period." Second, he says that "it is a false simplification to base the various arts on any one sensation." Sculpture is not, then, essentially a "palpatory" art. However, sculpture is to be distinguished from painting as the art that gives *preference* to tactile, as against visual, sensations; the *best* sculpture always involves tactile sensations.

Although he criticizes Berenson's dismissal of all painting prior to Giotto as negligible because it did not stimulate the tactile imagination, Read's own argument nonetheless would seem similar to Berenson's. Might not Read be answered in the words he uses against Berenson?: "I cannot so lightly dismiss the sculpture of the Egyptian, Greek, Roman, Medieval, Renaissance, and Baroque periods, or, in general, all sculpture down to our own period. It seems to me that the evaluation of an art according to whether it can be satisfactorily touched and handled is a curiously materialistic procedure."

What lands Read in this predicament is his initial assumption that there are two kinds of space, "touch-space" and "sight-space," and that they cannot be the same. Of course, Berkeley was right when he said that the tangible "feel" of a thing and the "look" of it to the eye are "specifically distinct." But does it follow that the touching and handling of objects is "the only way we can have direct sensation of the three-dimensional shape of an object"? Whatever the genesis of our sense of three-dimensional shape may be, is it true that, as William James put it, "touch-space is one world; sight-space is another world"—that is, are the space we see and the space we feel *different* spaces? Why can't we appreciate the *same* three-dimensional features of objects—bulk, mass, volume, etc.—with our eyes as well as with our hands?

Consider "ponderability." According to Read, we can have an "intuition" of an object's ponderability simply by looking at it, but this intuition comes from a knowledge of the relative weights of different materials, which can be appreciated "directly" only by lifting, feeling, fondling, and so on. But what particular ponderability is important to a piece of sculpture? Its mass or weight as measured by a pair of scales, say, or its mass or weight as an aesthetic object? These are not the same. Many sculptures, particularly those made of metal, are hollow inside; if they are cast of aluminum, they are indeed relatively light. Does this prevent them from having a heavy "look"? And isn't it the heavy "look" of a sculpture that counts artistically, not its physical mass or weight?

So much for Read's strong or exaggerated view of sculpture. His moderate view is that sculpture owes its individuality as an art to its appeal to the "specifically plastic sensibility." This involves an appreciation of three main factors: the tactile quality of surfaces, volumes as defined by planes, and the ponderability of the object. This appreciation may be purely visual or both visual and tactile at once.[9] The main point is that it is an appreciation of a three-dimensional mass.

Can any reasonable exception be taken to this view? Why not? Because it states a fact about sculpture? Or because it reflects what we mean by "sculpture," or what we mean when we say that someone does, or does not, appreciate sculpture?

Architecture. Is the Statue of Liberty sculpture or architecture? The Washington Monument? The Eiffel Tower? The pyramids of Egypt? The Arc de Triomphe? Though one could make his home in any one of these objects, they are not architecture, Zevi says, but huge pieces of sculpture that happen to have large hollow places inside.

Architecture, like sculpture, Zevi argues, owes its individuality as an art to its appeal to a plastic or spatial sensibility, and most pieces of architecture have "sculptural" qualities. Indeed, just as some sculpture is best appreciated as pictures, so the main appeal of some buildings is sculptural. Other buildings, however, call for a sensitivity to internal spaces in which a man can move about.

Being able to move about in a building is thus for Zevi a primary feature of it as architecture. Notice how *in miniature* a building loses architectural distinctiveness. If we were a hundred or more times our present size, would our buildings have more architectural significance than a doll house does now? To appreciate a building as architecture must we not actually move about in it or be able to imagine its internal spaces from an external view of it? If so, how do we explain the fact that for most people the *outsides* of buildings have the most architectural interest? Are such people somehow mistaken? How? Are they ignorant of building techniques? Do they not know what the word "architecture" means? What is it to *know what to look for* in a piece of architecture?

Notes

1. See, for example, M. C. Beardsley, *Aesthetics,* Ch. III. That the view, as stated, is vague, is nothing against it. It might be said to reflect the actual vagueness of the concept of literature.

2. For further discussion of these properties and of *how* music can be sad or joyful, see O. K. Bouwsma's "The Expression Theory of Art," Section IV of this book.

3. How do we know, for example, that Botticelli's Venus or Manet's Olympia are not angry or terrified?

4. "Editor's Introduction," pp. x, xii, Eduard Hanslick, *The Beautiful in Music,* New York, Liberal Arts Press, 1957. The most elaborate defense of the position here outlined by Weitz has been given by Susanne Langer. See her essay in Section I above and *Philosophy in a New Key,* Cambridge, Mass., Harvard University Press, 1942, Ch. VIII.

5. Cf. Paul Ziff, "Reasons in Art Criticism," #II, Section VII of this book.

6. See especially Susanne K. Langer, *Feeling and Form,* New York, Charles Scribner's Sons, 1953, and E. H. Gombrich, *Art and Illusion; A Study in the Psychology of Pictorial Representation,* New York, Pantheon Books, 1960.

7. See Erwin Panofsky's "Iconography and Iconology" in Section V of this book.

8. A standard diagnostic test in the psychological study of personality is the Thematic Apperception Test. For a description, see Henry A. Murray, *Explora-*

tions in Personality, New York, Oxford University Press, 1938, 530-545. In this test a subject is presented with a series of pictures each of which depicts "a dramatic event of some sort," and he is instructed "to interpret the action in each picture and make a plausible guess as to the preceding events and the final outcome." The test rests on the supposition that "in the performance of this task a subject would necessarily be forced to project some of his own fantasies into the material and thus reveal his more prevailing thematic tendencies." *Op. cit.,* p. 531. But how does a psychologist administering the TAT know when a subject has ceased to describe the pictures presented to him and has begun to project his own fantasies into them? And is *this* a question of psychology?

9. Note that in Henry Moore's description of this sensibility, quoted by Read, Moore speaks of visualizing and looking, not merely of handling.

Suggestions for Additional Reading

On aesthetics and the arts:

Monroe C. Beardsley, "The Definition of the Arts," *J.A.A.C.,* XX (1961), 175-187; T. M. Greene, *The Arts and the Art of Criticism* (Princeton, 1940); Susanne K. Langer, *Feeling and Form* (New York, 1953); Paul Weiss, *Nine Basic Arts* (Carbondale, Ill., 1961): Morris Weitz, *Philosophy of the Arts* (Cambridge, 1950); Virgil C. Aldrich, *Philosophy of Art* (Englewood Cliffs, N.J., 1963), Ch. 3.

On the nature of literature, especially poetry:

Lascelles Abercrombie, *The Theory of Poetry* (London, 1924); Owen Barfield, *Poetic Diction* (London, 1952); Monroe C. Beardsley, *Aesthetics* (New York, 1958), Chs. III, V, IX; Cleanth Brooks, *The Well Wrought Urn* (New York, 1947); Kenneth Burke, *The Philosophy of Literary Form* (Baton Rouge, La., 1941); A. E. Housman, *The Name and Nature of Poetry* (New York, 1933); Laurence Lerner, *The Truest Poetry* (London, 1960); Bernard Mayo, "Poetry, Language and Communication," *Philosophy,* XXXIX (1954), 131-145; Thomas C. Pollock, *The Nature of Literature* (Princeton, 1942); Ezra Pound, *ABC of Reading* (London, 1934); I. A. Richards, *Science and Poetry* (2nd. ed., London, 1935); Charles L. Stevenson, "On 'What is a Poem?,'" *Phil. Rev.,* LXVI (1957), 329-362; Allen Tate ed., *The Language of Poetry* (Princeton, 1942); René Wellek and Austin Warren, *Theory of Literature* (New York, 1949).

On music and its "meaning":

Monroe C. Beardsley, *Aesthetics* (New York, 1958), Ch. VII; Deryck Cooke, *The Language of Music* (London, 1959); Edmund Gurney, *The Power of Sound* (London, 1880); Paul Hindemith, *A Composer's World* (Cambridge, 1952); Susanne K. Langer, *Philosophy in a New Key* (Cambridge, 1942), Ch. VIII; Carroll C. Pratt, *The Meaning of Music* (New York, 1931); Roger Sessions, *The Musical Experience of Composer, Performer, Listener* (Princeton, 1950); J. W. N. Sullivan, *Beethoven: His Spiritual Development* (London, 1927; New York, 1949); Donald F. Tovey, *Essays in Musical Analysis* (New York, 1935-39), *The Forms of Music* (New York, 1956).

On the aesthetics of painting:

Albert C. Barnes, *The Art in Painting* (New York, 1937); Monroe C. Beardsley, *Aesthetics,* Ch. VI; Clive Bell, *Art* (London, 1914; New York, 1958); *Since Cézanne* (London, 1922); Bernard Berenson, *The Italian Painters of the Renaissance* (Oxford, 1930); Kenneth Clark, *Looking at Pictures* (London, 1960); Roger Fry, *Vision and Design* (London, 1920; New York, 1956), *Transformations* (London, 1926); Helen Knight, "Aesthetic Experience in Pictorial Art," *Monist,* XL (1930), 74-83; Erwin Panofsky, *Meaning in the Visual Arts* (New York, 1955); Paul Ziff, "On What a Painting Represents," *J. Phil.,* LVII (1960), 647-654; E. H. Gombrich, *Art and Illusion* (New York, 1960); Virgil C. Aldrich, "Picture Space," *Phil. Rev.,* LXVII (1958), 342-352; Rudolf Arnheim, *Art and Visual Perception* (Berkeley, 1954).

On sculpture:

Kenneth Clark, *The Nude: A Study of Ideal Form* (New York, 1956); J. C. Rich, *Materials and Methods of Sculpture* (New York, 1947); Auguste Rodin, *Art* (Boston, 1912).

On architecture:

Bruce Allsopp, *Art and the Nature of Architecture* (London, 1952); Robert Byron, *The Appreciation of Architecture* (London, 1932); W. R. Greeley, *The Essence of Architecture* (New York, 1927); Geoffrey Scott, *The Architecture of Humanism* (New York, 1925); H. R. Hitchcock, *Architecture* (Baltimore, 1958); F. L. Wright, *The Natural House* (New York, 1954).

IV

Expression, Creativity, Truth, and Form

Introduction

THE ESSAYS of this section attempt to clarify, occasionally to criticize, concepts of aesthetics such as expression, creativity, truth, fiction, and form.

Do works of art express emotions? Many aestheticians say that they do. Bouwsma examines this claim, not to show that it is true, or false, but to show what prompts it and to clarify the concept of expression.

"What goes on when a man creates a work of art?" is a question of psychology; "What do we mean when we speak of creative art?" is a question of philosophy. An answer to the second has nevertheless often been thought to entail an answer to the first. Tomas is interested in the second question, but he holds that when we speak of creative art, we have in mind certain general facts about the activity of creation.

Some philosophers contend that in writing fiction an author always says what is true; more contend that he always says what is false. Miss Macdonald demonstrates how a clarification of the concept of fiction leads to the view that fictional statements are neither true nor false.

May a work of fiction contain truths about the world? If a work of art can say nothing about the world or human behavior, then belief and disbelief are always inappropriate responses to art. Hospers contends that some works of literature at least contain putative truths; he attempts to show *how* they do. Isenberg, though he admits that there may be truths in literature, argues that belief is always *aesthetically* irrelevant and that the phenomena which belief and disbelief are invoked to explain can be accounted for without them.

Debates about the relative independence of form and content in art are of ancient origin. Weitz analyzes the form-content distinction in both nonaesthetic and aesthetic contexts and then argues that this distinction should be abandoned because it misrepresents the organic character of art.

Sibley maintains that a host of concepts applicable to art are not condition-governed; their use requires an exercise of taste.[1]

Note

1. In connection with Bouwsma's essay, see the selections from Tolstoy, Croce, and Mrs. Langer in Section I of this book; and from Hanslick in Section III. Relevant to the problem of creativity are the selections from Croce and Maritain in Section I and from Freud in Appendix C. The selection from Plato in Appendix A bears on the problems of truth and belief.

O. K. BOUWSMA

The Expression Theory of Art

THE EXPRESSION THEORY of art is, I suppose, the most commonly held of all theories of art. Yet no statement of it seems to satisfy many of those who expound it. And some of us find all statements of it baffling. I propose in what follows to examine it carefully. In order to do this, I want first of all to state the question which gives rise to the theory and then to follow the lead of that question in providing an answer. I am eager to do this without using the language of the expression theory. I intend then to examine the language of that theory in order to discover whether it may reasonably be interpreted to mean what is stated in my answer. In this way I expect to indicate an important ambiguity in the use of the word "expression," but more emphatically to expose confusions in the use of the word "emotion." This then may explain the bafflement.

I

And now I should like to describe the sort of situation out of which by devious turnings the phrase "expression of emotion" may be conceived to arise.

Imagine then two friends who attend a concert together. They go together untroubled. On the way they talk about two girls, about communism and pie on earth, and about a silly joke they once laughed at and now confess to each other that they never understood. They were indeed untroubled and so they entered the hall. The music begins, the piece ends, the applause intervenes, and the music begins again. Then comes the intermission and time for small talk. Octave, a naïve fellow, who loves music, spoke first. "It was lovely, wasn't it? Very sad music,

From *Philosophical Analysis,* edited by Max Black, Cornell University Press, Ithaca, N.Y. Copyright 1950 by Cornell University.

though." Verbo, for that was the other's name, replied: "Yes, it was very sad." But the moment he said this he became uncomfortable. He fidgeted in his seat, looked askance at his friend, but said no more aloud. He blinked, he knitted his brows, and he muttered to himself. "Sad music, indeed! Sad? Sad music?" Then he looked gloomy and shook his head. Just before the conductor returned, he was muttering to himself, "Sad music, crybaby, weeping willows, tear urns, sad grandma, sad, your grandmother!" He was quite upset and horribly confused. Fortunately, about this time the conductor returned and the music began. Verbo was upset but he was a good listener, and he was soon reconciled. Several times he perked up with "There it is again," but music calms, and he listened to the end. The two friends walked home together but their conversation was slow now and troubled. Verbo found no delight in two girls, in pie on earth, or in old jokes. There was a sliver in his happiness. At the corner as he parted with Octave, he looked into the sky, "Twinkling stars, my eye! Sad music, my ear!" and he smiled uncomfortably. He was miserable. And Octave went home, worried about his friend.

So Verbo went home and went to bed. To sleep? No, he couldn't sleep. After four turns on his pillow, he got up, put a record on the phonograph, and hoped. It didn't help. The sentence "Sad, isn't it?" like an imp, sat smiling in the loud-speaker. He shut off the phonograph and paced the floor. He fell asleep, finally, scribbling away at his table like any other philosopher.

This then is how I should like to consider the use of the phrase "expression of emotion." It may be thought of as arising out of such situations as that I have just described. The use of emotional terms—sad, gay, joyous, calm, restless, hopeful, playful, etc.—in describing music, poems, pictures, etc., is indeed common. So long as such descriptions are accepted and understood in innocence, there will be, of course, no puzzle. But nearly everyone can understand the motives of Verbo's question "How can music be sad?" and of his impulsive "It can't, of course."

Let us now consider two ways in which one may safely escape the expression theory.

Imagine Verbo at his desk, writing. This is what he now writes and this gives him temporary relief. "Every time I hear that music I hear that it's sad. Yet I persist in denying it. I say that it cannot be sad. And now what if I were wrong? If every day I met a frog, and the frog said to me that he was a prince, and that there were crown jewels in his head ('wears yet a precious jewel in his head'), no doubt I should begin by calling him a liar. But the more I'd consider this the more troubled I should be. If I could only believe him, and then treat him like a prince, I'd feel so much better. But perhaps *this* would be more like the case of this music: Suppose I met the frog and every day he said to me, 'I can talk,' and then went on talking and asked me, 'Can I talk?' then what would I do? And that's very much how it is with the music. I hear the music, and there it is again, sad, weeping. It's silly to deny this. See, now, how it is? There's a little prince, the soul of a prince, in the frog, and so there's the soul in this music, a princess, perhaps. See then how rude I was denying this princess her weeping. Why shouldn't music have a soul too? Why this prejudice in favour of lungs and livers? And it occurs to me that this is precisely how people have talked about music and poems. Art lives, doesn't it? And how did Milton describe a good book? Didn't Shelley pour out his soul? And isn't there soul and spirit in the music? I remember now that the poet Yeats recommended some such thing. There are spirits; the air is full of them. They haunt music, cry in it. They dance in poems, and laugh. Pan-psychism for the habitation of all delicacies! So this is how it is, and there is neither joke nor puzzle in this sad music. There's a sad soul in it."

And then it was that Verbo fell asleep. His resistance to the music had melted away as soon as he gave up his curious prejudice in favor of animal bodies, as soon as he saw that chords and tones, like rhymes and rhythms, may sigh and shed invisible tears. Tears without tear glands— oh, I know the vulgar habit! But surely tones may weep. Consider now how reasonable all this is. Verbo is suddenly surprised to discover something which he has always known, namely that music is sad. And the discovery startles him. Why? Because in connection with this, he thinks of his sister Sandra (Cassie to all who saw her cry). And he knows what her being sad is like. She sobs, she wipes her eyes, and she tells her troubles. Cassie has a soul, of course. So Cassie is sad and the music is sad. So the question for Verbo is "How can the music be like Cassie?" and he gives the answer "Why shouldn't there be a soul of the music, that flits in and flits out (People die too!) and inhabits a sonata for a half-hour? Or why shouldn't there be a whole troupe of them? 'The music is sad' is just like 'Cassie is sad,' after all. And Octave who was not disturbed was quite right for he must have a kind of untroubled belief in spirits. He believes in the frog-prince, in the nymphs in the wood, and in the psyche of the sonnet."

This then is one way of going to sleep. But there is another one, and it is based upon much the same sort of method. Both accept as the standard meaning for "The music is sad," the meaning of "Cassie is sad." We saw how Verbo came to see that the meaning is the same, and how then it was true in the case of the music. He might however have decided that the meaning was certainly the same, but that as applied to the music it simply made no sense at all, or was plainly false. Souls in sonnets! Don't be silly. There is the story about Parmenides, well-known to all readers of Dionoges,[1] which will illustrate the sort of thing I have in mind. According to the story, Parmenides and his finicky friend Zeno once went to a chariot race. The horses and chariots had been whizzing past and the race had been quite exciting. During the third round, at one turn a chariot broke an axle and horse and chariot and rider went through the fence. It was a marvelous exhibition of motion done to a turn at a turn. Parmenides was enjoying himself thoroughly. He clutched at the railing and shouted at the top of his voice, "Go, Buceph! Run!" The race is close. But at about the seventh round, with Buceph now some part of a parasang behind, Parmenides began to consider: "Half the distance in half the time; a quarter of the length of a horse in a quarter of the pace it takes. . . ." Suddenly, before the race was half over, Parmenides turned to Zeno. "Zeno," he said, "this is impossible." Zeno, who was ready for his master, retorted, "I quit looking a long time ago." So they left the chariot race, a little embarrassed at their nonexistence showing as they walked, but they did not once look back to see how Buceph was doing.

This then is the story about Parmenides. It may be, of course, that this story is not true; it may be one of Dionoges' little jokes. But our concern is not with Parmenides. The point is that it illustrates a certain way of disposing of puzzles. Parmenides has been disciplined to a certain use of such words as "run," "go," "turn," "walk," etc., so that when he is thoughtful and has all his careful wits about him, he never uses those words. He is then fully aware that all forms of motion are impossible. Nevertheless the eyes are cunning tempters. In any case as soon as Parmenides reflects, he buries himself in his tight-fitting vocabulary, and shuts out chariots and horses, and Buceph, as well. "Motion is impossible, so what am I doing here? Less than nothing. N'est pas is not." This disposition of the puzzle is, of course, open only to very strong men. Not many of those people who believe in the impossibility of motion are capable of leaving a horse race, especially when some fleet favorite is only a few heads behind.

Now something like this was a possibility also for Verbo. When, puzzled as he was, asking, "How can that be?" he hit upon the happy solution "Why not?" But he might surely have said, stamping his foot, "It can't be." And in order then to avoid the pain of what can't be, he might have sworn off music altogether. No more concerts, no more records! The more radical decision is in such cases more effective. One can imagine Parmenides, for instance, sitting out the race, with his eyes closed, and every minute blinking and squinting, hoping he'd see nothing. So too Verbo might have continued to listen to music, but before every hearing invigorating his resolution never to say that the music was sad. Success in this latter enterprise is not likely to be successful, and for anyone who has already been puzzled it is almost certainly futile.

We have now noticed two ways in which one may attempt to rid oneself of the puzzle concerning "The music is sad," but incidentally we have also noticed the puzzle. The puzzle is identified with the question "How can music be sad?" We have also noticed how easy it is, once having asked the question, to follow it with "Well, it can't." I want now to go on to consider the expression theory in the light of the question "How can it be?" In effect, the expression theory is intended to relieve people who are puzzled by music, etc. They listen and they say that the music is sad. They ask, troubled and shaking their heads, "How can it be?" Then along comes the expression theory. It calms them, saying, "Don't you see that the music expresses sadness and that this is what you mean by its being sad?" The puzzled one may be calmed too, if he isn't careful. In any case, I propose to consider the question "How can it be?" before going on further.

This question "How can it be?" is apparently then not a question primarily about the music. One listens to the music and hears all that there is to hear. And he is sure that it is sad. Nevertheless when he notices this and then returns to the music to identify just what is sad in it, he is baffled. If someone, for instance, had said that there is a certain succession of four notes on the flute, in this music, and he now sought to identify them, he could play the music, and when they came along, he would exclaim, "There they are," and that would be just what he aimed at. Or again if someone had said that a certain passage was very painful, and he explained that he meant by this that when it is heard one feels a stinging at one's finger tips, then again one could play the music and wait for the stinging. Neither is it like the question which leaped out of the surprise of the farmer at the birth of his first two-headed calf. He looked, amazed, and exclaimed, "Well, I'll be switched! How can that be?" He bedded the old cow, Janus, tucked in the calf, and went to consult his book. He did not stand muttering, looking at the calf, as Verbo did listening to the record on the phonograph. He took out his great book, *The Cow*, and read the chapter entitled "Two Heads Are Better than One?" He read statistics and something about the incidence of prenatal collusion and decided to keep an eye on collaborators among his herd. And that was all. When now it comes to "The music is sad," there's no such easy relief. What is there to listen for? What statistics are there?

We have noticed before how Verbo settled his difficulty. He did this, but not by examining the music further. He simply knew that the music was sad, and supplied the invisible tears, the unheard sobs, the soul of the music. If you had asked him to identify the tears, the unheard sobs, the soul of the music, he could not have done this. He might have tried, of course, and then he would have been baffled too. But the point is that he tries to think of the sadness of the music in the way in which he thinks of Cassie's sadness. Now we may be ready to explain the predicament, the bafflement. It arises from our trying to understand our use of the sentence "The music is sad" in terms of our uses of other sentences very much like this. So Verbo understands in terms of the sentence "Cassie is sad." One can imagine him saying to himself, "I know what sadness is, of course, having Cassie in the house, so that must be how it is with the music." Happily, as in the case of Parmenides, he thought of only one use, and as with a sharp knife he cut the facts to suit the knife. But suppose now that there are several uses of sentences much like "The music is sad"; what then? Is it like this use or this use or this use? And supposing sometimes it's like this and at other times like this, and sometimes like both. Suppose further that one is only vaguely aware that this is so, and that one's question "How can that be?" is not stated in such a way as to make this possibility explicit, would it then be any wonder that there is bafflement?

Let us admit then that the use of "The music is sad" is baffling, and that without some exploration, the question "How can that be?" cannot be dealt with. Merely listening to the music will not suffice. We must then explore the uses of other sentences which are or may be similar to this, and we may hope that in this process we may see the expression theory emerge. At any rate, we'll understand what we are about.

II

What now are some of these other types of sentences which might be helpful? Well, here are a few that might serve: "Cassie is sad," "Cassie's dog is sad," "Cassie's book is sad," "Cassie's face is sad." Perhaps, one or other of these will do.

Though we have already noticed how Verbo came to use "Cassie is sad," I should like to consider that sentence further. Verbo understood this. When, as he remembered so well, the telephone call came and little Cassie answered—she had been waiting for that call—she was hurt. Her voice had broken as she talked, and he knew that the news had been bad. But he did not think she would take it so hard. And when she turned to him and he asked her what the man had said, at first her chin quivered and she didn't speak. Then she moved towards him and fell into his arms, sobbing: "Poor Felicia, poor Felicia!" He stroked her hair and finally when she was calm, she began to pour out her confidences to him. She loved her cat so; they had been brought up together, had had their milk from the same bottle, and had kept no secrets from each other. And now the veterinary had called to say that she had had another fit. And she burst into tears again. This was some years ago. Cassie is older now.

But this is not the only way in which "Cassie is sad" is used. Verbo had often heard his father and mother remark that it was good that Cassie could cry. They used to quote some grandmother who made a proverb in the family. It went: "Wet pillows are best." She had made this up many years ago when some cousin came to sudden grief. This cousin was just on the verge of planned happiness, when the terrible news came. (Her picture is the third in the album.) She received the news in silence and never spoke of it or referred to it as long as she washed the dishes in her father's house, for, as you may have guessed, she never married. She never cried either. No one ever heard her sniffling in the middle of the night. She expressed no regrets. And she never told cat or mirror anything. Once she asked for a handkerchief, but she said she had a cold. All the family knew what had happened, of course, and everyone was concerned, but there was nothing to do. And so she was in many ways changed. She was drooping, she had no future, and she tried to forget her past. She was not interested. They all referred to her as their sad cousin, and they hoped that she would melt. But she didn't. Yet how can Cassie's cousin be sad if she never cries?

Well, there is a third use of "Cassie is sad." Tonight Cassie, who is eighteen now, quite a young lady, as the neighbours say, goes up to her room with her cat, her big book, and a great bowl of popcorn. She settles into her chair, tells kitty to get down, munches buttery corn, and reads her book. Before very long she is quite absorbed in what she reads and feels pretty bad. Her eyes fill with tears and the words on the page swim in the pool. It's so warm and so sweet and so sad! She would like to read this aloud, it's so wonderful, but she knows how the sadness in her throat would break her words in two. She's so sorry; she's so sad. She raises her eyes, closes them, and revels in a deep-drawn sigh. She takes up a full hand of popcorn and returns to her sadness. She reads on and eats no more corn. If she should sob in corn, she might choke. She does sob once, and quite loud, so that she is startled by it. She doesn't want to be heard sobbing over her book. Five minutes later she lays her book aside, and in a playful mood, twits her cat, pretending she's a little bird. Then, walking like old Mother Hubbard, she goes to the cupboard to get her poor cat a milk.

Cassie is sad, isn't she? Is she? Now that you consider it, she isn't really sad, is she? That cozy chair, that deliberate popcorn, that playing sparrow with her cat, that old Mother Hubbard walk—these are not the manners of a sad girl. She hasn't lost her appetite. Still one can see at once how we come to describe her in this way. Those are not phony tears, and she's as helpless in her sobs and in keeping her voice steady and clear as she was years ago when her dear cat had that fit. And she can, if you are so curious, show you in the book just what made her feel so sad. So you see it is very much like the case in which Cassie was sad. There's an obvious difference, and a similarity too. And now if you balk at this and don't want to say that Cassie in this situation is sad, your objection is intelligible. On the other hand if Cassie herself laughingly protests, "Oh, yes, I was sad," that will be intelligible too. This then may serve as an illustration of the way in which a puzzle which might become quite serious is fairly easily dealt with. How can Cassie be sad, eating popcorn and playing she's a sparrow?

In order to make this clear, consider Cassie now a grown woman, and an accomplished actress. She now reads that same passage which years ago left her limp as a willow, but her voice is steady and clear, and there are no tears. She understands what she reads and everyone says that she reads it with such feeling—it's so sad!—but there isn't a sign of emotion except for the reading itself, which as I said, goes along smoothly and controlled even to each breath and syllable. So there are no wet eyes, no drunken voice, and not a sob that isn't in the script. So there. Is she sad? I take it not. The spoken words are not enough. Tears, real tears, a voice that breaks against a word, sighs that happen to one, suffered sobs—when the reading occasions these, then you might say that Cassie was sad. Shall we say however, that the reading is sad? How can that be? Well, you see, don't you?

Let us now attend to a sentence of a different type: "Cassie's dog is sad." Can a dog be sad? Can a dog hope? Can a dog be disappointed? We know, of course, how a Cartesian would answer. He might very well reply with this question, "Can a locomotive be sad?" Generous, he might allow that a locomotive might look sad, and so give you the benefit of a sad look for your dog. But can a dog be sad? Well, our dog can. Once during the summer when Cassie left her for three weeks, you should have seen her. She wouldn't look at the meatiest bone. She'd hang her head and look up at you as woebegone as a cow. And she'd walk as though her four hearts would break. She didn't cry, of course, and there were no confidences except those touching ones that come by way of petting and snuggling and looking into those wailing eyes. In any case our dog acted very much like that sad cousin who couldn't cry. She had plenty of reason, much too much, but she kept her wellings-up down. It's clear in any case what I mean when I say that our dog was sad. You mustn't expect everything from a sad dog.

So we pass to another type of sentence: "Cassie's book is sad." Well, obviously books don't cry. Books do not remember happier days nor look upon hopes snuffed out. Still, books that are sad, must have something to do with sadness, so there must be sadness. We know, of course. Books make people sad. Cassie reads her book and in a few minutes if she's doing well, she's sad. Not really sad, of course, but there are real tears, and one big sob that almost shook the house. It certainly would be misleading to say that it was imaginary sadness, for the sadness of Cassie isn't imagined by anyone, not even by herself. What she reads on the other hand is imaginary. What she reads about never happened. In this respect it's quite different from the case in which she is overwhelmed by the sad news over the telephone. That was not imaginary, and with the tears and sobs there was worry, there was distress. She didn't go twittering about, pretending she was a little bird five minutes after that happened. So a sad book is a book that makes Cassie, for instance, sad. You ask, "Well, what are you crying about?" And she says, "Booh, you just read this." It's true that that is how you will find out, but you may certainly anticipate too that it will be a story about a little boy who died, a brave little boy who had stood up bravely for his father, about a new love and reconciliation come almost too late, about a parting of friends and tender feelings that will die, and so on. At any rate, if this is what it is like, you won't be surprised. It's a sad book.

There is one further sentence to consider: "Cassie's face is sad." The same sort of thing might be said about her speaking, about her walk, about her eyes, etc. There is once again an obvious way of dealing with this. What makes you say her face is sad? Anyone can tell. See those tear stains and those swollen eyes. And those curved lines, they all turn down. Her face is like all those sad faces in simple drawings where with six strokes of my neighbor's pencil I give you "Sad-Eye, the Sorry Man." The sad face is easily marked by these few unmistakable signs. Pull a sad face, or droop one, and then study it. What have you done? In any case, I am supposing that there is another use of "Cassie's face is sad," where this simplicity is absent. Oh, yes, there may be certain lines, but if you now ask, "And is this all you mean by Cassie's face being sad," the answer may very well be "No." Where then is the sadness? Take a long look and tell me. Cassie, hold still. The sadness is written all over her face, and I can't tell you it's here and not there. The more I look, the more I see it. The sadness in this case is not identified with some gross and simple signs. And you are not likely to find it there in some quick glance. Gaze into that face, leisurely, quietly, gently. It's as though it were composed not of what is sad in all sad faces, but rather of what is sad only in each sad face you've ever known. This sad face is sad but when you try now to tell someone what is sad in it, as you might with the drawing I made, you will have nothing to say. But you may say, "Look, and you will see." It is clear, of course, that when Cassie's face is sad, she need not be sad at all. And certainly when you look as you do, you need not be sad.

We have noticed briefly several types of sentences similar to "The music is sad," and we have seen how in respect to several of these the same sort of puzzling might arise that arose in respect to "The music is sad." We have also seen how in respect to these more obvious cases this puzzling is relieved. The puzzling is relieved by discerning the similarity between the offending use and some other use or uses. And now I should like to ask whether the puzzle concerning "The music is sad" might not also be relieved in some similar fashion. Is there not a use of some type of sentence, familiar and relatively untroubled, which is like the use of "The music is sad"?

We have these types of sentences now ready at our disposal: There are two uses of "Cassie is sad," in the first of which she is concerned about her cat, and in the second of which she is cozy and tearful, reading her book. We have "Cassie's cousin is sad," in which Cassie's cousin has real cause but no tears, and "Cassie's dog is sad," in which her dog is tearless as her cousin, but with a difference of course. You could scarcely say that Fido restrained his tears. Then there were the uses of "Cassie's face is sad" and "Cassie's reading is sad." And, of course, there is the use of "Cassie's book is sad." I am going to take for granted that these uses are also intelligible. Now then is the use of "The music is sad" similar to any of these?

I suppose that if the question is stated in this way, one might go on by pointing out a similarity between it and each one of these other types of sentences. But what we must discover is enough similarity, enough to relieve the puzzle. So the question is: To which use is the use of "The music is sad" most similar? Certainly not to "Cassie is sad (about her cat)," nor to "Cassie's cousin is sad," nor to "Cassie's dog is sad."

There are two analogies that one may hopefully seize upon. The first is this: "Cassie is sad, reading a book," is very much like "Verbo is sad, listening to music." And this first is also very much like "Cassie is sad, hearing the news over the telephone." And just as the first involves "The book is sad," so the second involves "The music is sad," and the third involves "The news is sad." Now let us consider the first. Reading the book is one thing, and feeling sad is quite another, and when you say that the book is sad, you mean by this something like this: When Cassie reads, she feels sad about what she reads. Her feeling sad refers to her tears, her sobs, etc. So too listening to the music and hearing it is one thing, and feeling sad is another, and when you say that the music is sad, you mean that while Verbo listens to the music, he feels sad. And shall we add that he feels sad about it? This might, if you like, refer to something like his half-tears, sub-sobs, etc.

Suppose now we try to relieve Verbo in this way. We say, "Don't you see? 'This music is sad' is like 'The book is sad.' You understand that. That's very much like 'The news is sad.'" Will that satisfy him? I think that if he is very sharp, it won't. He may say, "I can see how 'The book is sad' is like 'The news is sad.' But when it comes to these you can easily point out the disturbance, the weeping, but the music—that's different. Still there might be something." What now bothers him?

I think what bothers him may be explained in this way. When you say that a book is sad, or a certain passage in a book is sad, you may mean one or other or both of two things. You may mean what has already been defined by the analogy above. But you may also mean something else. The following illustration may exhibit this. Imagine Cassie, then, in her big chair, reading, and this is the passage she reads:

"I say this in case we become bad," Alyosha went on, "but there's no reason why we should become bad, is there, boys? Let us be, first and above all, kind, then honest, and let us never forget each other! I say that again. I give you my word, for my part, that I'll never forget one of you. Every face looking at me now I shall remember even for thirty years. Just now Kolya said to Kartashov that he did not care to know whether he exists or not. But I cannot forget that Kartashov exists and that he is blushing now as he did when he discovered the founders of Troy, but is looking at me with his jolly, kind, dear little eyes. Boys, my dear boys, let us all be generous and brave like Ilusha, clever, brave and generous like Kolya (though he will be ever so much cleverer when he grows up), and let us all be as modest, as clever and sweet as Kartashov. But why am I talking about those two! You are all dear to me, boys, from this day forth I have a place in my heart for you all, and I beg you to keep a place in your hearts for me! Well, and who has united us in this kind, good feeling which we shall remember, and intend to remember all our lives? Who, if not Ilusha, the good boy, the dear boy, precious to us forever! Let us never forget him. May his memory live forever in our hearts from this time forth."

Cassie reads this and Cassie cries. Let us call this Cassie's sadness. But is there now any other emotion, any other sadness, present? Well, there may very well be. There may be the Alyosha emotion. Whether that is present however depends upon how the passage in question is read. It may be read in such a way, that though Cassie understands all she reads, and so knows about the Alyosha emotion, yet she will miss it. This will be the case if she cries through the reading of it. If she reads the passage well, controlled, clear, unfalteringly, with feeling, as we say, which does not mean with crying, then the Alyosha emotion will be present. Other-wise only signs of it will be present. Anyone who has tried to read such a passage well, and who has sometimes failed and sometimes succeeded, will understand what I have in mind. Now then we have distinguished the Cassie emotion and the Alyosha emotion. They may be present to-gether, but only, I think, when the Cassie emotion is relatively weak. And so when someone says that the passage in question is sad, then in order to understand we must ask, "Is it sad in the Cassie emotion or is it sad in the Alyosha emotion?"

And now we are prepared again to examine the analogy: "The music is sad" is like "The book is sad," where it is sad with the Alyosha emotion. This now eliminates the messiness of tears. What we mean by Alyosha's emotion involves no tears, just as the sadness of the music in-volves no tears. And this now may remind us of Cassie reading the passage, cool, collected, reading with feeling. But more to the point it suggests the sentence "Cassie's face is sad." For see, when the music is sad, there are no tears, and when the passage is read, well read, there are no tears. And so when I look into this face and find it sad, there are no tears. The sadness in all these cases may be unmistakable, and yet in none of these is there anything to which I might now draw your at-tention, and say, "That's how I recognize it as sad." Even in the case of the reading, it isn't the sentences, it isn't the subject, that make it sad. The sadness is in the reading. Like a musical score, it too may be played without feeling. And it isn't now as though you both read and have these feelings. There is nothing but the reading, and the feeling is nothing apart from this. Read the passage with and without feeling, and see that the difference consists in a difference in the reading. What baffles in these cases is that when you use the word "sadness" and the phrase "with feeling," you are certain to anticipate sadness and feeling in the ordinary sense. But if the sadness is in the sounds you make, reading or playing, and in the face, once you are forewarned you need no longer anticipate anything else. There is sadness which is heard and sadness which is seen.

This then is my result. "The music is sad" is like "the book is sad," where "The book is sad" is like "The face is sad." But "The music is sad" is sometimes also like "The book is sad," where "The book is sad" is like "The news is sad." If exhibiting these analogies is to be helpful, then, of course, this depends on the intelligibility of such sentences as "The book is sad," "The face is sad," "The news is sad," etc.

III

So far I have tried to do two things. I have tried to state the problem to which the expression theory is addressed, and then I have gone on to work at the solution of that problem in the way in which this statement of the problem itself suggests that it be worked out. In doing this I have sought deliberately to avoid the language of the expression theory.

Here then is the phrase to be studied. The expression theory maintains: The music is sad means: The music is the expression of sadness or of a certain sadness. The crucial word is the word "expression." There are now at least two contexts which determine the use of that word, one is the language of emotion, and the other is the language of or about language.

Let us consider first the use of the word "expression" in the language of emotion. In the discussion of the types of sentences above, it will be remembered that Cassie's cousin is sad, but doesn't cry. She does not "express" her emotion. Cassie on the other hand carries on, crying, sobbing, and confiding in everyone. She "expresses" her emotion, and the expression of her emotion is tears, noises, talk. That talk is all about her cat, remember. When she reads her book, she carries on in much the same way. In this latter case, there was some question as to whether there was really any emotion. She was so sad, remember, and ate popcorn. But in terms of what we just now said, whether there is emotion or not, there certainly is "expression" of emotion. These tears are just as wet as other tears, and her sobs are just as wet too. So in both cases there is expression of emotion, and in the first case there is emotion, thick as you please, but in the second case, it's not that thick. It appears then that you might find it quite natural to say that there is expression of emotion but no emotion, much as you might say that there was the thought of an elephant, but no elephant. This may not seem so strange, however, if we reflect that as in the case of Cassie's cousin, there may be emotion, but no or very little expression of emotion.

In order to probe the further roots of the uses of this phrase, it may be useful to notice that the language of emotion is dominantly the language of water. So many of our associations with the word "emotion" are liquid. See then: Emotions well up. Children and young girls bubble over. There are springs of emotion. A sad person is a deep well. Emotions come in waves; they are like the tides; they ebb and flow. There are floods and "seas of passion." Some people gush; some are turbulent. Anger boils. A man blows up like a boiler. Sorrow overwhelms. The dear girl froze. We all know the theory of humors. In any case, it is easy enough, in this way, to think of a human being as like a reservoir and an ever flowing pool and stream of emotions. All flow on toward a dam, which may be raised or lowered, and over and through which there is a constant trickle. Behind the dam are many currents, hot, cold, luke-warm, swift, slow, steady, rippling, smooth. And there are many colors. Perhaps we should say that currents are never exhausted and do not altogether trickle away. Emotions, like our thoughts, are funded, ready to be tapped, to be rippled, to be disturbed.

Let us see how the term "expression" fits into this figure. How was it with Cassie's cousin? Well, once there was a clear, smoothflowing cur-rent of affection, and it flowed, trickle, trickle, over the dam in happy anticipation and a chestful of hope's kitchen and linen showers. And suddenly a planet falls, in the form of a letter, into that deep and flowing pool. Commotion follows, waves leap, eddies swirl. The current rushes on to the dam. And what happens? The dam rises. Cassie's cousin resists, bites her lip, intensifies her fist. She keeps the current back. Her grief is impounded. She does not "express" her emotion. And what hap-pens to Cassie, when she felt so bad about the cat? That's easy. Then too there was a disturbance. The current came down, splashed over the dam which did not rise at all, and it flowed away in a hurly-burly of "Oh! It's awful! My poor kitty!" Cassie let herself go. She "expressed" her emotion.

The use of the word "expression" in the light of this figure is, I take it, clear enough. And the use of the word in this way describes a familiar difference in the way in which good news and bad news may affect us. And now we may ask, "And is it something like this that people have in mind when they say that art is the expression of emotion?" Certainly something like this, at least part of the time. Consider how Wordsworth wrote about poetry: "Poetry is the spontaneous overflow of powerful emotions." Overflow! This suggests the pool and the dam and the "power-ful" current. An emotion, lying quiet, suddenly gets going and goes over. There is spontaneity, of course. No planet falls and no cat is sick. The emotion is unprovoked. There is also the common view that artists are people who are more emotional than other people. They are temperamental. This once again suggests the idea that they have particular need of some overflow. Poetry is a little like blowing off steam. Write poetry or explode!

This isn't all that Wordworth said about poetry. In the same context he said: "Poetry is emotion recollected in tranquility." Again this suggests a hiding place of emotion, a place where past heartaches are stored, and may be taken up again, "recollected." We store ideas. We also put away emotions. So we have the pool as we had the pool before in describing Cassie's cousin and Cassie. But now we have something else, "the spontaneous overflow" and the "recollection in tranquility."

Let us consider this for a moment, again in order to notice the use of the word "expression." Cassie hears bad news and cries. She "expresses" her emotion. The emotion is aroused and out it flows. What now happens in the case of the poet? Ostensibly in his case too emotions are aroused, but they do not flow out. Poets do not cry enough. Emotions are stored up, blocked. Emotions accumulate. And what happens now? Well, one of two things may happen. Emotions may quite suddenly leap up like spray, and find a way out, or again a poet may dip into the pool with his word dipper, and then dip them out. It's as though the emotions come over the dam in little boats (the poems) and the little boats may be used over and over again to carry over new surges. And this too may be described in this way: The poet "expresses" his emotion. Cassie cries. The real incident is sufficient. The poet does not cry. The real incident is not sufficient. He's got to make poems in order to cry. All men must cry. This may seem a bit fantastic, but this sort of phantasy is common in explaining something as old, for instance, as Aristotle's use of the word "catharsis."

The analogy which we have tried to exhibit now is this one: As Cassie "expresses" her emotion at hearing the news, so the poet or reader "expresses" his emotion at reading the poem. The news and the poem arouse or evoke the respective emotions. Now most people who expound the expression theory are not content with this analogy. They say that Cassie merely vents or discharges her emotion. This is not "expression" of emotion. Cassie merely gets rid of her emotion. And what does the poem do? Perhaps in terms of our figure we may say: It ripples it, blows a gentle wind over it, like a bird skimming the water. At any rate the emotion stays. And so the theory seeks a more suitable analogy and finds it conveniently in the language about language.

I should like first to notice certain distinctions which lead to this shift from the first to the second analogy. In the first place poems and music are quite different from the occasions that make Cassie and Cassie's cousin so sad. Tones on a piano and a faithless lover or dying cat are not much alike, and this is enough to disturb the analogy. But there is also an unmistakable difference in the use of the word "emotion" in the two cases. An "emotion recollected in tranquility" is, after all, as I suggested before, more like a ripple than like a tempest. It is, accordingly, these distinctions that determine the shift. It may be useful to notice that the general form of the first analogy is retained in the second. For the poem and the music are still conceived as "arousing," as "evoking," the emotion.

The new analogy accordingly is this one: Music "expresses" sadness (art expresses emotion) as sentences "express" ideas. And now, I think, it is easy to see why this analogy should have been seized upon. In the first place so much of art involves symbols, sentences themselves, and representations. There are horses in pictures. It is quite easy then to fall into regarding art as symbolic, that is, as like sentences. And now just as sentences symbolize ideas and serve to evoke them as distinguished from real things, of which ideas are more like shadows, so too music and poems serve to evoke emotions of a peculiar sort, emotions which are like the shadows of real emotions. So this analogy is certainly an improvement. Art is after all an artifice, like sentences, and the emotions involved are related to the real things in much the way that ideas are to real things, faint copies. All this fits in very well with the idea that art is like a dream, a substitute of real life, a vicarious more of what you cannot have, a shadowland.

And now how does this analogy succeed?

Before answering this question, I should like to notice the use of the words "evoking" and "arousing." Sentences "evoke" ideas. As one spieler I know, says: "When I read a sentence, an idea pops into my head." Pops! This is something like what, according to the analogy, is meant by sentences "expressing" ideas. I am not interested in criticizing this at this point. I wish only to clarify ideas. Pop! Consider the sentence "The elephant ate a jumbo peanut." If at the moment that you read this sentence you see in your mind's eye a big elephant nuzzling around a huge peanut, this will illustrate what "evoking" is like. The sentence evokes; the idea pops. There is the sentence and there is this unmistakable seeing in your mind's eye. And if this happened, surely you would have got the idea. What I wish to point out is that it is this view or some similar view of how sentences work, that underlies this present analogy. They "evoke." But the word "evoke" has other contexts. It suggest spirits, witchcraft. The spirit of Samuel appearing at the behest of the witch of Endor is an "evocation." Spiritualistic mediums "evoke" the living spirits of the dead. And the point of this association is that the spirits are waiting, in the second or third canto of Dante's *Comedy*, perhaps, to be called. They are in storage like our ideas, like our emotions. And the word "arouse" is like the word "evoke." Whom do you arouse? The sleeper. And so, sleeping ideas and sleeping emotions lie bedded in that spacious dormitory—hush!—we call the mind. Waiting to be called! And why now have I made a point of this? Because this helps to fill out this analogy by which in particular we are led to use the word "feeling" or "emotion" in the language of the expression theory. The music "evokes," "arouses" feelings.

The difficulty then does not arise concerning experiences of this sort. The puzzle arises and remains most stubbornly where the sadness is dry-eyed. And here the analogy with language seems, at least, to be of no use. Cassie may read the passage with feeling, but without the flicker of an eyelash. And she may listen to sad music as cool and intent as she is gazing at a butterfly. She might say that it was more like watching, fascinated, the pain in a suffering face, herself quite undistressed. Santayana identifies the experience in this way: "Not until I confound the impression (the music; the sentences) and suffuse the symbols with the emotions they arouse, and find joy and sweetness in the very words I hear, will the expressiveness constitute a beauty. . . ."² I propose now to study this sentence.

Now notice how curious this is. Once more we have the sentences or the music. And these arouse emotions. This describes Cassie reading her book. So we might expect that Cassie would cry and would sob and so on. But this isn't all. Cassie is confused. Actually she is crying but she thinks the words are crying. She wipes her tears off those words. She sighs but the words heave. The sentence of Santayana suggests that she sees the sentences she reads through her tears and now her tears misserve her much as blue moods or dark glasses do. So Cassie looks through sadness and the sentence is tearful. What a pathetic fallacy! From confusion to suffusion! Are there misplaced emotions? Imagine what this would be like where sentences aroused not emotions but a toothache. And now you confused the toothache with the sentence, and before someone prevented you, you sent the sentence to the dentist.

Nevertheless, Santayana has almost certainly identified an experience that is different from that in which Cassie is sad over her book. We find "joy and sweetness in the very words" we hear. Certainly, too, Santayana has been misled by these words "joy and sweetness." For if there is joy and sweetness, where should these be but where they usually are? Where is joy then and where is sweetness? In the human breast, in the heart ("my heart leaps up when I behold"), in the eye. And if you say this, then indeed there must be some illusion. The sentence is like a mirror that catches and holds what is in the heart. And so artful are poets' sentences that the best readers are the best confused. I want now, however, to suggest that indeed joy and sweetness, and sadness too, are in the very words you hear. But in that case, joy and sweetness must be of the sort that can be in sentences. We must, accordingly, try to figure out what this "joy and sweetness in the very words" is like. For even though, making a mistake, one imagined they were in the words, their being there must make some sense. And Santayana too does not imagine that sentences cry.

Let me return now to the analogy: The music is sad is like: The sentence expresses an idea. We saw before how the sentence "The elephant ate a jumbo peanut" might be accompanied by an image and how this was like sentences or music arousing emotions. We want now to see how we might use the phrase "joy and sweetness in the very words." Do we have a meaning for "The idea in the very words you hear." Where is the idea of the elephant eating a jumbo peanut? Suppose we say, "It's in the very words you hear." Have you ever seen, in your mind's eye, that is, an elephant eating a peanut in the very words you hear? A sentence is like a circus tent? I do not suppose that anyone who said that joy and sweetness are in the very words you hear would be likely to say that this was like the way in which you might also see an image in the very sentence which you hear—a bald head in the word "but." I should like in any case to try something different.

I do not intend to abandon the analogy with language yet. Music is expression of emotion as sentences are expression of ideas. But now how do sentences express ideas? We have noticed one way in which sentences do sometimes have meaning. Sentences, however, have been described in many ways. Sentences are like buzzers, like doorbells, like electric switches. Sentences are like mirrors, like maps, like pictures; sentences are like road signs, with arrows pointing the way. And so we might go on to ask, "Is music like buzzers, like pictures, like road sign arrows?" I do not however intend to do this. It will be noticed that the same analogy by which we have been trying to understand music, art, etc., may serve us also to understand what language is like. The analogy pre-supposes that we do know something about music, and so turning the analogy to this use may be fruitful. It might show us just how enlightening and how unenlightening the analogy is.

In order to study the analogy between music and the sentence and to try in this way to find out what the sentence is like, I now intend to offer a foolish theory. This may throw into clearer relief what Santayana says. What is understanding a sentence like? Understanding a sentence is speaking the sentence in a certain way. You can tell, listening to your- self talk, that you are understanding the sentence, and so can anyone else who hears you speak. Understanding has its rhythm. So the meaning of the sentence consists in a certain reading of the sentence. If, in this case, a sentence is spoken and not understood by someone, there would be only one thing to do, namely, speak the sentence again. Obviously this account will not do for there are other ways of clarifying what we mean. Nevertheless in some cases it may be all that is necessary.

Now notice. If this were what the meaning of a sentence is like, we should see at once what was meant if someone said that the meaning or the idea is in the sentence. For if there is meaning, where could it be but in the sentence, since the sentence is all there is. Of course, it is true that the sentence would have to be spoken and, of course, spoken in some way or other. And with every variation in reading it might then be said to have a different meaning. If anyone asked, "And what does the sen- tence mean?" expecting you to point to something or to elaborate the matter in gestures or to translate, it would be clear that he quite mis-understood what meaning is like. One might even correct him, saying it is even misleading to say that the meaning is in the sentence, as though it were only a part of the sentence, or tucked away somehow under over-lapping syllables. A sentence having meaning in a case like this would be something like a living thing. Here too one might ask, "Where is the life in a squirrel and in a geranium?" Truly the life is the squirrel and is the geranium and is no part of either nor tucked away in some hidden fold or tiny vein. And so it is with the sentence, according to our imagi-nary theory. We might speak of the sentence as like a living thing.

And now let us see whether we have some corresponding use for "The joy and sweetness are in the very words you hear." People do ask about the meaning of poems and even about the meaning of music. Let us first of all say that the meaning is "the joy and sweetness," and the sadness. And where are these? In the very words you hear, and in the music. And now notice that what was admittedly a foolish theory in respect to sen-tences is not a foolish theory in respect to poems or music. Do you get the poem? Do you get the music? If you do not, pointing, gestures, trans-lations will not help. (Understanding the words is presupposed.) There will be only one thing to do, namely, read the verses again, play the music once more. And what will the joy and sweetness and the sadness be like? They will be like the life in the living thing, not to be distin-guished as some one part of the poem or music and not another part, or as some shadow that follows the sounded words or tones. "In the very words you hear," like the squirrel in fur!

I infer now that the analogy between the "joy and sweetness" in words and the meaning in sentences is misleading and is not likely to be help-ful. The meaning of sentences is translatable, but the "meaning" of poems, of music is not. We have seen how this is so. There may, of course, be something in the sounding of all sentences which is analogous to the "joy and sweetness in the very words," but it is not the meaning of those sentences. And now this is an interesting consequence. It makes sense to ask, "What does the sentence express?" It expresses a meaning, of course, and you may have some way of showing what this is, without using the sentence to do so. But it now makes no sense to ask, "What does the poem express?" or "What does the music express?" We may say, if we like, that both are expressive, but we must beware of the analogy with language. And we may prevent the helpless searching in this case, by insisting that they "express" nothing, nothing at all.

And now let us review. My assumption has been that the expression theory is plagued with certain analogies that are not clearly distinguished, and none of which finally is helpful without being misleading. The first analogy is that in terms of which we commonly think of emotions. The second is that in terms of which we think of language, the doorbell view. Besides this there are two different types of experience that arise in connection with art. One of these types may be fairly well described by the analogy with doorbell language. The similarity of our language, however, in respect to both these types of experience, conceals the difference between those two types. Santayana's sentence reveals the agony that follows the recognition of this difference in these types of experience and the attempt to employ the language which describes the one to describe the other. The language requires very interesting translation. My conclusion, accordingly is this: The analogy drawn from language may be useful in describing one type of experience. It is practically useless in describing the other. Since, then, these two analogies dominate the use of the word "expression," I suggest that, for the sake of clarity and charity, they be abandoned in seeking to describe that "expressiveness" which Santayana says constitutes "a beauty."

If we now abandon these analogies, are we also to abandon the use of the word "expression"? Not unless we please to do so. But we do so at our risk, for these analogies are not easily abandoned. We may, however, fortify our use of this word by considerations such as these. We use the word "expressive" to describe faces. And we use "expressive" in much the same way that we use the phrase "has character." A face that is expressive "has character." But when we now say that a face has character, this may remind us that the letters of the alphabet are characters. Let us suppose for a moment that this is related to "He's a character!" I suppose that he's a character and he has a character do not mean quite the same thing. There are antics in he's a character. Try again: The zigzag line has character and the wavy line has character. Each letter of the alphabet is a character, but also has character. The number tokens, 1 2 3 4 5 6 7 8 9—each has its character. In the same way sounds have character. Let me see whether we can explain this further. You might say that if some dancing master were to arrange a dance for each of the numbers, you might see how a dance for the number one would not do at all for number five. Or again if the numbers were to be dressed in scarfs, again a certain color and a certain flimsy material would do for six but would not suit five at all. Now something of the same sort is true of words, and particularly of some. Words have character. I am tempted to say that all these things have their peculiar feel, but this then must be understood on the analogy with touch. If we, for instance, said that all these things have their peculiar feeling, then once again it might be supposed that in connection with them there is a feeling which is aroused by them.

Let your ears and your eyes, perhaps, too, feel these familiar bits of nonsense:

> Hi diddle diddle!
> Feel fi, fo, fum!
> Intery, mintery.
> Abra ca da bra.

Each has its character. Each is, in this sense, expressive. But to ask now "What is its character or what does it express?" is to fall into the pit. You may, of course, experiment to exhibit more clearly just what the character, in each case, is. You may, for instance, contrast the leaping, the stomping, the mincing, the shuffle, with what you get if you change the vowels. Try:

Ho! doodle doodle!
Fa, fo, fu, fim!
Untery, muntery.
Ay bray cay day bray.

One also might go on to change consonants in order again to exhibit character by giving the words new edges and making their sides steeper or smoothing them down.

I do not intend, in proposing illustrations of this sort, to suggest that art is nonsense and that its character is simple as these syllables are. A face, no doubt may bear the impress, the character, of a life's torment and of its hope and victory. So too words and phrases may come blazing out of the burning past. In art the world is born afresh, but the travail of the artist may have had its beginnings in children's play. My only point is that once the poem is born it has its character as surely as a cry in the night or intery, mintery. And this character is not something that follows it around like a clatter in a man's insides when he reads it. The light of the sun is in the sun, where you see it. So with the character of the poem. Hear the words and do not imagine that in hearing them you gulp a jigger to make yourself foam. Rather suppose that the poem is as hard as marble, ingrained, it may be, with indelible sorrow.

If, accordingly, we now use the sentence "Art is expression," or "Art is expressive," and the use of this sentence is determined by elucidations such as I have just now set out, then, I think, that our language may save us from some torture. And this means that we are now prepared to use freely those sentences that the expression theory is commonly inclined to correct. For now, unabashed, we shall say that the music is sad, and we shall not go on to say that this means that the music expresses sadness. For the sadness is to the music rather like the redness to the apple, than it is like the burp to the cider. And above all we shall not, having heard the music or read the poem, ask, "What does it express?"

IV

And now it's many words ago since we left Verbo and his friend at the corner. Verbo was trying to figure out, you remember, how the music was related to his grandmother. How can music be sad? I suggested then that he was having word trouble, and that it would be necessary to probe his sentences. And so we probed. And now what shall we tell Verbo?

Verbo, we will say, the music is sad. And then we will remind him that the geranium is living, and that the sun is light. We will say these things so that he will not look away from the music to discover the sadness of it. Are you looking for the life in the geranium? Are you looking for the light in the sun? As then the life and the light describe the geranium and the sun, so too does sadness describe the music. And then we shall have to go on to tell him about these fearful analogies, and about Santayana's wrestle on the precipice. And about how we cut the ropes! And you may be sure that just as things are going along so well, Verbo will ask, flicking the ashes from his cigarette, "And what about the sadness?"

And now it's time to take the cat out of the bag, for so far all that has been exposed is the bag. The sadness is a quality of what we have already described as the character, the expressive. One piece of music is like and unlike some other pieces of music. These similarities and these differences may be perceived. Now then, we have a class of sad music. But why sad, that is, why use this word? It must be remembered, of course, that the use of this word is not precise. So there may be some pieces of music which are unmistakably sad, and others which shade off in gradations to the point where the question "Is it sad?" is not even asked. Suppose we ask our question "Why sad?" in respect to the unmistakable cases. Then, perhaps, some such answer as this will do. Sad music has some of the characteristics of people who are sad. It will be slow, not tripping: it will be low, not tinkling. People who are sad move more slowly, and when they speak, they speak softly and low. Associations of this sort may, of course, be multiplied indefinitely. And this now is the kitten in whose interest we made so much fuss about the bag. The kitten has, I think, turned out to be a scrawny little creature, not worth much. But the bag was worth it.

The bag was worth it? What I have in mind is that the identification of music as the expressive, as character, is crucial. That the expressive is sad serves now only to tag the music. It is introspective or, in relation to the music, an aside. It's a judgment that intervenes. Music need not be sad, nor joyous, nor anything else. Aestheticians usually account for this by inventing all sorts of emotions without names, an emotion for every piece of music. Besides, bad music, characterless music, the unexpressive, may be sad in quite the same way that good music may be. This is no objection, of course, to such classifications. I am interested only in clarifying the distinction between our uses of these several sentences.

And now that I have come to see what a thicket of tangle-words I've tried to find my way through, it seems to me that I am echoing such words as years ago I read in Croce, but certainly did not then understand. Perhaps if I read Croce again now I shouldn't understand them either. "Beauty is expression."

Notes

1. An author of no repute at all, not to be confused with Diogenes.
2. *The Sense of Beauty* (1896), p. 149.

VINCENT TOMAS

Creativity in Art

WHEN A RIFLEMAN AIMS at his target, he knows what he wants to do. He wants to hit the bull's-eye. Before he shoots, he knows what the target is; he knows that the black circle in the center of it is the bull's-eye; and he knows that hitting the bull's-eye consists in causing a bullet to pass through that black circle. He also knows, before he has squeezed the trigger, that if, after he has squeezed it, a hole appears in the black circle, he will have succeeded in doing what he wanted to do; and that if there isn't a hole there, he will have failed.

Furthermore, the rifleman knows what he ought to do to hit the bull's-eye. He knows what position he ought to assume, how he ought to adjust the sling, where exactly he ought to place his left hand, where he ought to place the butt so that it fits his shoulder and cheek, what the sight picture ought to be, how he ought to exhale a little and then hold his breath when the sight picture is correct, and how he ought to squeeze off the shot without knowing exactly when the explosion will come, so that he won't flinch until after it is too late to spoil his aim.

If, after the rifleman has attempted to obey all these rules, he fails to hit the bull's-eye, any sergeant can tell him, and the rifleman will agree, that he did fail; and that, since he did, he had not obeyed all the rules. For, if he had obeyed them, there necessarily would have been a hole in the bull's-eye. If, on the other hand, he does hit the bull's-eye, the white disc is displayed and the rifleman is congratulated. He is congratulated, whether the people who congratulate him realize it or not, for having been able to learn and obey all the rules.

When we congratulate an artist for being creative, however, it is not because he was able to obey rules that were known before he painted his picture or wrote his novel or poem, so that thereby he succeeded in doing what had been done before. We congratulate him because he embodied in colors or in language something the like of which did not exist before,

Reprinted from *The Philosophical Review,* Vol. LXVII (1958).

and because he was the originator of the rules he implicitly followed while he was painting or writing. Afterwards, others may *explicitly* follow the same rules and thereby achieve similar successes. But the academic painter or writer is like the rifleman. He, too, aims at a known target, and he hits his bull's-eye by obeying known rules. As Sir Joshua Reynolds wrote:

> By studying carefully the works of great masters, this advantage is obtained; we find that certain niceties of expression are capable of being executed, which otherwise we might suppose beyond the reach of art. This gives us a confidence in ourselves; and we are thus incited to endeavor at not only the same happiness of execution, but also at other congenial excellencies. Study indeed consists in learning to see nature, and may be called the art of using other men's minds.[1]

Unlike either the rifleman or the academic painter or writer, the creative artist does not initially know what his target is. Although he seems to himself to be "aiming" at something, it is not until just before he affixes his signature or seal of approval to his work that he finds out that *this* was the way to bring it into being. Creative activity in art, that is to say, is not a paradigm of purposive activity, that is, of activity engaged in and consciously controlled so as to produce a desired result. In the paradigmatic case, the agent envisages the result he desires to produce and has it consciously in view, and he believes that if he acts in a certain way the result desired will be produced. Although we may say that his activity is "teleologically controlled," to explain it we do not appeal to a final cause, but only to an efficient cause, namely, to his desire for the result he envisages and his beliefs. But when he is impelled to engage in creative activity, the artist, as has been said, does not already envisage the final result. He does not therefore already have an idea or image of it. And his activity therefore is not "controlled," as in the paradigm case, by a desire for an envisaged result and beliefs about how to obtain it.

If, however, creative activity differs from clear-cut cases of purposive activity in the ways mentioned, it resembles purposive activity in other ways. As has been said, the creative artist has a sense that his activity is directed—that it is heading somewhere. Now the cash value of the statement that the artist has a sense of being engaged in a directed activity, of going somewhere despite the fact that he cannot say precisely where he is going while he is still on the way, is that he *can* say that certain directions are not right. After writing a couplet or drawing a line, he will erase it because it is "wrong" and try again. If there were in him no tendency to go in a certain direction, he would not resist being pulled in just any direction. This element of conscious resistance to the lure of beckoning side paths, or the exercise of critical judgment, is what sets creative activity apart from the activity that is acquiescent to the leadership of revery. In the latter, anything goes and nothing is rejected. Here we ought not to say that nothing is rejected because everything that the imagination suggests is consented to as "right," but only that all is accepted without criticism. Coleridge and the idealists were correct, therefore, in so far as they distinguished creative activity from the exercise of passive imagination, or fancy. Essential to the former, while absent from the latter, are critical judgment and fastidiousness.

Creative activity in art, then, is activity subject to critical control by the artist, although not by virtue of the fact that he foresees the final result of the activity. That this way of construing creativity reflects part of what we have in mind when we speak of creative art can be shown if we contrast what results from creative activity so construed with what results from other activities that we do not call creative.

Thus we do not judge a painting, poem, or other work to be a work of creative art unless we believe it to be original. If it strikes us as being a repetition of other paintings or poems, if it seems to be the result of a mechanical application of a borrowed technique or style to novel subject matter, to the degree that we apprehend it as such, to the same degree we deny that it is creative. There are men who have trained themselves to paint in the manner of Rembrandt, and some have become so good at it that even an expert aided by X-rays may find it hard to decide that their pictures were *not* painted by Rembrandt. Whatever other merits we attribute to such a painter or to his work, we do not judge him to be creative. He is like the rifleman. He knows what his bull's-eye is, and he knows how to hit it. Even in the case of a painter who has created a style of his own, we do not say that he is creating his style when he is painting his thirtieth or fortieth picture in that style. We may judge the style to be a good one, and the painting as a whole to be good. Yet we will grant that with respect to style the painter is no longer creative but is only repeating himself. To create is to originate. And it follows from this that prior to creation the creator does not foresee what will result from it. As T. E. Hulme put it, "to predict it would be to produce it before it was produced."[2]

Hulme's remark may sound odd, but it really isn't. To predict the result of his creative activity, the artist would have to envisage that result. He would have to have the idea of it in mind. But if he already had the idea in mind, all that would remain to be done is to objectify the idea in paint or in stone, and this would be a matter of skill, or work. That is why sculptors who do not need to work their material before they can envisage the determinate statue they want to make, but who can describe exactly what it should be like before the first blow of the mallet is struck, often hire stone-cutters to execute their plan. By the time they have the idea, the creative act, which in this case is the production of the idea, is finished. But to produce that original idea, the sculptor does not first have to produce an idea of it.

Although we do not judge a work to be a work of creative art unless we believe it to be original, it is not enough that we should judge it to be merely different or novel. In discourse about art, we use "creative" in an honorific sense, in a sense in which creative activity always issues in something that is different in an interesting, important, fruitful, or other *valuable* way. If what the artist produces is a novelty, yet indifferent or bad, we do not regard him as a creator. It is granted that, as R. G. Collingwood points out, there is a sense of the word in which we say that a man creates a nuisance or a disturbance. Yet if we believe, for example, that all that the Dadaists "created" was a nuisance and a disturbance, we will not judge them to have been creative artists.

Since "creative" as applied to art has this honorific sense, we will tend not to apply the term to any activity which does not result in a product having positive aesthetic or artistic value. To the degree that a work lacks coherence and lucidity, to the degree that it is not a unified whole the relations between whose parts are felt by aesthetic intuition as necessary, not fortuitous, connections, to that degree will it fail to be a work of creative art. Now a reason or ground for a judgment that something is not a work of creative art, I suggest, is not merely that the work as we see it lacks coherence and lucidity. Rather, this lack in the work is taken as evidence of a lack of control by the artist over the activity to which the work owes its origin, or of coherence and lucidity in him. And if this were so, then what he produced would not be a work of creative art. This is why, I suggest, we distinguish works of creative art from products of passive imagination on the one hand, and from the art of the insane on the other.

To illustrate the sort of works that we can expect to be produced under the guidance of passive imagination, I will use two extreme examples. These were deliberately chosen because of their bearing on a theory of artistic creativity, one thesis of which is that "Poetic creation, like the dream, is governed by strict psychic laws."[3]

In 1823, Ludwig Börne published an essay entitled "The Art of Becoming an Original Writer in Three Days." According to Ernest Jones, it was his reading of this essay that gave Sigmund Freud his "trust in the validity of free associations."[4] Börne writes:

> Here follows the practical prescription I promised. Take a few sheets of paper and for three days in succession write down, without any falsification or hypocrisy, everything that comes into your head. Write what you think of yourself, of your women, of the Turkish war, of Goethe, of the Fonk criminal case, of the Last Judgment, of those senior to you in authority— and when the three days are over you will be amazed at what novel and startling thoughts have welled up in you. This is the art of becoming an original writer in three days.[5]

No doubt someone who follows this prescription will, when the three days are over, be amazed when he reads what novel and startling things he has written. And it is not impossible that some of the statements will be judged by him to be adequate formulations of what he thinks—of himself, of his women, of Goethe, or of the Last Judgment, difficult subjects every one of them about which most of us don't know what we think unless, by a creative act, as distinguished from free association, we have found out. But it is much more probable that what was so written would be rejected by the writer as an inadequate expression of his thought. In any case, if everything were left exactly as it was just because it happened to come into the writer's head, we would not take it seriously as creative literature. Rather, to borrow another quotation from Reynolds, we would say, "When [the] desire of novelty has proceeded from mere idleness or caprice, it is not worth the trouble of criticism."[6]

The second horrible example is drawn from an essay in many ways similar to the one by Ludwig Börne. It is by Alva Johnson, and the title is "How to Become a Great Writer."[7] Virtually all of this essay is the biography of a great writer. Johnson tells of a young man who, as Freud says of the artist, like other men longed "to attain honor, power, riches, fame, and the love of women,"[8] but to whom reality denied all these things. After graduating from a university, full of ambition, he accepted a job which he soon gave up in favor of another, paying less money but offering better prospects. The prospects proved to be illusory, so he changed jobs again, drawn by further illusory prospects. This was repeated several times. After some years he found himself burdened with a family, and with an income smaller than his allowance as a student had been. Goaded by frustration, he did not take to drink but instead indulged in ritualistic daydreaming. For some years he devoted an hour each day to spinning castles in the air, and by inhabiting them in the role of hero he achieved a make-believe gratification of his desires. One day, when he was returning home, he bought a pulp magazine and read one of the stories. This opened his eyes. That evening, instead of daydreaming, he sat down with some sheets of paper and began to write one of his phantasies down. What he wrote was rejected by an extraordinary number of publishers. They gave such reasons as that the setting lacked authenticity, the style was atrocious, and the plot was infantile. But at length the manuscript was accepted and published, and the book proved to be a tremendous commercial success. By 1935 it and its sequels had sold twenty-five million copies and had been translated into fifty-six languages; and the author was living in a luxurious mansion in the Southwest. Thus he has won, as Freud says, "through his phantasy—what before he could win only in phantasy: honor, power, and the love of women."[9] The name of the writer is Edgar Rice Burroughs, and the title of his first book is *Tarzan of the Apes*.[10]

Its being subject to critical control sets creative art apart not only from the sort of thing just described, but from the art of the insane. There is an ancient tradition that the creative artist is a man possessed. To give once more the familiar quotations from Plato:

For the poet is a light and winged and holy thing, and there is no invention in him until he has been inspired and is out of his senses, and the
mind is no longer with him: when he has not attained to this state, he is
powerless and is unable to utter his oracles. [*Ion*, 534].

But he who, having no touch of the Muses' madness in his soul, comes to
the door and thinks that he will get into the temple by art—he, I say,
and his poetry are not admitted; the sane man disappears and is nowhere
when he enters into rivalry with the madman [*Phaedrus*, 245].

Shakespeare says:

> The lunatic, the lover, and the poet
> Are of imagination all compact.
>   [*Midsummer Night's Dream*, V, i.]

Despite this impressive tradition, we cannot accept the view that creative artists must literally be madmen. The pictures they paint and the
poetry they write make sense, whereas this is not true of the art of the
insane. When we gaze in succession upon a series of pictures by psychotics, we see that in them all there is a note of nightmare, delirium, or
mania which is not present in, for instance, da Vinci's drawings of mon-
sters or even in surrealist paintings. The difference may be described by
saying that in surrealist painting, delusion or nightmare is portrayed or
objectified, whereas no matter what an insane man portrays or objectifies
—be it "Mother" or "God"—his psychosis is revealed. If the art of the
insane makes sense to us, it is in the manner of a sign or symptom of
psychosis, not in the manner of an expression of it.

Here it may occur to the reader to raise the question of Van Gogh,
whose later works, we may suppose, are works of creative art, but in which
there is a kind of stridency signifying madness. The answer, I suggest, is
that it is only in so far as there is more in them than a stridency signifying
madness that we regard them as products of creative art. Those paintings
were not done, that is to say, in the complete absence of conscious control
and criticism. In psychiatric language, which I borrow from Ernst Kris,
those paintings were not completely tied to Van Gogh's delusional system.
As Kris says, in Van Gogh

> the disorder manifests itself in a change of style, but even though the style
> has changed, the connections with the artistic tendencies of the individual
> and his environment are preserved.[11]

Creativity and madness have traditionally been associated mainly
though not entirely because of the phenomenon of inspiration. In the
creative process, two moments may be distinguished, the moment of inspiration, when the new suggestion appears in consciousness, and the mo-

ment of development or elaboration. The moment of inspiration is sometimes accompanied by exalted feelings, and this is why, according to
Charles Lamb, it is confused with madness. According to Lamb,

> men, finding in the raptures of the higher poetry a condition of exaltation,
> to which they have no parallel in their own experience, besides the
> spurious resemblance of it in dreams and fevers, impute a state of dreami-
> ness and fever to the poet. But the true poet dreams being awake. He is
> not possessed by his subject but has dominion over it.[12]

The "moment" of development may last a long time, of course, even
years. During that more or less long moment the artist is striving to find
out what his inspiration is. As in the cases of Flaubert and Hemingway,
he may write and rewrite and hone and polish until at last he can look
upon what he has done and say, "There! That's what I wanted to say,
just as I wanted to say it." Before that, he knew only that what he had so
far done was *not* quite what he wanted to say, or quite how he wanted to
say it. It seems obvious that Flaubert, during that long moment of elaboration during which he fashioned *Madame Bovary,* was critically controlling what he was doing. He was neither mad nor free-associating nor
spinning daydreams. However, as Plato reminds us, if Flaubert had had
no touch of the Muses' madness in his soul, there would have been no
invention in him. He would have had no inspiration and therefore nothing to elaborate. In that case, however long he wrote and rewrote, honed
and polished, nothing would have come of it.

Now inspiration, as far as we know, is not subject to our will. We cannot decide to have an inspiration, nor can we by reasoning conclude our
way into it. And if by "art" we mean, as Plato did, skill—an activity consciously controlled so as to produce an already envisaged result—then art
is not enough to produce an inspiration. When, therefore, Plato says that
"there is no invention in him until he has become inspired and is out of
his senses, and the mind is no longer in him"; or when he says, "he who,
having no touch of the Muses' madness in his soul, comes to the door and
thinks that he will get into the temple by the help of art—he, I say, and
his poetry are not admitted," he may mean what I have just said, though
he says it in a less prosaic way. If he does mean that inspiration is necessary for creative art, and that it is not by reasoning or by the exercise of
skill that artists become inspired, we may agree. At the same time we
should observe that this does not entail that when an artist has been inspired he becomes incapable of exercising skill in developing his inspiration, or that reason in the sense of a capacity for critical control "is no
longer in him," or that the artist is literally a "madman."

Here it may be objected that cases of dramatically sudden and apparently fully determinate inspiration are being left out of the account, cases
such as the one Nietzsche describes in *Ecce Homo* in the following words:

something profoundly convulsive and disturbing suddenly becomes visible and audible with indescribable definiteness and exactness. One hears—one does not seek; one takes—one does not ask who gives. . . .There is the feeling that one is utterly out of hand. . . .Everything occurs without volition. . . .The spontaneity of the images and similes is most remarkable. . . .If I may borrow a phrase of Zarathustra's it actually seems as if the things themselves came to one, and offered themselves as similes.[13]

In such cases, the two moments of inspiration and elaboration collapse into one, and the poem issues forth in the complete absence of critical control. Or so it would seem. It is such cases that lend support to such truth as there is in the view that the creative artist is out of his mind, and in the Romanticist theory that art is the spontaneous overflow of powerful feelings. But was the manner in which Nietzsche wrote *Thus Spake Zarathustra* completely blind and automatic, or was there after all some critical control? I submit that there probably was. My reasons for thinking that there probably was may perhaps not have very much weight; but I am inclined to think that they have some weight—the weight of common sense.

C. S. Peirce refers to a man, who, when he was asked what he thought of the fact that the sun obeyed Joshua's command to stand still, replied, "Well, I'll bet that the sun wiggled just a bit when no one was looking." Similarly, I'll bet that Nietzsche edited just a bit while he wrote down *Thus Spake Zarathustra.* Should we accept reports of fully determinate inspiration at their face value as being about cases in which the moving finger writes, and, having writ, moves on? Is it absurd to suspect that such cases are in fact more like the parody of Omar's famous line?

> The moving finger writes, and having writ
> Moves on. But lo! It stops a bit.
> Moves back to cross a T, insert a word.
> The moving finger's acting quite absurd.

Even if Nietzsche didn't deliberately change a thing, even if all came out just right from the very first line, was there not a relatively cool hour when Nietzsche (and the same goes for Coleridge and "Kubla Khan") read what he had written and judged it to be an adequate expression of his thought? Haven't we all had the experience of being seized by the Muse in the middle of the night and writing as if possessed, only to read what we had written the next morning and to consign it not to a publisher but to the wastebasket?

If there was such a cool hour and such a critical judgment in Nietzsche's case, this is all that is needed to have made him create *Zarathustra* on the view of creation presented above. C. J. Ducasse has stated the point precisely in his *The Philosophy of Art.* Ducasse writes:

To say that art is conscious . . . or . . . critically controlled . . . does not mean that it need be conscious or so controlled either antecedently to or contemporaneously with the expressive act. . . .But it does mean that a *critical judgment is an intrinsic, essential constituent of the productive activity called art*; and indeed, not merely a critical judgment, but a *favorable* one. . . .One must be able to acknowledge the product as an adequate statement of oneself. . . .The telic character, which truly belongs to art since a critical moment is an intrinsic part of it, may be said to accrue to the expressive activity which is its first moment ex post fact. That activity is telically construed and criticized *after* it has occurred. And the work of art is not the product of that activity simply, but of that activity telically construed and criticized, and if need be repeated until correction of the product results, i.e., until objectivity of the expression is obtained.[14]

Given the concepts of conscious critical control and inspiration, we are in a position, I think, to set aside certain theories about creativity in art. Whether this can be done, by the way, should be of interest not only to philosophers of art but to metaphysicians and others as well.

Eliseo Vivas, in *Creation and Discovery*, finds in artistic creativity a difficulty for any "naturalistic" theory of mind. According to Vivas, what a naturalistic theory has to explain, but so far cannot explain, is

The control that the new whole, which from the standpoint of consciousness has not yet been fully born, exercises over the artist's mind as he proceeds to bring it to birth . . . [We need to explain] the purposive thrust of the mind, the mind's ability to follow the lead of something which is not pushing it from behind, so to speak, since it is not-yet-there. It is this fact, the control of the not-yet-there total situation over the present, that leads the idealist to insist that a factor is here at work of an essentially teleological nature.[15]

When the problem is formulated in this way, we are asked to explain how artistic creation is guided or controlled by an object that is "not-yet-there," that is, by something that does not exist, since it has not yet been created. And we may be tempted to say that, since it exercises an influence, the to-be-created object *is*, somehow, "there." It is an ideal or subsistent object which, perhaps in the manner of Aristotle's prime mover, does not push the artist's mind from behind, but attracts it from in front. It is, that is to say, not a kick, but a carrot, which the artist follows until the subsistent object stands revealed to him. Hence, creation is discovery.

But what needs to be explained is not, as Vivas formulates it, "the control that the new whole exercises over the artist's mind as he proceeds to bring it to birth." What needs to be explained is the fact that creative activity is controlled, but not by virtue of the fact that the artist already envisages the result he will create. That the artist's choices are controlled by a whole that is not-yet-there is not a fact but a theory. On the alternative theory that has been presented in this paper, what control consists in is the making of critical judgments about what has so far been done. There may be a great many of these judgments, or, in the limiting cases, just one.

But how, when he makes his critical judgments, does the artist know what is right and what is wrong? On the alternative theory, he knows because there is something pushing him from behind. Whenever the artist goes wrong, he feels himself being kicked, and he tries another way which, he surmises, trusts, or hopes, will not be followed by a kick. What is kicking him is "inspiration," which is already there. What he makes must be adequate to his inspiration. If it isn't, he feels a kick. We have all felt similar kicks when we have tried to put into words something we mean that we have not formulated before. On many such occasions, and they are always occasions on which we are *listening* to what we are saying as well as talking, we have uttered a sentence and then withdrawn it because it did not express what we meant, and we have sought to substitute for it another sentence which did.

Admittedly, the concept of inspiration we have been making use of is in need of clarification. Fortunately, it is not essential to our present purpose to attempt this task, since no matter whether the inspiration that appears on the threshold of the artist's reflexive consciousness is an impression, an emotion, a phantasy, an unclear idea, or whatnot, it is something that is "already there" in the creative process. That it should be already there is, for our purpose, the essential point.

In conclusion, let us consider briefly the view that when the moment of inspiration is distinct from the more or less long moment of its development or elaboration, during this second moment the mind of the artist is directed by his apprehension of "aesthetic necessity."

According to Brand Blanshard,

> Invention turns on a surrender to the workings of necessity in one's mind. [There is in the artist] a surrender of the will to an order whose structure is quite independent of it and whose affirmation through the mind is very largely so.[16]

In writing the last act of *Othello,* Blanshard continues, Shakespeare wrote what he did

> for the same reason that we, in reading or hearing it, find it satisfying, namely that with the given dramatic situation in mind "he could no other". . . .Given the character of Othello, his prevailing mood, his habits of speech, the situation in which he was placed, and given the need to round out the whole in accordance with the implicit demands of the aesthetic ideal, there was only one course for the Moor to take; and that he did.[17]

On this view, when an artist is inspired, what is given to him is analogous to a set of postulates and definitions in logic or mathematics; and what he does when he develops his inspiration is analogous to what a logician does when he deduces theorems from the postulates. Another analogy which is sometimes used is that inspiration is like an acorn. If the artist is inspired by an acorn, he can nurture it properly and develop an oak; or he may nurture it improperly and develop a stunted oak; but he can by no means develop an elm.

Such analogies, while they express how it feels to the artist when he is creating, can I believe be very misleading, especially when they lead us to postulate an ideal order of aesthetic necessity. Granted that we intuit "aesthetic necessity" in works of art, a lot of missing premises must be supplied before we can conclude that artistic creation is in important respects similar to logical deduction. When searching for these premises, we do well to tread warily.

For instance, from the fact that we feel (assuming that we do so feel) that the last act of Othello perfectly coheres with the preceding acts, it does not follow that a different last act, in which the Moor takes a different course, would not also be felt to cohere with them. With a different last act, we should have a different play, to be sure; but it might be an equally coherent one. Someone acquainted with it, and not with the play that we have, might well say about it that given the preceding acts, there was in the last act "only one course for the Moor to take; and that he did."

If this possibility is denied, what is the reason for the denial? The reason cannot be, "Aesthetic necessity is like logical necessity," since that is the thesis at issue.

Notes

1. From a fragment. Published in Elizabeth Gilmore Holt, *Literary Sources of Art History,* (Princeton, 1947), p. 504.

2. "Speculations," in *The Problems of Aesthetics,* ed. by Eliseo Vivas and Murray Krieger (New York, 1953), p. 126.

3. A. Bronson Feldman, "Reik and the Interpretation of Literature," *Explorations in Psychoanalysis,* ed. by Robert Lindner and Clement Staff (New York, 1953), p. 103.

4. *The Life and Works of Sigmund Freud,* I (New York, 1953), 245. See also p. 246.

5. *Ibid.,* p. 246.

6. *Discourses.* In Holt, *op. cit.,* p. 510.

7. *Saturday Evening Post,* July 25, 1935.

8. *A General Introduction to Psychoanalysis,* tr. by Joan Riviere (New York, 1935), p. 327.

9. *Ibid,* p. 328.

10. Johnson, who was writing a popular article, makes no mention of Freud. But it is worth remarking that, if his account is accurate, Burroughs is a perfect case study in support of what Freud said about artists in "The Relation of the Poet to Daydreaming" (1908) and elsewhere. Ernst Kris is the only Freudian writer on art I have read who is not blind to the distinction between creative and noncreative art.

11. *Psychoanalytic Explorations in Art* (New York, 1952), p. 94.

12. "The Sanity of True Genius," *The Works of Charles and Mary Lamb,* ed. by E. V. Lucas, (New York, 1903), II, 187.

13. *The Philosophy of Nietzsche,* introduction by W. H. Wright, (New York, no date), pp. 896-897.

14. New York, 1929, pp. 115-116.

15. New York, 1955, pp. 151-152.

16. *The Nature of Thought* (New York, 1940), II, 139, 166.

17. *Ibid.,* p. 145.

MARGARET MACDONALD

The Language of Fiction

I

"EMMA WOODHOUSE, handsome, clever and rich, with a comfortable home and happy disposition seemed to unite some of the best blessings of existence and had lived nearly twenty-one years in the world with very little to distress or vex her."

The opening sentence of Jane Austen's novel *Emma* is a sentence from fiction. *Emma* is a work in which the author tells a story of characters, places and incidents almost all of which she has invented. I shall mean by "fiction" any similar work. For unless a work is largely, if not wholly, composed of what is invented, it will not correctly be called "fiction." One which contains nothing imaginary may be history, science, detection, biography, but not fiction. I want to ask some questions about how an author uses words and sentences in fiction. But my interest is logical, not literary. I shall not discuss the style or artistic skill of any storyteller. Mine is the duller task of trying to understand some of the logic of fictional language; to determine the logical character of its expressions. How do they resemble and differ from those in other contexts? What are they understood to convey? Are they, e.g. true or false statements? If so, of or about what are they true or false? If not, what other function do they perform? How are they connected? These are the questions I shall chiefly discuss.

First of all, "fiction" is often used ambiguously both for what is fictitious and for that by which the fictitious is expressed. Thus "fiction" is opposed to "fact" as what is imaginary to what is real. But one must emphasize that a work of fiction itself is not imaginary, fictitious or unreal. What is fictitious does not exist. There are no dragons in the Zoo. But the novels of Jane Austen do exist. The world, fortunately, contains them just as it contained Jane Austen. They occupy many bookshelves. Works

Reprinted from *Proceedings of the Aristotelian Society*, Supplementary Vol. XXVIII (1954) by courtesy of the Editor of the Aristotelian Society.

of fiction, stories, novels are additions to the universe. Any unreality attaches only to their subject matter.[1]

Secondly, everyone understands the expressions of fiction. Or, if they do not, the reason is technical, not logical. One may find it hard to understand some of the expressions of Gertrude Stein or *Finnegan's Wake* but this is due to the peculiar obscurity of their style and not to the fact that they occur in works of fiction. No one who knows English could fail to understand the sentence quoted from *Emma*. That Emma Woodhouse was handsome, clever and rich is understood just as easily as that Charlotte Brontë was plain, sickly and poor. Both are indicative sentences which appear to inform about their subjects. But while the sentence containing "Charlotte Brontë" expresses a true statement of which Charlotte Brontë is the subject, that containing "Emma Woodhouse" cannot work similarly, since Jane Austen's Emma did not exist and so cannot be the logical subject of any statement. "Emma Woodhouse" does not and cannot designate a girl of that name of whom Jane Austen wrote. This has puzzled philosophers.[2] If apparent statements about Emma Woodhouse are about no one, of what is Jane Austen writing and how is she to be understood? Perhaps a subsistent wraith in a logical limbo is her subject? This will not do; or, at least, not in this form. Jane Austen is certainly "pretending" that there was a girl called Emma Woodhouse who had certain qualities and adventures. According to one view she is understood because we understand from non-fictional contexts the use of proper names and the general terms in which she describes Emma Woodhouse and her adventures. There is no Emma Woodhouse, so Jane Austen is not writing about her; rather she is writing about a number of properties, signified by the general terms she uses, and asserting that they belonged to someone. Since they did not "Emma Woodhouse" is a pseudo-designation and the propositions are false, though significant. Readers of *Emma* need not, and usually do not, believe falsely that its propositions are true. A work of fiction is, or is about, "one big composite predicate" and is so understood by readers who need neither to know nor believe that any subject was characterized by it. If, however, there had been, by chance, and unknown to Jane Austen, a girl called Emma Woodhouse who conformed faithfully to all the descriptions of the novel, its propositions would have been about and true of her and Jane Austen would have "accidentally" written biography and not fiction.[3]

This seems a somewhat strained account of a story. As Moore says,[4] it does not seem false to deny that Jane Austen wrote about Emma Woodhouse, even though she did not exist. There are many senses of "about." The common reader would be mystified to be told that *Emma* is not about Emma Woodhouse, Harriet Smith, Miss Bates, Mr. George Knightley and the rest, but is, instead, about such a peculiar object as a "composite predicate." He would, surely, find this quite unintelligible. It is also false to say that a work of fiction may be "accidentally" history or biography. For if there were ten girls called "Emma Woodhouse" of whom all that Jane Austen wrote were true, they are not the subject of *Emma,* for Jane Austen is not telling a story of any of them, but of a subject of her own invention. Moreover, it would not only be necessary that Emma Woodhouse should have a real counterpart but that such counterparts should exist for every other element of her novel. You cannot separate Emma from Highbury, her companions and the ball at the Crown. They all belong to the story. Such a coincidence would be almost miraculous. So Moore seems to be right when he says:[5]

"I think that what he [Dickens] meant by 'Mr. Pickwick,' and what we all understand is: 'There was only one man of whom it is true both that *I am going to tell you about him* and that he was called "Pickwick" *and that,* etc.' In other words, he is saying from the beginning, that he has one and only one man in his mind's eye, about whom he is going to tell you a story. That he has is, of course, false: it is part of the fiction. It is this which gives unique reference to all subsequent uses of 'Mr. Pickwick.' And it is for this reason that Mr. Ryle's view that if, by coincidence, there happened to be a real man of whom everything related of Mr. Pickwick in the novel were true then 'we could say that Dickens' propositions were true of somebody' is to be rejected . . . *since Dickens was not telling us of him*: and that this is what is meant by saying that it is only 'by coincidence' that there happened to be such a man."

I think this can be seen to be true even in circumstances which might appear to support Ryle's view. *Jane Eyre* and *Villette* are known to contain much biographical material. Charlotte Brontë knew her original as Dickens did not know of a "coincidental" Mr. Pickwick. Yet *Jane Eyre* and *Villette* are still works of fiction, not biography. They are no substitute for Mrs. Gaskell's *Life of Charlotte Brontë.* For although she may be *using* the facts of her own life, Charlotte Brontë is not writing "about" herself, but "about" Jane Eyre, Helen Burns, Mr. Rochester, Lucy Snowe, Paul Emmanuel and the rest. Or, she is writing about herself in a very different sense from that in which she is writing about the subject matter of her novels.

Ryle and Moore agree, with many others, that the sentences of fiction express false statements and Moore adds, I think rightly, that, so far, at least, as these are fictional, they could not be true. But there is a more radical view for which there is also some excuse. If a storyteller tells what he knows to be false, is he not a deceiver and his work a "tissue of lies"? That storytelling is akin to, if not a form of, lying is a very common view. "To make up a tale," "to tell a yarn" are common euphemisms for "to tell a lie." A liar knows what is true, but deliberately says what is false. What else does the storyteller who pretends that there was a girl called "Emma Woodhouse," etc., when she knows this is false? A liar intends to, and does, deceive a hearer. Does not a storyteller do likewise? "Poets themselves," says Hume, "though liars by profession, always endeavour to

give an air of truth to their fictions."[6] Hume is contrasting all other expressions as indifferently lies or fiction, with those which are true of matter of fact. Hume is quite wrong to classify all poetry with fiction, though
some stories may be told in verse. But no one could correctly call, e.g.
Shakespeare's Sonnets, Keats' Odes or Eliot's Four Quartets, works of fiction. Nor are they statements of fact, but their analysis is not my task
here. I wish only to protest against a common tendency to consign to one
dustbin all expressions which do not conform to the type of statement
found in factual studies. Even though they are not factual statements, expressions in literature may be of many different logical types. It is clear,
however, that for Hume storytelling is a form of lying. And, indeed, a
storyteller not only says what he knows to be false but uses every device
of art to induce his audience to accept his fancies. For what else are the
ancient incantatory openings, "Once upon a time . . . ," "Not yesterday,
not yesterday, but long ago . . . ," and their modern equivalents, but to
put a spell upon an audience so that the critical faculties of its members
are numbed and they willingly suspend disbelief to enter the state which
Coleridge called "illusion" and likened to dreaming?[7] All this is true.
Everyone must sometimes be informed, instructed, exhorted by others.
There are facts to learn and attitudes to adopt. However dull, these processes must be endured. But no one is obliged to attend to another's fancies. Unless, therefore, a storyteller can convince, he will not hold an
audience. So, among other devices, he "endeavours to give an air of truth
to his fictions." It does not follow that what he says *is* true, nor that he is
a deceiver. One must distinguish "trying to convince" from "seeking to
mislead." To convince is a merit in a work of fiction. To induce someone
to accept a fiction, however, is not necessarily to seduce him into a belief
that is real. It is true that some people may be deceived by fiction. They
fail to distinguish conviction from deception. Such are those who write to
the B.B.C. about Mrs. Dale and the Archers as if they believe themselves
to be hearing the life histories of real families in these programmes. But
this does not show that the B.B.C. has deliberately beguiled these inno-
cents. Finally, a liar may be "found out" in his lie. He is then discredited
and his lie is useless. Nor is he easily believed again. But it would be
absurd for someone to complain that since *Emma* was fiction he had
"found out" Jane Austen and could never trust her again. The conviction
induced by a story is the result of a mutual conspiracy, freely entered
into, between author and audience. A storyteller does not lie, nor is a
normal auditor deceived. Yet there are affinities between fiction and lying
which excuse the comparison. Conviction, without belief or disbelief, as
in art, is like, but also very different from, unwitting deception. And a
liar, too, pretends but not all pretending is lying.

A fictional sentence does not, then, express a lying statement. Does it
express a false statement which is not a lie? False statements are normally
asserted from total or partial ignorance of the facts. Those who assert

them mistakenly believe they are true. This is not true of the storyteller. Neither he nor his auditor normally believes that his statements are true. Moreover, though a proposition may be false, it must make sense to say that it might be true. It is false that Jane Austen wrote *Pickwick Papers* but it is not nonsense to suggest that it might have been true. As already seen, however, no factual discovery can verify a fictional statement. It can then never be true. So it would seem to be necessarily false or logically impossible. But the expressions of fiction are neither self-contradictory nor nonsensical. Most of them are perfectly intelligible. Those which are not are so for reasons quite unconnected with truth and falsity. It is not because James Joyce's statements are all false that they are unintelligible. For those of Jane Austen and Dickens are equally false, but not obscure.

Alternatively, it might be said that the propositions of fiction are false, but neither believed nor asserted. Their fictional character consists in the fact that they are merely proposed for consideration, like hypotheses. "Let us suppose there was a girl called Emma Woodhouse, who . . . etc." For a proposition may be entertained, but yet be false. So an author puts forward and his audience considers, but neither affirm, the false propositions of fiction.[8] Now, a storyteller does invite his audience to "Imagine that . . . ," "Pretend that . . ." and even "Suppose that . . ." or "Let it be granted that . . ." He does not often preface his story with just these remarks, but he issues a general invitation to exercise imagination. So far one may liken his attitude to that of someone proposing an hypothesis in other fields. An hypothesis, like a lie or a story, requires some invention; it is not a report of observed fact. But these suggested fictional hypotheses are also very different from all others. Non-fictional hypotheses are proposed to explain some fact or set of facts. "If the picture is by Van Dyck, then . . ."; "Suppose that malaria is transmitted by mosquitoes, then. . . ." They suggest, e.g., the origin of a painting or the cause of a disease. But a story is not told to solve any such problem. Moreover, a non-fictional hypothesis must be testable or be mere speculation without explanatory value. But, obviously, nothing can count as evidence in favour of a fictional story. And what no fact can confirm none can disconfirm either. So, if a story consists of propositions entertained for consideration, the purpose of such entertainment must be for ever frustrated since they can never be asserted as true, false, probable or improbable. I conclude, therefore, that the expressions of fiction do not function either as propositions or hypotheses.

Nevertheless, as I have said, one can easily understand why people are tempted to identify fictional expressions with lies, falsehoods, unverifiable hypotheses. For what it is worth, the English dictionary appears to support this view. "Fiction," it says, "the act of feigning, inventing or imagining: that which is feigned, i.e. a fictitious story, fable, fabrication, falsehood." If the last four terms are intended as synonyms, this certainly suggests that all fiction is falsehood. Both rationalist and religious parents have forbidden children to read fairy stories and novels lest they be led astray into false and immoral beliefs. Yet its logical difference from these seems to show that fiction is not false, lying, or hypothetical statement. It is clear that "S pretends that *p*" cannot entail *p*. This is, again, the point of saying that the truth of *p* must be "coincidental." When discovered, no future S (or storyteller) could pretend that *p*, for one cannot pretend that a proposition is true when it is, and is known to be, true. But neither, in fiction, can "S pretends that *p*" entail "not-*p*," or even "Perhaps-*p*." So, fictional expressions must be of a different type from statements.

An alternative is the familiar emotive answer. This is associated chiefly with the name of I. A. Richards. I can mention it only briefly. According to it, sentences in fiction, as in all non-informative contexts, express an emotional state of their author and seek to induce a similar state in his audience. A work is judged better or worse according to the amount of harmonious mental adjustment by which it was caused and which it effects. This view is difficult to estimate because of its vague use of the word "express." It tends to suggest that the expressions of fiction are disguised exclamations such as "Hurrah!" or "Alas!" Or that these could be substituted for them. This, of course, is impossible. No one could tell the story of *Emma* in a series of smiles, sighs, tears, shouts or the limited vocabulary which represents such emotive expressions. Most stories, one must reiterate, are told in normal English sentences which are common to fact and fiction and appropriately understood. This is, indeed, just the problem. If the expressions of Jane Austen were as easily distinguishable from factual statement as exclamation from articulate utterance no one would be puzzled. "Emotive expression" must, therefore, be compatible with understood sense.[9] It is true that emotional relationships play a large part in most fiction, but so does much else. Nor need these subjects coincide with the experience of either author or audience. No story, even though told in the first person, can be completely autobiographical without ceasing to be fiction. And whether or not a work of fiction uses autobiographical material, the actual, or suspected, direct intrusion of personal feeling by the author is liable to be fatal to the work.

"I opened it at chapter twelve and my eye was caught by the phrase 'Anybody may blame me who likes.' What were they blaming Charlotte Brontë for, I wondered? And I read how Jane Eyre used to go up on the roof when Mrs. Fairfax was making jellies and look over the fields at the distant view. And then she longed—and it was for this that they blamed her—that 'then I longed for a power of vision which might overpass that limit . . . I desired more of practical experience . . . more of intercourse with my kind. . . . I believed in the existence of other and more vivid kinds of goodness and what I believed in I wished to behold. . . . Who blames me? Many no doubt and I shall be called discontented. . . . When thus alone I not infrequently heard Grace Poole's laugh.'

"That is an awkward break, I thought. It is upsetting to come upon Grace Poole all of a sudden. The continuity is disturbed. One might say,

I continued, . . . that the woman who wrote these pages had genius . . . but if one reads them over and marks that jerk in them, that indignation, one sees . . . that her books will be deformed and twisted." (Virginia Woolf; *A Room of One's Own*, p. 104.)

In short, Charlotte Brontë will, or will appear to, express her own feelings too nakedly through her heroine, in order to induce a sympathetic emotional response in her readers, instead of telling her story. Someone may protest that this amounts to *describing*, not expressing, her emotions. But this is not ostensibly so. The passage is still a soliloquy by Jane Eyre, not an introspective report by Charlotte Brontë. Virginia Woolf is giving an interpretation of the passage, but this would not be necessary if it were a simple description of Charlotte Brontë's feelings. If her critic is right and if, nevertheless, the passage is not what is meant by an expression of the author's emotion by fiction, this cannot be because it is a straightforward description of fact. Another objection might be that this is a crude example of expression and does not prove that the task of fiction is not to express emotion. Skilful expression is impersonal, almost anonymous. One cannot tell from their works what Shakespeare or Jane Austen felt. Hence the floods of speculation by critics. One knows only too well from her novels what Charlotte Brontë felt, so she is not truly expressing, but merely venting, her emotions. But then, if one so often cannot tell whose, or even what, emotion is being expressed, what is the point of saying that all fictional expressions are emotive? Should the criterion be solely the effect on their audience? Certainly, a tale may amuse, sadden, anger, or otherwise move a hearer. But is the fact that *Emma* may cause one to laugh or sigh what distinguishes it as a work of fiction from a statement of fact? This must be false for much that is not fiction has the same effect. The answer of the theory is that a work of fiction, like any work of literary art, causes a very special emotional effect, an harmonious adjustment of impulses, a personal attitude, not otherwise obtainable. But no independent evidence of any such pervasive effect is offered, nor can I, for one, provide it from experience of reading fiction. So, if one cannot distinguish fiction from fact by the normal emotional effects which fiction sometimes causes, nor by the pervasive changes it is alleged to cause, the theory only reformulates and does not explain this distinction.

But the theory does emphasize that language has less pedestrian uses than those of the laboratory, record office, police court and daily discourse. Also, that to create and appreciate fiction requires more than intellectual qualities. Most fiction would be incomprehensible to a being without emotions. One must be able to enter imaginatively into its emotional situations though its emotions need not be felt. One need not *feel* jealousy either to construct or understand Mr. Knightley's censorious attitude to Frank Churchill, but someone who had never felt this might find an account of it unconvincing. Authors differ, too, in what may be vaguely called "climate" or "atmosphere," which is emotional and moral as well as intellectual. The "worlds" of Jane Austen and Henry James, e.g., differ considerably from those of Emily Brontë and D. H. Lawrence. Also, much of the language of fiction is emotionally charged. For it depicts emotional situations which are part of its story. But none of these facts is positively illuminated by a theory which limits the language of fiction to the expression of an emotion transferred from author to auditor even if such a transaction were fully understood. It does not seem to be the feeling which generates them nor that which they cause which wholly differentiates the ironies of Gibbon from those of I. Compton Burnett. Nor is it either Tolstoy or ourselves in whom we are primarily interested when reading *War and Peace*. Rather it is the presentation of characters, actions and situations. The vast panorama of the novel shrinks into triviality as the instrument of the emotional adjustments of Tolstoy and his readers. I conclude, therefore, that the characteristic which differentiates fictional sentences from those which state facts is not that the former exclusively express anybody's emotions, though many of them have a very vital connection with emotion.

II

When someone reports a fact he may choose the language or symbolism of his report. He may choose to use this carefully or carelessly. But there is a sense in which he cannot choose what he will say. No one could report truly that Charlotte Brontë died in 1890; that she wrote *Villette* before *Jane Eyre*; that she was tall, handsome and a celebrated London hostess. No biography of Charlotte Brontë could contain such statements and remain a biography. For what is truly said of Charlotte Brontë must be controlled by what she was and what happened to her. But Jane Austen was under no such restraints with Emma Woodhouse. For Emma Woodhouse was her own invention. So she may have any qualities and undergo any adventures her author pleases. It is not even certain that these must be logically possible, i.e. not self-contradictory. For some stories, and not the worst, are extremely wild. There is *Finnegans Wake* as well as *Emma*. A storyteller chooses not only the words and style but also, and I suggest with them, provides the material of a fictional story. I want to stress this fact that in fiction language is used to *create*. For it is this which chiefly differentiates it from factual statement. A storyteller performs; he does not—or not primarily—inform or misinform. To tell a story is to originate, not to report. Like the contents of dreams, the objects of fiction may presuppose, but do not compete with, those of ordinary life. Unlike those of dreams, however, they are deliberately contrived. Hence, they differ too from lunatic frenzies. A lunatic unintentionally offends against fact and logic. He intends to respect them. He thinks he is right, however wild his fancies, when he is always wrong. But a storyteller, though equally wild, is never deluded. He invents by choice, not accident.

As I have already said, most of a storyteller's words and sentences are understood to have the same meanings as the same words and grammatical forms in non-fictional contexts. For all who communicate use the same language, composed mainly of general terms. But language may be used differently to obtain different results. When a storyteller "pretends" he simulates factual description. He puts on an innocent air of informing. This is part of the pretence. But when he pretends, e.g. that there was a Becky Sharp, an adventuress, who finally came to grief, he does not inform or misinform about a real person called "Becky Sharp" or anyone else: he is creating Becky Sharp. And this is what a normal audience understands him to be doing. Of course, he does not thereby add to the population of the world. Becky Sharp is not registered at Somerset House. But this, too, is shown by language. A storyteller, like a dramatist, is not said to create persons, human beings, but *characters*. Characters, together with their settings and situations, are parts of a story. According to Ryle, although "it is correct to say that Charles Dickens created a story, it is wholly erroneous to speak as if Dickens created Mr. Pickwick."[10] But Dickens *did* create Mr. Pickwick and this is not equivalent to saying, as Ryle does, that what Dickens created was a "complex predicate." No one would ever say this. But it is perfectly ordinary and proper to say that an author has created certain characters and all that is required for them to function. "In Caliban," said Dryden, "Shakespeare seems to have *created* a being which was not in nature." He was not in nature because he was part of *The Tempest*. To create a story is to use language to create the contents of that story. To write "about" Emma Woodhouse, Becky Sharp, Mr. Pickwick, Caliban, and the rest is to "bring about" these characters and their worlds. Human beings are not normally called "characters." If they are, it is by analogy with art. One might say, "I met a queer character the other day; he might have been created by Dickens." This does not show that Dickens wrote or tried to write about such a person, but that his readers now view their fellows through Dickens' works. So may one now see Constable and Cézanne pictures in natural landscapes, which would not have been seen without these artists. A character, like all else in pure fiction, is confined to its rôle in a story. Not even the longest biography exhausts what could be told of any human person, but what Jane Austen tells of Emma Woodhouse exhausts Emma Woodhouse. A character may be completely understood, but the simplest human being, if any human being is simple, is somewhere opaque to others. A character has no secrets but what are contained within five acts or between the covers of a book or the interval from supper to bedtime.[12] A story may, indeed, have a sequel, but this is a new invention, not a report of what was omitted from the original.

This may be challenged. Surely, it will be said, many characters in fiction are as complex as human beings? Do not critics still dispute about the motives of Iago and the sex of Albertine? But to say that a character is limited to what is related of it in a story does not imply that this must always be indisputably obvious. All it implies is that the only way to find out about a character is to consult the author's text. This contains all there is to discover. No one can ever find independent evidence which the author has missed. Not even Dr. Ernest Jones for the alleged "complexes" of Hamlet. Assuming that the text is complete and authentic, there may be different interpretations of it and thus of a character but no new evidence such as may render out of date a biography. No one will find a diary or a cache of letters from Hamlet to his mother which will throw light upon his mental state. Nor must this be for ever secret in the absence of such evidence. For Hamlet is what Shakespeare tells and what we understand from the text, and nothing more.

What is true of characters is true also of other fictional elements of a story. "Barchester" does not name a geographical place. It is the setting or scene of a number of Trollope's characters. So is his magic island for Prospero and his companions. The words used to "set the scene" of a story paint as it were the backcloth to its incidents. "Scene" is a term of art, a word from the language of the theatre. One would naturally say "The scene of Archdeacon Grantly's activities is laid in Barchester," but not, unless affecting histrionics, "The scene of this Conference is laid in Oxford." It would be more normal to say "This Conference is being held in Oxford." "Scene" is used of natural situations only when these are being treated artificially. Finally, the situation and incidents of a story form its plot. They conform to a contrived sequence of beginning, middle and end—or have some modern variety of this shape. But human life and natural events do not have, or conform to, a plot. They have no contrived shape.

It is thus, then, that we talk of works of fiction and their fictional contents. They are contrivances, artefacts. A story is more like a picture or a symphony than a theory or report. Characters, e.g. might, for a change, be compared with musical "themes" rather than with human flesh and blood. A composer creates a symphony, but he also creates all its several parts. So does a storyteller, but his parts are the characters, settings and incidents which constitute his story. The similarity is obscure just because the storyteller does, and must, use common speech with its general terms, so that he appears to assert propositions about an independent reality in a manner similar to that of one who does or fails to report what is true. So, philosophers conclude, since pure fiction cannot be about physical objects, it must be about wraith-like simulacra of real objects or equally attenuated "predicates." I do not, however, want to claim a special mode of existence for fictional objects as the contents of fiction. And though it is obvious that fiction writers use our common tongue I do not think that what they do is illuminated by saying that they write about predicates or properties. It is agreed that a storyteller both creates a story, a verbal construction, and the contents of that story. I want to say that these activities are inseparable. Certainly, no one could create pure fiction without also creating the contents which are its parts. One cannot separate Emma

Woodhouse from *Emma* as one can separate Napoleon from his biography. I do not say that Emma is simply identical with the words by which she is created. Emma is a "character." As such she can, in appropriate senses, be called charming, generous, foolish, and even "lifelike." No one could sensibly use these epithets of words. Nevertheless, a character is that of which it makes no sense to talk except in terms of the story in which he or she is a character. Just as, I think, it would make no sense to say that a flock of birds was carolling "by chance" the first movement of a symphony. For birds do not observe musical conventions. What is true of characters applies to the settings and incidents of pure fiction. To the questions "Where will they be found?"; "Where do they exist?," the answer is "In such and such a story," and that is all. For they are the elements or parts of stories and this is shown by our language about them.

But the content of very little fiction is wholly fictitious. London also forms part of the setting of *Emma* as it does of many of Dickens' novels; Russia of *War and Peace* and India of *A Passage to India*. Historical persons and events also seem to invade fiction. They are indeed the very stuff of "historical" novels. Do not the sentences in which the designations or descriptions of such places, persons and incidents occur express true or false statements? It is true that these real objects and events are mentioned in such fictional expressions. Nevertheless, they certainly do not function wholly as in a typographical or historical record. They are still part of a story. A storyteller is not discredited as a reporter by rearranging London's squares or adding an unknown street to serve his purpose. Nor by crediting an historical personage with speeches and adventures unknown to historians. An historical novel is not judged by the same standards as a history book. Inaccuracies are condemned, if they are, not because they are bad history or geography, but because they are bad art. A story which introduces Napoleon or Cromwell but which departs wildly from historical accuracy will not have the verisimilitude which appears to be its object and will be unplausible and tedious. Or if, nevertheless, interesting will provoke the question, "But why call this character Oliver Cromwell, Lord Protector of England?" Similarly, for places. If somewhere called "London" is quite unrecognizable, its name will have no point.

So I am inclined to say that a storyteller is not making informative assertions about real persons, places and incidents even when these are mentioned in fictional sentences. But rather that these also function like purely fictional elements, with which they are always mingled in a story. Russia as the setting for the Rostovs differs from the Russia which Napoleon invaded which did not contain the Rostovs. There was a battle of Waterloo, but George Osborne was not one of the casualties, except in Thackeray's novel. Tolstoy did not create Russia, nor Thackeray the battle of Waterloo. Yet one might say that Tolstoy did create Russia-as-the-background-of-the-Rostovs and that Thackeray created Waterloo-as-the-scene-of-George-Osborne's-death. One might say that the mention of realities plays a dual role in fiction; to refer to a real object and to contribute to the development of a story. But I cannot pursue this, except to say that this situation differs from that in which, e.g. Charlotte Brontë uses the real events in her life in *Jane Eyre*. For she does not *mention* herself nor the real places and incidents upon which her story is modelled.

I have tried to say how the expressions of fiction operate and to show that they differ both from statements and emotive expressions. I also began by asking how they are connected. It is clear that their order need not be dictated by that of any matter of fact. Nor are they always even bound by the principles of logic. Do their connections, then, follow any rule or procedure? Is there a conception by which their transitions may be described? Since a work of fiction is a creative performance, however, it may be thought senseless to ask for such rules or such a conception. Is not the creation of that which is new and original, independent of logic and existence, just that to which no rules are appropriate and no conception adequate? But the creation of a work of fiction, however remarkable, is not a miracle. Nor is its author's use of language entirely lawless and vagabond but is directed by some purpose. Certainly, no set of rules will enable anyone to write a good novel or produce a good scientific hypothesis. But a scientist employs his ingenuity to invent a hypothesis to connect certain facts and predict others. He provides an organizing concept related to the facts to be organized and governed by the probability that it provides the correct explanation. As already emphasized, the situation of the storyteller is different.

In his Preface to *The Portrait of a Lady*, Henry James recalls that in organizing his "ado" about Isobel Archer, having conceived the character, he asked, "And now what will she *do*?" and the reply came immediately, "Why, the first thing she will do will be to come to Europe." He did not have to infer, guess, or wait upon observation and evidence; he *knew*. He knew because he had thus decided. He so decided, no doubt, for a variety of artistic reasons; to develop his conception of a certain character in relation to others, against a particular background, in accordance with his plot. His aim was to produce a particular, perhaps a unique, story; a self-contained system having its own internal coherence. There is certainly a sense in which every work of fiction is a law unto itself. Nevertheless, I think there is a general notion which governs these constructions though its application may give very different results. This is the Aristotelian notion which is usually translated "probability" but which I prefer to call "artistic plausibility." This is not an ideal phrase but is preferable to "probability" which suggests an evidential relation between premises and conclusion and "possibility" which suggests a restriction to logical conceivability which might exclude some rare, strange, and fantastic works. It is, moreover, a notion which applies only to what is verbal. Though some comparable notion may apply to them, one does not normally talk of "plausible" pictures, statues and symphonies, but does talk of "plausible stories." A plausible story is one which convinces; which induces acceptance. But since the plausibility is artistic plausibility, the conviction induced will not be the belief appropriate to factual statement. Nevertheless, one drawback to the notion is that it may suggest that all fiction is, or should be, realistic or naturalistic. It is true that although fiction does not consist of statements about life and natural events, yet much fiction does take lived experience as a model for its own connections. Sometimes, as with Charlotte Brontë's novels, using autobiographical material. Such stories convince by being "lifelike." But by no means all fiction is thus naturalistic. Nor is a story allegedly founded on fact necessarily fictionally convincing. To repeat the Aristotelian tag, "a convincing impossibility is better than an unconvincing possibility." There is, in fact, a range of plausible connections in fiction, varying from the purest naturalism to the wildest fantasy. If any convinces then it is justified. Much should obviously be said about who is convinced and whether he is a reliable judge, but I can do little more here than indicate the type of connection which differentiates works of fiction from descriptions of fact. It is the task of the literary critic to analyse the different types of plausibility exemplified by, e.g. *Emma, War and Peace, The Portrait of a Lady, Wuthering Heights, Moby-Dick, Alice in Wonderland* and *Grimm's Fairy Stories*. And though, perhaps, no rules can be given for attaining any particular type of plausibility, yet it is sometimes possible to say what does or would make a work unplausible. A mixture of elements from different plausible systems would, e.g., have this result. It is quite plausible that Alice should change her size by drinking from magic bottles, but it would be absurd that Emma Woodhouse or Fanny Price should do so. Or, to make such an incident plausible, Jane Austen's novels would need to be very different. For it would have needed explanation in quite different terms from the conventions she uses. This also applies to more important plausibilities. Emma Woodhouse could not suddenly murder Miss Bates after the ball, or develop a Russian sense of sin, without either destroying the plausibility of the novel or bringing about a complete revolution in its shape, though these incidents are in themselves more likely than that which befell Alice. But such examples raise questions about fiction and fact, art and life which I cannot now discuss.

Notes

1. Cf. also "Art and Imagination," *Proc. Aris. Soc.*, 1952-53, p. 219.
2. See earlier Symposium on "Imaginary Objects," *Proc. Aris. Soc.*, Supp. Vol. 12, 1933, by G. Ryle, R. B. Braithwaite and G. E. Moore.
3. *Loc. cit.*, G. Ryle, pp. 18-43.
4. *Ibid.*, p. 59.

5. *Loc. cit.*, p. 68.
6. *Treatise of Human Nature,* Bk. 1, Pt. 3, Sec. 10.
7. Cf. Notes on *The Tempest* from *Lectures on Shakespeare.*
8. I understood Professor Moore to hold such a view in a discussion in 1952. I do not, however, claim his authority for this version. Nor do I know if he is still of the same opinion.
9. Cf. also Empson, *The Structure of Complex Words,* London, 1951, ch. 1.
10. *Loc. cit.*, p. 32.
11. Quoted by Logan Pearsall Smith. S. P. E. Tract XVII, 1924.
12. See also *Aspects of the Novel,* E. M. Forster, chs. 3 and 4.

JOHN HOSPERS

Implied Truths in Literature

M ANY THINGS have been identified as "the function of art": to express emotions, to edify or ennoble mankind, to promote communism, to bring about a moral society. But among the functions it has often been supposed to have is to give us *truth*. This claim for art was made by Aristotle when he said that art (poetry) gives us universal truth; and a long line of critics and philosophers since Aristotle has defended this view.

When one examines this claim, however, it seems highly peculiar. One would have thought that the task of the natural sciences was to give us truth in the form of general laws and theories about the physical universe; of history, to give us truth about what has happened in the past; and of philosophy, to give us truth about—well, opinions differ on this point. Perhaps even aesthetics gives us truth about the arts; but what is it that the arts give us truth about?

I

One of the arts at any rate, literature, uses words as its medium, and thus it can make statements; therefore, it would seem, it is in an excellent position to make true statements, that is, to state truths. Whether true or false, statements do indeed occur in literature,

> Life is real! Life is earnest!
> And the grave is not its goal.
> "Dust thou art, to dust returneth"
> Was not spoken of the soul.

If a poem is defined as whatever doesn't extend all the way across the page, the above passage may be called poetry. But whether or not one

Reprinted from the *Journal of Aesthetics and Art Criticism*, Vol. XIX (1960).

decides to call it poetry, one could not ask for a more outright statement anywhere. Many statements occurring in poetry are undoubtedly true; so it can hardly be denied that poetry gives us truth in this sense.

Of course, it is not always clear what the sentences in poems mean:

> Life, like a dome of many-colored glass,
> Stains the white radiance of eternity.

True or false? We must first know what is being stated. Some would say that nobody can tell for sure what is being stated; others would say that this is not a statement at all, that we are merely being regaled with exotic images. No doubt this sometimes occurs; whether the above couplet is a case of it is for critics to determine. When it does occur, no question of truth, of course, arises. Nor does it arise in the case of sentences which contain only exclamations, suggestions, commands, or questions.

Such sentences, however, constitute only a small minority of the sentences in literature, as in daily discourse. For the vast remainder, questions of truth do arise. Some of these questions, as we shall see, are extremely puzzling. But it is important at the outset that we should not dismiss literature as "non-cognitive." (1) First, we cannot easily relegate poetry to the category of "emotive language."

> Stars, I have seen them fall.
> And when they drop and die,
> No star is lost at all
> From all the star-sown sky.
> The tears of all that be
> Help not the primal fault.
> It rains into the sea,
> And still the sea is salt.

These lines of Housman are, to be sure, deeply moving. But to understand their meaning we do not suddenly have to "shift gears" from ordinary discourse into an entirely different domain (or "function") of language. We understand what these sentences mean as we understand any other sentences in the language. They have meaning—or, if one wants the usual qualifying adjective, "descriptive meaning"—just as non-poetic sentences do. Perhaps the author of them is expressing a feeling, but this does not prevent him from making statements which he believes to be true. In daily life also we often express feelings by making true-or-false statements: "I wish the war would end," "She's changed so much in the last few years," and so on. Whether the author uses the sentences to express a feeling (or to arouse feeling in others) is something we would have to ask the author to discover. Whether the sentence contains a true or false statement, however, is something for which we examine not the author but the sentence itself. The words, especially in the combinations and juxtapositions we find them in the poem, may, then, move us emotionally, as do many expressions of deep feeling, but this does not prevent them from being true or false. (2) Nor do they fall into the category that has sometimes been called "pictorial meaning." It is true that a poem may present us with an interesting array of mental pictures, but this is something that may or may not occur, depending on the pictorial capacities of the reader; and many readers who have no mental pictures at all while reading poems still claim that they get the full impact of the poems. Even the use of metaphor, which is so important in poetry that poetry has often been defined in terms of it, does not imply that language is being used pictorially. Some metaphors evoke no pictures whatever, and even if one claims that they should, the fact is that metaphor is not to be defined in terms of mental pictures but in terms of linguistic devices. The whole attempt to relegate poetry to the realms of "emotive meaning" or "pictorial meaning" is, I believe, a mistake.

To be sure, the sentences in poetry are richer in suggestion than most of the sentences we utter, but this does not make them "mean" in a different way; it only shows that we respond to them somewhat differently. We are moved, but not (usually) to action. When we read that "Poor Tom's a-cold," we do not go out to fetch a blanket, nor do we gather flowers to put on Cordelia's casket. But the problem of how we do or should *respond* to various linguistic utterances (to religious language, to political speeches, to statements in textbooks, etc.)—and our responses are varied indeed—is not to be confused with understanding the *meaning* of these utterances. The meaning of a sentence does not vary with the use to which it happens to be put on a particular occasion. In particular, the meaning does not vary with either (a) the feelings of the speaker, which it may express, or (b) the response which it evokes in the listener. If two readers respond differently to the same sentence, this does not show that the sentence has two different meanings. Talk about "emotive meaning" would be far less misleading if the term "meaning" were scrapped in favor of the term "effects." A sentence in a poem may powerfully affect the emotions, but it does not follow that its *meaning* is "emotive." (The term "emotive" is misleading even in describing the effects. As the term "emotive" is ordinarily used, at any rate, I would suggest that the language of poetry is considerably more emotive in its effects than the telephone directory, somewhat more emotive than scientific treatises, not quite as emotive as day-to-day conversations—consisting as they usually do of an inelegant mixture of assertion, persuasion, suggestion, and loaded language—and not nearly as emotive as propaganda or the language of political and moral persuasion.)

Let us say no more about the explicit statements that occur in literature. Some of them may well be true, and may thus give us knowledge we did not previously possess, whether or not the imparting of such knowledge was the intent of the author when he wrote.¹ The main problem that confronts us now has to do not with explicit statements, but with statements which the author nowhere makes.

We are probably convinced that the novels of Balzac give us a reasonably accurate picture of certain aspects of life in Paris in the early nineteenth century, that in fact they were intended to do this; but whether or not they were so intended, they do. Yet we do not encounter, on reading any of these novels, any sentence such as "This is a true picture of life in Paris in my time; I do hereby assert it." Nor do the novels of Thomas Hardy contain sentences telling us what Hardy's view of life and human destiny was; yet, from the way the novels are plotted, and the chance character of the events upon which the major developments turn, even the least perceptive reader, before he finishes even one of the novels, has a pretty good idea of what the view was. Psychological novels customarily contain many remarks describing the psychological traits of the characters; these are stated, but what seems actually to be the concern of such novels is not singular propositions about the characters but general, even universal, propositions about human nature; yet none of these general propositions is stated outright.² These statements often seem to contain the most important things in the novel, and are often the novel's chief excuse for existing; yet they seem to operate entirely behind the scenes. The most important statements, views, theories in a work of literature are seldom stated in so many words. What is more natural, then, than to say that they are *implied*?

We can say it, and doubtless it is true. The difficulty, however, is to track down the relevant meaning of the term "imply." The logic-book senses of implication will not suffice here. There are, of course, statements in works of literature which imply other statements, just as they do anywhere else. If the sentence "Jones is a father" occurred in a novel, it would surely imply "Jones is a male." And if we read "If Smith was surprised, he gave no sign of it" and were later told that Smith was surprised (on this same occasion) but gave no sign of it, we could accuse the author of inconsistency in his narrative. But this is hardly the kind of case we are interested in here. What those who talk about implied truths in literature are referring to is seldom individual propositions at all; they talk about large segments of a work of literature, sometimes an entire novel or drama, as altogether implying certain propositions. But what is the meaning of such a claim? What sense of "imply" is being used?

II

Let us try a few obvious candidates. Perhaps what you imply is what you *meant* to say, or intended to say, even though you did not actually say it. If someone says to a student in a somewhat sarcastic tone of voice

after an examination, "Some people don't do their own work," the student may retort, "Are you implying that I cheat?" The proposition "You
cheat" is the one he *meant* to convey to the student, though without
having said it. Similarly, when I say during a miserable rain, "Lovely
weather, isn't it?" I may be said to imply (intend) the opposite of what
I said—what I meant to communicate to my hearer is that the weather
is foul. So, it may be said, it can be the same in a work of literature.
When we say that the author implied this proposition even though he
did not state it, perhaps we mean simply that this is the proposition he
wanted or intended to get across to his hearers through his work.

Why should people say one thing and mean (intend) another, either
in daily conversation or in works of literature? Why should the proposition they most want to impress upon their hearers or readers be never
stated? Because, surely, they can often impress it on their readers with
greater force and effectiveness by this means. When Jonathan Swift wrote
A Modest Proposal, his words would not have been so devastatingly
effective had he said outright what he meant; he said, with multiplied
examples, just the opposite. Sometimes, indeed, when an author has
meant to communicate something throughout an entire work, and then
goes on to say it explicitly, we are pained and disappointed. "The President of the Immortals had had his sport with Tess," wrote Thomas
Hardy, thus spoiling at the end (as Collingwood quite rightly, I think,
points out in a different connection) the effect of what was otherwise a
fine novel. The reader who has not surmised for himself by page 300
that this is what Hardy wants to communicate to us, hardly deserves to
be told it at the end.

But this sense of "imply" is subject to an interesting objection. The
test of whether a given proposition is implied in a work of art, as thus
far explained, is simply whether the artist meant to communicate it to
his audience by means of the work. If p is the proposition he meant to
convey, then p is the proposition implied in the work. But can't the
artist be wrong? Suppose he meant to convey one proposition, p, but
didn't succeed, or succeeded in conveying to his readers another one, q,
which he never intended or even thought of. And if all readers agree
that q is the proposition implied, are we still to say that it is p that is
implied because the author said so?

The main trouble here is that what is implied (in this sense) seems
to require no connection with the words and sentences that are actually
to be found in the work of literature. If Hardy (in a document just discovered) were to tell us that what he meant to convey in his novels is
that humanity is nearing perfection, then this is implied in the novels,
even though the novels seem to contradict such an assertion utterly at
every point. If the poet says sincerely that what he meant to say in the
poem is that reality is circular (and artists have said stranger things than
this about their work), then this proposition is what is implied in the
poem; and if the poet changes his mind and says that what he meant

to convey is that blue is seven, then this (if it can be called a proposition at all) is implied. He said that he meant *p* or *q*; but does it follow that *p* or *q* is implied? Is he the final test? We might read the poem till doomsday without any such notion entering our heads as that reality is circular; but, one might say, this only shows that the poet did not *succeed* in communicating this proposition to us, not that he did not mean to communicate it; and thus far what he meant to communicate has been the test of what proposition or propositions are implied.

III

Let us, then, try to find a criterion of implication other than what the artist meant or wanted to convey; following the hint just given, why not say that the criterion is what proposition he *succeeded in conveying*? What he meant to convey and what he did actually convey to his readers may, after all, be two different things.

But now another objection occurs at once: here the criterion of what is implied does not depend on the author, but it does depend on his readers. If the poem does not succeed in communicating to the readers proposition *p*, then the poem does not imply *p*. Moreover, it would follow that the poem may imply one proposition to one reader and a very different one (or none at all) to another reader, or even to the same reader at a different time. If the audience is dull, stupid, or sleepy, no proposition is implied no matter how much the poet meant to convey one and how much care he took to convey it, while if the audience is sensitive, alert, and imaginative, that same poem may imply a whole host of propositions, including many that never occurred to the poet at all or to any reader but one. This is, to say the least, an extremely relativistic kind of implying. Surely, one is tempted to say, a proposition is implied or it is not, and whether it is or is not doesn't vary with the intelligence or imaginative capacity of the audience or whether they have just been fed tranquillizing pills and taken the road to Miltown. I do not deny that we *can*, if we please, use the word "imply" in this sense, but I doubt very much whether it is a sense which anyone ever gives the word in practice, and it is certainly not a sense which (once we realize what it involves) would be at all acceptable to those who speak of propositions as being implied in works of literature.

IV

The trouble with the attempts at pinpointing the notion of implication we have considered thus far is that whether or not something is implied is determined by the artist's intention or by the audience's response, but not by the work of art itself. We want to be able to say that something is implied even though the author may not intend it and be quite unaware of it, and even though the audience may be so unperceptive as not to grasp it. In that way we shall at least be released from having to know the author's intentions to know what is implied.

Let us begin again with our previous example. "Some people don't do their own work," the person says to the student in an accusing tone of voice. Doubtless he intended to accuse him of cheating. But one might well allege that quite apart from this, he implied it: by what he said, by his tone of voice, by the whole context of the utterance (in connection with having finished an examination, and so on). A speaker uttering these words in this tone and in this context *does*, we would say, imply this, and if he later says that he didn't imply it because he didn't intend to, this does not exonerate him from the charge of implying it just the same.

It is surely this sense that G. E. Moore had in mind when he gave his classic example of implication: when I say that I went to the pictures last Tuesday, I thereby imply that I believe that I went. Of course I did not *say* that I believed it; this is no part of the statement I made, and one cannot formally deduce the proposition that I believed I went (*q*) from the proposition that I went (*p*). It is not the proposition *per se* that implies this, but my *utterance* of the proposition, in a normal tone of voice, without evidence of joking or playing tricks on my listener. I do imply *q* when I utter *p* in this way, in that anyone who knows the language and can interpret facial expression and manner is *entitled*, by virtue of all these, to infer *q*. If I later disavow this and claim that I was only exercising my vocal cords, I would not be excused (say, in a court of law) from having implied *q* in my utterance. "But you implied that you believed it by what you said and the way you said it. So you did imply it, whether you intended to or not."

Can we apply this kind of implication to works of literature? There is one difficulty at the outset: there is an enormous difference between literature and the examples we have just considered from everyday conversation, in that when Jones speaks to us, we have not only his spoken utterance to go by but all the other cues such as his facial expression and gestures and tone of voice and the environmental circumstances accompanying the utterance. When Jones writes us a letter, however, we have only his written word as a guide. There are many inferences we might make if we *saw* him speaking that we are unable to make when we have before us only the sentences he has recorded. There are not as many clues in the written word alone. This makes things more difficult; but still, it is not as if there were *no* clues. What a person writes *may* give us good evidence of what he thinks or believes, even though he nowhere tells us that he thinks or believes these things.

Works of literature, of course, are a special case of the written word, and we can sometimes make inferences from them. We can infer many things about Theodore Dreiser's beliefs, without knowing anything about him as a man, by reading his novels: that his view of life was (roughly) materialistic; that he saw man as a pawn of destiny, caught in a tangled web of circumstances not of his own making which nevertheless lead him to his doom; that he was a champion of the underdog and the down-trodden, a humanitarian, even a sentimentalist. How can we infer these things? By observing carefully which passages contain the greatest passion and intensity, which themes are most often reiterated, how the plot is made to evolve, which characters are treated with the greatest sympathy, and so on. There are countless clues in the novels themselves that we could cite as evidence for the author's beliefs. (Not for the truth of the beliefs, but for the truth of the proposition that the author entertained them.) And there are no contrary clues. From observing all this, we can say with considerable confidence that the work implies that the author had these beliefs. We are entitled to make this inference, even if by some chance it should turn out that he actually did not have these beliefs. The belief-clues are still there, even if (though this would be surprising, for normally they would not get there if he had not purposely put them there) the beliefs in this case did not exist. (A somewhat analogous kind of case is well-known in discussions of scientific method: our judgment that the next raven will be black is one we are entitled to make on the basis of the thousands of ravens already observed to be black and the absence of any contrary cases; and we are justified in making this inference, even if the next raven should turn out to be an albino.)

"Perhaps, however," an objector may say, "the point is not so much that the author believed this as that he wants *us* to believe it. As long as he can make us believe it, his own beliefs are irrelevant." This introduces the topic of the aesthetic relevance of belief, which is not my subject now. But I would venture this suggestion: Perhaps it doesn't matter whether the author believed *p*. But neither is it necessary, for understanding a work of literature, that *we* believe what the author may have wanted us to believe. Some would say that if we are in a state of belief or conviction, we are already far removed from a state of aesthetic receptivity. Do we know what beliefs Shakespeare had, or what beliefs (if any) he was trying to instill in us? And as far as the appreciation of his plays is concerned, who cares? There are many beliefs stated by the *characters* in Shakespeare's plays; but these cannot all be Shakespeare's beliefs, unless Shakespeare was pathologically addicted to changing his mind, for they constantly conflict with one another; nor can they all be our beliefs, unless we are so irrational as to believe whatever we hear regardless of whether it contradicts what we heard just before. Rather, it is necessary that we *understand* the beliefs to which the characters give voice, that we appreciate why they believe it, and what difference it makes to their motivation and behavior in the drama.

Whatever we may conclude, then, about the relevance of the author's beliefs, we can sometimes make highly probable inferences as to what they were; and when we do so, we can correctly say that the author was, in his written work, implying that he had these beliefs. But if we can infer what his beliefs were, why not his feelings, his attitudes, his intentions? Such inferences again are vulnerable, but they can often be made—perhaps not with Shakespeare, but with Dreiser. The written word often contains intent-clues as well as belief-clues.

Much of the writing of literary critics is given over to discovering, from these clues, what the author's intentions were (sometimes exclusively from these, and not from independent sources outside the work). The critic becomes a kind of sleuth, and from a careful reading of the work he tells us what the author probably felt or intended. Is this going back to intentions again? Not in the same way as before. Here we are not concerned with what he intended—i.e. in his intentions apart from the work—but with what he implied *in* the work *about* his intentions. (Not that there is anything sinful about discovering his intentions through outside sources, such as his autobiography. If we want to know what his intentions were, the work itself may offer no clues to this, and we have to discover it in other ways. There is no "fallacy" involved in this. We are in no position to cut ourselves off *a priori* from sources of information which may turn out to be useful, and if the author—outside his work— can enlighten us, we are cheating only ourselves if we refuse to accept this source of enlightenment. And if one objects, "But if you have to go outside the work to the artist to find such clues, the work is not self-sufficient, autonomous, etc., for the intentions should be embodied in the work and be wholly inferrable from it," we can reply that this is a counsel of perfection. Works of art may not be entirely self-sufficient— whatever exactly that is—and moreover there appears to be no compelling reason why they should be. Can we deny that some works, at any rate, mean more to us than they would if we had no such outside knowledge?)

A work of literature may also provide clues about the author's *unconscious* intentions, and a critic well-versed in psychiatry may discover them. Just as we say in daily life that a man does not intend, consciously, to be unpleasantly aggressive, he nevertheless has many such unconscious intentions (he says things in a hostile manner without meaning to, and unconsciously chooses situations for saying them that would strike any observer as calculated to arouse resentment), so we may make similar discoveries from the written word, though it takes someone who is both a sensitive critic and an astute psychiatrist to do this. (When Ernest Jones attempts it with *Hamlet,* I find his conclusions convincing, but when Ella Freeman-Sharpe attempts it with *King Lear,* I do not.) When this is well done, we have not merely a series of inferences about the author's personality—which would be of interest principally to clinicians —but clues to the interpretation of a work, or at least *an* interpretation of a work, which might otherwise have puzzled us forever.

One final point: although we sometimes draw inferences from works of literature to their authors, it may happen that we *think* we are doing this when we are actually doing something else.[3] Suppose that on walking through an empty building I see written on the blackboard a great many incendiary remarks and obscene epithets. I do not know who the author is, and presumably the words were not intended specifically for me. I may suspect that the author had vitriolic feelings when he wrote it, but this is not the inference that I normally make. He may have written it as a joke, or at random as a kind of verbal doodling, or seriously for someone's attention; I do not know. Accordingly I do not infer anything at all about the author. I conclude only that inflammatory language is being used—no matter by whom or for what purpose. Nor do I *infer* this; this language *is* inflammatory, and I do not so much infer this as *recognize* it as such; I make no inferences from it whatever.

We are sometimes in this situation with regard to works of literature. When we see the line "I fall upon the thorns of life! I bleed!" whether or not we know that Shelley wrote it, we can say that the lines are despairing in character. This is what they are, and they remain so even if neither Shelley nor the reader was despairing. We simply recognize them as lines of a certain character; the word "despairing" refers to a property of the poem, not of its author. Often what may first pass as inductive inference to propositions about the author is not only not inductive but is not inference at all.

V

But let us have an end of intentions. We have considered how an author's work, or parts thereof, can be said to imply that the author had certain beliefs, attitudes, or intentions. But this is not the end of the matter. Does not a work of literature often imply propositions, not about its author, but about the world, about human life, human traits, the human situation, the cosmos? Through reading the work we somehow arrive at these propositions—*not* the rather incidental proposition that the author believed them, although we may infer this also. (We might say in such cases, not that the *author* implied this or that in his work, but that *the very words* imply it. But this distinction is not a sharp one, and I am not sure how far we would have to stretch our ordinary use of such expressions in order to make such a distinction sharp.)[4]

Before trying to be more precise about this, I shall give a few examples of sentences implying propositions which are never stated and which have nothing to do with the speaker's beliefs. A reporter asks an anthropologist, "Would you say that the Bongoese are a clean people?" and the anthropologist replies, "I would not say that the Bongoese are clean." Note that he did not say that they were *not* clean; he said only what he would *not* say—he would not say that they were clean, but he would not say that they were not clean either; perhaps he knew nothing one way or the other about the Bongoese. But though he did not say they were not clean, it does seem plausible to hold that the sentence *implies* this to anyone who is at all aware of the English idiom (whether or not the speaker intended any such thing). Or, the physician says, "Yes, of course the patient died. I wasn't his physician." He does not *say* that the patient would have lived if he had been the patient's physician, but this certainly seems to be what is implied. (Note that what the sentence implies is that the patient died because this man was not his physician, *not* that the physician *believed* that the patient died because he was not the physician.)

There is surely a relation here which in daily life we do not hesitate to call implication. Nor is it bizarre or mysterious; it is a garden variety sort of thing which we constantly recognize. What exactly does it consist in? There does not seem to be any term (other than "implication" itself) that describes it precisely; it seems to be closest to what, in one sense, we call *suggestion*.[5] Statements often suggest other statements, which need not at all be about the person who utters them. "They had children and got married" suggests that they had illegitimate children, even though the utterance was a slip of the tongue and the order of the two clauses should have been reversed. "He saw the dragon and fell down dead" suggests, though it does not state, that he fell down dead because he saw the dragon. What is actually *said* is usually very limited, and when pressure is applied it tends to narrow still further: "Did he actually *say* he was going to kill you? True, he said he was going to make mincemeat out of you, but . . . ." And as our conception of what was actually said narrows, our conception of what was implied (suggested) tends to expand.

Why not conclude, then, that literature implies many propositions in the sense of suggesting them? The word "suggest," however, as it is presently employed, is not quite tailor-made for this job:

(1) The word "suggest" ordinarily has a far wider range than that of "imply" as we are now considering it. "To me this poem suggests the sounding surf, tropical islands, wine-red sunsets. . . ." This is a perfectly legitimate sense of "suggest," one in which what is suggested is not a proposition at all, and it is not at all synonymous with "imply." Is this because what the poem suggests here is not a proposition? No, for most of the cases in which what is suggested *is* a proposition will not do either: "To me this play suggests that the hero was struggling, afraid to face the truth about himself, trying to repress it without knowing it himself. . . ." This may indeed be what the play suggests to a particular reader, and it may do so even if the reader is just "imagining things" and there is not the slightest textual basis for such a claim. What a line suggests to you, it may not suggest to me; in our ordinary use of "suggest"

there is virtually unlimited subjectivity, whether what is suggested is or is not a proposition. But this is not true of the cases we are now concerned with. I want to say that a line suggests this or that, not to you or to me, but suggests, period; or at least that it suggests it to anyone who understands the words and is acquainted with the idiom of the language. "They had children and got married," though it does not *say* that they had illegitimate children, *does* suggest this, and if a person does not catch the suggestion (whether it is an intentional one on the part of the speaker or not), he is stupid or blind to any subtlety of linguistic expression. If we continue to use "suggest," then, we shall have to limit its application rather arbitrarily to these "objective" cases, excluding the to-you-but-not-to-me cases. And in view of our common use of this term, it is difficult to make this stricture stick.

(2) Even when the stricture is accepted, the term "suggest" seems unsatisfactory for another reason: it is far too pallid, too vanilla-flavored. The term "suggestion" suggests (!) something not quite there, lurking in the background, or visible through the trees if one squints. But works of literature, as well as sentences in daily discourse, may suggest in a far stronger way than this. The implied proposition, or thesis, or moral, of the work (where there is one), far from being "suggested" in this way, may be the most prominent thing in it; it may leap out at you, scream at you, bowl you over. Shall we say that Ibsen's *A Doll's House* only *suggests* that a woman should develop her personality and have a life of her own as much as her husband, or that Swift's *A Modest Proposal* only *suggests* that perhaps England was not treating Ireland in a humane manner? Perhaps we should say, not that these propositions are suggested by the work, but that they are *intimated* by it.[6] Or perhaps simply, "He said it all right, but not in so many words!"

Still, subject to these severe limitations, and because "imply" seems to have no ready synonym for this context, let us proceed with "suggest." Swift's *A Modest Proposal* is an instance of irony. Must irony be defined intentionalistically, as saying the opposite of what one intends? The disadvantage of this is, of course, that to know whether a given work was ironical, one would have to know whether it was so intended. It seems preferable to define "irony" as implying (suggesting) the opposite of what one says. One can even apply this to parody, which is often used as an incontrovertible example of a genre in which reference to the author's intention is indispensable. "To know that something is a parody, you have to know whether the author *meant* to parody this or that. If he didn't, you can hardly criticize him for failing to do something he didn't intend to do." In the intentionalistic sense, this is true; but we *can* criticize the work for not suggesting an interpretation other than the one it bears on its face. A good parody always contains countless such marks, whether or not the author so intended.

A frustrating and at the same time fascinating aspect of complex works of literature is their resistance to a single interpretation, in that many propositions seem to be implied, some of them contradicting others. The work would be far less rich in texture without this feature. Nor need any of the conflicting interpretations be wrong; both of two contradictory propositions may really be suggested by a work of literature, and though of course they cannot both be true, they may both really be implied, and both may live in aesthetic harmony in the same work, giving it a kind of piquancy by the very tension which is thus set up. How is *Paradise Lost* to be interpreted? There is some evidence in the text that man's fall is a dire catastrophe, a work of Satan in defiance of God; there is other evidence that the entire series of events was foreordained by omnipotence, and thus, in view of divine benevolence, not a catastrophe at all; and there is some evidence that man's state after the Fall is much better, in that he has free-will in a sense which he lacked before ("a paradise within thee, happier farr"). It is, I think, only of marginal interest to ask, What did Milton believe? or what did Milton intend? The question is: Regardless of what he believed or intended, what beliefs got embodied in the poem? Which propositions are stated, and what further ones are implied?

One fruitful field of suggested propositions is the following: Works of literature are able, through the delineation of character and the setting forth of situations which are followed through in the details of the plot, to suggest *hypotheses* about human behavior, human motivation, human actions, and sometimes about the social structure. In doing so it doubtless enters upon the domain of the social sciences; but in the present undeveloped state of these sciences, I do not think that a bit of supplementation from the literary artists (who are, at the least, excellent observers of the human scene) will be thought to crowd the scientists unduly. In any event, many writers have believed themselves, and with good reason, to be commentators on and interpreters of human behavior and the social situation in their time. Zola certainly considered himself to be one, and John Dos Passos another. Works of literature may suggest hypotheses of various kinds. Some are empirical in character—for example, Tolstoy's *War and Peace*, even apart from the explicitly stated philosophy of history at the end, suggests a hypothesis about the genesis of great events in history in relation to their leaders; and Dreiser's novels suggest semi-empirical and semi-metaphysical hypotheses about the helplessness of human beings caught in a web of circumstances beyond their control and carried on willy-nilly to their destruction. Many works of literature suggest what one might call *moral* hypotheses—Dostoyevsky, George Eliot, Victor Hugo. Works of literature do not, of course, *verify* these hypotheses; that is the task of the empirical sciences. But they can suggest hypotheses which may be empirically fruitful; and this is, of course, a far more difficult task than verification.

Now, what has all this to do with the topic of truth in literature, with which we began? Simply this: we were looking for propositions, and especially true propositions, in works of literature, other than explicitly stated ones. And we have found, first, that works of literature may provide us with evidence for propositions about the author's beliefs, attitudes, and intentions, thus entitling us to infer these propositions; and, second, that quite apart from any reference to their authors, these works may suggest or intimate (say without saying) numerous propositions which are not about the author but about the world, about the subject-matter of the work itself. And since some of these suggested propositions are doubtless true, we have here, surely, an important sense of truth in literature, and one which it seems to me that many critics who have made claims for truth in literature have had in mind without being fully aware of it.

Two final precautions: (1) I am not saying that truth in literature is an important feature of these works *aesthetically*. On this point, as far as the present paper is concerned, I am quite content to agree with Professor Arnold Isenberg when he says, "What is so glorious about truth? Why should a quality which all except the demented commonly attain in the greater number of their ideas be considered so precious as to increase the stature of a Milton or a Beethoven if it can be ascribed to him?"[7] Though in fact I would not go so far as this, the matter would have to be separately argued. (Roughly, I would hold that the thesis implied in a work of literature may be the most important single feature of that work, and that it may be an important thesis, never before thought of by anyone; but not that we must accept the thesis as *true*.) (2) Nor am I saying that the author of the work of literature means to *assert* the propositions he implies. He may, and in most cases he certainly does, wish to assert them, or he would not have taken such pains to suggest them; but this has to be discovered by checking the relevant data (including the work itself) and will enlighten us about the author's beliefs. I am saying only that a work of literature may imply certain propositions and that these implied propositions may be true; it is not even necessary that the author mean to *assert* that they are true. This too is a separate consideration.

Notes

1. The language of fiction seems to raise special problems: Is it true that Hamlet was the Prince of Denmark? Of course; just read the play. But how can it be true, since there never was a Hamlet at all? But then it's false. Still, Shakespeare's Hamlet *was* Prince of Denmark, wasn't he? These have been dealt with abundantly in the recent literature. (See Monroe C. Beardsley, *Aesthetics*,

pp. 411-414, and the numerous references on the topic listed on pp. 441-443, 446-447.) Once the peculiar logic of fictional sentences has been cleared up, no *special* problem of truth, I think, arises.

2. For example, the psychological observations of Marcel Proust are excellently described by Morris Weitz in his paper "Truth in Literature," *Revue Internationale de Philosophie,* IX (1955), 116-129.

3. This point was suggested to me by Professor Isabel Hungerland.

4. See Max Black, "Presupposition and Implication," in S. Uyeda (ed.), *A Way to the Philosophy of Science* (Tokyo, 1958), pp. 443-448.

5. See Monroe C. Beardsley, *Aesthetics,* p. 123.

6. This term was suggested to me by Professor Max Black.

7. *JAAC,* XIII (March 1955), 3, 400. (This paper appears next in this Section. Ed.)

ARNOLD ISENBERG

The Problem of Belief

PEOPLE ARE INFLUENCED in their responses to works of art by the beliefs which they hold on all sorts of questions and by the ways in which the works seem to impinge upon those beliefs. It might well be an object of interest to psychologists to study these influences. Critics and aestheticians, however, find themselves raising the strange question of the "legitimacy" or "relevance" of these belief reactions.[1] Some think them improper and intrusive while others hold them to be quite in order. The question, though not excessively clear, has been much debated; and it is possible to speak of "sides." I take one side, holding as I do the extreme view that belief and aesthetic experience are mutually irrelevant. I shall marshal some of the arguments that support this side, then state one fairly serious objection and reply to it. But, first, there are three ways in which the subject is to be limited; and I must take a few minutes to explain what they are.

i. "Belief" and "disbelief" are closely connected with problems of mimicry and illusion, psychic distance, topics in the theory of painting and of drama—in a word, with many problems in aesthetics. But I shall be considering as prime examples only lines of poetry and sentences of prose and, among those, only straightforward statements of fact—of which, as I am not the first to remark, imaginative literature is full: "The rainbow comes and goes," "From fairest creatures we desire increase," and so on without end. In other words, I am keeping (for the most part) to propositions which *can* be believed and *are* believed or disbelieved; for here, if anywhere, belief should count. The revival of interest in our present subject which started with Mr. Richards thirty years ago, like the original statement of the problem in the philosophy of Plato, began with the observation that much poetry that we all think very fine is incredible while much that we believe to be true is mediocre or bad. And this remains for most people the central conundrum—for how can

Reprinted from the *Journal of Aesthetics and Art Criticism*, Vol. XIII (March 1955).

we love and enjoy what we doubt or reject? Let us remind ourselves of
this paradox by recalling some beautiful lines from *Hyperion*. One of
the old hierarchy of gods and Titans, now deposed by Zeus and the
Olympians, speaks these consoling words to Saturn:

> So on our heels a fresh perfection treads,
> A power more strong in beauty, born of us
> And fated to excel us, as we pass
> In glory that old Darkness: nor are we
> Thereby more conquer'd, than by us the rule
> Of shapeless Chaos . . . .
> . . . . for 'tis the eternal law
> That first in beauty should be first in might.

I should think it a fair paraphrase to say that this asserts a constant and
unending progress from lower to higher in nature. Herbert Spencer may
have believed something of the sort. We do not believe anything of the
sort.

   ii. Each of us has millions of beliefs, not one of which is left behind
when we go to the theater or open a volume of poems. But no work of
art will impinge on more than a few of these beliefs. The *Nightingale
Ode* does not impinge on my belief that Sirius is very large; it may, however, impinge on various beliefs about the sadness of life or the lon-
gevity of nightingales. When this happens, the belief is called out of its
subliminal grotto and becomes what some would call a state of consciousness and others an active set. It grapples with the poem that
aroused it and, as often as not, strangles it. (I have also heard tell of
poems that slew grisly beliefs in single combat; but I have not known
whether to believe these stories.) What shall we call this aroused state
of the belief? I would call it assent, or dissent, or by one of the names—
like "doubt"—that stand for equally lively states in between. Let us take
assent and dissent as typical. But now we should observe that the poem
need not impinge directly on the belief or the belief respond to something directly stated in the poem. The reader may dissent from some
idea that is, in any of a thousand ways, "implied" by the poem. The
tone of the poem may evoke in him the idea of a belief that he dislikes.
For that matter, he can respond to a belief that he thinks is held by all
who brush their hair as the poet does. The poem need not give offense
for the belief to take offense. Beliefs and believers are more and less
sensitive. I need only speak the phrase "red grass," or paint some red
grass, and some people will bristle with dissent, though it be hard to
say just what they are dissenting from. Hence a vague, circumambient
displeasure, the source of which the reader hardly knows, or a mood
of diffuse but genial consent. This might be called the cognitive penum-
bra of the poetic experience; and I mention it only to dismiss it and

return to the central statements of poetry, the direct response of the reader. If it were our task to sweep every last shred of belief from the nooks and crevices of aesthetic experience, these lurking insinuations might be of greater concern than the open clash between poet and reader; but such a labor might well be of infinite magnitude.[2] I am helped in my present resolve by this reflection: no matter how far we should penetrate the cognitive recesses of poetry, there would still subsist for us and our argument the question of assent or dissent. If belief in the manifest doctrine of the poem is not relevant, we should hardly consider relevant a belief in some elusive intimation. I can thus hope to circumscribe the entire problem by reasoning "from the stronger."

iii. If a man should take exception to something that a poet says and at the same time express a dislike for the poetry, or if he should give his disagreement as a ground for his dislike, I do not know how we can separate his "cognitive" from his "aesthetic" reaction. In critical theory we are not competent experimentalists. And I do not know that we are in a position to *moralize.* Does it make good sense to ask whether beliefs, considered as psychological states, *should* influence tastes? They do; and that may well be the end of the matter! It is not clear, therefore, how we should understand such a phrase as "the aesthetic relevance of belief."

But beliefs, like poems, are subject to criticism. The criticism of a belief follows a standardized method, commonly termed "verification," and terminates in a verdict of "probable" or "improbable," "true" or "false." Our snap judgments and stubborn prejudices are compelled by this method to follow the courses to which they have previously committed themselves. They come out into the open field and can be spotted for what they are. Now if the criticism of poetry also follows a method by which, it is hoped, genuine values can be distinguished from spurious ones, it should be possible to compare that method with the characteristic criticism of belief, and to determine their identity or difference in character and result. Factors in human response which, as states of mind, are imponderable and mutually inextricable become distinguishable in terms of their several commitments. In other words: even though we should be unable to say how far the *liking* for a poem depended on *agreement* with the poem, we could quite intelligibly ask whether the *criticism* of a poem coincided with the *verification* of its statements and so, in the end, whether beauty depends upon truth. I shall, at any rate, assume that the question of the place of belief in the appreciation of poetry leads us over into the question of the role of truth as a criterion of aesthetic value. Let us dwell for another minute on this point as to how the psychological and the criteriological questions are bound together.

In modern philosophy since the time of Peirce, beliefs have been treated as a class of motor dispositions. Assent and dissent are, or involve, motor sets. And these motor sets are, in the well-chosen word of Eliseo Vivas, "transitive": that is, they look beyond the present to its sequel, beyond the meaning of the poem to its truth. Hence they distract us from the values given to contemplation and set up a tension between what is seen and what is foreseen. Now I am inclined to think that aestheticians on my side of the fence have made too much of these motor attitudes. It is true that, with refined methods of study, we might find it possible and worthwhile to distinguish carefully between one kind of covert impulse and another. The suspense of music and of drama is *not* the suspense of waiting for news from the hospital. The neural and muscular impulses, if investigated, would not be found to be alike. But we need not jealously guard the aesthetic experience and reprimand every faint muscle tremor of the wrong sort. Small belief reactions are harmless if they are enveloped and controlled by a dominant aesthetic set. Mention *criticism*, however, and belief can no longer remain snugly coiled, or half unfurled, in some kind of causal interaction with the enjoyment of poetry. Criticism takes belief on an open and explicit review of all that it has committed itself to, including evidence it may never yet have taken into account. And there we see it manifestly parading not only far beyond the casual aesthetic experience but beyond all those considerations which the *criticism of the poem* has found it necessary to review. The most detailed criticism of the passage I quoted from Keats will not begin to notice the major points that everyone would consider "relevant" for an evaluation of the doctrine of progress.

Now for our main points. These are not steps in consecutive argument but successive aspects of the problem that, along with others, would need to be taken into a rounded survey.

1. Whatever is believed must at least be understood; and this suggests that there is such a thing as understanding, detachable from belief. When something is said to us, we understand *before* we can assent and to accept or reject must take further steps in search of evidence; but then it should be possible to understand without being concerned with truth or falsity. I said that when a poem impinges on a belief, the belief is aroused. But this does not always happen, and, in principle, need not happen. I should think that all of you in this room had read the lines from *Hyperion* many times before and that few of you had ever asked yourselves whether you agreed with them—and this not from any slackness of attention but from the very fullness and fineness of your preoccupation with the meaning. You were making a different use of the proposition, which became for you simply an "aesthetic object." To be preoccupied with the aesthetic object implies no disregard of the "content" of the poem—only a disregard of one function of that content, namely, its relationship to observable fact. Someone has said that "ideas have consequences." Well, ideas have values—many besides their truth values, many even besides their aesthetic values. Gottlob Frege, in his famous essay on "Sense and Denotatum," said that "in listening to an epic, we are fascinated by the euphony of the language and *also by the*

sense of the sentences. . . . Whether the name 'Odysseus' has a denotatum," he goes on, "is therefore immaterial to us as long as we accept the poem as a work of art."[3]

Readers of poetry are capricious in their habits of dissent. We do not dissent from everything we think false but, perhaps, from statements we think *wildly* false, silly and preposterous, false on points of doctrine we think *important* or false, again, on petty points of information learned in school, such as that it was stout Balboa and not stout Cortéz who discovered the Pacific. Poetry drugs the dragon of disbelief, who can be rearoused only by counteracting features of provocation in the poem, such as sensational error. On the other hand, if something is so obviously false that it could not take anybody in, we do not dissent; for some of us are concerned primarily that others should not believe what we think is false.—But if these extra determinants are needed to make us raise the question of truth, we may at least wonder whether it is truth and falsity as such that are relevant.

Belief *adds* nothing to what is proposed. It only affirms the proposition. But a proposition first affirmed and then denied remains the same aesthetic object.

When we have once seen the understanding of the poem as something independent of belief, we begin to ask whether it does not account for everything in the experience of poetry that has been ascribed to the influence of belief. Language often *plays* upon the environment and demands, therefore, for its understanding, some attention to the environment. Someone says, "Here comes old Winston." I turn and see a dog. Instead of confirming my friend's words, this might well alter my understanding of them; then I may or may not take up the new question of truth. Critics often turn from a poet's text to discuss the things he is talking about and sound as if they were rating his lines by their truth. But if they keep coming back to the passage and turn all their observations to the clarification of its meaning, it becomes obvious that the world is being treated as an illustrated supplement to the poem, and not the other way round. We hear it said sometimes that we cannot enjoy the Greek plays as the Greeks did because we do not have the same beliefs. But those beliefs posited an environment; and that environment may have been needed to give the right shades of sense to passages in the play. How, in other words, do we know that we *understand* the plays as the Greeks did? Before we say that believing is relevant to value, we should be sure we know what is being valued and what is being believed.

2. The understanding can encompass anything that has been found to be true, as well as much that has not. It is nothing against a proposition, considered as an idea, that it should describe the world as it is; but then it is the world described that matters to us and not the fact that it is the real world that is being described. If the real world is in-

teresting, it is still no better than many imagined worlds. In a fine chapter on Intuition in *The Realm of Spirit,* Santayana explained how "intuition . . . sublimates knowledge into vision." "Then a body of positive knowledge of fact acquires the values of fiction." Reality surrenders its ontological prerogative when it is treated as one spectacle among many; but it may gain something in return.[4]

3. Truth is not sufficient for beauty nor belief for enjoyment. Thousands of propositions that we believe to be true we also deem perfectly trivial. Truths about the human heart are no *truer,* and no more firmly believed, than truths about the human pancreas. And this suggests at once that when we have "a great truth about the heart," what makes it *great* and what makes it a truth *about the heart* are not what makes it true. Perhaps it is not the truth but what the truth is about, i.e., the content of the proposition, that makes it great.

Men of letters who insist upon some version of the idea that beauty is truth would never accept as an example of their meaning the truth of the proposition, "There are not less than three people in this room." Their "truth" is not plain truth. Theirs is a fancy truth or, to speak more respectfully, a higher truth. But they are not unwilling to appropriate the prestige of the plain truth. And this prompts a query, which I must leave it to you to answer, about the sources of that prestige. What is so glorious about truth? Why should a quality which all except the demented commonly attain in the greater number of their ideas be considered so precious as to increase the stature of a Milton or a Beethoven if it can be ascribed to him? Perhaps it is because of the prevalence of liars or because our propensity to error in matters of difficulty and importance creates a reactive emphasis on truth, which then spreads itself over the rest of the cognitive field. Or perhaps there is some other reason.

Again. We do not consider the fact that we believe something a good enough reason for saying it. If we did, we should be uttering stupid truths all day long. A belief, to deserve utterance, must be to the point or purpose; or it must have some quality of interest and originality. There are distinctive cognitive values in ideas over and above their truth; and these are what warrant their publication. Now, poets too are silent about most of their beliefs. And when they pick some out for expression, it is through some sense of their exceptional value. It would be foolish to think that Dante did not know that the Christian view of things was not waiting for him to set it forth, or that Milton thought that until his time the ways of God had not been justified to man. These poets knew they were original; but they did not for a minute suppose they were original thinkers. Hence it looks as if the poem existed for some other reason than to enunciate the belief it may express.

Yet, you say, these poets did believe what they wrote. What would you have? Where should a poet get his material—if not from his fancy—

but from the world he believes himself to be living in? What should he write about but the things he knows? That does not mean that knowing something is a sufficient reason for writing it down. As well say that if a painter paints a tree, he must be inflamed by the conviction that there are trees.

4. Next, I should hold with those who say that truth and belief are not *negative* conditions either of beauty or of the perception of beauty except insofar as an active dissent may disrupt the entire aesthetic consciousness. In other words, falsity is not a negative aesthetic value but an accident, like a noise in the theater, the awareness of which may displace aesthetic values, good, bad, and indifferent.

There is a famous sentence by Coleridge which has for its grammatical subject a phrase so arresting that many people stop right there. I do not claim to be the first to have reached the predicate—only an independent discoverer. "That *illusion*, contra-distinguished from *delusion*, that negative faith, which simply permits the images presented to work by their own force, without either denial or affirmation of their real existence by the judgment," said Coleridge, "is rendered impossible by their immediate neighborhood to words and facts of known and absolute truth. . . . What would otherwise have been yielded to as pleasing fiction, is repelled as revolting falsehood."

Say: "Mr. Eisenhower is aged six hundred." That is all right, according to Coleridge; that is a mere *jeu d'esprit*. But add: "—and he is President in 1954," and the whole thing becomes revolting. There is something odd in this: why should falsity be innocuous in itself and become offensive only when accompanied by truth? Didn't Coleridge see how strange it is that truth should *damage* the mixture into which it enters—as if a man who can swallow cyanide in any amount should perish in agony if you add a few proteins? I think perhaps he did. For Coleridge is not saying that the neighborhood of truth somehow makes falsity for the first time objectionable. That is not so: truth can only redeem or balance falsity. Coleridge is saying that the awareness of truth makes us aware of falsity. It converts fiction into assertion of fact; and assertion of fact can be erroneous. By a kind of psychological infection, a sentence held to be true communicates to its neighbor the cognitive concern which lies behind it; and so, if the neighboring sentence is false, creates a contrast effect on the plane of cognition.—Coleridge, then is so far on the side of us who say that dissent is an intruder on the domain of poetic experience.

But there is still something that Coleridge has overlooked: infection can be reciprocal. If fact can elbow harmless fiction into becoming something fiercer and more ambitious, why should not fiction in turn hypnotize fact so that it lapses into fiction? If we have a sentence *a*, which is neither asserted nor denied, and another sentence *b*, which is asserted, why shouldn't *a* throw its cloak of neutrality over *b*, instead of adopting *b*'s partisanship? Why should illusion be rendered *impossible* by "the neighborhood of truth" if truth itself is passing for illusion?

I think Coleridge would have accepted an example like this. We have, in a novel by Samuel Butler, the description of a wholly fantastic system of law and of medicine. That's fine; that passes. But if a naturalistic novel, or a movie, should present medical practice very largely as it is but with deviations in detail, then that—according to Coleridge—would be held erroneous and provoke objection. The touch of reality allergizes us to mere fancy. But that is not true. *The Tempest* has much in it of the world as it really is, along with its fantasy and magic. Everything fabulous has in it, as the early empiricists stoutly contended, much that is real and true. All fiction combines ideas of what is with ideas of what is not. And we swallow the composition in one gulp, without sifting its ingredients.

Coleridge has taken a mere contingency and blown it up into a principle. We are *apt* to be disturbed by what we take to be an error, just as we are apt to be distracted by something that we think may be true. And—if I am permitted an ordinary generalization not weaker than Coleridge's—we are the more apt to be disturbed if we are not entranced by a work wherein fact and fable, "truths" and "untruths," have been melted into a single vision. But if it is the power of the aesthetic idea which helps to decide whether we shall submit to the illusion or look for little cognitive blemishes, then it is hard to see how those blemishes should enter into that power or detract from it.

5. Those whom I may call the Believers, in aesthetics, have a certain burden of analysis if not of proof. They will admit that people who are warmed by agreement with a poem or disturbed by disagreement are always mistaking those reactions for perceptions of value. Belief and disbelief *can* be baneful influences. The Believers, then, instead of arguing that belief is relevant should try to mark off the relevant kind of belief. But wherever they draw their line, what is to keep someone else from saying of them in their turn that they are "arbitrary," make "artificial distinctions," "emasculate art," "cushion it from reality," "reduce the significance of poetry," or erect a "phantom aesthetic state"? Everyone likes to have the advantage of seeing the subject in its concrete fullness and protesting against schematic divisions. But if at the same time you believe that distinctions are necessary, you should be able to show why one is to be preferred to another.

Now we come to a major difficulty. I do not know that it has ever been framed as an objection to the analysis that I have been defending; but it stirs in the minds of people otherwise well disposed and makes them uneasy.

I could rephrase some of my previous remarks by starting from certain speeches in plays and novels, which proclaim opinions or express moral judgments. Settembrini and Naptha in *The Magic Mountain,* with their long arguments, make a good example; or you could think of Polonius, of Portia with her sentiments about the quality of mercy. One remarks a certain indulgence in our response to these speeches. We do not rate them by what we believe to be their truth. A false speech can be a great speech, just as an evil character can be a great character. We take these "doctrines" as so much action and character, like the bodies and physical motions of the persons in the play. We enjoy the interplay of thesis with antithesis as we do the clashing of swords in a duel. We are satisfied with the aspect recorded, the point of view. And this is not to be confused with the dialectical interest of the themes in Plato, where, though we may not reach a conclusion, we are always pressing toward a conclusion. One who sits back and admires the give-and-take in the *Protagoras* is aestheticizing the dialogue. He does not share the main concern of the author and the characters, who are interested in the truth and who stop at the point of view only because the truth of the matter, embracing so many aspects, is so hard to get at. But in Shakespeare the points of view are somehow final.

I would then go on to say that we can and to some degree do extend this same toleration to lyric poetry and to prose. Opinions become ideas, which are enjoyed simply as contents. Certain poems by Swinburne, for example, which sound as if they bespoke the poet's outlook on life— as, indeed, perhaps they did, despite his subsequent disclaimers—are an expression of "a weary pagan aestheticism" or of "a decadent sensuality." Since "weary sensuality" and the like are to be denounced or rejected and since the poems are distinguished—and distinguished *as wholes,* their philosophy and all—the critic with an ounce of logic in his head finds himself confounded. But we discover that Swinburne, in a note to the really perverse and unwholesome *Dolores,* says, "I have striven here to express that transient state of spirit through which a man may be supposed to pass, foiled in love and weary of loving, but not yet in sight of rest; seeking refuge in those 'violent delights' which 'have violent ends,' in fierce and frank sensualities . . . ," with more to the same effect. Taking the poet's cue, we find suddenly that what was a vicious sentiment becomes a histrionic moment, a picture of thought and feeling, a "speech," and a fine one. But surely we did not require instruction from the poet. His note is not decisive: it will not disarm the moralist and it did not help the intelligent Victorian reader, who took the proper attitude from the beginning, as witness his consent to the poet's "genius," despite a residual consternation.

I do not mean to suggest that drama is to be taken as exemplary for literature in general. Our ability to set a sermon, an argument, a piece of information, a cry for help in a dramatic frame shows how flexible, in principle if not in fact, is our response to language, how independent of any rigorous control by the contents presented. And if as I contended above there is an aesthetic mode of commerce with human speech, no utterance of whatever cast or complexion need be ultimately refractory to this mode.

But now comes the antagonist, who takes me up at my own words. He says: Begin with the simplest case. Imagine a person in the play. Suppose he is a slanderer. He says something about Desdemona; and what he says about Desdemona is not true. Suppose he is a trickster. He says something about Birnam Wood's coming to Dunsinane; and Birnam Wood both does and does not come. Before he can so much as characterize himself by his speech, you must know at least *some of the rest of the play*. But references in the play do not always restrict themselves to the play. Oswald Alving, the hero of *Ghosts*, goes mad at the end. How do we know this? Because he asks for the sun. "Give me the sun, mother. I want the sun. The sun. The sun." It is only because we know that he cannot have the sun that we take him for one who has lost his mind— and this is knowledge about the real world. If we were to consider speeches of ethical import, it would soon appear that they cannot characterize either unless the audience has at least some ethical convictions, some perception of ethical truth. Cordelia is not good and Goneril is not bad unless something is good or bad. You could not detect a weary aestheticism, in Swinburne or elsewhere, you could not relish that "aspect of things," unless you had first judged it by standards of goodness and virtue.

The antagonist continues: You said, "Belief does not add anything to what is proposed." But belief has its own linguistic counterparts: usually, the declarative and categorical form of the verb. The poet, if he wished to entertain you with "ideas," was at liberty to use gerunds or subordinate 'that' clauses—as diarists who are not confident of their opinions in fact do. Or he could (and sometimes does) weaken the force of his verbs with "maybe's" and "possibly's." If he comes right out and asserts something, he seems to be demanding assent or challenging dissent as he need not have chosen to do. But surely that does make a difference to the aesthetic content.

The position here is rather novel. It does not say that poetry must be true or that it must be believed. On the contrary, it may be false, it may be disbelieved, and be good almost for that reason. But its contents, and hence its merits, are *relative* to knowledge or at least to opinion about the truth. Hence belief and truth are "relevant."

Before replying to this objection, I would like to display something of its scope and its ramifications. The following examples are in apposition with those just considered.

Frederick, the hero of *The Pirates of Penzance,* was to have been apprenticed as a child to a pilot; but his nurse, misunderstanding her instruction, brought him to a pirate, with whom he remained until the opening of the play. And Alfred Doolittle, the cockney dustman of *Pygmalion*, returns in the last act a wealthy toff; for he had been recommended to an American millionaire as the most original moralist in Great Britain. Such incidents, it might be said, are farcical just because they are so wildly improbable; and without the belief in their improbability, no farce. The point might be extended beyond farce to fantasy, and further. The shock of surrealist extravagance comes just from the intrusion of the unreal upon some natural setting, where it is not expected: it is this deliberate offense to our knowledge that makes the devices of these artists so weird. And a critic has said of the Shakespeare tragedies that "their improbability is the price of their effectiveness"; but some might insist that it is more than a price. Cognition is constitutive of the aesthetic fact.[5]

This argument certainly gives us much to think about and opens many new opportunities for confusion. One who has assumed the burden of a universal negative, as I have in this paper, now finds it increased; for he must show, it would seem, that belief is not *in any way* relevant. In such circumstances one can "answer" the opposing case only by offering a simpler and better explanation of the facts on which it rests. Such an explanation may be sketched out as follows.

i. In plays and novels we are apt to have something assumed or identified as "reality," operating as a framework against which the beliefs and assertions of the characters mark themselves off as "appearances" or "illusions." This "reality" and this "appearance" stand to each other much as "real" objects and "mirror" objects do in a painting, both comprised within the fundamental illusion. We in the audience can identify the "real truth" of the play even when this "real truth" is really false. In a horror story you often have one character who at the beginning is a sceptic and who is instantly put down by the reader as a fool simply because he does *not* believe in black magic. Sooner or later he is confounded by the unspeakable "truth." So in serious literature: you and I may think there are many fewer things in heaven and earth than are dreamed of in Shakespeare's *Hamlet*; but we have or should have no doubt that the Ghost is "real." Jocasta, the second personage of *Oedipus the King*, by making light of oracles and their forecasts, displays an offensive "levity." This is a part of the "tragic flaw" which, in the eyes of stern classicists who believe no more in oracles then they do in leprechauns, "justifies" the terrible fate that befalls her. And, indeed, if we regard her as an enlightened, far-seeing woman, we mistake her character; but this mistake is easily avoided. So with Antigone and her projection of the Greek burial taboo into the very heavens, Isabella with her fanatical chastity, and so many others: we judge them in the framework of beliefs and values provided by the play and not by our own serious convictions. And so with the "assertions" of the poet. It does indeed make a difference that he should state and declare rather than suppose or inquire. But the *tone* of assertion, which has become associated with the verb, does not necessarily denote real assertion—any more than the mere word "fire" or the words "nine o'clock" must *fail* to express an assertion. The idea of an assertion is not the assertion of an idea; and it may well be that in poetry it is the idea—the bracketed, fictive "assertion" —that matters.

ii. But of course I do not say that there are no serious assertions and no real truths in poetry. The "reality" of the poem may coincide with reality itself or overlap with it in any measure; and we agree with the poets and their beliefs in every manner and degree. But then truth and reality become illusion. There is no reason why the real sun, in the world outside of Ibsen's play, should not be an assumed "reality" in *Ghosts*, as much as the law of gravitation which is obeyed by the characters. It will then be the case that "truth" is a particular and special issue in the play, on a par with any other.

iii. Among the terms which we apply to objects in painting and incidents of the drama are some which denote frequency, incidence, distribution, causal determination, deviation from or conformity to a rule. There are "common" wild flowers and "rare" tropical ones, "prodigious" happenings like the birth of a two-headed child and "commonplace" or "average" ones. Some events in fiction are "accidental," others "inevitable," still others "miraculous" or "magical." When such statistical and causal characters are presented as actual qualities of the aesthetic object, we must of course note them, as we note red and green, large and small, or proud and humble. And I have just argued, by implication, that we need not bring our own opinions to bear in doing so. The downfall of Oedipus is not "expected" by the protagonist; in the larger frame of the play it is, however, "predestined"; but whether the action as a whole is in the eyes of the audience "probable" or "improbable" is still another question. The underlying question of aesthetic principle is whether what *we* find artistically original, or surprising, or trite, or incredible is relative to our own serious beliefs and anticipations.

One could urge, on many strong and varied grounds, that the frequency and causality adjectives are not often useful or essential. To paint a cat with its tail where its head should be is to produce something as unusual as a Gargantua or a Caliban—but with none of the brilliance of artistic fantasy or of farce. Caliban is grotesque: is he also "unique"? Is that important? Does it make a difference how many of him there are? If men were always biting dogs, journalists would lose interest; but would it become inherently less absurd? We get used to prodigies like the two-headed child; after a while, the smallest shred of incredulity that remains in us as an echo of serious doubt disappears and with it any real surprise. But are they then less monstrous? Or were they better sights to begin with because they were extraordinary? And we get used to the Surrealists: does that deprive them of any genuine eeriness they may have achieved? Apparently, it makes a great difference *what* the event may be that is qualified as "improbable"; for what is utterly unique and unexpected may be aesthetically humdrum and trivial. We may imagine even that Calibans were as common as imbeciles; that events should normally fall out as in Gilbert's operas; or that the universe of Hieronymus Bosch should be our familiar surrounding. Men would then develop a protective imperviousness; for they could not afford to marvel at a Caliban who faced them on every street corner. But, even as things are, we must be exhorted by a Wordsworth, an Emerson, or a Rilke to the recovery of perception. And when, heeding them, we pierce the film of familiarity that has spread itself over objects, we find that roses are red and violets blue, though there be millions of them. Nothing changes its character on account of its prevalence—unless that very character, frequency or rarity, should become an object of experience (much as "universality" becomes a thing actually considered in the Keatsian lines about joy "whose hand is *ever* at his lips/Bidding adieu"); and then, as with any other character, the question of value, far from being settled, is still to be raised.

But conceding as much merit as we can to this group of critical concepts: they still do not entail the relevance of *belief* and *disbelief*. Experience provides us with most of our beliefs. It also makes things familiar or leaves them unfamiliar; and it lends them their meanings and secondary associations. That does not mean that when we evoke and utilize past experience, we are utilizing beliefs. Cross eyes, which many of us thought comical when we were young, carry the suggestion that the bearer is trying to look two ways at once. Nobody believes this. Nobody acts *as if* he believed it. It is quite enough that we should possess the "connotation." Before we adopt a strong principle of explanation like belief, we should see what can be done with a weak one like association.[6] In my opinion, that would always suffice. And criticism confirms this opinion by a justifiable laxity in pressing the questions of frequency, generality, probability; for though one can recall hundreds of passages in which critics have said "this occurs" or "that does not occur," one cannot think of any critic who ever bothered to find out whether it really does or does not.

iv. I have not made these last points as convincing as, with a more thorough study of a larger number of examples, they could be made. It is enough that they should indicate the *possibility* of dispensing with the concept of belief in the aesthetics of poetry. There remains now only the very special class of statements within the poem which refer to other parts of the poem. I believe that with time for detailed consideration we should come to see that these, too, do not require the reader's assent or dissent or any perception of truth or falsity on his part. And I would leave with you as a suggestive model the idea, suitable perhaps as a cover painting for the *Saturday Evening Post*, of a front gate with the sign BEWARE THE DOG while behind the fence parades a small dachshund. I do not think that our way of judging the "falsity" of this sign is properly to be called "disbelief." But I do not mind it if you say that this last remnant of belief does figure quite significantly in the experience of poetry. For a belief whose confirmation terminates within the poem will neither destroy the psychological illusion nor compete with the judgment of aesthetic value. It will act as a minor cognitive phase within a controlling aesthetic purpose.

I come to a last word about the problem of belief in aesthetics. Those of us who offer purified conceptions of the field of aesthetics give reasons, some of which I think you must admit are plausible. But you can probably detect in us an animus which goes beyond those reasons: a desire to sweep the field clean of the traces of cognition. We do indeed have motives which prompt us to draw a sharp line between art and knowledge and to dispose as best we can of objections to that proceeding. Of these motives I may mention two. First, we believe that when aesthetic experience is freed of its entanglement with belief, everything comes out as it should; that is, works of art are seen upon reflection to take the various places in the scale of values that they have already forced mankind, by their own power, to concede to them. When beliefs are admitted as a proper element in valuation, we are not only prone to distortion of values but we are *committed* to greater distortions still, from which we are saved only by blessed inconsistency.—In the second place, we believe that aesthetics is full of problems of the greatest interest, as are too the psychology of belief and the theory of knowledge. But the kind of interest which exists in these two latter disciplines has never transferred itself, along with their categories, to aesthetics; on the contrary, these categories have blocked progress and account in large part for the "dreariness" of the subject, on which a writer in *Mind* lately commented. Is it not strange that after 2500 years during which cognitive conceptions of art have dominated the field of criticism,—endorsed as they are at the present time by accomplished logicians, semioticians, and epistemologists,—no one has ever thought of asking whether a law of excluded middle applies to art: can there be statements in poetry which are neither "poetically true" nor "poetically false"? No one has ever thought of drawing and *following up* a distinction between artistic truth and artistic probability. No one has so much as asked whether the concept of degree of probability might not be useful in the aesthetics of the drama. Nobody speaks of inductive and deductive processes in aesthetic experience. Nobody asks whether the truths of art are not known inferentially and if so, whether they rest on immediate truths. The most elementary ramifications of the problem of knowledge are ignored, for it is very properly felt that their application would be barren. "Truth" and "Knowledge" dignify the subject but do not illuminate it. As for belief, I could offer parallel examples. Epistemology and the psychology of belief furnish poor *models* for use in aesthetics; for these models do not yield principles and details which prove applicable in aesthetic inquiry. That is another reason for avoiding them. . . .

Notes

1. Henry Aiken, "The Aesthetic Relevance of Belief," JAAC, 1951. See also Arnold Isenberg, "The Aesthetic Function of Language," *Journal of Philosophy*, 1949.

2. Since secondary meanings—"overtones" or "connotations"—of which poet and reader are scarcely conscious, unquestionably do figure in the experience, who is to say what other occult forces may not be working in the abyss? A specious case can be made for the role of unconscious beliefs simply by *argumentum ad ignorantiam.*

3. My italics.

4. This point, which in spite of much discussion still lacks a proper theoretical development, has been variously adumbrated as follows:

"The aesthetic experience is imaginative not in the sense that all its objects are fictitious, but in the sense that it treats them indifferently, whether they are fictitious or real; its attitude, whether towards a real object or a fictitious, is the attitude which neither asserts reality, truly or falsely, nor denies it, but merely imagines."—R. G. Collingwood, *Speculum Mentis.*

"Nothing that man has ever reached by the highest flights of thought or penetrated by any probing insight is inherently such that it may not become the heart and core of sense."—John Dewey, *Art as Experience.*

"The whole course of a life is raised to a present datum possessed virtually in all its details by the dramatic imagination. . . . And in that case it would be indifferent that this truth happened to be true rather than mere poetry, since it would be only as poetry that the spirit would entertain it."—Santayana, *The Realm of Spirit.*

Then there are well-known remarks by Sidney, Goethe, Coleridge, Wordsworth, Hardy, *et al.*

5. When we begin to deal with objects which are not propositional in form, we no longer have sure footing. We do not understand how a picture or a dramatic episode can be an "object" of belief. Hence, there is as much temerity in denying as in affirming that belief is relevant. It is only in an endeavor to meet the critical tradition on its own ground that I venture to discuss such examples.

6. Henry Aiken, *loc. cit.,* p. 313: "No doubt Prokofiev's *Classical Symphony* is capable of giving a certain pleasure to persons who have never heard a classical symphony. But the charm which this work has for one who is aware of the classical symphonic forms and devices lies very largely in the composer's witty play with them. To perceive this, however, is . . . to respond immediately, through anticipation and surprise, to his allusions as a felt quality of what is heard."—I cannot see how any scrap of *belief* comes into this.

MORRIS WEITZ

The Form-Content Distinction

Analysis of the Form-Content Distinction

... I should like to propose an empirical theory of art that will resolve the basic issues between formalism and its critics. A number of analyses are required. Let us begin with the analysis of a distinction that, I think, is responsible for more of the difficulties in contemporary aesthetic thought than any other—the form-content distinction.

Now, in order to understand the significance of this distinction in aesthetic (and critical) theory, it may be well to consider the various ways in which the distinction appears in ordinary, common-sense language and in technical logical analysis.

Common sense, to begin with, regards form as a synonym of shape, and content as synonymous with matter in much of its talk. We say, for example, that two pennies, one copper, the other lead, have the same form, meaning shape, and different content, meaning matter. Or we say of two pieces of silver jewelry, where one is round and the other square, that they differ in form but not in content. Or, if we are in the presence of two round tables, one of which is made of oak, the other of mahogany, we may remark that whereas they have the same shape, meaning form, they differ in their matter, meaning content.

But this is not the only way in which common sense distinguishes between form and content. It also employs form as a synonym of appearance, as when it says of a dilapidated house, for example, that its outward form or appearance is ugly.

Further, the distinction manifests itself in ordinary speech in the distinction between the "what" as against the "how" of certain complexes or states of affairs. Consider the presence of four children's playing blocks, called A, B, C, and D. These blocks may be arranged in many different ways, as BACD or ACDB, and so on. In this situation, we could say that

Reprinted by permission of the publishers from Morris Weitz, *Philosophy of The Arts,* Cambridge, Mass.: Harvard University Press, Copyright 1950, by The President and Fellows of Harvard College.

the blocks, the "what" of the complex, are the content, and the serial order arrangement, the "how" of the complex, is the form.

The "what-how" usage, however, usually occurs in the distinction between certain elements and the organization of them. Consider the statement of the four freedoms of the Atlantic Charter. The four sentences of the total statement, complete with their meanings, we call the content, the elements, of the total statement. We further recognize that these elements, these individual sentences, the content, can be arranged or organized in different ways. That is, in one case we may write the sentence about freedom of religion above the sentence about freedom from fear; or we may reverse that order and get a new organization of elements. In these two cases the organization of, the relations between, the elements differ; but the elements—the individual sentences—remain the same. The form changes while the content is constant.

Serial order, however, is not always present in the "how-what" variety of the form-content distinction. Consider the message, "Come home!" We may write it, wire it, telephone it, yell it, or gesture it. Here the content remains the same throughout the different modes of expressing it. The form usage in this example is not rooted in "how" as serial order but "how" as the *way* in which something is said, the mode of expression, the medium.

Common sense also means by form in some of its linguistic usages class, kind, or species; and in this context it means by content the members of the class. We say, for example, that England and America have the same kind or form of government; or that the dance and music as art forms are similar, or that the movies are a form of escape; or that Russia is a form of totalitarianism. Now, in all of these cases, England, America, the dance, music, the movies, and Russia are members of certain classes, the content of certain forms.

The final way that we shall consider in which common sense uses the form-content distinction is in its distinction between abstract pattern and the completion of the pattern. All magazines have in their pages at various times what they call "subscription forms." These are patterns, partly blank, partly filled in. In its original state, each of these has form but no content. It is a variable; we say in logic, a propositional function. When we fill it in, i.e., give values to its variables, we give a content to it; and we may then say it has both a form and a content.

Contemporary logical theory has itself contributed much toward the understanding of the form-content distinction, even as it obtains in aesthetic and critical usage. Bertrand Russell has dealt extensively with the concept of logical form and has elucidated its fundamental meaning. The best way to define form, he declares, is in terms of propositions.

> In every proposition . . . there is, besides the particular subject matter concerned, a certain *form,* a way in which the constituents of the proposi-

tion . . . are put together. If I say, "Socrates is mortal," "Jones is angry," "The sun is hot," there is something in common in these three cases, something indicated by the word "is." What is in common is the *form* of the proposition, not an actual constituent.[1]

From any of these propositions we can derive the others, by a process of substitution; and that which remains unchanged when we replace constituents and get different propositions is the form of these propositions. Form is thus the variable invariant of a number of specific propositions. And the content may be designated as the specific values of any of these propositions. The form of the above propositions is subject-predicate, which mathematical logic symbolizes by Px, where P stands for the predicate and x for the subject. From the variable function Px we can derive, by substituting subject values like "Socrates" or "Jones" or "the sun" and predicate values like "hot" or "angry" or "mortal," the propositions, "Socrates is mortal," "Jones is angry" and "The sun is hot."

Besides the variable function Px there are *relational* variable functions; e.g., aRb or $aRbc$, which are the forms of numerous dyadically and triadically relational propositions like "Socrates loves Plato" or "Mary hates John" and "John gives Joan a book." Mathematical logicians have enumerated others of these logical forms which can be abstracted from our language and actual states of affairs; these include molecular, existential, general, and completely general forms. However, detailed considerations of these belong to more technical discussions in mathematical logic and are not relevant to this aesthetic context.

We may now consider the form-content distinction in contemporary aesthetic theory. In the first place, the common-sense usage of form as shape appears in concrete discussions of the arts. Many aestheticians and artists use shape as a synonym of form. Henry Moore and Alexander Calder, for example, talk about certain natural and human forms.[2]

It is difficult to understand the meaning of content in this linguistic context. Presumably, it has both a narrow and an extended meaning. Narrowly, it refers to *what* is shaped, be it the representation of a man, a horse, or a tree. But in its more extended reference, it denotes the entire work, in which case the forms comprise only part of the total content. Consequently, on this first extended adaptation of the form-content distinction, content and form are not taken as coördinate values of the work of art, but as its genus and species.

Aestheticians (including artists and critics) also mean by form and content the "how" as against the "what" of a work of art. And, so far as I can determine, this usage has at least three distinct variations.

(1) The what of a work of art is its theme, "what it is about," the subject, the "Idea"; and the how is the way in which the Idea or theme is expressed. Artist-critics like A. E. Housman and aestheticians like C. J. Ducasse sometimes talk this way.[3]

In this linguistic context, the content is but one element in the work of art, *the most abstract*; and the form becomes everything else: the lines, colors, even the specific representations of people and events! For example, consider two famous "Crucifixions," one by El Greco, the other by Grünewald. One could say, and quite in keeping with aesthetic usage, that the content of both pictures is similar, namely, the crucifixion, which is the theme of both paintings, "what they are about"; and that the form, which is the manner in which the crucifixion is exhibited, is very different because of the colors, the design, *and* the representations near Christ—in the El Greco, the Virgin weeping on the right of Jesus, with no one on His left; and in the Grünewald, the Virgin again on the right of Jesus, but with John the Baptist on His left, pointing his finger at Him.

The form here includes not only the specific individuals represented, but also all the emotions associated with them. Furthermore, on this view, the content may be said to be repeatable from picture to picture, so that all the "Crucifixions" that there are could be said to have the same content. Also, in this context, aesthetic formalism is the doctrine that it is *how* something is said, not *what* is said, that is all-important.[4]

(2) The what, or content, of a work of art is its terms or elements, which may include dramatic entities like people as well as colors, lines, or shapes, tones, etc., in the case of the arts other than painting; and the how, or form, is all the relations—spatial, temporal, or causal—among the elements.

This usage, I suppose, is the most generally accepted one in contemporary aesthetic analysis and corresponds pretty much to the way in which form and content are mostly used in ordinary linguistic contexts. Content is the terms; form, the organization of them.

In present aesthetic theory Ducasse, although he is diversified and even ambiguous in his usage, is the champion of this interpretation of the distinction. "By form is meant simply *arrangement* or order; and by content . . . whatever it happens to be that is arranged, ordered."[5]

Formalism, in this usage, is the view that in art only the relations are important, not the terms related. Such a theory was held by Herbart and Zimmermann.

(3) The what, or content, is the Idea or theme; and the how, or form, is the medium in which it is presented. Hanslick offers us an excellent example of this usage. He is arguing that in music there is no distinction between form and content which, he continues,

> presents a sharp contrast to poetry, painting, and sculpture, inasmuch as these arts are capable of representing the same idea and the same event in different forms. The story of William Tell supplied to Florian the subject for a historical novel, to Schiller the subject for a play, while Goethe began to treat it as an epic poem. The substance [content] is everywhere the same . . . and yet the form differs in each case.[6]

A third way in which discussions of the arts employ the distinction between form and content is similar to species (2) of the second, except that it is more specific and normative. The content of the work of art is regarded as the elements and the form as a certain kind of *successful* arrangement, i.e., as an arrangement of elements in which certain principles of balance, proportion, and harmony are realized. This usage is as old as Pythagoras; and both Plato and Aristotle sometimes construed artistic form in this way. In present aesthetics, Parker has also advanced such a doctrine.

Formalism, in this tradition, is the view that in art it is harmony, balance, and proportion that are all-important.

The final way that we shall consider in which the distinction between form and content occurs in contemporary theory leads us away from the common-sense usages to the logical one that we discussed above. Aestheticians speak of the sonata form or the sonnet form or fugal forms. What they mean by these terms are certain generic invariants of structure that can be abstracted from many different works of art in the same way in which mathematical logicians abstract invariant patterns from different propositions and facts by substituting variables for values. The musical aesthetician speaks of the classical ABA sonata form, and he means by it what Russell means by the classical subject-predicate form: a pattern that is shared by many different things in the world. The ABA sonata form is that abstract "musical propositional function" which becomes a "musical statement," so to speak, when the three variables, A, B, A, are filled in with the concrete values: exposition, development, recapitulation. When we say, therefore, that Haydn and Mozart, for example, compose in the sonata form, we mean at least that their symphonies have first movements which are alike in that they all have an exposition section, followed by a development section, in which the themes are expanded, inverted, contracted, etc., and a concluding recapitulation section in which the exposition returns to the tonic.

What is true of the meaning of sonata form obtains in the usage of sonnet form as well. Here, too, we are dealing with an abstract pattern, or series of patterns, if we distinguish between the Italian, Shakespearian, and Spenserian sonnet forms, that is, with the variable invariants of a number of different poems.

In this usage, we may say that many works of art have the same form but differ in their content; which usage is the exact opposite of that in which the content of a work of art is said to be the Idea and the form the way in which the Idea is expressed.

In the light of this discussion of the form-content distinction, let us return to the interpretation of the distinction offered by Bell and Fry. Bell construes artistic form as an aesthetically moving combination of lines and colors. This is a simple enough definition; and yet the more one examines it, the less it seems to be in accord with any of the above usages.

His conception of form is not that of shape, mode of expression, relations, organization, or medium. Rather, Bell means by the form of a work of art *certain elements in certain relations*; that is, lines and colors in combinations that excite us. Form does not include certain other elements in relation, namely, the so-called representational ones. These Bell calls the content of the art object.

There is at least one linguistic difficulty with this conception of the distinction between form and content. Consider once more Cézanne's "Italian Girl." When all the representations of objects and the girl are resolved into line and color combinations, the picture, strictly speaking, no longer has a content, but only a form. Now, it seems rather odd, linguistically speaking, to say that this painting and, in fact, all great painting has form but no content. This is, I think, only one of the difficulties aestheticians get into by using the form-content distinction altogether.[7]

In spite of this linguistic oddity, Bell's conception of form is rather good in that he understands by it elements in relation instead of relations versus elements. This usage at least emphasizes the organic character of a work of art, which the mathematical usage of relations versus elements does not.

In Bell's aesthetics, each art object has a "whatness" and a "howness," but both of these include elements in relation, i.e., an *organic complex* of elements and relations. The what, or the content, of a work of art is all the dramatically representative elements in certain causal relations; and the how, or the form, all the lines and colors in spatial relations. Bell's formalism, then, is the doctrine that in painting it is the plastic elements in relations that are all-important, and the nonplastic elements in relations that are totally irrelevant.

Fry also distinguishes between, and even, in his third period, separates form and content. Content includes those elements in the work of art that represent people or events and the associations attached to them, as all of these relate to each other. In Raphael's "Transfiguration," for example, Fry designates as the content all the Christian narrative element in their causal relations to each other, the main one being that of mutual dependency.

Form (in the second period) is all the plastic elements—line, color light, volume, etc.—as they relate spatially to compose a unity in variety or (in the third period) it is mere spatial relations as against *any* of the elements. Thus, in his second period, Fry is a formalist in Bell's sense: It is certain elements in certain relations that count for everything in art In his third period, he returns to the traditional mathematical formalism of Herbart: It is the arrangement, the relations, the how, not the elements, the what, that is all-important in art.

The great importance of both Bell and Fry (at least in his second period) lies in the fact that they offered a new conception of the distinction between form and content, one which comprehended the art object in more organic terms. In rejecting the mathematical approach to art—specifically, in repudiating the form-content distinction in terms of relations versus elements—and in suggesting that the form of a work of art comprises certain elements in relation, as the content includes certain other elements in relation, they brought us closer to an empirical conception of art.

Resolution of the Distinction

One of the overwhelming characteristics of contemporary aesthetic theory—and, I daresay, of past aesthetic theory as well—is its insistence upon the form-content distinction. It is, I suppose, one of the basic categories of aesthetic thought, analogous in its fundamental character to the substance-attribute distinction in metaphysical and logical thought. In our previous section we offered a rather extended sampling of the ways in which the form-content distinction has been construed in aesthetic theory. All of these usages have their historical, linguistic roots; hence they cannot be rejected in any cavalier fashion. But what we can do—and this has its parallel in contemporary metaphysics and logic in their repudiation of the substance-attribute, subject-predicate philosophy—is to recommend the rejection of all of these usages on the grounds that none of them does full justice to the nature of the art object; and, furthermore, that they lead to misdirected or specious aesthetic disputes.

I propose now to offer a new usage of form and content which is rooted in a more empirical consideration of the actual nature of works of art. This total analysis is based, in part, upon the writings of Bell, Fry, Parker, A. C. Bradley and Dewey in aesthetics and, more importantly, upon the articulated or suggested doctrines of practicing critics and artists like Cleanth Brooks, Albert Barnes, Martha Graham, Frank L. Wright, Elizabeth Selden, Henry Moore, Hanslick, Picasso and Matisse, to mention only a very few.

The hypothesis in terms of which the form-content distinction will be considered has to do with the definition of art. Every work of art, the hypothesis states, is an organic complex, presented in a sensuous medium, which complex is composed of elements, their expressive characteristics and the relations obtaining among them. I hold that this is a *real* definition of art: i.e., an enumeration of the basic properties of art.[8]

In many works of art, namely, those traditionally called representational, those which include what Ducasse refers to as "dramatic entities" or Parker "spiritual values," we must single out one element and give it a name: the "subject."

The subject is that element in a work of art that stands for, denotes, represents, means, a specific person, thing, scene, or event which exists *outside* of the work, and which is what we say the work is about. Semantically, the subject functions as a sign of specific entities—i.e., persons, events, etc.

That which the work of art is about, let us call the "referent" or "object" of the work.

Some examples will make clear our terminology. Consider, to begin with, Cézanne's "Mont Sainte-Victoire." The subject is the lines and colors that constitute certain volumes within the art object which stand for, denote, represent, mean, the actual mountain. Semantically, the subject is an iconic sign of its object, for it is like that which it means. It is to the mountain what a photograph is to the person it represents.

The object in this case is real, but it need not be. The object may be imaginary, as it probably is in Rousseau's "The Sleeping Gypsy." In cases of this sort, the object is an idea in the artist's or spectator's mind, which is being represented by the subject.

There is an intimate connection between objects and titles of works of art. In most paintings, at any rate, the title refers to the object of the work, "what it is about."

Consider, next, Milton's *Paradise Lost*. Its object or referent is the Fall of Man as it exists in the minds of the readers of the Bible or as it existed in the past, if it actually did. The subject of *Paradise Lost* is those elements in it that specify the characters and events involved in the Fall. These include God, Satan, the angels, the revolt of the angels, and so on.

It is worth noting that the subject of *Paradise Lost* is unique in the sense that Milton's God, Satan, etc., are like no one else's; whereas the object of the work may be the referent of many other works of art. Semantically, the subject, in its dimension as words, functions as symbols, i.e., signs that have become fixed to connotations through established usage. It is only when the words conjure up images that the subject assumes an iconic significance to its readers.

In music the problem is more complex. The object or referent of the *Eroica*, for example, it is claimed, is heroism. The subject, then, is all of those sounds in the symphony that stand for heroism. However, some aestheticians have argued that music cannot have a referent, in which case, it can have no subject. They conclude from this that music (with the exception of onomatopoetic elements) has no meaning or cannot represent anything. But, . . . this is not a correct conclusion since elements other than subjects can mean and represent in art, including music.

Finally, the recent Koestler novel, *Arrival and Departure*, is about the problem of modern salvation, which problem exists quite independently of any work of art. The problem is specified as the conflict between the life of social action and the life of egocentric preoccupation with guilt. In the novel the subject is the hero, Peter, whose inner and outer struggles signify, in semantical terms, the externally existing conflict in modern society.

All of these works of art are similar in that their referents can provide material for many other art objects. As we would say, there are many works of art on the same Idea or theme; they refer to the same thing; they are *about* the same thing. And, as A. C. Bradley pointed out, but with a different terminology, the Idea is primarily outside of the work of art.[9] He is incorrect, however, in supposing that this is the sole existence of the theme (or Idea, referent, object). These *also* exist in the art object in the sense that the subject partakes of the same universal which is embodied in the referent. In fact, and I should regard this as central in any adequate theory of communication, the subject is capable of meaning the object to some person precisely because of the universal that is present in both.[10]

Besides the referent, what Dewey calls the "matter for" the work of art, there are the *associations* of the referent. These comprise all of those experiences that the artist had before or while creating his work of art which are relevant to it. Milton's reflections on the Fall of Man; Koestler's experiences as a Communist (which he narrates so effectively in his *Scum of the Earth*); Beethoven's reactions to democracy and heroism; and Cézanne's feelings for the mountain, Sainte-Victoire, are examples of associations. We get our knowledge of these from the letters, diaries, and autobiographies of artists or from other similar sources left by their contemporaries, or even from Freudian or sociological analyses of their art works.[11] The associations, like the referents, exist primarily outside the art object, but may also exist within, as subjects or other elements.

We come now to the *content* of a work of art. If we are to employ this concept at all, then, in order to avoid getting into the many specious disputes which traditional conceptions of content have inspired, and in order to come to grips with the essentially organic character of art, we ought to interpret the content of a work of art as *all* that is in it: all the elements, expressive characteristics and the relations that obtain among them.[12] This interpretation is in keeping with one ordinary usage of content in which we say that the content of anything is what is in it; and is much more satisfactory in its results than interpreting content as theme, subject, or elements as against relations.

On this usage, then, we can speak of our previous examples in the following way. In Cézanne's "Mont Sainte-Victoire," the content can be said to be all the lines, colors, masses, volumes, drawing, design, space—in other words, the plastic—plus the subject and the expressive characteristics, as all of these relate together. In Parker's terminology, the content of the picture is all the linguistic, plastic, and spiritual values as they organically relate to make a total artistic complex.

In *Paradise Lost*, the content includes the subject terms, the images, metaphors, attitudes, ideas, diction, versification, and their expressive characteristics, as they organically relate to each other.

In the *Eroica*, the content comprises all the tones, chords, melodies, harmonies, rhythms, perhaps the subject, their expressive characteristics, also as all of these organically relate to each other.

The content or substance[13] or subject matter[14] of or matter in[15] the work of art is the work itself, the whole thing. It is something that cannot be said in any other way. Many works may have the same theme or referent, be about the same thing, but every work has only one content. Donne, Shakespeare, Shelley, Eliot all speak *of* love, but the content of each of their poems is unique. Nowhere is the Leibnizian principle of the identity of indiscernibles more secure than in the realm of art!

Actual artistic production probably begins with the artist's experiences as they converge upon a theme or Idea. Then he selects and unifies in an imaginative way his material while embodying it in a sensuous medium. He creates an artistic content, to which he usually gives a name. But the name or title is a mere label, not to be confused with the work itself. Most spectators unfortunately regard the content of art as a springboard to the referent, and eventually, to *their* associations. Here Bell and Fry and Bradley are right: Do not respond to the referent or the associations of the referent, but to the content.

If the content of a work of art is conceived as all of its expressive elements organically related to each other, what, then, is the form? Form, I submit, ought to be construed as exactly the same thing: *the organic unification of the several expressive constituents of the work of art.* Concrete artistic form, that is, the form of an individual work of art, ought not to be regarded merely as the relations or mode of expressing an Idea or shape or proportion of the work but as all of the expressive elements in relation. Form and content are to be regarded not as coördinates in art but as constituting the same coördination of elements, characteristics, and relations. Thus, there is *no* distinction on this usage between form and content in art.

There are elements and there are relations. But there are no elements, relations, or even grouping of them that can be singled out and designated as the content or the form except in an arbitrary and vitiating way.[16]

Our proposal to eliminate the form-content distinction as applied to concrete works of art and to construe them as synonyms is no *mere* stipulation as to the way in which we wish to use terms, no *mere* recommendation to effect an alteration of our aesthetic language in an attempt to abuse the language of common sense. The positivists and the Wittgensteinians are undoubtedly correct in their assertion that much of philosophy is of this character, but it is not our intention either to stipulate usage or commit linguistic abuse. Rather, we are offering a new way of talking about art which will not give rise to unnecessary aesthetic disputes and will be more consonant with its actual organic character. An aesthetic language that does not employ terms like form and content—which, let us be the first to admit, are essential for some philosophical and ordinary modes of discourse—or, if it does use them, regards them as synonyms, so our hypothesis about the nature of art implies, is a more adequate language than those languages found in the aesthetic systems considered thus far.

It is more adequate ultimately in the same sense that Russell's relational logic is more adequate in interpreting reality than the traditional Aristotelian subject-predicate logic: that is, it is a truer language because it corresponds to the facts.

Now, in the sense that art is an organic complex of elements, expressive in character, embodied in a sensuous medium, it is significant form. But to say that art is significant form is to say that it is also significant content. The two statements mean the same thing: that art may include as its constituents lines, colors, tones, words, emotions, concepts, feelings, meanings, representations, and subjects. Just as there is no artistic distinction between form and content, so there is no antithesis between form and ideas, representations and emotions. The problem, raised by Bell and Fry of the legitimacy of these constituents remains, and it will be equivalent to asking whether or not these elements can *integrate* successfully with each other. . . .

Notes

1. Bertrand Russell, *Our Knowledge of the External World*, p. 45 (italics in original) ; see also his *Introduction to Mathematical Philosophy*, p. 199.
2. See, e.g., Moore's essay, "The Sculptor's Aims," in Herbert Read (ed), *Unit One*, reprinted in *Henry Moore: Sculpture and Drawings;* and Calder's painting, "The Alphabet of Forms."
3. A. E. Housman, *The Name and Nature of Poetry*, pp. 35 ff; and Ducasse, *Art, the Critics, and You*, esp. pp. 42-43. This usage is at least as old as Cicero; see his *On the Character of the Orator*, bk. I, chap. xiv.
4. This is certainly *one* way in which aestheticians have interpreted formalism. See, e.g., A. C. Bradley, "Poetry for Poetry's Sake," *Oxford Lectures on Poetry*, pp. 7-8. Also, Ducasse, *Art, the Critics, and You*, p. 81.
5. Ducasse, *Philosophy of Art*, p. 202 (italics in original) .
6. Eduard Hanslick, *The Beautiful in Music*, pp. 166-167.
7. Erwin Panofsky, the great exponent of Iconology in the study of the history of art, also unwittingly commits himself to a theory which, because of his initial acceptance of the form-content distinction, entails the view that there are works of art with all form and no content. He does this by distinguishing between form and meaning. By meaning Panofsky understands representational meanings, like objects in nature or stories or allegories; and by form, certain elements like lines and colors in configurations. Such a distinction will work so long as we are dealing with nonabstract art, but it breaks down when we apply it to abstract art—for example, one of Kandinsky's "Improvisations"—unless we offer an extended theory of artistic meaning or representation (which, of course, Panofsky does not do) in which lines and colors have meanings just as surely as representations of natural objects or historical events. And the reason the distinction breaks down, and especially for Panofsky, when we apply it to abstract art, is that, on his assumptions, it makes of that art one in which there is all form and no content, i.e., meanings; which makes of Iconology a science that cannot, upon its stated principles, encompass the whole history of art. Iconologists, of course, do deal with modern art, and one might add, rather

brilliantly, too, but they do so by transcending the semantical foundations of their discipline as these have been set forth by Panofsky. See *Studies in Iconology: Humanistic Themes in the Art of the Renaissance,* chap. i. (Reprinted in Section V below. Ed.)

8. For an analysis and justification of real definition as against nominal or contextual, see my "Analysis and the Unity of Russell's Philosophy," P. A. Schilpp (ed.), *The Philosophy of Bertrand Russell,* pp. 110-121.

9. A. C. Bradley, "Poetry for Poetry's Sake," *Oxford Lectures on Poetry,* pp. 9 ff.

10. No Platonic theory is intended, necessarily. The main point is that nominalism cannot explain communication and that universals are not mere words or "legisigns." Charles Peirce recognized this long ago in his conception of "thirdness" or "law" as essential to communication, although some of his supposed followers have forgotten it.

That nominalism cannot deal adequately with the facts of communication was demonstrated by Russell in 1912, in *The Problems of Philosophy,* chap. ix. His arguments are still cogent.

11. See, e.g., Freud's *Leonardo da Vinci; a Psychosexual Study of an Infantile Reminiscence.*

12. Cf. A. C. Bradley, "Poetry for Poetry's Sake," p. 12.

13. *Ibid.*

14. A. C. Barnes, *The Art in Painting,* bk. II, chap. ii.

15. John Dewey, *Art as Experience,* p. 110.

16. Cf. Cleanth Brooks, "The New Criticism: A Brief for the Defense," *The American Scholar,* XIII (Summer 1944), No. 3, pp. 294-295.

FRANK SIBLEY

Aesthetic Concepts

THE REMARKS WE MAKE about works of art are of many kinds. For the purpose of this paper I wish to indicate two broad groups. I shall do this by examples. We say that a novel has a great number of characters and deals with life in a manufacturing town; that a painting uses pale colors, predominantly blues and greens, and has kneeling figures in the foreground; that the theme in a fugue is inverted at such a point and that there is a stretto at the close; that the action of a play takes place in the span of one day and that there is a reconciliation scene in the fifth act. Such remarks may be made by, and such features pointed out to, anyone with normal eyes, ears, and intelligence. On the other hand, we also say that a poem is tightly-knit or deeply moving; that a picture lacks balance, or has a certain serenity and repose, or that the grouping of the figures sets up an exciting tension; that the characters in a novel never really come to life, or that a certain episode strikes a false note. It would be natural enough to say that the making of such judgments as these requires the exercise of taste, perceptiveness, or sensitivity, of aesthetic discrimination or appreciation; one would not say this of my first group. Accordingly, when a word or expression is such that taste or perceptiveness is required in order to apply it, I shall call it an *aesthetic* term or expression, and I shall, correspondingly, speak of *aesthetic* concepts or *taste* concepts.[1]

Aesthetic terms span a great range of types and could be grouped into various kinds and sub-species. But it is not my present purpose to attempt any such grouping; I am interested in what they all have in common. Their almost endless variety is adequately displayed in the following list: *unified, balanced, integrated, lifeless, serene, somber, dynamic, powerful, vivid, delicate, moving, trite, sentimental, tragic.* The list of course is not limited to adjectives; expressions in artistic contexts like *telling contrast,*

Reprinted from *The Philosophical Review,* Vol. LXVIII (1949) and revised by the author.

sets up a tension, conveys a sense of, or holds it together are equally good illustrations. It includes terms used by both laymen and critic alike, as well as some which are mainly the property of professional critics and specialists.

I have gone for my examples of aesthetic expressions in the first place to critical and evaluative discourse about works of art because it is there particularly that they abound. But now I wish to widen the topic; we employ terms the use of which requires an exercise of taste not only when discussing the arts but quite liberally throughout discourse in everyday life. The examples given above are expressions which, appearing in critical contexts, most usually, if not invariably, have an aesthetic use; outside critical discourse the majority of them more frequently have some other use unconnected with taste. But many expressions do double duty even in everyday discourse, sometimes being used as aesthetic expressions and sometimes not. Other words again, whether in artistic or daily discourse, function only or predominantly as aesthetic terms; of this kind are *graceful, delicate, dainty, handsome, comely, elegant, garish*. Finally, to make the contrast with all the preceding examples, there are many words which are seldom used as aesthetic terms at all: *red, noisy, brackish, clammy, square, docile, curved, evanescent, intelligent, faithful, derelict, tardy, freakish*.

Clearly, when we employ words as aesthetic terms we are often making and using metaphors, pressing into service words which do not primarily function in this manner. Certainly, also, many words *have come* to be aesthetic terms by some kind of metaphorical transference. This is so with those like "dynamic," "melancholy," "balanced," "tightly-knit" which, except in artistic and critical writings, are not normally aesthetic terms. But the aesthetic vocabulary must not be thought wholly metaphorical. Many words, including the most common (*lovely, pretty, beautiful, dainty, graceful, elegant*), are certainly not being used metaphorically when employed as aesthetic terms, the very good reason being that this is their primary or only use, some of them having no current non-aesthetic uses. And though expressions like "dynamic," "balanced," and so forth *have come* by a metaphorical shift to be aesthetic terms, their employment in criticism can scarcely be said to be more than quasi-metaphorical. Having entered the language of art description and criticism as metaphors they are now standard vocabulary in that language.[2]

The expressions I am calling aesthetic terms form no small segment of our discourse. Often, it is true, people with normal intelligence and good eyesight and hearing lack, at least in some measure, the sensitivity required to apply them; a man need not be stupid or have poor eyesight to fail to see that something is graceful. Thus taste or sensitivity is somewhat more rare than certain other human capacities; people who exhibit a sensitivity both wide-ranging and refined are a minority. It is over the application of aesthetic terms, too, that, notoriously, disputes and differences sometimes go helplessly unsettled. But almost everybody is able to exercise taste to some degree and in some matters. It is surprising therefore that aesthetic terms have been so largely neglected. They have received glancing treatment in the course of other aesthetic discussions; but as a broad category they have not received the direct attention they merit.

The foregoing has marked out the area I wish to discuss. One warning should perhaps be given. When I speak of taste in this paper, I shall not be dealing with questions which center upon expressions like "a matter of taste" (meaning, roughly, a matter of personal preference or liking). It is with an ability to *notice* or *see* or *tell that* things have certain qualities that I am concerned.

<h1 style="text-align:center">I</h1>

In order to support our application of an aesthetic term, we often refer to features the mention of which involves other aesthetic terms: "it has an extraordinary vitality because of its free and vigorous style of drawing," "graceful in the smooth flow of its lines," "dainty because of the delicacy and harmony of its coloring." It is as normal to do this as it is to justify one mental epithet by other epithets of the same general type, *intelligent* by *ingenious, inventive, acute,* and so on. But often when we apply aesthetic terms, we explain why by referring to features which do *not* depend for their recognition upon an exercise of taste: "delicate because of its pastel shades and curving lines," or "it lacks balance because one group of figures is so far off to the left and is so brightly illuminated." When no explanation of this latter kind is offered, it is legitimate to ask or search for one. Finding a satisfactory answer may sometimes be difficult, but one cannot ordinarily reject the question. When we cannot ourselves quite say what non-aesthetic features make something delicate or unbalanced or powerful or moving, the good critic often puts his finger on something which strikes us as the right explanation. In short, aesthetic terms always ultimately apply because of, and aesthetic qualities always ultimately depend upon, the presence of features which, like curving or angular lines, color contrasts, placing of masses, or speed of movement, are visible, audible, or otherwise discernible without any exercise of taste or sensibility. Whatever kind of dependence this is, and there are various relationships between aesthetic qualities and non-aesthetic features, what I want to make clear in this paper is that there are no non-aesthetic features which serve in *any* circumstances as logically *sufficient conditions* for applying aesthetic terms. Aesthetic or taste concepts are not in *this* respect condition-governed at all.

There is little temptation to suppose that aesthetic terms resemble words, which, like "square," are applied in accordance with a set of necessary and sufficient conditions. For whereas each square is square in virtue of the *same* set of conditions, four equal sides and four right angles, aesthetic terms apply to widely varied objects; one thing is graceful because of these features, another because of those, and so on almost endlessly. In recent times philosophers have broken the spell of the strict necessary-and-sufficient model by showing that many everyday concepts are not of that type. Instead, they have described various other types of concepts which are governed only in a much looser way by conditions. However, since these newer models provide satisfactory accounts of many familiar concepts, it might plausibly be thought that aesthetic concepts are of some such kind and that they similarly are governed in some looser way by conditions. I want to argue that aesthetic concepts differ radically from any of these other concepts.

Amongst these concepts to which attention has recently been paid are those for which no *necessary-and-sufficient* conditions can be provided, but for which there are a number of relevant features, A, B, C, D, E, such that the presence of some groups or combinations of these features is *sufficient* for the application of the concept. The list of relevant features may be an open one; that is, given A, B, C, D, E, we may not wish to close off the possible relevance of other unlisted features beyond E. Examples of such concepts might be "dilatory," "discourteous," "possessive," "capricious," "prosperous," "intelligent" (but see below p. 358). If we begin a list of features relevant to "intelligent" with, for example, ability to grasp and follow various kinds of instructions, ability to master facts and marshall evidence, ability to solve mathematical or chess problems, we might go on adding to this list almost indefinitely.

However, with concepts of this sort, although decisions may have to be made and judgment exercised, it is always possible to extract and state, from cases which have already clearly been decided, the sets of features or conditions which were regarded as sufficient in those cases. These relevant features which I am calling conditions are, it should be noted, features which, though not sufficient *alone* and needing to be combined with other similar features, nevertheless carry some weight and can count only in one direction. Being a good chess player can count only *towards* and not *against* intelligence. Whereas mention of it may enter sensibly along with other remarks in expressions like "I say he is intelligent because . . ." or "the reason I call him intelligent is that . . . ," it cannot be used to complete such negative expressions as "I say he is *un*intelligent because. . . ." But what I want particularly to emphasize about features which function as conditions for a term is that *some* group or set of them *is* sufficient fully to ensure or warrant the application of that term. An individual characterized by some of these features may not yet qualify to be called lazy or intelligent, and so on, beyond all question, but all that is needed is to add some further (indefinite) number of such characterizations and a point is reached where we have enough. There are individuals possessing a number of such features of whom one cannot deny, cannot but admit, that they are intelligent. We have left necessary-and-sufficient conditions behind, but we are still in the realm of sufficient conditions.

But aesthetic concepts are not condition-governed even in this way. There are no sufficient conditions, no non-aesthetic features such that the presence of some set or number of them will beyond question logically justify or warrant the application of an aesthetic term. It is impossible (barring certain limited exceptions, see below p. 360) to make any statements corresponding to those we can make for condition-governed words. We are able to say "If it is true he can do this, and that, and the other, then one just cannot deny that he is intelligent," or "if he does A, B, and C, I don't see how it can be denied that he is lazy," but we cannot make *any* general statement of the form "If the vase is pale pink, somewhat curving, lightly mottled, and so forth, it will be delicate, cannot but be delicate." Nor again can one say *any* such things here as "Being tall and thin is not enough *alone* to ensure that a vase is delicate, but if it is, for example, slightly curving and pale colored (and so forth) as well, it cannot be denied that it is." Things may be described to us in non-aesthetic terms as fully as we please but we are not thereby put in the position of having to admit (or being unable to deny) that they are delicate or graceful or garish or exquisitely balanced.[3]

No doubt there are some respects in which aesthetic terms *are* governed by conditions or rules. For instance, it may be impossible that a thing should be garish if all its colors are pale pastels, or flamboyant if all its lines are straight. There may be, that is, descriptions using only non-aesthetic terms which are incompatible with descriptions employing certain aesthetic terms. If I am told that a painting in the next room consists solely of one or two bars of very pale blue and very pale grey set at right angles on a pale fawn ground, I can be sure that it cannot be fiery or garish or gaudy or flamboyant. A description of this sort may make certain aesthetic terms *in*applicable or *in*appropriate; and if from this description I inferred that the picture was, or even might be, fiery or gaudy or flamboyant, this might be taken as showing a failure to understand these words. I do not wish to deny therefore that taste concepts may be governed *negatively* by conditions.[4] What I am emphasizing is that they quite lack governing conditions of a sort many other concepts possess. Though on *seeing* the picture we might say, and rightly, that it is delicate or serene or restful or sickly or insipid, no *description* in non-aesthetic terms permits us to claim that these or any other aesthetic terms must undeniably apply to it.

I have said that if an object is characterized *solely* by certain sorts of features this may count decisively against the possibility of applying to it certain aesthetic terms. But of course the presence of *some* such features need not count decisively; other features may be enough to outweigh those which, on their own, would render the aesthetic term inapplicable. A painting might be garish even though much of its color is pale. These facts call attention to a further feature of taste concepts. One *can* find general features or descriptions which in some sense count in one direction only, only *for* or only *against* the application of certain aesthetic terms. Angularity, fatness, brightness, or intensity of color are typically *not* associated with delicacy or grace. Slimness, lightness, gentle curves, lack of intensity of color are associated with delicacy, but not with flamboyance, majesty, grandeur, splendor or garishness. This is shown by the naturalness of saying, for example, that someone is graceful *because* she's so light, but, *in spite of* being quite angular or heavily built; and by the corresponding oddity of saying that something is graceful *because* it is so heavy or angular, or delicate *because* of its bright and intense coloring. This may therefore sound quite similar to what I have said already about conditions in discussing terms like "intelligent." There are nevertheless very significant differences. Although there is this sense in which slimness, lightness, lack of intensity of color, and so on, count only towards, not against, delicacy, these features, I shall say, at best count only *typically* or *characteristically* towards delicacy. They do not count towards in the same sense as condition-features count towards laziness or intelligence; that is, no group of them is ever logically sufficient.

One way of reinforcing this is to notice how features which are characteristically associated with one aesthetic term may also be similarly associated with other and rather different aesthetic terms. "Graceful" and "delicate" may be on the one hand sharply contrasted with terms like "violent," "grand," "fiery," "garish," or "massive" which have characteristic non-aesthetic features quite unlike those for "delicate" and "graceful." But on the other hand "graceful" and "delicate" may also be contrasted with aesthetic terms which stand much closer to them, like "flaccid," "weakly," "washed out," "lanky," "anaemic," "wan," "insipid"; and the range of features characteristic of *these* qualities, pale color, slimness, lightness, lack of angularity and sharp contrast, is virtually identical with the range for "delicate" and "graceful." Similarly many of the features typically associated with "joyous," "fiery," "robust," or "dynamic" are identical with those associated with "garish," "strident," "turbulent," "gaudy," or "chaotic." Thus an object which is described very fully, but exclusively in terms of qualities characteristic of delicacy, may turn out on inspection to be not delicate at all, but anaemic or insipid. The failures of novices and the artistically inept prove that quite close similarity in point of line, color, or technique gives no assurance of gracefulness or delicacy. A failure and a success in the manner of Degas may be generally more alike, so far as their non-aesthetic features go, than either is like a successful Fragonard. But it is not necessary to go even this far to make my main point. A painting which has only the kind of features one would associate with vigor and energy but which even so fails to be vigorous and energetic *need* not have some other character, need not be instead, say, strident or chaotic. It may fail to have any particular character whatever.

It may employ bright colors, and the like, without being particularly lively and vigorous at all; but one may feel unable to describe it as chaotic or strident or garish either. It is, rather, simply lacking in character (though of course this too is an aesthetic judgment; taste is exercised also in seeing that the painting has no character).

There are of course many features which do not in these ways characteristically count for (or against) particular aesthetic qualities. One poem has strength and power because of the regularity of its meter and rhyme; another is monotonous and lacks drive and strength because of its regular meter and rhyme. We do not feel the need to switch from "because of" to "in spite of." However, I have concentrated upon features which are characteristically associated with aesthetic qualities because, if a case could be made for the view that taste concepts are in any way governed by sufficient conditions these would seem to be the most promising candidates for governing conditions. But to say that features are associated only *characteristically* with an aesthetic term *is* to say that they can never amount to sufficient conditions; no description however full, even in terms characteristic of gracefulness, puts it beyond question that something is graceful in the way a description may put it beyond question that someone is lazy or intelligent.

It is important to observe, however, that in this paper I am not merely claiming that no sufficient conditions can be stated for taste concepts. For if this were all, taste concepts might not be after all really different from one kind of concept recently discussed. They could be accommodated perhaps with those concepts which Professor H. L. A. Hart has called "defeasible"; it is a characteristic of defeasible concepts that we cannot state sufficient conditions for them because, for any sets we offer, there is always an (open) list of defeating conditions any of which might rule out the application of the concept. The most we can say schematically for a defeasible concept is that, for example, A, B, and C together are sufficient for the concept to apply *unless* some feature is present which overrides or voids them. But, I want to emphasize, the very fact that we *can* say this sort of thing shows that we are still to that extent in the realm of conditions.[5] The features governing defeasible concepts can ordinarily count only one way, *either* for or against. To take Hart's example, "offer" and "acceptance" can count only towards the existence of a valid contract, and fraudulent misrepresentations, duress, and lunacy can count only against. And even with defeasible concepts, if we are told that there are no voiding features present, we can know that some set of conditions or features, A, B, C, . . . is enough, in this absence of voiding features, to ensure, for example, that there is a contract. The very notion of a defeasible concept seems to require that some group of features *would* be sufficient *in certain circumstances*, that is, in the absence of overriding or voiding features. In a certain way defeasible concepts lack sufficient conditions then, but they are still, in the sense described, condition-governed. My claim about taste concepts is stronger; that they are not, except negatively, governed by conditions at all. We could not conclude even *in certain circumstances,* e.g., if we were told of the absence of all "voiding" or uncharacteristic features (no angularities, and the like), that an object *must* certainly be graceful, no matter how fully it was described to us as possessing features characteristic of gracefulness.

My arguments and illustrations so far have been rather simply schematic. Many concepts, including most of the examples I have used (*intelligent,* and so on, p. 354), are much more thoroughly open and complex than my illustrations suggest. Not only may there be an open list of relevant conditions; it may be impossible to give precise rules telling how many features from the list are needed for a sufficient set or in which combinations; impossible similarly to give precise rules covering the extent or degree to which such features need to be present in those combinations. Indeed, we may have to abandon as futile any attempt to describe or formulate anything like a complete set of precise conditions or rules, and content ourselves with giving only some general account of the concept, making reference to samples or cases or precedents. We cannot fully master or employ these concepts therefore *simply* by being equipped with lists of conditions, readily applicable procedures or sets of rules, however complex. For to exhibit a mastery of one of these concepts we must be able to go ahead and apply the word correctly to new individual cases, at least to central ones; and each new case may be a uniquely different object, just as each intelligent child or student may differ from others in relevant features and exhibit a unique combination of kinds and degrees of achievement and ability. In dealing with these new cases mechanical rules and procedures would be useless; we have to exercise our judgment, guided by a complex set of examples and precedents. Here then there is a marked *superficial* similarity to aesthetic concepts. For in using aesthetic terms too we learn from samples and examples, not rules, and we have to apply them, likewise, without guidance by rules or readily applicable procedures, to new and unique instances. Neither kind of concept admits of a simply "mechanical" employment.

But this is *only* a superficial similarity. It is at least noteworthy that in applying words like "lazy" or "intelligent" to new and unique instances we say that we are required to exercise *judgment*; it would be indeed odd to say that we are exercising *taste.* In exercising judgment we are called upon to weigh the pros and cons against each other, and perhaps sometimes to decide whether a quite new feature is to be counted as weighing on one side or on the other. But this goes to show that, though we may learn from and rely upon samples and precedents rather than a set of stated conditions, we are not out of the realm of general conditions and guiding principles. These precedents necessarily embody, and are used by us to illustrate, a complex web of governing and relevant conditions which it is impossible to formulate completely. To profit by precedents we have to understand them; and we must argue consistently from case to case. This is the very function of precedents. Thus it is possible, even with these very loosely condition-governed concepts, to take clear or paradigm cases of X and to say "this is X because . . . ," and follow it up with an account of features which logically clinch the matter.

Nothing like this is possible with aesthetic terms. Examples undoubtedly play a crucial role in giving us a grasp of these concepts; but we do not and cannot derive from these examples conditions and principles, however complex, which will enable us if we are consistent, to apply the terms even to some new cases. And when, with a clear case of something which *is* in fact graceful or balanced or tightly-knit, someone tells me why it is, what features make it so, it is always possible for me to wonder whether, in spite of these features, it really is graceful, balanced, and so on. No such features logically clinch the matter.

The point I have argued may be reinforced in the following way. A man who failed to realize the nature of aesthetic concepts, or someone who, knowing that he lacked sensitivity in aesthetic matters, did not want to reveal this lack might by assiduous application and shrewd observation provide himself with some rules and generalizations; and by inductive procedures and intelligent guessing, he might frequently say the right things. But he could have no great confidence or certainty; a slight change in an object might at any time unpredictably ruin his calculations, and he might as easily have been wrong as right. No matter how careful he has been about working out a set of consistent principles and conditions, he is only in a position to think that the object is very possibly delicate. With concepts like *lazy, intelligent,* or *contract,* someone who intelligently formulated rules that led him aright appreciably often *would* thereby show the beginning of a grasp of those concepts; but the person we are considering is not even beginning to show an awareness of what delicacy is. Though he sometimes says the right thing, he has not seen, but guessed, that the object is delicate. However intelligent he might be, we could easily tell him wrongly that something was delicate and "explain" why without his being able to detect the deception. (I am ignoring complications now about negative conditions.) But if we did the same with, say, "intelligent" he could at least often uncover some incompatibility or other which would need explaining. In a world of beings like himself he would have no use for concepts like delicacy. As it is, these concepts would play a quite different role in his life. He would, for himself, have no more reason to choose tasteful objects, pictures, and so on, than a deaf man would to avoid noisy places. He could not be praised for exercising taste; at best his ingenuity and intelligence might come in for mention. In "appraising" pictures, statuettes, poems, he would be doing something quite different from what other people do when they exercise taste.

At this point I want to notice in passing that there are times when it may look as if an aesthetic word could be applied according to a rule.

These cases vary in type; I shall mention only one. One might say, in using "delicate" of glassware perhaps, that the thinner the glass, other things being equal, the more delicate it is. Similarly, with fabrics, furniture, and so on, there are perhaps times when the thinner or more smoothly finished or more highly polished something is, the more certainly some aesthetic term or other applies. On such occasions someone might formulate a rule and follow it in applying the word to a given range of articles. Now it may be that sometimes when this is so, the word being used is not really an aesthetic term at all; "delicate" applied to glass in this way may at times really mean no more than "thin" or "fragile." But this is certainly not always the case; people often *are* exercising taste even when they say that glass is very delicate because it is so thin, and know that it would be less so if thicker and more so if thinner. These instances where there appear to be rules are peripheral cases of the use of aesthetic terms. If someone did merely follow a rule we should not say he was exercising taste, and we should hesitate to admit that he had any real notion of delicacy until he satisfied us that he could discern it in other instances where no rule was available. In any event, these occasions when aesthetic words can be applied by rule are exceptional, not central or typical, and there is still no reason to think we are dealing with a logical entailment.[6]

It must not be thought that the impossibility of stating any conditions (other than negative) for the application of aesthetic terms results from an accidental poverty or lack of precision in language, or that it is simply a question of extreme complexity. It is true that words like "pink," "bluish," "curving," "mottled," do not permit of anything like a specific naming of each and every varied shade, curve, mottling, and blending. But if we were to give special names much more liberally than either we or even the specialists do (and no doubt there are limits beyond which we could not go), or even if, instead of names, we were to use vast numbers of specimens and samples of particular shades, shapes, mottlings, lines, and configurations, it would still be impossible, and for the same reasons, to supply any conditions.

We do, indeed, in talking about a work of art, concern ourselves with its individual and specific features. We say that it is delicate not simply because it is in pale colors but because of *those* pale colors, that it is graceful not because its outline curves slightly but because of *that* particular curve. We use expressions like "because of *its* pale coloring," "because of *the* flecks of bright blue," "because of *the* way the lines converge" where it is clear we are referring not to the presence of general features but to very specific and particular ones. But it is obvious that even with the help of precise names, or even samples and illustrations, of particular shades of color, contours and lines, any attempt to state conditions would be futile. After all, the very same feature, say a color or shape or line of a particular sort, which helps make one work may quite spoil another. "It would be quite delicate if it were not for that pale color there" may be said about the very color which is singled out in another picture as being largely responsible for its delicate quality. No doubt one way of putting this is to say that the features which make something delicate or graceful, and so on, are combined in a peculiar and unique way; that the aesthetic quality depends upon exactly this individual or unique combination of just these specific colors and shapes so that even a slight change might make all the difference. Nothing is to be achieved by trying to single out or separate features and generalizing about them.

I have now argued that in certain ways aesthetic concepts are not and cannot be condition- or rule-governed.[7] Not to be so governed is one of their essential characteristics. In arguing this I first claimed in a general way that no non-aesthetic features are possible candidates for conditions, and then considered more particularly both the "characteristic" *general* features associated with aesthetic terms and the individual or *specific* features found in particular objects. I have not attempted to examine what relationship these specific features of a work do bear to its aesthetic qualities. An examination of the locutions we use when we refer to them in the course of explaining or supporting our application of an aesthetic term reinforces with linguistic evidence the fact that we are certainly not offering them as explanatory or justifying *conditions*. When we are asked why we say a certain person is lazy or intelligent or courageous, we are being asked in virtue of what we *call* him this; we reply with "because of the way he regularly leaves his work unfinished," or "because of the ease with which he handles such and such problems," and so on. But when we are asked to say why, in our opinion, a picture lacks balance or is somber in tone, or why a poem is moving or tightly organized, we are doing a different kind of thing. We may use similar locutions: "his verse has strength and variety *because of the way* he handles the meter and employs the caesura," or "it is nobly austere *because of* the lack of detail and the restricted palette." But we can also express what we want to by using quite other expressions: "it is the handling of meter and caesura which is *responsible for* its strength and variety," "its nobly austere quality is *due to* the lack of detail and the use of a restricted palette," "its lack of balance *results from* the highlighting of the figures on the left," "those minor chords *make it* extremely moving," "those converging lines *give it* an extraordinary unity." These are locutions we cannot switch to with "lazy" or "intelligent"; to say *what makes* him lazy, what is *responsible for* his laziness, what it is *due to*, is to broach another question entirely.

One after another, in recent discussions, writers have insisted that aesthetic judgments are not "mechanical": "Critics do not formulate general standards and apply these mechanically to all, or to classes of, works of art." "Technical points can be settled rapidly, by the application of rules," but aesthetic questions "cannot be settled by any mechanical method." Instead, these writers on aesthetics have emphasized that there is no "substitute for individual judgment" with its "spontaneity and speculation" and that "The final standard . . . [is] the judgment of personal taste."[8] What is surprising is that, though such things have been repeated again and again, no one seems to have said what is meant by "taste" or by the word "mechanical." There are many judgments besides those requiring taste which demand "spontaneity" and "individual judgment" and are not "mechanical." Without a detailed comparison we cannot see in what particular way aesthetic judgments are not "mechanical," or how they differ from those other judgments, nor can we begin to specify what taste is. This I have attempted. It is a characteristic and essential feature of judgments which employ an aesthetic term that they cannot be made by appealing, in the sense explained, to non-aesthetic conditions.[9] This, I believe, is a logical feature of aesthetic or taste judgments in general, though I have argued it here only as regards the more restricted range of judgments which employ aesthetic terms. It is part of what "taste" means.

II

A great deal of work remains to be done on aesthetic concepts. In the remainder of this paper I shall offer some further suggestions which may help towards an understanding of them.

The realization that aesthetic concepts are governed only negatively by conditions is likely to give rise to puzzlement over how we manage to apply the words in our aesthetic vocabulary. If we are not following rules and there are no conditions to appeal to, how are we to know when they are applicable? One very natural way to counter this question is to point out that some other sorts of concepts also are not condition-governed. We do not apply simple color words by following rules or in accordance with principles. We see that the book is red by looking, just as we tell that the tea is sweet by tasting it. So too, it might be said, we just see (or fail to see) that things are delicate, balanced, and the like. This kind of comparison between the exercise of taste and the use of the five senses is indeed familiar; our use of the word "taste" itself shows that the comparison is age-old and very natural. Yet whatever the similarities, there are great dissimilarities too. A careful comparison cannot be attempted here though it would be valuable; but certain differences stand out, and writers who have emphasized that aesthetic judgments are not "mechanical" have sometimes dwelt on and been puzzled by them.

In the first place, while our ability to discern aesthetic features is dependent upon our possession of good eyesight, hearing, and so on, people normally endowed with senses and understanding may nevertheless fail to discern them. "Those who listen to a concert, walk round a gallery, read a poem may have roughly similar sense perceptions, but some get a great deal more than others," Miss Macdonald says; but she adds that she is "puzzled by this feature 'in the object' which can be seen only by a specially qualified observer" and asks, "What is this 'something more'?"[10]

It is this difference between aesthetic and perceptual qualities which in part leads to the view that "works of art are esoteric objects . . . not simple objects of sense perception."[11] But there is no good reason for calling an object esoteric simply because we discern aesthetic qualities in it. The *objects* to which we apply aesthetic words are of the most diverse kinds and by no means esoteric: people and buildings, flowers and gardens, vases and furniture, as well as poems and music. Nor does there seem any good reason for calling the *qualities* themselves esoteric. It is true that someone with perfect eyes or ears might miss them, but we do after all say we *observe or notice* them ("Did you notice how very graceful she was?" "Did you observe the exquisite balance in all his pictures?"). In fact, they are very familiar indeed. We learn while quite young to use many aesthetic words, though they are, as one might expect from their dependence upon our ability to see, hear, distinguish colors, and the like, not the earliest words we learn; and our mastery and sophistication in using them develop along with the rest of our vocabulary. They are not rarities; some ranges of them are in regular use in everyday discourse.

The second notable difference between the exercise of taste and the use of the five senses lies in the way we support those judgments in which aesthetic concepts are employed. Although we use these concepts without rules or conditions, we do defend or support our judgments, and convince others of their rightness, by talking; "disputation about art is not futile," as Miss Macdonald says, for critics do "attempt a certain kind of explanation of works of art with the object of establishing correct judgments."[12] Thus even though this disputation does not consist in "deductive or inductive inference" or "reasoning," its occurrence is enough to show how very different these judgments are from those of a simple perceptual sort.

Now the critic's talk, it is clear, frequently consists in mentioning or pointing out the features, including easily discernible non-aesthetic ones, upon which the aesthetic qualities depend. But the puzzling question remains how, by mentioning these features, the critic is thereby justifying or supporting his judgments. To this question a number of recent writers have given an answer. Stuart Hamphire, for example, says that "One engages in aesthetic discussion for the sake of what one might see on the way. . . . [I]f one has been brought to see what there is to be seen in the object, the purpose of discussion is achieved. . . . The point is to bring people to see these features."[13] The critic's talk, that is, often serves to support his judgments in a special way; it helps us to *see* what he has seen, namely, the aesthetic qualities of the object. But even when it is agreed that this is one of the main things that critics do, puzzlement tends to break out again over *how* they do it. How is it that by talking about features of the work (largely non-aesthetic ones) we can manage to bring others to see what they had not seen? "What sort of endowment is this which *talking* can modify? . . . Discussion does not improve eyesight and hearing" (my italics) .[14]

Yet of course we do succeed in applying aesthetic terms, and we frequently do succeed by talking (and pointing and gesturing in certain ways) in bringing others to see what we can see. One begins to suspect that puzzlement over the "esoteric" character of aesthetic qualities too, arises from bearing in mind inappropriate philosophical models. When someone is unable to see that the book on the table is brown, we cannot get him to see it is by talking; consequently it seems puzzling that we might get someone to see that the vase is graceful by talking. If we are to dispel this puzzlement and recognize aesthetic concepts and qualities for what they are, we must abandon unsuitable models and investigate how we actually employ these concepts. With so much interest in and agreement about *what* the critic does, one might expect decriptions of *how* he does it to have been given. But little has been said about this, and what has been said is unsatisfactory.

Miss Macdonald,[15] for example, subscribes to this view of the critic's task as presenting "what is not obvious to casual or uninstructed inspection," and she does ask the question "What sort of considerations are involved, *and how,* to justify a critical verdict?" (my italics) . But she does not in fact go on to answer it. She addresses herself instead to the different, though related, question of the interpretation of art works. In complex works different critics claim, often justifiably, to discern different features; hence Miss Macdonald suggests that in critical discourse the critic is bringing us to see what he sees by offering new interpretations. But if the question is "what (the critic) does and how he does it," he cannot be represented either wholly or even mainly as providing new interpretations. His task quite as often is simply to help us appreciate qualities which other critics have regularly found in the works he discusses. To put the stress upon *new* interpretations is to leave untouched the question how, by talking, he can help us to see *either* the newly appreciated aesthetic qualities *or* the old. In any case, besides complex poems or plays which may bear many interpretations, there are also relatively simple ones. There are also vases, buildings, and furniture, not to mention faces, sunsets, and scenery, about which no questions of "interpretation" arise but about which we talk in similar ways and make similar judgments. So the "puzzling" questions remain: how do we support these judgments and how do we bring others to see what we see?

Hampshire,[16] who likewise believes that the critic brings us "to see what there is to be seen in the object," does give some account of how the critic does this. "The greatest service of the critic" is to point out, isolate, and place in a frame of attention the "particular features of the particular object which *make* it ugly or beautiful"; for it is "difficult to see and hear all that there is to see and hear," and simply a prejudice to suppose that while "things really do have colours and shapes . . . there do not exist literally and objectively, concordances of colours and perceived rhythms and balances of shapes." However, these "extraordinary qualities" which the critic "may have seen (in the wider sense of 'see') " are "qualities which are of no direct practical interest." Consequently, to bring us to see them the critic employs "an unnatural use of words in description"; "the common vocabulary, being created for practical purposes, obstructs any disinterested perception of things"; and so these qualities "are normally described metaphorically by some transference of terms from the common vocabulary."

Much of what Hampshire says is right. But there is also something quite wrong in the view that the "common" vocabulary "obstructs" our aesthetic purposes, that it is "unnatural" to take it over and use it metaphorically, and that the critic "is under the necessity of building . . . a vocabulary *in opposition to the main tendency of his language*" (my italics). First, while we do often coin new metaphors in order to describe aesthetic qualities, we are by no means always under the necessity of wresting the "common vocabulary" from its "natural" uses to serve our purposes. There does exist, as I observed earlier, a large and accepted vocabulary of aesthetic terms some of which, whatever their metaphorical origins, are now not metaphors at all, others of which are at most quasi-metaphorical. Second, this view that our use of metaphor and quasi-metaphor for aesthetic purposes is unnatural or a makeshift into which we are forced by a language designed for other purposes misrepresents fundamentally the character of aesthetic qualities and aesthetic language. There is nothing unnatural about using words like "forceful," "dynamic," or "tightly-knit" in criticism; they do their work perfectly and are exactly the words needed for the purposes they serve. We do not want or need to replace them by words which lack the metaphorical element. In using them to describe works of art, the very point is that we are noticing aesthetic qualities related to their literal or common meanings. If we possessed a quite different word from "dynamic," one we could use to point out an aesthetic quality unrelated to the common meaning of "dynamic," it could not be used to describe that quality which "dynamic" does serve to point out. Hampshire pictures "a colony of aesthetes, disengaged from practical needs and manipulations" and says that "descriptions of aesthetic qualities, which for us are metaphorical, might seem to them to have an altogether literal and familiar sense"; they might use "a more directly descriptive vocabulary." But if they had a new and "directly descriptive" vocabulary lacking the links with non-aesthetic properties and interests which our vocabulary possesses, they would have to remain silent about many of the aesthetic qualities we can describe; further, if they were more completely "disengaged from practical needs" and other non-aesthetic awarenesses and interests, they would perforce be blind to many aesthetic qualities we can appreciate. The links between aesthetic qualities and non-aesthetic ones are both obvious and vital. Aesthetic concepts, all of them, carry with them attachments and in one way or another are tethered to or parasitic upon non-aesthetic features. The fact that many aesthetic terms are metaphorical or quasi-metaphorical in no way means that common language is an ill-adapted tool with which we have to struggle. When someone writes as Hampshire does, one suspects again that critical language is being judged against other models. To use language which is frequently metaphorical might be strange for some *other* purpose or from the standpoint of doing something else, but for the purpose and from the standpoint of making aesthetic observations it is not. To say it is an unnatural use of language for doing *this* is to imply there is or could be for this purpose some other and "natural" use. But these *are* natural ways of talking about aesthetic matters.

To help understand what the critic does, then, how he supports his judgments and gets his audience to see what he sees, I shall attempt a brief description of the methods we use as critics.[17]

(1) We may simply mention or point out non-aesthetic features: "Notice these flecks of color, that dark mass there, those lines." By merely drawing attention to those easily discernible features which make the painting luminous or warm or dynamic, we often succeed in bringing someone to see these aesthetic qualities. We get him to see B by mentioning something different, A. Sometimes in doing this we are drawing attention to features which may have gone unnoticed by an untrained or insufficiently attentive eye or ear: "Just listen for the repeated figure in the left hand," "Did you notice the figure of Icarus in the Breughel? It is very small." Sometimes they are features which have been seen or heard but of which the significance or purpose has been missed in any of a variety of ways: "Notice how much darker he has made the central figure, how much brighter these colors are than the adjacent ones," "Of course, you've observed the ploughman in the foreground; but had you considered how he, like everyone else in the picture, is going about his business without noticing the fall of Icarus?" In mentioning features which may be discerned by anyone with normal eyes, ears, and intelligence, we are singling out what may serve as a kind of key to grasping or seeing something else (and the key may not be the same for each person).

(2) On the other hand we often simply mention the very qualities we want people to see. We point to a painting and say, "Notice how nervous and delicate the drawing is," or "See what energy and vitality it has." The use of the aesthetic term itself may do the trick; we say what the quality or character is, and people who had not seen it before see it.

(3) Most often, there is a linking of remarks about aesthetic and non-aesthetic features: "Have you noticed this line and that, and the points of bright color here and there . . . don't they give it vitality, energy?"

(4) We do, in addition, often make extensive and helpful use of similes and genuine metaphors: "It's as if there are small points of light burning," "as though he had thrown on the paint violently and in anger," "the

lights shimmer, the lines dance, everything is air, lightness and gaiety," "his canvases are fires, they crackle, burn, and blaze, even at their most subdued always restlessly flickering, but often bursting into flame, great pyro-technic displays," and so on.

(5) We make use of contrasts, comparisons, and reminiscences: "Suppose he had made that a lighter yellow, moved it to the right, how flat it would have been," "Don't you think it has something of the quality of a Rembrandt?", "Hasn't it the same serenity, peace, and quality of light of those summer evenings in Norfolk?" We use what keys we have to the known sensitivity, susceptibilities, and experience of our audience.

Critics and commentators may range, in their methods, from one extreme to the other, from painstaking concentration on points of detail, line and color, vowels and rhymes, to more or less flowery and luxuriant metaphor. Even the enthusiastic biographical sketch decorated with suitable epithet and metaphor may serve. What is best depends on both the audience and the work under discussion. But this would not be a complete sketch unless certain other notes were added.

(6) Repetition and reiteration often play an important role. When we are in front of a canvas we may come back time and again to the same points, drawing attention to the same lines and shapes, repeating the same words, "swirling," "balance," "luminosity," or the same similes and metaphors, as if time and familiarity, looking harder, listening more carefully, paying closer attention may help. So again with variation; it often helps to talk round what we have said, to build up, supplement with more talk *of the same kind*. When someone misses the swirling quality, when one epithet or one metaphor does not work, we throw in related ones; we speak of its wild movement, how it twists and turns, writhes and whirls, as though, failing to score a direct hit, we may succeed with a barrage of near-synonyms.

(7) Finally, besides our verbal performances, the rest of our behavior is important. We accompany our talk with appropriate tones of voice, expression, nods, looks, gestures. A critic may sometimes do more with a sweep of the arm than by talking. An appropriate gesture may make us see the violence in a painting or the character of a melodic line.

These ways of acting and talking are not significantly different whether we are dealing with a particular work, paragraph, or line, or speaking of an artist's work as a whole, or even drawing attention to a sunset or scenery. But even with the speaker doing all this, we may fail to see what he sees. There may be a point, though there need be no limit except that imposed by time and patience, at which he gives up and sets us (or himself) down as lacking in some way, defective in sensitivity. He may tell us to look or read again, or to read or look at other things and then come back again to this; he may suspect there are experiences in life we have missed. But these are the things he does. This is what succeeds if anything does; indeed it is all that can be done.

By realizing clearly that, whether we are dealing with art or scenery or people or natural objects, this is how we operate with aesthetic concepts, we may recognize this sphere of human activity for what it is. We operate with different kinds of concepts in different ways. If we want someone to agree that a color is red we may take it into a good light and ask him to look; if it is viridian we may fetch a color chart and make him compare; if we want him to agree that a figure is fourteen-sided we get him to count; and to bring him to agree that something is dilapidated or that someone is intelligent or lazy we may do other things, citing features, reasoning and arguing about them, weighing and balancing. These are the methods appropriate to these various concepts. But the ways we get someone to see aesthetic qualities are different; they are of the kind I have described. With each kind of concept we can describe what we do and how we do it. But the methods suited to these other concepts will not do for aesthetic ones, or vice versa. We cannot prove by argument or by assembling a sufficiency of conditions that something is graceful; but this is no more puzzling than our inability to prove, by using the methods, metaphors, and gestures of the art critic, that it will be made in ten moves. The questions raised admit of no answer beyond the sort of decription I have given. To go on to ask, with puzzlement, how it is that *when* we do these things people come to see, is like asking how is it that, when we take the book into a good light, our companion agrees with us that it is red. There is no place for this kind of question or puzzlement. Aesthetic concepts are as natural, as little esoteric, as any others. It is against the background of different and philosophically more familiar models that they seem queer or puzzling.

I have described how people justify aesthetic judgments and bring others to see aesthetic qualities in things. I shall end by showing that the methods I have outlined are the ones natural for and characteristic of taste concepts from the start. When someone tries to make me see that a painting is delicate or balanced, I have some understanding of these terms already and know in a sense what I am looking for. But if there is puzzlement over how, by talking, he can bring me to see these qualities in this picture, there should be a corresponding puzzlement over how I learned to use aesthetic terms and discern aesthetic qualities in the first place. We may ask, therefore, how we learn to do these things; and this is to inquire (1) what natural potentialities and tendencies people have and (2) how we develop and take advantage of these capacities in training and teaching. Now for the second of these, there is no doubt that our ability to notice and respond to aesthetic qualities is cultivated and developed by our contacts with parents and teachers from quite an early age. What is interesting for my present purpose is that, while we are being taught in the presence of examples what grace, delicacy, and so on are, the methods used, the language and behavior, are of a piece with those of the critic as I have already described them.

To pursue these two questions, consider first those words like "dynamic," "melancholy," "balanced," "taut," or "gay" the aesthetic use of which is quasi-metaphorical. It has already been emphasized that we could not use them thus without some experience of situations where they are used literally. The present inquiry is how we shift from literal to aesthetic uses of them. For this it is required that there be certain abilities and tendencies to link experiences, to regard certain things as similar, and to see, explore, and be interested in these similarities. It is a feature of human intelligence and sensitivity that we do spontaneously do these things and that the tendency can be encouraged and developed. It is no more baffling that we should employ aesthetic terms of this sort than that we should make metaphors at all. Easy and smooth transitions by which we shift to the use of these aesthetic terms are not hard to find. We suggest to children that simple pieces of music are hurrying or running or skipping or dawdling, from there we move to lively, gay, jolly, happy, smiling, or sad, and, as their experiences and vocabulary broaden, to solemn, dynamic, or melancholy. But the child also discovers for himself many of these parallels and takes interest or delight in them. He is likely on his own to skip, march, clap, or laugh with the music, and without this natural tendency our training would get nowhere. Insofar, however, as we do take advantage of this tendency and help him by training, *we do just what the critic does.* We may merely need to persuade the child to pay attention, to look or listen; or we may simply *call* the music jolly. But we are also likely to use, as the critic does, reiteration, synonyms, parallels, contrasts, similes, metaphors, gestures, and other expressive behavior.

Of course the recognition of similarities and simple metaphorical extensions are not the only transitions to the aesthetic use of language. Others are made in different ways; for instance, by the kind of peripheral cases I mentioned earlier. When our admiration is for something as simple as the thinness of a glass or the smoothness of a fabric, it is not difficult to call attention to such things, evoke a similar delight, and introduce suitable aesthetic terms. These transitions are only the beginnings; it may often be questionable whether a term is yet being used aesthetically or not. Many of the terms I have mentioned may be used in ways which are not straightforwardly literal but of which we should hesitate to say that they demanded much yet by way of aesthetic sensitivity. We speak of warm and cool colors, and we may say of a brightly colored picture that at least it is gay and lively. When we have brought someone to make this sort of metaphorical extension of terms, he has made one of the transitional steps from which he may move on to uses which more obviously deserve to be called aesthetic and demand a more obviously aesthetic appreciation. When I said at the outset that aesthetic sensitivity was rarer than some other natural endowments, I was not denying that it varies in degree from the rudimentary to the refined. Most people learn easily to make the kinds of remarks I am now considering. But when someone can call bright canvases gay and lively without being able to spot the one which is really vibrant, or can recognise the obvious outward vigor and energy of a student composition played *con fuoco* while failing to see that it lacks inner fire and drive, we do not regard his aesthetic sensitivity in these areas as particularly developed. However, once these transitions from common to aesthetic uses are begun in the more obvious cases, the domain of aesthetic concepts may broaden out, and they may become more subtle and even partly autonomous. The initial steps, however varied the metaphorical shifts and however varied the experiences upon which they are parasitic, are natural and easy.

Much the same is true when we turn to those words which have no standard non-aesthetic use, "lovely," "pretty," "dainty," "graceful," "elegant." We cannot say that these are learned by a metaphorical shift. But they still are linked to non-aesthetic features in many ways and the learning of them also is made possible by certain kinds of natural response, reaction, and ability. We learn them not so much by noticing similarities, but by our attention being caught and focussed in other ways. Certain phenomena which are outstanding or remarkable or unusual catch the eye or ear, seize our attention and interest, and move us to surprise, admiration, delight, fear or distaste. Children begin by reacting in these ways to spectacular sunsets, woods in autumn, roses, dandelions, and other striking and colorful objects, and it is in these circumstances that we find ourselves introducing general aesthetic words to them, like "lovely," "pretty," and "ugly." It is not an accident that the first lessons in aesthetic appreciation consist in drawing the child's attention to roses rather than to grass; nor is it surprising that we remark to him on the autumn colors rather than on the subdued tints of winter. We all of us, not only children, pay aesthetic attention more readily and easily to such outstanding and easily noticeable things. We notice with pleasure early spring grass or the first snow, hills of notably marked and varied contours, scenery flecked with a great variety of color or dappled variously with sun and shadow. We are struck and impressed by great size or mass, as with mountains or cathedrals. We are similarly responsive to unusual precision or minuteness or remarkable feats of skill, as with complex and elaborate filigree, or intricate wood carving and fan-vaulting. It is at these times, taking advantage of these natural interests and admirations, that we first teach the simpler aesthetic words. People of moderate aesthetic sensitivity and sophistication continue to exhibit aesthetic interest mainly on such occasions and to use only the more general words ("pretty," "lovely," and the like). But these situations may serve as a beginning from which we extend our aesthetic interests to wider and less obvious fields, mastering as we go the more subtle and specific vocabulary of taste. The principles do not change; the basis for learning more specific terms like "graceful," "delicate," and "elegant" is also our interest in and admiration for various non-aesthetic natural properties ("She seems to move *effortlessly*, as if floating," "So very *thin* and *fragile,* as if a breeze might destroy it," "So *small* and yet so *intricate*," "So *economical* and perfectly *adapted*").[18] And even with these aesthetic terms which are not metaphorical themselves ("graceful," "delicate," "elegant"), we rely in the same way upon the critic's methods, including comparison, illustration, and metaphor, to teach or make clear what they mean.

I have wished to emphasize in the latter part of this paper the natural basis of responses of various kinds without which aesthetic terms could not be learned. I have also outlined what some of the features are to which we naturally respond: similarities of various sorts, notable colors, shapes, scents, size, intricacy, and much else besides. Even the non-metaphorical aesthetic terms have significant links with all kinds of natural features by which our interest, wonder, admiration, delight, or distaste is aroused. But in particular I have wanted to urge that it should not strike us as puzzling that the critic supports his judgments and brings us to see aesthetic qualities by pointing out key features and talking about them in the way he does. It is by the very same methods that people helped us develop our aesthetic sense and master its vocabulary from the beginning. If we responded to those methods then, it is not surprising that we respond to the critic's discourse now. It would be surprising if, by using this language and behavior, people could *not* sometimes bring us to see the aesthetic qualities of things; for this would prove us lacking in one characteristically human kind of awareness and activity.

Notes

1. I shall speak loosely of an "aesthetic term," even when, because the word sometimes has other uses, it would be more correct to speak of its *use* as an aesthetic term. I shall also speak of "non-aesthetic" words, concepts, features, and so on. None of the terms other writers use, "natural," "observable," "perceptual," "physical," "objective" (qualities), "neutral," "descriptive" (language), when they approach the distinction I am making, is really apt for my purpose.

2. A contrast will reinforce this. If a critic were to describe a passage of music as chattering, carbonated, or gritty, a painter's coloring as vitreous, farinaceous, or effervescent, or a writer's style as glutinous, or abrasive, he *would* be using live metaphors rather than drawing on the more normal language of criticism. Words like "athletic," "vertiginous," "silken" may fall somewhere between.

3. In a paper reprinted in *Aesthetics and Language,* ed. by W. Elton (Oxford, 1954), pp. 131-146, Arnold Isenberg discusses certain problems about aesthetic concepts and qualities. Like others who approach these problems, he does not isolate them, as I do, from questions about verdicts on the *merits* of works of art, or from questions about *likings* and *preferences.* He says something parallel to my remarks above: "There is not in all the world's criticism a single purely descriptive statement concerning which one is prepared to say beforehand, 'if it is true, I shall *like* that work so much the better'" (p. 139, my italics). I should think *this* is highly questionable.

4. Isenberg (*op. cit.*, p. 132) makes a somewhat similar but mistaken point: "If we had been told that the colours of a certain painting are garish, it would be *astonishing* to find that they are *all* very pale and unsaturated" (my italics). But if we say "all" rather than "predominantly," then "astonishing" is the wrong word. The word that goes with "all" is "impossible"; "astonishing" might go with "predominantly."

5. H. L. A. Hart, "The Ascription of Responsibility and Rights" in *Logic and Language,* First Series, ed. by A. G. N. Flew (Oxford, 1951). Hart indeed speaks of "conditions" throughout, see p. 148.

6. I cannot in the compass of this paper discuss the other types of apparent exceptions to my thesis. Cases where a man *lacking* in sensitivity might learn and follow a rule, as above, ought to be distinguished from cases where someone who *possesses* sensitivity might know, from a non-aesthetic description, that an aesthetic term applies. I have stated my thesis as though this latter kind of case never occurs because I have had my eye on the logical features of *typical* aesthetic judgments and have preferred to over- rather than understate my view. But with certain aesthetic terms, especially negative ones, there may be perhaps some rare genuine exceptions when a description enables us to visualize very fully, and when what is described belongs to certain restricted classes of things, say human faces or animal forms. Perhaps a description like "One eye red and rheumy, the other missing, a wart-covered nose, a twisted mouth, a greenish pallor" may justify in a strong sense ("must be," "cannot but be") the judgments "ugly" or "hideous." If so, such cases are marginal, form a very small minority, and are uncharacteristic or atypical of aesthetic judgments in general. Usually when, on hearing a description, we say "it *must* be very beautiful (graceful, or the like)," we mean no more than "it surely must be, it's only remotely possible that it isn't." Different again are situations, and these are very numerous, where we can move quite simply from "bright colors" to "gay," or from "reds and yellows" to "warm," but where we are as yet only on the borderline of anything that could be called an expression of taste or aesthetic sensibility. I have stressed the importance of this transitional and border area between non-aesthetic and obviously aesthetic judgments below (p. 369).

7. Helen Knight says (Elton, *op.cit.*, p. 152) that "piquant" (one of my "aesthetic" terms) "depends on" various features (a *retroussé* nose, a pointed chin, and the like) and that these features are *criteria* for it; this is what I am denying. She also maintains that "good," when applied to works of art, depends on *criteria* like balance, solidity, depth, profundity (my aesthetic terms again; I should place piquancy in this list). I would deny this too, though I regard it as a different question and do not consider it in this paper. The two questions need separating: the relation of non-aesthetic features (*retroussé,* pointed) to aesthetic qualities, and the relation of aesthetic qualities to "aesthetically good" (verdicts). Most writings which touch on the nature of aesthetic concepts have this other (verdict) question mainly in mind. Mrs. Knight blurs this difference when she says, for example. " 'piquant' is the same kind of word as 'good.' " [Mrs. Knight's paper appears in Section VII of this book. Ed.]

8. See articles by Margaret Macdonald and J. A. Passmore in Elton, *op. cit.,* pp. 118, 119, 40, 41. [The principal portion of Miss Macdonald's article appears in Section VII of this book. Ed.]

9. As I indicated, p. 000 above, I have dealt only with the relation of *non-aesthetic* to aesthetic features. Perhaps a description in *aesthetic* terms may occasionally suffice for applying another aesthetic term. Johnson's Dictionary gives "handsome" as "beautiful with dignity"; Shorter O. E. D. gives "pretty" as "beautiful in a slight, dainty, or diminutive way."

10. Macdonald in Elton, *op. cit.,* pp. 114, 119. See also pp. 120, 122.

11. Macdonald, *ibid.*, pp. 114, 120-123. She speaks of non-aesthetic properties here as "physical" or "observable" qualities, and distinguishes between "physical object" and "work of art."

12. *Ibid.*, pp. 115-116; cf. also John Holloway, *Proceedings of the Aristotelian Society*, Supplementary Vol. XXIII (1949), pp. 175-176.

13. Stuart Hampshire in Elton, *op. cit.*, p. 165. Cf. also remarks in Elton by Isenberg (pp. 142, 145), Passmore (p. 38), in *Philosophy and Psycho-analysis* by John Wisdom (Oxford, 1953), pp. 223-224, and in Holloway, *op. cit.* p. 175. [Hampshire's paper appears in Section VII of this book. Ed.]

14. Macdonald, *op. cit.*, pp. 119-120.

15. *Ibid.* See pp. 127, 122, 125, 115. Other writers also place the stress on interpretations, cf. Holloway, *op. cit.*, p. 173 ff.

16. *Op. cit.*, pp. 165-168.

17. Holloway, *op. cit.*, pp. 173-174, lists some of these briefly.

18. It is worth noticing that most of the words which in current usage are primarily or exclusively aesthetic terms had earlier non-aesthetic uses and gained their present use by some kind of metaphorical shift. Without reposing too great weight on these etymological facts, it can be seen that their history reflects connections with the responses, interests, and natural features I have mentioned as underlying the learning and use of aesthetic terms. These transitions suggest both the dependence of aesthetic upon other interests, and what some of these interests are. Connected with liking, delight, affection, regard, estimation or choice—*beautiful, graceful, delicate, lovely, exquisite, elegant, dainty*; with fear or repulsion—*ugly*; with what notably catches the eye or attention—*garish, splendid, gaudy*; with what attracts by notable rarity, precision, skill, ingenuity, elaboration—*dainty, nice, pretty, exquisite*; with adaptation to function, suitability to ease of handling—*handsome*.

Expression, Creativity, Truth, and Form

Expression. We sometimes employ adjectives, such as "sad," "joyful," "gay," "wistful," and "agitated," to describe works of art.[1] But there is a "puzzle" about saying that a melody is sad: How *can* music be sad?

The puzzle, according to Bouwsma, is generated by our trying to understand sentences like "The music is sad" in terms of statements such as "Cassie is sad," failing to note that it might be more like other uses of "X is sad." We must, therefore, try to find a use of "X is sad" to which "The music is sad" is similar "enough to relieve the puzzle." Bouwsma explores different types of situations in which we use sentences of the form "X is sad" either without puzzlement—what we say is the natural thing to say—or where there is a ready way to "relieve" any puzzlement that may arise.

The most striking feature of Bouwsma's essay is its method, which is a consequence of his view of the origin of the problem. He is surely right in noting that "How can music be sad?" cannot be answered by listening to music or reading scores, or by reading the lives of composers. And is his technique for "relieving the puzzle" not the only plausible one?

The "expression" theory of art attempts to solve the puzzle by saying that "The music is sad" means the same as "The music expresses sadness."[2] But this will not do unless we know what "expression" means. The word has a place in discourse about emotions—Cassie expresses her emotions; her stoical cousin does not. If we try, however, to talk about works of art in this way, aren't we driven to speaking nonsense? Can a melody express, or suppress, sadness in the way a person does?

It is sometimes said that music expresses a composer's sadness, and that this is what it means to say the music is sad. When Cassie is sad she expresses her sadness by crying; when a composer is sad he writes music. But can a composer express his sadness by writing music? When I receive bad news, if I go for a swim or play chess, am I "expressing" my sadness, although in an unusual way? Will any activity substituted for the "natural" expression of sadness count nonetheless as an expression of sadness? If not, then why should writing music so count? Can't a happy composer write sad music?

The word "expression" is also used in regard to language. Music is sometimes believed to express emotion just as a sentence expresses a thought: Art, it has often been said, is the language of the emotions. But this presupposes a view about the ways sentences express ideas. The view that sentences express ideas by evoking images or concepts and that poems or songs express emotions by evoking feelings offers an unrewarding—if uncontroversial—view of art. For all it says is that poems and songs sometimes—"always" would make it empirically false—make people feel sad or gay. The problem arises, as Bouwsma puts it, "where the sadness is dry-eyed," where we don't feel sad at all but still want to say that the music is sad.

According to Bouwsma's "foolish theory"—that the meaning of a sentence is in the sentence as life is in a squirrel or geranium—the sadness is *in* the music. Bouwsma rejects this analogy as misleading, but are his reasons for doing so sufficient? "The meaning of sentences is translatable," he says, "but the 'meaning' of poems, of music, is not."

An English sentence can be translated into a French sentence having the same meaning. But can the *meaning* of an English sentence be translated? Into what? The meaning of a French sentence? If so, why can't the "meaning" of a poem or song be translated?[3] If I have a poem whose joy and sweetness is in its very words, and I write a different poem with joy and sweetness in its very words, will this not, on the analogy, do? What I have produced is not a translation but a "translation"; I have done something analogous to translating an English poem into French.

Again, Bouwsma says, it makes sense to ask, "What does the sentence express?" ("It expresses a meaning, of course . . ."), but it makes no sense to ask, "What does the poem express?"

But does a sentence *express* a meaning, not just *have* a meaning? I may, in a certain sentence, express my thoughts clearly or obscurely; the sentence accurately expresses, or doesn't quite express, what *I mean*. If *my* meaning is what the sentence expresses or does not express, then why doesn't it make sense to ask what "meaning," *i.e.* feeling, emotion, or attitude, the poem expresses? Might it not be unclear, for example, just what attitude a lyric poet adopts towards his subject?

Expressive faces have character. Words and sentences, melodies, lines and colors also have a character and to this extent are expressive. A line may be nervous, a blue serene. But if we understand this analogy, we are not led to ask *what* lines, colors, and melodies are expressive *of*. "The sadness is to the music . . . like the redness to the apple"; it is simply a property of the melody.

Now, Bouwsma asks, why do we use the word "sad" here? This question may be more central to the "puzzle" about expression than is often allowed. Suppose someone said, "Why 'sad'? Because that's the word we use to describe melodies of this sort. Why call a chair 'a chair'?"[4] Why wouldn't this answer do? Isn't to reply, as Bouwsma does, that "sad music has some of the characteristics of people who are sad" to invite trouble? How can a tune have any of the characteristics of a person? Does a tune move slowly in the way I do? Does it speak softly and low as I do? There may be "associations" of this sort attached to sad music, but is this why we call it sad?

Creativity. Tomas supposes that "what we have in mind when we speak of creative art" is something about the way it came into being.[5] To be creative, Tomas argues, a work of art must satisfy six conditions: it must be (1) something "the like of which did not exist before"; (2) different in "an interesting, important, fruitful, or other *valuable* way"; (3) produced according to rules originated by the artist and implicitly followed by him during the process of production; (4) something the artist did not know he was "aiming at" until he was finished; (5) inspired; (6) a product of exercised critical control.

These are presumably *necessary* conditions of creativity; it is not clear if they are also supposed to be *sufficient* conditions.[6] But if they are necessary conditions, then when we know that a work of art is creative, we also know four facts about the artist: that he originated the rules he followed in making it; that he did not know *this* was what he was aiming at until he was finished; that he was inspired; that he exercised critical control over his work.

Yet is it not a fact that we can know whether a work of art is creative while knowing nothing about the psychology of creation generally and even nothing about the artist? Are these, then, necessary conditions?

The first two conditions do, however, seem to be necessary conditions of creativity—but with one proviso. Had a contemporary of Cézanne, working in Siberia and wholly unacquainted with what was going on elsewhere in the art world, produced canvases just like the late canvases of Cézanne, would we have any reason not to describe his work as creative? Judgments of creativity are implicitly comparative, like saying that a man is tall, or short. But the comparison is not unrestricted. A work of art is creative only in comparison with works with which it is properly comparable, *i.e.* with what the artist might reasonably be expected to have been acquainted with. If one is familiar with only one work of art, is he qualified to say whether that work is creative, as opposed to being an imitation?

Words such as "creative," "imaginative," and "original" are honorific when applied to works of art. We can imagine a culture— ancient Egypt is sometimes thought to have been one—in which creativity and originality are not prized, in which the imitator takes precedence over the innovator. But are these not normally terms of praise, applicable not merely to what is different but to what is also valued?

Must an artist, implicitly or explicitly, follow rules while painting or writing? What rules? Those we might formulate *after* he has finished? If so, can there be a distinction between rule-following actions and other actions? Or is it logical that all actions in creating a work of art be rule-following? Isn't it *possible* that an artist, by doing something spontaneously, or even accidentally, mistakenly, or inadvertently, might produce a work of art, just as one might stumble on a discovery?[7]

Is to envisage a certain result in art to have completed the creative act? If so, *what* has been created? True, the paralyzed sculptor who does not work his own materials but gives orders to others is the creative artist, not the stonecutter. Does it follow from this that to create a statue is merely to envisage one?[8]

The case of poetry may seem different. To predict a poem might be to write it, if by "predicting a poem" we meant predicting that one would write "When," then "to," then "the," then "sessions," then "of," then "sweet," then "silent," then "thought," and so on. Had Shakespeare predicted that he would do this, we might want to say that he had already composed his sonnet. But could we then say that the poet did not know what he was aiming at? Writing about his poem, "The Old Woman and the Statue," Wallace Stevens says, "It is what I wanted it to be without knowing before it was written what I wanted it to be, even though I knew before it was written what I wanted to do."[9] Does this mean that Stevens did not know what he was aiming at—in the usual sense of this phrase—before he wrote his poem, even though before the poem was written he did not know just what it would be, and knew only what he wanted to do?

When we say that an artist's work is creative, are we saying that he was inspired— when by "inspiration" we mean, as Tomas does, the appearance of a new idea in his consciousness? A work of art must have an artist; an inspired work an inspired artist. But to say that an artist was inspired, isn't it sufficient to know that his work is inspired; and can't this be known while knowing nothing about his consciousness? When we speak of inspiration we may have a picture of divine afflatus, of the Muse breathing into the artist; but is this what we *mean* by "inspiration"?

According to Tomas, being subject to critical control sets creative art apart not only from books like *Tarzan of the Apes* but also from the art of the insane. Suppose, however, that Alva Johnson's story were not about Burroughs but about Tolstoy or Jane Austen. Are we prepared to say that this is logically impossible?

The late paintings of Van Gogh may not have been executed "in the complete absence of conscious control and criticism"; but how do we know? Is this an empirical inference based on biographical data or psychological theory; or is it a logical inference? Can we infer from Van Gogh's late paintings that he exercised critical control over them just as we can infer from Kant's being a bachelor that he was unmarried?[10]

That Tomas is unsure in what sense he means that critical control is a necessary condition of creativity is reflected in his response to Nietzsche's description of the composition of *Zarathustra*: he thinks it *probable*, he *bets*, that Nietzsche edited a bit. Yet almost immediately he cites with approval Ducasse's remark that criticism is *"an intrinsic, essential constituent"* of the production of art. But if critical control is intrinsic and essential, why assess probabilities or bet? Does one bet that a bachelor is unmarried?

It has been suggested earlier that the first two of Tomas' conditions are necessary to creativity and that the other four are not. If this is right, then to say that a work of art is creative is to say or imply nothing about the psychology of the artist or about the so-called "creative process." And is it not possible to go even further than this: aren't the first two conditions not merely necessary but *sufficient* to justify judgments of creativity?

Fiction, Truth and Belief. A "fictional sentence" says something about an imaginary person, place, thing, or event.[11] Do fictional sentences express propositions that are either true or false? Miss Macdonald says that they do not.

She rejects the idea that fictional sentences express lies. To lie is to say what is false with intent to deceive. But although storytellers try to make their stories "plausible"—and by a plausible story Miss Macdonald means "one which convinces; which induces acceptance"—they do not intend to deceive, and hence do not lie. This argument is acceptable, but it raises problems about the concept of plausibility. *Of what* does the storyteller try to convince us; *what* does he induce us to accept, if not the truth or probability of what he says?

Do fictional sentences express false statements which are not lies? It would appear that they do. For the sentence "Emma Woodhouse was rich" says in effect, "There was a person named 'Emma Woodhouse' and she was rich"; but since the first part of this statement is false, the whole statement is false.[12]

"As already seen," Miss Macdonald says, "no factual discovery can verify a fictional statement. It can never be true." In that case, it must be (1) necessarily false, (2) empirically false, or (3) necessarily neither true nor false. It can't be necessarily false, for fictional statements are not self-contradictory. It can't be empirically false, for "what no fact can confirm none can disconfirm either." Thus, it must be neither true nor false.

The phrase "as already seen," however, must refer to Moore's rejoinder to Ryle. But doesn't Moore hold that fictional statements are false? If so, doesn't Miss Macdonald's argument rest on a view she rejects? *Why*, in other words, can no factual discovery verify or disconfirm a fictional statement? (This premise is central to Miss Macdonald's argument.) Because it is false? That view is rejected. Because fictional statements are necessarily, by virtue of the fact that they are fictional, neither true nor false? But that begs the question.[13]

Apart from this argument, it might still be the case that fictional sentences do not express true or false propositions. Many other kinds of sentences do not, *e.g.* those that express questions or commands. But if they do not, how do we know this? Does it follow from the meaning of "fictional"? If so, how are we to explain the fact that philosophers such as Moore and Ryle, who know very well what "fictional" means, have held that fictional statements do express false propositions? Were they unwittingly contradicting themselves?

On the positive side, Miss Macdonald argues that fictional sentences are not used to communicate truths, because "in fiction language is used to *create*. . . . [I]t is this which chiefly differentiates it from factual statement." But will this argument do? A liar often makes up what he says; he need not simply deny what is true. What is the difference, then, between one who makes up false stories and the writer of fiction? Does the answer to this reside perhaps in Miss Macdonald's view that "a story-teller performs"? What is it to "perform" with language?

"Are there truths in literature?" is not like the question "Are there blackberries in the woods?"; we can't just look and see if there are. Or, if it is held that we can, how are we to explain the fact that some philosophers see them there though others do not?

For Hospers, there are two kinds of truths—or, more accurately, two kinds of statements with a truth-value—in literature: explicit truths of the "Life is real! Life is earnest!" variety, and implied truths.[14] His concern is solely with the sense in which literature "implies" (a) statements about the author's beliefs, intentions, feelings, etc., and (b) statements "about the world, about human life, human traits, the human situation, the cosmos."

Truths of the first kind, Hospers holds, are "implied" in the sense that from what an author says and how he says it we are *entitled to infer* what he believed or felt. Features of his work are *evidence* of his beliefs and feelings. But what warrants such inferences? Hospers likens this kind of inference to that in which, if a man asserts that *s*, we have the right to infer that he knows or believes that *s*—even if in fact he is lying. Will this do, however, for literature? There is a kind of paradox involved in asserting "I went to the pictures last Tuesday, but I believe that I didn't." Is a similar paradox involved in an atheist's writing religious poetry?[15] Are we entitled to infer, simply from the fact that he wrote materialistic and fatalistic novels, that Dreiser was a materialist and fatalist? We know from his work that the philosopher Hobbes was a materialist; do we know in the same way that Dreiser was a materialist?

According to a counter-view, every work of literature has "an implicit *speaker*, or voice: he whose words the work purports to be."[16] This implicit speaker is no more to be identified with the author than Hamlet,

Macbeth, and Othello are to be identified with Shakespeare. "Once we learn from the work itself the character of the speaker, we can, if we wish, ask how similar he is to the author." But to make this comparison we need independent evidence about the character of the author.

Is this view correct? Do all, or only some, works of literature have an "implicit speaker" who is not the author? How do we know? And if this view is correct, does it negate, or merely complicate, Hospers' view?

The implicit-speaker theory does not touch the second class of truths Hospers is interested in, those about the world. Even a fictional character's words—Hamlet's or Emma's—might intimate or imply propositions about the world. Suppose, however, that we distinguish between the world of a literary work, which is an imaginary world, and the real world. Clearly the world of fairy stories or of science fiction is not the world we live in. Even Dickens' London and Tolstoy's Moscow are, as Miss Macdonald notes, at least partly imaginary. How then would a work of literature *imply* truths about the real world?[17]

Finally, why, and how, do Dreiser's or Zola's works imply or intimate propositions about their author and about the world in a way that Shakespeare's or Jane Austen's do not?[18] Is it perhaps a triumph of art *not* to intimate truths about one's self or the world?

"Belief and aesthetic experience," says Isenberg, "are mutually irrelevant." What Coleridge called "a willing suspension of disbelief"—and, he might have added, belief—is necessary to aesthetic appreciation. There is "an aesthetic mode of commerce with human speech," and any utterance may become an aesthetic object only if we disregard its relation to fact. Belief is, in this sense, irrelevant to literature.

Is this so? If so, why? Because of the meaning of "aesthetic"? Some philosophers claim that this is *arbitrarily* to limit the meaning of "aesthetic." But if "aesthetic" is to mark a distinction between one "mode of commerce" with things and others, must it not exclude certain kinds of response? If it does not exclude assent, dissent, and related responses, what does it exclude?[19]

Is belief not also irrelevant to aesthetic appraisal, and for the same reason? Is "Because I believe it" or "Because it is believable" ever an acceptable reason for a work of literature to be aesthetically worthwhile?

Is not belief, however, relevant to aesthetic experience in at least one way? To understand, and hence aesthetically to appreciate some works of art, is not knowledge required, and to that extent belief? To appreciate *The Divine Comedy*, for example, isn't it necessary to know many things about medieval theology, astronomy, etc.—which is why modern editions of the poem are supplied with copious footnotes? Contrary to what Isenberg says, can such knowledge be written off as "association," as can the suggestion that a cross-eyed person is trying to look two ways at once? How do beliefs about antiquity or the Middle Ages effect our understanding, and hence our appreciation, of ancient and medieval literature?

Form, Content, and Other Aesthetic Concepts. Although the form-content distinction is in some sense a "category" of aesthetic thought, some philosophers and critics recommend that we abandon it in favor of new and better ways of talking about art. Weitz is among them. After analyzing the form-content distinction as it appears in extra-aesthetic as well as aesthetic contexts, he recommends "the rejection of all these usages," proposing "a new usage of form and content which is rooted in a more empirical consideration of the actual nature of works of art."

Weitz criticizes Bell's use of "form" to mean certain elements-in-relation on the grounds that on this use "all great painting has form but no content." Consider, however, Weitz's "new" use of these terms. "The content of a work of art is *all* that is in it . . . all of its expressive elements organically related to each other." And the form? It is "exactly the same thing"! There is thus no distinction at all between form and content. Isn't this as "odd, linguistically speaking," as Bell's view?

Although Weitz claims that the form-content distinction generates specious difficulties, how does his proposed use of the words avoid them? He asks that the words be used to mean the same thing. But doesn't this obliterate a distinction that is useful in talking about art? As long as *how* the words are being used remains clear—and isn't Weitz's analysis of the distinction an aid to such clarity?—is there really anything wrong with so using them?

Weitz says that his proposal fits the actual "organic" character of works of art. Is this the case? Or is Weitz offering "a new way of talking about art" that has no justification, either in language or in the nature of art? Is his proposal not, in short, despite his protest to the contrary, a "mere stipulation"? How can we tell if one use of words is closer than another to "the actual nature" of something? Is a work of art "an organic complex of elements," as Weitz says it is? If so, is this an empirical claim? Are *all* works of art organic complexes, and do we know this in the way we know that all water contains oxygen? Moreover, would it follow from the fact that a work of art is an organic complex, that the form-content distinction is inapplicable to it?

Aestheticians sometimes use the word "form" to refer to properties such as unity, balance, and coherence. These are sometimes called "supervenient" or "second-order" properties for the following reason: if two things are exactly alike, *e.g.* two impressions of the same etching, one of them cannot be unified while the other is not. If only one is unified, it *must* have features which the other does not have; this unity (and balance and coherence) supervene, or depend, upon these "other" features.

Are these features, however, *conditions* of unity? Sibley claims not only that they are not, but that they *cannot* be. Unity, balance, and all other "aesthetic concepts are not and cannot be condition- or rule-governed." One might agree with Sibley that as a matter of linguistic fact the correct application of words such as "unified" and "delicate" is not governed by formulable sufficient conditions, but how does he know that it is *impossible* that they are? Has he given any argument to show this? If someone asserted that aesthetic concepts are condition-governed would he be contradicting himself?

Sibley holds that *no* description of a work of art in nonaesthetic terms, "however full," warrants our saying that it is coherent or powerful; "even with the help of precise names, or even samples and illustrations, of particular shades of color, contours, and lines, any attempt to state conditions would be futile." On the other hand, he holds that "on *seeing* the picture we might say, and rightly," that it is coherent or powerful. Now what does seeing a picture give the viewer that no description, however full, *can* give, as far as the correct application of aesthetic terms is concerned? If what we see in the picture are the features that "make" it coherent or powerful, why *can't* a description of these features warrant our saying that it is? Can't anything that is visible be described? If not, what is the obstacle? If it can, then we can describe what makes a picture coherent, and what is that but a sufficient condition?

The use of aesthetic terms, Sibley says, "requires an exercise of taste," "an ability to *notice* or *see* or *tell* that things have certain qualities." He admits, however, that not everyone has taste, not even everyone with normal intelligence and good eyesight and hearing. How do we tell if someone does, or does not, have this ability? By his capacity to *use* aesthetic terms? This cannot be enough, for Sibley himself admits that a man may lack taste, and yet by shrewd observation and induction he may formulate rules or generalizations and "he might frequently say the right things." In short, he not only uses aesthetic terms; he frequently uses them correctly. But, Sibley says, he only *thinks* that the object is, say, delicate; he doesn't *know* that it is. He is merely *guessing*. How do we tell whether he is merely guessing? How do we distinguish between knowledge and mere opinion in aesthetic matters?

One might say that those who have taste can tell. But isn't this to beg the question? For who has taste, and how can we tell? A blind man can use color words; he might even apply them correctly. But, barring the use of some special device by which he knows the colors of things, we would say that he is guessing correctly. But we have tests for blindness. Have we any comparable, or even analogous, tests for taste? Sibley admits that "it is over the application of aesthetic terms . . . that, notoriously, disputes and differences sometimes go helplessly unsettled"; and this, presumably, among people who *have* taste. But if of two people, both of whom are equally sensitive, one says that a picture is tightly-knit because he sees that it is, and the other says that it isn't because he sees that it isn't, how *could* their dispute be settled if Sibley is right? *Must* one of them lack taste? If so, how can we know which one does?

Notes

1. It is interesting to note, however, that such terms are more often applied to music, poetry, and dance than they are to painting, sculpture, and architecture. There are depressing statues and buildings, but are there melancholy ones?

2. Still another attempt is that examined by Hanslick in Section III: "The music is sad" means the same as "The music depicts or is about sadness."

3. Note that it is the "meaning" of a poem, the emotion purported to be expressed, not the meaning of a poem that is at issue here.

4. "But why do we use 'sad' in reference to both people and melodies?" "Well, why do we apply the word 'table' to both logarithmic tables and pieces of furniture? Isn't this simply a question of etymology?"

5. This supposition was also operative in the thought of Plato, formed the basis of Coleridge's criticism and theory of art, and is found prominently in the writings of such diverse philosophers as Croce and Maritain. For the views of Croce and Maritain on "the creative process," see Section I of this book.

6. If x is a necessary condition of y, then something cannot be y unless it is also x. Being unmarried is a necessary condition of being a bachelor. If x is a sufficient condition of y, then if something is x it is also y. Having a standard I.Q. of 110 is a sufficient condition of being of normal intelligence.

7. That an artist follows rules while painting or writing is suggested to Tomas by his analogy of the rifleman. If a rifleman tries to hit the bull's-eye and fails, he has not obeyed all the rules (presumably of marksmanship). "If he had obeyed them, there necessarily would have been a hole in the bull's-eye." Hence, we congratulate a marksman not for hitting the bull's-eye, as one might suppose, but for obeying the rules.

But if I try to hit the bull's-eye and fail, *must* I have failed to obey at least one of the rules of marksmanship? Can't one hit the bull's-eye by chance (have good luck)? If so, can't he fail to hit it by mischance (have bad luck)? He stands properly, holds the gun properly, aims properly, etc.—his form is perfect—but just as he pulls the trigger, someone bumps him, or the wind blows in his eyes and distracts him. Is there anything paradoxical in saying "I obeyed all the rules, but I failed to hit the bull's-eye"?

8. Cf. the discussion of Collingwood in the concluding essay of Section II above.

9. Wallace Stevens, "The Irrational Element in Poetry," *Opus Posthumous,* New York, Alfred Knopf, 1957, p. 220.

10. "The art of the insane" is an ambiguous phrase. It may mean either (1) the art of people who are insane, or (2) insane art, art that does not "make sense," a kind of art usually produced by insane people. Van Gogh's late pictures are the art of an insane man, but they are not insane art. We tell if something is insane art by looking at it, not by inquiring into the psychology of its maker; we tell if something is the art of an insane person only by inquiring into the psychology of its maker.

11. This is not to say that a work of fiction, *e.g.* a novel, contains nothing but fictional sentences.

12. See Suggestions for Additional Reading at the end of this section for a short bibliography on the disputed logic of this point.

It has been objected to this view that if "Emma Woodhouse was rich" is false, so also is "Emma Woodhouse was not rich," and for the same reason.

But the two statements are contradictory; hence, one of them must be true (M. C. Beardsley, *Aesthetics,* p. 413.) According to the view under discussion, however, the two statements are *not* contradictory. For each is analyzable into a conjunction, and "p and q" and "p and not-q" are not contradictories: both of them cannot be true, but both can be false.

13. The claim that a fictional, or even a false, statement cannot be verified (shown to be true) is ambiguous, and her neglect of this ambiguity may be responsible for Miss Macdonald's difficulty here. "If a statement is fictional (or false), it can't be verified" may mean either (a) "It is logically impossible for a statement to be both fictional (or false) and verified," or (b) "If a statement is fictional (or false), it is logically impossible for it to be verified." Miss Macdonald apparently takes the sentence to mean (b). But (b) is a non-sequitur, unless we *mean* by a fictional statement one that cannot be verified. (But do we?) For even if *s* is false, it does not follow that it cannot be verified that "S has been verified" is self-contradictory; although it is necessarily the case that *s* cannot be both false and verified at the same time. Cf. "If Boots is a dog, he can't be a cat." This doesn't mean that if Boots is a dog, then it's logically impossible for him to be a cat. What is logically impossible is that Boots be both a dog and a cat at the same time.

14. Does Hospers successfully justify this claim? He says "it is important . . . that we should not dismiss literature as 'non-cognitive.' " But why is it important? And does it follow from the fact that literature is not merely emotive and does not have simply "pictorial meaning" that it does contain truths?

15. "Religious" in the sense in which Shelley's lines, quoted by Hospers, are despairing.

16. M. C. Beardsley, *op. cit.,* p. 238.

17. Literature may, of course, *suggest* to us propositions about the real world which have nothing to do with the literary work. But are these suggested propositions effectively *in* the work in the way that Oedipus's implied beliefs and intimated statements about Thebes are in Sophocles' play?

18. Cf. Miss Macdonald, "One cannot tell from their works what Shakespeare or Jane Austen felt."

19. For a fuller discussion of this issue, see Section VI of this book.

Suggestions for Additional Reading

On the concept of expression:

Rudolph Arnheim, *Art and Visual Perception* (Berkeley, 1954), Ch. 10; R. G. Collingwood, *The Principles of Art* (Oxford, 1938), Chs. VI, IX; John Dewey, *Art as Experience* (New York, 1934), Chs. IV, V; C. J. Ducasse, *The Philosophy of Art* (New York, 1929), Chs. 2, 8; John Hospers, *Meaning and Truth in the Arts* (Chapel Hill, 1946), Ch. III; D. W. Prall, *Aesthetic Judgment* (New York, 1929), Ch. 11, *Aesthetic Analysis* (New York, 1936), Ch. 5; Henry D. Aiken, "Art as Expression and Surface," *J.A.A.C.,* IV (1945), 87-95; Stuart Hampshire, *Feeling and Expression* (London, 1961); John Hospers, "The Concept of Artistic Expression," *P.A.S.,* LV (1954-55), 314-344; Vincent Tomas and Douglas N. Morgan, "Symposium: The Concept of Expression in Art," *Science,*

Language and Human Rights, American Philosophical Association, Eastern Division, Vol. I (Philadelphia, 1952), 127-165.

On creativity and the psychology of creation:

S. Alexander, *Beauty and Other Forms of Value* (London, 1933), Ch. IV; Rhys Carpenter et al., *The Bases of Artistic Creation* (New Brunswick, 1942); R. G. Collingwood, *The Principles of Art* (Oxford, 1938), Chs. VI-XI; June Downey, *Creative Imagination* (London, 1929); R. Guggenheimer, *Creative Vision in Artist and Audience* (New York, 1950); H. B. Lee, "The Creative Imagination," *Psychoanalytic Quarterly,* XVIII (1949), 351-360; Douglas Morgan, "Creativity Today," *J.A.A.C.,* XII (1953), 1-24; Milton C. Nahm, *The Artist as Creator* (Baltimore, 1956); Julius Portnoy, *The Psychology of Art Creation* (Philadelphia, 1942); H. E. Rees, *The Psychology of Artistic Creation* (New York, 1942); I. A. Richards, *Coleridge on Imagination* (New York, 1935); Eliseo Vivas, *Creation and Discovery* (New York, 1955).

On the logic of fictional statements:

Monroe C. Beardsley, *Aesthetics* (New York, 1958), Ch. IX; Michael Scriven, "The Language of Fiction," *P.A.S.,* Suppl. Vol. XXVIII (1954), 185-196; Bertrand Russell, "On Denoting," *Mind,* XIV (1905), 479-493, reprinted in *Logic and Knowledge* (New York, 1956); W. V. Quine, "On What There is," *Rev. Met.,* II (1948), 21-38, reprinted in *From a Logical Point of View* (Cambridge, 1953); P. F. Strawson, "On Referring," *Mind,* LIX (1950), 320-344; H. L. A. Hart, "A Logician's Fairy Tale," *Phil. Rev.,* LX (1951), 198-212; Wilfred Sellers, "Presupposing," *Phil. Rev.,* LXIII (1954), 197-215; Gilbert Ryle, R. B. Braithwaite, and G. E. Moore, "Imaginary Objects," *P.A.S.,* Suppl. Vol. XII (1933), 18-70.

On truth in art:

Monroe C. Beardsley, *Aesthetics,* Ch. VIII; R. G. Collingwood, *The Principles of Art,* Ch. XIII; Bernard C. Heyl, *New Bearings in Aesthetics and Art Criticism* (New Haven, 1943), Ch. III, "Artistic Truth Reconsidered," *J.A.A.C.,* VIII (1950), 397-407; John Hospers, *Meaning and Truth in the Arts* (Chapel Hill, 1946), Chs. V-VIII, "Literature and Human Nature," *J.A.A.C.,* XVII (1958), 45-57; H. D. Lewis, "Revelation and Art," *P.A.S.,* Suppl. Vol. XXIII (1949), 1-29; Kingsley B. Price, "Is There Artistic Truth?", *J. Phil.,* XLVI (1949), 285-291; J. W. R. Purser, *Art and Truth* (Glasgow, 1957); Alexander Sesonske, "Truth in Art," *J. Phil.,* LIII (1956), 345-353; Dorothy Walsh, "The Cognitive Content of Art," *Phil. Rev.,* LII (1943), 433-451; Morris Weitz, *Philosophy of the Arts* (Cambridge, 1950), Ch. 8.

On the aesthetic relevance of belief:

Literature and Belief, English Institute Essays, M. H. Abrams ed. (New York, 1958); Henry D. Aiken, "The Aesthetic Relevance of Belief,"

J.A.A.C., IX (1951), 301-315; Monroe C. Beardsley, *Aesthetics*, Ch. IX; Cleanth Brooks, "The Problem of Belief and the Problem of Cognition," *The Well Wrought Urn* (New York, 1947); Ronald W. Hepburn, "Literary and Logical Analysis," *Phil. Quart.*, 8, (1958), 342 ff.; I. A. Richards, *Science and Poetry* (2nd ed., London, 1935).

On form, content, and related concepts:

Virgil C. Aldrich, *Philosophy of Art* (Englewood Cliffs, 1963), Ch. 2; Rudolf Arnheim, *Art and Visual Perception* (Berkeley, 1954), Ch. 1, "Gestalt Psychology and Artistic Form," *Aspects of Form*, Lancelot Law Whyte ed. (Bloomington, Ind., 1961), 196-208; Monroe C. Beardsley, *Aesthetics*, Chs. IV, V; Bernard Berenson, *Aesthetics and History* (New York, 1948); C. D. Birkhoff, *Aesthetic Measure* (Cambridge, 1933); John Dewey, *Art as Experience* (New York, 1934), Chs. VI-VIII; D. W. Gotshalk, *Art and the Social Order* (Chicago, 1947), Ch. 5; T. M. Greene, *The Arts and the Art of Criticism* (Princeton, 1940), Pt. II; Arnold Isenberg, "Perception, Meaning, and the Subject-Matter of Art," *J. Phil.*, XLI (1944), 561-575; Thomas Munro, "Form in the Arts," *J.A.A.C.*, II (1943), 5-26; DeWitt H. Parker, *The Analysis of Art* (New Haven, 1926), Chs. 2, 3; Stephen C. Pepper, *Aesthetic Quality* (New York, 1938), Chs. 5-8; Meyer Shapiro, "Style," *Anthropology Today*, A. L. Kroeber ed. (Chicago, 1953).

V

Problems of Interpretation

Introduction

CRITICISM OF THE ARTS consists largely of two related activities: interpretation and evaluation. Although the term "criticism" is often
restricted to the latter, we find that critics devote much of their time and
effort to interpretation. For before one can reasonably evaluate a work
of art he must understand it, and understanding often requires interpretation.

Interpretation is a verbal activity that consists in explaining works of
art, or parts of them.¹ It takes various forms depending on the kind of
art being interpreted. In music, architecture, and the abstract visual arts,
it is formal in character, pointing out how the parts of a work are
formally related. Literature and representational painting and sculpture
are also subject to formal interpretation, but in these arts questions of
meaning and significance arise, as they do not elsewhere. Columns,
pilasters, windows, and vaults, harmonic progressions, cadenzas, arpeggios,
and chords, save where they can be shown to be symbolic, have literally
no meaning. They have a place in the formal pattern of a work and
contribute to its tone—joyfulness, sobriety, nobility, melancholy, etc.—
but this is not meaning or significance. In the case of allegory, symbolism,
and metaphor, however, and of the significance of the gestures and
actions of human beings in literature, drama, or the visual arts, questions of meaning and significance do arise, the answers to which are
interpretations.

The essays in this section deal with problems in the "logic" of interpretation, *i.e* with questions about the meaning and justification of
interpretive statements. Are they empirical statements and hence open
to objective confirmation? Or subjective reports of feeling and association? Or directives on how to read a poem or look at a picture? What
role does information about the intentions of the artist play in interpretation? To what can we appeal other than the intentions of the artist
to substantiate or justify an interpretation? How can we tell if something
in a work of art is a symbol and what it symbolizes? Can a paraphrase of

a poem—metaphor is the test case—adequately convey the meaning of a poem, or does a poem always mean more than it can be said to mean? These are some of the questions faced in the following selections.

Panofsky distinguishes different strata of "meaning" in a work of art and describes the powers requisite for apprehending them. Aiken, after carefully distinguishing between interpretation, appreciation, and appraisal, demonstrates how a consideration of the artist's intentions relates to each of these activities. Kris and Kaplan raise the problem of the adequacy of interpretations and how conflicts in them can be resolved.

Symbols and metaphors pose two of the chief problems of interpretation, the former in all of the arts, the latter in literature. Mrs. Hungerland discusses what a symbol is in literature and how it is to be construed. Although Black's essay is about philosophy, it has important consequences for literature, *e.g.* that at least some metaphors cannot adequately be paraphrased.

Stevenson argues that the interpretation of art is always other-than-scientific because interpretive statements contain a directive or imperative element.[2]

Notes

1. "Interpretation" has a different application in the performing arts. A pianist who performs Beethoven's Eroica Variations interprets them in so far as he plays them in a distinctive way marked by certain features of tonality, rhythm, tempo, and emphasis which reflect the performer's deliberate or studied intention so to play them.

2. The material of Section III of this book, the selections by Bouwsma, Weitz, Isenberg, and Macdonald in Section IV, Miss Macdonald's essay in Section VII, and the selection from Freud in Appendix C also have a bearing on problems of interpretation.

ERWIN PANOFSKY

Iconology and Iconography

ICONOGRAPHY is that branch of the history of art which concerns itself with the subject matter or meaning of works of art, as opposed to their form. Let us, then, try to define the distinction between subject matter or meaning on the one hand and form on the other.

When an acquaintance greets me on the street by lifting his hat, what I see from a formal point of view is nothing but the change of certain details within a configuration forming part of the general pattern of color, lines and volumes which constitutes my world of vision. When I identify, as I automatically do, this configuration as an object (gentleman), and the change of detail as an event (hat-lifting), I have already overstepped the limits of purely formal perception and entered a first sphere of subject matter or meaning. The meaning thus perceived is of an elementary and easily understandable nature, and we shall call it the factual meaning; it is apprehended by simply identifying certain visible forms with certain objects known to me from practical experience, and by identifying the change in their relations with certain actions or events.

Now the objects and events thus identified will naturally produce a certain reaction within myself. From the way my acquaintance performs his action I may be able to sense whether he is in a good or bad humor, and whether his feelings towards me are indifferent, friendly or hostile. These psychological nuances will invest the gestures of my acquaintance with a further meaning which we shall call expressional. It differs from the factual one in that it is apprehended, not by simple identification, but by "empathy." To understand it, I need a certain sensitivity, but this sensitivity is still part of my practical experience, that is, of my everyday familiarity with objects and events. Therefore, both the factual

From *Studies in Iconology,* by Erwin Panofsky, copyright 1939, by Oxford University Press, Inc., included in *Meaning in the Visual Arts* by Erwin Panofsky. Reprinted by permission of Doubleday & Co., Inc.

and the expressional meaning may be classified together: they constitute the class of primary or natural meanings.

However, my realization that the lifting of the hat stands for a greeting belongs in an altogether different realm of interpretation. This form of salute is peculiar to the Western world and is a residue of mediaeval chivalry: armed men used to remove their helmets to make clear their peaceful intentions and their confidence in the peaceful intentions of others. Neither an Australian bushman nor an ancient Greek could be expected to realize that the lifting of a hat is not only a practical event with certain expressional connotations, but also a sign of politeness. To understand this significance of the gentleman's action I must not only be familiar with the practical world of objects and events, but also with the more-than-practical world of customs and cultural traditions peculiar to a certain civilization. Conversely, my acquaintance could not feel impelled to greet me by lifting his hat were he not conscious of the significance of this act. As for the expressional connotations which accompany his action, he may or may not be conscious of them. Therefore, when I interpret the lifting of a hat as a polite greeting, I recognize in it a meaning which may be called secondary or conventional; it differs from the primary or natural one in that it is intelligible instead of being sensible, and in that it has been consciously imparted to the practical action by which it is conveyed.

And finally: besides constituting a natural event in space and time, besides naturally indicating moods or feelings, besides conveying a conventional greeting, the action of my acquaintance can reveal to an experienced observer all that goes to make up his "personality." This personality is conditioned by his being a man of the twentieth century, by his national, social and educational background, by the previous history of his life and by his present surroundings; but it is also distinguished by an individual manner of viewing things and reacting to the world which, if rationalized, would have to be called a philosophy. In the isolated action of a polite greeting all these factors do not manifest themselves comprehensively, but nevertheless symptomatically. We could not construct a mental portrait of the man on the basis of this single action, but only by co-ordinating a large number of similar observations and by interpreting them in connection with our general information as to his period, nationality, class, intellectual traditions and so forth. Yet all the qualities which this mental portrait would show explicitly are implicitly inherent in every single action; so that, conversely, every single action can be interpreted in the light of those qualities.

The meaning thus discovered may be called the intrinsic meaning or content; it is essential where the two other kinds of meaning, the primary or natural and the secondary or conventional, are phenomenal. It may be defined as a unifying principle which underlies and explains both the visible event and its intelligible significance, and which determines even the form in which the visible event takes shape. This intrinsic meaning or content is, normally, as much above the sphere of conscious volition as the expressional meaning is beneath this sphere.

Transferring the results of this analysis from everyday life to a work of art, we can distinguish in its subject matter or meaning the same three strata:

1. *Primary or Natural Subject Matter*, subdivided into *factual* and *expressional*. It is apprehended by identifying pure forms, that is: certain configurations of line and color, or certain peculiarly shaped lumps of bronze or stone, as representations of natural objects such as human beings, animals, plants, houses, tools and so forth; by identifying their mutual relations as events; and by perceiving such expressional qualities as the mournful character of a pose or gesture, or the homelike and peaceful atmosphere of an interior. The world of pure forms thus recognized as carriers of primary or natural meanings may be called the world of artistic motifs. An enumeration of these motifs would be a pre-iconographical description of the work of art.

2. *Secondary or Conventional Subject Matter*. It is apprehended by realizing that a male figure with a knife represents St. Bartholomew, that a female figure with a peach in her hand is a personification of veracity, that a group of figures seated at the dinner table in a certain arrangement and in certain poses represents the Last Supper, or that two figures fighting each other in a certain manner represent the Combat of Vice and Virtue. In doing this we connect artistic motifs and combinations of artistic motifs (compositions) with themes or concepts. Motifs thus recognized as carriers of a secondary or conventional meaning may be called images, and combinations of images are what the ancient theorists of art called *invenzioni*; we are wont to call them stories and allegories.[1] The identification of such images, stories and allegories is the domain of what is normally referred to as "iconography." In fact, when we loosely speak of "subject matter as opposed to form," we chiefly mean the sphere of secondary or conventional subject matter, viz., the world of specific themes or concepts manifested in images, stories and allegories, as opposed to the sphere of primary or natural subject matter manifested in artistic motifs. "Formal analysis" in Wölfflin's sense is largely an analysis of motifs and combinations of motifs (compositions) ; for a formal analysis in the strict sense of the word would even have to avoid such expressions as "man," "horse," or "column," let alone such evaluations as "the ugly triangle between the legs of Michelangelo's David" or "the admirable clarification of the joints in a human body." It is obvious that a correct iconographical analysis presupposes a correct identification of the motifs. If the knife that enables us to identify a St. Bartholomew is not a knife but a corkscrew, the figure is not a St. Bartholomew. Furthermore, it is important to note that the statement

"this figure is an image of St. Bartholomew" implies the conscious intention of the artist to represent St. Bartholomew, while the expressional
qualities of the figure may well be unintentional.

3. *Intrinsic Meaning or Content.* It is apprehended by ascertaining
those underlying principles which reveal the basic attitude of a nation,
a period, a class, a religious or philosophical persuasion—qualified by one
personality and condensed into one work. Needless to say, these principles are manifested by, and therefore throw light on, both "compositional methods" and "iconographical significance." In the fourteenth
and fifteenth centuries, for instance (the earliest examples can be dated
around 1300), the traditional type of the Nativity with the Virgin Mary
reclining in bed or on a couch was frequently replaced by a new one
which shows the Virgin kneeling before the Child in adoration. From
a compositional point of view this change means, roughly speaking, the
substitution of a triangular scheme for a rectangular one; from an
iconographical point of view, it means the introduction of a new theme
to be formulated in writing by such authors as Pseudo-Bonaventure and
St. Bridget. But at the same time it reveals a new emotional attitude
peculiar to the later phases of the Middle ages. A really exhaustive
interpretation of the intrinsic meaning or content might even show that
the technical procedures characteristic of a certain country, period, or
artist, for instance Michelangelo's preference for sculpture in stone instead of in bronze, or the peculiar use of hatchings in his drawings, are
symptomatic of the same basic attitude that is discernible in all the other
specific qualities of his style. In thus conceiving of pure forms, motifs,
images, stories and allegories as manifestations of underlying principles,
we interpret all these elements as what Ernst Cassirer has called "symbolic" values. As long as we limit ourselves to stating that Leonardo da
Vinci's famous fresco shows a group of thirteen men around a dinner
table, and that this group of men represents the Last Supper, we deal
with the work of art as such, and we interpret its compositional and
iconographical features as its own properties or qualifications. But when
we try to understand it as a document of Leonardo's personality, or of
the civilization of the Italian High Renaissance, or of a peculiar religious attitude, we deal with the work of art as a symptom of something
else which expresses itself in a countless variety of other symptoms, and
we interpret its compositional and iconographical features as more particularized evidence of this "something else." The discovery and interpretation of these "symbolic" values (which are often unknown to the
artist himself and may even emphatically differ from what he consciously intended to express) is the object of what we may call "iconology"
as opposed to "iconography."

The suffix "graphy" derives from the Greek verb *graphein*, "to write";
it implies a purely descriptive, often even statistical, method of procedure. Iconography is, therefore, a description and classification of

images much as ethnography is a description and classification of human races: it is a limited and, as it were, ancillary study which informs us as to when and where specific themes were visualized by which specific motifs. It tells us when and where the crucified Christ was draped with a loincloth or clad in a long garment; when and where He was fastened to the Cross with four nails or with three; how the Virtues and Vices were represented in different centuries and environments. In doing all this, iconography is an invaluable help for the establishment of dates, provenance and, occasionally, authenticity; and it furnishes the necessary basis for all further interpretation. It does not, however, attempt to work out this interpretation for itself. It collects and classifies the evidence but does not consider itself obliged or entitled to investigate the genesis and significance of this evidence: the interplay between the various "types"; the influence of theological, philosophical or political ideas; the purposes and inclinations of individual artists and patrons; the correlation between intelligible concepts and the visible form which they assume in each specific case. In short, iconography considers only a part of all those elements which enter into the intrinsic content of a work of art and must be made explicit if the perception of this content is to become articulate and communicable.

It is because of these severe restrictions which common usage, especially in this country, places upon the term "iconography" that I propose to revive the good old word "iconology" wherever iconography is taken out of its isolation and integrated with whichever other method, historical, psychological or critical, we may attempt to use in solving the riddle of the sphinx. For as the suffix "graphy" denotes something descriptive, so does the suffix "logy"—derived from *logos,* which means "thought" or "reason"—denote something interpretative. "Ethnology," for instance, is defined as a *"science of human races"* by the same *Oxford Dictionary* that defines "ethnography" as a *"description* of human races," and Webster explicitly warns against confusion of the two terms inasmuch as "ethnography is properly restricted to the purely descriptive treatment of peoples and races while ethnology denotes their comparative study." So I conceive of iconology as an iconography turned interpretative and thus becoming an integral part of the study of art instead of being confined to the role of a preliminary statistical survey. There is, however, admittedly some danger that iconology will behave, not like ethnology as opposed to ethnography, but like astrology as opposed to astrography.

Iconology, then, is a method of interpretation which arises from synthesis rather than analysis. And as the correct identification of motifs is the prerequisite of their correct iconographical analysis, so is the correct analysis of images, stories and allegories the prerequisite of their correct iconological interpretation—unless we deal with works of art in which the whole sphere of secondary or conventional subject matter is eliminated and a direct transition from motifs to content is effected, as is the case with European landscape painting, still life and genre, not to mention "non-objective" art.

Now, how do we achieve "correctness" in operating on these three levels, pre-iconographical description, iconographical analysis, and iconological interpretation?

In the case of a pre-iconographical description, which keeps within the limits of the world of motifs, the matter seems simple enough. The objects and events whose representation by lines, colors, and volumes constitutes the world of motifs can be identified, as we have seen, on the basis of our practical experience. Everybody can recognize the shape and behavior of human beings, animals and plants, and everybody can tell an angry face from a jovial one. It is, of course, possible that in a given case the range of our personal experience is not wide enough, for instance when we find ourselves confronted with the representation of an obsolete or unfamiliar tool, or with the representation of a plant or animal unknown to us. In such cases we have to widen the range of our practical experience by consulting a book or an expert; but we do not leave the sphere of practical experience as such, which informs us, needless to say, as to what kind of expert to consult.

Yet even in this sphere we encounter a peculiar problem. Setting aside the fact that the objects, events and expressions depicted in a work of art may be unrecognizable owing to the incompetence or malice aforethought of the artist, it is, on principle, impossible to arrive at a correct pre-iconographical description, or identification of primary subject matter, by indiscriminately applying our practical experience to the work of art. Our practical experience is indispensable, as well as sufficient, as material for a pre-iconographical description, but it does not guarantee its correctness.

A pre-iconographical description of Roger van der Weyden's "Three Magi" in the Kaiser Friedrich Museum at Berlin would, of course, have to avoid such terms as "magi," "Infant Jesus," etc. But it would have to mention that the apparition of a small child is seen in the sky. How do we know that this child is meant to be an apparition? That it is surrounded with a halo of golden rays would not be sufficient proof of this assumption, for similar halos can often be observed in representations of the Nativity where the Infant Jesus is real. That the child in Roger's picture is meant to be an apparition can only be deduced from the additional fact that he hovers in mid-air. But how do we know that he hovers in mid-air? His pose would be no different were he seated on a pillow on the ground; in fact, it is highly probably that Roger used for his painting a drawing from life of a child seated on a pillow. The only valid reason for our assumption that the child in the Berlin picture is meant to be an apparition is the fact that he is depicted in space with no visible means of support.

But we can adduce hundreds of representations in which human beings, animals, and inanimate objects seem to hang loose in space in violation of the law of gravity, without thereby pretending to be apparitions. For instance, in a miniature in the *Gospels of Otto III* in the Staatsbibliothek of Munich, a whole city is represented in the center of an empty space while the figures taking part in the action stand on solid ground.[2] An inexperienced observer may well assume that the town is meant to be suspended in mid-air by some sort of magic. Yet in this case the lack of support does not imply a miraculous invalidation of the laws of nature. The city is the real city of Nain where the resurrection of the youth took place. In a miniature of around 1000 "empty space" does not count as a real three-dimensional medium, as it does in a more realistic period, but serves as an abstract, unreal background. The curious semicircular shape of what should be the base line of the towers bears witness to the fact that, in the more realistic prototype of our miniature, the town had been situated on a hilly terrain, but was taken over into a representation in which space had ceased to be thought of in terms of perspective realism. Thus, while the unsupported figure in the van der Weyden picture counts as an apparition, the floating city in the Ottonian miniature has no miraculous connotation. These contrasting interpretations are suggested to us by the "realistic" qualities of the painting and the "unrealistic" qualities of the miniature. But that we grasp these qualities in the fraction of a second and almost automatically must not induce us to believe that we could ever give a correct pre-iconographical description of a work of art without having divined, as it were, its historical "locus." While we believe that we are identifying the motifs on the basis of our practical experience pure and simple, we really are reading "what we see" according to the manner in which objects and events are expressed by forms under varying historical conditions. In doing this, we subject our practical experience to a corrective principle which may be called the history of style.[3]

Iconographical analysis, dealing with images, stories and allegories instead of with motifs, presupposes, of course, much more than that familiarity with objects and events which we acquire by practical experience. It presupposes a familiarity with specific themes or concepts as transmitted through literary sources, whether acquired by purposeful reading or by oral tradition. Our Australian bushman would be unable to recognize the subject of the Last Supper; to him, it would only convey the idea of an excited dinner party. To understand the iconographical meaning of the picture he would have to familiarize himself with the content of the Gospels. When it comes to representations of themes other than Biblical stories or scenes from history and mythology which happen to be known to the average "educated person," all of us are Australian bushmen. In such cases we, too, must try to familiarize ourselves with what the authors of those representations had read or otherwise knew. But again, while an acquaintance with specific themes and concepts transmitted through literary sources is indispensable and sufficient material for an iconographical analysis, it does not guarantee its correctness. It is just as impossible for us to give a correct iconographical analysis by indiscriminately applying our literary knowledge to the motifs, as it is for us to give a correct pre-iconographical description by indiscriminately applying our practical experience to the forms.

A picture by the Venetian seventeenth-century painter Francesco Maffei, representing a handsome young woman with a sword in her left hand, and in her right a charger on which rests the head of a beheaded man, has been published as a portrayal of Salome with the head of John the Baptist.[4] In fact the Bible states that the head of John the Baptist was brought to Salome on a charger. But what about the sword? Salome did not decapitate St. John the Baptist with her own hands. Now the Bible tells us about another handsome woman in connection with the decapitation of a man, namely Judith. In this case the situation is exactly reversed. The sword in Maffei's picture would be correct because Judith beheaded Holofernes with her own hand, but the charger would not agree with the Judith theme because the text explicitly states that the head of Holofernes was put into a sack. Thus we have two literary sources applicable to our picture with equal right and equal inconsistency. If we should interpret it as a portrayal of Salome the text would account for the charger, but not for the sword; if we should interpret it as a portrayal of Judith the text would account for the sword, but not for the charger. We should be entirely at a loss were we to depend on the literary sources alone. Fortunately we do not. As we could supplement and correct our practical experience by inquiring into the manner in which, under varying historical conditions, objects and events were expressed by forms, viz., into the history of style, just so can we supplement and correct our knowledge of literary sources by inquiring into the manner in which, under varying historical conditions, specific themes or concepts were expressed by objects and events, viz., into the history of types.

In the case in hand we shall have to ask whether there were, before Francesco Maffei painted his picture, any unquestionable portrayals of Judith (unquestionable because they would include, for instance, Judith's maid) with unjustified chargers; or any unquestionable portrayals of Salome (unquestionable because they would include, for instance, Salome's parents) with unjustified swords. And lo! while we cannot adduce a single Salome with a sword, we encounter in Germany and North Italy, several sixteenth-century paintings depicting Judith with a charger;[5] there was a "type" of "Judith with a Charger," but there was no "type" of "Salome with a Sword." From this we can safely conclude that Maffei's picture, too, represents Judith, and not, as had been assumed, Salome.

We may further ask why artists felt entitled to transfer the motif of the charger from Salome to Judith, but not the motif of the sword from Judith to Salome. This question can be answered, again by inquiring into the history of types, with two reasons. One reason is that the sword was an established and honorific attribute of Judith, of many martyrs, and of such virtues as Justice, Fortitude, etc.; thus it could not be transferred with propriety to a lascivious girl. The other reason is that during the fourteenth and fifteenth centuries the charger with the head of St. John the Baptist had become an isolated devotional image (*Andachtsbild*) especially popular in the northern countries and in North Italy; it had been singled out from a representation of the Salome story in much the same way as the group of St. John the Evangelist resting on the bosom of the Lord had come to be singled out from the Last Supper, or the Virgin in childbed from the Nativity. The existence of this devotional image established a fixed association of ideas between the head of a beheaded man and a charger, and thus the motif of a charger could more easily be substituted for the motif of a sack in an image of Judith, than the motif of a sword could have penetrated into an image of Salome.

Iconological interpretation, finally, requires something more than a familiarity with specific themes or concepts as transmitted through literary sources. When we wish to get hold of those basic principles which underlie the choice and presentation of motifs, as well as the production and interpretation of images, stories and allegories, and which give meaning even to the formal arrangements and technical procedures employed, we cannot hope to find an individual text which would fit those basic principles as John 13:21 ff. fits the iconography of the Last Supper. To grasp these principles we need a mental faculty comparable to that of a diagnostician—a faculty which I cannot describe better than by the rather discredited term "synthetic intuition," and which may be better developed in a talented layman than in an erudite scholar.

However, the more subjective and irrational this source of interpretation (for every intuitive approach will be conditioned by the interpreter's psychology and *"Weltanschauung"*), the more necessary the application of those correctives and controls which proved indispensable where only iconographical analysis and pre-iconographical description were concerned. When even our practical experience and our knowledge of literary sources may mislead us if indiscriminately applied to works of art, how much more dangerous would it be to trust our intuition pure and simple! Thus, as our practical experience had to be corrected by an insight into the manner in which, under varying historical conditions objects and events were expressed by forms (history of style); and as our knowledge of literary sources had to be corrected by an insight into the manner in which, under varying historical conditions, specific themes and concepts were expressed by objects and events (history of types); just so, or even more so, must our synthetic intuition be corrected by an

	OBJECT OF INTERPRETATION	ACT OF INTERPRETATION	EQUIPMENT FOR INTERPRETATION	CORRECTIVE PRINCIPLE OF INTERPRETATION (*History of Tradition*)
I	Primary or *natural* subject matter—(A) factual (B) expressional—constituting the world of artistic motifs.	*Pre-iconographical description* (and pseudo-formal analysis).	*Practical experience* (familiarity with *objects* and *events*).	History of *style* (insight into the manner in which, under varying historical conditions, *objects* and *events* were expressed by forms).
II	*Secondary* or *conventional* subject matter, constituting the world of *images, stories* and *allegories*.	*Iconographical analysis*	*Knowledge of literary sources* (familiarity with specific *themes* and *concepts*.)	History of *types* (insight into the manner in which, under varying historical conditions, specific *themes* or *concepts* were expressed by *objects* and *events*).
III	*Intrinsic meaning or content,* constituting the world of "*symbolical*" values.	*Iconological interpretation*	*Synthetic intuition* (familiarity with the essential tendencies of the human mind), conditioned by personal psychology and "*Weltanschauung*."	History of *cultural symptoms* or "*symbols*" in general (insight into the manner in which, under varying historical conditions, *essential tendencies of the human mind* were expressed by specific *themes* and *concepts*).

insight into the manner in which, under varying historical conditions, the general and essential tendencies of the human mind were expressed by specific themes and concepts. This means what may be called a history of cultural symptoms—or "symbols" in Ernst Cassirer's sense—in general. The art historian will have to check what he thinks is the intrinsic meaning of the work, or group of works, to which he devotes his attention, against what he thinks is the intrinsic meaning of as many other documents of civilization historically related to that work or group of works, as he can master: of documents bearing witness to the political, religious, poetical, philosophical, and social tendencies of the personality, period or country under investigation. Needless to say that, conversely, the historian of political life, poetry, religion, philosophy, and social situations should make analagous use of works of art. It is in the search for intrinsic meanings or content that the various humanistic disciplines meet on a common plane instead of serving as handmaidens to each other.

In conclusion: when we wish to express ourselves very strictly (which is of course not always necessary in our normal talk or writing, where the general context throws light on the meaning of our words), we have to distinguish between three strata of subject matter or meaning, the lowest of which is commonly confused with form, and the second of which is the special province of iconography as opposed to iconology. In whichever stratum we move, our identifications and interpretations will depend on our subjective equipment, and for this very reason will have to be supplemented and corrected by an insight into historical processes the sum total of which may be called tradition.

I have summarized in a synoptical table what I have tried to make clear thus far. But we must bear in mind that the neatly differentiated-categories, which in this synoptical table seem to indicate three independent spheres of meaning, refer in reality to aspects of one phenomenon, namely, the work of art as a whole. So that, in actual work, the methods of approach which here appear as three unrelated operations of research merge with each other into one organic and indivisible process.

Notes

1. Images conveying the idea, not of concrete and individual persons or objects (such as St. Bartholomew, Venus, Mrs. Jones, or Windsor Castle), but of abstract and general notions such as Faith, Luxury, Wisdom, etc., are called either personifications or symbols (not in the Cassirerian, but in the ordinary sense, e.g., the Cross, or the Tower of Chastity). Thus allegories, as opposed to stories, may be defined as combinations of personifications and/or symbols. There are, of course, many intermediary possibilities. A person A. may be portrayed in

the guise of the person B. (Bronzino's Andrea Doria as Neptune: Dürer's Lucas Paumgärtner as St. George), or in the customary array of a personification (Joshua Reynolds' Mrs. Stanhope as "Contemplation"); portrayals of concrete and individual persons, both human or mythological, may be combined with personifications, as is the case in countless representations of a eulogistic character. A story may convey, in addition, an allegorical idea, as is the case with the illustrations of the *Ovide Moralisé*, or may be conceived as the "prefiguration" of another story, as in the *Biblia Pauperum* or in the *Speculum Humanae Salvationis*. Such superimposed meanings either do not enter into the content of the work at all, as is the case with the *Ovide Moralisé* illustrations, which are visually indistinguishable from non-allegorical miniatures illustrating the same Ovidian subjects; or they cause an ambiguity of content, which can, however, be overcome or even turned into an added value if the conflicting ingredients are molten in the heat of a fervent artistic temperament as in Rubens' "Galerie de Médicis."

2. G. Leidinger, *Das sogenannte Evangeliar Ottos III*, Munich, 1912, Pl. 36.

3. To correct the interpretation of an individual work of art by a "history of style," which in turn can only be built up by interpreting individual works, may look like a vicious circle. It is, indeed, a circle, though not a vicious, but a methodical one (cf. E. Wind, *Das Experiment und die Metaphysik*, Tubingen, 1934; *idem*, "Some Points of Contact between History and Natural Science," *Philosophy and History, Essays Presented to Ernst Cassirer*, Oxford, 1936, p. 255 ff.). Whether we deal with historical or natural phenomena, the individual observation assumes the character of a "fact" only when it can be related to other, analogous observations in such a way that the whole series "makes sense." This "sense" is, therefore, fully capable of being applied, as a control, to the interpretation of a new individual observation within the same range of phenomena. If, however, this new individual observation definitely refuses to be interpreted according to the "sense" of the series and if an error proves to be impossible, the "sense" of the series will have to be reformulated to include the new individual observation. This *circulus methodicus* applies, of course, not only to the relationship between the interpretation of motifs and the history of style, but also to the relationship between the interpretation of images, stories and allegories and the history of types, and to the relationship between the interpretation of intrinsic meanings and the history of cultural symptoms in general.

4. G. Fiocco, *Venetian Painting of the Seicento and the Settecento*, Florence and New York, 1929, Pl. 29.

5. One of the North Italian pictures is ascribed to Romanino and is preserved in the Berlin Museum, where it was formerly listed as "Salome" in spite of the maid, a sleeping soldier, and the city of Jerusalem in the background; another is ascribed to Romanino's pupil Francesco Prato da Caravaggio (quoted in the Berlin Catalogue), and a third is by Bernardo Strozzi, who was a native of Genoa but active at Venice about the same time as Francesco Maffei. It is very possible that the type of "Judith with a Charger" originated in Germany. One of the earliest known instances (by an anonymous master of around 1530 related to Hands Baldung Grien) has been published by G. Poensgen, "Beiträge zu Baldung und seinem Kreis," *Zeitschrift für Kunstgeschichte*, VI, 1937, p. 36 ff.

HENRY DAVID AIKEN

The Aesthetic Relevance of Artists' Intentions

LIKE MOST TITLES, this one is likely to prove misleading unl ss an initial disclaimer is made. In speaking of the aesthetic relevance of artists' intentions I want to come down rather lightly on the word "aesthetic." It is works of art that I want to discuss, and the cluster of questions concerning the relevance of intentions to their appraisal, appreciation, and interpretation.

There is one way of construing such questions which makes it very easy to dispose of them. If they are taken to concern the relevance of artists' intentions to appraisals and interpretations of *their* work, then it is apparent that such intentions are entirely relevant. What would it mean to speak of appraising your work, what it is that you have done or accomplished, apart from any consideration of what you are trying to do? The success or failure of your accomplishment depends upon the degree to which it fulfills your purpose; that is part of what is implied in calling it "your accomplishment." From such a standpoint, moreover, there is no important difference between appraising and appreciating. Both are estimates of your accomplishment, what it is that you have achieved. I cannot be said to appreciate your accomplishment if I totally ignore what you intended to do. The logic of appreciations of this sort leaves me no option in the matter. And for much the same reason I cannot ignore your intentions in trying to interpret what it is that you have accomplished. For the latter are part and parcel of the accomplishment, the thing achieved or done. You can't split off a man's intentions from what he has done in the way you can split off the branch from a tree. Change the intention and you change the act performed, the thing done or accomplished.

Evidently, then, we have something else in mind, if we are serious, in

Reprinted from *The Journal of Philosophy*, Vol. LII (1955).

raising questions about the relevance of artists' intentions to appraisals, appreciations, and interpretations of the works they have produced. What this may be begins to come out when we substitute for "the artist's work" the phrase "work of art." I can ask, with some show of a point, what the relevance of your intentions may be to the appraisal of the works of art you have happened to produce. It is here, therefore, that we must make our beginning: What is the role of the expression "work of art" in talking about the products of human ingenuity and imagination?

Notice, first of all, that questions concerning the relevance of an artist's intentions to the appraisal or interpretation of something he has produced *as a work of art* strongly suggest that the artist himself is not responsible for the fact that his production is a work of art. As an accomplishment, the artist's work is his own; but he alone does not and can not make it a work of art. This is not to say that in calling something a work of art we do not normally presuppose that it is a human artifact. But this is not what we are explicitly talking about when we refer to it as a work of art. Because of this, some aestheticians have supposed that the analysis of the expression "work of art" must be sought in the characteristics of the objects which we dignify by this title. And they have been mistaken. Like the term "happiness," the phrase "work of art" is not amenable to ordinary descriptive definitions, and the effects of so trying to define it are not what the definer may suppose: they do not clarify its use, but rather modify its range of application, and in so doing serve merely to redirect our attitudes toward the things to which the expression is subsequently applied. Moreover, the characteristics of the object to which we may point in giving reasons for calling it a work of art become reasons for so regarding it only because it is assumed that they help to make it worth contemplating in a certain way. Any feature of a work may provide a reason for speaking of it as a work of art, but only if that feature helps to make the whole of which it is a part something which is to be admired or appreciated for its own sake. It is for this reason that no particular symbolic form, no theme or subject-matter, no material or arrangement of materials, as such, can be definitive of what it is to be a work of art.

It is nevertheless possible to provide a characterization of the sort of thing that is being said when we call something a work of art. Works of art are so-called primarily because it is thought that when approached or handled in certain ways they tend to give satisfaction or pleasure to those who so handle them. But there is no one activity, no one way of approaching or handling works of art which is indispensable or which alone is appropriate to them all. Some aestheticians have tried to make such words as "contemplation" do the trick, and with disastrous results. Among other things, we contemplate pictures; but we read poetry, listen to music, witness plays, smell perfume, and taste fine wine or food. And when we do any of these things appreciatively and discriminatingly we are apt to call the things in question works of art. If we do not appreciate them, or if

ve find that our discriminations are not worth the candle, we resist any
emptation to speak of them as works of art.

At this point it may be useful to compare the concept of a work of art
vith that of a tool. Both are what I sometimes call "functional concepts."
By this I mean that they are used not to describe the physical attributes
of things but rather to specify their roles in human life and the activities
vhich are appropriate to them. A tool is an artifact that is used in certain
characteristic ways to accomplish a certain kind of result, to get a certain
ort of thing done. Tools, in short, have certain appropriate, conventional
uses; they are also subject to misuse and have improper uses. Now works
of art, like tools, are subject to improper uses; and, although in a some-
vhat different sense than that which we have in mind in speaking of the
misuse of a tool, they may be misused. Unlike tools, however, works of
rt, as such, are not used to accomplish a certain result or to get some-
hing done. There are certain things which it is proper to do with works
of art; but these are not done for the sake of a result, but, as we say, for
he pleasure or satisfaction of the doing. The result of doing what is appropriate to a work of art may be anything under the sun from emotional
atharsis to wish fulfillment. But such results are accidental; they have
nothing to do with the function of a work of art as such.

Before concluding these remarks, it is necessary to bring out more emphatically an aspect of the concept of a work of art which affects the na-
ure of any controversy as to the relevance of an artist's intentions to the
ppraisal, appreciation, or interpretation of his art. The point is that
"work of art" is an expression of commendation. This becomes obvious
vhen we think of what is being said when a rainbow or any other natural
bject is called a work of art. A work of art is something which is admirable, which is worthy of admiration, and which, perhaps, ought to be
dmired. This being so, any denial of the relevance of the artist's inten-
ions to what he has accomplished as a work of art is bound to have the
orce of a prescription which enjoins us to disallow any consideration of
uch intentions in attempting to give reasons why it is worthy of admira-
ion. Such denials, in short, do not so much state a fact as modify the
vays in which we approach or handle the objects we are prepared to call
vorks of art; they limit the scope of the considerations we may take into
ccount in judging, appreciating, and interpreting, and in so doing pro-
oundly affect our entire conception of what our artistic activities ought
o be or become. This is why the debate over questions of the sort with
vhich we have here to do is bound to be intense and acrimonious, and
vhy any appeal to the "facts" concerning the character of the objects
hemselves or concerning our actual transactions with such objects is
kely to be inconclusive. Nor do I deny that in trying to spell out some
f the proprieties governing our discourse about works of art, I myself
m at the same time protecting the activities of which such discourse is a
art. Forms of words, it has been said, reflect forms of life. In characteriz-

ing, with approval, the logical amenities that govern the use of a form of
words, I am doing something more than describing them; I am also re-
ënforcing the modes of behaviour to which the forms of words belong.

It is time, now, to turn to other matters. We cannot successfully understand the cluster of questions with which we are concerned without some
preliminary discussion of the concepts of appraisal, appreciation, and interpretation, as these are employed in talking about works of art.

To appraise a work of art, plainly, is to judge it, to estimate its worth.
It must be borne in mind, however, that the things we call works of art
are not merely such, that they often have other functions and interest us
for other reasons. It is therefore essential to distinguish appraisals of pictures, musical compositions, or literary productions which judge them as
works of art from those which estimate them from the standpoint of some
other role or capacity. Our concern, here, is only with the former. It
should be observed, also, that appraisals of works of art as such are properly and reasonably made only after the completion of other acts which
are performed in dealing with works of art as such. Such acts, which
would include reading, listening, witnessing, contemplating, and the like,
may conveniently be called the "primary" or "aesthetic" activities required in dealing with works of art. Among such acts we would not include acts of judgment or appraisal; the latter are secondary, dependent
acts which are performed subsequently to and in consequence of reading,
listening, witnessing, and contemplating. You can't appreciate a piece of
music as a work of art if you won't listen to it; but you can appreciate it
without judging it; nor is it essential to the proper handling of any work
of art that it be judged. But what we find when we perform the primary
acts called for by a work of art provides the basis for a proper performance of such secondary acts as judging. How we appraise a work of art as
such depends upon our appreciation of it and upon the performance of
the primary acts upon which appreciation itself depends. Any reasons we
may adduce for highly appraising a work of art which are not based upon
what is found in performance of the primary activities are irrelevant to
our appraisal or else, if we persist in them, transform the appraisal into a
judgment which is not concerned with the object as a work of art.

The term "appreciate" is equivocal. In one sense, as we have seen, its
meaning is like that of "appraise." But there is another important sense
of the term which must be contrasted with this. When we speak of art
appreciation or of appreciating a work of art as such, we are talking not
about estimations and judgments, but rather about pleasurable or satisfying discrimination. In this sense, my capacity for appreciation is not my
power to appraise but my sensitivity, my ability to discriminate and to be
moved by the qualities of the work as a work of art. To appreciate a
man's work, as we have seen, it is necessary to take into account his intentions; but it is not necessary, even though it may be desirable, to have
regard to an artist's intentions in appreciating his product as a work of

art. The question, here, concerns the fullness of our appreciation, not appreciation as such. In order adequately to appreciate a work of art, to discriminate and relate its qualities, to discern its full expressive content, one may have to consider the artist's intentions. But the latter, by the nature of the case, can have no authoritative claim upon us as appreciators or upon the subsequent judgments we may make as appreciators.

The term "interpretation" is used with abominable looseness by critics and philosophers of art. Sometimes, apparently, it is used in a way which seems to refer to the primary activities of reading, listening, and contemplating. I should regard this as a misuse of the expression. More properly it is employed to refer to the activities of a critic in paraphrasing, describing, explaining, explicating, analysing, and the like. In this sense, interpretation is clearly an ancillary activity, undertaken in order to accomplish something beyond itself. How great is the confusion latent in this equivocation becomes evident when we observe how different are the primary activities of looking or contemplating from those of explaining or explicating, and how different are their relations to the work of art itself. In effect, interpretations are tools for the use of an audience in readying itself for the activities involved in appreciation. But the appreciative reading of a poem is not a tool and is not undertaken to get something done; it does not ready us for something else and its adequacy is not judged by its effects.

The role of interpretation, then, is advisory. It serves to guide, direct, and in general to improve the facility with which the primary acts which are proper to works of art are performed. Interpretations of works of art are properly judged on this basis. But just as we frequently do other things, often very well, without advice or counsel, so on occasion we may appreciate a work of art very fully without the help of an interpretation, or without interpreting it at all. Interpretations are useful or necessary precisely because not everything in most works of art is immediately perceivable, and we resort to them, as a rule, because we fail to understand what we read or see or because its relevance to other things in the work is not adequately appreciated.

Interpretation and judgment obviously are not the same thing, any more than interpretation and appreciation are the same thing. Judgment presupposes appreciation; it does not presuppose interpretation. It is usually assumed, however, and with some basis, that appraisals that are based upon interpretation are sounder than those that are not. The reason for this is that interpretations are presumed to enable the artist's audience to gain a more adequate appreciation of the qualities of his art. But in speaking of appraisals "based" upon interpretations it is possible to be misleading, precisely because of the equivocation mentioned above. In the sense here under consideration, the appraisal of a work of art is only indirectly based upon interpretation; it is directly based only upon what we find in performing the primary acts proper to appreciation of a work of art. The relevance of any interpretation of a work of art, in short, is always through appreciation. It is only as it affects appreciation, through the modification of what we see, hear, or feel, that any interpretation provides a basis for and is relevant to the judgment of a work of art as such.

All interpretations of a work of art are bound to be selective and are bound to be slanted toward a certain mode of appreciation. And because in most cases alternative modes of appreciation are possible, there can be, as a rule, no such thing as a definitive interpretation. The aesthetic relevance of a particular interpretation, therefore, can be established only with respect to a certain mode of appreciation, a certain way of approaching and handling the work of art. We cannot just say that the thing as interpreted is "there" and have done. In speaking of a particular work of art, we are not talking about something that has a certain single definitive shape or pattern. Actually any particular work of art includes a considerable variety of such patterns which cannot all be appreciated in a single reading or view of the work. Each such pattern, moreover, answers to a particular mode of appreciation which is possible only if the work is approached and handled in a certain way. Nor is any one of these patterns the only objective one, the one that is constitutive of the work as it is "in reality." For this reason, any prolonged debate over what is there in the work itself is bound to be futile; and it will be so, in many cases, not just because our individual experiences of a work are not the same, but because the work itself is capable of a number of modes of appreciation, one of which, in principle, may be as proper to it as another.

This inescapable and innocuous relativity of interpretations does not, however, preclude the possibility of saying that one interpretation is more adequate than another. The adequacy of any interpretation may be judged in at least two ways, according either to the adequacy with which it prepares us for a particular mode of appreciation or else to the comparative satisfactoriness of the mode of appreciation to which it leads. The question concerning the aesthetic relevance of an interpretation, therefore, is likely to be somewhat complicated. Nor can it be properly answered without regard to the complexities which unavoidably enter into our conception of a particular work of art.

A few words must now be said about the use of the word "intention." Here, also, much avoidable trouble has resulted from the failure to distinguish carefully among the several senses in which aestheticians and critics employ the word. In speaking of an artist's intentions, some writers appear to be thinking of the ends or goals for which the artist may undertake his work. Frequently, however, this is confused with what the artist intends to say or do in some part of the work. Manifestly, what I intend to accomplish in saying something is not the same thing as what I mean when I say it. And what answers to questions about the former does not at all answer to questions concerning the latter. Unfortunately there are also other and different notions that are frequently introduced when questions concerning an artist's intentions are raised, which have to do neither with questions of ends nor with questions of what the artist intended to say or do in the work, but rather with the attitudes, conscious or otherwise, which cause him to choose his subject-matter or which condition his selection of themes, genres, or materials and determine the way in which he handles them. Such attitudes, so to say, affect the "personality" of the work of art as a whole, and our awareness of them is likely to affect our own view of it when we approach the work as appreciators and as interpreters.

It should be abundantly clear, by this time, that to raise questions as to the relevance of an artist's intentions to the appraisal, appreciation, and interpretation of works of art that he has produced is to raise a series of questions of very different sorts. In the remaining space I can merely indicate some of the considerations that are involved in trying to answer a few of them.

It is evident from what has already been said that in any of the above-mentioned senses, artists' intentions do not provide a standard for judging their productions as works of art. The only intrinsic standard afforded those who profess to judge the merits of works of art as such is the satisfaction that results when we engage in the primary activities that are proper to particular works. But it is too easily concluded from this that an artist's intentions are of no use to a potential judge. For by taking account of an artist's intentions we are frequently able to avoid the serious mistake of solemnly judging as works of art productions whose only interest, either to the artist or to ourselves, lies elsewhere. Properly regarded, artist's intentions are advisory: they help us to know what to expect and hence how to approach a particular artifact. They do not provide the criterion from which a work is to be judged as a work of art; but they are of help in deciding whether such a criterion is to be invoked in judging a work. This, I think, is their primary relevance, and no confusion of values or fallacy is involved in acknowledging the fact. Quite the contrary.

From the standpoint of appreciation, it is of the first importance not to confuse the various things which philosophers tend to lump together under the heading of "intentions." Consider, first, the artist's ulterior goals. Now as Hume long ago pointed out, one of the sources of our appreciation in contemplating a work of art is our awareness of the fitness of the work to the end for which it was produced. This functional beauty of a work of art can only be appreciated, however, if the artist's ulterior intentions are understood and borne in mind. Many works of art, of course, have no such interest; my only point in mentioning it is to show that you can't say out of hand that an artist's ulterior aims are irrelevant to the appreciation of his art. It depends upon the character of the individual work, upon the central focus of its artistic interest.

The same is true, in another way, of the relevance of an artist's attitudes, the factors we lump together under the heading of his "person-ality." Now it is certainly possible to appreciate many works of art, some of them quite fully, without regard to the attitudes which, consciously or unconsciously, the artist may express in them. But works of art differ enormously with respect to the central focus of their interest. Some works are virtually anonymous; nothing is added to our interest from the knowl-edge of their authors' characters. Others are intensely personal. I have found, for example, that when I read the novels of Dickens or Dostoyevski with some awareness of their authors' personalities much becomes clear that I could not previously understand or appreciate. The very dramatic dimension of their art is measurably intensified thereby, and the whole takes on a new dimension of significance it did not have before. The re-sult is not a distraction from what the author himself tells us, but rather an amplification of what he says or does, or, better, an amplification of what his work conveys to us as we read it. In short, a considerable part of our interest in many works of art arises from the fact that they express to us in a poignant and affecting way recurrent patterns of human behav-iour whose independent interest to us is funded into the artistic trans-action which transpires as we read or look or listen.

It will doubtless be replied that when an artist's attitudes are relevant to the appreciation of his work as art they will be manifest to us in the act of appreciation so that it is unnecessary to go outside the work for additional information. And it will be urged that, if we have to go out-side the work to discover what it may express, the work itself is *ipso facto* deficient as a work of art. I should reply, however, that just as no man is an island, so no work of art is an island, and that the integrity of a work of art, like the integrity of a person, is quite compatible with this fact. The phrase "going outside the work" is a treacherous one, responsible for no end of confusion and misconception as to the nature of works of art and the process whereby they are appreciated. For example, everyone knows that it is possible to go outside what one initially or immediately perceives in a work and yet not "read into" it something which is not there. Everyone knows also that it is frequently necessary to go outside the work as it immediately presents itself in order to gain access to its underlying meanings and depth values. The only serious question, there-fore, is whether, having gone outside, what we find when we return is more meaningful, more satisfying, more moving. If so, then what we have "read into" the work as a consequence is "really" there in the only sense in which, in the present context, such a question has any interest.

We have still to consider the relevance of an artist's intentions in the more limited sense which has to do with what he means to say or do *in* the work of art. Now it will be argued, no doubt, that although such in-tentions may be relevant if our concern is to measure his achievement, they have no bearing upon the appreciation of the work of art as such. In one sense, I agree. I agree also that in the sense now being considered, an artist's intentions, unlike his motives or attitudes, do not comprise a distinguishable expressive or functional aspect of the work. If what the poet meant or intended to say does not finally coincide with what the work itself means it is irrelevant to the work and to our appreciation of it.

These banalities, however, have frequently misled aestheticians into the mistaken conclusion that consideartion of an artist's intentions is irrelevant to the *interpretation* of his work. When I read a great work of art with full appreciation, the farthest thing from my mind is what he may have intended to say or what he means in a particular passage or by a particular allusion or figure of speech. The fact is, however, that full appreciation rarely occurs, and that with most complex works of art repeated study, with the aid of dictionaries, glossaries, mythologies, footnotes, and God knows what else, is necessary in order to place oneself in a position to perform successfully the primary acts required for the appreciation of a given work. In short, most works of art have to be interpreted, and it is because of this that consideration of what an artist intended to say or do in a work becomes relevant, although indirectly, to appreciation and to appraisal.

Just as we are all guilty, at one time or another, of the "one and only one meaning fallacy" so we are guilty of the fallacy of "fixed meaning." Words have meaning; they also acquire them. And for the purpose of understanding the subtle nuance, overtone, or association which may explain a poet's use of a given word or figure we have to go outside what the dictionary is able tell us. We must go somewhere. In ordinary discourse we make allowances for a person's intentions in construing what he has said. In the case of works of literary art we need not make allowances, but we are simply foolish not to accept any clue, however we may gain access to it, which will enable us to read a passage as intelligently as the work as a whole requires. Every interpretation, in one sense, goes outside the work as we immediately find it. This being so, it is of no importance whatever how an interpretation is come by, so long as the advice it gives us for the purpose of reading appreciatively actually serves that purpose. Whether the artist himself is in a privileged position to know what his work means I do not care. I care only that knowledge of his intentions sometimes enables me to construe a passage I could not otherwise adequately comprehend, and that when I follow such directions as he may give me for reading, looking, or listening, I commonly read, look, or listen in a way which is more satisfying.

There is nothing mysterious about the artists' intentions, as some theorists have argued. They are not private entities to which no one else can gain access. With artists as with less gifted folk, access to their intentions is gained in dozens of ways, from explicit, although by no means infallible, statements of intentions, from titles, stage directions, and other such paraphernalia. We gain such knowledge, frequently, by examining other works of the artist himself or other works in the style, idiom, or tradition of the work under consideration. We gain it also from the internal evidence afforded by other parts of the particular work. All this we sift and fit together as best we can into the most coherent, most satisfactory interpretation of which we, with the artist's help, are capable.

The point is that we approach the interpretation of works of art not as omniscient observers who can always distinguish what an artist means from what he says, and who know in advance what is relevant or irrelevant. We consider an artist's intentions because we have questions about his work that we cannot always answer without his guidance, without knowledge of what he was trying to do or say. And we arrive at our interpretations not by gaping at the "work itself," but by a complex process of trial and error involving many things besides looking at the work. Anyone who has sought to interpret a work belonging to a culture other than his own knows how true this is.

As I have found from the examination of a great many pieces of criticism, references to the artist's intentions usually do not and are not meant to go outside the work. Nor do they in the least indicate that the critic who uses them is not interested in the work as a work of art or that he has been overcome by preoccupations with history or biography. On the contrary, in most cases, they are references to what, as the critic believes, is "really there," and are introduced only in order to provide us with the means to a fuller, more adequate appreciation. The function of critical references to an artist's intentions, nine times out of ten, is simply to go behind immediate appearances to underlying artistic realities that we otherwise stand no chance of appreciating. They do not take us away from the work, but, rather, bring us in the end closer to it. They do not divert attention from the "aesthetic object" but provide the opportunity to appreciate what is really there. And if, overwhelmed by the noisy cries of "fallacy" and "heresy" that surround us, we refuse to make use of them, the consequence will not be a purification of our aesthetic experience of art, but merely an impoverishment of our resources for having such experience—if there is any such thing.

ERNST KRIS and ABRAHAM KAPLAN

Aesthetic Ambiguity

II

. . . Aesthetic creation, as Dewey has convincingly set forth in his *Art as Experience,* may be looked on as a type of problem-solving behaviour. The contrast between scientist and artist as "man of thought" and "man of feeling" has no more merit than the parent dualism between "reason" and "emotion." Ratiocinative processes are embedded in a manifold of feeling of various degrees of intensity. Emotions, as they are embodied in aesthetic activity, are not blind, but incorporated in structures of a complex patterning which result only from taking thought.

But problem-solving in the arts differs characteristically from its counterpart in scientific inquiry. For one thing, the artist works in a medium consisting of sensory materials, not the intellectualistic concepts and propositions of the scientist. The poet, to be sure, employs, like the scientist, linguistic symbols. But for the poet, language itself has a sensory form, a sound and rhythm; and he exploits the full range of responses to language, including imagery and excitation, not some operationally limited area of abstract significance.

A problem can be constituted as such only by the existence of conditions in terms of which it is to be solved. We shall refer to these conditions in a general way as *stringencies*: they restrict the possible modes of behavior by which the problem is "legitimately" dealt with. These stringencies further differentiate the problems of aesthetic creation (and re-creation) from other sorts. In mathematics, the stringencies are maximal; the permissible operations on given symbols are rigidly specified by what Carnap calls rules of formation and transformation. A derivation or demonstration is valid or invalid in terms of its strict adherence to such rules. In the inductive sciences, stringencies are not so extreme. At a given stage of inquiry, various hypotheses may be equally warranted by the data and known laws. Stringencies themselves emerge in the process of inquiry, and are subject to modification according to their workings in inquiry.

In the arts, stringencies in this sense are minimal. A given aesthetic problem may be solved (and indeed, even formulated) in a wide variety of ways. Hence arises the possibility of art as a means of expression. Two mathematicians, two scientists, will deal with their respective problems in much the same ways; but aesthetic solutions bear to a much higher degree (at least in many historical periods) the stamp of the solver, his individuality—his style.

Stringencies are minimal in the arts, however, only as compared with other sorts of problem-solving; in themselves, they are not inconsiderable. Materials have their own properties, and the transformation of physical material to aesthetic medium requires recognition of and adaptation to these properties. And of equal importance (greater, in the case of poetry) are a set of stringencies more or less independent of the requirements of the material: the *conventions* of the particular art form at a given period. Here is the point at which ambiguity enters into aesthetic creation—it is a means of expressing style within the limits of the conventions.

For rigid adherence to stringencies defines the academic in art, as will be elaborated below. And the extreme of stringency domination carries us back from art to ritual. In ritual, form and content are strictly patterned, and repeated again and again with minimal deviation, on pain of losing the ritualistic efficacy. The ritualistic act is one of *participation* rather than creation: the response which the members of the group are required or expected to have is rigidly limited. As ritual becomes secularized, the priest gives way to the bard or poet. Conformity of reaction vanishes: interpretations are not rigidly confined to the institutional or doctrinal requirements, but proliferate in accord with the creative impulse of the individual artist. Poetry becomes ambiguous concomitantly with its emergence from ritual.[1]

Art, in short, is a product of inspiration as well as skill. The satisfaction of stringencies provides only for the element of skill, which culminates in mastery of technique. Expressiveness, as contrasted with mere technical excellence, lies just in what is not determined by the stringencies, and involves the workings of a distinctive psychic process in which ambiguities frequently play a central rôle.

A detailed discussion of inspiration is outside the scope of this essay.[2] What is relevant here is its relation to external stringencies and internal ambiguities. The psychic activities or functions devoted to the adaptation to reality are comprised in the psychoanalytic concept of *ego*. Central to artistic—or, indeed, any other—creativeness is a relaxation ("regression") of ego functions. The word "fantasy" conveys just this disregard of external stringencies in its reference to the process and product of creative imagination. In fantasy and dream, in states of intoxication and fatigue, such functional regression is especially prominent; in particular, it characterizes the process of inspiration.[3]

But the regression in the case of aesthetic creation—in contrast to these other cases—is purposive and controlled. The inspired creativity of the artist is as far from automatic writing under hypnosis as from the machines recently marketed for "composing" popular songs. The process involves a continual interplay between creation and criticism, manifested in the painter's alternation of working on the canvas and stepping back to observe the effect. We may speak here of a *shift in psychic level*, consisting in the fluctuation of functional regression and control. When regression goes too far, the symbols become private, perhaps unintelligible even to the reflective self; when, at the other extreme, control is preponderant, the result is described as cold, mechanical, and uninspired. Poetry is, to be sure, related to trance and dream, as aestheticians since Plato have never tired of observing. But it is also related to rigorous and controlled rationality. No account of the aesthetic process can be adequate without giving due weight to this "intellectual" component.

It is the other component, however—the well of inspiration or so-called "primary process"—that is of most immediate interest. For it is in this aspect of aesthetic creation that ambiguity is most prominent. The symbols functioning in the primary process are not so much vague and indeterminate as "overdetermined," loaded down with a variety of meanings. An action (including an act of producing symbols) is said to be overdetermined when it can be construed as the effect of multiple causes. Such overdetermination is characteristic of almost all purposive action; but it is especially marked when the psychic level from which the behavior derives is close to the primary process. Words, images, fancies come to mind because they are emotionally charged; and the primary process exhibits to a striking degree the tendency to focus in a single symbol a multiplicity of references and thereby fulfill at once a number of emotional needs. This is most clearly exemplified in the dream, but can be traced as well in the production of poetry, as was shown, for instance, in John Livingston Lowes' *Road to Xanadu*. Overdetermination and consequent ambiguity is central to the understanding of poetry as self-expression—i.e, as the distinctive product of an individual artist. But it is equally important when we transfer attention to the reader of poetry.

Aesthetic creation is aimed at an audience; only that self-expression is aesthetic which is communicated (or communicable) to others. This is not to be taken as implying the existence of a content separable from the aesthetic form—a message, in other words—which the work of art must get across. To speak of art as communication does not involve a commitment to such positions as Matthew Arnold's, where poetry is valued for precisely what is *not* characteristic of it, i.e., what can be translated into prose. What is made common to artist and audience is

the aesthetic experience itself, not a prëexistent content. Dewey's warn-
ings of the confusion between eventual function and antecedent existence
are very much to the point. Communication lies not so much in the
prior intent of the artist as in the consequent re-creation by the audience
of his work of art. And re-creation is distinguished from sheer *reaction*
to the work precisely by the fact that the person responding himself
contributes to the stimuli for his response.[4]

What is required for communication, therefore, is similarity between
the audience process and that of the artist. But it is clear that only
certain aspects of the artist's process are relevant to this comparison. As
T. S. Eliot has observed:

> Impressions and experiences which are important for the man may take
> no place in the poetry, and those which become important in the poetry
> may play quite a negligible part in the man, the personality.

We cannot, that is to say, simply assume that what is emotionally
charged for the artist will evoke a comparable response in the audience.
Effect is a function of intent but not of intent only; it must be separately
considered.

Accordingly, we may introduce the concept of the *potential* of a
symbol as the obverse side of its overdetermination: a symbol has a high
potential in the degree to which it may be construed as cause of
multiple effects (rather than being taken as effect of multiple causes).
While the two are obviously related to one another, potential does not
necessarily correspond to overdetermination. The tyro may have an
intense experience and employ for its communication symbols which—
for him—are highly charged with multiple significance. But, in fact, this
overdetermination may be purely private; the symbols lack potential and
communication fails to take place. Conversely, symbols may have a
higher potential for a particular audience than was involved in the
artists's intent; Virgil, for instance, was for some centuries read as being
in effect a Christian author—a particular religious significance was *projected* into his writings.

Now the potential of a symbol contributes to a specifically aesthetic
experience only if the interpretation of the symbol evokes the resources
of the primary process. It is a commonplace that communication, of
whatever sort, requires a sharing of interests, knowledge and experience.
What is being said here is that aesthetic communication requires as
well a sharing of *psychic level*.

A few pages earlier we indicated the effect on artistic creation of the
extremes of psychic level: on the one hand the unintelligible, on the
other the uninspired. The process of re-creation exhibits a corresponding
effect if the interpretation does not involve shifts in level. Where ego
control in the audience is high, the result is not re-creation but recon-

struction. The experience is, in the common locution, "intellectualized."
The aesthetic response is replaced by pedantic connoisseurship or his-
toricism, and the trained incapacity which knows all about art but
doesn't know what it likes. It is not without reason that A. E. Housman
cautions in his *Name and Nature of Poetry* that "perfect understanding
will sometimes almost extinguish pleasure."

On the other hand, when the psychic level of interpretation involves
too little ego control, the meanings responded to are projective and
lacking in integration. The aesthetic response is overwhelmed in blind
raptures, the ecstasies of the "art lover." At best, the experience may be
characterized—in terms of Dewey's useful distinction—as one of enjoyment rather than appreciation.

While shift in psychic level is a necessary condition, it is not a sufficient condition for aesthetic communication to take place. The response
is not aesthetic at all unless it also comprises a shift in *psychic distance,*
that is, fluctuation in the degree of involvement in action.[5] The aesthetic
illusion requires, as was emphasized by Kant, a detachment from the
workings of the practical reason. In the drama and novel failure to
attain such detachment is manifested in that extreme of identification
with the characters which focusses interest and attention solely on "how
it all comes out." In poetry, the Kantian emphasis on detachment can
be expressed by Coleridge's formula of "willing suspension of disbelief."
More generally, when distance is minimal the reaction to works of art
is pragmatic rather than aesthetic. Art is transformed to pin-up and
propaganda, magic and ritual, and becomes an important determinant
of belief and action. The ambiguities with which interpretations must
deal are disjunctive and additive: meanings are selected and abstracted
in the service of practical ends.

When psychic distance is maximal, the response is philistine or
intellectualistic. At best, the experience is one of passive receptivity
rather than active participation of the self. No contribution comes from
the side of the audience because the interpretation follows the principle
of the dictionary, as determined by the current conventions of the
genre. Or, indeed, there may be no effort at interpretation at all, and the
work rejected out of hand as unintelligible and worthless.

Shifts of both distance and level are, of course, matters of degree.
There is nothing fixed and unalterable in the patterns of aesthetic response. Instruction, even though it is itself operative at a high ego level,
may succeed in facilitating a relaxation of ego controls. Technical
understanding may release energies otherwise employed in the reconstruction of the art work. Similarly, familiarity may serve to increase
distance, liberating attention for other aspects of the work than its
outcome or its practical applications. The function of criticism may be
characterized concisely as that of contributing to such instructed familiarity, so as to induce the requisite shifts of psychic distance and level.

We are now in a position for a more adequate statement of the rôle of ambiguity in the aesthetic process. A distinction can be drawn between the decorative and expressive occurrences of ambiguity in the arts. Ambiguity is *decorative* when its interpretation is relatively independent of the psychic shifts just discussed. It is embodied in specific devices interpretable as such from a distance and in intellectual terms—the explicit pun, conceit, allegory, and similar artifices of style. The multiple meanings thus signified are limited in scope, having no bearing beyond the immediate context of occurrence—as is true, for instance, of so many of Shakespeare's plays on words. Or if, like the allegory, they extend throughout the work, they apply to it as a whole, rather than distributively in each of its parts, and so fall short of full integration.[6]

Ambiguity is *expressive* when shifts of psychic level and distance are involved in its interpretation, i.e., when it is distinctly aesthetic (in psychological, not valuational terms). Expressive ambiguity provides a good instance of what Allen Tate has called the "tension" of poetry:

> the full organized body of all the extension and intension that we can find
> in it. The remotest figurative significance that we can derive does not
> invalidate the extensions of the literal statement. Or we may begin with
> the literal statement and by stages develop the complications of metaphor:
> at every stage we may pause to state the meaning so far apprehended, and
> at every stage the meaning will be coherent [integrative].

This "tension" may thus be equated with what we have called the potential of poetic symbols; it is the richness of integrated significance emerging in the process of aesthetic re-creation. The distinction between "classicist" precision of language and "romantic" exploitation of vagueness and symbolism has reference, therefore, only to the extent to which decorative ambiguities are employed. Expressive ambiguity is less limited to the style of a particular school or genre, though it, too, of course, is subject to variations of degree.

One function of poetic form may now be considered as that of pointing to the existence of latent ambiguities. Metre, rhyme, and poetic construction indicate that the symbols are to be construed as aesthetic, i.e., responded to at shifting distances. And they also constitute stringencies that force language from the channels of the prosaic, and in so doing create a problem of interpretation and hence a possibility of re-creation.[7]

The rôle of metaphor in poetry may be analysed, we suggest, in similar terms. Metaphor serves as a stimulus to functional regression because the primary process is itself metaphoric and imagistic. The dream life, for instance, is predominantly visual, and shows a marked tendency to note similarities (especially by way of similar emotional responses) that escape the practical orientation of waking life. Metaphor serves, not to bring poetry close to the dream, but rather close to the psychic processes underlying both art and fantasy.

More specifically, metaphor may also serve as an instrument for multiplying ambiguity: the relation between elements themselves ambiguous to some degree, generates a new and larger range of significance. And the relation serves at the same time as a mechanism of integration, indicating the direction along which unification of the multiple meanings is to be achieved. For example, Donne's simple metaphor "Find/what wind/serves to advance an honest mind" (in the poem "Go, and catch a falling star") not only admits of multiple interpretations within the main purport of an impossible task—the honest man is continually buffeted by adverse winds; the honest man finds no advancement on the seas of life; honesty already represents the highest level of advancement; there are paths of advancement open to the honest, but the difficulty is in finding them; etc., etc.—but these various meanings, centering around the idea that "advancement" depends on forces external to man and controlled by the gods, provides a focal point for integration of the poem in terms of a contrast between sacred and profane love, between the supernatural world of mandrakes, mermaids, and Faith, and the mundane realm of the purely human and inconstant.

In short, ambiguity functions in poetry, not as a carrier of a content which is somehow in itself poetic, but as the instrument by which a content is made poetic through the process of re-creation.[8]

We must emphasize, on the other hand, that ambiguity is only one of the resources of poetic effectiveness, on which more or less reliance may be placed. The "music" of poetry, for instance, would have to be given as much weight as its ambiguity in a full analysis of poetic effectiveness.[9] We are not saying, therefore, that the enjoyment of the aesthetic experience is altogether traceable to the pleasures of interpreting ambiguities, to what Mallarmé calls "the satisfaction of guessing little by little." But ambiguity is a frequent and important, though not the sole stimulus, to aesthetic response—the re-creation, at shifting psychic levels and distances, of the work of art.

III

In so far as poetry is taken to emerge in the process of re-creation of the artist's work, there arises the problem of the standards of interpretation to which this process is subject. But first a word of explanation to avoid a possible misunderstanding. As has been said earlier, it is not to be supposed that the multiple meanings of which we have been speaking are clearly and distinctly present to the mind of either artist or audience. For the most part they remain "pre-conscious"—i.e., though not conscious they can become so with comparatively little effort if the interpretation becomes problematic at that point. It is just because they are in the "back of the mind" in this sense that they contribute so much to poetic effectiveness.[10] Hence a concern with the problem of standards must not confuse the aesthetic experience with an intellectualistic reconstruction of the poem. The artist and audience are not themselves preoccupied with such standards. But standards are nevertheless important for a subsequent appraisal of the content of the experience.

One reason for their importance is the variation from person to person in the interpretation of the poem. Often, however, the varying interpretations correspond to equivalent effects in the respective readers; and again, the variation may be due, not to incompatibilities in the interpretations, but to the fact that each is only partial, and supplements the others. A more fundamental difficulty which requires consideration of standards is the possibility of projection, of reading into the poem meanings not present to others. This difficulty is brought into prominence by the art of the psychotic, and by the occasional success enjoyed by "fakes." Max Eastman, in his *Literary Mind*, quotes a sample of "Gertrude Stein's prose" which he then reveals to the unsuspecting reader as in fact having been written by a psychotic. And the Australian literary magazine *Angry Penguins* recently published with enthusiastic praise the work of a new "poet" which was in fact concocted in jest from a miscellany of reference works. Cases of this kind bring to a focus the question whether poetic re-creation is not in fact simply a form of "recreation," a game like finding shapes in the clouds and stars.

Interpretation, therefore, must have its stringencies just as does the original creation of the art work. Most obvious are the stringencies of subject matter, or, as we may call them, *standards of correspondence*. T. S. Eliot's reference to Agamemnon in the poem from which we previously quoted ["Sweeney Among the Nightingales"] provides warrant for certain interpretations on the basis of knowledge about the myth in question. In the Donne example, a knowledge of the relation of inconstancy, in the poetic tradition of the seventeenth century, to the theme of sacred and profane love substantiates the re-creation of the poem along certain lines rather than others.[11]

Another set of stringencies of interpretation have reference to the genesis of the art work, and so may be called genetic standards or *standards of intent*. Here knowledge about the artist—whether directly in the form of biographical material or indirectly in terms of his society—serves as a test of adequacy of interpretation. Here the familiar materials of literary history play their part. It must be pointed out, however, that interpretation resting chiefly on application of the standards of intent assumes an underlying similarity between the artist's basic desires, beliefs, values, and our own; or rather, the adequacy of interpretation depends on our adopting his standpoint. Where cultural differences are too great to make this possible, therefore, interpretation based on standards of intent is largely projective. This is true, for instance, of many parts of the Bible "viewed as literature."

A third set of stringencies has reference to the interrelation of the elements of the interpretation. We may refer to these as *standards of coherence*: an interpretation of a particular part of the work is tested by the coherence with the rest of the work it gives to this part. Whereas the standards of intent limit potential to known determinations, the coherence standards expand potential to include all possible determinations—whatever "fits in" is assumed to have been intended. This does not imply that the intent was fully conscious, but only that it was not wholly private: the genius characteristically "builds better than he knows."[12]

These three types of standards—others could perhaps be distinguished—are interactive. An interpretation may begin with any of them and seek confirmation from the others. Some fact about the subject matter may suggest a particular interpretation, which can then direct a search for evidence of such intent, or which can be further tested by its degree of integration with the rest of the work. Data about intent are checked by subject matter correspondences and internal coherence. An interpretation arrived at by considerations of coherence may be verified by knowledge about intent or subject matter. Thus the three sets of standards are jointly operative in the appraisal of a particular interpretation—as in the case of coherence, correspondence, and pragmatic conceptions of truth, to which, indeed, these standards could perhaps be related. The more clearly an interpretation is substantiated by one sort of consideration, the less confirmation is required from the others, and conversely.

In effect, the standards discussed test an interpretation by its *completeness*, the degree to which it takes account of all the elements of the work, and its *power of synthesis*, the degree of integration which it gives these elements—in classical terms, by the "unity in variety" disclosed in the work by the interpretation. Cases where the ambiguities are primarily projective usually fail in both respects. Even if the work of the psychotic contains some intelligible elements, these are ordinarily integrated only in the psychotic's delusional system, and there must be recognized besides the presence of other elements having no public significance at all; similar considerations apply to the "fake." It must be said, however, that the aesthetic can sometimes occur without an aesthetic intent; work created in the service of magic and religion, for example, may regularly evoke in another culture aesthetic responses. But generally speaking, where such a response is frequent and widespread, the three sets of standards tend to converge: the meanings achieving coherence in terms of subject matter are those intended.

We conclude with a brief consideration of the social setting of ambiguity; the following remarks are to be viewed only as hypotheses in the sociology of art. The level of stringency in works of art—their degree of interpretability—varies markedly from period to period. In some cases ambiguity is fully exploited, and correspondingly great demands are made on the audience: in other cases, there is no more ambiguity than is involved in the work's being aesthetic at all; the demands on the audience are minimal; the interpretations called for are rigidly limited. We may suggest that art is likely to be characterised by low stringency (i.e., high ambiguity and interpretability) where systems of conduct ideals are in doubt or social values are in process of transition.[13] Poetry produced under such circumstances will perhaps reflect in its own high ambiguousness the uncertainties and equivocations in the culture of which it is a part. Such poetry is at the same time more likely to evoke a favorable response in the culture.

When stringencies are very high the art form either approximates ritual or may be spoken of as academic. Artistic achievement may consist in solving the traditional problems of the genre in traditional ways. Or the great artist may be revolutionary, working on the basis of new stringencies. Initially, his work is obscure; gradually, however, it becomes intelligible in terms of the new stringencies. Obscurity gives way to ambiguity; what was formerly unclear now appears richly significant. In turn the ambiguities become more and more stylized; works of the new type become increasingly interpretable on the dictionary principle; the revolutionary becomes conventional and the academic once more flourishes. This cycle in the history of art has been frequently commented on. We are suggesting that it might fruitfully be investigated in terms of the changing rôle and character of ambiguity.[14]

Such an approach, finally, might also have important bearings on the problem of survival. This problem is of special interest because of its putative relevance to aesthetic merit. Survival has been frequently invoked as an index of aesthetic merit ever since Longinus's enunciation of the maxim that "that is truly great which bears repeated examination." Regardless of the weight of this principle of criticism, the question of what characteristics of the work of art make for its survival as an object of aesthetic value is of independent interest.

Among these characteristics ambiguity would seem to be not the least important. For one thing, high ambiguity allows for a wide range of interpretation, so that the work may be prized throughout various changes in cultural interests and values by being interpretable in a corresponding variety of ways. More important is the fact that ambiguity stimulates, as we have seen, the workings of the primary process. Now the primary process has been considered so far only in its bearings on the form of poetry rather than its content—i.e., on the occurrence of ambiguity, imagery, metaphor in poetry, rather than on the subject matters with which poetry most frequently deals. But the subject matters of poetry are as closely related to the primary process as the form of poetry; for they may be traced—in large part, if not solely—to the fundamental needs and desires of the personality, to the "id" in Freud's sense. Functional regression makes available as poetic material themes, like love and death, which are directly related to basic needs and desires, and which approach cultural universality far more closely than the patterns of satisfying such needs or the value of structures controlling these satisfactions.[15]

The effectiveness of ambiguity for survival is limited, however, by the dependence which it involves on knowledge of subject matter and of intent as conditions of coherence. The less ambiguous work is correspondingly less dependent on such external knowledge. Survival may thus be presumed to be maximal for those works which have as high a degree of interpretability as is compatible with containing within themselves their own sources of integration. Other factors than ambiguity, of course, are also important for survival—e.g., the range of experience with which the work is concerned. And still others are to be taken into account in appraisals of aesthetic merit.

Notes

1. For a fuller account of the relation between art and ritual from this viewpoint, see Ernst Kris, *Psychoanalytic Explorations in Art,* New York, International Universities Press, Inc., 1952, pp. 40 ff.

2. See R. E. M. Harding, *An Anatomy of Inspiration and an Essay on the Creative Mood,* Third Edition, Cambridge, W. Heffer & Sons, 1948; and Ernst Kris, *op. cit.,* Ch. 13.

3. See Ernst Kris, "Art and Regression," *Transactions of the New York Academy of Sciences,* VI, Series II, No. 7; and *Psychoanalytic Explorations in Art,* Chs. 3, 6 and 14. The term "functional regression" is here and in the following used equivalent with topographical regression.

4. In so doing he reduces the ambiguity of the original stimulus: we say that the work has "become" clear or intelligible, i.e., it has become so as a result of his work of interpretation. But a rich core of ambiguity remains as constitutive of the poetic substance. See below, pp. 418f.

5. See Edward Bullough's *"Physical Distance" as a Factor in Art and an Aesthetic Principle,* Section VI of this book. Ed.

6. For an extensive discussion of the decorative style, see for instance E. K. Kane, *Gongorism and the Golden Age: A Study of Exuberance and Unrestraint in Art,* Chapel Hill, University of North Carolina Press, 1928.

7. Compare William Empson, *Seven Types of Ambiguity,* New York, Harcourt, Brace & Co., p. 39: "The reason that ambiguity is more elaborate in poetry than in prose, other than the fact that the reader is trained to expect it, seems to be that the presence of metre and rhyme, admittedly irrelevant to the straightforward process of conveying a statement, makes it seem sensible to diverge from the colloquial order of statement, and so imply several colloquial orders from which the statement has diverged." Here we construe poetic form not as the "reason" but as one condition of poetic ambiguity; the "reason" we have sought in the nature of aesthetic experience.

8. Just this is the function assigned to the language of poetry by Lascelles Abercrombie, *Theory of Poetry,* New York, Harcourt, Brace & Co., 1926, pp. 82-83: "Language is not the vehicle of inspiration in the sense of being a re-

ceptacle into which the poet pours his mind for purposes of transmission, and out of which the reader then extracts what is contained. Language in poetry is a transmission of energy rather than of substance. It sets the reader's mind working and directs the tendency of the work. It urges us to live for a time in a particular style of imagination—the style of the poet's imagination: but it is our own imagination that really does the business of poetry. In other words, the symbolic nature of language in poetry means just this: that it is a *stimulus* for our minds, though a stimulus of a very determining character."

9. Empson suggests, however, that even here ambiguities are operative: "Apart from the ambiguities in the fully-developed language . . . one would have also to consider the ambiguities (of the same sort, but entirely different in their details) which are always latent in the fundamental symbolism of the sound." *Op. cit.,* p. 20.

10. Compare Empson, *op. cit.,* p. 74: "I do not think that all these meanings should pass through the mind in an appreciative reading. . . , what is gathered is the main sense, the main form and rhythm, and a general sense of compacted intellectual wealth, of an elaborate balance of variously associated feeling." An analysis of the effectiveness of poetry must also take into account the proximity of preconscious mentation to the high potentials of unconscious, repressed materials.

11. Of special interest is the case where the subject matter gives rise to psychological considerations (about the reactions of the characters or of the poet himself). Examples of this type of check over interpretations could be multiplied endlessly; a particularly striking one, perhaps, is Ernest Jones' famous essay on *Hamlet* from a psychoanalytic viewpoint (*Hamlet and Oedipus,* London, S. Gollancz, 1949; "The Death of Hamlet's Father," *International Journal of Psycho-Analysis,* XXXI, 1950). It is to be understood that the standards of correspondence with psychological fact do not necessarily involve technical scientific knowledge, but may rest on the sort of understanding of motivation which is directly available to the perceptive reader or critic, as it was to the insight of the poet.

12. The matter may be reformulated in terms of Croce's distinction between the "empirical" personality of the artist, with which standards of intent are concerned, and his "aesthetic" personality—which is manifested in and accessible through the art work considered in itself and not as a fact about the artist as a person. It is the aesthetic personality with which the standards of coherence deal.

13. The present period seems to be of this kind. It is perhaps for this reason that there is today such a widespread interest in the art of children and psychotics, and such striking successes of "fakes." The predisposition to deal with high ambiguity dominates over stimuli from the work itself, so that projective interpretations are the more likely to occur.

14. In particular, this approach could account for the changes in stringencies on the basis of its bearings on the process of re-creation, which is impossible if conventions are too rigidly adhered to. This is to be contrasted with such metaphysical positions as that of, say, Bergson, for whom art "has no other object than to brush aside the utilitarian symbols, the conventional and socially accepted generalities, in short, everything that veils reality from us, in order to bring us face to face with reality itself." From the present standpoint, it would be more correct, perhaps, to say that art brushes aside the conventional in order to bring us face to face with the artist—and with ourselves.

15. Similar viewpoints are presented, for instance, by W. Muschgg, "Dichtung als archaisches Erbe," *Imago,* XIX, 1933; Herbert Read, *Collected Essays in Literary Criticism,* London, Faber & Faber, 1938; and others.

ISABEL C. HUNGERLAND

Symbols in Poetry

THE PROBLEMS that confront us in dealing with symbols are much like those encountered in dealing with figures of speech and images. "Symbol," like "image," is a semitechnical term of literary criticism. The common man uses it rarely in connection with poetry, partly no doubt because he rarely reads poetry, but also partly because when he does indulge in literary criticism he doesn't talk much about symbols. Moreover, although critics employ the term frequently, they are not agreed about the proper manner of its employment. Accordingly, my task in this chapter cannot be merely that of exhibiting the use or uses of "symbol"; I must also propose one and justify the proposal.

There is, however, an additional task in dealing with "symbol," the task of deflation. The psychological conditions and effects of employing "symbol," both in criticism and in philosophy, afford a splendid example of what has been called "emotive meaning." The doctrine of emotive meaning, we have seen, is mistaken in taking the psychological effects of language as its meaning. But it is not at all mistaken in supposing that some words become peculiarly emotion-producing, and that this can happen when the words have no clear-cut referential use. The sociological explanation of the current power of "symbol" to produce excitement and reverence lies outside the scope of this work. I am concerned here only with the fact that the word has this power. I hope to reduce it somewhat for readers of this chapter. Among philosophers of art, we find the claim that all works of art are symbols, accompanied by the notion that this characterization makes clear to us at last the profundity and wonder of art. Workers in the arts often welcome the claim. "Here is a philosopher who understands us!" But when we try to learn either from philosophers or artists of this bent what constitutes being a symbol or why it is so wonderful to be one, no clear account is given.

In literary criticism, a similar situation exists. Mary McCarthy, one of

First published in the *University of California Publications in Philosophy,* Vol. 33 (1958).

the few good writers today completely immune to symbol emotionalism, writes about the literary scene as follows:

> . . . I thought these notions were peculiar to progressive education: it was oldfashioned or regressive to read a novel to find out what happens to the hero or to have a mere experience empty of symbolic pointers. But I now discover that this attitude is quite general, and that readers and students all over the country are in a state of apprehension, lest they read a book or story literally and miss the presence of a symbol. And like everything in America, this search for meanings has become a socially competitive enterprise: the best reader is the one who detects the most symbols in a given stretch of prose. And the benighted reader who fails to find any symbols humbly assents when they are pointed out to him; he accepts his mortification.[1]

My intention, of course, is not to show that good writers do not use symbols, or that symbols are unimportant in art. But I do wish to approach the topic of symbols without awe, and I do not wish to add to the current mystification.

I

At the outset of our inquiry into symbols it will be helpful to dispose of irrelevant meanings of "symbol" and to take a look at the methodological considerations that will guide us.

"Symbol" has meanings in both ordinary and technical language that are not relevant to literary symbols. We all speak of the "symbols" of mathematics and of other disciplines. Here, "symbol" has the sense of an abbreviation, a shorthand sign, employed in place of words. On the other hand, some philosophers have, quite legitimately, I think, called words "symbols" in order to distinguish them from signals, such as traffic lights. These uses of the term need not concern us here.

My search for a sensible use of "symbol" in connection with literature will be guided by the following considerations. An account which confines symbols to some particular school of writing, say, French Symbolism, is inconveniently narrow for literary criticism. Also, any account which takes over either the Freudian or Jungian applications of the term, dogmatically prejudges the issue whether symbols in literature always represent either sexual objects or archetypal patterns. Furthermore, if we are to have a sufficiently flexible account of symbols, we must start, not with looking at certain kinds of linguistic expression, but rather with a certain kind of experience which may be formulated in language in a variety of ways. However, if we start with dreams and similar experiences, we start too far away from the artistic use of symbols. Where, then, shall we start? The following description of a symbol in a movie affords a central example from which we can move easily back and forth to daily life, to literature, to dreams and myths.

> . . . most of us have seen *Lost Horizon* and remember the death of the High Lama of Shangri La. The writer and director of the movie could have simply left the camera on the Lama, allowing us to see his breath cease and his eyes close. Instead, they chose (with no great originality, of course) to let the camera rest upon a candle flickering before an open window. We watch the flame flicker as a cold gust of air fills the curtain and lets it fall, and then we see the flame go out. We know that the Lama has died. But more than that, we are presumably made to feel countless suggestions about the connection between the soul and the flux and change, warmth and light, impermanence and yet eternalness of fire.[2]

What is involved in this illustration? In the first place, the extinction of the candle flame functions as a sign of the High Lama's death. That is to say, knowledge is conveyed. We infer from a perceived process one that is not perceived. In the example, what we perceive is, strictly speaking, a moving picture, and the context is fictional, but these circumstances do not invalidate the points I am making. It is possible to make things function as signs in art, because of the way things function in real life. One could, in another movie, convey the fact of a character's death by, say, showing a flag at half-mast, his weeping friends, or someone drawing a sheet over the man's face, or the man himself, clutching his heart. What is exhibited in these examples is the familiar relationship of daily life, whereby the presence of one thing is a basis for our inferring the existence, impending or contemporaneous, of something else. Thus, clouds may signify rain; a certain gesture, dress, or choice may signify something about a person's character or personality or momentary state. Are these signifying things symbols? We hesitate, because neither ordinary nor technical usage draws a clear line here. I propose that we draw one by saying "no." (The reasons for the proposal will emerge in the discussion.) The mere functioning as a sign, then, will not in my account suffice to make a thing a symbol, though a sign may become also a symbol.

In the movie example, we do not, of course, have, as we do with clouds, gestures, and so forth, a natural sign. Human deaths are not regularly preceded or accompanied by candles going out. Nor is there a signifying relationship established by convention, as there is between a flag at half-mast and death. But the maker of the movie could use the extinction of the candle to signify death without fear of misunderstanding, because the going out of a flame easily suggests—that is, reminds us of, makes us think of—dying. (The ambiguities of "suggestion" explored in chapter I,* should be recalled here. In particular, we should remember that "to be

---

* [Chapter I of Mrs. Hungerland's book appears as "Language and Poetry," Section III above. Ed.]

reminded of *x*" does not mean the same as "to expect *x*" or "to believe in the existence of *x*.") The associations of the candle in the movie work on the basis of certain analogies, but spatiotemporal relations (part-whole, causality) or convention working alone or together with the other bases, can determine suggestion. A breast may suggest maternal care; a burning candle might, according to one convention (literary or more broadly cultural) suggest virility, or just human life. But a flag or emblem may be chosen more or less arbitrarily, as far as analogy or contiguity are concerned.

The question now arises: are all things that suggest others, in one or all of the above ways, symbols? Again, I shall do about as much proposing as exhibiting of a use. The relation of suggestion alone, I shall say, does not establish a symbol. A man may remind me of my father, a kitchen bowl of a certain recipe; neither, according to my proposal, is *ipso facto* a symbol.

What is lacking? If we recall what was said in the preceding chapter about the kinds of experience that lead, not inevitably, but understandably, to the employment of figures, we shall find the missing circumstance. It is the transference of trains of thought and the accompanying attitude and feelings (which may work mainly in one or in both directions) from one object to another. If I begin to think and feel about a man, in certain respects, as I did about my father, and to treat him as I treated my father, then he becomes a father symbol for me. Analogously, in fictional contexts, when we transfer trains of thought and the related attitudes and feelings from one object to another, a symbol is established.

The reason for introducing the notion of transference into our account of symbols is that transference provides the only kind of justification one can give for the employment of symbols in art. Consider the example of the candle in the movie. Unless the candle's presence made us think and feel about fire and life, death and darkness (for example, the precariousness and brevity of both candle flame and the High Lama's life may be suggested to us) in ways that neither it alone nor the dying man alone would, there is no artistic justification for the shift of the camera. The device, without these effects becomes either extraneous ornament or pretentious mystification. I shall return at the end of this section to the artistic use of symbols; for the present, I wish to take stock of the position reached and then determine further the concept of the symbol.

From the account given thus far, it is plain that there is no class of things which can be called "symbols" apart from the ways people respond to and treat them in relation to other things. From this it follows that, in general, almost anything can become a symbol of something. However, when we study a particular culture or social situation, we may find that certain objects are better fitted than others to become symbols of certain other things for the people concerned. (It is possible, too, that certain objects—the sun, for example—might be fitted to symbolize similar things to almost all human beings.) It follows also that symbols can be either idiosyncratic or communal, and that in the course of time they can change from one class to the other. Finally, my account, like that of figures of speech, has not turned a vague concept into a precise one. The concepts of transference and suggestion, which I have used in explaining that of symbol, are themselves not very precise. Although I have tried to reduce the vagueness a little, my main attempt has been to show why and how "symbol" is not a precise term, and could not usefully be made one. However, there remain certain questions the answers to which will determine somewhat further the boundaries of the application of "symbol." Let us raise them here.

In the example of the movie symbol, the context makes it clear to a spectator what the candle is a symbol of. Suppose, now, that we are moved by fear, awe, sadness in watching a guttering candle, but do not know what so moves us. "It is not just the flickering flame," we might say, for we find nothing sad about that. In this post-Freudian era, most of us, I think, would be prepared to say that in these circumstances, the candle probably is a symbol of something of which we are unconscious, that is, that association and transference work without our being aware of what the associated object is. The example, at any rate, is not fanciful. Experiences of this sort appear to be rather common. (In reading literature, the analogous experience is equally common: we are often moved by a poem without at all knowing what in the poem moves us, or, as we say, "really understanding the poem.") There seems to be no good reason either to exclude these experiences from the application of "symbol" or to confine the term to cases of this sort. And there is a good reason, for our purposes, in having a term which is neutral in regard to Freudian theory. Accordingly, I propose a use which will permit us to say that something is a symbol for someone, both when the person concerned has a high degree of knowledge about and awareness of the symbolic relation and when he has not.

Another question is raised by the notion, common among literary people, that symbols are always concrete objects, and what they symbolize is an abstraction of some sort. It is easy enough to fall into this way of thinking—the notion appears to fit many literary passages. But critical reflection shows that what is at issue is merely a locution appropriate in many instances, but in others misleading. For example, the same symbolic relations might be described equally well in the following ways: "Mrs. A is a symbol to B of his mother," "Mrs. A's maternal qualities symbolize B's mother to him," "Mrs. A is a symbol to B of maternal qualities." Also, number superstitions, which usually involve symbolism, present examples in which the symbol term would normally be described as "being . . . in number." The possibility of shifting the form of description depends on the fact that objects become linked by association through some of their qualities. The whole matter is of importance only so far as the literary notion blinds us to certain possibilities of symbolism in literature. The symbol-hunting reader of today scrutinizes literature for the mention of concrete objects, ignoring the fact that rhythmic and sound patterns, the general structure of a plot, and even a conventional stanza form, may function as symbols.

Finally, the question arises whether we would call the flickering candle in the movie "a symbol" if it were shown set beside the dying man, and we saw both processes, the flickering out and the dying, together. The decision would be somewhat arbitrary, and this very fact raises interesting issues. Figures of speech are sometimes discussed as *merely* rhetorical linguistic devices, while symbols are given an aura of mystery, of inexplicable expression of profundities not attributed to figures. It is obvious that figures of speech must be defined in terms of linguistic devices, whereas, as we have seen, symbols are more conveniently approached by a consideration of certain kinds of experience which may or may not receive linguistic expression. But these kinds of experience are very similar to those that lead us to use certain figures. In both cases associations based on similarity or contiguity are operating, and in both cases there is some sort of transference of attitudes and feelings. Should we consider the experience of the compresence of candle flickering out and dying man, as more clearly related to metaphor or to symbol? Is "Out, out, brief candle . . ." a condensed metaphor, or an example of the linguistic expression of symbolic experience? Ordinarily, we seem to make the somewhat arbitrary condition that an object functions symbolically only if the related object is absent. This condition is reflected in the following set of definitions given by Cleanth Brooks and Robert Penn Warren in *Understanding Poetry*:

> . . . Closely related to the metaphorical process is the process by which a poet creates or makes use of a SYMBOL. The symbol may be regarded as a metaphor from which the first term has been omitted. For example: "Queen of the rosebud garden of girls" is a metaphor, but if the poet simply refers to the rose in order to suggest the qualities of love which he is treating, and does not indicate the metaphorical framework, he has turned the rose into a symbol.[3]

Although it may be admitted that there are differences between figures and symbols in literature, these differences are not basic, and the use of a figure, "Life is (or is like) a brief candle," or the use of a symbol, "The candle flickers out" (in a context in which dying is suggested), can be said to be linguistic formulations of similar processes of association and transference.

There is still one important question the answer to which will help to determine further the boundaries of the concept of symbol. How can a single incident, plot, situation, person, or character become symbolic of others like them, and of whole ranges of context? Does not the going out of the candle in the movie symbolize, not just the High Lama's death, but the death of all men? This question, however, will be more easily answered if we return first to the justification or reason for employing symbols in art.

That reason, we have seen, is that the symbol reveals something to the spectator or reader that cannot so well or easily be revealed without it. (An ornamental function might also be admitted.) The justification is certainly not that the symbol conceals something from the spectator or reader! Yet certain writers and literary critics appear to have adopted this odd doctrine. It results, I think, from a further twist of the confusion involved in holding that by the use of symbols one "says the unsayable" or "says what cannot otherwise be said." This confusion is a very close relative of the one examined in chapter ii in connection with a poem and its paraphrase. No more need be said about it here.

As we shall see in more detail later, some writers—and great ones—do use allegory or fable, what might be called a "double-order" symbolic scheme. This kind of scheme can be justified if each order illuminates the other, or if, when the presented one is not in itself of importance, it serves to reveal well the outlines of the other. The function of allegory is hardly to present an unimportant story which conceals a story that might be important to us if we could find out what it is. Turning now to what I shall call a "single-order" symbol, let us look first at Mary McCarthy's excellent account of the train symbol in Tolstoy's *Anna Karenina*.

> At the beginning of the novel, Anna meets the man who will be her lover, Vronsky, on the Moscow-St.Petersburg express; as they meet, there has been an accident; a workman has been killed by the train coming in to the station. This is the beginning of Anna's doom, which is completed when she throws herself under a train and is killed; and the last we see of Vronsky is in a train, with a toothache; he is being seen off by a friend to the wars. The train is necessary to the plot of the novel, and I believe it is also symbolic, both of the iron forces of material progress that Tolstoy hated so and that played a part in Anna's moral destruction, and also of those iron laws of necessity and consequence that govern human action when it remains on the sensual level.
>
> One can read the whole novel, however, without being aware that the train is a symbol; we do not have to "interpret" to feel the import of doom and loneliness conveyed by the train's whistle—the same import we ourselves can feel when we hear a train go by in the country, even today. . . . I suspect that he [Tolstoy] did not think of the train as a symbol but that it sounded "right" to him, because it was, in that day, an almost fearsome emblem of ruthless and impersonal force, not only to a writer of genius but to the poorest peasant who watched it pass through the fields. And in Tolstoy's case, I think it would be impossible, even for the most fanciful critic, to extricate the train from the novel and try to make it bear a meaning that the novel itself does not proclaim, explicitly and tacitly, on every page.[4]

This account, while it disposes of the notion that mystification is a virtue of symbols, will, for some readers, raise the questions: "But how do these fictional characters, Anna and Vronsky, and their situation, become symbols for us of a certain type of human being in a certain predicament?" "And how does it happen that, although these individuals symbolize unrestricted ranges of other individuals, our attention is concentrated on the symbol, not on what is symbolized?" Paradoxes about the concrete individual and symbols that symbolize themselves are easily generated from these questions. . . .

Consider the fairly common experience which we describe as "recognizing an individual as a type," or "seeing him as a symbol of a kind of person." Sometimes we may not have been aware that there was such a type or kind until we became acquainted with the person in question. He possesses in high degree, or in striking outline, a complex of character and personality traits with which we are familiar. In him we recognize and notice the complex, all at once. This experience, we saw in chapter ii, is a kind of extension of ordinary perception. It is connected with scientific knowledge, and, if you like, is a stage of "knowing," but it is not scientific generalization. It can, we have seen, be utilized in different ways and directions. If my interests are those of a psychologist, I shall begin to list the traits I notice, to form generalizations and hypotheses about them, and proceed to test them. The individual then ceases to have importance except as a good specimen of a class. Even here, however, it should be noticed, I concentrate on the individual specimen because it presents so well the characteristics of a group I am studying. If my interests are those of a writer, I shall begin, perhaps, to sketch a character in a story, patterned after the real individual. While I may generalize or comment, I shall also put my character in dramatic situations in which his traits will be revealed in behavior and talk and perhaps inner thoughts. It is not necessarily my task to generalize, but it is my task to keep the reader noticing and recognizing traits in connection with some central theme or point that emerges from my story. Whenever any element of my story (character, object, setting, or episode) is so treated as to accomplish a transference of trains of thought, attitudes, and feelings between it and the range of objects it suggests, then that element is (according to our account) a symbol. If my symbol is a single-order one, I continue to direct the reader's attention upon it. The reader can only notice and recognize, in ways relevant to the point of my story, by paying attention to characters acting and reacting. In the case of a double-order symbol, the reader's attention may be divided between the two orders. But in both cases, it should be noted, the symbol does not "refer to" something else in the way that the word "cows" (in appropriate contexts) refers to cows. Nor is it a sign of something else as clouds are a sign of rain. However, words can become symbols, word magic being an extreme instance of this, and signs, too, we have seen, can become symbols. When the same word, "means," is used for all these different relations, paradoxes arise. When the relations are distinguished, there is no puzzle or mystery about the fact, although an artistic symbol suggests other things, our attention continues to focus on the symbol itself. Of course, during or after the reading of a story, I may pause to think of the likeness between the characters and their situation and people and circumstances I have known in real life. This is why I can understand the effect on me of the fate of an individual who is a stranger to me or even a fictional character. But when I thus pause in my reading about or perception of a single person, to trace his likeness in others, then he does become a representative of others for me. He functions in much the same way that a good specimen does for a scientist. He plays the role, for me, of a kind of map, what philosophers have called an "iconic sign." He is no longer a symbol. In contrast, when a person, real or fictional, is a symbol of others for me, then my past experiences of similar people are mobilized in my experience of him. These past experiences function as what used to be called my "apperception"—they enable me to notice and recognize and be stirred by traits in the individual which otherwise might escape me or leave me indifferent. (This is an aspect of transference which was not explicitly treated earlier.)

One more, fairly minor, point, and our introduction to symbols will be completed. We do, I think, in the interests of stability, of naming, call objects "symbols" which usually function in the required way in certain situations or for many people, even though they do not for ourselves or do not for many other persons at some times or in some situations. Thus, I may call Buddha a "symbol" of such and such, even though he is never one for me, nor, in some situations, for his followers.

II

What is the relationship between the kind of symbols discussed in psychoanalysis and the symbols that appear in poetry? Psychoanalytic theory offers an account of symbolic thinking not only as it occurs in primitive myth and magic, but also as it occurs in contemporary culture in childhood, in normal adults who are tired, asleep, or intoxicated, and in psychotic individuals. Attempts have been made both by experts and by amateurs in psychoanalytic theory to extend this account to symbolism as it appears in artistic products. But theory here is still in an incomplete state and insufficiently supported by carefully collected empirical evidence.[5] (Freud himself thought that there was something about the artistic process that defied analysis.) Under these conditions it will be best for our purposes merely to present a summary of a standard psychoanalytic account of symbolism as it occurs outside the field of art, and then, on the basis of evidence of a common-sense sort, ask what relevance the account might have to the use of symbols in poetry. No attempt will be made to criticize the theory itself; this is a job for an expert.

In *The Psychoanalytic Theory of Neurosis*, Otto Fenichel points out that there are two distinct and independent characteristics of symbolic thinking: it is a method of distortion; a conscious idea not in itself objectionable, replacing and disguising an unconscious idea which is objectionable; and, second, it is an aspect of archaic pictorial thinking.[6] (In dream symbols, both characteristics are present.) Thus, if the idea of, say, breasts is objectionable, it may be replaced in consciousness by the idea of apples. In archaic thinking, however, the distinction between symbol and symbolized does not apply, the two being merged into one object. For primitive, prelogical thought, Fenichel holds:

> The object and the idea of the object, the object and a picture or model of the object, the object and a part of the object are equated; similarities are not distinguished from identities; ego and nonego are not yet separated. What happens might (by identification) be experienced as happening to the ego, and what happens to the ego causes the same thing to happen to the object, a "transitivism" which makes the technique of "magical gestures" possible; by making a gesture someone forces another person to do the same thing.[7]

Inadequate as primitive thought is as a means of understanding and dealing with reality, it is ". . . more adequate than immediate discharge [of impulses] . . ." and, like more developed thought, is a "preparation and an attempt to master reality."[8] The primitive level and processes are not annihilated, however, by the new development; persons who are tired, asleep, intoxicated, or psychotic, may regress to the primitive level. Further, "even in healthy, good thinkers who are wide-awake, every single thought runs through initial phases that have more similarity with dream-thinking than with logic."[9]

Fenichel states that, although regression to prelogical, prelinguistic thought serves, for modern man, as a substitute for unpleasant reality, and logical, linguistically expressed thought as a means of controlling reality, ". . . this co-ordination of types of thinking with different functions is valid in general only. Practically, there are certain ways of returning from daydreaming to reality (art) as well as of using word thinking for withdrawal from reality (compulsive thinking)."[10]

With this general background of theory in mind, let us return to Fenichel's account of symbols and the explanation he offers for the connection between symbol and what is symbolized. Here, with one possible exception, the ordinary principles of association, that is, similarity and spatio-temporal relation, suffice. (Similarity, of course, includes similarity of function, and of attitudinal response as in the case of *king* symbolizing *father*. Also, a number of relations may be operative. In the case of *house* symbolizing *woman*, there is the obvious container function in common, but also, possibly, the feelings of being sheltered and protected, as well as spatiotemporal relation in a culture in which women spend most of their time at home.) The possible exceptions to the ordinary principles of association are those that seem to depend on relations empirically unknown to the user of the symbol. Fenichel leaves open the explanation of such symbols.

Before we ask what the relevance of this account of symbols has for poetry, one point needs clarification. Certain statements made by Freud have led to the impression that, according to psychoanalytic theory, the interpretation of a dream can be automatically read off by the analyst on the basis of knowledge of constant symbolic relationships, holding for all persons. But, in spite of the fact that Freud spoke of constant relations between symbol and symbolized, the most that he claimed for interpretation in *A General Introduction to Psycho-Analysis* is stated as follows:

> If the symbols commonly appearing in dreams are known, and also the personality of the dreamer, the conditions under which he lives, and the impressions in his mind after which his dream occurred, we are often in a position to interpret it straightaway. . . .But do not let this lead you away: . . .that method of interpretation which is based on knowledge of symbolism [is not] one which can replace, or even compare with, that of free association.[11]

The danger that there would be in automatically interpreting the unconscious dream thought is illustrated in the case cited by Fenichel: "A patient used to dream exclusively about food and the analysis apparently made no progress. It turned out that he actually did not have enough to eat. After he succeeded in getting a job, the 'oral' dreams disappeared and the analysis went on normally."[12] The tendency since Freud has been to stress more the pattern of symbols in dreams and the whole context in which the dream occurs. Further, the ambiguity of "meaning" ("to represent," "to have certain emotional effects," and so forth) has led to confusion about what psychoanalytic theory states concerning symbols. It is one thing to say that *king* commonly symbolizes ("means") *father*, and another thing to say that the concept of father, in every social context and for every individual, has the same emotional reverberations. Psychoanalytic theory is obviously not committed to the latter assertion. The individual character of the Oedipus complex and its effect on any person depend on a vast number of variables.

Psychoanalytic theory is, of course, much more than a theory of symbols. The relevance, in general, of the theory to the interpretation of literature will be considered. . . . But there are certain obvious relevancies which it will be well to state here before we turn to the limited topic of symbolism. First, any complete system of psychology (and psychoanalytic theory is that) may help us to understand the processes of enjoying and making works of art. Second, since literature, in its own way, deals with human motivation, human conflicts, ideals, feelings, and attitudes, any theory about human behavior may throw light on the structure of a drama, a novel, a poem. (Psychoanalysis has paid particular attention to myth, folk tale, and literature in developing its theory.) Third, many modern writers have consciously and deliberately drawn upon psychoanalytic theory in constructing plots, in presenting conflicts of attitudes, and in selecting certain objects for symbols. An understanding of psychoanalysis will help us to understand this kind of literary work in precisely the same way in which, say, an understanding of seventeenth-century science will help us to understand Donne's poetry. Lastly, for the analyst interested in psychoanalyzing a literary artist, the literary products may afford valuable clues to unconscious conflicts. In other words, the use of literature to find out what is wrong with the artist is a perfectly legitimate use, from the viewpoint of psychoanalysis. But the job of the literary critic is to find out what is right or wrong artistically with the literary work, and there is no necessary, invariable connection between what is wrong with a poet and what is wrong with his poem. Also, according to psychoanalytic theory itself, there is no invariable, direct resemblance relation between the content of a literary work and the content of the neurosis of its creator (for example, the relation might be that of compensation).

Accordingly, there is no direct relevance, for literary interpretation and evaluation, in the use of literature for clinical purposes. Further, the literary critic who is not a qualified expert in psychoanalysis has no business trying to psychoanalyze anyone. Although literary journals occasionally contain sad examples of amateur and incompetent psychoanalysis of the artist, parading as literary criticism, still, on the whole, the points made here are accepted among literary critics. But there are two less obviously fallacious uses of psychoanalytic theory by literary critics which appear in the interpretation of symbolism in poetry. These fallacies consist in a misapplication of the characteristics which Fenichel attributes to symbolic thinking occurring in states of psychosis, sleep, fatigue, and intoxication. The first of these fallacies to be considered I shall call "the misapplication of the disguise character of symbols in dreams, intoxication, and so on."

There are many variations of the fallacy, but in brief it consists in the following procedure. The critic, disavowing any attempt to psychoanalyze the poet through his poetry, nevertheless patterns his interpretation of symbolic images after the formula "conscious unobjectionable idea disguising unconscious objectionable idea" ("objectionable" being taken as synonymous with "sexual"). The formula appears to work well in certain kinds of poems. For example, in interpreting Eliot's "Sweeney Among the Nightingales," the literary critic who works in this fashion can point out the sexual symbolism of fruit in the lines:

> The waiter brings in oranges,
> Bananas, figs and hothouse grapes.[13]

Since Sweeney is, on the level of realistic narrative in the poem, rather obviously among prostitutes, the sexual interpretation of the symbolism of the fruit images fits the context. But the larger symbolic aspect of the poem (more important in relation to the total artistic structure) is that Sweeney and the prostitutes and their environment are symbols for a certain kind of life in the modern world, a kind of life that stands in ironic contrast to (as well as being analogous to) the kind of life symbolized by Agamemnon, the nightingale of Greek myth, and the Christian version of salvation. The "hothouse" sex, on the level of realistic narrative, is itself a symbol of artificiality, lack of vital connection with nature, which from the viewpoint of the poem characterize modern life. Thus, the direct application of the "disguise" formula to the poem yields only a minor part of the symbolism, and the formula must be reversed if we are to get at the larger symbolic structure of the poem. The larger symbolism concerns ideas which are more inclusive than the directly sexual ones and which are not at all "objectionable." Further, while Eliot's method is indirect (he refrains from explicit statements of evaluation), the direction of the larger symbolism is quite plain, and readers familiar with Eliot's work are quite conscious of the direction. The method of indirection, which is an aspect of Eliot's poetic style, should not be confused with the fact that for an analyst interested in discovering Eliot's unconscious sexual conflicts, the poem can quite legitimately be considered as a disguised expression of them.

At this point, in order to avoid misunderstanding, it should be remembered that what I am concerned with here is the misapplication of the disguise character of symbols in dreams, intoxication, and so forth. If we look at psychoanalytic theory as a whole, it is plain that, far from denying that sexual objects and situations can suggest objects and situations not directly or exclusively sexual, it offers us an explanation why they can. Psychoanalytic theory takes early family life (and hence sexual experience in a wide sense) as a causally important determinant in the character of later attitudes and interests that do not have a directly sexual object—political, social, and religious attitudes and interests, for example. Further, many of the "desexualized" goals of affection and interest of normal adults are explained as a sublimation of pregenital libido.[14] These aspects of the theory, then, do not conflict with, but rather, make understandable, the fact that the poet may select erotic objects and relations as symbols for religious objects and relations. If there were no kind of connection between erotic and religious experience, it would be hard to explain the effectiveness of Donne's "Batter My Heart," which is addressed to God, and ends: ". . . for I/Except you enthrall me, never shall be free,/Nor ever chaste, except you ravish me."

To return to the misapplication of the disguise formula, the point which is strangely ignored is that the direction of symbolism which is important for the clinical treatment of a neurosis, is not necessarily the most important direction for understanding the artistic structure of a poem.

Since the fallacy is a persistent one, it will be worth while to examine it further in some detail in an actual case. The case I have selected is not one of those extreme examples of the misuse of the disguise formula which, bcause of their patent absurdity, may be ignored; it is, rather, an example of a psychoanalytic interpretation of a poem which is not so much misleading as incomplete.

Roy P. Basler, in *Sex, Symbolism and Psychology in Literature,* has disavowed any attempt to psychoanalyze the author, maintaining that "the most fruitful employment of Freudian theory by the student of literature lies in the interpretation of literature itself."[15] In particular, Basler points out that many comments on the treatment of sex in Eliot's poetry "seem to miss the center of the target, the poetry itself, which seems more often dramatic than lyric . . . and provides . . . representation of a character's experience rather than a subjective outpouring of the poet's own psyche."[16] Basler then sets to work on Eliot's "The Love Song of J. Alfred Prufrock" and, instead of trying to psychoanalyze Eliot, tries to psychoanalyze Prufrock, as though he were a real person suffering from a real neurosis. There is no doubt that psychoanalytic theory can throw a great deal of light on the poem. The dramatic structure of the work is analogous to the general pattern of many dreams; the speaker, Prufrock, is undergoing a conflict which he cannot solve; he suffers from fear of growing old, fear of women and sex, possibly fear of impotence and castration; he is incapable of "object love," and at the end of the poem there appears a symbol which, in the context, can plausibly be interpreted as a "return to the womb," suggesting a dependent, infantile kind of existence. While the many interpretations made of the poem differ in various respects, those that are psychoanalytically oriented agree rather well on the foregoing points, and there is much in the poem which supports these interpretations. Basler's analysis in general follows this line, and there is nothing wrong with it, so far as it goes. If Prufrock were a patient on an analyst's couch, the sexual direction of the symbolism would be perhaps the most important (though not the only) one to follow out for understanding the cause of his neurotic conflict. But if, as literary critics, we confine ourselves to this direction, we miss, as Basler does, the more inclusive symbolism which differently oriented interpretations have brought out. Prufrock's state, which is also that of the society around him, is one of spiritual torpor, lack of ability to will, to act, to love in general. The indications of sexual timidity, impotence, and so on, are symbolic of a more inclusive timidity and impotence. To take a specific example of the missing, by Basler, of much of the symbolic structure as well as dramatic pattern of the poem, consider the following account of the references to Hamlet and others in the poem:

> This association of love and death underlies the sinister meaning of women to Prufrock, and accounts for the revulsion and disgust which

accompanies his too-close-for-comfort acquaintance with feminine appur-
tenances. . . . Likewise it accounts in a measure for the allusions to John
the Baptist and Lazarus, as well as to Hamlet, each of whom is associated
in Prufrock's mind with sex, women, and death, for the obvious reason
that each had his sorrow of a woman who was more or less directly responsible for his death. . . . In brief, woman means death to Prufrock's
"I."[17]

The functions in the poem of the reference to Hamlet are too complex to
list at all completely here, but the following functions are essential to the
development of the theme. When the line "No! I am not Prince Hamlet,
nor was meant to be" occurs, the reader has already been prepared to find
analogies as well as ironic contrasts between the character and predicament of Prufrock and those of Hamlet. The earlier lines, for example, are
part of this preparation:

> And time yet for a hundred indecisions,
> And for a hundred visions and revisions,
> Before the taking of a toast and tea.[18]

There are, first, the obvious similarity of indecision and conflict in the
two characters, and the obvious contrast between Hamlet's final action
and Prufrock's inability to act. Further, Hamlet, through his final action,
takes on a tragic stature which Prufrock, "Almost, at times, the Fool,"
cannot achieve, though he too is caught in forces which doom him. Then,
there is the contrast between the heroic world of Shakespeare's play (and
the Elizabethan society which was its setting) and the arty, tea-party society in which Prufrock exists; and, in spite of the contrasts, the same
problems and forces are found in both worlds. The figure of Prufrock
may be said to become in the poem a symbol of a certain kind of existence, individual and social, which contrasts with as well as resembles the
kind of person, way of life, and society symbolized by the character of
Hamlet.

There is an additional difficulty in taking exclusively the doctor-patient
attitude toward Prufrock. At the end of Basler's analysis Prufrock appears
to be so neurotic that the reader will hesitate to take at their face value
Prufrock's comments about himself and his surroundings. Although it is
possible, of course, for an extremely neurotic or even psychotic individual
to make true and perceptive remarks about himself and other people, we
quite naturally are skeptical about the objective bases of the appraisals of
mentally ill persons. But if Prufrock's appraisal of himself (for example,
"NO! I am not Prince Hamlet, nor was meant to be;/Am an attendant
lord, one that will do/To swell a progress, start a scene or two") and of
his society ("I know the voices dying with a dying fall") cannot within
the fictional context of the poem be taken seriously, then the poem has

little, if any, point. Part of the tragedy of Prufrock is that while he can see what is lacking in his society and to some extent what is lacking in himself, he is unable to do anything which would free himself from his predicament.

The second fallacy in the use of psychoanalytic accounts of symbolic thinking I shall call "the fallacy of misplaced archaic character." Very few people, if any, would attempt to "reduce" the thought activity of, say, an atomic scientist to the archaic phase which his thinking may go through before it emerges in explicit, conscious form. And very few, if any, would try to characterize the thought of a modern scientist in terms appropriate only to primitive man's first attempts to deal with reality, even though science is historically a development of primitive thought processes. But in the contemporary criticism of poetry, and of art in general, there exist tendencies, somewhat vague in character, to "reduce" the product to its primitive origins, either in the individual or in society at large. These tendencies usually result in a view which neglects the conscious-design aspect of artistic activity and finds the highest merit in its "unconscious sources," the unconscious being associated with the "primitive," or "archaic." Those who hold this view overlook the fact that there are few things with less artistic merit than automatic writing, the outpourings of a drunkard or psychotic, records of dreams, and so on—all the results of mental activity in which there is a minimum of conscious control and regulation. In this connection, the reproduction of manuscripts and work sheets of modern poets in *Poets at Work* is of interest.[19] In particular, the work sheet of "The Ballad of the Long-legged Bait," by Dylan Thomas, shows changes which are plainly based on considerations of diction, rhythm, sound, and structure of idea and feeling. (For example, "Land, land, land, there is nothing left" is changed to "Land, land, land, nothing remains," and "Of the deep famous sea but its speech" is changed to "Of the stalking famous sea," which in turn is changed to "Of the pacing famous sea."[20]) It is precisely because of these considerations that Thomas writes a fine poem, rather than merely recording an eruption of unconscious material, boring and disorganized (except from a medical viewpoint) to all but the one person in whom the eruption takes place. The sea, as a symbol in the poem, may well have an archaic source, but the control and regulation of the symbol, in the medium of language, can scarcely be thought of as exercised by archaic processes. This kind of control constitutes a skill—that is, a set of habits developed as the result of practice and native endowment. The possessor of a skill, whether he be a golfer or a poet, is ordinarily, as he engages in skilled activity, aware neither of the past experiences of acquiring the skill, nor of just why he does this or that at any one moment. However, usually the past experiences can be recalled easily, and reasons for performing one operation rather than another made plain. Neither deeply repressed material nor primitive material is directly involved in the operation of a skill.[21]

The reader who will accept what I have said above may nevertheless make the following kind of objection. Granted the importance of non-primitive skills in shaping the art product, is it not the relation of the theme and symbolism of a literary work to archaic impulses and ideas common to all humanity, that gives the work a deeply moving quality, that makes us call it "great" rather than merely "competent"? This question is ambiguous and cannot be answered by a simple "yes" or "no." The best way to deal with it will be to examine the claims made by Jung and his followers in regard to the presence of archaic patterns of symbols (called by Jungians "archetypal patterns," "primordial images") in literature.

III

In certain respects the Jungian account of symbols appears to many people to be applicable to literature with fewer additions and changes than the Freudian account of symbols in dreams and in other mental states. The sex impulse is not as basic in the Jungian system as in the Freudian, and the deepest level of the unconscious contains, according to Jung, not only animal, but also "spiritual" instincts and impulses. On the other hand, Jung's mode of exposition, as well as that of his followers, is at times so metaphysical and mystic as to repel the empirically minded. Thus, the archetypal patterns are spoken of not only as similarities in the direction of symbolism, found in the myths, literature, dreams, and visions of many geographically and temporally separated groups, but also as individual forces of a substantial nature. It lies beyond the scope of this work to deal with the philosophical difficulties in Jung's various formulations of his system. The least offensive (to the empirically minded) formulation which one can gather from the writings of Jung and his expositors is, roughly, as follows.

As the result of the evolution of the human nervous system (involving, apparently, inheritance of acquired characteristics) there have been formed in human beings dispositions to produce certain patterns of symbols, these dispositions being realized in certain human situations. Since these dispositions have not been formed by our own personal experience, they are located by Jung on a level of the psyche called "the collective unconscious," which, as it were, lies "below" the personal unconscious, containing our personal memories and repressed material from our own experience. It should be emphasized that the archetype, or archetypal pattern, is not an individual image or set of them, but rather consists in the general structure and direction of symbols. Any individual example of an archetype in poetry or in a dream will have features explainable only by reference to the individual poet's or dreamer's experience and cultural environment. Further, the images that exhibit archetypal patterns are images drawn from "outer perception," while what they symbolize is psychic situations and events. "All the mythologized occurrences of nature . . . ," writes Jung, "are . . . symbolic expressions for the inner and unconscious psychic drama that becomes accessible to human consciousness by way of projection—that is, mirrored in the events of nature."[22] Finally, the archetypes are, by Jung, assigned the role of transformers and directors of psychic energy. That is to say, it is not just regression to more primitive levels of thought that produces the archetypes, but the need for further psychic development. For example, images of going down into the darkness, under the water, into the belly of a monster, or even into the womb of a mother, are not, in the Jungian system, expressions of a wish for any infantile state of existence, but of a need for "spiritual" transformation and "rebirth." This transformation can only be accomplished by a turning to and "immersion" in the unconscious levels of the psyche from which, in the course of evolution, the conscious level emerged.

It would be unfair to Jung and his followers to attribute to them, as an explicitly held view, the naïve assumption that the presence of archetypal patterns in literature automatically confers artistic merit. As a matter of fact, Jung appears to be clearly aware, at the outset of an essay, "Psychology and Literature," that features of a work important from a literary point of view are not important from a psychological viewpoint and vice versa.[23] Further, Jung makes a distinction, stated as descriptive rather than evaluative, between *psychological* artistic creation and *visionary*. In the former kind of art, ". . . materials drawn from the realm of human consciousness . . . [are] . . . psychically assimilated by the poet, raised from the commonplace to the level of poetic experience, and given an expression which forces the reader to greater clarity and depth of human insight. . . ."[24] But, toward the end of the essay, in writing of the art that uses materials from the collective unconscious, Jung begins to talk of "great art" and of the poet who has ". . . drawn upon the healing and redeeming forces of the collective psyche that underlies consciousness with its isolation and its painful errors."[25] And in another work, we find the following:

> Who, however, speaks in primordial images speaks as with a thousand tongues, he grips and overpowers, and at the same time he elevates that which he treats out of the individual and transitory into the sphere of the eternal, he exalts the personal lot to the lot of man, and therewith he releases in us too all those helpful forces that have ever enabled humanity to rescue itself from whatever distress and to live through even the longest night. . . . That is the secret of the artistic effect.[26]

If this were indeed the secret of the artistic effect, we would have to find artistic merit, for example, in the awkwardly drawn and often unintentionally funny depictions of the archetype of the *mandala* (a circular form with many variations) produced by Jung's patients. To return to literature, I doubt that anyone with some familiarity with the medium would find either artistic merit or any deeply moving quality about the writings in poetry and prose which form the basis for Jung's researches in *The Psychology of the Unconscious.*[27] These writings by an American, a Miss Miller (who later became psychotic), are shown, quite convincingly, to contain themes similar to themes frequently found in myth and religion. However, since the themes are filtered through a derivative and inexpert style of writing, to competent critics the result will be both artistically bad and unmoving, except for the pathetic quality of the products seen in relation to their seriously disturbed author.

In brief, then, one may grant that many of the symbols in literature have an archetypal character in the sense of showing features common to many myths and religions, visions and dreams, and, further, that these symbols are connected with deep and strong feelings in all or most of us, without falling into the fallacy of assuming that the mere presence of these primordial images guarantees either a deeply moving experience or a work of artistic merit. The most that can be asserted about common themes and symbols is the truistic statement that where an artist uses materials connected with deep and strong feelings, there exists the potentiality for deeply moving art. Whether or not the potentiality is realized depends on considerations that have nothing to do with the archaic or the collective unconscious. (That Jungian material can be fallaciously used does not, of course, imply that the material cannot be used in a legitimate way to illumine certain kinds of literary work. For example, Elizabeth Drew, in a discerning book, *T. S. Eliot: The Design of His Poetry,* has, I think, applied some of Jung's findings with good sense to Eliot's work.) [28]

IV

There is a multitude of ways in which poets can formulate in language the experiences in which objects become symbols. It will be well to conclude this chapter by looking at some examples that, according to our account, come under the broad heading of "symbols in poetry."

Symbols in the form of figures of speech—condensed metaphors—are found in the following lines from the end of T. S. Eliot's "Little Gidding":

> All manner of thing shall be well
> When the tongues of flame are in-folded
> Into the crowned knot of fire
> And the fire and the rose are one.[29]

Here, if we take the meanings literally (that is, employ the words according to the customary rules), the result is obviously nonsense. We can hardly suppose that Eliot is saying that everything will be fine when we are no longer able to distinguish what glows on our hearth from what grows in our rose garden. Rather, we interpret the lines in much the same way that we interpret figures of speech. We know, from the whole poem, that "fire" and "rose" refer to objects which, in the context, are symbols for certain aspects and features in the process of attaining the state of salvation. (There are also, of course, sexual overtones—or should one say, "undertones"?—of the religious experience and its symbols.)

By contrast, in cases of clear-cut allegory, a poem makes sense taken literally, but, in one way or another, forces us into another reading. What we have is a double order of correlated meanings. Consider, for example, Christina Rossetti's "Uphill." (That this specimen of allegory is trite should not lead us to suppose that the form cannot be excellently handled.) The poem begins:

> Does the road wind uphill all the way?
>   Yes, to the very end.
> Will the day's journey take the whole long day?
>   From morn to night, my friend.

Almost all readers will, from the very outset, correlate the road "winding uphill all the way" with the struggle of human beings from birth to death, and the "day's journey" with a lifetime. The indication of a double order of meanings is given not only within the context of the poem, but also by the fact that life has so often been metaphorized as a journey. It is this fact which indicates for most readers that T. S. Eliot's "Journey of the Magi" has an allegorical character, and that it is not only an imaginitive account of the journey referred to in the Bible, but also an account of the "journey of the soul" toward religious salvation. However, while there is not much point to Christina Rossetti's poem, unless the symbolic level is grasped, Eliot's poem, read only on the literal level, remains an interesting and well-told story—also, the indications, within Eliot's poem, of a double order of meanings, are not so clear as in Christina Rossetti's. On the other hand, one can follow through Eliot's poem, to a considerable extent, on the hypothesis of a double meaning, correlating incident to incident in the two sorts of journeys.

In Robert Frost's "Stopping by Woods on a Snowy Evening," the speaker lets us know that, driving on a snowy evening, he has stopped to watch the woods of a neighbor fill up with snow. Casually, he remarks that his little horse "must think it queer" to have the driver stop in the lonely place. Then, in the last stanza, the speaker says:

> The woods are lovely, dark and deep,
> But I have promises to keep,
> And miles to go before I sleep,
> And miles to go before I sleep.[30]

The situation has been so described (darkness, snow falling, isolation), and appraised (both attractive and dangerous), and the connection between journey and life, sleep and death, is so usual that there is at the end of the poem a strong suggestion of a kind of death-wish, combated by considerations of the practical duties and obligations of living. But one cannot follow through the poem from beginning to end to get two parallel stories; and the emphasis, as almost always in Frost, remains on the incident realistically described. Hence, it would be a mistake to say that the poem has a double meaning, literal and symbolic. However, the repeated "And miles to go before I sleep" does approach, in its second occurrence, a double-meaning expression.

Thomas Hardy's "Neutral Tones" is clearly a nonallegorical poem which is of interest on two scores. In it, the poet steps on stage to point out the symbols, and the symbolism which is effected as well as commented on, is of the sort which we considered at the end of section I. The entire poem follows.

> We stood by a pond that winter day,
> And the sun was white, as though chidden of God,
> And a few leaves lay on the starving sod;
>   —They had fallen from an ash, and were gray.
> Your eyes on me were as eyes that rove
> Over tedious riddles of years ago;
> And some words played between us to and fro
>   On which lost the more by our love.
> The smile on your mouth was the deadest thing
> Alive enough to have strength to die;
> And a grin of bitterness swept thereby
>   Like an ominous bird a-wing . . .
> Since then, keen lessons that love deceives,
> And wrings with wrong, have shaped to me
> Your face, and the God-curst sun, and a tree,
>   And a pond edged with grayish leaves.[31]

Brooks, Purser and Warren have described the symbolic aspects of the poem, and I wish to quote them, not only for the aptness of the analysis, but also as evidence that literary criticism needs a sense of "symbol" as wide as the one I have made out.

> . . . what really lifts the content of the poem above the commonplace poetic effect of mere pathos at broken love, and what defines the real theme of the poem is the last stanza. . . . Why have "keen lessons that love deceives" etc., always shaped for the speaker the face of the first beloved in that particular background. . . ? The answer may run something like this: that early, and perhaps first, quarrel and disappointment in love have become a symbol for all the later disappointments and frustrations of his life; but it is more than that, being, as it were, in conjunction with the

"God-curst" landscape also a *symbol* of all the curse of evil that hangs over man and nature. Therefore, this poem does in a very clear and apparently simple and direct way, what all poetry tries to do: it takes a single incident, fact, or observation (the quarrel) and manages to link it with, or fuse it with, other things out of experience (the "starving sod," the dead leaves, the misty sun, etc.) to make a new kind of experience and perception of some kind of coördination or ordering of separate things. That is to say, the poet creates a *symbolic* experience. . . .[32]

Finally, I wish to examine two cases of symbolism which illustrate, respectively, a kind of symbolic object and a certain way of developing a symbol, both often overlooked.

Walter de La Mare's "The Listeners" is an overanthologized poem which, to judge from the responses of students, has a wide appeal, largely because they feel in it an atmosphere of romantic mystery. There is enough of a narrative in the poem for the average reader to follow without feeling unpleasantly baffled. The Traveler knocks at the moonlit door in the silent forest; there are only phantom listeners within. "Tell them that I came, and no one answered, /That I kept my word," the Traveler says, and then, his pledge kept, though futilely, he rides off. For the rest, the average reader is content with the vague and mystifying comment of Louis Untermeyer.

It ["The Listeners"] can be interpreted in many ways, as the record of an actual quest or as a symbol, a fable of man's eternal attempt to answer life's riddle or as a courageous challenge to terror. But no contemporary poem is more provocative, more purely a work of the imagination, a work that does not explain but never fails to illumine.[33]

If the reader is not satisfied to be pleasantly mystified, however, he wants to know what is illumined. Yet, if he starts off, trying to correlate forest, bird, horse, and so on, each with another, symbolized object, he remains baffled. There is, however, a perfectly obvious dramatic structure to the narrative, and one that is suggestive of a wide range of experiences. The story is one of an attempt, motivated by a sense of obligation, to return to a past scene and to persons known in the past; the promise is kept, but only phantoms are there to listen. The theme is, then, a "you can't go home again" theme, with supernatural over-tones. It is in this direction that the symbolic aspect of the poem is to be sought. Freudian and Jungian material might be helpful in further exploring the direction of symbols, but it will suffice here to point out that the dramatic structure of the poem is clear, and that there is no need to make an impenetrable mystery of its symbolism, if a broad sense of symbol is kept in mind.

The second case of symbolism which I wish to examine illustrates the point that symbolic relations may be gradually developed, not given in main outline from the start (as in Christina Rossetti's "Uphill"), but worked out in a process in which a series of images are interrelated. Yeats's "Sailing to Byzantium" contains, as a main line of symbolism, references to bird and song.[34]

The poem is too complex to analyze with any thoroughness here, but one can indicate briefly how the golden bird, prominent in the last stanza, becomes a symbol of various qualities as a result of a process of interrelating images in the preceding stanzas.[35] The first two stanzas present a contrast between youth and age, each having contrasting properties of both positive and negative value. Youth (and the first stanza relates living birds and their song to youth) has sensual enjoyment, beauty, vitality, but neglects intellect. Age, which lacks these values, is capable of intellectual activity. In the first two stanzas, art (as contrasted with the spontaneous song of birds) is represented as "monuments," inanimate artifacts. In the third stanza, there is a suggestion that art embodies soul, passion, as well as intellect. In the last stanza we are presented with an object, sensuously beautiful and singing, like the living birds of the first stanza, but also an artifact, not subject to biological decay, and embodying intellect and passion. Thus, the golden bird incorporates all that was of positive value in youth and age, and the transition from the spontaneous song of the natural bird to the constructed song of the artificial bird (with their similar yet partly different themes) suggests the kind of transformation of nature that is effected in art—the kind of escape from oblivion that the "dying animal" can achieve through artifice.

Notes

1. Mary McCarthy, "Settling the Colonel's Hash," first published in *Harper's Magazine*, Vol. CCVIII, No. 1245 (February, 1954), pp. 68-75. Copyright 1954 by Harper & Brothers. Reprinted by permission of the publishers.

2. Everett Carter, in an unpublished paper, "Norris and the Modern Novel."

3. Cleanth Brooks and Robert Penn Warren, *Understanding Poetry* (New York, Henry Holt and Company, 1951), p. 688.

4. McCarthy, *op. cit.*, pp. 72-73.

5. For interesting and always tentative speculations about art, see Ernst Kris, *Psychoanalytic Explorations in Art* (New York, International Universities Press, Inc., 1952).

6. Otto Fenichel, *The Psychoanalytic Theory of Neurosis* (New York, W. W. Norton and Company, 1945), p. 48.

7. *Ibid.*, pp. 47-48.

8. *Ibid.*, p. 49.

9. *Ibid.*, p. 47.

10. *Ibid.*, p. 50.

11. Sigmund Freud, *A General Introduction to Psycho-Analysis*, trans. by Joan Riviere (New York, Liveright Publishing Corporation, 1935), p. 135.

12. Fenichel, *op. cit.*, p. 24.

13. T. S. Eliot, *Collected Poems of.* . . . (New York, Harcourt, Brace and Company, 1936), p. 65.

14. Fenichel, *op. cit.*, pp. 141-143.

15. Roy P. Basler, *Sex, Symbolism and Psychology in Literature* (New Brunswick, Rutgers University Press, 1948), p. 11. Copyright 1948.

16. *Ibid.*, p. 205.

17. *Ibid.*, pp. 213-214.

18. Eliot, *op. cit.*, pp. 11-17.

19. Rudolf Arnheim, W. H. Auden, Karl Shapiro, and Donald A. Stauffer, *Poets at Work, Essays Based on the Modern Poetry Collection at the Lockwood Memorial Library, University of Buffalo* (New York, Harcourt, Brace and Company, 1948).

20. *Ibid.*, work sheet facing p. 165.

21. See Kris, *op. cit.*, chap. xiv.

22. C. G. Jung, *The Integration of the Personality*, trans. by Stanley Dell (New York and Toronto, Farrar and Rinehart, 1939), pp. 54-55.

23. C. G. Jung, *Modern Man in Search of a Soul*, trans. by W. S. Dell and Cary F. Baynes (New York, Harcourt, Brace and Company, 1933), pp. 175-199.

24. *Ibid.*, p. 179.

25. *Ibid.*, p. 198.

26. C. G. Jung, *Contributions to Analytical Psychology*, trans. by H. G. and C. F. Baynes (London, Kegan Paul, Trench, Trubner and Co., 1928), p. 248.

27. C. G. Jung, *The Psychology of the Unconscious*, trans. by Beatrice M. Hinkle (New York, Dodd, Mead and Company, 1947).

28. Elizabeth Drew, *T. S. Eliot: The Design of His Poetry* (New York, Charles Scribner's Sons, 1949).

29. T. S. Eliot, *Four Quartets* (New York, Harcourt, Brace and Company, 1943), p. 39.

30. Robert Frost, *Complete Poems of.* . . . (New York, Henry Holt and Company, 1949), p. 275. Copyright 1930, 1949, by Henry Holt and Company, Inc. Copyright 1936, 1948, by Robert Frost. By permission of the publishers.

31. Thomas Hardy, *Collected Poems of.* . . . (New York, The Macmillan Company, 1931), p. 9. Reprinted by permission of the publishers.

32. Cleanth Brooks, Jr., John Thibaut Purser, and Robert Penn Warren, *An Approach to Literature* (3rd ed.; New York, Appleton-Century-Crofts, Inc., 1952), p. 329. Copyright 1952.

33. *A Treasury of Great Poems, English and American*, ed. by Louis Untermeyer (New York, Simon and Schuster, 1942), p. 1073.

34. W. B. Yeats, from *The Tower*, in *The Collected Poems of.* . . . (New York, The Macmillan Company, 1940), pp. 223-224. Copyright 1928, reprinted by permission of The Macmillan Company.

35. See Elder Olson, "An Outline of Poetic Theory," Appendix, in *Critiques and Essays in Criticism*, selected by R. W. Stallman (New York, The Ronald Press Company, 1949), pp. 284-288.

MAX BLACK

Metaphor

"Metaphors are no arguments, my pretty maiden."
(*The Fortunes of Nigel*, Book 2, Ch. 2.)

TO DRAW ATTENTION to a philosopher's metaphors is to belittle him—like
praising a logician for his beautiful handwriting. Addiction to metaphor
is held to be illicit, on the principle that whereof one can speak only
metaphorically, thereof one ought not to speak at all. Yet the nature of
the offence is unclear. I should like to do something to dispel the
mystery that invests the topic; but since philosophers (for all their
notorious interest in language) have so neglected the subject, I must get
what help I can from the literary critics. They at least do not accept
the commandment, "Thou shalt not commit metaphor," or assume
that metaphor is incompatible with serious thought.

I

The questions I should like to see answered concern the "logical
grammar" of "metaphor" and words having related meanings. It would
be satisfactory to have convincing answers to the questions: "How do
we recognize a case of metaphor?", "Are there any criteria for the detection of metaphors?", "Can metaphors be translated into literal expressions?", "Is metaphor properly regarded as a decoration upon 'plain
sense'?", "What are the relations between metaphor and simile?", "In
what sense, if any, is a metaphor 'creative'?", "What is the point of using
a metaphor?". (Or, more briefly, "What do we *mean* by 'metaphor'?"
The questions express attempts to become clearer about some uses of
the word "metaphor"—or, if one prefers the material mode, to analyze
the notion of metaphor.)

The list is not a tidy one, and several of the questions overlap in fairly

Reprinted from *Proceedings of the Aristotelian Society*, LV (1954-5) by courtesy of the Editor of the Aristotelian Society.

obvious ways. But I hope they will sufficiently illustrate the type of inquiry that is intended.

It would be helpful to start from some agreed list of "clear cases" of metaphor. Since the word "metaphor" has some intelligible uses, however vague or vacillating, it must be possible to construct such a list. Presumably, it should be easier to agree whether any given item should be included than to agree about any proposed analysis of the notion of metaphor.

Perhaps the following list of examples, chosen not altogether at random, might serve:

   (i) "The chairman ploughed through the discussion."
   (ii) "A smoke-screen of witnesses."
   (iii) "An argumentative melody."
   (iv) "Blotting-paper voices" (Henry James).
   (v) "The poor are the negroes of Europe" (Baudelaire).
   (vi) "Light is but the shadow of God" (Sir Thomas Browne).
   (vii) "Oh dear white children, casual as birds,
       Playing amid the ruined languages" (Auden).

I hope all these will be accepted as unmistakable *instances* of metaphor, whatever judgments may ultimately be made about the meaning of "metaphor." The examples are offered as clear cases of metaphor, but, with the possible exception of the first, they would be unsuitable as "paradigms." If we wanted to teach the meaning of "metaphor" to a child, we should need simpler examples, like "The clouds are crying" or "The branches are fighting with one another." (Is it significant that one hits upon examples of personification?) But I have tried to include some reminders of the possible complexities that even relatively straightforward metaphors may generate.

Consider the first example—"The chairman ploughed through the discussion." An obvious point to begin with is the contrast between the word "ploughed" and the remaining words by which it is accompanied. This would be commonly expressed by saying that "ploughed" has here a metaphorical sense, while the other words have literal senses. Though we point to the whole sentence as an instance (a "clear case") of metaphor, our attention quickly narrows to a single word, whose presence is the proximate reason for the attribution. And similar remarks can be made about the next four examples in the list, the crucial words being, respectively, "smoke-screen," "argumentative," "blotting-paper," and "negroes."

(But the situation is more complicated in the last two examples of the list. In the quotation from Sir Thomas Browne, "Light" must be supposed to have a symbolic sense, and certainly to mean far more than it would in the context of a text-book on optics. Here, the metaphorical sense of the expression, "the shadow of God" imposes a meaning richer than usual upon the subject of the sentence. Similar effects can be noticed in the passage from Auden [consider for instance the meaning of "white" in the first line]. I shall have to neglect such complexities in this paper.)

In general, when we speak of a relatively simple metaphor, we are referring to a sentence or another expression, in which *some* words are used metaphorically, while the remainder are used non-metaphorically. An attempt to construct an entire sentence of words that are used metaphorically results in a proverb, an allegory, or a riddle. No preliminary analysis of metaphor will satisfactorily cover even such trite examples as "In the night all cows are black." And cases of symbolism (in the sense in which Kafka's castle is a "symbol") also need separate treatment.

II

"The chairman ploughed through the discussion." In calling this sentence a case of metaphor, we are implying that at least one word (here, the word "ploughed") is being used metaphorically in the sentence, and that at least one of the remaining words is being used literally. Let us call the word "ploughed" the *focus* of the metaphor, and the remainder of the sentence in which that word occurs the *frame*. (Are *we* now using metaphors—and mixed ones at that? Does it matter?) One notion that needs to be clarified is that of the "metaphorical use" of the focus of a metaphor. Among other things, it would be good to understand how the presence of one frame can result in metaphorical use of the complementary word, while the presence of a different frame for the same word fails to result in metaphor.

If the sentence about the chairman's behaviour is translated word for word into any foreign language for which this is possible, we shall of course want to say that the translated sentence is a case of the *very same* metaphor. So, to call a sentence an instance of metaphor is to say something about its *meaning*, not about its orthography, its phonetic pattern, or its grammatical form.[1] (To use a well-known distinction, "metaphor" must be classified as a term belonging to "semantics" and not to "syntax"—or to any *physical* enquiry about language.)

Suppose somebody says, "I like to plough my memories regularly." Shall we say he is using the same metaphor as in the case already discussed, or not? Our answer will depend upon the degree of similarity we are prepared to affirm on comparing the two "frames" (for we have the same "focus" each time). Differences in the two frames will produce *some* differences in the interplay[2] between focus and frame in the two cases. Whether we regard the differences as sufficiently striking to warrant calling the sentences *two* metaphors is a matter for arbitrary decision. "Metaphor" is a loose word, at best, and we must beware of attributing to it stricter rules of usage than are actually found in practice.

So far, I have been treating "metaphor" as a predicate properly applicable to certain expressions, without attention to any occasions on which the expressions are used, or to the thoughts, acts, feelings, and intentions of speakers upon such occasions. And this is surely correct for *some* expressions. We recognise that to call a man a "cesspool" is to use a metaphor, without needing to know who uses the expression, or on what occasions, or with what intention. The rules of our language determine that some expressions must count as metaphors; and a speaker can no more change this than he can legislate that "cow" shall mean the same as "sheep." But we must also recognise that the established rules of language leave wide latitude for individual variation, initiative, and creation. There are indefinitely many contexts (including nearly all the interesting ones) where the meaning of a metaphorical expression has to be reconstructed from the speaker's intentions (and other clues) because the broad rules of standard usage are too general to supply the information needed. When Churchill, in a famous phrase, called Mussolini "that *utensil*," the tone of voice, the verbal setting, the historical background, helped to make clear *what* metaphor was being used. (Yet, even here, it is hard to see how the phrase "that utensil" could ever be applied to a man except as an insult. Here, as elsewhere, the general rules of usage function as limitations upon the speaker's freedom to mean whatever he pleases.) This is an example, though still a simple one, of how recognition and interpretation of a metaphor may require attention to the *particular circumstances* of its utterance.

It is especially noteworthy that there are, in general, no standard rules for the degree of *weight* or *emphasis* to be attached to a particular use of an expression. To know what the user of a metaphor means, we need to know how "seriously" he treats the metaphorical focus. (Would he be just as content to have some rough synonym, or would only *that* word serve? Are we to take the word lightly, attending only to its most obvious implications—or should we dwell upon its less immediate associations?) In speech we can use emphasis and phrasing as clues. But in written or printed discourse, even these rudimentary aids are absent. Yet this somewhat elusive "weight" of a (suspected or detected[3]) metaphor is of great practical importance in exegesis.

To take a philosophical example. Whether the expression "logical form" should be treated in a particular frame as having a metaphorical sense will depend upon the extent to which its user is taken to be conscious of some supposed analogy between arguments and other things (vases, clouds, battles, jokes) that are also said to have "form." Still more will it depend upon whether the writer wishes the analogy to be active in the minds of his readers; and how much his own thought depends upon and is nourished by the supposed analogy. We must not expect the "rules of language" to be of much help in such enquiries. (There is accordingly a sense of "metaphor" that belongs to "pragmatics," rather than to "semantics"—and this sense may be the one most deserving of attention.)

III

Let us try the simplest possible account that can be given of the meaning of "The Chairman ploughed through the discussion," to see how far it will take us. A plausible commentary (for those presumably too literal-minded to understand the original) might run somewhat as follows:—

"A speaker who uses the sentence in question is taken to want to say *something* about a chairman and his behaviour in some meeting. Instead of saying, plainly or *directly*, that the chairman dealt summarily with objections, or ruthlessly suppressed irrelevance, or something of the sort, the speaker chose to use a word ('ploughed') which, strictly speaking, means something else. But an intelligent hearer can easily guess what the speaker had in mind."[4]

This account treats the metaphorical expression (let us call it "*M*") as a substitute for some other literal expression ("*L*", say) which would have expressed the same meaning, had it been used instead. On this view, the meaning of *M*, and its metaphorical occurrence, is just the literal meaning of *L*. The metaphorical use of an expression consists, on this view, of the use of that expression in other than its proper or normal sense, in some context that allows the improper or abnormal sense to be detected and appropriately transformed. (The reasons adduced for so remarkable a performance will be discussed later.)

Any view which holds that a metaphorical expression is used in place of some equivalent *literal* expression, I shall call a *substitution view of metaphor*. (I should like this label to cover also any analysis which views the entire sentence that is the locus of the metaphor as replacing some set of literal sentences.) Until recently, one or another form of a substitution view has been accepted by most writers (usually literary critics or writers of books on rhetoric) who have had anything to say about metaphor.

To take a few examples. Whately defines a metaphor as "a word substituted for another on account of the Resemblance or Analogy between their significations."[5] Nor is the entry in the Oxford Dictionary (to jump to modern times) much different from this: "Metaphor: The figure of speech in which a name or descriptive term is transferred to some object different from, but analogous to, that to which it is properly applicable; an instance of this, a metaphorical expression."[6] So strongly entrenched is the view expressed by these definitions that a recent writer who is explicitly arguing for a different and more sophisticated view of metaphor, nevertheless slips into the old fashion by defining metaphor as "saying one thing and meaning another."[7]

According to a substitution view, the focus of a metaphor, the word or expression having a distinctively metaphorical use within a literal frame, is used to communicate a meaning that might have been expressed literally. The author substitutes M for L; it is the reader's task to invert the substitution, by using the literal meaning of M as a clue to the intended literal meaning of L. Understanding a metaphor is like deciphering a code or unravelling a riddle.

If we now ask why, on this view, the writer should set his reader the task of solving a puzzle, we shall be offered two types of answer. The first is that there may be, in fact, no literal equivalent, L, available in the language in question. Mathematicians spoke of the "leg" of an angle because there was no brief literal expression for a bounding line; we say "cherry lips," because there is no form of words half as convenient for saying quickly what the lips are like. Metaphor plugs the gaps in the literal vocabulary (or, at least, supplies the want of convenient abbreviations). So viewed, metaphor is a species of *catachresis,* which I shall define as the use of a word in some new sense in order to remedy a gap in the vocabulary. Catachresis is the putting of new senses into old words.[8] But if a catachresis serves a genuine need, the new sense introduced will quickly become part of the *literal* sense. "Orange" may originally have been applied to the colour by catachresis; but the word is now applied to the colour just as "properly" (and unmetaphorically) as to the fruit. "Osculating" curves don't kiss for long, and quickly revert to a more prosaic mathematical contact. And similarly for other cases. It is the fate of catachresis to disappear when it is successful.

There are, however, many metaphors where the virtues ascribed to catachresis cannot apply, because there is, or there is supposed to be, some readily available and equally compendious literal equivalent. Thus in the somewhat unfortunate example,[9] "Richard is a lion," which modern writers have discussed with boring insistence, the literal meaning is taken to be the same as that of the sentence "Richard is brave."[10] Here, the metaphor is not supposed to enrich the vocabulary.

When catachresis cannot be invoked, the reasons for substituting an indirect, metaphorical, expression are taken to be stylistic. We are told that the metaphorical expression may (in its literal use) refer to a more concrete object than would its literal equivalent; and this is supposed to give pleasure to the reader (the pleasure of having one's thoughts diverted from Richard to the irrelevant lion). Again, the reader is taken to enjoy problem-solving—or to delight in the author's skill at half-concealing, half-revealing his meaning. Or metaphors provide a shock of "agreeable surprise"—and so on. The principle behind these "explanations" seems to be: When in doubt about some peculiarity of language, attribute its existence to the pleasure it gives a reader. A principle that has the merit of working well in default of any evidence.[11]

Whatever the merits of such speculations about the reader's response, they agree in making metaphor a *decoration*. Except in cases where a metaphor is a catachresis that remedies some temporary imperfection of literal language, the purpose of metaphor is to entertain and divert. Its use, on this view, always constitutes a deviation from the "plain and strictly appropriate style" (Whately).[12] So, if philosophers have something more important to do than give pleasure to their readers, metaphor can have no serious place in philosophical discussion.

IV

The view that a metaphorical expression has a meaning that is some transform of its normal literal meaning is a special case of a more general view about "figurative" language. This holds that any figure of speech involving semantic change (and not merely syntactic change, like inversion of normal word order) consists in some transformation of a *literal* meaning. The author provides, not his intended meaning, m, but some function thereof, $f(m)$; the reader's task is to apply the inverse function, f^{-1}, and so to obtain $f^{-1}(f(m))$, i.e., m, the original meaning. When different functions are used, different tropes result. Thus, in irony, the author says the *opposite* of what he means; in hyperbole, he *exaggerates* his meaning; and so on.

What, then, is the characteristic transforming function involved in metaphor? To this the answer has been made: either *analogy* or *similarity*. M is either similar or analogous in meaning to its literal equivalent L. Once the reader has detected the ground of the intended analogy or simile (with the help of the frame, or clues drawn from the wider context) he can retrace the author's path and so reach the original literal meaning (the meaning of L.)

If a writer holds that a metaphor consists in the *presentation* of the underlying analogy or similarity, he will be taking what I shall call a *comparison view* of metaphor. When Schopenhauer called a geometrical proof a mousetrap, he was, according to such a view, *saying* (though not explicitly): "A geometrical proof is *like* a mousetrap, since both offer a delusive reward, entice their victims by degrees, lead to disagreeable surprise, etc." This is a view of metaphor as a condensed or elliptical *simile*. It will be noticed that a "comparison view" is a special case of a "substitution view." For it holds that the metaphorical statement might be replaced by an equivalent literal *comparison*.

Whately says: "The Simile or Comparison may be considered as differing in form only from a Metaphor; the resemblance being in that case *stated*, which in the Metaphor is implied."[13] Bain says that: "The metaphor is a comparison implied in the mere use of a term" and adds, "It is in the circumstance of being confined to a word, or at most to a phrase, that we are to look for the peculiarities of the metaphor—its advantages on the one hand, and its dangers and abuses on the other."[14] This view of the metaphor, as condensed simile or comparison, has been very popular.

The chief difference between a substitution view (of the sort previously considered) and the special form of it that I have called a comparison view may be illustrated by the stock example of "Richard is a lion." On the first view, the sentence means approximately the same as "Richard is brave"; on the second, approximately the same as "Richard is *like* a lion (in being brave)," the added words in brackets being understood but not explicitly stated. In the second translation, as in the first, the metaphorical statement is taken to be standing in place of some *literal* equivalent. But the comparison view provides a more elaborate paraphrase, inasmuch as the original statement is interpreted as being about lions as well as about Richard.[15]

The main objection against a comparison view is that it suffers from a vagueness that borders on vacuity. We are supposed to be puzzled as to how some expression (M), used metaphorically, can function in place of some literal expression (L) that is held to be an approximate synonym; and the answer offered is that what M stands for (in its literal use) is *similar* to what L stands for. But how informative is this? There is some temptation to think of similarities as "objectively given," so that a question of the form, "Is A like B in respect of P?" has a definite and pre-determined answer. If this were so, similes might be governed by rules as strict as those controlling the statements of physics. But likeness always admits of degrees, so that a truly "objective" question would need to take some such forms as "Is A more like B than like C in respect of P?"—or, perhaps, "Is A closer to B than to C on such and such a scale of degrees of P?" Yet, in proportion as we approach such forms, metaphorical statements lose their effectiveness and their point. We need the metaphors in just the cases when there can be no question as yet of the precision of scientific statement. Metaphorical statement is not a substitute for a formal comparison or any other kind of literal statement, but has its own *distinctive* capacities and achievements. Often we say, "X is M," evoking some imputed connexion between M and an imputed L (or, rather, to an indefinite system, L_1, L_2, L_3, . . .) in cases where, prior to the construction of the metaphor, we would have been hard put to find any *literal* resemblance between M and L. It would be more illuminating in some of these cases to say that the metaphor *creates* the similarity than to say that it formulates some similarity antecedently existing.[16]

V

I turn now to consider a type of analysis which I shall call an *interaction view* of metaphor. This seems to me to be free from the main defects of substitution and comparison views and to offer some important insight into the uses and limitations of metaphor.[17]

Let us begin with the following statement: "In the simplest formulation, when we use a metaphor we have two thoughts of different things active together and supported by a single word, or phrase, whose meaning is a resultant of their interaction."[18]

We may discover what is here intended by applying Richards' remark to our earlier example, "The poor are the negroes of Europe." The substitution view, at its crudest, tells us that something is being *indirectly* said about the poor of Europe. (But what? That they are an oppressed class, a standing reproach to the community's official ideals, that poverty is inherited and indelible?) The comparison view claims that the epigram *presents* some comparison between the poor and the negroes. In opposition to both, Richards says that our "thoughts" about European poor and (American) negroes are "active together" and "interact" to produce a meaning that is a resultant of that interaction.

I think this must mean that in the given context the focal word "negroes" obtains a *new* meaning, which is *not* quite its meaning in literal uses, nor quite the meaning which any literal substitute would have. The new context (the "frame" of the metaphor, in my terminology) imposes *extension* of meaning upon the focal word. And I take Richards to be saying that for the metaphor to work the reader must remain aware of the extension of meaning—must attend to both the old and the new meanings together.[19]

But how is this extension or change of meaning brought about? At one point, Richards speaks of the "common characteristics" of the two terms (the poor and negroes) as "the ground of the metaphor" (*op. cit.*, p. 177), so that in its metaphorical use a word or expression must connote only a *selection* from the characteristics connoted in its literal uses. This, however, seems a rare lapse into the older and less sophisticated analyses he is trying to supersede.[20] He is on firmer ground when he says that the reader is forced to "connect" the two ideas (p. 125). In this "connexion" resides the secret and the mystery of metaphor. To speak of the "interaction" of two thoughts "active together" (or, again, of their "interillumination" or "co-operation") is to *use* a metaphor emphasizing the dynamic aspects of a good reader's response to a non-trivial metaphor. I have no quarrel with the use of metaphors (if they are good ones) in talking about metaphor. But it may be as well to use several, lest we are misled by the adventitious charms of our favourites.

Let us try, for instance, to think of a metaphor as a *filter*. Consider the statement, "Man is a wolf." Here, we may say, are *two* subjects—the *principal subject*, Man (or: men) and the *subsidiary subject*, Wolf (or: wolves). Now the metaphorical sentence in question will not convey its intended meaning to a reader sufficiently ignorant about wolves. What is needed is not so much that the reader shall know the standard dictionary meaning of "wolf"—or be able to use that word in literal senses—as that he shall know what I will call the *system of associated commonplaces*. Imagine some layman required to say, without taking special thought, those things he held to be true about wolves; the set of statements resulting would approximate to what I am here calling the system of commonplaces associated with the word "wolf." I am assuming that in any given culture the responses made by different persons to the test suggested would agree rather closely, and that even the occasional expert, who might have unusual knowledge of the subject, would still know "what the man in the street thinks about the matter." From the expert's standpoint, the system of commonplaces may include half-truths or downright mistakes (as when a whale is classified as a fish); but the important things for the metaphor's effectiveness is not that the commonplaces shall be true, but that they should be readily and freely evoked. (Because this is so, a metaphor that works in one society may seem preposterous in another. Men who take wolves to be reincarnations of dead humans will give the statement "Man is a wolf" an interpretation different from the one I have been assuming.)

To put the matter in another way: Literal uses of the word "wolf" are governed by syntactical and semantical rules, violation of which produces nonsense or self-contradiction. In addition, I am suggesting, literal uses of the word normally commit the speaker to acceptance of a set of standard beliefs about wolves (current platitudes) that are the common possession of the members of some speech community. To deny any such piece of accepted commonplace (*e.g.*, by saying that wolves are vegetarians—or easily domesticated) is to produce an effect of paradox and provoke a demand for justification. A speaker who says "wolf" is normally taken to be implying in some sense of that word that he is referring to something fierce, carnivorous, treacherous, and so on. The idea of a wolf is part of a system of ideas, not sharply delineated, and yet sufficiently definite to admit of detailed enumeration.

The effect, then, of (metaphorically) calling a man a "wolf" is to evoke the wolf-system of related commonplaces. If the man is a wolf, he preys upon other animals, is fierce, hungry, engaged in constant struggle, a scavenger, and so on. Each of these implied assertions has now to be made to fit the principal subject (the man) either in normal or abnormal senses. If the metaphor is at all appropriate, this can be done—up to a point at least. A suitable hearer will be led by the wolf-system of implications to construct a corresponding system of implications about the principal subject. But these implications will *not* be those comprised in the commonplaces *normally* implied by literal uses of "man." The new implications must be determined by the pattern of implications associated with literal uses of the word "wolf." Any human traits that can without undue strain be talked about in "wolf-language" will be rendered prominent, and any that cannot will be pushed into the background. The wolf-metaphor suppresses some details, emphasizes others—in short, *organizes* our view of man.

Suppose I look at the night sky through a piece of heavily smoked glass on which certain lines have been left clear. Then I shall see only the stars that can be made to lie on the lines previously prepared upon the screen, and the stars I do see will be seen as organised by the screen's structure. We can think of a metaphor as such a screen, and the system of "associated commonplaces" of the focal word as the network of lines upon the screen. We can say that the principal subject is "seen through" the metaphorical expression—or, if we prefer, that the principal subject is "projected upon" the field of the subsidiary subject. (In the latter analogy, the implication-system of the focal expression must be taken to determine the "law of projection.")

Or take another example. Suppose I am set the task of describing a battle in words drawn as largely as possible from the vocabulary of chess. These latter terms determine a system of implications which will proceed to control my description of the battle. The enforced choice of the chess vocabulary will lead some aspects of the battle to be emphasized, others to be neglected, and all to be organised in a way that would cause much more strain in other modes of description. The chess vocabulary filters and transforms: it not only selects, it brings forward aspects of the battle that might not be seen at all through another medium. (Stars that cannot be seen at all, except through telescopes.)

Nor must we neglect the shifts in attitude that regularly result from the use of metaphorical language. A wolf is (conventionally) a hateful and alarming object; so, to call a man a wolf is to imply that he too is hateful and alarming (and thus to support and reinforce dislogistic attitudes). Again, the vocabulary of chess has its primary uses in a highly artificial setting, where all expression of feeling is formally excluded: to describe a battle as if it were a game of chess is accordingly to exclude, by the choice of language, all the more emotionally disturbing aspects of warfare. (Similar by-products are not rare in philosophical uses of metaphor.)

A fairly obvious objection to the foregoing sketch of the "interaction view" is that it has to hold that some of the "associated commonplaces" themselves suffer metaphorical change of meaning in the process of transfer from the subsidiary to the principal subject. And *these* changes, if they occur, can hardly be explained by the account given. The primary metaphor, it might be said, has been analyzed into a set of subordinate metaphors, so the account given is either circular or leads to an infinite regress.

This might be met by denying that *all* changes of meaning in the "associated commonplaces" must be counted as metaphorical shifts. Many of them are best described as *extensions* of meaning, because they do not involve apprehended connexions between two systems of concepts. I have not undertaken to explain how such extensions or shifts occur in general, and I do not think any simple account will fit all cases. (It is easy enough to mutter "analogy," but closer examination soon shows all kinds of "grounds" for shifts of meaning with context—and even no ground at all, sometimes.)

Secondly, I would not deny that a metaphor may involve a number of subordinate metaphors among its implications. But these subordinate metaphors are, I think, usually intended to be taken less "emphatically," *i.e.*, with less stress upon *their* implications. (The implications of a metaphor are like the overtones of a musical chord; to attach too much "weight" to them is like trying to make the overtones sound as loud as the main notes—and just as pointless.) In any case, primary and subordinate metaphors will normally belong to the same field of discourse, so that they mutually reinforce one and the same system of implications. Conversely, where substantially new metaphors appear as the primary metaphor is unravelled, there is serious risk of confusion of thought (*cf.* the customary prohibition against "mixed metaphors").

But the preceding account of metaphor needs correction, if it is to be reasonably adequate. Reference to "associated commonplaces" will fit the commonest cases where the author simply plays upon the stock of common knowledge (and common misinformation) presumably shared by the reader and himself. But in a poem, or a piece of sustained prose, the writer can establish a novel pattern of implications for the literal uses of the key expressions, prior to using them as vehicles for his metaphors. (An author can do much to suppress unwanted implications of the word "contract," by explicit discussion of its intended meaning, before he proceeds to develop a contract theory of sovereignty. Or a naturalist who really knows wolves may tell us so much about them that *his* description of man as a wolf diverges quite markedly from the stock uses of that figure.) Metaphors can be supported by specially constructed systems of implications, as well as by accepted commonplaces; they can be made to measure and need not be reach-me-downs.

It was a simplification, again, to speak as if the implication-system of the metaphorical expression remains unaltered by the metaphorical statement. The nature of the intended application helps to determine the character of the system to be applied (as though the stars could partly determine the character of the observation-screen by which we looked at them). If to call a man a wolf is to put him in a special light, we must not forget that the metaphor makes the wolf seem more human than he otherwise would.

I hope such complications as these can be accommodated within the outline of an "interaction view" that I have tried to present.

VI

Since I have been making so much use of example and illustration, it may be as well to state explicitly (and by way of summary) some of the chief respects in which the "interaction" view recommended differs from a "substitution" or a "comparison" view.

In the form in which I have been expounding it, the "interaction view" is committed to the following seven claims:

(1) A metaphorical statement has *two* distinct subjects—a "principal" subject and a "subsidiary" one.[21]

(2) These subjects are often best regarded as "*systems* of things," rather than "things."

(3) The metaphor works by applying to the principal subject a system of "associated implications" characteristic of the subsidiary subject.

(4) These implications usually consist of "commonplaces" about the subsidiary subject, but may, in suitable cases, consist of deviant implications established *ad hoc* by the writer.

(5) The metaphor selects, emphasizes, suppresses, and organizes features of the principal subject by *implying* statements about it that normally apply to the subsidiary subject.

(6) This involves shifts in meaning of words belonging to the same family or system as the metaphorical expression; and some of the shifts, though not all, may be metaphorical transfers. (The subordinate metaphors are, however, to be read less "emphatically.")

(7) There is, in general, no simple "ground" for the necessary shifts of meaning—no blanket reason why some metaphors work and others fail.

It will be found, upon consideration, that point (1) is incompatible with the simplest forms of a "substitution view," point (7) is formally incompatible with a "comparison view"; while the remaining points elaborate reasons for regarding "comparison views" as inadequate.

But it is easy to overstate the conflicts between these three views. If we were to insist that only examples satisfying all seven of the claims listed above should be allowed to count as "genuine" metaphors, we should restrict the correct uses of the word "metaphor" to a very small number of cases. This would be to advocate a persuasive definition of "metaphor" that would tend to make all metaphors interestingly complex.[22] And such a deviation from current uses of the word "metaphor" would leave us without a convenient label for the more trivial cases. Now it is in just such trivial cases that "substitution" and "comparison" views sometimes seem nearer the mark than "interaction" views. The point might be met by classifying metaphors as instances of substitution, comparison, or interaction. Only the last kind are of importance in philosophy.

For substitution-metaphors and comparison-metaphors can be replaced by literal translations (with possible exception for the case of catachresis) —by sacrificing some of the charm, vivacity, or wit of the original, but with no loss of *cognitive* content. But "interaction-metaphors" are not expendable. Their mode of operation requires the reader to use a system of implications (a system of "commonplaces"—or a special system established for the purpose in hand) as a means for selecting, emphasizing, and organizing relations in a different field. This use of a "subsidiary subject" to foster insight into a "principal subject" is a distinctive *intellectual* operation (though one familiar enough through our experiences of learning anything whatever), demanding simultaneous awareness of both subjects but not reducible to any *comparison* between the two.

Suppose we try to state the cognitive content of an interaction-metaphor in "plain language." Up to a point, we may succeed in stating a number of the relevant relations between the two subjects (though in view of the extension of meaning accompanying the shift in the subsidiary subject's implication system, too much must not be expected of the literal paraphrase). But the set of literal statements so obtained will not have the same power to inform and enlighten as the original. For one thing, the implications, previously left for a suitable reader to educe for himself, with a nice feeling for their relative priorities and degrees of importance, are now presented explicitly as though having equal weight. The literal paraphrase inevitably says too much—and with the wrong emphasis. One of the points I most wish to stress is that the loss in such cases is a loss in *cognitive* content; the relevant weakness of the literal paraphrase is not that it may be tiresomely prolix or boringly explicit— or deficient in qualities of style; it fails to be a translation because it fails to give the *insight* that the metaphor did.

But "explication," or elaboration of the metaphor's grounds, if not regarded as an adequate cognitive substitute for the original, may be extremely valuable. A powerful metaphor will no more be harmed by such probing than a musical masterpiece by analysis of its harmonic and melodic structure. No doubt metaphors are dangerous—and perhaps especially so in philosophy. But a prohibition against their use would be a wilful and harmful restriction upon our powers of inquiry.[23]

Notes

1. *Any* part of speech can be used metaphorically (though the results are meagre and uninteresting in the case of conjunctions) ; any form of verbal expression may contain a metaphorical focus.

2. Here I am using language appropriate to the "interaction view" of metaphor that is discussed later in this paper.

3. Here I wish these words to be read with as little "weight" as possible!

4. Notice how this type of paraphrase naturally conveys some implication of *fault* on the part of the metaphor's author. There is a strong suggestion that he ought to have made up his mind as to what he really wanted to say—the metaphor is depicted as a way of glossing over unclarity and vagueness.

5. Richard Whately, *Elements of Rhetoric* (7th revised ed., London, 1846), p. 280.

6. Under "Figure" we find: "Any of the various 'forms' of expression, deviating from the normal arrangement or use of words, which are adopted in order to give beauty, variety, or force to a composition; *e.g.* Aposiopesis, Hyperbole, Metaphor, etc." If we took this strictly we might be led to say that a transfer of a word not adopted for the sake of introducing "beauty, variety, or force" must necessarily fail to be a case of metaphor. Or will "variety" automatically cover *every* transfer? It will be noticed that the O.E.D.'s definition is no improvement upon Whately's. Where he speaks of a "word" being substituted, the O.E.D. prefers "name or descriptive term." If this is meant to restrict metaphors to nouns (and adjectives?) it is demonstrably mistaken. But, if not, what *is* "descriptive term" supposed to mean? And why has Whately's reference to "Resemblance or Analogy" been trimmed into a reference to analogy alone?

7. Owen Barfield, "Poetic Diction and Legal Fiction" in *Essays Presented to Charles Williams* (Oxford, 1947), pp. 106-127. The definition of metaphor occurs on p. 111, where metaphor is treated as a special case of what Barfield calls "tarning." The whole essay deserves to be read.

8. The O.E.D. defines catachresis as: "Improper use of words; application of a term to a thing which it does not properly denote; abuse or perversion of a trope or metaphor." I wish to exclude the pejorative suggestions. There is nothing perverse or abusive in stretching old words to fit new situations. Catachresis is merely a striking case of the transformation of meaning that is constantly occurring in any living language.

9. Can we imagine anybody saying this nowadays and seriously meaning anything? I find it hard to do so. But in default of an authentic context of use, any analysis is liable to be thin, obvious and unprofitable.

10. A full discussion of this example, complete with diagrams, will be found in Gustaf Stern's *Meaning and Change of Meaning* (Göteborgs Högskolas Arsakrift, vol. 38, 1932, part I) pp. 300 ff. Stern's account tries to show how the reader is led by the context to *select* from the connotation of "lion" the attribute (bravery) that will fit Richard the man. I take him to be defending a form of the substitution view.

11. Aristotle ascribed the use of metaphor to delight in learning; Cicero traces delight in metaphor to the enjoyment of the author's ingenuity in overpassing the immediate, or in the vivid presentation of the principal subject. For references to these and other traditional views, see E. M. Cope, *An Introduction to Aristotle's Rhetoric* (London, 1867), "Appendix B to Book III, Ch. II: *On Metaphor.*"

12. Thus Stern (*op. cit.*) says of all figures of speech that "they are intended to serve the expressive and purposive functions of speech better than the 'plain statement'" (p. 296). A metaphor produces an "enhancement" (*Steigerung*) of the subject, but the factors leading to its use "involve the expressive and effective (purposive) functions of speech, not the symbolic and communicative functions" (p. 290). That is to say, metaphors may evince feelings or predispose others to act and feel in various ways—but they don't typically *say* anything.

13. Whately, *loc. cit.* He proceeds to draw a distinction between "Resemblance, strictly so called, *i.e. direct* resemblance between the objects themselves in question (as when we speak of '*table*-land,' or compare great waves to *mountains*)"

and "Analogy, which is the resemblance of Ratios—a similarity of the relations
they bear to certain other objects; as when we speak of the '*light* of reason,' or of
'revelation'; or compare a wounded and captive warrior to a stranded ship."

14. Alexander Bain, *English Composition and Rhetoric* (Enlarged edition,
London, 1887) p. 159.

15. Comparison views probably derive from Aristotle's brief statement in the
Poetics: "Metaphor consists in giving the thing a name that belongs to something else; the transference being either from genus to species, or from species
to genus, or from species to species, or on grounds of analogy" (1457*b*). I have
no space to give Aristotle's discussion the detailed examination it deserves. An
able defence of a view based on Aristotle will be found in S. J. Brown's *The
World of Imagery* (London, 1927, especially pp. 67 ff).

16. Much more would need to be said in a thorough examination of the comparison view. It would be revealing, for instance, to consider the contrasting
types of case in which a formal comparison is preferred to a metaphor. A comparison is often a prelude to an explicit statement of the grounds of resemblance;
whereas we do not expect a metaphor to explain itself. (Cf. the difference
between *comparing* a man's face with a wolf mask, by looking for points of
resemblance—and seeing the human face *as* vulpine.) But no doubt the line
between *some* metaphors and *some* similes is not a sharp one.

17. The best sources are the writings of I. A. Richards, especially Chapter 5
("Metaphor") and Chapter 6 ("Command of Metaphor") of his *The Philosophy
of Rhetoric* (Oxford, 1936). Chapters 7 and 8 of his *Interpretation in Teaching* (London, 1938) cover much the same ground. W. Bedell Stanford's *Greek
Metaphor* (Oxford, 1936) defends what he calls an "integration theory" (see
especially pp. 101 ff) with much learning and skill. Unfortunately, both writers
have great trouble in making clear the nature of the positions they are defending. Chapter 18 of W. Empson's *The Structure of Complex Words* (London,
1951) is a useful discussion of Richards' views on metaphor.

18. *The Philosophy of Rhetoric*, p. 93. Richards also says that metaphor is
"fundamentally a borrowing between and intercourse of *thoughts*, a transaction
between contexts" (p. 94). Metaphor, he says, requires two ideas "which co-
operate in an inclusive meaning" (p. 119).

19. It is this, perhaps, that leads Richards to say that "talk about the identification or fusion that a metaphor effects is nearly always misleading and pernicious" (*op. cit.*, p. 127).

20. Usually, Richards tries to show that similarity between the two terms is
at best *part* of the basis for the interaction of meanings in a metaphor.

21. This point has often been made. E.g.:—"As to metaphorical expression,
that is a great excellence in style, when it is used with propriety, for it gives
you two ideas for one." (Samuel Johnson, quoted by Richards, *op. cit.*, p. 93).
The choice of labels for the "subjects" is troublesome. See the "Note on
terminology" appended to this paper.

22. I can sympathize with Empson's contention that "The term ['metaphor']
had better correspond to what the speakers themselves feel to be a rich or
suggestive or persuasive use of a word, rather than include uses like the *leg*
of a table" (*The Structure of Complex Words*, p. 333). But there is the opposite
danger, also, of making metaphors too important by definition, and so narrowing
our view of the subject excessively.

23. (*A note on terminology*:) For metaphors that fit a substitution or comparison view, the factors needing to be distinguished are: (i) some word or
expression E; (ii) occurring in some verbal "frame" F; so that (iii) $F(E)$ is the
metaphorical statement in question; (iv) the meaning $m'(E)$ which E has in
$F(E)$; (v) which is the same as the literal meaning $m(X)$, of some literal

synonym, *X*. A sufficient technical vocabulary would be: "metaphorical expression" (for *E*) "metaphorical statement" (for *F (E)*), "metaphorical meaning" (for m') and "literal meaning" (for *m*).

Where the interaction view is appropriate, the situation is more complicated. We may also need to refer (vi) to the principal subject of *F (E)*, say *P* (roughly, what the statement is "really" about), (vii) the subsidiary subject, *S* (what *F (E)* would be about if read literally); (viii) the relevant system of implications, *I*, connected with *S*; and (ix) the resulting system of attributions, *A*, asserted of *P*. We must accept at least so much complexity if we agree that the meaning of *E* in its setting *F* depends upon the transformation of *I* into *A* by using language, normally applied to *S*, to apply to *P* instead.

Richards has suggested using the words "tenor" and "vehicle" for the two *"thoughts"* which, in his view, are "active together" (for "the two *ideas* that metaphor, at its simplest, gives us," *Op. cit.*, p. 96, my italics) and urges that we reserve "the word 'metaphor' for the whole double unit" *(ib.)* But this picture of two *ideas* working upon each other is an inconvenient fiction. And it is significant that Richards himself soon lapses into speaking of "tenor" and "vehicle" as "things" (*e.g.* on p. 118). Richards' "vehicle" vacillates in reference between the metaphorical expression *(E)*, the subsidiary subject *(S)* and the connected implication system *(I)*. It is less clear what his "tenor" means: sometimes it stands for the principal subject *(P)*, sometimes for the implications connected with that subject (which I have not symbolized above), sometimes, in spite of Richards' own intentions, for the *resultant* meaning (or as we might say the "full import") of *E* in its context, *F (E)*.

There is probably no hope of getting an accepted terminology so long as writers upon the subject are still so much at variance with one another.

CHARLES L. STEVENSON

Interpretation and Evaluation
in Aesthetics

I

LET US SUPPOSE that a critic is in doubt about the meaning of a certain poem. He is inclined to take it as an allegory, for if he were content with its literal meaning, he suspects, he would be understanding it too passively—he would be bringing too little to it. Yet the poem sometimes resists the allegory; so he fears that in his efforts to avoid bringing too little to it he has gone to the other extreme: he has read meanings into it. Whether or not the poem is allegorical, then, presents him with a problem, one that is familiar throughout literary criticism.

His decision will be closely related to his evaluation of the poem; but it will not in itself be a decision about the poem's value. If he subsequently concludes that the poem is allegorical, for instance, he may or may not conclude that the allegory enhances its beauty. His problem is one of *interpretation*, and we can conveniently use that term to distinguish it from any problem of aesthetic *evaluation* that normally attends it.

We shall encounter the same distinction, though in a somewhat altered form, in this further example: Suppose that a critic is studying a non-objective painting. In certain of his moods, on attentively regarding it, he has experienced a subtle emotion and has felt that its lines form a unified design. These moods have been rare, however, and for the most part it has seemed emotionally weak, with lines moving awkwardly and pointlessly. So which reaction is he to trust—which reveals the emotion that the painting actually expresses or the design that it actually embodies? Are his rarer moods those of special discernment, enabling him to bring to the painting a proper sensibility; or are they forced, overwrought moods, causing him to project into the painting various elements that are foreign to it?

In this case the *relation* of the problem to an evaluative one is even

From *Philosophical Analysis,* edited by Max Black, Cornell University Press, Ithaca, N.Y. Copyright 1950 by Cornell University.

more obvious. If the critic decides that the painting expresses a subtle emotion or that it has a unified design, we shall expect him to evaluate it favorably. But the relation is presumably a contingent one. If he should go on to make an unfavorable evaluation, we should be surprised at his unusual taste; but we should not, I think, be inclined to say that he had contradicted himself. Or even if we should be so inclined—for the vagueness of our language does not permit a categorical decision about such a matter—we should not want to say that "subtle emotion" and "unified design" are *limited* to an evaluative function. We should want to separate, by abstraction, two aspects of their meaning. First they designate certain nonevaluative qualities of emotion or design; and then, as an independent step, they say that these qualities *possess* value or are *attended by* value. Hence the emotion and design are not *identical* with value, and questions about them can be considered as presenting distinct, nonevaluative problems.

Shall we say that the nonevaluative problems are concerned with an "interpretation" of the painting? If we do we shall perhaps be using the word in an extended sense. In our first example the use of "interpretation" was strictly conventional; but in the second, where emphasis on the cognitive meaning of a work of art gives place to emphasis on its expressiveness and design, the term has a way of seeming half-metaphorical. But however that may be, I propose to say that an "interpretive" problem is presented by the second example no less than by the first. For the examples have much in common: both require a decision about the way in which we are to experience a work of art—a decision about nonevaluative but aesthetically relevant elements that the work "has," as distinct, from those that are "read into it" or are "forcibly projected into it." The word "interpretive," no other familiar word being available, is convenient for emphasizing this important point of analogy.

We must be careful to distinguish this use of the term from another that is somewhat more familiar. An "interpretation" is often given by a *secondary artist*, such as a virtuoso or an actor, who re-creates the work of a primary artist by performing it. But as the term will here be used, an "interpretation" is given by a *critic*, whose aim is not to recreate the work but to decide how to react to it in an appropriate way and to guide others in doing so. In the first sense, which introduces topics that the present paper cannot discuss, one may interpret Beethoven or Shakespeare but not El Greco or Donatello; but in the second sense one may interpret the work of any artist whatsoever.

These remarks permit me to indicate, though still somewhat roughly, the scope of the present paper. It will be concerned with both interpretive and evaluative questions—though it will emphasize the former, the latter having had more than their share of attention in aesthetics. It will not attempt to *answer* these questions, however, since that is the task not of analytical philosophy but of art criticism. Its aim, which can be realized only in a partial way, will be to *clarify* the questions—to define the terms in which they are formulated. And it will draw certain conclusions, for which the study of terms will prepare the way, about the extent to which interpretation and evaluation involve matters of taste that are "not to be disputed."

II

If we generalize from the examples that have been given, we shall find that any problem of art criticism, whether interpretive or evaluative, can scarcely be formulated without reference to a fivefold distinction.

There is always (*a*) *a work of art*, which for the sense of words here in question will be a physical object or event. Let us assume that it undergoes no change during the time that it is being observed and criticized. In literature, music, and the ballet, the work of art can be identified with the physical events involved in various readings or performances. Let us assume that these undergo no change in the sense that any two readings or performances will be exactly alike. For although false, the assumption will conveniently exclude any question about "interpretation" of a secondary artist, which the limited scope of this paper (it will be remembered) does not permit us to consider. Now the work of art will be contemplated by (*b*) *an observer*, and it will be obvious that (*c*) *the conditions of observation* under which he contemplates it will not be constant. For if there is no change in the more obvious physical conditions, there will at least be changes in the observer's state of mind—in his sensitiveness, his manner of paying attention, and so on. (It is convenient to include the latter under (*c*) even though they might, alternatively, have been included under a separate heading.) With these changes, even though the work of art undergoes no changes at all, there will be correlated certain changes in (*d*) *the appearances* that the work presents to the observer, where this term is to be understood quite broadly, designating not only visual and auditory experiences, but many others, including those that attend cognitive and emotional reactions. We may tacitly ignore, however, the appearances that obviously have no bearing on aesthetic appreciation. It is these changes in the appearances, and various other changes in them that may reasonably be expected to occur later on, that introduce the problem of art criticism. For the observer is trying to make a decision about (*e*) *the aesthetic properties that are possessed by the work of art itself*, such as its grace, spatial rhythm, beauty, and so on; and he does not wish to say that it has all the properties that are suggested, at one time and another, by its appearances. In some sense or another he must distinguish appearances that are "deceptive" from those that are not. It is on that account, as the introductory examples have emphasized, that he finds the problem of interpreting or evaluating the work of art (of deciding what aesthetic properties it "really has") a difficult one.

The exact basis of this fivefold distinction, familiar though it is, could become the topic of a difficult and sophisticated analysis. It raises questions that fall within the problem of perception—of "appearance and reality"—which is only a little less perplexing to modern philosophers than it was to Socrates and Theaetetus. For our limited purposes, however, we may leave the earlier parts of the distinction unexamined, dealing only with the last one.

The reason is simply this: In aesthetics there is first of all the need for a middle degree of clarity—one that goes beyond common sense without yet aspiring to epistemolgy. For if epistemology must say the last word, it is not likely to say it tomorrow; and in the meanwhile, by accepting distinctions that in some sense must be recognized and by following out their implications, we can hope for a clarity which, if partial, is at least within our grasp.

Nor will the first four elements that we have recognized be suspected, on any familiar view of perception, of involving a distinction without a difference. If the physical work of art is repudiated as a Lockean substance, it is likely to be reinstated as a Berkeleyan sensible object. And if it is then identical with all its appearances, it is not identical with that particular set of its appearances in which we shall be principally interested. Thus our distinction continues to hold, as it does, *mutatis mutandis,* for other theories of perception. The controversy has not been about *whether* the distinction can be made, but about *precisely how* it can be made; and the latter question, important though it is, leads far beyond the middle degree of clarity that we must seek.

With regard to the last factor in our fivefold distinction, however—the aesthetic properties possessed by the work of art itself—we must proceed with greater care. For any misunderstanding there will be a misunderstanding of what is peculiar and central to interpretation and evaluation.

What can a critic be reasonably understood to mean, then, when he predicates this or that aesthetic term *of a work of art*—when he says (to take new examples) that it is "satirical" or that it "expresses nostalgia" or that "its perpendicular planes set up an internal tension" or that "in spite of its artistic imperfections, it achieves sublimity"? (Note that the first three terms emphasize interpretation and the last, evaluation.) We shall not be able to give separate attention to each of the many terms that are used in this way, but perhaps we can find the aspects of meaning that they have in common and that distinguish them from other terms.

III

Although factor (*e*) of our distinction is obviously different from the other factors taken separately, it may nevertheless be defined with reference to some combination of them: it may be defined, for instance, with reference to (*b*), (*c*), and (*d*). As we shall progressively see, that is a

tenable assumption on which to proceed. A part of what we shall be assuming, then, is this: Whenever a term is predicated of a work of art, and
assigns to it a property that is interpretive or evaluative, it will prove on
analysis to refer to the *appearances* that the work of art presents to an
observer. But it will not refer to all of these appearances; for, as has been
indicated, the varying appearances simply *raise* questions of interpretation and evaluation, whereas a term predicated of a work of art is expected to *answer* them. So a further part of what we shall be assuming is
this: The term will refer only to those appearances that arise under certain *conditions of observation*, and will itself implicitly specify what these
conditions are. Thus a work of art must be capable of seeming as it is, but
need not actually do so when the conditions of observation are *other* than
those specified.

Should this assumption be made for all terms whatsoever and not just
for those typical of aesthetics, it would imply that to be is to be per-
ceiv*able* and would introduce epistemological issues that we must be content to avoid. When restricted to aesthetics, however, it cannot easily be
questioned. A work of art that is beautiful but under no conditions can
seem beautiful or that is unified, poignant, and true to life, but under no
conditions can be seen, felt, or understood to have these characteristics,
may be a fitting object of contemplation, if you will, for speculative
minds; but for artists and critics it is devoid of interest.

How will our assumption work out on a concrete case? Since any interpretive or evaluative term will provide an example, let us arbitrarily select "cheerful," as it might be used in describing a musical theme. Now it
will be obvious that our assumption is itself sufficient to suggest the *form*
that the definition of this term must assume, namely, (*A*) "The theme is
cheerful" has the same meaning as "The theme appears cheerful to those
who listen to it under conditions *X*." And this in turn suggests where the
next steps of analysis must lead.

Although "cheerful" is the term to be defined, it reappears in the definiens with a change of context. So we have the question: (1) What does
"cheerful" mean as it occurs in the definiens? And there will obviously be
this further question: (2) What terms, specifying the conditions of observation, must be put in place of the variable, "*X*"? Let us discuss these
questions in turn.

The first question sounds paradoxical, giving the impression that any
definition of the form (*A*) is destined to circularity. But the paradox is
easily resolved. Like so many terms in our language, including all those
that here concern us, "cheerful" changes its sense with certain changes in
its context—an ambiguity that is not unfortunate, by the way, since its
contribution to linguistic economy outweighs any perplexities that it may
temporarily occasion. To see the nature of the ambiguity we need only
examine (*A*) a little more closely.

In the definiendum the reference to an observer, the conditions of observation, and the appearances is only implicit; and the burden of the reference rests on "cheerful" itself. But in the definiens the reference is explicit; there "cheerful" does no more than assign a quality to certain appearances, the reference to the observer and to the conditions of observation being made by *other* words. So the definition implies (and in a way that many epistemological theories will sanction)[1] that there are at least two senses of "cheerful": there is a complicated sense which assigns a property to a theme (or painting, etc.), and there is a relatively simple sense which assigns a quality to *certain appearances* of the theme. The net effect of (*A*), then, is to show how the simple sense can be used in defining the complicated sense.

Let us use the term with the subscripts "*c*" and "*s*," depending on whether its complicated or its simple sense is in question. We can then rewrite (*A*) in the following way: (*B*) "The theme is cheerful$_c$" has the same meaning as "The theme appears cheerful$_s$ to those who listen to it under conditions X." Hence question (1) does not indicate that the definition of "cheerful$_c$" is circular, but simply goes on to ask about the meaning of "cheerful$_s$."

A study of (1) and parallel questions would be of great interest, for it would locate and perhaps minimise a troublesome vagueness in the language of criticism. But, having now seen its relation to the rest of our problem, we must be content to leave it without further discussion. We must pretend, in fact, that not only "cheerful$_s$" but also a great many other *s*-terms, including the controversial term, "beautiful$_s$," can safely be used without being clarified. This will be pardonable, so long as we *know* that we are pretending. And it will be practicable; for terms are characteristically interpretive or evaluative only when used in their complicated senses, and all that is common to their meanings can be seen by examining how they are related to their simple senses, no matter what the latter may subsequently prove to be.

Our attention must focus, then, on question (2). With regard to schema (*A*) or its reformulation (*B*), we must ask what terms, specifying the conditions of observation, can replace the variable, "X." Or rather, since the cheerfulness of a theme interests us only as an example, we must ask about "X" in the general schema: (*C*) "The work of art is Q_c" has the same meaning as "The work of art appears Q_s when observed under conditions X," where "Q_c" is to be replaced, initially, by *any* of our interpretive or evaluative terms, and "Q_s" by the same term, used in its simple sense. It is this question that will be discussed in the following section and, more indirectly, in those that follow it. So for preliminary purposes I need only say this: The value assigned to "X" must contribute to a satisfactory analysis of the definiendum. And a satisfactory analysis (if I may speak with undue simplicity about a complicated topic) is one that is faithful to common usage without being bound by its confusions and without being insensitive to its flexibilities. In the present case we shall want to make the definiendum clearer than it normally is, but we shall not want to divert it from the purposes for which critics are accustomed to use it.

IV

Let us begin with a definition which makes only a slight, almost imperceptible advance, but which is nevertheless of interest: (D) "The work of art is Q_c." has the same meaning as "The work of art appears Q_s when observed in the proper way." It is obvious that in some sense, and so far as it goes, this can be accepted. It is equally obvious that "proper" is not much better than the "X" that it replaces. It will be useful only if it can be defined, or at least partially clarified, in its turn.

And yet "proper" must not be dismissed as unworthy of our attention. Like its near synonyms, "appropriate," "fitting," and "correct," it has a normative sound, and hence seems to belong to the same family as "good." Now the meaning of "good" has long been a subject of controversy; so we must not assume that a clearer version of (D) will be easily obtained.

Even "good," however, has *certain* senses that are not at all perplexing. Good soil is fertile soil, good money is money backed by a solvent government, and so on. It is just possible, then, that we can define "proper" in an equally straightforward way, if not for all contexts then for the special context that (D) provides. Let us try this, experimentally.

If we bear in mind the phrase, "Time will tell," remembering that time tells nothing without the help of critics, we may be inclined to propose the following definition: (1) The "proper" way of observing a work of art is the way in which it will be observed, in the long run, by the majority of critics who have studied it. But to this there are many objections, of which I can here take time to mention only the one that is most important to the later parts of this paper.

If in ordinary conversation a man should say, "In the long run the majority of critics who have studied a work of art will always observe it properly," he would be taken as an aesthetic optimist, maintaining that criticism is *progressing*. An aesthetic pessimist would immediately disagree. And the disagreement, in any usual sense of words, would be one that involved many complexities. It could not be settled in the way that (1) would appear to settle it—merely by making the optimist's statement, in its essential respects, true by definition and the pessimist's self-contradictory. So if definition (1) is to be considered at all, it must be with the understanding that it is irrelevant to such an issue: it leaves out from the meaning of "proper" any suggestion of optimism, or any suggestion that what is proper is in some degree good or desirable or worth cultivating. Having accepted the definition, a man is free to say, if he wishes, that the proper way of observing a work of art is one that no sensitive person, no matter how justified he may be in cherishing the arts, ever ought to respect. And with that restriction the definition becomes pointless for the purpose of this paper.

We are interested in "proper" only for contexts provided by (D) at the beginning of this section, one of the logical consequences of (D), for example, being, "A work of art is beautiful$_c$ if and only if it appears beautiful$_s$ when observed in the proper way." But if the "proper" way may be one that no sensitive person ought to respect, etc., then neither this instance of (D) nor any other will be acceptable. Meanwhile there is obviously some other sense of "proper" that *will* make (D) acceptable; and that we have still to find.

Note that the element that (1) disregards is normative.[2] To return to our earlier parallel, (1) is comparable less to a definition equating good soil with fertile soil, where any normative force of "good" is gratuitous, than to a definition equating good laws with those that the legislators, judges, and juries will eventually establish. The latter is either a way of using words to forward (perhaps inadvertently, due to a confusion) a legal optimism[3] or else, when it deprives "good" of its normative force, a thoroughly misleading way of changing the meaning of a useful term.

Let us now turn to a further example. It is sometimes said, and often implied, that the intentions of the artist must be the critic's constant guide.[4] If we let our definition reflect this view we shall have: (2) The "proper" way of observing a work of art is the way that the artist intended. This is initially somewhat plausible, but is nevertheless open to serious objections. One of the objections, in fact, is similar to that just given for (1).

As ordinarily used, the statement, "The proper way of observing it is the way the artist intended," has the effect of suggesting that the artist's decision is authoritative—of a sort that *ought* to be taken, for aesthetic purposes, as beyond appeal. And that is a controversial suggestion. Certain critics might repudiate it, pointing out that not all artists are great artists and that some are impossibly vain and pretentious, intending us to observe their work in ways that are absurd. Now no matter what stand we ourselves may care to take on this issue, we must realize that the authoritative position of the artist, so long as it is to bring with it an obligation of other people to respect it, is nothing that can be established as a definition. So we may conclude, as before, that (2) is neutral on such an issue, allowing anyone to say, if he wishes, that the proper way of observing a work of art is one that no sensitive person ought to respect. And seeing this, we are no longer inclined to accept the definition as suitable to the context provided by (D).

Let me add that (2) is open to a further objection. Suppose that a painter, looking at a work that he has just completed, finds it strong and dignified; and suppose that later on he can discern neither of these qualities. He does not wholly trust his later reaction; but he also wonders whether he should trust his earlier one—his creative enthusiasm may have caused him to think he had succeeded in expressing what he had actually failed to express. He must now make a critical judgment of his own work, and there can be no doubt that the problem will often be as difficult for him as for others. What will happen, then, if he makes use of (D) supplemented by (2) and draws the conclusion: "My painting is strong$_c$ and dignified$_c$ if and only if it appears strong$_s$ and dignified$_s$ when observed in the way I intend"? He will only be perplexed, and simply because he *has* no fixed intentions. He may, to be sure, acquire them later on; but it is also true that he may not. Each year he may see his painting with new eyes, never quite certain that his present way of observing it is to be his ultimate one.

This second objection, is, however, less important than the first. For we are not so much interested in examining this or that particular definition as in examining definitions of a certain *kind*: and the first objection to (2), which parallels, as we have seen, the objection to (1) holds equally well for many other definitions—for all those, in fact, that make "proper" a scientific or naturalistic term. So let me return to this objection, showing why it becomes relevant.

When used in contexts like (D), "proper" has a normative function which any naturalistic definition fails to make evident. In considering the definition, however, our familiarity with the term leads us to supply this element: we understand the definiendum in some other sense than the definiens provides. And then, in order to make the best of the definition, we take it less as a definition than as a judgment—one that weds the normative force of "proper" to the conditions mentioned in the definiens and thus favorably evaluates them. That is why (1) appeals only to optimists about the future of criticism, and (2) only to those who trust in the self-criticism of artists. But note that the definition, if we continue to call it that, now requires us to consider whether or not the naturalistic conditions, specified by the definiens *deserve* the favorable evaluation that "proper" gives them. And like any normative question about the arts, this belongs not to analysis but to criticism. A well-founded answer to it cannot be obtained merely from a study of language. Since we want the definition to clarify criticism, not to legislate to its conclusions, we immediately proceed, as soon as we see this, to understand the definition in a strict way, taking it as ascribing to "proper" neither more nor less meaning than the word is to have. That is to say, we inhibit our tendency to supply the word, independently of the definition, with its usual normative force. And we then see that the analysis proposed by any such definition is not acceptable.

What we must do, then, is to emphasize the normative force of the term. We must not tacitly use its normative force without analyzing it, nor must we leave it out. Rather, we must make clear what it is. And from the above discussion we may conclude—though not without the caution that this tangled issue demands—that we shall not be successful so long as we insist that "proper" be equated with purely scientific terms.

V

Although the above remarks have been negative, they have important implications. If they are correct—if "proper" is an other-than-scientific term and if (D), which defines the Q_c terms with reference to "proper," is in accordance with established usage—then this much is evident: All those questions of art criticism that are concerned with interpretation and evaluation, their nature being established by their key terms, will be (in part, at least) other-than-scientific questions. The critics who attempt to answer them will not be pure scientists; and the answers that they give, in the very nature of the case, will be of a sort that the methods of science cannot wholly establish.

This will be evident if we contrast the Q_c terms, which introduced "proper," with such a term as "red$_c$." Although the latter has an incidental use in criticism, I should classify it as neither interpretive nor evaluative, since it leads to a different sort of issue than any that "unified$_c$," "poignant$_c$," "beautiful$_c$," and so on, are likely to occasion. We may presumably accept, for "red$_c$" a schema like (C), page 471: "This is red$_c$" has the same meaning as "This appears red$_s$ when observed under conditions X." But here there is little doubt that "X" can be replaced by *scientific* terms—those referring to lighting conditions similar to daylight, to average eyesight, and so on. The vagueness of the term will allow us a certain freedom in replacing "X," to be sure; but the vagueness is like that of many other common terms and in this case causes no serious perplexity. So, "This is red$_c$" is directly open to empirical tests, both with regard to (a) whether the specified conditions of observing obtain, and (b) whether, under these conditions, the object appears red. For any interpretive or evaluative judgment, however, we have a different situation. The conditions of observation are there specified by "proper," which resists a purely scientific definition; the test corresponding to (a) above will accordingly not be empirical in any ordinary way; and the judgment, to that extent, will be other than scientific.

This conclusion should not be surprising. A critic is not altogether unlike a creative artist; for if he does not re-create a work of art in a literal sense, as does an actor or a virtuoso, he does so in a figurative sense: he re-creates it in his own experience, constantly selecting, from the various ways in which it can be seen, heard, felt, or understood, those that are to be actualized and perpetuated. Now scientific knowledge is not "the" concern (even though it is often "a" concern) of a creative artist; so may we not fairly suspect that it is not "the" concern of a critic? Although not decisive, this analogy suggests that our conclusion is free from paradox.

We must make sure, however, that we do not leave a scientific conception of criticism too hastily. And we must make doubly sure that the other-than-scientific aspects of criticism, if we are indeed to recognize them, are free from chaotic implications. Should they make reflective criticism impossible—should they require us to say, for instance, that interpretation and evaluation depend on caprice or depend on some "insight" that defies intersubjective test and hence is the practical equivalent of caprice—then for that very reason we should have to consider the possibility of rejecting them. We should have to question the previous steps in our analysis, seeking with greater care for definitions that were free of these implications. For an analysis that, to such an extent, undermined our everyday convictions would in all probability do so at its own peril and not at the peril of reflective criticism.

So our conclusion—that the key terms of art criticism introduce a problem which is partly other-than-scientific—can so far be accepted only in a provisional, tentative way. . . .

VII

What are the essential parts of a critic's problem, then, when he is interpreting or evaluating some given work of art? In the initial stages of his inquiry and perhaps, though in lesser degree, throughout all its stages, a critic is attempting to become familiar with the *possibilities* that lie before him. He is sampling, as it were, the apparent qualities of a work of art, seeking to determine the various ways in which it *can* be experienced. For if he ignores some of the possible Q_s's he will later ignore the corresponding Q_c's; hence certain interpretations or evaluations, of a sort that he might wish to accept, will not even occur to him. So he observes the work under varying conditions, attending to this rather than that, weakening these associations and strengthening those, and so on. In doing this he is not, *ipso facto*, deciding which of the conditions of observations are "proper." He is doing something preliminary to that and separable from it, if in no other way, at least by abstraction.

To this extent the critic's problem is obviously a scientific one: it is a problem of psychophysics. As dealt with by a professional psychologist, to be sure, it would lead to matters of great complexity. The last word of scientific explanation, if it were obtainable, would involve a tabulation of *all* the apparent qualities that a work of art can present, each of them specifically correlated with the conditions of observation under which it occurs. And it would involve knowledge not only of the remote conditions that determine aesthetic experience, but also of the immediate ones, including the physical and chemical states of the observer's nervous system. These are matters that lie well beyond the critic's interests or needs. But it does not follow that the critic is engaged in something foreign to psychology. He is engaged in the relatively simple, though still difficult, parts of it. In the same way a fisherman, learning about the weather from his own varied experience, is not doing something foreign to meteorology.

Having roughly familiarized himself with the ways in which a work of art *can* be experienced, a critic must proceed to make a selection from among them—a *decision* about how he is to observe the work in the course of his subsequent appreciation. There is no doubt that interpretation and evaluation require such a decision, in some sense of the word, and that it is a process of the utmost complexity. It involves a channeling, so to speak, of the critic's aesthetic sensibilities. The states of mind that he "brings to" the work he is appreciating—these in turn being among the factors that determine how he reacts to it—progressively become less subject to variation, certain of them becoming his own and others alien to him.

Although I use the word "decision" to refer to this process, let me say that I do so for want of a better one. For "decision" is likely to emphasize only those factors which immediately respond to volition and are relatively open to introspection, as when a man "decides" to walk to his office rather than to drive there. Now these factors by no means predominate when a critic "decides" to observe a work of art in this way rather than that. In certain cases, to be sure, they are not absent. Thus a critic of music can usually attend "at will" to the inner voices in a contrapuntal composition; and in listening to program music, he can deliberately control, within certain limits, the extent to which he permits himself to become preoccupied with the program rather than with the sounds. But in many cases—particularly in those where the channeling of the critic's sensibilities involves his receptiveness to certain emotions—the changes cannot be made "at will." They are subject to control only by indirect steps, in which voluntary effort is directed not to them but to certain factors which, cumulatively, may bring them about in the course of time. When I speak of the critic's characteristic *decision*, then, with reference to cases of the latter sort no less than the former, I must ask the reader to remember that I am using the term in a half-technical, forcibly extended sense.

The critic's decision is related to his problem in a very important way, as will be evident from this observation: Suppose that of the several possible conditions, C_1, C_2, C_3, under which a work of art can be observed, a critic decides to accept C_1; and suppose that under conditions C_1 the work of art appears Q_{s1}. In that case the critic will be inclined, so long as his decision does not alter, to say that the work of art has (or "really has") the property Q_{c1}. This last remark *presents* in verbal form his interpretation or evaluation. So between the critic's decision and his interpretation or evaluation there is a direct, intimate relation. (I shall return to this point in subsequent sections.)

So far we have seen that the critic must (*a*) learn about the *possible* C's and the Q_s's correlated with them; and we have seen that he must (*b*) make a *decision* between the C's. Now (*b*) immediately suggests a further part of the critic's problem. He will not wish (normally, that is) to make his central decision in ignorance. Hence he must (c) bring to mind or acquire knowledge that will serve to *guide* his decision. Let me explain by example.

In one of his elegies, John Donne writes,

> . . . my love is slaine, I saw him goe
> O'r the white Alps alone. . . .[5]

Do these lines represent the lover's death as serene and noble or as horrible? We may be temporarily uncertain, since the reference to the "white Alps" suggests the former interpretation, whereas the accompanying context (which I do not quote) suggests the latter. So we must make a decision; and we can here make use of knowledge, as mentioned above in (c), in order to *guide* our decision. An instance of relevant knowledge is easily given: The Alps, which to us are a relatively accessible region and a symbol of natural beauty, were in the seventeenth century virtually unexplored and a symbol of a forbidding barrier between one people and another. This knowledge, when called to mind, is likely to lead us to avoid an anachronistic reading of the poem and hence guide our decision in a way that favors the second of the two interpretations mentioned.

In just what sense can such knowledge "guide" a decision? We must not suppose that a logical relation is involved. For a decision is a *process*, in which certain ways of responding to a work of art are accepted and others rejected. It is not, then, the assertion of a proposition (this being true for *any* usual sense of "proposition"). And only if it involved a proposition could it meaningfully be said to stand in a logical relation to knowledge.

Rather, the guiding relation is a *causal* one. The situation, when viewed with deference to the principle of parsimony, is simply this: Like any psychological process, the critic's decision has a great many causes; and among these causes we must include the critic's beliefs, which will not, of course, remain compartmentalized in a purely cognitive "portion" of his mind, but will influence him both conatively and affectively. Similarly, we must include among these causes the critic's knowledge; for his beliefs, when strongly confirmed, are the same as his knowledge. Now when his knowledge acts as a psychological *cause* of his decision—when it is *one* of the factors, that is to say, that determines him to make this decision rather than that—then it may also be said to "guide" his decision.

In many problems of interpretation or evaluation, it will be evident that the critic's characteristic decision can be guided by knowledge, and by knowledge of various sorts. In the above case, and in others roughly parallel to it, his decision can be guided by a knowledge of cultural history or of philology. In other cases it can be guided by a knowledge of psychology. Thus a critic may find that certain associations, though they intensify the mood of a work of art, do so in a way that is ephemeral; so he may decide to counteract these associations, preferring a mood that is less intense but more enduring. Note that the ephemeral or enduring character of a mood is one which psychology, often in its nontechnical aspects, can establish. Let me add that the critic may be guided, in part, by an inquiry into the artist's intentions (no matter whether these are fixed or variable) or by an inquiry into what the majority of critics are likely to say in the long run; for, although we have rejected these factors as unsuitable for a definition of "proper," we have not banished them from criticism altogether. Knowledge about them can serve, that is to say, as a part cause of the critic's decision. But since my general point will now be clear, I need not multiply examples.

Now here the critic's problem has again its scientific aspects. The beliefs that guide his decision will be open to empirical tests and hence to scientific methods. Nor is it possible to overemphasize the extent to which science, in this special way, becomes relevant. In the part of the critic's problem that was first mentioned, where he is surveying the various alternatives (the various C's with their correlated Q_s's) between which he must decide, we have seen that his problem is essentially one of psychophysics. But in the part of his problem that was last mentioned, where he is seeking knowledge that will guide him in deciding upon this alternative rather than that, he can confine himself to no one science. Potentially, all sciences have a bearing on his problem.

VIII

Among these many scientific aspects of criticism, then, where are we to find something that is more than scientific? There are two sharply different ways in which we might hope to answer this question. We might hold either that criticism involves some more-than-scientific *knowledge* or that it involves some more-than-scientific *aim*. And the second of these possibilities, in my opinion, is far more promising than the first.

For if we should develop the first, we should find, sooner or later, that our recognition of more-than-scientific knowledge requires us to postulate some special entity—some unique object or quality, or some unique, synthetic, *a priori* relation—which this knowledge is about. And such a view, even if it could be stated in an intelligible way, would run the risk of multiplying entities beyond necessity. It would be tenable only as a last resort.

If we develop the second possibility, however, we shall be able to avoid this objection. For the critic's more-than-scientific aim need not be one that a scientist cannot describe. It may simply be one that a scientist, in his professional capacity, does not *share*. It may be a noncognitive aim, not in the sense that it is unknowable, and not, in the sense that it is unguided by knowledge, but only in the sense that it is not directed *to* the acquirement of knowledge. Thus it need not involve any unique subject matter. The principle of parsimony can be retained without compromise.

So let us consider only this second possibility, working it out in detail. And our first and central observation in doing so is an obvious one; in fact it is so very obvious that we have made it, almost inadvertently, in the preceding section. We were there trying to emphasize the aspects of the critic's problem that are scientific; but these lay so near to the non-scientific aspect that we could not help but notice the latter as well.

More specifically, we noted the presence of what I called the critic's "decision"—the channeling of his sensibilities in which he comes to accept certain ways of observing a work of art, when appreciating it, and to reject others. And this very decision introduces an aim that is not a pure scientist's aim. For the critic's task is not limited, in scientific fashion, to one of accepting or rejecting, as true or false, certain *descriptions of* the conditions under which works of art are observed; it is concerned with accepting or rejecting these very conditions. His decision culminates not in a new scientific *belief about* aesthetic sensibility, but in a new aesthetic sensibility. It culminates not in an "I shall" but in an "I will," not in a prediction but in a resolution. A scientist may wish to *study* the critic's decision and all the factors that make it possible or determine its outcome; but he is not called upon, in his professional capacity, to *make* it. His study is one thing and the decision that he studies is another, to say otherwise being a particularly transparent instance of the "psychologist's fallacy."[6]

We have, then, in the critic's efforts to make his characteristic decision, an aim which is "noncognitive" in the sense previously indicated; it is neither unknowable nor unguided by knowledge, but it is directed *to* something other than knowledge. And in contrasting it with a scientist's aim, let me add, we need not fear that we are misdescribing the work of a scientist, implying that he is a purely cognitive being. The scientist too must make certain "decisions" in the very course of his studies; he must decide, for instance, what topics are *worth studying.*[7] But note that *his* decision bears directly on his knowledge; it requires him to accept or reject certain topics of cognitive inquiry and not, like the characteristic decision of a critic, to accept or reject certain ways of responding to a work of art.

So there is little that is controversial, so long as we hold that a special kind of decision is *one* factor that distinguishes criticism from science. The essential question, then, is whether or not this point of difference is the one that we have been seeking. Does it really color the critic's problem in an important way; and will it help us, once it is noticed, to find acceptable definitions of "proper" and of our interpretive and evaluative terms?

These questions will be answered presently and in the affirmative. We must begin by examining the critic's decision more closely, with attention to the scientific issues that surround it.

IX

Although we have just seen that the critic's decision is noncognitive, we have previously seen that it can be guided by knowledge. And it will be evident that for reflective critics, in whose work we are likely to be most interested, the decision will be guided in an elaborate way. It may be asked, then, why is it necessary to emphasize the decision at all. Could we not take it for granted and attend only to the knowledge that guides it?

Let me put the question more concretely. Suppose that a man, having for some years been a critic, now wishes to change his vocation and to devote his attention to purely scientific questions about the arts. He will no longer deliberately attempt, then, to make any aesthetic decision; but he will still be acquiring scientific knowledge that can guide a decision. Will there be any real change? Will not his decision, even though he is not concerned about it, attend his scientific inquiries as a kind of epiphenomenon?

A part of the answer is simply this: Since neither a critic nor a pure scientist can hope for complete knowledge, even about some individual work of art, each must emphasize certain beliefs and neglect others. Now a critic emphasizes those that bear upon his special aim—that of deciding how to observe a work of art aesthetically. Beliefs that he thinks will influence his decision are accepted as relevant and tested, the others being ignored as irrelevant. Although his decision is not immediately directed *to* knowledge, it has this *effect* on the sort of knowledge he seeks. A pure scientist, however, emphasizes beliefs for a less specific purpose: he is neither exclusively nor primarily concerned with selecting and testing just those beliefs that will alter his own aesthetic sensibilities or the sensibilities of others. So although the critic and the pure scientist may be alike in having beliefs that are empirically testable, they will differ in their manner of organizing them. And only when they are organized in the critic's fashion will they be likely to have a marked effect on aesthetic sensibilities. Even if an answer to all scientific questions were found and made available in a vast encyclopedia, a critic would still have the task of gathering together the limited part of this knowledge that is relevant to his interpretive and evaluative decisions and of bearing it in mind while deciding.

Thus the critic's decision is not epiphenomenal to his inquiries into pure science. It has its own effects, determining the extent and direction of his studies. We may conclude, then, that between the critic's aim and the scientist's there is not only a difference, but an important difference.

It remains the case, of course, that whenever criticism is reflective it is still closely related to science. Indeed, one might speak of it as an applied science. For in any applied science—in surgery, in bridgebuilding, or even in billiards—the same need arises for a special organization of knowledge, used for the purpose of influencing a *decision*. And if the term "decision," in such cases, has not the technical sense that has here been assigned to it, it nevertheless retains a sense that suggests interesting parallels.

But if we refer to criticism as an applied science—and I am not recommending that way of speaking, but only indicating that I have no strong objection to it—we must be careful to prevent the term "applied" from being deceptive. Now it will be deceptive, and strongly so, if it leads us to forget that we can say of most applied science precisely what is here being said of criticism: it is *more* than science. And it is more than science for the same reason. It requires a decision about what is to be done—and about what is to be done not merely for the purpose of acquiring further scientific knowledge, but for purposes that extend beyond the pursuit of knowledge. It requires a decision to make this surgical operation rather than that, or to build this kind of bridge rather than that, and so on. So, as before, the decision is guided by knowledge without being directed to knowledge; it is more than cognitive and hence more than scientific. But let us continue.

We must emphasize the critic's decision partly for the reason just given: it directs his inquiries, giving his knowledge a special scope and organization. And we must emphasize it for this further reason: it helps us to see that his knowledge, however carefully selected and organized it may be, does not guide him with the impersonal demands of logic. Between his beliefs and his decisions (as we have previously seen) there is not a logical but only a causal, psychological relation. Hence his beliefs guide him in a way that permits his decision to be colored by his own individuality.

Given certain beliefs about a painting, for instance, a critic may in fact decide to accentuate its colors and lines, letting its subject matter, with its various associations, occupy only the periphery of his attention. But if he had been of another temperament he might, with the same beliefs, have made the opposite decision. And the latter would have been neither more nor less "logical," neither more nor less "scientific," than the former. He is taking a step *from* knowledge *to* a way of observing—a step to which these terms, in any literal sense, simply do not apply.

We shall see this more clearly if we view the issue not as a personal but as an interpersonal one, as an issue that arises when two or more critics, interpreting or evaluating the same work of art, are attempting to come to a *mutual* decision about how to observe it. In the course of their discussion the critics will tend to extend and correct their beliefs, and in the light of their new beliefs some or all of them may be guided to new decisions. It is for that reason, in good measure, that they find discussion so profitable. But let us ask this question: Suppose that they should come to agreement about *all* beliefs that can in any way affect their decision, omitting no evidence and making no mistakes in logic. Will they, *ipso facto*, make the same decision? Clearly, their beliefs will not be the only factors that guide them, for their training and native sensibility will also be relevant. So they will make the same decision only if these other factors, too, are the same. And that is not at all likely. We must take account of individual differences; and in such a complicated matter as this we cannot suppose that nature has been miserly in distributing them.

No matter how scientific criticism may become, then, no matter how inexorably its scientific aspects are subject to the canons of inductive and deductive logic, it will bring with it no conclusions that impose a uniformity on the way in which a work of art must be observed. It may—indeed, it *does*—rule out certain of these ways, since no one, in the light of knowledge, is content to decide in their favor. But it will not rule out all ways but one. For knowledge influences each critic's decision through the mediation of factors that are peculiarly his own; it guides him but does not constrain him.

X

We have been led to these observations, it will be remembered, by questions about the meaning of certain terms, such as "allegorical," "unified," and "beautiful." Taking these instances of Q_c, we saw that they could presumably be defined by the schema: (D) "This work of art is Q_c." has the same meaning as "This work of art appears Q_s when observed in the proper way." But with regard to the meaning of "proper" in this context we were as yet able to draw only a negative conclusion: that it does not lend itself to a purely naturalistic definition. That suggested, in turn, that criticism involves an element that is other than scientific. We were unwilling to accept this conclusion, however, unless we could locate the other-than-scientific element as it arose in the critic's problem and could show that it does not undermine the possibility of a reflective criticism, in close touch with the sciences. So having first examined the aspects of criticism that clearly *are* scientific we concluded that the other-than-scientific element lies not in some knowledge or subject matter that is peculiar to criticism, but simply in the critic's special aim and, more specifically, in his characteristic decision. And we have since considered this decision more closely to see why it requires emphasis.

Our inquiry has not led us, I think it will be agreed, to ignore or underestimate the reflective elements in criticism. Although the critic's decision is not uniquely determined by his knowledge—although he is free to express his own temperament—the fact that he can be guided by knowledge is sufficient to show that his decision need not be capricious. And with this suspicion allayed, we are now in a position to return to the word "proper," in the hope of indicating the other-than-scientific aspect of its meaning in some more positive way.

We must obviously establish a relation between "proper" and the critic's decision. And yet we cannot assign the term a sense that merely *describes* the decision. For in that case it would remain a scientific term (the principle of parsimony excluding, save as a last resort, any subject matter that "transcends" science) and would be open to the objections that we encountered in our earlier efforts to define "proper" (see section 4).

Shall we say, then, that "proper" introduces the beliefs that *guide* the decision? That, too, would make it a scientific term. And it would raise still other difficulties: The beliefs that guide a decision are enormously varied; they are not the same for one work of art as they are for another; and those that one critic considers relevant, for any given work of art, may be considered irrelevant by another critic. So any definition, if it dealt with these matters, would have to recognize a complexity and ambiguity in the meaning of "proper" which—though it might conceivably exist—is scarcely to be accepted, so long as some simpler analysis can be given.[8]

There remains an alternative that we have yet to explore, and one that promises to lead to constructive results. It is possible that "proper" functions less as a *descriptive* term, giving information that bears on the decision, than as an *imperative* or *quasi-imperative* term, directly evincing such a decision or influencing it. This alternative has immediately two points in its favor. In the first place, it is in accord with our observation that "proper" bears upon the critic's decision in some other-than-scientific way. For an imperative, used to influence a decision (in our special sense of the term), is not an expression that is needed in a purely scientific study of the arts. In the second place, it helps us to locate the *normative* element which we found lacking (section 4) in the definitions we have discarded. For a norm exerts an influence, usually of a sort that extends beyond cognition. And exactly the same may be said of an imperative.

Let us begin the analysis, then, in some such fashion as this: (3) The "proper" way of observing a work of art is the way that *is to be* cultivated and maintained. . . . Although this is *only* a beginning—an additional clause being needed to give "proper" a specifically aesthetic meaning—it is at least serviceable in emphasizing the term's imperative force. The latter is preserved by the phrase "is to be," whose meaning will be evident from this example: When *A*, speaking to *B*, says that the task on which they are working "is to be" completed before they attempt anything else, he is not making a prediction about the task, nor is he merely giving an introspective description of his feelings about it. Rather, he is taking steps to *get* the task completed. In the first place, he is building up his own resolve, strengthening his decision. So, as it were, he is addressing an imperative to himself. In the second place, he is influencing *B*'s decision by addressing an imperative to him.

Before continuing let me remark that "is to be" is somewhat harsh and when addressed to another person tends to exert a unilateral influence, whereas "proper" is less harsh, proposing rather than commanding, and often permitting or positively inviting a counterproposal. If I were to remedy this inaccuracy, however, I should have to enter into an elaborate discussion of the *emotive meaning* of "proper," showing that its subtleties must be "characterized" rather than defined;[9] and that I cannot develop, even schematically, in the present paper. Nor is it wholly necessary. If the reader will bear in mind that (3) is rough and approximate, he will see, I trust, that it helps to disclose the cognizable but noncognitive element that we have been seeking.

We must now "test" (3) to make sure that it is correct. This is to say, we must observe how "proper" occurs in familiar contexts and determine whether or not our analysis of its meaning is faithful to common usage.

Suppose that a critic is temporarily *unable* to decide on a way of observing a work of art: he is in a state of conflict, half inclined to accept C_1, which is correlated with Q_{s1}, and half-inclined to accept C_2, which is correlated with Q_{s2}. Under these conditions he will say, in any usual sense of the word, that he cannot make up his mind which way of observing it is "proper." Now is that what we would expect him to say, if we take "proper" as having the quasi-imperative meaning of "is to be cultivated and maintained"? There can be no doubt that it is; hence (3), so far, is "confirmed." In fact our analysis helps us to supply an explanation: The critic withholds the term "proper" because, when about to use its quasi-imperative force to strengthen his decision in one way, he finds that a counterimpulse leads him in another way. He is uncertain not about how to *describe* his conflict, but about the direction in which to *resolve* it. He cannot make up his mind, then, about which sort of "is to be" expression he will address to himself. And for much the same reason he withholds "proper" when speaking to others. Should he assure them that C_1 (with its correlated Q_{s1}) is proper, for instance, he would be *recommending* C_1 to them; and he does not wish to advise others about a decision that he cannot as yet make for himself.[10]

Let us now test definition (3) in a further way. We have seen that it takes account of the element in criticism that is other than scientific; but will it take account of the element that is scientific?

Suppose that our critic has tentatively resolved his conflict: he has decided upon C_1 with its correlated Q_{s1} and has accordingly judged this way of observing the work of art to be "proper." Now he will probably not feel secure about this judgment unless he has *reasons* to support it; and can we account for these *reasons* if we take "proper" to be quasi-imperative? There is no difficulty about this, since any sort of imperative can be supported by reasons. When we say, for instance, "Let's schedule the meeting for Wednesday," we may give as a reason for our imperative, "Since there are no other meetings then, we shall have a larger attendance." Here the imperative exerts a direct influence, and the reason supports it by exerting a supplementary but indirect influence—one that is mediated by cognition. That is to say, a belief of the reason is likely to *cause* one to be more willing to do what the imperative recommends.

We can find a simple example of a reason in aesthetics if we return

to our question from Donne, as given on page 478. We there saw that a
critic might decide to read the lines as expressing horror, being guided
by the knowledge that any other way of reading it would involve a cultural anachronism. And we can now say much the same thing by using
the terms "proper" and "reason." Thus the critic may judge, "One reads
the lines *properly* (i.e. in the way they *are to be* read) only when he reacts to them with horror." And he may give as a *reason* for his judgment,
"Any other way of reading it would involve a cultural anachronism."

The example clearly shows that our *reasons* introduce nothing new into
our study; they simply point once more to the beliefs that *guide* the critic's decision. Hence they immediately restore the scientific aspects of criticism that our quasi-imperative conception of "proper" may at first seem
to exclude. And they bear out our previous conclusions: In the first place,
the reasons will take on a special organization, which is precisely the organization we have mentioned in section 9 when distinguishing criticism
from pure science. In the second place, the reasons will not serve to eliminate the critic's personal sensibilities; for their relation to the quasi-imperative judgment they support (which is the same, in essentials, as the
relation between knowledge and the decision that knowledge guides) is
causal rather than logical; hence they "guide without constraining."

It will be obvious that the imperative force of "proper" has far less effect, in influencing a decision, than the reasons that accompany it. That
does not imply, however, that definition (3) is injudicious in its emphasis, attending to the element that is unimportant and ignoring the elements that are important. For in itself "proper" actually *has* a modest
function. If we should encounter a critic who did no more than reiterate
that so-and-so is proper, we should feel that we were being advised dogmatically—advised without being illuminated. We should ask him for his
reasons, expecting illumination to come from *them*.

And yet "proper" has a borrowed importance, for it introduces a situation to which the reasons become relevant. Only by recognizing its imperative force, in fact, can we understand why the reasons that accompany
it are so varied in content. Only by taking it as noncognitive can we
become fully sensitive to the cognitive elements that surround it. The
reasons that support an ordinary descriptive statement of physics, for instance, are usually limited to the subject matter of that specialized scientific field and hence are not (relatively speaking) varied in content;
whereas the reasons that support an imperative sentence, that potentially
involve literally *any* kind of knowledge that may indirectly cause a person to do what the imperative recommends, can be highly varied in content and will fall within no one specialized scientific field.

There are two other tests of definition (3) that deserve attention. The
first concerns the "survey of possibilities," which attends the critic's decision and which, at the beginning of section 7, we classified as psychophysics. Will this survey be relevant, if the critic is determining what
decision is "proper," in our quasi-imperative sense? The answer is obvi-

ously yes; for in using any imperative—in strengthening or influencing *any* decision—one will wish to know about the alternatives that are open. To resolve upon the impossible, or to advise it, is futile; and to resolve on one alternative in ignorance of another, or to advise it, is to run the risk of subsequent regret.

Our final test introduces a somewhat different point. When a critic says, "Observed under conditions that are proper, this work of art seems Q_s," he will normally be unable to enumerate, in scientific terms, just what the conditions of observation are. He will have no doubt that there are such conditions and that they could be enumerated; but the actual enumeration, he will feel, will take him well beyond anything that he has already indicated by the term "proper" itself. He will occasionally have no other explicit knowledge of the conditions of observation than that given by the description, "the conditions that are correlated with Q_s." Now this observation, which holds true when "proper" is used in its ordinary, unselfconscious way, also holds true when the term is used as we have defined it. Its quasi-imperative reference to the conditions of observation does not enumerate them; it leaves that to be done, when necessary, by *other* terms.[11] Let me add that if a critic *does* go on to enumerate the conditions of observation—when he says that C_1, C_2, and C_3 are proper—he is not explaining what he means, as a preliminary to making a judgment. (That is the point on which definitions [1] and [2], which we rejected in section 4, became confused.) He is actually *making* a judgment, in which "proper" has its quasi-imperative force of resolving or recommending. So far, then, we have found several respects in which definition (3) is satisfactory and, save for its excessive harshness, no respect in which it is unsatisfactory.

XI

I have remarked that definition (3) is incomplete—that it requires an added clause if it is to assign "proper" a meaning that is relevant to the special contexts of aesthetics. The definition can readily be completed in this way: (4) The "proper" way of observing a work of art is the way that *is to be* cultivated and maintained—though only by those who wish to observe the work with care and in an attitude of aesthetic absorption. The added clause prevents the imperative force of "is to be" from being too extensive; it shows that "C is proper" recommends C only to certain people under certain circumstances. To those who are content not to appreciate the work of art in question, for instance, and hence do not wish to observe it for aesthetic purposes, the statement does not recommend C— even though it does, of course, put a vector in that direction which may influence them should they wish to observe the work for aesthetic purposes later on.

The restriction provided is rough; but I doubt that an attempt to im-

prove it would yield interesting results. The need of *some* such restriction
will be evident. Concern with the arts, even if it should have no other
effects, always takes time, and therefore competes with other activities—
with business, politics, and so on. Now when a critic judges that C (correlated with Q_s) is the proper way to observe a work, he is not, obviously,
recommending that people cultivate and maintain C in preference to all
other things they might do. He is scarcely in a position to estimate the
importance of cultivating C as compared with other activities, for the latter are by no means the same for all people or at all times. So he simplifies his problem, which is difficult at best, by letting others decide as they
will about *whether* to observe, for aesthetic purposes, the work of art in
question. Or if he does discuss that question he considers it a broader one
than any that falls within aesthetic interpretation or evaluation. For the
most part he is content to limit his influence to "those who wish" to observe the work for aesthetic purposes, discussing *how* it is to be observed
by them. And his interests, of course, are reflected by his central terms.

XII

Let us now return to such terms as "unified$_o$," "sentimental$_o$," and
"beautiful$_o$," with which our study began. Since these have been related
to "proper" by (D), page 472, and since "proper" has been defined by
(4), page 487, we have only to put (D) and (4) together; and the result,
for the special case of "unified$_o$," for instance, will be this: (E) "The
work of art is unified$_c$," has the same meaning as "The work of art appears
unified$_s$ when observed in the way that *is to be* cultivated and maintained
—though cultivated and maintained only by those who wish to observe
the work with care and in an attitude of aesthetic absorption. Thus "uni-
fied$_c$" (and any other Q_o term that is interpretive or evaluative) is disclosed to have a meaning that, in part, is quasi-imperative. If the previous
steps in our analysis are correct, we must accept this conclusion as their
consequence. But it will be well to "test" definition (E) independently,
to make sure there has been no mistake. Let us see whether we can locate
the quasi-imperative element in a simple context.

When a work of art seems disunified$_s$ to us, and when a certain critic,
A, says that it is actually unified$_c$, we wonder whether or not to change
our way of observing it; for his remark induces us (very slightly or somewhat strongly, depending on our respect for A as a critic) to see it as he
presumably does, and we can do this only by changing our aesthetic decision. And it is precisely here that the quasi-imperative force of "unified$_c$,"
becomes manifest. We do not change our aesthetic decision immediately,
since we do not want to yield to A's influence without deliberation; nor
would we always be *able* to change our decision immediately, even *if* we
wanted to. But at least A's influence leads us to take the possibility of

changing more seriously—and that, normally, is all that is accomplished by *any* imperative, so long as the imperative has no legal or physical sanction.

If we now go on to discuss the matter with A, we may temporarily stop using the term "unified$_c$," and instead make an overt use of "proper" or "is to be" or their near synonyms. We may tell A, for instance, that he is making "too much" of the work, i.e., more than is *proper*. Or he may tell us that we observe it "too passively," i.e., passively to a degree that *is to be* avoided. These words occur so readily in the discussion that it is hard to believe that they introduce an imperative element for the first time; it is easier to believe that they intensify the imperative element that "unified$_c$," introduced at the beginning—an imperative element that (E), then, has been correct in recognizing. And perhaps "unified$_c$" will disclose its imperative force, once again, at the end of the discussion. If we finally accept A's decision as our own (for instance) and if the work then seems unified$_s$ to us, we are likely to say, as A does, that it is unified$_c$. Here the word "imperatively" expresses our new decision and reassures A in his old one. (Compare this with the overtly imperative expression, "Yes, let's observe it in the way that makes it appear unified$_s$.")

We may "test" (E) in this further way: If the definition is faithful to common usage, we should expect the *reasons* for or against the judgment, "The work of art is unified$_c$," to be the same as those we have discussed previously (section 8) in connection with "proper"—reasons causally rather than logically related to the judgment. Now I think they are in fact the same, as will be evident from this further observation: When we at first object, as in the above example, to A's judging that the work of art is unified$_c$, we may give some such *reason* as this: "It can appear unified$_s$ only when observed in a state of mind that is tense and strained. Is that anything which it is proper to cultivate?" To which A may reply: "A certain amount of habituation is required, as for any new work of art. After that, there is no tension or strain." Note that these remarks, which obviously provide instances of the *reasons* that were mentioned in connection with "proper," here appear, and in a quite ordinary context, as *reasons for or against A's interpretive judgment about unity$_c$.*

Definition (E) is "confirmed," then, by the way in which "unified$_c$" is used in ordinary discourse; and the same can be said, *mutatis mutandis*, for the definition of any other Q_c term that follows the same pattern.

Let us note, before proceeding, that in any problem of interpretation or evaluation a judgment of the form, "The work of art is Q_c," will have a central place. Our analysis has emphasized it for that reason. When a critic hesitates to make such a judgment, or when two or more critics make it in diffeernt ways, then there is a problem to be resolved. When a critic makes it without hesitation or conflict, or when critics make it in the same way, then—from *their* point of view, of course, and not from ours if we tacitly diverge from them—the problem is no longer troublesome. We should expect that to be true; for the Q_c judgment introduces, by implication, all of the essential factors of interpretation and evaluation: the work of art, the conditions of observation, the appearances of the work, and the critic's decision as to which conditions of observation (with the appearances correlated with them) are proper. And indirectly, through the reasons that support it, the judgment introduces the *knowledge* that may *guide* the critic's decision.

XIII

Our analysis of the Q_c terms must end at this point, even though it is manifestly incomplete. We can readily see how "beautiful$_c$" and "unified$_c$," for instance, resemble each other in meaning and how they differ from purely factual terms. But how do they *differ from each other* in meaning? We have provided, by implication, this kind of answer: They differ from each other to whatever extent "beautiful$_s$" and "unified$_s$," differ from each other. And the answer, of course, is not sufficient. But a sufficient answer would lead to a study of the Q_s terms; and as previously stated (page 471) that cannot be attempted here. We must be content with having taken a first step in clarifying the interpretive and evaluative terms, even though so many other steps remain to be taken.

In this section and the following one, then, I shall be concerned less with developing or testing the analysis of the Q_c terms than with emphasizing some of its implications; I shall attempt to free these implications from certain sources of confusion. In particular, I shall say something more about the way in which interpretive and evaluative judgments can be supported by *reasons*.

We have just seen how reasons can be given for the interpretive judgment, "The work of art is unified$_c$"; and we have seen that these reasons are no different from those that support a judgment about what is proper, as discussed in section 8, and hence are intimately related to the knowledge that guides a critic's characteristic decision, as discussed in section 6. The same considerations arise, of course, not only for judgments about unity$_c$ but for all judgments of the form, "The work of art is Q_c," and thus for all interpretive and evaluative judgments. The reasons that support one of these judgments need not be identical, in factual content, with those that support another; but they are all alike in that they are comparable to reasons supporting an imperative: they are related causally rather than logically to the judgments they support and "guide without constraining."

Now in this connection there are two points that deserve further attention: In the first place, the reasons that support Q_c judgments should be more adequately illustrated; for otherwise their variety may be imperfectly evident, with the result that their importance may be underestimated. In the second place, these reasons must be contrasted with supporting statements of a quite different kind—supporting statements that, in a familiar sense, may also be called "reasons" for an interpretive or evaluative judgment and, if left unmentioned, might be confused with the reasons that have previously been discussed.

It will be convenient to begin with the second of these points—which is of interest, let me add, not only for avoiding confusion but also in its own right. We can then return to the first point in section 14.

To prevent ambiguity let us hereafter refer to the reasons that have previously been discussed as "primary reasons," and let us refer to those that are about to be discussed as "secondary reasons."

The nature of the secondary reasons can best be indicated by an example. In criticizing the landscapes of Rubens, Mr. A. C. Barnes[12] finds them "as a rule, inferior to" those of Claude of Lorraine. This is of course an evaluative judgment, "inferior to" having much the same meaning as "less beautiful$_c$ than." And Barnes supports his evaluative judgment with the remark, "because the animation and movement which are intrinsic to Rubens' technique are not adapted to the placidity so often characteristic of landscape." Now in some sense, this latter remark is a "reason" for the former. But note that it is not a primary reason. For a primary reason is always a *factual* statement. Here the reason is not a factual statement but is itself an interpretive judgment—such terms as "animation," "movement," and "placidity" being obvious examples of interpretive Q_c terms. I call it, then, a "secondary reason"; and in general I speak of a "secondary reason" whenever one Q_c judgment is used to support another.

Since the secondary reason in the above example is itself an interpretive judgment, it could be supported by primary reasons in its turn. Barnes provides it with no such support, and his omission is scarcely one that we shall wish to censure. For primary reasons lead to very complicated questions (as we shall see better in the following section), and a practical critic cannot always take time to make them explicit. And perhaps Barnes assumed that the primary reasons would be gratuitous—perhaps he assumed that the conditions of observation under which Rubens' paintings appear to have animation$_g$ and movement$_g$, and under which landscapes appear to have placidity$_g$, are so commonly accepted as *proper* that his own interpretation, concurring with the general one, required no defense. But however that may be, the interpretation given by the secondary reasons *could* have been supported (or attacked, of course) by primary reasons. And should any controversy arise about whether or not the secondary reason gives a correct interpretation of the works in question, it would lead back to the primary reasons, which would be essential in settling the issue, so far as it could be settled. It is on that account that the terms "secondary" and "primary" seem to me to be appropriate.

To explain the *modus operandi* of secondary reasons, when these are viewed in relation to an evaluative judgment that they support, it will first be necessary to make this observation about the Q_s qualities. Between beauty$_s$ and various other Q_s's, of which animation$_g$, movements$_s$, and placidity$_s$ are examples, there is often an intimate relation. Should we have an experience in which the first two of the latter qualities clash$_s$ with the third, we should be likely to have a relatively low degree of beauty$_s$ characterizing the experience. The relation between the Q_s's is contingent and subject to exceptions, but it holds often enough to be of interest. Bearing this in mind, let us continue the above example, at first paying less attention to the Q_s terms than to the quasi-imperative effect introduced by the Q_c terms:

By his initial evaluative judgment, Barnes tends to make us accept, as *proper*, the conditions of observation under which Rubens' landscapes seem less beautiful$_s$ than Claude's. But we shall not want to give assent to his judgment—unless, of course, we are content to set him up as our ultimate authority in such matters—until we have tried these conditions of observation ourselves, to make sure that we too consider them proper. And here we may encounter a difficulty. We may have very little knowledge about what these conditions are, being able to describe them, perhaps, only as "the conditions which, for these paintings, will be correlated with the relative degrees of beauty$_s$ that Barnes has presumably experienced." So our efforts to try out these conditions may be unsuccessful, since we are unable to locate them. We may accordingly suspend judgment, feeling that we do not want to make a final decision about what is proper until we have taken these conditions, which elude us, into account. Barnes's secondary reason, however, may not be attended by this difficulty. His reason, being an interpretive judgment, will tend to make us accept, as proper, the conditions of observation under which qualities of animation$_s$, movement$_s$, and placidity$_s$ are experienced; and we shall again not want to give assent to it until we have tried these conditions out. But we may now be more successful in locating the conditions; for in general we have a better idea as to what we must do—how we must attend to the pictures, encouraging these reactions and discouraging those, etc.—when we are looking for animation$_s$, movement$_s$, and placidity$_s$ than when we are looking for the highly generic quality of beauty$_s$. With regard to the interpretation given by the secondary reason, then, we may *not* feel that we have to suspend judgment.

By putting together the observations of the last two paragraphs, we can now see why the secondary reason is helpful. I shall consider only the case in which our reflections might lead us to agree with Barnes—i.e., lead us to make the same sort of *decision* that he does—without discussing the many ways in which we might be led to disagree.[13] Let us assume that, having initially suspended judgment on his evaluation, we later come to accept the interpretation provided by his secondary reason. We then maintain, as proper, the conditions of observation that lead us to experience an animation$_s$ and movement$_s$ clashing$_s$ with placidity$_s$ in the landscapes of Rubens, but not in those of Claude. Now these qualities, as we have seen, are intimately related to beauty$_s$, so when experiencing them we also experience, let us assume, the relative degrees of beauty$_s$ to which

Barnes has implicitly referred. And being confident that the conditions of observation that are proper for interpreting the pictures are also proper for evaluating them, we conclude that the landscapes of Rubens seem less beautiful$_s$ than those of Claude when observed properly—or in other words, that they are less beautiful$_c$.

So the secondary reason is instrumental in leading us to accept the evaluative judgment. And it frees us (partially, at least) from the fear of having made an evaluative judgment prematurely; for it helps us to explore certain possible conditions of observation which we might otherwise have been unable to take into account.

Had I space to do so I should say much more about secondary reasons. I should like to give a more complete account of their *modus operandi*, the above account being in several respects incomplete. I should like, moreover, to discuss them in connection with norms.[14] And I should like to show how they affect the meaning of many interpretive terms—explaining how these terms, being so often used in secondary reasons that support evaluations, come to acquire, by association, an evaluative function of their own.[15] But these are matters that I must leave until another time.

Enough has here been said, I trust, to prevent the secondary reasons from being confused with primary reasons and to show that the present analysis can recognize a place for both. And let me especially emphasize this point: the secondary reasons in no way make the primary reasons unnecessary; for, being interpretive judgments, they can be supported by primary reasons in their turn.

XIV

I have said that my discussion of the primary reasons, to which we must now return, is in need of further examples. Occasional examples have been given, of course, dealing with philological or cultural anachronisms, with the comparative permanence of certain moods (see page 479), with the intentions of the artist, and so on. But in addition to these somewhat obvious primary reasons there are others that, in promise, seem to me more interesting. I refer to reasons that point out the *consequences* of that channeling of sensibilities that I have called the critic's "decision"— consequences that bear not merely on subsequent artistic experience but upon various aspects of practical life. But perhaps this suggestion will immediately provoke a question.

It is widely held that beauty$_s$ is experienced only when patterns$_s$, emotions$_s$, and meanings$_s$ are dwelt upon for their own sake, rather than as cues to practical action or theoretical speculation. When appreciating, one dwells upon the "aesthetic surface." It may be asked, then, how the reasons that I have envisaged—reasons that deal expressly with practical consequences—can help but be foreign to aesthetics.

The answer is simply this: It is the task of a critic not merely to dwell upon an aesthetic surface, but to make up his mind, and to help others make up their minds, *which* aesthetic surface is to be dwelt upon. For an aesthetic surface is an experience; and as we have repeatedly seen, a given work of art brings with it not some one experience, but many possibilities of experience, the possibility that is in fact realized depending upon one's aesthetic decision. So if we acknowledge that the contemplation of an aesthetic surface, once selected, involves a non-speculative, nonpractical state of mind, we need not acknowledge, and in sanity we must wholly deny, that the same state of mind attends the decision governing its selection.

When a critic is making his characteristic decision, how *can* he be non-speculative and nonpractical? It is true that he can temporarily avoid *certain* practical matters. I have myself remarked (section 11) that in interpretation and aesthetic evaluation a critic will address his suggestions to "those who wish" to observe a given work for aesthetic purposes, thereby avoiding the often practical problem of indicating who should or should not, amid competing activities, actually appreciate it. But *other* practical matters are likely to influence the decision even of those who definitely *do* wish to observe the work for aesthetic purposes, and these virtually cannot be ignored.

For example, should a man react to a poem in a way that involves many stock responses, even though the poem permits more subtle reactions—and Mr. I. A. Richards has cited examples of this[16]—we might wish to say that he is approaching it improperly. What primary reasons could we give for our judgment, particularly if his reactions are immediately agreeable to him? We could say what Richards himself has said: the stock responses transfer to practical life, with effects that the man will not welcome. He will then avoid them, should we establish our point, only as a means of avoiding their practical effects, not as unpleasant "surfaces" to dwell upon. But in any case he may be led to a new channeling of his sensibilities and gradually come to dwell upon another sort of surface. So the fact that his decision was *guided by* practical matters does not deprive his experience, when he returns to the poem, of its aesthetic character. Let me add that he is likely, later on, to find stock responses (I refer only to crude ones, of course) unrewarding even to dwell upon; for what is first avoided as a means of escaping certain effects often comes, by a process of conditioning, to be distasteful in itself. If aesthetic experience is different from the experience that attends practical activity, it does not follow that the two are causally unrelated.

Let me take a further example. Camille Bellaigue once wrote of Debussy's *Pelléas and Mélisande*, "Art such as this is unhealthy and harmful. . . . Its hardly perceptible vitality tends to the lowering and the ruin of our existence. It contains germs, not of life and progress, but of decadence and death."[17] To this one might wish to reply, on the basis of observations that time has since made possible, that the fears are groundless, that one can immunize himself to the "unhealthy" aspects of the music and progressively grow sensitive to other aspects that are "healthy."

But would such an issue be aside from the point—irrelevant to pure criticism? To say so is to run the risk of making criticism altogether too pure for comfort. One's effort to immunize himself to the "unhealthy" aspects of the music, though practically motivated, is not hostile to aesthetic experience. As in the preceding example, it simply alters one's sensibility; it still permits him, when later appreciating the music, to dwell with aesthetic immediacy upon the new forms and moods that the music then occasions. And in this case we have a further consideration: a man who has practical fears of the music is insistently *prevented* from dwelling on its forms and moods. So if we refuse to discuss his fears and engage only in "pure" criticism, we narrow our considerations in a curious way. In insisting on the demands of aesthetic experience we neglect the factors that make it possible.

So there is no irrelevance in the variety of the practical, primary reasons by which an aesthetic decision may be guided. There is a genuine problem, of course, in establishing the reasons as true—one that is all too genuine. No one can be perfectly sure, for instance, just how much stock responses to poetry actually transfer elsewhere, or just how much one can actually immunize himself to "unhealthy" aspects of music; nor are intuitive convictions an adequate substitute for controlled experiment and intersubjective evidence. But that is only to say that criticism is difficult, and all the more difficult when it ceases to be superficial.

Throughout all history critics have wanted a philosophical basis for their judgments. They have profited little, however, by vast speculative generalizations, cut off from the sciences and set up in rivalry to them. So perhaps, in their place, critics can find a basis in the form of a more comprehensive, more carefully organized body of empirically verified primary reasons, *guiding* their judgments in the way I have described. Their results, to be sure, will always fall short of finality; for their reasons will be elusive, manifold, never more than probable; and their tastes, which in part will depend on factors *other* than these reasons, will be likely to diverge in this way or that and remain subject to variation. But let us not forget this: these critics will always have a direction in which to travel and a not unreasonable hope that discussion and inquiry, whether it provokes agreement or dissent, will progressively be attended by a greater enlightenment and a richer reward.

Notes

1. See C. I. Lewis's distinction between properties and qualia, *Mind and the World Order* (1929), pp. 121 ff. Note that in *some sense* the distinction will reappear in epistemological theories that differ sharply from Lewis's. A materialist, for instance, can distinguish between properties of objects and qualities of their appearances, even though he takes the appearances as physiological

reactions caused by the object in an observer's body. Once again, the question is not *whether* the distinction can be made, but *just how* it can be made, the latter lying beyond our present interests.

2. This "normative" element has so far been indicated by the words "optimist," "progress," "worth cultivating," "ought," etc. Do they actually disclose an element which definition (1) of "proper" has omitted? My argument can appeal only to introspection on this point; and I think that no other argument, on such an issue, can avoid such an appeal. Indeed, it is less an "argument" than a way of directing attention: it supplies contexts which help the reader to become aware of his linguistic habits and to notice how the proposed definition would require him to change them.

3. For a discussion of the semantic principles involved in such cases see my *Ethics and Language* (1944), ch. ix, or my paper "Persuasive Definitions," *Mind*, XLVII (1938), 331-350.

4. A penetrating criticism of this view has been given by W. K. Wimsatt and M. C. Beardsley, "The Intentional Fallacy," *Sewanee Review*, LIV (1946), 468-488. They are discussing a different form of the view, however, from the one I am discussing. They ask: Must a critic compare what an artist actually expressed with what he intended to express, and judge his work accordingly? Whereas I am concerned only with what the artist's work actually expressed, and am asking, in effect, whether certain intentions of the artist are relevant even in determining that.

5. "Elegie XVI," Nonesuch Press ed. of Donne's works, edited by John Hayward (1929), p. 90.

6. See William James, *Principles of Psychology* (1890), vol. I, ch. vii, last section. One is said to commit the "psychologist's fallacy" when, in describing a given state of mind, he erroneously ascribes to *it* the characteristics that attend his own state of mind as he studies it—when he confusedly assumes, as it were, that the proper study of mankind is man studying man.

7. A judgment about what is *worth* studying, though one that a scientist makes, is not, as I see it, a scientific judgment. I should classify it as an evaluative judgment about science. Or should anyone wish to classify it as "scientific" in some broader sense of that term, then at least I should want to point out that it is not directly testable by inductive methods, but requires indirect and less definitive methods of the sort I have discussed in my *Ethics and Language*. So the similarity between a scientist's decision and a critic's (which is generic only) does not, in my opinion, show that a direct use of induction pervades science and criticism alike. It shows, rather, that an *indirect* use of induction, of a sort that will presently be recognized here for criticism, also attends certain problems of evaluation that are particularly interesting to scientists.

8. I do not wish, however, positively to exclude this type of definition from aesthetics. When "proper" is allowed to refer to the factors that guide a decision, much the same considerations arise that I have discussed in my *Ethics and Language,* ch. ix and ch. x, where I deal with "the second pattern of analysis." For those familiar with those chapters let me simply say that second-pattern definitions are persuasive, and although persuasive definitions have often an important use, they are not of the sort that can be defended within analysis itself, but lead directly to questions that are normative. When merely analyzing, one can do no more than give "samples" of the many persuasive definitions that are linguistically possible. But for the "first pattern of analysis," which in effect I am about to follow here for "proper," a normatively neutral characterization of meaning, yielding a sense that *could* be used in all typical contexts, becomes possible.

9. See *Ethics and Language*, ch. iii and ch. iv, particularly p. 82.

10. Let me reiterate the following point, even though I may seem to belabor it: The distinguishing feature of "proper" lies not in its exerting an influence, but in exerting an influence that is not immediately *directed* to cognition. *All* words have *some* influence, both on those who use them and those who hear them. The essentially cognitive term, "true," for instance, influences beliefs. In fact it may be withheld when the speaker has *conflicting* inclinations to believe; for he then wishes to avoid expressing his own beliefs prematurely, and to avoid exerting a premature influence on the beliefs of others. But it is one thing to influence beliefs and another thing to influence the characteristic decision that attends aesthetic interpretation and evaluation: and "proper" remains distinct from any scientific term in that it has the latter function in a direct, quasi-imperative way.

11. If I were not deliberately ignoring the possibility of a "second-pattern" analysis of "proper" (see note 8) I should here have to introduce a number of qualifying remarks.

12. *The Art in Painting* (1937), p. 279.

13. When people make the same sort of decision, their agreement is analogous, in important respects to the "agreement in attitude" that I have discussed in *Ethics and Language,* particularly ch. 1.

14. For an interesting discussion of evaluations, reasons, and norms, see Arnold Isenberg's paper, "Critical Communication," in *Phil. Rev.* LVIII (1949), 330-344. Isenberg presumably regards the reasons he discusses as factual; but many of his conclusions, including those about the practicability of criticizing without the use of articulate norms, would hold if the reasons were taken, in my own fashion, as "secondary," and hence interpretive and quasi-imperative.

15. In other words, we must recognize "two aspects of their meaning," as already mentioned in passing. I have subsequently ignored the evaluative element in some of my "interpretive" terms, finding it necessary to sacrifice accuracy to simplicity.

16. *Practical Criticism* (1930), particularly pp. 240-242; and *Principles of Literary Criticism* (1924), pp. 202 f.

17. An early criticism, quoted by Edward Lockspeiser in *Debussy* (1936).

Interpreting Works of Art

Although the two may sometimes overlap, there is a difference between *describing* a work of art and *interpreting* it. To say that Manet's "Olympia" contains a nude woman is to describe that picture, in part, but not to interpret it. So also for saying that the atmosphere of a Dutch interior is peaceful and homelike.[1] Hence Panofsky is in general right to speak of statements about "primary" or "natural" subject matter and about "expressional meanings" as descriptions rather than interpretations.

Statements about the obvious in a work of art, about what Aiken calls the "immediately perceivable," we classify as descriptions. An interpretation, however, is a species of explanation whose function is to aid understanding and appreciation. For example, in the case of pictures the "motifs" of which are not all readily recognizable, to identify a certain shape as this rather than that is to interpret. Hence, even statements about natural subject matter or expressive characteristics, that is, about what Panofsky calls "first stratum meanings," can be interpretations. Think of all that has been said about the Mona Lisa's smile.

Similarly, statements about "secondary or conventional subject matter" are sometimes descriptions. Not all iconographical identifications are interpretations. That a figure in a picture is St. Bartholomew might be just as obvious as that it is the figure of a man. Would saying that the figure is St. Bartholomew be interpreting the picture or the "motif" in question? Panofsky's example of the picture by Francesco Maffei is a good one to illustrate what is meant by an interpretation, for here it is not obvious just what the picture is a picture of. But this does not mean that where it is obvious—as it is, for example, in most pictures of the crucifixion—an iconographical statement is not a description but always an interpretation.

What Panofsky means by "iconological interpretation" is unclear. The fact that a mental patient draws certain motifs in a certain way may indicate to a psychiatrist that he is suffering from a form of schizophrenia; the drawings are symptomatic of the disease. On the other hand, the psychiatrist may use his knowledge of the patient's sickness to identify the motifs of those drawings. These are two distinct activities.[2] The same holds for works of art as "cultural symptoms"; the art of a period or country contains certain motifs rendered in certain ways that reveal—are "symptomatic" of—"the basic attitudes of a nation, a period, a class, a religious or philosophical persuasion." But to speak of works of art as "symptoms," as Panofsky does, is to suggest that iconological interpretation consists of using works of art as evidence of basic attitudes, etc., rather than of using our knowledge of basic attitudes, etc., to understand works of art. But which of these kinds of interpretation is relevant to aesthetic appreciation? Are both relevant? Or is the former chiefly of interest to archeologists, historians, and anthropologists, for whom a work of art is mainly an aid to understanding something else, not something to be understood in its own right? And is therefore only the former relevant?

Aiken considers the artist's intentions in relation to interpretation, appreciation, and appraisal.[3] We are concerned only with the relevance of information about the artist's intentions to the interpretation of his work, that is, to our *understanding* of it. We must agree with Aiken, however, on the distinction between the "ends or goals for which the artist may undertake his work"—his ulterior aims— and "what the artist intends to say or do in some part of his work"—his artistic intentions. These two are not the same, and only the latter is of interest here.

What sort of dispute is the "intentionalist," who says, "Considerations of artistic intentions are sometimes relevant to understanding a work of art," having with the "anti-intentionalist," who says, "Considerations of artistic intentions are never relevant to understanding a work of art"? Could observations, experiments, and the like, prove that the intentionalist is right and the anti-intentionalist wrong, or vice versa? Are their contentions, in short, empirical? If their disagreement is about the way works of art *are* often dealt with, then the intentionalist is surely right: considerations of the artist's intentions frequently are relevant to understanding his work, in the same way that certain observations are relevant to understanding the behavior of gasses at very low temperatures.[4]

On the other hand, if the dispute is not one that can be settled by seeing what we actually do with works of art, what sort of dispute is it? One possibility is this: the anti-intentionalist is *recommending* another way of dealing with works of art; the intentionalist is *defending* our present practices. Since both are concerned with what *is to be* done, or not done, we should expect their dispute to be irresolvable by ordinary empirical means.

Aiken's statement of the intentionalist position is not, however, free from a reformative element of its own. This emerges in his treatment of the question of the *adequacy* of an interpretation of a work of art.

"The relevance of any interpretation of a work of art," he says, "is always through appreciation." "Appreciation," he notes, is ambiguous, but in the sense relevant to the interpretation of art it has to do not with "my power to appraise but my sensitivity, my ability to discriminate and to be moved by the qualities of the work as a work of art." Appreciation is thus not the same as understanding. Understanding involves our sensibilities, our capacities for discrimination, but not our abilities to be moved by what we find. We can understand works of art that we cannot appreciate. Efforts to understand a work of art are only sometimes undertaken in the interests of appreciation.[5] In view of this, should Aiken's statement not read: "The relevance of any interpretation of a work of art is always through understanding or appreciation"?

"All interpretations of a work of art," Aiken says, "are bound to be selective and are bound to be slanted towards a certain mode of appreciation. And because in most cases alternative modes of appreciation are possible, there can be, as a rule, no such thing as a definitive interpretation." Is this so? Why are all interpretations *bound* to be selective, *bound* to be slanted? Is it simply because of the fallibility of human powers, or something else? What is the point of denying that there can be a definitive interpretation of a work of art? Do we know what a definitive interpretation would be? Would we recognize one if we found it? If the answer is "Yes," then what are the obstacles to our ever finding one? One obstacle can't be that every interpretation of a work of art is slanted towards a certain mode of *appreciation*, for this is false. Some interpretations are "slanted" only towards understanding. Why can we not understand a work of art "as definitively" as we can understand many other things?[6]

The adequacy of an interpretation of a work of art, Aiken maintains, is to be judged in one of two ways: by the adequacy with which it prepares us for a certain mode of appreciation, or by the relative satisfactoriness of the sort of appreciation to which it leads. But it is possible to find *Oedipus Rex*, say, a "more meaningful, more satisfying, more moving" drama if one adopts the misinterpretation of it according to which the gods punish Oedipus for his impious pride. Does it permit the assumption that this is what really happens in Sophocles' play, that what I have "read into" his play "is 'really' there in the only sense in which . . . such a question has any interest"? Isn't one interesting question not whether we should prefer this to happen in Sophocles' play, but whether it does happen? The misinterpretation is adequate preparation for a particular mode of appreciation. Is it perhaps an unsatisfactory mode of appreciation? But how is it unsatisfactory? *Ex hypothesi*, it is more meaningful, more satisfying, more moving. Does it matter if the interpretation is simply false?

Kaplan and Kris are also interested in the adequacy of interpretations and how conflicting ones are to be reconciled. If it is not to be a free-association game, the interpretation of a work of art presupposes "stringencies." It requires standards of correspondence, intent, and coherence, and these three types of standards, they note, are "inter-active," in that "an interpretation may begin with any one of them and seek confirmation from the others." But at this point a question arises if we suppose that the confirmation is not forthcoming: what happens when there is a conflict between interpretations warranted by different standards? Or is such a conflict impossible?

It is hard to see how an interpretation warranted by standards of correspondence and one warranted by standards of intent could conflict. Such a conflict would require, for example, that the Agamemnon mentioned in T. S. Eliot's "Sweeney Among the Nightingales" be the Agamemnon of Greek legend even while Eliot intended the name "Agamemnon" to refer to some other man. But if Eliot did intend "Agamemnon" to refer to someone other than the hero of Greek legend, then the Agamemnon of Eliot's poem does not "correspond" to the hero of Greek legend. To suppose otherwise is to "project" something into the poem that is not there. Standards of correspondence are thus controlled by standards of intent. If an interpretation, apparently warranted by standards of correspondence, logically conflicts with one warranted by standards of intent, then the first interpretation is wrong.

If there can be no conflict between interpretations warranted by standards of correspondence and those warranted by standards of intent, the same is not true for interpretations warranted by correspondence and intent and those warranted by standards of coherence. By the standards of coherence, "whatever 'fits in' is assumed to be intended." But surely many things might "fit in" an interpretation that could not have been intended. Virgil could not have intended any allusion in his poems to the coming of Christ, yet such an allusion might well fit in an interpretation of his poems. Christian readers of Virgil in the Middle Ages were clearly projecting things into his poems that were not there. This means that the standards of coherence must be controlled by those of correspondence and intent; or, as Kris and Kaplan put it towards the end of their discussion of survival, "The effectiveness of ambiguity for survival is limited . . . by the dependence which it involves on knowledge of subject-matter and of intent as conditions of coherence." Only in some such way can we avoid contradictions among equally warranted interpretations or remove conflicts among them. Which is not to say that *in practice* all such conflicts are resolvable; the requisite knowledge of subject matter and of intent may simply be unavailable.

How does one recognize a symbol in a work of art and tell what it symbolizes? According to Mrs. Hungerland, one thing is a symbol of another if the first suggests the second and if we transfer trains of thought along with related attitudes and feelings from the second to the first. But will this do?

Perhaps in the psychiatrist's consulting room this is how something is recognized as a symbol, but it is not how we recognize symbols in art. If we do not transfer our feelings about the forces of material progress and the laws of consequence in human affairs to the train in *Anna Karenina*, this does not mean that the train is not a symbol to us of those forces and laws. Even if we made the transference in question, this would not be the reason why the train is a symbol.[7]

A symbol is something that *stands for* something else.[8] Some symbols are conventional. According to one convention, white stands for purity, red for courage, blue for loyalty. The keys may stand for the powers delegated by Christ to St. Peter and his successors, the lamb for Jesus as the innocent sacrifice for the sins of the world. Many, if not all, iconographical "images" are symbols of this sort. If one knows the convention in question and has reason to believe it is being followed, he can recognize the symbol and tell what it is a symbol of. No transference of attitudes and feelings is necessary to recognize a conventional symbol or to tell what it symbolizes.

Conventional symbols present no serious theoretical problems, but nonconventional symbols are another matter. In interpreting works of art, we assume that everything in a work makes sense until we can show that it doesn't. Some things in a work of art are readily recognized as symbolic because they make sense only if they are symbolic. Christina Rossetti's poem and Eliot's "Little Gidding" are cases in point. But if everything in a work of art makes sense on the "literal" level, is there any reason to suppose that it contains symbols? Sometimes there is.

Anna Karenina makes sense apart from our recognizing the train as symbolic. Why suppose, then, that the train is a symbol? Because of its *prominence* in the story; what calls for explanation is the appearance of a train at crucial points. Is this appearance mere coincidence? If not, another explanation must be found; perhaps the train is symbolic in the way Mary McCarthy says it is. Similarly, the journey of the poet in the *Divine Comedy* is symbolic—and we have Dante's word that it is—and so are the hardships of Aeneas in Virgil. But what about the journey of the magi in Eliot's poem? Some works of literature can be read on two different levels, the literal and the symbolic. What is to be done with these? Barring evidence of intent to the contrary, can't the reader read them as he pleases? The only relevant standard of interpretation is that of coherence. But coherence, as we have seen, is not sufficient to settle a question of interpretation, if the question is one of fact. If, however, it is simply a question of how a work *is to be* read, Aiken's standards of adequacy are the only ones to which we can appeal.

Whether and how metaphor is interpretable would seem to depend on what we take metaphor to be. Black rejects two popular views of the nature of metaphor and offers a view of his own.

Is Black entirely fair to the "substitution view" of metaphor? Interpreting a metaphor *might* be like deciphering a code or unravelling a riddle, but how so? For a person reared on only literal uses of language, it might be very like deciphering a code; but a person acquainted with metaphor, like a man reading a message in a code he already knows, does not have to stop and think and puzzle his brains about the meaning of many metaphors.

Aren't there other reasons for the use of metaphor than mere decoration? In metaphors "for which the literal interpretation refers us to a broader class of things than does the characterizing term of the figure," says Mrs. Hungerland,[9] "there exists the potentiality for achieving stronger feeling and attitudinal effects by means of the figurative expression." Is this mere decoration? And by thwarting customary or stock responses to language, metaphors can encourage now efforts of thought, can stimulate new, unfamiliar, and potentially important lines of thinking. Is this mere decoration?

Black's objection to the "comparison view" is that it is so vague as to be vacuous, for two reasons: (1) one thing is not simply like another but is like it in certain respects; (2) prior to employing a metaphor we are often unable to find any resemblance between the subject of the metaphorical attribution and the literal referent of the metaphor.[10]

Suppose that (1) is true; does it constitute a criticism of the comparison view? Is that view committed to the claim that to say Richard is a lion is merely to say that Richard is like a lion? Richard is obviously like a lion in some respects and not others: he is brave, intrepid, and fierce; but he does not roar, have a tawny skin and mane, or eat raw meat. In almost any use of the metaphor, the context would make this clear, through what Black calls "the system of associated commonplaces." Nor need a comparison view hold that the resemblance or similarity in question must be "antecedently given," but only that there be a specifiable resemblance or similarity. Metaphors can "create" similarities only metaphorically: they sometimes call attention to similarities not noted before. But if a similarity exists, it exists independently of the use of the metaphor.

Can't everything Black says about metaphor in support of his "interaction view" be turned to account by a comparison view? Black lists seven claims to which the interaction view is committed. Only the seventh is "formally incompatible" with a comparison view; the others merely give reasons for regarding comparison views as inadequate. But do the first six claims do even this? Can no comparison view survive if these claims are true? As for the seventh, a comparison view does hold that there is, in general, a ground—whether "simple" or not—for a metaphor, *viz.* analogy, resemblance, or similarity.[11] Black admits that a metaphor is grounded on certain *relations* between the subject of the metaphorical attribution, *e.g.* man, and the referent of the metaphor, *e.g.* wolf. But what relations other than analogy or similarity are there for the metaphor to rest on? Does Black give us any reason to suppose that there are others? Until some relation other than analogy or similarity can be exhibited, the seventh claim remains conjectural.

Conflicts between different views of metaphor, Black admits, can be overstated. Instead of thinking of three logically conflicting theories covering all metaphors, metaphors can be classified as instances of substitution, comparison, or interaction. The main difference between them is, that whereas substitution and comparison metaphors can be paraphrased without loss of cognitive content, interaction metaphors cannot.

But how can we tell if any given metaphor is an interaction-metaphor? By seeing whether it can successfully be paraphrased? But what is the standard of success? If the paraphrase does not have "the same power to inform and enlighten as the original," are we then dealing with an interaction metaphor? How can we tell if it does not have the same power?

The interaction view tells us that "the literal paraphrase inevitably says too much—and with the wrong emphasis." Why "inevitably"? If a reader can educe implications for himself, can these implications not be educed for him by a critic by means of a paraphrase? And can't the critic explicitly indicate relative priorities and degrees of importance? Why must he present them as though they all had equal weight?

The relation between a metaphorical expression and its paraphrase is not the same as that between *definiendum* and *definiens* or between *synonyms*; nor is a paraphrase a translation—except metaphorically.[12] It must, therefore, "leave something out." But this does not mean that it must leave out some "cognitive content," that a sentence containing a metaphor and a paraphrase of that sentence cannot *say the same thing*.[13]

For Stevenson, interpretive and evaluative statements contain an imperative or quasi-imperative element and hence criticism, which consists largely or entirely of interpretations and evaluations, is an "other-than-scientific" activity. The procedure by which he arrives at this position, however, is filled with difficulties.

He takes as cases for analysis four apparently different kinds of statements: (1) "X is allegorical"; (2) "X is cheerful"; (3) "X is graceful"; (4) "X is beautiful."[14] Stevenson assumes that all four are subject to the same analysis, but is this a plausible assumption?

Although he admits that only statements of type (1) are, strictly speaking, interpretations, he extends the meaning of "interpretation" to cover statements of type (2) and proceeds to analyze these statements, as if whatever holds for them must also hold for statements of type (1). He would thus seem to base his case on the analysis of examples which he admits are not strictly cases of interpretation at all.

His examples of situations in which he imagines the statements he analyzes being used, are equivocal or border-line cases, *e.g.* situations in which pictures appear, only in certain moods or lights, to be unified. Are these the cases from which one would want to generalize about all interpretations of works of art?

Consider, for example, Stevenson's second case, that of the critic who, in some moods, feels that a nonobjective painting is unified, while in other, more frequent, moods he feels that it is not. Stevenson represents his problem as one of deciding which reaction to trust. But why should the critic "trust" either reaction? Should he discover that other sensitive observers have the reaction to the painting he has, must he not conclude that the painting is just one of those—and there are such paintings— that look unified sometimes and not others? If, on the other hand, other observers unanimously agree that the painting is unified, must the critic not conclude that those moods in which he felt that the painting was not unified were deceptive? In either case, is the critic's problem one of *deciding* how to react to the painting and of how to guide others in doing so?

The fivefold distinction which Stevenson claims must be recognized in any problem of interpretation is based on a model of visual perception. But how adequate is this model for understanding what is involved in interpretation? Do we literally *observe* poems and symphonies, or even pictures and statues when our concern with them is interpretation? And what are the "conditions of observation" in interpretation?[15] Having enough light to read by, enough light to see a picture; looking at a picture in white rather than red or violet light; not being so agitated or upset that one cannot attend to what he is reading, hearing, or seeing? Stevenson's references to moods, etc., suggest that this is what he means, but are these the "conditions of observation" in the interpretive problem connected with Donne's "Elegie XVI"?

Similar questions arise in connection with the notion of the "appearances" of a work of art; and these questions are important in view of Stevenson's "assumption" that the aesthetic properties actually possessed by a work of art can be defined with reference to the observer, to the conditions of observation, and to the appearances the work presents to the observer. On first reading *The Faerie Queene*, a college freshman might say, "There appears to be an allegory here."[16] After having been shown that there is an allegory, however, it would be quite inappropriate for him to continue to say that there *appears* to be an allegory. Hence, Stevenson's "assumption" *can* "easily be questioned."

To meet the charge that his initial analysis of "The theme is cheerful" is circular, Stevenson claims that words like "cheerful" have two senses, a simple one and a complicated one, and that the latter can be defined in terms of the former without circularity. Is this so?

Clearly the word "cheerful" can be used twice, once to describe a theme and once to describe how it sounds or "appears." But does that mean that there are *two different uses*, or *senses*, of the term? The term "red" might be used to describe an apple and again to describe a ball. But despite the fact that the word is used twice there are not two different senses of the word involved. Why should it be supposed, then, that there are two different senses involved in "The apple is red" and "The apple looks red"?

Which, moreover, is the "cheerful" in "That sounds cheerful, but is it"? According to Stevenson, it is "cheerful$_s$," for the cheerfulness here is what he calls "a quality of a certain appearance."[17] But the theme does *not* sound cheerful$_s$; it sounds cheerful$_c$. The doubt is about whether the theme is cheerful$_c$, and the doubt could not arise unless the theme sounded, or appeared to be, cheerful$_c$, not cheerful$_s$. Objects appear to have only those qualities they can really have; if an object cannot really have a quality, it cannot appear to have it.

"A satisfactory analysis," Stevenson says, "is one that is faithful to common usage without being bound by its confusions and without being insensitive to its flexibilities." If this is the case, is Stevenson's analysis of statements such as "The theme is cheerful" satisfactory? If not, does this not invalidate—or at least seriously weaken—the whole of his subsequent argument?

It is commonly thought that works of art have the properties they "appear" to have when they are "observed" in the *proper* way. "Proper," however, is a problematic term. Stevenson offers two definitions of it, both of which he rejects on the ground that they are "naturalistic": " 'proper' has a normative function which any naturalistic definition fails to make evident." But does "proper" always have a normative function in contexts like those considered by Stevenson?

Suppose a painter is commissioned to paint a picture for the ceiling or dome of a lofty church. In order to make his picture convincing or "realistic," he will have to make certain adjustments in the drawing of the figures or in the perspective generally. He intends the picture to be seen from a great distance and from an unusual angle. Here the *proper* way to see the picture is to see it from the distance and angle it was meant to be seen from; which means that you cannot see it in perspective *unless* you see it from a certain distance and angle. The proper light in which to see most pictures is white light or daylight, in the sense that you can't see them at all in the dark and can't make certain discriminations in them in colored light. The lines Stevenson quotes from Donne are to be read as expressive of horror: this is the proper way to read them; for unless they are read this way, as opposed to the alternative suggested, a cultural anachronism will be involved. You can *choose* to read them any way you please, but unless you read them in a certain way you will miss Donne's meaning.[18]

Why must a critic's statements always be normative? The answer to this brings us to the heart of Stevenson's picture of what a critic is and does. Stevenson envisions the critic making himself familiar with the ways in which a work of art can be "observed" and then choosing from among these ways or deciding on how he is going to continue to "observe" it. Having decided to "observe" it in a certain way, *i.e.* under certain "conditions of observation," the critic then ascribes to the work of art the properties it appears to have under these "conditions." His ascription or claim, put in verbal form, is his interpretation. This brings out what is "other-than-scientific" in the critic's enterprise: his job is to *decide* how to "observe" a work of art, and this decision is inevitably "non-cognitive."

This may describe the activities of some critics, but does it describe the "essential parts" of a critic's job? Could a man properly be called a critic if he did not behave as Stevenson suggests? Or would he be an atypical critic if he did not so behave?

Erwin Panofsky is generally admitted to be an expert interpreter of Renaissance art.[19] Contrary to Stevenson, Panofsky's activities give us the picture of someone engaged in an enterprise that is certainly empirical and governed by "stringencies" analogous to, if not identical with, those of the sciences. The characteristic activities of such interpreters are the sifting and weighing of historical evidence. Their "decisions" are indeed not like decisions to walk to the office rather than driving there, for they are "cognitive" decisions no different in kind from those of a detective deciding, on the basis of the evidence before him, who the murderer is. Hence we must ask if Stevenson's definition is not, to use his own expression, a "persuasive definition." Is he describing what critics and art historians actually do, telling us what is meant by "criticism"? Or is he assigning a task to critics, saying what he thinks they ought to do? Whether one wishes to call interpretive criticism a science or not, has Stevenson shown that interpreting works of art *cannot* be a scientific or near scientific enterprise?

Notes

1. Stevenson would classify statements like the latter as interpretations, but he admits that the word "interpretation" here "has a way of seeming half-metaphorical."

2. There may be a tendency to conflate them owing to the fact that both rest on the same empirical generalizations. If I know, for example, that only schizophrenic patients of a certain type produce drawings containing certain motifs, either I can infer from the fact that a given patient produces drawings containing these motifs that he has that type of schizophrenia, or I can infer from the fact that the patient has that type of schizophrenia that his drawings must be "read" as containing these motifs and not others.

3. Aiken's essay is in effect a reply to an earlier paper by W. K. Wimsatt and Monroe C. Beardsley, "The Intentional Fallacy," *Sewanee Review*, LIV (1946), 468-88, reprinted in Wimsatt's *The Verbal Icon*, Lexington, Ky., University of

Kentucky Press, 1954, Ch. 1. It is not entirely clear from Wimsatt's and Beardsley's paper just what *fallacy* is committed by one who commits the "intentional fallacy," but it appears to be one or both of two things: (1) supposing, erroneously, that information about an artist's intentions vis-à-vis his work is relevant to an understanding of his work; (2) supposing, erroneously, that such information is relevant to, or can provide a criterion for, appraising, judging, or evaluating his work.

4. To take a simple case, we sometimes want to know if a line of verse contains a pun. But can an expression contain a pun if no pun was meant, intended? Can you detect a pun simply from reading a printed sentence? If you think someone has made a pun and laugh at what he says, and he, catching the point of your laughter, says "There was no pun intended," was there any pun made at all? Or is the point of his remark to show you that you have made a mistake, that what you took to be a pun was in fact not a pun, despite the fact that the very words he used could have been used to make a pun? Can we make a man mean what he doesn't mean?

5. A professional art historian or critic, for example, might have no ability to be moved by some of the materials he works with; still, interpretation of those materials will be of direct concern to him.

6. If we attend only to "great" works of art, like the *Iliad* or *Hamlet,* our skepticism with respect to a definitive interpretation may seem to be justified. But are there not also quite simple works of art, such as an epigram or a ballad, which can be thoroughly understood?

7. That something is a symbol to someone may not be separable, in psychological diagnosis, from the emotional significance it has for him—why he feels that way about trains—but it is separable in the interpretation of art. The emotional significance something has for someone may explain why he *chooses* it as a symbol—why Tolstoy chose the train to symbolize the forces of materialism and human destiny—but it does not explain the fact that it *is* a symbol in a novel or painting.

8. This is not a rigorous definition of "symbol." The letters "U.S.A." stand for "The United States of America," but they are not a symbol of "The United States of America" or of the United States of America.

9. *Poetic Discourse,* Ch. IV.

10. Black says "between M and L," but this must be a slip of the pen. The resemblance is not supposed to hold between the metaphorical expression (M) and the literal expression (L), but between, say, Richard and the lion.

11. Whether this is also the reason why some metaphors "work" and others "fail" is another question, having to do with the job a metaphor is supposed to accomplish. And what is that?

12. See Isabel C. Hungerland, *op. cit.,* pp. 109-110.

13. To put the point another way: it is not a necessary or logical truth that no paraphrase has the same cognitive content as the metaphor it paraphrases. Hence, a metaphor can, in principle, be adequately paraphrased, however difficult it may be to paraphrase a given metaphor in practice.

14. For a different analysis of statements of type (2), see O. K. Bauwsma's "The Expression Theory of Art," and for a different analysis of statements of type (3), see Frank Sibley's "Aesthetic Concepts," both reprinted in Section IV of this book. On statements of type (4), see Section VI.

15. This question is of vital importance to the argument of Section 8.

16. Note, however, that a poem's seeming or appearing to be an allegory is different from a painting's *looking* unified or a theme's *sounding* cheerful, both of which might also be called "appearances."

17. " 'The work of art is Q_c,' " he says, "has the same meaning as 'The work

of art appears Q$_s$ when observed under conditions X." This means that "The theme is cheerful$_c$," is equivalent to "The theme sounds cheerful$_s$ under conditions X"; which means that "The theme sounds cheerful, but is it?" is equivalent to "The theme sounds cheerful$_s$, but is it cheerful$_c$?"

18. "*W* is the proper way to observe a work of art" often means no more than "Unless you observe the work of art in way *W*, you cannot see it in perspective (or you will be involved in a cultural anachronism, or you will miss the poet's meaning, etc.)." This is a straightforward naturalistic definition of "proper" which does not fail to make evident the normative function of "proper" in the cases cited, because in those cases, and others like them, "proper" has no normative function. It has a negative conditional function—"If not. . ., then. . ." —which is quite different and is capable of naturalistic analysis.

19. See his *Studies in Iconology*, New York, Oxford University Press, 1939; *The Life and Art of Albrecht Dürer*, Princeton, Princeton University Press, 1943; and *Meaning in the Visual Arts*, Garden City, N. Y., Doubleday Anchor Books, 1955.

Suggestions for Additional Reading

On interpretation:

Monroe C. Beardsley, *Aesthetics* (New York, 1958), 17-29, 114-147, 267-309, 318-352, 400-419; Campbell Crockett, "Psychoanalysis in Art Criticism," *J.A.A.C.*, XVII (1958), 34-44; William Empson, *Seven Types of Ambiguity* (London, 1930), *Some Versions of Pastoral* (London, 1935), *The Structure of Complex Words* (London, 1950); John Hospers, *Meaning and Truth in the Arts* (Chapel Hill, 1946), Pt. I; Isabel C. Hungerland, *Poetic Discourse* (Berkeley, 1958), Ch. VI; Abraham Kaplan, "Referential Meaning in the Arts," *J.A.A.C.*, XII (1954), 457-474; G. Wilson Knight, *The Wheel of Fire* (New York, 1949); Joseph Margolis, "Describing and Interpreting Works of Art," *Phil. and Phen.*, XXII (1961), 537-542; William Phillips ed., *Art and Psychoanalysis* (New York, 1957); I. A. Richards, *The Philosophy of Rhetoric* (London, 1936), *How to Read a Page* (New York, 1942), *Speculative Instruments* (London, 1955); W. K. Wimsatt, Jr., *The Verbal Icon* (Lexington, Ky., 1954).

On metaphor:

Monroe C. Beardsley, *Aesthetics*, Ch. III; Martin Foss, *Symbol and Metaphor in Human Experience* (Princeton, 1949); Paul Henle, ed., *Language, Thought and Culture* (Ann Arbor, 1958), 173-195; R. Herschberger, "The Structure of Metaphor," *Kenyon Review*, V (1943); C. S. Lewis, "Bluspels and Flalansferes: A Semantic Nightmare," *Rehabilitations and Other Essays* (New York, 1939); I. A. Richards, *The Philosophy of Rhetoric*, Chs. 5, 6; J. Szrednicki, "On Metaphor," *Phil. Quart.*, 10 (1960), 228-237; Gustav Stern, *Meaning and Change of Meaning* (Goteborg, 1931); Andrew P. Ushenko, "Metaphor," *Thought*, XXX (1955),

421-439; René Wellek and Austin Warren, *Theory of Literature* (New York, 1949), Ch. 15.

On symbols in literature and the visual arts:

Monroe C. Beardsley, *Aesthetics*, 288-293, 406-408; Richard Bernheimer, "Concerning Symbols," *Art: A Bryn Mawr Symposium* (Bryn Mawr, 1940); Maud Bodkin, *Archetypal Patterns in Poetry* (New York, 1934); Paul Henle, ed., *Language, Thought and Culture*, 196-257; Douglas Morgan, "Icon, Index, and Symbol in the Visual Arts," *Phil. Studs.*, VI (1955), 49-54; J. Schnier, "Art Symbolism and the Unconscious," *J.A.A.C.*, XII (1953), 67-75; Philip Wheelwright, *The Burning Fountain* (Bloomington, Ind., 1954).

VI

Beauty and the Aesthetic Experience

Introduction

———

THE CHIEF AESTHETIC QUESTION of antiquity and the Middle Ages was "What is beauty?" Since the eighteenth century, along with "What is art?" the question has been, "What is the aesthetic experience?"

Theories of beauty are of two kinds. Subjective theories hold that beauty, like pleasure, is relative to a percipient or subject; judgments of beauty are, despite their grammatical form, logically analogous to statements like "That is pleasing." And just as something cannot be pleasing without being pleasing *to* someone, so it cannot be beautiful without being beautiful to someone. From this it follows that there can be no genuine disagreements about beauty; the same thing can please one man and displease another; nor does Peter, who says that X pleases him, contradict Paul, who says that X does not please him. The fact that aesthetic tastes vary from time to time and from place to place is often cited in support of this view.

Objective theories maintain that beauty is a property of things as much as is color or shape; judgments of beauty are logically analogous to statements like "That is red." Beauty is no more relative to a percipient or subject than is any other property of things. If Peter says that X is beautiful, he contradicts Paul, if Paul says that it is not beautiful.

The subjectivist position is represented in this Section by a selection from Santayana's *The Sense of Beauty*. T. E. Jessop's essay presents a defense of objectivism.

To those who think of the aesthetic as synonymous with the beautiful, the aesthetic experience is adequately accounted for, once beauty has been defined. For those who think of the aesthetic in broader terms, the distinctive features of aesthetic experience must be sought elsewhere. Edward Bullough is one of many who have construed the question about the nature of the aesthetic experience as a psychological one. Bullough argues that it is a function of what he calls "psychical distance." Urmson examines the ways in which people explain their reactions to things for clues to the nature of the aesthetic.

Also relevant to the problems of this Section are the essays of Section I, the essays of Bouwsma and Sibley in Section IV, and Stevenson's essay in Section V.

GEORGE SANTAYANA

The Nature of Beauty

The Differentia of Aesthetic Pleasure
Not Its Disinterestedness

THE DISTINCTION between pleasure and the sense of beauty has sometimes been said to consist in the unselfishness of aesthetic satisfaction.
In other pleasures, it is said, we gratify our senses and passions; in the
contemplation of beauty we are raised above ourselves, the passions are
silenced and we are happy in the recognition of a good that we do not
seek to possess. The painter does not look at a spring of water with the
eyes of a thirsty man, nor at a beautiful woman with those of a satyr.
The difference lies, it is urged, in the impersonality of the enjoyment.
But this distinction is one of intensity and delicacy, not of nature, and
it seems satisfactory only to the least aesthetic minds.[1]

In the second place, the supposed disinterestedness of aesthetic delights is not very fundamental. Appreciation of a picture is not identical
with the desire to buy it, but it is, or ought to be, closely related and
preliminary to that desire. The beauties of nature and of the plastic arts
are not consumed by being enjoyed; they retain all the efficacy to
impress a second beholder. But this circumstance is accidental, and those
aesthetic objects which depend upon change and are exhausted in time,
as are all performances, are things the enjoyment of which is an object
of rivalry and is coveted as much as any other pleasure. And even plastic
beauties can often not be enjoyed except by a few, on account of the
necessity of travel or other difficulties of access, and then this aesthetic
enjoyment is as selfishly pursued as the rest.

The truth which the theory is trying to state seems rather to be that
when we seek aesthetic pleasures we have no further pleasure in mind;
that we do not mix up the satisfactions of vanity and proprietorship
with the delight of contemplation. This is true, but it is true at bottom
of all pursuits and enjoyments. Every real pleasure is in one sense disinterested. It is not sought with ulterior motives, and what fills the mind

From *The Sense of Beauty* (1896) pp. 30-41, by George Santayana, used by
permission of Charles Scribner's Sons.

is no calculation, but the image of an object or event, suffused with emotion. A sophisticated consciousness may often take the idea of self as the touchstone of its inclinations; but this self, for the gratification and aggrandizement of which a man may live, is itself only a complex of aims and memories, which once had their direct objects, in which he had taken a spontaneous and unselfish interest. The gratifications which, merged together, make the selfishness are each of them ingenuous, and no more selfish than the most altruistic, impersonal emotion. The content of selfishness is a mass of unselfishness. There is no reference to the nominal essence called oneself either in one's appetites or in one's natural affections; yet a man absorbed in his meat and drink, in his houses and lands, in his children and dogs, is called selfish because these interests, although natural and instinctive in him, are not shared by others. The unselfish man is he whose nature has a more universal direction, whose interests are more widely diffused.

But as impersonal thoughts are such only in their object, not in their subject or agent, since all thoughts are the thoughts of somebody: so also unselfish interests have to be somebody's interests. If we were not interested in beauty, if it were of no concern to our happiness whether things were beautiful or ugly, we should manifest not the maximum, but the total absence of aesthetic faculty. The disinterestedness of this pleasure is, therefore, that of all primitive and intuitive satisfactions, which are in no way conditioned by a reference to an artificial general concept, like that of the self, all the potency of which must itself be derived from the independent energy of its component elements. I care about "myself" because "myself" is a name for the things I have at heart. To set up the verbal figment of personality and make it an object of concern apart from the interests which were its content and substance, turns the moralist into a pedant, and ethics into a superstition. The self which is the object of *amour propre* is an idol of the tribe, and needs to be disintegrated into the primitive objective interests that underlie it before the cultus of it can be justified by reason.

The Differentia of Aesthetic Pleasure
Not Its Universality

The supposed disinterestedness of our love of beauty passes into another characteristic of it often regarded as essential—its universitality. The pleasures of the senses have, it is said, no dogmatism in them; that anything gives me pleasure involves no assertion about its capacity to give pleasure to another. But when I judge a thing to be beautiful, my judgment means that the thing is beautiful in itself, or (what is the same thing more critically expressed) that it should seem so to everybody. The claim to universality is, according to this doctrine, the essence of the aesthetic; what makes the perception of beauty a judgment rather than a sensation. All aesthetic precepts would be impossible, and all criticism arbitrary and subjective, unless we admit a paradoxical universality in our judgment, the philosophical implications of which we may then go on to develop. But we are fortunately not required to enter the labyrinth into which this method leads; there is a much simpler and clearer way of studying such questions, which is to challenge and analyse the assertion before us and seek its basis in human nature. Before this is done, we should run the risk of expanding a natural misconception or inaccuracy of thought into an inveterate and pernicious prejudice by making it the centre of an elaborate construction.

That the claim of universality is such a natural inaccuracy will not be hard to show. There is notoriously no great agreement upon aesthetic matters; and such agreement as there is, is based upon similarity of origin, nature and circumstance among men, a similarity which, where it exists, tends to bring about identity in all judgments and feelings. It is unmeaningful to say that what is beautiful to one man ought to be beautiful to another. If their senses are the same, their associations and dispositions similar, then the same thing will certainly be beautiful to both. If their natures are different, the form which to one will be entrancing will be to another even invisible, because his classifications and discriminations in perception will be different, and he may see a hideous detached fragment or a shapeless aggregate of things, in what to another is a perfect whole—so entirely are the unities of objects unities of function and use. It is absurd to say that what is invisible to a given being *ought* to seem beautiful to him. Evidently this obligation of recognizing the same qualities is conditioned by the possession of the same faculties. But no two men have exactly the same faculties, nor can things have for any two exactly the same values.

What is loosely expressed by saying that any one ought to see this or that beauty is that he would see it if his disposition, training, or attention were what our ideal demands for him; and our ideal of what anyone should be has complex but discoverable sources. We take, for instance, a certain pleasure in having our own judgments supported by those of others; we are intolerant, if not of the existence of a nature different from our own, at least of its expression in words and judgments. We are confirmed or made happy in our doubtful opinions by seeing them accepted universally. We are unable to find the basis of our taste in our own experience and therefore refuse to look for it there. If we were sure of our ground, we should be willing to acquiesce in the naturally different feelings and ways of others, as a man who is conscious of speaking his language with the accent of the capital confesses its arbitrariness with gaiety, and is pleased and interested in the variations of it he observes in provincials; but the provincial is always zealous to show that he has reason and ancient authority to justify his oddities. So people who have no sensations, and do not know why they judge, are always trying to show that they judge by universal reason.

Thus the frailty and superficiality of our own judgments cannot brook contradiction. We abhor another man's doubt when we cannot tell him why we ourselves believe. Our ideal of other men tends therefore to include the agreement of their judgments with our own; and although we might acknowledge the fatuity of this demand in regard to natures very different from the human, we may be unreasonable enough to require that all races should admire the same style of architecture, and all ages the same poets.

The great actual unity of human taste within the range of conventional history helps the pretension. But in principle it is untenable. Nothing has less to do with the real merit of a work of imagination than the capacity of all men to appreciate it; the true test is the degree and kind of satisfaction it can give to him who appreciates it most. The symphony would lose nothing if half mankind had always been deaf, as nine-tenths of them actually are to the intricacies of its harmonies; but it would have lost much if no Beethoven had existed. And more: incapacity to appreciate certain types of beauty may be the condition *sine qua non* for the appreciation of another kind; the greatest capacity both for enjoyment and creation is highly specialized and exclusive, and hence the greatest ages of art have often been strangely intolerant.

The invectives of one school against another, perverse as they are philosophically, are artistically often signs of health, because they indicate a vital appreciation of certain kinds of beauty, a love of them that has grown into a jealous passion. The architects that have pieced out the imperfections of ancient buildings with their own thoughts, like Charles V, when he raised his massive palace beside the Alhambra, may be condemned from a certain point of view. They marred much by their interference; but they showed a splendid confidence in their own intuitions, a proud assertion of their own taste, which is the greatest evidence of aesthetic sincerity. On the contrary, our own gropings, eclecticism, and archaeology are the symptoms of impotence. If we were less learned and less just, we might be more efficient. If our appreciation were less general, it might be more real, and if we trained our imagination into exclusiveness, it might attain to character.

The Differentia of Aesthetic Pleasure: Its Objectification

There is, however, something more in the claim to universality in aesthetic judgments than the desire to generalize our own opinions. There is the expression of a curious but well-known psychological phenomenon, viz., the transformation of an element of sensation into the quality of a thing. If we say that other men should see the beauties we see, it is because we think those beauties *are in the object*, like its colour, proportion, or size. Our judgment appears to us merely the perception and discovery of an external existence, of the real excellence that is without. But this notion is radically absurd and contradictory. Beauty, as we have seen, is a value; it cannot be conceived as an independent existence which affects our senses and which we consequently perceive. It exists in perception, and cannot exist otherwise. A beauty not perceived is a pleasure not felt, and a contradiction. But modern philosophy has taught us to say the same thing of every element of the perceived world; all are sensations; and their grouping into objects imagined to be permanent and external is the work of certain habits of our intelligence. We should be incapable of surveying or retaining the diffused experiences of life, unless we organized and classified them, and out of the chaos of impressions framed the world of conventional and recognizable objects.

How this is done is explained by the current theories of perception. External objects usually affect various senses at once, the impressions of which are thereby associated. Repeated experiences of one object are also associated on account of their similarity; hence a double tendency to merge and unify into a single percept, to which a name is attached, the group of those memories and reactions which in fact had one external thing for their cause. But this percept, once formed, is clearly different from those particular experiences out of which it grew. It is permanent, they are variable. They are but partial views and glimpses of it. The constituted notion therefore comes to be the reality, and the materials of it merely the appearance. The distinction between substance and quality, reality and appearance, matter and mind, has no other origin.

The objects thus conceived and distinguished from our ideas of them, are at first compacted of all the impressions, feelings, and memories, which offer themselves for association and fall within the vortex of the amalgamating imagination. Every sensation we get from a thing is originally treated as one of its qualities. Experiment, however, and the practical need of a simpler conception of the structure of objects lead us gradually to reduce the qualities of the object to a minimum, and to regard most perceptions as an effect of those few qualities upon us. These few primary qualities, like extension which we persist in treating as independently real and as the quality of a substance, are those which suffice to explain the order of our experiences. All the rest, like colour, are relegated to the subjective sphere, as merely effects upon our minds, and apparent or secondary qualities of the object.

But this distinction has only a practical justification. Convenience and economy of thought alone determine what combination of our sensations we shall continue to objectify and treat as the cause of the rest. The right and tendency to be objective is equal in all, since they are all prior to the artifice of thought by which we separate the concept from its materials, the thing from our experiences.

The qualities which we now conceive to belong to real objects are for the most part images of sight and touch. One of the first classes of effects to be treated as secondary were naturally pleasures and pains, since it could commonly conduce very little to intelligent and successful action to conceive our pleasures and pains as resident in objects. But emotions are essentially capable of objectification, as well as impressions of sense; and one may well believe that a primitive and inexperienced consciousness would rather people the world with ghosts of its own terrors and passions than with projections of those luminous and mathematical concepts which as yet it could hardly have formed.

This animistic and mythological habit of thought still holds its own at the confines of knowledge, where mechanical explanations are not found. In ourselves, where nearness makes observation difficult, in the intricate chaos of animal and human life, we still appeal to the efficacy of will and ideas, as also in the remote night of cosmic and religious problems. But in all the intermediate realm of vulgar day, where mechanical science has made progress, the inclusion of emotional or passionate elements in the concept of the reality would be now an extravagance. Hence our idea of things is composed exclusively of perceptual elements, of the ideas of form and of motion.

The beauty of objects, however, forms an exception to this rule. Beauty is an emotional element, a pleasure of ours, which nevertheless we regard as a quality of things. But we are now prepared to understand the nature of this exception. It is the survival of a tendency originally universal to make every effect of a thing upon us as a constituent of its conceived nature. The scientific idea of a thing is a great abstraction from the mass of perceptions and reactions which that thing produces; the aesthetic idea is less abstract, since it retains the emotional reaction, the pleasure of the perception, as an integral part of the conceived thing.

Nor is it hard to find the ground of this survival in the sense of beauty of an objectification of feeling elsewhere extinct. Most of the pleasures which objects cause are easily distinguished and separated from the perception of the object; the object has to be applied to a particular organ, like the palate, or swallowed like wine, or used and operated upon in some way before the pleasure arises. The cohesion is therefore slight between the pleasure and the other associated elements of sense; the pleasure is separated in time from the perception, or it is localized in a different organ, and consequently is at once recognised as an effect and not as a quality of the object. But when the process of perception itself is pleasant, as it may easily be, when the intellectual operation, by which the elements of sense are associated and projected, and the concept of the form and substance of the thing produced is naturally delightful, then we have a pleasure intimately bound up in the thing, inseparable from its character and constitution, the seat of which in us is the same as the seat of the perception. We naturally fail, under these circumstances, to separate the pleasure from the other objectified feelings. It becomes, like them, a quality of the object, which we distinguish from pleasures not so incorporated in the perception of things, by giving it the name of beauty.

The Definition of Beauty

We have now reached our definition of beauty, which, in the terms of our successive analysis and narrowing of the conception, is value positive, intrinsic, and objectified. Or, in less technical language, Beauty is pleasure regarded as the quality of a thing.

This definition is intended to sum up a variety of distinctions and identifications which should perhaps be here more explicitly set down. Beauty is a value, that is, it is not a perception of a matter of fact or of a relation: it is an emotion, an affection of our volitional and appreciative nature. An object cannot be beautiful if it can give pleasure to nobody: a beauty to which all men were forever indifferent is a contradiction in terms.

In the second place, this value is positive, it is the sense of the presence of something good, or (in the case of ugliness) of its absence. It is never the perception of a positive evil, it is never a negative value. That we are endowed with the sense of beauty is a pure gain which brings no evil with it. When the ugly ceases to be amusing or merely uninteresting and becomes disgusting, it becomes indeed a positive evil: but a moral and practical, not an aesthetic one. In aesthetics that saying is true—often so disingenuous in ethics—that evil is nothing but the absence of good: for even the tedium and vulgarity of an existence without beauty is not itself ugly so much as lamentable and degrading. The absence of aesthetic goods is a moral evil: the aesthetic evil is merely relative, and means less of aesthetic good than was expected at the place and time. No form in itself gives pain, although some forms give pain by causing a shock of surprise even when they are really beautiful: as if a mother found a fine bull pup in her child's cradle, when her pain would not be aesthetic in its nature.

Further, this pleasure must not be in the consequence of the utility of the object or event, but in its immediate perception; in other words, beauty is an ultimate good, something that gives satisfaction to a natural function, to some fundamental need or capacity of our minds. Beauty is therefore a positive value that is intrinsic; it is a pleasure. These two circumstances sufficiently separate the sphere of aesthetics from that of ethics. Moral values are generally negative, and always remote. Morality has to do with the avoidance of evil and the pursuit of good: aesthetics only with enjoyment.

Finally, the pleasures of sense are distinguished from the perception of beauty, as sensation in general is distinguished from perception; by the objectification of the elements and their appearance as qualities rather of things than of consciousness. The passage from sensation to perception is gradual, and the path may be sometimes retraced: so it is with beauty and the pleasures of sensation. There is no sharp line between them, but it depends upon the degree of objectivity my feeling has attained at the moment whether I say "It pleases me," or "It is beautiful." If I am self-conscious and critical, I shall probably use one phrase; if I am impulsive and susceptible, the other. The more remote, interwoven, and inextricable the pleasure is, the more objective it will appear; and the union of two pleasures often makes one beauty. In Shakespeare's LIVth sonnet are these words:

> O How much more doth beauty beauteous seem
> By that sweet ornament which truth doth give!
> The rose looks fair, but fairer we it deem
> For that sweet odour which doth in it live.
> The canker-blooms have full as deep a dye
> As the perfumèd tincture of the roses,
> Hang on such thorns, and play as wantonly
> When summer's breath their maskèd buds discloses.
> But, for their beauty only is their show,
> They live unwooed and unrespected fade;
> Die to themselves. Sweet roses do not so:
> Of their sweet deaths are sweetest odours made.

One added ornament, we see, turns the deep dye, which was but show and mere sensation before, into an element of beauty and reality; and as truth is here the co-operation of perceptions, so beauty is the co-operation of pleasures. If colour, form, and motion are hardly beautiful without the sweetness of the odour, how much more necessary would they be for the sweetness itself to become a beauty! If we had the perfume in a flask, no one would think of calling it beautiful: it would give us too detached and controllable a sensation. There would be no object in which it could be easily incorporated. But let it float from the garden, and it will add another sensuous charm to objects simultaneously recognized, and help to make them beautiful. Thus beauty is constituted by the objectification of pleasure. It is pleasure objectified.

Note

1. Schopenhauer, indeed, who makes much of it, was a good critic, but his psychology suffered much from the pessimistic generalities of his system. It concerned him to show that the will was bad, and, as he felt beauty to be a good

if not a holy thing, he hastened to convince himself that it came from the suppression of the will. But even in his system this suppression is only relative. The desire of individual objects, indeed, is absent in the perception of beauty. but there is still present that initial love of the general type and principles of things which is the first illusion of the absolute, and drives it on to the fatal experiment of creation. So that, apart from Schopenhauer's mythology, we have even in him the recognition that beauty gives satisfaction to some dim and underlying demands of our nature, just as particular objects give more special and momentary pleasure to our individualized wills. His psychology was, however, far too vague and general to undertake an analysis of those mysterious feelings.

T. E. JESSOP

The Definition of Beauty

IT IS THE WAY of a newly quickened science to claim that it supplies a philosophical viewpoint. Physics did this in the seventeenth century and biology did the same in the last few decades of the nineteenth. Nowadays, it is psychology that claims to prove the all-seeing eye. Aesthetic theory and art-criticism alike are accepting and elaborating this claim. The study of beautiful objects has become the study of their origination in a mind and of their effect on a mind. I want first to argue that such contraction of interest to subjective considerations is a mistake, and then to discuss certain difficulties which seem to lie in the way of the objective definition of beauty.

It is certainly a relief to turn away from those older aesthetic theories that were mere deductions from general metaphysical principles which drew neither content nor inspiration from aesthetic experience, deductions drawn simply to complete the circuit of a system. Besides being in this sense oblique they were so general as to have no close and clear relation to the realm of actual aesthetic objects, and supplied little help for a principled discrimination of these. But if metaphysical aesthetics was harmless because it simply remained aloof from the peculiar difficulties of the concrete field, psychologically biased aesthetics is harmful because it leads us away from those difficulties. Where, at any rate, a work of art is in question, the inquiry is deflected to an examination of either creation or appreciation.

In the emphasis on creation the product is lost in the producer. We are made to jump from the poem to the poet. When we ask for an analysis of a statue we are given a piece of conjecture about the sculptor. The inseparability of the work of art from the artist is the justifying principle. It is, of course, a true one, but the respect in which it is true is the respect in which it is a commonplace, for all that its truth in-

Reprinted from *Proceedings of the Aristotelian Society,* Vol. XXXIII (1932-3) by courtesy of the Editor of the Aristotelian Society.

volves is that the work of art is an element in a system of causes and effects. Aesthetics begins only when this point of view has been transcended. Its relevance for the critic is to the preliminary business of understanding a work of art—more particularly an elaborate, obscure or eccentric work—not to the task of judging this aesthetically; and for the theorist it is a principle of purely psychological interest. However hard it may sound, both for the immediate aesthetic judgment and for the philosophical analysis of such judgment, the nature of the artist need not be considered. A judgment about an artist cannot always be transferred to the thing he has made, the reason being that most of what happens in him does not happen afresh, or have any direct correspondence, in his work. He may, for example, be insincere, and yet we may find no trace of this in his work. Insincerity, moreover, is a moral quality. Motive, too, is irrelevant: in art, as in conduct, there is often a disparity between aim and achievement, and often a pure difference. The judgment of motive is a moral affair; the judgment of the relation of motive to achievement requires only predicates such as success and failure; an achievement alone can accept an aesthetic predicate, and, in fact, it is to achievements—to poems, pictures, statues, buildings—that aesthetic predicates are applied. A work of art may realise a motive, but this is not its defining characteristic. Even when causally considered, its deeper relation is to sensibility, which is not a motive, nor even an emotion, but just a sense which very commonly runs through to the finger-tips of the painter without any conscious or describable intermediary, leaving on the canvas a passage of so-called accidental beauty of which the painter himself becomes aware not as creator but simply as beholder. Beauty arises in a thousand ways, even with a bread-and-butter motive; to trace these out is an interesting essay in conjecture; but the story of the mental genesis of beauty is not aesthetics. Those who think it is are thrown into the curious position of making natural beauty a special and specially difficult problem. However produced, a beautiful object is what it is, and its beauty, whencesoever derived, is a part of what it is. If in order to judge a work of art or to vindicate the aesthetic predicate in my judgment I had to know anything of the creative experience of the artist a palsy would fall upon my sensibility. In fact, however, I roundly call the line-work of a prehistoric bone-graving beautiful, although I neither know nor ever will know what sort of experience originated it. My judgment, being about the engraving, is based on the engraving. It cannot decently have any other ground. By "beautiful" I mean, not that the thing has been produced in a certain way, but that it is in a certain state. I have in mind only what is in it, not what lay behind it. The causal explanation of beauty is not a definition of its nature, which is the only peculiar problem I can find for aesthetics as a philosophical science.

Perhaps the bias against which I am here arguing is not entirely psychological, but springs in part from that emphasis on origins which arose with the rebirth of the theory of evolution, an emphasis which has brought with it the odd principle, implied in a great deal of current quasi-philosophical thinking, that a thing is not really what it is but only what it sprang from: man is an animal, religion is fear, this vast frame of things is but an assemblage of star-dust. Even where this egregious principle is not insinuated, we have a diversion of interest from what a thing is to how it came to be what it is. The neglect of essence, the cult of causality, is one of the chief distinguishing marks of modern as compared with Greek and medieval philosophy; and its being later does not make it better. Phenomenology is a timely recall to the Platonic ideal of knowledge.

The other pole of subjectivism—interest in appreciation—is more enticing. It has the considerable scientific advantage that the connection between appreciation and the object appreciated is more open to inspection than is the connection between creation and the object created. Appreciation is a more conscious process, also a more common one, for while few of us are artists we are all appreciators. But if, in this commerce of object and appreciation, we concentrate on the appreciative side, we do no more than prepare the approaches to aesthetics. To differentiate aesthetic experience from other forms of experience by comparing its subjective aspect with theirs, seeking its peculiarity in a characteristic attitude or emotion, is to conduct an entirely psychological inquiry. So far, it is legitimate, but all too commonly the boundary is passed with a bias which leads to the further step of defining the aesthetic object in terms of that attitude or emotion.

When this step is taken we are left in the air with a purely formal definition. The aesthetic object is reduced to a mere correlate: it is simply whatever we respond to in the supposed aesthetic manner. We are even discouraged from trying to fill the empty form with any content of its own. Objects *quâ* aesthetic are said to be simply objects related to aesthetic feeling. Anything can be made aesthetic by adopting the aesthetic attitude towards it; some object is needful to provide a focus, but otherwise it is indifferent. This seems to me to be an error of fact. It amounts to saying that an entire section or function of experiencing consistently lies under no restraint whatever from the objective side. I believe in the spirit's freedom as firmly, though not so ardently, as those aestheticians to whom it is the most dear of all things, but I cannot find in myself a freedom of the kind asserted. When I attribute beauty to an object the tribute seems to be wrung from me by the object, and if on reflection I conclude that I have misapprehended the object, I am unable to retain the attribution, at any rate in the form of a judgment (I may retain it in the form of emotion, but emotion is the most conservative part of our nature, much more quick than judgment to slip into a habit). I cannot at pleasure give it, withhold it, or change it.

Under the influence of a mood beauty may lose its savour, but not its beauty; in a reflective person the judgment remains the same so long as the object does.

The practical consequence of defining beauty as just what we greet with the supposed aesthetic attitude is that every aesthetic response would be right, or rather neither right nor wrong, but merely natural. Even the most discerning piece of art-criticism would be no more than a personal confession, to be read, if read at all, only in order to know what the critic feels about his object, not whether he has detected in this some aspect or relation which I may have overlooked. I must accept his judgment as final for himself and irrelevant to me. On this view the aesthetic judgment disappears, becomes a synonym for a judgment of introspection, being reducible without any loss of meaning to "I feel in such and such a way towards this object." To say conversely, "This object makes me feel in such and such a way"—which, though not an aesthetic judgment, is on the way towards one—would be to destroy the subjectivism I have in view, for by imputing a potency to the object it prescribes an investigation into the general nature and particular forms of that potency.

The reasoned way of escape from all this subjectivism which is due to onesided concern with appreciation seems to me to consist in reminding ourselves of two very elementary distinctions. The first is the distinction between object and thing. It is sufficient for our present purpose to say that the thing is what is really there, whereas the object is so much of it, or of anything else, as comes effectively before the mind. Now what may be indifferent to the aesthetic feeling is the thing. In the presence of any thing I may under subjective causation adopt an aesthetic attitude, but only because I apprehend the thing either in one of its intrinsic aspects or in a certain context of images and ideas. Subjective conditions may determine the perceptual discrimination (as they do, indeed, even in perception with a scientific interest) or the movement of imagination, but it is the perceived or imagined object that determines the appreciation. When in certain conditions of light I see a foul slum-alley as beautiful, I am not asserting an unrestricted liberty of judgment and feeling. The only freedom I am asserting is from my olfactory sensations and from my knowledge of the ghastliness of slum-life. For the rest I am submitting to my mind's immediate object—to the patterned incidence of light, the mercy of concealing shadow, the balance of the two, the continuity and contrast of lines, and the coherent arrangement of masses. When the object is constituted by imagination instead of by perception, the situation is the same: however the object is produced, it is the object that produces the appreciation. Presumably, then, it has specific properties, of which the appreciation is a recognition.

But the term "appreciation" is ambiguous, and the second elementary distinction to be stressed is between appreciation as emotion and appreciation as judgment. The one is simply an event, and the other an event bearing a claim. The first savours beauty, the second asserts it. The one calls for causal study, the second for definition and testing. The distinction is not a merely analytical one. Unreluctantly and unaffectedly I can admit an object to be beautiful without liking it (even without having liked it, so that the judgment is not explicable by memory or habit). This may be shocking to those subjectivists whose ruling desire is to enjoin that the aesthetic objective shall be greeted with an emotion at once vibrant and authentic. The requirement is in place in a *Lebensanschauung*, but not in aesthetics. Anyhow, I do meet objects with the judgment that they are beautiful, and all that is theoretically required of judgment is that it shall be true; the emotion that accompanies it is logically irrelevant, irrelevant because it is bound up with an individual set of mental and bodily conditions. Reverting now to our previous point, I would say that what enjoys a considerable degree of independence of the aesthetic object is the emotion, or the attitude of which the emotion is part. I cannot neatly balance this statement by saying that contrariwise every judgment is wholly determined by the object. Nevertheless, the ideal is that they should be. Determination in this sense, however, is not the right word to use. What matters about a judgment is not what causally determines it, but what it logically determines. Its judgmental character consists in a claim to be *relevant* to an object, and it is by reference to the object that the claim has to be understood and tested. I see no reason for exempting aesthetic judgments from this requirement.

From the foregoing considerations I venture to draw the following conclusions: (1) That the constant form of aesthetic experience is the aesthetic judgment. It is, moreover, the perfect form, the entelechy, the experience gathered up, articulated, and brought to the clear level of cognitive awareness and intention. If, then, I may be allowed to follow Plato, Aristotle and Hegel in holding that philosophy is distinguished by its studying everything in its most organised form, I must hold that aesthetics as a philosophical science is primarily concerned with the aesthetic judgment, not with its subjective accompaniments and conditions. (2) That the aesthetic judgment cannot be reduced without remainder to an introspective one. It is not about me but about the object. Nor is it a blank assertion of the object's potency over me, but about some feature in it that wields that potency. And the potency it primarily wields is not over my feelings, but over my powers of judgment. The minimum and distinctive quality of beauty is that it wins for itself admission; whatever else it wins is largely a matter of accident, the accident of association, of mood and of taste. (3) That aesthetic experience needs to be studied normatively (*i.e.* leaving room for a right and a wrong), and that the only feature of it that allows of an aesthetic norm is the aesthetic judgment interpreted objectively. If "This is beautiful" meant *simply* "I like it," it would be impossible to pass to "All people ought to like it"; a purely subjective judgment cannot be generalized and elevated into a norm. Even if it could be, a canon that enjoins us to adopt a certain attitude to beauty loses all its canonical character if beauty be defined as that to which this attitude *is* adopted, and all sense except that of tautology if beauty be defined as that to which this attitude *ought to be* adopted. And in either of these two senses the canon dogmatically brushes aside as meaningless the perfectly sensible question: What kind of object am I to respond to aesthetically? But in any case a norm or canon of feeling belongs to ethics, not to aesthetics. The right attitude to beauty is no more the affair of aesthetics than is the right attitude to truth the affair of epistemology. What we require, in aesthetics as in practice, is a canon of judgment; the only canon of the aesthetic judgment is a definition of its predicate, beauty; and the only definition of beauty that preserves the aesthetic judgment in its integrity (that is, from being a synonym for an altogether different kind of judgment, an introspective or lyrical one) is a statement of certain properties of objects.

As Plato pointed out, the paradox of all search for definition is that we already know what we are seeking to define. The paradox is not resolved by simply restating it in the form that we already perceive what we want to conceive, for the conception is prior. The paradox is that while psychologically the denotation comes first, providing the material over which the defining activity analytically and synthetically plays, logically the connotation is prior because it prescribes the denotation. We only escape from the paradox by admitting that conception has an embryonic stage in the perception. It is just because the concept is already involved in our immediate apprehensions that it can be evolved from these by reflexion. Our spontaneous application of the same term to many things rests on a basis of unconscious recognition of that common quality which is to be abstractly expressed in the definition. In defining we do but raise to clarity, purity and organization a precedent knowledge that was obscure, confused and inarticulate.

Where, then, there is consistency in our perceptions the business of defining is in principle easy. An accepted denotation seems to be the condition of reaching an acceptable connotation. Now the absence of this condition is the practical difficulty in the way of defining beauty. We haven't the agreed instances from which to generalize, nor by which to check our tentative generalizations. Where there is no homogeneous group there can be no common quality.

It may be urged that beauty, being an ideal, is insusceptible of inductive definition, and that the difficulty here is that we have not yet devised a logic for the definition of ideals. But I am by no means certain that beauty is an ideal in the sense in which good is; the most striking respect in which they are alike is that we differ heartily about their meaning, and this does not make beauty an ideal. Whether it is or not we meet it as a fact. But an ideal is a *summum*, and the expression *summum pulchrum* is nothing more than a grammatically correct collocation of words. It is meaningful to speak of a more beautiful and a less beautiful, but there is a heavy limitation to this quasi-quantitative comparison. One painting may be more beautiful than another, and yet two others may be incomparable in respect of degree, being, like a daffodil and a rose, like a statue and a piece of music, just different. Beauty, unlike goodness, has various orders—visual, auditory and so on—and in no one of these orders, still less in all of them taken together, is there one perfect degree or form, a *summum pulchrum*. It is not a hierarchy of subordinate and superordinate degrees, but a galaxy of brilliant individuals. Of each of these we ask only if it is beautiful: to ask how beautiful it is is trivial even where it is possible. Beauty as value is equally unintelligible to me. It *has* value; what it *is* is my present concern.

To return to the difficulty of the inductive definition of beauty. The wide disagreement about the denotation of the term is one of the grounds of subjectivism. I now want to protest that the disagreement has been exaggerated. We must at once discount the large number of second-hand judgments which, being determined neither by the judger's own sensibility nor by the character of his object but by modesty, laziness, desire to be counted perspicacious, up-to-date, or well-informed, are not properly aesthetic judgments but only verbally identical with these. Turning from the diffusion and persistence of disagreements to their origination, we have to note that many people are unskilled or careless in discerning which of the stimuli is effective, exactly which aspect of the total object occupies the focus of attention. This ineptitude shows itself in many ways. Before a picture an onlooker is frequently excited by the painter's name, by the special reputation of the picture, by its rarity as a specimen, its market value, its history, its title, its mere subject-matter; and because a picture is admittedly an aesthetic thing he mistakes his excitement for aesthetic response and applies to a non-aesthetic aspect an aesthetic predicate. When "How beautiful!" really means "How rare!", "At last!", "Lucky owner!" and so on, it is not, of course, an aesthetic judgment. Disagreements here have no bearing on the question of the objectivity of beauty. Nor have the disagreements that arise through the efficacy of purely casual associates which are linked with the aesthetic object by nothing more than the accidents of individual experience, and which displace from the foreground of awareness the aesthetic stimulus that introduced them.[1]

The amount of disagreement, then, is considerably reduced if it be granted that not all judgments about a beautiful thing are really about its beauty, even though they verbally purport to be so. A single thing can strike at many a chord of our nature, touch many a need, show many an aspect of itself to cognition, and not every person is skilled enough to frame either spontaneously or reflectively a judgment which accurately expresses his dominant reaction or his dominant object. And the disagreement is even further reduced if we do in aesthetics what we do in all other spheres of study, namely, refuse to put everybody's judgment on one plane of equal worth. There is more concord among experts than among lay minds, one reason being that they are able to state their judgments in objective terms.

To these complaints about the ways in which the problem of the definition of beauty is treated I have to add two more. The first concerns the assumption that beauty is one. Doubtless there is a sense in which it is, but if the concept is reached quickly it is likely to be too narrow, empty enough not to gainsay a single kind of beauty instead of rich enough to comprehend them all. The concept of harmony is of this kind, the *abstractum* left when all differences have been left out. We may avoid this abstract form of unification by identifying all beauty with one of its concrete forms. This is very commonly done, and the form taken as standard is literary beauty. I feel increasingly sure that this exaltation of the literary type has an ultimate justification and yet not an aesthetic one. Keeping to beauty I find one difference which I cannot overcome, the difference between sensory and what, through inability to find a better term, I will call ideo-sensory beauty. The first has an obvious exemplification in painting, the other in literature.

In literature the medium is not, and cannot be, regarded as purely sensory. Words, phrases, sentences are not mere sounds, but sounds appointed to be and operative as vehicles of determinate images and meanings and of the emotional evocations of these. The auditory aspect offers many possibilities of design, but all this various form and texture of sound-pattern has to be contributory to or concordant with the ideal burden which is the inalienable essence of the words. The so-called pure poetry desiderated by some of the moderns is not poetry, not literature, because its medium is not words but simply sounds; nor is it even music, for music is minimally a pattern of musical sounds, different both sensorily and physically from spoken sounds. Important, then, as sound-beauty may be in verbal art, it is subordinate; its whole office is not to present itself, but to introduce and reinforce a system of images and meanings and emotions; and since images and meanings and emotions are the distinctive stuff and life of human experience, verbal beauty is indefeasibly humanistic; not only properly but inescapably ideal, representative, expressive and evocative—which is another way of saying that it is inescapably related to that system of needs, interests and evaluations which make us practical and moral beings.

This is not the case in painting. Here the medium can be apprehended in its purely sensory aspect without mutilation. It can stand alone entire. It is not a necessary part of colour, line, and space to represent, express, or evoke. The sensory medium itself has a beauty all its own. Certain colours sit quietly side by side, others enhance each other; certain lines are graceful, directive, and organizing; certain masses are mutually supporting, coherent. These are the specific excellences of colour in its spatial setting, its own aesthetic aspect. With nothing more than these, a picture is beautiful, and so, too, is an evening sky, for I can detect no difference of kind between a natural scene and a painted one: both consist of congruent visual elements. In no case is it necessary to know what a colour-object stands for in order to appreciate its own beauty; as beautiful, it is non-significant. I could still apprehend beauty in a sunset even if I did not know it to be a sunset, and without contemplating it imaginatively as the death-moment of day, as an emblem or monition of our mortality, or as an intimation that a passing so gorgeously attended is not extinction but translation. Paint may be used to represent, but the mere representing of things will not make beauty unless the things are beautiful. When what is represented is not centrally a visual thing, but some fragment of life's joy or pathos, itself perhaps beautiful, we have a supervenient beauty, that of the subject of the painting, not of the medium, of the painting as paint. If, then, painting and the other visual arts, and probably music, too, may be beautiful quite apart from what they represent or express, there is a beauty distinct from that of which alone literature is capable. To approach painting, sculpture, architecture and music from the side of literature and require there what is always to be found here is to overlook the nature of the difference between the two kinds of media, one of which may, the other of which may not, forgo all representative or expressive character. A word ceases to be a word and therefore loses the beauty of a word when its signification and significance are not apprehended; a colour is most a colour when apprehended apart from what it may happen to represent, and then most reveals its own beauty. Between the homogeneous beauty of a colour-pattern and the ideo-sensory beauty of a poem I can find no likeness, for the latter is not a pattern of mere images, still less of visual images, but an organic concretion of every kind of experienceable element. This "Persian carpet" account of painting may be a poor theory of art, but it is the only just theory of visual beauty.

This leads me to my final grumble, one against the tendency to define beauty as whatever can be achieved in the arts. This gives us the absurdity of calling the comic beautiful. Aesthetics and the philosophy of art are made to coincide instead of to overlap. Art is capable of, and achieves, more than beauty—this is the secret of its thrall. The minimal task of each art is a manipulative emphasis on the peculiar virtues of its medium, but if, when this first duty has been cared for, the medium can be further exploited without prejudice to its basic excellence, the result is a richer and therefore more acceptable gift. I see no reason why a painter should not represent things, express his attitude towards them, preach, teach and move, provided he does so from a rostrum of beautiful paint. Nor do I see any reason why a painter should be required to do these additional tasks, since the discipline and craft of painting have no magic to give its practitioners insight into human character, moral values, and non-phenomenal truth. The school that would limit art to the creation of its proper beauty is trying to reduce it to its minimal task; the school that would force an art with a material medium to expression and the like, is requiring of the artist what his special skill does not of itself enable him to give. In the sphere of aesthetics this conflict has its correspondence in the controversy between formalism and, in the widest sense of the term, expressionism. For the first, all beauty is sensory, for the second ideo-sensory. For me there are both these kinds, irreducible to each other. But if, under a verbal scruple, under the desire to define beauty univocally, I have a leaning, it is towards formalism, for sound and sight that self-effacingly present a world of significant and emotive ideas appeal not to a part of man but to the whole of him; he meets them as a practical, moral and religious personality. Beauty is too poor a predicate to apply to anything expressive. From which I deduce that an expressive work of art, not being exhaustively describable as beautiful, falls under the approval and law of our moral judgments. Only senses are non-moral. But the sphere of moral judgments is to be circumscribed in ethics; aesthetics can only mark out its own realm.

Note

1. Sometimes, of course, the associate, or the complex now formed of it and its introducing object is a new aesthetic object. When Keats contemplated his Grecian urn, he apprehended neither the beauty of its shape nor the specific beauty of the painting on it. What he noticed was the subject of the painting and the silence and immobility of the representation, and then, with a sweep of imagination, he idealized and eternalized it. The unheard melodies of the painted piper are sweeter than those that strike the sensual ear; the painted tree has happy boughs that cannot shed their leaves; the painted damsel will never age nor her painted lover ever cease his wooing. The visual beauty of the vase is curtained over with a new object, also beautiful, but in a different way. Here we have the distinction between sensory and ideo-sensory beauty.—Cf. above.

EDWARD BULLOUGH

"Psychical Distance" as a Factor in Art and an Aesthetic Principle

I

THE CONCEPTION of "Distance" suggests, in connection with Art, certain trains of thought by no means devoid of interest or of speculative importance. Perhaps the most obvious suggestion is that of *actual spatial* distance, i.e. the distance of a work of Art from the spectator, or that of *represented spatial* distance, i.e. the distance represented within the work. Less obvious, more metaphorical, is the meaning of *temporal* distance. The first was noticed already by Aristotle in his *Poetics*; the second has played a great part in the history of painting in the form of perspective; the distinction between these two kinds of distance assumes special importance theoretically in the differentiation between sculpture in the round, and relief-sculpture. Temporal distance, remoteness from us in point of time, though often a cause of misconceptions, has been declared to be a factor of considerable weight in our appreciation.

It is not, however, in any of these meanings that "Distance" is put forward here, though it will be clear in the course of this essay that the above-mentioned kinds of distance are rather special forms of the conception of Distance as advocated here, and derive whatever *aesthetic* qualities they may possess from Distance in its *general* connotation. This general connotation is "Psychical Distance."

A short illustration will explain what is meant by "Psychical Distance." Imagine a fog at sea: for most people it is an experience of acute unpleasantness. Apart from the physical annoyance and remoter forms of discomfort such as delays, it is apt to produce feelings of peculiar anxiety, fears of invisible dangers, strains of watching and listening for distant and unlocalised signals. The listless movements of the ship and

Reprinted from the *British Journal of Psychology*, Vol. V (1912).

her warning calls soon tell upon the nerves of the passengers; and that special, expectant, tacit anxiety and nervousness, always associated with this experience, make a fog the dreaded terror of the sea (all the more terrifying because of its very silence and gentleness) for the expert seafarer no less than for the ignorant landsman.

Nevertheless, a fog at sea can be a source of intense relish and enjoyment. Abstract from the experience of the sea fog, for the moment, its danger and practical unpleasantness, just as every one in the enjoyment of a mountain-climb disregards its physical labour and its danger (though it is not denied that these may incidentally enter into the enjoyment and enhance it); direct the attention to the features "objectively" constituting the phenomenon—the veil surrounding you with an opaqueness as of transparent milk, blurring the outline of things and distorting their shapes into weird grotesqueness; observe the carrying-power of the air, producing the impression as if you could touch some far-off siren by merely putting out your hand and letting it lose itself behind that white wall; note the curious creamy smoothness of the water, hypocritically denying as it were any suggestion of danger; and, above all, the strange solitude and remoteness from the world, as it can be found only on the highest mountain-tops; and the experience may acquire, in its uncanny mingling of repose and terror, a flavour of such concentrated poignancy and delight as to contrast sharply with the blind and distempered anxiety of its other aspects. This contrast, often emerging with startling suddenness, is like a momentary switching on of some new current, or the passing ray of a brighter light, illuminating the outlook upon perhaps the most ordinary and familiar objects—an impression which we experience sometimes in instants of direst extremity, when our practical interest snaps like a wire from sheer over-tension, and we watch the consummation of some impending catastrophe with the marvelling unconcern of a mere spectator.

It is a difference in outlook, due—if such a metaphor is permissible—to the insertion of Distance. This Distance appears to lie between our own self and its affections, using the latter term in its broadest sense as anything which affects our being, bodily or spiritually, e.g. as sensation, perception, emotional state or idea. Usually, though not always, it amounts to the same thing to say that the Distance lies between our own self and such objects as are the sources or vehicles of such affections.

Thus, in the fog, the transformation by Distance is produced in the first instance by putting the phenomenon, so to speak, out of gear with our practical, actual self; by allowing it to stand outside the context of our personal needs and ends—in short, by looking at it "objectively," as it has often been called, by permitting only such reactions on our part as emphasise the "objective" features of the experience, and by interpreting even our "subjective" affections not as modes of *our* being but rather as characteristics of the phenomenon.

The working of Distance is, accordingly, not simple, but highly complex. It has a *negative*, inhibitory aspect—the cutting-out of the practical sides of things and of our practical attitude to them—and a *positive* side—the elaboration of the experience on the new basis created by the inhibitory action of Distance.

2. Consequently, this distanced view of things is not, and cannot be, our normal outlook. As a rule, experiences constantly turn the same side towards us, namely, that which has the strongest practical force of appeal. We are not ordinarily aware of those aspects of things which do not touch us immediately and practically, nor are we generally conscious of impressions apart from our own self which is impressed. The sudden view of things from their reverse, usually unnoticed, side, comes upon us as a revelation, and such revelations are precisely those of Art. In this most general sense, Distance is a factor in all Art.

3. It is, for this very reason, also an aesthetic principle. The aesthetic contemplation and the aesthetic outlook have often been described as "objective." We speak of "objective" artists as Shakespeare or Velasquez, of "objective" works or art-forms as Homer's *Iliad* or the drama. It is a term constantly occurring in discussions and criticisms, though its sense, if pressed at all, becomes very questionable. For certain forms of Art, such as lyrical poetry, are said to be "subjective"; Shelley, for example, would usually be considered a "subjective" writer. On the other hand, no work of art can be genuinely "objective" in the sense in which this term might be applied to a work on history or to a scientific treatise; nor can it be "subjective" in the ordinary acceptance of that term, as a personal feeling, a direct statement of a wish or belief, or a cry of passion is subjective. "Objectivity" and "subjectivity" are a pair of opposites which in their mutual exclusiveness when applied to Art soon lead to confusion.

Nor are they the only pair of opposites. Art has with equal vigor been declared alternately "idealistic" and "realistic," "sensual" and "spiritual," "individualistic" and "typical." Between the defence of either terms of such antitheses most aesthetic theories have vacillated. It is one of the contentions of this essay that such opposites find their synthesis in the more fundamental conception of Distance.

Distance further provides the much needed criterion of the beautiful as distinct from the merely agreeable.

Again, it marks one of the most important steps in the process of artistic creation and serves as a distinguishing feature of what is commonly and loosely described as the "artistic temperament."

Finally, it may claim to be considered as one of the essential characteristics of the "aesthetic consciousness," if I may describe by this term that special mental attitude towards, and outlook upon, experience, which finds its most pregnant expression in the various forms of Art.

II

Distance, as I said before, is obtained by separating the object and its appeal from one's own self, by putting it out of gear with practical needs and ends. Thereby the "contemplation" of the object becomes alone possible. But it does not mean that the relation between the self and the object is broken to the extent of becoming "impersonal." Of the alternatives "personal" and "impersonal" the latter surely comes nearer to the truth; but here, as elsewhere, we meet the difficulty of having to express certain facts in terms coined for entirely different uses. To do so usually results in paradoxes, which are nowhere more inevitable than in discussions upon Art. "Personal" and "impersonal," "subjective" and "objective" are such terms, devised for purposes other than aesthetic speculation, and becoming loose and ambiguous as soon as applied outside the sphere of their special meanings. In giving preference therefore to the term "impersonal" to describe the relation between the spectator and a work of Art, it is to be noticed that it is not impersonal in the sense in which we speak of the "impersonal" character of Science, for instance. In order to obtain "objectively valid" results, the scientist excludes the "personal factor," i.e. his personal wishes as to the validity of his results, his predilection for any particular system to be proved or disproved by his research. It goes without saying that all experiments and investigations are undertaken out of a personal interest in the science, for the ultimate support of a definite assumption, and involve personal hopes of success; but this does not affect the "dispassionate" attitude of the investigator, under pain of being accused of "manufacturing his evidence."

1. Distance does not imply an impersonal, purely intellectually interested relation of such a kind. On the contrary, it describes a *personal* relation, often highly emotionally coloured, but *of a peculiar character*. Its peculiarity lies in that the personal character of the relation has been, so to speak, filtered. It has been cleared of the practical, concrete nature of its appeal, without, however, thereby losing its original constitution. One of the best-known examples is to be found in our attitude towards the events and characters of the drama: they appeal to us like persons and incidents of normal experience, except that that side of their appeal, which would usually affect us in a directly personal manner, is held in abeyance. This difference, so well known as to be almost trivial, is generally explained by reference to the knowledge that the characters and situations are "unreal," imaginary. . . . But, as a matter of fact, the "assumption" upon which the imaginative emotional reaction is based is not necessarily the condition, but often the consequence, of Distance; that is to say, the converse of the reason usually stated would

then be true: viz. that Distance, by changing our relation to the characters, renders them seemingly fictitious, not that the fictitiousness of the characters alters our feelings towards them. It is, of course, to be granted that the actual and admitted unreality of the dramatic action reinforces the effects of Distance. But surely the proverbial unsophisticated yokel, whose chivalrous interference in the play on behalf of the hapless heroine can only be prevented by impressing upon him that "they are only pretending," is not the ideal type of theatrical audience. The proof of the seeming paradox that it is Distance which primarily gives to dramatic action the appearance of unreality and not vice versa, is the observation that the same filtration of our sentiments and the same seeming "unreality" of *actual* men and things occur, when at times, by a sudden change of inward perspective, we are overcome by the feeling that "all the world's a stage."

2. This personal, but "distanced" relation (as I will venture to call this nameless character of our view) directs attention to a strange fact which appears to be one of the fundamental paradoxes of Art: it is what I propose to call "the antinomy of Distance."

It will be readily admitted that a work of Art has the more chance of appealing to us the better it finds us prepared for its particular kind of appeal. Indeed, without some degree of predisposition on our part, it must necessarily remain incomprehensible, and to that extent unappreciated. The success and intensity of its appeal would seem, therefore, to stand in direct proportion to the completeness with which it corresponds with our intellectual and emotional peculiarities and the idiosyncrasies of our experience. The absence of such a concordance between the characters of a work and of the spectator is, of course, the most general explanation for differences of "tastes."

At the same time, such a principle of concordance requires a qualification, which leads at once to the antinomy of Distance.

Suppose a man, who believes that he has cause to be jealous about his wife, witnesses a performance of *Othello*. He will the more perfectly appreciate the situation, conduct and character of Othello, the more exactly the feelings and experiences of Othello coincide with his own— at least he *ought* to on the above principle of concordance. In point of fact, he will probably do anything but appreciate the play. In reality, the concordance will merely render him acutely conscious of his own jealousy; by a sudden reversal of perspective he will no longer see Othello apparently betrayed by Desdemona, but himself in an analogous situation with his own wife. This reversal of perspective is the consequence of the loss of Distance.

If this be taken as a typical case, it follows that the qualification required is that the coincidence should be as complete as is compatible with maintaining Distance. The jealous spectator of Othello will indeed appreciate and enter into the play the more keenly, the greater the resemblance with his own experience—*provided* that he succeeds in keeping the Distance between the action of the play and his personal feelings: a very difficult performance in the circumstances. It is on account of the same difficulty that the expert and professional critic make a bad audience, since their expertness and critical professionalism are *practical* activities, involving their concrete personality and constantly endangering their Distance. [It is, by the way, one of the reasons why Criticism is an art, for it requires the constant interchange from the practical to the distanced attitude and vice versa, which is characteristic of artists.]

The same qualification applies to the artist. He will prove artistically most effective in the formulation of an intensely *personal* experience, but he can formulate it artistically only on condition of a detachment from the experience *qua personal*. Hence the statement of so many artists that artistic formulation was to them a kind of catharsis, a means of ridding themselves of feelings and ideas the acuteness of which they felt almost as a kind of obsession. Hence, on the other hand, the failure of the average man to convey to others at all adequately the impression of an overwhelming joy or sorrow. His personal implication in the event renders it impossible for him to formulate and present it in such a way as to make others, like himself, feel all the meaning and fullness which it possesses for him.

What is therefore, both in appreciation and production, most desirable is the *utmost decrease of Distance without its disappearance*.

3. Closely related, in fact a presupposition to the "antinomy," is the *variability* of Distance. Herein especially lies the advantage of Distance compared with such terms as "objectivity" and "detachment." Neither of them implies a *personal* relation—indeed both actually preclude it; and the mere inflexibility and exclusiveness of their opposites render their application generally meaningless.

Distance, on the contrary, admits naturally of degrees, and differs not only according to the nature of the *object*, which may impose a greater or smaller degree of Distance, but varies also according to the *individual's capacity* for maintaining a greater or lesser degree. And here one may remark that not only do *persons differ from each other* in their habitual measure of Distance, but that the *same individual differs* in his ability to maintain it in the face of different objects and of different arts.

There exist, therefore, two different sets of conditions affecting the degree of Distance in any given case: those offered by the object and those realised by the subject. In their interplay they afford one of the most extensive explanations for varieties of aesthetic experience, since loss of Distance, whether due to one or the other, means loss of aesthetic appreciation.

In short, Distance may be said *to be variable both according to the distancing-power of the individual, and according to the character of the object.*

There are two ways of losing Distance: either to "under-distance" or to "over-distance." "Under-distancing" is the commonest failing of the *subject*, an excess of Distance is a frequent failing of *Art*, especially in the past. Historically it looks almost as if Art had attempted to meet the deficiency of Distance on the part of the subject and had overshot the mark in this endeavour. It will be seen later that this is actually true, for it appears that over-distanced Art is specially designed for a class of appreciation which has difficulty to rise spontaneously to any degree of Distance. The consequence of a loss of Distance through one or other cause is familiar: the verdict in the case of under-distancing is that the work is "crudely naturalistic," "harrowing," "repulsive in its realism." An excess of distance produces the impression of improbability, artificiality, emptiness or absurdity.

The individual tends, as I just stated, to under-distance rather than to lose Distance by over-distancing. *Theoretically* there is no limit to the decrease of Distance. In theory, therefore, not only the usual subjects of Art, but even the most personal affections, whether ideas, percepts or emotions, can be sufficiently distanced to be aesthetically appreciable. Especially artists are gifted in this direction to a remarkable extent. The average individual, on the contrary, very rapidly reaches his limit of decreasing Distance, his "Distance-limit," i.e. that point at which Distance is lost and appreciation either disappears or changes its character.

In the *practice*, therefore, of the average person, a limit does exist which marks the minimum at which his appreciation can maintain itself in the aesthetic field, and this average minimum lies considerably higher than the Distance-limit of the artist. It is practically impossible to fix this average limit, in the absence of data, and on account of the wide fluctuations from person to person to which this limit is subject. But it is safe to infer that, in art practice, explicit references to organic affections, to the material existence of the body, especially to sexual matters, lie normally below the Distance-limit, and can be touched upon by Art only with special precautions. Allusions to social institutions of any degree of personal importance—in particular, allusions implying any doubt as to their validity—the questioning of some generally recognised ethical sanctions, references to topical subjects occupying public attention at the moment, and such like, are all dangerously near the average limit and may at any time fall below it, arousing, instead of aesthetic appreciation, concrete hostility or mere amusement.

This difference in the Distance-limit between artists and the public has been the source of much misunderstanding and injustice. Many an artist has seen his work condemned and himself ostracised for the sake of so-called "immoralities" which to him were bona fide aesthetic objects. His power of distancing, nay, the necessity of distancing feelings, sensations, situations which for the average person are too intimately bound up with his concrete existence to be regarded in that light, have often quite unjustly earned for him accusations of cynicism, sensualism, morbidness or frivolity. The same misconception has arisen over many "problem-plays" and "problem novels" in which the public have persisted in seeing nothing but a supposed "problem" of the moment, whereas the author may have been—and often has demonstrably been—able to distance the subject-matter sufficiently to rise above its practical problematic import and to regard it simply as a dramatically and humanly interesting situation.

The variability of Distance in respect to Art, disregarding for the moment the subjective complication, appears both as a general feature in Art, and in the differences between the special arts.

It has been an old problem why the "arts of the eye and of the ear" should have reached the practically exclusive predominance over arts of other senses. Attempts to raise "culinary art" to the level of a Fine Art have failed in spite of all propaganda, as completely as the creation of scent or liqueur "symphonies." There is little doubt that, apart from other excellent reasons of a partly psycho-physical, partly technical nature, the actual, *spatial distance* separating objects of sight and hearing from the subject has contributed strongly to the development of this monopoly. In a similar manner *temporal remoteness* produces Distance, and objects removed from us in point of time are *ipso facto* distanced to an extent which was impossible for their contemporaries. Many pictures, plays and poems had, as a matter of fact, rather an expository or illustrative significance—as for instance much ecclesiastical Art—or the force of a direct practical appeal—as the invectives of many satires or comedies—which seem to us nowadays irreconcilable with their aesthetic claims. Such works have consequently profited greatly by lapse of time and have reached the level of Art only with the help of temporal distance, while others, on the contrary, often for the same reason have suffered a loss of Distance, through *over*-distancing.

Special mention must be made of a group of artistic conceptions which present excessive Distance in their form of appeal rather than in their actual presentation—a point illustrating the necessity of distinguishing between distancing an object and distancing the appeal of which it is the source. I mean here what is often rather loosely termed "idealistic Art," that is, Art springing from abstract conceptions, expressing allegorical meanings, or illustrating general truths. Generalisations and abstractions suffer under this disadvantage that they have too much general applicability to invite a personal interest in them, and too little individual concreteness to prevent them applying to us in all their force. They appeal to everybody and therefore to none. An axiom of Euclid belongs to nobody, just because it compels everyone's assent; general conceptions like Patriotism, Friendship, Love, Hope, Life, Death, concern as much Dick, Tom and Harry as myself, and I, therefore, either feel unable to get into any kind of personal relation to them, or, if I do so, they become at once, emphatically and concretely, *my* Patriotism, *my* Friendship, *my* Love, *my* Hope, *my* Life and Death. By mere force of generalisation, a general truth or a universal ideal is so far distanced from myself that I fail to realise it concretely at all, or, when I do so, I can realise it only as part of my *practical actual being*, i.e. it falls below the Distance-limit altogether. "Idealistic Art" suffers consequently under the peculiar difficulty that its excess of Distance turns generally into an *under*-distanced appeal—all the more easily, as it is the usual failing of the subject to *under*- rather than to *over*-distance.

The different special arts show at the present time very marked variations in the degree of Distance which they usually impose or require for their appreciation. Unfortunately here again the absence of data makes itself felt and indicates the necessity of conducting observations, possibly experiments, so as to place these suggestions upon a securer basis. In one single art, viz. the *theatre*, a small amount of information is available, from an unexpected source, namely the proceedings of the censorship committee,[1] which on closer examination might be able to yield evidence of interest to the psychologist. In fact, the whole censorship problem, as far as it does not turn upon purely economic questions, may be said to hinge upon Distance; if every member of the public could be trusted to keep it, there would be no sense whatever in the existence of a censor of plays. There is, of course, no doubt that, speaking generally, theatrical performances *eo ipso* run a special risk of loss of Distance owing to the material presentment[2] of its subject-matter. The physical presence of living human beings as vehicles of dramatic art is a difficulty which no art has to face in the same way. A similar, in many ways even greater, risk confronts *dancing*: though attracting perhaps a less widely spread human interest, its animal spirits are frequently quite unrelieved by any glimmer of spirituality and consequently form a proportionately stronger lure to under-distancing. In the higher forms of dancing technical execution of the most wearing kind makes up a great deal for its intrinsic tendency towards a loss of Distance, and as a popular performance, at least in southern Europe, it has retained much of its ancient artistic glamour, producing a peculiarly subtle balancing of Distance between the pure delight of bodily movement and high technical accomplishment. In passing, it is interesting to observe (as bearing upon the development of Distance) that this art, once as much a fine art as music and considered by the Greeks as a particularly valuable educational exercise, should—except in sporadic cases—have fallen so low from the pedestal it once occupied. Next to the theatre and dancing stands *sculpture*. Though not using a *living* bodily medium, yet the human form in its full spatial materiality constitutes a similar threat to Distance. Our northern habits of dress and ignorance of the human body have enormously increased the difficulty of distancing Sculpture, in part through the gross misconceptions to which it is exposed, in part owing to a complete lack of standards of bodily perfection, and an inability to realise the distinction between sculptural form and bodily shape, which is the only but fundamental point distinguishing a statue from a cast taken from life. In *painting* it is apparently the form of its present-ment and the usual reduction in scale which would explain why this art can venture to approach more closely than sculpture to the normal Distance-limit. As this matter will be discussed later in a special con-nection this simple reference may suffice here. *Music* and *architecture* have a curious position. These two most abstract of all arts show a re-markable fluctuation in their Distances. Certain kinds of music, especially "pure" music, or "classical" or "heavy" music, appear for many people over-distanced; light, "catchy" tunes, on the contrary, easily reach that degree of decreasing Distance below which they cease to be Art and become a pure amusement. In spite of its strange abstractness which to many philosophers has made it comparable to architecture and mathe-matics, music possesses a sensuous, frequently sensual, character: the undoubted physiological and muscular stimulus of its melodies and harmonies, no less than its rhythmic aspects, would seem to account for the occasional disappearance of Distance. To this might be added its strong tendency, especially in unmusical people, to stimulate trains of thought quite disconnected with itself, following channels of subjective inclinations—day-dreams of a more or less directly personal character. *Architecture* requires almost uniformly a very great Distance; that is to say, the majority of persons derive no aesthetic appreciation from archi-tecture as such, apart from the incidental impression of its decorative features and its associations. The causes are numerous, but prominent among them are the confusion of building with architecture and the predominance of utilitarian purposes, which overshadow the architec-tural claims upon the attention.

4. That all art requires a Distance-limit beyond which, and a Distance within which only, aesthetic appreciation becomes possible, is the *psy-chological formulation of a general characteristic of Art*, viz. *its anti-realistic nature*. Though seemingly paradoxical, this applies as much to "naturalistic" as to "idealistic" Art. The difference commonly expressed by these epithets is at bottom merely the difference in the degree of Distance; and this produces, so far as "naturalism" and "idealism" in Art are not meaningless labels, the usual result that what appears obnoxiously "naturalistic" to one person, may be "idealistic" to another. To say that Art is anti-realistic simply insists upon the fact that Art is not nature, never pretends to be nature and strongly resists any confusion with nature. It emphasises the *art*-character of Art: "artistic" is synony-mous with "anti-realistic"; it explains even sometimes a very marked degree of artificiality.

"Art is an imitation of nature," was the current art-conception in the eighteenth century. It is the fundamental axiom of the standard work of that time upon aesthetic theory by the Abbé du Bos, *Réflexions critiques sur la poésie et la peinture, 1719*; the idea received strong support from the literal acceptance of Aristotle's theory of μίμησις and produced echoes everywhere, in Lessing's *Laokoön* no less than in Burke's famous statement that "all Art is great as it deceives." Though it may be assumed that since the time of Kant and of the Romanticists this notion has died out, it still lives in unsophisticated minds. Even when formally denied, it persists, for instance, in the belief that "Art idealises nature," which means after all only that Art copies nature with certain improvements and revisions. Artists themselves are unfortunately often responsible for the spreading of this conception. Whistler indeed said that to produce Art by imitating nature would be like trying to produce music by sitting upon the piano, but the selective, idealising imitation of nature finds merely another support in such a saying. Naturalism, pleinairism, impressionism, even the guileless enthusiasm of the artist for the works of nature, her wealth of suggestion, her delicacy of workmanship, for the steadfastness of her guidance, only produce upon the public the impression that Art is, after all, an imitation of nature. Then how can it be anti-realistic? The antithesis, Art *versus* nature, seems to break down. Yet if it does, what is the sense of Art?

Here the conception of Distance comes to the rescue. The solution of the dilemma lies in the "antinomy of Distance" with its demand: utmost decrease of Distance without its disappearance. The simple observation that Art is the more effective, the more it falls into line with our predispositions which are inevitably moulded on general experience and nature, has always been the original motive for "naturalism." "Naturalism," "impressionism" is no new thing; it is only a new name for an innate leaning of Art, from the time of the Chaldeans and Egyptians down to the present day. Even the Apollo of Tenea apparently struck his contemporaries as so startlingly "naturalistic" that the subsequent legend attributed a superhuman genius to his creator. A constantly closer approach to nature, a perpetual refining of the limit of Distance, yet without overstepping the dividing line of art and nature, has always been the inborn bent of art. To deny this dividing line has occasionally been the failing of naturalism. But no theory of naturalism is complete which does not at the same time allow for the intrinsic idealism of Art: for both are merely degrees in that wide range lying beyond the Distance-limit. To imitate nature so as to trick the spectator into the deception that it is nature which he beholds, is to forsake Art, its anti-realism, its distanced spirituality, and to fall below the limit into sham, sensationalism or platitude.

But what, in the theory of antinomy of Distance, requires explanation is the existence of an *idealistic, highly distanced* Art. There are numerous reasons to account for it; indeed in so complex a phenomenon as Art, *single* causes can be pronounced almost *a priori* to be false. Foremost among such causes which have contributed to the formation of an idealistic Art appears to stand the subordination of Art to some extraneous purpose of an impressive, exceptional character. Such a subordination has consisted—at various epochs of Art history—in the use to which Art was put to subserve commemorative, hieratic, generally religious, royal or patriotic functions. The object to be commemorated had to stand out from among other still existing objects or persons; the thing or the being to be worshipped had to be distinguished as markedly as possible from profaner objects of reverence and had to be invested with an air of sanctity by a removal from its ordinary context of occurrence. Nothing could have assisted more powerfully the introduction of a high Distance than this attempt to differentiate objects of common experience in order to fit them for their exalted position. Curious, unusual things of nature met this tendency half-way and easily assumed divine rank; but others had to be distanced by an exaggeration of their size, by extraordinary attributes, by strange combinations of human and animal forms, by special insistence upon particular characteristics, or by the careful removal of all noticeably individualistic and concrete features. Nothing could be more striking than the contrast, for example, in Egyptian art between the monumental, stereotyped effigies of the Pharaohs, and the startlingly realistic rendering of domestic scenes and of ordinary mortals, such as "the Scribe," or "the Village Sheikh." Equally noteworthy is the exceeding artificiality of Russian ikon-painting with its prescribed attributes, expressions and gestures. Even Greek dramatic practice appears to have aimed, for similar purposes and in marked contrast to our stage-habits, at an increase rather than at a decrease of Distance. Otherwise Greek Art, even of a religious type, is remarkable for its *low* Distance value; and it speaks highly for the aesthetic capacities of the Greeks that the degree of realism which they ventured to impart to the representation of the gods, while humanising them, did not, at least at first,[3] impair the reverence of their feelings towards them. But apart from such special causes, idealistic Art of great Distance has appeared at intervals, for apparently no other reason than that the great Distance was felt to be essential to its *art*-character. What is noteworthy and runs counter to many accepted ideas is that such periods were usually epochs of a low level of general culture. These were times, which, like childhood, required the marvellous, the extraordinary, to satisfy their artistic longings, and neither realised nor cared for the poetic or artistic qualities of ordinary things. They were frequently times in which the mass of the people were plunged in ignorance and buried under a load of misery, and in which even the small educated class sought rather amusement or a pastime in Art; or they were epochs of a strong practical common sense too much concerned with the rough-and-tumble of life to have any sense of its aesthetic charms. Art was to them what melodrama is to a section of the public at the present time, and its wide Distance was the safeguard of its artistic character. The flowering periods of Art have, on the contrary, always borne the evidence of a narrow Distance. Greek Art, as just mentioned, was realistic to an extent which we, spoilt as we are by modern developments, can grasp with difficulty, but which the contrast with its oriental contemporaries sufficiently proves. During the Augustan period—which Art historians at last are coming to regard no longer as merely "degenerated" Greek Art—Roman Art achieved its greatest triumphs in an almost naturalistic portrait-sculpture. In the Renaissance we need only think of the realism of portraiture, sometimes amounting almost to cynicism, of the *désinvolture* with which the mistresses of popes and dukes were posed as madonnas, saints and goddesses apparently without any detriment to the aesthetic appeal of the works, and of the remarkable interpenetration of Art with the most ordinary routine of life, in order to realise the scarcely perceptible dividing line between the sphere of Art and the realm of practical existence. In a sense, the assertion that idealistic Art marks periods of a generally low and narrowly restricted culture is the converse to the oft-repeated statement that the flowering periods of Art coincide with epochs of decadence: for this so-called decadence represents indeed in certain respects a process of disintegration, politically, racially, often nationally, but a disruption necessary to the formation of larger social units and to the breakdown of outgrown national restrictions. For this very reason it has usually also been the sign of the growth of personal independence and of an expansion of individual culture.

To proceed to some more special points illustrating the distanced and therefore anti-realistic character of art: both in subject-matter and in the form of presentation Art has always safeguarded its distanced view. Fanciful, even fantastic, subjects have from time immemorial been the accredited material of Art. No doubt things, as well as our view of them, have changed in the course of time: *Polyphemus* and the *Lotus-Eaters* for the Greeks, the *Venusberg* or the *Magnetic Mountain* for the Middle Ages were less incredible, more realistic than to us. But *Peter Pan* or *L'Oiseau Bleu* still appeal at the present day in spite of the prevailing note of realism of our time. "Probability" and "improbability" in Art are not to be measured by their correspondence (or lack of it) with actual experience. To do so had involved the theories of the fifteenth to the eighteenth centuries in endless contradictions. It is rather a matter of *consistency* of Distance. The note of realism, set by the work as a whole, determines *intrinsically* the greater or smaller degree of fancy which it permits; and consequently we feel the loss of Peter Pan's shadow to be infinitely more probable than some trifling improbability which shocks our sense of proportion in a naturalistic work. No doubt also, fairy-tales, fairy-plays, stories of strange adventures were primarily invented to satisfy the craving of curiosity, the desire for the marvellous, the shudder of the unwonted and the longing for imaginary experiences.

But by their mere eccentricity in regard to the normal facts of experience they cannot have failed to arouse a strong feeling of Distance.

Again, certain conventional subjects taken from mythical and legendary traditions, at first closely connected with the concrete, practical, life of a devout public, have gradually, by the mere force of convention as much as by their inherent anti-realism, acquired Distance for us today. Our view of Greek mythological sculpture, of early Christian saints and martyrs must be considerably distanced, compared with that of the Greek and medieval worshipper. It is in part the result of lapse of time, but in part also a real change of attitude. Already the outlook of the Imperial Roman had altered, and Pausanius shows a curious dualism of standpoint, declaring the Athene Lemnia to be the supreme achievement of Phidias's genius, and gazing awe-struck upon the roughly hewn tree-trunk representing some primitive Apollo. Our understanding of Greek tragedy suffers admittedly under our inability to revert to the point of view for which it was originally written. Even the tragedies of Racine demand an imaginative effort to put ourselves back into the courtly atmosphere of red-heeled, powdered ceremony. Provided the Distance is not too wide, the result of its intervention has everywhere been to enhance the *art*-character of such works and to lower their original ethical and social force of appeal. Thus in the central dome of the Church (Sta Maria dei Miracoli) at Saronno are depicted the heavenly hosts in ascending tiers, crowned by the benevolent figure of the Divine Father, bending from the window of heaven to bestow His blessing upon the assembled community. The mere realism of foreshortening and of the boldest vertical perspective may well have made the naïve Christian of the sixteenth century conscious of the Divine Presence—but for us it has become a work of Art.

The unusual, exceptional, has found its especial home in tragedy. It has always—except in highly distanced tragedy—been a popular objection to it that "there is enough sadness in life without going to the theatre for it." Already Aristotle appears to have met with this view among his contemporaries clamouring for "happy endings." Yet tragedy is not sad; if it were, there would indeed be little sense in its existence. For the tragic is just in so far different from the merely sad, as it is distanced; and it is largely the exceptional which produces the Distance of tragedy: exceptional situations, exceptional characters, exceptional destinies and conduct. Not of course characters merely cranky, eccentric, pathological. The exceptional element in tragic figures—that which makes them so utterly different from characters we meet with in ordinary experience—is a consistency of direction, a fervour of ideality, a persistence and driving-force which is far above the capacities of average men. The tragic of tragedy would, transposed into ordinary life, in nine cases out of ten, end in drama, in comedy, even in farce, for lack of steadfastness, for fear of conventions, for the dread of "scenes," for a hundred-and-one petty faithlessnesses towards a belief or an ideal: even if for none of these, it would end in a compromise simply because man forgets and time heals.[4] Again, the sympathy which aches with the sadness of tragedy is another such confusion, the under-distancing of tragedy's appeal. Tragedy trembles always on the knife-edge of a *personal* reaction, and sympathy which finds relief in tears tends almost always towards a loss of Distance. Such a loss naturally renders tragedy unpleasant to a degree: it becomes sad, dismal, harrowing, depressing. But real tragedy (melodrama has a very strong tendency to speculate upon sympathy), truly appreciated, is not sad. "The pity of it—oh, the pity of it," that essence of all genuine tragedy is not the pity of mild, regretful sympathy. It is a chaos of tearless, bitter bewilderment, of up-surging revolt and rapturous awe before the ruthless and inscrutable fate; it is the homage to the great and exceptional in the man who in a last effort of spiritual tension can rise to confront blind, crowning Necessity even in his crushing defeat.

As I explained earlier, the form of presentation sometimes endangers the maintenance of Distance, but it more frequently acts as a consider-able support. Thus the bodily vehicle of *drama* is the chief factor of risk to Distance. But, as if to counterbalance a confusion with nature, other features of stage-presentation exercise an opposite influence. Such are the general theatrical *milieu*, the shape and arrangement of the stage, the artificial lighting, the costumes, *mise en scène* and make-up, even the language, especially verse. Modern reforms of staging, aiming primarily at the removal of artistic incongruities between excessive decoration and the living figures of the actors and at the production of a more homogeneous stage-picture, inevitably work also towards a greater emphasis and homogeneity of Distance. The history of staging and dramaturgy is closely bound up with the evolution of Distance, and its fluctuations lie at the bottom not only of the greater part of all the talk and writing about "dramatic probability" and the Aristotelian "unities," but also of "theatrical illusion." In *sculpture*, one distancing factor of presentment is its lack of colour. The aesthetic, or rather in-aesthetic, effect of realistic colourings is in no way touched by the controversial question of its use historically; its attempted resuscitation, such as by Klinger, seems only to confirm its disadvantages. The distanc-ing use even of pedestals, although originally no doubt serving other purposes, is evident to anyone who has experienced the oppressively crowded sensation of moving in a room among life-sized statues placed directly upon the floor. The circumstance that the space of statuary is the same space as ours (in distinction to relief sculpture or painting, for instance) renders a distancing by pedestals, i.e. a removal from our spatial context, imperative.[5] Probably the framing of *pictures* might be shown to serve a similar purpose—though paintings have intrinsically a much greater Distance—because neither their space (perspective and imaginary space) nor their lighting coincides with our (actual) space or light, and the usual reduction in scale of the represented objects prevents a feeling of undue proximity. Besides, painting always retains to some extent a *two*-dimensional character, and this character supplies *eo ipso* a Distance. Nevertheless, life-size pictures, especially if they possess strong relief, can occasionally produce the impression of actual presence which is a far from pleasant, though fortunately only a passing, illusion. For decorative purposes, in pictorial renderings of vistas, garden-perspectives and architectural extensions, the removal of Distance has often been consciously striven after, whether with aesthetically satisfactory results is much disputed.

A general help towards Distance (and therewith an anti-realistic feature) is to be found in the "unification of presentment"[6] of all art-objects. By unification of presentment are meant such qualities as symmetry, opposition, proportion, balance, rhythmical distribution of parts, light-arrangements, in fact all so-called "formal" features, "composition" in the widest sense. Unquestionably, Distance is not the only, nor even the principal function of composition; it serves to render our grasp of the presentation easier and to increase its intelligibility. It may even in itself constitute the principal aesthetic feature of the object, as in linear complexes or patterns, partly also in architectural designs. Yet, its distancing effect can hardly be underrated. For, every kind of visibly intentional arrangement or unification must, by the mere fact of its presence, enforce Distance, by distinguishing the object from the confused, disjointed and scattered forms of actual experience. This function can be gauged in a typical form in cases where composition produces an exceptionally marked impression of artificiality (not in the bad sense of that term, but in the sense in which all art is artificial); and it is a natural corollary to the differences of Distance in different arts and of different subjects, that the arts and subjects vary in the degree of artificiality which they can bear. It is this sense of artificial finish which is the source of so much of that elaborate charm of Byzantine work, of Mohammedan decoration, of the hieratic stiffness of so many primitive madonnas and saints. In general the emphasis of composition and technical finish increases with the Distance of the subject-matter: heroic conceptions lend themselves better to verse than to prose; monumental statues require a more general treatment, more elaboration of setting and artificiality of pose than impressionistic statuettes like those of Troubetzkoi; an ecclesiastic subject is painted with a degree of symmetrical arrangement which would be ridiculous in a Dutch interior, and a naturalistic drama carefully avoids the tableau impression characteristic of a mystery play. In a similar manner the variations of Distance in the arts go hand in hand with a visibly greater predominance of composition and "formal" elements, reaching a climax in architecture and music. It is again a matter of "consistency of Distance." At the same time, while from the point of view of the artist this is undoubtedly the case, from the point of view of the public the emphasis of composition and technical finish appears frequently to relieve the impression of highly distanced subjects by *diminishing the Distance of the whole.* The spectator has a tendency to see in composition and finish merely evidence of the artist's "cleverness," of his mastery over his material. Manual dexterity is an enviable thing to possess in everyone's experience, and naturally appeals to the public *practically*, thereby putting it into a directly personal relation to things which intrinsically have very little personal appeal for it. It is true that this function of composition is hardly an aesthetic one: for the admiration of mere technical cleverness is not an artistic enjoyment, but by a fortunate chance it has saved from oblivion and entire loss, among much rubbish, also much genuine Art, which otherwise would have completely lost contact with our life.

5. This discussion, necessarily sketchy and incomplete, may have helped to illustrate the sense in which, I suggested, Distance appears as a fundamental principle to which such antitheses as idealism and realism are reducible. The difference between "idealistic" and "realistic" Art is not a clear-cut dividing line between the art-practices described by these terms, but is a difference of degree in the Distance-limit which they presuppose on the part both of the artist and of the public. A similar reconciliation seems to me possible between the opposites "sensual" and "spiritual," "individual" and "typical." That the appeal of Art is sensuous, even sensual, must be taken as an indisputable fact. Puritanism will never be persuaded, and rightly so, that this is not the case. The sensuousness of Art is a natural implication of the "antinomy of Distance," and will appear again in another connection. The point of importance here is that the whole sensual side of Art is purified, spiritualised, "filtered" as I expressed it earlier, by Distance. The most sensuous appeal becomes the translucent veil of an underlying spirituality, once the grossly personal and practical elements have been removed from it. And—a matter of special emphasis here—*this spiritual aspect of the appeal is the more penetrating, the more personal and direct its sensual appeal would have been* BUT FOR THE PRESENCE OF DISTANCE. For the artist, to trust in this delicate transmutation is a natural act of faith which the Puritan hesitates to venture upon: which of the two, one asks, is the greater idealist?

6. The same argument applies to the contradictory epithets "individual" and "typical." A discussion in support of the fundamental individualism of Art lies outside the scope of this essay. Every artist has taken it for granted. Besides it is rather in the sense of "concrete" or "individualised," that it is usually opposed to "typical." On the other hand, "typical," in the sense of "abstract," is as diametrically opposed to the whole nature of Art, as individualism is characteristic of it. It is in the sense of "generalised," as a "general human element" that it is

claimed as a necessary ingredient in Art. This antithesis is again one which naturally and without mutual sacrifice finds room within the conception of Distance. Historically the "typical" has had the effect of counteracting *under*-distancing as much as the "individual" has opposed *over*-distancing. Naturally the two ingredients have constantly varied in the history of Art; they represent, in fact, two sets of conditions to which Art has invariably been subject: the personal and the social factors. It is Distance which on one side prevents the emptying of Art of its concreteness and the development of the typical into abstractness; which, on the other, suppresses the directly personal element of its individualism; thus reducing the antithesis to the peaceful interplay of these two factors. It is just this interplay which constitutes the "antinomy of Distance." . . .

Notes

1. Report from the Joint Select Committee of the House of Lords and the House of Commons on Stage Plays (Censorship), 1909.

2. I shall use the term "presentment" to denote the manner of presenting, in distinction to "presentation" as that which is presented.

3. That this practice did, in course of time, undermine their religious faith, is clear from the plays of Euripides and from Plato's condemnation of Homer's mythology.

4. The famous "unity of time," so senseless as a "canon," is all the same often an indispensable condition of tragedy. For in many a tragedy the catastrophe would be even intrinsically impossible, if fatality did not overtake the hero with that rush which gives no time to forget and none to heal. It is in cases such as these that criticism has often blamed the work for "improbability"— the old confusion between Art and nature—forgetting that the death of the hero is the convention of the art-form, as much as grouping in a picture is such a convention and that probability is not the correspondence with average experience, but consistency of Distance.

5. An instance which might be adduced to disprove this point only shows its correctness on closer inspection: for it was on purpose and with the intention of removing Distance, that Rodin originally intended his *citoyens de Calais* to be placed, without pedestals, upon the market-place of that town.

6. See note 2.

J. O. URMSON

What Makes a Situation Aesthetic?

PHILOSOPHERS HAVE HOED OVER the plot of aesthetics often enough, but the plants that they have raised thereby are pitifully weak and straggling objects. The time has therefore not yet come for tidying up some corner of the plot; it needs digging over afresh in the hope that some sturdier and more durable produce may arise, even if its health be rather rude. I therefore make no excuse for reopening what seems to me to be the central problem of aesthetics: I hope that by a somewhat new approach I may succeed in making a contribution, if but a small one, towards its solution.

We may refer to a person as, in a given situation, getting an aesthetic thrill or aesthetic satisfaction from something, or of his finding something aesthetically tolerable, or aesthetically dissatisfying, or even aesthetically hateful. In a suitable context the adjective "aesthetic" and the adverb "aesthetically" may well be superfluous, but it is sometimes necessary to introduce one of these words in order to make it clear that when we refer, say, to a person's satisfaction we are not thinking of moral satisfaction, economic satisfaction, personal satisfaction, intellectual satisfaction, or any satisfaction other than aesthetic satisfaction. If we merely know that someone gained satisfaction from a play we do not know for sure that we are in the aesthetic field. Thus a play may give me moral satisfaction because I think it likely to have improving effects on the audience; economic satisfaction because it is playing to full houses and I am financing it; personal satisfaction because I wrote it and it is highly praised by the critics; intellectual satisfaction because it solves a number of difficult technical problems of the theatre very cleverly. But the question will still be open whether I found the play aesthetically satisfying. Though these various types of satisfaction are not mutually exclusive, it is clear that when we call a satisfaction aesthetic the purpose must be to mark it off from the other types.

Reprinted from *Proceedings of the Aristotelian Society*, Supplementary Vol. XXXI (1957) by courtesy of the Editor of the Aristotelian Society.

The philosophical task to be tackled in this paper is therefore this: to make explicit what it is that distinguishes aesthetic thrills, satisfactions, toleration, disgust, etc., from thrills, satisfactions, etc., that would properly be called moral, intellectual, economic, etc. I put the question in this form because I think that it is tempting to consider the aesthetic as an isolated matter and within the field of the aesthetic to concentrate unduly upon the most sublime and intense of our experiences; but I am convinced that it is important to ensure that our account of the aesthetic should be as applicable to toleration as to our most significant experiences and should make it clear that in characterising a reaction or judgment as aesthetic the point is to distinguish it from other reactions and judgments that are moral, economic, and so on. Only thus can we hope to bring out the full forces of the term "aesthetic."

This is not intended to be a problem especially about the appreciation of works of art. No doubt many of our most intense aesthetic satisfactions are derived from plays, poems, musical works, pictures and other works of art. But to me it seems obvious that we also derive aesthetic satisfaction from artifacts that are not primarily works of art, from scenery, from natural objects and even from formal logic; it is at least reasonable also to allow an aesthetic satisfaction to the connoisseur of wines and to the gourmet. I shall therefore assume that there is no special set of objects which are the sole and proper objects of aesthetic reactions and judgments, and which are never the objects of an economic, intellectual, moral, religious or personal reaction or judgment. We may judge a power-station aesthetically and find economic satisfaction in a work of art that we own. We may take it, then, that we are not exclusively concerned with the philosophy of art, and that whatever the criteria of the aesthetic may be they cannot be found by trying to delimit a special class of objects.

If the aesthetic cannot be identified by its being directed to a special class of objects, it might be more plausibly suggested that the criteria of the aesthetic are to be sought by looking for some special features of objects which are attended to when our reaction or judgment is aesthetic; beauty and ugliness have often been adduced as the features in question. Alternatively it has often been suggested that aesthetic reactions and judgments contain or refer to some unique constituent of the emotions of the observer, either a special "aesthetic emotion" or an "aesthetic tinge" of some other emotion. I think that most commonly theories elicited by our problem have been variations on one or other of these two themes, a variation on the first theme being called an objectivist theory and a variation on the second being called subjectivist. I propose to give some reasons in this paper for finding both these theories unsatisfactory as answers to our problem, even if neither is wholly false as a mere assertion; in their place, I shall suggest that the correct answer is to be given in terms of the explanation of the reaction or the grounds of the judgment. I shall make some tentative remarks about what sort of grounds for a judgment make that judgment aesthetic, but cannot even begin the systematic treatment of the subject.

Let us revert to an illustration already casually used, and suppose that we observe a man in the audience at a play who is obviously beaming with delight and satisfaction. If I now maintain that his delight is purely economic, what have I to do in order to establish this contention? If the question at issue were whether he was delighted or merely contented it would no doubt be necessary to ascertain fairly accurately his emotional state; but if it be agreed that he is delighted and the only issue is whether his delight is properly to be called economic, it is surely clear that phenomenological study of his emotions is not necessary. If, however, we find him to be the impresario, and he agrees that the complete explanation of his delight is that there is a full house, and the reaction of his audience indicates a long run, what more could possibly be needed to justify us in describing his delight as economic? It seems hard to dispute that in the case of economic delight, satisfaction, disappointment and the like the criterion of the reaction's being economic lies in the nature of the explanation of that reaction. Similarly it would be beyond dispute that a man's delight was wholly personal if it were conceded that its explanation was entirely the fact that his daughter was acquitting herself well in her first part as a leading lady; again his delight will be moral if wholly explained by the belief that the play will have a good effect on the conduct of the audience. It would, I suggest, be very surprising if the way of establishing that delight, satisfaction and other reactions were aesthetic turned out to be quite different from the way in which we establish them to be moral, personal, economic, intellectual, etc. Nor would it be surprising merely as a novelty; it would be logically disturbing to find that one had suddenly to depart from a single *fundamentum divisionis*, which had sufficed for all the other types, when one came to the aesthetic.

We must now note a further point about the logical relation between the concepts of the moral, the aesthetic, the economic, the intellectual, and the personal, as applied to reactions, both because it is of some logical interest and because a misunderstanding of it has led to some silly theories. *Triangular, square* and *pentagonal,* as applied to surfaces, are clearly species of a single genus and as such are mutually exclusive; there is a single *fundamentum divisionis* which is the number of sides that the rectilinear surface has. The same applies, *mutatis mutandis,* to *bachelor, married* and *widowed* as applied to men. On the other hand *triangular, red* and *large* are three logically unconnected predicates of surfaces, and *bachelor, bald* and *wealthy* are similarly unconnected predicates of men. What then are we to say about the predicates *moral, economic* and *aesthetic* as applied to, say, satisfactions? Clearly they are not technically species of a genus for they are not mutually exclusive as are species of a single genus; I may be simultaneously satisfied by a single object aesthetically, morally and economically, just as well as a man may be simultaneously bald, wealthy and a widower. But on the other hand to ask whether a satisfaction is moral or aesthetic makes as good sense as to ask whether a surface is square or triangular, whereas only in a very odd context can one ask whether a man is bald or a widower; furthermore, if a satisfaction is wholly moral it is not at all aesthetic; whereas being wholly bald does not prevent a man from being a widower. Thus moral, aesthetic and economic satisfactions seem neither to be logically disconnected nor to be true species of a genus.

Aesthetic and moral satisfactions thus seem to be related as are business and sporting associates. A man may be both a business and a sporting associate, yet the point of calling a man a business associate is to distinguish his status from that of a sporting or other type of associate, as it does not distinguish him from, say, an associate first met at Yarmouth. In the same way, to call a satisfaction aesthetic has the point of distinguishing its status from that of being a moral or economic satisfaction, though a satisfaction may be both aesthetic and moral. It surely follows that the criteria for a reaction's being aesthetic cannot be wholly unrelated to the criteria for its being moral or economic—they must be connected in such a way that we can see how being wholly one excludes being also another and yet how a single reaction can be both moral and aesthetic.

If we find the criterion for distinguishing aesthetic from kindred reactions in the nature of the explanation of the reactions we can readily account for this logical situation. To say that a satisfaction is wholly aesthetic, for example, will be to say that the explanation or grounds of the satisfaction are wholly of one sort, which will necessitate that the satisfaction cannot rest also on moral grounds; on the other hand there is clearly nothing to prevent our satisfaction from being multiply-grounded and thus simultaneously aesthetic and moral, aesthetic and economic, and so on.

But if we were to accept different kinds of criteria of the aesthetic, the moral and the economic we should be in difficulties here. Thus if a philosopher were to hold (and some apparently do) that a moral judgment is one that asserts an object to have a certain character and an aesthetic judgment to be one that announces or expresses the special emotional state of the speaker he would be maintaining views which, however plausible when consistently adhered to in isolation, are poor bed-fellows. For one would expect a wholly moral judgment interpreted as ascribing a moral character, to deny implicitly the presence of a special aesthetic or special economic character; similarly a wholly aesthetic judgment, interpreted as expressing a special aesthetic emotion, should deny implicitly the presence of a special moral or economic emotion. Consistency is required here.

So much for the logical point of being clear on the relation between the aesthetic, the moral, the economic, etc. Unclarity on the point can lead to other less philosophical confusions. Thus the belief that moral considerations are relevant to a thing's aesthetic rank seems to stem from an awareness that appreciation may be simultaneously based on aesthetic and moral considerations coupled with a blindness to the fact that to call an appreciation aesthetic has as part of its point the effect of ruling out the moral as irrelevant. At the opposite extreme those who rage at any moral comment on a work of art are so conscious that the moral is irrelevant to the aesthetic that they suppose some error in allowing one's general satisfaction to have both a moral and an aesthetic component.

I have illustrated sufficiently the dangers of considering aesthetic reactions and judgments in abstraction from moral, economic and other kindred reactions and judgments. Similarly we must not concentrate on aesthetic delight and neglect other aesthetic reactions. The view that delight is aesthetic when that emotion has some special aesthetic tinge is not unplausible in isolation; we can no doubt bring aesthetic disgust under the same theory easily enough. But what if I am asked for an aesthetic judgment on what seems to me a very ordinary building and I reply truthfully that I find it merely tolerable? Am I reporting an emotion of toleration which has an aesthetic tinge, or perhaps an absolute tinge with no emotion to be tinged? But if I be taken to report merely the absence of any emotion or tinge by what criterion can we say that I am making an aesthetic judgment at all? It is surely important that we should be able to distinguish an aesthetic judgment of toleration from merely refraining from any aesthetic judgment at all; to regard a thing with mere aesthetic toleration is quite different from not considering it in an aesthetic light at all.

Thus the view that what distinguishes the aesthetic reaction and judgment is the presence of a special emotion or a special emotional tinge has already proved unsatisfactory on two counts. First, we have seen that we require a similar type of criterion of the aesthetic, the moral, the intellectual and the economic reaction, whereas the emotional criterion is very unplausible in some of these cases. Secondly, we have seen that however plausible with regard to strong emotional reactions, the emotional view is most unplausible when we consider such cool aesthetic reactions as that of bare toleration. Even if these difficulties were overcome, it is perhaps worth noticing that on this view a single reaction which involved, say, simultaneous economic, moral, aesthetic and intellectual satisfaction might well be required to involve an emotion having a quite kaleidoscopic variety of tinges.

But apart from these more logical points it is surely clear that when we experience emotions that we should wish to call aesthetic they are often very different from each other. Thus Tovey (*Essays in Musical Analysis*, Vol. I, p. 200) speaks of a theme "which gives Mozart's most inimitable sense of physical well-being" precisely because most of even the most delightful musical themes are so different in emotional effect.

Or again, is it so clear that aesthetic emotions are different in kind from others? Tovey, we have seen, compares a Mozart theme to a quite non-aesthetic delight, and Housman can be adduced as a still more striking, since unwilling, witness. Enumerating three types of "symptoms" of poetical delight in his lecture, "The Name and Nature of Poetry," he says, "One of these symptoms was described in connexion with another object by Eliphaz the Temanite: 'A spirit passed before my face; the hair of my flesh stood up' "; another he describes by using Keats's words about his feelings for Fanny Brawne, "everything that reminds me of her goes through me like a spear"; the third, he says, "consists in a constriction of the throat and a precipitation of water to the eyes," an experience which is surely common to many emotional situations, and not confined to the aesthetic.

The objection to the view that what distinguishes the aesthetic judgment or reaction from others is that it alone involves the recognition or awareness of beauty and ugliness, if offered as a solution to our problem, is rather different. As a minor objection it is worth pointing out that we should hesitate to call many things for which we have a great aesthetic admiration "beautiful," that "beautiful" is a relatively specialised word of aesthetic appraisal, though this will inevitably elicit the answer that here "beauty" is being used with a wider meaning than is currently assigned to it. But granted that "beauty" and "ugliness" are being used with a wide enough significance, the trouble with this answer to our problem is not that it is false but that it is futile. Of course if I admire a thing aesthetically I must be aware of its beauty, or of its charm, or of its prettiness or some other "aesthetic characteristic"; this is true in the same way as it is platitudinously true that moral admiration must involve awareness of a thing's moral goodness or rectitude or of some other "moral characteristic." But the trouble is that we have no independent way of telling whether we are aware of beauty or ugliness on the one hand or rightness or wrongness on the other; to know this we must know whether our admiration is aesthetic or moral, or, more accurately, to try to discover whether our admiration is aesthetic or moral and to try to discover whether we are aware of beauty or rightness are not two distinct enquiries but a single enquiry described in two ways neither of which is more luminous than the other. To identify the aesthetic judgment by the aesthetic characters of which it involves awareness is therefore not helpful.

Let me now set out more generally and completely the view that I wish to urge. The terms, "good," "bad" and "indifferent" are, I take it, among the widest terms of appraisal that we possess, and we do appraise things on the basis of criteria, criteria to be formulated in terms of the "natural" features of the things appraised. But usually we wish at any time to appraise a thing only from a restricted point of view. We may, for instance, wish to appraise a career from the restricted point of view of its worth as a means of earning a livelihood; to do so we restrict our attention to a special set of the criteria of a good career, all others being for the purpose irrelevant. I wish to suggest that the moral, the aesthetic, the economic, the intellectual, the religious and other special appraisals should all be understood as being appraisals distinguished by their concentration on some special sub-set of criteria of value. To say that something is good as a means is not to say that it is good in some special sense distinct from that of "good as an end" but to appraise it from a special point of view; similarly to judge a thing aesthetically good or first-rate is not to call it good in a sense different from that in which we call a thing morally good, but to judge it in the light of a different sub-set of criteria. We may if we wish choose to invent a special meaning for "beautiful" in which it becomes shorthand for "good from the aesthetic point of view," but that is only a dubious convenience of no theoretical significance. The central task of the philosopher of aesthetics is, I take it, to clarify the principles on which we select the special set of criteria of value that are properly to be counted as relevant to aesthetic judgment or appraisal. We may recognise an aesthetic reaction by its being due to features of the thing contemplated that are relevant criteria of the aesthetic judgment, and the aesthetic judgment is one founded on a special sub-set of the criteria of value of a certain sort of thing.

It may justly be said that so far I have done little more than to assert this view dogmatically, though I should wish to claim that I have given it some *a priori* probability by showing that it is a view which will enable us to deal with some of the difficulties that other views cannot surmount. Certainly, I have as yet done nothing to indicate on what principles the criteria of value relevant to the aesthetic judgment are selected.

This lacuna can only be properly filled by field-work, and then only filled completely by a full-scale work on aesthetics. By doing field-work I mean studying examples of people actually trying to decide whether a certain judgment is or is not aesthetic and observing how they most convincingly argue the matter. Unfortunately to do this on an elaborate scale in one paper of a symposium is hardly possible; I can but ask you to believe that this paper has been written only after a considerable amount of such work, and produce one or two examples of it to show more clearly what I have in mind.

In his more philosophical moments A. E. Housman tried to account for the peculiar nature of the aesthetic in terms of emotional, and even physical, reactions; but here is an example of what he has to say at a more literary and less philosophical level: "Again, there existed in the last century a great body of Wordsworthians, as they were called. It is now much smaller; but true appreciation of Wordsworth's poetry has not diminished in proportion: I suspect that it has much increased. The Wordsworthians, as Matthew Arnold told them, were apt to praise their poet for the wrong things. They were most attracted by what may be called his philosophy;

they accepted his belief in the morality of the universe and the tendency of events to good; they were even willing to entertain his conception of nature as a living and sentient and benignant being; a conception as purely mythological as the Dryads and the Naiads. To that thrilling utterance which pierces the heart and brings tears to the eyes of thousands who care nothing for his opinions and beliefs they were not noticeably sensitive; and however justly they admired the depth of his insight into human nature and the nobility of his moral ideas, these things, with which his poetry was in close and harmonious alliance, are distinct from poetry itself."

It does not matter whether we agree with Housman about Wordsworth; but I do hope that all will agree that this is the right sort of way to set about showing that an appreciation is not aesthetic. Clearly Housman does not deny that what the nineteenth century admired in Wordsworth was admirable; but he says that if your admiration of Wordsworth is based on certain grounds (the philosophical truth and moral loftiness of the content of the poetry) it is not aesthetic admiration, whereas if it is based on what Housman calls the "thrilling utterance," by which the surrounding paragraphs abundantly show him to mean the sound, rhythm and imagery of the words used, then it is aesthetic admiration. Whether Housman is right about Wordsworth or not, whether he has selected the most important criteria of poetical merit or not, this is the type of argument to be expected in a competent discussion; but to have argued the case by adducing the claim that Wordsworthians tended to concentrate rather on traits other than beauty would in fact have been to have restated the case rather than to have argued it. Moreover, if some Wordsworthian had maintained that Wordsworth's pantheism did bring tears to his eyes it would clearly have made no difference to the argument; it is concentration on the utterance, rather than having tears in your eyes, that makes you truly appreciative of the poetry.

Housman's *The Name and Nature of Poetry* is a mine of similar examples. Though he says in a theoretical moment: "I am convinced that most readers, when they think that they are admiring poetry, are deceived by inability to analyse their sensations, and that they are really admiring, not the poetry of the passage before them, but something else in it, which they like better than poetry," in fact all the concrete examples are in accordance with my theory and not his own. Thus the later seventeenth century writers are said by Housman to have but rarely true poetic merit not on the basis of any analysis of sensations but because, for example, they aimed to startle by novelty and amuse by ingenuity whereas their verse is inharmonious.

If, then, Housman's practice is sound it vindicates my view and stultifies his; nor is the obvious fact that we would not rate highly poetry that did not move us, relevant to the question how we are to distinguish a high aesthetic rating from another type of high rating. If field work and reflection in general vindicate my contention as do these examples from Housman I cannot see what else can be relevant; but I freely own that it is the cumulative weight of a large collection of examples from a variety of fields that is necessary, and these I have not supplied; nor could we ever attain a strict proof.

But all this being granted we are still only on the periphery of our subject and the most difficult question remains to be dealt with. It is comparatively easy to see that there must be general principles of selection of evaluative criteria which determine whether our evaluation is to be counted as aesthetic, moral, intellectual or of some other kind; nor is it at all difficult to give examples of what anyone, who is prepared to accept this way of looking at the matter, can easily recognise as being a criterion falling under one or another principle. It would be a very odd person who denied that the sound of the words of a poem was one of the criteria of the aesthetic merit of a poem, or who maintained that being scientifically accurate and up to date was another; similarly it is clear that the honesty of a policy is a criterion of its moral goodness whereas, even if honesty is the best policy, honesty is not a direct criterion of economic merit. But it is by no means easy to formulate these general principles.

This difficulty is by no means peculiar to aesthetics. Part of the general view of which the aesthetic doctrine given here is a fragment is that what determines whether a judgment is moral is what reasons are relevant to it; but everyone knows the difficulty of answering the question what makes a judgment a moral judgment. (In my terminology Kant's answer would be that the reasons must refer to the rationality or otherwise of consistently acting in a certain way.) Certainly it would be over-optimistic to expect to find very precise principles; probably there will be some overlap of criteria between the various spheres of evaluation in anybody's practice; certainly there are some overt border-line disputes whether this or that criterion is relevant to, say, aesthetic evaluation.

I think, however, that there is one peculiar difficulty in trying to find the principle, however vague, that determines what sort of reasons are relevant to a judgment if it is to be counted as aesthetic. When we think of giving reasons for an aesthetic judgment we tend at once to call to mind what we would give as reasons for our appreciation of some very complex works of art; rightly considering, for example, that the plays of Shakespeare are things intended especially for consideration from the aesthetic point of view (I believe that a work of art can most usefully be considered as an artifact primarily intended for aesthetic consideration), we tend to think that we can most usefully tackle our problem by examining what would be relevant to an appreciation of, say, *Hamlet,* merely leaving aside obvious irrelevancies like cost of production. But this is most unfortunate, because, dealing with things intended primarily for aesthetic appreciation, we are inclined to treat as relevant to aesthetic appreciation very much more than we would in the case of things not so officially dedicated to aesthetic purposes; for practical purposes it would be pedantic to do otherwise. Moreover it is obviously very difficult to get straight our grounds for appreciating anything so complex. I am inclined to think that if *Hamlet* were rewritten to give the essential plot and characterisation in the jargon of the professional psychologist there could still be a lot to admire that we at present mention in our aesthetic appreciations, but we would no longer regard it as aesthetic appreciation but rather as intellectual appreciation of psychological penetration and the like.

For these and other reasons, it seems to me hopeless to start an enquiry into the nature of aesthetic grounds by concentrating our attention on great and complex works of art. Among other reasons is that in evaluating great works of art the reasons proximately given will almost inevitably already be at a high level of generality and themselves evaluative —we will refer to masterly style, subtle characterization, inevitability of the action and so on. If we are to have any hope of success we must first set our sights less high and commence with the simplest cases of aesthetic appreciation; in this paper, at least, I shall try to look no further.

If we examine, then, some very simple cases of aesthetic evaluation it seems to me that the grounds given are frequently the way the object appraised looks (shape and colour), the way it sounds, smells, tastes or feels. I may value a rose bush because it is hardy, prolific, disease-resistant and the like, but if I value the rose aesthetically the most obvious relevant grounds will be the way it looks, both in colour and in shape, and the way it smells; the same grounds may be a basis for aesthetic dislike. Though I might, for example, attempt to describe the shape to make you understand what I see in it these grounds seem to me to be really basic; if I admire a rose because of its scent and you then ask me why I admire its scent I should not in a normal context know what you want. These grounds are also those that we should expect to be basic in aesthetics from an etymological point of view, and while one can prove nothing philosophically from etymologies, etymological support is not to be despised. Things, then, may have sensible qualities which affect us favourably or unfavourably with no ulterior grounds. Surely there is no need to illustrate further these most simple cases of aesthetic evaluation.

But there are some slightly more sophisticated cases which need closer inspection. I have in mind occasions when we admire a building not only for its colour and shape but because it looks strong or spacious, or admire a horse because it looks swift as well as for its gleaming coat. These looks are not sensible qualities in the simple way in which colour and shape are. It is clear that in this sort of context to look strong or spacious or swift is not to seem very likely to be strong or spacious or swift. I might condemn a building for looking top-heavy when I knew very well it was built on principles and with materials which ensured effectively that it would not be top-heavy. It is no doubt a plausible speculation that if a building looks top-heavy in the sense relevant to aesthetics it would probably seem really to be top-heavy in the untutored eye; but if an architect, who knows technically that a building is not top-heavy, judges it to look top-heavy when he considers it aesthetically he is in no way estimating the chances of its being blown over.

We are now considering the facts which, exclusively emphasized, lead to the functional view of aesthetics. The element of truth in that view I take to be that if a thing looks to have a characteristic which is a desirable one from another point of view, its looking so is a proper ground of aesthetic appreciation. What makes the appreciation aesthetic is that it is concerned with a thing's looking somehow without concern for whether it really is like that; beauty we may say, to emphasize the point, is not even skin-deep.

We have, then, isolated two types of aesthetic criteria, both of which are cases of looking (sounding, *etc.*) somehow; in the simpler type it is the sensible qualities, in the narrowest sense, that are relevant; in the slightly more complex type it is looking to possess some quality which is non-aesthetically desirable that matters. We like our motor-cars in attractive tones and we like them to look fast (which does not involve peering under the bonnet) ; we like, perhaps, the timbre of a bird's note and we like it also for its cheerful or nobly mournful character, but would not be pleased if it sounded irritable or querulous; the smell of a flower may be seductive in itself but it will be better still if it is, say, a clean smell. Both these elementary types of criteria go hand in hand and are constantly employed.

The most obvious criticism of these suggestions is not that they are wrong but that they are incapable of extension to the more complicated situations in which we appraise a work of art. I cannot try now to deal with this sort of objection in any full way. But I should like to make two small points. First, I would repeat my suggestion that we are inclined to allow in non-aesthetic criteria "by courtesy" when we are evaluating a work of art, so that we may even include intellectual merit. Secondly, the fact that such things as intellectual understanding are essential to an aesthetic appreciation of a work of art does not in itself establish the criticism. If, for example, we enjoy listening to a fugue it is likely that a part of our appreciation will be intellectual; no doubt intellectual understanding of what is going on is also necessary to aesthetic appreciation; but the fact that I cannot enjoy the sound of a theme being continually employed, sometimes inverted or in augmentation or in diminution, unless I have the theoretical training to recognise this, does not prevent my aesthetic appreciation from being of the sound. I am still appreciating the way a thing sounds or looks even when my intellect must be employed if I am to be aware of the fact that the thing does look or sound this way.

There remain many difficulties; above all the notion of "looking in a certain way," especially in such cases as when we say something looks strong or swift, needs more elaboration. But to carry out this task is beyond the scope of this paper. Apart from a short appendix, I shall now close with a brief summary, a summary of a paper which is intended to do no more than to distinguish the aesthetic judgment and reaction from others and perhaps to indicate the best way in which to proceed to the further problems of the philosophy of aesthetics.

Summary

1. The problem raised is how an aesthetic judgment, reaction or evaluation is to be distinguished from others.
2. We should expect to find a criterion which allows us to distinguish the aesthetic, the moral, the economic, the intellectual and other evaluations by a single *fundamentum divisionis*.
3. All evaluations are made on the basis of criteria for the merit of the kind of thing in question.
4. An aesthetic evaluation is one which is made on the basis of a selection from the total body of relevant criteria of merit.
5. In at least the simpler cases of aesthetic evaluation the relevant criteria appear to be those which are concerned with the way the object in question looks or presents itself to the other senses.
6. It is impossible to distinguish the aesthetic by a special object, by a special characteristic attended to, or by a special emotion.

Appendix

It may appear to some that too little importance has been accorded to the emotions in this paper. To avoid misunderstanding I will mention one or two ways in which I recognise the importance of considering the emotions in aesthetics.

First, I recognise that we would be very little interested in the aesthetic aspect of things but for their emotional effect upon us.

Secondly, I acknowledge that if we experience an emotional thrill when we look at a picture or hear a piece of music we do not normally have to examine our grounds and reasons to know that we are reacting aesthetically in a favourable way. But I do want to maintain that it is the nature of the grounds that makes our appreciation aesthetic and that if on an examination of our grounds we find, as sometimes happens, that our reasons are appropriate rather to moral evaluation or are erotic, or what you will, we will, if we are honest, recognise that our reaction was not after all aesthetic. Of course we have trained ourselves to a great extent to approach pictures and music from the aesthetic angle so that we shall not in general be mistaken if we rely on an unanalysed impression.

Thirdly, there are a great number of terms that we use in aesthetic evaluation—*pleasant, moving, pretty, beautiful, impressive, admirable* and *exciting* among others. I do not know what makes one more appropriate than another in a given context; partly, perhaps, they are more or less laudatory, or are based on a still more restricted selection of criteria than a mere judgment of goodness or badness; but I suspect that the choice of word is at least in part determined by the precise character of the emotion experienced.

For these and other reasons I do not wish to belittle the importance of the emotions in the philosophy of aesthetics; but I do wish to deny most emphatically that the aesthetic field can be distinguished from others by an attempt to analyse the emotions involved therein: and that is all that the thesis of this paper requires.

Beauty and the Aesthetic Experience

BEAUTY HAS OFTEN BEEN considered a purely aesthetic concept. This presupposes, however, that "beauty," "beautiful," and "beautifully" are used only in aesthetic contexts, which is not so. Aiken, above, refers to the "functional beauty of a work of art"; this is one kind of nonaesthetic beauty possessed by many things. Something is "functionally beautiful" if it is exceptionally fit for the achievement of an end. A beautifully designed machine is not necessarily aesthetically admirable; it may be merely efficient and economical; to a dentist, a beautiful set of teeth is one that is regular, sound, and cavity-free. Closely related to this sense of "beautiful" are two others: (1) that in which we speak of passes in football or serves and returns in tennis as beautiful; and (2) the beauty of a case, specimen, or example, as when something exhibits in a particularly clear way the characteristic features of the species to which it belongs.

Aestheticians are concerned with aesthetic beauty only. They want to know what the nature of aesthetic beauty is, what it means to say that something is aesthetically beautiful.

Beauty as Pleasure Objectified. According to subjective theories of beauty, the *esse* of beauty is *percipi.* Just as something cannot be pleasing, disgusting, or titillating without pleasing, disgusting, or titillating someone, or at least tending to do so, it cannot be beautiful without being beautiful *to* someone.

"The sense of beauty," Santayana says, is a kind of pleasure.[1] But since not all pleasures are aesthetic, what distinguishes aesthetic pleasure from other kinds? Santayana rejects the Kantian solution, that the aesthetic differs from other kinds of pleasure in its unselfishness, impersonality, disinterestedness, and universality. Instead, he appeals to what he calls a "well-known psychological phenomenon," that of "projection" or "objectification," "the transformation of an element of sensation into the quality of a thing." When we say that something is beautiful, we construe the pleasing effect it has upon us as a quality of it.

Although Santayana initially draws a distinction between beauty and properties such as color, he ends by putting them on all fours with one another. Beauty is first *contrasted* with color, proportion, and size; we are then told that it is *just like* color, proportion, and size—"all are sensations." But if the latter is the case, what happens to the distinction between properties that are "in" things and properties that are not "in" things? Does it not vanish? Do we know what it is for a quality to be "in" something, for something to have a quality independent of its being sensed by someone? If not, then there is no difference between the objective and the subjective, between what is "in" objects and what is "in" us. Beauty is no more a subjective property than color; color is no more objective than beauty; what sense then can the word "objectify" have? Santayana appears to want it both ways: beauty is not a property of things like color and size, and yet, like color and size, it is only the "objectification" of a sensation. Is this a coherent position?

Is there not another confusion in his notion of beauty as pleasure objectified? Objectifying a sensation of color consists in treating a feature of the sensation as a feature of the object causing the sensation. Thus, if an apple *looks* red to me, I say it *is* red. But how do we objectify our pleasures and pains? Presumably in the same way: when something pleases me, I do not say that it pleases me but that it is beautiful. Meaning what? That the pleasure is "resident in" the object. But this, it would seem, can mean only one of two things: (1) that the object is pleased—which is absurd; (2) that the object pleases us—which is not to objectify pleasure at all!

What *does* beauty have to do with our pleasures, satisfactions, approvals, and the like? A man who *judges* something to be beautiful (says that it is beautiful and is not lying, joking, speaking ironically, etc.) does not *say*, nor does he usually *mean*, that it pleases him, that he likes or admires it.[2] He *implies* that it pleases him aesthetically or in some other way satisfies his aesthetic interests, in the same way that one who asserts that he was born in 1930 implies that he believes or knows that he was born in 1930. Would it not be as paradoxical for a man to say, by way of judging, "That is a beautiful picture but I find it aesthetically displeasing, dissatisfying" as it would for a man to say, "I was born in 1930 but I don't believe that I was" or "I know that I wasn't"?

An affirmative answer would not rule out the possibility that one might *admit* that something is beautiful but add that it leaves him cold. Here his admission has the effect of saying that he has reason to suppose that it is beautiful but that he does himself not find it beautiful. One may be insensitive to the beauties of atonal music but may have reason to suppose that a certain Schönberg quartet is beautiful; though the quartet sounds to him like a lot of unpleasant noise, this does not prevent his admitting that it may be beautiful. To judge that something is beautiful, must not one be able to appreciate *why* it is beautiful?

If to judge something is beautiful is to imply that one finds it aesthetically pleasing, does this in turn imply that something can be beautiful to one man but not to another? Is "beautiful to" a meaningful English idiom any more than is "a yard long to"?[3] Is the so-called "relativity of beauty" a relativity of *beauty*? Or is it just a misleading way of referring to differences in taste or powers of appreciation?

The Definition of Beauty as a Canon of Aesthetic Judgment. Subjectivist theories of beauty err, according to Jessop, in saying that (1) our judgments of beauty lie "under no restraint whatever from the objective side"—we can "make" anything beautiful by having certain feelings about it; and they err further in implying that (2) every judgment of beauty is "no more than a personal confession"; it is of the same logical type of statement as "I have a headache," which means (a) that the judgment is not about the thing said to be beautiful but about the person making the judgment, and (b) that any judgment of beauty honestly made is true.

We have already raised questions about (1). However, (2), and particularly (2b), raises a further interesting point. Are all honest and sincere judgments of beauty true? Aren't such judgments amenable to reassessment, and hence, in this sense at least, objective?[4]

The reasoned way of escape from subjectivism, Jessop says, is to remind ourselves of "two very elementary distinctions": (1) between object and thing, and (2) between appreciation as emotion and appreciation as judgment. The latter distinction is the simpler one. Is there not a difference between enjoying something that is beautiful and judging it to be beautiful? Confusion between the two might lead us to suppose that when we judge something to be beautiful we are saying how we feel towards it.

The distinction between object and thing, though elementary, is not so simple. "The thing," says Jessop, "is what is really there, whereas the object is so much of it . . . as comes effectively before the mind." What we judge to be beautiful, then, are not "things" but "objects." What is Jessop's point?

Consider his own example of the foul slum-alley that is beautiful in a certain light from a certain vantage point.[5] What is beautiful about the alley is the *patterned* incidence of light and shadow, the *balance* of the two, the *continuity and contrast* of lines, and the *coherent arrangement* of the masses. Are not these features of the alley "really there" as much as any of its features are? Yet two people may look at the same alley and not notice the same features; one sees beauty, the other does not. They see the same "thing" (the same alley), but they do not see the same "object" (the same features of the same alley). One who does not notice the appropriate features of the alley will not see its beauty.[6]

But how do we tell whether, and when, something *is beautiful*? According to Jessop, only by means of a "canon" of aesthetic judgment, *i.e* a definition of its predicate, beauty.[7] And the only acceptable definition of beauty "is a statement of certain properties of objects."

To see Jessop's point, we must remark on an important aspect of the concept of beauty. It makes perfectly good sense to say of two things, X and Y (*e.g.* two cars coming off an assembly line), that they are exactly alike, except that X is red while Y is green. Does it make equally good sense to say of two things, A and B (*e.g.* two impressions of the same etching), that they are exactly alike, except that A is beautiful while B is not? Must there not be some *other* difference between them? If so, then the beauty of something logically depends on certain other properties that it has. These other properties are those by reference to which we justify our judgment that it is beautiful. They are its beauties, the things that are beautiful about it.

When Jessop speaks of a canon of aesthetic judgment and a definition of beauty, he refers to a statement about "that common quality" which all beautiful things must share. What he wants, in short, is a true statement of the form, "Something is beautiful if and only if it has the property f," where "f" may stand for a single property or a collection of properties. He discusses several obstacles to our finding a satisfactory definition of beauty, and what he says about these is interesting. Of greater moment, however, is his assumption that there is and must be a canon of beauty, a property shared by all beautiful things that makes them beautiful. Is this assumption true? Do we apply the adjective "beautiful," in its aesthetic sense, to such diverse things as a shade of red, a line, a painting by Rembrandt, a sunset, a Mozart symphony, a diamond, a gesture, a tone of voice, and a proof in mathematics, by virtue of their possessing some property in common? What property?

The ancient Neoplatonic philosopher Plotinos offered an argument against an earlier version of Jessop's assumption, that "the symmetry of parts towards each other and towards a whole . . . constitutes the beauty recognized by the eye, that in visible things, as indeed in all else, universally, the beautiful thing is essentially symmetrical." If this were true, Plotinos argues, then

> only a compound can be beautiful, never anything devoid of parts; and only a whole; the several parts will have beauty, not in themselves, but only as working together to give a comely total. . . . All the loveliness of color and even the light of the sun, being devoid of parts and so not beautiful by symmetry, must be ruled out of the realm of beauty. And how comes gold to be a beautiful thing? And lightning by night, and the stars, why are these so fair?[8]

Can Plotinos' argument not be applied, in principle, to any supposed canon of beauty? Take any property on which the beauty of all beautiful things is supposed to depend; can't we always find, or imagine, something beautiful which does not possess that property? If so, there is no canon of beauty in the sense required, and logically there can be none.

The alternative to Jessop's assumption is that we apply the term "beautiful" to different things for different reasons; the properties that make a Mozart symphony beautiful are not necessarily the same as those that make Virgil's *Aeneid* beautiful. Indeed, in his argument against the existence of a *summum pulchrum*,[9] Jessop seems to imply that there is no canon of beauty. One painting or one rose may be more beautiful than another, but a painting and a rose, Jessop holds, are incomparable with respect to beauty; they are "just different." If this is so, is it not because a rose is beautiful for reasons very different from those for which a painting is beautiful? And does this not also explain Jessop's impression that beauty is "one" and at the same time "many"— that there is but one aesthetic sense of the adjective "beautiful" and yet many different reasons why different things are beautiful?

What Makes an Experience Aesthetic? So far we have used the words "aesthetic" and "aesthetically" many times. What do they mean? They are qualifying expressions used to modify other expressions. We speak of something's being aesthetically gratifying *as opposed to* its being morally, religiously, personally, or politically gratifying, as well as of aesthetic pleasures *as opposed to* those that are sensual, or intellectual; and so on. Now pleasures, delights, disgusts, disappointments, gratifications, and the like, are all "experiences." But what makes them *aesthetic* experiences, when they are?

Philosophers have tried to define the aesthetic: (1) by reference to a special class of objects; (2) by reference to certain psychological features of our reactions to objects. No definition of either type is generally accepted, which leads us to wonder if any such definition can be successful.

Are aesthetic experiences restricted to a specifiable class of objects? What objects? Works of art? Can flowers, scents, and sunsets, then, not be objects of aesthetic delight? Or is it rather the case that no matter what class an object belongs to, it may be the object of an aesthetic experience? There may be certain sorts of objects of more aesthetic interest than others, but is there any kind of object that *could* not provide one with an aesthetic experience?

Since aesthetic experiences are experiences, and hence subjective or psychological phenomena, one might suppose that the way to find out what all aesthetic experiences have distinctively in common is introspection. Unfortunately, those who have employed this method have not come up with the same results. Even if they had, would this be of any more philosophical interest than the fact—if it were a fact—that all and only men named "Smith" have blue eyes? Would it say what *makes* an experience aesthetic, unless it is assumed that the term "aesthetic" is applied to experiences by virtue of their having some introspectable feature in common? But is this assumption true?

If it were, then must not anyone who knows how to apply the term "aesthetic" correctly to the description of experiences know *before* he begins his investigation what the common psychological feature of such experiences is? And if he already knows this, is it not pointless for him to search, by introspection or in any other way, for the common feature in question? In Saul Bellow's novel, *Henderson the Rain King*, Henderson says of himself, "Certain emotions make my teeth itch. Aesthetic appreciation especially does it to me. Yes, when I admire beauty, I get these tooth pangs, and my gums are on edge."[10] It is *possible* that we should all have Henderson's itch and identify an aesthetic experience by its presence. But do we so identify the aesthetic experience? Do we so tell whether we ourselves, or other people, have had one? Don't we manage successfully to identify an aesthetic experience and to distinguish it from other experiences without introspection and without asking other people to engage in introspection? If so, how so?

Psychical Distance. One of the more famous answers to this question is Bullough's theory of "psychical distance." "Psychical distance" is a metaphor which Bullough uses to refer to similar phenomena. If one is *physically* too close to something, he cannot get a good view of it; so also if he is too far away. And if one cannot get a good view, certain features fail to be discerned. *Psychical* distance is a function of our capacity to appreciate certain features of something that would otherwise not be noted, either because one is "too close" or "too far away" from it.

But what is psychical distance *from*? It is, according to Bullough, distance from *practical* needs and concerns—moral, religious, personal, economic, and so on. But does this explain the aesthetic? Isn't the "distanced" view of things simply the aesthetically appreciative view of them?[11] Consider, for example, the discussion of the "distance-limit," "that point at which distance is lost and appreciation either disappears or changes its character." What *kind* of appreciation? Surely, only *aesthetic* appreciation. Is this not simply to say, then, that the point at which one ceases to appreciate something aesthetically he ceases to appreciate it aesthetically? To make sense of the concept of psychical distance, must we not introduce the notion of the aesthetic, thereby reducing Bullough's thesis to a tautology?

Bullough appears to offer us a psychological account of aesthetic experience, namely, that it is a function of psychical distance. But if this is a genuine psychological hypothesis, must we not have an *independent* means of measuring psychical distance and of recognizing aesthetic experience, to see if the one is in fact a function of the other? Does Bullough supply this?

Aesthetic Explanations. Departing from tradition, Urmson says, "We find the criterion for distinguishing aesthetic from kindred reactions in the nature of the explanation of the reaction." An aesthetic object, in other words, is an object of aesthetic experience; an aesthetic experience is an experience, the explanation of which is aesthetic. But what constitutes an aesthetic explanation?

It is tempting at this point to look for a simple definition of aesthetic explanation. Urmson suggests that there is a single principle, however vague, that determines the sort of explanation necessary for an experience to be counted as aesthetic; he thinks this principle has something to do with the *appearances* of things. References to the appearances of things doubtless can often serve as the required explanation, but can they always so serve? Works of literature provide us with some of our richest aesthetic experiences, but is to find a poem or novel aesthetically pleasing, or displeasing, to find it so solely because of how it looks or sounds?

If almost anything can be the object of an aesthetic experience, can we not reasonably expect aesthetic explanations to be as heterogeneous as objects? One admires something aesthetically for its . . . , or because of its . . . , or because it is . . . , where the blank is to be filled by the name or description of a property of an object. Obviously, not just any property of the object will do. Some properties, "typically aesthetic properties" such as beauty, grace, elegance, prettiness, handsomeness, daintiness, and exquisiteness, are however obvious candidates, in the sense that to be pleased by something because it possesses one of them will usually mark the pleasure as aesthetic.

When we leave the "typically aesthetic properties," however, the problem becomes more complicated. Consider why one might admire, or be displeased by, the following: a color, scent, or shape; a rose,[12] a sunset, or a stone; an animal's coat, the surface of a table, a person's face. Which reasons are clearly nonaesthetic? Aesthetic? Which are hard to classify? Can you discern a principle by which the aesthetic are separated from the nonaesthetic?[13]

Now turn to some works of art and try to separate these reasons into aesthetic and nonaesthetic. Consider the following: "I like it because it's funny"; "I admire that picture for its clarity, power, and richness"; "It's the grace and delicate gayety of the theme that pleases me"; "It's optimistic, shows the bright side of things; that's why I like it"; "It's about God (children, love, the sea)";[14] "The poem bores me; it's lifeless, flat, colorless"; "That Vermeer is one of the most moving pictures I know; it's so exquisitely organized, the colors so delicately balanced and contrasted; it's soft and subtle, and yet as clear and vivid as bright light."

Is this delineation of the aesthetic more feasible than alternative approaches? Why, or why not? How would you characterize the problem at issue here? How would you recognize a solution?

Notes

1. This echoes the Scholastic definition of beauty as "that which pleases when seen"—*id quod visum placet.*

2. And certainly *what* he says, namely, "That is beautiful," does not mean the same as "That pleases me" or "I like that," even if *he* means *by* what he says "That pleases me" or "I like that."

3. Something can, of course, appear or seem to be beautiful to one person and not to another, just as it may appear to be or look a yard long to one and not to another. But can it *be* beautiful to one and not to another?

4. See Albert Tsugawa, "The Objectivity of Aesthetic Judgments," *The Philosophical Review,* LXX (1961) , 3-22. Tsugawa does not discuss judgments of beauty, but much of what he says can be applied to them.

5. Note that the alley *is* beautiful in a certain light and from a certain vantage point; it does not merely *look* beautiful. Even if it merely looked beautiful, it would have to be *possible* for it to *be* beautiful, and this is all Jessop needs.

6. Cf. Frank Sibley's "Aesthetic Concepts," Section IV above.

7. Jessop assumes that the only genuinely aesthetic predicate is "beautiful," and hence that an aesthetic judgment is one of the form "X is beautiful." This is not the case. There is a wide range of aesthetic predicates; "pretty," "charming," "exquisite," and a host of others can be used aesthetically. Granting this point, however, Jessop would claim that his argument holds *mutatis mutandis* for these other predicates as well as for "beautiful."

8. *The Enneads,* trans. by Stephen MacKenna, London, Faber and Faber, Ltd., 1930, I, 6, 1.

9. The most famous argument for the existence of a *summum pulchrum* is to be found in Plato's *Symposium.*

10. Saul Bellow, *Henderson the Rain King,* New York, The Viking Press, 1959, p. 79.

11. The aesthetically appreciative view, note; not just the aesthetic view. Bullough's examples strongly suggest that one who does not appreciate something aesthetically, who does not react to it positively in an aesthetic way, does not take a "distanced" view of it.

12. Urmson says, "If I admire a rose because of its scent and you ask me why I admire its scent I should not in a normal context know what you mean." Is this quite right? Suppose you do ask why I admire its scent; might I not reply that I admire it for its delicate sweetness? Of course, aesthetic, like any other kind of explanation, comes to an end; beyond a certain point the question "Why?" becomes otiose.

13. For an excellent essay on this problem, see Frank Sibley's "Aesthetics and the Looks of Things," *The Journal of Philosophy,* LVI (1959) , 905-915.

14. Think, in this connection, of Clive Bell's remark that "The representative element in a work of art may or may not be harmful; always it is [aesthetically] irrelevant." Can admiration for the subject or subject matter of a work of art, unqualified, ever count as aesthetic?

Suggestions for Additional Reading

On the concept of beauty:

Virgil C. Aldrich, "Beauty as Feeling," *Kenyon Review,* I (1939) , 300-307; S. Alexander, *Beauty and Other Forms of Value* (London, 1933), Pt. I; Monroe C. Beardsley, *Aesthetics* (New York, 1958), 502-512; E. F. Carritt, *The Theory of Beauty* (London, 1928); C. J. Ducasse, "What Has Beauty to do with Art?", *J. Phil.,* XXV (1928), 181-195; T. M. Greene, "Beauty in Art and Nature," *Sewanee Review,* LXIX (1961),

236-268; G. P. Henderson, "An 'Orthodox' Use of the Term 'Beautiful' ", *Philosophy*, XXXV (1960), 114-121; C. E. M. Joad, "The Objectivity of Beauty," *Matter, Life and Value* (London, 1929), 266-283; G. Katkov, "The Pleasant and the Beautiful," *P.A.S.*, XL (1940), 177-206; Vernon Lee, *The Beautiful* (Cambridge, 1913); H. Osborne, *Theory of Beauty* (London, 1952); W. T. Stace, *The Meaning of Beauty* (London, 1929); Jerome Stolnitz, " 'Beauty': History of an Idea," *Journal of the History of Ideas*, XXIII (1961), 185-204; Andrew P. Ushenko, "Beauty in Art," *Monist*, XL (1932), 627-629.

On the nature of aesthetic experience:

Virgil C. Aldrich, *Philosophy of Art* (Englewood Cliffs, N.J., 1963), Ch. 1; Monroe C. Beardsley, *Aesthetics* (New York, 1958), Ch. XI; Bernard Bosanquet, *Three Lectures on Aesthetic* (London, 1959); Laurence Buermeyer, *The Aesthetic Experience* (Merion, Pa., 1929); Marshall Cohen, "Appearance and the Aesthetic Attitude," *J. Phil.*, LVI (1959), 915-926; John Dewey, *Art as Experience* (New York, 1934), Ch. III; Pepita Haezrahi, *The Contemplative Activity* (New York, 1956); H. S. Langfeld, *The Aesthetic Attitude* (New York, 1920); George H. Mead, "The Nature of Aesthetic Experience," *Int. Jour. of Ethics*, XXXVI (1925-26), 382-393; Milton C. Nahm, *Aesthetic Experience and Its Presuppositions* (New York, 1946); C. K. Ogden, I. A. Richards, and James Wood, *The Foundations of Aesthetics* (New York, 1922); DeWitt H. Parker, *The Principles of Aesthetics* (New York, 1946); Stephen C. Pepper, *Aesthetic Quality* (New York, 1938); D. L. Pole, "Varieties of Aesthetic Experience," *Philosophy*, XXX (1955), 238-248; D. W. Prall, *Aesthetic Judgment* (New York, 1929), Ch. 15; I. A. Richards, *Principles of Literary Criticism* (London, 1925), Chs. 2, 32; Frank Sibley, "Aesthetics and the Looks of Things," *J. Phil.*, LVI (1959), 905-915; Vincent Tomas, "Aesthetic Vision," *Phil. Rev.*, LXVIII (1959), 52-67; Eliseo Vivas, "A Definition of the Aesthetic Experience," *J. Phil.*, XXXIV (1937), 628-634, reprinted in *Creation and Discovery* (New York, 1955), "A Natural History of the Aesthetic Transaction," *Naturalism and the Human Spirit*, Y. H. Krikorian ed. (New York, 1944).

VII

Art Criticism

Introduction

THE WORDS "good" and "bad" have no inherent connection with criticism, which could be carried on without them. They are, however, perhaps the most common critical terms; the central problems of criticism have arisen in connection with their use. Indeed, nothing else has occasioned more widespread disagreement in philosophy.

The following selections, representative of recent research in this area of philosophy, are principally about the meaning and justification of statements such as "That is a good painting." What does it mean to say that a painting is good? Why is it good? And what is the relation between reason and judgment? Closely connected with these issues is the question of the function of criticism. Is art criticism, like moral appraisal, directed at affecting the practice of artists and the choices of spectators? Or is it rather directed at enlightening the spectator's looking, reading, and listening?

Hampshire and Miss Macdonald deal mainly with the function of criticism. Critical appraisal, according to Hampshire, is not analogous to moral judgment; there are no principles of criticism as there are standards of right conduct. The aim of criticism is to display the unique features of works of art. Miss Macdonald agrees, arguing that critical judgments are essentially what J. L. Austin called "performatives," forms of words with which we do something other than state what is the case.

Mrs. Knight and Ziff deal primarily with the role of reasons in criticism. According to Mrs. Knight, critical judgments presuppose criteria, and the relation between the goodness of a work of art and the criteria of its goodness is one of meaning: the reasons offered for saying that a painting is good show what one means by "good." For Ziff, the reason why a painting is good must always be a reason why it is worth contemplating, and he explores the relation between the goodness of a work of art and the interests associated with it.

Also relevant to the problems of this Section are the selections to be found in Section I.

STUART HAMPSHIRE

Logic and Appreciation

IT SEEMS THAT there *ought* to be a subject called "Aesthetics." There is an alexandrianism which assumes that there are so many classified subjects waiting to be discussed and that each one ought to have its place in the library and in the syllabus. There is moral philosophy—the study of the nature of the problems of conduct—in every library and in every syllabus; there ought surely to be a philosophical study of the problems of Art and Beauty—if there are such problems; and this is the question which comes first. That there are problems of conduct cannot be doubted; people sometimes wonder what they ought to do and they find reasons for solving a moral problem to their own satisfaction; one can discuss the nature of these problems, and the form of the arguments used in the solution of them; and this is moral philosophy. But what is the subject-matter of aesthetics? Whose problems and whose methods of solution? Perhaps there is no subject-matter; this would fully explain the poverty and weakness of the books. Many respectable books can be, and have been, written on subjects which have no subject-matter; they may be written for the sake of system and completeness, to round off a philosophy, or simply because it is felt that there ought to be such a subject.

There is a simple and familiar way of finding the subject-matter of aesthetics, by begging the question. One may invent a kind of judgment called a value judgment, and let it be either a judgment about conduct or a judgment about Art and Beauty: a single genus with two species. From this beginning, one may go on to distinguish value judgments from other kinds of judgment. But the existence of the genus has been assumed, the assimilation of moral to aesthetic judgment taken for granted. One has certainly not isolated the subject-matter of aesthetics by this method; the original material has simply been dropped from view. What questions under what conditions are actually answered by aesthetic judgments? This must be the starting-point. I shall argue that aesthetic judg-

Reprinted from *The World Review*, October 1952.

ments are not comparable in purpose with moral judgments, and that there are no problems of aesthetics comparable with the problems of ethics.

There are artists who create and invent, and there are critics and a wider audience who appraise and enjoy their work. An artist has the technical problems of the medium in which he works; he may discuss these technical problems with other artists working in the same medium and with those who intimately understand the difficulties of his material. As an artist, he has his own conception of what his own work is to be; clearly or confusedly, he has set his own end before himself; even if his work must satisfy some external demand, he has his own peculiar conception of it, if he is to be regarded as more than a craftsman in some applied art. He has therefore created his own technical problems; they have not been presented to him; they arise out of his own conception of what he is to do. He did not set himself to create Beauty, but some particular thing. The canons of success and failure, of perfection and imperfection, are in this sense internal to the work itself, if it is regarded as an original work of art. In so far as the perfection of the work is assessed by some external criterion, it is not being assessed as a work or art, but rather as a technical achievement in the solution of some presented problem. A work of art is gratuitous. It is not *essentially* the answer to a question or the solution of a presented problem. Anyone may dance for any reason and to achieve any variety of purposes; but a spectator may attend to the movements of the dance for the sake of their own intrinsic qualities, and disregard the purposes which lie outside; and, so regarded, the dance becomes gratuitous; it ceases to be an action, and becomes a set of movements; the subject of the spectator's attention has changed.

Compare the subject-matter and situation of moral judgment. Throughout any day of one's life, and from the moment of waking, one is confronted with situations which demand action. Even to omit to do anything positive, and to remain passive, is to adopt a policy; Oblomov had his own solution to the practical problems confronting him; his was one possible solution among others. One can suspend judgment on theoretical questions and refuse either to affirm or deny any particular solution; but no one can refuse to take one path or another in any situation which confronts him; there must always be an answer to the question "What did you do in that situation?" even if the answer is: "I ignored it and did nothing; I went to bed and to sleep." If that is the answer, that was the solution adopted. One can always describe, first, the situation and the possibilities open, and, secondly, the solution of the problem which the agent adopted. Action in response to any moral problem is not gratuitous; it is imposed; that there should be some response is absolutely necessary. One cannot pass by a situation; one must pass *through* it in one way or another.

When there are unavoidable problems, a rational man looks for some general method of solving them; a rational man may be defined as a man who adheres to general methods, allotting to each type of problem its own method of solution. Unless general methods of solution are recognized, there can be no grounds for distinguishing a valid from an invalid step in any argument in support of any solution. To be irrational is either to have no reasons at all for preferring one solution to another, or to give utterly different reasons in different cases of the same type; to refuse any general method of solving problems of a particular type is to accept either caprice or inconsistency in that domain. "Must there be some general method of solving problems of conduct?" Or "Must to act rightly be to act rationally and consistently?"—these have always been the principal questions in moral philosophy. Aristotle, the most accurate of moral philosophers, gave a carefully ambiguous answer, Kant an unambiguous "Yes," Hume a qualified "No"; for Hume held that morality was ultimately a matter of the heart and not of the head, of sympathy and not of consistency. But none of these philosophers denied that it always makes sense to ask for the reasons behind any practical decision; for constant ends may be served by a variety of different means. Actions (unlike works of art) do not bear their justification on the face of them; one must first inquire into reasons and purposes. Even if it is not necessary, at least it is always possible, to adopt some general ends of action, or (it is ultimately the same) to acknowledge some universal principles. Since any action susceptible of moral judgment can be viewed as the solution of a problem presented, one can always criticize and compare different methods of solution. Consistent policies are needed in order to meet common human predicaments; men may discuss the reasons which have inclined them to solve the same problem in different ways. Their arguments (since arguments must be consistent) will lead them to general principles; anyone, therefore, who moralizes necessarily generalizes; he "draws a moral"; in giving his grounds of choice, he subsumes particular cases under a general rule. Only an aesthete in action would comfortably refuse to give any grounds of decision; he might refer the questioner to the particular qualities of the particular performance; precisely this refusal to generalize would be the mark of his aestheticism. Virtue and good conduct are essentially repeatable and imitable, in a sense in which a work of art is not. To copy a right action is to act rightly; but a copy of a work of art is not necessarily or generally a work of art.

In a moralizing climate there will always be a demand, based on analogy, for principles of criticism, parallel with principles of conduct. But this analogy must be false. Where it makes sense to speak of a problem, it makes sense to speak of a solution of it; and where solutions are offered, it makes sense to ask for reasons for preferring one solution to another; it is possible to demand consistency of choice and general principles of preference. But if something is made or done gratuitously, and not in response to a problem posed, there can be no question of preferring one solution to another; judgment of the work done does not involve a choice, and there is no need to find grounds of preference. One may, as a spectator, prefer one work to another, but there is no *necessity* to decide between them; if the works themselves are regarded as free creations, to be enjoyed or neglected for what they are, then any grading is inessential to the judgment of them; if they are not answers to a common problem, they do not compete and neither need be rejected, except on its own merits. A critical judgment is in this sense noncommital and makes no recommendation; the critic may reject the work done without being required to show what the artist ought to have done in place of the work rejected. But the moralist who condemns an action must indicate what ought to have been done in its place; for something had to be done, some choice between relative evils made. All practical decision is choice between relative evils or relative goods; if what was done was wrong, the agent must have failed to do what he ought to have done. Any moral comment has therefore some force of recommendation and is itself a practical judgment. A moral censor must put himself in the place of the agent and imaginatively confront the situation which the agent confronted; the censor and the agent censored have so far the same problem. But a critic is not another artist, as the moral censor is another agent; he is a mere spectator and he has the spectator's total irresponsibility; it is only required that he should see the object exactly as it is. Nothing which he says in judgment and description necessarily carries any exclusions with it, or necessarily reflects upon the merit of other work; the possible varieties of beautiful and excellent things are inexhaustible. He may therefore discuss any work on its merits alone, in the most strict sense of this phrase; he need not look elsewhere and to possible alternatives in making his judgment. On the contrary, his purpose is to lead people *not* to look elsewhere, but to look here, at precisely this unique object; not to see the object as one of a kind, but to see it as individual and unrepeatable.

One engages in moral argument in order to arrive at a conclusion—what is to be done or ought to have been done; one had the practical problem to begin with, and the conclusion ("this is better than that") is always more important than the route by which one arrives at it; for one *must* decide one way or the other. But a picture or poem is not created as a challenge or puzzle, requiring the spectator to decide for or against. One engages in aesthetic discussion for the sake of what one might see on the way, and not for the sake of arriving at a conclusion, a final verdict for or against; if one has been brought to see what there is to be seen in the object, the purpose of discussion is achieved. Where the logicians' framework of problem and conclusion does not apply, the notion of "reason" loses some of its meaning also; it is unnatural to ask "*why* is that picture or sonata good?" in parallel with "why was that the right thing to do?" There are no reasons why some object is ugly in the sense that there are reasons why some action is wrong. Perhaps it may be said that there are

particular features of the particular object which *make* it ugly or beautiful, and these can be pointed out, isolated, and placed in a frame of attention; and it is the greatest service of the critic to direct attention in this
analytical way. But when attention is directed to the particular features
of the particular object, the point is to bring people to see these features,
and not simply to lead them to say: "That's good." There is no point in
arguing that the object is good *because* it possesses these qualities, if this
involves the generalization that all objects similar in this respect are good;
for if one generalizes in this manner, one looks away from the particular
qualities of the particular thing, and is left with some general formula or
recipe, useless alike to artist and spectator. One does not need a formula
or recipe unless one needs repetitions; and one needs repetitions and rules
in conduct, but not in art; the artist does not need a formula of reproduction and the spectator does not need a formula of evaluation.

The spectator-critic in any of the arts needs gifts precisely the opposite
of the moralist's; he needs to suspend his natural sense of purpose and
significance. To hold attention still upon any particular thing is unnatural; normally, we take objects—whether perceived by sight, touch, hearing, or by any combination of the senses—as signs of possible actions and
as instances of some usable kind; we look through them to their possible
uses, and classify them by their uses rather than by sensuous similarities.
The common vocabulary, being created for practical purposes, obstructs
any disinterested perception of things; things are (in a sense) recognized
before they are really seen or heard. There is no practical reason why
attention should be arrested upon a single object, framed and set apart;
attention might always be practical attention, and therefore always passing from one thing to the next; in the sense in which thunder "means"
rain, almost everything means something else; "what does it mean?" is
the primitive reaction which prevents perception. One may always look
through a picture as if it were a map, and look through a landscape towards a destination; for everything presented through the senses arouses
expectations and is taken as a signal of some likely reaction. Nothing but
holding an object still in attention, by itself and for its own sake, would
count as having an aesthetic interest in it. A great part of a critic's work,
in any of the arts, is to place a frame upon the object and upon its parts
and features, and to do this by an unnatural use of words in description.
Perception, of any kind and on any level, has degrees; some perceive
more than others, and it is difficult to see and hear all that there is to see
and hear. There is a metaphysical prejudice that the world consists of so
many definite objects possessing so many definite qualities, and that, if
we perceive and attend to the objects, we necessarily notice their qualities; as if the things and their qualities were somehow already isolated
and labelled for us, ready for the camera-brain to record. So it seems that
in principle a vast inventory might be made of all the things in the world
with their qualities, passively received and recorded; when one had gone

through the inventory of literal description, any further statements about the furniture of the world would be subjective impression and metaphor. There is the prejudice that things really do have colours and shapes, but that there do not exist, literally and objectively, concordances of colours and perceived rhythms and balances of shapes; these are supposed to be added by the mind. It seems that the more recondite qualities of form, expression, style, atmosphere, cannot properly be entered in the inventory of the world, alongside the weights and measures of things; the relations of stress and balance between masses in sculpture or building cannot *really* be seen in any literal sense; the expression of a voice is not as much a perceptible reality as its loudness. The qualities which are of no direct practical interest are normally described metaphorically, by some trans-ference of terms from the common vocabulary; and the common vo-cabulary is a vocabulary of action, classifying by use and function. The assumption is that only these literal descriptions are descriptions of reali-ties; so descriptions of aesthetic qualities become subjective impressions. But a colony of aesthetes, disengaged from practical needs and manipula-tions, would single out different units of attention (things), and they would see different resemblances and make different comparisons (quali-ties). Descriptions of aesthetic qualities, which for us are metaphorical, might seem to them to have an altogether literal and familiar sense. They might find complete agreement among themselves in the use of a more directly descriptive vocabulary, singling out different units of attention. A critic in any one of the arts is under the necessity of building such a vo-cabulary in opposition to the main tendency of his language; he needs somehow to convince himself that certain isolated objects of his attention really do have the extraordinary qualities which they seem to have; to this end he will need to discuss his perceptions with others, and to try to bring others to notice these qualities. He may have seen (in the wider sense of "see") more than there is to be seen; and the only test of whether the qualities are really there must be some agreement among careful and dis-interested observers. This is the point at which an aesthetic judgment is made—what are the relationships of elements here? What pattern or ar-rangement of elements is there to be seen, when one attends to the thing carefully and disinterestedly? Anything may be seen or heard or read in many different ways, and as an arrangement of any number of elements of different kinds. The picking out of the elements and of their pattern, in defiance of habit and practical interest, is a work of practice and skill; and the use of words in description is an aid to this perception. Anything whatever may be picked out as an object of aesthetic interest—anything which, when attended to carefully and apart altogether from its uses, pro-vides, by the arrangement of its elements and their suggestion to the im-agination, some peculiar satisfaction of its own. An aesthetic judgment has to point to the arrangement of elements, and to show what constitutes the originality of the arrangement in this particular case; what one calls originality in one case may bear little analogy to originality found elsewhere; for there was no common problem to be solved and the achievements were essentially different.

But a moralist in criticism (and there exist such critics) will always be making unnecessary choices and laying down principles of exclusion, as a moralist must. He will make "value judgments," and a value judgment is essentially a grading of one thing as better than another. If the judgment is an assessment of the particular excellences of works which are very similar, it may be enlightening and useful; but there can be larger comparisons of scale and greatness between things which are in themselves very different. Judgments of this second kind may be taken as practical advice that certain things ought to be read, seen, and heard, and the advice must involve some reference to the whole economy of human needs and purposes; but at this point the critic has actually become a moralist, and the arguments supporting his recommendations are the subject-matter of ethics. "Is this thing more worth attention than other objects of its kind?" is one question, and "What is the peculiar arrangement of elements here and what are the effects of this arrangement?" is another. Most aesthetic theories have involved a confusion of answers to these two very different questions; no positive answer to the second by itself entails any answer to the first. One would need to add some further premises about changing human needs and interests; and there is no reason to assume that all works of art satisfy the same needs and interests at all times and for all people. The objects themselves, and the artists who made them, make no unavoidable claim on the spectator's interest, and anyone may neglect the work done when it is of no interest to him. But the peculiar features of particular objects, with their own originality of arrangement, remain constant and unaffected by the spectator's choices and priorities; and there can be no place for exclusive theories and general principles in identifying their originality; they must be seen as they are, individually, and not judged as contestants in a single race called Art or The Novel or Painting.

I conclude that everyone needs a morality to make exclusions in conduct; but neither an artist nor a critical spectator unavoidably needs an aesthetic; and when in Aesthetics one moves from the particular to the general, one is travelling in the wrong direction.

HELEN KNIGHT

The Use of "Good" in
Aesthetic Judgments

I

I INTEND TO SPEAK about "good" in such judgments as "Most of Cézanne's pictures are good," "*Howard's End* is a good novel," "This is a good film." But the main points apply to "beautiful" as much as to "good." It is largely a matter of choosing different illustrations for the same general point, and I have chosen "good" in preference to "beautiful" as I want to speak about works of art, and, in particular, about pictures. On the whole we commend the works of man for their goodness, and the works of nature for their beauty.

I am raising a philosophic question. When we get into philosophic difficulty about the use of "good" we are puzzled by the difference between goodness and its criteria, the reasons for goodness—the difference, for example, between "this is good" and "this object balances that," "this line repeats that," "the placing of this figure brings out the psychological significance of the event." We become interested in what differentiates the use of "good" from the use of expressions for its criteria, we become interested in its generality.

This is the problem, and I shall try to show that we can only get light on it by considering the goodness-criteria relation. But this involves a significant denial. Many people have tried to solve their difficulty by giving a naturalistic analysis of "good" or "beautiful." It is suggested, for example, that when anyone says that a work of art is good he means that he likes it, or that it satisfies a desire, or that it gives him a feeling of "objectified self-affirmation." But analysis throws no light at all on the goodness-criteria relation, and I shall try to show that no analysis will give us what we want. We shall also see that all naturalistic analyses misrepresent the situation in one way or another.

Reprinted from *Proceedings of the Aristotelian Society,* Vol. XXXVI (1935-6) by courtesy of the Editor of the Aristotelian Society.

I will introduce my view by asking you to consider two different uses of "good," one of which is also a group of uses. There is the use exemplified by "good tennis player," "good knitter," "good Pekingese," "good piece of steak," etc. We use "good" in these cases for what is good of its kind. The goodness of these things depends on their satisfying the criteria of goodness for things of their kind. So this use embraces a group of *specific* uses. On the other hand, we have the *general* use exemplified in "aesthetic experience is good," "philosophic discussion is good." We can bring out the contrast by comparing "philosophic discussion is good" with "that was a good philosophic discussion," we should use quite different arguments to establish each of these statements.

These uses are different—but in what respects? Certainly not because "good" occupies different positions in the sentence. It makes no difference to our meaning whether we say "that tennis player is good" or "that's a good tennis player." Whereas we do get the difference when we say "that discussion was good" (as ordinarily used) and "discussion is good" (but we might use "that discussion was good" to exemplify the general use). The difference does not lie in the position of "good," nor in another and far more important fact. For in *each* case we show the meaning of "good" by considering its criteria—and by not giving an analysis. There is, however, this difference. Whenever we get a specific "good" we can always use a certain type of expression—"is a good *picture*," "is a good *knitter*," "is a good *Pekingese*," etc.; and the words "picture," "knitter," and "Pekingese" contribute to the meaning of the sentence. But if we try to put the general "good" into this form we can only get "is a good *thing*"; and "is a good thing" means exactly the same as "is good." But I want in particular to notice another (though related) difference. It is highly plausible to suppose that my desire for aesthetic experience or philosophic discussion is the criterion for their goodness in the general sense; and, indeed, that my desire for x is a criterion for the goodness of x in this sense, whatever x may be. But it is not plausible to suppose that any of my mental states is a criterion for the goodness of Helen Wills' tennis. The contrast I am pointing to is this: On the one hand we get my desire as a criterion for the goodness of everything that is good in the general sense. On the other hand we get a number of completely different sets of criteria—criteria for tennis, for knitting, for Pekingese dogs, for pieces of steak, and so on. And this is a point I want to emphasize when I class the "good" of aesthetic judgments among the specific uses.

When we say "Cézanne's 'Green Jar' is good," we are not using "good" in the general, but in one of the specific senses. It belongs to the group exemplified by "good tennis playing" and "good Pekingese." I shall try to show that this is the natural view to take. And I shall try to say as much as I can about what it involves. The main thing to consider is the goodness-criteria relation. This is the central fact, and explains the generality of "good." On the other hand, we must also consider the criteria specific to aesthetic goodness. I propose to discuss the goodness-criteria relation in a relatively simple case, and conclude this discussion with some general observations about the use of "good." But all this is extremely difficult, and I know that the discussion is most inadequate; I then hope to show that aesthetic goodness involves this relation. But why, it may be asked, has the point been overlooked? This is not surprising. The aesthetic situation is very complicated, and its complications have obscured the main structure of aesthetic reasoning. But if we see the structure in a simple case we may recognize it in a more complicated one. And accordingly I lay great stress on the analogy.

Suppose I am looking at a game of tennis and say "that's a good player." If someone asks me "why?" or "what do you mean?" I answer by pointing out features of his playing. I say, for example, that his strokes are swift, that his placing is accurate, and point to the speed of his footwork. In making these remarks I am showing that he satisfies the criteria. I am indicating features of his playing that are criteria for its goodness. And this is what my questioner expected. It is the only answer that any of us expects in our ordinary conversations. We give our meaning by pointing out criterion-characters.

But suppose that my questioner wants a philosophic discussion, and says that this answer neglects the generality of "good." It is clear that "he's a good player" is not equivalent to any one of the reasons suggested above, nor to a group of such reasons. The mere fact of their being *reasons* shows that they are not equivalent, as no proposition is a reason for itself. But it is also obvious that "he's a good player" says in a sense far less than "his aim is accurate," and "she's a good knitter" says far less than "her knitting is even." But though "he's a good player" says less than *one* reason, yet in a sense it stretches over all.

It is at this point that analysis crops up. Suppose we persist in asking "But what do we mean when we say his playing is good? what are we saying?" We no longer expect the normal answer. We want someone to say: "I mean by 'his playing is good' that so-and-so" where "so-and-so" is a set of words that provides an analysis. But such an answer, if it could be found, would not really satisfy us. For we want to understand the generality of "good," and the key to this lies in the goodness-criteria relation. Thus at this point the question: what do we mean? is misleading. For neither an enumeration of criteria nor an analysis will give us what we want.

But let us consider what analysis might be suggested. We shall find the case of knitting quite instructive, for here I can see no candidate at all. It is plain that there just are different criteria, evenness, speed, capacity to do intricate patterns etc. In the case of tennis, someone might suggest "his winning ability." It would then be natural to retort: "and what about style?" This is of course a criterion of goodness, though a steady and reliable player would be good without it. In winning ability and style we have simply found two criteria of a very general type. A player is good *because* of his style and *because* he is able to win. Let us suppose we are looking at two stylish players, neither of whom is able to win. One of them, we can see, is unlikely to improve, in spite of his style he is bad. But the other is promising, "Look at his style," we say, "he is good even though he can't win." These cases show us something about the goodness-criteria relation. Style is a criterion, but a player may be good without it; and a knitter may be good without speed. On the other hand, a player may have style and not be good, a knitter may be quick and not be good. And consider this: One player is good because of his smashing service and speed of returns, another because of his careful and unexpected placing of the ball, another because of his smashing service and spectacular backhand strokes, another because he never misses a ball. These variations are typical. We sometimes get one set of criteria, sometimes another; and the sets overlap, providing a number of different combinations. It is through considering such examples, and the more of them the better, that we get to know what the goodness-criteria relation is like. It is not, however, just a matter of collecting facts, but of seeing how elastic the relation is.

I shall now attempt to sum up some general points that I think have emerged about the use of "good," and these contain as much as I can say about its generality. We have seen that the meaning of "good" is determined by criteria. And this is to say: that the truth and falsity of "he is a good so-and-so" depends on whether he possesses criterion-characters or not; and that the natural answer to the question, "What do you mean?" lies in pointing out these characters. But, on the other hand, "he is a good so-and-so" is not equivalent to any proposition which asserts the possession of a criterion-character, nor to a group of such propositions. This lack of equivalence is marked by the use of "because" which introduces the criterion propositions. A clear way of stating the difference would be to give a great many cases in which goodness and criterion propositions are differently used. For example: "he is good, but his placing is not accurate"; "he is not good, but has a smashing service"; "he is good, his service is smashing and his returns are speedy"; "he is good, he is steady and reliable, his service is not smashing, and his returns are not speedy."

On different occasions, as we have seen, we judge by different criteria—"he is good because his service is smashing and his returns are speedy"; "he is good because he is steady and reliable." This is certainly not ambiguity. There are not several meanings of "good" as there are two meanings of "plain" or two meanings of "see" when we distinguish "seeing a physical object" from "seeing a sense-datum." The situation, as I have tried to show, is totally different. But nonetheless I should like to speak about variations in the meaning of "good," to say that its meaning varies when we use different criteria. Some of the differences, I suggest, are striking enough to merit this description. I shall raise the point later on in connection with aesthetic judgments.

Let us now see how the meaning of "good" in aesthetic judgments is determined by its criteria. It will be useful to look at a word like "piquant." Suppose I say that a certain woman is beautiful, and someone replies "Not beautiful, but piquant." I am quite likely to accept this correction; why? Because I see that her features are piquant as distinct from beautiful. And we might point out the marks of piquancy. We might say that her nose is *retroussé*, her chin pointed, her expression vivacious. But in any case we can see that her piquancy depends on her features or expression. And in distinguishing piquancy from beauty we imply that beauty depends on other features (though there may be over-lapping).

This example is useful because "piquant" is the same kind of word as "good." But the range of criteria is narrower, and this makes its dependence on them easier to see. "Good" is exactly the same kind of word as "piquant" and "beautiful," but its use is far wider. It is used with *this* set of criteria and with *that*; and so on through an extremely wide range of overlapping sets. On any *one* occasion it is used with one set only, but on this occasion with this set, on that occasion with that, and so on. This in a way drains it of meaning, it is empty as compared with "piquant." So we see the relation between "piquant" and its criteria more readily, but with a little more attention we can see it just as clearly in the case of "good."

Suppose I say that Cézanne's "Green Jar" is a good picture and someone asks me "why?" or "what do you mean?" I should answer by describing it. I should point out a number of facts about its organization, for example: that apple is placed so that it exactly balances the main mass on the right; the lines of tablecloth, knife, and shadows repeat each other; the diagonal of the knife counteracts the diagonals of the shadows. All these objects, I might continue, are exceedingly solid and the shadows exceedingly deep—each thing "is infallibly in its place." I might point out a number of important problems that Cézanne has solved; for example, that he combines a geometrical scheme with the variety we get in natural appearances. And finally I might allude to the profundity and gravity of the picture. In this description I have pointed out criterion-characters, the "Green Jar" is good because it possesses them.

This is the type of reasoning that runs through critical writings. I shall give a few illustrations. Consider Reynolds' discussion of the principal lights in a picture.[1] He praises the "Bacchus and Ariadne" of Titian. The figure of Ariadne dressed in blue and the sea behind her form a cold contrast to the mellow colours of the principal group. But by giving Ariadne a red scarf and one of the Bacchante some blue drapery Titian prevents a division of the picture into separate sections. On the other hand, Le Brun in "The Tent of Darius" mismanages the light. The picture has a heavy air because the principal light falls on Statira who is dressed in pale blue. Reynolds then gives the "Landscape in Moonlight" by Rubens as an example of modifying natural appearance for the sake of harmony. On the one hand Rubens introduces more colour contrast, and on the other hand modifies the natural brightness of the moon. The natural brightness could only be preserved by making everything else dark. Rembrandt in his "Man in Armour" preserves the natural brightness of the armour, and as a result the picture is too black. We get a similar type of criterion when Berenson praises Giotto for representing just those lines, those lights and shadows which convey solidity,[2] and when Fry points out how Cézanne emphasizes just those aspects of colour which convey plastic form.[3] We get quite another type when Reynolds condemns Bernini's "David" for the meanness of its expression,[4] and Delacroix points out that Millet's peasants are a little too ambitious—this, he explains, is because Millet only reads the Bible.[5]

We find in these cases the same kind of reasoning as in discussions about tennis—he is good because his returns are speedy, it is good because the red scarf and blue drapery preserve the balance. And the question "what do you mean by saying it's good?" provokes the same kind of answer, "I mean that the lines balance each other, that it combines geometric structure with variety, that it is profound."

Let us now consider some cases in which I change my judgment. I decide that a picture is bad. Then someone points out its construction, and I see the picture in a new way. The figures had seemed a mere haphazard collection. I now see a diagonal movement in which the figures participate, and as I follow this movement the space recedes, giving a strong impression of depth. And I reverse my judgment. What determines the change? My perception of how the picture is constructed, my recognition of a criterion-character. Or take these cases. I believe that the "Death of Chatterton" and the "Last Goodbye" are good, the one because of its dramatic presentation, the other because of its pathos. But someone convinces me that the one is theatrical and the other sentimental. And now I decide that these pictures are bad.

It is worth while to notice that my *liking* a picture is never a criterion of its goodness. We never say "this picture is good because I like it." I fully admit that we value aesthetic experience because it includes enjoyment. It is obvious that liking is important, but we must not mistake its role. It is not a criterion. Nor is it true, as we may be inclined to think, that we always like what we judge to be good, and dislike what we judge to be bad. It is common to find indifference combined with approval—"I can't see anything in so-and-so, but I believe it's good." And we also find liking combined with disapproval. I may have a taste for the sentimental, and like *East Lynne*, even if I know that *East Lynne* is sentimental, and that sentimentality is bad. Or I may like a novel because it deals with a problem that interests me, and because I agree with its views. But I may believe that its treatment of the problem is unsuited to the novel form. And in both these cases I condemn the novels for the very characters I like.

I have tried to show that the goodness of pictures depends on their possession of criterion-characters. We give reasons for goodness by pointing them out. The judgment "this is good" or "this is bad" depends on their presence or absence. And this means that we understand the "good" of aesthetic judgments by understanding the goodness-criteria relation. Its meaning is determined by criterion-characters, but the proposition "this is good" is not equivalent to any criterion proposition. And there are rules which determine the truth of the former in relation to the truth of the latter.

And now a few last words about analysis. It is irrelevant to our problem because it tells us nothing about the goodness-criteria relation. I believe we become increasingly convinced of this the more we consider this relation, and that desire for analysis dwindles away. We have indeed found a third alternative, previously overlooked. Our puzzle started when we became convinced that "good" does not name an indefinable quality, and we tried to remove the puzzle by defining "good" in naturalistic terms. We now see that "good" may be indefinable and yet not stand for an indefinable quality, and that it has significance even though in one sense it stands for nothing.

We also see how naturalistic analyses distort the situation. Most of them select a state of mind such as our liking which is not even a criterion of goodness. In looking for such an analysis we tend to look for a mental state which constantly accompanies the judgment that a work of art is good or beautiful. We are struck by some one or other experience such as liking, satisfaction of desire, increased vitality, and analyse aesthetic judgments in terms of this experience. But let us suppose that we *do* find a mental state that constantly accompanies the judgment that a work of art is good or beautiful. What then? It will only provide us with a psychological generalization: whenever anyone judges a work of art to be good he always likes it or it always satisfies a desire, or it always increases his vitality. It does not solve any philosophic problem about the use of "good."

II

There are many points to notice about the criteria of aesthetic merit, and many problems to consider. I am passing over many of these, but certainly not because I think them of little importance. I shall first give examples to show the diversity of aesthetic criteria, and then consider variations in the use of "good" to which this diversity leads. If we look at certain cases of disagreement from this point of view we shall be inclined to interpret them as linguistic differences.

One picture is good for one sort of thing, and another for something quite different. We may praise a water colour for its translucency and an oil for the thickness and richness of its impasto. We praise the brightness and clarity of an Impressionist painting, but do not condemn a Rembrandt for lacking these qualities. It is clear that we look for something different in each case. We praise a Botticelli for the poetry of its theme and a Degas for its realism. And how do we praise a realistic picture? We say that the artist has caught the exact pose, the kind of thing one might see at any moment. And the very banality of that pose (in the case of Degas) is a merit. But we do not condemn Botticelli because we fail to meet his goddesses and nymphs as we walk through the street. On the contrary, we praise him for imagination of the ideal. And we praise him for his flowing rhythm, but do not condemn Byzantine art for being rigid, nor Cézanne for being ponderous. Suppose we are considering the work of a colourist, a member, let us say, of the Venetian school. We praise it for subtle nuances of colour and for atmospheric unity, the kind that obscures the contour of things. We praise it for richness of paint, for richness and vitality of effect. And if it fails in these respects we condemn it. But of course we do not condemn a fresco painting of the fifteenth century because it has none of these qualities. In this kind of painting we look for something quite different, for perfection in each part, for unity achieved by the balance of independent wholes, for simplicity in colour and thinness of paint, for its simple and dignified effect.

These examples show that there are a great many alternative standards. To a large extent these are set by the artist or school. An artist tries to produce a certain effect, and his purpose is shaped by a number of factors: the use of a certain medium (oil, tempera etc.), interest in a certain kind of appearance (sunlight, depth etc.), in a certain kind of form (classical, baroque etc.), in a certain kind of subject (the poetic, the commonplace etc.). All these factors provide criteria. I do not say that the artist's aim is our only critical measure, but it is extremely important and mainly responsible for the diversity of standards.

It is natural to suggest that we can classify criteria, or at least a great many of them, under the headings of form and representation. This classification is convenient and enlightening. But it may suggest misleading ideas. We may think, for example, that we class all formal criteria together because of a common property to which "formal" refers. But the class of formal properties is heterogeneous. We praise a picture because the parts balance each other, because the colours are orchestrated, because the figures are solid, because the colours are brilliant. These are all formal criteria, but we do not class them together because of a common property. Classification is important, but it does not reduce the diversity of criteria.

I now want to discuss the diversity from the linguistic point of view. We have seen that different pictures are good for different reasons. Accordingly when we say "this picture is good" we are often judging by different criteria. We can translate this into a statement about language: when we say "this picture is good" we are often using "good" with different meanings. Only we must remember that "good" is not ambiguous, and that the variations of meaning are distinctive.

These variations occur very frequently. We have already seen one reason for this; namely, that pictures are good by different criteria. But there is another reason, that some people *habitually* judge by certain criteria and not by others. It is a commonplace that some people always praise a picture for its form and others for its subject. Each set habitually selects criteria from another group, and, as we shall see, there are other cases. It may be a matter of ignorance. Without historical and technical training we do not know what artists are aiming at, and accordingly are ignorant of a great many criteria. But there is a far more curious reason. We *refuse* to use criteria of which we are well aware. And this is by no means uncommon. Suppose I say to someone that "After Office Hours" is a good film, and he denies it. I then point out its competent acting, its slickness and smartness. He does not deny that it has these qualities, but answers "that's not goodness." But there are many different criteria of goodness in films and these are among them. His answer amounts to saying "I don't want to accept these criteria of goodness—I don't want to use 'good' in this way." We also get more serious cases of this refusal. Thus Delacroix complains of the "modern schools" who look on colour as an inferior and "earthy" aspect of painting, and exhort artists to reject the technique of the colourist. Again what does this come to? "We don't want to accept these criteria of goodness." Even Reynolds maintains that the highest art requires simplicity, in fact monotony of colour, and must renounce the harmony of subtle nuances. This partly explains his depreciation of Tintoretto, Veronese and Rubens. And what does his criticism come to? "I have *decided* to degrade these criteria, and in consequence these artists only paint 'ornamental' pictures."

The point then is this. Either through ignorance or prejudice many people habitually use "good" with certain meanings and not with others. And when we look at the matter in this light we see that a great deal of aesthetic disagreement is linguistic. It is disagreement in the use of "good." Suppose that two people are looking at a picture by Picasso, the kind in which we get abstract treatment of actual objects. One of them says "this is good" and the other "this is bad." The first is judging by its form, and the other points scornfully to the representation (or lack of it). The appropriate comment is, I suggest, "They are using 'good' with different meanings." And this also applies to the dispute about "After

Office Hours." But we need not only consider such complete disagreement. Delacroix, for example, places Rubens much higher than Reynolds places him, and this is partly because Delacroix is willing, in fact anxious, to accept colour criteria at their full value.

It is important to notice that when people disagree in this way they may completely agree about the nature of what they are discussing. The filmgoers may agree that "After Office Hours" is competent in acting, smart and slick. Reynolds fully agrees with Delacroix that Rubens excels in colour technique. This agreement is significant, and fits in very happily with the linguistic explanation. Suppose, on the other hand, that Reynolds was disputing Rubens' excellence as a colourist. This would be a dispute of quite another kind. It would be a factual dispute about Rubens' technique.

There are two more points I must raise before concluding. I shall treat them both in a very sketchy manner, but cannot leave the subject without indicating the lines along which my answer to them would run.

The first is concerned with comparative judgments, "This picture is better than that." Such judgments are most profitable when we compare pictures that resemble each other pretty closely, two water colours, two Impressionist paintings, two Baroque paintings, etc. In such cases we judge both pictures by the same criteria.

But what about the comparison of pictures which are good for different reasons? I believe that in some cases this would be nonsensical. It is nonsense to ask whether Raphael or Rembrandt is the better artist, whether rugged scenery is better than soft, or Gothic architecture better than Norman. In these cases we can only state a preference for one or the other. But we *do* make comparative judgments where the criteria are different. Raphael's "School of Athens" is better than a water colour by Crome or a cartoon by Max Beerbohm. But Crome and Beerbohm were aiming at completely different ends from Raphael, and their pictures may be perfect of their kind. The explanation of these comparative judgments is, I believe, that some criteria are higher than others. I mean by this simply that when pictures excel by some criteria we say they are better than if they excel by others. The criteria by which Raphael excels, such as space, composition, organization of groups, expressiveness, dignity, are among the very highest.

The second question is closely connected, and has probably been provoked by many of my statements. What is the guarantee of a criterion? What determines the truth of "so-and-so is a criterion for goodness in pictures"? The guarantee, I would answer, lies in its being used as a criterion. Organization of groups, space composition, profundity, etc., are criteria of goodness because they are used as such. But we must face a difficulty. Who is it that uses them? It is true that some are in general use. A large number of people would praise a picture for its profundity. There is also the important fact that we often use criteria without being able to name or distinguish them. But we must acknowledge that some are only used by critics, and not even by all of them. We must admit that criteria are not firmly fixed, like the points (at any one time) of a Pekingese. But it completely misrepresents the situation to say they are not fixed at all.

Perhaps I should also point out that the fixing of criteria is one thing, and their use another. When we make aesthetic judgments we are using criteria, and not talking about the circumstances in which they are fixed. They are fixed by certain people who no doubt have their reasons for preferring some to others. But we do not refer to these facts in our aesthetic judgments.

I have been constantly harping in this paper on the judicial office of aesthetic judgments, and feel that I must supply an antidote, for I have no desire to exalt this office. I believe, it is true, that the judgments we make in pointing out criteria are the most profitable judgments to make. But we need not make them with judicial intent. It is far better to say "Cézanne was interested in this and that, we can find so-and-so in his pictures." The great thing is to discover what a work of art is like.

Notes

1. *Discourses*, Seeley & Co., London, 1905, pp. 245-52.
2. *The Italian Painters of the Renaissance.* The Clarendon Press, Oxford, 1930, pp. 70-71.
3. *Cézanne*, Hogarth Press, London, 1927, pp. 39-40.
4. *Discourses*, p. 71.
5. *Journal*, Librairie Plon, Paris, 1893, vol. 2, p. 61.

MARGARET MACDONALD

Some Distinctive Features of
Arguments Used in
Criticism of the Arts

. . . THE LOGICAL TYPE of value judgments affects the question whether critical discussion is argument to prove true and false propositions. I shall assume it to be generally agreed that value judgments are not simply descriptions of physical or psychological fact. For the statement that an object has certain physical qualities or an observer certain states is not an evaluation. "This is good" does not *say* either "This has certain observable qualities" or "I admire this." Nor shall I recapitulate the arguments against the view that judgments of aesthetic value assert the presence in an object of the non-natural quality "aesthetic goodness" or "beauty." Moreover, while those who affirm value judgments take favourable or unfavourable attitudes to what is evaluated, value judgments seem to do more than express personal attitudes. They are "objective" at least to the extent that those who agree or disagree with them do so without necessarily referring to any private feeling or sentiment. "I admit that Raphael is a great painter but I do not like his work; it does not move me." Such a statement is not self-contradictory, and very often true. If so, it is hard to believe that "Raphael is a good painter" expresses a favourable attitude which the speaker denies. To suppose that he is expressing the attitude of no one in particular (if, indeed, this makes sense) is to remove the chief charm of the theory. "This is good" is ostensibly similar to "this is red." If "good" does not name a simple quality like "red" then the sole alternative, it has been supposed, is that it names a simple feeling in the assertor. But "This is good" also has the form of the impersonal verdict "He is guilty" with which it may perhaps be more profitably compared.

Reprinted from *Proceedings of the Aristotelian Society*, Supplementary Vol. XXIII (1949) by courtesy of the Editor of the Aristotelian Society.

For a verdict does not describe the accused nor express the feelings of judge and jury. It affirms a decision reached by a definite procedure but unlike that of relating evidence to conclusion in deductive and inductive inference.[1] This is a situation which extends far beyond law courts, to show rings, examiners' meetings, selection boards. All these estimate qualifications and indicate a decision by certain signs, a prize, diploma, appointment. It is this activity, far more than those of logicians and scientists, which resembles the critic's. For he, too, adjudicates; he affirms merit or demerit. By calling a work "good" he places the hall mark on an artistic performance. But he does not describe it or himself. So that to affirm a work good is more like bestowing a medal than naming any feature of it or of the states of its creators and audience. Verdicts and awards are not true or false. They may be reversed but not disproved. But they can be justified and unjustified. Both the verdict and the competence of the judges may be contested. The opposition protests that the verdict was wrong or unjust; not that it was false or invalid.

If this account is accepted then it follows that critical discussion cannot establish value judgments by deductive and inductive inference. They are neither deduced nor confirmed by empirical evidence. So no one, as Wordsworth said, can be *argued* into a favourable verdict on the Lyrical Ballads. Does it follow that such a verdict can be obtained only by graft, sales talk, wheedling or whatever other device will influence a capricious fancy? No, for though these may obtain, they do not *justify*, a decision. The word "judge" does not properly apply to those, like the Duchess in *Alice in Wonderland,* who indulge a liking for cutting off heads. Nor to those, more amiable, like the Dodo, who give prizes to everyone. Even a bad judge makes some pretence of observing a procedure other than mere caprice. So, too, a critic is worthy of the name only if he distributes verdicts with discrimination. But discrimination about what, and what sort of procedure justifies a value judgment about art? What sort of considerations are invoked, and how, to justify a critical verdict?

I have said that we ordinarily distinguish a work of art from a physical object. That we use these terms differently. "That," exclaims A triumphantly, pointing to his newly acquired canvas, "is a great picture!" "I should not call it a picture," retorts B, "but only a pot of paint flung in the face of a gullible public!"[2] It seems clear that both have located the same physical object but that not both have located a work of art. Nor will it be of much use to tell B to look more closely and carefully when he will find the work of art hidden in the paint, like the monkey in the branches of a child's puzzle. He may look as hard as you please, but he will not succeed, for in *that* sense there is nothing more to find. It is not perceptual tricks which distinguish a painted canvas from a work of art. Remember Reynolds and the Venetians. What B lacks is not observation but that which A must supply as a critic to support his judgment, instruction, and interpretation. The distinction between physical object and work of art is even more complicated for the non-plastic arts. Even if one *can* locate "Cremorne Lights" on the wall of a certain room in the National Gallery, where can one locate Shakespeare's plays or Beethoven's symphonies? I have an object on my bookshelf, of the same type as the shelf, a copy of Shakespeare's Works; I have the score and a set of records of a Beethoven symphony. So have thousands of others, and they have the same works. When I talk of these works I do not refer only to my particular copies. But by "Cremorne Lights" I mean the original by Whistler in the National Gallery of which anything resembling it is a mere copy and *not* the same work. The type/token distinction applies to literary and musical but not to works of the plastic arts. I do not propose to discuss this further except to say that it shows that while a work of the plastic arts cannot, logically, be in more than one place at one time, this is not true of literary and musical works. Hence it is much more plausible to suppose that in painting and sculpture one refers simply to a physical object when talking of a work of art. But this is not true of any works of art. Because it is not, certain idealist aesthetic philosophers, e.g. Croce[3] and Collingwood,[4] have held that a work of art is a mental image, an imaginary or "ideal" object for which its physical expression in words, paint, stone, sounds, etc., is a mere vehicle, a stimulus to the reproduction of the "real" work in an observer's mind. For Alexander[5] the work of art is a material thing magically endowed with mysterious life by the artist and so turned into an illusion, though a beautiful illusion. For Sartre, too, the work of art is "something unreal" for which the artist constructs a material analogue in the external world.[6] There is obviously a very strong temptation to treat the work of art as a mysterious entity, somewhat like a genie in its physical bottle. But if a work of art is not a physical object, it does not follow that it is a mental state or ghost. These do not exhaust the possibilities for not all discourse which uses substantival words and phrases need be "about" objects. If one wished to be metaphysically paradoxical one might say that a work of art is not an object of any sort but only, as it were, a manner of speaking, though this, of course, is also highly misleading if taken seriously. But aesthetic, like all other philosophical problems, are those of how words are used rather than of what kinds of objects exist.

The problem of how "work of art" is used, which I confess I cannot satisfactorily solve and may even be wrong in considering a problem, does at present seem to me connected with the question of how value judgments in art are justified and hence with that of critical interpretation. "Work of art" is a cultural, not an everyday term. Like "electron" its use is learned by a more sophisticated process than that of "table." Someone may object that this is only because "work of art" is a general term and these should be avoided in philosophy. Everyone knows the difference between a poem, a play, a picture, a statue, a symphony. These are "works of art" so why so much fuss? I can only say that even in particular cases there sometimes seems to be difficulty about what is being discussed and evaluated in art.

I shall introduce my difficulties by referring to some points in Mrs. Helen Knight's discussion of "The Use of 'Good' in Aesthetic Judgments." Mrs. Knight compares the use of "good" in "*Persuasion* is a good novel," "Cézanne's 'Green Jar' is a good picture" with its use in such judgments as " 'Serena' is a good Persian cat," " 'Lady Jane' is a good arum lily," "Joan is a good knitter," etc. The similarity in all such uses is the existence of a set of criteria-qualities for good novels, good Persian cats, good knitters, etc., which, when indicated, justify the use of "good" for each type of performance. Works of art may be good for many such "reasons." There are many different criteria of merit recognized by critics. They form an indefinite and increasing family. Their exemplification can, however, be recognized in particular works of art which may be judged accordingly.

Mrs. Knight's interesting account does not quite satisfy me, for two reasons. (1) Two Persian cats, two tennis players, two roses, two knitters, may tie for first place. There may be "nothing to choose between them." They exemplify the agreed criteria-characters to an indistinguishable degree. But I am not sure that it makes sense to say that *Emma* and *Persuasion* might compete for the same place; that two works, even by the same artist, might excel by exhibiting certain meritorious characters in a way which makes them qualitatively indistinguishable. There could be twin prize cats, but it seems to me logically impossible that there should be twin masterpieces in art. Works of art are unique. Their performance cannot be repeated even by the artist. In this they seem to differ from certain other performances in which what is produced, though numerically different, may be qualitatively exactly similar. This is not a mysterious natural fact, but simply a characteristic of the way in which we talk about works of art. No doubt the borrower from a circulating library who just wants a "good" novel for the weekend will accept any standard work. But then he is not interested in art. For those who are, though *The Portrait of a Lady* has much in common with *The Wings of the Dove* and both are good novels, it would seem absurd to list their characteristics and suppose them to add up to the same sum. One would not be content to lose either so long as the other were retained. They are not simply substitutable for each other. This would be admitted by any competent critic. (2) My second objection to Mrs. Knight's account is that it seems to assume that a work of art is an object rather like a cake, whose meritorious features may be picked out, like plums, and exhibited. The model suggested to me is of a combination of ingredients which it is the business of the critic to exhibit to justify his approval of the work. There is, e.g., one object, the play of *Hamlet*, whose features can be revealed once and for all by expert interpretation and the result evaluated. Mrs. Knight gives an example of this in the description of its characters by which she would support a favourable verdict on Cézanne's "Green Jar."

If this is the correct story, it is strange that the task of interpreting and evaluating a work of art seems to be never completed. In art, the dead are never finally buried. The re-interpreting and revaluating of established, and the resurrecting of forgotten, works is a favourite activity of critics. One need only think of the procession of critics of Shakespeare. Yet many of them from Johnson to the latest name may still be read with profit. Is it because the features of Shakespeare's plays are so inexhaustible that no one critic can ever finally list them as adequate grounds for value judgments? Or is it because the plays are not simple objects whose features can be presented for listing? To suppose that they are is, again, to be misled by the methods of science. Scientists observe and explain the behavior of objects. Whether bodies are observed to fall by X in Italy in the sixteenth century or by Y in London in the twentieth does not affect the result, unless new facts are relevant. I have suggested that new facts in this sense about works of art are discovered only by scholars and historians whose methods are scientific. There are few such facts about Shakespeare's plays known to-day which were unknown to Dr. Johnson, though later interpretations of the plays and perhaps their evaluation have differed. It is often said that a great artist is reinterpreted in every age and no doubt by some of these interpretations he would be much astonished. Yet even the apparently bizarre interpretations are often illuminating. It seems to follow that interpretation is partly subjective invention, but about this there could be endless argument of the sort that would hardly be necessary about the description of a chair or horse, except perhaps in extreme borderline cases. Certainly, the critic claims to be interpreting the work, not supplying his own fancies. But the work is what it is interpreted to be, though some interpretations may be rejected. There seems to be no work apart from *some* interpretation.

This critical function may be illustrated by another form of interpretation. The presentation of the character of "Hamlet" by actors from Richard Burbage to John Gielgud is of "the same character." Each actor impersonates "Hamlet" and speaks the lines given in any text of the play. Yet the effect of each interpretation may be very different but, apart from presentation through someone, what is *the* character "Hamlet"? Does each actor find something in "Hamlet" missed by the rest or is it not rather that the character is a construction from this series of interpretations upon a text and evaluated by means of its members? Music and its executants are another example of interpretations which seem to constitute a work of art. A musical work is composed for performance but each performance while playing the notes of the same score varies, often widely, from any other. A great conductor, with a responsive orchestra, may give an entirely fresh meaning to a hackneyed composition. Yet, again, the composition does not exist as a *musical* work apart from some performance. It is a construction from such performances. Nor need such performances be actual. In reading *Hamlet* or following a score one imagines a performance, gives a certain interpretation to the words and notes even though this may be a very poor relation of that given by a great actor or executant. The point is that there is no object which is "the real" play or sonata which exists independently of any interpretation. If it be said that there is such an object, *viz.* the play or sonata as it existed in the minds of Shakespeare or Mozart, then the reply must surely be that if this is so we must remain not only ignorant of, but literally *without* these works, since we cannot restore the dead. I do not think we are condemned to such a pessimistic conclusion. Nor does this view conflict with the statement that a work of art is unique. For the fact that there could not be another play of exactly the same merit as *Hamlet* is not incompatible with its construction from many interpretations. This is an attempt to explain what is meant when we say that there is such a play, or any work of art.

I suggest that the task of the critic resembles those of the actor and executant rather than those of the scientist and logician. Another fruitful comparison might be with that of a good Counsel. The Counsel, too, has the "facts" but from them he "creates" his client's case. So the critic must present what is not obvious to casual or uninstructed inspection, *viz.* a work of art. Of course, he is not to be identified with an actor, executant or Counsel. He differs from these in one very important respect, in being also a judge of what he presents. That a critic is "creative" is not very revolutionary doctrine and most great critics have been great showmen of their subjects. Such were Ruskin on Turner, Clive Bell and Roger Fry on Cézanne and the Post-Impressionists, Coleridge on Shakespeare and, finally, Wordsworth on the Lyrical Ballads. Should we have the works we value, without these and other advocates? But to a lesser degree we are all critics in relation to art. Some construction must precede serious judgment.

To judge a work of art, therefore, is to give a verdict on something to which the judge has contributed and this also "justifies" the verdict. It is an odd sort of justification, perhaps more like that by which we try to "justify" our affections and antipathies. For a work of art appeals to more than the intellect. People often develop for their favourite works an almost personal relationship for which "reasons" seem irrelevant. This should not be exaggerated, but is an element in the attitude to art which makes an account of "proving" a value judgment by the listing of criteria-characters seem inappropriately mechanical. Not in that way, one protests, is conviction induced.

But if each interpretation is individual how is one to explain the fact that different ages or even different persons in any age evaluate the "same" work of art? One might suggest that "same" here is used analogously to its use in "same function" and *Hamlet* is a function of which individual interpretations are values as "x is a man" is a function of which individual men are values. Of course, they are not exactly similar for *Hamlet* is not a universal or set of universals of which its interpretations are instances as "Man" is a universal of which individual men are instances. My reading of *Hamlet* is not an "instance" of *Hamlet* though it is one of a vast number of more or less similar performances without which, I suggest, it would make no sense to speak of the play. The idea of a "work of art-in-itself" which can never be conceivably experienced is as mythical as a "material object-in-itself" which can never conceivably be perceived. But neither are its interpretations connected in the construction of a work of art as sense data are connected in the construction of a physical object on the phenomenonalist thesis. If the work of art is such a construction as I have suggested, it is unique and not to be identified with any others with which it may be compared. The history of the arts, of criticism and evaluation, does seem to show that "work of art" is not used for simple, identifiable objects which can be indicated like a pebble on a beach or a book on a shelf, but rather for something like a set of variations on a basic theme.

I wonder whether aesthetic philosophers do not make too much fuss about "sameness" and "objectivity" in art. Art is different from morals. It may be important that for Shakespeare as for us stealing a purse is theft, and wrong; wrong, perhaps, for all rational beings who acknowledge private property. I am much less sure that the play which Shakespeare's audience enjoyed as *Hamlet* is identical with that enjoyed now. Not only in matters such as text, which scholarship can rectify, but as a work of art. Since our circumstances and background are utterly different from those of the first Elizabethans, such an identity seems most unlikely. A simple, but important, difference is that the work would have *sounded* very different in Elizabethan English. As different as Bach's music would sound on the instruments for which it was originally composed. If we and our ancestors could change places each might loathe the other's version and we might wrangle interminably about which was the "real" work. The answer is, surely, *both* and that there are and will continue to be innumerable members of the family. This may also be part of the answer to our differences with Reynolds about the Venetians. The problem becomes one of choosing an emphasis: same work but *different versions*; different versions but the *same work*. Either alternative is valid.

So, to affirm that a work of art is good or bad is to commend or condemn, but not describe. To justify such a verdict is not to give general criteria as "reasons" but to "convey" the work as a pianist might "show" the value of a sonata by playing it. Critical talk about a work is, as it were, a construction of it by someone at a particular time, and in a certain social context. Thus criticism does not, and cannot, have the impersonal character and strict rules, applicable independently of time and place, appropriate to science and mathematics. A mathematician who claimed to have squared the circle, a scientist who announced a law for which he could give no empirical evidence, would be justly ridiculed. But to attempt to legislate for art is to invite successful infringement of any law, as the "Unities" showed. Criticism is, therefore, I suggest, an indefinite set of devices for "presenting" not "proving" the merits of works of art. It has none of the stability of logical truth, scientific method, legal and moral law. It varies with time, place and audience, while not being completely subject to these limitations. For it is certainly possible to appreciate the work of artists and critics of other ages and cultures. But the differences are as important as any common characters and must be equally respected. It is mythical to suppose that one can distil some "eternal essences" which are works of art and some uniform method of their appraisal from the vast and complex system of relationships between artists and their audiences throughout the history of art. Art is creation, not discovery. Criticism and appraisal, too, are more like creation than like demonstration and proof.

Does it follow from this that all judgments about art are of equal value, which I began by denying? I do not think so. But they are not measured by correspondence with the qualities of some mythical object, the "real work of art" independent of all interpretation. Instead, they are generally appraised in relation to qualities of the critic. The judgments of a skilful, sympathetic, widely experienced critic are better than those of one without these, and other appropriate qualities. But "better" and "worse" judgments are probably all that can be achieved in this field. No critic, even the best, is infallible and sometimes we may be well advised to trust our own judgment rather than that of any expert.

Notes

1. Cf. also J. Wisdom, "Gods," *Logic and Language,* p. 187, and M. Macdonald, "Natural Rights," *Proc. Aris. Soc.,* 1946-47, esp. pp. 242-50.

2. Cf. Ruskin *v.* Whistler.

3. *Aesthetic,* trans. D. Ainslie, London, Macmillan, 1922. [The relevant passages of Croce's *Aesthetic* are to be found in Section I above. Ed.]

4. *Principles of Art.* Oxford University Press, 1938. [See the selection from Collingswood's *Principles* in Section II of this book. Ed.]

5. Cf. *Beauty and Other Forms of Value,* London, Macmillan, 1933; also Paul Ziff on "Art and the 'Object of Art,' " *Aesthetics and Language,* ed. by William Elton (Oxford, 1954), p. 170.

6. *The Psychology of Imagination,* trans. New York, Philosophical Library, 1948. Conclusion, Section 2, "The Work of Art."

PAUL ZIFF

Reasons in Art Criticism

Hsieh Ho said one of the principles of painting is that "through organization, place and position should be determined." Le Brun praised Poussin's paintings to the French Academy, saying the figures were faithful copies of Roman and Greek statues.

If someone now says "P.'s painting is a faithful copy of a Roman statue," he is not apt to be offering a reason why the work is either good or bad. "The painting has a touch of blue," ". . . is a seascape," ". . . a picture of peasants," ". . . conforms to the artist's intentions," ". . . will improve men's morals": these too are not apt to be offered, and if offered cannot be accepted as reasons why the painting is good or bad.

But if someone says "P.'s painting is disorganized," he is apt to be offering a reason why the work is bad (he need not be; this might be part of an answer to "Which one is P.'s?"). Even if it is right to say "P.'s painting is disorganized," it may be wrong to conclude "P.'s painting is bad," or even "P.'s painting is not good." Some good paintings are somewhat disorganized; they are good in spite of the fact that they are somewhat disorganized. But no painting is good because it is disorganized and many are bad primarily because they are disorganized.

To say "P.'s painting is disorganized" may be to offer a good reason why P.'s painting is bad. It is a consideration. It need not be conclusive. But it is a reason nonetheless. Much the same may be said of reference to the balance, composition, proportions, etc., of a painting; but much the same may not be said of certain references to the subject matter, of any reference to the size, shape, effect on morals, etc., of a painting. Why is this so? Is this so?

From *Philosophy and Education*, Israel Scheffler, ed., pp. 219-36. Copyright, 1958, by Allyn and Bacon, Inc., Boston. Reprinted by permission of the publisher.

I

Someone might say this: "If a painting were disorganized and had no redeeming features, one would not call it 'a good painting.' To understand the relevant uses of the phrase 'a good painting' is to understand, among other things, that to say 'P.'s painting is disorganized' may be to offer a reason in support of an unfavorable opinion of P.'s painting."

This won't do at all even though it is plainly true that someone would not—I would not—call a painting "a good painting" if it were disorganized and had no redeeming features.

Maybe certain persons use the phrase "a good painting" in such a way that they would call a painting "a good painting" even if it were disorganized and had no redeeming features. Maybe some or even many or most in fact use the phrase "a good painting" in a way that no painting is good if it is not a seascape. Many people probably use the phrase "a good painting" in many different ways.

It is true that I and my friends would not call a painting "a good painting" if it were merely disorganized, unredeemed. That is no reason why anyone should accept the fact that a painting is disorganized as a reason in support of an unfavorable opinion of it. To say one would not call it "a good painting" if it were disorganized and had no redeeming features is primarily a way of indicating how strongly one is committed to the acceptance of such a fact as a reason, it is a way of making clear precisely what attitude one has here: it does not show the attitude is reasonable.

Why use the phrase in one way rather than another? Why bother with organization? Why not concentrate on seascapes? on pictures of peasants? Is it merely a linguistic accident that one is concerned with organization? This is not a matter of words. (And this is not to say that the words do not matter: "That is a good painting" can be queried with "According to what standards?"; "That is a magnificent painting" cannot be so queried and neither can "That is an exquisite painting," ". . . a splendid painting," etc.)

Only some of the remarks sometimes made while discussing a work of art are reasons in support of a critical evaluation of the work: to evaluate a work one must understand it, appreciate it; much of what is said about a work is directly relevant only to an appreciation of it.

Any fact is relevant to an appreciation of a work if a knowledge of it is likely to facilitate, to enhance, the appreciation of the work. A critic may direct attention to many different facts: the role of the supporting continuo is the central point in Tovey's discussion of Haydn's chamber music. Tovey points out that the supporting continuo was used to fill a crucial gap in the musical structure:

The pioneers of instrumental music in the years 1600-20 showed an accurate instinct by promptly treating all groups of instruments as consisting of a firm bass and a florid treble, held together by an unobtrusive mass of harmony in the middle. Up to the death of Handel and beyond, throughout Haydn's boyhood, this harmonic welding was entrusted to the continuo player, and nobody ever supposed that the polyphony of the "real" orchestral parts could, except accidentally or by way of relief, sound well without this supplement.[1]

When Tovey then says: in the later chamber music Haydn abandoned the use of a supporting continuo, he is saying something of relevance to an appreciation of any one of Haydn's chamber works: who can then listen to an early Haydn quartet and not hear it in a new way? The supporting continuo acquires a new prominence in the structure of the whole work. But the end product of this process of re-examining the interrelations of the various parts, to which one has been impelled by the critic's information, is a keener feeling for the texture of the whole.

This is one instance of how historical information can be of value in directing and enlightening the appreciation of a work; there are others: the music of Bach has been compared with that of Schütz, Donne's poetry with that of Cavalcanti, Matisse's work with Egyptian wall paintings. Comparative studies are useful; they provide fresh means of directing and arousing interest in certain aspects of the works under consideration. When a critic shows that work *A* is intimately related or similar in some important respects to work *B*, this is of interest not only in that one is then aware of this particular relation between *A* and *B*, but more significantly, one may then see both *A* and *B* in a different way: *A* seen in the light of its relation to *B* can acquire a new lucidity.

Any fact may be relevant to an appreciation of a work, may thereby be indirectly relevant in evaluating it. Presumably every fact directly relevant in evaluating the work is also relevant to an appreciation of it. But the converse is not true, e.g. that the work was executed while the artist was in Rome may be relevant to an appreciation of it but is likely to be relevant in no other way to an evaluation of it. What further requirements must a fact relevant to an appreciation of a work satisfy if it is also to be relevant in evaluating the work?

To say a painting is a good painting is here simply to say it is worth contemplating. (Strictly speaking, this is false but for the time being I am not concerned to speak strictly, but only for the time being. See II below.) Nothing can be a reason why the painting is good unless it is a reason why the painting is worth contemplating. (One can add: for its own sake, but that is redundant.)

Suppose we are in a gallery with a friend looking at P.'s painting; he somewhat admires the work, is inclined to claim that it is good; we wish to deny this, to claim it is a bad painting. We might attempt to support our counter claim by saying "The painting is clearly disorganized," offering this as a reason in support of our opinion of the work.

Saying this to him would be a way of drawing his attention to the organization of the painting, to the lack of it, a way of pointing to this aspect of the painting, saying "Notice this, see the disorder," not merely this, of course, but at least this.

> ("Here you see a single great curving diagonal holds together in its sweep nearly everything in the picture. And this diagonal is not built up by forms that are at the same distance from the eye. The forms are arranged so as to lead the eye gradually backwards until we pass out of the stable into the open air beyond. Here . . ."[2]

said Roger Fry, discussing a painting by Rubens, focusing the listening eye on the single great curving diagonal, drawing it back and forth across the picture plane, levelling the attention, directing it freely throughout the painting.)

This pointing is a fundamental reason why "The painting is clearly disorganized" is a reason, and the fact that it is indicates why "The work was executed while the artist was in Rome," ". . . conforms to the artist's intentions," ". . . is liked by Bernard," even though possibly relevant to an appreciation of the work, are not reasons why the painting is good or bad; for all this is not directly relevant. One cannot contemplate the fact that the work was done while the artist was in Rome in the painting; this is not an aspect of the painting, not a characteristic of it which one can either look at or look for. Suppose one were told: "Notice that the work was done while the artist was in Rome," one could only reply: "But what am I supposed to look at?"

Of course one could do this: I say to you "Think of Rome; then look for things in the picture that will fit in with what you've just been thinking"; you might find a great deal in some pictures, little in others. If I want you to make out a lion in the picture which you seem not to have seen I could say this: "Remember the work was done in Africa," "The artist was much interested in animals," etc. So it won't do, in one sense, to say that remarks like "Notice that the work was done while the artist was in Rome" are not reasons because they do not direct or guide one in the contemplation of the work. But in another sense it is obvious that such remarks do not guide or direct one in the contemplation of a work; to suppose that they do is to suppose certain familiar locutions to be signifying in somewhat extraordinary ways.

What is important here is this: one looks at paintings; nothing can be a reason why a painting is good or bad unless it is concerned with what can be looked at in the painting, unless it is concerned with what can, in some sense, be seen.

If it be asked: "Why insist on this? How does this show that 'The work was done while the artist was in Rome' is not a reason why the painting is good?," a sufficient answer is: only in this way can the reason direct or guide one in the contemplation of the work; a "reason" that failed to do this would not be worth asking for, not worth giving; there would be no reason to be concerned with such a "reason."

But this is not to say that "The work was done while the artist was in Rome," ". . . is liked by Bernard," etc., are necessarily, apart from questions of appreciation, altogether irrelevant; these matters may in many ways be indirectly relevant to an evaluation of a work.

That the work was done while the artist was in Rome, is liked by Bernard, was done in the artist's old age, is detested by people of reputed good taste . . . may be indications, signs, that it is a poor work; these may be very good and important reasons to suppose the work is defective. It is for such reasons as these that one decides not to see a certain exhibition, not to read a certain book, not to hear a certain concert. But such facts as these do not in themselves constitute reasons why the painting is a poor work: indications or signs are never reasons why the painting is good or bad, but at best only reasons to suppose it is good or bad. The fact that C cannot remember D's name is often an indication or a sign of the fact that C dislikes D; it is a reason to suppose C dislikes D; in odd cases it may also be a reason why C dislikes D in that it is a contributing cause of the dislike: an indication or a sign is a reason why only when it is a cause. But one is not here concerned with causes: "What causes this to be a good painting?" has no literal meaning; "What makes this a good painting?" asks for the reason why it is a good painting, and this kind of question cannot be answered by citing indications or signs.

This pointing is not the only reason why certain facts are, and others are not, reasons why a painting is good or bad: "The painting is a seascape" points to a characteristic of the painting, directs one's attention to certain features of the work; for saying this to him could be a way of saying "Notice this, see that it is a seascape," yet this is not a reason why the painting is either good or bad.

To say to him "The painting is a seascape" could be a way of directing his attention to the subject matter of the painting, indicating that the painting was of a certain kind. While contemplating a painting one may consider what kind of work it is, who painted it, what kind of organization it has, what kind of subject matter (if any), what kind of pigmentation, etc. To learn that a painting is by a certain artist, has a certain kind of organization, subject matter, pigmentation, etc., may be relevant to an appreciation of the work; it may enable one to recognize, discern, make out, identify, label, name, classify things in the painting, aspects of the painting; such recognition, identification, classification, may be important in the appreciation of a painting; one who failed to recognize or discern or make out the man in Braque's *Man with a Guitar*, the printed letters in a cubist painting, a horse in *Guernica*, would be apt to misjudge the balance and organization of these works, would fail to appreciate or understand these works, would be in no position to evaluate them.

That a painting is of a certain kind may be an excellent reason to suppose it is good or bad. But is it ever a reason why the painting is good or bad? Is the fact that the painting is of a certain kind directly relevant to the contemplation of the painting? Does "The painting is a seascape" direct or guide one in the contemplation of the painting?

Being of a certain kind matters here primarily in connection with the recognition, identification, classification, etc., of various elements of the work. Shall we then say: "Contemplating the subject matter of a painting (or its organization, or its pigmentation, etc.) is not merely a matter of recognizing, identifying, the subject matter, not merely a matter of labelling, naming, classifying"?

That is not enough; it is not that contemplating a painting is not merely a matter of this or that, it is not a matter of recognizing or identifying or classifying or labelling at all.

Contemplating a painting is something one does, something one may be engaged in; one can and does say things like "I am contemplating this painting," "I have been contemplating this painting for some time." But in this sense, recognizing is not something one does; even though it may be true that while contemplating a painting (which has subject matter) I may recognize, or fail to recognize, or simply not recognize, the subject matter of the painting, it is never true that I am recognizing the subject matter; and this is a way of saying one cannot say "I am recognizing the subject matter of this painting," or "I am recognizing this painting," or "I have been recognizing it for some time," etc.

Recognition is like an event, whereas contemplation is like an activity (much the same may be said of identification, classification, etc., in certain relevant senses, though not in all senses, of these terms) ; certain events may occur during the course of an activity, recognition may or may not take place during the course of contemplation. While contemplating Braque's *Man with a Guitar* one may suddenly (or slowly and at great length) recognize, discern, make out, a figure in the painting; analytical cubistic works often offer such difficulties. If on Monday one recognizes a figure in the Braque painting, on Tuesday there is ordinarily no question of recognition; it has occurred, is over and done with, for the time being; "I recognize it every time I see it" would be sensible if each time it appeared in a fresh disguise, if I suffered from recurrent amnesia, if it appeared darkly out of a haze. (In the sense in which one can speak of "recognizing" the subject matter of an abstract or semi-abstract work, one often cannot speak of "recognizing" the subject matter of a characteristic Chardin still-life: one can see, look at, study, examine the apple in the Chardin painting, but there is not likely to be any "recognition.")

This is not to deny that if a work has recognizable elements, recognition may occur during the course of contemplation, nor that if it does occur then the contemplation of the work is, for some people at least, likely to be somewhat enhanced. If recognition is ever a source of delight, that is certainly true; this, too, would be true: the second time one contemplates the work the contemplation of it may be less worthwhile. But whether this is true or not does not really matter here. It appears to be of interest owing only to an ambiguity of "contemplating."

"Contemplating" may be employed to refer simply to contemplating, or to someone's contemplation of a work at a certain time and place and under certain conditions. "In contemplating the work one attends to the organization" is about contemplating, about what one is doing in contemplating the work; to speak of "contemplating a work," or of "the contemplation of a work," is a way of referring only to certain aspects of one's contemplation of a work at a certain time and place and under certain conditions; it is a way of abstracting from considerations of person, place and time. "In contemplating the work one recognizes a figure in the foreground" is not about contemplating the work; it is not about what one is doing in contemplating the work; it is about something like an event that may occur while someone is contemplating the work for the first or second time under certain conditions. (Contrast "In walking one's leg muscles are continually being tensed and relaxed" with "In walking one finds an emerald.")

To say "Since the work has recognizable elements, recognition is likely to occur while contemplating the work and thus the contemplation of the work will be enhanced" would not be to refer to the contemplation of the work, it would not be to abstract from considerations of time; for it is not the contemplation of the work that would be enhanced, but only and merely the contemplation of the work on that particular occasion when recognition occurred. It is for this reason the fact that the work has recognizable elements—and thus admits of the possibility of recognition occurring during the course of contemplation, so enhancing the contemplation—is not a reason why the work is worth contemplating. To say "The work is worth contemplating," or "Contemplating the work is worthwhile," is here and ordinarily to speak of contemplating the work, it is here and ordinarily to abstract from considerations of person, place and time.

Were *Guernica* hung in Hell, contemplating it would hardly be worthwhile, would there be altogether tedious; yet it is not the work that would be at fault, rather the contemplation of the work in the galleries of Hell. But whether this would be the case has no bearing on whether *Guernica* is worth contemplating. It would ordinarily be at best foolish to reply to "*Guernica* is well worth contemplating" by asking "When?" or "Where?" or even "For whom?" That a certain person, at a certain time and place, finds *Guernica* not worth contemplating may be a slight reason to suppose *Guernica* is not worth contemplating, but it is not a reason why the work is not worth contemplating. If one knows that no one ever has found, or ever will find, *Guernica* worth contemplating, one has excellent reason to suppose *Guernica* is not worth contemplating; one can be absolutely sure it is not worth contemplating; yet this is not even the most trifling reason why *Guernica* is not worth contemplating. This does not ever entitle anyone to say "I know *Guernica* is not worth contemplating." All this is but an elaborate way of saying that in saying "The work is worth contemplating" one is abstracting from considerations of person, place and time.

What has been said of "recognition" could be said, in one way or another, of "identification," "classification," "labelling," "naming," etc.; thus identification, as well as recognition, may occur during the course of contemplation, may enhance the contemplation, is over and done with after a time. But this is never a reason why the painting is good or bad. If recognition, identification, classification, etc. all fail, as they do in fact all fail, to be such a reason, and if nothing can be such a reason unless it is a fact about the work that directs or guides one in the contemplation of the work—thus comparisons, associations, etc., are out of order—it follows that the fact that a work is of a certain kind is also incapable of being a reason why the work is worth contemplating. "There can be no objective rule of taste by which what is beautiful may be defined by means of concepts," said Kant,[3] and he was right (but for the wrong reasons).

Let it be clear that nothing has been said to deny that one can be concerned only with recognition, or identification, or classification, or comparisons, etc., when contemplating paintings; one can treat a painting in the way an entomologist treats a specimen spider, or be concerned only with puzzle pictures, with conundrums. Nor has it been maintained that to say "The work is worth contemplating" is necessarily to abstract from considerations of person, place, and time; that this is what is here and ordinarily intended in speaking of "contemplating a painting" is primarily (though not exclusively) a verbal point and does not signify. There are other ways of speaking: a person may choose to say "The work is worth contemplating" and abstract only from considerations of person, or of place, or of time, or not at all. But if so, he cannot then say what one now wants to say and does say about paintings; for if a person fails or refuses to abstract from such considerations at all, it will be impossible either to agree or disagree with him about the worth of paintings; refusing to abstract from considerations of person, place, and time is tantamount to refusing ever to say, as one now says, "The work is worth contemplating," but insisting always on saying things like "The work is worth contemplating for me, here and now," or ". . . for him, yesterday, at two o'clock," etc. One can speak in this way if one chooses; one can do what one wills with paintings. But none of this has anything to do with art.

To state that a painting is a seascape, if it is simply to state that the work is of a certain kind, is not to state a reason why it is good or bad; for that the painting is of a certain kind cannot be such a reason. What can?

Contrast "The painting is a seascape" with "The painting is disorganized." To say the former to someone could be a way of directing his attention to the subject matter of the painting, indicating that it had a certain kind of subject matter; to say the latter not only could but would be a way of directing his attention to the organization of the painting, but it would not be indicating that it had a certain kind of organization.

The sense of "organization" with which one is here primarily concerned is that in which one can say of any painting "Notice the organization" without thereby being committed to the view that the painting is in fact organized; one can and does say things like "The main fault to be found with Pollock's paintings is in the organization: his work is completely disorganized." (Just so one can on occasion say "Notice the balance" of a certain painting, and yet not be committed to saying the painting is balanced.) Every work has an organization in the sense that no matter what arrangement there may be of shapes, shades, etc., there is necessarily a particular configuration to be found in the painting. In this sense, the organization is an aspect, a feature, of every painting; something that may be contemplated, studied, and observed, in every painting.

There are various kinds of organization, for the organization of a work is something which may be described, classified, analyzed:

> The chief difference between the classical design of Raphael and the Baroque lay in the fact that whilst the artists of the high Renaissance accepted the picture plane and tended to dispose their figures in planes parallel to that—Raphael's cartoons, for instance, almost invariably show this method—the Baroque designers disposed their figures along lines receding from the eye into the depths of the picture space.[4]

"Horizontally, crossing the picture plane," or "Primarily rectangular," or "Along a single curving diagonal," could be answers to the question "What kind of organization does it have?" in a way that "Organized" or "Disorganized" could not. "Organized" and "Disorganized" are more like states than like kinds of organization ("organized" is more like "happy" than like "healthy," and more like "healthy" than like "human").

Yet this is not to deny what cannot be denied, that a sensible answer to "What kind of painting is it?" might be "A fairly well organized seascape, somewhat reminiscent of the Maine coast." "What kind of painting is it?" is often a request not only to describe the painting, to identify it, name it, classify it, point out its similarities and dissimilarities to other paintings, but also to evaluate the painting, to say whether it is worth bothering with, etc.

But seascapes are a kind of painting in a way disorganized or organized paintings are not; crocodiles are a kind of animal in a way healthy animals are not: unlike "seascape" and "crocodile," "organized" and "healthy" admit of questions of degree; one can say "He is quite healthy," "It is somewhat disorganized," "It would be less well organized if that were done," etc.; there are and can be no corresponding locutions employing the terms "seascape" and "crocodile." (One could introduce the terms "seascapish" and "crocodilish," but this is to say: one could invent a use for them.) One cannot discriminate between seascapes on the basis of their being seascapes, whereas one can and does discriminate between disorganized paintings on the basis of their being disorganized, for some are more and some are less.

That "organized," and "disorganized," unlike "seascape," admit of questions of degree is important (thus Tolstoi, who knew what art was, and knowing crucified it, spoke of ". . . those infinitely minute degrees of which a work of art consists");[5] here it indicates that determining whether a painting is disorganized, unlike determining whether it is a seascape, is not a matter of recognition or identification, though it may, on occasion, presuppose such recognition or identification. In order to determine whether a painting is disorganized, it is necessary to contemplate the organization of the painting. To determine whether a painting is a seascape, it is sufficient to recognize or identify the subject matter of the work; it is not necessary to contemplate the subject matter. To say to someone "The painting is a seascape" could be a way of drawing his attention to the subject matter of the painting, but it would be a way of inviting recognition or identification of certain things in the painting, not a way of inviting contemplation of an aspect of the painting.

"Disorganized," unlike "seascape," reports on an aspect of the painting; one might also say: it refers to a point in a dimension, the particular dimension being that of organization; another point in this dimension is referred to by "clearly organized," another by "an incoherent organization," etc.; to say "The organization of the painting is defective," or "The painting has a defective organization," or "The painting is defectively organized," are ways—different ways—of attributing approximately the same location to the painting in the dimension of organization. To say "The painting is a seascape" is not to direct attention to a certain dimension, that of subject matter; it may direct attention to the subject matter, but not to the dimension of subject matter: such a dimension is found when one considers not the kind but the treatment or handling of subject matter (contrast "The painting is a seascape" with "The figures are too stiff, too impassive") ; for it does not refer to a point in that dimension; it does not locate the painting in that dimension. (Just so to say "The painting has a diagonal organization" is not to direct attention to a certain dimension.)

But not any report on any aspect of the painting can be a reason why the painting is good or bad; "The painting is quite green, predominantly green" reports on an aspect of the painting, yet it is not a reason why the work is good or bad.

To say "The painting is quite green" could be somewhat like saying "Notice the organization of the painting" for it could serve to direct attention to an aspect of the painting; but it is not apt to be the relevant kind of report on this aspect. It is not such a report if it does not lead one either to or away from the work: if it were a reason, would it be a reason why the painting is a good painting or a reason why the painting is a bad painting?

But it would not be correct to say it is never a report, in a relevant sense; it is not apt to be, but it might; if someone were to claim that a painting were good and if, when asked why, replied, "Notice the organization!" it could be clear he was claiming that the painting was organized, perhaps superbly organized, that the organization of the work was delightful, etc.; just so if he were to claim "The painting is quite green, predominantly green," it could be quite clear he was claiming that the greenness of the painting was delightful, that the work was "sufficiently green," etc. "The painting is quite green" would here be a report on an aspect of the painting, a report leading in one direction. Even so, it is not a reason why the painting is good or bad.

This is not to deny that someone might offer such a statement as the statement of a reason why the painting is good. Nor is it to deny that "The painting is quite green" has all the marks of such a reason: it points to the painting: it directs one's attention to an aspect of the painting, an aspect that can be contemplated; it reports on this aspect of the painting and thus directs one to the contemplation of the painting. It could be a reason why the painting is good. But it is not. Is it because one simply does not care whether the painting is quite green? because it makes no difference?

One would not ordinarily say to someone "The painting is clearly disorganized" unless one supposed he had somehow not sufficiently attended to the organization of the work. But more than this: ordinarily one would not attempt to draw his attention to the organization of the painting, to the lack of it, unless one took for granted that if he did sufficiently attend to the organization and did in fact find the work to be disorganized, he would then realize that the painting was indeed defective.

One sometimes takes for granted that the absence of organization in a painting, once it is attended to, will in fact make much difference to a person; that he will be less inclined and perhaps even cease to find the work worth contemplating. And this is in fact sometimes the case; what one sometimes takes for granted is sometimes so.

This is one reason that a reference to the organization of the work may be a reason, and why a reference to the greenness of the painting is not; one ordinarily neither finds nor takes for granted one will find the fact that the painting is or is not quite green will make any such difference.

Being green or not green is not likely to make any difference to anyone in his contemplation of the painting; but the same is not true of being huge, or of having a sordid subject. Suppose a work were three miles high, two miles long: one simply could not contemplate it; suppose the subject matter of a work were revolting; certainly many could not contemplate it; or again, what if one knew that contemplating a work would have an insidious and evil influence: could one, nonetheless, contemplate it calmly?

There are many factors that may prevent and hinder one from contemplating a work; there are also certain factors that may facilitate the contemplation of a work; e.g., figure paintings, the Italian treatment of the figure, Raphael's, Signorelli's, Piero's handling, smoothes the path of contemplation.

> Therefore the nude, and best of all the nude erect and frontal, has through all the ages in our world—the world descended from Egypt and Hellas—been the chief concern of the art of visual representation.[6]

One is inclined to contemplate the nude (though not the naked—there is a difference).

That a painting has revolting subject matter, may seduce the beholder, is too large, too small, etc., does make much difference, but a difference of a different kind. That a painting is too large is in fact a reason why the painting is not good; yet it is a reason of a different kind, for it is also a reason why the painting is not bad: that the painting is too large is not a reason why the contemplation of the work is not worthwhile; rather it is a reason why one cannot contemplate the painting, a reason why one simply cannot evaluate the work.

That a painting is not too large, not too small, is not apt to seduce and is even apt to improve one, has splendid subject matter, etc., are not, in themselves, or in isolation, reasons why a work is a good work, why the work is worth contemplating. Yet such factors as these, by rendering the work accessible to contemplation, can tend to enhance its value. (Memling's *Lady with a Pink* would be less lovely were it larger; *Guernica* would be less majestic were it smaller.) Such factors as these cannot stand alone; alone they are not reasons why the painting is a good painting. That the neighbouring woods are nearby does not prove them lovely, but if lovely, then by being nearby they are that much lovelier, and if ugly, that much uglier.

It is here, perhaps, that the locus of greatness, of sublimity, is to be found in art; a painting with a trivial subject, a shoe, a cabbage, may be a superb work, but its range is limited: even if it succeeds, it is not great, not sublime; and if it fails, its failure is of no consequence; it may be trivial, it may be delightful—nothing more. But a figure painting, Signorelli's Pan, was a great, a sublime painting; had it failed, its failure would have been more tragic than trivial.

Such factors as these often do make a difference, but unlike the fact that the work is well or poorly organized, they do not indicate that the work is or is not worth contemplating: they indicate only that if the work is worth contemplating, it will be well worth contemplating; and if it is not worth contemplating, then possibly it will be not merely not worth contemplating, but distressing.

One sometimes takes for granted that the presence or absence of organization will make a difference to the person. But what if it does not?

It is quite possible that it will not. It is possible that to some people it makes no difference at all whether a painting is disorganized. It may even be that some people prefer what are in fact disorganized paintings (though they might not call them "disorganized"). Perhaps some people greatly admire quite green paintings; the fact that a painting is or is not quite green will make much difference to them.

Someone might now want to say this: "even though you may happen to like a disorganized painting at a time, you won't like it after a time; disorganized paintings do not wear well." Or this: "Even though you may happen to like a disorganized painting, your liking of it will interfere with and narrow the range of your appreciation of many other paintings." Or even this: ". . . your liking of it is unlike that of someone who likes an organized painting; for such a person will not only like it longer, but will like it in a different and better way: 'not merely a difference in quantity, but a difference in quality.' Thus the satisfaction, the value, he finds in contemplating an organized painting is unlike and better than that you find in contemplating a disorganized painting."

It is sometimes true that disorganized paintings do not wear well, but it sometimes is not true; some people persist in liking unlikable paintings. Will perseverance do to transmute vice to virtue? It is sometimes true that a taste for disorganized paintings is apt to interfere with and narrow the range of one's appreciation of other paintings; but is it not likely that one who likes both organized and disorganized paintings will have the more catholic taste? Is it wise to be a connoisseur of wine and cut one's self off from the pleasures of the poor? There is a sense in which it is certainly true that the satisfaction one finds in contemplating an organized painting is unlike and superior to that one finds in contemplating a disorganized painting, but in the sense in which it is, it is here irrelevant: for of course it is certainly true that the satisfaction and value found in connection with a good painting is superior to that found in connection with a bad painting—this of course being a necessary statement. But apart from the fact that the satisfaction found in connection with a good painting is of course superior to that found in connection with a bad painting, what reason is there to suppose in fact—and not merely of course—this is the case? I find no satisfaction in connection with a bad painting, so how shall I compare to see which is superior?

One sometimes says: "Last year I found satisfaction in connection with what I now see to be a bad painting. Now I can see that my satisfaction then was inferior to my satisfaction now found in connection with a good painting." So you might predict to someone: "Just wait! Cultivate your taste and you will see that the satisfaction found in connection with good-*A* will be superior to the satisfaction, value, you now find in connection with bad-*B*."

And what if he does not? (Is it not clear that here aesthetics has nothing to do with consequences?) A man might say: "I find the very same kind of satisfaction in this 'disorganized' painting that you find in that 'organized' one: I too am greatly moved, greatly stirred. You may say of course your satisfaction, the value you find, is superior to mine; in fact it is not." He might be lying, but could he be mistaken?

There is then an inclination to say this: "If being organized or being disorganized does make much difference to a person then for him it is a reason, whereas if it does not make any such difference, it is not." This would be to say that instead of speaking of "the reasons why the painting is good," one would have to speak of "his reasons why" and "my reasons why" and "your reasons why" if one wished to speak precisely. This will not do at all.

I or you or he can have a reason to suppose (think, believe, etc.) the work is worth contemplating; but neither I nor you nor he can have a reason why the work is worth contemplating; anyone may know such a reason, discover, search for, find, wonder about such a reason, but no one can ever have such a reason; even when one has found such a reason, one can only point to it, present it, never appropriate it for one's own; "What are your reasons?" makes sense in reply to "I believe it is worth contemplating," but it has no literal sense if asked of "I know it is worth contemplating." "My reasons why the work is worth contemplating . . . ," "The reason for me the work is worth contemplating . . . ," are also here without relevant literal meaning.

(It would be absurd to describe this fact by saying that what is a reason for me must be a reason for everyone else—as though what no one ever could own must therefore be owned by all alike. What one could say here is that a reason must be as abstract as the judgment it supports.)

If being organized or being disorganized does make much difference to a person then, not "for him" nor "in that case," nor "then and there," it is apt to be a reason, for in that case, then and there, one can forget about him then and there; whereas if it does not make any such difference then, for him, in that case, then and there, it is not apt to be a reason, for in that case, then and there, one cannot forget about him then and there.

To say "The work is worth contemplating" is here and ordinarily to abstract from considerations of person; but such abstraction is, as it were, a minor achievement, an accomplishment possible only when there either is or can be a community of interest. I can ignore the ground I walk on so long as it does not quake. This fact cannot be ignored: contemplating a painting is something that people do, different people.

Paradise gardens are not ever simply a place (one could not be there not knowing it, and it is in part because I know I am not there that I am not there) ; not being simply a place, paradise gardens are proportioned to everyman's need, even though these requirements may at times be incompatible. But these lesser perfections that paintings are are less adaptable, answer only to some men's need.

Reasoning about works of art is primarily a social affair, an attempt to build and map our common Eden; it can be carried on fruitfully only so long as there is either a common care or the possibility of one. But Kant was wrong in saying aesthetic judgments presuppose a common sense: one cannot sensibly presuppose what is often not the case. A community of interest and taste is not something given, but something that can be striven for.

II

And now I can be more precise, and that is to say, more general, for we speak of "good poems," "good quartets," "good operas," etc., as well as "good painting." But the problem is always the same. A good anything is something that answers to interests associated with it. In art, this is always a matter of performing certain actions, looking, listening, reading, etc., in connection with certain spatio-temporal or temporal entities, with paintings, poems, musical compositions, etc.

Formulaically, there is only this: a person p_i, performs an action, a_i, in connection with an entity, e_i, under conditions, c_i; e.g. George contemplates Fouquet's *Madonna* in the gallery at Antwerp. e_i is good if and only if the performance of the relevant a_i by p_i under c_i is worthwhile for its own sake. To state a reason why e_i is good is simply to state a fact about e_i in virtue of which the performance of the relevant a_i by p_i under c_i is worthwhile for its own sake.

Someone says, pointing to a painting, "That is a good painting." There is (at least) a triple abstraction here, for neither the relevant persons, nor actions, nor conditions, have been specified. Is it any wonder we so often disagree about what is or is not a good painting.

Persons: George and Josef disagree about a Breughel. Say Josef is color-blind. Then here I discount Josef's opinion: I am not color-blind. But if they were concerned with a Chinese ink drawing, color-blindness would be irrelevant. George is not a peasant, neither does he look kindly on peasants, not even a Breughel painting of peasants. Well, neither do I, so I would not, for that reason, discount his opinion. Josef is a prude, that is, a moralist, and he looks uncomfortably at the belly of a Titian nude. I would discount his opinion, for I am not. (This is why it is horrible nonsense to talk about "a competent observer" in matters of art appreciation: no one is competent or not competent to look at the belly of a Titian nude.) But George has no stomach for George Grosz's pictures of butchers chopping up pigs, and neither do I, so I would not discount his opinion there. George has a horror of churches: his opinion of stained glass may be worthless. Not having an Oedipus complex, George's attitude towards Whistler's Mother is also eccentric. And so on.

If e_i is good then the performance of a_i by p_i under c_i is worthwhile for its own sake. But this obviously depends on the physical, psychological, and intellectual, characteristics of p_i. If p_i and p_j are considering a certain work then the relevant characteristics of p_i depend on the particular p_j, e_i, a_i and c_i involved. It is worse than useless to stipulate that p_i be "normal": what is that to me if I am not normal? and who is? To be normal is not necessary in connection with some limited works, and it is not enough to read *Finnegan's Wake*. Different works make different demands on the person. The popularity of "popular art" is simply due to the fact that it demands virtually nothing: one can be as ignorant and brutish as a savage and still deal with it.

But there is no point in worrying about persons for practically nothing can be done about them. Actions are what matter. Art education is a matter of altering the person's actions, and so, conceivably the person.

Actions: here we have a want of words. Aestheticians are fond of "contemplate," but one cannot contemplate an opera, a ballet, a cinema, a poem. Neither is it sensible to contemplate just any painting, for not every painting lends itself to contemplation. There is only one significant problem in aesthetics, and it is not one that an aesthetician can answer: given a work e_i under conditions c_i what are the relevant a_i? An aesthetician cannot answer the question because it depends on the particular e_i and c_i: no general answer exists.

Roughly speaking, I survey a Tintoretto, while I scan an H. Bosch. Thus I step back to look at the Tintoretto, up to look at the Bosch. Different actions are involved. Do you drink brandy in the way you drink beer? Do you drive a Jaguar XKSS in the way you drive a hearse?

A generic term will be useful here: "aspection," to aspect a painting is to look at it in some way. Thus to contemplate a painting is to perform one act of aspection; to scan it is to perform another; to study, observe, survey, inspect, examine, scrutinize, etc., are still other acts of aspection. There are about three hundred words available here in English, but that is not enough.

Generally speaking, a different act of aspection is performed in connection with works belonging to different schools of art, which is why the classification of style is of the essence. Venetian paintings lend themselves to an act of aspection involving attention to balanced masses; contours are of no importance, for they are scarcely to be found. The Florentine school demands attention to contours, the linear style predominates. Look for light in a Claude, for color in a Bonnard, for contoured volumes in a Signorelli.

George and Josef are looking at Van der Weyden's *Descent from the Cross*. Josef complains, "The figures seem stiff, the Christ unnatural." George replies, "Perhaps. But notice the volumes of the heads, the articulation of the planes, the profound movement of the contours." They are not looking at the painting in the same way, they are performing different acts of aspection.

They are looking at the *Unicorn Tapestry.* Josef complains "But the organization is so loose!" So Spenser's great *Faerie Queene* is ignored because fools try to read it as though it were a sonnet of Donne, for the *Queene* is a medieval tapestry, and one wanders about in it. An epic is not an epigram.

George says "A good apple is sour" and Josef says "A good apple is sweet," but George means a cooking apple, Josef means a dessert apple. So one might speak of "a scanning-painting," "a surveying-painting," etc., and just so one speaks of "a Venetian painting," "a sonata," "a lyric poem," "an improvisation," etc.

If e_i is good then the performance of a_i by p_i under c_i is worthwhile for its own sake. If p_i performs a_i under c_i in connection with e_i, whereas p_j performs a_j under c_i in connection with e_i, p_i and p_j might just as well be looking at two different paintings (or poems, etc.). It is possible that the performance of a_i under c_i in connection with e_i is worthwhile for its own sake, while the performance of a_j under c_i in connection with e_i is not worthwhile for its own sake.

There is no easy formula for the relevant actions. Many are possible: only some will prove worthwhile. We find them by trial and error. The relevant actions are those that prove worthwhile in connection with the particular work, but we must discover what these are.

Imagine that *Guernica* had been painted in the time of Poussin. Or a Mondrian. What could the people of the time have done with these works? The question the public is never tired of asking is: "What am I to look at? look for?" and that is to say: what act of aspection is to be performed in connection with e_i?

Before 1900, El Greco was accredited a second-rate hack whose paintings were distorted because he was blind in one eye. Who bothered with Catalonian frescoes? The Pompeian murals were buried.

Modern art recreates the art of the past, for it teaches the critics (who have the ear of museum and gallery directors who pick the paintings the public consents to see) what to look for and at in modern works. Having been taught to look at things in a new way, when they look to the past, they usually find much worth looking at, in this new way, that had been ignored. So one could almost say that Lehmbruck did the portal of Chartres, Daumier gave birth to Hogarth, and someone (unfortunately) did Raphael in.

Artists teach us to look at the world in new ways. Look at a Mondrian, then look at the world as though it were a Mondrian and you will see what I mean. To do this, you must know how to look at a Mondrian.

And now I can explain why a reason why a work is good or bad is worth listening to. One reason why a (good) Mondrian is good is that it is completely flat. If that sounds queer to you, it is because you do not know how to look at a Mondrian. And that is why the reason is worth considering.

A reason why e_i is good is a fact about e_i in virtue of which the performance of a_1 by p_1 under c_i is worthwhile for its own sake. So I am saying that the fact that the Mondrian is completely flat indicates that the performance of a_1 by p_1 under c_i is worthwhile in connection with the Mondrian painting. In telling you this, I am telling you something about the act of aspection to be performed in connection with the work, for now you know at least this: you are to look at the work spatially, three-dimensionally. (Without the painting to point to, I can only give hints: look at it upside down! Right side up, each backward movement into space is counterbalanced by an advancing movement. The result is a tense, dynamic, and dramatic picture plane held intact by the interplay of forces. Turn the painting upside down and the spatial balance is destroyed: the thing is hideous.)

Reasons in criticism are worthwhile because they tell us what to do with the work, and that is worth knowing. Yao Tsui said:

> It may seem easy for a man to follow the footsteps of his predecessors, but he does not know how difficult it is to follow the movements of curved lines. Although one may chance to measure the speed of the wind which blows through the Hsiang Valley, he may have difficulty in fathoming the water-courses of the Lü-liang mountain. Although one may make a good beginning by the skilful use of instruments, yet the ultimate meaning of an object may remain obscure to him until the end. Without knowing the song completely, it is useless to crave for the response of the falling dust.

Notes

1. *Essays and Lectures on Music*, pp. 3-4.
2. *French, Flemish and British Art*, p. 125.
3. *Critique of Aesthetic Judgment*, Bk. I, sec. 17.
4. R. Fry, *op. cit.*, p. 22.
5. *What is Art?*, Oxford Univ. Press, p. 201.
6. B. Berenson, *Aesthetics and History*, pp. 81-82.

Art Criticism

Moralists and Critics. Many philosophers have supposed that there is an analogy between judging a work of art to be good or bad, and judging an action to be right or wrong. Hampshire, however, says that "aesthetic judgments are not comparable in purpose with moral judgments." He claims that there are no principles of art criticism comparable with the principles of right conduct; hence there are no reasons why a work of art is good comparable with the reasons why an action is right. This claim rests in turn on the assumption that "a work of art is gratuitous. It is not *essentially* the answer to a question or the solution of a presented problem."

Hampshire sometimes moves toward the stronger thesis that anyone who says that a painting is good or that one poem is better than another is being "a moralist in criticism"; value judgments are in effect practical advice about what to read, look at, or listen to. Since such advice "must involve some reference to the whole economy of human needs and purposes," the critic is actually a moralist.

That works of art are gratuitous in Hampshire's sense does not mean, of course, that no work of art provides an answer to a problem. Artists set problems for themselves and have problems set for them by others, *e.g.* art teachers and sponsors of competitions. In the light of these problems their work may be judged as succeeding or failing. But these are what Hampshire calls *technical* problems, and criticism based on them is technical criticism, which is to imply that there is a difference between the technical criticism of something and criticism of it as a work of art. What is this difference?

One type of technical criticism has to do with the way an artist does something—how he achieves, or why he fails to achieve, certain results or effects. Might not the techniques employed in fashioning a work of art— those of painting, etching, building, casting, etc.—be faultless and yet the work of art be a poor one for all that? Technique may be a *condition* of artistic excellence in the sense that, unless an artist meets certain

623

technical standards, it is unlikely that he will achieve satisfactory artistic results. But is there not a difference between *conditions of* and *reasons for* artistic excellence or failure? "Because the glazes are improperly applied" may explain why a painting is a failure, but is it a reason why it is not a good work of art?

A second type of technical criticism has to do with technical accomplishment. One might try to draw a study in perspective, write a sestina, or compose a fugue, and there would be a question as to how well he had succeeded. But might not something be a good or accomplished sestina, fugue, or perspective drawing and not a good work of art?

The same applies to technical problems in an even wider sense. Tolstoy urged artists to create works which would "unite men with God and with one another"; other artists—Virgil, Dante, Goya, and Daumier among them—have created works to stir men's consciences, to make them aware of social injustices, or to mobilize their energies toward political or religious ends. Apart from the fact that art may be incapable of doing what some men have wanted it to do, is it not one thing to judge a work of art as morally, religiously, or politically efficacious, and another to judge it as a work of art?[1]

Now what is it to criticize art *as art*? First, to criticize it apart from any problems—the artist's or the spectator's—which the work of art is purported to solve. Does this imply that value judgments, unless they are simply indicative of particular features of unique works of art, are out of place in criticism? Or that they are essentially moral judgments?

All natural objects are gratuitous in Hampshire's sense. Apples, lakes, fishes, trees, and rubies are not *essentially* the solution to a problem. Many of them, of course, we use to solve problems, and we judge them in that light; but many we do not. One ruby may be superior to another apart from any task to be accomplished by the use of rubies. Does this not suggest that Hampshire implicitly misrepresents the function of value judgments, by construing them as relevant only to problem-solving? Do we make value judgments only in the light of problems to be solved? Even if a value judgment is essentially a grading of one thing as better than another, is it always in effect a piece of practical advice, or a moral judgment? If to judge that a painting is good is to be a moralist in criticism, isn't to judge typewriters, hunting dogs, and mathematicians also to be a moralist? And in that case doesn't the notion of a critical moralist lose its meaning?

Hampshire's main target is not value judgments as such, however, but generalized judgments of works of art: there are no universal *principles* of art criticism.[2] If this is so, is it because art is gratuitous; or is it rather because not all works of art "satisfy the same needs and interests at all times and for all people"?

To satisfy or answer an interest is not the same as to solve a problem. An interest in cats may be met by cats, pictures of cats, books about cats, etc.; the problem of ridding a barn of mice is solved by a good mouser. Now are not different interests taken in different works of art; and do not different works of art answer different interests? Do a sonnet of Shakespeare, a symphony of Mozart, and a painting by Rubens meet the same interests? Can we reasonably expect them to? If they do not, can we sensibly judge them by the same general standards, any more than we can judge cats and diamonds as indiscriminately meeting the interests of the cat lover and the gem collector?

We might want to say that all works of art should answer aesthetic interests. But isn't "aesthetic" a generic term covering a wide diversity of distinct interests? Are the reasons why one work of art is good, bad, or superior to another always the same as the reasons why another work of art is good, bad, or superior to another, even in those contexts, *e.g.* a competition for prizes, where works are judged comparatively?

Unity, coherence, and the like, are often considered properties which we can reasonably expect all works of art to possess, presumably because no interest in art can be met by anything that does not possess them; such qualities have thus been favored by those who desire universal principles of criticism. However, is a work of art good only if it is unified? If it is not unified, is it not good? Or if it is unified, is it good? If any of these statements is true, why is it true? Because "good" in this context *means* unified? Or for some other reason? Can no work of art be good in spite of the fact that it is not unified, or bad in spite of the fact that it is unified?

Finally, does not critical moralism presuppose the existence of a nonmoralistic art criticism? To advise people to devote their time and energies to certain works of art as opposed to others may be a moral judgment, but does it not assume that we can distinguish in art the good from the bad, or the better from the worse, irrespective of how we ought to spend our time?

Criteria. Isn't it always possible to query a statement such as "That is a good picture" by "What's good about it?" If so, then goodness, like beauty, depends on other properties. Referring to these other properties as "criteria," Mrs. Knight is concerned with the relation between them and goodness; with the relation, that is, between statements such as, "That is a good picture," and statements such as "The objects in this portion of the picture exactly balance those in that portion, and the placing of the figures brings out precisely the psychological significance of the event depicted."

Some philosophers have tried to solve this problem through a "naturalistic" analysis of value judgments, according to which such judgments are essentially reports—in some versions of Naturalism, expressions—of the speaker's approval in respect to whatever the judgment is about. Some Naturalists also allow that value judgments may on occasion be reports, or predictions, of the approval of someone other than the speaker. In all cases, however, the meaning of words such as "good" is logically connected with preferences, approvals, enjoyments, and the like: "That is a good . . ." is logically equivalent to something like "I approve of that . . ."; or this plus an imperative element, "You do so too."

Is it not clear, however, that "That is a good . . ." is not logically equivalent to anything like "I approve of that . . ."? Can one not, without contradiction, assert the one and deny the other? If so, does this not also show that a value judgment is not simply an expression, as opposed to a report, of a preference or enjoyment, on the grounds that where I do not approve of something and yet say that it is good, my judgment cannot express my nonexistent approval? This would not rule out the fact that we can sometimes *infer* from a man's judging something to be good, or from the way he does it, that he approves of it or enjoys it. But here the relation between his approval and what he says is not one of *meaning*.

Some Naturalists may grant this but say either (1) that the *criterion* of the goodness of something is the speaker's, or someone else's, approval of it; or (2) that the *reason why* one employs certain criteria of goodness is that he always approves of whatever satisfies them. Is Mrs. Knight not right, however, when she says that "my liking a picture is never a criterion of its goodness"? Will "Because I like it" ever count as a reason why a picture is good? Or can the reason why one employs certain criteria be that he approves of whatever satisfies them? Will this always serve as a *causal* explanation of why we employ certain criteria? Or will it even serve as a *justification* of our employment of criteria?

Mrs. Knight calls attention to two different uses of "good," a specific one and a general one. Only the first is used for what is good of its kind,[3] and to be good in this sense depends on satisfying criteria of goodness for things of a certain kind. But isn't Mrs. Knight's distinction between a specific and general use of "good" a false one? Is there anything more general in the use of "good" in "Philosophic discussion is good" than there is in "That was a good philosophic discussion"? Does the generality enter in the use of "good," or is it rather that the second statement is about a specific philosophic discussion, while the first is about philosophic discussion in general? And is the first statement any more immune to being queried by "Good for what?" or "What's good about it?" than is the second? Or is it plausible to suppose that my desire for philosophic discussion is a criterion of its goodness, any more than it is to suppose that my liking Helen Wills's tennis is a criterion of the goodness of her playing?

Mrs. Knight claims that the goodness-criteria relation is one of meaning: "The meaning of 'good' is determined by criteria." If we judge tennis players, even the same player, by different criteria, we are using "good" with different meanings. At the same time, she wishes to avoid "naturalism": there are not several meanings of "good" as it is used in reference to tennis players, Pekingese, and poems; and a statement that something is good is not logically equivalent to any reason for its being good.

Is Mrs. Knight's position confused? Let *s* represent any statement like "That is a good picture"; doesn't Mrs. Knight mistakenly identify "What do *you mean by s*?" and "What does *s* mean?" If someone asks me what I mean by *s*, I might reply by giving my reasons for *s*. But what *s* means is not properly answered by citing criteria. What you mean by *s* may not be what I mean by it, but that does not imply that *s*, when I use it, means one thing, and when you use it, another. Doesn't this explain why Mrs. Knight is dissatisfied with analyses? If you ask what I mean by *s*, an analysis will not answer your question. An analysis answers the question "What does *s* mean?" Hence, analysis throws no light on the goodness-criteria relation. A great deal of aesthetic disagreement may be linguistic, but is that because "it is disagreement in the use of 'good' "?

Critical Appraisals as Performatives. Miss Macdonald raises two objections to Mrs. Knight's approach to criticism:

(1) If what Mrs. Knight says is true, two works of art could compete for the same place, tie for first place. But, while there may be nothing to choose between two Persian cats or two knitters, the same is not true of *Emma* and *Persuasion*. "Works of art are unique"; they are "not simply substitutable for each other."

But are works of art alone in being unique? If one Persian cat is as good as another, does that mean that it is substitutable for the other for all purposes? If I enter my Persian in a cat show, does it make no difference which cat is returned to me, my own or the one that tied with it for first place? Two men might be equally good husbands and fathers; does it make no difference to their wives and children who comes home at night? Assuming that *Emma* and *Portrait of a Lady* are equally good novels, *would* there be anything to choose between them in contexts where only their worth is at issue?

(2) Mrs. Knight assumes that "a work of art is an object rather like a cake, whose meritorious features may be picked out, like plums, and exhibited." But we interpret works of art, not cakes; and what we call a work of art is a "construction" of the interpretations made of it. Works of art are thus "not simple objects whose features can be presented for listing."

That a work of art is a construction of its interpretations is dubious. If it were true, then before a sonata is performed or a poem interpreted could there be any sonata to play or poem to interpret? But even if Miss Macdonald is right, doesn't a performance or a poem interpreted in a certain way have features that can be listed?

Miss Macdonald chiefly objects to the claim that critical discussion is an argument to show that something is the case. Statements like "That is a good picture," she maintains, are more profitably compared with verdicts, awards, performances, prizes, diplomas, medals, and appoint-ments, none of which is true or false, than with scientific statements.

Miss Macdonald offers so many comparisons, however, that it is hard to see how to apply them. A medal differs from a verdict, the activities of a judge from those of an actor. Is a critical estimate of a work of art more like a medal than it is a verdict, the activities of a critic more like those of a judge than those of an actor? Miss Macdonald must pursue her analogies further if we are to have anything but her word that critical estimates resemble medals and verdicts more than they do scientific statements.

Whatever similarities may exist between critical judgments and medals, are there not equally important analogies between them and scientific statements? What is said about art can be challenged in a way a medal or performance cannot be:

A: "That is a good picture."
B: "Is it?"
C: "It is not."
D: "What's good about it?"

There are reasons why Vermeer's "View of Delft" is a good picture, and these reasons have no analogue in the awarding of medals or the playing of sonatas. To be sure, there are reasons for awarding a medal to some-one, for playing a sonata in a certain way, but are these analogous to the reasons why Vermeer's picture is good? Or are they rather analogous to reasons for *saying* that Vermeer's picture is good, *e.g.* to get people to look at the picture again?

" 'True' and 'false'," says J. L. Austin, "are just general labels for a whole dimension of different appraisals which have something or other to do with the relation between what we say and the facts."[4] But is the relation between the facts and an appraisal of a work of art such that our appraisals cannot be said to be true, or false?

Good Reasons. "What," asks Mrs. Knight, "is the guarantee of a criterion?" What makes something a criterion of goodness in pictures or poems? "The guarantee," she answers, "lies in its being used as a criterion." Is this answer satisfactory?

If someone says that Vermeer's "View of Delft" is good because it is a picture of Delft, is he using its being a picture of Delft as a criterion of its goodness? Is this a reason why Vermeer's picture is good?

Ziff would say "No." To say that a painting is good is to say that it is worth contemplating; hence, "Nothing can be a reason why the painting is good unless it is a reason why the painting is worth con-templating." Is this so? If it is, how do we know that it is? Do we know it is the way we know that nothing can be a triangle unless it has three sides? Or in the way we know that no animal can survive without air?

Does Ziff imply a view of the nature of art—that a work of art is something to be contemplated (using "contemplated" in an extended sense)? Compare this view with those represented in Section I of this book. Is Ziff's view more satisfactory than any of those? Why, or why not? Does any theory about what counts as a good reason why a work of art is good presuppose a theory of the nature of art? We do, of course, distinguish between criticizing something *as* art and criticizing it as something else, *e.g.* a vehicle of moral or religious instruction. Doesn't this commit us to a view of the nature of art?

"A good anything," Ziff says, "is something that answers to interests associated with it."[5] Is this the case? If so, is it because "That is a good X" means the same as, or is logically equivalent to, "That X answers to such-and-such interests"; or for some other reason? Interests are of different sorts—religious, ethical, economic, etc. If something is a good work of art if and only if it answers to interests associated with it, what are those interests? Aesthetic interests? If so, isn't the definition circular?

Ziff says that these interests are "always a matter of performing certain actions, looking, listening, reading, etc. . . ." Always? How so? And aren't there different ways of looking, listening, reading, etc., some of which have nothing to do with paintings and poems as works of art? (Ziff admits that there are many ways of looking at a painting as a work of art and introduces the term "aspection" to cover them.) Does this explain why disputes about whether a painting is good are more frequent and more resistant to settlement than are disputes about who painted it and when? Does it also account for "relativism" in criticism and taste, and illuminate the confusing history of both?

Notes

1. For an illuminating discussion of this issue, see R. G. Collingwood, *The Principles of Art*, Oxford, The Clarendon Press, 1938, Chs. II-V. More modest problems, to which works of art are sometimes solutions, are those of interior decorators, program planners, designers of memorials, etc. To judge a work of art as good or bad, appropriate or inappropriate for any of these purposes is also to judge it "externally."

2. By a principle, or canon, of criticism is usually meant a true statement of one of the following forms: "Something is a good work of art if and only if it possesses the property p"; "If something does not possess the property p, then it is not a good work of art"; "If something is a work of art and possesses the property p, it is a good work of art"; where "p" represents either a single property or a conjunction of properties.

3. Is "good of its kind" not ambiguous, however? "An ancient error takes 'good' as shorthand for 'good of its kind' and this in turn as meaning the same as 'good specimen of its kind.' Now, the goodness of a specimen is related to classifying purposes. A good specimen of a species is one in which the differentiae

are strikingly present or, where degree is possible, present in high degree. The best specimen is one with the clearest or highest degree of distinguishing features." (Isabel C. Hungerland, *Poetic Discourse*, pp. 69-70.) But is a good specimen of Venetian painting necessarily a good painting, even a good Venetian painting? Is it not one thing to be a good specimen or example of a certain kind, another to be good according to the criteria of goodness for things of a certain kind?

4. *Philosophical Papers,* ed. by J. O. Urmson and G. J. Warnock, Oxford, The Clarendon Press, 1961, pp. 237-238.

5. For an extensive defense of this view, see Ziff's *Semantic Analysis*, Ithaca, N. Y., Cornell University Press, 1960, especially Ch. VI.

Suggestions for Additional Reading

On the meaning of "good":

A. J. Ayer, *Language, Truth, and Logic* (2nd ed., London, 1946), Ch. 6; John Dewey, *Theory of Valuation* (Chicago, 1939); R. M. Hare, *The Language of Morals* (Oxford, 1952); Ray Lepley, ed., *The Language of Value* (New York, 1957) ; C. I. Lewis, *An Analysis of Knowledge and Valuation* (La Salle, Ill., 1946); G. E. Moore, *Principia Ethica* (Cambridge, 1903); P. H. Nowell-Smith, *Ethics* (Baltimore, 1954); J. O. Urmson, "On Grading," *Mind*, LIX (1950), 145-168, reprinted in *Logic and Language*, 2nd series, A. G. N. Flew, ed. (Oxford, 1953); Paul Ziff, *Semantic Analysis* (Ithaca, 1960).

On art criticism:

Henry D. Aiken, "A Pluralistic Analysis of Aesthetic Value," *Phil. Rev.*, LIX (1950), 493-513; Virgil C. Aldrich, *Philosophy of Art* (Englewood Cliffs, N.J., 1963), Ch. 4; Monroe C. Beardsley, *Aesthetics* (New York, 1958) , Chs. X, XI; George Boas, *A Primer for Critics* (Baltimore, 1937), *Wingless Pegasus* (Baltimore, 1950); R. W. Church, *An Essay on Critical Appreciation* (Ithaca, 1938); C. J. Ducasse, *Art, The Critics, and You* (New York, 1944); T. M. Greene, *The Arts and the Art of Criticism* (Princeton, 1940); A. H. Hannay, John Holloway, and Margaret Macdonald, "What Are the Distinctive Features of Arguments Used in Art Criticism?", *P.A.S.*, Suppl. Vol. XXIII (1949), 165-194; R. Harré, "Quasi-Aesthetic Appraisals," *Philosophy*, XXXIII (1958), 132-137; B. Harrison, "Some Uses of 'Good' in Criticism," *Mind*, LXIX (1960), 206-222; Bernard C. Heyl, *New Bearings in Aesthetics and Art Criticism* (New Haven, 1943); Isabel C. Hungerland, *Poetic Discourse* (Berkeley, 1958), Ch. III; Arnold Isenberg, "Critical Communication," *Phil. Rev.*, LVIII (1949), 330-344, reprinted in *Aesthetics and Language,* W. Elton ed. (Oxford, 1954); Mortimer R. Kadish and Albert Hofstadter, "Symposium: The Evidence for Esthetic Judgment," *J. Phil.,* LIV (1957) ,

670-688; Joseph Margolis, "Proposals on the Logic of Aesthetic Judgments," *Phil. Quart.*, 9 (1959), 208-216; R. Meager, "The Uniqueness of a Work of Art," *P.A.S.*, LIX (1959), 49-70; H. Osborne, *Aesthetics and Criticism* (London, 1954) ; Stephen C. Pepper, *The Basis of Criticism in the Arts* (Cambridge, 1945); Theodore Redpath, "Some Problems of Modern Aesthetics," *British Philosophy in the Mid-Century*, C. A. Mace ed. (London, 1957); I. A. Richards, *Principles of Literary Criticism* (London, 1925); Albert Tsugawa, "The Objectivity of Aesthetic Judgments," *Phil. Rev.*, LXX (1961), 3-22.

Appendices

PLATO

Republic X

OF THE MANY excellences which I perceive in the order of our State, there is none which upon reflection pleases me better than the rule about poetry.

To what do you refer?

To our refusal to admit the imitative kind of poetry, for it certainly ought not to be received; as I see far more clearly now that the parts of the soul have been distinguished.

What do you mean?

Speaking in confidence, for you will not denounce me to the tragedians and the rest of the imitative tribe, all poetical imitations are ruinous to the understanding of the hearers, unless as an antidote they possess the knowledge of the true nature of the originals.

Explain the purport of your remark.

Well, I will tell you, although I have always from my earliest youth had an awe and love of Homer which even now makes the words falter on my lips, for he seems to be the great captain and teacher of the whole of that noble tragic company; but a man is not to be reverenced more than the truth, and therefore I will speak out.

Very good, he said.

Listen to me, then, or rather, answer me.

Put your question.

Can you give me a general definition of imitation? for I really do not myself understand what it professes to be.

A likely thing, then, that I should know.

There would be nothing strange in that, for the duller eye may often see a thing sooner than the keener.

Very true, he said; but in your presence, even if I had any faint notion, I could not muster courage to utter it. Will you inquire yourself?

From *The Dialogues of Plato,* Vol. II, translated by B. Jowett, 4th edition, 1953. Reprinted by permission of The Clarendon Press, Oxford.

Well, then, shall we begin the inquiry at this point, following our usual method: Whenever a number of individuals have a common name, we assume that there is one corresponding idea of form: do you understand me?

I do.

Let us take, for our present purpose, any instance of such a group; there are beds and tables in the world—many of each, are there not?

Yes.

But there are only two ideas or forms of such furniture—one the idea of a bed, the other of a table.

True.

And the maker of either of them makes a bed or he makes a table for our use, in accordance with the idea—that is our way of speaking in this and similar instances—but no artificer makes the idea itself: how could he?

Impossible.

And there is another artificer,—I should like to know what you would say of him.

Who is he?

One who is the maker of all the works of all other workmen.

What an extraordinary man!

Wait a little, and there will be more reason for your saying so. For this is the craftsman who is able to make not only furniture of every kind, but all that grows out of the earth, and all living creatures, himself included; and besides these he can make earth and sky and the gods, and all things which are in heaven or in the realm of Hades under the earth.

He must be a wizard and no mistake.

Oh! you are incredulous, are you? Do you mean that there is no such maker or creator, or that in one sense there might be a maker of all these things but in another not? Do you see that there is a way in which you could make them all yourself?

And what way is this? he asked.

An easy way enough; or rather, there are many ways in which the feat might be quickly and easily accomplished, none quicker than that of turning a mirror round and round—you would soon enough make the sun and the heavens, and the earth and yourself, and other animals and plants, and furniture and all the other things of which we were just now speaking, in the mirror.

Yes, he said; but they would be appearances only.

Very good, I said, you are coming to the point now. And the painter too is, as I conceive, just such another—a creator of appearances, is he not?

Of course.

But then I suppose you will say that what he creates is untrue. And yet there is a sense in which the painter also creates a bed? Is there not?

Yes, he said, but here again, an appearance only.

And what of the maker of the bed? were you not saying that he too makes, not the idea which according to our view is the real object denoted by the word bed, but only a particular bed?

Yes, I did.

Then if he does not make a real object he cannot make what *is*, but only some semblance of existence; and if any one were to say that the work of the maker of the bed, or of any other workman, has real existence, he could hardly be supposed to be speaking the truth.

Not, at least, he replied, in the view of those who make a business of these discussions.

No wonder, then, that his work too is an indistinct expression of truth.

No wonder.

Suppose now that by the light of the examples just offered we inquire who this imitator is?

If you please.

Well then, here we find three beds: one existing in nature, which is made by God, as I think that we may say—for no one else can be the maker?

No one, I think.

There is another which is the work of the carpenter?

Yes.

And the work of the painter is a third?

Yes.

Beds, then, are of three kinds, and there are three artists who superintend them: God, the maker of the bed, and the painter?

Yes, there are three of them.

God, whether from choice or from necessity, made one bed in nature and one only; two or more such beds neither ever have been nor ever will be made by God.

Why is that?

Because even if He had made two, a third would still appear behind them of which they again both possessed the form, and that would be the real bed and not the two others.

Very true, he said.

God knew this, I suppose, and He desired to be the real maker of a real bed, not a kind of maker of a kind of bed, and therefore He created a bed which is essentially and by nature one only.

So it seems.

Shall we, then, speak of Him as the natural author or maker of the bed?

Yes, he replied; inasmuch as by the natural process of creation He is the author of this and of all other things.

And what shall we say of the carpenter—is not he also the maker of a bed?

Yes.

But would you call the painter an artificer and maker?

Certainly not.

Yet if he is not the maker, what is he in relation to the bed?

I think, he said, that we may fairly designate him as the imitator of that which the others make.

Good, I said; then you call him whose product is third in the descent from nature, an imitator?

Certainly, he said.

And so if the tragic poet is an imitator, he too is thrice removed from the king and from the truth; and so are all other imitators.

That appears to be so.

Then about the imitator we are agreed. And what about the painter?— Do you think he tries to imitate in each case that which originally exists in nature, or only the creations of artificers?

The latter.

As they are or as they appear? you have still to determine this.

What do you mean?

I mean to ask whether a bed really becomes different when it is seen from different points of view, obliquely or directly or from any other point of view? Or does it simply appear different, without being really so? And the same of all things.

Yes, he said, the difference is only apparent.

Now let me ask you another question: Which is the art of painting designed to be—an imitation of things as they are, or as they appear—of appearance or of reality?

Of appearance, he said.

Then the imitator is a long way off the truth, and can reproduce all things because he lightly touches on a small part of them, and that part an image. For example: A painter will paint a cobbler, carpenter, or any other artisan, though he knows nothing of their arts; and, if he is a good painter, he may deceive children or simple persons when he shows them his picture of a carpenter from a distance, and they will fancy that they are looking at a real carpenter.

Certainly.

And surely, my friend, this is how we should regard all such claims: whenever any one informs us that he has found a man who knows all the arts, and all things else that anybody knows, and every single thing with a higher degree of accuracy than any other man—whoever tells us this, I think that we can only retort that he is a simple creature who seems to have been deceived by some wizard or imitator whom he met, and whom he thought all-knowing, because he himself was unable to analyse the nature of knowledge and ignorance and imitation.

Most true.

And next, I said, we have to consider tragedy and its leader, Homer; for we hear some persons saying that these poets know all the arts; and all things human; where virtue and vice are concerned; and indeed all divine things too; because the good poet cannot compose well unless he knows his subject, and he who has not this knowledge can never be a poet. We ought to consider whether here also there may not be a similar illusion. Perhaps they may have come across imitators and been deceived by them; they may not have remembered when they saw their works that these were thrice removed from the truth, and could easily be made without any knowledge of the truth, because they are appearances only and not realities? Or, after all, they may be in the right, and good poets do really know the things about which they seem to the many to speak so well?

The question, he said, should by all means be considered.

Now do you suppose that if a person were able to make the original as well as the image, he would seriously devote himself to the image-making branch? Would he allow imitation to be the ruling principle of his life, as if he had nothing higher in him?

I should say not.

But the real artist, who had real knowledge of those things which he chose also to imitate, would be interested in realities and not in imitations; and would desire to leave as memorials of himself works many and fair; and, instead of being the author of encomiums, he would prefer to be the theme of them.

Yes, he said, that would be to him a source of much greater honour and profit.

Now let us refrain, I said, from calling Homer or any other poet to account regarding those arts to which his poems incidentally refer: we will not ask them, in case any poet has been a doctor and not a mere imitator of medical parlance, to show what patients have been restored to health by a poet, ancient or modern, as they were by Asclepius; or what disciples in medicine a poet has left behind him, like the Asclepiads. Nor shall we press the same question upon them about the other arts. But we have a right to know respecting warfare, strategy, the administration of States and the education of man, which are the chiefest and noblest subjects of his poems, and we may fairly ask about them. "Friend Homer," then we say to him, "if you are only in the second remove from truth in what you say of virtue, and not in the third—not an image maker, that is, by our definition, an imitator—and if you are able to discern what pursuits make men better or worse in private or public life, tell us what State was ever better governed by your help? The good order of Lacedaemon is due to Lycurgus, and many other cities great and small have been similarly benefited by others; but who says that you have been a good legislator to them and have done them any good? Italy and Sicily boast of Charondas, and there is Solon who is renowned among us; but what city has anything to say about you?" Is there any city which he might name?

I think not, said Glaucon; not even the Homerids themselves pretend that he was a legislator.

Well, but is there any war on record which was carried on successfully owing to his leadership or counsel?

There is not.

Or is there anything comparable to those clever improvements in the arts, or in other operations, which are said to have been due to men of practical genius such as Thales the Milesian or Anacharsis the Scythian?

There is absolutely nothing of the kind.

But, if Homer never did any public service, was he privately a guide or teacher of any? Had he in his lifetime friends who loved to associate with him, and who handed down to posterity an Homeric way of life, such as was established by Pythagoras who was especially beloved for this reason and whose followers are to this day conspicuous among others by what they term the Pythagorean way of life?

Nothing of the kind is recorded of him. For surely, Socrates, Creophylus, the companion of Homer, that child of flesh, whose name always makes us laugh, might be more justly ridiculed for his want of breeding, if what is said is true, that Homer was greatly neglected by him in his own day when he was alive?

Yes, I replied, that is the tradition. But can you imagine, Glaucon, that if Homer had really been able to educate and improve mankind—if he had been capable of knowledge and not been a mere imitator—can you imagine, I say, that he would not have attracted many followers, and been honoured and loved by them? Protagoras of Obdera, and Prodicus of Ceos, and a host of others, have only to whisper to their contemporaries: "You will never be able to manage either your own house or your own State until you appoint us to be your ministers of education"—and this ingenious device of theirs has such an effect in making men love them that their companions all but carry them about on their shoulders. And is it conceivable that the contemporaries of Homer, or again of Hesiod, would have allowed either of them to go about as rhapsodists, if they had really been able to help mankind forward in virtue? Would they not have been as unwilling to part with them as with gold, and have compelled them to stay at home with them? Or, if the master would not stay, then the disciples would have followed him about everywhere, until they had got education enough?

Yes, Socrates, that, I think is quite true.

Then must we not infer that all these poetical individuals, beginning with Homer, are only imitators, who copy images of virtue and the other themes of their poetry, but have no contact with the truth? The poet is like a painter who, as we have already observed, will make a likeness of a cobbler though he understands nothing of cobbling; and his picture is good enough for those who know no more than he does, and judge only by colours and figures.

Quite so.

In like manner the poet with his words and phrases may be said to lay on the colours of the several arts, himself understanding their nature only enough to imitate them; and other people, who are as ignorant as he is, and judge only from his words, imagine that if he speaks of cobbling, or of military tactics, or of anything else, in metre and harmony and rhythm, he speaks very well—such is the sweet influence which melody and rhythm by nature have. For I am sure that you know what a poor appearance the works of poets make when stripped of the colours which art puts upon them, and recited in simple prose. You have seen some examples?

Yes, he said.

They are like faces which were never really beautiful, but only blooming, seen when the bloom of youth has passed away from them?

Exactly.

Come now, and observe this point: The imitator or maker of the image knows nothing, we have said, of true existence; he knows appearances only. Am I not right?

Yes.

Then let us have a clear understanding, and not be satisfied with half an explanation.

Proceed.

Of the painter we say that he will paint reins, and he will paint a bit?

Yes.

And the worker in leather and brass will make them?

Certainly.

But does the painter know the right form of the bit and reins? Nay, hardly even the workers in brass and leather who make them; only the horseman who knows how to use them—he knows their right form.

Most true.

And may we not say the same of all things?

What?

That there are three arts which are concerned with all things: one which uses, another which makes, a third which imitates them?

Yes.

And the excellence and beauty and rightness of every structure, animate or inanimate, and of every action of man, is relative solely to the use for which nature or the artist has intended them.

True.

Then beyond doubt it is the user who has the greatest experience of them, and he must report to the maker the good or bad qualities which develop themselves in use; for example, the flute-player will tell the flute-maker which of his flutes is satisfactory to the performer; he will tell him how he ought to make them, and the other will attend to his instructions?

Of course.

So the one pronounces with knowledge about the goodness and badness of flutes, while the other, confiding in him, will make them accordingly?

True.

The instrument is the same, but about the excellence or badness of it
the maker will possess a correct belief, since he associates with one who
knows, and is compelled to hear what he has to say; whereas the user
will have knowledge?

True.

But will the imitator have either? Will he know from use whether or
no that which he paints is correct or beautiful? or will he have right
opinion from being compelled to associate with another who knows and
gives his instructions about what he should paint?

Neither.

Then an imitator will no more have true opinion than he will have
knowledge about the goodness or badness of his models?

I suppose not.

The imitative poet will be in a brilliant state of intelligence about
the theme of his poetry?

Nay, very much the reverse.

And still he will go on imitating without knowing what makes a thing
good or bad, and may be expected therefore to imitate only that which
appears to be good to the ignorant multitude?

Just so.

Thus far then we are pretty well agreed that the imitator has no
knowledge worth mentioning of what he imitates. Imitation is only a
kind of play or sport, and the tragic poets, whether they write in iambic
or in heroic verse, are imitators in the highest degree?

Very true.

And now tell me, I conjure you,—this imitation is concerned with an
object which is thrice removed from the truth?

Certainly.

And what kind of faculty in man is that to which imitation makes its
special appeal.

What do you mean?

I will explain: The same body does not appear equal to our sight when
seen near and when seen at a distance?

True.

And the same objects appear straight when looked at out of the water,
and crooked when in the water; and the concave becomes convex, owing
to the illusion about colours to which the sight is liable. Thus every
sort of confusion is revealed within us; and this is that weakness of the
human mind on which the art of painting in light and shadow, the art
of conjuring, and many other ingenious devices impose, having an effect
upon us like magic.

True.

And the arts of measuring and numbering and weighing come to the rescue of the human understanding—there is the beauty of them—with the result that the apparent greater or less, or more or heavier, no longer have the mastery over us, but give way before the power of calculation and measuring and weighing?

Most true.

And this, surely, must be the work of the calculating and rational principle in the soul?

To be sure.

And often when this principle measures and certifies that some things are equal, or that some are greater or less than others, it is, at the same time, contradicted by the appearance which the objects present?

True.

But did we not say that such a contradiction is impossible—the same faculty cannot have contrary opinions at the same time about the same thing?

We did; and rightly.

Then that part of the soul which has an opinion contrary to measure can hardly be the same with that which has an opinion in accordance with measure?

True.

And the part of the soul which trusts to measure and calculation is likely to be the better one?

Certainly.

And therefore that which is opposed to this is probably an inferior principle in our nature.

No doubt.

This was the conclusion at which I was seeking to arrive when I said that painting or drawing, and imitation in general, are engaged upon productions which are far removed from truth, and are also the companions and friends and associates of a principle within us which is equally removed from reason, and that they have no true or healthy aim.

Exactly.

The imitative art is an inferior who from intercourse with an inferior has inferior offspring.

Very true.

And is this confined to the sight only, or does it extend to the hearing also, relating in fact to what we term poetry?

Probably the same would be true of poetry.

Do not rely, I said, on a probability derived from the analogy of painting; but let us once more go directly to that faculty of the mind with which imitative poetry has converse, and see whether it is good or bad.

By all means.

We may state the question thus:—Imitation imitates the actions of men, whether voluntary or involuntary, on which, as they imagine, a good or bad result has ensued, and they rejoice or sorrow accordingly. Is there anything more?

No, there is nothing else.

But in all this variety of circumstances is the man at unity with himself—or rather, as in the instance of sight there was confusion and opposition in his opinions about the same things, so here also is there not strife and inconsistency in his life? Though I need hardly raise the question again, for I remember that all this has been already admitted; and the soul has been acknowledged by us to be full of these and ten thousand similar oppositions occurring at the same moment?

And we were right, he said.

Yes, I said, thus far we were right; but there was an omission which must now be supplied.

What was the omission?

Were we not saying that a good man, who has the misfortune to lose his son or anything else which is most dear to him, will bear the loss with more equanimity than another?

Yes, indeed.

But will he have no sorrow, or shall we say that although he cannot help sorrowing, he will moderate his sorrow?

The latter, he said, is the truer statement.

Tell me: will he be more likely to struggle and hold out against his sorrow when he is seen by his equals, or when he is alone in a deserted place?

The fact of being seen will make a great difference, he said.

When he is by himself he will not mind saying many things which he would be ashamed of any one hearing, and also doing many things which he would not care to be seen doing?

True.

And doubtless it is the law and reason in him which bids him resist; while it is the affliction itself which is urging him to indulge his sorrow?

True.

But when a man is drawn in two opposite directions, to and from the same object, this, as we affirm, necessarily implies two distinct principles in him?

Certainly.

One of them is ready to follow the guidance of the law?

How do you mean?

The law would say that to be patient under calamity is best, and that we should not give way to impatience, as the good and evil in such things are not clear, and nothing is gained by impatience; also, because no human thing is of serious importance, and grief stands in the way of that which at the moment is most required.

What is most required? he asked.

That we should take counsel about what has happened, and when the dice have been thrown, according to their fall, order our affairs in the way which reason deems best; not, like children who have had a fall, keeping hold of the part struck and wasting time in setting up a howl, but always accustoming the soul forthwith to apply a remedy, raising up that which is sickly and fallen, banishing the cry of sorrow by the healing art.

Yes, he said, that is the true way of meeting the attacks of fortune.

Well then, I said, the higher principle is ready to follow this suggestion of reason?

Clearly.

But the other principle, which inclines us to recollection of our troubles and to lamentations, and can never have enough of them, we may call irrational, useless, and cowardly?

Indeed, we may.

Now does not the principle which is thus inclined to complaint, furnish a great variety of materials for imitation? Whereas the wise and calm temperament, being always nearly equable, is not easy to imitate or to appreciate when imitated, especially at a public festival when a promiscuous crowd is assembled in a theatre. For the feeling represented is one to which they are strangers.

Certainly.

Then the imitative poet who aims at being popular is not by nature made, nor is his art intended, to please or to affect the rational principle in the soul; but he will appeal rather to the lachrymose and fitful temper, which is easily imitated?

Clearly.

And now we may fairly take him and place him by the side of the painter, for he is like him in two ways: first, inasmuch as his creations have an inferior degree of truth—in this, I say, he is like him; and he is also like him in being the associate of an inferior part of the soul; and this is enough to show that we shall be right in refusing to admit him into a State which is to be well ordered, because he awakens and nourishes this part of the soul, and by strengthening it impairs the reason. As in a city when the evil are permitted to wield power and the finer men are put out of the way, so in the soul of each man, as we shall maintain, the imitative poet implants an evil constitution, for he indulges the irrational nature which has no discernment of greater and less, but thinks the same thing at one time great and at another small— he is an imitator of images and is very far removed from the truth.

Exactly.

But we have not yet brought forward the heaviest count in our accusation:—the power which poetry has of harming even the good (and there are very few who are not harmed), is surely an awful thing?

Yes, certainly, if the effect is what you say.

Hear and judge: The best of us, as I conceive, when we listen to a passage of Homer or one of the tragedians, in which he represents some hero who is drawling out his sorrows in a long oration, or singing, and smiting his breast—the best of us, you know, delight in giving way to sympathy, and are in raptures at the excellence of the poet who stirs our feelings most.

Yes, of course, I know.

But when any sorrow of our own happens to us, then you may observe that we pride ourselves on the opposite quality—we would fain be quiet and patient; this is considered the manly part, and the other which delighted us in the recitation is now deemed to be the part of a woman.

Very true, he said.

Now can we be right in praising and admiring another who is doing that which any one of us would abominate and be ashamed of in his own person?

No, he said, that is certainly not reasonable.

Nay, I said, quite reasonable from one point of view.

What point of view?

If you consider, I said, that when in misfortune we feel a natural hunger and desire to relieve our sorrow by weeping and lamentation, and that this very feeling which is starved and suppressed in our own calamities is satisfied and delighted by the poets;—the better nature in each of us, not having been sufficiently trained by reason or habit, allows the sympathetic element to break loose because the sorrow is another's; and the spectator fancies that there can be no disgrace to himself in praising and pitying any one who while professing to be a brave man, gives way to untimely lamentation; he thinks that the pleasure is a gain, and is far from wishing to lose it by rejection of the whole poem. Few persons ever reflect, as I should imagine, that the contagion must pass from others to themselves. For the pity which has been nourished and strengthened in the misfortunes of others is with difficulty repressed in our own.

How very true!

And does not the same hold also of the ridiculous? There are jests which you would be ashamed to make yourself, and yet on the comic stage, or indeed in private, when you hear them, you are greatly amused by them, and are not at all disgusted at their unseemliness;—the case of pity is repeated;—there is a principle in human nature which is disposed to raise a laugh, and this, which you once restrained by reason because you were afraid of being thought a buffoon, is now let out again; and having stimulated the risible faculty at the theatre, you are betrayed unconsciously to yourself into playing the comic poet at home.

Quite true, he said.

And the same may be said of lust and anger and all the other affections, of desire and pain and pleasure, which are held to be inseparable from every action—in all of them poetry has a like effect; it feeds and waters the passions instead of drying them up; she lets them rule, although they ought to be controlled if mankind are ever to increase in happiness and virtue.

I cannot deny it.

Therefore, Glaucon, I said, whenever you meet with any of the eulogists of Homer declaring that he has been the educator of Hellas, and that he is profitable for education and for the ordering of human things, and that you should take him up again and again and get to know him and regulate your whole life according to him, we may love and honour those who say these things—they are excellent people, as far as their lights extend; and we are ready to acknowledge that Homer is the greatest of poets and first of tragedy writers; but we must remain firm in our conviction that hymns to the gods and praises of famous men are the only poetry which ought to be admitted into our State. For if you go beyond this and allow the honeyed Muse to enter, either in epic or lyric verse, not law and the reason of mankind, which by common consent have ever been deemed best, but pleasure and pain will be the rulers in our State.

That is most true, he said.

And now since we have reverted to the subject of poetry, let this our defence serve to show the reasonableness of our former judgment in sending away out of our State an art having the tendencies which we have described; for reason constrained us. But that she may not impute to us any harshness or want of politeness, let us tell her that there is an ancient quarrel between philosophy and poetry; of which there are many proofs, such as the saying of the "yelping hound howling at her lord," or of one "mighty in the vain talk of fools," and "the mob of sages circumventing Zeus," and the "subtle thinkers who are beggars after all"; and there are innumerable other signs of ancient enmity between them. Notwithstanding this, let us assure the poetry which aims at pleasure, and the art of imitation, that if she will only prove her title to exist in a well-ordered State we shall be delighted to receive her—we are very conscious of her charms; but it would not be right on that account to betray the truth. I dare say, Glaucon, that you are as much charmed by her as I am, especially when she appears in Homer?

Yes, indeed, I am greatly charmed.

Shall I propose, then, that she be allowed to return from exile, but upon this condition only—that she make a defence of herself in some lyrical or other metre?

Certainly.

And we may further grant to those of her defenders who are lovers of poetry and yet not poets the permission to speak in prose on her behalf: let them show not only that she is pleasant but also useful to States and to human life, and we will listen in a kindly spirit; for we shall surely be the gainers if this can be proved, that there is a use in poetry as well as a delight?

Certainly, he said, we shall be the gainers.

If her defence fails, then, my dear friend, like other persons who are enamoured of something, but put a restraint upon themselves when they think their desires are opposed to their interests, so too must we after the manner of lovers give her up, though not without a struggle. We too are inspired by that love of such poetry which the education of noble States has implanted in us, and therefore we shall be glad if she appears at her best and truest; but so long as she is unable to make good her defence, this argument of ours shall be a charm to us, which we will repeat to ourselves while we listen to her strains; that we may not fall away into the childish love of her which captivates the many. At all events we are well aware that poetry, such as we have described, is not to be regarded seriously as attaining to the truth; and he who listens to her, fearing for the safety of the city which is within him, should be on his guard against her seductions and make our words his law.

Yes, he said, I quite agree with you.

Yes, I said, my dear Glaucon, for great is the issue at stake, greater than appears, whether a man is to be good or bad. And what will any one be profited if under the influence of honour or money or power, aye, or under the excitement of poetry, he neglect justice and virtue?

Yes, he said; I have been convinced by the argument, as I believe that anyone else would have been.

ARISTOTLE

Poetics

I PROPOSE to treat of Poetry in itself and of its various kinds, noting the essential quality of each; to inquire into the structure of the plot as requisite to a good poem; into the number and nature of the parts of which a poem is composed; and similarly into whatever else falls within the same inquiry. Following, then, the order of nature, let us begin with the principles which come first.

Epic poetry and Tragedy, Comedy also and Dithyrambic poetry, and the music of the flute and of the lyre in most of their forms, are all in their general conception modes of imitation. They differ, however, from one another in three respects,—the medium, the objects, the manner or mode of imitation, being in each case distinct.

For as there are persons who, by conscious art or mere habit, imitate and represent various objects through the medium of colour and form, or again by the voice; so in the arts above mentioned, taken as a whole, the imitation is produced by rhythm, language, or "harmony," either singly or combined.

Thus in the music of the flute and of the lyre, "harmony" and rhythm alone are employed; also in other arts, such as that of the shepherd's pipe, which are essentially similar to these. In dancing, rhythm alone is used without "harmony"; for even dancing imitates character, emotion, and action, by rhythmical movement.

There is another art which imitates by means of language alone, and that either in prose or verse—which verse, again, may either combine different metres or consist of but one kind—but this has hitherto been without a name. For there is no common term we could apply to the mimes of Sophron and Zenarchus and the Socratic dialogues on the one hand; and, on the other, to poetic imitations in iambic, elegaic, or any similar metre. People do, indeed, add the word "maker" or "poet" to the name of

From *Aristotle's Theory of Poetry and Fine Art*, 4th edition, 1911, translated by S. H. Butcher, and reprinted by permission of Macmillan & Co., Ltd, London.

the metre, and speak of elegiac poets, or epic (that is, hexameter) poets, as if it were not the imitation that makes the poet, but the verse that entitles them all indiscriminately to the name. Even when a treatise on medicine or natural science is brought out in verse, the name of poet is by custom given to the author; and yet Homer and Empedocles have nothing in common but the metre, so that it would be right to call the one poet, the other physicist rather than poet. On the same principle, even if a writer in his poetic imitation were to combine all metres, as Chaeremon did in his Centaur, which is a medley composed of metres of all kinds, we should bring him too under the general term poet. So much then for these distinctions.

There are, again, some arts which employ all the means above mentioned,—namely rhythm, tune, and metre. Such are Dithyrambic and Nomic poetry, and also Tragedy and Comedy; but between them the difference is, that in the first two cases these means are all employed in combination, in the latter, now one means is employed, now another.

Such, then, are the differences of the arts with respect to the medium of imitation.

Since the objects of imitation are men in action, and these men must be either of a higher or a lower type (for moral character mainly answers to these divisions, goodness and badness being the distinguishing marks of moral differences), it follows that we must represent men either as better than in real life, or as worse, or as they are. It is the same in painting. Polygnotus depicted men as nobler than they are, Pauson as less noble, Dionysus drew them true to life.

Now it is evident that each of the modes of imitation above mentioned will exhibit these differences, and become a distinct kind in imitating objects that are thus distinct. Such diversities may be found even in dancing, flute-playing, and lyre-playing. So again in language, whether prose or verse unaccompanied by music. Homer, for example, makes men better than they are; Cleophon as they are; Hegemon the Thasian, the inventor of parodies, and Nicochares, the author of the Deiliad, worse than they are. The same thing holds good of Dithyrambs and Nomes; here too one may portray different types, as Timotheus and Philoxenus differed in representing their Cyclopes. The same distinction marks off Tragedy from Comedy; for Comedy aims at representing men as worse, Tragedy as better than in actual life.

There is still a third difference—the manner in which each of these objects may be imitated. For the medium being the same, and the objects the same, the poet may imitate by narration—in which case he can either take another personality as Homer does, or speak in his own person, unchanged—or he may present all his characters as living and moving before us.

These, then, as we said at the beginning, are the three differences which distinguish artistic imitation,—the medium, the objects, and the manner.

So that from one point of view, Sophocles is an imitator of the same kind as Homer—for both imitate higher types of character; from another point of view, of the same kind as Aristophanes—for both imitate persons acting and doing. . . .

Poetry in general seems to have sprung from two causes, each of them lying deep in our nature. First, the instinct of imitation is implanted in man from childhood, one difference between him and other animals being that he is the most imitative of living creatures, and through imitation learns his earliest lessons; and no less universal is the pleasure felt in things imitated. We have evidence of this in the facts of experience. Objects which in themselves we view with pain, we delight to contemplate when reproduced with minute fidelity: such as the forms of the most ignoble animals and of dead bodies. The cause of this again is, that to learn gives the liveliest pleasure, not only to philosophers but to men in general; whose capacity, however, of learning is more limited. Thus the reason why men enjoy seeing a likeness is, that in contemplating it they find themselves learning or inferring, and saying perhaps, "Ah, that is he." For if you happen not to have seen the original, the pleasure will be due not to the imitation as such, but to the execution, the colouring, or some such other cause.

Imitation, then, is one instinct of our nature. Next, there is the instinct for "harmony" and rhythm, metres being manifestly sections of rhythm. Persons, therefore, starting with this natural gift developed by degrees their special aptitudes, till their rude improvisations gave birth to Poetry. . . .

Comedy is, as we have said, an imitation of characters of a lower type,— not, however, in the full sense of the word bad, the Ludicrous being merely a subdivision of the ugly. It consists in some defect or ugliness which is not painful or destructive. To take an obvious example, the comic mask is ugly and distorted, but does not imply pain. . . .

Epic poetry agrees with Tragedy in so far as it is an imitation in verse of characters of a higher type. They differ, in that Epic poetry admits but one kind of metre, and is narrative in form. They differ, again, in their length: for Tragedy endeavours, as far as possible, to confine itself to a single revolution of the sun, or but slightly to exceed this limit; whereas the Epic action has no limits of time. This, then, is a second point of difference; though at first the same freedom was admitted in Tragedy as in Epic poetry.

Of their constituent parts some are common to both, some peculiar to Tragedy: whoever, therefore, knows what is good or bad Tragedy, knows also about Epic poetry. All the elements of an Epic poem are found in Tragedy, but the elements of a Tragedy are not all found in the Epic poem. . . .

Tragedy, then, is an imitation of an action that is serious, complete, and of a certain magnitude; in language embellished with each kind of artistic ornament, the several kinds being found in separate parts of the play; in the form of action, not of narrative; through pity and fear effecting the proper purgation of these emotions. By "language embellished," I mean language into which rhythm, "harmony," and song enter. By "the several kinds in separate parts," I mean, that some parts are tendered through the medium of verse alone, others again with the aid of song.

Now as tragic imitation implies persons acting, it necessarily follows, in the first place, that Spectacular equipment will be a part of Tragedy. Next, Song and Diction, for these are the medium of imitation. By "Diction" I mean the mere metrical arrangement of the words: as for "Song," it is a term whose sense every one understands.

Again, Tragedy is the imitation of an action, and an action implies personal agents, who necessarily possess certain distinctive qualities both of character and thought; for it is by these that we qualify actions themselves, and these—thought and character—are the two natural causes from which actions spring, and on actions again all success or failure depends. Hence, the Plot is the imitation of the action:—for by plot I here mean the arrangement of the incidents. By Character I mean that in virtue of which we ascribe certain qualities to the agents. Thought is required wherever a statement is proved, or, it may be, a general truth enunciated. Every Tragedy, therefore, must have six parts, which parts determine its quality—namely, Plot, Character, Diction, Thought, Spectacle, Song. Two of the parts constitute the medium of imitation, one the manner, and three the objects of imitation. And these complete the list. These elements have been employed, we may say, by the poets to a man; in fact, every play contains Spectacular elements as well as Character, Plot, Diction, Song, and Thought.

But most important of all is the structure of the incidents. For Tragedy is an imitation, not of men, but of an action and of life, and life consists in action, and its end is a mode of action, not a quality. Now character determines men's qualities, but it is by their actions that they are happy or the reverse. Dramatic action, therefore, is not with a view to the representation of character: character comes in as subsidiary to the actions. Hence the incidents and the plot are the end of a tragedy; and the end is the chief thing of all. Again, without action there cannot be a tragedy; there may be without character. The tragedies of most of our modern poets fail in the rendering of character; and of poets in general this is often true. It is the same in painting; and here lies the difference between Zeuxis and Polygnotus. Polygnotus delineates character well: the style of Zeuxis is devoid of ethical quality. Again, if you string together a set of speeches expressive of character, and well finished in point of diction and thought, you will not produce the essential tragic effect nearly so well as with a play which, however deficient in these respects, yet has a plot and artistically constructed incidents. Besides which, the most powerful elements of emotional interest in Tragedy—Peripeteia or Reversal of the

Situation, and Recognition scenes—are parts of the plot. A further proof is, that novices in the art attain to finish of diction and precision of portraiture before they can construct the plot. It is the same with almost all the early poets.

The Plot, then, is the first principle, and, as it were, the soul of a tragedy: Character holds the second place. A similar fact is seen in painting. The most beautiful colours, laid on confusedly, will not give as much pleasure as the chalk outline of a portrait. Thus Tragedy is the imitation of an action, and of the agents mainly with a view to the action.

Third in order is Thought,—that is, the faculty of saying what is possible and pertinent in given circumstances. In the case of oratory, this is the function of the political art and of the art of rhetoric: and so indeed the older poets make their characters speak the language of civic life; the poets of our time, the language of the rhetoricians. Character is that which reveals moral purpose, showing what kind of things a man chooses or avoids. Speeches, therefore, which do not make this manifest, or in which the speaker does not choose or avoid anything whatever, are not expressive of character. Thought, on the other hand, is found where something is proved to be or not to be, or a general maxim is enunciated.

Fourth among the elements enumerated comes Diction; by which I mean, as has been already said, the expression of the meaning in words; and its essence is the same both in verse and prose.

Of the remaining elements Song holds the chief place among the embellishments.

The Spectacle has, indeed, an emotional attraction of its own, but, of all the parts, it is the least artistic, and connected least with the art of poetry. For the power of Tragedy, we may be sure, is felt even apart from representation and actors. Besides, the production of spectacular effects depends more on the art of the stage machinist than on that of the poet.

These principles being established, let us now discuss the proper structure of the Plot, since this is the first and most important thing in Tragedy.

Now, according to our definition, Tragedy is an imitation of an action that is complete, and whole, and of a certain magnitude; for there may be a whole that is wanting in magnitude. A whole is that which has a beginning, a middle, and an end. A beginning is that which does not itself follow anything by causal necessity, but after which something naturally is or comes to be. An end, on the contrary, is that which itself naturally follows some other thing, either by necessity, or as a rule, but has nothing following it. A middle is that which follows something as some other thing follows it. A well-constructed plot, therefore, must neither begin nor end at haphazard, but conform to these principles.

Again, a beautiful object, whether it be a living organism or any whole composed of parts, must not only have an orderly arrangement of parts, but must also be of a certain magnitude; for beauty depends on magnitude and order. Hence a very small animal organism cannot be beautiful; for the view of it is confused, the object being seen in an almost imperceptible moment of time. Nor, again, can one of vast size be beautiful; for as the eye cannot take it all in at once, the unity and sense of the whole is lost for the spectator; as for instance if there were one a thousand miles long. As, therefore, in the case of animate bodies and organisms a certain magnitude is necessary, and a magnitude which may be easily embraced in one view; so in the plot, a certain length is necessary, and a length which can be easily embraced by the memory. The limit of length in relation to dramatic competition and sensuous presentment, is no part of artistic theory. For had it been the rule for a hundred tragedies to compete together, the performance would have been regulated by the water-clock,—as indeed we are told was formerly done. But the limit as fixed by the nature of the drama itself is this:—the greater the length, the more beautiful will the piece be by reason of its size, provided that the whole be perspicuous. And to define the matter roughly, we may say that the proper magnitude is comprised within such limits, that the sequence of events, according to the law of probability or necessity, will admit of a change from bad fortune to good, or from good fortune to bad.

Unity of plot does not, as some persons think, consist in the unity of the hero. For infinitely various are the incidents in one man's life which cannot be reduced to unity; and so, too, there are many actions of one man out of which we cannot make one action. Hence the error, as it appears, of all poets who have composed a Heracleid, a Theseid, or other poems of the kind. They imagine that as Heracles was one man, the story of Heracles must also be a unity. But Homer, as in all else he is of surpassing merit, here too—whether from art or natural genius—seems to have happily discerned the truth. In composing the Odyssey he did not include all the adventures of Odysseus—such as his wound on Parnassus, or his feigned madness at the mustering of the host—incidents between which there was no necessary or probable connexion: but he made the Odyssey, and likewise the Iliad, to centre round an action that in our sense of the word is one. As therefore, in the other imitative arts, the imitation is one when the object imitated is one, so the plot, being an imitation of an action, must imitate one action and that a whole, the structural union of the parts being such that, if any one of them is displaced or removed, the whole will be disjointed and disturbed. For a thing whose presence or absence makes no visible difference, is not an organic part of the whole.

It is, moreover, evident from what has been said, that it is not the function of the poet to relate what has happened, but what may happen,—what is possible according to the law of probability or necessity. The poet and the historian differ not by writing in verse or in prose. The work of Herodotus might be put into verse, and it would still be a species of history, with meter no less than without it. The true difference is that one relates what has happened, the other what may happen. Poetry, therefore, is a more philosophical and a higher thing than history: for poetry tends to express the universal, history the particular. By the universal I mean how a person of a certain type will on occasion speak or act, according to the law of probability or necessity; and it is this universality at which poetry aims in the names she attaches to the personages. The particular is—for example—what Alcibiades did or suffered. In Comedy this is already apparent: for here the poet first constructs the plot on the lines of probability, and then inserts characteristic names;—unlike the lampooners who write about particular individuals. But tragedians still keep to real names, the reason being that what is possible is credible: what has not happened we do not at once feel sure to be possible: but what has happened is manifestly possible; otherwise it would not have happened. Still there are even some tragedies in which there are only one or two well known names, the rest being fictitious. In others, none are well known,—as in Agathon's Antheus, where incidents and names alike are fictitious, and yet they give none the less pleasure. We must not, therefore, at all costs keep to the received legends, which are the usual subjects of Tragedy. Indeed, it would be absurd to attempt it; for even subjects that are known are known only to a few, and yet give pleasure to all. It clearly follows that the poet or "maker" should be the maker of plots rather than of verses; since he is a poet because he imitates, and what he imitates are actions. And even if he chances to take an historical subject, he is none the less a poet; for there is no reason why some events that have actually happened should not conform to the law of the probable and possible, and in virtue of that quality in them he is their poet or maker.

Of all plots and actions the epeisodic are the worst. I call a plot "epeisodic" in which the episodes or acts succeed one another without probable or necessary sequence. Bad poets compose such pieces by their own fault, good poets, to please the players; for, as they write show pieces for competition, they stretch the plot beyond its capacity, and are often forced to break the natural continuity.

But again, Tragedy is an imitation not only of a complete action, but of events inspiring fear or pity. Such an effect is best produced when the events come on us by surprise; and the effect is heightened when, at the same time, they follow as cause and effect. The tragic wonder will then be greater than if they happened of themselves or by accident; for even coincidences are most striking when they have an air of design. We may instance the statue of Mitys at Argos, which fell upon his murderer while he was a spectator at a festival, and killed him. Such events seem not to be due to mere chance. Plots, therefore, constructed on these principles are necessarily the best.

Plots are either Simple or Complex, for the actions in real life, of which the plots are an imitation, obviously show a similar distinction. An action which is one and continuous in the sense above defined, I call Simple, when the change of fortune takes place without Reversal of the Situation and without Recognition.

A Complex action is one in which the change is accompanied by such Reversal, or by Recognition, or by both. These last should arise from the internal structure of the plot, so that what follows should be the necessary or probable result of the preceding action. It makes all the difference whether any given event is a case of *propter hoc* or *post hoc*.

Reversal of the Situation is a change by which the action veers round to its opposite, subject always to our rule of probability or necessity. Thus in the Oedipus, the messenger comes to cheer Oedipus and free him from his alarms about his mother, but by revealing who he is, he produces the opposite effect. Again in the Lynceus, Lynceus is being led away to his death, and Danaus goes with him, meaning to slay him; but the outcome of the preceding incidents is that Danaus is killed and Lynceus saved.

Recognition, as the name indicates, is a change from ignorance to knowledge, producing love or hate between the persons destined by the poet for good or bad fortune. The best form of recognition is coincident with a Reversal of the Situation, as in the Oedipus. There are indeed other forms. Even inanimate things of the most trivial kind may in a sense be objects of recognition. Again, we may recognise or discover whether a person has done a thing or not. But the recognition which is most intimately connected with the plot and action is, as we have said, the recognition of persons. This recognition, combined with Reversal, will produce either pity or fear; and actions producing these effects are those which, by our definition, Tragedy represents. Moreover, it is upon such situations that the issues of good or bad fortune will depend. Recognition, then, being between persons, it may happen that one person only is recognised by the other—when the latter is already known—or it may be necessary that the recognition should be on both sides. Thus Iphigenia is revealed to Orestes by the sending of the letter; but another act of recognition is required to make Orestes known to Iphigenia.

Two parts, then, of the Plot—Reversal of the Situation and Recognition—turn upon surprises. A third part is the Scene of Suffering. The Scene of Suffering is a destructive or painful action, such as death on the stage, bodily agony, wounds and the like. . . .

As the sequel to what has already been said, we must proceed to consider what the poet should aim at, and what he should avoid, in constructing his plots; and by what means the specific effect of Tragedy will be produced.

A perfect tragedy should, as we have seen, be arranged not on the simple but on the complex plan. It should, moreover, imitate actions which excite pity and fear, this being the distinctive mark of tragic imitation. It follows plainly, in the first place, that the change of fortune presented must not be the spectacle of a virtuous man brought from prosperity to adversity: for this moves neither pity nor fear; it merely shocks us. Nor, again, that of a bad man passing from adversity to prosperity: for nothing can be more alien to the spirit of Tragedy; it possesses no single tragic quality; it neither satisfies the moral sense nor calls forth pity or fear. Nor, again, should the downfall of the utter villain be exhibited. A plot of this kind would, doubtless, satisfy the moral sense, but it would inspire neither pity nor fear; for pity is aroused by unmerited misfortune, fear by the misfortune of a man like ourselves; such an event, therefore, will be neither pitiful nor terrible. There remains, then, the character between these two extremes,—that of a man who is not eminently good and just, yet whose misfortune is brought about not by vice or depravity, but by some error or frailty. He must be one who is highly renowned and prosperous,—a personage like Oedipus, Thyestes, or other illustrious men of such families.

A well constructed plot should, therefore, be single in its issue, rather than double as some maintain. The change of fortune should be not from bad to good, but, reversely, from good to bad. It should come about as the result not of vice, but of some great error or frailty, in a character either such as we have described, or better rather than worse. The practice of the stage bears out our view. At first the poets recounted any legend that came in their way. Now, the best tragedies are founded on the story of a few houses,—on the fortunes of Alcmaeon, Oedipus, Orestes, Meleager, Thyestes, Telephus, and those others who have done or suffered something terrible. A tragedy, then, to be perfect according to the rules of art should be of this construction. Hence they are in error who censure Euripides just because he follows this principle in his plays, many of which end unhappily. It is, as we have said, the right ending. The best proof is that on the stage and in dramatic competition, such plays, if well worked out, are the most tragic in effect; and Euripides, faulty though he may be in the general management of his subject, yet is felt to be the most tragic of the poets.

In the second rank comes the kind of tragedy which some place first. Like the Odyssey, it has a double thread of plot, and also an opposite catastrophe for the good and for the bad. It is accounted the best because of the weakness of the spectators; for the poet is guided in what he writes by the wishes of his audience. The pleasure, however, thence derived is not the true tragic pleasure. It is proper rather to Comedy, where those who, in the piece, are the deadliest enemies—like Orestes and Aegisthus—quit the stage as friends at the close, and no one slays or is slain.

Fear and pity may be aroused by spectacular means; but they may also result from the inner structure of the piece, which is the better way, and indicates a superior poet. For the plot ought to be so constructed that, even without the aid of the eye, he who hears the tale told will thrill with horror and melt to pity at what takes place. This is the impression we should receive from hearing the story of the Oedipus. But to produce this effect by the mere spectacle is a less artistic method, and dependent on extraneous aids. Those who employ spectacular means to create a sense not of the terrible but only of the monstrous, are strangers to the purpose of Tragedy; for we must not demand of Tragedy any and every kind of pleasure, but only that which is proper to it. And since the pleasure which the poet should afford is that which comes from pity and fear through imitation, it is evident that this quality must be impressed upon the incidents.

Let us then determine what áre the circumstances which strike us as terrible or pitiful.

Actions capable of this effect must happen between persons who are either friends or enemies or indifferent to one another. If an enemy kills an enemy, there is nothing to excite pity either in the act or the intention,—except so far as the suffering in itself is pitiful. So again with indifferent persons. But when the tragic incident occurs between those who are near or dear to one another—if, for example, a brother kills, or intends to kill, a brother, a son his father, a mother her son, a son his mother, or any other deed of the kind is done—these are the situations to be looked for by the poet. He may not indeed destroy the framework of the received legends—the fact, for instance, that Clytemnestra was slain by Orestes and Eriphyle by Alcmaeon—but he ought to show invention of his own, and skilfully handle the traditional material. Let us explain more clearly what is meant by skilful handling.

The action may be done consciously and with knowledge of the persons, in the manner of the older poets. It is thus too that Euripides makes Medea slay her children. Or, again, the deed of horror may be done, but done in ignorance, and the tie of kinship or friendship be discovered afterwards. The Oedipus of Sophocles is an example. Here, indeed, the incident is outside the drama proper; but cases occur where it falls within the action of the play: one may cite the Alcmaeon of Astydamas, or Telegonus in the Wounded Odysseus. Again, there is a third case,—to be about to act with knowledge of the persons and then not to act. The fourth case is when some one is about to do an irreparable deed through ignorance, and makes the discovery before it is done. These are the only possible ways. For the deed must either be done or not done,—and that wittingly or unwittingly. But of all these ways, to be about to act knowing the persons, and then not to act, is the worst. It is shocking without being tragic, for no disaster follows. It is, therefore, never, or very rarely, found in poetry. One instance, however, is in the Antigone, where Haemon threatens to kill Creon. The next and better way is that the deed should be perpretated. Still better, that it should be perpetrated in ignorance, and the discovery made afterwards. There is then nothing to shock us, while the discovery produces a startling effect. The last case is the best, as when in the Cresphontes Merope is about to slay her son, but, recognising who he is, spares his life. So in the Iphigenia, the sister recognises the brother just in time. Again in the Helle, the son recognises the mother when on the point of giving her up. This, then, is why a few families only, as has been already observed, furnish the subjects of tragedy. It was not art, but happy chance, that led the poets in search of subjects to impress the tragic quality upon their plots. They are compelled, therefore, to have recourse to those houses whose history contains moving incidents like these.

Enough has now been said concerning the structure of the incidents, and the right kind of plot.

In respect of Character there are four things to be aimed at. First, and most important, it must be good. Now any speech or action that manifests moral purpose of any kind will be expressive of character: the character will be good if the purpose is good. This rule is relative to each class. Even a woman may be good, and also a slave; though the woman may be said to be an inferior being, and the slave quite worthless. The second thing to aim at is propriety. There is a type of manly valour; but valour in a woman, or unscrupulous cleverness, is inappropriate. Thirdly, character must be true to life: for this is a distinct thing from goodness and propriety, as here described. The fourth point is consistency: for though the subject of the imitation, who suggested the type, be inconsistent, still he must be consistently inconsistent. As an example of motiveless degradation of character, we have Menelaus in the Orestes: of character indecorous and inappropriate, the lament of Odysseus in the Scylla, and the speech of Melanippe: of inconsistency, the Iphigenia at Aulis,—for Iphigenia the suppliant in no way resembles her later self.

As in the structure of the plot, so too in the portraiture of character, the poet should always aim either at the necessary or the probable. Thus a person of a given character should speak or act in a given way, by the rule either of necessity or of probability; just as this event should follow that by necessary or probable sequence. It is therefore evident that the unravelling of the plot, no less than the complication, must arise out of the plot itself, it must not be brought about by the *Deus ex Machina*—as in the Medea, or in the Return of the Greeks in the Iliad. The *Deus ex Machina* should be employed only for events external to the drama,—for antecedent or subsequent events, which lie beyond the range of human knowledge, and which require to be reported or foretold; for to the gods we ascribe the power of seeing all things. Within the action there must be nothing irrational. If the irrational cannot be excluded, it should be outside the scope of the tragedy. Such is the irrational element in the Oedipus of Sophocles.

Again, since Tragedy is an imitation of persons who are above the common level, the example of good portrait-painters should be followed. They, while reproducing the distinctive form of the original, make a likeness which is true to life and yet more beautiful. So too the poet, in representing men who are irascible or indolent, or have other defects of character, should preserve the type and yet enoble it. In this way Achilles is portrayed by Agathon and Homer.

These then are the rules the poet should observe. Nor should he neglect those appeals to the senses, which, though not among the essentials, are the concomitants of poetry; for here too there is much room for error. But of this enough has been said in our published treatises.

What Recognition is has been already explained. We will now enumerate its kinds.

First the least artistic form, which, from poverty of wit, is most commonly employed—recognition by signs. Of these some are congenital,—such as "the spear which the earth-born race bear on their bodies," or the stars introduced by Carcinus in his Thyestes. Others are acquired after birth; and of these some are bodily marks, as scars; some external tokens, as necklaces, or the little ark in the Tyro by which the discovery is effected. Even these admit of more or less skilful treatment. Thus in the recognition of Odysseus by his scar, the discovery is made in one way by the nurse, in another by the swineherds. The use of tokens for the express purpose of proof—and, indeed, any formal proof with or without tokens—is a less artistic mode of recognition. A better kind is that which comes about by a turn of incident, as in the Bath Scene in the Odyssey.

Next come the recognitions invented at will by the poet, and on that account wanting in art. For example, Orestes in the Iphigenia reveals the fact that he is Orestes. She, indeed, makes herself known by the letter; but he, by speaking himself, and saying what the poet, not what the plot requires. This, therefore, is nearly allied to the fault above mentioned:-—for Orestes might as well have brought tokens with him. Another similar instance is the "voice of the shuttle" in the Tereus of Sophocles.

The third depends on memory when the sight of some object awakens a feeling: as in the Cyprians of Dicaeogenes, where the hero breaks into tears on seeing the picture; or again in the "Lay of Alcinous," where Odysseus, hearing the minstrel play the lyre, recalls the past and weeps; and hence the recognition.

The fourth kind is by process of reasoning. Thus in the Choëphori:—"Some one resembling me has come: no one resembles me but Orestes: therefore Orestes has come." . . .

But, of all recognitions, the best is that which arises from the incidents themselves, where the startling discovery is made by natural means. Such is that in the Oedipus of Sophocles, and in the Iphigenia; for it was natural that Iphigenia should wish to dispatch a letter. These recognitions alone dispense with the artificial aid of tokens or amulets. Next come the recognitions by process of reasoning. . . .

Every tragedy falls into two parts,—Complication and Unravelling or *Dénouement*. Incidents extraneous to the action are frequently combined with a portion of the action proper, to form the Complication; the rest is the Unravelling. By the Complication I mean all that extends from the beginning of the action to the part which marks the turning-point to good or bad fortune. The Unravelling is that which extends from the beginning of the change to the end. . . .

It remains to speak of Diction and Thought, the other parts of Tragedy having been already discussed. Concerning Thought, we may assume what is said in the Rhetoric, to which inquiry the subject more strictly belongs. Under Thought is included every effect which has to be produced by speech, the subdivisions being,—proof and refutation; the excitation of the feelings, such as pity, fear, anger, and the like; the suggestion of importance or its opposite. Now, it is evident that the dramatic incidents must be treated from the same points of view as the dramatic speeches, when the object is to evoke the sense of pity, fear, importance, or probability. The only difference is, that the incidents should speak for themselves without verbal exposition; while the effects aimed at in speech should be produced by the speaker, and as a result of the speech. For what were the business of a speaker, if the Thought were revealed quite apart from what he says?

Next, as regards Diction. One branch of the inquiry treats of the Modes of Utterance. But this province of knowledge belongs to the art of Delivery and to the masters of that science. It includes, for instance,—what is a command, a prayer, a statement, a threat, a question, an answer, and so forth. To know or not to know these things involves no serious censure upon the poet's art. For who can admit the fault imputed to Homer by Protagoras,—that in the words, "Sing, goddess, of the wrath," he gives a command under the idea that he utters a prayer? For to tell some one to do a thing or not to do it is, he says, a command. We may, therefore, pass this over as an inquiry that belongs to another art, not to poetry. . . .

As to that poetic imitation which is narrative in form and employs a single metre, the plot manifestly ought, as in a tragedy, to be constructed on dramatic principles. It should have for its subject a single action, whole and complete, with a beginning, a middle, and an end. It will thus resemble a living organism in all its unity, and produce the pleasure proper to it. It will differ in structure from historical compositions, which of necessity present not a single action, but a single period, and all that happened within that period to one person or to many, little connected together as the events may be. For as the sea-fight at Salamis and the battle with the Carthaginians in Sicily took place at the same time, but did not tend to any one result, so in the sequence of events, one thing sometimes follows another, and yet no single result is thereby produced. Such is the practice, we may say, of most poets. Here again, then, as has been already observed, the transcendent excellence of Homer is manifest. He never attempts to make the whole war of Troy the subject of his poem, though that war had a beginning and an end. It would have been too vast a theme, and not easily embraced in a single view. If, again, he had kept it within moderate limits, it must have been over-complicated by the variety of the incidents. As it is, he detaches a single portion, and admits as episodes many events from the general story of the war—such as the Catalogue of the ships and others—thus diversifying the poem. All other poets take a single hero, a single period, or an action single indeed, but with a multiplicity of parts. . . .

Again, Epic poetry must have as many kinds as Tragedy: it must be simple, or complex, or "ethical," or "pathetic." The parts also, with the exception of song and spectacle, are the same; for it requires Reversals of the Situation, Recognitions, and Scenes of Suffering. Moreover, the thoughts and the diction must be artistic. In all these respects Homer is our earliest and sufficient model. Indeed each of his poems has a twofold character. The Iliad is at once simple and "pathetic," and the Odyssey complex (for Recognition scenes run through it), and at the same time "ethical." Moreover, in diction and thought they are supreme.

Epic poetry differs from Tragedy in the scale on which it is constructed and in its meter. As regards scale or length, we have already laid down an adequate limit:—the beginning and the end must be capable of being brought within a single view. This condition will be satisfied by poems on a smaller scale than the old epics, and answering in length to the group of tragedies presented at a single sitting.

Epic poetry has, however, a great—a special—capacity for enlarging its dimensions, and we can see the reason. In Tragedy we cannot imitate several lines of actions carried on at one and the same time; we must confine ourselves to the action on the stage and the part taken by the players. But in Epic poetry, owing to the narrative form, many events simultaneously transacted can be presented; and these, if relevant to the subject, add mass and dignity to the poem. The Epic has here an advantage, and one that conduces to grandeur of effect, to diverting the mind of the hearer, and relieving the story with varying episodes. For sameness of incident soon produces satiety, and makes tragedies fail on the stage. . . .

Homer, admirable in all respects, has the special merit of being the only poet who rightly appreciates the part he should take himself. The poet should speak as little as possible in his own person, for it is not this that makes him an imitator. Other poets appear themselves upon the scene throughout, and imitate but little and rarely. Homer, after a few prefatory words, at once brings in a man, or woman, or other personage; none of them wanting in characteristic qualities, but each with a character of his own.

The element of the wonderful is required in Tragedy. The irrational, on which the wonderful depends for its chief effects, has wider scope in Epic poetry, because there the person acting is not seen. Thus, the pursuit of Hector would be ludicrous if placed upon the stage—the Greeks standing still and not joining in the pursuit, and Achilles waving them back. But in the Epic poem the absurdity passes unnoticed. Now the wonderful is pleasing: as may be inferred from the fact that every one tells a story with some addition of his own, knowing that his hearers like it. It is Homer who has chiefly taught other poets the art of telling lies skilfully. The secret of it lies in a fallacy. For, assuming that if one thing is or becomes, a second is or becomes, men imagine that, if the second is, the first likewise is or becomes. But this is a false inference. Hence, where the first thing is untrue, it is quite unnecessary, provided the second be true, to add that the first is or has become. For the mind, knowing the second to be true, falsely infers the truth of the first. There is an example of this in the Bath Scene of the Odyssey.

Accordingly, the poet should prefer probable impossibilities to improbable possibilities. The tragic plot must not be composed of irrational parts. Everything irrational should, if possible, be excluded; or, at all events, it should lie outside the action of the play (as, in the Oedipus, the hero's ignorance as to the manner of Laius' death) ; not within the drama,—as in the Electra, the messenger's account of the Pythian games; or, as in the Mysians, the man who has come from Tegea to Mysia and is still speechless. The plea that otherwise the plot would have been ruined, is ridiculous; such a plot should not in the first instance be constructed. But once the irrational has been introduced and an air of likelihood imparted to it, we must accept it in spite of the absurdity. Take even the irrational incidents in the Odyssey, where Odysseus is left upon the short of Ithaca. How intolerable even these might have been would be apparent if an inferior poet were to treat the subject. As it is, the absurdity is veiled by the poetic charm with which the poet invests it.

The diction should be elaborated in the pauses of the action, where there is no expression of character or thought. For, conversely, character and thought are merely obscured by a diction that is over brilliant.

With respect to critical difficulties and their solutions, the number and nature of the sources from which they may be drawn may be thus exhibited.

The poet being an imitator, like a painter or any other artist, must of necessity imitate one of three objects,—things as they were or are, things as they are said or thought to be, or things as they ought to be. The vehicle of expression is language,—either current terms or, it may be, rare words or metaphors. There are also many modifications of language, which we concede to the poets. Add to this, that the standard of correctness is not the same in poetry and politics, any more than in poetry and any other art. Within the art of poetry itself there are two kinds of faults,—those which touch in essence, and those which are accidental. If a poet has chosen to imitate something, but has imitated it incorrectly through want of capacity, the error is inherent in the poetry. But if the failure is due to a wrong choice—if he has represented a horse as throwing out both his off legs at once, or introduced technical inaccuracies in medicine, for example, or in any other art—the error is not essential to the poetry. These are the points of view from which we should consider and answer the objections raised by the critics.

First as to matters which concern the poet's own art. If he describes the impossible, he is guilty of an error; but the error may be justified, if the end of the art be thereby attained (the end being that already mentioned) ,—if, that is, the effect of this or any other part of the poem is thus rendered more striking. A case in point is the pursuit of Hector. If, however, the end might have been as well, or better, attained without violating the special rules of the poetic art, the error is not justified: for every kind of error should, if possible, be avoided.

Again, does the error touch the essentials of the poetic art, or some accident of it? For example,—not to know that a hind has no horns is a less serious matter than to paint it inartistically.

Further, if it be objected that the description is not true to fact, the poet may perhaps reply,—"But the objects are as they ought to be": just as Sophocles said that he drew men as they ought to be; Euripides, as they are. In this way the objection may be met. If, however, the representation be of neither kind, the poet may answer,—"This is how men say the thing is." This applies to tales about the gods. It may well be that these stories are not higher than fact nor yet true to fact: they are, very possibly, what Xenophanes says of them. But anyhow, "this is what is said." Again, a description may be no better than the fact: still, it was the fact"; as in the passage about the arms: "Upright upon their butt-ends stood the spears." This was the custom then, as it now is among the Illyrians.

Again, in examining whether what has been said or done by some one is poetically right or not, we must not look merely to the particular act or saying, and ask whether it is poetically good or bad. We must also consider by whom it is said or done, to whom, when, by what means, or for what end; whether, for instance, it be to secure a greater good, or avert a greater evil. . . .

In general, the impossible must be justified by reference to artistic requirements, or to the higher reality, or to received opinion. With respect to the requirements of art, a probable impossiblity is to be preferred to a thing improbable and yet impossible. Again, it may be possible that there should be men such as Zeuxius painted. "Yes," we say, "but the impossible is the higher thing; for the ideal type must surpass the reality." To justify the irrational, we appeal to what is commonly said to be. In addition to which, we urge that the irrational sometimes does not violate reason; just as "it is probable that a thing may happen contrary to probability."

Things that sound contradictory should be examined by the same rules as in dialectical refutation—whether the same thing is meant, in the same relation, and in the same sense. We should therefore solve the question by reference to what the poet says himself, or to what is tacitly assumed by a person of intelligence.

The element of the irrational, and, similarly, depravity of character, are justly censured when there is no inner necessity for introducing them. Such is the irrational element in the introduction of Aegeus by Euripides and the badness of Menelaus in the Orestes.

Thus, there are five sources from which critical objections are drawn. Things are censured either as impossible, or irrational, or morally hurtful, or contradictory, or contrary to artistic correctness. The answers should be sought under the twelve heads above mentioned.

The question may be raised whether the Epic or Tragic mode of imitation is the higher. If the more refined art is the higher, and the more refined in every case is that which appeals to the better sort of audience, the art which imitates anything and everything is manifestly most unrefined. The audience is supposed to be too dull to comprehend unless something of their own is thrown in by the performers, who therefore indulge in restless movements. . . .

So we are told that Epic poetry is addressed to a cultivated audience, who do not need gesture; Tragedy, to an inferior public. Being then unrefined, it is evidently the lower of the two.

Now, in the first place, this censure attaches not to the poetic but to the histrionic art; for gesticulation may be equally overdone in epic recitation, as by Sosistratus, or in lyrical competition, as by Mnasitheus the Opuntian. Next, all action is not to be condemned—any more than all dancing—but only that of bad performers. Such was the fault found in Callippides, as also in others of our own day, who are censured for representing degraded women. Again, Tragedy like Epic poetry produces its effect even without action; it reveals its power by mere reading. If, then, in all other respects it is superior, this fault, we say, is not inherent in it.

And superior it is, because it has all the epic elements—it may even use the epic metre—with the music and spectacular effects as important accessories; and these produce the most vivid of pleasures. Further, it has vividness of impression in reading as well as in representation. Moreover, the art attains its end within narrower limits; for the concentrated effect is more pleasurable than one which is spread over a long time and so diluted. What, for example, would be the effect of the Oedipus of Sophocles, if it were cast into a form as long as the Iliad? Once more, the Epic imitation has less unity; as is shown by this, that any Epic poem will furnish subjects for several tragedies. Thus if the story adopted by the poet has a strict unity, it must either be concisely told and appear truncated; or, if it conform to the Epic canon of length, it must seem weak and watery. Such length implies some loss of unity, if, I mean, the poem is constructed out of several actions, like the Iliad and the Odyssey, which have many such parts, each with a certain magnitude of its own. Yet these poems are as perfect as possible in structure; each is, in the highest degree attainable, an imitation of a single action.

If, then, Tragedy is superior to Epic poetry in all these respects, and, moreover, fulfils its specific function better as an art—for each art ought to produce, not any chance pleasure, but the pleasure proper to it, as already stated—it plainly follows that Tragedy is the higher art, as attaining its end more perfectly.

Thus much may suffice concerning Tragic and Epic poetry in general; their several kinds and parts, with the number of each and their differences; the causes that make a poem good or bad; the objections of the critics and the answers to these objections.

SIGMUND FREUD

Creative Writers and Day-Dreaming

WE LAYMEN have always been intensely curious to know—like the Cardinal who put a similar question to Ariosto[1]—from what sources that strange being, the creative writer, draws his material, and how he manages to make such an impression on us with it and to arouse in us emotions of which, perhaps, we had not even thought ourselves capable. Our interest is only heightened the more by the fact that, if we ask him, the writer himself gives us no explanation, or none that is satisfactory; and it is not at all weakened by our knowledge that not even the clearest insight into the determinants of his choice of material and into the nature of the art of creating imaginative form will ever help to make creative writers of *us*.

If we could at least discover in ourselves or in people like ourselves an activity which was in some way akin to creative writing! An examination of it would then give us a hope of obtaining the beginnings of an explanation of the creative work of writers. And, indeed, there is some prospect of this being possible. After all, creative writers themselves like to lessen the distance between their kind and the common run of humanity; they so often assure us that every man is a poet at heart and that the last poet will not perish till the last man does.

Should we not look for the first traces of imaginative activity as early as in childhood? The child's best-loved and most intense occupation is with his play or games. Might we not say that every child at play behaves like a creative writer, in that he creates a world of his own, or, rather, re-arranges the things of his world in a new way which pleases him? It would be wrong to think he does not take that world seriously; on the contrary, he takes his play very seriously and he expends large amounts of emotion on it. The opposite of play is not what is serious

From *The Standard Edition of the Complete Psychological Works of Sigmund Freud,* Vol. IX, translated by James Strachey, 1959. Reprinted by permission of The Hogarth Press and the Institute of Psychoanalysis, London, 1959.

but what is real. In spite of all the emotions with which he cathects his world of play, the child distinguishes it quite well from reality; and he likes to link his imagined objects and situations to the tangible and visible things of the real world. This linking is all that differentiates the child's "play" from "phantasying."

The creative writer does the same as the child at play. He creates a world of phantasy which he takes very seriously—that is, which he invests with large amounts of emotion—while separating it sharply from reality. Language has preserved this relationship between children's play and poetic creation. It gives [in German] the name of *"Spiel"* ["play"] to those forms of imaginative writing which require to be linked to tangible objects and which are capable of representation. It speaks of *"Lustspiel"* or *"Trauerspiel"* ["comedy" or "tragedy": literally, "pleasure play" or "mourning play"] and describes those who carry out the representation as "Schauspieler" ["players": literally "show-players"]. The unreality of the writer's imaginative world, however, has very important consequences for the technique of his art; for many things which, if they were real, could give no enjoyment, can do so in the play of phantasy, and many excitements which, in themselves, are actually distressing, can become a source of pleasure for the hearers and spectators at the performance of a writer's work.

There is another consideration for the sake of which we will dwell a moment longer on this contrast between reality and play. When the child has grown up and has ceased to play, and after he has been labouring for decades to envisage the realities of life with proper serious-ness, he may one day find himself in a mental situation which once more undoes the contrast between play and reality. As an adult he can look back on the intense seriousness with which he once carried on his games in childhood; and, by equating his ostensibly serious occupations of today with his childhood games, he can throw off the too heavy burden imposed on him by life and win the high yield of pleasure afforded by *humour*.[2]

As people grow up, then, they cease to play, and they seem to give up the yield of pleasure which they gained from playing. But whoever understands the human mind knows that hardly anything is harder for a man than to give up a pleasure which he has once experienced. Actu-ally, we can never give anything up; we can only exchange one thing for another. What appears to be a renunciation is really the formation of a substitute or surrogate. In the same way, the growing child, when he stops playing, gives up nothing but the link with real objects; instead of *playing*, he now *phantasies*. He builds castles in the air and creates what are called *day-dreams*. I believe that most people construct phantasies at times in their lives. This is a fact which has long been overlooked and whose importance has therefore not been sufficiently appreciated.

People's phantasies are less easy to observe than the play of children.

The child, it is true, plays by himself or forms a closed psychical system with other children for the purposes of a game; but even though he may not play his game in front of the grown-ups, he does not, on the other hand, conceal it from them. The adult, on the contrary, is ashamed of his phantasies and hides them from other people. He cherishes his phantasies as his most intimate possessions, and as a rule he would rather confess his misdeeds than tell anyone his phantasies. It may come about that for that reason he believes he is the only person who invents such phantasies and has no idea that creations of this kind are wide-spread among other people. This difference in the behaviour of a person who plays and a person who phantasies is accounted for by the motives of these two activities, which are nevertheless adjuncts to each other.

A child's play is determined by wishes: in point of fact by a single wish—one that helps in his upbringing—the wish to be big and grown up. He is always playing at being "grown up," and in his games he imitates what he knows about the lives of his elders. He has no reason to conceal this wish. With the adult, the case is different. On the one hand, he knows that he is expected not to go on playing or phantasying any longer, but to act in the real world; on the other hand, some of the wishes which give rise to his phantasies are of a kind which it is essential to conceal. Thus he is ashamed of his phantasies as being childish and as being unpermissible.

But, you will ask, if people make such a mystery of their phantasying, how is it that we know such a lot about it? Well, there is a class of human beings upon whom, not a god, indeed, but a stern goddess—Necessity—has allotted the task of telling what they suffer and what things give them happiness.[3] These are the victims of nervous illness, who are obliged to tell their phantasies, among other things, to the doctor by whom they expect to be cured by mental treatment. This is our best source of knowledge, and we have since found good reason to suppose that our patients tell us nothing that we might not also hear from healthy people.

Let us now make ourselves acquainted with a few of the characteristics of phantasying. We may lay it down that a happy person never phantasies, only an unsatisfied one. The motive forces of phantasies are un-satisfied wishes, and every single phantasy is the fulfilment of a wish, a correction of unsatisfying reality. These motivating wishes vary according to the sex, character and circumstances of the person who is having the phantasy; but they fall naturally into two main groups. They are either ambitious wishes, which serve to elevate the subject's personality; or they are erotic ones. In young women the erotic wishes predominate almost exclusively, for their ambition is as a rule absorbed by erotic trends. In young men egoistic and ambitious wishes come to the fore clearly enough alongside of erotic ones. But we will not lay stress on the opposition between the two trends; we would rather emphasize the fact that they are often united. Just as, in many altar-pieces, the portrait of the donor is to be seen in a corner of the picture, so, in the majority of ambitious phantasies, we can discover in some corner or other the lady for whom the creator of the phantasy performs all his heroic deeds and at whose feet all his triumphs are laid. Here, as you see, there are strong enough motives for concealment; the well-brought-up young woman is only allowed a minimum of erotic desire, and the young man has to learn to suppress the excess of self-regard which he brings with him from the spoilt days of his childhood, so that he may find his place in a society which is full of other individuals making equally strong demands.

We must not suppose that the products of this imaginative activity—the various phantasies, castles in the air and day-dreams—are stereotyped or unalterable. On the contrary, they fit themselves in to the subject's shifting impressions of life, change with every change in his situation, and receive from every fresh active impression what might be called a "date-mark." The relation of a phantasy to time is in general very important. We may say that it hovers, as it were, between three times—the three movements of time which our ideation involves. Mental work is linked to some current impression, and provoking occasion in the present which has been able to arouse one of the subject's major wishes. From there it harks back to a memory of an earlier experience (usually an infantile one) in which this wish was fulfilled; and it now creates a situation relating to the future which represents a fulfilment of the wish. What it thus creates is a day-dream or phantasy, which carries about it traces of its origin from the occasion which provoked it and from the memory. Thus past, present and future are strung together, as it were, on the threat of the wish that runs through them.

A very ordinary example may serve to make what I have said clear. Let us take the case of a poor orphan boy to whom you have given the address of some employer where he may perhaps find a job. On his way there he may indulge in a day-dream appropriate to the situation from which it arises. The content of his phantasy will perhaps be something like this. He is given a job, finds favour with his new employer, makes himself indispensable in the business, is taken into his employer's family, marries the charming young daughter of the house, and then himself becomes a director of the business, first as his employer's partner and then as his successor. In this phantasy, the dreamer has regained what he possessed in his happy childhood—the protecting house, the loving parents and the first objects of his affectionate feelings. You will see from this example the way in which the wish makes use of an occasion in the present to construct, on the pattern of the past, a picture of the future.

There is a great deal more that could be said about phantasies; but I will only allude as briefly as possible to certain points. If phantasies become over-luxuriant and over-powerful, the conditions are laid for an onset of neurosis or psychosis. Phantasies, moreover, are the immediate mental percursors of the distressing symptoms complained of by our patients. Here a broad by-path branches off in pathology.

I cannot pass over the relation of phantasies to dreams. Our dreams at night are nothing else than phantasies like these, as we can demonstrate from the interpretation of dreams.[4] Language, in its unrivalled wisdom, long ago decided the question of the essential nature of dreams by giving the name of "day-dreams" to the airy creations of phantasy. If the meaning of our dreams usually remains obscure to us in spite of this pointer, it is because of the circumstance that at night there also arise in us wishes of which we are ashamed; these we must conceal from ourselves, and they have consequently been repressed, pushed into the unconscious. Repressed wishes of this sort and their derivatives are only allowed to come to expression in a very distorted form. When scientific work had succeeded in elucidating this factor of *day-distortion*, it was no longer difficult to recognize that night-dreams are wish-fulfilments in just the same way as day-dreams—the phantasies which we all know so well.

So much for phantasies. And now for the creative writer. May we really attempt to compare the imaginative writer with the "dreamer in broad daylight,"[5] and his creations with day-dreams? Here we must begin by making an initial distinction. We must separate writers who, like the ancient authors of epics and tragedies, take over their material ready-made, from writers who seem to originate their own material. We will keep to the latter kind, and, for the purposes of our comparison, we will choose not the writers most highly esteemed by the critics, but the less pretentious authors of novels, romances and short stories, who nevertheless have the widest and most eager circle of readers of both sexes. One feature above all cannot fail to strike us about the creations of these story-writers: each of them has a hero who is the centre of interest, for whom the writer tries to win our sympathy by every possible means and whom he seems to place under the protection of a special Providence. If, at the end of one chapter of my story, I leave the hero unconscious and bleeding from severe wounds, I am sure to find him at the beginning of the next being carefully nursed and on the way to recovery; and, if the first volume closes with the ship he is in going down in a storm at sea, I am certain, at the opening of the second volume, to read of his miraculous rescue—a rescue without which the story could not proceed. The feeling of security with which I follow the hero through his perilous adventures is the same as the feeling with which a hero in real life throws himself into the water to save a drowning man or exposes himself to the enemy's fire in order to storm a battery. It is the true heroic feeling, which one of our best writers has expressed in an inimitable phrase: "Nothing can happen to *me*!"[6] It seems to me, however, that through this revealing characteristic of invulnerability we can immediately recognize His Majesty the Ego, the hero alike of every day-dream and of every story.[7]

Other typical features of these egocentric stories point to the same kinship. The fact that all the women in the novel invariably fall in love with the hero can hardly be looked on as a portrayal of reality, but it is easily understood as a necessary constituent of a day-dream. The same is true of the fact that the other characters in the story are sharply divided into good and bad, in defiance of the variety of human characters that are to be observed in real life. The "good" ones are the helpers, while the "bad" ones are the enemies and rivals, of the ego which has become the hero of the story.

We are perfectly aware that very many imaginative writings are far removed from the model of the naïve day-dream; and yet I cannot suppress the suspicion that even the most extreme deviations from that model could be linked with it through an uninterrupted series of transitional cases. It has struck me that in many of what are known as "psychological" novels only one person—once again the hero—is described from within. The author sits inside his mind, as it were, and looks at the other characters from outside. The psychological novel in general no doubt owes its special nature to the inclination of the modern writer to split up his ego, by self-observation, into many part-egos, and, in consequence, to personify the conflicting currents of his own mental life in several heroes. Certain novels, which might be described as "eccentric," seem to stand in quite special contrast to the type of the day-dream. In these, the person who is introduced as the hero plays only a very small active part; he sees the actions and sufferings of other people pass before him like a spectator. Many of Zola's later works belong to this category. But I must point out that the psychological analysis of individuals who are not creative writers, and who diverge in some respects from the so-called norm, has shown us analogous variations of the day-dream, in which the ego contents itself with the role of spectator.

If our comparison of the imaginative writer with the day-dreamer, and of poetical creation with the day-dream, is to be of any value, it must, above all, show itself in some way or other fruitful. Let us, for instance, try to apply to these authors' works the thesis we laid down earlier concerning the relation between phantasy and the three periods of time and the wish which runs through them; and, with its help, let us try to study the connections that exist between the life of the writer and his works. No one has known, as a rule, what expectations to frame in approaching this problem; and often the connection has been thought of in much too simple terms. In the light of the insight we have gained from phantasies, we ought to expect the following state of affairs. A strong experience in the present awakens in the creative writer a memory of an earlier experience (usually belonging to his childhood) from which there now proceeds a wish which finds its fulfilment in the creative work. The work itself exhibits elements of the recent provoking occasion as well as of the old memory.[8]

Do not be alarmed at the complexity of this formula. I suspect that in fact it will prove to be too exiguous a pattern. Nevertheless, it may contain a first approach to the true state of affairs; and, from some experiments I have made, I am inclined to think that this way of looking at creative writings may turn out not unfruitful. You will not forget that the stress it lays on childhood memories in the writer's life— a stress which may perhaps seem puzzling—is ultimately derived from the assumption that a piece of creative writing, like a day-dream, is a continuation of, and a substitute for, what was once the play of childhood.

We must not neglect, however, to go back to the kind of imaginative works which we have to recognize, not as original creations, but as the re-fashioning of ready-made and familiar material. Even here, the writer keeps a certain amount of independence, which can express itself in the choice of material and in changes in it which are often quite extensive. In so far as the material is already at hand, however, it is derived from the popular treasure-house of myths, legends and fairy tales. The study of constructions of folk-psychology such as these is far from being complete, but it is extremely probable that myths, for instance, are distorted vestiges of the wishful phantasies of whole nations, the *secular dreams* of youthful humanity.

You will say that, although I have put the creative writer first in the title of my paper, I have told you far less about him than about phantasies. I am aware of that, and I must try to excuse it by pointing to the present state of our knowledge. All I have been able to do is to throw out some encouragements and suggestions which, starting from the study of phantasies, lead on to the problem of the writer's choice of his literary material. As for the other problem—by what means the creative writer achieves the emotional effects in us that are aroused by his creations—we have as yet not touched on it at all. But I should like at least to point out to you the path that leads from our discussion of phantasies to the problems of poetical effects.

You will remember how I have said that the day-dreamer carefully conceals his phantasies from other people because he feels he has reasons for being ashamed of them. I should now add that even if he were to communicate them to us he could give us no pleasure by his disclosures. Such phantasies, when we learn them, repel us or at least leave us cold. But when a creative writer presents his plays to us or tells us what we are inclined to take to be his personal day-dreams, we experience a great pleasure, and one which probably arises from the confluence of many sources. How the writer accomplishes this is his innermost secret; the essential *ars poetica* lies in the technique of overcoming the feeling of repulsion in us which is undoubtedly connected with the barriers that rise between each single ego and the others. We can guess two of the methods used by this technique. The writer softens the character of his egoistic day-dreams by altering and disguising it, and he bribes us by the purely formal—that is, aesthetic—yield of pleasure which he offers us in the presentation of his phantasies. We give the name of an *incentive bonus*, or a *fore-pleasure*, to a yield of pleasure such as this, which is offered to us so as to make possible the release of still greater pleasure arising from deeper psychical sources.[9] In my opinion, all the aesthetic pleasure which a creative writer affords us has the character of the fore-pleasure of this kind, and our actual enjoyment of an imaginative work proceeds from a liberation of tensions in our minds. It may even be that not a little of this effect is due to the writer's enabling us thenceforward to enjoy our own day-dreams without self-reproach or shame. This brings us to the threshold of new, interesting and complicated enquiries; but also, at least for the moment, to the end of our discussion.

Notes

1. [Cardinal Ippolito d'Este was Ariosto's first patron, to whom he dedicated the *Orlando Furioso*. The poet's only reward was the question: "Where did you find so many stories, Lodovico?"]

2. [See Section 7 of Chapter VII of Freud's book on jokes (1905c).]

3. [This is an allusion to some well-known lines spoken by the poet-hero in the final scene of Goethe's *Torquato Tasso*:
"Und wenn der Mensch in seiner Qual verstummt,
Gab mir ein Gott, zu sagen, wie ich leide."
"And when mankind is dumb in its torment, a god granted me to tell how I suffer."]

4. Cf. Freud. *The Interpretation of Dreams* (1900a).

5. ["*Der Träumer am hellichten Tag.*"]

6. ["Es kann dir nix g'schelen!" This phrase from Anzengruber, the Viennese dramatist, was a favourite one of Freud's. Cf. "Thoughts on War and Death" (1915b). *Standard Ed.*, 14, 296.]

7. [Cf. "On Narcissism" (1914c), *Standard Ed.*, 14, 91.]

8. [A similar view had already been suggested by Freud in a letter to Fliess of July 7, 1898, on the subject of one of C. F. Meyer's short stories (Freud, 1950a) Letter 92.]

9. [This theory of "fore-pleasure" and the "incentive bonus" had been applied by Freud to jokes in the last paragraphs of Chapter IV of his book on that subject (1905c). The nature of "fore-pleasure" was also discussed in the *Three Essays* (1905d). See especially *Standard Ed.*, 7, 208 ff.]

The Personal Distribution of Income and Wealth

National Bureau of Economic Research

Conference on Research in Income and Wealth

The Personal Distribution of Income and Wealth

James D. Smith, Editor

Pennsylvania State University

Studies in Income and Wealth

Volume Thirty-nine

by the Conference on Research

in Income and Wealth

National Bureau of Economic Research

New York 1975

Distributed by Columbia University Press

New York and London

Printed in the United States of America

Relation of the National Bureau Directors to
Publications Reporting Conference Proceedings

Since the present volume is a record of conference proceedings, it has been exempted from the rules governing submission of manuscripts to, and critical review by, the Board of Directors of the National Bureau.

(Resolution adopted July 6, 1948,
as revised November 21, 1949,
and April 20, 1968)

Prefatory Note

This volume of Studies in Income and Wealth contains the papers presented at the Conference on Personal Distributions of Income and Wealth, held on October 3 and 4, 1972, at Pennsylvania State University. We are indebted to the University for making its facilities available to us, to the National Science Foundation for its support, and to the Program Committee, which consisted of James D. Smith (chairman), Edward C. Budd, F. Thomas Juster, and Robert J. Lampman. H. Irving Forman drew the charts and Ruth Ridler prepared the manuscript for press.

Funds for the economic research conference program of the National Bureau of Economic Research are supplied by the National Science Foundation

Contents

Prefatory Note   *vii*

Introduction
   James D. Smith   *1*

PART I

Chapter 1   The Pursuit of Equality
       Kenneth E. Boulding   *11*

PART II

REDISTRIBUTIVE MECHANISMS

Chapter 2   Social Accounting for Transfer
       Robert J. Lampman   *31*

Chapter 3   Individual Taxes and the Distribution of Income
       Benjamin A. Okner   *45*

Chapter 4   On the Comparison of Income Redistribution Plans
       Harold W. Watts and Jon K. Peck   *75*

PART III

INCOME DISTRIBUTIONS WITH LONG AND SHORT ACCOUNTING PERIODS

Chapter 5   Capital Gains and Individual Income—Evidence on Realization and Persistence
       Martin David and Roger Miller   *121*

Chapter 6   Income Instability Among Young and Middle-Aged Men
       Andrew I. Kohen, Herbert S. Parnes,
       and John R. Shea   *151*

Chapter 7   Time Period, Unit of Analysis, and Income
             Concept in the Analysis of Income Dis-
             tribution
                Jacob Benus and James N. Morgan   *209*

Chapter 8   Comments on Part III
                Martin David   *225*

PART IV

THE DISTRIBUTION OF PERSONAL WEALTH

Chapter 9   The Wealth, Income, and Social Class of Men in
             Large Northern Cities of the United States in
             1860
                Lee Soltow   *233*

Chapter 10   The Distribution of Wealth in Britain in the
             1960s—the Estate Duty Method Reexamined
                A. B. Atkinson   *277*

Discussion   Wealth in Britain—The Estate Duty Method
             Reexamined
                Kathleen M. Langley   *321*

Chapter 11   White Wealth and Black People: The Distribu-
             tion of Wealth in Washington, D.C., in 1967
                James D. Smith   *329*

Discussion   White Wealth and Black People: The Distribu-
             tion of Wealth in Washington, D.C., in 1967
                Vito Natrella   *365*

PART V

The Quality of Income Data

Chapter 12   Measurement of Transfer Income in the Current Population Survey
       Dorothy S. Projector and Judith Bretz   *377*

Chapter 13   The Bureau of Economic Analysis and Current Population Survey Size Distributions: Some Comparisons for 1964
       Edward C. Budd and Daniel B. Radner   *449*

Index of Names and Titles   *560*

Subject Index   *567*

The Personal Distribution of Income and Wealth

Introduction

James D. Smith

This volume contains papers presented at the annual meeting of the Conference on Research in Income and Wealth held on the campus of Pennsylvania State University in the fall of 1972.

The meeting and the one to follow it in 1974 reflect a renewed interest in the distributions and determinants of income and wealth. The papers in this volume focus on income and wealth defined in traditional monetary terms. The 1974 follow-up conference will extend the scope of inquiry to include non-monetary dimensions.

In large measure, the resurgence of researcher interest in personal distributions of income and wealth has resulted from increased availability of microdata and the sustained method-ological efforts by Orcutt and others demonstrating the superior-ity of microdata approaches to the estimation of many socially relevant or intellectually interesting models of behavior.

With respect to data, the decade of the sixties saw a rich harvest of microdata, reflecting the desire of policymakers to estimate in advance and measure in retrospect the consequences of social programs. Early in the sixties, the Board of Governors of the Federal Reserve System produced the Survey of Financial Charac-teristics of Consumers and the Survey of Changes in Financial Characteristics. By mid-decade, the Department of Labor was at work on the National Longitudinal Surveys, and the Office of Economic Opportunity had begun work on the Surveys of Economic Opportunity (1966 and 1967). The Office of Economic Opportunity, in conjunction with the Survey Research Center of the University of Michigan, also began collecting data from an ongoing panel of families in an effort known as the Panel Study of Income Dynamics. Microdata from all of these studies were made available to researchers. Near the end of the decade, Internal Revenue Service (IRS) tapes of income tax returns (without names or street addresses) became available to researchers who needed them. By the beginning of the decade of the 1970s, the IRS had made available microdata from estate tax returns, and the Census Bureau was creeping toward the release of a standard version of

1

the Current Population Survey which could be purchased by researchers who were not among the superrich.

The release of public data by government agencies has not been achieved easily, but the benefits, as evidenced by the papers in this volume, justify the effort. The push to make microdata available came from many researchers inside and outside of government. Raymond Bowman in his many years at the Bureau of the Budget contributed to this effort, as did Richard Ruggles, Guy Orcutt, Joseph Pechman, Benjamin Okner, Robert Levin, Harold Watts, and Ralph Nader, among others, outside of government.

Opposition to the release of microdata often has been argued in terms of confidentiality. The principle of confidentiality has both positive and negative aspects. We can easily agree that the protection of individuals is often well served by priviledged information, but when applied to the innocuous data of Census and tax records after names and street addresses have been removed, the argument rings false. Indeed, secrecy may harbor worse evils than those it is intended to prevent. One of the serious consequences of microdata privy only to the government agency collecting it is that the situation offers a tremendous incentive for "Watergating" errors which, understandably enough, occur in large-scale data-collection efforts. The social benefits of accessible microdata include an incentive to agencies to do first-rate work, many eyes to uncover elusive, but often serious, errors which can escape even very careful workers, and greater use of information that is usually collected at great cost. In any event, it is clear that research using microdata is on the ascendency, and that government agencies and private researchers are finding ways to reap the social benefits of microdata without injury to citizens who provide information.

The first chapter in this volume has very little to do with data per se but, rather, is concerned with economic methodology in the broadest sense—that is to say, with meta-economics. It is characteristic Boulding, piercing through the fine polish of technique to the important questions: What is it all about? What does it mean? The author forces reflection:

> Considering the enormous symbolic importance of the concept [equality], surprisingly little work has been done on it, philosophically, theoretically, or empirically. Perhaps the reason for this is that it is too painful, too contradictory, too confusing, and too important to be the object of anything but rhetoric.

And what of the complement of equality: inequality? Is there a meaningful quantitative interpretation of that? Boulding suggests that we have named the measure rather than measured the named. Gini coefficients, standard deviations, means of algebraic sums or absolute differences, ranges—bah, humbug! It is all a myth. The inequality of a distribution is a psychological phenomenon, a measurable but unmeasured perception of beholders. He suggests mental mapping may be the path to a better understanding. Social psychology in the Sherifian tradition may or may not provide the conceptual basis of quantitative measures, but, in any event, reading the essay is delightful medicine for cerebral sclerosis.

Part II of the volume contains three papers on redistributive mechanisms. The first paper (Chapter 2) by Robert Lampman, deals with measuring the redistributive impact of tax and transfer systems within the National Income Accounts framework. Starting with the basic proposition that every economy has within it mechanisms for redistributing its national product among consumers, he asks how the redistributive process can be more meaningfully monitored within the National Income Accounts than it currently is. In answer, he suggests that the household sector be subdivided to show insurance and pensions, philanthropic organizations, and families' subsectors, and that direct interfamily transfers be identified. These changes would permit the accounts to quantify the relative importance of transfers between years and between nations.

He urges government to make such changes in the official accounts, but suggests the profession should be prepared to move forward on its own.

In Chapter 3, Ben Okner imaginatively manipulates a synthetic population (the MERGE File) created from the 1966 personal income-tax model and the 1967 Survey of Economic Opportunity. Using an assortment of income concepts, Okner addresses a number of questions dealing with the distribution of tax burden a la Musgrave ("The Distribution of Tax Burden by Income Group: A Case Study for 1949," *National Tax Journal,* Vol. 4, March 1954), and with the combined redistributive impact of taxes and transfers.

Looking only at the tax burden, his results are similar to those of Musgrave, which appeared two decades ago: essentially, there is little progressivity in federal, state, and local tax systems taken as a group. Such progressivity as does exist is to be found far out in the right tail. Thus, the combined personal tax structure tends to be proportional with respect to income and, consequently, does not per se contribute significantly to income redistribution.

Transfers, on the other hand, significantly improve the income position of persons in the lower tail of the pretransfer income distribution, but they also contribute importantly to the upper tail.

Using an income concept which comes close to being consumption minus taxes plus changes in net worth, he found a 13 percent reduction in the Gini coefficient due to the combined influence of taxes and transfers.

In his early work on tax burdens, Musgrave had been forced to work with aggregated data, which precluded estimation of the tax burden for subpopulations. Using the microdata developed from the tax and survey data mentioned above, Okner was able to demonstrate that there are substantial differences in the effect of tax-transfer systems on subpopulations. For instance, where he found a 13 percent reduction in the Gini coefficient for all families, a 30 percent reduction for families with a head age 65 or over was discovered.

In Chapter 4, Harold Watts and Jon Peck use the MERGE File to simulate the redistributive consequences of a number of variants of a tax function combining a constant marginal rate and a fixed credit. They compare the before and after well-being of a set of six "family" types. The family typology, obviously selected for its relevance to the problem of welfare reform, consisted of:

1. aged individuals;

2. families with aged heads;

3. families with female heads;

4. nonaged individuals;

5. families with nonaged male heads and 2 to 5 members; and

6. families with nonaged male heads and 6 or more members.

The authors examine the before and after tax, income status of these units, and more interestingly, the before and after tax distribution of the welfare ratio (income/poverty threshold).

They conclude that the extant tax structure is differentially beneficial to the aged and to female-headed units, and that working poor families headed by males are significantly overtaxed or undertransferred. This is a finding of both economic and political significance.

Part III deals with accounting periods of lengths other than the traditional one-year period. It is noteworthy that two of the chapters in this part use large microdata sets assembled outside the federal government, and that the third uses microdata produced cooperatively by the government and Herbert Parnes.

Martin David and Roger Miller, relying on a decade of professional investment in the development of a file of Wisconsin tax returns which links families between years and individuals to their parental families, examine the importance of capital gains on the size distribution of income. They find little difference in long versus shorter accounting periods, which can be explained by the inclusion of capital gains. The reason adduced is that capital gains tend to be a recurring form of income for those who receive them.

Kohen, Parnes, and Shea (Chapter 6) examine income instability among two groups of men: those aged 14 to 24 in 1966 and a group aged 45 to 59 in the same year. The microdata used by them was collected in a joint effort by Parnes, the Department of Labor, and the Bureau of the Census and has become known as the National Longitudinal Surveys. They develop a measure of relative income instability (RIC) which is intended to measure the relative instability of an individual's income change vis-á-vis the mean change in income of his cohort.

They found that the instability of income rank was greater for blacks and for younger men generally than for whites and men in the 45 to 59 year age group.

Among whites, earnings were more stable than total family income. While the same relation was found among the older black group, the reverse was true for young blacks.

As has been found in other studies, a regression toward the mean was found when changes in income rank were compared to initial rank.

Jacob Benus and James Morgan use three sets of panel data collected by the Survey Research Center to study the influence of the unit of analysis, the accounting period, and the income concept on the size distribution of income. The first of these data sets was produced in a study of the response of consumers to the 1964 tax cut. Families were interviewed quarterly in that study and thus provided a basis for looking at short-term changes in income. The second set of data were collected from about 1,400 respondents in four interviews spaced approximately a year apart. The third data set was the Panel Study of Income Dynamics, a panel study now in its fifth year and still going on. The authors find that the unit of analysis and the concept of income have greater influence on the size distribution than does the length of the accounting period. In terms of the influence of other factors on income stability, occupation, age, and race—in that order—were found to be important.

There were no formal discussants in the session from which these papers came, but each participant was asked to provide, within the time allotted to him, such observations upon the papers of the other participants as he felt would be useful. Martin David provided a set of comments reflecting on his own joint effort with Roger Miller and on the other two papers presented in this part. David's comments are included as Chapter 8.

The three chapters of Part IV are concerned with the distribution of wealth. Lee Soltow presents estimates of the distribution of wealth, income, and social class of men in large northern cities in 1860 (Chapter 9); A. B. Atkinson writes of the distribution of wealth in England in 1968; and James Smith presents a study of the distribution of wealth in Washington, D.C., in 1967.

The Soltow piece starts with the microdata of the 1860 Census and incorporates it into a model which permits one to predict the probability of escape from a state of propertylessness—a state which was not as uncommon as one might suspect. According to Soltow's data, slightly over half of the adult males were without assets; and according to his model, the probability of remaining in a propertyless condition in a given year was .96.

Soltow also presents a model which employs a Pareto-rectangular income distribution and a conventional savings function to determine the 1860 wealth distribution.

Atkinson (Chapter 10) provides the latest available statistics of the distribution of wealth in Britain. He uses the estate multiplier method of estimating the number of wealth holders and their asset holdings in 1968.

His paper is particularly valuable not simply because it extends a long series of wealth estimates for Britain which have been made using the estate multiplier method, but because it examines the sensitivity of the estimates to a methodology which has been increasingly employed in the United States and in other parts of the world.

Atkinson presents evidence that the concentration of British wealth is not decreasing: the conventional wisdom that the richest 1 percent own one-third, and the richest 5 percent one-half, of the total wealth is more nearly correct than some recently published estimates which suggest that there has been a significant decrease in inequality of wealth in Britain. A discussion of Atkinson's paper by Kathleen Langley, herself one of the pioneers in British wealth estimates, is included at the end of Chapter 10.

Using the same technique as Atkinson, but concerning himself with Washington, D.C., Smith (Chapter 11) estimates that the total wealth of all residents of the District of Columbia was $5.5 billion in 1967. However, his focus is not upon the aggregate level of wealth or its size distribution among all residents, but upon the differences in wealth holdings of whites and blacks. He found blacks to have an average net worth of $1,000, while whites averaged $19,000. He also found that 96 percent of the black population had a net worth of under $5,000, about the same figure that Soltow's work suggests for the population as a whole in 1860.

A discussion of Smith's paper by Vito Natrella is included at the end of Chapter 11.

In Part V, two papers which served as the focal point of a session on the quality of data on income and wealth are presented. One of the papers deals with a retooled model of the former OBE income distribution series, which for many years presented family-income size distributions aligned to personal income aggregates in the National Income Accounts (NIA), but which was subjected to a major overhaul in 1962. The other paper is a test of the quality of transfer income data reported in the *Current Population Reports.* The two papers are related by the fact that they both have the Current Population Survey (CPS) as a focal point; the latter paper directly and the former indirectly, because the CPS is the basic source of income information in the redesigned OBE series.

In Chapter 12, Dorothy Projector and Judith Bretz present the results of tests of the reliability of three types of transfer reported in the CPS: (1) Social Security and railroad retirement; (2) public assistance; and (3) unemployment and workmen's compensation. They compared the incidence of reported incomes of each type of the CPS against a simulated incidence based upon the character-istics of families and individuals in the CPS file. They also compared the CPS reported receipts of transfers to administrative tallies of the numbers of persons receiving such transfers and their value.

Projector and Bretz found the characteristics of CPS respon-dents reporting transfer incomes to be consistent—or at least not inconsistent—with eligibility criteria established for specific pro-grams. They concluded, using personal income in the National Income Accounts as a standard, that all types of transfer payments were understated in the Current Population Survey. Comparing program aggregates, the CPS was found to understate the value of transfer payments by about 8 percent. The understatement was found to be greater for younger age groups than for those over 65.

In Chapter 13, Edward Budd and Daniel Radner provide a guided tour of the statistical labyrinth they negotiate in producing the BEA income size-distribution series. The BEA series is intended to produce income size-distributions which are concep-tually consistent with personal income in the National Income Accounts and such that the sum of the distributed incomes is equal to the personal income aggregate in the NIA.

The old OBE (now BEA) income size-distribution series was discontinued in 1962 because benchmark data used to relate tax and survey data had become suspect, and because the art of income size-distribution estimating was trailing far behind the science of data processing.

Budd and Radner have spent several years incorporating microdata techniques into the BEA series. They have been hampered by lack of access to direct matches of tax return and survey data, but they have made imaginative use of statistical matching procedures to overcome this impediment.

PART I

CHAPTER 1

The Pursuit of Equality

Kenneth E. Boulding

University of Colorado

In the last few generations, the pursuit of equality has had a high value for large portions of mankind. How far back the idea of equality as an ideal goes is hard to say, and it would take a good deal of historical and anthropological research to document the origins and the immense complexities of this idea. A tentative hypothesis is that it is an offshoot of monotheistic religion. An intricate polytheistic religion, such as Hinduism, is more apt to take on the social function of legitimating inequality through caste, Karma, and other devices, for where there are many gods there can be many levels of mankind. Under the trenchant monotheism of a jealous God, however, human differences diminish in the overpowering perspective of the Lord, and all men become equal in the sight of God, no matter what they are in the sight of their neighbors.

One sees much of the upheaval of the present age as a result of the mingling of two great religious traditions of mankind: one stemming from Moses and producing in turn Christianity, Islam, and Marxism; and the other stemming from the Vedas, with perhaps an independent contribution from China, producing Buddhism and present-day Hinduism. These social genetic strains, of course, are never pure. Christianity has its Trinity and the cult of the saints; mysticism everywhere has moved toward unity and the adoration of the One. Nonetheless, though this distinction may be fuzzy, it does, indeed, exist.

The pursuit of equality in some form characterizes nearly all modern secular ideologies. The United States was ushered onto the stage of history with the trumpet call, "We hold these truths to be self-evident, that all men are created equal." The democratic ideology pushes constantly toward the principle of one person, one vote; and in that sense, at least, equality of political weight. Marxism dreams, however unsuccessfully, of a classless society.

The pursuit of freedom and the pursuit of equality are equally significant ideals for the Enlightenment, even though they may not be wholly compatible. Yet the pursuit remains as elusive as the pursuit of happiness, and our different interpretations of what we mean by equality are even threatening to destroy us. Considering the enormous symbolic importance of the concept, surprisingly little serious work seems to have been done on it, philosophically, theoretically, or empirically. Perhaps the reason for this is that it is too painful, too contradictory, too confusing, and too important to be the object of anything but rhetoric.

One can see these confusions in considering the impact of the rise of the biological sciences, especially of genetics, on the idea of human equality. On the one hand, in the light of genetics, it is by no means self-evident that all men are created equal. The fertilized eggs which are the first products of the act of human creation come endowed with a great deal of common genetic material, but also with very significant differences. One thing that genetics has taught us, of course, it that a large proportion of this genetic material is common to all of us. We are as equal before deoxyribonucleic acid as we are before God. Genetics also dispels certain illusions about inequality. We know that the genetic differences within the races of mankind are greater than the differences between them, and this has undermined what might be called the "folk" genetic theory of racism.

The enormous complexity of the human genetic structure, however, still stands before us as a continent on which we have barely landed, and it is still too early to say how significant for social systems are the genetic differences among individuals. At the extremes, they are clearly significant; in the large middle range, they seem not to be highly significant; but it is very hard to identify the significant extremes—especially the extremes on the side of excellence. We know much more about genetic defects than we do about genetic superiority. In the human species, indeed, it is extraordinarily hard to disentangle biological genetics from social genetics, that is, transmission of culture. The heretics, like Professor Shockley, at least point to the depth of our ignorance in these matters. On the surface of this ignorance, however, we do seem to have a very broad consensus that in the larger dynamics of society, biological genetics has made a relatively small contribution, simply because of the widespread variety of genetic endowments. The learned obstacles to human learning, which are essentially cultural, seem far more significant than the genetic obstacles, and it is human learning that dominates social dynamics.

Equality, of course, is not the same thing as identity. A set of identical elements are equal in all respects, but we can have a set of equal elements which are equal in only some respects, not in all, and hence are not identical. It is crucial to the idea of political or social equality that men can be equal when they are different. The difficulty comes in defining what aspects of a set of human beings can be identified in which the concepts of equality or inequality are significant. In the biological species, for instance, all the adult members in good standing, as it were, are presumably equal in their capacity to interbreed. They are not all equal in survival value; otherwise, evolution would never have taken place.

The extraordinary evolutionary success of the invention of sex is due to the fact that it creates genetic inequality within the members of a single species. Unisexual species which reproduce by budding, cloning, or mitosis tend to have great genetic uniformity in individuals. This militates against genetic change, and a species either survives indefinitely in a suitable niche with practically no changes in genetic structure, like the amoeba—or if its niche is destroyed, these species likewise will perish. In sexual species there are constant redistributions of the gene pool, which is larger than that possessed by any individual, among the members of the species. This gives opportunity for much more rapid genetic mutation and introduces new patterns for survival, like sexual display.

I have argued, indeed, that the extraordinary rapidity of social evolution, by comparison with genetic evolution, is precisely because, with the development of the human nervous system, evolution passed into the field of human knowledge and became, as it were, multisexual instead of merely bisexual. The genetic structures of society, such as ideas, constitutions, organization charts, ideologies, and so on, are the result of the interaction of large numbers, not only of individual people, but of individual knowledge components. This very multisexual character of social evolution, however, makes for enormous diversity, which makes the concept of equality difficult, as we seek to identify the attributes for which equality makes sense among enormous diversity and complexity—not only of individuals but of social structures and organizations. If it is hard to identify significant equalities and inequalities, it is still harder to evaluate and prescribe along this dimension.

Equality or inequality is always, of course, a property of a distribution. A distribution implies that we can identify some aspects of each element in a set which can either be represented by a cardinal number; or in a somewhat limiting case, by an ordinal rank. We cannot get really far in this regard with ordinal numbers. We can distinguish a case of perfect equality in which all the elements of a set are bracketed in rank order, and hence all count as "first." Any deviation from this, in which more than one cardinal number has to be used to rank the elements of the set, introduces inequality. Possibly the simplest measure of inequality here would be the number of ordinal numbers necessary to rank a set, perhaps divided by the number of elements in the set. Thus, suppose we have a set of five elements. If we were to rank these first, first, first, first, and first, this is clearly perfect equality. Ranking them first, second, second, second, and second, or first, first, first, first, and second, would represent the first level of inequality. Various combinations of first, second, and third would be a higher degree of inequality, and so on. This does not seem to be satisfactory intuitively, and we reach almost instinctively for cardinal numbers; that is, when we have a rank ordering, we want to know by how much the first in rank exceeds the second, or the second the third, and so on.

Once we can identify each element of the set with a cardinal number by which a common property of all the elements is measured, many concepts of distribution and measures of inequality are possible. Suppose we take weight as our cardinally measurable quality or aspect. If we have five individuals each weighing 180 pounds, we clearly have perfect equality in weight. If the range between the highest and lowest is only 5 pounds, they are still fairly equal and might well be classified as middleweights. If the range is between 300 pounds and 100 pounds, they are obviously very unequal and could not be put in any meaningful pigeonhole assigned by weight categories. This relationship which appears between equality and taxonomy is by no means accidental. Indeed, the very possibility of taxonomy depends on the discovery of certain sets of objects in the world which are "reasonably" equal in some regard. It may be only the need for economy in language that forces us into taxonomy, but we cannot get along without it. We do not have time to specify every rose that we talk about. We develop the idea of a general class of roses, in which all roses are approximately equal, at least in their "roseness." Stereotyping is a pathological form of this taxonomic urge. If we assume that all blacks or all whites or all Jews are alike, we will be missing the richness and variety of the inhabitants of these pigeonholes and are, therefore, likely to fall into serious error.

Even when we can identify a cardinally measurable aspect of a set of elements, like weight, the problem of the measurement of inequality remains difficult, indeed, in some sense, insoluble, except as an approximation. The problem is that equality can usually be identified fairly easily. When the set with which we are concerned is a set of identically equal numbers, we know we have perfect equality. As soon as we diverge from this, however, we diverge into a vast set of sets of numbers—each of which has a certain individuality and character of its own—in which it is hard to develop a significant taxonomy and still harder to identify any index which unequivocally measures cardinally the inequality property of these sets. Thus, we know that the set 5, 5, 5, 5, 5 is equal, but is the set 1, 2, 3, 4, 5 more or less equal than the set 1, 1, 1, 1, 5? The first of these has smaller differences among pairs, the second has a subset of equality within it and then a wide difference. The difficulty here is that the significant classification, or taxonomy, of these unequal sets may not correspond to any cardinal measure that we could devise. Any measure will create a taxonomy of sets of equal inequality according to the measure, but in each of the boxes of this taxonomy we may have to put sets which are very different or significantly different from certain points of view, while sets which are significantly similar from certain points of view may find themselves in different boxes. Thus, suppose we took what is perhaps the simplest possible measure—the difference between the highest and the lowest number in the set—divided perhaps by the mean if we wish to compare sets of different sizes. An equal set will, of course, come out with an inequality of zero, which would be a property of any of these measures, but the two sets mentioned above will be equally unequal, although they are very different, even in certain properties that suggest inequality. That this is not a trivial consideration may be perceived if we consider the two sets above to be typical of two different kinds of societies, in each of which the difference between the richest and the poorest member is about the same; but in one of which, one person is rich and everybody else is equally poor, whereas in the other, there are about equal numbers of individuals in all the income classes.

A measure which concentrates simply on the two extreme members of the set dismisses, in effect, all those between them as irrelevant. It is not surprising, therefore, that more elaborate and sophisticated measures of inequality have been devised. The standard deviation takes into account the deviation of all members of the set from the mean, though in a rather peculiar way: by taking the square root of the sum of the squares of the deviations, rather than by taking the sum of the absolute values of the deviations themselves. As far as I have been able to see, the only reason for this is algebraic elegance, and there certainly seems to be nothing to suggest that as a measure of inequality the standard deviation is any better than the means of the absolute values of the deviations themselves. Again, in order to compare distributions of different sizes, both of these are usually expressed as a proportion of the mean itself, though the information that is lost by this process is sometimes quite interesting.

These principles are illustrated in Table 1, which shows five different sets of numbers, each with five elements, in line 1. Line 2 is labeled Measure I, which is the crudest and simplest possible measure in quality, the absolute difference between the largest and smallest numbers. Case 1 represents perfect equality in which all the measures are zero. Case 6 is extreme inequality. By Measure I, Cases 2, 3, and 4 are perceived as equally unequal; 5 and 6 are much more unequal than these. Line 3 is Measure II, which is the largest number minus the smallest number, divided by the mean. By this measure, Case 4 is now perceived to be more unequal than Cases 2 or 3, because of its smaller mean. Line 4 shows the mean and line 5 the deviations from the mean; line 6 is Measure III, which is the mean of the absolute deviations divided by the mean. Line 7 is Measure IV, which is the standard deviation. Line 8 shows the cumulative distribution. Line 9 shows the cumulative distribution if each number were the mean, that is, the line of equal cumulation. Line 8 corresponds to the Lorenz curve, and Line 9 to the 45° line in the Lorenz diagram if these numbers are expressed as percentages of the total. Line 10 is the deviation of the cumulative distribution from the line of equal cumulation, and line 11 is the Gini index, which is the sum of deviations of line 10

TABLE 1

		1	2	3	4	5	6
1	Case	(3,3,3,3,3[15])	(1,3,3,3,5[15])	(1,2,3,4,5[15])	(1,1,1,1,5[9])	(1,1,1,1,11[15])	(0,0,0,0,15[15])
2	Measure I (Highest − lowest)	0	4	4	4	10	15
3	Measure II $\left(\dfrac{\text{Largest − smallest}}{\text{Mean}}\right)$	0	$\dfrac{4}{3} = 1.33$	$\dfrac{4}{3} = 1.33$	$\dfrac{4}{1.8} = 2.22$	$\dfrac{10}{3} = 3.33$	$\dfrac{15}{3} = 5$
4	Mean	3	3	3	1.8	3	3
5	Deviations from mean	0,0,0,0,0	−2,0,0,0,2	−2,−1,0,1,2	−.8,−.8,−.8,−.8,3.2	−2,−2,−2,−2,8	−3,−3,−3,−3,12
6	Measure III $\left(\dfrac{\text{Mean}}{\text{Deviation}}\right)$	0	$\dfrac{4}{5 \times 3} = 0.27$	$\dfrac{6}{5 \times 3} = 0.40$	$\dfrac{0.4}{5 \times 1.8} = 0.71$	$\dfrac{16}{5 \times 3} = 1.07$	$\dfrac{24}{5 \times 3} = 1.60$
7	Measure IV $\left(\dfrac{\sqrt{\Sigma x^2}}{nM}\right)$	0	$\dfrac{\sqrt{8}}{5 \times 3} = 0.19$	$\dfrac{\sqrt{10}}{5 \times 3} = 0.21$	$\dfrac{\sqrt{12.8}}{5 \times 1.8} = 0.40$	$\dfrac{\sqrt{80}}{5 \times 3} = 0.60$	$\dfrac{180}{5 \times 3} = 1.20$
8	Cumulative distribution	3,6,9,12,15(45)	1,4,7,10,15(37)	1,3,6,10,15(35)	1,2,3,4,9(19)	1,2,3,4,15(25)	0,0,0,0,15(15)
9	Equal cumulative distribution	3,6,9,12,15(45)	3,6,9,12,15(45)	3,6,9,12,15(45)	1.8,3.6,5.4,7.2,9(27)	3,6,9,12,15(45)	3,6,9,12,15(45)
10	Cumulative deviation	0,0,0,0,0	2,2,2,2,0(8)	2,3,3,2,0(10)	.8,1.6,2.4,3.6,0(8.4)	2,4,6,8,0(20)	3,6,9,12,0(30)
11	Measure V Gini index $\left(\dfrac{\Sigma(10)}{\Sigma(9)}\right)$	0	$\dfrac{8}{45} = 0.18$	$\dfrac{10}{45} = 0.22$	$\dfrac{8.4}{27.0} = 0.31$	$\dfrac{20}{45} = 0.44$	$\dfrac{30}{45} = 0.67$

divided by the sum of the equal cumulations of line 9. The Lorenz curves for the five distributions are shown in Figure 1.

Each of these measures has some plausibility; they give rather similar results: for each measure, the order of inequality is the same if we accept the bracketing in Measures I and II—but none of them necessarily correspond to what we would find if we asked people to rate a large number of different sets on a subjective scale of inequality. This indeed would be an interesting subject for an experiment, which could easily be done with the techniques of Kenneth Hammond's Cognograph.[1] We really do not know much about what the actual cues are which people pick up from given distributions in assessing the degree of inequality which they represent. One way of approaching this problem would be to calculate the higher moments of distribution and see how far these affected people's judgments of inequality. It might well be judged,

[1] K. R. Hammond, "Computer Graphics as an Aid to Learning," *Science* 72 (1971):903-8.

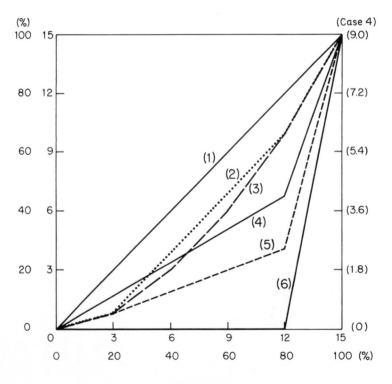

FIGURE 1

for instance, that distributions with the same standard deviation, but which differed in skewness, would be perceived as having greater inequality—with perhaps the more skewed distribution being perceived as more unequal. Other characteristics of distributions, however, which may not even be describable by the higher moments may also come into play. It would be extremely interesting to ask people to classify different distributions and see if there is anything like a subjective taxonomy of these things. A whole field of fascinating psychological experiments seems to be opening up at this point.

An even more fundamental question than the measurement of inequality is its evaluation. We could expand the psychological experiment suggested in the preceding paragraph and ask people to choose out of the six distributions shown in line 1, Table 1, which of each possible pair they prefer. This is by no means impossible. If we can get people to express their preferences between North and South Dakota,[2] we can surely get them to express their preferences between Case 1 and Case 2.

It will be rightly objected that the preferences will depend on what people think the distributions are distributing. Suppose, for instance, in Table 1 that each unit represented 50 pounds of weight. Case 1 would then be five people each weighing 150 pounds. Case 2 would be one kindergartner, three young men, and a fatty. Case 3 could well be a kindergartner, a schoolboy, a young man, an adult, and a fatty. Case 4 would be four kindergartners and a fatty. Case 5 would be four kindergartners and a circus freak, and Case 6 would be four ghosts and a freak. It would certainly be quite reasonable to ask people which group they would prefer to be with, and to extend this inquiry to a large number of other cases.

This illustrates the problem that every distribution is not simply a set of numbers but is a gestalt, and that no matter how many descriptive moments of the distribution we formulate, we will never be able to capture its peculiar gestalt property. What we are pursuing, therefore, is not really equality, except in the very special case in which Case 1, Table 1, is the gestalt which happens to be highest on everybody's value ordering. This seems unlikely, unless everybody happens to be looking for a peer group.

[2] Peter R. Gould, "On Mental Maps," in Roger M. Downs and David Stea, eds., *Cognitive Mapping and Spatial Behavior* (Chicago: Aldine, 1973).

It is not surprising that the problem of the optimum degree of inequality is difficult and perhaps insoluble. The value ordering of the different cases in Table 1 may not correspond to the ordering of our judgment of the amount of inequality simply because our value ordering depends on other things besides inequality, and depends, indeed, on our perception of the whole set of properties of the distribution, some of which we may not even be aware of except subconsciously. Thus, suppose in Table 1 that our subjective ordering of the six cases according to the degree of inequality (from low to high) was 1, 4, 2, 3, 5, 6, and that our ordering according to preference or value (low to high), was 6, 1, 5, 4, 2, 3. (We dislike teenagers and ghosts, and like a warm variety of people.) These seem to be not wholly implausible valuations, assuming that these are parties of people with which one might want to spend a day. If, however, we plot value against inequality, as in Figure 2, there seems to be hardly any linear relationship. There may be evidence of an "Aristotelian mean" at medium inequality (Case 3), but even this may be spurious. We may like Cases 2 and 3 for reasons not connected with inequality.

If now the judgment of equality were the only factor in determining our judgment of value, we would have something like Figure 3, with perfect correlation between equality and value. We very often assume situations like that depicted in Figure 3 almost unconsciously when we are trying to set a value on single components or dimensions of the system, yet one suspects that the condition shown in Figure 2 is much more common than that shown in Figure 3.

The above considerations should have some impact on our consideration of economic equality or inequality. Here we do seem to have a measure, indeed at least two measures—one of wealth and the other of income—which have the appearance of cardinality in the sense that for each individual we can usually attach some sort of number in dollar terms to measure his wealth and income. We can then get distributions of these numbers which we can express, for instance, in a frequency diagram or in a Lorenz curve, and we could apply any of the five measures outlined above—and no doubt half a dozen others that we could think up on fairly short notice. In economics, we are accustomed to thinking of a "theory of distribution" (which usually seems to apply only to the distribution of income), in which we discuss the forces which lead to personal distribution of income and its

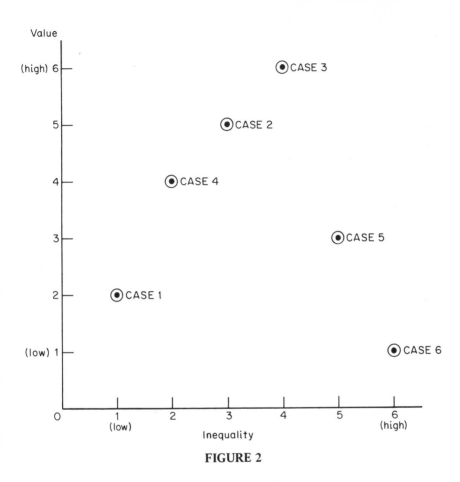

FIGURE 2

equality or inequality. A good deal of social policy is justified on the grounds that it changes the distribution of income, the usual justification being that it makes this distribution more equal. Progressive taxation is usually defended on these grounds, and so are welfare payments, agricultural subsidies, public housing, the war on poverty, and so on. It is almost always assumed that there is a high correlation between some measure of equality and some estimate of social value.

I find myself in profound sympathy with much of the social-value function which underlies the pursuit of equality. I have no liking for feudal societies (Case 4 in Table 1), still less liking for slave societies (Case 5 in Table 1), and still less for totally mechanized utopias (Case 6 in Table 1). I must confess, however,

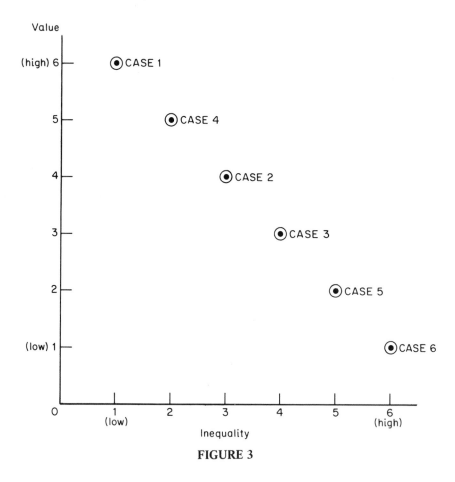

FIGURE 3

that I am bothered by the apparent simplicity of the picture which is presented, largely because the quantification in terms of dollars is, in part, at any rate, an illusion. The dollars that we write down to represent somebody's income (or wealth), in fact represent a very long heterogeneous list of quantities of commodities. Income (or wealth) is not, therefore, a number of homogeneous "dollars," in which all the units are alike, but a vast array of heterogeneous things. A $5,000 a year income for one person may represent genteel poverty, living in grandfather's big old house, eating very little meat, not having a car, wearing last year's clothes, and so on. For another person, $5,000 might mean a large alcohol consumption, neglect of his family, considerable expenditure on prostitutes, and skimping on medical care. We make pigeonholes labeled, say, $5,000–$6,000 or

$30,000–$31,000, and proceed to put all people who have the stated incomes into these pigeonholes. Then, when we look inside each box, we find that we have a fantastically heterogeneous collection of people. In the lower one, we note ministers, graduate students, factory workers, owners of corner groceries, small farmers, landlords, little old ladies living on a pension in Miami, welfare families, and so on. In the upper one, we come upon professors, corporation executives, politicians, gamblers, real estate speculators, coupon clippers. Each list appears endless.

This is not to deny that there are important differences between the $5,000 group and the $30,000 group. The differences within each group, however, may be just as interesting as the differences between them and possibly even more significant. Thus, we are apt to fall into an "income prejudice" very similar to the fallacy of race prejudice. That is, we assume that because people are alike in one quality or measure, they are alike in others. Income prejudice is even worse in some sense, because whereas all black people do presumably have rather similar chromosomes producing melanin, people having $5,000 a year may not even have any special genetic qualities or any consumption pattern in common.

One justification for the great illusive simplicities of economics is perhaps that by simplifying things we may make it easier to do something about them. The concept of income poverty is particularly appealing in this respect. At any one time, we can define a level of income in dollar terms which marks the lower limits of what is socially acceptable and the upper limits of what is defined as poverty. We can then calculate how much we have to redistribute to people with incomes below this level in order to bring them up to it. In a rich society like the United States, it usually turns out that the amount we have to redistribute in order to eliminate income poverty is well within our fiscal resources, generally on the order of ten or twenty billion dollars. This seems like doing a great deal of good with a relatively small proportion of the GNP. Following the principle that the size of the grants economy is largely dependent on the grantor's perceptions of its efficiency—that is, how much good it does per dollar—economics of this kind would certainly seem to lead to a rhetoric for doing good which one would hate to question.

Nevertheless, somebody has to bear in mind, even if he keeps quiet about it, that the distribution of income is not really very much like the cutting up of a pie. This "pie," so beloved of popular expositors of economics, is a very dangerous image. It suggests that somebody makes the pie and then somebody else cuts it and distributes it. The truth is that the pie is a vast heterogeneous mass of artifacts and activities, so that it is an almost grotesque abstraction to suppose that we can put a single number on it and call it the GNP or national income, and an even greater abstraction to suppose that this single number can be divided among the population. What is really divided is not dollars but Volkswagons and dinners in a nightclub, church services and pants suits, in a medley that makes shoes, ships, and sealing wax look relatively homogeneous. There is no "division of the pie." Instead, there is a vast free school with everybody doing his own thing and making his own tartlets in his own little corner.

I am almost tempted to say that there is no such thing as the distribution of income. I cannot go quite that far, because it is a useful abstraction, but it is very dangerous to forget what a very abstract abstraction it is. I am prepared to give at least one cheer when the Gini index goes down, but my second cheer is paralyzed by the reflection that societies with the same Gini index, or even the same Lorenz curve, may be enormously different in quality, in the sense of community and the overall patterns of life and consumption. At what point then, one asks oneself, is it better to put effort into making a better society with the same income distribution rather than changing the distribution in the hope that such a change automatically makes things better? One worries also about the costs of greater equality in terms of the sacrifice of other social values, such as freedom, variety, and so on.

The pursuit of equality, which looks on first inspection like a very decent and well-ordered chase, has, on closer inspection, alarming tendencies to turn into a caucus race with everybody running off in all directions. We should take a brief look, therefore, at some of the different equalities that might be pursued. A favorite one in American society is, of course, equality of opportunity. It is often implied that if we have equality of opportunity without achieving equality of income, it will be because some people were virtuous and took advantage of their opportunities, whereas others were lazy no-goods who did not take advantage of opportunities open to them, i.e., laggards who richly deserve their poverty. Equality of opportunity, therefore, all too easily becomes a device like Karma for justifying existing inequalities of status and income. The doctrine of Karma is, indeed, an extreme expression of cosmic equality of opportunity; every soul presumably starts from scratch, and if you happen to find yourself in 1972 as a starving manure collector, it is no doubt because you missed some opportunities in an earlier incarnation. Nevertheless, the equality of opportunity ideal is not to be repudiated outright. It is a weapon in the attack on something which everybody despises unless he has it—that is, privilege. The struggle against what have been felt to be unfair privileges has been an important element in human history for a long time, and we cannot deny there is a great deal of validity in it.

Now, however, we run into another hornet's nest, which is the problem of equality in luck, or uncertainty. Suppose the State of New York, in a fit of madcap generosity, gave everybody in the state a ticket for the state lottery free of charge. What could be more equal? Yet the result, once the tickets are drawn, is a vast inequality, with the winners becoming rich and the losers perhaps a little poorer. The delicate line between the excitement of gambling and the staid respectabilities of insurance is one of the trickiest questions in the evaluation of societies. Would we really want a society in which there was no luck, no uncertainty—one in which everything bad that happened to you was clearly and unmistakably your own fault? Where there is luck, however, there will be inequality, and a society of total cradle to grave no-fault insurance on everything begins to look a little bit like a spiritual Great Plains. We cannot really say peaks Yes, and valleys No, for the only way to get rid of the valleys is to bulldoze the peaks into them. These are moral dilemmas of a high order which underlie, largely subconsciously, a good deal of current discussion, and they contain so much dynamite that one hesitates even to bring them out of the cave.

In a recent paper,[3] I compared the search for justice to the search for the Holy Grail, something which might never be found, and perhaps might even be nonexistent, but the search for which created enormous side benefits. The pursuit of equality is perhaps the most important single part of the search for justice. The quarry is elusive and it is manifold, sometimes seeming like a great herd of pure white unicorns who shoot off in all directions.

[3] K. E. Boulding, "Social Justice as a Holy Grail: The Endless Quest," in Melvin J. Lerner and Michael Ross, eds., *The Quest For Justice: Myth Reality, Ideal* (Toronto: Holt, Rinehart and Winston of Canada, forthcoming).

Nevertheless, what we are pursuing is something real. It cannot be dismissed as a will-o'-the-wisp.

The most satisfactory human relationships are those which are based on some kind of equality—equality of status if nothing else. The unequal hierarchical relationship of superior and subordinate always seems to be corrupting. It corrupts the information system, for the subordinate is apt to tell a superior what he thinks will please him rather than the truth. It is likewise apt to give the superior delusions of grandeur and the subordinate delusions of inferiority, both of which corrupt the process of human learning and development.

The pursuit of equality is also an important component of the search for what might be called "disalienation," the development of a society from which nobody feels excluded, and in which everybody feels that he has value as a person. The net moral worth, that is, the sum of each person's evaluation of himself as a person, is a much more fundamental measure of the value of the society than the gross national product, which can never be more than a collection of intermediate goods.

The pursuit of equality is likely to become more urgent and more important as we move toward the "spaceship earth" and the more stationary society which seems to lie ahead as the human race expands to the capabilities of its niche. The progressive state, as Adam Smith says, is both "hearty and cheerful," partly, at least, because it helps in the legitimation of existing inequalities if those at the bottom end of the scale feel that they have a good chance of rising. In a progressive state, everybody can rise absolutely, if not relatively. In a stationary state, the only way in which the poor can get richer is for the rich to get poorer. This is by no means an agreeable state of affairs. Unless there is a strong legitimation for downward mobility—this is perhaps the real significance of the counterculture—the slowdown toward the stationary state opens up grim possibilities: either increasing social disorganization as a society becomes incapable of legitimating existing inequalities, or a retreat into a kind of Hobbesian tyranny and an attempt to end the war of all against all by a new Leviathan. It may be that the real significance of the radical egalitarian societies, such as Cuba and China, is that they may be at least one means of legitimating stagnation. It is clear that in the next five hundred years, the challenge of finding the right kinds of equality, and the optimum degrees of equality, will be perhaps the greatest confronting the political and social thought of the human race.

The pursuit of equality is a metaphor and the pursuit of any metaphor, if carried too far, will lead us over a cliff. In this case, the quarry is itself the hunter. One is reminded of Pogo's great principle, "We have met the enemy and he is us." I have formulated what I have called "D'Arcy Thomson's law," for the great biologist and author of *Growth and Form*. It states that "everything is what it is because it got that way." The state of affairs today is the result of the whole process of the universe through time. If any distribution is unequal today, it is because the dynamic processes which produced it made it that way. The inequality of genetic endowment is the result of the whole process of evolutionary mutation and selection. Inequality of capital endowments is the result of a rather similar process by which property grows, declines, is redistributed, and inherited. The distribution of income is largely a function of the distribution of property, including property in bodies and minds, modified by the "grants economy," that is, by one-way transfers or redistributions. The grants economy is also a result of a long historical process, the building up of integrative structures, families, communities, nations, or of threat structures.

When we pursue equality, therefore, we are not pursuing something which is different from ourselves. We are, however, attempting to introduce conscious objectives into the overall dynamic process of society. All we can ever hope to change is parameters. Often, we cannot change them much. Nevertheless, we can change them significantly. We can introduce progressive taxation, inheritance taxes, inheritance regulations, subsidies to rectify inherited deficiencies, Head Start, educational subsidies, boarding schools for the children of the poor, birth control propaganda, and so on. Any one of these things changes the parameters of the dynamics of the system, moving it either toward or away from greater equality, or toward or away from other desirable objectives. Understanding the relations between the parameters of the dynamic process is a great task in the social sciences. Without such understanding public policy is virtually blind and inexorably subject to what I have called the "law of political irony"—that almost everything we do to help people hurts them, and everything we do to hurt them helps them.

The virtues and the excitement of the pursuit of equality,

however, must never blind us to the fact that what we are ultimately pursuing is the good. This is the real Holy Grail, and equality is only one of the arguments, although a very significant one, in the total goodness function. Putting equality in its place, finding out what its costs are, is again part, and perhaps the largest part, of the great task which lies ahead.

PART II

REDISTRIBUTIVE MECHANISMS

CHAPTER 2

Social Accounting for Transfer

Robert J. Lampman
University of Wisconsin

What is the nature and scope of the "system" for redistribution—that set of positive and negative transfers, some public and some private, some in the form of money and some nonmoney—in the contemporary political economy of the United States? What kind of social accounting for that system could serve best the task, as Paul Fisher sees it, of "devising a more rational ordering of priorities among competing demands for programs directed to the betterment of society?"[1] Can the economic accounts be revised to show us more about redistribution, in order, as Arthur Okun puts it, to "evaluate the extent to which our society fulfills its egalitarian objectives."[2]

This paper is addressed to these questions and has been written in the belief that the broad frame of the national income and product account, and of the sectoral income and outlay accounts, is necessary to (though not sufficient for) a full appreciation of the transfer process. At the same time, I find that some revised sectoring and additions to the list of transfers in the official accounts would clarify the response to the questions stated above. That such revision may be necessary will not surprise those who have been taught that the income and product account's representation of the nation as a coherent behavioral entity is restricted in scope to the goods and services "throughput" of the market sector of the economy. All would agree with Edgar S. Dunn, Jr., that there are policy and management issues for which this account does not yield an appropriate set of integrated statistics.[3]

---

[1] Paul Fisher, "Social Reports of the German Federal Republic, 1970-71," *Social Security Bulletin* (July 1972):16.

[2] Arthur Okun, "Social Welfare Has No Price Tag," *Survey of Current Business* 51, no. 7, part 2 (July 1971):133.

[3] Edgar S. Dunn, Jr., "The National Economic Accounts: A Case Study of the Evolution Toward Integrated Statistical Information Systems," *Survey of Current Business* 51, no. 7, part 2 (July 1971):49.

However, I move cautiously in suggesting revisions, seeking to follow George Jaszi's guideline that changes should be based upon a clear perception of fundamental historic processes and useful predictive processes rather than upon "the fancies of isolated research subcultures."[4] I recognize limitations in the one-year accounting period but see merit in the discipline of the double-entry system and in the paradigm of the circular flow of spending and income in which—to paraphrase Kendrick—the "final" production of goods and services that men want gives rise to the primary income flows which, together with income redistribution, provide the incomes that the various sectors and subsectors spend and invest either directly or through financial or other types of intermediaries.[5] I accept the distinction, which is implicit in the accounts, between transfer receipts and income generated by production, and the separation of secondary or redistributive flows from primary or distributive ones. I seek to improve analysis of the transfer process while retaining the basic frame of the accounting system. It is my belief that this offers the best hope of understanding how our political economy answers several interlocking questions: Who gets the product? What is the composition of that product? What is the level of activity?

In the discussion that follows, we first look at how the existing system of accounts portrays the process of transfer. Second, we suggest how a more inclusive identification of transfer and consequent additions to GNP, and some deconsolidation of the household sector, would modify that portrayal. Third, we explore the issues involved in going inside a family sector to find how positive and negative transfers may affect the sharing of final income.

Two disclaimers must be put forward. The transfers we are studying are identified with, and are a part of, a particular institutional setting within which individuals act and react, and economic accounting offers us little insight into the modifications of price, effort, saving, and family responsibility which might follow from a change in transfers. Hence, the counterfactual of an income distribution which would exist in the absence of transfer, or with a very different scheme for transfer, is scarcely a credible

---

[4] George Jaszi, "An Economic Accountant's Ledger," *Survey of Current Business* 51, no. 7, part 2 (July 1971):227.

[5] John W. Kendrick, *Economic Accounts and Their Uses* (New York: McGraw-Hill, 1972), p. 21.

concept. The other caution is that economic accounting cannot pierce the money veil and tell us whether transferring increases the community's total of satisfactions or welfare. Perhaps, however, better recording of such transfers will stimulate further research into these questions, which accountants can suggest but cannot answer.

I. TRANSFERS IN EXISTING SYSTEM OF ACCOUNTS

To begin with, let us see how far the present income and product account, and the income and outlay accounts for the several sectors, take us in our pursuit. A transfer is generally defined as a payment or receipt for which less than fully reciprocal specific payment is made or good or service is exchanged in the current period. The payment may be voluntary or coerced. This means that all taxes are transfers, as are gifts and, it may be argued, insurance contributions intended to benefit third parties. Transfers may be received via government agencies or private intermediaries or directly from a personal giver in the form of an interfamily transfer. Conversely, negative transfers may be made from any sector to another.

The statement of national product, of course, shows no trace of transfer—only the purchase of final product by sectors. We can loosely translate that purchasing as consumption by households, investment by business, and public use by government. The parallel income statement, however, reveals what we will identify as transfers to be an important component of charges against the gross national product. Those transfer items that involve the business sector as a payer or receiver include the following nonfactor charges: indirect business taxes, subsidies to business, current losses of government enterprises, and business transfer payments to households (which comprise write-off of consumer bad debts and contributions to philanthropic organizations). Business transfers also include three factor-cost items: corporate profit taxes, employer contributions for social insurance, and similar contributions for private insurance (carried under the heading "other labor income").

To find other transfer items, one must look to secondary flows recorded in the sectoral accounts, but not in the national income and product account. These are nonbusiness items and include personal tax and nontax payments and personal contributions for social insurance (but not those for private insurance), and government transfer payments to persons. They also include net interest paid by government and interest paid by consumers; these, for several reasons, I would elect to leave out of the list of transfer items. Net interest paid by government is considered a transfer, since it is largely a payment for service on a debt incurred in past wars and, hence, has no counterpart in current product. Consumer interest is justified as other than primary income because no imputation to product is made for the services of lenders. Both of these items seem to defy the ordinary definition of transfer in the sense that the *recipients* have supplied a reciprocal service in the current period. For this reason, I would elect to leave them out.

The transfer items now recorded in the accounts, aside from the two mentioned, may be related systematically to one another in the fashion shown by Table 1. In it are enumerated the items listed above and the movement of each across sectors. In this simplified version, I leave out "the rest of the world" and assume that business is the only employer. Transfers flow from and to the business sector, as well as from and to governments and

TABLE 1   Transfers (Positive and Negative) by Sector

| | Sectors | | |
Transfer Item	Busi- ness	Govern- ment	House- holds
Charges against GNP			
Indirect business taxes	–	+	
Subsidies to business	+	–	
Current loss of government enterprises	+	–	
Business transfer payments to households	–		+
Employer contributions for social insurance	–	+	
Other labor income	–		+
Corporate profits tax	–	+	
Other than charges against GNP			
Personal tax and nontax payments		+	–
Personal contributions for social insurance		+	–
Government transfer payments to persons		–	+
Balancing			
Transfer receipts less transfer payments	–	+	–

households. Households are defined to include not only families but insurance carriers and philanthropic organizations such as churches, private schools, and charitable foundations. The system of transfers reflected in the table does not produce a balance of transfers paid and transfers received, since there is no requirement that transfer receipts must be respent for transfer purposes. In particular, government will ordinarily spend its receipts of transfers largely for purchases (none of which is now identified as transfer to other sectors). The flow of transfer is back and forth among the sectors, with governments serving as intermediary. Transfers may be seen as emerging out of the primary income in the form of business receipts from the sale of final product. This primary income less capital consumption is disbursed to the nonbusiness sectors, some of it as transfer (as shown in Table 1) and some of it as nontransfer (not shown). The transfer and nontransfer income of the nonbusiness sectors is, in turn, moved back and forth (only transfers are shown in Table 1) among the several sectors with residual amounts (not shown) available for the next round of final purchases (not shown).

II. SUGGESTED REVISIONS OF EXISTING ACCOUNTS

How could we improve upon Table 1 and the present accounts which it reflects? One way would be to deconsolidate the households sector to show families as distinct from financial intermediaries and philanthropic organizations. Establishing a separate "insurance and pension" subsector would enable us to show employer and employee contributions to fringe-benefit insurance and pension funds, and outpayments from those funds to families. Setting out a separate subsector for philanthropies would identify the business and nonbusiness contributions to, and the outpayments from, such organizations. Both insurance and philanthropies make payments on bases quite different from return for current service and hence are part of a transfer system. However, philanthropies, unlike insurance intermediaries, may operate like governments in having residuals for nontransfer purposes. This deconsolidation is pictured in Table 2, which assumes that the current receipts and current outpayments of insurance and pension funds are equal.

Further questions about the adequacy of Table 1 take us to reconsideration of the definition of the term transfer. The existing

TABLE 2   Revisions to Table 1, Transfers (Positive and Negative) by Sector[a]

Transfer Item[b]	Sectors				
	Business	Government	Insurance and Pensions	Philanthropic Organizations	Families
Business transfers to households					
In money	−			+	+
In kind	−			+	+
Other labor income	−		+		
Government transfers to persons					
In kind		−			+
Personal tax and nontax payments					
In kind		+			−
Personal contribution to insurance			+		−
Personal contribution to philanthropic organizations				+	−
Insurance payments to persons					
In money			−		+
In kind			−		+
Philanthropic organizations contribution to persons					
In money				−	+
In kind				−	+
Balancing					
Receipts of transfer less payment of transfer			0[c]	+[d]	

[a] The household sector is resectored into the insurance and pensions sector, the philanthropic organizations sector, and the families sector.
[b] Items not presently shown as transfers in the National Income Accounts.
[c] Zero, by definition, as discussed in text.
[d] Positive, by definition, as discussed in text.

accounts restrict the use of the term to quite explicit transactions, such as taxes and social insurance contributions. We have already suggested that it takes only a small leap to consider employer and employee contributions to collectively bargained insurance funds as transfers. It may not be a great leap from that to think of certain other types of pure insurance (as opposed to saving) contracts as being in the nature of transfers. Certainly, from the point of view of many beneficiaries (commonly somewhat removed from the contractor), insurance proceeds are similar to government transfer payments.

It is likely that businesses make some transfers that are now counted as factor payments and others that are "lost" in intermediate product. Consider the following: wages are paid to an employee during the time he is sick;[6] a good or service is sold below cost to some customers with the loss recouped by higher charges to others (this practice, as followed by doctors with sliding scales of fees or public utilities, is akin to private means testing); the services of an executive, while he is on the company payroll, are made available to a philanthropic agency; free on-the-job training is extended to employees; radio and TV broadcasts are made available to consumers at zero price (this could be identified as a transfer to the family sector, or, as Ruggles and Ruggles[7] suggest, it could be carried as a nontransfer in the form of consumption by business). On the assumption that all these are properly identified as transfers, they should be included in Table 2.

Also not recorded in the existing accounts are certain transfers from households to the other sectors. Thus, it can be argued that the opportunity cost of being frictionally unemployed—and thereby contributing to the overall efficiency of the economy—is a transfer from families to business.[8] Similarly, military conscripts who supply labor at less than opportunity cost are party to a transfer.

But probably the most significant quantity of nonrecorded transfer is transfers in kind by government to private beneficiaries.

[6] David L. Grove calls for OBE to produce an addendum item on compensation for time not worked in "Survey Readers at IBM," *Survey of Current Business,* 51, no. 7, part 2 (July 1971):92.

[7] Richard Ruggles and Nancy Ruggles, *The Design of Economic Accounts* (New York: National Bureau of Economic Research, 1970).

[8] Kendrick, *Economic Accounts and Their Uses,* p. 123.

To say that all government purchases are part of final product and hence beyond the count of income is, of course, correct in an accounting sense, but the statement overlooks the fact that, in many instances at least, government buys goods or services for specific persons. The line between giving a person money to make a consumer purchase and making, on his behalf, the purchase (or a fraction of it) of a good he consumes is not a meaningful line. But, some may object, if we admit that some purchases by governments (or philanthropies or health insurance carriers) are properly counted as transfers to households, there may be no logical dividing line separating purchases for transfer from other purchases. The guideline for such a separation is, we assert, to identify those publicly purchased goods which have a broad analogue in private markets and which, potentially at least, have a largely exclusive benefit to a single person or family.[9] Incidentally, this same test, if applied to purchases for business firms, might produce a substantial list of what should be called transfers in kind to business. The word *exclusive* implies that we are talking about items that are not pure public goods. The principal items in this category are purchases of health and education services, along with food and housing. Nontransfer purchases by government are, of course, financed by the difference between transfers received and transfers made by government.

The government income and outlay account could show a transfer in kind simply by dividing purchases into those for "transfers in kind" and those for "other purposes." This shows the employment-generating purchase in the government sector. The personal sector account could carry entries in parentheses, crediting (transfers in kind) and debiting (consumption of transfers in kind).

This seems plausible enough when the transfer takes the form of food or housing, but not so plausible when it is education, which is more in the nature of an investment good which may not yield returns for some years. To account for education as a capital transfer, the accounting of each sector should be divided into

---

[9] For a discussion of this issue and one resolution of it, see *Social Welfare Expenditures, 1929-1966*, Social Security Administration Research Report No. 25, 1972, pp. 11-16. Also see Alfred M. Skolnik and Sophie R. Dales, "Social Welfare Expenditures, 1971-72," *Social Security Bulletin* (December, 1972):3-17.

current and capital accounts.[10] The personal sector's capital account would then show a credit of transfer of capital from government and a debit of accumulation through capital transfer of education. The current account of the personal sector would enter human capital consumption as a deduction from income.

Until the substantial revision of accounts referred to is accomplished, there is no option open to us but to carry education along with other transfers in kind as "income" to the beneficiaries. Training financed by business presents a similar consumption versus investment problem. Kendrick suggests that the "costs of rearing children to working age" is in the same category.[11] The latter would be a transfer if paid for by government.

Table 2 presents all the revisions to the existing accounts discussed above. (This table needs to be read in conjunction with Table 1.) No division of transfer into current and capital is suggested, but resectoring is indicated, and new transfer items in money and in kind are included. A residual for nontransfer purposes is indicated for the philanthropic organizations sector.

Table 1, along with the revisions in Table 2, gives a complete picture of intersectoral transfer. We can, without conceptual difficulties, regroup the tax and transfer items listed in Tables 1 and 2 and attribute each of them to "all families" in the manner suggested in Table 3. (Only broad headings for groups of transfer items are shown. The complete table should carry a detailed list of money and in-kind items.) To get a total of all transfers exclusive of intrafamily transfer, we need to add interfamily transfers. One can pretend that these transfers move into and out of an imaginary "interfamily transfer fund."

The discrepancy between transfer payments and transfer receipts in the "all families" column quantifies one result of the transfer process, namely, the giving up of income to government and philanthropic sectors. The total of transfer receipts has special interest as an indicator of the importance of transfer. This is the part of families' final income which has been shuffled about through intermediaries rather than coming directly to them in the form of factor income. This particular total—or, rather, something

---

[10] Kendrick, *Economic Accounts and Their Uses,* pp. 128-30. Also see Dudley Seers and Richard Jolly, "The Treatment of Education in National Accounting," *Review of Income and Wealth* (1966):195-208.

[11] Kendrick, *Economic Accounts and Their Uses,* p. 124.

TABLE 3 Transfer Payments and Receipts Attributed to Families, by Groups of Families

			Family Sector			
	All Families		*Group A Families*		*Group B Families*	
Item	*Payments*	*Receipts*	*Payments*	*Receipts*	*Payments*	*Receipts*
Business taxes and transfers						
Intersectoral nonbusiness taxes and transfers						
Interfamily transfers						
Total transfer receipts and total transfer payments						
Balancing						
Receipts less payments						

close to it—is sometimes related to GNP to suggest the relative significance of transfers. Note that if this is done with the expanded list of transfer items listed here, we must be careful to add certain of the transfers, e.g., the training paid for by business, to official GNP. Also note that the apparent significance of transfers would be altered if one were to gross up GNP to include such nontransfer items as home production of housewives and rental value of consumer durables. But perhaps it would make more sense to relate total transfers to GNP less capital consumption and less governmental and philanthropic outlays for non-transfer purposes. In other words, relate the transfer receipts of families to what might have been available as factor income after financing consumption by business, government, and philanthropies.

The transfer receipts and payments by "all families" conveys a good deal of information about the functions and sources of transfer. However, these data could be rearranged to show how much of the "nation's transfer budget" goes to such functions as those detailed in the Social Budget of the German Federal Republic as sickness, invalidity, death, unemployment, old age, large families, training, employment, housing, and restitution. The sources in that budget are government, nongovernment for certain "social security-related measures," and indirect measures such as tax relief.[12] We should note that our "all families" totals will not allow a separate presentation of tax relief by function. However, when families are divided into groups as discussed below, the differential tax payments will reflect tax preferences by group.

We have deliberately spread our net wide in order to catch all the transfer in a modern mixed economy having several identifiable sectors. This should mean that it is also wide enough to serve for comparative study of quite differently structured economies. Consider first an economy where the market sector is less important and home production is more important, and where there is no separate insurance nor private philanthropy sector. In such an economy, one would expect most transfer to be done within the family sector. The key problem for social accountants is to distinguish factor income from transfer income and to standardize across countries the definition of the primary family. The interfamily transfers via the extended family may be largely in kind.

[12] Fisher, "Social Reports," p. 16.

The challenge to the accountant may be even greater in the case of another structure: namely, an economy that is advanced in the sense that there is little home production, but where production is largely socialized and government is unitary. In such an economy, most transfer goes on between an undifferentiated government sector and a family sector, yet such transfer may be hidden by a failure to account for the distinction between transfer and producer income or between taxes and prices (as reflections of costs) paid. In actuality, most socialist economies do have some institutions and accounts which make possible some estimates of communal consumption and of payments to nonproducers.

III. ACCOUNTING FOR REDISTRIBUTION WITHIN THE FAMILY SECTOR

Although considerable interest attaches to the listing of total transfer receipts for "all families," we still do not have a good indication of how the transfer system enters into the determination of the distribution of final income *among* families. To make any inroads on that topic we need to make some big leaps away from present practices of national income accountants.[13] Let us divide all families into two socially significant groups, A and B. Then, by careful survey of money income and valuation of items in kind, determine the total amount of final income (including undistributed corporation profits), after all transfer, positive and negative, which is received by all families. Divide the total between group A and group B. Next, add back each positive and negative transfer to arrive at a total of pretransfer income for each group. This process requires, of course, considerable estimation and imputation and must rely on information from household surveys and from records of business firms, government agencies, and others supplying transfers in kind. Key decisions must be made with regard to tax incidence. In undertaking to do this, one finds that one of the more troublesome issues has to do with the balancing item shown in Table 3. This is equal to nontransfer

[13] At least this is the case in the United States. However, in the United Kingdom, official estimates have been produced over the last decade of the redistributive effects, by income class, of all taxes and of all cash and noncash government and social service benefits. See "The Incidence of Taxes and Social Service Benefits in 1971," *Economic Trends*, no. 229 (November, 1972).

outlays by governments and philanthropies and is the difference between total pretransfer income, less capital consumption, and posttransfer income for all families.

How is one to apportion this "discrepancy" between groups A and B? One way is to ignore it in the same way we handle capital consumption. In other words, simply assert that the pretransfer income is the income left after consumption by business, government, and philanthropies has been financed. That is not altogether satisfying because the taxes and contributions financing that consumption are transfers and they must have redistributive impact. The other way to handle it is to include the nontransfer outlays and to apportion them between group A and group B so as to have no redistributive impact. That is, give each group as a receipt the same proportion of this total as it has of final income. This particular method of apportionment as it applies to government consumption has been objected to by Henry Aaron and Martin McGuire on the ground that people in group A may like public goods more than do those in group B.[14] One might raise the same point with regard to capital consumption, since some people have more interest in future output than do others. This objection calls for extending income accounting beyond the measurement of money flows and the money value of flows in kind to the measurement of satisfactions, something which we do not know how to do. However, the objection is well taken as a caution in interpreting the findings with regard to income redistribution accomplished. Those findings can be stated in terms of how the share of pretransfer income received by group A relates to its share of posttransfer income.

One important matter for decision by the social accountant has to do with division of the population into groups. Here, as in the decision with regard to functional breakdown of transfer receipts,

---

[14] Henry Aaron and Martin McGuire, "Public Goods and Income Distribution," *Econometrica*, 38, no. 6 (November 1970):907-20. L. Stiefel, E. Smolensky, and M. Schmundt make a similar point with reference to the possibility that recipients of transfers in kind may value them at less than cost but that donors of such transfers may get satisfaction from making the transfer, which offsets some of the dissatisfaction from paying for it. One implication of this insight is that a straightforward money accounting may be said to overstate the redistribution of satisfactions from rich to poor ("Modifications for In-Kind Transfer Entries in the National Income Accounts," processed, Madison, Wisconsin, Working Paper No. 7, 1972).

one should have in mind broad social goals. Income classes or welfare-ratio[15] groups are undoubtedly important, but a well-rounded study will include divisions by such characteristics as age, sex, education, work status of head, and location of residence. Such a diversity of breakdowns would do a great deal to enlighten us concerning the consequences of the system of transfers.

We have asserted that social accounting for transfer should develop in two stages. One would bring us a picture of all types of tranfer across a revised sectoring of the economy. The second would describe how transfer modifies the share of total product going to various groups of families within the population.

[15] For rough estimates of how much the pretransfer poor gain from the American system of transfers, see Robert Lampman, "Transfer Approaches to Distribution Policy," *American Economic Review* 60 (May 1970):270. Earlier estimates along these lines are cited therein.

CHAPTER 3

Individual Taxes and the Distribution of Income

Benjamin A. Okner
The Brookings Institution

Most economists agree that the most appropriate way to measure the burden or incidence of taxes is in terms of their effect on the distribution of income. There is so little dispute, in fact, that incidence is usually defined simply as the effect of taxes on the distribution of income available for private use.

In order to determine empirically the burden of any tax, some assumption must be made about whose real income it reduces and about the amount of before-tax income that would have been received in its absence. Since taxes affect the total level of economic output as well as the distribution of real income through their impact on both factor prices (the sources of income) and commodity prices (the uses of income), a full-fledged study of the overall burden of taxes is exceedingly complex.

In this paper, I am concerned only with the distributional effects of the personal income and employment taxes. Since these two levies amounted to more than 50 percent of total government tax receipts in 1966,[1] their incidence is of considerable importance for any overall study of tax burdens. In addition, there is

---

The views presented are those of the author and not necessarily those of the officers, trustees, or other staff members of The Brookings Institution. All computer operations described in the paper were performed at the Brookings Social Science Computation Center and the programming was done by Andrew D. Pike, whose efforts are gratefully acknowledged. The work described is part of a research program supported by a grant from the U.S. Office of Economic Opportunity.

[1] Total government tax receipts in the study are equal to federal, state, and local government receipts as measured in the National Income Accounts, adjusted to exclude nontaxes, intergovernmental grants-in-aid, and social insurance contributions for civilian government retirement funds and veterans' life insurance.

little disagreement as to how these taxes should be allocated among persons.[2]

Once one has decided how a given tax should be allocated among individuals in the population, its incidence—or impact on the distribution of income—might be presumed to be a rather straightforward calculation. However, this is not necessarily the case, because there are a number of ways in which income might be defined. Although we prefer a particular income definition, at the beginning of the analysis some attention is given to alternative income concepts which might be used in an incidence study.

In addition to the overall distributions of before- and after-tax income, we also examine and compare the incidence of individual taxes for specific subgroups of the population. And since we interpret individual taxes broadly to include transfer payments received from the government as well as taxes paid, we assess the extent to which both individual taxes and transfers affect the distribution of income in our analysis.

METHODOLOGY AND DATA

The results presented are all based on the Brookings MERGE File which contains demographic and financial data for a sample of 72,000 families and single individuals in calendar year 1966. This file was created by combining information from the 1967 Survey of Economic Opportunity (SEO) and data from the 1966 Tax File, which contains income and tax information from federal individual income tax returns filed for 1966. The basic unit of analysis in the MERGE File is the Census family or unrelated individual.[3]

[2] While it is possible that individuals might change their allocation of time between work and leisure because of the individual income tax, there are few economists who believe that this would be a significant factor. Therefore, we follow the traditional practice of allocating personal income taxes directly among individuals on the basis of their incomes under the assumption that we need not take account of tax-induced changes in the distribution of before-tax income. In the case of employment taxes, even though there is not unanimous agreement as to the incidence of such levies, we follow the prevalent modern practice of allocating both the employer and employee shares of these taxes among persons on the basis of their compensation from earnings. For a detailed discussion of the reasoning and various views on this subject, see John A. Brittain, *The Payroll Tax for Social Security* (Washington, D.C.: Brookings Institution, 1972).

[3] A detailed description of the MERGE File and how it was created is given in Benjamin A. Okner, "Constructing a New Data Base from Existing

Since all the calculations are based on microunit data in the MERGE File, the methodology used here differs considerably from previous empirical tax burden studies. In the past, individual taxes were allocated to broad income classes on the basis of a large number of statistical series which were used as proxies for the tax distributions.[4] The major disadvantage of such methodology is that it requires that taxes be distributed on the basis of the average income and behavior of all households in a particular income class, rather than on the basis of the income and behavior of the individual microunits in the class.

Although we could not make all the distinctions that are relevant for estimating tax liabilities, the MERGE File provides us with a very rich source of information for this purpose. Among the characteristics that are particularly important for estimating tax payments are sources of income, marital status and family composition, consumption patterns, and home ownership. Since this information is available for each unit in the file, whenever it is necessary to make assumptions about the economic behavior of households, we are not limited to a single assumption for all families in a given income class. This frees us from the uniformity assumption which has been the hallmark of all past studies.

In addition to this major improvement in methodology, the MERGE File permits us to prepare tax burden distributions on the basis of various alternative incidence assumptions and income definitions. In the past, these were impossible because of the sheer magnitude of the computational job. As illustrated below, the new file, along with present electronic computer capabilities, gives us great flexibility in this respect.

BEFORE-TAX DISTRIBUTION OF INCOME

There is no single concept of income that is acceptable and useful for all analytical purposes. However, for analyzing the incidence of taxes it is clearly inappropriate to compare tax payments with income subject to tax; we are interested in a comparison between taxes paid and total incomes. To provide this type of information, we adopted a comprehensive income defini-

---

Microdata Sets: The 1966 MERGE File," *Annals of Economic and Social Measurement* 1 (July 1972):325-42.

[4] The classic study along these lines is by Richard A. Musgrave and others, "Distribution of Tax Payments by Income Groups: A Case Study for 1948," *National Tax Journal* 4 (March 1951):1-54.

tion that is intended to correspond as closely as is practical to an economic concept of income, viz., consumption plus tax payments plus (or minus) the net increase (or decrease) in the value of assets during the year. This concept, called family income (FI), is the sum of national income (as defined in the National Income Accounts)[5] plus transfer payments plus accrued gains on farm assets and nonfarm real estate.[6] In keeping with the national income concept, FI includes corporation income before tax. This procedure has the advantage not only of consistency but also of providing a complete account of the accrued income claims of the household sector. Retained earnings of corporations, which are included in family income, may be regarded as an approximation of accrued capital gains on corporate stock during the year.[7] FI includes only income which accrues directly to families and individuals, and thus excludes the income received by fiduciaries and persons in the institutional population not represented in the SEO File.

Other income concepts that might be employed are money factor income, Census money income, and total money receipts. The relationship among these four concepts is illustrated in Table 1. Money factor income includes the $484 billion of money income received by individuals from production. To this we add wage supplements, net imputed rent, accrued capital gains on farm assets and nonfarm real estate, corporate retained earnings and the

---

[5] The major departure from the official definition of income is the omission of interest imputed to individuals for the services rendered to them by the banking system.

[6] For a detailed description, see Benjamin A. Okner, "Adjusted Family Income: Concept and Derivation," Brookings Technical Working Paper II, for the Distribution of Federal, State and Local Taxes Research Program, rev., processed (Washington, D.C.: Brookings Institution, August 1972), which is available on request.

[7] We used this approximation because the annual fluctuations in the value of corporate stock are very large and even three- to five-year averages may not give an adequate representation of accrued capital gains. Martin J. Bailey and Martin David have shown that over very long periods of time, capital gains on corporate securities are roughly equal to retained earnings. See Martin J. Bailey, "Capital Gains and Income Taxation," in Arnold C. Harberger and Martin J. Bailey, eds., *The Taxation of Income from Capital* (Washington, D.C.: Brookings Institution, 1969), pp. 15-26; and Martin David, *Alternative Approaches to Capital Gains Taxation* (Washington, D.C.: Brookings Institution, 1968), pp. 242-46.

TABLE 1   Comparison of Various Income Concepts, 1966

(billions of dollars)

Item	Amount
Money factor income[a]	484
Plus: Wage supplements[b]	41
Net imputed rent	11
Retained corporate profits	22
Corporation income tax	26
Accrued gains on farm assets and nonfarm real estate	37
Interest on life insurance policies	6
Subtotal	142
Equals family income before transfers	627
Less total nonmoney income	−142
Plus: Private pensions	6
Civilian and military government pensions	6
Other income	7
Subtotal	−124
Equals Census money income before transfers	503
Plus realized gains on asset sales	19
Equals total money receipts before transfers	523
Memorandum: transfer payments[c]	34

[a] Money factor income is the sum of wages and salaries, interest, dividends, rents and royalties, and farm and nonfarm proprietors' income.

[b] Wage supplements include employer contributions to private pension and welfare funds, Social Security, workmen's compensation, unemployment insurance, and civilian government retirement systems.

[c] Transfer payments include Social Security benefits, public assistance, veterans' disability compensation and pensions, workmen's compensation, and unemployment insurance payments received by individuals.

corporation income tax allocated to individual stockholders,[8] and interest on life insurance policies to obtain total FI before transfers of $624 billion. Since the Census income concept does not include nonmoney items, it is necessary to subtract the $141 billion of such income from FI before transfers and then add receipts from private pensions and civilian government and

[8] This excludes the portion of the tax attributable to fiduciaries and organizations not represented in the SEO universe.

military retirement pay to derive the $502 billion of Census money income before transfers.[9] Finally, because the Bureau of the Census does not include profits from the sale of assets in its income concept, we add $19 billion of realized capital gains to derive $521 billion of total money receipts before transfers.

These four different concepts vary considerably in their coverage. Family income is the most comprehensive concept, while money factor income is least inclusive. And as might be expected, the before tax and transfer distribution of income is quite different, depending on which concept is used. In Table 2 we present the distribution of income by size class under each of the four different definitions. (In Table 2, the income classes are defined in terms of each of the specific income definitions; therefore, the same family units *are not* included in the same income class under the various definitions.)

In Table 3, we show the same distributions by population quintiles under the different income definitions. Based on the data in Table 3, it is obvious that one can reach very different conclusions about the distribution of income depending upon what income concept is used. For example, under the FI concept, the lowest quintile includes families with incomes under $2,799; under the least comprehensive money factor income (MFI) concept, the lowest quintile includes those with incomes of less than $2,368, At the other end of the income distribution, the top quintile under the FI concept is comprised of families with incomes of $14,564 and over, whereas under the MFI definition, the highest quintile starts at $12,446. The absolute differences in income increase even more at the very highest levels; the top one percent of units are those with $44,318 of MFI while the top percentile under the FI concept begins at $50,000.

As measured by the Gini coefficient,[10] the distributions also

[9] Under our definition, only social insurance benefits financed by payroll taxes are treated as transfer payments. Benefits paid under government retirement programs are treated like private pensions and annuities and, therefore, are excluded from transfers. Government contributions, if any, to these programs are considered income during the current year and benefit payments received are viewed as representing only a change in the form of asset holding by individuals (i.e., cash is increased and a prepaid insurance asset is reduced).

[10] The Gini coefficient of inequality is a statistical measure of overall equality or inequality in the distribution of income. Pictorially, it is equal to the ratio of the area between the Lorenz curve and the line of equal distribution to the entire area below the line of equal distribution. The value

TABLE 2 Distribution of Income Before Taxes and Transfers Under Various Income Definitions, by Income Class, 1966

(millions of dollars and percent)

Income Classes*a* ($000)	Money Factor Income	Family Income	Census Money Income	Total Money Receipts
Under 3[b]	10,724	10,784	11,386	11,286
3- 5	28,053	23,563	29,578	29,450
5- 10	151,516	133,594	152,566	151,284
10- 15	138,406	162,444	139,953	139,286
15- 20	61,959	101,637	68,538	69,924
20- 25	24,304	50,054	26,679	28,017
25- 50	43,712	72,894	46,784	51,782
50- 100	15,937	28,881	16,665	20,112
100- 500	8,153	29,470	8,643	14,224
500-1,000	655	4,854	681	2,051
1,000 and over	632	6,658	645	3,178
All classes	484,050	624,833	502,118	520,594

Percentage Distributions

Under 3[b]	2.2	1.7	2.3	2.2
3- 5	5.8	3.8	5.9	5.7
5- 10	31.3	21.4	30.4	29.1
10- 15	28.6	26.0	27.9	26.8
15- 20	12.8	16.3	13.6	13.4
20- 25	5.0	8.0	5.3	5.4
25- 50	9.0	11.7	9.3	9.9
50- 100	3.3	4.6	3.3	3.9
100- 500	1.7	4.7	1.7	2.7
500-1,000	0.1	0.8	0.1	0.4
1,000 and over	0.1	1.1	0.1	0.6
All classes	100.0	100.0	100.0	100.0

NOTE: Details may not add to totals because of rounding.

[a] The income class is defined in terms of the income distribution for each of the concepts.

[b] Includes negative incomes.

of the Gini coefficient varies between 0 (indicating perfect equality) and 1 (indicating perfect inequality). A decrease in the value of the coefficient signifies a more equal distribution; an increase signifies a more unequal distribution.

TABLE 3   Shares of Income Before Taxes and Transfers Received by Each Fifth of the Population Under Various Income Definitions, 1966

Population Quintile	Money Factor Income		Family Income		Census Money Income		Total Money Receipts	
	Income Range	Percent of Income Received	Income Range	Percent of Income Received	Income Range	Percent of Income Received	Income Range	Percent of Income Received
Lowest 5th	Under $2,368	1.41	Under $2,799	1.90	Under $2,482	2.05	Under $2,502	2.01
Second 5th	2,368- 5,389	9.50	2,799- 6,534	9.30	2,482- 5,582	9.79	2,502-5,630	9.54
Middle 5th	5,389- 8,383	17.07	6,534- 9,982	16.07	5,582- 8,567	17.00	5,630-8,634	16.53
Fourth 5th	8,383-12,446	24.57	9,982-14,564	23.29	8,567-12,736	24.22	8,634-12,884	23.72
Highest 5th	12,446 and over	47.39	14,564 and over	49.44	12,736 and over	46.94	12,884 and over	48.30
Top 5 percent	19,576 and over	20.23	24,459 and over	23.48	19,848 and over	20.05	20,714 and over	21.80
Top 1 percent	44,318 and over	7.56	50,000 and over	11.02	44,565 and over	7.42	46,152 and over	9.01
Gini coefficient of inequality[a]		.4601		.4746		.4489		.4622

[a] The Gini coefficient of inequality is a statistical measure of overall equality or inequality in the distribution of income. It may vary between 0 (indicating perfect equality) and 1 (indicating perfect inequality). A decrease in the value therefore signifies a more equal after-tax distribution of income and a more progressive tax structure.

differ substantially in the degree of inequality exhibited under the various income definitions. Census money income is distributed among families most nearly equal (Gini coefficient = .4489). In order of decreasing equality (increasing inequality), this is followed by money factor income (Gini coefficient = .4601); total money receipts (Gini coefficient = .4622); and finally, family income (Gini coefficient = .4746). All of the preceding coefficients refer to the distributions of income exclusive of transfer payments.

DISTRIBUTION OF INDIVIDUAL TAXES AND TRANSFERS

As has been indicated, the analysis is confined to the effects of personal income and employment taxes on the distribution of individual income. Since in this paper, we are dealing only with individual taxes, the amount of the corporation income tax allocated to each family is *excluded* from family income in all the effective tax-rate tables. However, in each table, families are classified by the amount of total income before taxes and transfers, i.e., total FI less transfer payments.

The income taxes include federal and state and local taxes. Payroll taxes include employee and employer Social Security contributions plus employer contributions for unemployment insurance and workmen's compensation. Other employer social insurance contributions—such as those for pension and health funds—are not considered taxes and are excluded from the analysis. Transfer payments include all benefits paid to individuals under government programs, regardless of whether they are financed by general revenue or by payroll taxes.[11]

Personal Income Taxes

The MERGE File contains the federal individual income tax reported by each taxpaying unit in 1966, so there is no need to allocate these taxes among families in the file.

State and local income taxes reported as itemized deductions on tax returns amounted to approximately 70 percent of the total collections reported for 1966. However, for units that did not

---

[11] Business transfer payments, as defined in the National Income Accounts, are not included in our transfer payment (or income) definition.

itemize their deductions, we estimated the state and local income tax liability on the basis of income, family size, and place of residence.[12]

Total personal income tax collections (less refunds) in the National Income Accounts were $64.0 billion in 1966; this was comprised of $58.6 billion in federal collections and $5.4 billion in state and local government collections. The $55.4 billion of federal tax collections in the MERGE File amounts to about 90 percent of the national income amount. We did not attempt to adjust the MERGE figures to the national income total and accepted the amount reported.[13] State and local income taxes allocated to MERGE File units were $5.4 billion. The total amount of personal income taxes allocated among families in the file is therefore $60.8 billion.

Total federal income taxes amount to 9.2 percent of income, while total state and local income taxes equal 0.9 percent of FI. These taxes as a percentage of total FI in each income class are shown in Table 4.[14] As can be seen, both federal and state and local income taxes are progressive throughout most of the income distribution. However, for most families, total personal income tax rates are quite low. The federal income tax never exceeds 20.7 percent of total income, and the highest effective rate of state and local income taxes is only 1.9 percent. The effective tax rate is 10 percent or less for all families with incomes below $20,000 and exceeds 20 percent only for those with incomes of $100,000 and above. The highest effective rate of tax—22.7 percent—is reached in the $500,000 to $1 million FI class; beyond this income level, the effective income tax rate declines, because nontaxable income is highly concentrated among those with incomes at the very top of the income distribution.

---

[12] The last criterion is needed because not all states have an individual income tax. While it is used extensively, in 1966 there were still seventeen states that did not levy a personal income tax.

[13] An unknown, but probably small, part of the difference can be attributed to the fact that the SEO population differs from the national income covereage.

[14] Similar tables, with effective income tax rates based on the other income concepts, are presented in Appendix Tables A.1 to A.3. In order to aid the reader, families are classified by family income less transfers in all the Appendix Tables so that the effects of the income definition changes for the same families may be followed.

TABLE 4   Effective Rates of Federal and State and Local Individual Income Taxes,[a] by Family Income Classes, 1966

(percent)

Family Income Before Transfers ($000)	Federal Individual Income Tax	State and Local Individual Income Taxes	Total Individual Income Taxes
0- 3[b]	2.7	0.2	3.0
3- 5	4.6	0.4	5.0
5- 10	6.7	0.6	7.2
10- 15	8.1	0.8	8.9
15- 20	9.1	0.9	10.0
20- 25	9.9	1.1	11.0
25- 50	11.4	1.2	12.6
50- 100	17.3	1.7	19.0
100- 500	19.6	1.9	21.5
500-1,000	20.7	1.9	22.7
1,000 and over	19.0	1.8	20.8
All classes	9.2	0.9	10.2

NOTE: Details may not add to totals because of rounding.

a Effective tax rates are calculated on the basis of family income before transfers, excluding the amount of corporation income tax allocated to families in the MERGE File.

b Excludes families with negative incomes.

It is well known that average effective rates, such as those shown in Table 4, often obscure large variations in taxes paid by different kinds of families within the same income class. The differences between those who derive their incomes primarily from wages and those who are primarily recipients of property income were reported in a recent paper by Joseph A. Pechman.[15] There are a very large number of other population subgroups that might be examined: two of these which are of particular interest are families of different size and those headed by aged and nonaged persons. The effective income tax rates for these subgroups are shown in Table 5.

[15] See Joseph A. Pechman, "Distribution of Federal and State Income Taxes by Income Classes," Papers and Proceedings of the Thirtieth Annual Meeting of the American Finance Association, *Journal of Finance* 27, no. 2 (May 1972):179-91. Brookings Reprint 234.

TABLE 5   Effective Rates of Individual Income Taxes[a] by Age of Family Head and Size of Family, by Family Income Classes, 1966

(percent)

Family Income Before Transfers ($000)	All Families							Nonaged Families[b]							Aged Families[b]						
	All Sizes	Family Size						All Sizes	Family Size						All Sizes	Family Size					
		1	2	3	4	5+			1	2	3	4	5+			1	2	3	4	5+	
0- 3[c]	3.0	4.1	2.5	2.0	1.8	1.7		3.9	5.5	3.7	2.3	1.9	1.9		1.7	2.0	1.7	0.7	1.1	d	
3- 5	5.0	8.5	4.3	4.2	2.9	1.6		5.6	10.0	5.4	4.4	2.7	1.5		3.1	3.8	2.7	2.8	4.8	2.2	
5- 10	7.2	11.5	8.2	7.4	6.1	3.9		7.4	12.4	8.9	7.5	6.1	3.9		5.5	4.9	5.7	6.0	5.4	4.5	
10- 15	8.9	13.8	10.6	9.7	8.2	6.7		9.0	15.1	10.9	9.7	8.2	6.7		8.2	7.4	8.3	8.8	8.7	6.1	
15- 20	10.0	12.6	11.4	10.4	9.8	8.6		10.1	14.2	12.0	10.7	9.8	8.6		8.3	8.2	7.8	8.6	9.8	8.5	
20- 25	11.0	12.7	12.7	11.1	10.8	9.9		11.3	16.8	13.5	11.6	10.9	9.9		7.6	5.0	7.7	6.9	9.2	10.5	
25- 50	12.6	11.4	12.5	13.4	12.8	12.5		13.1	16.1	13.8	13.7	12.8	12.5		8.0	6.1	7.2	10.3	12.6	6.0	
50- 100	19.0	21.7	17.1	18.9	20.2	20.0		20.2	23.3	20.7	19.0	20.3	20.0		4.6	9.6	4.3	d	3.5	–	
100- 500	21.5	16.4	22.0	24.7	24.1	20.3		21.6	16.4	22.1	24.7	24.1	20.3		10.3	–	10.4	–	–	–	
500-1,000	22.7	19.4	23.1	23.7	25.9	23.0		22.7	19.4	23.1	23.7	25.9	23.0		–	–	–	–	–	–	
1,000 and over	20.8	19.8	20.3	23.8	21.0	21.7		20.8	19.8	20.3	23.8	21.0	21.7		–	–	–	–	–	–	
All classes	10.2	11.6	11.3	10.5	9.8	8.7		10.5	13.3	12.5	10.7	9.8	8.7		6.2	5.0	5.8	7.7	8.5	6.6	

a Effective tax rates are calculated on the basis of family income before transfers, excluding the amount of corporation income tax allocated to families in the MERGE File.

b Families headed by an individual age 64 or under are considered nonaged; those headed by an individual age 65 or over are classified as aged.

c Excludes families with negative incomes.

d Less than half of 1 percent.

For aged families, income taxes as a percentage of income are substantially below the rates paid by the nonaged at all income levels. On the average, the aged pay income taxes at about 60 percent of the rates paid by families headed by an individual under age 65.

While the same general pattern of lower tax rates is found by income class for each family-size group, we see a very different overall pattern of effective income tax rates among the aged and nonaged as family size increases. For nonaged families, effective tax rates fall as family size increases, whereas just the opposite occurs among aged families. This occurs because a large family headed by a person age 65 or over is very likely comprised of the head plus other, younger, family members still in the labor force, whereas an aged one-person family is likely to be a widow or widower. In general, as family size increases among aged families, there are likely to be more earners, larger incomes, and therefore higher tax payments.[16] On the other hand, among nonaged families, larger family size more typically represents more dependents and a lower likelihood of additional earners other than the family head (or head and spouse) than is the case among the aged.[17]

Employment Taxes

Employer and employee payroll taxes amounted to $31.8 billion in 1966. As indicated above, the employer payroll taxes are defined to include only the portion of social insurance contributions for Social Security and unemployment insurance in the National Income Accounts. In addition, employer workmen's compensation costs, which are excluded from wage supplements in the National Income Accounts, are included here as an employer payroll tax.

Since neither the employee nor employer payroll tax data were available from the SEO or Tax Files used in constructing the MERGE File, these amounts were allocated to workers on the

[16] The average income for aged single persons is about $2,400. This rises sharply as family size increases up to an average of almost $8,900 for aged families with five or more persons.

[17] The average income for nonaged single persons is about $5,800. This rises to about $11,200 for two-person families and then remains in the $11,500 to $12,600 range for all other family sizes.

basis of their earnings, industry and occupation, and the statutory requirements in effect in 1966.[18] Employer Social Security contributions for self-employed individuals were available directly from the federal individual income-tax data.

Since we accept the assumption that employer payroll taxes are ultimately borne by employees, we follow the national income procedure and include such levies as part of employee compensation in FI. The effective rate of such taxes is then correctly computed as the ratio of the tax to income before tax.[19] There is little disagreement over who pays the employee share of the payroll tax, and using the standard assumption, it was allocated among wage and salary earners. The effective payroll tax rates under these assumptions are shown in Table 6. As in the case of total individual income taxes, these are shown for all families and also by family size for aged and nonaged families.

The overall pattern of employment taxes shows the expected regressive pattern by income class. Although for both aged and nonaged families, tax rates ultimately fall as income rises, the effective tax rate is lower for those with incomes under $3,000 than it is at incomes of $3,000 to $5,000. Since the payroll taxes are essentially proportional to earnings in covered employment (up to the $6,600 maximum of taxable wages in 1966), the pattern of effective rates indicates that families in the lowest income class have a low proportion of covered earnings to total income. For the aged, this occurs because a large proportion of income is derived from property and is not subject to the payroll tax. Among nonaged families, low effective payroll tax rates at the bottom of the income scale result primarily from working in

[18] For details on the allocation process, see Benjamin A. Okner, "The Imputation of Missing Income Information," Technical Working Paper III, for the Distribution of Federal, State and Local Taxes Research Program, processed (Washington, D.C.: Brookings Institution, April 1971), which is available on request.

[19] Under this incidence assumption, employer payroll taxes should be added to reported money earnings in order to correctly assess the impact of these taxes under other income definitions. Alternative incidence assumptions are not included in this paper, since the distributional effects tend to become very complex. For example, if it is assumed that employer taxes are shifted forward in the form of higher commodity prices, it is necessary to move from the sources to the uses of income side in the analysis. This, in turn, requires that net national product (which includes indirect business taxes) be used as the tax base instead of the "national income" concept used here.

TABLE 6   Effective Rates of Employment Taxes[a] by Age of Family Head and Size of Family, by Family Income Classes, 1966

(percent)

Family Income Before Transfers ($000)	All Families							Nonaged Families[b]							Aged Families[b]						
	All Sizes	Family Size						All Sizes	Family Size						All Sizes	Family Size					
		1	2	3	4	5+			1	2	3	4	5+			1	2	3	4	5+
0- 3[c]	5.4	5.1	4.4	6.2	7.7	8.8		7.6	7.5	7.2	7.0	8.0	9.0		2.3	1.5	2.6	3.5	6.5	5.8
3- 5	7.1	6.9	6.3	7.5	8.1	8.0		8.2	8.4	8.3	7.9	8.2	8.0		3.3	2.2	3.2	5.3	6.7	7.1
5- 10	7.3	6.8	6.9	7.6	7.5	7.6		7.5	7.3	7.6	7.7	7.5	7.6		4.8	3.1	4.6	6.8	7.3	7.4
10- 15	6.2	4.4	6.4	6.8	6.2	6.2		6.4	5.0	6.6	6.8	6.2	6.2		4.6	1.3	4.4	6.0	6.9	7.2
15- 20	5.2	3.0	5.2	5.3	5.5	5.3		5.4	3.4	5.5	5.5	5.4	5.3		3.9	1.9	3.0	4.1	8.0	6.8
20- 25	4.6	1.9	3.8	5.3	4.9	4.7		4.7	2.9	4.0	5.4	4.8	4.7		3.0	d	2.4	3.7	5.9	4.4
25- 50	2.8	1.0	1.8	3.3	3.4	3.1		2.9	1.4	2.0	3.2	3.3	3.1		2.0	0.5	1.1	3.6	7.0	4.1
50- 100	0.9	0.5	0.7	0.8	1.2	1.0		0.9	0.6	0.8	0.8	1.2	1.0		0.3	d	0.4	d	2.2	–
100- 500	0.3	d	0.3	0.4	0.5	0.4		0.3	0.1	0.3	0.4	0.5	0.4		d	–	0.4	–	–	–
500-1,000	d	d	0.1	0.1	0.1	0.1		d	d	0.1	0.1	0.1	0.1		–	–	–	–	–	–
1,000 and over	d	d	d	d	d	d		d	d	d	d	d	d		–	–	–	–	–	–
All classes	5.3	4.9	4.9	5.8	5.5	5.3		5.5	5.7	5.2	5.8	5.5	5.3		3.6	1.8	3.2	5.0	7.0	6.4

[a] Effective tax rates are calculated on the basis of family income before transfers, excluding the amount of corporation income tax allocated to families in the MERGE File.
[b] Families headed by an individual age 64 or under are considered nonaged; those headed by an individual age 65 or over are classified as aged.
[c] Excludes families with negatives incomes.
[d] Less than hafl of 1 percent.

occupations not covered by Social Security and the other programs, which tends to lower the proportion of taxable wages to total income for these units. For nonaged families with incomes of $3,000 to $5,000, the effective tax rate on family income is about 8 percent, and this falls steadily as income rises above that level. There is very little difference in this pattern among nonaged families of different sizes. The burden of employment taxes among aged families is generally low, because a much smaller proportion of such units are in the labor force and subject to the payroll levies.

Because larger families in this category tend to have more earners, we find that effective payroll tax rates rise as family size increases for families headed by an aged person. Among nonaged families in the $10,000 to $20,000 income range, there is a sharp rise in effective payroll taxes paid by two-person families as compared with single individuals. This undoubtedly represents a move from single-earner to two-earner status for units in this income range.

Total Individual Taxes

When we examine the combined effect of the regressive employment taxes and the progressive income taxes, we find that the overall pattern of total tax burdens is slightly progressive. The effective tax rates by income classes for both taxes combined are given in Table 7. Those figures suggest that the progressivity involved in the combined data comes almost totally from the effect of the individual income tax near the top of the income distribution.

For the vast bulk of families, the combined effect of the individual income and employment taxes is pretty much proportional with respect to income. For example, among families headed by a nonaged individual, the combined effective tax rate is between 15 percent and 16 percent for all income levels between $5,000 and $50,000. This group comprises about 68 percent of all family units and receives almost 80 percent of all income (before taxes and transfers).

Families headed by a person age 65 and over pay lower tax rates on the average, but again there is not a great deal of variation in the combined effective rates of tax. Among the aged families, the effective tax rate ranges from about 10 percent to 13 percent of

TABLE 7 Combined Effective Rates of Individual Income and Employment Taxes[a] by Age of Family Head and Family Income Classes, 1966

(percent)

Family Income Before Transfers ($000)	All Families	Nonaged Families[b]	Aged Families[b]
0- 3[c]	8.4	11.5	4.0
3- 5	12.1	13.8	6.4
5- 10	14.5	15.0	10.3
10- 15	15.2	15.3	12.8
15- 20	15.2	15.5	12.2
20- 25	15.6	16.0	10.6
25- 50	15.5	16.0	9.9
50- 100	19.8	21.1	4.9
100- 500	21.8	21.9	11.2
500-1,000	22.7	22.7	—
1,000 and over	20.8	20.8	—
All classes	15.4	16.0	9.8

[a] Effective tax rates are calculated on the basis of family income before transfers, excluding the amount of corporation income tax allocated to families in the MERGE File.
[b] Families headed by an individual age 64 or under are considered nonaged; those headed by an individual age 65 or over are classified as aged.
[c] Excludes families with negative incomes.

income for all units between the $5,000 and $50,000 income levels. Since there are no aged families at the very top of the income distribution in the MERGE File sample, the small degree of progressivity for the aged all comes from the lower taxes paid by those near the bottom of the income distribution.

Transfer Payments

Since transfer payments have a direct impact on the distribution of income available for private use, it seems clear that they should also be included in this analysis. Our definition of transfers is quite similar to that used in the National Income Accounts. The major differences are that we do not count either civilian or government retirement receipts as transfers but we do include workmen's compensation benefits in transfer income.

Under this definition, total transfers to individuals amounted to $34 billion in 1966. This was primarily comprised of the $21.5 billion of Social Security benefits paid; it also included unemployment insurance, public assistance, veterans' disability compensation and pensions, and workmen's compensation receipts.

Since the most relevant distinctions among families with transfer receipts are age and income, we omit the family-size classification in showing the effect of transfer payments in Table 8. Transfer payments have their greatest impact on low-income families and especially the aged. In fact, for aged persons with incomes below $3,000, transfers average more than double the amount of income from production. Transfer income amounts to

TABLE 8   Transfer Payments as a Percentage of Income[a] by Age of Family Head and Family Income, 1966

(percent)

Family Income Before Transfers ($000)	All Families	Nonaged Families[b]	Aged Families[b]
0- 3[c]	124.2	74.4	203.0
3- 5	17.9	11.5	39.6
5- 10	5.1	3.5	19.9
10- 15	2.2	1.6	10.9
15- 20	1.8	1.3	9.0
20- 25	1.4	1.1	5.2
25- 50	0.9	0.6	4.2
50- 100	0.2	d	2.6
100- 500	d	—	1.9
500-1,000	—	—	—
1,000 and over	—	—	—
All classes	5.7	3.0	33.3

[a] Percentages are calculated on the basis of family income before transfers, excluding the amount of corporation income tax allocated to families in the MERGE File.

[b] Families headed by an individual age 64 or under are considered nonaged; those headed by an individual 65 or over are classified as aged.

[c] Excludes families with negative incomes.

[d] Less than half of 1 percent.

almost 40 percent of before-transfer income for the aged with incomes of $3,000 to $5,000 and close to 20 percent of FI for those with incomes of $5,000 to $10,000. As expected, transfers are much less important in influencing the distribution of income among nonaged families except at the very bottom of the income scale. Transfer payments are a very small proportion of total income for nonaged families with incomes of $5,000 or more.

DISTRIBUTION OF INCOME AFTER TAXES AND TRANSFERS

In this section, we combine the partial results discussed above to assess the overall impact of individual taxes and transfers on the distribution of before-tax income. The most expeditious way to summarize the large amount of information already presented is in terms of Lorenz curves showing the various income distributions. The before-tax and after-tax and transfer Lorenz curves for all families are shown in Chart 1[20] and the Gini coefficients and percentage reductions in the areas of inequality for each of the population subgroups examined are given in Table 9.[21] (The cumulative distributions of before- and after-tax income for all families and for each of the population subgroups are given in Appendix Tables A.5 to A.7.)

For all families, the Gini coefficient computed on the basis of the before-tax distribution of income is .4595; the coefficient for income after transfer payments is .4155; for income less transfers and income taxes, it is .3959; for income less transfers and employment taxes combined, it is .4200; and the Gini coefficient for the income distribution after both taxes and transfers is .3998. Translating these figures into more commonly used terms, they

[20] Before-tax income for the distribution in Chart 1 is equal to FI before transfers and excluding the amount of corporation income tax allocated to each family in the MERGE File. This is also the basis used for computing the before-tax and transfer Gini coefficients in Table 9.

[21] The percentage reduction in the area of inequality is equal to the ratio of the area between the before- and after-tax Lorenz curves (B) to the total area of inequality, i.e., the area between the line of equal distribution and the before-tax Lorenz curve (A). This ratio can be computed directly from the Gini coefficients associated with the before- and after-tax Lorenz curves. If the before-tax Gini coefficient is equal to G, and the after-tax Gini coefficient equals G', the percentage reduction in the area of inequality is equal to $(G - G')/G$.

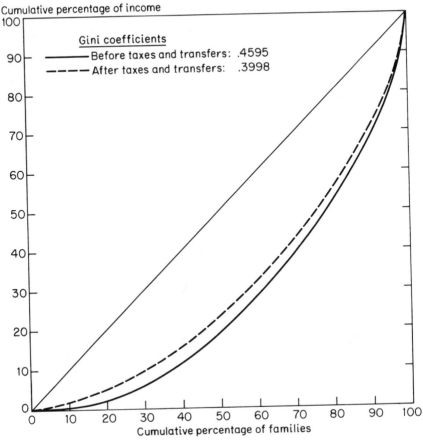

Cumulative percentage of income

CHART 1: Comparison of the Distribution of Family Income Before and After Individual Taxes and Transfers, All Families, 1966

indicate that in the aggregate, income taxes are progressive; employment taxes are regressive; the total of income and employment taxes is progressive; and that transfer payments are very progressive.

In general, income before taxes and transfers is more equally distributed among nonaged families than among those headed by someone age 65 or over. The group with the most unequal distribution of before-tax income consists of aged single individuals; they are closely followed by aged couples. At the other end of "the equality scale" are the "standard" four-person families headed by a person under age 65.

Based on the changes in the area of inequality shown in Table 9,

TABLE 9   Gini Coefficients for the Distributions of Income Before Taxes and Transfers, Income After Transfers, and Income After Taxes and Transfers, 1966

| Population Group | *Gini Coefficient*[a] | | | *Percentage Change in Area of Inequality*[b] *Due to:* | |
	Income Before Taxes[c]	*Income After Transfers*	*Income After Taxes and Transfers*	*Transfers*	*Individual Taxes and Transfers*
All families	.4595	.4155	.3998	9.6	13.0
Nonaged families[d]	.4099	.3886	.3774	5.2	7.9
1 person	.5102	.4717	.4570	7.5	10.4
2 persons	.4310	.4059	.3919	5.8	9.1
3 persons	.3628	.3427	.3297	5.5	9.1
4 persons	.3385	.3255	.3126	3.8	7.6
5+ persons	.3639	.3433	.3277	5.2	9.9
Aged families[d]	.6278	.4573	.4367	27.2	30.4
1 person	.6799	.4263	.4097	37.3	39.7
2 persons	.5842	.4129	.3944	29.3	32.5
3 persons	.4598	.3744	.3595	18.6	21.8
4 persons	.4869	.3916	.3647	19.6	25.1
5+ persons	.4231	.3470	.3309	18.0	21.8

[a] The Gini coefficient of inequality is a statistical measure of overall equality or inequality in the distribution of income. It may vary between 0 (indicating perfect equality) and 1 (indicating perfect inequality). A decrease in the value therefore signifies a more equal after-tax distribution of income and a more progressive tax structure.

[b] The percentage reduction in the area of inequality is equal to the ratio of the area between the before-tax and the after-tax (after-transfer) Lorenz curves to the total area of inequality, i.e., the area between the line of equal distribution and the before-tax Lorenz curve.

[c] Income before taxes is equal to family income less transfers, excluding the amount of corporation income tax allocated to families in the MERGE File.

[d] Families headed by an individual age 64 or under are considered nonaged; those headed by an individual age 65 or over are classified as aged.

we find that transfer payments have a much greater effect on the after-tax and transfer distribution of income than do tax payments. For all families, transfer payments account for about three-quarters of the reduction in the area of inequality, whereas taxes account for one-fourth of the total change. Approximately the same proportions of total change are also attributable to the effects of transfers and taxes for one-person nonaged families. For two- and three-person nonaged families, about 60 percent of the total reduction in inequality can be attributed to transfers and 40 percent to taxes; the proportions are about 50 percent each for taxes and transfers among larger nonaged families.

Transfer payments are extremely important in reducing inequality in the distribution of income among the aged. For such units, transfers account for a minimum of about 80 percent of the total reudction in the area of inequality (among four-person families) and they are responsible for 94 percent of the total change among single individuals over age 65. It should also be noted that the total percentage changes in inequality between the before-tax and the after-tax and transfer distributions for aged families are all substantially larger than they are for the nonaged group.

CONCLUSIONS

On the basis of the data presented here, it is clear that (1) the net effect of direct federal taxes and transfers has an important impact on the distribution of individual incomes in the economy; and (2) of the two parts, transfers play a far more important role in redistributing income among families than do taxes.[22] Since there have been two federal income tax reductions since 1966, it is possible that we are understating the redistributive effects of taxes in this analysis. However, there have also been significant increases in public assistance and Social Security benefits (plus payroll tax increases) during the period which would tend to offset some of the tax reduction effects. The data needed to assess the impact of these changes are not available, but I do not believe that the major conclusions would be very different if these new features were taken into account. On balance, I would guess that taxes now account for a little bit more of the total redistribution, while transfers account for a slightly smaller degree of redistribution. Thus, if further income redistribution is an important national

---

[22] The major finding of a study of overall tax burdens in 1966 was that total taxes—federal, state, and local—are proportional to income for almost 90 percent of all U.S. families. (See Joseph A. Pechman and Benjamin A. Okner, *Who Bears the Tax Burden* [Washington, D.C.: Brookings Institution, 1974]). As a result, the total tax system had a very small effect on the overall distribution of income.

objective, we must either adopt changes that will increase the progressivity of existing taxes.[23] and/or expand transfer payments to individuals using financing arrangements which are not regressive.

APPENDIX

TABLE A.1 Effective Rates of Total Individual Income Taxes Based on Census Money Income[a] by Age of Head and Family Income Classes, 1966

(percent)

Family Income Before Transfers ($000)	All Families	Nonaged Families[b]	Aged Families[b]
0- 3[c]	3.0	4.2	1.6
3- 5	6.0	6.6	3.8
5- 10	8.6	8.8	6.8
10- 15	10.6	10.6	10.0
15- 20	11.8	12.0	10.2
20- 25	13.1	13.4	9.5
25- 50	15.6	16.0	11.5
50- 100	24.5	25.8	6.8
100- 500	33.8	33.9	18.6
500-1,000	45.5	45.5	—
1,000 and over	47.4	47.4	—
All classes	12.1	12.6	7.4

[a] Effective tax rates computed on the basis of Census money income excluding transfers.

[b] Families headed by an individual age 64 or under are considered nonaged; those headed by an individual age 65 or over are classified as aged.

[c] Excludes families with negative income.

[23] For ways to increase federal income tax progressivity, see Joseph A. Pechman and Benjamin A. Okner, "Individual Income Tax Erosion by Income Classes," in *The Economics of Federal Subsidy Programs,* A Compendium of Papers submitted to the Joint Economic Committee, Part 1, *General Study Papers,* 92 Cong., 2 sess., 1972, pp. 13-40. Brookings Reprint 230. For a discussion of measures that would reduce the regressivity of payroll taxes, see Joseph A. Pechman, Henry J. Aaron, and Michael K. Taussig, *Social Security: Perspectives for Reform* (Washington, D.C.: Brookings Institution, 1968), pp. 214-27.

TABLE A.2   Effective Rates of Total Individual Income Taxes Based on Money Factor Income, by Age of Head and Family Income Classes, 1966

(percent)

Family Income Before Transfers ($000)	All Families	Nonaged Families[a]	Aged Families[a]
0- 3[b]	4.7	5.3	3.4
3- 5	6.5	6.9	4.8
5- 10	8.8	9.0	7.6
10- 15	10.8	10.8	10.7
15- 20	12.1	12.2	10.8
20- 25	13.4	13.7	10.1
25- 50	16.0	16.3	12.0
50- 100	24.9	26.3	7.0
100- 500	34.6	34.7	18.6
500-1,000	46.4	46.4	—
1,000 and over	47.9	47.9	—
All classes	12.6	12.9	8.7

[a] Families headed by an individual age 64 or under are considered nonaged; those headed by an individual age 65 or over are classified as aged.

[b] Excludes families with negative income.

TABLE A.3   Effective Rates of Total Individual Income Taxes Based on Total Money Receipts,[a] by Age of Head and Family Income Classes, 1966

(percent)

Family Income Before Transfers ($000)	All Families	Nonaged Families[b]	Aged Families[b]
0- 3[c]	2.3	4.0	1.5
3- 5	5.9	6.5	3.6
5- 10	8.5	8.7	6.3
10- 15	10.5	10.5	9.3
15- 20	11.6	11.8	9.6
20- 25	12.6	12.9	9.1
25- 50	14.9	15.2	10.8
50- 100	22.1	23.2	6.6
100- 500	27.3	27.4	18.6
500-1,000	32.8	32.8	—
1,000 and over	32.2	32.2	—
All classes	11.7	12.1	7.0

[a] Effective tax rates computed on the basis of total money receipts excluding transfers.

[b] Families headed by an individual age 64 or under are considered nonaged; those headed by an individual age 65 or over are classified as aged.

[c] Excludes families with negative income.

TABLE A.4　Combined Effective Rates of Individual Income and Employment Taxes[a] by Age of Family Head and Size of Family, by Family Income Classes, 1966

(percent)

Family Income Transfers ($000)	All Families						Nonaged Families[b]						Aged Families[b]					
	All Sizes	Family Size					All Sizes	Family Size					All Sizes	Family Size				
		1	2	3	4	5+		1	2	3	4	5+		1	2	3	4	5+
0- 3[c]	8.4	9.1	6.9	8.2	9.5	10.5	11.5	13.0	10.9	9.4	9.9	10.9	4.0	3.4	4.3	4.2	7.6	5.8
3- 5	12.1	15.3	10.6	11.7	11.0	9.6	13.8	18.4	13.7	12.2	11.0	9.6	6.4	6.0	5.8	8.1	11.5	9.3
5- 10	14.5	18.2	15.1	15.0	13.6	11.5	15.0	19.7	16.4	15.2	13.6	11.5	10.3	8.0	10.3	12.9	12.7	11.8
10- 15	15.2	18.3	17.0	16.4	14.4	12.9	15.3	20.1	17.6	16.6	14.4	12.9	12.8	8.7	12.7	14.8	15.6	13.3
15- 20	15.2	15.6	16.5	15.8	15.3	13.9	15.5	17.6	17.5	16.2	15.3	13.9	12.2	10.1	10.9	12.8	17.8	15.3
20- 25	15.6	14.6	16.5	16.4	15.7	14.6	16.0	19.6	17.6	17.0	15.7	14.5	10.6	5.0	10.1	10.6	15.1	14.8
25- 50	15.5	12.4	14.3	16.6	16.2	15.6	16.0	17.5	15.8	16.9	16.0	15.6	9.9	6.7	8.3	13.9	19.6	10.1
50- 100	19.8	22.2	17.8	19.7	21.4	21.0	21.1	23.9	21.5	19.9	21.4	21.0	4.9	9.6	4.6	d	5.7	—
100- 500	21.8	16.5	22.3	25.1	24.6	20.7	21.9	16.5	22.5	25.1	24.6	20.7	11.2	—	10.9	—	—	—
500-1,000	22.7	19.4	23.2	23.8	26.0	23.1	22.7	19.4	23.2	23.8	26.0	23.1	—	—	—	—	—	—
1,000 and over	20.8	19.8	20.3	23.8	21.1	21.7	20.8	19.8	20.3	23.8	21.1	21.7	—	—	—	—	—	—
All classes	15.4	16.5	16.1	16.2	15.4	14.0	16.0	18.9	17.7	16.6	15.4	14.0	9.8	6.7	9.1	12.7	15.5	13.0

[a] Effective tax rates are calculated on the basis of family income before transfers, excluding the amount of corporation income tax allocated to families in the MERGE File.

[b] Families headed by an individual age 64 or under are considered nonaged; those headed by an individual age 65 or over are classified as aged.

[c] Excludes families with negative incomes.

[d] Less than half of 1 percent.

TABLE A.5 Cumulative Distribution of Before-Tax[a] and After-Tax[b] Income for All Families, 1966

(in cumulative percentages of income)

Income Decile[a]	All Sizes		1-Person Family		2-Person Family		3-Person Family		4-Person Family		5+-Person Family	
	Before-Tax	After-Tax	Before-Tax	After-Tax	Before-Tax	After-Tax	Before-Tax	After-Tax	Before-Tax	After-Tax	Before-Tax	After-Tax
Lowest	0.31	1.98	0.59	3.13	0.39	2.54	1.05	2.67	1.79	2.85	1.34	2.63
Second	1.96	4.93	1.19	6.26	1.79	5.80	4.74	7.06	6.16	7.61	5.45	7.23
Third	5.74	9.48	1.78	9.39	5.01	10.37	10.06	12.64	11.99	13.63	11.01	13.10
Fourth	11.49	15.51	4.84	13.85	10.03	16.28	16.86	19.57	19.03	20.75	17.96	20.21
Fifth	18.96	23.02	9.81	19.86	16.97	23.45	25.00	27.69	27.09	28.83	25.90	28.22
Sixth	28.11	31.96	17.31	27.63	25.61	31.88	34.37	36.92	36.42	38.13	35.12	37.43
Seventh	39.04	42.50	27.94	37.47	36.15	41.80	45.10	47.37	46.97	48.68	45.51	47.76
Eighth	52.15	55.13	41.47	49.49	48.74	53.48	57.80	59.73	59.26	60.88	57.67	59.74
Ninth	68.36	70.67	59.61	65.13	64.69	68.12	72.87	74.45	73.93	75.34	72.23	74.02
Highest	100.00	100.00	100.00	100.00	100.00	100.00	100.00	100.00	100.00	100.00	100.00	100.00
Lowest 95 percent	78.70	80.52	71.58	75.37	75.09	77.72	82.18	83.45	82.96	84.14	81.48	82.99
Lowest 99 percent	91.03	92.16	85.56	87.66	88.49	90.19	92.88	93.70	93.38	94.17	92.83	93.67
Gini coefficient of inequality	.4595	.3998	.5875	.4496	.4958	.4049	.3740	.3322	.3439	.3145	.3656	.3279
Percentage reduction in area of inequality		13.0		23.5		18.3		11.2		8.5		10.3

a Based on distribution of family income before transfers, excluding the amount of corporation income tax allocated to families in the MERGE File.
b Based on family income including transfers and excluding corporation income tax and after individual income and payroll taxes.

TABLE A.6   Cumulative Distributions of Before-Tax[a] and After-Tax Incomes[b] for Nonaged[c] Families, 1966

(in cumulative percentages of income)

Income Decile[a]	All Sizes		1-Person Family		2-Person Family		3-Person Family		4-Person Family		5+-Person Family	
	Before-Tax[b]	After-Tax[c]	Before-Tax	After-Tax	Before-Tax	After-Tax	Before-Tax	After-Tax	Before-Tax	After-Tax	Before-Tax	After-Tax
Lowest	0.78	1.85	0.49	1.81	0.92	2.04	1.42	2.65	1.99	2.88	1.41	2.64
Second	3.91	5.48	1.66	4.11	3.99	5.83	5.47	7.15	6.48	7.71	5.59	7.29
Third	8.83	10.66	4.58	7.77	8.77	11.02	10.96	12.88	12.40	13.80	11.18	13.17
Fourth	15.16	17.14	9.42	13.08	14.94	17.39	17.84	19.91	19.43	20.91	18.12	20.26
Fifth	22.95	24.95	16.15	19.97	22.31	24.84	25.95	28.07	27.48	29.00	26.04	28.27
Sixth	31.95	33.95	24.77	28.48	30.95	33.46	35.20	37.27	36.80	38.31	35.23	37.45
Seventh	42.48	44.38	35.08	38.41	40.75	43.09	45.71	47.59	47.29	48.83	45.58	47.73
Eighth	54.79	56.54	47.86	50.49	52.41	54.50	58.12	59.77	59.47	60.95	57.69	59.69
Ninth	69.92	71.44	63.64	65.49	66.71	68.41	72.87	74.20	74.00	75.33	72.20	73.94
Highest	100.00	100.00	100.00	100.00	100.00	100.00	100.00	100.00	100.00	100.00	100.00	100.00
Lowest 95 percent	79.44	80.74	73.76	75.06	75.81	77.25	81.99	83.10	82.98	84.05	81.44	82.92
Lowest 99 percent	91.06	91.99	85.23	86.04	88.74	89.81	92.61	93.37	93.33	94.11	92.84	93.65
Gini coefficient of inequality	.4099	.3774	.5102	.4570	.4310	.3919	.3628	.3297	.3385	.3126	.3639	.3277
Percentage reduction in area of inequality		7.9		10.4		9.1		9.1		7.7		9.9

a Based on distribution of family income before transfers, excluding the amount of corporation income tax allocated to families in the MERGE File.
b Based on family income including transfers and excluding corporation income tax and after individual income and payroll taxes.
c Families headed by an individual age 64 or under.

TABLE A.7 Cumulative Distributions of Before-Tax[a] and After-Tax Incomes[b] for Aged Families,[c] 1966

(in cumulative percentages of income)

Income Decile[a]	All Sizes		1-Person Family		2-Person Family		3-Person Family		4-Person Family		5+-Person Family	
	Before-Tax	After-Tax	Before-Tax	After-Tax	Before-Tax	After-Tax	Before-Tax	After-Tax	Before-Tax	After-Tax	Before-Tax	After-Tax
Lowest	0.69	3.48	1.09	4.68	0.77	3.78	0.53	2.83	0.26	2.78	0.39	2.70
Second	1.39	7.00	2.18	9.36	1.54	7.62	1.53	6.06	1.55	6.22	2.32	6.12
Third	2.08	10.52	3.27	14.05	2.89	11.83	4.24	10.48	4.32	11.08	5.86	11.32
Fourth	3.73	14.73	4.36	18.73	5.76	17.04	9.39	16.70	8.88	16.72	10.88	17.27
Fifth	7.30	20.35	5.45	23.42	10.27	23.52	16.09	23.75	14.99	23.80	18.73	25.53
Sixth	13.25	27.65	9.45	29.69	17.18	31.38	25.82	33.24	23.59	32.69	28.71	35.41
Seventh	22.05	36.98	17.07	38.06	26.69	41.16	38.55	44.74	34.69	43.34	42.12	47.99
Eighth	35.57	49.38	29.01	48.99	40.05	53.02	54.24	58.93	50.39	57.77	56.86	62.33
Ninth	56.77	66.48	48.11	64.34	59.27	68.25	72.99	76.07	71.03	75.81	74.94	78.11
Highest	100.00	100.00	100.00	100.00	100.00	100.00	100.00	100.00	100.00	100.00	100.00	100.00
Lowest 95 percent	72.60	78.92	63.97	75.87	73.08	79.07	84.27	86.32	84.39	87.07	86.35	88.00
Lowest 99 percent	91.01	93.01	87.21	91.60	90.90	92.89	95.98	96.40	96.45	96.91	96.48	96.95
Gini coefficient of inequality	.6287	.4367	.6799	.4097	.5842	.3944	.4598	.3595	.4869	.3647	.4231	.3309
Percentage reduction in area of inequality	30.5		39.7		32.5		21.8		25.1		21.8	

a Based on distribution of family income before transfers, excluding the amount of corporation income tax allocated to families in the MERGE File.
b Based on family income including transfers and excluding corporation income tax and after individual income and payroll taxes.
c Families headed by an individual age 65 or over.

CHAPTER 4

On the Comparison of Income Redistribution Plans

Harold W. Watts
University of Wisconsin

and

Jon K. Peck
Yale University

In this paper, we develop a microsimulation to assess the distributional consequences of the existing system of taxes and transfers and to compare those consequences with the impacts of several alternative credit income-tax systems for the 1970 population and income distributions. Then we use this microsimulation to explore the properties of proportional tax schedules combined with lump-sum credits as a simple form of redistribution that can be used as a reference standard against which other redistributive mechanisms can be assessed.

Our analysis begins with a concept we call "primary" income, which is the money income accruing to families and individuals from their current productive activities and other private transactions. Tax and transfer systems modify this primary income to produce what we call "final" income, which measures the claims of individuals and families on resources. Our analysis examines a variety of final income distributions. Any tax and transfer system redistributes some of the gross revenue it raises, using the rest (the *net* revenue) to finance the direct expenditure programs of the public sector (defense, education, highways, and so on) in combination with other public revenue sources. The alternative systems we specify can be considered comparable to the status quo in the sense that we require them to raise the same net revenue as the current system. Within this constraint, we make drastic alterations in the present system by imagining that almost all the current programs—Social Security taxes and benefits, public assistance, federal individual income tax, state and local income, sales, and property taxes—are replaced simultaneously by one simplified credit income tax operating on a comprehensive tax base.[1] In doing this, we give no recognition to political or administrative constraints that would make the realization of such a scheme impossible or unwise. We also make no allowance for possible changes in the distribution of primary income due to the level or nature of redistributive activities, although the greater the deviations from the current system, the more likely such changes would be.

Before we proceed with our analysis we would like to consider briefly the "cost" of redistribution—a concept given prominence by discussions of the welfare reform plans introduced during President Nixon's first term. There is no concept of cost obviously appropriate for application to income redistribution questions. If we had a social-welfare function in which we and you really believed, we could simply maximize it with respect to the income distribution and would not need a notion of cost. This question is considered further below. Since we do not have such a function, concepts of cost must be considered. At one extreme, there is a strong a priori basis for expecting total output to be sensitive to the level and type of redistribution; the change in total output is one concept of cost that appeals to an economist. For nonmarginal changes, however, the measurement of real output changes is difficult. Labor-supply elasticities of various kinds are required, and lack of firm estimates of such magnitudes has motivated negative-income-tax experiments in New Jersey and elsewhere. At the other extreme, the cost might be reckoned as simply the total dollar amount the Treasury would be obliged to write checks for in a given year. This "Treasury-throughput" measure of cost has some appeal because of its concreteness and its bearing on the extent of redistribution, but it has the disadvantage of making a program paying out gross benefits that are then partially taxed away appear spuriously costly relative to one which pays only net benefits and collects only net taxes. It is, thus, of little interest or relevance except as it bears upon the cost of administration, i.e., how many bureaucrats, clerks, machines,

[1] We have left in place some public transfer programs which are not primarily redistributive in nature but have made the receipts taxable.

lawyers, and accountants would be engaged in the mechanics—paper work and legal work—connected with the system. This notion of administrative costs, though not the subject of this paper, is certainly legitimate and the amount involved may be significant.

Insofar as the administrative and output costs are ignored, a zero sum redistribution, by definition, gives to one group the same number of dollars that it takes from another. The group of households as a whole has the same amount as before to spend on shoes, and ships, and sealing wax. An individual taxpayer, of course, has a great deal of interest in how much redistribution is going to cost him; this depends on his particular circumstances and may be a negative amount. It is possible to make some sense out of the cost question if one defines a specific group of families, e.g., those with red hair or, more relevantly, those with high incomes, and then asks how a specified change in redistribution policy affects their net tax bill.

The question of how much a particular redistribution costs, then, can only be answered either (1) by discussing the imponderables involved in foregone output or changed administrative costs; or (2) by asking for clarification as to *whose* cost you are interested in, a rich man's or a poor man's. We take a rather different approach to the issue of producing one statistic that defines a group of tax-and-transfer schemes with comparable impact on the income distribution for the entire population. Rather than calculating either of these notions of cost, we compare redistributions on the basis of the fraction of personal income explicitly intended for redistribution, i.e., distributed on a basis without regard to income. This share of income may be distributed, as in a credit income tax,[2] on a per capita basis; or according to schedules based on personal and family demographic characteristics. The balance of individual or family income, of course, is either extracted as net revenue for public uses or left in the hands of the people who received it under the primary distribution. Under certain administrative arrangements, this figure could be the same as the Treasury-throughput concept mentioned above.

[2] The credit income tax was proposed by Earl Rolph, "The Case for a Negative Income Tax Device" [15]. See also James Tobin, "Raising the Incomes of the Poor" [18].

FRAMEWORK FOR ANALYSIS

The underlying theme of this paper is the need for better understanding and wider discussion of distributional issues and policies. For this, a better framework of analysis and more explicit standards of comparison than those presently in use would be valuable. While we are convinced that such a framework, or standard, necessarily involves normative judgments, we do not believe that broad concurrence in a minimal set of judgments is impossible. We have, therefore, utilized a redistributional device which, in our view, falls within many people's definition of *fairness*—a simple credit income tax, consisting of a lump-sum grant and a tax schedule linear in income—as a standard form of taxation against which actual systems of taxes and transfers or specific variations can be compared.

The first part of the mechanism is a flat-rate proportional tax. This has a superficial evenhandedness, since it is neither progressive nor regressive and can be derived from the application of the principle of equal sacrifice applied to a utility function that is proportional to the logarithm of income: the Bernouilli assumption about utility. Although there seems to exist a general acceptance of the idea of progressive taxation, we have chosen the proportional rule as a minimum standard of fairness in the belief that virtually no one would seriously press the merits of a less-than-proportional (regressive) formula. However, we have not considered here the question of what kinds of income should be included in the tax base. The other part of the mechanism is the credits, and here again we have aimed at a principle of equal treatment in absolute terms of all persons or equivalent families, regardless of their level of income. This principle provides, at least, a starting point which may be useful in evaluating alternative plans, even though the definition of an equivalent family is not self-evident. (Note that the redistribution issue is here separated into a debate about principles of taxation and a debate about the actual amount of redistribution which should be effected under such principles.[3]) The resulting tax and transfer system is extremely easy to work with and easy to describe both for analysts and taxpayers. In addition, several authors have recently suggested that linear or nearly linear tax structures may have important optimality properties over a range of assumptions.[4]

[3] See Rawls [14] and Lerner [6].
[4] See Mirrlees [7] and Sheshinski [16].

Nevertheless, this linear tax scheme is capable of substantial amounts of redistribution and with a 100 percent tax is capable of achieving whatever notion of equality is built into the credit plan. Average net taxes can be quite progressive, varying from negative values toward an asymptotic rate equal to the marginal or gross tax rate.

With all these considerations in mind, it is proposed that a linear credit tax using poverty-standard credits be adopted as a "canonical" form of redistribution against which alternatives may be compared. It embodies a simple and easily grasped notion of equity, which need not be regarded as final or optimal or even popular; it is, however, a convenient standard that enables us to focus attention more precisely on the case for and against specific departures from it.

An alternative to comparing redistributions on the basis of the fraction of total income given out via the credit is to measure the total change in an income distribution induced by a redistribution plan with a net revenue of zero as

$$C = \frac{\sum_i \left| Y_{Bi} - Y_{Ai} \right|}{\sum_i \left| Y_{Bi} \right|}$$

where Y_{Bi} is the income of the ith unit before taxes and transfers, and Y_{Ai} is its income afterward. The sum is taken over all units in the population. C does not measure a total cost, but it does reflect the magnitude of the overall redistribution. For a linear tax system, this statistic is directly related to the fraction of the before-tax personal income which is redistributed independently of income. To see this, suppose that the tax system has a constant marginal tax rate, t (applied only to positive incomes), and a constant lump-sum grant, a. Then for Y_{Ai} nonnegative:

$$Y_{Ai} = (1 - t) Y_{Bi} + a$$

and

$$\left| Y_{Bi} - Y_{Ai} \right| = \left| t Y_{Bi} - a \right|.$$

Since the total net tax is zero, $t = Na \bigg/ \sum_{i \in p} Y_{Bi}$, where the population is of size N, and p is the set of indexes of the N_p units with positive pretax income. Therefore,

$$C = N|a| \left[\sum_{i \in p} \frac{NY_{Bi} - \sum_{i \in p} Y_{Bi}}{\left(\sum_{i \in p} Y_{Bi}\right)\sum_{i=1}^{N} |Y_{Bi}|N} + \frac{N - N_p}{\sum_{i=1}^{N} |Y_{Bi}|N} \right].$$

Since the term in brackets is constant by assumption, C is directly proportional to $|a|$ for any given population. If we had defined C in terms of squared changes instead of their absolute values, C would be proportional to a^2. When the demogrant[5] differs for different population units, however, C and the sum of the grants are not uniquely related to each other. (Constraining two different demogrant systems to have the same value of C as well as to yield zero net revenue is, unfortunately, too expensive a computational task for us.)

The choice of a scale on which to base the credits is crucial. A simple and appealing possibility is to allocate equal credits to all persons. This would be a more satisfactory choice if it were possible to deal realistically with individual lifetime incomes either for statistical analysis or for actual tax administration. In fact, we must deal with income over shorter periods, usually one year, and recognize that the family or household is the smallest unit to which many kinds of income can be allocated. Since families are very diversely constituted, some means to standardize them must be found. Although they have many drawbacks, the poverty thresholds for various sizes and kinds of families represent the most widely used and recognized scale of equivalence. We shall therefore use this scale to normalize family incomes; that is, we shall use the ratio of income to the poverty threshold[6] appropriate for each family, termed the welfare ratio, as the basis for comparing families' needs. This normalization is particularly questionable for high-income families, but in those calculations which assume diminishing marginal utility, inaccuracies in the normalization become less important as income rises. Tax credits

[5] The term demogrant is used here as synonymous with the credit part of a credit income tax. It emphasizes the property that the credits are lump-sum amounts which may be related to demographic and family characteristics but not to income or wealth status.

[6] For a definition and explanation of the current poverty ("low income") thresholds, see *Characteristics of the Low Income Population 1970* [4].

in the standard redistribution are allocated in proportion to these thresholds.

In summary then, we are concerned with the variety of redistributions that are, by assumption, "costless." No allowance is made for output or administrative costs. The question is, simply, who recieves what proportion of a fixed total of final income. We will consider specific population groups, defined both in terms of their demographic characteristics and in terms of their income status. We evaluate the cost to such groups, or the benefits, relative either to the status quo or relative to a zero-redistribution norm. For readers with highly developed a priori notions about an equitable income distribution, the relatively raw and disaggregated distributions of final income for various groups will be the most interesting results. We have attempted, however, to supply several alternative redistributions. For this, we have adopted a group of primitive utility-based inequality measures that can be readily evaluated. These will be shown both in fully aggregated form and with breakdowns which show the impact on various demographic groups and on the poor and nonpoor subpopulations.

First of all, as mentioned before, we use a family income welfare-ratio measure to normalize different family compositions. In the utility analysis, we assume that this ratio is the argument of each person's utility function. Utility can then be suitably aggregated for each family and for groups of families.[7] The class of utility functions and inequality measures we consider, which has been suggested by Atkinson [1], includes a wide range of assumptions about the rate of decline of marginal utility with increases in the welfare index. This class of functions includes as special cases a linear utility function (with constant marginal utility) and a logarithmic function, where marginal utility declines in proportion to the inverse of the welfare index. It also includes measures with more rapidly falling marginal utility, two of which we have used.

Let us now turn to further discussion of the tax base we are using. We refer to this as primary income. In so doing, we are trying to use a term which does not connote close conformity with any of the commonly used income concepts and to signal the possibility that some of our approximations may be inaccurate.

[7] In order to deal with negative and zero incomes we do not allow the argument of the utility function to fall below 0.1.

We are aiming at a concept which measures the flow of income to families and individuals prior to any tampering by the public sector. We cannot, however, undo all the real allocational and distributional consequences of public sector activities, as this would require an elaborate general equilibrium analysis.

For the present calculations, we have used the Current Population Survey (CPS) money income concept as adjusted in the MERGE File to conform to aggregate control totals, minus public transfers from Social Security, public assistance, unemployment insurance benefits, workmen's compensation, and income-conditioned veterans' benefits. To this, we have added realized capital gains. This income concept totals $679 billion for the simulated 1970 population in the MERGE File, which is nearly $125 billion less than total personal income in the national accounts for 1970, both because of the transfer payments that have been deducted and because of various imputations in the national accounts that are not in the MERGE File. We have, however, in our calculations retained those public transfers with the exception of Old-Age, Survivors, and Disability Insurance (OASDI) that are not primarily designed to affect the size distribution of income.

The basic strategy is first to calculate a "final" income based on the status quo of taxes and transfers as they existed in 1970, and then to compare the redistribution effected by those policies with a group of alternative redistributions produced by simple credit-income-tax formulas, which differ from each other in the formula for the credit and in the amount of income redistributed. An attempt has been made to be quite inclusive as regards taxes at all levels. A disproportionate interest is always taken in the federal individual income tax, because it is the largest single tax program affecting households directly and because it is a universal program subject to debate and change at the federal policy level; but other taxes, in the aggregate, constitute a similar proportion of the difference between primary and final income and need to be accounted for in any comprehensive assessment of overall redistribution. Hence, from primary income we have subtracted federal individual income taxes, employee contributions for Social Security, property taxes, state individual income taxes, and sales taxes.[8] Finally, the transfers that were subtracted from CPS

---

[8] For the assumption made about the incidence of the property tax, see the appendix.

income are added back in. We take no account of the federal
corporate income tax in this analysis. Thus we must interpret our
status quo final income as the total money receipts—after taxes
and transfers—available for spending on goods and services, with
prices adjusted for both the elimination of sales taxes and the
payment of housing expenses other than the property tax.[9]

This final income must be clearly distinguished from the usual
concept of disposable income, which only deducts income and
payroll taxes but includes such items as imputed rental income of
households; hence, disposable income is the amount available for
expenditure on goods and services as actually priced. The rationale
for using final instead of disposable income is that states regard
property and sales taxes as substitutes for income taxes. So
calculated, status quo final income totals $566 billion, which is
$113 billion, or 16.6 percent, less than the $679 billion of primary
income reckoned for 1970. In other words, the net aggregate
effects of current tax and transfer policies—federal, state, and local
—are to redistribute income in ways to be discussed below and
to extract $113 billion of purchasing power for financing various
direct-expenditure programs. Some of these programs, of course,
are deliberately redistributive, such as food stamps and housing
subsidies. Others, such as education, highways, and national
defense, are not, although they have some redistributive effects.
However, these are not the subject of our inquiry.

In gross terms, the existing taxes we take account of actually
collect $54 billion more than the $113 billion described above,
but those dollars are returned to the purchasing power of
households in the form of transfers. The simplified credit-tax
schemes that we introduce for comparison are treated as complete
replacements for this entire tax and transfer system. They have all
been calibrated to yield the same $113 billion of net revenue—or
(equivalently) to reduce primary income down to the final income
of $566 billion—as do the status quo policies. In gross terms, the
tax is a simple proportional one applied to primary income as the
base. If one were concerned only to raise the required net revenue,
leaving the primary relative distribution unaltered—which is a
hypothetical policy of zero redistribution—a tax of 16.6 percent
on primary income would be sufficient. We vary the level of
redistribution from this point by increasing the fraction of

---

[9] In the alternative redistributions, this results in some overstatement of
the final income for owners of rental property who report such income on
the 1040 federal form and equivalent understatement for renters.

the gross tax by a given proportion—say, 10 percent—and then distributing the resulting added gross revenue—$68 billion in this case—as refundable tax credits, on a basis which is not a function of income.

In addition to varying the level of redistribution, i.e., the fraction of primary income which is distributed as tax credits, we examine six different credit structures. The plans investigated are summarized in Table 1. The first structure is for tax credits that are proportional to family poverty thresholds. It is assumed that relative "needs" are measured by these thresholds, and that it is, therefore, reasonable to allocate credits against gross taxes in proportion to the needs or responsibilities of the family. This is consistent with the choice of poverty thresholds for normalizing family incomes.

The poverty threshold structure of credits is used with four different levels of redistribution, viz., 10 percent, 20 percent, 30 percent, and 50 percent. As explained above, these imply gross proportional taxes ranging from 26.6 percent to 66.6 percent of primary income. This covers a range from relatively weak to quite drastic redistribution. At one end, 12 percent of final income reflects the uniform distribution of credits and 88 percent reflects the initial distribution of primary income. At the other end, only 40 percent of final income reflects the initial income distribution. The table indicates the fraction of the poverty standard that the four levels of distribution afford. Also indicated are the dollar amounts due the prototypical urban male-headed family of four.

The five other structures used are replicated for only two levels of redistribution: 10 percent and 30 percent. The first of these is a simple per capita demogrant with credits of $341 at the 10 percent level, and $1,022 at the 30 percent level, allocated to each person in a family. Next is a per adult allowance which pays $520 or $1,559 at the two redistribution levels to each person over 18. A simple child allowance was considered as a contrast but was rejected because the adverse effect on aged persons, who are left without Social Security, makes the case uninteresting. Instead we have explored a pair of hybrid plans: At the 10 percent level, the same Social Security benefits as the status quo are paid, and the remainder of the $68 billion is allocated as tax credits equally among all persons under 18. At the 30 percent level of redistribution, Social Security benefits are doubled and again the remaining balance is distributed equally among all children. This

TABLE 1   Alternative Credit Income Taxes

	Tax Rates (percent)			
	26.6	36.6	46.6	66.6
Redistribution rate[a]	10	20	30	50
Credit structures:				
1. Poverty standard (fraction of poverty level)	.319	.637	.956	1.593
Mean amount	$1,266	$2,529	$3,795	$6,324
2. Per capita	$341	—	$1,022	—
3. Per adult	$520	—	$1,559	—
4. Social Security plus child allowances	Current Social Security rates plus $504 per child	—	Double current Social Security rates plus $1,995 per child	—
5. Age scale 1: 65 and over, 18 to 64, 0 to 17	$578:$385:$193	—	$1,734:$1,156:$578	—
6. Age scale 2: 65 and over, 18 to 64, 10 to 17, 0 to 9	$613:$408:$204:$102	—	$1,838:$1,225:$613:$306	—

[a] This rate is measured as the percentage of pretax or primary income devoted to redistribution.

results in child allowances of approximately $500 and $2,000 respectively. The last two plans employ credits that are graduated according to age. In the first instance (age scale 1), the population is divided into aged (65 and over), other adults (18 to 64), and children (17 and under), and these three groups get credits with relative values 3:2:1. In the second instance (age scale 2), four groups are distinguished, including two categories of children: aged 10 to 17 and 0 to 9. The younger children receive only half as much as the older ones. The combination of the six alternative structures with the redistribution level variations results in fourteen tax systems. These variations were chosen to show how the actual distributions of income for the United States would be altered by different levels or degrees of redistributional activity, and to explore the consequences of alternative structures for the tax credits.

THE EFFECT OF ALTERNATIVE REDISTRIBUTIONS ON INCOME SHARES

As mentioned earlier, we have adopted a "welfare-ratio" normalization of income, and hence we do not display the traditional distribution by dollar-income brackets. While this normalization is useful in securing comparability among families of different size, it does not render fully comparable categories of families which are treated as distinct in our existing tax and transfer system. Indeed, there are important differences with regard to the equity of income shares among these categories.

We distinguish, instead, six mutually exclusive and exhaustive groups. Individuals 65 and over form one group, and families headed by an aged person form the second. These two groups together contain nearly 92 percent of all aged persons and relatively few persons under 65. The remaining groups are all headed by nonaged persons. Individuals form the third group, families with female heads form the fourth, and the last two groups are small to moderate-sized male-headed families (2 to 5 persons)[10] and large male-headed families (6 or more). Within these groups, the welfare ratio is more reliable as an indicator of economic or income status. We have chosen these groupings for

---

[10] This is the modal family: more than 55 percent of all persons live in such families.

several reasons. The aged and female-headed categories are presently recognized as having a differential basis for income support. Individuals of all ages are difficult to compare with families in terms of income needs. Finally, large families are often overlooked in our tendency to focus on the four-person archetype.

Section B of Table 2 displays the distribution of total need, as measured by the poverty thresholds, and the distribution of persons in total and by age status across the six groups listed above. Section A of the same table shows how income is distributed among these groups—both primary income and the fifteen versions of final income. It should be noted here that the status quo redistributed a substantial amount of income to the aged and female-headed categories, most of which is offset by reductions in the shares going to nonaged individuals and male-headed families of small to moderate size. By contrast, the poverty-standard redistribution adds to the shares of all groups except the modal group, which is the only one that now gets a larger share of primary income than its share of (poverty-standard) need. With a poverty-standard credit structure, less is provided to the aged and female-headed units than the status quo up to a level of 30 percent redistribution. None of the structures at the 10 percent level does as well by these categories as does the status quo. They all, however, allocate more to the large families and nonaged individuals. Not surprisingly, the Social-Security-plus-child-allowance plan conforms most closely to the current outcome; it differs mainly in giving more to large male-headed families than is currently the case. Clearly the poverty standard and the age-scaled credits are similar in their impact, and both yield less redistribution from individuals or small families to large families than does a flat per capita credit.

However, we are most directly interested in income redistribution among welfare strata. Table 3 contains the basic outcome in terms of primary- and final-income shares. The first three columns indicate how income is distributed among the lowest 20 percent of the population of persons ranked by the welfare ratio of primary income. This group is approximately equivalent to the poor. The next stratum contain 50 percent of the population and ranges from the near-poor at 110 percent of the poverty level up to the moderately comfortable at 375 percent of poverty. The third group, the top 30 percent, is all above 375 percent of poverty level and ranges from the upper middle class through the superrich. In

TABLE 2   Percent Distribution of Income and Persons Among Subgroups of Units for Alternative Redistributions

| | Aged | | Nonaged | | | |
	Individuals	Family Heads	Individuals	Female-Headed Families	Male-Headed Families 2 to 5	Male-Headed Families 6+
Section A:						
Primary income	2.1	8.6	7.2	3.1	65.01	13.1
Final income						
Status quo	3.2	10.5	6.5	4.1	62.5	13.2
Poverty standard						
10[a]	2.5	8.8	7.4	3.4	64.5	13.4
20[a]	3.0	9.0	7.6	3.7	63.0	13.7
30[a]	3.4	9.3	7.8	4.0	61.5	14.0
50[a]	4.3	9.8	8.1	4.6	58.5	14.7
Per capita 10[a]	2.3	8.8	6.9	3.4	64.7	13.9
Per adult 10[a]	2.5	9.3	7.2	3.3	64.9	12.8

Social Security + child						
allowance	10[a]	3.2	10.3	6.7	3.7	62.2	13.9
Age scale 1	10[a]	2.5	9.4	7.0	3.3	64.4	13.4
Age scale 2	10[a]	2.6	9.5	7.1	3.3	64.3	13.2
Per capita	30[a]	2.6	9.2	6.3	4.1	62.1	15.7
Per adult	30[a]	3.2	10.9	7.1	3.7	62.6	12.5
Social Security + child						
allowance	30[a]	4.1	11.2	5.3	4.9	56.7	17.8
Age scale 1	30[a]	3.4	11.0	6.5	3.8	61.2	14.1
Age scale 2	30[a]	3.5	11.4	6.6	3.8	61.1	13.6
Section B:						
"Need"		5.7	10.8	8.6	5.5	53.6	15.8
Persons		3.3	10.5	4.6	5.8	55.4	20.4
Less than 18		—	1.9	.2	8.1	52.6	37.2
18 to 64		—	5.4	8.3	5.2	67.4	13.7
65 and over		29.4	62.4	—	1.4	5.5	1.3

[a] Redistribution rate. This rate is measured as the percentage of pretax or primary income devoted to redistribution.

TABLE 3   Shares of Primary and Final Income Going to Selected Strata of Units Ranked by Primary Welfare Ratio
(percent)

	Low 20 Percent ($w_0 < 1.1$)[a]	Mid 50 Percent ($w_0 = 1.1\text{-}3.75$)	High 30 Percent ($w_0 > 3.75$)	Top 5 Percent ($w_0 > 8.3$)	Aged Individuals and Families ($w_0 < 1.1$)	Female-Headed Families ($w_0 < 1.1$)	Male-Headed Families ($w_0 < 1.1$)	Male-Headed Families ($w_0 = 1.1\text{-}3.75$)
Primary income	2.8	34.6	62.5	21.6	0.8	0.3	1.4	27.2
Final income								
Status quo	6.9	35.1	58.0	18.7	3.4	1.0	2.0	26.7
Poverty standard								
10[b]	5.0	36.3	58.7	19.7	1.7	0.6	2.1	28.5
20[b]	7.2	37.9	54.9	17.7	2.7	0.8	2.8	29.4
30[b]	9.4	39.5	51.1	15.8	3.6	1.1	3.5	30.9
50[b]	13.8	42.8	43.4	11.8	5.5	1.7	4.8	33.3
Per capita 10[b]	4.8	36.5	58.7	19.6	1.5	0.6	2.2	28.9
Per adult 10[b]	4.9	36.0	59.1	19.8	1.9	0.4	2.0	28.1
Social Security + child allowance 10[b]	6.5	36.1	57.4	19.3	3.0	0.8	2.3	27.9
Age scale 1 10[b]	5.1	36.2	58.7	19.7	2.0	0.5	2.1	28.3
Age scale 2 10[b]	5.1	36.1	58.8	19.7	2.1	0.5	2.0	28.2
Per capita 30[b]	8.8	40.2	51.0	15.7	3.0	1.2	3.9	32.3
Per adult 30[b]	8.9	38.7	52.4	16.3	4.1	0.8	3.1	29.7
Social Security + child allowance 30[b]	12.1	40.3	47.6	14.8	5.2	1.9	4.4	31.8
Age scale 1 30[b]	9.6	39.2	51.2	15.9	4.3	1.0	3.4	30.5
Age scale 2 30[b]	9.6	38.9	51.5	16.0	4.6	0.9	3.3	30.0

[a] w_0 is the welfare ratio based on primary income.
[b] Redistribution rate. This rate is measured as the percentage of pretax or primary income devoted to redistribution.

the fourth column, the top 5 percent is shown separately—the lowest income in this group is 8.3 times the poverty level before tax and transfers. The last four columns show several subgroups of these strata—the aged, female-headed families, and male-headed families.

It is important to notice that the status quo redistributes a substantial amount toward the lowest 20 percent of the income distribution. Their share increases from 2.8 percent of primary income to nearly 7.0 percent of final income. This is nearly as much as the 7.2 percent achieved by the poverty-standard credit tax at a 20 percent redistribution level. However, the middle 50 percent, in contrast, receive only 35 percent under the current tax system, as compared with the nearly 38 percent they would get under that same 20 percent linear tax scheme. The extra 3 percent is retained by the highest 30 percent with the top 5 percent getting one-third of the extra. Moreover, as the level of redistribution is increased, the share going to the middle 50 percent continues to increase. Indeed, looking further down to the different tax-credit structures, there is no structure at the 10 percent level which is not noticeably more generous to the middle 50 percent than is our present policy. At given redistribution levels, the Social-Security-plus-child-allowance plans provide the largest gains to the poor, but even here there is no tendency for the extra gains to be at the expense of the middle majority.

If one compares the treatment of aged and female-headed families, it is clear that the poverty-standard law at the 30 percent redistribution rate is most comparable with the status quo. But that law would increase the share going to poor male-headed families from 2 percent to 3.5 percent and raise the transfer going to male-headed families in the middle 50 percent from 26.7 percent to 30.9 percent. This phenomenon is the result of current neglect of the working poor, as well as some squeezing of the lower middle class wage-earning group. The top 30 percent now receive nearly 7 percent more of total final income than they would under this "fair" redistribution. Clearly, the United States already engages in substantial redistribution; and for the groups that are "poorest," the amount is equivalent to a level of nearly 30 percent on a poverty-standard credit tax. However, it is also clear that the male-headed families of modest means have not been given comparable treatment, and that it would not be necessary to penalize the families near the median welfare-ratio level in order to be more generous—and more uniformly so—to the poor and the near-poor.

Table 4 shows how the distribution of persons by welfare ratio is altered by redistribution. The current policies reduce the fractions below the poverty level and the fraction more than four times above it. The effect of high redistribution levels is to concentrate more and more persons in the 2 to 4 range of the welfare ratio, which includes the mean (2.7). The strongly redistributive poverty-standard law at the 50 percent redistribution rate completely eliminates poverty; it also decimates the stratum above eight times the poverty level and concentrates 70 percent of the population in the 2 to 4 range, which now contains only 35 percent. The Social-Security-plus-child-allowance plans are

TABLE 4   Percent Distribution of Persons by Welfare Ratio of Unit for Alternative Redistributions

		0 to 1	1 to 2	2 to 4	4 to 8	8+
Primary income		18.1	21.0	33.9	21.4	5.5
Final income						
Status quo		15.5	31.1	35.3	15.3	2.8
Poverty standard	10[a]	17.1	28.6	37.0	14.8	2.5
	20[a]	11.5	31.0	42.1	13.7	1.7
	30[a]	5.0	33.5	48.5	11.8	1.2
	50[a]	0.0	22.4	70.5	6.6	0.5
Per capita	10[a]	16.3	28.5	37.8	14.9	2.5
Per adult	10[a]	17.8	28.4	36.3	14.9	2.6
Social Security + child allowance	10[a]	14.0	31.2	38.0	14.5	2.3
Age scale 1	10[a]	16.8	29.0	36.8	14.9	2.5
Age scale 2	10[a]	17.0	28.9	36.7	14.8	2.6
Per capita	30[a]	5.7	28.0	52.8	12.3	1.2
Per adult	30[a]	7.8	33.3	44.4	13.1	1.4
Social Security + child allowance	30[a]	5.4	24.1	57.6	11.8	1.1
Age scale 1	30[a]	5.0	32.9	48.6	12.2	1.3
Age scale 2	30[a]	5.4	33.9	46.9	12.5	1.3

[a] Redistribution rate. This rate is measured as the percentage of pretax or primary income devoted to redistribution.

seen here to be the most effective in reducing dispersion at any given level of redistribution.

Figure 1 shows how the distribution of persons as ranked by welfare ratios is altered by redistribution. The cumulative distribution is plotted on log-probability scales (a log-normal distribution would provide a straight line). It is evident here that the status quo system reduces dispersion and poverty; it is also clear that the higher levels of redistribution, 30 percent to 50 percent, produce a noticeable amount of added equalization.

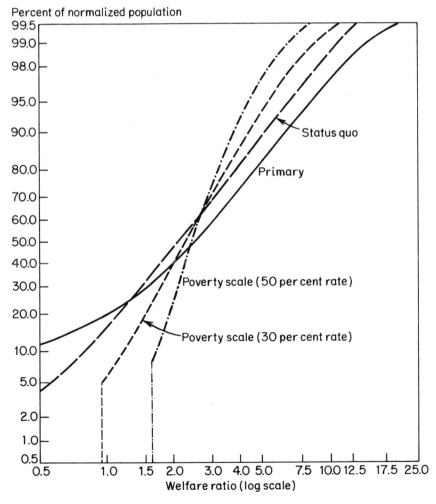

FIGURE 1: Cumulative Distributions of Persons by Welfare Ratio of Family

Figures 2 through 6 display the Lorenz curves for the status quo and various alternative redistributions. Once again we see that current policies do tend to equalize the distribution, and that the alternatives that we have worked with cover a broad range of shift in the curves. It should be repeated here, however, that we have not allowed for any labor-force response by the economy to the tax and transfer system.

ANALYSIS AND RESULTS OF SUMMARY MEASURES OF THE WELFARE DISTRIBUTION

While it is useful, and for many purposes adequate, to observe the impact of redistribution on shares of different groups and

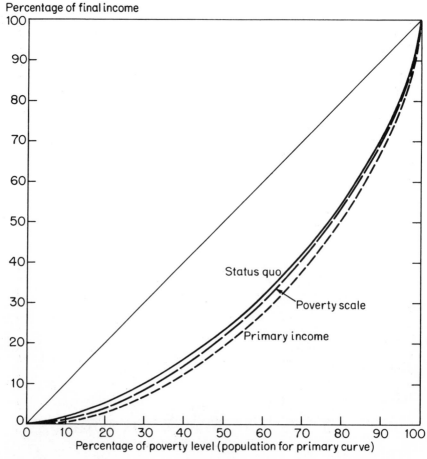

FIGURE 2: Lorenz Curves for Primary Income, Status Quo, and Poverty Scale Redistribution at 10 Percent

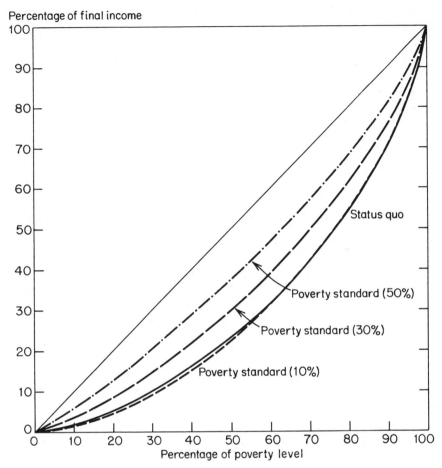

FIGURE 3: Lorenz Curves for Status Quo and Alternative Levels of Redistribution Using Poverty Standard Credits

strata, it is also of interest to evaluate more summary descriptions which attempt to condense the plethora of numbers into a few, more comprehensible indicators. As we view this problem, it is again one of embodying some standard of "fairness" in a formula that enables us to rank and compare final distributions.

The problem of what summary statistics to use in describing an income distribution and what measures of inequality are appropriate is an ancient one. The most commonly used measures are the mean or median income and the Gini coefficient. However, as has been observed, most recently by Atkinson [1] and earlier by Dalton [5], we should be concerned with some notion of social welfare and, therefore, should choose statistics which are directly

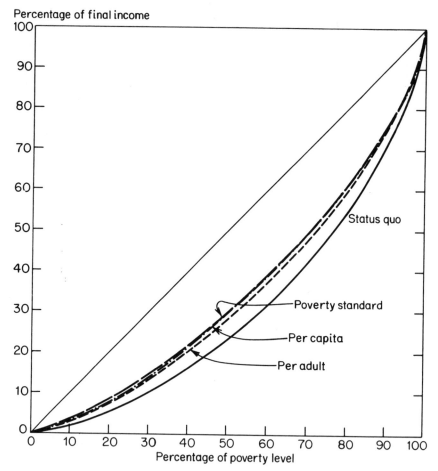

Percentage of final income

FIGURE 4: Lorenz Curves for Alternative Tax Credit Structures Using 30 Percent Redistribution

related to some social welfare measures. What follows includes a summary of Atkinson's solution to this problem.

Our goal is to rank the alternative income distributions by social welfare. For this purpose, we use a simple social welfare function, W, described below. Many factors which affect social welfare are not taken into account in the formulation we use. Our W might, perhaps, be called a partial social-welfare function to emphasize that other factors are also important. However, we only use W to compare alternative income distributions under ceteris paribus assumptions. It could still be argued that the assumptions about utility and W lead to the omission of important factors which are

Percentage of final income

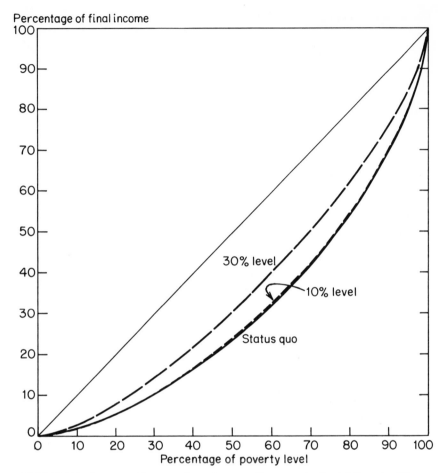

FIGURE 5: Lorenz Curves for Status Quo and Social-Security-Plus-Child-Allowance Plan

not constant as the distribution changes, but we do not pursue more complex formulations. Assume that there exists a social welfare function, W, which is symmetric and additively separable,

$$W = \sum_i U(w_i) f(w_i),$$

where U is the individual utility function which is assumed to be identical for all persons and f is the probability function for the (finite) population. Assume further that the individual utility function, U, is increasing and concave. Under these assumptions two distributions, say f and f^*, with the same mean, can be ranked

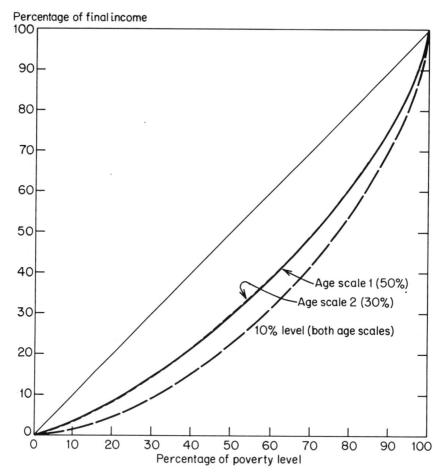

FIGURE 6: Lorenz Curves for Age-Related Plans

without further assumptions about utility functions if, and only if, the two Lorenz curves do not cross. When the means differ, the distribution with the higher mean will be preferred if its Lorenz curve is everywhere above the Lorenz curve of the other distribution.[11]

When the distributions cannot be ranked without further information on the utility function, we choose certain particular functional forms for U which are unique up to a linear

---

[11] Our exercise might be thought always to result in distributions whose means are equal; however, since we have normalized income by the poverty level, redistributions which preserve the aggregate incomes can change the mean of the welfare ratios.

transformation and have one argument—the family's welfare ratio. Any choice of functions is necessarily subjective. Value judgments must be made sometime, however, and our treatment has the virtue of making these judgments explicit.

Once a utility function is chosen, a measure of inequality can be constructed by analogy with the certainty-equivalent calculations in risk theory.[12] To do this, define the equally distributed-equivalent level of normalized income, w_{ede}, as the per capita amount which would give the same total utility as the actual distribution gives if each person received w_{ede}. That is, $U(w_{ede})$ is the expected value of the utility function over the distribution of w. More formally,

$$U(w_{ede}) = \sum U(w_i) f(w_i).$$

Clearly, w_{ede} depends on the particular utility function chosen. Then the inequality measure defined is $I_U = 1$ $(wede/\mu)$, where μ is the mean of the distribution of w. The index I appears similar to a Gini coefficient, because it lies in the interval $[0, 1]$, with zero corresponding to perfect equality, and one, maximum inequality; but, as will be seen below, the index I will generally give a ranking of distributions by inequality different from the Gini coefficient ranking. Under our assumptions about U, social welfare is maximized when all incomes are equal, but we would not assert that complete equality is the ideal distribution. Our analysis is too unrealistic to support such a conclusion, but w_{ede} does suggest an upper bound on the efficiency losses which could be suffered as a consequence of redistribution without producing a decrease in total social welfare.[13]

What reasonable restrictions should be put on the class of possible utility functions? One criterion, suggested by Atkinson and adopted by us, is what he terms "constant relative inequality aversion," i.e., if we transform a distribution by a change of

[12] We also report Gini coefficients, but as Newbery [9] has shown, there exists no additive utility function which ranks distributions in the same order as the Gini coefficient.

[13] It is not obvious that the linear tax systems we investigate are inferior to our current tax system in terms of allocative efficiency. Indeed, this is one of the arguments usually cited in favor of a demogrant system.

location and scale, the inequality measure should not change. This, plus concavity, requires that $U(w)$ be of the form:

$$U(w) = \begin{cases} A + B\dfrac{w^{1-\epsilon}}{1-\epsilon} & \epsilon \neq 1, \\ A + B \ln w & \epsilon = 1. \end{cases}$$

This is a one-parameter family indexed by ϵ, since A and B are arbitrary. When ϵ is zero, marginal utility is constant; as ϵ rises, marginal utility falls more rapidly, $dU/dw = Bw^{-\epsilon}$.

Using this family of utility functions, we are led to the family of inequality measures,

$$I_\epsilon = 1 - \left[\sum \left(\frac{w_i}{\mu} \right)^{1-\epsilon} f(w_i) \right]^{\frac{1}{1-\epsilon}}.$$

These measures are invariant under linear transformations.

We have performed our calculations for four different utility functions corresponding to values for ϵ of 0 (linear), 1 (logarithmic), 1.5 (reciprocal square root), and 2 (reciprocal). Some respondents report negative or zero income. Since we do not believe that this really represents the claims of these units on resources, we have arbitrarily chosen to calculate the welfare ratio as either the reported ratio or .1, whichever is larger. That is, no one is allowed to have a claim on resources of less than 10 percent of his poverty level.[14]

These are individual utility functions, but the argument of the functions is the welfare ratio of the family. To find the utility for a family, individual utility is multiplied by family size. In summary, we (1) assume all persons' utility functions are identical; (2) take some account of economies realized by families living together through the normalization process; (3) assume that there is no inequality within a family; and (4) assume that each family member's utility counts equally in the total welfare of society.

---

[14] The exact choice of a minimum w is not crucial for the plans we investigate, although a minimum of zero would give very different answers. In the status quo income distribution, only about 1.5 percent of the population report a welfare ratio of less than .1; and in the other distributions, the percentage is also very small. In fact, many of these cases come from families reporting a negative w, and their permanent income is likely to be much larger than the reported amount.

In Table 5, we have assembled several averages and inequality measures describing the various final distributions. The first column contains the average individual welfare ratio, where the individual ratio for a person is equal to the welfare ratio of his family. The next three columns contain the "equally distributed-equivalent" welfare ratios corresponding to ϵ values of 1.0, 1.5, and 2.0, respectively. The first column is, of course, $w_{ede}(0)$. It is worth pointing out that these can be regarded as averages—$w_{ede}(1)$ is simply the geometric mean of individual welfare ratios and $w_{ede}(2)$ is their harmonic mean, while $w_{ede}(1.5)$ is some parametric hybrid average—and we can appeal to theorems about the relative size of these means (applied to positive numbers) to infer that the equivalent income will be smaller, the larger is ϵ for any given distribution. Alternatively, observe that $w_{ede}(\epsilon)$ falls as ϵ rises, because the faster marginal utility falls, the greater is the amount of income which can be redistributed away from high-income families for any given utility loss.

Columns 5 through 7 contain the inequality index values for $\epsilon = 1.0$, 1.5, and 2.0. I_0 is identically zero and is, therefore, not shown. As explained above, these values indicate the fraction of current (unequally distributed) income that would be required to achieve the same total utility if distributed equally. Equivalently, it places an upper bound on the income loss that could be "afforded" by a redistribution without lowering average welfare. These values can be readily calculated from the numbers on the left as:

$$I_\epsilon = 1 - \frac{w_{ede}(\epsilon)}{w_{ede}(0)} .$$

Finally, the Gini coefficient is shown in the last column. In comparing our estimates of the Gini coefficients with others in the literature, it must be recalled that the population is measured in units of need. The average utilities have not been shown, but they can be derived by substituting the appropriate w_{ede} into the formula given above.

The means and inequality measures are shown for the overall distribution, separately for the poor and nonpoor ($w < 1, w \geqslant 1$), and for each of the six subgroups of the population. The inequality measures for such subgroups reflect only internal dispersion; between-group dispersion is reflected in the all-unit measures.

TABLE 5   Averages and Inequality Measures From Actual and Transformed Distribution of Welfare Ratios

	Average Welfare	$W_e(1)$	$W_e(1.5)$	$W_e(2.0)$	$I(1.0)$	$I(1.5)$	$I(2.0)$	Gini Coefficient
Primary income:								
All	3.23	2.01	1.35	.82	.379	.581	.746	.4601
Poor	.42	.30	.25	.21	.293	.420	.513	.3600
Nonpoor	3.88	3.12	2.85	2.63	.197	.266	.323	.3767
Aged								
Individuals	1.22	.40	.26	.20	.675	.786	.837	.7305
Heads	2.59	1.06	.64	.41	.589	.754	.843	.6249
Nonaged								
Individuals	2.70	1.49	.93	.57	.447	.654	.790	.4943
Female heads	1.73	.74	.45	.30	.570	.742	.827	.6079
Male head 2-5	3.89	2.88	2.32	1.67	.259	.403	.571	.3938
Male head 6+	2.64	1.91	1.51	1.08	.277	.429	.590	.3943
Status quo final income:								
All	2.70	2.00	1.65	1.29	.259	.387	.523	.3957
Poor	.84	.67	.57	.46	.205	.325	.448	.1863
Nonpoor	3.13	2.58	2.37	2.19	.175	.242	.300	.3380
Aged								
Individuals	1.52	1.09	.93	.77	.280	.387	.490	NA
Heads	2.64	1.87	1.59	1.29	.289	.398	.511	NA
Nonaged								
Individuals	2.04	1.36	1.01	.71	.333	.503	.650	NA
Female heads	1.93	1.41	1.19	.97	.270	.387	.497	NA

Male head 2-5	3.09	2.38	2.02	1.58	.229	.348	.489	NA
Male head 6+	2.23	1.71	1.43	1.13	.233	.356	.491	NA
Poverty standard (10)[a]:								
All	2.68	1.96	1.62	1.30	.270	.394	.516	.4088
Poor	.60	.55	.49	.44	.094	.192	.262	.2075
Nonpoor	2.16	2.63	2.48	2.33	.168	.214	.262	.3321
Aged								
Individuals	1.18	.69	.59	.51	.419	.503	.565	.5477
Heads	2.20	1.33	1.02	.83	.395	.537	.621	.5400
Nonaged								
Individuals	2.29	1.60	1.31	1.06	.300	.427	.536	.4243
Female heads	1.58	1.06	.85	.72	.328	.462	.543	.4744
Male head 2-5	3.16	2.50	2.21	1.31	.208	.300	.421	.3462
Male head 6+	2.24	1.79	1.57	1.31	.203	.299	.416	.3338
Poverty standard (20)[a]:								
All	2.67	2.14	1.91	1.64	.197	.286	.387	.3538
Poor	.87	.83	.75	.68	.046	.140	.224	.0815
Nonpoor	3.09	2.67	2.56	2.44	.135	.170	.208	.3074
Aged								
Individuals	1.38	1.03	.95	.89	.258	.309	.356	.4091
Heads	2.26	1.64	1.37	1.21	.274	.393	.467	.4542
Nonaged								
Individuals	2.34	1.85	1.65	1.44	.209	.295	.385	.3587
Female heads	1.73	1.39	1.23	1.13	.194	.291	.349	.3779
Male head 2-5	3.09	2.58	2.36	2.04	.165	.235	.341	.3063
Male head 6+	2.30	1.96	1.79	1.56	.148	.219	.319	.2828

TABLE 5   *(Continued)*

	Average Welfare	$W_e(1)$	$W_e(1.5)$	$W_e(2.0)$	$I(1.0)$	$I(1.5)$	$I(2.0)$	Gini Coefficient
Poverty standard (30)[a]:								
All	2.67	2.28	2.11	1.88	.143	.209	.295	.2980
Poor	2.14	1.11	1.00	.89	.029	.124	.224	.0198
Nonpoor	3.02	2.70	2.63	2.54	.105	.129	.159	.2801
Aged								
Individuals	1.58	1.32	1.28	1.23	.163	.190	.220	.3011
Heads	2.32	1.89	1.65	1.49	.187	.290	.359	.3722
Nonaged								
Individuals	2.39	2.04	1.89	1.70	.145	.208	.286	.2964
Female heads	1.88	1.67	1.53	1.46	.112	.185	.222	.2949
Male head 2-5	3.02	2.63	2.47	2.19	.128	.181	.275	.2639
Male head 6+	2.35	2.10	1.98	1.78	.106	.158	.243	.2326
Poverty standard (50)[a]:								
All	2.66	2.48	2.38	2.21	.066	.103	.167	.1844
Poor	1.69	1.66	1.49	1.28	.017	.117	.242	.3261
Nonpoor	2.88	2.72	2.71	2.66	.055	.061	.076	.1831
Aged								
Individuals	1.98	1.86	1.85	1.83	.063	.065	.076	.1470
Heads	2.45	2.28	2.08	1.94	.068	.149	.207	.2199
Nonaged								
Individuals	2.48	2.33	2.25	2.10	.063	.095	.154	.1750
Female heads	2.17	2.12	2.02	2.00	.022	.067	.079	.1578

Male head 2-5	2.88	2.68	2.61	2.41	.067	.094	.161	.1715
Male head 6+	2.46	2.33	2.25	2.06	.052	.084	.163	.1352
Per Capita (10)ᵃ:								
All	2.70	1.96	1.60	1.25	.272	.405	.537	.4103
Poor	.61	.53	.46	.41	.129	.242	.324	.2419
Nonpoor	3.18	2.66	2.51	2.36	.165	.210	.257	.3306
Aged								
Individuals	1.05	.51	.40	.34	.518	.617	.680	.6093
Heads	2.20	1.33	1.01	.82	.398	.542	.628	.5423
Nonaged								
Individuals	2.14	1.38	1.04	.77	.358	.515	.641	.4526
Female heads	1.61	1.12	.91	.78	.307	.436	.517	.4645
Male head 2-5	3.18	2.52	2.24	1.85	.205	.296	.417	.3439
Male head 6+	2.34	1.91	1.71	1.44	.184	.271	.385	.3200
Per capita (30)ᵃ:								
All	2.72	2.32	2.12	1.86	.148	.222	.318	.3067
Poor	1.16	1.08	.95	.83	.072	.182	.287	.1136
Nonpoor	3.09	2.77	2.70	2.61	.102	.126	.155	.2712
Aged								
Individuals	1.18	.88	.82	.76	.255	.307	.358	.4007
Heads	2.32	1.88	1.63	1.47	.192	.298	.369	.3793
Nonaged								
Individuals	1.95	1.53	1.36	1.20	.211	.299	.385	.3621
Female heads	1.97	1.78	1.64	1.56	.097	.168	.206	.2805
Male head 2-5	3.06	2.69	2.52	2.24	.123	.176	.270	.2591
Male head 6+	2.65	2.41	2.29	2.05	.090	.136	.226	.2069

TABLE 5 *(Continued)*

	Average Welfare	$W_e(1)$	$W_e(1.5)$	$W_e(2.0)$	$I(1.0)$	$I(1.5)$	$I(2.0)$	Gini Coefficient
Per adult (10)[a]:								
All	2.67	1.91	1.55	1.18	.284	.421	.558	.4150
Poor	.58	.50	.43	.38	.134	.252	.341	.2281
Nonpoor	3.16	2.61	2.45	2.30	.174	.223	.273	.3352
Aged								
Individuals	1.15	.64	.54	.46	.443	.532	.594	.5646
Heads	2.33	1.50	1.17	.98	.358	.496	.581	.5148
Nonaged								
Individuals	2.23	1.50	1.18	.90	.327	.471	.596	.4366
Female heads	1.52	.85	.58	.42	.445	.620	.722	.5195
Male head 2-5	3.18	2.50	2.21	1.82	.212	.305	.427	.3492
Male head 6+	2.16	1.67	1.43	1.16	.228	.336	.460	.3552
Per adult (30)[a]:								
All	2.66	2.20	1.97	1.71	.173	.257	.358	.3229
Poor	1.08	.98	.86	.75	.087	.202	.307	.1137
Nonpoor	3.02	2.65	2.55	2.43	.124	.157	.196	.2912
Aged								
Individuals	1.47	1.20	1.15	1.10	.182	.214	.248	.3237
Heads	2.71	2.29	2.00	1.79	.156	.261	.341	.3331
Nonaged								
Individuals	2.20	1.80	1.59	1.32	.182	.277	.401	.3237
Female heads	1.70	1.24	1.02	.86	.269	.403	.492	.4183

Male head 2-5	3.06	2.63	2.45	2.16	.140	.199	.294	.2792
Male head 6+	2.09	1.78	1.64	1.46	.149	.214	.300	.2889
Social Security plus child allowance (10)[a]:								
All	2.69	2.03	1.71	1.36	.244	.363	.495	.3900
Poor	.80	.69	.58	.49	.142	.278	.393	.1981
Nonpoor	3.13	2.61	2.47	2.32	.165	.210	.258	.3303
Aged								
Individuals	1.49	.98	.82	.67	.346	.449	.549	.4710
Heads	2.56	1.81	1.46	1.20	.293	.430	.530	.4579
Nonaged								
Individuals	2.08	1.31	.95	.65	.370	.544	.687	.4559
Female heads	1.75	1.28	1.05	.89	.268	.400	.492	.4294
Male head 2-5	3.06	2.40	2.11	1.72	.214	.310	.438	.3506
Male head 6+	2.35	1.93	1.72	1.44	.178	.267	.389	.3121
Social Security plus child allowance (30)[a]:								
All	2.75	2.34	2.07	1.68	.151	.247	.389	.2911
Poor	1.60	1.29	.99	.72	.192	.383	.553	.2473
Nonpoor	3.02	2.68	2.58	2.45	.112	.146	.189	.2543
Aged								
Individuals	1.88	1.45	1.25	.98	.228	.335	.477	.3379
Heads	2.78	2.33	1.97	1.64	.163	.291	.410	.3267
Nonaged								
Individuals	1.65	1.09	.81	.58	.339	.507	.650	.4274
Female heads	2.42	2.19	1.98	1.78	.093	.182	.262	.2600
Male head 2-5	2.82	2.42	2.21	1.87	.143	.216	.338	.2738
Male head 6+	3.02	2.78	2.62	2.94	.080	.132	.241	.1836

TABLE 5   *(Concluded)*

	Average Welfare	$W_e(1)$	$W_e(1.5)$	$W_e(2.0)$	$I(1.0)$	$I(1.5)$	$I(2.0)$	Gini Coefficient
Age scale 1 (10)[a]:								
All	2.68	1.96	1.63	1.29	.269	.394	.518	.4091
Poor	.62	.56	.49	.44	.104	.209	.286	.2121
Nonpoor	2.16	2.63	2.48	2.33	.168	.215	.263	.3333
Aged								
Individuals	1.18	.68	.59	.51	.423	.509	.570	.5509
Heads	2.34	1.53	1.22	1.03	.346	.479	.560	.5082
Nonaged								
Individuals	2.17	1.41	1.07	.80	.350	.505	.630	.4488
Female heads	1.56	1.00	.78	.64	.357	.501	.588	.4895
Male head 2-5	3.16	2.50	2.20	1.82	.210	.302	.424	.3478
Male head 6+	2.25	1.80	1.58	1.32	.202	.297	.412	.3354
Age scale 1 (30)[a]:								
All	2.69	2.29	2.11	1.87	.146	.215	.303	.3028
Poor	1.20	1.13	1.01	.88	.053	.157	.262	.0776
Nonpoor	3.03	2.70	2.62	2.53	.109	.135	.166	.2788
Aged								
Individuals	1.56	1.30	1.26	1.21	.166	.194	.226	.3059
Heads	2.75	2.36	2.09	1.88	.140	.240	.317	.3193
Nonaged								
Individuals	2.01	2.60	1.43	1.25	.202	.288	.375	.3521
Female heads	1.82	1.55	1.39	1.30	.146	.233	.284	.3334

Male head 2-5	3.01	2.61	2.44	2.16	.132	.186	.280	.3699
Male head 6+	2.37	2.11	1.99	1.79	.109	.160	.245	.2390
Age scale 2 (10)[a]:								
All	2.68	1.95	1.62	1.28	.271	.397	.522	.4100
Poor	.62	.55	.48	.44	.107	.214	.292	.2122
Nonpoor	3.16	2.62	2.47	2.32	.170	.218	.266	.3344
Aged								
Individuals	1.20	.70	.60	.53	.413	.496	.558	.5430
Heads	2.37	1.56	1.25	1.06	.339	.471	.553	.5031
Nonaged								
Individuals	2.18	1.43	1.10	.83	.345	.496	.620	.4465
Female heads	1.55	.97	.73	.59	.378	.530	.622	.4973
Male head 2-5	3.15	2.49	2.19	1.81	.212	.305	.426	.3494
Male head 6+	2.27	1.76	1.54	1.28	.209	.306	.423	.3411
Age scale 2 (30)[a]:								
All	2.68	2.27	2.08	1.85	.151	.222	.310	.3067
Poor	1.19	1.12	.99	.87	.059	.164	.267	.0924
Nonpoor	3.02	2.68	2.59	2.49	.114	.142	.176	.2831
Aged								
Individuals	1.62	1.36	1.32	1.27	.159	.185	.214	.2953
Heads	2.82	2.44	2.17	1.97	.136	.232	.303	.3123
Nonaged								
Individuals	2.04	1.64	1.47	1.30	.196	.279	.366	.3463
Female heads	1.79	1.48	1.31	1.20	.171	.269	.328	.3551
Male head 2-5	3.00	2.59	2.42	2.14	.136	.193	.286	.2756
Male head 6+	2.30	2.02	1.90	1.70	.119	.174	.258	.2540

NA = not available.

[a] Redistribution rate. This rate is measured as the percentage of pretax or primary income devoted to redistribution.

Figure 7 shows how the overall inequality measures vary with the level of redistribution, that is, the fraction of primary income distributed in proportion to the poverty standard. We note that the three utility-based measures show a curvilinear relation to the level such that successive fractions of redistribution contribute less to reduction of inequality. The Gini coefficient, on the other hand, declines in a linear way. All these measures should converge at zero when the level reaches 83.4 percent, since that fraction plus the net revenue fraction of 16.6 percent exhaust primary income.

The asterisks on the curves of Figure 7 indicate the levels of inequality that characterize the status quo distribution of final income. Thus, our present policies correspond to a redistribution level of approximately 10 to 12 percent.

Table 6 presents the rankings of the several tax-credit structures according to the various inequality measures. The measures have been normalized to make the current law equal 100 percent. Separate rankings are provided for the 10 and 30 percent levels of redistribution, and the inequality relative to the status quo of the primary distribution is shown separately. As can be seen, the choice of an inequality measure does affect the rankings, which also change with the level of redistribution. The Social Security-plus-child-allowance plan ranks first at the linear level and falls to last at the higher level of redistribution for $\epsilon = 2$.

The Gini coefficient, here, as in Figure 7, shows less sensitivity and dispersion with respect to the variations introduced. For example, the primary distribution is only 16 percent worse than the status quo final distribution on the Gini scale, while it is 40 to 50 percent worse by the utility-based measures.

FINAL REMARKS

At the level of a basically arithmetic exercise to see what happens when highly simplified credit-tax redistributions are applied to a relatively comprehensive pretransfer income base, the work reported above requires no further interpretation, but there are also more ambitious objectives lying behind the study. One is to clarify the notion of cost and to supply a framework within which more relevant equivalence classes of households could be identified for comparative analysis. Toward this objective, a linear credit income tax with credits scaled to the poverty standard has

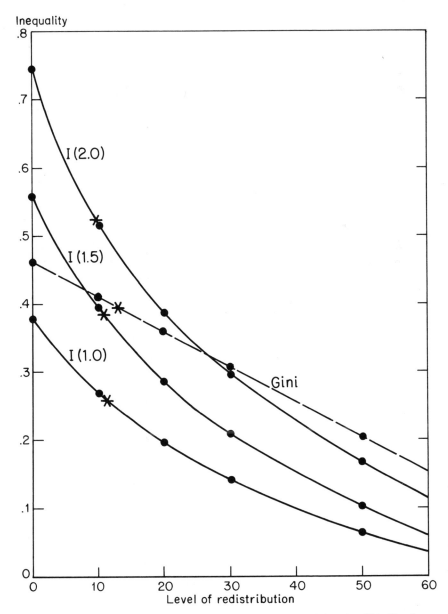

FIGURE 7: Relation Between Inequality Measures and Levels of Redistribution for Poverty-Standard Credits

NOTE: The asterisk denotes level of status quo inequality.

TABLE 6   Ranking of Credit Structures in Relation to Status Quo on the Basis of Alternative Inequality Measures

	Gini Coefficient	I(1.0)	I(1.5)	I(2.0)	
10 percent redistribution:					
Social Security plus child allowance	.99	.94	.94	.95	Social Security plus child allowance
Status quo	1.00	1.00	1.00	.99	Poverty standard
Poverty standard	1.03	1.04	1.02	.99	Age scale 1
Age scale 1	1.03	1.04	1.02	1.00	Age scale 2
Age scale 2	1.04	1.05	1.03	1.00	Status quo
Per capita	1.04	1.05	1.05	1.03	Per capita
Per adult	1.05	1.10	1.09	1.07	Per adult
30 percent redistribution:					
Social Security plus child allowance	.74	.55	.54	.56	Poverty standard
Poverty standard	.75	.57	.56	.58	Age scale 1
Age scale 1	.77	.57	.57	.59	Age scale 2
Per capita	.78	.58	.58	.61	Per capita
Age scale 2	.78	.58	.64	.68	Per adult
Per adult	.82	.67	.66	.74	Social Security plus child allowance
Status quo	1.00	1.00	1.00	1.00	Status quo
No redistribution—same shares as primary income	1.16	1.46	1.50	1.43	

been taken as a reference benchmark. The credit tax is required to generate the same net revenue for nontransfer uses of the public sector and to redistribute a variable fraction of primary income as credits on a uniform basis. The fraction of income so redistributed provides a convenient standardization for comparing alternative credit structures. Equivalence with nonlinear or other more complex structures such as the status quo depends on specifying additional criteria. For example, it was noted that in terms of the various overall indicators of inequality, the status quo corresponds to a credit tax at around 10 to 12 percent redistribution. In terms of the impact on the poor, considered as a homogeneous group, the current law does almost as well as a 20 percent redistribution. Focusing on the aged and female heads, the status quo is more nearly comparable to a 30 percent—say, 27 percent—level of redistribution. By contrast, the allocation to poor male family heads corresponds approximately to a 9 percent redistribution, and the share for male heads in the middle 50 percent category appears to be closer to a 4 to 5 percent redistribution.

Under the assumptions of this paper, the conclusion that relative to the norm provided by the poverty credit tax, the male-headed working poor and lower middle class have been heavily overtaxed or undertransferred is unmistakable. Current benefits are tilted strongly in the direction of the aged and the female-headed; and while one can usually think of reasons why these groups of the poor should be favored over others, it is difficult to find adequate rationalizations for the disparities we find, particularly in view of the large number of children to be found in those male-headed poor and near-poor families. It is also clear that a more active redistributive policy, by moving toward the kind of equity embodied in the credit-tax formula, would not work to the disadvantage of the large middle majority of taxpayers as has often been assumed.

Under the 30 percent poverty-standard plan, the archetypical small family with a male head would enjoy lower taxes up to an income of $11,750; this accounts for 63 percent of such families. Similarly, nearly 70 percent of the larger families with male heads would benefit up to a pretax income of more than $15,500. As indicated before, that plan would allocate more to each of the categories of poor than does the status quo.

These results all assume a strictly proportional gross tax, but it is clear that a more progressive structure for obtaining gross revenue would be more advantageous to that broad middle group.

We have found the framework of a standard reference point for distributional analysis to be a useful one. In an area where value judgments are necessarily the final determinants, there can be no analytically definitive argument for the set we have chosen. The use of some such standard is, however, illuminating; the most useful form of criticism, in our view, should take the form of specifying plausible alternatives. Our application of the inequality measures proposed by Atkinson has confirmed their usefulness. We find them more sensitive than the Gini coefficient, and they have the added advantage of being logically related to a plausible family of utility specifications.

Finally, we must say that our exploration into the arithmetic of income distribution has produced a large volume of numbers; the heavy burden of tables in this paper is only the tip of the iceberg. A substantial amount of interpretation and assessment remains to be done, but we hope that the findings presented here will move the debate on issues of tax and welfare reform forward.

DATA APPENDIX

The data source for all calculations in this paper is the 1966 Brookings Institution Family MERGE File, adjusted to 1970 population and income levels.

The Brookings MERGE File

This file was created by Ben Okner under a grant from the Office of Economic Opportunity from two sets of data, the 1967 Survey of Economic Opportunity and the 1966 Federal Individual Income Tax File. It contains observations on a family basis, combining survey information from the SEO with tax return data from the Tax File. MERGE is in two sections: the first part, the FAM subfile, contains the survey and tax return data for 26,192 Interview Units (families and single individuals) whose Current Population Survey (CPS) income was less than $30,000 in 1966; while the second part, the FAT subfile, has Internal Revenue Service tax-return data only for 46,946 tax-return-filing units with income of at least $30,000. The units in the FAT file represent less than 2 percent of the total number of families, although they represent a much larger percentage of total income; therefore, it is adequate for our purposes to treat the units of the FAT file as if they were Interview Units (IU) and to use estimates for the missing demographic data we need. In particular, this requires us to estimate the number of persons and children in the Interview Units from the number of exemptions, and to assume that none of these returns are filed by persons who are not the head or wife of an IU. When secondary members of an IU file returns separately from the head's return, their income is not included in the IU's income total, but they are not likely to be counted as dependents. We have used the FAM file plus a 20 percent subsample of the FAT file in our calculations.

The details of the creation of the SEO, Tax, and MERGE files are reported in Okner [10], [11], [12]; SEO Codebook; and Brookings Institution Computer Center [2]. Only a few remarks need to be made here. The MERGE File is intended to represent the noninstitutional CPS population in calendar year 1966, but it is far removed from the original tax and SEO data. Since the two data sources used do not contain data on the same individuals, a complex matching procedure was used by Okner and his associates to associate one or more tax returns with each Interview Unit. The resulting "sample" can be no better than this procedure. Some of the difficulties with the matching procedure have been analyzed by Sims [17], Budd [3], and Peck [13]. It is likely that some of the relationships and distributions in MERGE are distorted measures of reality. We have tried to avoid relying on particularly suspect joint distributions and, therefore, we do not report any results on the impact of the various plans by race, for example.

In addition to the changes introduced by the merging process itself, there are three other ways in which the data were modified: (1) Extensive adjustments for nonreporting and underreporting were made. These are discussed in the Okner papers cited above. (2) Imputations were made for a number of items for which there were no data in the file, particularly the amounts of property, sales, and state and local income taxes paid by individuals, either directly or indirectly via shifting to consumers or owners of capital. (3) The 1966 MERGE File was projected forward to 1970, using routines written at Brookings and control totals from the 1970 Census.

Imputations and Adjustments Made to the MERGE File

Three types of state and local taxes were imputed to all IUs in the file, using routines devised by Okner. The taxes imputed were property tax, state and local income taxes, and sales taxes.

The procedure used for estimating property taxes was as follows. Property income was defined as the sum of interest received, rental income, royalties, estate and gift income, dividends, and 29 percent of income from farming and 14 percent of income from nonfarm business (estimated returns on capital) received by the IU. Negative amounts were not included. A tax rate was applied to this total. The remainder of the direct tax was found by taking percentages of the values of automobiles and owner-occupied housing. It was assumed, in addition, that property taxes levied on the nonland assets of businesses and farms are borne by consumers, and an adjustment was made based on the unit's total consumption. Finally, renters were assumed to bear all of the property tax on their housing, and this amount was estimated from their monthly rent. The procedure for calculating those taxes was modified for IUs who filed itemized tax returns in such a way as to accept the taxes claimed as deductions as the actual taxes paid (apart from the shifting estimates). It should be emphasized that the total property tax figure estimated includes both direct property taxes and indirect taxes assumed shifted to renters and consumers.

The amount of state and local income taxes paid had to be estimated for some IUs. If a tax return associated with an IU had itemized deductions, the amount deducted for state and local income taxes was accepted. Otherwise, the tax rate was estimated from adjusted gross income (AGI) and family size and applied to a "taxable income" defined as AGI minus exemptions of $1,000 each for the taxpayer and wife (if a joint return) and $500 for each dependent. The estimated taxes were added for each tax return in the IU to give the total state and local income tax. The amount of sales tax paid was estimated as a percentage of total consumption expeditures.

The last major adjustment to the data was to project the file forward to 1970. This was done in two steps. First, the sample weights associated with IUs were adjusted to bring the 1966 population to 1970 Census Bureau population figures. The adjustment factor was a function of four variables: (1) age (seventeen classes), (2) race (white/nonwhite), (3) type of area (urban, rural, nonfarm, farm), and the size of the family. Then, the means of the distributions of the amounts of fifteen sources of income and thirty-nine items in the tax returns were adjusted to 1970 levels. No attempt was made to take explicit account of changes in benefit schedules for such items as Social Security payments.

These procedures stop short of producing an estimate of the total tax burden borne by a family. Specific taxes, such as a gasoline tax, and fees charged for government services, such as motor-vehicle registration charges, are omitted. These taxes do not have income redistribution as an objective and they are small compared to the remainder of revenue collected under the present tax system; therefore, it is acceptable to ignore them.

A much more important omission is the federal corporate income tax. In a truly comprehensive assessment of the redistributive aspects of the taxation system, this tax would have to be considered. In comparing our linear tax-demogrant systems with the status quo, we have left the federal corporate tax unchanged and have made no assessment of who pays it. The adoption of a radically different tax system would surely affect corporate financial behavior, but we ignore this as well as all other responses of the economy.

REFERENCES

1. Atkinson, Anthony A. "On the Measurement of Inequality." *Journal of Economic Theory* 2(1970):244-63.
2. Brookings Institution Computer Center. "The 1966 Federal Individual Income Tax File." Memo no. 42, 1968, processed.
3. Budd, Edward C. "Comments." *Annals of Economic and Social Measurement* 1, no. 3 (July 1972):325-42.
4. *Characteristics of the Low Income Population 1970.* Current Population Reports, Series P-60, no. 81 (November 1971):19-21.
5. Dalton, H. "The Measurement of the Inequality of Incomes." *Economic Journal* 30 (September 1920):348-61.
6. Lerner, A. P. *The Economics of Control: Principles of Welfare Economics.* New York: Macmillan, 1944.
7. Mirrlees, J. A. "An Exploration in the Theory of Optimum Income Taxation." *The Review of Economic Studies* 38 (April 1971):175-208.
8. Morgan, James N.; David, Martin H.; Cohen, Wilbur J.; and Brazer, Harvey E. *Income and Welfare in the United States,* Part IV. New York: McGraw-Hill, 1962.
9. Newbery, David. "A Theorem on the Measurement of Inequality." *Journal of Economic Theory* 2 (1970):264-66.
10. Okner, Benjamin A. "Adjusted Family Income: Concept and Derivation." Working Paper 2, 1972, processed.
11. _____ . "Constructing a New Data Base from Existing Microdata Sets: The 1966 MERGE File." *Annals of Economic and Social Measurement* 1, no. 3 (July 1972):325 ff.

12. _____ . "The Imputation of Missing Income Information." Working Paper 3, 1971, processed.
13. Peck, Jon K. "Comments." *Annals of Economic and Social Measurement* 1, no. 3 (July 1972):347-48.
14. Rawls, John A. *Theory of Justice.* Cambridge: Belknap Press of Harvard University Press, 1972.
15. Rolph, Earl R. "The Case for a Negative Income Tax Device." *Industrial Relations* 6, no. 2 (February 1967):155-65.
16. Sheshinski, Eytan. "On the Theory of Optimal Income Taxation." Cambridge: Harvard Institute of Economic Research, Discussion Paper 172, February 1971.
17. Sims, Christopher A. "Comments." *Annals of Economic and Social Measurement* 1, no. 3 (July 1972):343-45.
18. Tobin, James. "Raising the Incomes of the Poor," in Kermit Gordon, ed., *Agenda for the Nation.* Washington, D.C.: The Brookings Institution, 1968.

PART III

INCOME DISTRIBUTIONS WITH LONG AND SHORT ACCOUNTING PERIODS

CHAPTER 5

Capital Gains and Individual Income— Evidence on Realization and Persistence

Martin David

University of Wisconsin

and

Roger Miller

University of Wisconsin

PREFACE

In this paper, we attempt to investigate one particular source of income over individuals, and through time, in order to see what affect this has on variation of income through time. A particular source of income which we have chosen is capital gains—and, particularly, realized capital gains, as reported on the income tax returns. Thus, the approach of our paper is in rather sharp contrast to that of the other two papers presented in this session. Consequently, it is appropriate for us to state the reasons for having chosen our approach, as well as to interject a comment or two on what we feel is valuable in the approaches taken in the other papers.

It is our belief that the most appropriate manner in which to study variations in the distribution of income among individuals through time is to employ a model of income determination. Such a model may have submodels of the determination of separate parts of total income as its components. We focus at this juncture on just one such component.

The other papers in this section, by Kohen, Parnes, and Shea, and by Benus and Morgan, each focus on the Lorenz curve of the distribution of income among individuals year by year or period by period, and also when the incomes of individuals are aggregated over two, three, or four or more subperiods or complete periods.

In each paper, the primary determinant of whether one distribution is more or less equal than another is the Gini coefficient, notwithstanding all of the recent criticism of that measure in the study of the inequality of income distributions. No logical structure of the determination of income and its variation is included in their analyses. Their focus is thus on the total distribution of income without regard to the placement of individuals within the distribution, whereas our focus is on what accounts for the movement of individuals up and down within a given distribution, even when that distribution is for two years or more.

In the paper by Kohen, Parnes, and Shea, our attention is not only drawn to the discrepancy between single year and panel surveys in studying income variability, but they also attempt to analyze the source of the discrepancy as an element of bias, as opposed to a real phenomena. Unfortunately their ability to carry through this analysis is somewhat hampered by the fact that they have, by the very nature of their panel, removed from the distribution those persons who are most mobile and, perhaps, most likely to have large income fluctuations.

Benus and Morgan are similarly concerned with discrepancies between analyses of single-year and panel surveys. However, they go further in noting the problems one has with definitions of "what is income" and "for whom" (for what "unit of analysis") when examining a time period that extends much farther than that of the Kohen group. They recognize that simple concepts become complex and ambiguous as the time period expands. They do not quite emphasize enough, however, the effect that this would have on simple measures—such as a Gini coefficient—which tend to lose their precision of meaning.

A secondary consideration which represents a principal departure of our analyses from those of the other papers is the discrepancy between survey panel data and administrative panel data, especially where the administrative panel data is for a shifting panel, in which people can move into, as well as out of, the data. Because of our use of administrative panel data, another departure of our paper involves the length of the period concerned. While we have not gone to the extreme of comparing distributions of lifetime income, we have considerably more than four years of data for many of the individuals in our sample.

One could perhaps criticize our study because it concentrates on realized reported capital gains from income tax returns. However, we see some justification for this in that the redistributive effects of the income tax, particularly at certain low levels of income, have received a great deal of publicity, especially in recent years. This does not mean that we would denigrate the importance of unrealized but accrued capital gains. Indeed, we have plans for attempting to assess, for the people in our sample, annual accrued gains which are not realized. Nor did we wish to make a simple imputation of unrealized accrued gains to individuals similar to that made by Ben Okner in his paper presented during an earlier session.

A final point to emphasize is that in our paper, in contrast to the others in this session, we make a comparison between what can be accomplished in terms of understanding human behavior when truly micro-time-series data are used, as opposed to the partially aggregated data that is inherent in cohort analysis, which is so much in vogue.

We end this preface with the following observation derived from our study of realized capital gains: (1) there is not overmuch distinction between the distributions of money income, long-run versus short-run, due to the realization of capital gains, owing to the persistence of such realization for individuals who realize; and (2) there is a large effect on either long-run or short-run distributions due to the differential incidences of realized capital gains over individuals.

INTRODUCTION

Analysis of single-period cross sections, and of successive cross sections, reveals that the tax subsidy to income in the form of realized capital gains is very large, very unevenly distributed among individual tax-paying units, and especially unevenly distributed among income classes.

Aside from the information summarized in the preceding paragraph, very little is known about the economic effect of the capital gains tax provisions. Perhaps the greatest single gap in our knowledge is the distribution through time of this tax subsidy for particular individuals. Even within a single high-income class, realized gains are unevenly distributed in any one year. Are those "left out" in one year able to reap the rewards of this special treatment in the following year? Or in the following five or even ten years? If not, are the differentials in impact systematically related to taxpayer characteristics over which the individual has control?

The analyses of our data which we present produce partial answers to these questions. We are limited because we have no direct information about the existence and amount of unrealized gains. (Such gains do not appear in the annual tax documents that are the basis for these data.) In all that follows, therefore, it should be understood that we are using data on taxable realized gains reported on tax returns by Wisconsin residents. The extent to which this limits our conclusions is indicated by Bhatia's finding that during the period 1948–64, only $147 billion were reported as capital gains on U.S. individual income tax returns out of a total of $682 billion of increases in wealth accruing to U.S. individuals.[1] While some of these unreported accrued gains will eventually be partially taxed when realized, a substantial fraction will be exempted from taxation altogether, because of transfer of appreciated assets at death. Estimates by David[2] on the mortality of wealth holders indicate that at least one-fifth of the accrued gains that are not reported on tax returns will be transferred at death. A similar calculation by the U.S. Treasury for the population of taxpayers with more than $100,000 of adjusted gross income in 1967 indicated that nearly half of the total income accruing to those taxpayers would escape capital gains taxation at death because of forgiveness.[3]

The information that we report is derived from a random sample of tax returns filed by Wisconsin taxpayers 1946-60. By law, husband and wife file independent returns, so that income sources of men and women can be separately studied. The tax return data include information on occupation; and we were able to obtain birth data from other sources.[4] We are thus able to

[1] Kul Bhatia, "Accrued Capital Gains, Personal Income and Saving in the United States, 1948-1964," *Review of Income and Wealth,* Series 16, no. 4 (December 1970).

[2] Martin David, *Alternative Approaches to Capital Gains Taxation* (Washington, D.C.: Brookings Institution, 1968), pp. 96-98.

[3] Committee on Ways and Means, *Tax Reform Studies and Proposals: U.S. Treasury Department* (91st Congress, 1st Sess., February 5, 1969), Part I, p. 110.

[4] Richard Bauman, Martin H. David, and Roger F. Miller, "The Wisconsin Assets and Incomes Studies Archive," *Social Science Information* (December

relate changes in income patterns to changes in wealth and aging over the lifetimes of taxpayers.[5] The value of the data are enhanced because all the tax returns for a particular individual in the sample are matched over the years that he has filed. Thus variability of income and changes in an individual's use of tax subsidies can be studied.

Wisconsin income tax provisions require the reporting of capital gains or losses by all resident taxpayers, and add the entire amount of gain to taxable income for the purpose of computing tax liability. The data we report therefore do not distinguish between gains on assets held for more than six months (long-term capital gains in the federal code during this period) and gains on assets held for shorter periods of time.

With these caveats behind us, we can begin our presentation. The analysis in this paper is divided into two parts. First, we investigate the characteristics of individuals (and the economy) that are associated with the realization of gains. Then, we assemble evidence on the importance of gains in the income streams of individuals over extended periods of time.

Being ever mindful of the opportunities we have to demonstrate the potentialities of microdata, we begin with a two-stage look at the data on realization in the context of a formal model. The basic features of the model are developed in Section I, which includes our "first look" at the data. In this stage, the cost of accessing microdata led us to concentrate on partially aggregated data. Our micro-time-series of individual data are grouped into age-sex cohorts, producing distinct time series of cohort means. In addition, nonproperty sources of income are lumped together (aggregated). The second type of aggregation, of variables, is at least partially due to the first type, of units, for the latter results in vastly fewer distinct observations, with resulting loss of degrees of freedom. This "first look" thus incorporates the types of

---

1967):49-70; also available as a chapter in Ralph Bisco, ed., *Data Bases, Computers, and the Social Sciences* (New York: Wiley, 1969). The method of the data collection is documented in Martin David et al., *Linkage and Retrieval of Microeconomic Data* (Lexington, Mass.: Heath-Lexington Books, 1974).

[5] Martin David and Roger F. Miller, "A Naive History of Individual Incomes in Wisconsin, 1947-1959," *Journal of Income and Wealth* (March 1970):79-116; also available as Social Systems Research Institute Reprint No. 223.

compromises ordinarily encountered in econometric time series analysis using data that are not ideally suited to the model. In keeping with the spirit of this comparison, the section is written as though (and should be read as though) these were the best and only data available.[6]

Section II estimates the same model with these "limited data" compromises relaxed. It is not necessarily the best model for the disaggregated data, but the essential point would be lost if we used a different model. Further explanation of the "second look" is postponed to the second section of the paper, in order to avoid distracting the reader from the substantive analysis presented in Section I. Indeed, much of Section II will be unintelligible without the background of Section I.

I. ANALYSIS OF THE PARTIALLY AGGREGATED DATA

Two propositions underlie the analysis below: (1) appreciation of property rights is the principal source of realized gains; and (2) property rights generate income that is reported on tax returns. These propositions imply that it is useful to look at samples of *taxpayers* to discover propositions about the realization of capital gains. The nexus between property rights and income implies that persons holding wealth are represented as part of the reporting population. Conversely, persons whose gross income falls below the filing limit and who thus do not file tax returns are unlikely to hold wealth that accrued potentially realizable gains.

Neither proposition is totally correct: some realized capital gains are derived from royalties on patents and sources other than appreciation of wealth; some property rights do not generate income that is taxable under Wisconsin law.[7] Nonetheless, if diversification of portfolios leads owners of property rights to hold several classes of assets, we may expect some taxable return to appear on tax returns of individuals who have the potential to realize gains.

We stress the relationship between ownership of appreciating wealth and the filing of tax returns, inasmuch as the proportion of

---

[6] These partially aggregated results were reported in the Joint Economic Committee, *Compendium on the Economics of Federal Subsidy Programs,* Part 3, pp. 269-85. The disaggregated results are presented here for the first time.

[7] U.S. securities are tax-exempt; vacant land and owner-occupied housing do not yield annual taxable receipts.

the *population* filing returns varies with age. Only 35 percent of men over 75 in 1960 filed a tax return; 59 percent of men aged 66 to 75 did so; and over 87 percent of men aged 31 to 65 filed returns.[8] The propositions above imply that the bulk of persons with a potential for realizing capital are embedded in this tax-return filing population. If we can discriminate those with a potential gain from the remainder of the taxpayers, useful statements about the relationship between potential for realization and the act of realizing gains can be made.

To study the behavior of wealth holders which causes them to realize gains, we constructed a simple model:

$$R_{it} = aW_{it} + bO_{it} + cA_{it} + d + u_{it} .$$

R_{it} is the probability that the ith individual realized gains in year t; W_{it} is the wealth of the individual in year t; O_{it} is income not associated with return on W_{it}, and A_{it} is age. W_{it} was estimated by the quotient of rent, interest, and dividends divided by the Baa rate on corporate bonds [Moody's index of yields]. O_{it} was defined as adjusted gross income (AGI) less capital gains, rent, interest, and dividends. Clearly W_{it} understates wealth; equity in owner-occupied homes and unincorporated enterprises is not included. For that reason, one would expect some propensity to realize capital gains to be associated with the mixture of self-employment and wage income included in O_{it}. Thus we would expect both a and b to be significantly positive.

The relationship between age and realization that should be expected is not clear. If advancing age causes a lock-in effect, c should be negative. However, failure to isolate the potential for gains occasioned by self-employment income causes a positive bias in c.[9] u_{it} is a random error term.

[8] Martin David, "Legislation, Enforcement and the Filing of Tax Returns," *National Tax Journal* (December 1971):519-20, and David and Miller, "A Naive History," p. 85.

[9] Suppose O declines as people retire, so that there is an inverse correlation of O with age. In addition, as O declines, assume that those with a potential to realize gains out of self-employment income continue to file returns. Then, the probability of realizing a gain is higher for the older group with smaller average incomes. This may be revealed by a spurious correlation of the probability of realizing gains with age.

Bias in the age coefficient does not occur if the explanatory variable for W is measured in a way that includes all potential for gains and O includes only labor-related income.

To explore variants of the model suggested and to handle the information more efficiently, the representative samples of tax returns for the years 1947–59 were aggregated to produce a time series of information on eight distinct birth cohorts for men and women. This produced a total of sixteen time series of observations on groups of virtually identical individuals for a period of thirteen years.[10] The relationships was then fitted to the average of each variable over the cohorts.

Results of the model are displayed in Table 1. Age, the wealth proxy, and other income all have significant positive impacts on realization. The model was also extended to determine whether global changes in market conditions contributed to, or detracted from, realization of gains. Table 1 indicates that the level of yields on Baa bonds had no influence on realizations, aside from its role in the wealth proxy. The appreciation accrued or reduction in property values accumulated during the year also failed to play a role in the probability of realizing gains.

Several aspects of the relationship require comment and interpretation. The age effect is large and significantly positive. This is to be expected. A natural correlation between age and the existence of appreciated assets occurs, inasmuch as an individual must first acquire the asset and then hold it for a period of time before the change in prices alters its value. Only after holding an asset for a time is realization of gain or loss possible. Indeed, this natural correlation is a principal justification for the cohort analysis. By studing what happens to a fixed group of people, we can observe how their assets and incomes change over time. We can avoid imputing an age effect due to historical differences between younger and older persons based on a comparison of individuals who are, in fact, different. Instead, our analysis

---

[10] Individuals who fail to file a return or migrate out of the Wisconsin tax jurisdiction will be included in the totals for some years but not for others. In any case, the average for each cohort in each year is representative of taxpayers.

The eight birth cohorts used are 1860-74, 1875-84, 1885-94, 1895-1904, 1905-14, 1915-24, 1925-29, and 1930-34. Each observation for a cohort in each year is treated identically, although some observations represent many more taxpayers than others. This treatment of the data does not bias coefficients in Table 1. Use of a linear probability model is discussed in John Neter and Scott Maynes, "On the Appropriateness of the Correlation Coefficient with a 0, 1 Dependent Variable," *Journal of the American Statistical Association* 65 (June 1970):501-9.

TABLE 1 A Model of the Realization Propensity of Wisconsin Taxpayers, 1947-59

(cohort data, 8 age groups)

	Regression Coefficients	
	Men	Women
Constant	−.00495	−.0986[a]
	(−0.30)	(−4.23)
Birth cohort variables		
Age	.00130[a]	.00262[a]
	(8.21)	(13.3)
Wealth proxy ($000)	.00105[a]	.000487[a]
	(4.48)	(5.00)
Labor and self-employment income ($000)	.00658[b]	.00994[b]
	(2.60)	(2.56)
Market variables		
Baa bond rate	−.480	.392
	(−1.06)	(0.62)
Accruing capital gains in the house-hold sector ($ billions)	−.0000935	.0000485
	(1.27)	(0.46)
R^2	.842	.803
Standard error of estimate	.0245	.0352

NOTE: Figures in parentheses are t-ratios.

Age is measured by the difference in calendar year and the average birth year of the cohort, except for those born 1860-74, where age is measured by the difference between the year and 1872.

Baa bond rate is Moody's index of yields on corporate bonds (Source: *Economic Report of the President,* 1971, p. 265).

Accrued gains are those reported by Kul Bhatia, "Accrued Capital Gains, Personal Income and Saving in the United States, 1948-1964," *Review of Income and Wealth,* Series 16, no. 4 (December 1970).

Other variables are defined in the text.

[a] Significant at the $p = .01$ level.

[b] Significant at the $p = .05$ level.

observes the changing character of income and its effects on the realization of gains for the same individual.

The natural correlation between age and accumulation of gains and the amount of gains realized confounds any effort to use the relationship to draw definitive conclusions about a lock-in effect.

The age effect in Table 1 was tested to determine whether a tapering off occurred for increasingly older individuals. None was detected. Holt and Shelton's analysis suggests that lock-in is related to the probability of dying during the year.[11] That probability rises more than in proportion to calendar age. Evidence of attenuation of the age affect would be consistent with the Holt-Shelton model. Augmentation of the age affect might be introduced by the attrition in the tax-paying population, since the model fails to distinguish capital gains arising from self-employment income. Thus, we are left with two interpretations of the result: (1) Lock-in exists but is masked by sufficient bias in the model to (a) make the age effect change sign and (b) to offset the expected nonlinearity associated with increasing mortality rates of older people. (2) Alternatively, no lock-in exists, and the observed increase in propensity to realize gains with increasing age is a real and powerful phenomenon. In either case, the age coefficient serves as a proxy for the period over which assets have been held; and this second role for the age variable confounds inferences about the importance of lock-in as a factor motivating portfolio behavior. It is still a fact that, ceteris paribus, older taxpayers have a greater propensity to realize gains than younger ones.

Although the wealth effect appears smaller in magnitude than the effect of labor and self-employment income, the two variables are not measured in comparable units; wealth is a stock; labor income is a flow. If wealth is converted back to an equivalent annual income flow, given interest rates during the period, the impact of a dollar of rent, interest, or dividends on realization of capital gains is three to four times that of other income for men and one to one and one-half times that of other income for women.

The meaning of the relationships estimated in Table 1 and evaluated in Table 2 can be better appreciated by comparing the difference in realization implied for different individuals in the tax-paying population. A man aged 50 with $20,000 of wealth and $10,000 of income has a probability of realizing gains that is eight percentage points higher than the probability of a man aged 30 with no wealth and $5,000 of income. The difference between

---

[11] Charles C. Holt and John P. Shelton, "The Lock-in Effect of the Capital Gains Tax," *National Tax Journal* 15 (December 1962):337-52.

TABLE 2   Mean Values and Standard Errors of Explanatory Variables in Table 1

	Means	
	Men	*Women*
Age	49.84	49.84
	(21.12)	(21.12)
Wealth (dollars)	8,687	22,700
	(14,270)	(59,500)
Self-employment and labor income		
(dollars)	3,356	1,484
	(1,082)	(1,363)
Baa bond rate	.0380	
	(.00593)	
Accrued gains	35.15	
($ billions)	(33.83)	

NOTE: Figures in parentheses are standard errors.

As each year's observation for a cohort is weighted equally in the regression, means and standard errors do not reflect population values. Also, the ages of men and women are identical despite differences in mortality. The results are shown only to indicate the relative importance of these variables in the relationships estimated in Table 1.

two women with those same characteristics is eleven percentage points.

The differences in the propensity to realize gains between men and women are highly significant and are not readily explained. Because many women work part time and aged women taxpayers are likely to be widows, the average wealth proxy for the women is nearly three times that of the men; the mean of other income for women is less than half as large. In addition, more men than women engage in self-employment or farming. Taken together, these characteristics imply that the failure to isolate the effect of self-employment in estimating b creates less upward bias in the age effect for women than for men. Nevertheless, we observe a propensity to realize gains that increases almost twice as rapidly with age in the case of women as it does for men. This finding supports our second interpretation of the relationship in Table 1, namely, individuals with wealth have an increasing propensity to realize capital gains as they get older.

II. DISAGGREGATION: THE "SECOND LOOK"

One of the most notable features of the preceding section is the extent to which we were forced into speculation regarding the manner in which the aggregations involved had masked some significant results that one might have expected on theoretical grounds. Table 3 presents the results of a similar regression using

TABLE 3 A Model of the Realization Propensity of Wisconsin Taxpayers Estimated with Microdata, 1947-64

	Regression Coefficients	
	Males	Females
Constant	.0237	−0.0998
	(2.81)	(−5.55)
Individual variables:		
Age { linear	.000909	.00257
	(6.47)	(15.1)
quadratic[a]	−.0000394	.0000490
	(21.4)	(5.26)
Wealth proxy ($000)	.00348	.00313
	(29.6)	(22.5)
Wages and salaries ($000)	.00168	−.00456
	(2.40)	(−2.81)
Self-employment income ($000)	.00717	.000492
	(8.11)	(0.09)
Other Income ($000)	.00293	.00100
	(0.76)	(0.14)
Market variables:		
Baa bond rate	0.767	0.483
	(2.57)	(1.32)
Accruing capital gains in the household sector ($ billions)	.0000866	.0000156
	(1.91)	(0.09)
R^2	.092	.152
Standard error of estimate	.286	.195

NOTE: Figures in parentheses are t-ratios. See notes to Table 1.
[a] Measured as $(x - 46)^2$ where x is age.

disaggregated data and somewhat disaggregated variables. The import of the first type of change is brought home by a realization that it involves a change from 104 to 5,992 degrees of freedom (at the onset) for females, 104 to 12,495 for males. The variable "labor and self-employment income" is now divided into three categories: "wages and salaries"; "self-employment income"; and "other income." The last category does not include interest, dividends, or rent since they are in the numerator of the wealth proxy. "Other income" also excludes capital gains (that will be included in adjusted gross income); gains are excluded to avoid tautological explanation of the dependent variable.

The list of regressors now includes both linear and quadratic terms for age. In the aggregated data, age—being averaged over cohorts for each year—became a close proxy for the simple passage of time, so it is not too surprising that the coefficient of age squared turned out to be insignificantly different from zero. For the disaggregated data, the quadratic term turns out to be highly significant for both sexes, but differs in sign from one to the other. For males, we get a negative coefficient, which is what would be expected if the locking-in hypothesis were true. The positive coefficient for females may be rationalized on other grounds. Presumably, older women are more likely to have their finances handled by others, such as lawyers or trust officers. Perhaps trustees, under the strictures of prudence of management, behave differently than they might in handling their own affairs. Clearly, in the case of a trust in which a widow has a life interest in the income only, and where capital gains are considered part of the income, there may be a definite incentive encouraging realizations. In addition, women live longer and have less income from other sources than men, and the need for cash income to cover expenditures could be considerably greater.

The coefficient for the linear effect of age is virtually the same as for the aggregated relationship for women. It remains substantially positive, increasing the probability of realizing gains by one-quarter of 1 percent per year of age. For men, the coefficient of the linear term is one-third smaller than in the aggregated relationship.

The wealth proxy, which indicates the potential ability to realize gains, increases in significance from the coefficients in the aggregated regression. The coefficients are nearly equal between the sexes in the disaggregated relationship, suggesting that the wealth proxy captures a real economic characteristic that induces the realization of gains.

One of the most interesting comparisons between the sexes in the disaggregated regression is the high significance of self-employment income for males, and the complete insignificance of this variable for females. This type of income is presumably more likely to involve some form of capital or goodwill, which, in the case of males, might yield a capital gain if the business is terminated or sold.

The coefficients for wage and salary income are signficant for both sexes, but here again there is a difference in sign. For males, the positive sign may indicate that this variable is capturing some residual effect from the wealth proxy. This seems likely in cases involving closely held corporations. For females, the negative sign again may indicate that realization of gains is a necessity for some, in lieu of other forms of income. This explanation is consistent with, and reinforces, that which we gave for the differential quadratic effect of age for men and women.

The macroeconomic variables gain some signficance for the male taxpayers. The coefficient of the bond-yield rate is positive but relatively small, increasing the probability of a realization by only .008 for a change of one percentage point in the interest rate. The positive relationship must be viewed as an indication that the prices of real assets rose with the nominal interest rate during this period.

We do not wish to belabor the obvious with further discussion of the regressions results in detail. However, we would be less than human if we did not mention the great pleasure we felt when the greater analytic power of the disaggregated regression was so dramatically demonstrated. The tremendous personal professional investment (over 10 years) that we have made in developing these microdata has not been for naught. In succeeding sections, we explore further insights into gains realization behavior that we have gleaned from disaggregated data.

III. A LONG-RUN VIEW OF CAPITAL GAINS

The assessment of propensity to realize capital gains provided in Table 1 gives a picture of taxpayer behavior in relation to taxpayer characteristics at the same point in time. To assess the persistence of realized capital gains, analysis of the realization of capital gains over a period of time is essential. One-period studies can not indicate to what extent realization of gains occurs widely in the population of taxpayers and to what extent realization is concentrated among a few individuals. One-period studies cannot distinguish taxpayers who never realize gains from those whose occasional realizations play a significant role in income in the long run. One-period studies cannot relate variability in capital gains to variability in income sources generally.

Conversely, existing one-period tabulations of capital gains in the *Statistics of Income*[12] provide a peculiar perspective on the role of capital gains in taxpayer income. Tabulations of the amount of capital gains and number of taxpayers reporting capital gains by adjusted gross income class confound the level of realized gains in a single year and the amount of income from other sources. A taxpayer realizing a large gain is classified in a high adjusted gross income class, while another with identical income from other sources and a realized loss may be classified in a relatively low AGI class. Tabulations that report on taxpayers who realize gains in a given year, single out a subgroup from the taxpayers who have potential for realizing capital gains.[13] Thus, a comparison of those who realize gains in one year with all taxpayers tends to understate the difference between those for whom capital gains provisions provide a tax subsidy and those for whom the provisions are irrelevant.

In the following tabulations, the shortcomings of one-period data are overcome in two ways. Information on sources of income refers to the average over a substantial period of time. Secondly, taxpayers are classified according to whether they ever realized gains during the period of observation. Use of the long-term averages avoids the confounding of gains and other income present in the *Statistics of Income.* Discrimination of taxpayers who never realize gains from those who realized gains at any time in the long-run comes closer to identifying the relevant population than the *Statistics of Income* tabulations of those who reported capital gains in a particular year.

To estimate average income, its variability, and the realization of capital gains over a period of time, men who filed tax returns in

---

[12] U.S., Treasury Department, Internal Revenue Service, *Statistics of Income, Individual Income Tax Returns,* various years.

[13] Martin David, "Alternative Approaches," p. 85.

at least four consecutive pairs of years were sampled from available tax returns for 1947–59. For each man, at least five tax returns were available; for many, thirteen were available. The average and standard error of each income source over the period reported were computed separately for each taxpayer. (If no income was reported from a particular source, its standard error was taken to be zero.)

The first findings that we report provide support for the relationship fit in the previous section and underscore the connection between income from wealth and the realization of capital gains in the long run. Table 4 classifies each of the men in the long-term sample according to the average level of dividends reported over the entire period. Those with no income from dividends are shown at the left; those with substantial income in the second column from the right. For each of the groups defined on average level of dividend income, the distribution of the average capital gain realized is reported. Four-fifths of those with no dividend income reported no capital gains; one-sixth of those will more than $300 of dividends on the average reported no capital gains. The distributions indicate an increasingly positive average gain as the average size of dividend increases.

The pattern shown in Table 4 is also typical of the relationship

TABLE 4   Distribution of Mean Gains by Mean Dividends Received During the Filing Period

(long-term sample, percent)

Mean Capital Gain (Dollars)	Mean Dividend (Dollars)				
	None	*1-100*	*101-300*	*301+*	*All*
Less than −100	1.8	3.3	3.1	6.8	2.2
−100–−1	3.8	7.5	10.4	11.3	4.7
0	78.2	52.0	33.3	16.9	71.4
1-100	8.4	18.5	18.8	17.7	10.4
101-200	2.7	5.6	9.4	8.8	3.5
201-500	3.1	9.4	11.5	12.0	4.5
501-1,000	1.4	2.9	8.3	11.3	2.1
1,001+	0.6	0.8	5.2	15.3	1.2
Total	100.0	100.0	100.0	100.0	100.0
Number of filers	3,001	519	96	124	3,740

between mean capital gain and mean interest, and mean capital gain and mean rent. We hypothesize that the relationship results from a strong positive relationship between wealth in all forms and the realization of income in the form of capital gains. Some support for this hypothesis comes from simultaneous consideration of mean dividends and mean rent in relation to mean capital gains. (See Table 5.) Those with no income from either type of property showed less propensity to realize gains than is the case when only dividends are taken into account. In addition, the size of the gains reported were, on the average, smaller.

Self-employment income is also clearly a key factor in the realization of capital gains in the long run (Table 6). While only one-sixth of those with no self-employment income reported capital gains at any time, more than two-fifths of those with any self-employment income reported capital gains. Since self-employment and income dividends and rent are correlated, this finding is not independent of that in Table 5. Nonetheless, the strength of the relationship indicates how unimportant realization of capital gains is for those who have no self-employment income and how strongly correlated the size of average gain is to the size of average self-employment income.

Some additional insights into the long-term consequences of the realization of capital gains come from a further analysis of the impact of capital gains on individuals classified by occupation. Table 7 shows the long-term sample of male taxpayers classified by both birth cohort and principal occupation during the reporting period.

TABLE 5 Mean Gains by Presence of Income from Rent or Dividends

(long-term sample, percent)

Mean Capital Gain (Dollars)	No Rent or Dividend Income	Some Rent or Dividend Income
Less than 0	4.7	11.4
None	83.3	46.9
1–100	7.1	17.2
More than 100	4.9	24.5
Total	100.0	100.0
Number of filers	2,511	1,229

TABLE 6   Mean Capital Gain Within Mean Self-employment

(long-term sample, percent)

Mean Capital Gain (Dollars)	Mean Self-employment Income (Dollars)						
	Negative	None	1- 1,000	1,000- 3,000	3,000- 7,000	Over 7,000	Total
Less than −100	6.9	1.1	3.9	2.4	3.2	7.0	2.2
−100—−1	10.0	3.0	7.9	5.0	8.1	11.3	4.7
None	54.7	84.3	55.3	54.5	39.5	12.7	71.4
1–100	14.5	6.3	14.4	18.3	20.5	22.5	10.4
100–200	5.7	2.0	6.0	5.6	5.4	8.5	3.5
200–500	3.8	2.1	7.2	8.0	14.6	15.4	4.5
500–1,000	0.6	0.8	3.2	4.5	5.4	12.7	2.1
More than 1,000	3.8	0.3	2.1	1.7	3.2	9.9	1.2
Total	100.0	100.0	100.0	100.0	100.0	100.0	100.0
Number of taxpayers	159	2,293	568	464	185	71	3,740

TABLE 7   Percent Ever Realizing Capital Gains, by Principal Occupation and Birth Cohort

(long-term sample)

	Principal Occupation	Birth Cohort			
		1860-1894	*1895-1904*	*1905-1914*	*All*
1.	Professional	47	54	51	44
2.	Semiprofessional	57	54	47	35
3.	Managers	41	53	39	39
4.	Businessmen	61	56	61	57
5.	Farmers	45	42	41	42
6.	Clerical	32	36	22	19
7.	Sales	45	64	43	40
8.	Service	26	24	23	22
9.	Skilled	25	34	24	23
10.	Semiskilled and unskilled	17	19	21	16
11.	Retired, students	54	50	–	34
	All	35	37	33	29

Reporting of realized capital gains is concentrated heavily on businessmen, professionals, farmers, sales workers, and managers, in that order. We return to the birth-cohort specific rates of realization in the following section.

The Importance of Capital Gains in the Long Run

The foregoing gives little feeling for the role of capital gains in relation to adjusted gross income as a whole. We assess that effect in two stages. First, how prevalent is the realization of capital gains? Second, what share of the adjusted gross income of those who realize gains is accounted for by the capital gains themselves? At the same time, to give a better insight into the age effect reported earlier, we present answers to these questions for six birth cohorts. Table 8 shows that just under a third of the taxpayers in the long-term sample realized gains at some time during the period for which they reported income. (That period averaged more than ten years for the sample of men selected.) At the same time, the average capital gain reported by those who realized gains accounted for only 4.1 percent of all the adjusted gross income reported.

Table 8 demonstrates an inverse relationship between the importance of capital gains and birth date. (For all but the youngest and oldest cohorts, the rate of filing tax returns was extremely high, so that differences in the realization of gains correspond roughly to population differences as well as to differences between taxpayers.) The older the cohort observed from 1947-59, the greater the likelihood that gains were realized at some time during the period. Among those realizing gains, the ratio of total gain realized to total adjusted gross income reported proved larger, the older the birth cohort observed.

Comparing the proportion ever realizing gains in Tables 7 and 8 makes it clear that a life-cycle, or cohort-related, pattern of realizations is far stronger in some occupations than in others. Farmers and businessmen show little more propensity to realize

TABLE 8   Importance of Realized Capital Gains by Birth Cohort

(long-term sample)

	Ever Realized Capital Gain	
Birth Cohort	*Proportion*	*Ratio of Total Gain to Total AGI*
1860-1894	.35 (10.0)	.074
1895-1904	.37 (11.2)	.061
1905-1914	.33 (11.1)	.027
1915-1924	.25 (10.4)	.020
1925-1929	.19 (9.6)	.010
1930-1934	.08 (7.0)	.007
All	.29 (10.1)	.041

NOTE: Figures in parentheses are average number of years filed.

gains when they are in the three oldest cohorts than when they are in the younger group. By contrast, in the cohort just prior to retirement (1895-1904), sales workers, managers, and semiprofessionals demonstrate an extremely high propensity to realize gains relative to the average over all cohorts. What factors lead to that effect is unclear.

The Dynamics of Receiving Capital Gains

Another way to view the realization of gains is to relate the taking of gains over a period of time to the growth in income over time. We have done this for the male taxpayers included in the long-term sample. Essentially the procedure amounts to fitting a trend line to the data reported by each individual.[14] To make the results easier to view against known trends in income due to inflation and changes in life cycle, we computed the trend of the AGI reported relative to the income of the birth cohort to which the individual belonged.

As a result of fitting trends to the 3,740 men in the long-term sample, we obtained a distribution of rates of growth in relative income position (see Table 9). Realization of capital gains was concentrated among those individuals who experienced either extreme growth (more than 5 percent per annum) or extreme decline (less than -10 percent). The least reporting of gains occurs where the rate of increase of relative income position is 1 to 2 percent. The amount of gains realized shows the same pattern.

Additional insight into dynamic analysis comes from classifying individuals by both relative income position in 1959 and rate of growth of relative position. The largest dollar amounts of realized capital gains were recorded by persons whose relative income position projected to 1959 could be expected to be at least 50 percent higher than the average for their birth cohort. Fifty-eight percent of all realized gains were concentrated in that group.

The combination of these findings indicates that more than one-fourth of capital gains are realized by relatively wealthy individuals with systematically increasing income. The tax subsidy to capital gains thus moderates progression on high and rapidly

---

[14] Martin David, "Lifetime Income Profiles," *Proceedings of the Social Statistics Section of the American Statistical Association, 1971*, pp. 285-92.

TABLE 9   Capital Gains in Relation to Rate of Growth of Income

(long-term sample)

Annual Rate of Growth of Income (Percent)	Distribution of All Long-Term Filers (Percent)	Filers Reporting Realized Gains at Some Time		
		As a Percent of Long-Term Filers	Average Gain Reported (Dollars)	Share of Realized Gains Reported (Percent)
Less than −10	10.9	33	570	30.4
−10 to −5	10.6	28	182	8.0
−5 to −2	16.5	28	166	11.8
−2 to −1	7.4	25	150	4.1
−1 to 1	17.9	24	119	7.6
1 to 2	7.6	23	65	1.7
2 to 5	17.2	26	106	5.8
5 to 10	9.0	34	205	9.2
More than 10	6.0	50	494	21.8
All	100.0	29	236	100.0

growing incomes. For those with declining incomes, the largest amounts of gains accrue to those with relatively high incomes (25 percent or more above the average of their birth group). Those individuals account for the large average gain reported by those with extreme declines in relative position in Table 9. Again, the tax subsidy is concentrated on those with an advantageous income position.

Another aspect of the dynamics of income is its variability over time. We can report one facet of that variability. For each taxpayer, the variance of both capital gains and adjusted gross income was computed. Table 10 indicates the relative importance of variation in the realization of capital gains relative to variation of all income sources. The column furthest left indicates the proportion of the long-term filers who realized no gains whatsoever. That proportion drops radically as mean AGI arises. For this group, no income variation was accounted for by capital gains.

Looking at taxpayers who realized some gains, we can compute the proportion of all income variation accounted for by capital gains. Only in the top income bracket do more than one-fifth of

TABLE 10   Distribution of Variance of Capital Gains Relative to Variance in AGI Within Mean AGI Groups

(long-term sample, percent)

Mean AGI (Dollars)	Ratio of Variance of Capital Gains to Variance in AGI								
	0	.00-.01	.01-.05	.05-.10	.10-.20	.20-.40	.40-.60	.60+	All
Less than 3,000	73.2	6.9	5.9	3.0	2.8	2.3	1.9	3.0	100.0
3,001-4,000	77.6	6.4	5.7	2.2	1.7	2.1	2.0	2.2	100.0
4,001-5,000	78.5	7.3	3.8	2.1	2.6	2.6	1.5	1.7	100.0
5,001-7,000	65.1	11.3	6.0	4.2	3.0	3.9	2.5	3.9	100.0
7,001 or more	28.9	30.4	11.8	4.2	8.0	6.5	4.2	6.1	100.0
All	71.2	9.7	5.9	2.9	2.9	2.8	2.1	3.2	100.0

all filers report that variations in capital gains amount to more than 5 percent of total income variation.

We conclude from this relationship that if capital gains provisions are intended as an ad hoc averaging device to deal with income variation, the provision has badly missed its mark. Only 3 percent of the sample report capital gains variance .6 as large as AGI variance; and it is only for this group that the reduced taxation on capital gains can begin to approach the magnitude of variations in tax progession due to income variability.

The foregoing material characterizes the impact of realized capital gains on taxpayers. Realized capital gains are concentrated on those with sizable incomes from self-employment and dividends. They are concentrated on those whose relative income positions are substantially above the average of their cohort, and to a large extent on the subgroups whose income position is changing rapidly.

Realized gains account for a remarkably small proportion of total adjusted gross income, and for a relatively small proportion of the income variation experienced by taxpayers over an extended period of time. It is still the case that capital gains tend to be relatively more volatile than other sources of income.

This description glosses over many of the characteristics of taxpayers that affect their potential to realize capital gains. In the following section, we highlight the differences between those who realize gains in the long run and those who do not.

Differences Between Recipients and Nonrecipients of Capital Gains in the Long Run

We can characterize the differences between taxpayers who use capital gains and those who do not in terms of the long-term income experience of the population. Table 11 indicates that

TABLE 11   Share of Long-Term Income, by Source

(long-term sample, percent)

	No Gains Reported at Any Time	*Received Gains at Some Time*
Adjusted gross income	62.5	37.5
Interest	34.0	66.0
Dividends	12.5	87.5
Rent	30.4	69.6

persons realizing capital gains at any time during the period received a large share of the total sample income from dividends, interest, and rent. This was certainly to be expected, given the positive correlations among wealth, age, and realization of gains. The share of income sources received by those who realized capital gains at any time during the period provides an interesting contrast with one-year data available from the *Statistics of Income*.[15] In 1962, the first year for which such data were published nationally, taxpayers realizing capital gains received 47.1 percent of interest, 74.6 percent of dividends, and 37.9 percent of rents. The difference between these statistics and those in Table 11 suggests that realizations of gains are undertaken by recipients of rents erratically; the long-term realizers indicate a far greater proportion of total rents than what would be anticipated from the one-year tabulation.

Mean values of rent, interest, and dividends in the long run are shown in Table 12. The large difference in adjusted gross income between those reporting realized gains and those not reporting gains far exceeds the amount of gains realized. The difference is also large by comparison to income from property ownership (rent, interest, and dividends). We must conclude that persons realizing capital gains have large wage and salary or self-employment incomes relative to those who do not.

[15] This comparison relates national data to the Wisconsin sample. Work by Moyer has shown that Wisconsin taxpayers have mean incomes close to the U.S. average but somewhat less broadly distributed.

Comparison of rates of reporting capital gains in the Wisconsin sample with that reported for the U.S. indicates little difference:

| Year | Wisconsin Sample | | U.S. |
	Women	Men	
1947	4	6	4.5
1948	4	7	4.4
1949	4	6	4.1
1950	5	7	4.8
1951	5	6	4.9
1952	4	5	4.8
1953	4	6	4.8
1954	5	7	5.4
1955	5	7	6.1
1956	5	7	6.6
1957	4	6	6.6
1958	5	5	7.4
1959	6	7	8.1

TABLE 12   Difference Between Gains Takers and Nontakers

(long-term sample)

Birth Cohort and Report of Gains	AGI	Capital Gains	Income Source (Mean Amount in Dollars)			
			Portfolio Income			
			Interest	Dividends	Rent	Total
1860-94						
No gains	3,215	–	36	46	38	120
Some gains	4,376	355	125	408	209	742
1895-1904						
No gains	3,793	–	17	12	56	85
Some gains	6,883	426	98	347	140	585
1905-14						
No gains	4,105	–	24	7	6	37
Some gains	6,098	140	74	79	59	212
1915-24						
No gains	4,116	–	5	4	4	14
Some gains	5,361	109	29	57	19	105
1925-29						
No gains	3,819	–	3	1	5	9
Some gains	4,134	42	4	39	a	43
1930-34						
No gains	3,390	–	3	3	2	8
Some gains	5,216	40	20	9	35	64
All						
No gains	3,767	–	15	11	17	43
Some gains	5,645	237	72	196	99	367

[a] Less than $1.

Scanning the cohort differences in realization of capital gains illustrates the increasing ratio of capital gains to adjusted gross income already cited in Table 8. More surprising is the finding that the ratio of the amount of realized gain declines in relation to the sum of income from rent, interest, and dividends as birth year declines.

To study this relationship more closely, we applied the same model used in the time series analysis of Section I to the aggregated data for the six cohorts in Table 12. While the proxy for wealth and other income both were positively and significantly related to the amount of gains taken, there was no additional variation that could be related to the date of birth of the taxpayer. We conclude that the decline in mean gains for the oldest cohort is adequately explained by declines in other income. Mean gains do not appear to be associated with age of taxpayer in this sample.

Differences between recipients and nonrecipients of capital gains are even more striking when viewed in the context of the principal occupation held by the individual (see Table 13). In the entire sample of long-term filers, recipients of capital gains average 50 percent more adjusted gross income than nonrecipients. In professional and managerial groups, the ratio is nearly two to one. Among farmers and blue collar workers the differentials were much smaller. What these findings suggest is that some occupations include a wealthy echelon that realizes capital gains and a lower-paid group with little or no potential for realizing gain.

This hypothesis is borne out to some extent by the amounts of rent, interest, and dividends received by taxpayers within each occupation group. Individuals who did not realize gains received, on the average, about one-eighth as much income from these sources as those who did realize. In the professional and managerial occupations, that ratio was smaller, while in farm and blue collar occupations it was substantially higher. Thus, realization of capital gains is more selective to the owners of assets that yield income in the former group than in the latter. For farmers, this can be explained by the sale of livestock for breeding purposes and the realization of gains on the sale of equipment, both of which occasion widely experienced sources of realized capital gains. It is not clear why these special provisions do not operate equally strongly for businessmen. Moreover, we can offer no explanation for the relatively nonselective realization of capital gains within the blue collar occupations.

The difference in income from wealth and level of income between individuals who realize gains and those who do not is striking. There can be no doubt that the advantages of the capital gains provisions benefit those with relatively high labor income in addition to their substantial portfolios.

TABLE 13   Difference in Mean AGI and Share of AGI Between Gains Takers and Nontakers by Principal Occupation

(long-term sample)

Principal Occupation and Report of Gains	Mean AGI (Dollars)	Share of AGI (Percent)	Percent of Filers	Mean Gains (Dollars)	Total of Rent, Interest, and Dividends (Dollars)
Professional					
None	5,733	39	56	—	53
Some	11,349	61	44	176	542
Semiprofessional					
None	4,448	43	67	—	180
Some	10,988	57	35	250	678
Managerial					
None	5,889	44	61	—	85
Some	11,578	55	39	977	1,101
Businessman					
None	3,200	30	43	—	71
Some	5,590	70	57	222	440
Farmer					
None	2,292	52	58	—	32
Some	2,978	48	42	258	145

Clerical					
None	3,762	78	81	—	23
Some	4,586	22	19	35	143
Sales					
None	4,385	54	60	—	26
Some	5,624	56	40	17	261
Service					
None	3,258	73	78	—	22
Some	4,251	27	22	88	158
Skilled					
None	4,362	76	77	—	32
Some	4,734	24	23	106	116
Semiskilled and unskilled					
None	3,529	83	84	—	22
Some	3,729	17	16	72	115
Retired					
None	2,162	52	66	—	305
Some	3,908	48	33	506	1,650
All					
None	3,767	62	71	—	43
Some	5,645	38	29	237	367

IV. CONCLUSIONS

The foregoing data support four generalizations about the realization of the capital gains and the concomitant tax subsidy:

1. Realization of gains is concentrated among persons with incomes that are far above average for their birth cohort.

2. To a great extent realization of gains is associated with substantial long-term growth or substantial decline in relative income position.

3. Realizations account for a small fraction of all income variance.

4. Other factors being equal, realizations do not appear to decline in frequency for women taxpayers over the age of 46. For men, ceteris paribus, realizations appear to decline in frequency beyond that age.

A study of this type cannot reveal the incentives to save and invest that are created by favorable treatment of capital gains. It can only assess the resulting distribution and utilization of the tax incentives. The data presented here clearly reveal the favorable income and wealth position of taxpayers realizing gains. The data suggest that gains play a different role in the incomes of men and women, and suggest that elderly women taxpayers are the recipients of income from professionally managed portfolios to a greater extent than men.

We urge further study of the data underlying this paper and attention to the changes in tax liability and portfolio structure that might be induced by a change in capital gains taxation.

CHAPTER 6

Income Instability Among Young and Middle-Aged Men

Andrew I. Kohen
Ohio State University

Herbert S. Parnes
Ohio State University

and

John R. Shea
Ohio State University

I. INTRODUCTION

Most of what is known about the size distribution of income is based upon measurements taken over the span of a single year. In several areas bearing on both theory and policy, single-year measures are inadequate. In the calculation of rates of return to human capital investments, for example, it is often critical to be able to differentiate age-earning profiles that start high and rise slowly from those that have a lower starting point but rise more steeply. Consider also a widely recognized problem in defining poverty status. Because of the generally temporary nature of their poverty, public policy responds somewhat differently to low-income graduate students than to the typical low-income family. Another example, recognized in law, is income averaging for tax purposes. To cite a final example, much of the literature on labor-force participation and consumer economics is built around notions of "transitory" and "permanent" components of income.

We are indebted to Daniel Hummer, Ken Henderson, Keith Stober, and Harvey Forstag for the computer work; to Dennis Bayley, our principal research assistant on the paper, and to Dortha Gilbert and Kandy Bell for typing the several versions of text and tables.

151

Purpose

In this paper we attempt: (1) to quantify the influence on measured income inequality of lengthening the accounting period; (2) to describe the mechanism through which income instability among male heads of households is manifested (e.g., changes in sources of income, hours worked, and wage rates); and (3) to identify some of the demographic and economic characteristics of those household heads whose income is "unstable" over a two- or three-year period, in the sense of changing at above-average or below-average rates. To the extent that their relative position in the income distribution changes from one year to the next, these are the individuals who cause the length of the accounting period to influence the measure of income inequality. When reranking occurs, measures of income concentration based on annual data (e.g., annual averages) necessarily show a higher degree of inequality than those based upon a longer accounting period.[1]

Nature of the Data

Data for the study are derived from the National Longitudinal Surveys.[2] Specifically, the information comes from personal interviews with two national probability samples of approximately five thousand individuals in two subsets of the civilian, noninstitutional population: young men who were 14 to 24 years of age when first interviewed in October 1966, and middle-aged men 45 to 59 years of age when contacted initially in mid-1966. In accordance with the sample design, blacks were overrepresented by a three-to-one ratio relative to whites. This was done to permit a reasonably confident analysis of the black experience. For this reason, most of our results are presented separately for whites and blacks,[3] although we use weighted sample cases throughout the analysis.

---

[1] Frank A. Hanna, "The Accounting Period and the Distribution of Income," Part III in Frank A. Hanna, Joseph A. Pechman, and Sidney M. Lerner, *Analysis of Wisconsin Income,* Volume 9, Conference on Research in Income and Wealth (New York: NBER, 1948), p. 212.

[2] For a detailed description of the samples and the data, see Herbert S. Parnes et al., *The Pre-Retirement Years,* U.S. Department of Labor Manpower Research Monograph No. 15, Vol. 1 (1970) and *Career Thresholds,* U.S. Department of Labor Manpower Research Monograph No. 16, Vol. 1 (1970).

[3] We have excluded non-Caucasians other than Negroes from the analysis, except in a few instances where the focus is on all individuals in a cohort, irrespective of race.

Information was collected at yearly intervals in the 1966 and 1967 surveys of older men, and in the 1966, 1967, and 1968 surveys of the younger men—a group often referred to as boys throughout the remainder of the paper. Before describing methods of analysis, a few words should be said about the income items and about measurement problems. Two units of observation are used in the analysis, depending on whether total family income or individual earnings is the focus of attention. When total family income is at issue, the unit is the family, specifically the respondent and any relatives (wife, children, and so forth) living with him.[4] Earnings from wages and salaries, on the other hand, apply only to the respondent.

In the first interview with the older men in mid-1966, respondents were asked a series of questions concerning sources of both individual and family income for calendar 1965. Similar questions were asked a year later referring to calendar 1966. Granting some imprecision, we use the survey year (1966, 1967) to designate these two periods. Separate inquiries each year elicited information on the gross value of wages, salaries, tips, commissions, and so on, of the respondent, his wife (if married), and of other adult family members (if living in household). Additional questions were asked to obtain net self-employment income of respondent and of other family members, and farm income of the family. This was followed by queries concerning unemployment compensation of respondent and other family members, rental income, interest and dividends, and so forth, disability or illness income, Social Security, public assistance or welfare, the value of food stamps, government and private pensions, and, finally, income not elsewhere specified.

When interviewed in October and November of each year, the younger men were asked to report their income and earnings over the twelve months immediately preceding each survey. We have designated each twelve-month period by the year in which the interview took place: 1966, 1967, or 1968. The set of income questions asked of the younger men was much shorter than the set asked of the older men. There were eight items in all, four for the

[4] An exception has been made within the younger cohort. Each young man must have been a head of household at the time of each interview. If married, spouse present, we have included the income of his wife in calculating total family income, but we have excluded possible income from other family members, because it cannot be separately estimated with any precision.

respondent and (if married) four for his wife. The questions, identical in form, asked about gross earnings (wages, salaries, tips, and commissions), net income from a business or farm, unemployment compensation, and all other income.[5]

As might be expected, nonresponse to various income items results in some bias. Nearly a third of the respondents in each cohort failed to provide complete answers to relevant income items in one or more of the years in question (see Appendix Tables A.1 and A.2). Much of the failure to provide full information on total family income occurred in the first year. Because repeated failure to answer income questions was not especially great, especially among the boys, we believe that much of the nonresponse in the first year occurred because respondents did not have some of the required information, and that they were better prepared in subsequent interviews. The reader can form his own judgment on the matter by examining Tables A.1 and A.2, which show nonresponse to the income items that add to total family income in 1966 and 1967 (men) and in 1966 and 1968 (boys), according to the response in the preceding (or subsequent) year. The pattern for the older group indicates somewhat higher-than-average nonresponse among those with relatively low (under $6,000 per year) and relatively high incomes ($12,000 or more for whites; $9,000 or more for blacks).[6] Nevertheless, nonresponse was only a few percentage points less common among those who reported middle-level incomes in one of the years. There is little, if any, systematic relationship between income level and nonresponse among the younger men. Thus, we are on relatively firm ground in generalizing from the income experience of the two-thirds of the respondents who reported fully on their income or wage and salary earnings in two or all three years.[7]

---

[5] This last question was worded as follows: "Did you (or your wife) receive any other income, such as rental income, interest or dividends, income as a result of disability or illness, etc.?"

[6] Vandome reported that response in the 1954 Reinterview Savings Survey was poor at both ends of the distribution. Peter Vandome, "Aspects of the Dynamics of Consumer Behavior: Income and Savings Over Two Years from the 1954 Reinterview Savings Survey," *Bulletin of the Oxford University Institute of Statistics* 20 (February 1958):71.

[7] The nonresponse rate on respondent's earnings from wages and salaries was much lower than nonresponse to at least one item making up total family income.

Methods of Analysis

We have examined the stability of income and earnings at both macro and micro levels. Comparison of Gini coefficients[8] for one-, two-, and three-year periods provides an indication at a macro level of the extent to which reranking—and, therefore, relative instability of position within the income distribution—has taken place from year to year. While most of our work has been in terms of each respondent's family income or personal earnings, for the older men we have also calculated Gini coefficients for family income per family member. In summing per capita family income over a two-year period, each year's per capita income has been calculated before adding the two figures together.

At the micro level we have gauged the way in which each respondent's family income (Y_i) or earnings (E_i) has moved relative to the total income or earnings of all respondents in each cohort. The measure, which we have dubbed a relative instability coefficient (or RIC) is equal to $100\,(\alpha_i - \bar{\alpha})$ where, in the case of total family income for the older men,

$$\alpha_i = \frac{Y_i^{67}}{\frac{1}{2}\,(Y_i^{66} + Y_i^{67})} \text{ and } \bar{\alpha} = \frac{1}{n}\sum_{i=1}^{n} \frac{Y_i^{67}}{\frac{1}{2}\,(Y_i^{66} + Y_i^{67})}.$$

[8] Gini's coefficient of concentration, expressed in terms of a percentage, is equal to the area between the Lorenz curve and a 45° line divided by the area of the entire triangle below that line, where the 45° diagonal shows equal cumulative percentages of income recipients and of income on the x and y axes. Arithmetically, the Gini coefficient "corresponds to the arithmetic average (*mean difference*) of the $n(n - 1)$ differences (taken in absolute value) which may be constituted between the n terms, divided by its maximum possible value (equal twice the arithmetic average of the n terms)." Corrado Gini, "On the Measure of Concentration with Special Reference to Income and Wealth," Proceedings of a Research Conference on Economics and Statistics held by the Cowles Commission, July-August 1936, *Colorado College Publication*, General Series No. 208, Study Series No. 21, p. 77. We have approximated the area below the Lorenz curve using the trapezoidal rule with 300 intervals.

$$\text{Area} = \sum_{i=2}^{n} \text{Area}_{i-1} + \left(\frac{x_i - x_{i-1}}{2}\right)(Y_i + Y_{i-1}),$$

where x_i is the percentage of the population at the ith interval, Y_i is the percentage of income at the ith interval, and $x_i - x_{i-1}$ is the length of the interval (a constant). The Gini coefficient is equal to 1 minus twice the area below the Lorenz curve.

Similarly for the younger men,

$$\alpha_i = \frac{Y_i^{67}}{Y_i^{66} + Y_i^{67}} + \frac{Y_i^{68}}{Y_i^{67} + Y_i^{68}} \text{ and } \bar{\alpha} = \frac{1}{n} \sum_{i=1}^{n} \left(\frac{Y_i^{67}}{Y_i^{66} + Y_i^{67}} + \frac{Y_i^{68}}{Y_i^{67} + Y_i^{68}} \right).$$

After examining the distribution of RIC, we decided to categorize each measure (family income and earnings separately) for each cohort as follows. *Highly unstable upward* is a value one or more standard deviations above the grand mean, which by definition is zero. *Moderately unstable upward* refers to a value of α_i between .25 and .99 S.D. above the grand mean. *Stable* means an α_i within ± .24 S.D. from the grand mean. *Moderately unstable downward* and *highly unstable downward* are defined analogously to the two upwardly unstable categories, but on the other side of the mean.

In the next section of this paper, we describe the results of our analysis of Gini coefficients. We also present a number of summary measures, including values of the RICs. This is followed in Section III by an examination of some of the demographic and economic correlates of instability of earnings. Section IV analyzes the sources (or components) of instability in income and earnings. A brief conclusion comprises Section V.

II. INSTABILITY OF INCOME AND EARNINGS: AN OVERVIEW

When the distribution of total family income, in absolute terms, is placed into 15 or 16 class intervals, a great deal of movement is evident between class intervals from one year to another (Tables 1 and 2). Among the older men, 33 percent of the whites and 38 percent of the blacks were in the same class interval in 1967 as in 1966. About two-fifths moved up, while just over one-fifth moved down. Even less stability is evident among the boys over a *three-year* period (1966-68), in which case only one in ten white and about one in seven blacks stayed in the same income class. Over seven-tenths of the respondents reported higher family incomes in 1968 than in 1966. Of course, movement per se need not result in reranking and, therefore, in greater measured equality over the longer time period. For reranking to occur, incomes must change at different rates or by different amounts. Leaving aside for the time being whether the changes are "real" or due to measurement error, some reranking doubtless occurred. After all,

...ge in Lower, Same, or Higher Total Family Income Class in 1967 as Compared With 1966: Middle-Aged Men

| | Whites | | | | Blacks | | | |
| | | Percent in[a] | | | | Percent in[a] | | |
Income Class	Total Number, 1966 (Thousands)	Lower Class, 1967	Same Class, 1967	Higher Class, 1967	Total Number, 1966 (Thousands)	Lower Class, 1967	Same Class, 1967	Higher Class, 1967
Total or average	12,842	23.6	32.8	43.5	1,225	21.7	37.9	40.4
Loss of income	47	0.0	25.7	74.3	5	0.0	0.0	100.0
$0-$1,999	496	0.8	58.6	40.6	159	1.0	70.2	28.8
2,000- 2,999	395	21.7	29.9	48.4	113	22.6	40.8	36.6
3,000- 3,999	431	16.3	35.4	48.3	126	25.3	36.5	38.2
4,000- 4,999	480	21.4	26.8	51.8	103	15.5	30.6	53.9
5,000- 5,999	655	17.2	29.2	53.6	91	15.6	38.2	46.2
6,000- 6,999	795	9.9	24.7	65.4	100	16.6	27.1	56.3
7,000- 7,999	1,021	23.8	27.4	48.8	85	34.4	28.3	37.3
8,000- 8,999	830	26.1	25.7	48.2	50	35.3	26.8	37.9
9,000- 9,999	817	21.6	31.0	48.4	31	41.3	9.1	49.6
10,000-10,999	716	24.9	23.0	52.1	20	45.0	18.6	36.4
11,000-11,999	657	27.5	23.7	48.8	19	52.3	26.1	21.6
12,000-12,999	608	35.5	18.2	46.3	24	40.0	22.3	37.7
13,000-14,999	639	34.6	32.3	33.1	17	48.1	15.6	36.0
15,000-19,999	788	34.1	47.2	18.7	20	35.6	55.6	8.8
20,000 or more	576	26.3	73.7	0.0	6	82.3	17.7	0.0
Not ascertained	2,891	—	—	—	256	—	—	—

[a] Number for whom income was not ascertained in one or both years is excluded from base in calculating percentages.

TABLE 2 Percentage in Lower, Same, or Higher Total Family Income Class in 1968 as Compared With 1966: Young Men

Income Class	Whites				Blacks			
	Total Number, 1966 (Thousands)	Percent in[a]			Total Number, 1966 (Thousands)	Percent in[a]		
		Lower Class, 1968	Same Class, 1968	Higher Class, 1968		Lower Class, 1968	Same Class, 1968	Higher Class, 1968
Total or average	2,628	16.7	10.5	72.8	237	14.8	14.2	71.0
Less than $1,000	22	0.0	9.8	90.2	4	0.0	0.0	100.0
$1,000-$1,999	39	0.0	0.0	100.0	14	0.0	9.5	90.5
2,000- 2,999	85	0.0	20.2	79.8	34	0.0	30.2	69.8
3,000- 3,999	163	8.8	9.5	81.7	29	4.7	28.6	66.7
4,000- 4,999	208	5.4	7.4	87.2	33	13.6	3.6	82.8
5,000- 5,999	279	3.4	9.2	88.4	6	0.0	0.0	100.0
6,000- 6,999	252	11.9	8.2	79.9	14	0.0	0.0	100.0
7,000- 7,999	212	19.9	10.6	69.5	6	50.2	0.0	49.8
8,000- 8,999	206	17.1	22.1	61.8	4	32.3	67.7	0.0
9,000- 9,999	137	25.6	6.5	67.9	8	0.0	0.0	100.0
10,000-10,999	117	37.4	4.4	58.2	17	91.6	0.0	8.4
11,000-11,999	59	53.0	6.3	41.7	0	—	—	—
12,000-12,999	61	38.2	21.6	40.2	0	—	—	—
13,000-14,999	8	0.0	0.0	100.0	0	—	—	—
15,000-19,999	30	100.0	0.0	0.0	0	—	—	—
20,000 or more	10	69.2	30.8	0.0	0	—	—	—
Not ascertained	740	—	—	—	68	—	—	—

a Number for whom income was not ascertained in one or both years is excluded from base in calculating percentages.

as indicated in Tables 1 and 2, there was movement in both directions, with movement to a higher income class more likely among those with relatively low incomes in the first year and movement to a lower income class more likely for the high-income group.

Gini Coefficients

The Gini coefficients of concentration presented in Tables 3 and 4 confirm the fact that reranking did occur, for Gini coefficients are lower when income and earnings are cumulated over a period of two or three years than when yearly coefficients are averaged. For all races combined, among the older men the yearly average coefficient for total family income is .3386, while the cumulative coefficient is 3.4 percent lower at .3271. Within the younger group of men, total family income is less unequally distributed. The yearly average coefficient for the three-year period is .2404, while the cumulative coefficient is 10.4 percent lower at .2154. These results are consistent with previous findings that the reduction in measured income equality resulting from increasing the accounting period to two or three years is relatively modest.[9]

Some of the literature on income dynamics attributes change in degree of equality over time to variation in the composition of income (e.g., earnings versus property income), because some components are more equally distributed than others.[10] Only in the case of older men were there sufficient numbers of self-employed respondents for separate analysis. Not only are their Gini coefficients much larger (yearly average, .4545; cumulative, .4298) than those for all class-of-worker categories combined, but the disparity between the yearly average and the cumulative figure is greater, suggesting that somewhat greater variation (with reranking) took place from one year to the next among the self-employed than among wage and salary workers.

[9] On the basis of British data for the early 1950s, Vandome reported a reduction in the Gini coefficient of 2.5 percent for a two-year period and of 4 percent for a three-year period. "Income and Savings," pp. 87-88. See also James Morgan, "The Anatomy of Income Distribution," *The Review of Economics and Statistics* 44 (August 1962):272.

[10] See, for example, Mary W. Smelker, "Shifts in the Concentration of Income," *Review of Economics and Statistics* 30 (August 1948):215-22.

TABLE 3 Gini Coefficients for Selected Measures of Income: Middle-Aged Men

Income Measure and Class of Worker	Number[a] (Thousands)	Gini Coefficient			
		Yearly 1966	1967	Average, 1966-67	Cumulative, 1966-67	Difference Between Cumulative and Average, as Percent of Average
		Whites, Blacks, and Others				
Total family income:						
Wage and salary workers, 1966-67	7,056	.2870	.2801	.28355	.2750	-3.0
Self-employed, 1966-67	1,397	.4674	.4416	.4545	.4298	-5.4
Total or average[b]	9,628	.3431	.3342	.33865	.3271	-3.4
Total family income per family member	9,628	.3894	.3895	.38945	.3727	-4.3
Earnings of wage and salary workers	9,617	.3015	.2900	.29575	.2834	-4.2

			Whites		
Total family income:					
Wage and salary workers, 1966-67	6,345	.2735	.2678	.27065	.2619	-3.2
Self-employed, 1966-67	1,342	.4624	.4365	.44945	.4246	-5.5
Total or average[b]	8,702	.3318	.3239	.32785	.3160	-3.6
Total family income per family member	8,702	.3794	.3706	.3750	.3632	-3.1
Earnings of wage and salary workers	8,665	.2923	.2813	.2868	.2741	-4.4
			Blacks		
Total family income:					
Wage and salary workers, 1966-67	672	.3242	.3102	.3172	.3064	-3.4
Self-employed, 1966-67	49	.5552	.4898	.5225	.4979	-4.7
Total or average[b]	866	.3705	.3565	.3635	.3518	-3.2
Total family income per family member	866	.4463	.4238	.43505	.4234	-2.7
Earnings of wage and salary workers	891	.3012	.2882	.2947	.2844	-3.5

[a] Excludes those with negative income or earnings in either or both years and those for whom total income or wage and salary earnings was not ascertained.

[b] Total includes those who changed class-of-worker status between the two years, not shown separately.

TABLE 4 Gini Coefficients for Total Family Income and Wage and Salary Earnings Respondents: Young Men

Income Measure and Class of Worker	Numbera (Thousands)	1966	1967	1968	Yearly Average 1966-67	Yearly Average 1967-68	Yearly Average 1966-68	Cumulative 1966-67	Cumulative 1967-68	Cumulative 1966-68	Difference 1966-67	Difference 1967-68	Difference 1966-68
Whites, Blacks, and Others													
Total family income:													
Wage and salary workers, 1966-68	1,754	.2509	.2334	.2252	.24215	.22935	.2365	.2253	.2165	.2121	−7.0	−5.6	−10.3
Total or averageb	1,892	.2589	.2350	.2272	.24715	.2311	.2404	.2299	.2181	.2154	−7.0	−5.6	−10.4
Earnings of wage and salary workers	2,483	.2485	.2292	.2137	.23885	.22145	.2305	.2224	.2110	.2075	−6.9	−4.7	−10.0
Whites													
Total family income:													
Wage and salary workers, 1966-68	1,590	.2385	.2251	.2157	.2318	.2204	.22643	.2147	.2079	.2020	−7.4	−5.7	−10.8
Total or averageb	1,729	.2480	.2273	.2185	.23765	.2229	.23127	.2203	.2100	.2062	−7.3	−5.8	−10.8
Earnings of wage and salary workers	2,257	.2380	.2176	.2024	.2278	.2108	.21933	.2115	.1998	.1964	−7.2	−5.2	−10.5
Blacks													
Total family incomec	164	.3282	.2872	.2794	.3077	.2833	.29827	.2903	.2646	.2706	−5.7	−6.6	−9.3
Earnings of wage and salary workers	223	.2973	.2998	.2736	.29855	.2367	.29023	.2789	.2710	.2634	−6.7	−5.5	−9.2

a Excludes those with negative income or earnings in any year and those for whom total income or wage and salary earnings was not ascertained.

b Total includes all other comparative class-of-worker categories not shown separately.

c All blacks who had not changed class-of-worker status were wage and salary workers all three years.

162

Four other relationships evident in Tables 3 and 4 deserve emphasis. First, family income per family member, at least in families headed by middle-aged men, is less equally distributed than total family income. Second, consistent with what one might suppose on the basis of Tables 1 and 2, cumulation of income makes a greater difference in the coefficient of concentration for boys than it does for men, even if attention is focused on a period of only two years. Third, among young men, lengthening the accounting period from two to three years continues to reduce the level of inequality evident in yearly data or yearly averages. Finally, income in both age groups is more unequally distributed among blacks than among whites.

Relative Instability Coefficients (RIC)

As a backdrop against which to examine our measure of income change, it is well to note that average family income, as well as wage and salary earnings, increased at a faster pace for the young than for the middle-aged men (Table 5). Within both age groups, the relative increase was greater for blacks than for whites. Moreover, among the blacks, average family income was actually higher for the young than for the middle-aged group in 1967.

TABLE 5 Means and Percentage Changes in Total Family Income: Middle-Aged and Young Men[a]

Item	Men 45-59		Men 16-24	
	Whites	Blacks	Whites	Blacks
Mean, 1966 (dollars)	9,756	5,394	6,718	4,655
	(7,055)	(3,810)	(3,086)	(2,792)
Mean, 1967 (dollars)	10,147	5,775	7,784	5,804
	(6,985)	(3,804)	(3,329)	(2,941)
Mean, 1968 (dollars)	—	—	8,908	6,495
			(3,748)	(3,336)
Percentage change:				
1967/1966	+4.0	+7.1	+15.9	+24.7
1968/1966	—	—	+32.6	+39.5

NOTE: Figures in parentheses are standard deviations.
[a]Persons reporting negative income in any year have been excluded.

Before examining the behavior of the relative instability coefficient it is desirable to reflect briefly on the nature of this measure of instability and its implications. Recall that the RIC measures each individual's change in income or earnings relative to the *average* change experienced by the entire cohort.[11] It may be useful to conceive of a given population as being distributed along an "income escalator," moving upward. The rate of upward movement is basically determined by changes in the level of factor productivity and in the price level. If all individuals remained motionless with respect to the escalator, everyone's income, by our measure, would be perfectly stable.

In addition to the upward movement of the escalator, however, changes take place in relative positions as some individuals climb the moving stairs while others move in the opposite direction. It is these shifts that our measure identifies as instability,[12] and the search for the correlates of instability amounts to an effort to ascertain whether such moves are essentially random among members of the population or whether they tend to be concentrated among those with particular demographic and employment characteristics. We hypothesize the latter; for it seems reasonable to suppose, to take but one example, that those subsets of the population most susceptible to unemployment will have unstable earnings if there are variations from year to year in their unemployment experience. This leads to a final observation, namely, that when one is considering only a two- or three-year period, it is difficult in many cases to predict the *direction* of instability, even for groups for whom there is good reason to hypothesize unstable earnings. For example, a person whose earnings are *upwardly* unstable between years x and $x + 1$ may, during that period, merely be recovering from an experience of *downward* instability between years $x - 1$ and x. Such an individual will show up as having unstable earnings over either of the two-year periods, but whether the direction is upward or

[11] The grand mean ratio, $\bar{\alpha}$, equals 1.035 for family income and 1.028 for earnings in the case of the middle-aged men. Among the boys, $\bar{\alpha}$ (for the period 1966-68) equals 1.076 for family income and 1.079 for earnings.

[12] The measure would, of course, also reflect increases in dispersion on the escalator even without alteration in relative positions to the extent that such spreading out actually occurred. However, there is no evidence of this phenomenon in the Gini coefficients for the individual years under consideration.

downward depends on when he happens to be observed. Of course, the level of income in the base period relative to such characteristics of the individual as his education or occupation may provide a basis for predicting direction of change.

Distribution of RIC: Wage and Salary Workers

The data in Table 6, which relate only to wage and salary workers, show that the relative instability of incomes among the young men is considerably greater than among the middle-aged group, which is, of course, consistent with the former's greater susceptibility to unemployment, their greater job mobility, and their greater likelihood of entering and withdrawing from the labor force as the result of variations in school status. There is also greater instability among blacks than among whites. Using individual earnings to illustrate both the intercolor and the intercohort differences, 56 percent of the older white men and 44 percent of the older black men are classified as stable, in contrast to only 30 percent of young whites and 25 percent of the young blacks. Substantially the same pattern prevails in the case of total family income.

In both age groups of whites, there is greater stability in earnings than in total family income. Among blacks, this relationship prevails for the men, but is reversed for the boys. In both color groups, the differences between stability of earnings and stability of income are more pronounced in the case of the older group than the younger, reflecting the fact that earnings is a smaller component of total family income for the older group.

There is a substantial relationship between the direction of income change and the level of income in the base year. Among the eight age-color-income measure cases, there is only one exception to the generalization that the direction of instability is monotonically related to the level of initial income. The sole exception is among the older black men, for whom the probability of downward income instability is actually somewhat higher for the lowest income group than for the intermediate group. Not only is there the indicated regularity in all other cases, but the relationship is very pronounced, especially among the boys. For example, among high-income whites, 7 percent had upwardly unstable earnings, whereas 66 percent were downwardly unstable. Of those with low base-year earnings, 58 percent were upwardly

TABLE 6   Stability of Annual Earnings and Family Income, by Color and Level of Base-Year Earnings and Income: Middle-Aged and Young Male Wage and Salary Workers[a]

Age Group, Income Measure, and Level of Base-Year Income	Number of Persons (Thousands)	Percent Whose Income is:				
		Highly Unstable Upward	Moderately Unstable Upward	Stable	Moderately Unstable Downward	Highly Unstable Downward
		Whites				
Men 16-24						
Family income:						
Total, all levels	1,590	12	23	25	30	11
High	505	2	13	19	49	18
Medium	491	4	20	37	31	8
Low	594	26	34	20	13	8
Earnings:						
Total, all levels	2,257	12	18	30	31	10
High	680	1	6	29	50	16
Medium	871	2	23	36	32	7
Low	706	34	24	23	11	7
Men 45-59						
Family income:						
Total, all levels	6,345	6	24	44	21	6
High	2,328	5	17	46	25	11
Medium	2,474	4	28	45	20	3
Low	1,544	16	26	40	14	3
Earnings:						
Total, all levels	8,665	5	15	56	19	5

	Number					
High	2,703	0	10	59	24	7
Medium	2,729	1	13	63	20	3
Low	3,235	13	20	47	14	5
Blacks						
Men 16-24						
Family income:						
Total, all levels	164	14	25	29	23	10
High	52	5	9	45	19	22
Medium	52	5	30	28	28	9
Low	58	32	34	13	21	0
Earnings:						
Total, all levels	223	14	22	25	30	10
High	56	0	6	46	35	13
Medium	85	5	32	17	37	10
Low	81	34	22	18	18	8
Men 45-59						
Family income:						
Total, all levels	672	12	23	36	19	9
High	262	2	19	40	28	11
Medium	244	13	27	41	14	4
Low	166	26	26	23	12	14
Earnings:						
Total, all levels	891	9	19	44	20	8
High	276	1	11	58	23	8
Medium	289	4	21	47	24	5
Low	326	22	25	29	14	10

a Persons reporting negative income in any year have been excluded.

unstable and 19 percent were downwardly unstable. Because of the stong correlation between initial income level and direction of change, the analysis in the remainder of the paper stratifies respondents according to initial income level. The strata were established by estimating from group data the cutting points which divide the distribution into equal thirds for total family income and for respondent's earnings within each cohort and color group. The estimated cutting points are presented in Appendix Table A.5.

III. VARIATION IN INCOME STABILITY

Stability of Total Family Income, by Class of Worker: Middle-Aged Men

Consistent with our previous interpretation of the Gini coefficients, families headed by middle-aged males who are self-employed have income that is far less stable from year to year than those whose heads are wage and salary workers (Table 7). According to our measure, stability of total family income is only half as prevalent among men who were self-employed in both years as among those who worked for others (21 percent versus 44 percent). The greater instability among the self-employed is evident in all three base-year income groups; in the low and high categories it prevails in both directions, but in the middle-income group it exists only in the downward direction.

Variation in Stability of Earnings: Wage and Salary Workers

We have performed multiple classification analyses (MCA) of earnings instability of the middle-aged and youthful wage and salary workers, using two dependent variables in turn: (1) a dichotomous variable representing stability of earnings (1, if stable; 0, otherwise); and (2) the relative instability coefficient (RIC) expressed in continuous form. The former yields for each category of each predictor variable the proportion of respondents with stable earnings. The latter yields the average RIC for the category. In each case, the value is adjusted to reflect the net influence of the predictor variable under consideration, given the other predictors in the regression.[13]

[13] For a detailed description of the technique, see Frank Andrews, James Morgan, and John Sonquist, *Multiple Classification Analysis* (Ann Arbor: University of Michigan Survey Research Center, May 1967).

TABLE 7 Stability of Total Family Income, by Class of Worker, Color, and Level of Base-Year Income: Middle-Aged Men

Class of Worker	Total			High Base Income			Medium Base Income			Low Base Income		
	Number (Thousands)	Percent Unstable Upward	Percent Unstable Downward	Number (Thousands)	Percent Unstable Upward	Percent Unstable Downward	Number (Thousands)	Percent Unstable Upward	Percent Unstable Downward	Number (Thousands)	Percent Unstable Upward	Percent Unstable Downward
Whites												
Wage and salary workers, 1966-67	6,345	29	26	2,328	19	36	2,474	32	23	1,544	42	18
Self-employed, 1966-67	1,341	43	36	325	26	50	291	30	48	726	56	26
Total[a]	8,703	32	30	2,810	19	38	2,972	31	27	2,923	46	23
Blacks												
Wage and salary workers, 1966-67	672	36	28	262	21	39	244	40	19	166	52	25
Self-employed, 1966-67	49	35	52	8	b	b	12	b	b	29	37	51
Total[a]	866	35	32	287	21	41	283	39	23	296	46	31

[a] Totals include cases in which class-of-worker status was not ascertained, as well as cases in which class-of-worker status changed between 1966 and 1967.
[b] Percentage not calculated where base represents fewer than 25 sample cases.

For the older cohort, the predictor variables that were entered into the MCA runs are age, marital status, education, health condition, size of community, occupation, industry, and degree of interfirm mobility. The more limited sample size of the younger cohort made it unfeasible to include all of the foregoing variables; only age, education, and mobility were entered. Because of the strong association between the direction of instability and the level of base-year earnings, we have stratified the samples and have run separate MCAs for each base-year income group, as well as for the total of all income groups. Tables 8 and 9 present the MCA results for all income groups combined, for the men and boys respectively, using the dichotomous dependent variable. Appendix Tables A.6 and A.7 present the results for each of the three income groups in terms of both the dichotomous and the continuous variables.

Before examining the relation between the predictor variables and measures of instability, it is well to note the regularity of the intercolor and the interincome group differences that are discernible in the tables. First, the greater stability of earnings of white men that has been observed in the aggregate prevails with only rare exceptions within all categories of the predictor variables. Second, within each category, black men tend to show a larger positive or smaller negative RIC than their white counterparts, probably reflecting their lower base incomes *within* each of the three income groups. Finally, the association between the *direction* of relative change in earnings and initial earnings level prevails in virtually all categories of both color groups.

Middle-Aged Men. Of the eight predictor variables included in the analysis, only city size failed to show a consistent relationship with either the extent or the direction of instability of earnings of the middle-aged men. Whereas the proportion with stable earnings does not vary systematically among the three five-year age categories, the *pattern* of instability does vary for white men, although not for blacks. In the case of the whites, the RIC is less favorable for older than for younger men. That is, with advancing age, the coefficient assumes a larger negative or a smaller positive value. Among both black and white men in the middle- and lower-income groups, limited education is likewise associated with less favorable RICs. In other words, the data confirm the expectation that the higher the education, the greater the probability that low earnings are the result of a transitory condition.

Men who were married and living with their wives at both survey dates had greater stability of earnings than those who were not married at either date (single, divorced, separated, widowed), which is consistent with what is known about the relationship between the labor-force participation and the marital status of men.[14] Moreover, among men with low base earnings, those who are married manifest greater upward movement than those who are not.

The relation between our measure of health and income stability is particularly interesting. Respondents were asked whether their health or physical condition prevented work or limited the amount or kind of work they could do. Those who reported that such limitations had existed for at least a year were classified as having chronic health problems. While these men are no more likely to have unstable incomes than those with no chronic problems, it is noteworthy that in the high- and low-income groups they are much more likely than their healthy counterparts to have high (negative or positive) RIC values. The tendency for men with chronic health problems to be concentrated in the lower-income groups and the fact that similar proportions of healthy and unhealthy men have stable earnings, suggest that chronic health problems frequently result in continuously low annual earnings. On the other hand, the behavior of the RIC values in the high- and low-income groups suggests that some men with chronic health problems experience flare-ups that adversely affect income in a given year, but then bounce back when the acute stage of the disability terminates.

There are differences in both the extent and direction of earnings instability among major occupation groups, but the pattern is not easily described.[15] Overall, in the case of white men,

---

[14] See William G. Bowen and T. Aldrich Finegan, *The Economics of Labor Force Participation* (Princeton: Princeton University Press, 1969), pp. 40-49.

[15] There are some anomalies in the MCA for black men that we are unable to explain. For example, on the basis of the unadjusted figures, the proportion of men with stable earnings is greatest for clerical workers (59 percent) and professionals (57 percent) and lowest for farm workers (19 percent), which is consistent with our expectations. In the adjusted proportions, however, the rank ordering of the stability of professionals and farm workers is reversed (36 versus 44 percent)! In the industry variable, agricultural workers—who are substantially the same group as the occupational category "farm workers"—have an adjusted stability proportion of 22 percent.

TABLE 8   Unadjusted and Adjusted Proportions[a] of Wage and Salary Workers With Stable Earnings, by Selected Characteristics: Middle-Aged Men

Characteristic	Whites			Blacks		
	Number (Sample Cases)[b]	Unadjusted Percent Stable	Adjusted Percent Stable	Number (Sample Cases)[b]	Unadjusted Percent Stable	Adjusted Percent Stable
Total sample[c]	2,217	56	56	962	44	44
Age:						
45-49	871	54	54	360	45	41
50-54	779	56	57	348	46	48
55-59	567	58	58	254	39	41
Marital status:						
Married spouse present, 1966-67	2,033	57	57	782	46	45
Nonmarried, 1966-67	155	48	50	143	30	32
Highest year of school completed:						
0-4	77	47	54	277	39	41
5-8	664	54	56	359	38	39
9-11	499	55	56	169	49	48
12	555	60	58	101	56	52
13+	417	57	53	52	57	54
Health:						
Chronic health problem	399	55	55	155	37	40
No chronic health problem	1,814	56	56	802	45	44
Major occupation group, 1966-67:						
Different occupation group each year	163	39	50	85	20	32
Professional, technical	246	64	64	31	57	36

Managers and officials	284	57	56	12	d	d
Clerical	135	69	65	52	59	42
Sales	103	56	58	5	d	d
Craftsmen, foremen	604	56	56	117	50	48
Operatives	422	54	52	273	52	50
Nonfarm laborers	100	48	48	204	41	45
Service workers	116	62	59	127	41	36
Farm workers	44	51	53	56	19	44
Major industry division, 1966-67:						
Different industry division each year	112	27	37	69	18	31
Agriculture	49	52	56	64	20	22
Mining, forestry, fisheries	32	57	57	15	d	d
Construction	203	49	50	101	35	36
Manufacturing	798	58	58	303	47	43
Transportation, utilities	253	57	56	116	44	44
Trade	259	54	54	87	54	55
Finance, insurance, real estate	79	55	54	19	d	d
Service	232	60	58	114	47	48
Public administration	200	69	65	74	68	65
Interfirm mobility, 1966-67:						
Same employer both years	1,978	58	57	860	47	44
Voluntary change	136	36	50	54	17	40
Involuntary change	103	40	49	48	27	40

[a] Adjusted for the effect of age, marital status, education, health, size of city, occupation, industry, and interfirm mobility. For method of adjustment see text, p. 168.

[b] Although the absolute numbers of sample cases are shown, calculations are based on weighted observations.

[c] Total includes cases in which characteristic was not ascertained. It also includes individuals whose marital status changed between the two survey dates. Persons with negative income in any year have been excluded from the data.

[d] Percentage not calculated where base is smaller than 25 sample cases.

TABLE 9 Unadjusted and Adjusted Proportions[a] of Wage and Salary Workers With Stable Earnings, by Selected Characteristics: Young Men

Characteristic	Whites			Blacks		
	Number (Sample Cases)[b]	Unadjusted Percent Stable	Adjusted Percent Stable	Number (Sample Cases)[b]	Unadjusted Percent Stable	Adjusted Percent Stable
Total sample[c]	584	29	29	124	25	25
Age:						
16-18	15	d	d	5	d	d
19-20	84	32	32	19	d	d
21-22	189	31	32	40	20	21
23-24	296	29	28	60	32	30
Highest year of school completed:						
0-8	57	28	29	25	17	16
9-11	115	28	29	42	21	22
12	261	34	33	45	24	29
13-15	77	20	20	10	d	d
16+	74	28	29	2	d	d
Interfirm mobility, 1966-68:						
Same employer all three dates	305	35	35	54	32	30
Two different employers	168	25	25	37	22	22
Three different employers	71	20	21	21	d	d

a Adjusted for the effect of age, education, and mobility. For method of adjustment, see text, p. 168.
b Although numbers refer to sample cases, calculations are based on weighted observations.
c Total includes cases in which characteristic was not ascertained. Persons with negative income have been excluded.
d Percentages not calculated where base is smaller than 25 sample cases.

the greatest stability is found among professional and clerical workers (64 and 65 percent) and the least among operatives and farm and nonfarm laborers (52, 53, and 48 percent, respectively), but the pattern varies among the several income groups. For example, among high-income whites, operatives have below-average stability and the downward instability as measured by RIC is large. Among low-income workers, however, operatives have slightly higher-than-average stability and are below average in degree of *upward* instability. Similarly, high-income managers have relatively great stability and exhibit only moderate downward instability as measured by RIC. On the other hand, managers in the low-income group have very low levels of stability and the degree of upward movement registered by their RIC is very high. In other words, both the probability of instability and the direction of change in relative income position depend upon the extent to which the base-year income is congruent with the individual's occupational class.

As expected, men employed in public administration enjoy substantially greater-than-average stability of earnings—greater than men in any other major industry division. The only other industry division that differs consistently from the average for both white and black men is construction, with a lower-than-average proportion of men with stable earnings. The other industrial difference worthy of mention is the prevalence of extreme fluctuations in trade among the white men. That is, in the high- and the low-income groups, respectively, the negative and positive RIC values are substantially higher for trade than for any other major industry division.

The data on occupation and industry indicate that earnings instability is especially pronounced among those individuals who changed from one major occupation group or from one major industry division to another between the two survey dates. Because industrial and occupational affiliation were measured as of the time of each survey, while the income data relate to the preceding calendar year, we cannot be certain of the direction of causation. It is clear, nonetheless, that income instability and job mobility are closely related. More direct evidence on the same point is provided by the measure of interfirm mobility. Men who changed employers between the two survey dates—whether voluntarily or involuntarily—were more likely to have unstable earnings.[16] It is interesting that in terms of RIC, involuntary job changes did not invariably produce less desirable results than voluntary changes. Specifically, among low-income whites, involuntary movers had an RIC of +9.0 as compared with +0.7 for voluntary movers.

Young Men.   As has been mentioned, the smaller number of observations for the youth has compelled us to confine our attention to only three of the variables used in the case of the older cohort of men: age, education, and mobility.[17] The relationships between these and income stability are analogous to those that prevail among the older men. With respect to age, the behavior of RIC becomes increasingly favorable as age increases. That is, it is the *youngest* men in this cohort who have the largest negative and the smallest positive values of RIC, just as this was true of the *oldest* group of middle-aged men.

Increasing educational attainment is likewise associated with more favorable *direction* of income change, even though there is no systematic relation with the *degree* of stability. Among those with high base-year earnings, the negative value of the RIC declines as educational attainment increases, although there is a slight reversal between the 12-year and the 13- to 15-year categories. Among those with low base-year earnings, RIC rises monotonically from −2.1 for those with less than nine years of education to +11.0 for those with sixteen or more years.

Young men who changed survey-week employer at least once were less likely to have stable earnings than those continuously employed in the same firm, although this relationship does not exist in the lowest income group. Moreover, the instability that prevailed among the mobile workers was, on the average, less favorable than that for those who were immobile. Within the high-income group, the job changers had greater negative RIC values; in the low-income group, they had smaller positive RIC values than their immobile counterparts.[18]

[16] It may be noted that the difference is less pronounced in the adjusted than the unadjusted data, because part of the difference in the unadjusted figures reflects the effect of occupational and industrial changes that are included in the MCA analysis.

[17] Specifically, there are too few sample cases of unhealthy and of nonmarried young men to permit an analysis of health and marital status, and only a few of the occupational and industrial categories within each of the income groups have as many as 25 observations.

[18] The data for the young men do not permit us to distinguish between voluntary and involuntary job changes.

IV. SOURCES OF INCOME INSTABILITY:
WAGE AND SALARY WORKERS

Several of the correlates of instability in earnings are suggestive of the mechanisms through which year-to-year change takes place. For example, we have speculated that differences in the stability of earnings by occupation, job mobility, and health status are probably attributable, in large measure, to differential changes from one year to the next in number of weeks worked. We now turn, therefore, to a direct examination of year-to-year variation in several components of total family income[19] and in the proximate determinants of personal earnings of wage and salary workers.[20] Each of these topics is discussed in turn, on the basis of both a cross-tabular and an MCA analysis.

Total Family Income

In the relative sense in which we are using the term instability, there is no *necessary* relation between instability in one or more of the components of family income and instability in the total. First, while none of the components of a family's income may be unstable relative to the mean change in the population, its total income may nevertheless be unstable as the result of interfamily differences in the relative importance of the several components. Secondly, total family income may remain stable even in the face of instability of the components if these are unstable in offsetting directions. Finally, family income may remain stable by our definition when one or more of its components is unstable, if these components comprise a sufficiently small proportion of the total.

Cross-Tabular Analysis. Table 10 and Appendix Table A.8 show the relationship between instability in total family income and instability in each of its components for wage and salary earners in both age cohorts. A few words of explanation, together with an illustration, may help to clarify the meaning of the data.

---

[19] For the older men, the components that are analyzed are earnings of respondent, earnings of wife, earnings of other family members, property income, and transfers. For the younger group, the data permit us to decompose aggregate income into only four categories: respondent's earnings, wife's earnings, unemployment compensation, and other income.

[20] Earnings are decomposed into hourly rate of pay and hours worked per year, with the latter further examined in terms of hours usually worked per week, weeks unemployed per year, and weeks out of the labor force.

TABLE 10 Mean Ratios of Change, 1966-67, in Selected Components of Total Family Income, by Age Group and Color: Middle-Aged and Young Male Wage and Salary Workers[a]

Component of Family Income	Whites				Blacks			
	Total or Average	Unstable Upward	Stable	Unstable Downward	Total or Average	Unstable Upward	Stable	Unstable Downward
Men 45-59 Years of Age								
Earnings of respondent	2.4	11.1	1.8	-6.1	3.7	16.4	1.4	-9.3
Earnings of wife	3.1	14.6	3.6	-10.3	3.3	17.5	-0.6	-9.9
Earnings of others	5.5	21.8	6.5	-14.5	9.3	19.4	10.9	-5.4
Property income	-3.5	7.5	-1.1	-19.6	-3.2	4.7	-4.9	-11.2
Transfer income	1.1	1.2	-0.3	3.0	-0.9	0.7	-1.7	-1.7
Total number (thousands)	6,345	1,867	2,791	1,683	672	239	243	190
Men 16-24 Years of Age								
Earnings of respondent	7.9	15.6	8.0	2.1	9.8	19.1	6.6	3.4
Earnings of wife	-13.8	-7.1	-8.9	-20.2	-2.4	2.2	2.4	-12.3
Unemployment compensation	-2.8	-0.7	-3.6	-3.9	-8.2	-9.8	-3.8	-10.1
Other income	-8.6	-0.7	-8.1	-15.3	-3.2	0.1	-9.9	-1.1
Total number (thousands)	1,590	551	394	657	164	64	47	53

[a] Persons reporting negative income in any year are excluded.

The change ratios that are presented for each component of total family income differ from the RICs defined earlier. Whereas the RIC represented an average *deviation* from a mean measure of relative change, the change ratio is simply a measure of relative change in the component for the subset of the sample under consideration.[21]

The change ratios for the total sample are shown in the first column of Tables 10 and A.8 for each component of income. These can be used as benchmarks for comparing the relative stability of a component of income from one income-stability group to another or from one base-year income group to another.

To illustrate, among the older white men, the entry of 11.1 in the second column of Table 10 for earnings of respondents in the upwardly unstable total-family-income group means that 1967 earnings of the average respondent in this category were 11.1 percent higher than the mean of his 1966 and 1967 earnings. Thus, the rate of earnings increase for this group was considerably above the overall mean rate of increase in earnings for all men employed as wage and salary workers (11.1 versus 2.4). For the same age-color group, men with downwardly unstable family income exhibited downwardly unstable earnings (−6.1 versus 2.4), and those with relatively stable family income experienced relative stability of earnings (1.8 versus 2.4).

Thus, there is a strong positive correlation between instability of total family income and instability of respondent's earnings. This is hardly surprising in view of the fact that among wage and salary workers, earnings of the household head constitute upwards of 70 percent of family income.[22]

[21] Specifically, for each component, the change ratio (CR) in the case of total family income for the older men is computed as follows:

$$CR = \frac{1}{n} \sum_{i=1}^{n} \left[\frac{Y_i^{67}}{\frac{1}{2}(Y_i^{66} + Y_i^{67})} \cdot 100 \right] - 100 .$$

The corresponding formula for the boys is

$$CR = \frac{1}{n} \sum_{i=1}^{n} \left[\left(\frac{Y_i^{67}}{Y_i^{66} + Y_i^{67}} + \frac{Y_i^{68}}{Y_i^{67} + Y_i^{68}} \right) \cdot 100 \right] - 100.$$

The change ratio is computed for each income-stability category and for every base-year income level. Data for the three base-year income levels are shown in Appendix Table A.8.

[22] Appendix Table A.9 shows the basic relationship between change in respondent's earnings and in total family income in somewhat greater detail. Five categories of relative instability in family income are cross-classified by five categories of change in respondent's earnings.

While the earnings of wives and of other family members (principally children) are not a large fraction of total family income, these sources are less stable from year to year than respondent's earnings. As a result, there is a strong positive association between the degree and direction of change in family income and change in the earnings of other family members. In other words, those middle-aged men with upwardly unstable total family income generally reported larger increases (or smaller reductions) in the earnings of other family members (including wives) than those with downwardly unstable family income.

Among the boys, all sources of income other than respondent's earnings declined over the three-year period. With respect to earnings of wives, this pattern may reflect in many cases a conscious family decision concerning which marriage partner will work, which one will attend school, and when to begin raising a family. In the case of older men, however, it is difficult to say on the basis of these data whether changes in the labor-force participation of wives and children are compensatory for those of respondents. Consider, for example, the downwardly unstable income group. In some instances, a drop in respondent's earnings—which, it will be recalled, constitutes the bulk of family income—may overwhelm an increase in the earnings of wives and children. Nevertheless, it is worth emphasizing that, on the average, all sources of income, except transfers, tended to rise more than average (or, fall less than average) for those with upwardly unstable income, whereas the reverse was generally the case for the downwardly unstable group.

Tabulations not shown here indicate that among the middle-aged men, positive association between instability of family income and instability of wife's earnings is produced in at least three ways. Relative to families with downwardly unstable income, families with upwardly unstable income were more likely to contain a wife who entered the labor force over the period and less likely to contain a wife who departed from the labor force. Regardless of level of base-year income, a substantial increase took place among the upwardly unstable group in the proportion with wives making a monetary contribution to total family income; the other groups experienced either small net increases or actual declines.[23] Furthermore, the rate of increase in earnings among

[23] Low-income black men constitute an interesting exception to the monotonic relationship. In the families of such men, the rate of labor-force

those wives who were in the labor force during both periods was higher than average in families with upwardly unstable income.

On the average, the earnings of family members (other than wives) are a much smaller proportion of family income than are the wife's earnings; the respective grand means in 1966 were $555 and $1,268 for whites, and $293 and $996 for blacks. Yet, upward instability of income seems to be at least as dependent upon increases in the earnings of other family members as upon increases in the wife's earnings. For example, among older white men in the top income group who had upwardly unstable family income, the average monetary contribution in the second year of other members was $1,859 (up from $806) as compared to $1,899 (up from $1,559) from earnings of the wife. Similar patterns obtain in the other five color–base-income groups.

Among men employed as wage and salary workers, property income comprises a very small proportion of family income. For example, it is less than 5 percent of the total among older whites in the top third of the income distribution. Consequently, for most respondents, even very wide fluctuations in this component cannot generate relative instability in total family income. However, the data indicate that among older wage and salary workers, patterns of change in property income tend to reinforce patterns of instability set by the other components. The mean ratio of change in property income is consistently above the grand mean among those with upwardly unstable income and well below the mean for the downwardly unstable.

As might be expected, there is some evidence that transfer payments are a "stabilizing" component of total family income. Among the families with low base-year incomes, transfer payments show the largest positive change ratio for those whose family income was unstable downward. For the only group which can be categorized as "poor" by conventional standards—black men in the lowest third of the income distribution—transfer-payment income exhibits substantial absolute and relative increases for both the upwardly and downwardly unstable. This suggests that transfer payments, such as disability benefits, unemployment and work-

---

entry by wives was about the same for the two instability groups and was higher than among families with stable family income. The relationships shown in Table A.8 for low-income black men is maintained, only in part, by a slightly higher labor-force departure rate among wives in families with downwardly unstable income.

men's compensation, both cushion backslides on the metaphorical escalator and provide an upward boost in periods subsequent to the backslide. Without performing an extensive decomposition of existing variables, we cannot be certain about the reason for the increase in transfer income among white men in the top income group, but it may reflect this group's increased eligibility for pensions associated with military service and other programs.

Multiple Classification Analysis. In order to examine simultaneously the relative contribution of change in each component to change (or stability) in total family income, an MCA analysis was performed. The MCA was restricted to the older cohort for two reasons. First, the number of data cases in each income group of young blacks is very small. Second, the number of data cases with nonzero values for unemployment compensation in either year or for "other income" is minute. The RIC for total family income (in continuous form) was regressed on a set of 25 dummy variables. The latter consisted of five categories of change ratios for each component of family income. These categories ranged from "highly unstable upward" to "highly unstable downward." The results are presented in Table 11. *Eta* is a simple correlation ratio between a given explanatory variable and the dependent variable and is analogous to a Pearsonian *r*. According to Andrews, Morgan, and Sonquist, the *beta* coefficients, on the other hand, are "moderately good substitute[s] for a partial correlation coefficient . . . , [but] must be interpreted with caution, and are useful only for indicating the relative importance of the various predictors."[24]

As would be expected from the definitional relationship between total family income and the sum of its components, the MCA produced R^2s that are unusually large for microdata.[25]

In each color-income group, instability of respondent's earnings stands out as the principal source of instability in family income. Moreover, the results indicate that the importance of the earnings of the head of the household in causing change in total family income is inversely related to the level of base-year income.

There is support for an observation made earlier on the basis of

[24] Andrews, Morgan, and Sonquist, *Multiple Classification Analysis*, pp. 117-18.

[25] They are, nevertheless, less than unity since, among other reasons, the method of measuring the dependent variable (continuous) is different from measurement of the explanatory variables (five categories each).

TABLE 11 MCA Results for Components of Total Family Income, by Color and Base-Year Income: Middle-Aged Male Wage and Salary Workers

Base-Year Income (N)	Component											
	Respondent's Earnings		Wife's Earnings		Other Earnings		Property Income		Transfer Income		R^2	$\bar{R}^2$
	η	β	η	β	η	β	η	β	η	β		
					Whites							
High (588)	.507	.489	.229	.212	.320	.295	.220	.172	.101	.076[a]	.432	.410
Medium (642)	.591	.610	.276	.271	.317	.322	.206	.151	.026	.105[a]	.558	.542
Low (404)	.631	.658	.266	.233	.261	.227	.218	.137[b]	.061	.189	.561	.536
					Blacks							
High (259)	.503	.508	.300	.261	.363	.335	.199	.172	.208	.125[a]	.506	.462
Medium (264)	.641	.641	.352	.233	.296	.308	.120	.124[a]	.137	.120[a]	.603	.568
Low (198)	.793	.790	.219	.198	.256	.192	.094	.063[a]	.130	.060[a]	.709	.674

NOTE: Significance was determined by an *F*-test suggested by Andrews, Morgan, and Sonquist, *Multiple Classification Analysis*, p. 100, equation (4-23). Unless otherwise indicated figures are significant at $\alpha \leqslant .01$.
[a] Not significant at $\alpha \leqslant .05$.
[b] Significant at $.01 \leqslant \alpha < .05$.

relationships shown in Table 10. Specifically, instability in the earnings of family members other than the wife contributes as much or more to instability in family income as instability of the wife's earnings. In the equations for the high- and middle-income families in both color groups, the *beta* coefficients are noticeably higher for "other earnings" than for "wife's earnings," whereas for the low-income families these two components have approximately equal coefficients.

As mentioned earlier, for wage and salary workers the small proportion of total family income attributable to property income makes it unlikely that this component can contribute substantially to relative instability in total income. The MCA results confirm this common-sense observation; the coefficients for property income are considerably below those for any of the earnings components and, in fact, are only statistically significant in three of the equations (i.e., for families with 1966 incomes above $6,500). The bivariate relationship between the change ratio in transfer payments and the RIC for total family income turns out to be illusory, except in the case of low-income whites. The net coefficients are very small and are significant only for whites in the bottom third of the income distribution.

Respondent's Earnings

In order to investigate the sources of relative instability in respondent's earnings, we have adopted a procedure analogous to that used to study instability of total family income. Annual earnings have been decomposed into their definitional components, i.e., hourly rate of pay and annual hours worked, with the latter component further decomposed into usual hours worked per week, weeks of unemployment, and weeks out of the labor force.[26]

Cross-Tabular Analysis. The data in Table 12 and Appendix Table A.10 depict the bivariate relationships between relative instability of earnings and its components in the same manner as was done for relative instability of total family income in Tables 10 and A.8.

---

[26] While definitional, hourly rate of pay and usual hours worked per week refer to current (or last) job. Thus, these figures may not be representative of the base-year period. Furthermore, the work experience measures for the older men refer to the 12-month period preceding each survey while earnings (and income) were reported on a calendar-year basis.

TABLE 12 Mean Ratios of Change, 1966-67, in Components of Respondent's Earnings, by Age Group and Color: Middle-Aged and Young Male Wage and Salary Workers[a]

Component of Respondent's Earnings	Whites				Blacks			
	Total or Average	Unstable Upward	Stable	Unstable Downward	Total or Average	Unstable Upward	Stable	Unstable Downward
	Men 45-59 Years of Age							
Hourly rate of pay	2.7	5.9	2.7	0.1	4.7	8.2	3.4	3.2
Hours worked per year	-0.5	3.2	-0.5	-3.7	0.8	4.1	0.4	-2.1
Usual hours per week	-0.9	-0.5	-0.7	-1.7	-0.8	-0.6	-0.5	-1.5
Weeks unemployed	-0.9	-10.8	0.0	5.1	-4.3	-10.6	-5.2	3.7
Weeks not in labor force	-0.7	-6.8	-0.5	3.8	-2.1	-6.6	-1.8	1.8
Total number (thousands)	8,665	1,750	4,842	2,076	891	254	389	247
	Men 16-24 Years of age							
Hourly rate of pay	3.5	3.6	4.7	2.3	5.1	3.1	7.1	5.6
Hours worked per year	-1.1	4.4	-2.0	-4.3	-1.6	2.9	-2.9	-4.9
Usual hours per week	-2.1	-0.1	-2.5	-3.0	-1.5	0.4	-2.5	-2.6
Weeks unemployed	-4.6	-8.2	-3.9	-2.5	-12.0	-9.4	-6.3	-18.1
Weeks not in labor force	-10.9	-23.2	-6.3	-5.3	-5.0	-11.1	1.9	-3.8
Total number (thousands)	2,257	673	676	914	223	80	55	88

[a] Persons reporting negative income in any year are excluded.

Among the older men who were employed as wage and salary workers, relative instability in both hourly earnings and annual hours of work exhibit positive associations with relative instability of annual earnings. However, the associations are regular and pronounced only among whites. For example, among black men with low incomes, there is no difference in the relative stability of rate of pay as between those with upwardly unstable earnings and those with downwardly unstable earnings. Likewise, among blacks in the upper two-thirds of the earnings distribution, the two groups with unstable earnings are virtually indistinguishable with respect to stability of total hours worked.

Among the younger men, only instability of annual hours of work appears to bear a discernible relationship to instability of annual earnings. Indeed, for whites and blacks alike, the mean ratio of change in the wage rate is at least as great among those with stable earnings as among those whose earnings changed faster or slower than the average. In fact, among the whites in the lowest base-year earnings category, there appears to be an inverse association between change in the wage rate and change in earnings. This may be a result of the fact that this group contains a disproportionate share of men who were students during part of the first year. These individuals would be expected to experience large increases in annual earnings after becoming full-time participants in the labor market, but without necessarily showing much increase in hourly rate of pay.

When we further examine the sources of instability in annual hours of work (usual hours per week, and so on), it is apparent that the impact of each component varies with color, age, and base-year earnings. Because virtually all of the men under study are full-time participants in the labor market, there is extremely little variation in weekly hours of work. Furthermore, since our measure is "usual" hours of work per week, we do not pick up the variation which sometimes results from overtime. Thus, it is not surprising that the relationship between relative stability of weekly hours and annual earnings is weak.

Relative instability of unemployment experience generally exhibits the expected association with relative instability of annual earnings. That is, over a period of improving economic conditions, weeks unemployed declined more than average among those men classified as having upwardly unstable earnings. Because of the concentration of unemployment among certain groups of workers, its change shows no relation to the stability of annual earnings among older white men in the high base-year earnings category. Further, there is no apparent relationship within the group which has the greatest recorded susceptibility to unemployment, i.e., young black men.

Change in the amount of time spent out of the labor force generally is associated with earnings instability in the anticipated way. As expected, respondents with upwardly unstable earnings reduced their time out of the labor force at an above average rate and the opposite was true of those with downwardly unstable earnings. Of course, to the extent that some of the increased time in the labor force is spent unemployed rather than working, the effect is attenuated. The relationship between stability of weeks out of the labor force and stability of earnings seems to be most pronounced among those in the low-earnings categories. The large coefficient of change (-32.8) for young white men with low base-year and upwardly unstable earnings is support for the conjecture expressed earlier regarding wage rate and earnings stability for those who may have been students at some time during the base year.

Multiple Classification Analysis.   In order to examine the "net" relationships of the several possible sources of relative instability of earnings, we have again employed multiple classification analysis. Once again, the dependent variable is expressed in continuous form, this time as the RIC for respondent's earnings. The regressors are categorical variables. However, only the change ratios of hourly rate of pay and usual hours worked per week were coded into five categories. The variables to measure stability of weeks unemployed and weeks out of the labor force were coded into only three categories each: unstable upward, stable, and unstable downward.[27] Results of the analysis for both cohorts appear in Table 13.

In general, our findings are consistent with the preceding discussion of the tables showing bivariate relationships.[28] First,

---

[27] We have departed somewhat from our earlier method of measuring stability in these two variables. The upwardly unstable were defined as those for whom the change ratio was above zero and the downwardly unstable were defined as those for whom the change ratio was below zero. This procedure was adopted because of the tremendously large concentration of cases in which the change ratio equaled zero.

[28] Because of small sample sizes among the young blacks, none of the F-tests show statistical significance. Consequently, the discussion below omits consideration of these results.

TABLE 13   MCA Results for Components of Respondent's Earnings, by Level of Base-Year Earnings, Age Group, and Color: Middle-Aged and Young Male Wage and Salary Workers

| | Stability of | | | | | | | | | | |
| | Wage Rate | | Hours/Week | | Weeks Unemployed | | Weeks OLF | | | | |
Cohort and Earnings Group (N)	η	β	η	β	η	β	η	β	R^2	$\bar{R}^2$	F
					Men 45-59 Years of Age						
					Whites						
High (689)	.233	.208	.192	.156	.094	.024[a]	.095	.125	.083	.063	4.07
Medium (698)	.251	.279	.167	.181	.099	.422	.053	.435	.120	.101	6.21
Low (848)	.162	.157	.088	.022[a]	.163	.206	.078	.092	.055	.038	3.25
					Blacks						
High (285)	.255	.281	.028	.064[a]	.093	.206	.095	.181	.093	.043	1.84
Medium (298)	.165	.196[a]	.075	.082[a]	.087	.460	.098	.439	.066	.017[a]	1.34

Low (384)	.161	.162[a]	.131	.156	.218	.170	.180	.168	.097	.060	2.63
Men 16-24 Years of Age											
Whites											
High (174)	.233	.193[a]	.276	.269	.314	.266	.113	.040[a]	.201	.125	2.64
Medium (206)	.285	.327	.353	.367	.178	.136[a]	.177	.118	.260	.197	4.78
Low (204)	.249	.228	.446	.438	.246	.200	.243	.253	.357	.306	6.96
Blacks[b]											
Medium (47)	.208	.365[a]	.388	.503[a]	.237	.202[a]	.151	.177[a]	.297	c	
Low (53)	.331	.263[a]	.412	.407[a]	.235	.251[a]	.265	.283[a]	.344	.078[a]	1.30

NOTE: Significance was determined by an *F*-test suggested by Andrews, Morgan, and Sonquist, *Multiple Classification Analysis*, p. 100, equation (4-23). Unless otherwise indicated figures are significant at $\alpha \leqslant .05$.

[a] Not significant at $\alpha \leqslant .05$.

[b] No results are shown for blacks in the high-earnings group because there are only 24 sample cases representing the 52,000 men in this group.

[c] Because of the small number of data cases and relatively large number of predictor categories, the R^2 adjusted for degrees of freedom is less than zero.

the instability of rate of pay, usual hours worked per week, weeks unemployed, and weeks out of the labor force explain a rather small proportion of the relative instability of annual earnings, especially among the older men.[29] Second, the instability in weeks unemployed and weeks out of the labor force exhibit the most consistently significant relationships to relative instability of annual earnings. Unemployment experience is nonsignificant only for the high-earnings group of older white men and for the medium-earnings group of young whites.

However, in contrast to the conjecture based on the data in Tables 12 and A.10, there is evidence that instability in weekly hours of work does bear a significant relationship to instability of annual earnings. This is a consistent result of the regressions for young white men and for three of the six equations for the older men. The rather unsystematic results concerning the association of instability in hourly wage rate and in annual earnings were presaged in the earlier discussion. Because of the substantial variation in the results across the 11 age–color–base-earnings groups, it does not seem prudent to draw any general conclusions about the relative importance of the several potential sources of relative instability in annual earnings. There is need for additional research on this question with improved measurement and somewhat different specifications (e.g., a multiplicative model).

V. CONCLUDING OBSERVATION

Collecting income data covering several years by means of repeated annual surveys rather than by a single retrospective interview has the advantage of reducing the problem of faulty recall by respondents and doubtless improves the validity of the data. On the other hand, when such data are used longitudinally to measure gross changes (i.e., instability) in income over time, as is the case in this paper, it is almost certain that spurious change is

---

[29] These regressions probably are less successful than those presented earlier because: (1) there is considerably less variation in the several components of earnings than in the components of total family income; (2) our measurement of the components of personal earnings is less precise than is the case for the components of family income; (3) the measures do not always relate to the time period for which earnings were reported; and (4) the components chosen are related multiplicatively to earnings, whereas they were additive in the case of total income.

registered as the result of reporting and clerical errors in one or more of the time periods. In cross-sectional analysis, such errors, if unsystematic, tend to average out; in longitudinal analysis they almost inevitably result in overstating the "true" amount of gross change in the variable under consideration.

If the year-to-year income instability that our data reveal were completely spurious, it would, or course, no longer follow that the length of the accounting period affects a "true" measure of income inequality. The modest reduction in the Gini coefficients that we have observed as the time period is lengthened would be merely reflecting noise in the data rather than a real-world phenomenon.

While we believe that our data almost certainly overstate the extent of income instability, there is no way of knowing by precisely how much. Nevertheless, we can be reasonably certain that a substantial amount of the change in relative position in the income distribution that we have measured is real, for the consistency of the relationships that we have found between income instability on the one hand and demographic and labor-market variables on the other hand admits of no other interpretation.

APPENDIX

TABLE A.1   Nonresponse Rates on Total Family Income, 1966 and 1967, by Income Class in 1966 and 1967: Middle-Aged Men

Income Class	Whites				Blacks			
	Number, 1966 (Thousands)	Nonresponse Rate, 1966 (Percent)	Number, 1967 (Thousands)	Nonresponse Rate, 1967 (Percent)	Number, 1966 (Thousands)	Nonresponse Rate, 1966 (Percent)	Number, 1967 (Thousands)	Nonresponse Rate, 1967 (Percent)
Total or average	12,842	22.5	12,842	15.6	1,225	21.0	1,225	12.0
Loss of income	47	11.7	34	6.4	5	25.0	4	60.0
$0-$1,999	496	20.3	580	8.2	159	17.6	170	5.7
2,000- 2,999	395	18.8	346	10.1	113	16.5	109	8.0
3,000- 3,999	431	21.6	486	11.8	126	20.4	108	11.9
4,000- 4,999	480	24.2	507	9.6	103	20.0	105	7.8
5,000- 5,999	655	20.6	649	9.6	91	21.5	121	8.8
6,000- 6,999	795	15.2	889	8.3	100	13.0	108	10.0
7,000- 7,999	1,021	14.7	931	7.8	85	17.4	86	8.2
8,000- 8,999	830	16.6	877	13.8	50	15.1	79	16.0
9,000- 9,999	817	17.7	920	12.2	31	27.7	47	9.6
10,000-10,999	716	16.0	751	11.2	20	27.9	43	15.0
11,000-11,999	657	16.1	707	11.7	19	23.1	26	21.0
12,000-12,999	608	19.0	593	14.5	24	10.5	19	20.8
13,000-14,999	639	20.4	971	12.5	17	13.3	15	11.8
15,000-19,999	788	25.7	951	14.9	20	21.8	32	10.0
20,000 or more	576	20.5	663	20.1	6	20.0	5	16.7
Not ascertained	2,891	41.7	1,997	28.9	256	35.3	147	20.8

TABLE A.2 Nonresponse Rates on Total Family Income, 1966 and 1968, by Income Class in 1966 and 1968: Young Men

	Whites				Blacks			
Income Class	Number, 1966 (Thousands)	Nonresponse Rate, 1968 (Percent)	Number, 1968 (Thousands)	Nonresponse Rate, 1966 (Percent)	Number, 1966 (Thousands)	Nonresponse Rate, 1968 (Percent)	Number, 1968 (Thousands)	Nonresponse Rate, 1966 (Percent)
Total or average	2,628	5.4	2,628	28.1	237	1.3	237	28.8
Less than $1,000	22	0.0	14	87.5	4	0.0	1	0.0
$1,000-$1,999	39	12.8	9	44.4	14	0.0	8	50.0
2,000- 2,999	85	0.0	63	31.7	34	2.9	15	40.0
3,000- 3,999	163	8.6	80	22.5	29	6.9	34	17.6
4,000- 4,999	208	1.9	105	34.3	33	0.0	23	39.1
5,000- 5,999	279	4.3	194	39.2	6	0.0	34	26.5
6,000- 6,999	252	4.8	298	33.9	14	0.0	36	33.3
7,000- 7,999	212	8.5	308	30.2	6	0.0	12	41.7
8,000- 8,999	206	4.4	312	23.1	4	0.0	19	5.3
9,000- 9,999	137	12.4	299	22.4	8	0.0	21	38.1
10,000-10,999	117	3.4	233	25.7	17	0.0	9	44.4
11,000-11,999	59	0.0	167	32.9	0	—	1	100.0
12,000-12,999	61	18.0	150	28.7	0	—	12	25.0
13,000-14,999	8	50.0	126	7.9	0	—	3	—
15,000-19,999	30	0.0	96	34.4	0	—	3	—
20,000 or more	10	0.0	32	28.1	0	—	0	—
Not ascertained	740	4.2	142	22.0	68	0.0	3	0.0

TABLE A.3 Percentage of Income and Earnings Received by Selected Fractions of Respondents: Middle-Aged Men[a]

Year and Fraction of Recipients Arrayed by Level of Income or Earnings	Total Family Income			Total Family Income per Family Member	Earnings of Wage and Salary Workers
	Total or Average	Wage and Salary Workers, 1966-67	Self-employed, 1966-67		
			Whites		
1966:					
Lowest 25 percent	9.1	12.1	5.9	7.9	10.7
Lowest 50 percent	27.8	31.6	19.9	24.3	30.6
Lowest 75 percent	53.9	57.3	42.8	49.7	56.7
Lowest 95 percent	83.9	86.1	76.1	82.6	85.8
1967:					
Lowest 25 percent	9.3	12.3	6.3	8.3	11.5
Lowest 50 percent	28.2	32.0	21.0	25.0	31.2
Lowest 75 percent	54.5	57.9	45.1	50.2	57.3
Lowest 95 percent	84.7	86.3	78.8	83.0	85.9
1966-67, cumulative:					
Lowest 25 percent	9.8	12.6	7.0	8.5	11.8

Lowest 50 percent	28.9	32.4	22.0	25.4	31.7
Lowest 75 percent	54.9	58.3	45.7	50.8	57.6
Lowest 95 percent	84.8	86.5	78.9	83.3	86.2
			Blacks		
1966:					
Lowest 25 percent	7.3	8.7	4.2	5.2	9.1
Lowest 50 percent	24.0	27.3	14.7	19.0	28.4
Lowest 75 percent	51.4	54.8	33.8	44.7	57.3
Lowest 95 percent	84.9	87.0	70.4	81.7	88.6
1967:					
Lowest 25 percent	7.2	9.2	3.4	5.6	9.8
Lowest 50 percent	24.9	28.5	15.6	20.4	29.6
Lowest 75 percent	52.7	55.7	40.9	46.8	57.9
Lowest 95 percent	86.1	87.2	82.0	83.3	88.6
1966-67, cumulative:					
Lowest 25 percent	7.7	9.4	5.2	5.8	9.9
Lowest 50 percent	25.2	28.6	17.0	20.4	29.6
Lowest 75 percent	52.9	56.0	38.3	46.5	58.2
Lowest 95 percent	86.2	87.6	79.0	83.3	88.9

[a] See text, Table 3, for universe restrictions and number of observations.

TABLE A.4   Percentage of Income and Earnings Received by Selected Fractions of Respondents: Young Men[a]

Year and Fraction of Recipients Arrayed by Level of Income or Earnings	Whites			Blacks	
	Total Family Income		Earnings of Wage and Salary Workers	Total Family Income	Earnings of Wage and Salary Workers
	All Respondents	Wage and Salary Workers, 1966-68			
1966:					
Lowest 25 percent	12.2	12.5	11.4	9.6	9.5
Lowest 50 percent	32.5	33.0	33.4	27.1	29.0
Lowest 75 percent	60.1	60.8	61.5	52.3	56.5
Lowest 95 percent	89.3	90.0	90.3	88.8	88.4
1967:					
Lowest 25 percent	13.2	13.4	12.9	9.9	10.1
Lowest 50 percent	34.3	34.4	34.9	28.8	28.6
Lowest 75 percent	61.2	61.3	62.6	58.1	56.0
Lowest 95 percent	89.7	89.7	90.8	89.8	88.3
1968:					
Lowest 25 percent	13.6	13.7	13.6	11.0	10.8
Lowest 50 percent	35.0	35.2	36.0	30.1	31.0
Lowest 75 percent	61.8	62.0	63.6	57.8	58.2
Lowest 95 percent	89.5	89.6	90.8	88.5	88.7
1966-68, cumulative:					
Lowest 25 percent	14.4	14.6	14.1	11.6	11.6
Lowest 50 percent	35.6	35.9	36.3	30.0	31.5
Lowest 75 percent	62.5	62.7	63.7	57.9	58.5
Lowest 95 percent	90.3	90.6	91.1	89.8	89.0

TABLE A.5   Cutting Points for Equal Thirds (Rounded to Nearest $100) of Total Family Income and Respondent's Earnings: Middle-Aged and Young Men

(dollars)

Third	*Men 45-59*		*Men 16-24*	
	Total Family Income, 1966	*Earnings of Wage and Salary Workers, 1966*	*Total Family Income, 1966*	*Earnings of Wage and Salary Workers, 1966*
			Whites	
1st third	7,000	6,100	5,400	4,600
2nd third	10,900	8,700	8,000	6,500
			Blacks	
1st third	3,300	3,400	3,100	2,800
2nd third	6,400	5,700	5,000	4,600

TABLE A.6   Adjusted Proportion[a] of Respondents with Stable Earnings and Adjusted Relative Instability Coefficient,[a] by Color, Level of Base-Year Earnings, and Selected Other Characteristics: Middle-Aged Men

Characteristic	High Base-Year Earnings			Medium Base-Year Earnings			Low Base-Year Earnings		
	Number (Sample Cases)[b]	Adjusted Percent Stable	Adjusted RIC	Number (Sample Cases)[b]	Adjusted Percent Stable	Adjusted RIC	Number (Sample Cases)[b]	Adjusted Percent Stable	Adjusted RIC
				Whites					
Total sample[c]	686	59	−4.8	691	64	−2.3	840	48	+5.4
Age:									
45-49	303	58	−4.2	283	62	−1.8	285	42	+6.8
50-54	228	61	−4.7	242	66	−2.2	309	48	+5.0
55-59	155	58	−6.0	166	64	−3.2	246	54	+4.0
Marital status:									
Married spouse present, 1966-67	657	59	−4.8	649	64	−2.2	727	48	+5.9
Nonmarried, 1966-67	25	54	−3.9	35	47	−4.4	95	48	+1.1
Highest year of school completed:									
0-4	4	d	d	12	d	d	61	47	−0.6
5-8	97	58	−5.4	206	64	−3.7	361	48	+3.6
9-11	128	57	−4.2	181	61	−2.5	190	50	+4.3
12	181	63	−5.7	210	63	−1.4	164	49	+8.0
13+	275	57	−4.2	80	66	−0.3	62	32	+18.4
Health:									
Chronic health problem	75	57	−8.5	116	64	−2.5	208	48	+8.6
No chronic health problem	610	59	−4.4	573	63	−2.2	631	48	+4.2
Major occupation group, 1966-67:									
Different occupation group each year	34	45	−7.5	38	67	−4.3	91	46	+5.7
Professional, technical	163	71	−3.4	49	52	−4.1	34	43	+2.5
Managers and officials	156	61	−5.8	69	68	−1.5	59	28	+13.2

Clerical	26	56	−1.6	68	73	−2.7	41	68	+1.6
Sales	44	48	−2.8	36	66	−2.1	23	d	d
Craftsmen, foremen	184	55	−4.8	242	64	−1.8	178	48	+6.0
Operatives	66	48	−7.4	156	58	−2.2	200	49	+3.1
Nonfarm laborers	3	d	d	16	d	d	81	39	+2.2
Service workers	10	d	d	15	d	d	91	56	+5.5
Farm workers	0	—	—	2	d	d	42	44	+13.3
Major industry division, 1966-67:									
Different industry division each year	21	d	d	25	49	−4.2	66	23	+8.9
Agriculture	0	—	—	3	d	d	46	49	+3.9
Mining, forestry, fisheries	7	d	d	10	d	d	15	d	d
Construction	55	51	−5.2	55	53	+0.2	93	48	+2.7
Manufacturing	281	60	−3.7	284	67	−1.0	233	46	+5.4
Transportation, utilities	88	59	−3.2	102	59	−2.4	63	51	+4.9
Trade	67	57	−8.2	69	65	−3.9	123	48	+11.3
Finance, insurance, real estate	36	62	−4.1	21	d	d	22	d	d
Service	56	56	−5.4	54	69	−7.1	122	56	+0.9
Public administration	75	69	−5.2	68	68	−2.7	57	58	+2.6
Interfirm mobility, 1966-67:									
Same employer both years	630	60	−4.7	634	64	−2.2	714	49	+5.7
Voluntary change	30	47	−4.6	27	76	−1.4	79	40	+0.7
Involuntary change	26	52	−7.7	30	48	−5.6	47	44	+9.0
					Blacks				
Total sample[c]	285	58	−4.1	296	47	−1.0	381	29	+5.9
Age:									
45-59	122	56	−3.9	120	44	−1.1	118	27	+6.0
50-54	99	60	−5.0	105	54	−2.0	144	30	+5.8
55-59	64	56	−3.0	71	41	−0.7	119	30	+5.9
Marital status:									
Married spouse present, 1966-67	244	57	−4.0	254	48	−1.4	284	32	+6.9

TABLE A.6 *(Concluded)*

Characteristic	High Base-Year Earnings			Medium Base-Year Earnings			Low Base-Year Earnings		
	Number (Sample Cases)[b]	Adjusted Percent Stable	Adjusted RIC	Number (Sample Cases)[b]	Adjusted Percent Stable	Adjusted RIC	Number (Sample Cases)[b]	Adjusted Percent Stable	Adjusted RIC
Nonmarried, 1966-67	33	54	−4.9	32	40	+1.3	78	18	+5.2
Highest year of school completed:									
0-4	33	56	−2.7	74	51	+0.7	170	28	+4.3
5-8	96	48	−7.0	122	43	−0.8	141	26	+7.8
9-11	72	64	−2.0	56	49	−2.2	41	25	+7.2
12	54	56	−3.3	29	55	−3.0	18	d	d
13+	29	71	−2.1	13	d	d	10	d	d
Health:									
Chronic health problem	36	52	−6.1	45	58	−1.1	74	21	+11.3
No chronic health problem	246	59	−3.8	249	44	−2.0	307	31	+4.6
Major occupation group, 1966-67:									
Different occupation group each year	12	d	d	17	d	d	56	26	+8.1
Professional, technical	16	d	d	6	d	d	9	d	d
Managers and officials	10	d	d	2	d	d	0	–	–
Clerical	29	59	−4.3	13	d	d	10	d	d
Sales	2	d	d	2	d	d	1	d	d
Craftsmen, foremen	56	60	−1.8	35	47	+3.0	26	24	+14.0

Operatives	95	61	−3.9	101	48	−1.8	77	38	+6.6
Nonfarm laborers	45	53	−6.7	62	56	−2.5	97	35	+3.6
Service workers	20	d	d	55	40	−1.4	52	23	+8.8
Farm workers	0	—	—	3	d	d	53	26	+0.0
Major industry division, 1966-67:									
Different industry division each year	8	d	d	13	d	d	48	24	+6.2
Agriculture	0	—	—	4	d	d	60	21	+2.6
Mining, forestry, fisheries	8	d	d	5	d	d	2	d	d
Construction	24	d	−3.8	30	24	−7.7	47	14	+11.1
Manufacturing	115	58	−7.4	104	40	+3.4	84	27	+13.7
Transportation, utilities	40	50	d	51	47	−2.3	25	30	+3.6
Trade	17	d	d	27	50	−7.6	43	58	+0.7
Finance, insurance, real estate	6	d	d	4	d	d	9	d	d
Service	18	d	d	39	77	+0.8	57	32	−0.7
Public administration	49	64	−1.9	19	d	d	6	d	d
Interfirm mobility, 1966-67:									
Same employer both years	274	59	−3.6	273	46	−1.6	313	30	+6.8
Voluntary change	5	d	d	12	d	d	37	34	+6.5
Involuntary change	6	d	d	11	d	d	31	18	−3.3

a See footnote *a* Text Table 8.
b See footnote *b* Text Table 8.
c See footnote *c* Text Table 8.
d See footnote *d* Text Table 8.

TABLE A.7   Adjusted Proportion[a] of Wage and Salary Workers With Stable Earnings and Adjusted Relative Instability Coefficient,[a] by Level of Base-Year Earnings and Other Selected Characteristics: White Young Men[b]

Characteristic	High Base-Year Earnings			Medium Base-Year Earnings			Low Base-Year Earnings		
	Number (Sample Cases)[c]	Adjusted Percent Stable	Adjusted RIC	Number (Sample Cases)[c]	Adjusted Percent Stable	Adjusted RIC	Number (Sample Cases)[c]	Adjusted Percent Stable	Adjusted RIC
Total sampled[d]	174	28	−4.3	206	38	−1.8	204	22	+6.0
Age:									
16-18	0	—	—	3	e	e	12	e	e
19-20	13	e	e	34	44	−2.2	37	18	+4.4
21-22	57	32	−4.6	53	40	−2.0	79	29	+6.1
23-24	104	23	−3.9	116	35	−1.2	76	20	+6.3
Highest year of school:									
0-8	6	e	e	21	e	e	30	27	−2.1
9-11	34	32	−6.7	39	38	−0.3	42	21	+3.0
12	75	25	−3.8	103	41	−1.1	83	29	+6.3
13-15	30	14	−4.1	21	e	e	26	12	+1.1
16+	29	49	−2.2	22	e	e	23	e	e
Interfirm mobility, 1966-68:									
Same employer all three dates	103	36	−2.9	122	45	−0.9	80	18	+8.8
Two different employers	49	16	−6.0	54	32	−0.5	65	23	+7.0
Three different employers	17	9	−6.9	23	e	e	31	25	+6.5

[a] See footnote a, Text Table 9.
[b] There are insufficient sample cases of blacks to permit analysis at this level of detail.
[c] Although numbers refer to sample cases, calculations are based on weighted observations.
[d] Total includes cases in which characteristic was not ascertained. Persons with negative income are excluded.
[e] Percentage or RIC not calculated where base is smaller than 25 sample cases.

TABLE A.8 Mean Ratios of Change, 1966-67, in Selected Components of Total Family Income, by Level of Base-Year Income, Age Group, and Color: Middle-Aged and Young Male Wage and Salary Workers[a]

Component of Family Income	Total Sample Average	High Base-Year Income				Medium Base-Year Income				Low Base-Year Income			
		Total or Average	Unstable Upward	Stable	Unstable Downward	Total or Average	Unstable Upward	Stable	Unstable Downward	Total or Average	Unstable Upward	Stable	Unstable Downward
White Men 45-59 Years of Age													
Earnings of respondent	2.4	0.5	9.1	1.4	-10.8	2.7	8.9	2.2	-5.0	4.9	15.0	1.8	-17.2
Earnings of wife	3.1	-1.1	9.4	2.2	-10.5	3.1	11.5	4.5	-11.1	10.6	23.1	4.5	-7.0
Earnings of others	5.5	3.4	23.9	10.9	-17.3	5.3	22.5	2.9	-13.4	8.9	19.6	5.6	-8.5
Property income	-3.5	-7.3	4.9	2.8	-26.6	-1.2	11.2	-3.0	-14.3	-1.5	4.9	-4.5	-9.8
Transfer income	1.1	4.8	7.3	5.0	3.3	-1.3	-1.3	-3.7	3.5	-0.9	0.2	-3.1	1.3
Total number (thousands)	6,345	2,328	437	1,056	830	2,474	782	1,116	576	1,544	648	619	277
Black Men 45-59 Years of Age													
Earnings of respondent	3.7	-0.6	7.2	2.2	-11.0	2.0	12.5	1.1	-15.2	8.8	11.4	0.1	-24.1
Earnings of wife	3.3	1.7	21.6	2.5	-10.9	4.8	19.1	-2.7	-12.5	3.8	11.1	-4.9	-3.1
Earnings of others	9.3	7.3	23.8	11.5	-5.8	15.2	24.1	14.2	-1.4	3.8	11.2	0.5	-10.6
Property income	-3.2	-6.5	13.1	-6.4	-17.3	-3.2	4.4	-7.9	-8.7	1.8	-0.2	7.5	1.0
Transfer income	-0.9	-2.4	-3.2	0.2	-4.5	-3.7	-2.2	-5.0	-4.1	5.7	6.4	1.6	7.7
Total number (thousands)	672	262	56	105	102	244	97	101	46	166	86	37	42
White Men 16-24 Years of Age													
Earnings of respondent	7.9	4.9	b	7.5	2.4	7.3	12.4	8.2	2.2	13.1	18.3	8.7	-0.3
Earnings of wife	-13.8	-13.0	b	0.1	-20.4	-16.6	-3.0	-15.8	-23.5	-11.1	-10.9	-5.5	-14.7
Unemployment compensation	-2.8	-4.0	b	-7.8	-3.8	-3.7	1.2	-3.7	-6.7	-0.9	-1.5	0.0	0.0
Other income	-8.6	-15.0	b	-14.5	-18.3	-5.1	3.4	-4.4	-11.0	-6.1	-2.4	-8.9	-14.0
Total number (thousands)	1,590	505	72	94	340	491	121	183	192	594	358	117	125

TABLE A.8 *(Concluded)*

Black Men 16-24 Years of Age

Component of Family Income	Total Sample Average	High Base-Year Income				Medium Base-Year Income				Low Base-Year Income			
		Total or Average	Unstable Upward	Stable	Unstable Downward	Total or Average	Unstable Upward	Stable	Unstable Downward	Total or Average	Unstable Upward	Stable	Unstable Downward
Earnings of respondent	9.8	b	b	b	b	7.6	b	b	b	18.7	23.5	b	b
Earnings of wife	-2.4	b	b	b	b	-8.5	b	b	b	6.8	10.8	b	b
Unemployment compensation	-8.2	b	b	b	b	-3.3	b	b	b	-9.7	-13.6	b	b
Other income	-3.2	b	b	b	b	-4.5	b	b	b	-0.5	0.0	b	b
Total number (thousands)	164	52	7	23	21	52	18	15	19	58	38	8	12

a Persons reporting negative income in any year are excluded.
b Percentages not shown where base represents fewer than 25 sample cases.

TABLE A.9   Relative Stability of Total Family Income by Relative Stability of Respondent's Earnings, Age Group, and Color: Middle-Aged and Young Male Wage and Salary Workers[a]

(percentage distribution)

Relative Stability of Respondent's Earnings	Men 14-24 Years of Age — Total Family-Income:					Men 45-59 Years of Age — Total Family Income:				
	Highly Unstable Upward	Moderately Unstable Upward	Stable	Moderately Unstable Downward	Highly Unstable Downward	Highly Unstable Upward	Moderately Unstable Upward	Stable	Moderately Unstable Downward	Highly Unstable Downward
Whites										
Highly unstable +	66	8	2	2	2	42	4	1	2	4
Unstable +	19	47	10	3	2	23	40	6	3	1
Stable	15	32	73	31	20	27	50	80	33	32
Unstable−	0	13	15	53	21	3	6	12	58	22
Highly unstable−	0	0	0	11	55	5	0	1	4	41
Total percent	100	100	100	100	100	100	100	100	100	100
Total number (thousands)	186	364	389	472	171	376	1,491	2,791	1,309	374
Blacks										
Highly unstable +	67	0	0	3	0	48	11	1	2	0
Unstable +	29	80	4	3	0	37	48	8	4	2
Stable	4	20	68	28	44	5	33	77	29	23
Unstable−	0	0	26	56	25	8	8	14	56	25
Highly unstable−	0	0	2	10	31	2	0	1	9	50
Total percent	100	100	100	100	100	100	100	100	100	100
Total number (thousands)	24	40	47	37	16	82	157	243	127	62

[a] Persons reporting negative income in any year are excluded.

TABLE A.10   Mean Ratios of Change, 1966-67, in Components of Respondent's Earnings, by Level of Base-Year Earnings, Age Group, and Color: Middle-Aged and Young Wage and Salary Workers[a]

Component of Respondent's Earnings	Total Sample	High Base-Year Earnings				Medium Base-Year Earnings				Low Base-Year Earnings			
		Total or Average	Unstable Upward	Stable	Unstable Downward	Total or Average	Unstable Upward	Stable	Unstable Downward	Total or Average	Unstable Upward	Stable	Unstable Downward
White Men 45-59 Years of Age													
Hourly rate of pay	2.7	2.4	6.6	3.1	1.9	2.3	6.9	2.3	-0.6	3.1	5.4	2.7	0.2
Hours worked per year	-0.5	-1.6	0.7	-0.4	-4.6	-1.3	1.0	-1.0	-3.6	1.0	4.9	-0.2	-2.3
Usual hours per week	-0.9	-1.1	0.5	-0.7	-2.6	-1.0	-0.4	-0.7	-2.2	-0.6	-0.9	-0.7	0.1
Weeks unemployed	-0.9	1.0	2.0	-0.3	3.3	1.2	-8.7	1.6	6.1	-4.4	-15.0	-1.5	6.6
Weeks not in labor force	-0.7	-1.4	-6.9	-1.8	1.2	1.3	-7.0	1.0	7.4	-1.9	-6.8	-0.7	-5.7
Total number (thousands)	8,665	2,703	283	1,584	836	2,729	379	1,727	623	3,235	1,087	1,531	617
Black Men 45-59 Years of Age													
Hourly rate of pay	4.7	3.0	8.5	2.5	2.0	3.7	7.0	4.2	0.0	7.0	8.7	3.8	7.8
Hours worked per year	0.8	-0.9	-2.5	0.0	-2.0	1.4	2.1	0.4	2.6	1.6	6.4	1.0	-7.1
Usual hours per week	-0.8	-0.9	-1.4	-0.6	-1.3	-0.2	-1.1	-0.4	0.9	-1.2	-0.2	-0.8	-3.7
Weeks unemployed	4.3	-2.3	3.6	-6.6	4.0	-2.5	-5.5	-2.6	0.4	-7.6	-15.8	-6.6	6.8

Weeks not in labor force	-2.1	-0.6	1.6	-4.6	6.2	-6.3	-2.1	-7.1	0.2	-5.1	3.3	6.2
Total number (thousands)	891	276	32	159	86	289	136	82	326	151	95	80

White Men 16-24 Years of Age

Hourly rate of pay	3.5	2.1	b	2.8	1.2	3.4	6.0	1.6	5.0	3.7	4.6	8.0
Hours worked per year	-1.1	-3.1	b	-2.0	-3.9	-2.9	-2.6	-4.2	3.1	8.1	-0.9	-5.9
Usual hours per week	-2.1	-2.7	b	-2.4	-3.2	-2.9	-2.8	-3.1	-0.3	1.4	-2.1	2.4
Weeks unemployed	-4.6	-3.8	b	-4.6	-3.0	-2.1	-1.6	-0.9	-9.8	-12.3	-7.6	-5.1
Weeks not in labor force	-10.9	-3.6	b	-3.4	-4.5	-7.3	-3.7	-8.1	-22.5	-32.8	-14.8	-1.2
Total number (thousands)	2,257	680	45	195	447	871	317	336	706	407	164	131

Black Men 16-24 Years of Age

Hourly rate of pay	5.1	b	b	b	b	10.6	7.1	b	5.7	2.5	0.5	b	b
Hours worked per year	-1.6	b	b	b	b	-1.1	2.8	b	1.3	-1.3	3.2	b	b
Usual hours per week	-1.5	b	b	b	b	-0.8	1.3	b	-0.4	-2.5	-0.2	b	b
Weeks unemployed	-12.0	b	b	b	b	-17.9	-26.1	b	-7.9	-5.0	1.2	b	b
Weeks not in labor force	-5.0	b	b	b	b	-11.9	-12.3	b	-11.0	-5.8	-11.0	b	b
Total number (thousands)	223	56	3	26	27	85	31	15	40	81	46	14	21

a Persons reporting negative income in any year are excluded.
b Percentages not shown where base represents fewer than 25 sample cases.

CHAPTER 7

Time Period, Unit of Analysis, and Income Concept in the Analysis of Income Distribution

Jacob Benus*
Stanford Research Institute

and

James N. Morgan
University of Michigan

The traditional focus of economic analysis has been more on the functional distribution of income than on the personal distribution of income, partly because the distribution between wages, rents, interest, and profits fits neatly into macromodels of the economy. In recent years, however, there has been a growing interest in the distribution of income among individuals or families, especially among those researchers concerned with evaluating and improving the personal distribution of welfare.

One dimension of welfare which has received little attention is the stability of income. This deficiency is partly due to the fact that microdata are usually available only for a single year. In order to study income stability, one needs data on income across several time periods. However, even when panel data are available, important questions remain. For example, what is an appropriate unit of analysis to examine? Given the importance of intrafamily transfers, individual income data are usually discarded in favor of family income data, yet the family may not be a stable unit over a lifetime, and the same income means different levels of well-being, depending on the size and structure of the family. The definition of income (before or after taxes and transfers, with or without nonmoney components) also affects the results. Finally, the

* Formerly of the University of Michigan.

instability or uncertainty of income and its temporal pattern are also important.

This paper focuses on the unit of analysis, the concept of income used, and the time period, leaving to another forum a discussion of instability as a dimension of welfare.[1] We focus on time periods ranging from three months to four years, not dealing with the lifetime-income problem directly.

MEASURES OF INCOME INEQUALITY

The question of whether the length of the accounting period affects the distribution of income may be answered by adopting a summary measure of inequality and comparing the results for various accounting periods. The two most widely used measures of inequality are the Gini concentration coefficient and the variance of the logarithms of income. The former is the ratio of the area between the Lorenz curve and the 45° line of equal distribution to the area under the 45° line. It ranges between zero and one, with zero representing perfect income equality and one representing perfect inequality (i.e., one person has all the income). If the size distribution on income is in fact log-normal, the two measures provide the same ranking of the distributions, since the Gini concentration coefficient is monotonically related to the variance of the logarithms of income.[2] If income is not log-normally distributed, the two measures may yield conflicting results.[3] Since the income distributions of some subgroups may not be log-normal, and since we will examine inequality for selected subgroups, the Gini concentration coefficient appears to be the more appropriate measure for our analysis.

The usual method of estimating the Gini concentration coeffi-

[1] Jacob Benus and James Morgan, "Income Instability as a Dimension of Welfare," *Proceedings of the American Statistical Association, 1972,* pp. 102-6.

[2] See J. Aitchison and J. A. C. Brown, *The Lognormal Distribution* (Cambridge, Mass.: Harvard University Press, 1957) pp. 111-15.

[3] An example of such discrepancies is found in a recent article by Schultz, where the Gini coefficient indicates lower inequality for white males, while the variance of logarithms of income indicates lower inequality for nonwhite males. See T. Paul Schultz, "Secular Trends and Cyclical Behavior of Income Distribution in the United States, 1944-1965," in L. Soltow, ed., *Six Papers on the Size Distribution of Wealth and Income* (New York: NBER, 1969). See especially the comment by Eleanor M. Snyder, pp. 101-6.

cient from data grouped by income intervals assumes that within each interval all incomes are equal. This assumption yields a lower bound for the Gini concentration coefficient.[4] However, since our main objective is to compare Gini coefficients for various accounting periods, the consistent underestimation due to grouping the data into deciles is unlikely to affect our results.

SINGLE-YEAR VERSUS PANEL SURVEYS

Single-year survey data often contain persons whose incomes are temporarily high and others whose incomes are temporarily low. As a result, the measures of income inequality derived from these studies may exaggerate the real lifetime-income inequality. Two solutions to the problems caused by temporary fluctuations in income suggest themselves. First, one may eliminate those individuals who report recent short-run fluctuations in income. This leaves for analysis a subsample of individuals whose incomes remained relatively stable over a period of time. A second approach involves the lengthening of the accounting period for measuring income. The implicit assumption in this approach is that temporary income fluctuations average out over a period of years. Thus, with a longer accounting period, an individual's income level is less likely to reflect the effect of a temporary phenomenon.

While both approaches theoretically require only a single interview survey, a panel study can provide greater accuracy in measuring the effect of lengthening the accounting period. A single interview can obtain, retrospectively, the respondent's income level over several accounting periods. Inequality measures for these accounting periods may then be compared to investigate the effect of lengthening the accounting period. The results, however, will reflect not only the effect of accounting period variation, but also the effect of diminishing recall for the more distant past. In a study of the reliability of income recall, Withey found that the greater the income change experienced, the greater the tendency to report a smaller amount of change (in the same direction).[5] The use of recall data in our analysis would, therefore,

[4] Joseph L. Gastwirth, "The Estimation of the Lorenz Curve and Gini Index," *Review of Economics and Statistics* 54 (August 1972): 306-16.

[5] Stephen B. Withey, "Reliability of Recall of Income," *Public Opinion Quarterly* 18 (Summer 1954):197-204.

lead to underestimation of the impact of lengthening the accounting period. The use of panel data, on the other hand, eliminates the difficulties caused by variable recall. What remains is the effect of lengthening the accounting period.

In the past few years the Survey Research Center (SRC) of the University of Michigan has conducted several panel surveys which may be useful in studying the effects of varying the accounting period. In 1964-65, the SRC conducted a four-wave panel to investigate the impact of the tax-cut provisions of the Revenue Act of 1964.[6] The panel members in this study (hereafter called the Tax Panel) were restricted to nonfarm families whose total family income before taxes was between $3,000 and $20,000 in 1963. Approximately 900 respondents remained in the panel through three interviews in 1964 and a fourth interview in 1965. Since these data were collected toward the end of the second, third, and fourth quarters in 1964, we have the opportunity to examine the effect of lengthening the accounting period by three-month intervals. In the final interview, conducted in May 1965, data were gathered on both the three-month period prior to the interview (i.e., March-May) and the entire calendar year 1964.

A second panel study, the Debt Panel, was conducted between early 1967 and early 1970 to investigate the factors that underlie the purchase of large household durables.[7] In this study, over 1,400 respondents completed four interviews approximately twelve months apart. Unlike the Tax Panel, this panel represents a national cross section of families with heads under 60 years old in 1967. As a result of the differences in the two samples, we would expect to find greater income inequality in the Debt Panel. Whether these differences will also lead to different responses to accounting period changes is open to question. We speculate, however, that the panel members of the Tax Study are more stable and, as a result, lengthening the accounting period will have less impact on income inequality.

The third, and perhaps the most useful panel for our analysis of income inequality, is the Office of Economic Opportunity (OEO)

[6] For details, see George Katona and Eva Mueller, *Consumer Response to Income Increases* (Washington, D.C.: The Brookings Institution, 1968).

[7] Details of this study will be found in Gary Hendricks and Kenwood C. Youmans, with Janet Keller, *Consumer Durables and Instalment Debt: A Study of American Households* (Ann Arbor: Survey Research Center, University of Michigan, 1973).

Panel.[8] In this panel, a national cross section of households have been interviewed annually since 1968, with the objective of studying family-income dynamics. The fifth wave of this study will be available before the end of 1972. The current availability of four waves of data, however, offers ample opportunity to analyze the impact of lengthening the accounting period by annual intervals. In addition, since the panel represents a national cross section, one may compare our results on inequality with the results of earlier single-year national cross-section studies.

UNIT OF ANALYSIS AND INCOME CONCEPT

While the organization of our data does not permit the analysis of inequality on an individual basis, we can examine income inequality for heads, wives, and families separately. As seen in Table 1, the addition of wife's labor income to that of the head's labor income reduces the inequality of labor income by approximately 2 percent. Similarly, the addition of taxable income of other family members to head and wife's taxable income further reduces the inequality by approximately the same amount. We conclude, therefore, that as the unit of analysis is broadened to include the earnings of all family members, the distribution of income becomes more equal.

A comparison of lines 2 and 3 of Table 1 also reveals another source of variation in income inequality. That is, altering the income concept from labor income to taxable income (i.e., labor

[8] Since the completion of this paper two more waves of data have been collected. For an analysis of the initial five years of data, see James Morgan et al., *Five Thousand American Families—Patterns of Economic Progress* (Ann Arbor: Survey Research Center, University of Michigan, 1974).

TABLE 1   Gini Concentration Coefficients for Various Units of Analysis, Office of Economic Opportunity Panel[a]

	1967	*1968*	*1969*	*1970*
Head's labor income	.45	.46	.46	.48
Head and wife's labor income	.44	.45	.45	.47
Head and wife's taxable income	.43	.44	.44	.45
Family taxable income	.42	.43	.43	.44

[a] Based on entire sample of 4,840 households in 1971.

income plus income from assets) leads to a reduction in inequality. This result, therefore, suggests that differences in income concept also affect the results on income inequality.

An examination of Table 2 confirms that differences in income concept have substantial impact on the Gini coefficients. The addition of transfer payments to family taxable income, for example, reduces the income inequality by raising the income level of those families in the low end of the income distribution while leaving others essentially unaffected. The distributional impact of the inclusion of transfer income is substantial, reducing income inequality by approximately 15 percent (i.e., from an average of .430 to an average of .365). The impact of taxes on the distribution of income is weaker, reducing the Gini coefficient by approximately 5 percent.[9] The relatively weaker impact of the tax adjustment in reducing income inequality reflects, perhaps, the fact that income taxes are less progressive than transfer payments. That is, the wealthy and the not-so-wealthy pay income taxes, while mostly the poor receive transfer payments.

[9] Other studies have estimated the effect of taxation to be slightly higher, with estimates of about 7 to 8 percent. Peter Vandome, "Aspects of the Dynamics of Consumer Behavior," *Bulletin of the Oxford University Institute of Statistics* 20 (February 1958):87. James N. Morgan, Martin H. David, Wilbur J. Cohen, and Harvey E. Brazer, *Income and Welfare in the United States* (New York: McGraw-Hill, 1962) p. 315.

TABLE 2   Gini Concentration Coefficient for Various Income Measures, Office of Economic Opportunity Panel[a]

	1967	1968	1969	1970
Family taxable income	.42	.43	.43	.44
Plus: transfer income =				
Family money income	.36	.36	.37	.37
Less: federal income taxes =				
Family disposable income	.34	.34	.35	.35
Less: cost of child care				
Less: union dues				
Plus: nonmoney income (including free food, housing, etc.) =				
Family net real income	.33	.33	.34	.34

[a] Based on entire sample of 4,840 households in 1971.

Finally, adjusting disposable money income by adding non-money incomes and deducting the cost of earning income (union dues and child-care cost) reduces the inequality still further, but only slightly. We may, therefore, conclude that the results on income inequality depend significantly on the choice of unit of analysis and income concept. Our analysis of the impact of accounting period variation on income inequality may also be affected by the choice of unit of analysis and income concept.

ACCOUNTING PERIOD VARIATION

In an early study, Hanna measured the impact of lengthening the accounting period by comparing the weighted average of annual distributions with distributions for two- and three-year accounting periods.[10] Since individual relative income positions shift from year to year, the Lorenz curve for several years taken as a single accounting period will lie between the "average" Lorenz curve and the line of equal distribution. Thus, the "average" Lorenz curve serves as an inequality limit against which the effect of lengthening the accounting period may be measured.

In the analysis that follows, we use the initial-year distribution rather than the average annual distribution as our benchmark. The results of Tables 1 and 2 indicate less income inequality in the initial year than in subsequent years of the panel. Thus, the use of the initial year as a benchmark probably underestimates the impact of lengthening the accounting period

Since the initial-year distribution does not serve as an inequality limit for the longer accounting period distributions, lengthening the accounting period may, in principle, lead to increased inequality. In practice, however, the inequality of the initial year does establish a limit for the lengthened accounting period. This result is largely due to the fact that data from any single period contain incomes that are influenced by temporary events. Lengthening the accounting period reduces the influence of these vagaries, raising the income level of those with unusually low incomes in a single period and vice versa.

Since income for a short accounting period is more likely to be

[10] See Frank A. Hanna, "The Accounting Period and the Distribution of Income," Part III in Frank A. Hanna, Joseph A. Pechman, and Sidney M. Lerner, *Analysis of Wisconsin Income*, Vol. 9, Conference on Research in Income and Wealth (New York: NBER, 1948), pp. 204-12.

influenced by temporary events or institutional arrangements (i.e., quarterly dividend, semiannual interest payment) than long accounting periods, lengthening short accounting periods should exhibit a greater impact on the distribution of income. As a result, we expect to observe a greater reduction in inequality for the Tax Panel than for either the Debt or OEO panels. However, as seen in Table 3, the impact of lengthening the accounting period is lower for the Tax Panel than for the Debt Panel. This unexpected result may partly reflect the unusual composition of the Tax Panel (i.e., the sample is restricted to nonfarm families with a total income between $3,000 and $20,000 in 1963).[11] However, as we discover later, greater homogeneity of the sample is expected to increase rather than decrease the impact of accounting period variation. Thus, we are left without an explanation for this result.

While lengthening the accounting period by constant intervals is expected to reduce inequality monotonically, the rate of inequality reduction is expected to decline. That is, since additional periods represent declining proportions of the total period, their impact in reducing inequality diminishes. This expectation is supported by the results of Table 3. In fact, lengthening the accounting period beyond three periods has almost no impact on the distribution of income. This result suggests that a limit may have been reached with the extension of the accounting period to three periods. Whether the periods are quarters or years seems insignificant, since similar results are obtained for all three panels. Only the number of periods combined appears to be important.

The overall conclusion that may be drawn from Table 3 is that lengthening the accounting period has only a slight effect on the distribution of income. The impact ranges from no reduction in inequality for head's labor income (OEO Panel) to a reduction of approximately 9 percent for family money income (Debt Panel).[12] Within each of the studies, the impact of lengthening the accounting period appears to be approximately the same for all the income concepts. Differences, however, appear between the

---

[11] This composition of the sample also accounts for the relatively low inequality level for the Tax Panel when compared to the OEO and Debt panels.

[12] Vandome estimated that the inequality of gross income declined by 4 percent (over the average for yearly distributions) when the years were taken as a single accounting period. "Dynamics of Consumer Behavior," p. 88.

TABLE 3   Gini Concentration Coefficients for Various Accounting Periods (same heads)[a]

Type of Income	Tax Panel (N = 844)				Debt Panel (N = 1,335)				OEO Panel (N = 3,743)			
	Jan.-June 1964	Jan.-Sept. 1964	Jan.-Dec. 1964	Jan.-Dec. 1964 + March-May 1965	1966	1966-67	1966-68	1966-69	1967	1967-68	1967-69	1967-70
Head's labor income	.33	.32	.32	.32	.41	.40	.39	.39	.45	.45	.45	.45
Family money income	.22	.21	.21	.21	.33	.31	.31	.30	.36	.35	.35	.35
Family disposable income	—	—	—	—	.30	.29	.28	.28	.34	.33	.33	.33

[a] In this analysis only those families with unchanged heads are included.

studies, with the Debt Panel exhibiting the largest impact of accounting period variation.

While the impact of lengthening the accounting period may not have a powerful effect on the income distribution of the entire sample, it may affect significantly the income distribution of selected subgroups. The groups most likely to be affected by accounting period variation are those groups with the highest income instability over the period of the panel. To search out these subgroups, we employ an Automatic Interaction Detection Program (AID) analysis on individual coefficients of variation,[13] $V_i = 100 \ (\sigma_i/\overline{Y}_i)$.[14] The results, presented in Chart 1, indicate that

[13] For a description of this procedure, see John A. Sonquist, Elizabeth Lau Baker, and James N. Morgan, *Searching for Structure* (Ann Arbor: Survey Research Center, University of Michigan, 1971. Revised, 1973.).

[14] The coefficient of variation may be thought of as a measure of relative

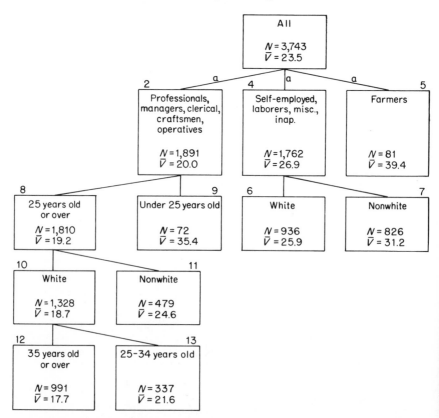

CHART 1: Coefficient of Variation on Family Money Income for Families With Same Head, 1968-71, OEO Panel

the most important determinant of income instability is occupation. Farmers, by far, have the highest instability; white collar and skilled occupations are at the other end of the spectrum; the self-employed, laborers, and so forth, are somewhere in between. Another important determinant of income instability is age, exhibiting an inverse relationship. The third important determinant is race, with nonwhite incomes exhibiting greater instability than that of whites. Demographic characteristics which proved to be less important determinants of income instability include sex, education, region, size of city, and family size.

To examine the differential impact of accounting period variation for groups of various instability levels, we present in Table 4 the seven final subgroups of the AID tree. As expected, accounting period variation tends to have greater impact on subgroups with relatively high income instability. For example, groups 5, 7, and 9 have both high instability levels and relatively large declines in inequality as a result of lengthening the accounting period from one to four years. The relation between instability and reduction in inequality, however, is not monotonic. Group 13 (25- to 34-year-old whites who were professionals, managers, clerks, craftsmen, or operatives), for example, has a relatively low instability level but the second highest decline in inequality. We may, therefore, conclude that there is a differential impact of accounting period variation for selected subgroups. The tendency is for groups with high instability levels to exhibit a greater impact of accounting period variation. The relationship, however, is not strong.

Intuitively, one would expect that the less homogeneous a group's income trajectories (or trends), the greater the reduction in inequality that results from lengthening the accounting period.[15] That is, differences in income trends within a group are

---

variance. Each individual's standard deviation is divided by his own average income level. If the standard deviation were one quarter the size of income, for example, $V_i = 25.0$.

[15] We define income trajectory or trend as the slope of a regression of income on "time." The equation for the slope reduces to:

$$b = \frac{\sum_{t=1}^{4} Y_t T_t}{\sum_{t=1}^{4} T_t^2} = \frac{1.5Y_4 + .5Y_3 - .5Y_2 - 1.5Y_1}{5},$$

where $T = -1.5, -.5, .5, 1.5$.

TABLE 4 Impact of Accounting Period Variation for Selected Subgroups, Office of Economic Opportunity Panel[a]

Group Number	Description	N	$\bar{V}$	One-Year Gini Coefficients	Four-Year Gini Coefficients	Relative Decline in Inequality, 1968-71
5	A. Farmers	83	39.4	.35	.32	8.6
	B. Self-employed, laborers, misc.					
6	1. White[b]	937	25.9	.43	.41	4.7
7	2. Nonwhite[c]	828	31.2	.41	.36	12.2
	C. Professionals, managers, craftsmen					
9	1. Under 25 years old	75	35.4	.33	.23	30.3
	2. 25 years old or over					
11	a. Nonwhite[c]	485	24.6	.29	.28	3.4
	b. White[b]					
13	(1) 25-34 years old	339	21.6	.25	.21	16.0
12	(2) 35 years old or over	992	17.7	.27	.26	3.7
1	All	3,739	23.5	.36	.35	2.8

[a] An examination of the nine extreme cases revealed that in four cases errors had been made in recording one year's income level. The remaining cases represented exceptional but legitimate income fluctuation. The latter cases are included in this analysis.
[b] Included in the white category are 32 cases coded "other" on race (i.e., Orientals, Filipinos).
[c] Included in the nonwhite category are 87 cases coded Spanish American, Puerto Rican, Mexican, or Cuban.

expected to reduce inequality. The results of Table 5, however, indicate that the opposite is true. Groups with relatively large trend variation (i.e., groups 6, 11, and 12) have the lowest relative decline in inequality. On the other hand, groups with more homogeneous trends (i.e., groups 7, 9, and 13) have the highest relative declines in inequality. These results partly reflect the fact that, within any group, those with high income levels tend to have the steepest trends, and those with low incomes the flattest trends. As a result of this positive correlation between trend and level, inequality may actually increase, rather than decrease, over time. At the same time, however, there is a tendency for incomes to regress from unusual initial income levels, thereby leading to reduced inequality over time. These two forces, operating in opposite directions, determine the extent of inequality reduction that results from lengthening the accounting period. Thus, for those subgroups with large variation in trends, trend differences are expected to dominate the regression effect. On the other hand, for subgroups with relatively homogeneous trends, the regression effect is expected to be the dominant force. We, therefore, expect to observe greater reduction in inequality for subgroups with relatively homogeneous trends.

In order to isolate subgroups with various levels of trend variation we run an AID analysis on income trend level. Since average trend is positively correlated with the variance of the trends within a group, the AID analysis, in effect, isolates

TABLE 5 Initial Income, Trend, Trend Variance, and Relative Change in Inequality for Selected Subgroups

Group Number	1967 Family Income (Dollars)	Family Income Trend (Dollars)	Trend Variance (10^6)	Relative Change in Inequality
5	6,670	764	5.1	−8.6
6	6,498	400	2.9	−4.7
7	4,517	337	1.4	−2.2
9	5,039	1,164	2.3	−30.3
11	7,720	1,204	2.6	−3.4
13	8,841	1,039	1.9	−16.0
12	11,667	1,042	2.9	−3.7
Total	8,612	779	2.8	−2.8

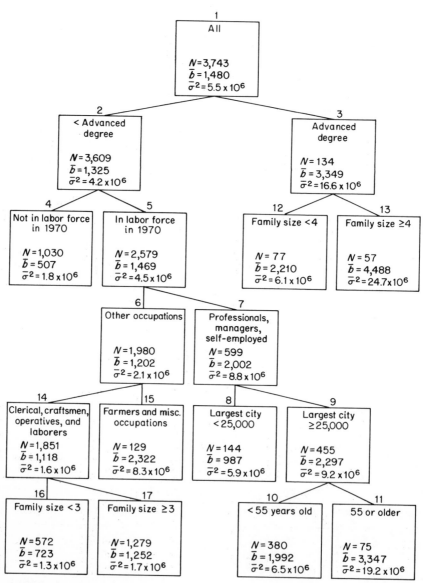

CHART 2: AID on Family Money Income Trend: Families With Same Head, 1968-71

TABLE 6   Impact of Accounting Period Variation for Selected Subgroups, Office of Economic Opportunity Panel

Group Number	Description	N	Trend Variance (10^6)	One-Year Gini Coefficient	Four-Year Gini Coefficient	Relative Change in Inequality
	A. Advanced degree					
12	1. Family size < 4	77	6.1	.31	.29	−6.5
13	2. Family size ⩾ 4	57	24.7	.25	.25	0.0
	B. No advanced degree					
4	1. Not in labor force (1970)	507	1.8	.42	.39	−7.1
	2. In labor force (1970)					
15	a. Farmers and miscellaneous occupations	129	8.3	.33	.29	−12.1
	b. Professionals, managers, self-employed					
8	(1) Largest city < 25,000	144	5.9	.31	.27	−12.9
10	(2) Largest city ⩾ 25,000 (a) Under 55 years old	380	6.5	.28	.24	−14.3
11°	(b) 55 years old or older	75	19.2	.30	.31	3.3
	c. Clerical, craftsmen, operatives and laborers					
16	(1) Family size < 3	575	1.3	.33	.30	−9.1
17	(2) Family size ⩾ 3	1,279	1.7	.25	.23	−8.0
1	All	3,743	5.5	.36	.35	−2.8

subgroups with different levels of variance in the trends. The results, presented in Chart 2, indicate that the group that has the highest trend level, as well as the highest trend variance, is composed of families with four or more members in which the family head has an advanced degree. The group with the lowest trend variance, but not the lowest trend level, is composed of one- or two-member families in which the head has less than an advanced degree and is employed in the clerical, craftsman, operative, or laborer classification.

In Table 6 we present the nine final subgroups and the impact of changing the accounting period from one year to four years. The results indicate that accounting period variation has less of an impact on subgroups with substantial variation in income trends than on subgroups with relatively homogeneous income trends. For example, groups 11 and 13, the groups with the highest trend variances, show either no reduction or a slight increase in inequality as the accounting period is lengthened from one to four years. The remaining subgroups exhibit reductions in inequality that range from 6.5 percent to 14.3 percent.

Thus, we may conclude that there are indeed two forces in operation: one that leads to increased inequality due to the permanent spreading of individual incomes, and another that leads to diminished inequality due to the regression of individual incomes toward a permanent level.

CONCLUSION

What we have been examining is still a far cry from an assessment of the distribution of well-being in a society. We said at the start that well-being depends on lifetime income level and its pattern (instability), but we have been dealing with distributions of income over shorter periods. We do not have the data to study income distributions over longer periods, but that is only the first problem. Families do not stay intact over lifetimes, price levels change, and levels of real income also change. Consequently, we must be careful in making evaluative judgments on the basis of the data presented. What we can say is that for the population as a whole, the unit of analysis and the measure of income seem to have more effect on measures of inequality than the length of the accounting period. For some subgroups, however, the impact of accounting period variation is substantial.

CHAPTER 8

Comments on Part III

Martin David

University of Wisconsin

The title of this session indicates that the authors were to deal with the impact of the accounting period on the distribution of income. All three of the papers have difficulty dealing with the topic and bringing it into a useful focus. Benus beings with a declaration that he will not deal with instability per se and concludes (Table 6) with an analysis that locates groups with large interpersonal differences in income trends—which appears to me to be an important feature of instability. Kohen begins with a measure that purports to refer to instability, but in fact cannot distinguish systematic changes in relative income position from random noise affecting the income position of an individual. The David paper concentrates on a phenomenon that has nothing to do with income in a Hicksian sense in either the short or long run, yet has more relevance to the session topic than either of the other papers.

I believe that there are two reasons for this: (1) one cannot deal with a concept of long-run income without a conceptual structure; and (2) the conceptual structure can be useful for understanding the *origins* of the income distribution or the *welfare consequences* of the distribution, but a failure to distinguish the focus of interest leads to data that cannot be assimilated by any intelligent user. The capital-gains paper has solved both of these problems: (1) necessarily, the conceptual structure for income is the Internal Revenue Code; and (2) the focus of the paper is to impart an understanding of the welfare consequences of the favorable tax treatment of capital gains for long-term vertical equity in the tax structure. As a coauthor, I am the first to admit that the evidence presented is not ideal; yet the conceptual unity of the questions being investigated cannot be faulted.

Let me elaborate on the conceptual structures that might be brought to bear on the Benus and Kohen papers. Any attempt to deal with a long-run concept of the origins of income must explicitly account for the persistent and obvious life-cycle pattern of income. The model may also account for endogenous changes in the demand for human labor, net accumulation of wealth due to increased productivity of both human and nonhuman assets, and compensatory features of the public sector that alter the outcomes of markets; but all of this is conceptualization that must be built on a model of the life cycle of incomes. Given a model, one can then answer numerous pertinent questions. For example:

1. What are the model parameters?
2. Is there evidence of stable interpersonal differences?
3. What is the stochastic process associated with the model, and what do its parameters tell us about income instability?

It is clear from these three questions that I believe that income instability can only be measured as the stochastic portion of a model of income determination. Lack of a model leads to precisely the confusion of concepts that appears in the Kohen paper. In the diagram below, observations of RIC for two individuals (indicated by x and t) are contrasted. One (x) has a highly variable rate of growth of income which averages 6 percent per annum. The other (t) has a steady rate of increase of 6 percent per annum. The two individuals cannot be distinguished in the Kohen analysis; both will be treated as positive deviations from the grand sample mean (o) of 4 percent per annum.

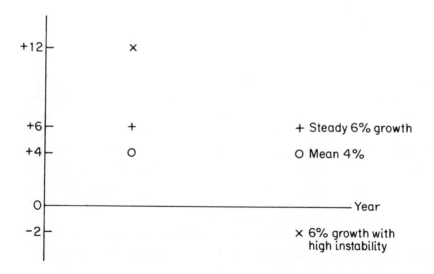

The use of a theoretical model permits inference on the basis of limited data. Fase (1971) demonstrated that the dynamic stochastic process determining earnings could be inferred from cross-section age-earnings ogives. Those who would quarrel with his conceptualization can only do so by specifying a model that clearly pinpoints the inadequacies of the pooling of data from a cross section of individuals. Our only clues about the differences in cross-section and panel information concerning the origin of income that is available in either the Benus or Kohen paper is contained in the differences between one- and multi-year Gini coefficients. This is clearly not an adequate description of the stochastic process producing instability or of the model of lifetime income ogives.

If the analysis is oriented toward the welfare consequences of income changes in the long run, then another set of considerations must be developed. An individual's welfare is determined by the flows of current services he receives from goods consumed or from stocks to which he has access. Variation in income translates into variation in welfare to the extent that the unit cannot average income flows. Borrowing, lending, or changing the household structure may all result in an averaging of real goods and services consumed in relation to income received. In addition, variation may set in motion particular tax or transfer mechanisms that compensate or exacerbate the change in flows of income from the market.

Interest in the latter kind of problem has sparked the concern over the negative income tax and its relation to wealth holdings, the studies of tax averaging (David et al., 1970), and the focus of the paper in this session on capital gains.

Neither the Kohen nor the Benus paper appear to have adopted a focus on individual welfare; by default, they appear to be dealing with the origins of the income distribution over a longer period of time. The Gini measures that both papers concentrate on focus on the difference in concentration of indivdual incomes depending on the period of observation. The only sense I can make of this question is that the authors are concerned with "layering" or the existence of heterogeneous income trajectories for individuals within a given well-defined demographic group. Measures of such trajectories can better be explicitly developed by reference to a model. I have done so in a paper that deals very crudely with the age-income-profile problem (David, 1971).

The thrust of the argument so far has been that the papers fail to address meaningful questions. However, there are meaningful results that can be drawn from the information presented, perhaps with little alteration in the analysis. What is required is a careful reading of past studies of income variation and an attempt to replicate, confirm, or contradict earlier findings. The principal sources with which I am familiar are: Friedman and Kuznets (1945), Hanna, Pechman, and Lerner (1948), Bristol (1958), Morgan and Kosobud (1964), Huang and Meyers (1964), David and Miller (1970), Fase (1971) and David (1971). The Kohen evidence can be restructured to give answers to the same questions that were addressed by Bristol, Huang, Morgan, and Friedman: What is the significance of regression of income toward the mean? What is the intertemporal covariance of different income sources? There is no need, indeed it is obfuscating, to invent a new conceptual structure to deal with those questions.

The Benus evidence ought to be restructured to give comparable results to those obtained in David (1971). Table 5 comes close, but there are important differences. First, in the David paper, variation in income is taken relative to the mean for the cohort, not for the individual, with the result that the David paper may be said to have an implicit model of lifetime income, whereas Table 5 does not. (Futhermore, the interpretation of findings in the two studies is startlingly different: farmers' income instability is small relative to the income for the cohort [David, 1971], yet large relative to the individual means [see Benus, Table 5].) The second major difference is that the David paper obtains a set of descriptive parameters that characterize long-run income variation over the life cycle for different occupation groups. The task of subsequent work is to challenge that description, not to go on fishing, or search, expeditions. The Automatic Interaction Detection Program (AID) technique that underlies Tables 5 and 6 is a search technique that assumes no prior information on the relationship between the dependent variable and the independent variables. The report in David (1971) indicates that an investigation based on no prior knowledge is an absurd starting point for an investigation.

One must conclude that the Benus and Kohen papers are internally imprecise and lacking in adequate references and corroboration of earlier work. These defects arise from the failure to view the question to be addressed either as a question of the origin of income instability or the welfare consequences of instability. The lack of an explicit model of the lifetime-income determination process flaws any attempt to speak of the sources of income instability. Lack of an explicit concern for the link between income instability and a specific mechanism that affects well-being limits the value of information for discussing welfare consequences. We can hope that further work on these valuable data sources will be better targeted to scientific and policy-related questions.

REFERENCES

1. Bristol, R. B. (1958). "Factors Associated with Income Variability." *American Economic Review* 48 (May 1958):279-90.
2. David, M. (1971). "Lifetime Income Variability and Income Profiles." *Proceedings of the Social Statistics Section of the American Statistical Association, 1971,* pp. 285-92.
3. David, M., and Miller, R. F. (1970). "A Naive History of Individual Incomes in Wisconsin, 1947-1959." *Review of Income and Wealth* Series 16, No. 1 (March 1970):79-116.
4. Fase, M. M. G. (1971). "On the Estimation of Lifetime Income." *Journal of the American Statistical Association* 66 (December 1971):686-92.
5. Friedman M., and Kuznets, S. (1945). *Income from Independent Professional Practice.* (New York: NBER, 1945), Chap. VII, "The Stability of Relative Income Status."
6. Hanna, F.; Pechman, J.; and Lerner, S. (1948). *Analysis of Wisconsin Income,* Studies in Income and Wealth, Vol. 9 (New York: NBER, 1948).
7. Huang, D. S., and Meyers, J. G. (1964). "Income Variability and the Analysis of Income Size." *Journal of Political Economy* 72 (June 1964):289-94.
8. Miller, R. F.; David, M.; Groves, H. M.; and Weigner, E. A. (1970). "Optimal Choices for an Averaging System—A Simulation Analysis of the Federal Averaging Formula of 1964." *National Tax Journal* 23 (September 1970):275-96.
9. Morgan, J., and Kosobud, R. (1964). *Consumer Behavior of Individual Families over Two and Three Years.* (Ann Arbor, Michigan: Institute for Social Research, 1964.)

PART IV

THE DISTRIBUTION
OF PERSONAL WEALTH

CHAPTER 9

The Wealth, Income, and Social Class of Men in Large Northern Cities of the United States in 1860

Lee Soltow
Ohio University

There is a need for an organized study of the wealth of men in urban areas which covers the full gamut from those with no wealth to those who are the most affluent. One would like to have a consistent compilation of the characteristics of men in various wealth classes, since wealth is thought to be such an important variable in helping to delineate social classes and social hierarchy in urban society. We are fortunate, indeed, to have records of wealth declarations and other characteristics for every free individual in the United States for the year 1860; the microfilms of the manuscripts of the Census enumerators are made available by the National Archives in Washington.

One finds Abraham Lincoln from entries for Springfield, Illinois, recorded in about June 1860, with age, occupation, birth state, personal estate, and real estate listed as 51, lawyer, Kentucky, $5,000, and $12,000. More affluence was shown further north in Chicago where William Ogden had entries of 55, lawyer, New York, $1,500,000, and $1,000,000; and Cyrus McCormick had entries of 50, reaper factory, Virginia, $278,000, and $1,750,000. It is certainly not difficult to find the entries of the many, many people with personal estate and real estate of $0 and $0. It is fascinating to study those individuals with large estates as they appear on the Census rolls because so much information is available. Entries are given for each member of the family, including the wife, children, servants, gardeners, and other individuals involved in maintaining the family unit. It is often possible to ascertain, with high probability, the mobility of the family by tracing the birth places of the oldest to youngest children. One loses some of his ardor for fine individual details of successful men when he realizes that certain large cities had more than half of their population declaring no wealth whatsoever.

This paper is concerned with the frequency distribution of wealth among men in ten large urban areas of the United States in 1860 and with two models approximating this distribution. We first present characteristics of the frequency curve, stressing relative inequality and the proportion who were propertyless. A descriptive binomial model of social classes will be developed almost solely on the basis of the proportion who were property-less. This model adequately depicts social classes in the sense that it yields both frequency tables similar to those of W. Lloyd Warner and, in one sense, the 1860 wealth distribution. The second approximation of wealth distribution is obtained by applying an orthodox consumption function to a realistic Pareto-type model of income distribution. The resulting relative distribution of saving is similar to relative distribution of wealth.

I. THE WEALTH STUDY OF TEN URBAN AREAS IN 1860

A probability sample of men in urban areas has been drawn from microfilm of the Census manuscripts of 1860 for the United States. Emphasis was placed on the wealth declarations for real and personal property. Very briefly, real estate value was reported wherever it was owned. The individual decided whether or not he wished to subtract debt. Personal estate value was defined as including all bonds, stock, mortgages, notes, livestock, plate, jewels, or furniture, but excluding wearing apparel. Aggregates for Northern states and our selected urban areas appear to be in excellent accord with the backward extrapolations and inter-polations of data of Goldsmith, Kuznets, and Easterlin. It is found that the data yield exciting configurations, including implications of strong economic growth from 1800 to 1860.

A sample of 8,966 adult males was obtained from the manuscripts in all of 10 urban counties in 1860 as listed in Table 1. This represents a population of 449,640 adult males, which was 36.3 percent of the adult males of the 22 counties in the United States having cities with a total population of 40,000 or more, and 5.6 percent of the adult males in the 2,105 counties of the entire country. The use of counties made it possible to check average wealth values in various counties, as explained in the note to Table 1. The arithmetic-mean wealth of individuals in the 10 counties was only 3.3 percent higher than that in the 22 counties. It was 25 percent larger than the arithmetic mean of all individuals in the states and territories. The results of Table 1 indicate consistency of average wealth of about $2,300 and remarkable consistency of level of inequality of slightly more than .9, as measured by the Gini coefficient of inequality.[1] The median age is also constant with but two exceptions. Only nativity varies significantly, with western cities having larger percentages of foreign born. It is reasonable to combine the ten distributions so that we may generalize urban holdings.

New York County presents a special problem, since its population was 50 percent of the population in the ten cities. It was decided not to include New York in the general analysis because of its size. A rather small sample of New York was drawn, however, and its results are reported separately in Table 1. It is contrasted with a sample for St. Paul, Minnesota, the youngest and most affluent city at that time. A judgment was made that the ten middle cities of the listed twelve probably convey a better picture of highly urbanized society at that time than do the twelve.

A. Wealth Distribution

The data of Table 2 show that there was extreme inequality in the distribution of wealth in 1860. The top one-tenth of 1 percent had 15 percent of the wealth in the urban areas. The richest 6,000 men had as much wealth as the poorest 450,000. A statistician might find it difficult to cite another example of similar skewness, one in which the arithmetic mean to median ratio was very large, if not infinite. The 50 percent who were propertyless truly had little material wealth. It is doubtful that many would have guessed that this level of inequality existed prior to the Civil War. The

---

[1] A measure of relative dispersion, Gini's coefficient of concentration, or R, is calculated by determining the area between the actual Lorenz curve and the straight-line curve of perfect equality. This area as a ratio of the triangular area under the line of perfect equality was .924 for the ten counties in 1860.

TABLE 1   The Number, Wealth, Nativity, and Age of Males 20 Years Old and Over in Each of Ten Urban Counties in 1860

Listing by Major City of Each County	Census Tabulation of Number of Adult Males	Number of Men[a]	Average Wealth of Men (Dollars)	Sample of Adult Men		
				Gini Coefficient of Concentration	Proportion That Are Foreign Born	Median Age
Boston	53,024	55,203	2,828	.944	.48	33
Philadelphia	145,172	148,216	2,679	.932	.47	34
Newark	25,893	28,377	1,894	.904	.52	38
Washington, D.C.	18,474	17,493	2,373	.898	.30	34
Pittsburgh	44,198	42,679	1,962	.894	.53	37
Cleveland	20,233	18,877	1,946	.859	.61	36
Cincinnati	60,330	62,090	2,200	.932	.70	35
Chicago	40,740	40,737	2,393	.920	.68	31
Milwaukee	15,897	15,382	2,371	.893	.82	35
San Francisco	25,679	27,633	1,137	.915	.65	33

All ten counties	449,640	456,687	2,346	.924	.55	36
Five Eastern	286,761	291,967	2,507	.927	.47	37
Five Western	162,879	164,720	2,062	.919	.69	36
Median of the ten	33,300	34,600	2,286	.909	.57	35
New York	219,642	219,600	1,911	.933	.64	36
St. Paul	3,523	3,523	3,423	.918	.61	33

SOURCES: The sample of the ten counties was taken from Schedule 1 of the 1860 Census. One line was chosen at random from each one, two, or four pages of the manuscripts, where one page contained forty lines. County populations are from Table 1 of the *Census of Population, 1860*. The sum of the individual wealth declarations was published for each county in Table 3 of *Mortality and Miscellaneous Statistics, 1860*. When these county sums are divided by the respective number of adult males, averages are obtained which are as much as 10 percent larger than those given above. The average of *Census* Table 3 values for the ten counties is $2,544, or 8.8 percent larger than the sample value of $2,346. The aggregates of *Census* Table 3 include the estates of women and a few young males under 20.

a These totals are obtained from weighting the sample items in each city. Thus, 148,216 for Philadelphia stems from $160 \times 923 + 4 \times 134$ where approximately one of every 160 men was sampled of those with wealth under the cutoff of $100,000 and approximately one of every four men was sampled of those with wealth above $100,000. The sample size for the ten cities was 8,966, including presumably all these 885 men above $100,000 in nine cities and 134 of the presumed 536 above $100,000 in Philadelphia. The New York sample is 588 in size, including 40 rich, and that of St. Paul is 391, including presumably all 43 rich above $100,000.

TABLE 2 The Distribution of Wealth Among Males 20 Years Old and Over in Ten Urban Counties in 1860

All the 456,687 Adult Men in the Ten Counties

Lower Limit of Wealth Class, in Dollars, X	Total Number of Males in the Wealth Class	Total Amount of Wealth, in Millions of Dollars, in the Wealth Class	Nx, or the Percent of Total Males Above the Lower Limit, X	Ax, or the Percent of Total Wealth Above the Lower Limit, X	Nx of the 207,422 Native Born in Ten Counties	Nx of the 679,810 Adult Men in the Twelve Counties
0	234,540	—	100.	100.	100.	100.
10	1,360	—	48.64	100.	48.86	45.88
20	10,280	—	48.35	100.	48.65	45.68
50	18,720	1	46.09	99.97	47.74	43.75
100	31,900	4	41.99	99.87	45.54	40.32
200	40,290	11	35.01	99.54	40.42	34.11
500	26,320	16	26.18	98.52	31.68	24.48
1,000	26,440	34	20.42	96.99	26.47	19.19

2,000	29,100	86	14.63	93.85	20.73	14.10
5,000	15,720	104	8.26	85.85	12.83	8.08
10,000	11,100	145	4.82	76.18	7.70	4.51
20,000	6,881	212	2.39	62.64	4.31	2.45
50,000	2,615	164	.88	42.83	1.76	.72
100,000	983	128	.31	27.53	.59	.27
200,000	361	105	.10	15.62	.17	.095
500,000	59	34	.017	5.85	.032	.022
1,000,000	18	25	.004	2.42	.006	.006
Total	456,687	1,072				
Arithmetic mean (dollars)	2,346				3,878	2,211
Median (dollars)	0				0	0
Gini coefficient	.924				.913	.927

SOURCE: The sample of sizes 8,966; 588; and 391 are from schedule 1 of the 1860 Census. See Table 1.

finding casts some doubt on the prevailing notion that inequality increased until the turn of the century.[2]

In spite of the inequality level in 1860, the literature of the time stressed not only the free play that one had for his talents; emphasis was also placed on the reward one would obtain for his abilities and efforts, rather than on the penalties for lack of abilities. One may well wonder how this reward "myth" could prevail if so few held so much wealth. Our problem, then, entails resolving the apparent conflict between the fact of extreme inequality and the belief in individual economic growth from effort. One must examine data from the standpoint of the age and background of the individual. By all measures, the best proxies for measuring the abilities, feelings, and accumulative ingenuity of the individual in the period are his age and whether he was born in the United States or emigrated from a foreign country. We shall begin by examining characteristics of the poor.

B. The Propertyless

The single most important parameter of wealth distribution is the proportion of men with no wealth, $P_{\$0}$. It depicts the proportion of persons in society at a point in time who are failing to participate in accumulation—the proportion of persons who are consuming at least their total incomes. These individuals may be young, they may be foreign born. They may be plagued by full or partial unemployment brought about by sickness, lack of knowledge of job opportunities, or general economic conditions dominated by seasonal or cyclical factors. It may have been true that there was some general queuing process, first for employment, and second for employment which provided income larger than some minimum consumption need.

---

[2] There would have been about 50 millionaires in large cities if our 18 millionaires represent 36 percent of the highly urban sector. Consider that the number of adult males in 1900 was 2.73 times the number in 1860, and that average wealth in 1900 would have been 2.20 times that in 1860 if compounded annually at 2 percent per capita. Thus, 135 individuals in 1900, each above $2,200,000, would be consistent with the mean and inequality of the 1860 distribution. The 77 individuals above $500,000 in Table 2 would have been consistent with 580 millionaires in 1900 in the United States. Prices in the two years were similar. Our focus here is on large cities. However, in 1860 in Louisiana alone, there were 36 large slaveholders with wealth above $500,000.

It has been determined that $P_{\$0}$ was .514 for the ten major cities in the North in 1860. Thus the have-nots were as many as the haves! The have-nots had little more than clothing and petty cash. The definition of personal estate presumably included such items as furniture, so we are considering the fact that median wealth value was close to being nothing. (Some might maintain that $10 to $40 would be a more appropriate figure. This would be roughly $40 to $160 at 1970 prices.) Table 3 indicates that $P_{\$0}$ was higher in the East and lower in the West, reaching 58 percent in New York City but only 34 and 39 percent in Milwaukee and Minneapolis, respectively. Part of these differences could be explained by the importance of nonurban populations in the counties.

W. Lloyd Warner's nomenclature of social classes prominently distinguishes persons with and without wealth. His lower class encompasses the lower-lower and the upper-lower categories, each of which contains people with essentially no wealth. This lower class constituted 58 percent of the population of Yankee City in the early 1930s. It is not surprising that the figure is similar to our $P_{\$0}$ of .514, since conditions of the early 1930s were part of the Great Depression, and since a rigid standard of $0 was not applied in delineating the lower group. The 1860 proportion of wealth-holders in the ten cities having less than $100 was $P_{\$0-99} = .58$, a figure which was the same as that stated by Warner.[3]

There is an appealing probability calculation involving $P_{\$0}$ and average age. The average age of males 20 and older in the ten cities in 1860 was about 35. If one assumed that individuals could accumulate wealth only during their adult years, say, $age - K = age - 20$, then they would have had on the average about 15 years exposure in the adult labor force. The probability of nonaccumulation, calculated for a year by assuming independent and constant annual probabilities, would be $(P_{\$0,year}) = (P_{\$0})^{1/(age - K)}$; .957 $= (.514)^{1/15}$. The probability of remaining in the zero class in a year might be estimated as .957. The probability of advancement in a year, $P_{\$1-,year} = 1 - (P_{\$0})^{1/(age\ K)}$, is calculated to be .043.

[3] W. Lloyd Warner and Paul S. Hunt, *The Social Life of a Modern Community*, Vol. I, Yankee City Series (New Haven: Yale University Press, 1941) p. 88; W. Lloyd Warner and Associates, *Democracy in Jonesville*, (New York: Harper Torchbook, 1964) pp. 24-25; W. Lloyd Warner, Marchia Meeker, Kenneth Eells, *Social Class in America* (New York: Harper Torchbook, 1960) pp. 14, 140-41, 165.

TABLE 3   The Proportion of Men 20 Years Old and Over With No Wealth for Each of the Ten Cities and New York and St. Paul in 1860

Listing by Major City of Each County	Census Tabulation of Number of Adult Males	Sample of Adult Males				
		Proportion With No Wealth				Proportion With Wealth Less Than $100 (P$0-99)
		All (P$0)	*Native-Born* (P$0, NB)	*Nonfarm* (P$0, NF)		
Boston	53,024	.520	.530	.522		.616
Philadelphia	145,172	.564	.539	.570		.594
Newark	25,893	.523	.454	.535		.568
Washington, D.C.	18,474	.466	.485	.465		.546
Pittsburgh	44,198	.400	.443	.423		.537
Cleveland	20,233	.441	.402	.494		.498
Cincinnati	60,330	.474	.503	.482		.614
Chicago	40,740	.489	.432	.500		.513
Milwaukee	15,897	.340	.415	.332		.425
San Francisco	25,679	.674	.662	.682		.674
All ten counties	449,640	.514	.511	.524		.580
Five Eastern	286,761	.524	.516	.531		.587
Five Western	162,879	.495	.497	.511		.568
Unweighted average of ten		.489	.486	.500		.559
New York	219,642	.601	.560	.602		.634
St. Paul	3,523	.392	.373	.363		.460

...mple of sizes 8,066; 588; and 391. See Table 1.

This might be interpreted as meaning that an individual without wealth faces the year with only a 4.3 percent chance of joining the group of people who save, who have wealth. An alternative interpretation might be that 4.3 percent of people in the lower class escape to the middle class or choose the middle class in a given year.

At least two qualifications should be applied to the notion of probability of escape, $P_{\$1-, year}$. We have an average figure for the population based on the experience of those who were young and old. It will be shown later that $P_{\$1-, year}$ varies with age, being greater when one is young, smaller in middle age and quite small in later life. The concept of adult age is also subject to criticism, particularly in dealing with social classes. Since family connections, family wealth, and inheritance are an important part of wealth accumulation, it might very well be argued that the K in $age-K$ should be 10, 0, or even a negative value. A calculation of $P_{\$1-, year, K = 0}$ gives $1 - (.514)^{1/(35 - 0)}$, or .019. Empirical testing of age-wealth configurations suggests that a K of 16 is often appropriate. This yields $P_{\$1-, year, K = 16} = .035$. In all these calculations, the product of the average age times the probability of escaping is about the same; thus, $.043(35-20) = .65$, $.019(35-0) = .66$, $.035(35-16) = .66$, and $(P_{\$1-, year, K})(age - K) \approx c$.

It might be thought that the have-not proportion would be larger for foreign-born than native-born. This, strangely enough, was not the case, since $P_{\$0, FB} = .515$ and $P_{\$0, NB} = .511$. A correction for the fact that there were relatively more native-born among the young and old camouflages a native-born advantage appearing among older age groups. The ten counties did have some farm populations, since there were rural areas in most of the counties. The farm group constituted about 5 percent of the population of adult males with $P_{\$0, farm} = .338$. This was substantially less than $P_{\$0, nonfarm} = .524$. Part of this difference could be explained by differences in age composition and nativity composition, but there certainly was a larger propertyless group in the cities. People must have elected, in part, to participate in urban rather than in rural life. This was in spite of the fact that it was more difficult to accumulate in cities. The difference, $P_{\$0, nonfarm} - P_{\$0, farm}$ might have been an indicator of an upper-lower class—a class which is able and willing to save in rural society but not in urban society.

II. A BINOMIAL MODEL RELATING SOCIAL AND WEALTH CLASSES

Suppose the probability of escaping the zero class in a year was $P_{\$0,\,year,\,K}$ = .04 where K is 20 (but could be as low as 16). If one of age 20 does advance in a year (i.e., at age 21) to the class which has saved, he is part of a select group. It seems reasonable to distinguish him from those who will become haves at age 22 or later. Surely his expected wealth will be larger than that of one entering the have class at age 22 if one considers the year in which he has been able to employ his wealth. The forces producing the 4 percent group at age 21 might, then, be expected to create a have-have group at age 22. This might very well be 4 percent of 4 percent or .16 percent of those 22 years of age. The argument could be extended to a have-have-have group of $(.04)^3 = (.04)^{23-20}$ at age 23. Alternatively, the proportion remaining in the have-not group at age 23 would be $(.96)^3$. A series of rungs would be established which would become increasingly difficult to reach. The probability of movement from rung to rung in a given year would be $P_{\Delta rung} = P_{\$1-,year}$.

A. *Binomial Probabilities*

The probability of success in a year would remain constant, and the process could be described with the binomial probability distribution, $B(X;N_t,P)$, where X is the rung level (X=0,1,2, . . . , N_t), N_t is $age_t - K_t$ or $age_0 - 20_0$ in year t=0, and P is $P_{\Delta rung}$. An example for a given age cohort is:

					$B(X,N_t.04)$		
t	age_t	N_t	X=0	X=1	X=2	X=3	X⩾4
1845	20	0	1.0000				
1846	21	1	.9600	.0400			
1847	22	2	.9216	.0768	.0016		
1848	23	3	.8847	.1106	.0046	.0001	
–	–	–	–	–	–	–	–
1860	35	15	.5421	.3388	.0988	.0179	.0024

If one were examining urban population in a given year, he would have to weight the $B(X,N_t,P)$ for each age group by its relative population.

The probabilities $B(X,N_{1860},.04)$ are given for the selected age group $N_{1860} = 35 - 20 = 15$ in columns 3 and 4 of Table 4. This is taken as an initial approximation for adult men in that year. (Poisson probabilities for $NP = 15$ (.04) = .6 are essentially the same as those presented, since P is relatively small and N is fairly large; other products of N and P of .6 give about the same binomial results.) The very interesting aspect of the probabilities is that they generate classes which have about the *same frequencies* as those found by W. Lloyd Warner for Yankee City! The similarities displayed in Table 4 for X of 1 and the lower-middle class, X of 2 and the upper-middle class, and X of 3 and the lower-upper class are remarkable. Even the $X = 4$ frequency is of the same general magnitude as the upper-upper class as quantified for Yankee City. Table 4 includes a column for $B(X,N,.05)$ as well as for $B(X,N,.04)$. This allows one to judge how sensitive the calculation is to changes in the probability of escape.

It might be claimed that knowledge of (1) the proportion of adults without wealth, and (2) the average of adult age, can be used to construct social classes by employing a binomial model. These two parameters suggest the proportions in the next four classes, LM, UM, LU, and UU classes. They also suggest a super fifth class at $X = 5$ for cities of size 10,000, a super-super class at $X = 6$ for cities of size 100,000, and a seventh class for an urban population[4] of 1,000,000. The first characteristic of the binomial classes is $P[X_t|(X-1)_{t-1}] = P_{\Delta rung}$. The probability of moving from any one class to the next higher class in the course of a year is constant for all classes. This includes movement from the lower class to the lower-middle class. No allowance is made for movement from a higher to lower class except insofar as $P_{\Delta rung}$ is a net upward movement. The second characteristic is $P_{\Delta rung} = 1 -$

---

[4] Theoretically, a village of 10 would have one individual in the UM class at $X = 2$ and none for $X \geqslant 3$, in the case of $B(X,N,.04)$. A town of 100 would have 2 persons in the LU class and none for $X \geqslant 4$. A population of 10^n would have a top class at $X = n + 1$. The relative dispersion of persons in classes in a given town would be $\sigma_X/\mu_X = \sqrt{NP(1-P)}/NP = \sqrt{(1-P)/NP} = \sqrt{(.96)/(.04N)} = \sqrt{(24)/N}$, where $P = .04$ and $N_t = age_t - K$. Thus, relative dispersion of persons distributed by social class would *not* be a function of size of city if average age and $P_{\Delta rung}$ were the same in each city.

TABLE 4   Status Hierarchy in Yankee City, Binomial Probabilities Based on Adult Age and Persons With No Property in the Ten Northern Cities in 1860, and Wealth in the Ten Northern Cities in 1860 for Classes Having These Binomial Probabilities

| Warner Classes for Yankee City | | | Binomial Probability B(X, N, P) — Cumulative Frequency | | Wealth, W, in the Ten Cities (Using $N_W = N_X$) | |
Class Name, YC (1)	Cumulative Frequency, N_{YC} (2)	Class Rung, X (3)	N_X for: B(X, 15, .04) (4)	N_X for: B(X, 15, .05) (5)	W Using Column 4 Frequencies (Dollars) (6)	W Using Column 5 Frequencies (Dollars) (7)
		7	.000001	.000004		2,900,000
		6	.00002	.00005	1,240,000	775,000
UU	.0144	5	.0002	.0006	450,000	250,000
LU	.0300	4	.0024	.0055	110,000	65,000
UM	.1322	3	.0203	.0362	22,000	12,400
LM	.4134	2	.1191	.1710	2,500	1,250
UL	.7394	1	.4579	.5367	50	0
LL	.9916	0	1.0000	1.0000	0	0

SOURCES: W. Lloyd Warner and Paul S. Hunt, *The Social Life of a Modern Community*, Vol. I, Yankee City Series (New Haven: Yale University Press, 1941), p. 88; W. Lloyd Warner and Associates, *Democracy in Jonesville* (New York: Harper Torchbook, 1964), pp. 24-25; W. Lloyd Warner, Marchia Meeker, Kenneth Eells, *Social Class in America*, (New York: Harper Torchbook, 1960), pp. 14, 140-41, 165. Wealth data are from the sample size 8,966 drawn from the manuscripts of the Census of 1860.

Cumulative frequencies for Yankee City are based on class frequencies of .0144, .0156, .1022, .2812, .3260, and .2522. Binomial values of N and P were chosen because the average adult age was $35 - 20 = 15$ and P's of .04 and .05 encompassed $P(\Delta rung) = .0434$. The proportion of individuals with no wealth was $P_{\$0} = .514 = (9.566)^{1/15}$ and $P(\Delta rung)$ is $1 - (P_{\$0})^{1/15}$.

Binomial probabilities are taken from U.S., Department of Commerce, National Bureau of Standards, Applied Mathematics Series 6, *Tables of Binomial Probabilities Distribution* (Washington, D.C., 1949) and Harry G. Romig, *50-100 Binomial Tables* (New York: John Wiley & Sons, 1952).

$(P_{\$0})^{1/(age-K)}$ where $P_{\$0}$ is the proportion of people without wealth, *age* is the average age of people, and $0 \leqslant K \leqslant 20$. Calculations are determined from the size of the lower class. The classes are not chosen arbitrarily. Probability of movement is the same for an individual throughout the system.

B. Transformation of Variables for the Binomial Model

The system is characterized not only by frequencies, $f(X)$, but by the various variate values $X = 0,1,2, \ldots, 7$. Let N_X be the cumulative frequencies above each X, that is, above each rung. What will be the dollar wealth value, W, at these various rungs? We let $N_X = N_W$, find the W of column (6) of Table 4, and speculate about the relationship of W and X. An example of a transformation might possibly be of the form $W = aX^b$ or $W = cd^X$ for $X > 0$ and $W = X$ for $X = 0$. Illustrations are:

X	$W = aX^b$		$W = cd^X$	
	$W = X^2$	$W = 50X^{5.6}$	$W = 2^X$	$W = 400\,(3.9)^X$
0	$ 0	$ 0	$ 0	$ 0
1	1	50	2	(1,600)
2	4	2,300	4	(6,100)
3	9	22,000	8	24,000
4	16	110,000	16	93,000
5	25	380,000	32	361,000
6	36	1,100,000	64	1,400,000
7	49	2,520,000	128	5,500,000

The elasticity form, $W = aX^b$, means that wealth ratios of two bordering classes would decrease as one climbs the social ladder; values of X would be considered as cardinal numbers with an origin value of zero embedded in the lower class. If the severe test of constant wealth ratios were applied, the climb from rung 1 to 2 is commensurate with the climb from rung 2 to 4, and this is commensurate with the climb from rung 4 to 8. It would mean that the quantitative jump from LM to UM is the same as the double jump from UM to UU, at least from the standpoint of wealth ratios. In Chart 1, it is shown that an elasticity coefficient

Wealth in dollars

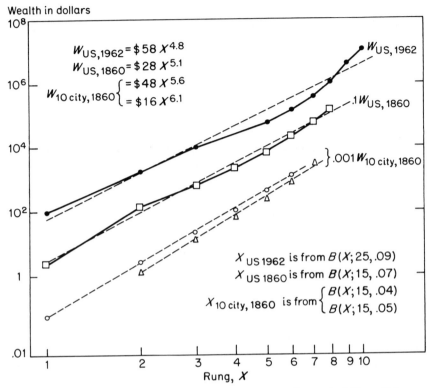

CHART 1: Indirect Elasticity Correlations Between Binominal Rung Values, X, and Wealth Values, W (Obtained by Letting $N_X = N_W$)

SOURCE: See Table 4.

of 5.6 accords very well with the data for $X > 0$. A 1 percent change in class rank, X, corresponds with a 5.6 percent increase in wealth. It is difficult to understand why one has a product concept where X is multiplied by itself five or six times. Perhaps an explanation lies in inheritances, generations, time in a social class, or economic power of a social class.

There is an appealing aspect of the model $W = cd^X$ since X may be considered as time and d is 1 plus a rung interest rate. If $W = 2^X$, then wealth would double at each rung, the interest or growth rate of wealth would be 100 percent for the length of time one remained in a given social class. Chart 2 demonstrates that there is some empirical evidence for believing that this configuration

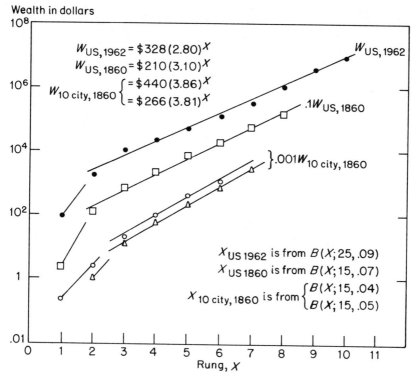

Wealth in dollars

$W_{US, 1962} = \$328(2.80)^X$
$W_{US, 1860} = \$210(3.10)^X$
$W_{10 \, city, 1860} \begin{cases} = \$440(3.86)^X \\ = \$266(3.81)^X \end{cases}$

$W_{US, 1962}$

$.1W_{US, 1860}$

$\}.001W_{10 \, city, 1860}$

$X_{US \, 1962}$ is from $B(X; 25, .09)$
$X_{US \, 1860}$ is from $B(X; 15, .07)$
$X_{10 \, city, 1860}$ is from $\begin{cases} B(X; 15, .04) \\ B(X; 15, .05) \end{cases}$

Rung, X

CHART 2: Exponential Correlations Between Binomial Rung Values, X, and Wealth Values, W (Obtained by letting $N_X = N_W$)

SOURCE: See Table 4.

holds for the four social classes $3 \leqslant X \leqslant 6$ for the cities in 1860 with the form $W = c(3.9)^X$. If the differential change in X each year were .04, then percentage growth in wealth for the individual would be approximated as $dW/W = .04 \log 3.9 = .05$.

It has been demonstrated that $B(cX^{5.6}, 15, .04)$ is an excellent description of the 1860 wealth data. It is essentially an excellent fit of Warner's social classes if no distinction is made between the lower-lower and upper-lower class. Some further evidence is offered in Table 5 for a Warner dollar index. He suggested that the size of the business could be used in placing proprietors and managers in one rating technique for occupation. The reader may agree that values of this size are about the same as the $W = cX^{5.6}$ for 1860.

TABLE 5   Average Value of Businesses of Proprietors and Managers in Yankee City and Average Wealth in the Ten Northern Cities in 1860, Classified by Status Hierarchy and Binomial Rung

Warner Classes for Yankee City		Wealth, W, in the Ten Cities (Using $N_W = N_X$)		
Class Name, YC	Average Value of Business (Dollars)	Class Rung, X	W, Using B(X, 15, .04) (Dollars)	W, Using B(X, 15, .05) (Dollars)
		7		2,900,000
		6		775,000
		5		250,000
		4		65,000
		3		12,400
		2		1,250
		1		0
UU	75,000[a]		1,240,000	
LU	26,000		450,000	
UM	1,960		110,000	
LM	12		22,000	
UL			2,500	
LL			50	
	0	0	0	0
		0	0	

SOURCES: W. Lloyd Warner, Marchia Meeker, Kenneth Eells, *Social Class in America*, (New York: Harper Torchbook, 1960) Table 7, pp. 140-41, and Table 9, p. 165. The Index of Status Characteristics ratings of Table 6, p. 127, imply linearity in social-class equivalents. Thus, lower-limit ratings of 17 for U, 33 for UM, 50 for LM, 62 for UL, and 84 for LL leave intervals of 16, 16, 17, 12, and 22; Table 19, p. 183, with lower limits of 17, 32, 46, 61, and 75 illustrates the same linearity with intervals of 14 or 15 points. The stated linear equation of $Y = .21X - 1.12$ (of page 183), with Y as social-class placement on the 15 point scale and X as the weighted total for status characteristics, could be adapted to $z = (60 - X)/15$ in giving binomial values of 3, 2, 1, 0 and −1.

a The average values are weighted geometric means obtained from the values $75,000; $20,000; $5,000; $2,000; $500; and (assumed) $1, as listed for occupational ratings 1, 2, 3, 4, 5, and 6. The weights are obtained from a table of the number of old Americans cross classified by ratings on occupation and social class (Evaluated Participation). An example is:

$$50\sqrt{(75,000)^{29} \times (20,000)^7 \times (5,000)^{11} \times (2,000)^1 \times (500)^2}.$$

C. The Binomial Distribution and Specific Age Classes

The binomial model yielding $P_{\Delta rung}$ and $W = cX^d$ fortunately gives results which are generally consistent with statistical data on wealth for specific age groups. The proportion with no wealth in an age group, $P_{\$0, age}$, can be estimated fairly well from $P_{\Delta rung}$ for all age groups; native-born probabilities, $P_{\$0, age, NB}$ are quite well represented by $P_{\Delta rung, NB}$. The linear relationship in logarithms of W and X for each age group produces a slope about the same as that produced among all age groups.

1. Probabilities of Advancement for Specific Age Groups. The proportion with wealth, $P_{\$1.} = .486 = 1 - .514$, is a population-weighted average of $P_{\$1-,age}$ figures varying from near zero at age 20 to between .67 and .75 for those of old age. The proportions given in Table 6 for all adult males in the ten counties show a rapid rise from .168 for ages 20-24 to a peak at .681 in the age group 55-59. Suppose the binomial model is applicable, with $P_{\Delta rung}$ of .04 (or, more specifically, .043). If $B(X, 35 - 20, .043)$, then presumably $B(X, age_t - 20, .043)$ would be applicable for $age_t = 20_{1860}, 21_{1860}, \ldots, 99_{1860}$. Results for this situation are given in the table in the column $1.0 - (.957)^{age - 20}$. The predicted values at each age are less than $P_{\$1-, age}$ for those under 40 and more than $P_{\$1-, age}$ for older ages. A better fit is achieved with a probability of advancement of .05 in the earlier stages and .03 in the later stages.

A theoretically more attractive model in this context is obtained from $P_{\Delta rung} = .034$ and $age - 16$, where accumulation is considered to begin at least a few years before age 20. The $P_{\$0, age}$ at ages 20, 21, and 22 were actually .10, .13, and .17. This suggests that $age - 16$ or $age - 17$ is a more appropriate year to start the process. If one is to make this consistent with the ten-county average of $P_{\$0} = .514$, then $P_{\Delta rung}$ would be $1 - (.514)^{1/(age - 16)} = .034$. The values generated from $B(0, age_{1860} - 16, .034)$ for $age_t = 20_{1860}, \ldots, 77_{1860}$ are given in Table 6. This series is particularly appealing since it generates values similar to those for native-born in the counties in 1860. The figures in Table 6 for $P_{\$1-, NB}$ are a little larger than the theoretical values at ages 32 and 37. However, consider those at ages 20-24, 25-29, 40-44, 45-49, 50-54, 55-59, and 60-64, of .16, .36, .61, .66, .67, .76, and .77; they are faithfully duplicated by .19, .32, .60, .66, .72, .76, and .80. It seems rather amazing that there was this consistency of probability movements from the have-not classes to have classes.

TABLE 6 The Proportion of Men 20 Years Old and Over With Wealth in the Ten Cities (Counties) for Various Age Groups and Suggested Binomial Values

Age	Proportion With Wealth			Probability Calculations Based on $P_{\$0} = .514^a$			
	All $(P_{\$1.})$	Native $(P_{\$1.,\ NB})$	Nonfarm $(P_{\$1.,\ NF})$	$1.000 - (.957)^{a-20}$ $= P'_{\$1.}$	$1.000 - (.966)^{a-16}$ $= P'_{\$1.}$	$1.000 - (.981)^{a-0}$ $= P'_{\$1.}$	$Age = a$
20-24	.168	.157	.168	.085	.189	.341	22
25-29	.386	.363	.358	.267	.320	.401	27
30-34	.535	.563	.528	.413	.429	.455	32
35-39	.596	.627	.584	.530	.521	.505	37
40-44	.577	.608	.561	.623	.598	.549	42
45-49	.651	.666	.634	.698	.662	.590	47
50-54	.641	.666	.636	.758	.716	.627	52
55-59	.681	.760	.674	.806	.762	.661	57
60-64	.667	.769	.637	.845	.800	.692	62
65-69	.660	.757	.602	.876	.832	.720	67
70-99	.516	.559	.474	.920	.882	.786	77
20-99	.486	.489	.476	.486	.486	.486	35

SOURCES: See Tables 1 and 2.

[a] The proportion with no wealth in the 10 counties was .514; $.514 = (.957)^{35-20} = (.966)^{35-16} = (.981)^{35-0}$.

There is some attractiveness in generating a series from $P_{\Delta rung} = .514^{1/(35-0)} = .981$. It would be assumed that an individual would begin at birth to inherit his ability to climb from class to class. Calculations would yield only potential class position in younger age. The potential class position would be realized only in later life when actual inheritances would materialize. It is seen in Table 6 that this series generates values consistent with actual values after age 40. The mystifying aspect of this is that $P_{\$0} = 1.0 - .981 = .019$. This implies a lifetime growth rate in advancement of .019 rungs per annum. Those of age 50 or 60 would have an expected value or NP of about $50(.019)$ or $60 (.019)$, that is, about 1.0 rungs. This, in turn, implies an annual growth rate of about .019 rungs per year/1.0 rungs, or a little less than 2 percent a year. This proposition will be tested again, using probabilities of dying.

2. Transformation of the Variable for Specific Age Groups.   It is to be expected that the power parameter d in $w = cX^d$ will be less than 5.6 in all but the youngest age class. It is perhaps surprising that the d values in Table 7 do not drop very much below the 5.6 value for all age groups. There is little evidence that the figure is less than 4.6. One concludes that the original formulation $B(cX^{5.6}, 35 - 20, .043)$ does not need to be qualified greatly in adapting it to specific age groups. Accumulation begins as early as 16 and the power 5.6 might be decreased to 5.0 for middle age groups.

D. Social Class Averages of Nativity Groups in 1860

The wealth limits, W, suggested by $B(X,15,.043)$ for the ten counties in 1860 at $X = 0, 1, 2, 3, 4, 5$, and 6 are given in Table 8. Let us turn the problem around by considering X as this step function of W. Substitute X for W in a computer run of the sample items to determine the number of persons in the various social groups. This procedure will yield information about nativity, occupation, and age for the various social classes. It is recalled that the population was half native-born. These native-born naturally dominate the higher social classes, including the upper-middle, upper-lower, upper-upper, and classes 5 and 6. The cumulative frequency columns almost show $N_{X, native-born} \geqslant N_{X-1, foreign-born}$ for these classes. The pattern would be consistent with the idea of moving one rung in a generation, since the children of foreign-born

TABLE 7 Indirect Exponential Correlations Between Binomial Rung Values, X, and Wealth Values, W, Classified by Age for the Ten Cities

(obtained by letting $N_X = N_{W, age}$)

Age	$(P_{\$1\text{-}, age})$	Implied $P_{\Delta Rung}$	Average $P_{\Delta Rung}$	Age Midpoint	Binomial Formula, for $X \geqslant 0$	Least-Squares Results for the Specification $W = cX^d$
20-29	.284	.065	.043	25	$B(X, 05, .06)$	$W = \$\ 39X^{6.2}$
				25	$B(X, 05, .05)$	$W = 91X^{5.8}$
				25	$B(X, 05, .04)$	$W = 128X^{5.8}$
30-39	.563	.054	.043	35	$B(X, 15, .05)$	$W = 66X^{5.3}$
				35	$B(X, 15, .04)$	$W = 28X^{5.4}$
40-49	.609	.037	.043	45	$B(X, 25, .04)$	$W = 40X^{5.0}$
				45	$B(X, 25, .03)$	$W = 102X^{4.8}$
50-59	.656	.030	.043	55	$B(X, 35, .04)$	$W = 118X^{5.5}$
				55	$B(X, 35, .03)$	$W = 53X^{5.1}$
				55	$B(X, 35, .02)$	$W = 233X^{4.8}$
60-69	.665	.024	.043	65	$B(X, 45, .03)$	$W = 30X^{5.3}$
				65	$B(X, 45, .02)$	$W = 77X^{5.3}$

| 70-99 | .516 | .013 | .043 | 75 | B(X, 55, .02) | W = $125X^{4.6}$ |
| | | | | 75 | B(X, 55, .01) | W = $293X^{5.2}$ |

NOTE: Details for fitting the above 14 equations are:

d	Number of Points	Range for X	Unadjusted Coefficient of Determination	Standard Error of d
6.2	4	1-4	.999	.072
5.8	4	1-4	.998	.176
5.8	4	1-4	.996	.254
5.3	6	1-6	.997	.138
5.4	6	1-6	.978	.399
5.0	6	2-7	.999	.076
4.8	6	1-6	.997	.132
5.5	7	2-8	.997	.136
5.1	6	2-7	.991	.237
4.8	6	1-6	.998	.109
5.3	6	2-7	.994	.202
5.3	6	1-6	.995	.198
5.6	7	1-7	.978	.309
5.2	5	1-5	.994	.223

SOURCE: See Table 4.

TABLE 8 The Distribution of Adult Native- and Foreign-Born Men in the Ten Cities in 1860, by Wealth and Social Class as Determined From the Binomial Distribution, $B(X, 15, .043)$

Class Rung, X	Cumulative Frequency, N_X, for $B(X, 15, .043)$	Wealth, W, Determined by Letting $N_W = N_X$ (Dollars)	Cumulative Frequencies Determined From W Values of Preceding Column		Average Age
			Native-Born $(N_X, {}_{NB})$	Foreign-Born $(N_X, {}_{FB})$	
7	.000001				
6	.000023	1,180,000	.000434	.000040	52.4
5	.000320	382,000	.000959	.000148	55.3
4	.003290	94,000	.006340	.000814	51.2
3	.025100	18,000	.046600	.008280	48.6
2	.136200	2,000	.207600	.095700	43.2
1	.486000	1	.488600	.484700	37.6
0	1.000000	0	1.000000	1.000000	33.0
Arithmetic mean, $\overline{X}$	.66		.75	.59	
Gini coefficient, R_X	.61		.62	.59	

SOURCE: See Tables 4 and 7, N_W is the proportion of all adult males above the wealth value, W.

would be essentially first-generation Americans. The average class rung for native-born, $\overline{X}_{NB}$, is only 25 percent larger than the foreign-born average, $\overline{X}_{FB}$. If we limit ourselves to those in classes 2 through 6, we find the difference is 11 percent. One might maintain that these differences are not substantial and that wealth accumulation provided the avenue of escape for the progeny of foreign-born.

There are substantial differences in average rung levels among age groups. Figures demonstrating $\overline{X}_{age}$ patterns are given in Table 9. One would expect a linear relationship between $\overline{X}$ and adult age, $age - K$, because the binomial model would have an almost constant $P = P_{\Delta \, rung}$. As $N = age - K$ increases in $B(X,N,P)$, $\Delta \overline{X} = P$, since $X = NP$. The best demonstration of linearity is the column for native-born. A plot of $\overline{X}_{age, \, NB}$ gives a satisfying verification of the model; the least-squares equation is $\overline{X}_{age,NB} = .0312 \, [(.0024)] \, (age - 11.5)$, $n = 9$, $R^2 = .96$, $20 \leqslant age \leqslant 64$. The predicted slope from $(age - K)P$ would be 4.3 percent a year. The

TABLE 9   Average Class Status of Adult Males in the Ten Cities in 1860, Classified by Age and Nativity (Using $B(X, 15, .0434)$ in Establishing $X = 0, 1, \ldots, 6$ in the Wealth Ranges $0; $1-1,999; \ldots ; $1,180,000 and Up)

		The Average[a] Social Class, Value $\overline{X}$			
Age	*All*	*Native-Born*	*Foreign-Born*	*Nonfarmers*	*Farmers*
20-24	.20	.20	.21	.20	.18
25-29	.45	.45	.45	.44	.64
30-34	.64	.72	.58	.62	.98
35-39	.78	.94	.68	.76	1.24
40-44	.83	1.01	.72	.80	1.38
45-49	.96	1.12	.81	.93	1.33
50-54	1.00	1.19	.83	.99	1.27
55-59	1.09	1.34	.88	1.08	1.22
60-64	1.15	1.59	.72	1.06	1.68
65 and up	.96	1.12	.72	.82	1.48
20 and up	.662	.749	.589	.638	1.048

[a] The ten-city (county) rungs are established from $B(X, 15, .0434)$ such that $X = 0$ for $W = \$0$; $X = 1$ for W of $1-1,999; $X = 2$ for $2,000-17,999; $X = 3$ for $18,000-93,999; $X = 4$ for $94,000-381,999; $X = 5$ for $382,000-1,179,999; and $X = 6$ for wealth of $1,180,000 or more. The method of letting $N_W = N_X$ is described in Tables 4 and 8.

actual slope of .0312 rungs, expressed as a proportion of X_{NB} = .75, is 4.2 percent. This is excellent verification. The relative slopes for all persons of 3.3 percent and that for foreign-born of 2.2 percent are less than the expected 4.3 percent.

E. Social Classes of the Deceased

One might entertain the bold hypothesis that the social status of the deceased could be given to the progeny. The reason is that the wealth provides the means for status; it is, as a minimum, a proxy for attainment. One dying with $\overline{X}$ = 1.10 *rungs* might figuratively leave to each of three children a little over a third of a rung. He certainly makes it possible for them to avoid the zero class.

Social-class data for deceased can be obtained in an indirect fashion by using death rates. Age-specific death rates for persons in Massachusetts are available for the year 1865. These may be treated in probability terms in generating death distributions for 1860. The transformation for frequencies would be $freq_{dead,age}$ = $death\ rate_{age} \times freq_{living,\ age}$. When this is applied to the 1860 urban sample, the following results are obtained:

	Number	Age	P$_{\$0}$	$\overline{X}$ All	NB	FB	R_X All	NB	FB
Living	456,687	36.3	.514	.662	.749	.589	.609	.621	.586
Deceased	6,860	42.3	.493	.729	.844	.624	.753	.782	.719

The number of adult deceased in the year was about 1.5 percent of the living population. Their average status relative to that of the living was (.729/.662) = 1.10. It could be asserted that the status value of the deceased was .0152 × 1.10 = .017 of the aggregate status of the living.

There is some rather meager evidence about growth in the status average over time. The growth in status points of 4.2 percent for the living is buoyed up in part by inheritances. Net growth might be .042 − .017, or 2.5 percent a year. If the population growth were not more than 2.5 percent, there could be growth per capita.

It has been determined that population in the ten counties was growing about 5 percent a year at that time.[5] Thus, it would be doubtful if there was per capita improvement in status. It should be remembered that we are dealing with the urban sector, and that this sector was strongly dominated by population growth.

F. Social Classes in the United States in 1860 and 1962

There are data available for the entire free population in the United States in 1860 and for all families in 1962. One could apply the binomial method to these data in a fashion similar to the method applied to the urban data. However, there is certainly no reason to believe that Warner classes are applicable to a labor force in 1860 which was half urban and half rural. It would be better to have wealth figures for the highly urban regions of the country. It is not the purpose of this paper to describe the United States data in any detail. Summary information is given in Charts 1 and 2 indicating that $B(c_1 X^{5.1}, 35 - 20, .07)$ for 1860 and $B(c_2 X^{4.8}, 45 - 20, .09)$ for 1962 are rough approximations. Better specifications for $X > 2$ are $B[c_3(3.1)^X, 35 - 20, .07]$ for 1860 and $B[c_4(2.8)^X, 45 - 20, .09]$ for 1962. The probability of advancement has increased a little but there is at least one more rung or super class. There is evidence of progress since $P_{\Delta rung}$ has increased. The have-nots constituted 33 percent of the population of all free men in 1860 and perhaps 10 percent of the population in 1962.[6] There has been an increase in the $X = 1$ class and probably the $X = 2$ class. The very elite at X of 7 and 8 in 1860 certainly has its counterpart[7] in 1962 at X of 9 and 10.

[5] The average annual percent of change in the number of adult males in the ten counties was 5.2 percent for the period from 1830 to 1860 and 4.5 percent for the period from 1850 to 1860.

[6] Dorothy S. Projector and Gertrude S. Weiss, *Survey of Financial Characteristics of Consumers* (Washington, D.C.: Federal Reserve Board, 1966) pp. 150, 151, 110; and John B. Lansing and John Sonquist, "A Cohort Analysis of Changes in the Distribution of Wealth," in Lee Soltow, ed., *Six Papers on the Size Distribution of Wealth and Income*, Vol. 33, Studies in Income and Wealth (New York: NBER, 1969) p. 42. Figures vary from 5 to 17 percent.

[7] Consider two possible bounds, $B(X, 15, .01)$, representing a very stagnant society, and $B(X, 15, .5)$, representing a very mobile society. The stagnant case for a manorial society of 100 men would have 86 men in the lower class, 14 in a lower-middle class and 1 lord in an upper-middle class. The stagnant

G. Summary

The most important figure revealed by study of 1860 urban wealth inequality is that 51.4 percent of the adult males were propertyless. Some might maintain that this lower-lower and upper-lower group provided the basis for the existence of other groups in the socioeconomic hierarchy. Indeed, a binomial model, $B(X, N, P)$, of the number of persons in the middle and upper classes can be constructed in which N is average adult age of $35 - 20$ and P is the probability of escaping the propertyless class in a given year, or $1 - (.514)^{1/N} = .043$. The frequency distribution generated by this model conforms closely to that offered by W. Lloyd Warner for social classes in Yankee City in the 1930s. It is also determined that $B(cX^{5.6}, 35 - 20, .043)$ and possibly $B[d(3.9)^X, 35 - 20, .043]$ represent urban wealth distribution in 1860 where coefficients are related to inheritance and annual economic growth. The model is consistent with wealth classifications for specific age groups.

III. AN INCOME-WEALTH MODEL FOR THE TEN CITIES

It is intriguing to try to construct an income distribution and consumption function which would yield saving and wealth distributions similar to the wealth distribution in the ten cities in 1860. I have been successful in developing a model which achieves this feat, but admittedly the desired results may arise, at least in part, because of compensating errors. Yet the model is sufficiently interesting to be presented, because it adds the dimension of distribution to the concepts of income, consumption, saving, and wealth. The stakes are high since an urban income distribution for the entire labor force would materially enhance the study of one-hundred-year changes in income distribution; it would in some ways be more attractive than one for the entire urban-rural economy. Historical comparisons could be made without the confounding influence of the urban movement.

A. Requirements for the Model

What characteristics should the model have? We first have requirements for have-nots and various averages: (1) The model

---

society of 1,000,000 men would have $0 \leqslant X \leqslant 4$ with a Gini coefficient $R[B(X^5,15,.01)] = .96$. The mobile society would have 16 classes with $R[B(X^5,15,.50)] = .56$.

should have about 50 percent of the population with wealth and about 50 percent without wealth. This necessarily means that half the people do not have net saving from the time they enter the labor force until the point in time when they are part of a census of wealth. (2) It should yield an average income, $\overline{Y}$, of about \$500 (\$450 to \$550). Kuznets has found[8] that product per worker in the United States in 1860 was \$526. (3) The average propensity to save, $\overline{S}/\overline{Y}$, should probably not be larger than 21 percent. Kuznets has found gross domestic capital formation was 21 percent of GNP.[9] Perhaps the saving average per person might not be too far from \$100-\$120 per annum. Most saving studies have shown that the personal gross saving ratio does not fall too much short of 20 percent.[10] It seems reasonable that the ratio might be substantial if one includes capital gains and savings through consumer durables. (4) The saving-wealth ratio, $\overline{S}/\overline{W}$, might not differ greatly from 5 to 6 percent. This is because the interest rate on government bonds was 5 percent at the time.[11] The wealth average of the ten cities was \$2,346. This would indicate that $\overline{S}$ was at least \$115-\$120. (5) There should be some rough correspondence between the wealth-saving ratio, $\overline{W}/\overline{S}$, and adult age. This could be $\overline{W} \approx \overline{S} (\overline{age} - 19)$ if wealth and adult age are linearly related. The average age of adult males in the ten cities of 36.1 and average wealth in the ten cities of \$2,346 lead to the expression \$138(36.1 − 19) = \$2,346, where $\overline{S}$ of 138 is slightly larger than the indicated range in point 3. We are assuming that the individual would save in some linear fashion during his productive life. The scatter diagram of wealth values for *different* individuals in various

[8] Simon Kuznets, *Economic Growth and Structure* (New York: W. W. Norton, 1965) p. 305.

[9] Simon Kuznets, *Modern Economic Growth* (New Haven: Yale University Press, 1966), p. 237; House Document No. 94-64, Part 1, *Institutional Investor Study Report of the Securities and Exchange Commission* (March 10, 1971), p. 91. Gross saving of households, including capital gain dividends, savings through consumer durable purchases, and capital consumption allowances, amount to 22 to 23 percent of personal disposable income since 1950. See also *Federal Reserve Bulletin* October 1971, p. A73.3.

[10] Dorothy S. Projector, *Survey of Changes in Family Finances* (Washington, D.C.: Federal Reserve System, 1968), pp. 7-10. She finds a saving rate of 17 percent for 1963.

[11] Sidney Homer, *A History of Interest Rates* (New Brunswick: Rutgers University Press, 1963), pp. 286-88.

ages in 1860 does substantiate the general plausibilities of the linear hypothesis. We have[12]

A. All adult males $W = \$175 \ (age - 22.9)$,

$$(14) \qquad W/W = .0747 \ (age - 22.9)$$

B. All with positive wealth $W = \$254 \ (age - 13.0)$,

$$(30) \qquad W/W = .0526 \ (age - 13.0)$$

All native-born and all native-born with positive wealth have forms of .0680 $(age - 21.6)$ and .0451 $(age - 18.8)$.

We next have requirements about distribution of income, consumption or saving, and wealth. (6) It is often felt that income is distributed as a Pareto curve among the upper 30 to 50 percent of income recipients. The income (and wealth) distribution is sometimes thought to be log-normal in shape. We shall find that income distribution in 1970 and 1962 was of the Pareto form for approximately the upper 30 percent of income earners and was approximately uniform in distribution among the lower 70 percent of income earners ($N_Y = \alpha Y^{-b}$ for $Y > Q_{70}$ and $N_Y = \kappa Y$ for $0 \leqslant Y \leqslant Q_{70}$). Evidence will also be presented that income in the upper tail in the 1860s was of the Pareto form. (7) Almost all saving from income must come from upper-income groups if only half the individuals have wealth. The implication is that there is some threshold income, T, at about the median income, above which saving occurs. Perhaps a consumption function $C = T + d(Y - T)^E$ is appropriate above median income.[13] The distribution of saving resulting from the application of the consumption function

---

[12] Standard errors from computer runs have been multiplied by the square root of $(456,687)/(8,966)$ since regression equations were fitted to weighted sample items.

[13] Consumption function data for 1874-75 and 1889-91 essentially have this form as do the consumption and income figures developed by the Federal Reserve wealth and saving studies of 1963. *Historical Statistics of the United States,* series C 315-316, 324-326; Projector, *Family Finances,* p. 9.

The threshold income, T, perhaps remained constant over time while incomes initially below T were increasing at a real rate of 1.3 percent per annum, a figure similar to the 1.4 percent growth rate found by Kuznets for per capita income in the period. Suppose that income is uniformly distributed below the median, that $P_{\$0, \ 1860 \ U.S. \ free} = .33$ or slave-adjusted is $P_{\$0, \ 1860 \ U.S. \ all} = .37$ and that $P_{\$0, \ 1962} = .10$. The implication is that incomes rise inversely as lower-tail frequencies decrease. The average annual percent of change is computed as $.37 = .10(1.013)^{1962-1860}$.

to income should have a relative distribution not materially different from wealth distribution; $R_S \approx R_W$ even though $R_S >$ R_Y.[14] (8) The Gini coefficient of the derived wealth (or saving) distribution should be between .91 and .93 since the coefficient in 1860 was .92. This coupled with the requirement that $P_{\$0} = .5$ means that the Gini coefficient for those with wealth should be about $R_{\$1-} = (.924 - .514)/.486 = .846$. (9) Far more important than any overall measure that the model might have is the exacting necessity that the Lorenz curve of the wealth model (and probably the saving model) must be the same as that for actual wealth. The $(N_X = N_W, A_W)$ points should be similar to those in Table 10 for wealth for the ten cities.

B. Income Distribution

The distribution of income among males in the United States in 1970 was of the Pareto form for about the top 30 percent of recipients and of a rectangular form for the bottom 70 percent of recipients. We are unable to state with certainty that this Pareto-rectangular form existed in 1860 for free men, because no complete income distributions for that period are extant.

Fortunately, there are some upper-tail income distributions available for Philadelphia in 1864, Milwaukee in 1864, Cleveland in 1865, and New York in 1863. These interesting figures purportedly include net income, as defined, to as low as an exemption level of $600. In spite of deficiencies of coverage, it seems clear that these upper-tail data are of the Pareto type. This shape will be extended below $600 to the point Y_{Nc} where frequency density is equal to that of uniform density from $0 to Y_{Nc}. The resultant Pareto-rectangular forms are not precise, but this does not detract from their usefulness. It will be shown that the Philadelphia income density function, coupled with a con-

[14] Projector and Weiss in *Survey of Financial Characteristics*, p. 30, list inequality of wealth among consumer units in the United States in 1962-63 as yielding a Gini coefficient of .76. Projector in *Family Finances*, pp. 6, 52, 214, and 321, gives a distribution of saving which yields $R_S = .74$ if dissavers are considered as having zero saving. The Lorenz curves for wealth and saving are very similar in 1962-63.

Distributions of savings of urban wage earners in Ontario were estimated from samples for the years 1884 to 1889. These too are highly suggestive of urban wealth inequality (*Annual Report of the Bureau of Industries for the Province of Ontario, 1887*, Toronto, 1888, p. 61).

TABLE 10   Relative Wealth Distribution in the Ten Cities and Its Derivation from a Pareto-Rectangular Distribution of Income and Saving

(relative distribution (N_X, A_X), where N_X is the proportion of all cases above the variate X, and A_X is the proportion of all wealth, income, or saving above the variate X)

Proportion of Cases (N_X)	Ten-City Wealth (A_W)	Income (A_Y)	The Pareto-Rectangular Model for $(b; c; N) = (.9; .473; 1,000)$ Saving From Income Where $(P_{\$1}; T/\overline{Y}) = (.50; .39)$	
			$(A_S$ for $E = .97)$	$(A_S$ for $E = .98)$
.001	.159	.099	.157	.158
.002	.224	.152	.238	.240
.005	.335	.240	.368	.371
.010	.452	.318	.418	.482
.020	.592	.405	.594	.597
.050	.769	.531	.747	.750
.100	.889	.635	.855	.857
.200	.968	.747	.945	.946
.300	.991	.816	.982	.983
.400	.998	.868	.996	.996
.500	1.000	.908	1.000	1.000
1.000	1.000	1.000	1.000	1.000
R	.924	.712	.912	.913
S/Y			.241	.172

SOURCES: See Tables 1 and 2. Consumption, C, is computed from $C = T + (Y - T)E$, $S = Y - C$, for $Y > T$ and $C = Y$ otherwise. The Gini coefficient ... tion is R and the saving ratio from income is $\overline{S}/\overline{Y}$.

sumption function, leads to a saving function that is not materially different from relative wealth distribution in the ten cities and in Philadelphia.

The same income-saving-wealth patterns of density functions, leading to $R_Y < R_S \approx R_W$, exist with less exactitude in the cases of Milwaukee, Cleveland, and New York City. Finally, there is some evidence, based on tabulations for five and six income classes for all persons in the United States for each of the years 1866 through 1872, that the upper tail is of the Pareto type. Its extrapolation to the point Y_{Nc} can be coupled with a uniform distribution below Y_{Nc}. A consumption function with a threshold can be applied to the resulting income distribution in generating a saving distribution which fairly well duplicates the 1860 wealth distribution.

1. The Pareto-Rectangular Form. Suppose we have 1,000 persons with the top 473 conforming to a Pareto distribution from the highest income, Y_1, to the lowest income, Y_{473}, and the bottom 527 conforming to a rectangular (uniform) distribution from Y_{474} to Y_{1000}, where Y_{1000} is effectively zero. We need only the inverse of the Pareto slope, b, to generate the values in a recursive fashion.

$$Y_1$$
$$Y_2 = Y_1 \, (1/2)^b$$
$$Y_3 = Y_2 \, (2/3)^b$$
$$\cdot$$
$$\cdot$$
$$\cdot$$

$$Y_{Nc} = Y_{473} = Y_{472} \, (472/473)^b$$
$$Y_{474} = Y_{473} \, (1{,}001 - 474)/(1{,}002 - 474)$$
$$Y_{475} = Y_{474} \, (1{,}001 - 475)/(1{,}002 - 475)$$
$$\cdot$$
$$\cdot$$
$$\cdot$$

$$Y_{1000} = Y_{999} \, (1{,}001 - 1{,}000)/(1{,}002 - 1{,}000)$$

If $Y_1 = \$10{,}000$, $b = .9$, and $c = .473$ in the Pareto portion of 473 items, then $\overline{Y}$ is calculated to be $\$101$, the Gini coefficient, R_Y, is calculated to be .712, and $Y_{473}/\overline{Y}$ is .39. The relative proportion of persons and income for this distribution are shown in Table 10. These could be fairly good representations of income distribution in the ten cities in 1860. Some other possibilities are:

Y_1	b	$c = \dfrac{b}{1+b}$	N–Nc	$\overline{Y}$	R_Y	$\dfrac{Y_{Nc}}{Y}$	*Perhaps Realistic of Income Distribution of Males in:*
10,000	.9	.473	527	101	.712	.39	Ten cities, 1860
10,000	.7	.411	589	219	.582	.68	U.S., 1860
10,000	.4	.286	714	857	.422	1.21	U.S., 1970

Of crucial importance is the portion of the upper tail which is of the Pareto form. Fortunately there is a simple relationship between b and c which has appeal in the location of Y_{Nc}. We wish similar frequency density just above and below Y_{Nc} so that one distribution blends into the other. We then obviate any embarrassing discontinuity. This is achieved by letting $Y_{Nc} - Y_{Nc-1} = Y_{Nc+1} - Y_{Nc}$ in generating the N values. Thus $[Nc/(Nc-1)]^b = (N - Nc + 2)/(N - Nc + 1)$, and $c = b/(1+b)$ when N is large. The greater is upper-tail concentration, the greater is b. The greater is b, the greater is c and the proportion in the Pareto sector. If concentration were relatively weak as in the case of $b = .4$, then only 28.6 percent would be in the upper tail. If it were very strong, then the Pareto portion approaches 50 percent. The maximum b will not usually be greater than 1 since the limiting slope[15] for a continuous density function is 1.0.

	Share of Total Income in Range		
Percentile Range	$b = .9$	$b = .7$	$b = .4$
90–100	.635	.481	.296
80– 90	.112	.140	.159
70– 80	.070	.096	.128
60– 70	.051	.076	.111
50– 60	.040	.063	.093
40– 50	.033	.052	.077
30– 40	.026	.040	.059
20– 30	.018	.029	.043
10– 20	.011	.017	.025
0– 10	.004	.006	.009
	1.000	1.000	1.000

[15] An extreme plutocracy might exist with a b of 1.0 or 2.0 and $N = 1,000$. Although many are in the Pareto sector, only a few would have almost

A decrease in b over time would mean that middle classes would gain relative to lower and upper classes. Consider the lowest, middle, and top third of people, using percentile ranges and $c = b/(1 + b)$. In going from $b = .9$ to $b = .4$, one notes that the poorest one-third would still receive a relatively small share, the middle one-third would have a dramatic increase to a share almost one-third of aggregate income, while the top group would lose; the break-even percentile would be between P_{90} and P_{92} with the top 10 percent losing one-half of its former share.[16]

2. Income in 1970 and a Slope, b, of .4. A plotting of the Pareto curve for males in 1970 reveals an upper tail that is a straight line with an inverse Pareto slope of about .4. We accordingly generate a model for $b = .4$ using an $N = 1,000$—a number sufficient to yield the figures in Table 11. The relative distribution from the model is adjusted to have a mean equal to that for male income in 1970 of $7,537. It is seen that there is remarkable similarity between $N_{Y, \text{U.S. males, 1970}}$ and $N_{Y, b = .4}$. An alternative procedure for testing is to examine percentages of income held above various percentiles. Some of these results are:

N_Y	A_Y *for 1970*	A_Y *for b = .4*
.003	.029	.028
.022	.109	.113
.090	.245	.277
.267	.558	.543
.399	.710	.693
.547	.825	.825
.614	.890	.873
1.000	1.000	1.000

The same procedures were used in determining that the $b = .4$ model was quite appropriate in characterizing income in 1962, as reported by the Federal Reserve Board. The 1970 data are offered only as a preface.

---

all the income. It is a coincidence for $.9 \leqslant b \leqslant 1.0$ that $.473 \leqslant c \leqslant .499$ is similar to $P_{\$1}. = .489$ for the ten cities.

[16] This break-even point has been found for century changes in both Norway and Scotland. See Lee Soltow, "An Index of the Poor and Rich of Scotland, 1861-1961," *Scottish Journal of Political Economy* 18 (February 1971), p. 58.

TABLE 11   Income Distribution for the United States in 1970 and Pareto-Rectangular Models Adjusted to the Same Mean

	N_Y, *the Cumulative Proportion of Males above* Y		
		Pareto-Rectangular Models	
Y, *Income in 1970* (Lower Class Limit) (Dollars)	*Males in 1970*	b = .40 c = .286 N = 1,000	b = .45 c = .310 N = 1,000
50,000	.003	.004	.004
25,000	.022	.023	.028
15,000	.090	.083	.087
10,000	.267	.229	.213
8,000	.399	.376	.346
6,000	.547	.532	.510
5,000	.614	.610	.592
4,000	.676	.688	.674
3,000	.744	.766	.755
2,000	.813	.845	.837
1,000	.896	.922	.919
0	1.000	1.000	1.000
$\overline{Y}$	$7,537	$7,537	$7,537
R	.436	.422	.443

SOURCE: U.S., Department of Commerce, Bureau of the Census, *Current Population Reports*, Series P-60, No. 80, "Income in 1970 of Families and Persons in the United States" (Washington, D.C., October 1971), p. 89, income of males 14 and up with income. Computations of R were made using midpoints of classes to $15,000 and then, $19,000 and $75,000. This gives a mean of $7,810. The model for b = .40 also fits the income distribution for 1962 income presented in Dorothy S. Projector and Gertrude S. Weiss, *Survey of Financial Characteristics of Consumers* .(Washington, D.C.: Federal Reserve Board, 1966), pp. 151, 149.

3. Philadelphia Income in 1864 and b = .9.   Incomes for the year 1864 for Philadelphia, as reported on income tax returns, have been published in book form. They include net incomes where income is defined quite comprehensively.[17] I recorded all

[17] See G. S. Boutwell, *The Taxpayer's Manual* (1866), p. 156; Rufus S. Tucker, "The Distribution of Income Among Taxpayers in the United States, 1863-1935," *Quarterly Journal of Economics* 52 (1938): 547-67; J. B. Hill, "Civil War Income Tax," *Quarterly Journal of Economics* 8 (1894):414-52, 491, 498; Philadelphia incomes are given in *Income Tax of Residents of Philadelphia and Bucks County* (Philadelphia: 1865) and those for New York

incomes to $5,600 and every fifth page for those incomes from $600 to $5,599. The estimated total number of returns above $600 was 22,080 or 15 percent of the 145,172 males 20 years old and over in the county in 1860 (see Table 12).

A plotting was made of 648 points representing 580 incomes above $20,600 and 68 classes from $600 to $20,600. A definite Pareto straight line appears with a slope *b* of about .9, but it is important to note that it does not extend methodically to the highest income at $617,000. There is a definite leveling above $50,000 (*b* is but .48 among the top 140 persons). The decision was made to fit a least-squares line to the 648 points, minimizing those at the top by weighting each point by its class frequency. This gives the equation $\log Y = 8.5749 - .9242 \log N_Y, r^2 = .98$. It was further decided to use a slope *b* = .924 and, since *c* = .924/1.924 = .48 $\approx$ .5, to extend the distribution below $600 to include half the total population. This gives a $Y_{Nc} \approx$ $200; the remaining half of the cases below $200 were distributed evenly[18] in 10 classes with a constant class interval of $20.

The resulting distribution is shown in Table 12. The arithmetic mean of $715 is relatively large, presumably because of the high average incomes of the wealthy persons in Philadelphia. This income becomes $406 when adjusted to 1860 prices and the wealth-income ratio is $2,679/$406, or 6 to 1. The income figure is deemed to be too small on the basis of standards already suggested. This is due in part to the definition of income, which did not include salary from federal employment; rent from owner-occupied housing was allowed as a deduction. It is the *relative* distribution of income which will be important.

4. Milwaukee Income in 1864 and b = .85. Cards were punched for all of the reported 1,874 incomes above $600 in Milwaukee County in 1864. Analysis again reveals that the Pareto-curve pattern terminates among the top 1/100 of 1 percent of the population, above $30,000 in this case. There is a definite Pareto shape from $30,000 to $600 and the least-squares equation

---

are given in American News Co., *Income Record* (New York: 1865). Milwaukee County data are from the *Milwaukee Sentinel,* August 5, 1865, p. 1, and August 7, 1865, p. 1. Those for Cleveland and Cuyahoga County are from the *Cleveland Leader,* August 13, 1866, p. 4, columns 2-6. United States data are given in Lee Soltow, "Evidence on Income Inequality in the United States, 1866-1965," *Journal of Economic History* 29 (June 1969):279-86.

[18] If the $600 extension were continued until all were included, the lower limit would be $100 and the overall average would be raised by only $17.

TABLE 12   Philadelphia Income in 1864 Above $600 and Its Pareto-Rectangular Extension to $0

(N_Y and A_Y are the proportions of persons and income above Y)

Y, Income in 1864 (Lower Class Limit) (Dollars)	Philadelphia With Extension Below $600		Pareto-Rectangular Models Adjusted to the Philadelphia Mean			
			b = .90 c = .473 N = 1,000		b = .95 c = .487 N = 1,000	
	N_Y	A_Y	N_Y	A_Y	N_Y	A_Y
100,000	.00025	.060				
50,000	.00096	.13	.0016	.13	.0018	.17
25,000	.0030	.22	.0032	.20	.0036	.24
15,000	.0063	.31	.0056	.25	.0061	.30
10,000	.010	.37	.0088	.30	.0094	.35
5,000	.021	.47	.019	.40	.020	.45
2,000	.053	.61	.052	.54	.051	.58
1,000	.11	.72	.11	.65	.11	.68
600	.15	.77	.20	.75	.18	.76
200	.50	.99	.62	.95	.56	.94
0	1.00	1.00	1.00	1.00	1.00	1.00
$\bar{Y}$	$716		$716		$716	
R	.766		.713		.742	

SOURCE: *Income Tax Residents of Philadelphia and Bucks County* (Philadelphia, 1865). The b = .90 model was generated from an initial $Y_1 = 10^7$; this gives a $Y = 101,155$. Each value was then multiplied by a factor $716/101,155$.

has a slope, b, of .849 and R^2 = .987. This pattern has been extended below $600 to 50 percent of the cases at Y_{Nc} = $176. This is coupled with a uniform distribution below Y_{Nc} in giving $\overline{Y}$ = $458, R_Y = .702, and a population of 15, 897. The average income from the extrapolation is disappointingly small, but the relative distribution is highly suggestive of actual relative distribution.

5. *Cleveland in 1865 and New York City in 1863.* A sampling was made of the 1,577 reported incomes above $600 in Cleveland in 1865. Results were combined in 68 classes which had an inverse Pareto slope of .863. Frequencies for New York in 1863 have been published for 9 income classes. A fitting to the seven points from $600 to $100,600 gives a slope of .928.

6. *An Estimate of b = .9 for the Ten Cities.* It seems that a slope of .9 might be appropriate as the parameter from which to build an income distribution. This is about the average one would obtain by weighting the Philadelphia b by the population of eastern cities and the Cleveland and Milwaukee b's by the population in the western five cities. In Table 12, the Philadelphia example for 1864 indicates that a model with a b of .92 or .93 might be better in terms of showing income dispersion if one uses an N of 1,000 in the model. It should be borne in mind that income in 1864 relates to a time after the 1860 date we wish to simulate.

C. Distribution of Saving

We now construct a distribution of saving which is remarkably similar to wealth distribution in 1860. This is done by assuming that the consumption function is $C = T + (Y - T)^E$ for $Y > T$, where C is consumption, Y is income, T is a threshold income below which there is no saving, and E is the elasticity of consumption with respect to income above the threshold. The value of T is placed at the median so that 50 percent save, the case for the ten cities. We also place a value of E at .97 or .98, so that the saving will be about 20 percent of income. The results in Table 10 quite adequately duplicate the distribution of wealth, presumably by having relative saving determine relative wealth.

The model is deficient in not explicitly dealing with age-specific groups. It would have been more challenging had we had an income distribution for each age group. Each in turn would have had its own consumption function and saving. Saving at various ages would be used to estimate long-run saving, and thus wealth accumulation at various ages. These groups would be combined, using population weights, in a grand wealth distribution for the ten cities. It is not possible to construct this model, since income data are not available for individual age groups. The author has constructed an interesting model of this type but assumptions about b_{age}, c_{age}, T_{age}, and E_{age} are questionable.

Our purpose has been to duplicate wealth distribution from income distribution, considering a saving function. The empirical evidence indicates that we have succeeded, and we shall now turn the procedure around.

D. Income Derived from Wealth Distribution

Wealth distributions for specific age groups are available. This means that it is possible to say something about income distribution where age is explicitly considered. The method we employ involves adjustment of wealth to saving and saving to income: (1) The wealth value of each individual in the ten-city sample is transformed into a saving figure, using $S = W/(age - 19)$. This involves the assumption that an individual saves the same amount in each of his adult years. Empirical verification of the reasonableness of this assumption has already been presented in the form of regression equations in wealth and age. Results of the transformation give:

Proportion of Men (N_X)	Wealth Distribution, $W = \$2,346$; $R_W = .932$ (A_W)	Saving Distribution, $S=W/(age-19)$, $S = \$122$; $R_S = .917$ (A_S)
.001	.159	.157
.002	.224	.240
.005	.335	.368
.010	.452	.475
.020	.592	.589
.050	.769	.755
.10	.889	.875
.20	.968	.959
.30	.991	.988
.40	.998	.998
.50	1.000	1.000

The saving average is about 5 percent of the wealth average. (2) Each individual income value was determined from $Y = S + C = S + T + (Y - T)^E$ for $Y > T$. Those with zero wealth were assigned a $C = Y$ value between 0 and T in order to insure a uniform income distribution. Computer runs were made for various T and E and an accurate approximation method was used in determining Y from S. Some of these runs give results of:

	T=0	T=100	T=200	T=300
E=.96				
Mean=Y	$432	$506	$581	$655
S/Y	.28	.24	.21	.19
R_Y	.897	.799	.726	.669
E=.95				
Mean=$\overline{Y}$	$366	$440	$514	$588
S/Y	.33	.28	.237	.21
R_Y	.896	.783	.703	.643

The Kuznets income-saving requirement that $\overline{Y}$ be about $500 and that S/Y be about 20 percent means that income distribution probably had a concentration coefficient of about .70 to .73. Interesting income distributions have been obtained for specific age and urban-rural groups, but they are subject to assumptions of T and E.

E. The Saving and Income of Social Classes

What does the procedure for measuring saving and income from wealth tell us when we apply it to the Warner-Binomial social classes of the first section of the paper? Saving classified by binomial-wealth categories is not quite as strongly confined to the upper classes. Younger individuals with less wealth may save as much as older persons in higher wealth classes. Income is even more weakly related to social class as previously defined. One must have income and consumption to subsist, even though he does not save. It is not surprising that Warner found that amount of income was somewhat tenuously related to social class in his multiple regression equations.[19] We conclude with estimates of the

[19] Warner, Meeker, and Eells, *Social Class in America*, pp. 180-81.

various variables (Table 13). It is the upper social classes which have had the wealth and have done the saving in our urban society. Had it not been necessary for have-nots to consume all of their income, wealth distribution might have been income distribution and urban inequality would not have been so glaring.

F. Summary

A frequency distribution of wealth among males 20 years old and older in ten large cities in the United States in 1860 has been presented. It has been determined that there was extensive inequality, since the Gini coefficient of concentration was .92. Among these adult males, whose average age was about 35, was a propertied group constituting 48.6 percent of the population; 51.4 percent were essentially propertyless. This latter proportion is about that found by W. Lloyd Warner for the lower class in Yankee City in the 1930s. The probability of remaining property-less in a given year of adult experience was about $(.957) = (.514)^{1/(35-20)}$. The probability of escape averaged 4.3 percent. It is found that the binomial probability distribution $B(X,N,P) = B(X,35 - 20, .043)$ yields a distribution of social classes very similar to that found by Warner for the lower-middle, upper-middle, lower-upper, and upper-upper classes. It is further determined that $B(cX^{5.6}, 35 - 20, .043)$ is a good representation of the 1860 distribution of wealth. The model holds well for specific age groups. Thus, knowledge of the proportion of people with no wealth is central and consistent with describing distribution among those having wealth. The magnitude of the lower class seems to govern the number of higher classes; low mobility means few classes and very large relative inequality of wealth.

A second model has been based on how saving, established from a Pareto-rectangular income distribution, could quantitatively determine the 1860 wealth distribution. Models of incomes distributed in Pareto fashion above the median and in rectangular fashion below the median seem to fit the available empirical data for all males in 1970 and for upper income groups in the 1860s. The model with an inverse Pareto slope of .9 can be coupled with an orthodox consumption function in deriving a density function of saving whose relative distribution is quite similar to that of wealth distribution in the ten cities in 1860. This procedure is

TABLE 13 Wealth, Saving, and Income Shares of Social Classes in the Ten Cities in 1860

Class Rung, X (1)	Cumulative Frequency, Nx (2)	Cumulative Percent of Wealth, Aw (3)	Cumulative Percent of Saving, As (4)	Cumulative Percent of Income, Ay (5)	(6)
7	.000001	—	—	.007	.008
6	.000022	.017	.014	.033	.036
5	.000320	.086	.059	.124	.137
4	.003120	.276	.207	.354	.391
3	.025500	.639	.514	.679	.735
2	.146000	.938	.911	.900	.929
1	.486000	1.000	1.000	.900	.929
0	1.000000	1.000	1.000	1.000	1.000
Mean		$2,346	$122	$514	$543

NOTE:

(2) These are obtained from the W limits of Table 8. There is bunching.

(4) Each sample item is transformed with $S = W/(age - 19)$.

(5) The equation $Y = S + T + (Y - T)E$ is employed for $Y > T$, where $E = .95$ and $T = 200$.

(6) Here $E = .97$ and $T = 150$.

SOURCE: See Table 8.

elaborated further in making estimates of saving and income for Warner-Binomial social classes. It is the relatively small number in the upper classes who accumulate the wealth, and who have performed almost all of the saving function in American urban society of the past.

CHAPTER 10

The Distribution of Wealth in Britain in the 1960s—the Estate Duty Method Reexamined

A. B. Atkinson
University of Essex

There seems little doubt that the distribution of wealth in Britain is highly concentrated; however, while this has been widely accepted, there has been remarkably little research in recent years to determine the degree of inequality with precision. The only statistics published for the 1960s are those prepared by the Inland Revenue, and these do not set out to cover the entire distribution. Moreover, no attempt has been made to reconcile these estimates with the National Balance Sheet data. This lack of interest is the more surprising in view of the fact that the estate method was pioneered in Britain, and that in the past there have been major studies of the size distribution of wealth by (among others) Clay [1], Daniels and Campion [2], Campion [3], Langley [4], [5], and Lydall and Tipping [6].

This paper describes the first results of a new investigation intended to provide more reliable estimates of the distribution of wealth in Britain in the 1960s.[1] The estimates presented here are based on the estate duty returns, but are adjusted in a number of major respects to take account of the deficiencies of this source. The paper builds on the work of earlier investigators, but departs from them in its extensive use of National Balance Sheet data

In preparing the revised version of this paper, I have been greatly helped by the comments of the discussant, as well as by the detailed criticism of the Statistics and Intelligence Division, Inland Revenue.

[1] The research is being undertaken at the University of Essex by Alan Harrison and myself and is supported by the Social Science Research Council. The full results of the study will be reported in a forthcoming monograph, *The Distribution of Wealth in Great Britain,* to which the reader is referred for further details.

which were not previously available and in its analysis of the sensitivity of the results to the different assumptions made.

The plan of the paper is as follows: Section I describes the estate duty method as presently employed by the Inland Revenue and examines the principal problems connected with this approach. Section II sets out the alternative approach to the use of the estate duty data adopted in this paper and presents new estimates on a more comprehensive basis for the year 1968. Section III examines the shape of the wealth distribution indicated by the estimates and the extent to which it may be represented by particular functions such as the Pareto and log-normal distributions. Section IV compares the estimates presented here with those prepared by the Inland Revenue and summarizes the main results.

I. THE ESTATE DUTY METHOD AND THE INLAND REVENUE STATISTICS

The estate duty method has a long history and was used by Baxter to estimate total personal wealth as early as 1869. Since then, the method has been refined, notably by the use of age-related multipliers pioneered by Mallet [8], and has been applied to the estimation of the size distribution of wealth by Clay [1] and subsequent writers. This section examines the use which has been made of this method in recent years by the Inland Revenue.

Since 1961, the Inland Revenue has published estimates of the distribution of wealth based on the estate duty method. As a result we now have an "official" series for the wealth distribution for the years 1960-70.[2] The Gini coefficients published by the Inland Revenue indicate that wealth in Britain is highly concentrated: in 1968, for example, the coefficient was .68, which is over twice that for the distribution of income.[3] As the Inland Revenue recognizes, however, there are a number of major problems with the use of estate duty data and, as a result, their estimates may provide an incomplete picture of the distribution of wealth in Britain. The most serious of these problems are described below.

---

[2] See, for example, *Inland Revenue Statistics*, 1972, Table 86.

[3] See Stark [9]. It should be noted that the wealth data relates to individuals, whereas the income data relates to tax units. This is unlikely, however, to explain this very large difference.

A. *Incomplete Coverage of Estates– "Missing" People*

The estate duty data covers only those estates which come to the notice of the estate duty office and, as a result, over half the estates are not included. Those omitted are those cases where no property has been left, or where the estate is not liable for estate duty[4] and the assets are of a type which may be transferred without probate: (1) property to which title can pass by delivery: e.g. cash, personal possessions, and household goods; (2) property where the owner can nominate a person to whom the asset should be transferred: e.g. industrial life assurance policies; and (3) property covered by statutory exemptions (Administration of Estates [Small Payments] Act, 1965)–e.g., sums up to £500 held in National Savings, buildings societies, cooperative societies and friendly societies. It is clear from this list that none of the people excluded from the Inland Revenue estimates are likely to possess large amounts of wealth; the wealth holders who are missing from the official estimates almost certainly belong to the lowest ranges.

In the main part of its work, the Inland Revenue makes no allowance for these "missing" wealth holders: the Gini coefficients quoted earlier, for example, are based only on those covered by the returns. In its most recent report, the Inland Revenue has presented a second set of Gini coefficients, based on the alternative extreme assumption that the remainder of the population has no wealth at all. As one would expect, the Gini coefficients are considerably higher: .87 in 1968, as opposed to .68. However, neither of these extreme assumptions is adequate for our purposes. To ignore the existence of half the adult population is clearly wrong, but at the same time, it is not reasonable to suppose that they possess no wealth at all. It is therefore necessary to investigate more closely the possible wealth of those who do not appear in the Inland Revenue's tables. An attempt to do this was made by Lydall and Tipping [6], who based their estimates for the whole population on the extrapolation (apparently by eye) of the estate duty data below the exemption limit, and on the results of the 1954 Oxford savings survey.[5] Since the savings survey has

---

[4] The exemption level was £3,000 at the beginning of the 1960s. It was increased to £4,000 in 1962, £5,000 in 1963, and £10,000 in 1969.

[5] Adjustments for the wealth of this group were also made by earlier writers, but since the estate duty exemption limit was very much lower (£100 until 1946) the amounts involved were smaller.

not been repeated, the second of these approaches is not open to us;[6] we do, however, have available the National Balance Sheet data used by Revell [10], which allow us to form an estimate of the likely holdings of the missing population. This balance-sheet approach will provide the main basis for the estimates described below, but in Section III we consider the alternative approach of estimating the holding of lower wealth groups by extrapolating wealth distributions fitted to the upper ranges.

B. *Incomplete Coverage of Wealth— "Missing" Wealth*

In addition to the wealth of those not covered by the Inland Revenue statistics, there are other important elements of "missing" wealth, which arise from the provisions in the estate duty law allowing wealth to be transferred in certain circumstances without duty being paid. As it is put by the Inland Revenue, "certain elements are omitted because no duty is payable on them either because of special exemptions or because they fall outside the scope of estate duty law." The most important items excluded are: (1) property settled on a surviving spouse (who has no power to dispose of the capital), which is exempt on the death of this spouse; (2) property held under discretionary trusts (exempt before the 1969 Finance Act); (3) items treated as estates by themselves, which do not appear if they do not exceed the exemption limit;[7] (4) growing timber, which is not aggregated with the rest of the estate and on which duty is not paid until the timber is sold; and (5) assets such as annuities and pensions, which disappear on death.

The Inland Revenue makes no attempt to adjust its estimates for this missing wealth, and as a result, the levels of wealth may be seriously understated. In their estimates for 1954, Lydall and Tipping made some very approximate adjustments and added to their total of £40,000 million for personal wealth, a further £2,000 million for pension funds, £3,000 million for property settled on a surviving spouse, and £1,000 million for discretionary

---

[6] Although it is hoped that at a later stage in the investigation we may be able to make use of data collected by Professors Abel-Smith and Townsend in their survey of living standards in 1968–69.

[7] This applied, for example, to certain life assurance policies and property settled otherwise than by the deceased, when the rest of the property did not exceed £10,000.

trusts. In this paper, we attempt to make more accurate adjustments, based on the National Balance Sheet data and with a series of assumptions about the allocation of the missing wealth by ranges.

C. *Choice of Mortality Multipliers*

The early discussions of the estate duty method demonstrated clearly that the choice of mortality multipliers is of crucial significance. (The overall multipliers used in the early estimates ranged from 25 to 65, with corresponding variations in the estimate of total personal wealth.) It is, therefore, important to examine the sources from which the multipliers are derived and the consequences of alternative assumptions. The Inland Revenue, following earlier investigators, uses mortality multipliers adjusted for social class (which is assumed to be correlated with wealth): (1) for estates over £3,000, those relating to social classes I and II (broadly the managerial and professional classes); and (2) for estates under £3,000, rates midway between those for social classes I and II and those for the population as a whole.[8] The relationship between these social-class mortality rates and that for the general population is obtained by relating the deaths recorded for the years 1959-63 to the population at risk, as enumerated in the Census of Population of 1961. This procedure suffers from a number of drawbacks; in particular, from the fact that there are serious discrepancies between the occupational statements at death registration and those at the Census. This has led Revell to reject this source and to adopt the alternative approach of using the mortality experience of life assurance offices as a basis for deriving estate multipliers (as used in the United States by Lampman [7]). In Section II, this question is considered at greater length and results are presented on a variety of assumptions.

D. *Sampling Problems*

The fundamental assumption underlying the estate duty method is that those dying in a given year may be regarded as a representative sample of the living population. This assumption is

---

[8]   The division has been made at £5,000 since 1970.

clearly open to question, and there are a number of reasons why it may lead to biased estimates of the size distribution. In particular, those with poorer health (and shorter life expectancy) are more likely to have taken steps to reduce their estate duty liability than others in the same age-sex group. The effect of such action depends on the form which avoidance takes.[9] In certain cases, such as the deathbed purchase of agricultural property (which bears a lower rate of duty), the full value of wealth is still reported in the estate statistics; in others, the effect of avoidance has already been discussed under the heading of missing wealth (e.g., settled property). One method which may lead to biased estimates, however, is the dispersion of property through gifts *inter vivos* (which are exempt from any tax if the donor lives for a further seven years). If both donors and recipients had the same life expectancy as others in their age-sex group, gifts would not lead to any understatement, since the wealth would appear in the estates of those recipients who died in a given period. However, there are good reasons to doubt whether this is likely to be so. As it was put by Lampman: ". . . it might seem reasonable to assume that persons, particularly at older ages, with shorter than average life expectancy for their age group, would be more likely to be donors than those with longer expectancies" ([7], p. 68n). There is no firm evidence to support this view, but it appears highly plausible. If it is correct, and if gifts are made largely by the wealthy (to avoid duty), then the degree of inequality is understated, although it is very difficult to make any estimate of the likely magnitude of this effect.[10]

In addition to the difficulties arising from the method by which the sample is selected, there are the problems of sampling error. For certain classes, particularly the largest estates and the youngest age groups, the number of cases is extremely small: in 1969–70, for example, only one man leaving an estate of over £200,000 died between the ages of 35 and 45. The Inland Revenue has attempted to reduce the error involved by: (1)

[9] *Evasion* of estate duty is not taken into account here. As is pointed out by Revell: "most people would probably agree that this is at a low level in Britain—if only because the legal methods of avoidance are so many" ([10], p. 112).

[10] A factor working in the opposite direction is that where the donor dies within seven years, the gift is included in his estate and hence may be counted twice.

combining the observations for the largest wealth groups for a number of years to produce a smoother series; and (2) in the case of other wealth groups, combining observations across age groups and applying a combined multiplier. The rationale for these adjustments is far from obvious. The reason for concern is not that errors may be introduced through variation in the total number of deaths in a particular age group, since this would be reflected in an exactly offsetting variation in the mortality multiplier. The problem arises with the distribution of estates among wealth classes. This suggests that any combination of observations before applying the multipliers should *not* be between age groups (which would introduce errors arising from variation in the overall mortality rate for each group) but between estate classes. In view of this, the Inland Revenue approach is not followed here and no adjustment is made for sampling error apart from the grouping of estate classes.

E. Method of Valuation

The valuation of assets in the estate data was discussed by Revell ([10], Chap. 4) in the context of National Balance Sheets, and he concluded that "in general the valuation of items for estate duty is just what we need—a valuation at market prices." He does not, however, bring out the ambiguities involved in such a definition for certain types of asset.[11] His own interpretation is framed in terms of valuation on a "going concern" basis, but in the case of household goods (for example) this could be very different from the price obtainable on the secondhand market. It may therefore be helpful to distinguish between a "going concern" value and a realization value (through sale or borrowing power). It is not clear which of the bases would be more appropriate for our purposes,[12] and although we shall consider only the former ("going concern" value), ideally both should be examined.

One class of assets where the problems of valuation are particularly acute is that of life policies and pension rights. In the estate duty statistics, life assurance policies on the deceased's own life are valued at the sum assured, whereas, in the hands of the

[11] This passage owes a great deal to Kathleen Langley's perceptive comments.

[12] I do not agree with Langley that a realization basis is clearly preferable.

living, they are worth less than this amount (even as a "going concern"). On the other hand, annuities may not appear at all, and the rights to occupational pensions are not included apart from any death benefit (and, in certain schemes, this may be held in trust). On a realization basis, no allowance should be made for pension rights (since one cannot in general borrow on the strength of these rights), and in the case of life policies the appropriate valuation—as has been suggested by Langley [5]—is the surrender value. However, Revell has pointed out that these methods of valuation are "inappropriate for the holder viewed as a 'going concern'. . . . For this there is no alternative but the present value of the future income stream or capital payment." In what follows, this method of valuation is adopted as far as possible. In the case of life policies and funded pension schemes, it is based on the total value of life and pension funds; in the case of unfunded pension schemes, the valuation is necessarily more approximate.[13] The detailed basis for the estimates is discussed further in Section II. The methods followed parallel those of Revell in his work on the National Balance Sheets, but there is the additional problem of allocating the assets by ranges of total wealth.

Summary

The most important problems connected with the Inland Revenue approach have been outlined above,[14] and Table 1 summarizes the main differences between its treatment and the approach adopted here. As will be clear, this paper is particularly concerned with the sensitivity of the results to the assumptions made, and it is hoped that it will provide a guide to those areas where further research is most needed.

---

[13] No account is taken here of the value of rights to state pensions or other state benefits. This follows earlier studies.

[14] A number of other problems have not been discussed, such as that stemming from the fact that estates only appear in the statistics with a delay (see Langley [5], pp. 2–3). It is assumed here that estates coming to the notice of the estate duty office in a given tax year relate to deaths in the preceding calendar year (the same assumption as that made by the Inland Revenue), but this is not entirely satisfactory.

TABLE 1 Comparison of Methods

	Inland Revenue	*Approach Adopted Here*
A. Incomplete coverage of estates	Estates not coming to notice of Estate Duty Office are omitted	All adult population included Wealth of missing adults estimated from: (1) National Balance Sheet data (Section II) (2) Extrapolation of wealth distribution (Section III)
B. Incomplete coverage of wealth	No adjustments made	Adjustments using National Balance Sheet data and assumptions about allocation by ranges (Section II)
C. Mortality multipliers	Based on Census of Population data	Alternative approaches based on Census of Population and life office data (Section II)
D. Sampling errors	Age groups are combined and observations for largest wealth groups smoothed over time	No adjustments made to basic data
E. Valuation	No adjustments made	Adjustments to a "going concern" basis (Section II)

II. NEW ESTIMATES FOR 1968

A. *Choice of Mortality Multipliers*

The choice of the multipliers to be applied to the estate data is clearly of central importance, and it is surprising that no attempt has been made to assess the sensitivity of the results to the assumptions made. In this section, we examine the two main sources of data—the Census of Population and the life office mortality investigation—and the differences in the results obtained. As can be seen from Table 2, the mortality rates vary considerably. The first two columns show the rates used by Lydall

TABLE 2   Social-Class Mortality Rates as Percentage of General Mortality Rates

(England and Wales [males])

		Census Data	
Age Group	Lydall and Tipping, 1951[a]	Registrar General, 1959-63; Social Classes I and II Combined	Life Office Data — Revell, 1953-58
15-19	–	92.6	98.7
20-24	96.4	76.1	
25-34	75.5	72.6	72.9
35-44	74.2	72.4	68.3
45-54	80.6	76.9	69.7
55-64	83.7	83.7	66.8
65-74	87.5	92.5	71.8
75-84	91.8	–	77.4
85 and over		–	84.5

SOURCES: Lydall and Tipping [6], Table A; Revell [10], Table 5.4; Registrar General for England and Wales, *Census 1961: Decennial Supplement, Occupational Mortality* (H.M.S.O), Table 3A(i).

[a] This data has been adjusted; see text.

and Tipping, whose approach has been followed by the Inland Revenue, and the rates derived from the census of 1961; the third column shows the life office data used by Revell. The differences are particularly marked in the case of those aged 45 and over, the life office mortality rates being 20 percent lower in some cases.

The Census of Population data suffer from a number of serious shortcomings for the purpose at hand:

1. As noted earlier, the data on deaths and on the population at risk are obtained from different sources, and there are major discrepancies between the occupational statements in the two sources. This has been demonstrated in successive censuses by special matching exercises, which in 1961 showed that only 63 percent of men were assigned to the same occupation unit on both occasions, and that the social class differed in 17 percent of cases surveyed. The Registrar General himself commented that "the lack of agreement between the occupation given at census and that at death reduces considerably the reliability of the analysis. . . . the

net discrepancies . . . are so large that the mortality estimates must be affected by them."

2. A substantial number of people (7 percent) were recorded as "unoccupied" in the Census but very few were so recorded at death (0.5 percent). As a result, the mortality rate for all social classes is overstated, particularly at older ages.

3. The analysis of female mortality does not include widows.[15]

4. The use of the Census data is based on the assumption of a high degree of correlation between social class and wealth, but this association is clearly far from perfect.

In their estimates for 1954, Lydall and Tipping made allowance for point 1 by reducing the estimates of "upper class" mortality by the percentage overrecording indicated by the matching study; and made approximate adjustments for point 2 by allocating the unoccupied proportionately to all social classes. The Inland Revenue has followed them in making this adjustment but otherwise has used the data as it stands.[16]

Revell considered the deficiencies of the Census data so serious as to render it "quite useless" for the derivation of estate multipliers and he accordingly rejected it in favor of the life office data. This latter is derived from the Continuous Mortality Investigation, based on the mortality experience of life offices in the United Kingdom and covering those accepted for ordinary life and endowment policies at standard rates of premium. As Revell points out, this source is attractive in that the population is known throughout, so that there is no problem of incorrect classification. He also argues that those holding life assurance policies are likely to be representative of wealth holders appearing in the estate duty returns, since life policies are subject to estate duty.[17]

There are, however, two major difficulties with the life office data: the problem of "selection" by health and the inadequate coverage of female lives. The first stems from the fact that

[15] Related to this point is the variation in mortality rates with marital status; see Smith [11].

[16] It should also be noted that the Inland Revenue makes no allowance for differential trends in mortality over time, and that it maintained the £3,000 division in applying the social-class multipliers throughout the 1960s, despite the fact that the number of estates above this level approximately doubled.

[17] Industrial branch claims are largely paid without probate, but these are not covered by the Continuous Mortality Investigation.

acceptance for life assurance at standard premiums depends on evidence of health. As a result, the data do not cover those excluded on account of ill health and hence the social-class multipliers are biased upwards. The likely extent of this bias is discussed by Revell and he makes corrections covering those excluded from the life office data. The only light which can be thrown on the second problem is the Continuous Mortality Investigation of male and female annuitants, which indicates that for the older age groups the ratio of female to male mortality is broadly the same as that for the general population. The assumption that this is true for all ages is adopted by Revell, although he describes it as "definitely *faute de mieux.*"

From this brief discussion, it is clear that neither the Census data nor data derived from the Continuous Mortality Investigation are ideal for our purposes. Instead of making any attempt to weigh up the relative advantages and disadvantages of the two sources, the procedure followed is to consider the results obtained with the following range of assumptions:

1. *Assumption A1.* Social-class multipliers based on the Census data adjusted in the same way as Lydall and Tipping (as employed by the Inland Revenue)

2. *Assumption A2.* Social-class multipliers based on the life office data (using the mortality ratios given in [10], Table 5.4) for estates of £3,000 and over, general mortality multipliers below this level

3. *Assumption A3.* General mortality multipliers

The multipliers described above have been applied to the estate data for 1968.[18] (The choice of this year was based on the availability of data required to make the balance sheet adjustments described below.) Table 3 summarizes the results for assumptions A1, A2 and A3 covering the adult population, where adult is defined as 18 and over.[19]

---

[18] The basic estate data and a number of supplementary analyses were made available by the Inland Revenue Statistics and Intelligence Division, and I am very grateful to them for their assistance with the investigation. They are not responsible in any way for the use to which the data has been put.

[19] Any definition of the adult population is essentially arbitrary, but 18 was chosen on the grounds that it is both the age of majority and likely to correspond to the average age at which children become financially independent of their parents. The use of 18 may be compared to that of 15 by the Inland Revenue, 20 by Lydall and Tipping, and 25 by Daniels and Campion, Campion, and Langley.

TABLE 3 Estimates Using Multipliers A1, A2, and A3: Great Britain, 1968

	A1: Census Multipliers		A2: Life Office Multipliers		A3: General Multipliers	
	Percent of Population	*Percent of Wealth*	*Percent of Population*	*Percent of Wealth*	*Percent of Population*	*Percent of Wealth*
Not covered by estate duty returns	56.126	—	55.847	—	61.480	—
Cumulative percentage above:						
£ 1,000	30.229	96.6	31.730	97.3	26.096	96.3
5,000	9.492	73.2	11.173	76.0	7.947	72.5
10,000	3.989	56.1	4.735	58.5	3.362	55.7
15,000	2.415	47.8	2.880	49.8	2.040	47.5
20,000	1.641	41.8	1.970	43.6	1.392	41.5
25,000	1.282	38.0	1.535	39.6	1.086	37.7
50,000	0.467	25.8	0.559	26.7	0.396	25.5
100,000	0.154	16.5	0.182	17.0	0.129	16.2
200,000	0.049	10.5	0.057	10.7	0.040	10.2

The first difference between the results concerns the proportion of the population not covered by the estate .duty returns. The "missing" population ranges from 61 percent with the general mortality multiplier to 56 percent with the social-class multipliers. The results for assumptions A1 and A2 are in fact very close and suggest that the proportion not covered is unlikely to fall below 50 percent on any assumptions. The second difference concerns the shape of the upper part of the distribution. In general terms, it appears that the use of social-class multipliers (as opposed to general multipliers) leads to a lower estimate of the share of top wealth holders. Comparing assumption A1 with the general mortality case (A3), the share in total personal wealth of those above £200,000 is higher, but the number in this group is also increased. Figure 1 shows that the net effect is that the Lorenz curve for assumptions A1 and A2 lies inside that for assumption A3, and that with social-class multipliers A2, the share of the top 1 percent may be 3½ percent lower than with the general mortality multipliers.

If we turn to a comparison of the two social-class multipliers, the differences are less marked: in terms of the share of the top 1 percent, for example, the difference is some 1 percent of total wealth. This difference is perhaps surprisingly small in view of the substantial differences in the multipliers for certain age groups. It should be noted that the differences between the two estimates are largest in proportionate terms at the top wealth levels (the top one-half percent and above) and that the life office multipliers give considerably higher estimates of the number of top wealth holders:

Numbers above (cumulative)	A1	A2
£1 million	610	714
£500,000	4,917	5,572
£200,000	18,835	22,178

B. Relationship to Balance Sheet Data

The estimates of personal wealth derived from the estate duty statistics are, as we have seen in Section I, deficient in three major respects: the property of "small" wealth holders is not covered, certain types of wealth (such as settled property) are excluded, and certain assets are not valued in an appropriate way (such as

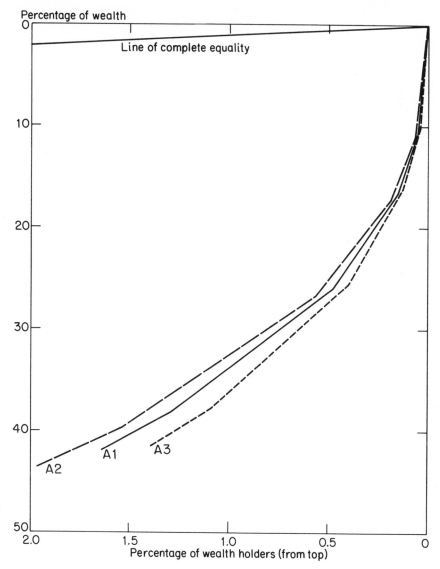

FIGURE 1: Upper Part of Lorenz Curve With Multipliers A1-A3

pension rights). These deficiencies cause the estimates of personal wealth derived by blowing up the estate data to fall considerably short of those reached by National Balance Sheet methods. The existence of the deficiencies may be illustrated by comparing the estimated holdings of government liabilities for which the totals in issue are known. All figures are in millions of pounds.

	Estate duty estimate			*Known total*[20]
	A1	A2	A3	
Unquoted U.K. government				
securities	3,157	3,500	2,688	4,293
Savings bank deposits	2,878	3,039	2,489	4,040

Even with the life office multipliers, the estimates for these assets fall considerably short of the known totals and adjustments are clearly necessary.

The relationship between estate duty estimates and National Balance Sheet totals was discussed by Revell with particular reference to 1961. In that year, the estimate of total personal wealth made by him on the basis of estate data was £63.9 billion, whereas the corresponding balance sheet total was £77.6 billion. The main sources of this discrepancy are shown in Table 4. Although the assets and liabilities listed there do not exhaust those for which there were discrepancies, they account for the main part of the difference; and in what follows, attention is focused on these categories. It must, of course, be recognized that the discrepancies may arise as much through errors in the balance sheet totals as through inadequacies of the estate duty estimates. In certain cases, the balance sheet totals for the personal sector are obtained as residuals and the divergence from the estate estimates may simply reflect errors in the totals for other sectors. In view of this, the policy adopted here has been to make adjustments only to those assets where there is an a priori reason to expect wealth to be missing from the estate duty estimates. In the case of quoted company shares, for example, there was no clear reason for the discrepancy between the estate duty estimates and Revell's figures obtained from register surveys, and no adjustment is made here. Moreover, it should be noted that the balance sheet totals used in this study are, in nearly all cases, classified by Revell as A (very reliable) or B (fairly reliable). It must, however, be borne in mind that the balance sheet totals quoted in Table 4 correspond to values at December 31, whereas the estate duty estimates are a weighted average for the year as a whole. If the value of assets is rising, then the discrepancy can be partly explained in this way. In view of this, the balance sheet totals have, wherever possible, been

---

[20] In each case allowance has been made for nonpersonal holdings. The total is an average for the year.

TABLE 4   Discrepancy Between Estate Duty Estimates and National Balance Sheet, 1961

(£ billion)

	Estate Duty	Balance Sheet	Adjust- ment
Assets:			
Unquoted U.K. government	3.4	4.2	1
Savings bank deposits	2.9	3.2	2
Building society deposits	3.6	3.1	3
Household goods, etc.	2.1	4.0	4
Trade assets	2.2	4.4	5
Exempt settled property	0	1.4	6
Expectant interests	2.5	0	6
Quoted U.K. shares	12.1	13.9	7
Unquoted U.K. shares	3.1	5.4	7
Life policies and pension rights	7.2	13.5	8
Land and buildings[a]	13.0	19.8	9
Liabilities:			
House mortagages	1.2	4.9	8
Debts	2.9	4.9	10
Net worth	63.9	77.6	

SOURCE: Revell [10], Table 7.1. This excludes holdings by overseas residents.
[a] The liability "other deductions from landed property" is subtracted from this item.

based on a weighted average of the figures for different dates in the year.[21]

Bearing these points in mind, we may use the balance sheet totals to make adjusted estimates for 1968. The first stage involves the construction of balance sheet totals; the basic method follows that of Revell and is described in the appendix. The second stage is one not undertaken by Revell and involves the allocation of missing wealth by ranges. In this allocation, two main factors are taken into account. First, in certain cases the nature of the asset suggests that it is likely to be held in certain wealth ranges: for example, those types of property covered by the Administration

[21] The weights employed correspond to the proportion of deaths in each period.

of Estates Act. Secondly, in a number of cases the discrepancies arise through differences in the method of valuation (e.g. physical assets) and the procedure followed is to increase the holding in each range by an appropriate factor. For this purpose, it is necessary to know the asset composition by wealth range, and use is made of unpublished tabulations provided by the Inland Revenue. Even allowing for these two factors, however, it is necessary to make a number of assumptions, and the practice followed has been to make four types of assumption:

1. *Assumption B1.* No adjustment
2. *Assumption B2.* Lower bound to inequality—where wealth is allocated as far as reasonable to lowest wealth groups
3. *Assumption B3.* A central estimate—inevitably arbitrary but a "best guess"
4. *Assumption B4.* Upper bound to inequality—where wealth is allocated as far as reasonable to upper wealth groups

The precise assumptions are described in greater detail in the appendix.[22]

The results obtained with these four assumptions in the case of the Census of Population multipliers are shown in Table 5. It is immediately clear that the outcome differs considerably according to which assumption is made: for example, the share of the bottom group ranges from 3.4 percent (no adjustment) to 13.2 percent (adjustment B2). Where the wealth is allocated as far as reasonable to the lowest wealth groups (B2), the effect of the adjustment is to shift the Lorenz curve inward at all points; but in the upper-bound case (B4), the Lorenz curve shifts outward at all points above £1,000. In the case of the central estimate (B3) the Lorenz curve is shifted outward for those in the top 0.5 percent and inward below this level. If anything, the Lorenz curve for this case is closer to assumption B2 than to assumption B4. In general, the results suggest the critical importance of the allocation of missing wealth by ranges and the need for further research designed to narrow the bounds placed on the allocation.

Table 6 shows the results obtained with the central assumption B3 and the range of mortality multipliers A1 through A3. We should expect that where the multipliers applied are lower, larger

[22] One further difficulty which should be mentioned here is that the adjustments for missing wealth may change the ranking by size of holding. No allowance has been made for this in the estimates presented below.

TABLE 5   Sensitivity to Assumptions B1–B4: Case of Census Multipliers

Range of Wealth^a	Percentage of Population	Assumption B1: Percentage of Total Wealth	Assumption B2: Percentage of Total Wealth	Assumption B3: Percentage of Total Wealth	Assumption B4: Percentage of Total Wealth
Below £1,000	70.17	3.4	13.2	9.2	4.1
Cumulative percentage above:					
£ 1,000	29.83	96.6	86.8	90.8	95.9
5,000	9.30	73.0	64.9	69.3	75.4
10,000	3.91	56.0	50.3	53.9	60.0
15,000	2.37	47.7	43.3	46.3	52.1
20,000	1.61	41.7	38.2	40.7	46.3
25,000	1.26	37.9	35.0	37.4	42.8
50,000	0.46	25.7	24.2	26.2	30.9
100,000	0.15	16.5	15.8	17.4	20.9
200,000	0.05	10.5	10.2	11.3	13.7

NOTE: The population figures and the "unadjusted" estimates (B1) differ from those in Table 3 in that allowance has been made for Northern Ireland and the holdings of overseas residents. See the appendix.
^a The ranges relate to wealth *before* adjustment.

TABLE 6 Adjusted Estimates: Assumptions B1 and B3 and Different Multipliers

	Assumption A1: Census Multipliers			Assumption A2: Life Office Multipliers			Assumption A3: General Mortality Multipliers		
		Percentage of Wealth			Percentage of Wealth			Percentage of Wealth	
	Percentage of Population	No Adjustment (B1)	Adjustment (B3)	Percentage of Population	No Adjustment (B1)	Adjustment (B3)	Percentage of Population	No Adjustment (B1)	Adjustment (B3)
Below £1,000	70.17	3.4	9.2	68.70	2.8	7.4	74.24	3.7	11.5
Cumulative percentage above:									
£ 1,000	29.83	96.6	90.8	31.30	97.2	92.6	23.76	96.3	88.5
5,000	9.30	73.0	69.3	10.95	75.8	73.0	7.79	72.3	66.6
10,000	3.91	56.0	53.9	4.64	58.3	56.9	3.30	55.6	51.8
15,000	2.37	47.7	46.3	2.82	49.7	48.9	2.00	47.3	44.4
20,000	1.61	41.7	40.7	1.93	43.5	43.2	1.37	41.4	39.1
25,000	1.26	37.9	37.4	1.50	39.5	39.5	1.06	37.6	35.8
50,000	0.46	25.7	26.2	0.55	26.7	27.6	0.39	25.4	25.2
100,000	0.15	16.5	17.4	0.18	16.9	18.1	0.13	16.1	16.6
200,000	0.05	10.5	11.3	0.06	10.7	11.6	0.04	10.1	10.7

NOTE: See Notes to Table 5.

adjustments will be required to bring the estate data into line with the balance sheet totals. This is borne out by the results, which show that the share of those below £1,000 is increased by considerably more in the case of the general mortality multipliers than for assumption A1, and that the same holds true when one compares A1 with A2. The general effect is to shift the Lorenz curves closer together. This may be seen by comparing the share of the top 1.9 percent (A2) and the top 2 percent (A3). Before the adjustment the difference is 3.8 percent, but afterwards it is narrowed to 1.2 percent.

In the results described above, no adjustment has been made for real property, for which the estate duty total falls considerably short of the balance sheet estimates. As is explained in the appendix, this difference reflects in large part the method of valuation, and it may therefore be interesting to see the results of increasing the estate duty estimates for this item proportionately, so that they are in line with the balance sheet figures (see Table 7). The Lorenz curve is clearly shifted inward at the top, and outward at the bottom, reflecting the fact that real property is held disproportionately in the middle ranges.

The adjustments described above have been based on very limited evidence and a large number of assumptions, and it is therefore important to consider the checks which can be made of the reasonableness of the estimates presented here. The figures for

TABLE 7 Effect of Adjustment for Land and Buildings

(percent)

	Assumptions A1 and B3	
Percentage of Population	As shown in Table 6	Adjusted for Land and Buildings
29.83	90.8	91.6
9.30	69.3	69.1
3.91	53.9	52.7
2.37	46.3	44.6
1.61	40.7	38.7
1.26	37.4	35.2
0.46	26.2	24.3
0.15	17.4	16.1
0.05	11.3	10.4

total personal wealth provide one such test. Although there are at present no balance sheet totals to provide a benchmark for 1968, we may examine the relationship between the estimates given here, the balance sheet totals for earlier years and the Inland Revenue figures (see Table 8). This suggests that the balance sheet totals in the past varied between 130 percent and 150 percent of the Inland Revenue total. Since the Revell/Roe figures were derived using the life office multipliers, we should expect the total to be closest in the case of assumption A2, and this is borne out by the results in Table 8. A second check on the plausibility of the estimates is to consider the implied average wealth of those not covered by the estate duty returns:

Per capita wealth (£)

	Assumption B2	Assumption B3	Assumption B4
Assumption A1	395	275	69
Assumption A2	343	245	66
Assumption A3	437	302	65

TABLE 8   Estimates of Total Personal Wealth

(£ billion)

	Revell/Roe (1)	Inland Revenue (2)	(1) as percent of (2)
1960	72.0	51.6	140
1961	77.4	54.9	141
1962	85.6	58.3	147
1963	92.4	63.7	145
1964	94.9	71.8	132
1965	102.8	74.3	138
1966	106.5	76.8	139

Estimates Given Here (Assumptions B3) for 1968[a]

A1 Census of Population	117.7	88.0	134
A2 Life office	123.9	88.0	141
A3 General	111.8	88.0	127

SOURCES: Column (1) from [13], column (2) from Inland Revenue Statistics, 1970 and 1972.

[a] Including adjustment for land and buildings.

Bearing in mind the conditions under which property may be transferred without probate (see page 279), and allowing for an average value for consumer durables and so on, the central assumption does not seem unreasonable.

III. THE SHAPE OF THE WEALTH DISTRIBUTION

The estimates presented in the previous sections provide some evidence about the shape of the wealth distribution in Britain, and in this section we take a preliminary look at how far it may be represented by a specific distribution function.[23] There are two main reasons for being interested in this question: (1) in the absence of complete information about the distribution, we may wish to use a fitted distribution to fill the gaps in our knowledge; and (2) we may wish to test theories of the generation of wealth which lead to predictions about the shape of the distribution.

In the former case, reference has already been made to the extrapolation of the data derived from the estate returns to cover lower wealth ranges. In the past, this extrapolation has often been made by eye, a procedure which is to a large extent arbitrary. As pointed out by Brittain "about the only solid reed Lampman had to lean on below the top 1.6 percent was his eye for a beautiful curve" ([14], p. 6). As an alternative, Brittain suggests the estimation of an explicit wealth distribution function and refers particularly to that proposed by Champernowne. This method, however, is only superior to that of Lampman if two conditions are met: (1) it provides a satisfactory fit to the upper tail; and (2) there are a priori grounds for supposing that the function provides a reasonable characterization of the lower part of the wealth distribution. The former is an obvious requirement, but the second is equally important, and unless it is satisfied we may simply be replacing a beautiful curve by a beautiful formula.[24]

---

[23]　A more detailed study of this question is at present in progress and will be the subject of a later paper.

[24] In addition to the *extrapolation* of the distribution to lower wealth ranges, we may also be concerned about the problem of interpolation. The distributions given earlier are based on grouped data, and it is not, in general, possible to compare points on the Lorenz curve: for example, in order to estimate the share of the top 1 percent, interpolation is required. In the past interpolation has frequently been based on graphical methods, but the Inland Revenue [15] has apparently used a specific distribution function (the Pareto

The requirement that there be a priori grounds for supposing that the distribution is of a particular form leads naturally to the testing of theories of wealth generation. The theories which have been put forward are of two main types. The first group consists of those which regard the distribution as the outcome of a Markov stochastic process. Such theories have been advanced in the case of wealth distributions by (among others) Sargan [16], Wold and Whittle [17], Steindl [18] and Shorrocks [19]. Without considering the plausibility of the assumptions made by these authors, we may simply note here that the models are capable of generating a range of asymptotic distributions (see Table 9). Secondly, there are theories which regard the distribution as essentially deterministic in nature and attach particular

---

distribution), and if conditions 1 and 2 described above are satisfied, this may well be preferable.

TABLE 9   Theories of Wealth Generation

Model	Equilibrium Distribution	Formula
Stochastic models:		
Sargan	Log-normal	$F = N(\log W/\mu, \sigma^2)$
Wold-Whittle	Pareto (type I)	$1 - F = \left(\dfrac{W}{W_0}\right)^{-\alpha}$
Steindl	Pareto	$1 - F = \left(\dfrac{W}{W_0}\right)^{-\alpha}$
Shorrocks	Yule	$f = A^W W^{-\alpha}$
Deterministic models:		
Stiglitz	Pareto (type II)	$1 - F = (1 - F_0)\left(\dfrac{W}{W_0} + 1\right)^{-\alpha}$
Atkinson	Range including sech^2	$1 - F = \dfrac{1}{\left(\dfrac{W}{W_0}\right)^{\beta} + 1}$

NOTE: F denotes the distribution function, f denotes the density function. W denotes wealth. N denotes the normal distribution. W_0 and F_0 are constants.

importance to economic and social forces. These have received very little attention, and reference is made only to the work of Stiglitz [20], as extended by the author [21], which shows how a range of equilibrium distributions may be generated as a result of the practice of primogeniture.[25] The comparison of the distributions predicted by the two groups of theories with that actually observed in Britain cannot necessarily be expected to allow us to discriminate between them, but it may well provide indications of the directions which further research should take.

There are a number of different methods which could be adopted to estimate the parameters of the distributions under consideration and to judge their goodness of fit, and these have been discussed by Quandt [24] in the context of measuring industrial concentration. For the present, attention will be confined to the very simplest graphical methods, but in view of the obvious deficiencies they should only be regarded as a preliminary "sorting" procedure. The data to be employed is that given in Table 3. There are two reasons for choosing these data rather than the adjusted data of Table 6: (1) the fitting of a distribution function is an alternative method of estimating the wealth of the "missing" population; and (2) the adjustments made in Table 6 mean that the data would have to be regrouped by ranges if conventional procedures were to be employed.[26]

Pareto (Type I) Distribution

Although use of this distribution is hallowed by tradition, there is remarkably little evidence in its support: the only British data, for example, referred to by Wold and Whittle is that relating to estates for 1907–11. A straightforward graphical test of the Pareto distribution is obtained from the fact that $\log 1/(1 - F) = \alpha \log (W/W_0)$. Figure 2 shows the data in this form for the range £1,000–£500,000 and suggests that a Pareto distribution with α approximately equal to 1.6 could provide a reasonable representation of the upper tail (above £25,000). Below this level,

[25] For an interesting analysis, comparing this assumption with the case where wealth is divided equally at death and discussing the role of marriage patterns, see Blinder [23]. This model is not listed in Table 9 since it leads to no definite predictions about the shape of the wealth distribution.

[26] We also confine our attention to the multipliers A1; the results for A2 produce very similar results.

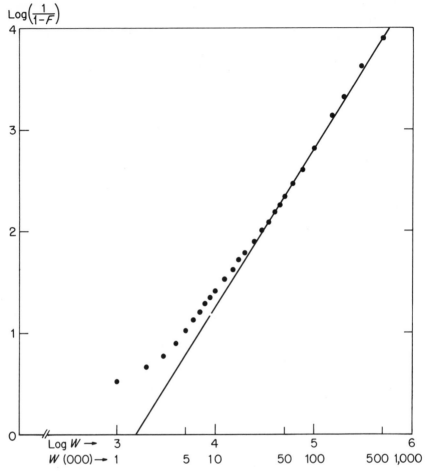

FIGURE 2: Graphical Test of Pareto Distribution

however, it is clearly inadequate, and even its strongest supporters would not want to claim that it could be used to extrapolate the wealth distribution downward. By the same token, the value of α does not provide a good index of the *overall* degree of inequality.

Log-normal Distribution

This distribution was found by Sargan to provide a good approximation to the British data for 1911–13, 1924–30, 1935–38 and 1946–47. The same method of estimation (using log probability paper) is used in Figure 3 for the 1968 data.[27] This suggests that the log-normal may give a reasonable fit in the middle ranges, but there are systematic deviations from linearity at the top and the bottom. Given the finding that the upper tail is approximately Paretian, we could not expect the log-normal to fit well to large wealth holdings and this is borne out by the excess of

[27] See Aitchison and Brown [25], Section 4.5. The straight-line fit is based on the "quantiles" corresponding to £5,000 and £100,000.

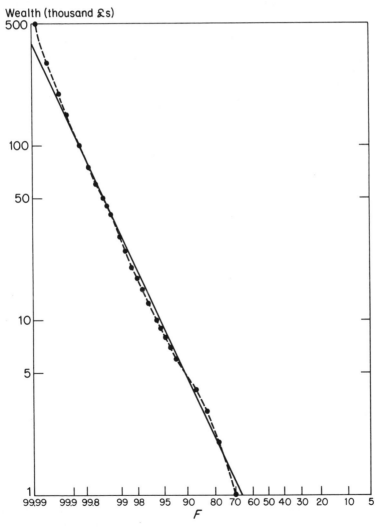

FIGURE 3: Graphical Test of Log-Normal Distribution

frequencies above £100,000. At the lower end (below £5,000) the deviations may well be explained by underrecording or missing estates, and it does not seem unreasonable to suppose that the log-normal might provide an adequate fit to the lower part of the distribution.

If we are seeking a distribution to provide a reasonable fit to the whole range, then we need to find a distribution combining a Pareto tail at the upper end with a shape closer to log-normal in the middle ranges. In addition we need to consider the lower tail. The Pareto distribution assumes a positive lower limit and the log-normal assumes that $W > 0$; whereas, in fact, some fraction of the population have negative net worth. One distribution which may go some way toward meeting these requirements is that given by:[28]

$$1 - F = (1 - F_0) \left[1 + \left(W/W_0 \right)^{\beta} \right]^{\alpha}. \tag{1}$$

There is no straightforward graphical method of fitting this distribution, but we may make some assessment of its possibilities by considering the following special case.

The Sech² Distribution

In the special case where $\alpha = 1$ and $F_0 = 0$, we obtain the sech² distribution (which is also a special case of the Champernowne distribution: see [29]). This may be transformed to yield:

$$\log \frac{F}{1 - F} = \beta(\log W - \log W_0),$$

which provides a convenient graphical test. From Figure 4, it can be seen that the distribution provides a quite good fit to the data over the range £5,000–£500,000. Although there are still systematic deviations from linearity, the curvature is less marked than in the Pareto case and there are grounds for being more confident that it can be extrapolated to the lower ranges. As in the case of the log-normal, there are discrepancies in the ranges below

---

[28] For discussion of this distribution, see Burr [28]. In an unpublished paper, a somewhat similar form was proposed and applied to income data by J. D. Sargan at the 1958 meetings of the Econometric Society.

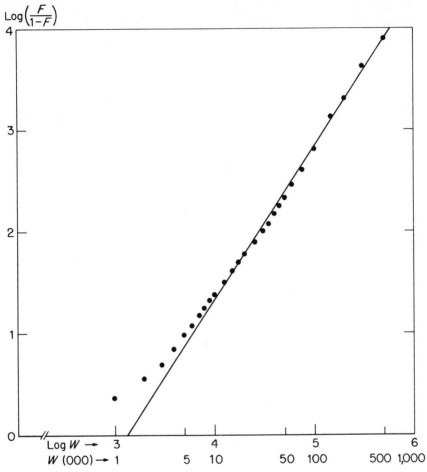

FIGURE 4: Graphical Test of Sech² Distribution

the estate duty limit (£5,000), but these may be explained by underrecording.

Table 10 shows the results obtained if the log-normal and sech² distributions fitted to the range above £5,000 are extrapolated downward to cover the whole distribution. It is clear that the results using the two distributions are quite different. The log-normal estimates indicate that some £5 billion must be added to allow for those not covered by the estate duty returns, which is £1 billion less than the amount added on assumption B3, using the balance sheet approach. On the other hand, the sech² estimates suggest that the amount added should

TABLE 10   Extrapolated Distribution (Multiplier Al)

	Log-normal	Sech²
Median (£)	472	1,318
Mode (£)	19	382
Mean (£)	2,380	2,801
Total wealth (£ billion)	95	109
Total wealth according to estate duty estimates (£ billion)[a]	90	90

[a] Corresponding to the distribution given in Table 3.

be £19 billion, which is higher than any of the assumptions B2 through B4. It is probably fair to say that neither distribution gives particularly reasonable results. The log-normal distribution attributes very little wealth to those not covered by the distribution[29] and the mode is somewhat implausible, but the location parameters of the sech² appear to err in the opposite direction.

Summary

As emphasized earlier, the primitive techniques employed here do not allow any definite conclusions to be reached about the relative merits of different distribution functions. It is clear, however, that the estimates derived using fitted distributions to extrapolate from the upper tail depend sensitively on the particular functional form adopted. Further research is needed to allow us to discriminate more finely between the alternative distributions (including ones not discussed here, such as the Pareto type II and the Yule distributions). Without this, the usefulness of fitted distributions in filling the gaps in our knowledge will be very limited, and it will not be possible to throw light on such questions as the relative importance of stochastic and deterministic factors in leading to the concentration of wealth.

[29] It is interesting to note that the Gini coefficient (.80) is approaching that calculated on the assumption that the excluded population have no wealth at all.

IV. COMPARISON WITH THE OFFICIAL ESTIMATES

In this section, we compare the results obtained here with the official Inland Revenue estimates. The correct method to be used for such a comparison is open to debate. The Inland Revenue chooses to summarize its results in the form of Gini coefficients, but as argued elsewhere [12], this has little apparent justification, and it seems preferable to adopt the time-honored approach of comparing points on the Lorenz curves. In order to present the results in this form, interpolation is, in general, necessary. The method used in the first part of the section is to take a log-linear interpolation of the Lorenz curves,[30] but the alternative approach using fitted distributions is also discussed. In comparing Lorenz curves, it is conventional to take the top 1 percent, 5 percent, 10 percent, and so on, but since we are particularly concerned with the top of the distribution, it seems more helpful to focus on the top 0.5 percent, 1 percent, 2.5 percent, and 5 percent. The top 10 percent, for example, extends as far as those worth £5,000, which is not exactly the kind of figure one has in mind when considering top wealth holders.

Table 11 shows the Inland Revenue distribution (expressed in terms of the total population aged 18 and over) and the adjusted estimates made here, and allows us to assess the contribution made by different adjustments. First, we may compare the Inland Revenue figures and those obtained using the Census of Population multipliers without any corrections for sampling error. As was pointed out in Section I, the rationale for the particular adjustments made by the Inland Revenue is unclear; and in the present study, we have not followed them in combining age groups and smoothing across years. The effect of the adjustments will vary from year to year, but it is clear that in 1968 they served to reduce the share of top wealth holders (comparing lines 1 and 2). If we continue with the Census of Population multipliers, the next main set of adjustments are those to allow for missing wealth. With the central assumption B3, this involves the addition to total personal wealth of £12 billion (not including the adjustment for land and buildings). Of this, £6 billion is allocated to those not covered by the estate duty returns (an average of £275 per head) and £1.2 billion to those with recorded estates of under £10,000.

---

[30] This is equivalent to assuming that a Pareto curve is fitted to each pair of points.

TABLE 11   Comparison of Results

(percent)

		Share in Total Personal Wealth: Top Percentages of Adult Population			
		0.5	*1*	*2.5*	*5*
1.	Inland Revenue[a]	24.9	33.1	47.2	59.3
2.	Census of Population multipliers (no other adjustments)	26.5	34.9	48.5	60.5
3.	Life office multipliers (no other adjustments)	25.7	33.8	47.6	59.7
4.	General multipliers (no other adjustments)	28.1	36.8	50.9	63.3
	Census of Population multipliers with:				
5.	Adjustment B2	24.9	32.3	44.0	54.2
6.	Adjustment B3	27.0	34.6	47.0	58.0
7.	Adjustment B4	31.7	39.8	52.9	64.2
8.	Log-normal distribution fitted to Census of Population data (unadjusted)	21.9	30.0	43.6	56.1

[a] The estimates given in *Inland Revenue Statistics,* 1972, expressed as a percentage of total population aged 18 and over.

As a result, the share in total wealth of those with recorded estates above £10,000—broadly the top 4 percent—is reduced, but at the same time the distribution within the top 4 percent becomes more unequal, so that the share of the very rich is actually increased (see line 6). In Section III, we explored the alternative approach of using distributions fitted to the upper wealth ranges to estimate total personal wealth, and the predicted shares, using the log-normal distribution, are shown in line 8. (The use of a fitted distribution also avoids the need for interpolation.) This method makes no allowance for the missing wealth of the rich and, for this reason, we should expect the distribution to appear less concentrated. Moreover, we have seen that the log-normal distribution does not provide a good fit to the upper tail. When these considerations are borne in mind, the results for the log-normal distribution provide broad support for the earlier estimates.

One of the main aims of the investigation is to examine the sensitivity of the results to different assumptions; and in this paper, we have concentrated on two important aspects: the choice of multipliers and the allowance for missing wealth. The analysis of the paper suggests that the results are likely to be particularly sensitive to the latter factor. The range of variation is illustrated by the fact that the share of the top 0.5 percent increases by nearly 7 percent if we move from assumption B2 to assumption B4 (see lines 5 through 7 of Table 11). In the same way, if a fitted distribution is used to extrapolate the distribution to cover the lower wealth ranges, the results depend sensitively on the functional form adopted. The choice of multipliers, on the other hand, appears to make less difference to the shares of upper wealth groups. The adoption of life office multipliers in place of the Census of Population multipliers used by the Inland Revenue would, for example, reduce the share of the top 0.5 percent by only 0.8 percent (compare lines 2 and 3 in Table 11), and the difference would be even smaller after the adjustment for missing wealth.

APPENDIX: ADJUSTMENTS USING BALANCE SHEET DATA[31]

A. Unquoted U.K. Government Securities

The totals in issue are known from official statistics. In most cases, the assets are owned exclusively by persons: the only major exception is tax reserve certificates, where nonpersonal holdings have been estimated extending the method applied by Roe [13]. The total is a weighted average of the December 1967, June 1968, and December 1968 figures.

The main reasons for the discrepancy between the estate duty estimates and the balance sheet totals are (1) the exclusion of small wealth holders; and (2) the understatement of holdings of those covered by the estate duty returns (particularly those below the exemption level). On the basis of a special analysis of death claims for 1960, Revell concluded that about 40 percent of the

---

[31] For further details see the forthcoming monograph, *The Distribution of Wealth in Great Britain.*

excess wealth should be allocated to the excluded population.[32] However, since that date, the limit for probate has been increased from £100 to £500. In view of this, the assumptions made are those set out in Table 12 (assumption B1 is that no adjustment be made).

B. Savings Bank Deposits

The totals in issue are known from official statistics and personal holdings are obtained in the same way as for unquoted government securities. The allocations by ranges is made under the same assumptions as unquoted government securities.

C. Building Society Deposits

The total deposits are known from the issuing body, and again nonpersonal holdings are small (about 1 percent). Personal holdings are estimated using the same method as Roe and averaged over the December 1967, June 1968, and December 1968 figures.

According to Revell's estimates for 1960, the value of deposits involved in estates not appearing in the estate data is likely to be small ([10], pp. 168–69). Since that data the Administration of Estates Act 1965 has increased the limit below which probate is not required and the amounts involved may be larger. At the same time, the proportion allocatable to the excluded population is probably smaller than in the case of unquoted U.K. government securities and savings bank deposits, and the assumptions shown in Table 12 reflect this.[33]

D. Household Goods, Etc.

The balance sheet totals given by Revell and Roe are based on a perpetual inventory method, and those used here are obtained in the same way. The total is an average of the December 1967 and December 1968 figures.

The difference between the balance-sheet and estate-duty estimates arises in this case because of the exclusion of small

[32] See [10], pp. 168–69.
[33] The reasons why the holdings appearing in the estate data may be understated include, for example, the fact that accrued interest may not always be credited where the estate is clearly not dutiable.

estates and because of the adoption here of a "going concern" basis for evaluation. The natural assumption under B2 is that the first factor accounts for the whole of the difference, although in certain situations the amount allocated per head would exceed the average for those covered by the estate duty estimates, in which case, the excluded population is allocated an amount equal to the average holdings. For assumption B4, we take the extreme case where the excluded population are allocated no part of the excess wealth. For assumption B3, we take the intermediate case where the average holdings of the excluded population are taken to be equal to the average for the range £0–£3,000 in the estate estimates (approximately half the average for the estate statistics as a whole). In each case, the remaining excess wealth is attributed to the difference in the method of valuation and allocated proportionately to holdings (including those of the excluded population).

E. Trade Assets

The balance sheet total for this item, which relates to the assets of unincorporated businesses, is obtained by Revell using a quite different method from the estate duty estimates, and his approach is followed here (see [10], pp. 141–4). The total is an average of the December figures. The main reason for the differences in this case is the adoption by Revell of a "going concern" valuation, and in view of this, the excess wealth is allocated proportionately to holdings.

F. Exempt Settled Property and Expectant Interests

Any adjustment for missing settled property is necessarily speculative, since no really firm evidence is available about its extent; it is, however, possible to make some approximate allowance. A starting point is provided by the estimates of Revell that in 1961 the amounts involved were:

(£ million)

Property settled on surviving spouse	1,250
Discretionary trusts	200
Property settled on minors	200
Total "missing" settled property	1,650

TABLE 12 Assumptions About Allocation by Ranges

Asset	B2	B3	B4
1. Unquoted U.K. government securities	All excess wealth allocated to EP[a]	70% allocated to EP; remainder equally to those below exemption level	40% allocated to EP, remainder proportional to estate holdings
2. Savings bank deposits		Same as 1	
3. Building society deposits	75% excess wealth allocated to EP; remainder equally to those below exemption level	50% allocated to EP; remainder proportional to holdings below exemption level	25% allocated to EP; remainder allocated proportionately to estate duty holdings
4. Household goods	See text	EP allocated holding equal to that in range £0–£3,000, remainder proportional to holdings	All excess wealth allocated proportionately to holdings

5. Trade assets	Allocated proportionately to holdings		
6. Settled property	Allocated in proportion to estate duty wealth above £5,000 (property settled on surviving spouse) or £50,000 (discretionary trusts and property settled on minors)		
7. Shares	No adjustment		
8. Life policies and pension rights	Industrial policies allocated to EP; death benefits allocated as pension rights; nonaggregable policies allocated proportionately to total estate duty wealth		
	Pension rights equally distributed among males	Pension rights distributed as life policies	Pension rights distributed as total wealth
9. Land and buildings	Allocated proportionately to holdings		
10. Debts	25% allocated to EP and those below exemption level; remainder proportionate to estate duty estimates	50% allocated to EP and those below exemption level; remainder proportionate to estate duty estimates	All debts allocated to EP and those below exemption level

These estimates may be on the low side. In the case of discretionary trusts, Revell himself commented that "many people who have practical experiences of settled property would claim that the figure . . . is far too low," and he goes on to say that "undoubtedly an enquiry on similar lines taken today [1967] would yield a much larger figure because corporate trustees all report a great increase in this form of trust ([10], p. 138)." The estimates made by earlier investigators were indeed considerably higher. Campion's figure for the settled property missing from the estate duty estimates in 1936 was between £750 million and £1,300 million ([3], p. 21). In 1954, Lydall and Tipping assumed that discretionary trusts accounted for £1,000 million and "settled property" (presumably that covered by the surviving spouse exemption) for £3,000 million.

It is hoped that in the course of the research being undertaken, it will be possible to provide more definite evidence about settled property,[34] but for the present we consider a range of estimates based on the earlier studies. A lower figure is provided by the estimates of Revell and an upper one by those of Lydall and Tipping, in each case extrapolated to 1968.[35] The central estimate lies in the middle of this range and represents broadly the same percentage of wealth as that estimated by Campion [3].

| | (£ million) | | |
	B2	B3	B4
Property settled on surviving spouse	1,250	3,000	6,000
Discretionary trusts Property settled on minors	1,200	1,700	2,000

It seems reasonable to assume that much of this missing property should be allocated to the higher wealth ranges. The investigations by Revell ([10] and [26]) provide some guide in this respect. It is assumed that all wealth in discretionary trusts and trusts settled on minors belongs to those with wealth of over £50,000, and that this should be allocated in proportion to wealth

---

[34] Among the questions which need further consideration is the correct method of valuing an interest in settled property.

[35] The extrapolation of the lower figure is based on the indications given by Revell ([10], p. 169) and that of the upper figure on the assumption that settled property has increased approximately in proportion to total wealth.

in excess of this amount as indicated by the estate duty estimates. Property settled on a surviving spouse may be held lower down the scale and is allocated in proportion to wealth in excess of £5,000.

There are two further problems concerning settled property. First, the inclusion of "expectant interests" involves double counting and this item is excluded. Second, the adjustments described in the previous two paragraphs may involve double counting if, at the same time, we are using the national balance sheet estimates to correct for missing wealth. In order to overcome this, it is assumed that the net addition of settled property (allowing for the exclusion of expectant interests) is distributed among different assets in the way shown below (which is based on the estimates in [10], Table 6.2):

	(*percent*)
Land and buildings	10
Quoted U.K. government securities	15
Quoted U.K. ordinary shares	70
Life policies	5

G. Quoted and Unquoted Company Shares

In the case of unquoted shares, the adjustment made by Revell was designed primarily to give a smoothed series over a number of years. Since the problem of sampling errors has already been considered, no further adjustment is made here. In the case of quoted securities, Revell obtained information from register surveys about personal holdings and used these estimates in place of the estate duty figures. As he comments "the reasons for the apparent errors . . . are by no means clear" (apart from the settled property already taken into account) and in view of this no adjustment is made here.

H. Life Policies and Pension Rights

There are three main problems which arise under this heading. First, the estate duty estimates of sums assured under life policies exclude a number of items, including death claims paid with production of probate (industrial branch claims), death benefits at the discretion of trustees, policies securing loans (e.g. for home purchase) and nonaggregable policies. Second, the method of valuation—sums assured—is not appropriate. Third, no allowance is made for the value of rights to occupational pensions apart from the death benefits. In order to deal with these problems, Revell replaces the estate duty figure by an estimate of the life funds and of the value of unfunded pensions rights, and the same approach is adopted here, with the total being a weighted average of the December figures.[36]

In allocating the missing items from the estate estimates, industrial branch policies are allocated to the excluded population; death benefits are allocated in the same way as pension rights (see below); policies securing loans are ignored on the grounds that we are not concerned with the asset composition of wealth (and the corresponding adjustment to mortgages is similarly ignored); and nonaggregable policies are allocated proportionately to wealth indicated by the estate duty estimates. The allocation of pension rights can only be based on guesswork in the absence of any firm information about the distribution of the value of rights. It does not seem implausible, however, to suppose that the rights would be distributed across wealth ranges in much the same way as life policies, and this forms the basis for the central assumption.[37] The lower bound is based on the assumption that rights are equally distributed among all male wealth holders; and the upper bound on the assumption that rights are distributed in proportion to total wealth as indicated by the estate duty estimates.

I. Land and Buildings

The balance sheet total for this item is derived primarily by multiplying up the ratable values (as an index of rents), and the figures used here are an extrapolation on the same basis (the total being a weighted average of the December figures). The balance sheet total is quite substantially higher than the estate duty estimate. It is not reasonable to suppose that this excess should be allocated to the excluded population since, according to Revell, it is unlikely that estates containing dwellings would be omitted from the Inland Revenue statistics. Part of the difference can be explained by the understatement of holdings of these assets

[36] An allowance is made for the policies held by personal trusts.

[37] For individuals, there may be a *negative* correlation between life insurance and pension rights (one being a substitute for the other); however, when we consider ranges of wealth, it is likely that they are positively correlated.

by unincorporated businesses and partly by the omission of trusts, but these are unlikely to account for the whole difference, which must reflect in particular the method of valuation. As Inland Revenue has pointed out, the estate data values separate interests in a property and the sum of separate interests may be less than the value for the property as a whole taken in the balance sheet total. On the other hand, the estate valuation is closer to a realization basis than to the "going concern" basis adopted here. In view of this, estimates are presented both with and without the adjustment to the balance sheet total.[38]

J. Debts (Apart from House Mortgages)

The balance sheet total for this item is constructed by Revell largely on the basis of information available from other sectors, and in the present case the same approach is followed.

The discrepancy between the balance sheet value and the estate duty estimate can be attributed to the inadequate coverage of unincorporated businesses, the netting out of debts when a life policy is held, and the estates below the duty exemption level. Revell emphasizes the last of these factors and points out that "when an estate is clearly not liable to duty, nobody has any incentive to do elaborate sums to compute the debts owing by the decreased and they will almost certainly be understated ([10], p. 159)." In view of this, it is assumed that the difference should be attributed in large part to the excluded population and those below the exemption level.

K. Allowance for Northern Ireland and Overseas Residents

The intention is to produce estimates for Great Britain, and we must, therefore, remove the elements of Northern Ireland wealth involved in the adjustments described above. This is assumed to be achieved by reducing the balance sheet totals by 1.7 percent (the percentage of U.K. personal wealth held by Northern Ireland in 1961). The adjustment for overseas residents has to be made to the estate duty figures, since they include property situated in the U.K. owned by overseas residents.[39] According to Revell, these

---

[38] An allowance is made for land held in settled property; see F above.

[39] Double-taxation relief usually means that duty is not paid, but the full value of the assets will nonetheless appear in the statistics.

constituted between 1.4 percent and 2.1 percent of the gross capital value of all estates of £3,000 and over in 1951–61, and about 1 percent of the estates below £3,000. The assumption made is that 1 percent of estates below £5,000 and 2 percent of estates above this level should be excluded.

REFERENCES

1. Clay, H. "The Distribution of Capital in England and Wales." *Transactions of the Manchester Statistical Society*, 1925.
2. Daniels, G. W., and Campion, H. *The Distribution of National Capital.* Manchester: Manchester University Press, 1936.
3. Campion, H. *Public and Private Property in Great Britain.* Oxford: Oxford University Press, 1939.
4. Langley, K. M. "The Distribution of Capital in Private Hands in 1936–38 and 1946–47." *Bulletin of the Oxford University Institute of Statistics* 12 (December 1950):339–59; and 13 (February 1951):33–54.
5. Langley, K. M. "The Distribution of Private Capital, 1950–51." *Bulletin of the Oxford University Institute of Statistics* 16 (January 1954):1–13.
6. Lydall, H. F., and Tipping, D. G. "The Distribution of Personal Wealth in Britain." *Bulletin of the Oxford University Institute of Economics and Statistics* 23 (1961): 83–104.
7. Lampman, R. J. *The Share of Top Wealth-Holders in National Wealth, 1922-1956.* Princeton: Princeton University Press, 1962.
8. Mallet, B. "A Method of Estimating Capital Wealth from the Estate Duty Statistics." *Journal of the Royal Statistical Society* 71 (March 1908): 65–84.
9. Stark, T. *The Distribution of Personal Income in the United Kingdom.* Cambridge: Cambridge University Press, 1972.
10. Revell, J. R. S. *The Wealth of the Nation.* Cambridge: Cambridge University Press, 1967.
11. Smith, J. D. "White Wealth and Black People: The Distribution of Wealth in Washington, D.C., in 1967." Paper presented at the Conference on Research in Income and Wealth, October 1972, and included in this volume.
12. Atkinson, A. B. "On the Measurement of Inequality." *Journal of Economic Theory* 2 (September 1970): 244–63.
13. Roe, A. R. *The Financial Interdependence of the Economy, 1957-1966.* London: Chapman and Hall, 1971.
14. Brittain, J. A. "The Intergenerational Transmission of Personal Wealth: Prospects for a Research Program." Discussion paper circulated December 1971.
15. House of Commons Committee on Income Tax, 1906, No. 365.
16. Sargan, J. D. "The Distribution of Wealth." *Econometrica* 25 (October 1957): 568–90.
17. Wold, H. O. A., and Whittle, P. "A Model Explaining the Pareto Distribution of Wealth." *Econometrica* 25 (October 1957): 591–95.

18. Steindl, J. "The Distribution of Wealth After a Model of Wold and Whittle." *Review of Economic Studies* 39 (July 1972): 263–80.
19. Shorrocks, A. T. "The Dynamics of Wealth Distribution." Unpublished paper, May 1971.
20. Stiglitz, J. E. "Distribution of Income and Wealth Among Individuals." *Econometrica* 37 (July 1969): 382–97.
21. Atkinson, A. B. "Inheritance and the Distribution of Wealth." Unpublished paper, 1972.
22. Allais, M. "Inegalité et Civilisation", in *Mélanges en l'honneur de Raymond Aron—Science et Conscience de la Societé.* Vol. II. Paris: Calmann-Lévy, 1971, pp. 71–97.
23. Blinder, A. "A Model of Inherited Wealth." Discussion paper circulated November 1971.
24. Quandt, R. E. "On the Size Distribution of Firms." *American Economic Review* 56 (June 1966): 416–32.
25. Aitchison, J., and Brown, J. A. C. *The Lognormal Distribution.* Cambridge: Cambridge University Press, 1957.
26. Revell, J. R. S. "Settled Property and Death Duties." *British Tax Review* (May-June 1961):177–82.
27. Champernowne, D. G. "The Graduation of Income Distribution." *Econometrica* 20 (October 1952): 591–615.
28. Burr, I. W. "Cumulative Frequency Function." *Annals of Mathematical Statistics* 13 (1942): 215–35.
29. Fisk, P. R. "The Graduation of Income Distributions." *Econometrica* 29 (April 1961): 171–85.

DISCUSSION: WEALTH IN BRITAIN—THE ESTATE DUTY METHOD REEXAMINED

Kathleen M. Langley
Boston University

Atkinson has made a masterly reappraisal of the estate duty method of estimating the distribution of wealth in Britain. It is a real advance to have subjected the two principal sources of error in this method of wealth calculation to a sensitivity analysis. It has long been appreciated by wealth calculators that a considerable opportunity for error arises from inappropriate multipliers and from the problem that decedents' reported estates may differ from the current capital holdings of the living in the same age-sex groups. It is, however, intriguing to learn that after the searching review of the different mortality rates and of "missing" data, conventional wisdom based on rule-of-thumb estimation is more or less confirmed. What is long overdue is the task of selecting a random drawing of living persons—and of their wealth—even if only to reveal the inadequacies of deriving wealth estimates from estate-duty tax returns.

The persistence of significant inequality in the distribution of wealth in Britain despite the existence since 1940 of confiscatory death duties does indeed suggest that either the underlying institutional forces making for inequality are particularly strong or that measurement of the wealth distribution is inadequate. Hicks,[1] in a recent examination of "equality" factors, points out that an estate of £400,000 has today a real value of no more than £100,000 in terms of 1939 pounds, and that since 1939 the rate of tax on such an estate has risen from 20 percent to more than 60 percent. Moreover, during that time span, most estates will have changed hands. As income and wealth are correlated, Hicks looks at the change in the distribution of the personal incomes of married persons (before tax) between 1954-55 and 1967-68 (in terms of "1967 pounds"), and his estimates show a reduction in the number of couples who fall into the top income group of above £10,000 from 43,000 to 33,000 (a 23.3 percent drop). He

---

[1] J. R. Hicks, *The Social Framework*, 4th edition (Oxford: Oxford University Press, 1971), Chap. XVIII, p. 246.

concludes that "it can hardly be doubted that the *fall* in the number of *large* properties, which is the result of death duties, is one of the causes of the decline."[2] He does, however, speculate that as more than half of income over £10,000 is "earned income," a number of income earners who would otherwise be top income earners have made arrangements to take income in a nontaxable form. "Too great reliance on income taxation to equalize incomes weakens the power of the income taxation itself to do what it is supposed to do."[3] It is possible that this is also the situation with regard to estate duty taxation. Revell[4] says that it has become customary in Britain to call estate duty a "voluntary tax" and to regard as "eccentric" an individual whose estate, through his own neglect to take advantage of legal methods of estate duty avoidance, does attract tax rates in the 60 to 80 percent range. The estate duty statistics must also be somewhat "eccentric," and we may have reached a point when we can no longer pretend that the estate duty statistics in any way represent a random sample of the living population.

I should like to comment, first, on the forces making for wealth preservation and on the problem of "missing" wealth; second, on usage of National Balance Sheet data; and third, on other aspects of the paper.

THE FORCES OF WEALTH PRESERVATION

The process of personal wealth generation and wealth transfer has received inadequate study by economists. Atkinson refers to two types of operational forces, namely, stochastic and deterministic ones. Further discussion of the a priori assumptions concerning the relative weighting of these respective forces within a specific society would have been, I believe, both interesting and pertinent in assessing the validity of his wealth calculations.

The economic and social forces making for both income and wealth distributions of inequality may well exist in a not easily disturbed fashion in Britain. Stiglitz[5] considers the main forces of

---

[2] Ibid.

[3] Ibid., p. 249.

[4] J. Revell, *The Wealth of the Nation* (Cambridge: Cambridge University Press, 1967), p. 110.

[5] J. E. Stiglitz, "Distribution of Income and Wealth Among Individuals," *Econometrica* 37 (July 1969): 394-97.

wealth inequality to be (a) heterogeneity of the labor force in terms of productivity, that is, I assume, in terms of acquired skills or of given natural abilities; (b) class saving behavior; and (c) primogeniture. A possible additional factor, namely life-cycle saving behavior has been previously investigated for the British case by Atkinson,[6] who concluded that these differences were not an important factor in explaining inequality. While primogeniture may be of importance in Britain and also heterogeneity of the labor force—in the words of George Bernard Shaw "It is impossible for an Englishman to open his mouth without making some other Englishman hate or despise him"[7]—I believe, that we should consider category (b) not in terms of differential savings ratios but in terms of social-class estate duty avoidance or mitigation behavior. System maintenance is alleged[8] to fall within the domain of "grants economics" and one-way transfers or gifts *inter vivos* have long troubled users of estate duty statistics for the purposes of wealth measurement. It is probable that although wealth may indeed be unequally distributed, it is more equally divided within a social group than is apparent from the statistical estimates.

Gifts *inter vivos* pay estate duty today if made within seven years of the death of the deceased. It has been assumed that the question of these "gifts" can be ignored, because as has often been pointed out, the recipients are also subject to the laws (or chances) of mortality and such wealth may be counted *twice* in the statistics. It has for some time been an article of faith to believe in the above thesis and hence to accept the validity of the estate-duty multiplier method of making wealth calculations. There have always been legal gift exemptions: gifts made for public or charitable purposes, or—of greater importance—"reasonable gifts" shown to be part of *normal* expenditure if these should ever be included in the estate. No attention has been given to the question of responsibility for family expenses, that is, to the possibility that gifts *inter vivos* may not be outright gifts—and thus liable to be revealed in the unexpected death of a person in a young rather

[6] A. B. Atkinson, "The Distribution of Wealth and the Individual Life Cycle," *Oxford Economic Papers,* July 1971.

[7] G. B. Shaw, "Preface to Pygmalion 1912," *Prefaces by Bernard Shaw* (London: Constable, 1934), p. 771.

[8] K. E. Boulding, M. Pfaff, and J. Horvath, "Grant Economics: A Simple Introduction," *American Economist* 16 (Spring 1972):21.

than an old age group—but the taking over by more affluent family members of expenses such as those for education or even for vacations or normal living expenses. These "gifts" would, by their very nature, be consumed by the recipient and never come to the attention of the tax inspector, yet in a very real sense they permit the buildup of human capital and of wealth potential to take place and thus help to preserve the social class. Further, is it reasonable to assume that tax inspectors question the payment of possibly (over a period of years) quite substantial sums to wives (or husbands) as normal living expenses—sums which are in effect, capital transfers? In addition to exempt settled property and discretionary and other trusts, significant sums could in this way escape the tax collector.

THE USAGE OF NATIONAL BALANCE SHEET DATA

Atkinson's paper uses extrapolations of the National Balance Sheet data on the basis of the estimates published by Revell in 1967 for the years 1957-61. It should be noted, however, that these estimates of the value of a number of the assets owned by the personal sector were made using the estate multiplier method. Revell considered that he could correct for certain deficiencies in the context of compiling an aggregate balance sheet for the personal sector but he wrote, "We do not go into *further* difficulties involved in trying to estimate the *concentration* of personal wealth."[9] Atkinson has been more ambitious and has allocated the "missing" wealth to specific wealth ranges; his assumptions appear to be based on good judgment—although, of course, an allocation which is simply proportional to estate holdings necessarily compounds any initial misallocation by class size.

The use of National Balance Sheet data means an acceptance of the methods of valuation used in making the estimates. An implicit assumption made by Revell is that of valuation based on a "going concern" basis, that is, that all economic units are continuing in their current line of economic activity. This assumption appears to be entirely appropriate at a national level—but while the state lives on, individuals arrive and depart.

What matters to an individual is his command over resources at

---

[9] Revell, *Wealth of the Nation*, p. 106.

any specific time. Both the poor and the very rich (at least in Britain) have been called profligate—both groups spend what they get, but the rich can afford to buy the services of tax lawyers, and the lawyers see that their client's status is maintained. A life interest in a trust means that provision is made to obtain (1) current purchasing power and thus command over immediately available goods and services; and (2) the ability to pass along to heirs entitlement to future goods and services. Trusts and the ownership of corporations have shielded the wealthy from many of the consequences of their spending follies. Insurance policies provide additional protection and can be of a form that need never appear in an estate. When a policy on the life of a person is owned by someone else (often for large sums), particularly when business interests are involved, an insurance company will pay out on a death claim, but no estate will pay estate duty. The poor can and do also obtain insurance protection, particularly for anticipated funeral expenses—but it is highly probable that the traditional weekly collection by insurance agents is a means whereby the poor transfer a total "savings" sum to the insurance companies which exceeds the benefits ultimately received. Such small policies do not provide immediate liquidity to the holders; but on the other hand, the wealthy can use their insurance policies to secure bank overdrafts or other loans.

On a personal rather than on a national level, the "going concern" valuation concept is not necessarily the most appropriate one. Personal wealth consists largely of paper "claims"[10] of varying degrees of liquidity. In 1969, on the basis of Inland Revenue's estimate of gross personal wealth (and—as the paper has pointed out—this is an underestimate), quoted shares and debentures and insurance policies alone accounted for 45 percent of the total. On the other hand, household goods and "other personalty" formed 13 percent of the total. Paper claims to wealth and to command over resources are not closely tied to either the flow or stock of real goods and the realization value at any given time can fluctuate for many reasons which are not associated with the productivity

---

[10] In 1938, in an early and very searching examination of the concept of national capital, Kuznets indicated that the "claims" approach to wealth estimation was "especially suited to be the basis of distribution of wealth among individuals." *Conference on Research in Income and Wealth*, Vol. 2 (New York: National Bureau of Economic Research, 1938), p. 7.

or real economic performance of a country. The interests of the holders of paper wealth do not necessarily lie in the same direction as the interests of the nation as a producer of real things. Carter has recently put forward the view that Britain considered as a "going concern" has suffered too often in the last twenty years from undue attention being given to the interests of those people who hold paper wealth.[11] Can we assert that the "true" capital value of a company on a given date is "correctly" determined by the securities market, when it is known that the specialists in specific stocks frequently encourage speculation? It is generally accepted that the capital market is imperfect and many securities may not be worth their going exchange prices in terms of the present discounted value of future expected earnings—but we must accept, when considering wealth in terms of its command over resources, the view that "a thing is worth what you can get for it"—either through outright sale or through its borrowing power. Inland Revenue does attempt to abide by the above principle. When, for example, the decedent has held an insurance policy on the life of another person, the estate is charged to duty on the surrender value of the policy. If an insurance policy is considered as a current asset, its value must be what can be raised against it or its current surrender value, even if the surrender value is computed so as to impose a penalty on the act of surrender; the poor, with few liquid assets, pay heavily in order to obtain a little additional immediate command over resources. Further, I would not dispute that it is a reasonable procedure in a National Balance Sheet context to take account of rights to funded or unfunded pension schemes and, logically, also of social security retirement benefits. Ultimately, the nation, considered as a "going concern," will have to meet these claims to future consumption in some manner, but if the value of these future "rights" is not at the current time realizable by an individual, can they be considered as part of his wealth? If these "rights" are included in the personal wealth estimates, the actual distribution of *realizable* wealth holdings becomes increasingly concealed. The provision of a pension by an institution is one form whereby an individual can avoid complete payment of current high income taxes; and as the need for personal saving is reduced, so also is control over personal wealth.

[11] Charles Carter, *Wealth, An Essay on the Purposes of Economics* (Baltimore: Penguin Books, 1971), Chap. 5.

SOME OTHER MATTERS

Sampling Error

Atkinson prefers combining observations by estate ranges to ensure a minimum sample size (p. 283) instead of following the Inland Revenue procedure of obtaining a smoother series by combining observations for a number of years. Neither procedure is particularly satisfactory; the decision making is arbitrary, and we can never be sure that the sample size is of minimum adequacy when there is no particular principle that governs the selection of estate class or age groupings.

Choice of Mortality Multipliers

If, as is very likely, the distribution of wealth in Britain owes much to social and economic deterministic factors then it is reasonable (despite an overall national trend of increased prosperity and lower mortality) to attempt to differentiate the mortality rates of wealth owners from those of the general public. The characteristics of the ease of life which wealth makes possible are likely to linger on over several generations and to reduce the hazards of exposure to physically demanding occupations or to occupations entailing a risk to health. Unfortunately, as is pointed out in the paper, the precise relationship between the level of social-class multipliers and the degree of wealth inequality is unclear. It would, however, have been interesting to have heard speculations concerning the not insignificant differences in the estimated number of top wealth holders based on multipliers A1 and A2. The cumulative number of people with over £1 million is 17 percent higher using assumption A2 rather than assumption A1, and the cumulative number of people with over £200,000 is 18 percent higher. Numbers are increased, but evidently per capita wealth decreases and the Lorenz curve shifts inward. The result must be related to the age and sex classification by estate grouping but precisely in what manner?

Wealth Distribution Functions

Atkinson is undoubtedly correct in insisting that much further research work is required before we can rely on a specific fitted distribution to fill the gaps in our knowledge concerning the overall distribution of wealth. It is, indeed, only too easy to substitute a beautiful formula for a beautiful "guesstimate." It would appear, in particular, that attention should be given to the problem of assessing the proportion of the adult population who have zero or negative net worth. We do not know, either on empirical or theoretical grounds, which of the many assumptions that can be made should be considered reasonable. At present, an assessment of the adequacy or inadequacy of any estimate of the implied average wealth of those not covered by the estate duty statistics is inevitably an arbitrary one.

On the question of the appropriateness of any particular fitted distribution, the basic issue of the functional form should perhaps be reconsidered. It is well known that an appropriate mathematical function to describe the actual frequency distribution of wealth (or income) has been difficult to find. Partly because of this problem, and partly because of Pareto's early discovery that the tail end of the cumulative distribution is linear in the log-log plane, the distribution function has been preferred to the frequency function in most economic research—but most distribution functions do not provide a description of the data over more than a small region of interest. It is possible that further research concerning the form of frequency function in addition to that of the cumulative distribution would be rewarding and help in the assessment of the relative weight of stochastic and/or deterministic wealth-generating factors.

In conclusion, since the results presented by Atkinson indicate that significant inequality of wealth persists in Britain, we might ask whether the publication of wealth estimates does not indeed encourage a continued search by the rich for new devices to ensure the preservation of their status.

CHAPTER 11

White Wealth and Black People: the Distribution of Wealth in Washington, D.C., in 1967

James D. Smith
Pennsylvania State University

I. INTRODUCTION

U.S. estimates of the distribution of wealth are scarce. Contemporary estimates using sound statistical methods, but limited data bases, have been made by Mendershausen (1944), Lampman (1953), Smith (1958, 1962, 1965, and 1969), and Projector and Weiss.[1] Beginning around the turn of the cen-

Support for this research was provided by the National Science Foundation under two grants. Particular thanks are due to James Blackman of that institution for his early suggestions and continuing interest in the study of the distribution of income and wealth.

Thanks are due Mary Hosterman for yeoman labor in abstracting and coding the original data and preparing the initial computer files. Mark Soskin, John Gregor, and Gretchen Kline contributed to the resolution of various substantive problems.

[1] Horst Mendershausen, "The Pattern of Estate Tax Wealth," in Raymond W. Goldsmith, ed., *A Study of Savings in the United States*, Vol. III (Princeton: Princeton University Press, 1956). Robert J. Lampman, *The Share of Top Wealth-Holders in National Wealth, 1922-56*, (New York: National Bureau of Economic Research, 1962). James D. Smith, *The Income and Wealth of Top Wealth-Holders in the United States, 1958* (Doctoral dissertation, University of Oklahoma, 1966). James D. Smith, "The Concentration of Personal Wealth in America, 1969," *Review of Income and Wealth*, Series 20, No. 2, June 1974. James D. Smith and Stephen D. Franklin, "The Concentration of Personal Wealth, 1922-69," *American Economic Review* 64 (May 1974):162-67. James D. Smith, Stephen D. Franklin, and Douglas A. Wion, "The Distribution of Financial Assets," in Fred R. Harris, ed., *In the Pockets of a Few: The Distribution of Wealth in America* (New York: Grossman, 1974). James D. Smith, Stephen D. Franklin, and Guy H. Orcutt, "The Intergenerational Transmission of Wealth: A Simulation Experiment,"

tury and continuing up to 1937, there were occasional attempts to estimate U.S. wealth distributions, but the only attempts were, for the most part, weak on statistics and short on data.[2] It is of little surprise then to find that there are no wealth distributions available for modern U.S. cities.[3] The reasons for the scarcity of estimates at all levels are believed to be the high cost of collecting original data and the bureaucratization of public information.[4] This paper presents the first findings from a study of the distribution of

---

forthcoming in Vol. 41, Studies in Income and Wealth, NBER. Dorothy Projector and Gertrude Weiss, *Survey of Economic Characteristics of Consumers* (Washington, D.C.: Board of Governors of the Federal Reserve System, 1966). *Statistics of Income . . . Personal Wealth* (Washington, D.C.: U.S. Treasury Dept., 1967).

[2] See, for instance, G. K. Holmes, "The Concentration of Wealth," *Political Science Quarterly* 3 (1893): 589-600; C. B. Spahr, *The Present Distribution of Wealth in the United States* (New York: Crowell, 1896); W. I. King, *Wealth and Income of the People of the United States* (New York: Macmillan, 1915); Federal Trade Commission, *National Wealth and Income*, Senate Document 126, 69th Congress, 1st Session (Washington, D.C., 1962); R. R. Doane, "Summary of the Evidence on National Wealth and Its Increasing Diffusion," *Analyst* (July 26, 1935): 115-18; Maxine Yaple, "The Burden of Direct Taxes Paid by Income Classes," *American Economic Revue* 26 (December 1936): 691-710; Fritz Lehmann, "The Distribution of Wealth," in Max Ascoli and Fritz Lehmann, *Political and Economic Democracy* (New York: W. W. Norton, 1937).

[3] There has been one estimate of the distribution of assets at the state level. See Richard French, "Estate Multiplier Estimates of Personal Wealth," *American Journal of Economics and Sociology* 29 (April 1970): 150-61. Also, see Daniel A. McGowan, "The Measurement of Personal Wealth in Centre County, Pennsylvania" (Doctoral dissertation, Pennsylvania State University, 1972).

[4] To its credit, the Board of Governors of the Federal Reserve System released the microdata from the Projector and Weiss study so that researchers could analyze the findings. The same credit can be given to the Office of Economic Opportunity (OEO) which insisted that the Surveys of Economic Opportunity belonged to the public and not only released them for research use, but has maintained a continuing interest in their updating. These examples are in sharp contrast to the general position taken by government agencies. Bureaucrats have often defended their denial of researcher access to public microdata (with names and street addresses deleted) on the grounds that by combining data in complex but unstated ways, the identity of respondents could be determined and thus their privacy violated. It appears, however, that an overwhelming case is emerging that government secrecy is for the benefit of those who govern and to the detriment of the governed.

wealth in Washington, D.C. Washington was selected because it offered an exploitable data base and because local administrators were receptive to the scientific use of administrative records.[5]

With three-quarters of a million inhabitants, Washington is the ninth largest city in the United States. It is 71 percent black, and the proportion and absolute number of blacks has increased monotonically from at least 1950, when the number stood at 280,000 and represented 35 percent of the total population.

The estimates presented here were generated by the estate multiplier technique. The methodology has been elaborated upon elsewhere (see Lampman,[6] Mendershausen,[7] and Smith and Calvert[8]). The broad outlines of the technique are mentioned below, and the section on methodology covers special modification peculiar to this application. Basically, it is assumed that death draws randomly within population strata defined by age, sex, and perhaps social class. Unbiased estimates of population parameters can be made from the observed characteristics of decedents by weighting decedents by the reciprocals of the mortality rate applicable to each sample strata. In most past uses of the method, age-sex-specific mortality rates have been "social-class adjusted" to account for the more favorable mortality experience enjoyed by

---

[5] In contrast to what many researchers have found the attitude of the federal bureaucracy to be toward the scientific use of public information, the research reported here was aided at almost every step by persons in various administrative posts below the federal level. Particular thanks are due to William Mason, the Director of the Washington, D.C., Inheritance and Estate Tax Section at the time the study was designed. Our work was assisted after Mason's retirement by Alfred R. Rector, who replaced him. John Crandall, Chief of the Vital Records Division of the District of Columbia, was indispensable to our understanding and use of vital statistics. Vernon Randall of the Office of Vital Statistics, State of Maryland, and Betty Rodger of the Health Department, State of Maryland, provided valuable assistance in the use of vital statistics information for District of Columbia residents dying in the state of Maryland. Albert Mindlin, Chief Statistician of the City of Washington, D.C., lent us his ear and his statistical insights as we moved toward closure in these estimates. He, of course, bears no responsibility for our errors.

[6] Lampman, *Share of Top Wealth-Holders.*

[7] Mendershausen, *Pattern of Estate Tax Wealth.*

[8] James D. Smith and Staunton Calvert, "Estimating the Wealth of Top Wealth-Holders from Estate Tax Returns," *Proceedings of the Business and Economics Section, American Statistical Association,* Philadelphia, 1965.

upper socioeconomic groups. However, weighting in U.S. estimates has failed to utilize available knowledge about mortality differentials fully, because the IRS has refused to release relevant though innocuous information from tax returns. In this study, an unusually rich body of data permits taking account of age, sex, race, and marital status, as well as social class.

Two major and several less important sources of data were utilized to make the estimates. The major sources were (a) estate tax returns filed in the District of Columbia for decedents who died in 1967; and (b) death certificates filed for the same decedents. Washington has its own estate tax. Unlike the federal tax with its relatively high filing exemption of $60,000, estates of residents with gross assets of $1,000 or more must file a District of Columbia estate tax return. The return used by the city requires itemized assets, including joint interests of the decedent and personal information about the decedent's age, occupation, and marital status.

Regardless of their domicile, a death certificate is required for all persons who die in the District of Columbia. Similarly, District residents who die outside the District cause a death certificate to be filed in the jurisdiction in which they die. For all residents dying in the District, death certificate information about their race, marital status, place of birth, and usual occupation was obtained from the registrar's office. For District of Columbia residents dying in the state of Maryland, assistance was received from the Maryland Office of Vital Statistics. For District of Columbia residents dying in other jurisdictions, use was made of a death-certificate tape file from the National Center for Health Statistics. The file contained information for all District of Columbia residents who died in any registration district of the United States.

Wealth in this paper is the sum of real estate, stocks and bonds, mortgages, notes, time deposits, checking account balances, currency, coin, consumer durables, works of art, automobiles, boats, personal clothing and jewelry, lifetime transfers at less than fair value, powers of appointment, and the present value of annuities and vested rights to retirement funds. The only assets conceptually excluded from the estimates are cash surrender value of life insurance policies and real estate owned by District of Columbia residents but located outside of the city.

II. METHODOLOGY

A. *The Estate Multiplier Technique*

Death is an intriguing phenomenon, not only to the philosopher and mystic who see it as a door to something beyond, but to scientists who see it as a mirror reflecting life unexaminable in process. Pathologists can trace backward the events that led to a human system's ultimate demise. Anthropologists enter the graves of the dead and emerge into the culture of another society, comfortable in their ability to infer from the bones and artifacts interred with its members not only the ritual and art but the physical and intellectual characteristics of a society long dead.

Economists were slow to appreciate the uses of death, though some, like Malthus, were aware of its economic implications. About the turn of the century, a number of American economists realized the transfer of property at death might provide a means of estimating the distribution of wealth, but it took nearly a century before they found the statistical bridge between the estates of the dead and the wealth of the living.[9] The bridge is that death draws a stratified sample of the living population whose weights are, as with any sample, the reciprocals of the sampling rates—in the case of death, mortality rates. Since the mortality rate for a population is the ratio of the number of deaths to living persons in the population,

$$R = \frac{M}{V} ,$$

where R is the mortality rate and M and V are the number of deaths and living persons respectively. It follows algebraically that the living population is

$$V = \frac{1}{R}(M).$$

To estimate a set of characteristics, C_k, for a living population

---

[9] The first published recognition that estates did not provide a direct estimation of the wealth of a society was by Sir. T. A. Coughlin in the *Journal of the Royal Statistical Society* 44, (1906) p. 736. For a review of early attempts to use probate records to estimate wealth, see G. H. Knibbs, *The Private Wealth of Australia and Its Growth* (Melbourne: McCarron, Bird, 1918).

from characteristics of decedents, using age-sex-specific mortality rates, the estimate would be:

$$C_k = \sum_{i=j}^{n} \sum_{j=1}^{2} C_k^{ij} \frac{1}{R_{ij}} \, ,$$

where C_k^{ij} is the value of the kth characteristic associated with decedents of the ith age and jth sex. R_{ij} is a set of age-sex-specific mortality rates. Mortality rates may, of course, be conditional on variables in addition to age and sex. Indeed the mortality rate stratification should encompass any variable which is to be estimated, and which at the same time is a determinant of mortality.

Actuaries, biologists, and demographers have invested a substantial amount of intellectual capital in the refinement of mortality statistics, and specific rates for various personal characteristics are available for the United States. In the Washington, D.C., estimates, we have employed rates based on age, sex, race, and marital status. The decision to use a complex set of rates follows from the fact that many variables have been shown to affect mortality rates.

Mortality rates by age, sex, and race are generally available on an annual basis. The most recent rates which combine marital status with age, sex, and race are for the three-year period 1959-61. The importance of marital differentials are pointed out in studies by Moriyama,[10] Shurtleff,[11] and Klebba.[12] They have shown that married men and women have at every age a substantially greater life expectancy than do single, widowed, or divorced persons of the same sex. Using age-standardized populations, Klebba found for the three-year period 1959-61 that single and widowed white males had a mortality rate 1.5 times that for married white males, and that divorced men had a rate twice that of married ones. The marital status differentials for nonwhite men follow the same pattern as for whites, but the absolute rates are higher than for whites. Marital status differentials are smaller for women, but nevertheless important.

[10] I. M. Moriyama, "Deaths from Selected Causes by Marital Status, by Age and Sex: United States, 1940," *Vital Statistics—Special Reports* 23 (November 1945):118-65.

[11] D. Shurtleff, "Mortality Among the Married," *Journal of the American Geriatrics Society* 4(7) (July 1956):654-55.

[12] A. Joan Klebba, "Mortality from Selected Causes by Marital Status," *Vital and Health Statistics*, Series 20, Nos. 8a and 8b, 1970.

Tables 1 and 2 show mortality rates by age, sex, race, and marital status for the period 1959-61 from Klebba. To derive marital-status-adjusted rates for 1967, the percent that each marital-status mortality rate within each age-race-sex group represented of the overall age and sex group was computed from the rates in Tables 1 and 2. These percentages were then applied to age-sex-race mortality rates in 1967 to generate the 1967 marital-status-adjusted rates. The derived rates were then converted to weights by calculating their reciprocals. The age-sex-race-marital status weights are shown in Tables 3 and 4.

Social class is a nebulous concept. It generally is used in reference to a life style for which education, income, and occupation are proxies. As is well known, these variables are correlated and the link between them and mortality is indirect, but they appear to affect life style in a way that changes the probability of death at given points in life. Houser and Kitagawa, as well as others, have measured with some success the association of these variables with mortality rates.[13]

In estate multiplier estimates for the United States, social-class mortality adjustments have been employed. Mendershausen used a "select" set of rates based upon the Metropolitan Life Insurance Company experience with a preferred-risk population. Lampman and Smith used age-sex-specific mortality rates with differentials which split the difference between high-status-occupation mortality rates and rates for holders of large insurance policies up to age 65, and between the large-policy-holder rate and white rates after age 65. The IRS, in its 1962 estimate, used rates based entirely on life insurance experience.

In past national wealth estimates for persons with gross assets of

---

[13] See Evelyn Kitagawa and Phillip Houser, "Methods Used in a Current Study of Social and Economic Differentials in Mortality," in *Emerging Techniques in Population Research* (New York: Milbank Memorial Fund, 1963), and "Educational Differentials in Mortality by Cause of Death, United States, 1960," *Demography* 5(1) (1968):315-53; Evelyn Kitagawa, "Social and Economic Differentials in Mortality in the United States, 1960," *Proceedings of the General Assembly and Conference of the International Union for Scientific Study of Population,* London, 1969; I. M. Moriyama and L. Guralnick, "Occupational and Social Class Differentials in Mortality" (New York: Milbank Memorial Fund, 1956); Lillian Guralnick, "Mortality by Occupation and Industry Among Men 20-64 Years of Age: United States, 1950," *Vital Statistics—Special Reports* 53 (September 1962).

TABLE 1 Mortality Rates by Age, Sex, Race, and Marital Status, 1959-61

(deaths per 100,000 population)

| | White | | | | | | | |
| | *Females* | | | | *Male* | | | |
Age	*Single*	*Married*	*Widow*	*Divorced*	*Single*	*Married*	*Widower*	*Divorced*
15-19	48.0	53.5	283.2	117.0	121.5	122.7	390.6	189.1
20-24	77.4	50.3	213.4	137.2	205.6	115.8	626.1	359.5
25-34	153.9	74.3	188.6	196.0	276.4	128.7	498.9	516.0
35-44	312.1	167.0	318.7	355.5	614.7	276.6	797.0	1,110.2
45-54	571.8	412.1	625.4	652.0	1,419.0	793.2	1,741.5	2,473.1
55-59	839.0	744.0	959.6	1,053.8	2,315.2	1,545.6	2,742.0	3,948.6
60-64	1,379.3	1,228.7	1,538.8	1,627.6	3,653.5	2,445.1	3,907.5	5,436.4
65-69	2,072.5	1,967.0	2,405.7	2,450.8	5,303.5	3,623.5	5,529.6	7,256.3
70-74	3,429.9	3,252.0	3,857.5	3,970.2	7,509.0	5,245.0	7,311.7	9,315.9
75 and over	10,247.8	6,891.2	10,920.0	9,574.4	13,889.8	10,133.2	15,670.1	16,031.6
15 and over	591.4	533.9	4,487.6	971.9	752.0	1,274.7	8,847.9	3,155.9

SOURCES: A. Joan Klebba, "Mortality from Selected Causes by Marital Status," in *Vital and Health Statistics*, Series 20, Nos. 8a and 8b, December 1970.

TABLE 2   Mortality Rates by Age, Sex, Race, and Marital Status, 1959-61

(deaths per 100,000 population)

	Nonwhite							
	Female				Male			
Age	Single	Married	Widow	Divorced	Single	Married	Widower	Divorced
15-19	78.3	100.3	245.9	121.8	157.3	209.5	396.8	60.1
20-24	165.9	118.4	329.0	192.3	314.1	208.8	737.2	455.8
25-34	392.6	212.5	531.0	323.5	627.7	286.8	1,113.3	747.1
35-44	836.5	451.5	934.9	710.4	1,357.3	554.8	1,740.4	1,543.4
45-54	1,351.4	909.2	1,795.8	1,245.9	2,285.3	1,205.5	3,251.2	3,012.8
55-59	1,851.3	1,439.6	2,666.4	1,934.5	3,049.5	1,990.1	4,537.9	4,185.7
60-64	2,769.5	2,122.3	3,879.7	2,740.3	4,658.1	3,214.8	6,418.4	6,334.9
65-69	3,015.9	2,436.4	4,147.1	3,413.6	5,496.4	4,134.0	7,467.4	7,951.9
70-74	4,186.5	3,237.7	5,315.3	4,322.0	7,223.6	5,128.0	8,734.8	9,146.9
75 and over	7,243.2	5,143.6	8,498.6	6,346.7	10,284.5	7,103.0	12,474.7	10,840.7
15 and over	405.4	684.4	3,893.1	1,072.4	743.6	1,335.9	7,004.8	2,972.4

SOURCES: A. Joan Klebba, "Mortality from Selected Causes by Marital Status," in *Vital and Health Statistics*, Series 20, Nos. 8a and 8b, December 1970.

TABLE 3   Reciprocals of White Age-Race-Sex-Marital-Status-Specific Mortality Rates (1967)

Age	Female				Male			
	Single	Married	Widow	Divorced	Single	Married	Widower	Divorced
15-19	1,855.3	1,666.7	315.3	762.2	734.8	724.6	228.5	470.8
20-24	1,213.6	1,876.2	439.2	682.6	456.2	809.7	150.1	261.3
25-34	644.7	1,331.6	525.8	505.8	358.4	768.6	198.3	191.7
35-44	311.0	579.0	306.0	274.7	158.8	351.7	122.2	87.7
45-54	180.1	248.9	164.1	157.2	72.5	129.9	59.0	41.6
55-59	119.2	133.6	104.7	94.5	43.3	64.6	36.5	25.3
60-64	74.9	84.8	68.0	63.8	28.5	42.7	26.6	19.1
65-69	50.5	52.9	43.5	42.4	19.6	28.9	18.9	14.4
70-74	29.7	31.3	26.5	25.9	13.7	19.5	14.0	11.0
75 and over	10.5	15.7	9.9	11.2	7.7	10.6	6.8	6.7

TABLE 4 Reciprocals of Nonwhite Age-Race-Sex-Marital-Status-Specific Mortality Rates (1967)

Age	Female				Male			
	Single	Married	Widowed	Divorced	Single	Married	Widowed	Divorced
15-19	1,190.5	937.2	380.5	772.8	594.9	446.2	236.5	1,562.5
20-24	546.4	766.9	276.7	470.1	289.6	432.9	123.2	199.6
25-34	233.5	428.1	172.2	282.5	145.6	317.4	82.1	122.3
35-44	115.1	213.8	103.2	136.0	70.9	174.0	55.4	62.6
45-54	77.6	114.2	57.9	83.5	45.7	86.3	32.1	34.7
55-59	55.4	71.0	38.2	52.8	33.4	104.3	22.5	24.4
60-64	42.4	55.0	30.2	42.4	25.0	36.4	18.2	18.4
65-69	28.6	35.6	20.7	25.4	15.7	20.9	11.5	10.8
70-74	22.3	28.9	17.4	21.5	12.9	18.2	10.7	10.2
75 and over	16.2	22.8	13.9	18.5	11.5	16.6	9.5	10.9

$60,000 or more, the assumption has been made that social-class differentials in mortality apply uniformly to all such individuals.

Some uneasiness is occasioned by this procedure. It is partly because the category assets of $60,000 and over includes persons with zero and negative net worth. Moreover, the $60,000 figure is also a point figure; it reveals little about the mortality-related conditions of life in the years prior to current financial status. Accumulated wealth is a function of income, time, and the propensity to consume. The same level of wealth may be generated by low income and low propensity to consume or by high income and high propensity to consume, time held constant. If out of a given income, lower propensities to consume mean foregoing health services, the $60,000 limit may be misleading.

It is also apparent from other studies of social-class mortality that differentials converge with age. Unlike the national estimates, which look only at the rich, this study estimates the entire wealth distribution. We are forced, therefore, to consider differential mortality rates over a much greater socioeconomic range than the national estimate handles.

The only measure of socioeconomic status on the death certificate is occupation. We, of course, have wealth from the tax records, but there are no available studies which relate wealth and mortality. An attempt by Kitagawa and Houser to use income as an independent variable proved only moderately successful because of data deficiencies.[14]

Lampman, in the most important study of U.S. wealth distribution, *The Share of Top Wealth-Holders in U.S. Wealth*, reviewed most of the social-class mortality literature up to 1962. Since the publication of his work, there have been a few additions, but they support the earlier literature rather than provide a significant quantitative refinement. In the most important of the new studies, Kitagawa and Houser[15] matched about 260,000 death certificates for persons dying in May, June, July, and August of 1960 with their 1960 Census records. The death certificates provided information on cause of death, marital status, place of birth, age and race, and usual occupation during life. The Census records, in addition to some of the above variables, provided information on occupation, work experience, income, and educa-

---

[14] Kitagawa and Houser, "Social and Economic Differentials."
[15] Ibid.

tion. Kitagawa and Houser's findings published to date show mortality rates to be inversely related to income, education, and occupational status. For purposes of this study, only occupational mortality differentials are of direct interest, inasmuch as income and education are not identifiable in our data. In Table 5, some of the Kitagawa–Houser findings for occupations are presented in the form of a mortality differential index. The base for the index is the overall age-adjusted mortality rate for white males age 25 to 64 or age 65 to 74, depending upon which age group one is examining. Within the age 25 to 64 group, there appears to be a reasonably smooth progression of the index value from high- to low-status occupations. The smooth relationship disolves, however, in the 65 to 74 age group. In order to determine if there was a dichotomous relationship between age, occupation, and mortality groups which disappeared when retirement was reached, or if the relationship followed a gradually weakening pattern, resort was made to the Moriyama-Guralnick data, which was older, but which contained occupational grouping by several age classes below 65.[16]

[16] Moriyama and Guralnick, "Occupational and Social Class Differentials."

TABLE 5 Occupation Mortality Differentials for Males With Work Experience Since 1950, May-August, 1960

| | | White | |
| | Nonwhite 25-64 | 25-64 | 65-74 |
Occupation Class	Years	Years	Years
Worked since 1950	1.00	1.00	1.00
White collar workers[a]	.93	.92	.98
Blue collar workers[b]	.95	1.07	1.02
Craftsmen and operatives[c]	.91	1.01	1.02
Service workers and laborers[d]	.98	1.28	1.04
Agricultural workers[e]		.76	.90

SOURCE: Evelyn M. Kitagawa, "Social and Economic Differentials in Mortality in the United States, 1960," *Proceedings, General Assembly and Conference of International Union for Scientific Study of Population,* London, September, 1969.

[a] Census Occupational Groups 1-3.
[b] Census Occupational Groups 4-9.
[c] Census Occupational Groups 4-5.
[d] Census Occupational Groups 6-7.
[e] Census Occupational Groups 8-9.

Moriyama-Guralnick grouped occupations into five categories:

1. Professional workers
2. Technical, administrative, and managerial workers
3. Proprietors, clerical, sales, and skilled workers
4. Semiskilled workers
5. Laborers, except farm and mine

Agricultural workers were excluded from the five categories, but farm owners and farm managers were included in category 2.

In Table 6, the Moriyama-Guralnick data have been cast into a set of mortality indexes by age group. The base of the index is the mortality rate for class 1 occupations within each age group. It is apparent that the impact of occupation on mortality depends upon age group. For men of all ages, there is an increase in mortality associated with decreased occupational status, but the strength of the association diminishes with age. For instance, for men aged 20-24, the mortality rate for those in the occupational class 5 is 388 percent of the rate for occupational class 1; but for the men 60-64, the occupational class 5 rate is only 133 percent of the class 1 rate. The decay of the relationship can be seen quite sharply in the lines of Chart 1. The mortality index tends to flatten out along the abscissa as age increases.

The social-class adjustments used on the estimates which follow are based entirely on occupation. The procedure used to make the adjustments to age-sex-race-marital-status-specific rates was as follows:

Decedents whose occupations fell within the *Dictionary of Occupational Titles*[17] codes 001 through 399 were assigned the average relative mortality differentials by which white male professional, technical, administrative, and managerial workers differed from all white males, age-class by age-class, as found by Moriyama and Guralnick.

Decedents whose occupations fell within the *Dictionary of Occupational Titles* codes 400 through 899 and housewives were assumed to enjoy average mortality and no adjustment was made to the age-sex-race-marital-status rates already assigned to them.

---

[17] U.S., Department of Labor, *Dictionary of Occupational Titles*, 3rd ed. (Washington, D.C., 1965).

TABLE 6 Occupational Mortality Rate Differential Shifts by Age-Class for Males of All Races, 1950

Age	Mortality Rate Occupation Class 1 (Deaths per 100,000)	Ratio of Occupational Class Mortality to Occupation Class 1 Mortality (Percent)				
		Class 1	Class 2	Class 3	Class 4	Class 5
20-24	95.9	100	153	146	184	388
25-29	92.6	100	153	156	205	473
30-34	135.1	100	125	136	179	426
35-44	288.9	100	115	131	156	330
45-54	946.9	100	99	109	118	205
55-59	1,922.3	100	99	108	105	156
60-64	2,886.0	100	99	109	101	133

SOURCE: The basic data from which the table was constructed are from I. M. Moriyama and L. Guralnick, *Trends and Differentials in Mortality, Proceeding, 1955 Annual Conference*, Milbank Memorial Fund, New York, p. 66.

Percent of occupation,
Class I mortality

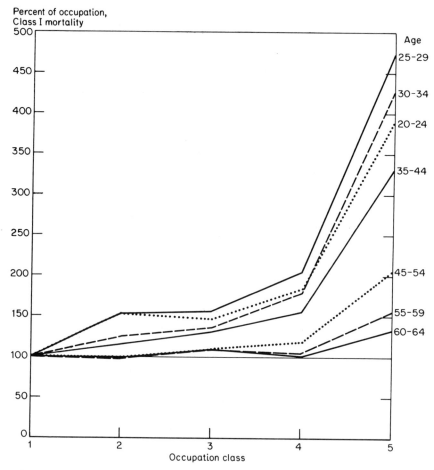

CHART 1: Occupation Class Mortality as a Percent of Occupational
Class I Mortality by Age

The occupations represented in this group include skilled and semiskilled and production and structural workers.[18]

Decedents whose occupations were listed as codes 900 or above in the *Dictionary of Occupational Titles* were assigned the average relative differential for male black laborers from all black males, age-class by age-class. The adjustment factors for the three classes are shown in Table 7.

[18] *The Dictionary of Occupational Titles* includes farmers within the code range 400 to 899, but none of the decedents was found to have had farming as his usual lifetime occupation, an occupation with particularly high mortality rates.

TABLE 7 Social-Class Adjustment Factors for Age-Sex-Race-Marital-Specific Mortality Rates

Occupation Class	Age					
	25–29	30–34	35–44	45–54	55–59	60–64
I	.71	.68	.81	.96	1.00	1.00
iI	1.00	1.00	1.00	1.00	1.00	1.00
III	1.64	1.65	1.68	1.50	1.48	1.38

Where occupation was missing from the death certificate or where a death certificate could not be located, the mean mortality rate after social-class adjustments for cases with complete occupation information was assigned to deficient cases within age-sex-race-marital-status classes.

B. Data and Its Sources

Two major and several ancillary data sources were used for the estimates. Most important and first in order of use was the 1967 District of Columbia estate tax return (FR-19). The second source was the death certificates filed for persons dying in the District of Columbia; and the third, the death certificates filed in the State of Maryland for residents of the District of Columbia dying there. Finally, a National Institute of Health (NIH) file of all District of Columbia residents dying in any state was used.

In outline, the data was assembled as follows:

1. All (3,303) estate tax returns filed for decedents who died in 1967 were examined and abstracted. The year 1967 was selected so that large estates which can take several years to settle would be in the closed files. Excellent cooperation was received from the District of Columbia Finance and Revenue Division.

2. Abstract sheets containing tax return information were matched with decedent's death certificates filed in the District of Columbia. The purpose of the match was to obtain additional information about the characteristics of decedents. The most important additional variables were race, place of birth, marital status, usual occupation during life, and death certificate number.

Because death certificates are filed in the political jurisdiction where death occurs, all District of Columbia taxpayers who died in the District presumably had a death certificate filed there. For 545 decedents who filed tax returns, no death certificate was located in the District of Columbia Vital Statistics Office. These decedents were then presumed to have died elsewhere.

3. Arrangements were made with the State of Maryland to purchase a card listing of all District of Columbia residents who died in Maryland (except in the city of Baltimore, which is an independent filing district). Of the 545 certificates not located in the District of Columbia files, 239 were found in the Maryland file.

4. A tape containing information for all District of Columbia residents who died anywhere and nonresidents who died in the District of Columbia in 1967 was purchased from the National Office for Health Statistics.

The tape was used in two ways:

(a) The death certificate contains information on cause of death which was desired for studies of differential mortality and to test hypothesis about sampling bias in the sample drawn by death. The certificate number coded from the death certificates in the Washington Vital Statistics Office and from the Maryland file was used to merge the wealth file with the NIH tape.

(b) For the remaining 329 decedents not dying in the District or the state of Maryland, excluding Baltimore City, no information was at hand on race, marital status, place of birth, or usual occupation, because a death certificate had not been found for these decedents. Therefore, a synthetic match was made on characteristics of decedents which were available both on our own file and the NIH file.

Common items were:

    i. Age
    ii. Date of death[19]
    iii. Sex
    iv. Partial information on marital status
    v. Place of death (partial)

The match procedure was as follows. All cases which had been matched exactly on death certificates were removed from the

[19] The date of death included the day, month, and year for deaths up to July 15, 1967; after that date only the month and year were included on the tape file.

working file of the NIH tape. The remaining cases, about 8,000 records, were sorted by date of death and sex. A listing of the file was then produced and a manual match was made on the full set of characteristics. When a perfect or near-perfect match was achieved, the death certificate number was entered into the wealth file and a computer merge was used to transfer the desired information. The quality of the match is believed to be very high. The probability of finding more than one person in 8,000 with the same date of death, sex, and age is not in itself very high, and in addition, 7,000 of the 8,000 records in the NIH file were for persons dying in the District and could be generally excluded from consideration because the certificates themselves had been searched. Further, in about a fifth of the cases the tax returns carried information on the place of death, which coupled with age and sex completely identified many persons dying outside the District. From tax information, it was known if a person left assets to a spouse, which permitted a further reduction in mismatches by testing for marital status on certificates. Where assets were not left to a spouse but to children, matches were ruled out by death certificate marital status: "never married."

For decedents who died after July 15, 1967, the date of death was limited to month of death. This resulted in a diminished ability to separate decedents into separate cells by a factor of 30 (360/12). In the end, 60 cases were assigned a random match from one or more certificates, which on the basis of limited information were plausible mates. These records were flagged for future attention. It is hoped that to reduce matching errors further the state of Virginia and the city of Baltimore will be able to provide assistance at a later time similar to that provided by Maryland.

5. Addresses of decedents were converted to 1970 Census tract codes. In nearly all cases, the address information supplied on the tax return and death certificate combined permitted a precise assignment of Census tract. In about 100 cases, the quadrant (NW, SW, NE, or SW) or some other part of the address was not available and the record could have fallen into more than one tract. The Bell system permitted use of their library facilities to identify the correct tracts. Where a phone listing for one person with the decedent's name appeared at a specific address in the 1966 or 1967 directory, that quadrant of that address was used to assign the tract. Where more than one phone listing for a person with the name of the decedent appeared and the listing appeared

in different tracts, it was determined if one name disappeared from the 1968 or 1969 listing. If it did, it was taken as prima facie evidence that that was the correct match for the decedent.

Although the concept of wealth is quite broad, estimates by type of asset are limited to those classes which are recorded as line items on the District of Columbia estate tax return. They are as follows:

1. *Real estate.* Real estate is limited to that situated in the District of Columbia. It is shown at its market value. Mortgages and debts against real estate are shown separately. In the case of rental real estate, accrued rents are included in the value.

2. *Stocks and bonds.* Included together are corporate issues of common and preferred stocks and corporate bonds, as well as bonds of all levels of government—foreign and domestic.

3. *Mortgages, notes, cash, deposits and other intangible property.* The category includes time and demand deposits, the present value of notes and mortgages, and interest accrued on any of them. It also includes less common items, such as tax sale certificates, refund coupons, and similar intangible wealth.

4. *Miscellaneous property.* Included are the net values of sole proprietorships and shares of partnership interests, interests in the estates of other decedents, currency and coins, works of art, personal effects, automobiles, consumer durables, and other real property not elsewhere included.

5. *Transfers during life.* Included are transfers of property at less than full money's worth during life in any of the following ways:

(a) to take effect at the death of the decedent;

(b) with the right retained by the decedent to enjoy the property during his lifetime;

(c) made in contemplation of death. (All transfers at less than money's worth within two years of death must be listed whether or not beneficiaries or agents of the estate consider the transfer in contemplation of death.)

6. *Powers of appointment.* A power of appointment is a set of rights with respect to an asset one does not own. Powers of appointment often come about because A wishes to permit B to transfer A's assets to a party to be designated at a later time by B.[20]

---

[20] The power may come about in the creation of a trust, the income of which was to be used to support an elderly parent until his death, then the

7. *Annuities and retirement funds.* Included here are the present market values of annuities or retirement funds which can be realized by the holder. Right to nonvested retirement funds or to Social Security benefits are not included, since those rights cannot be sold to another.

III. THE ESTIMATES

It is estimated that residents of the District of Columbia had a collective net worth of 5.5 billion dollars in 1967. This amounts to $7,200 for every man, woman, and child—a figure considerably below our rough estimate of $19,000 for the United States as a whole. The great difference is explainable by the low wealth position of blacks who made up about 67 percent of the District's population in 1967. The nonblack average net worth of District of Columbia residents, $19,300, compares favorably with the national figure, while the black average, $1,000, falls far below it.

The estimates of total wealth were made by fitting log-normal functions to estate multiplier estimates for persons with net worth of $5,000 or more and extrapolating them into the lower tail of the distribution. The process was applied separately for blacks and nonblacks. The tax data included persons with assets as low as $1,000 gross, but there is reason to believe that near the filing threshold, the quality of the data deteriorates because estates recognizing that they have zero tax liability opt not to file, though legally required to do so. Also, valuing small estates which consist largely of personal effects is likely to be imprecise, and it is suspected that executors may tend to err on the low side and not file.

Quite apart from the usefulness of the log-normal distribution

corpus to be distributed to such surviving relatives and friends of the grantor as the trustee deemed appropriate. When a trustee is free to appoint without constraint the persons to receive the corpus, the power of appointment is said to be general; if there are restrictions upon whom may be appointed, the power is special. In both property doctrine and tax law the distinction between general and special powers of appointment has become clouded. The use of the concept here follows its application in tax law which looks to the financial benefit which may potentially rebound to the person who has the power to appoint. Clearly, if one has the power to appoint himself as a beneficiary, whether he does so or not, he has wealth at his disposal. We have not made our own interpretation of the instruments which grant the power or determined their value but have used the interpretations of the tax officials and the courts as found in the records.

in filling in the wealth at the bottom of the distribution, it provides a succinct view of the overall distribution. In Chart 2 the separate functions for blacks and nonblacks have been plotted. The abscissa shows income levels on a log scale, while the ordinate is scaled to linearize a normal distribution. The points along the functions relate the percentages of the populations which have wealth equal to or less than specified amounts. The function for blacks shows that over 96 percent of the District's black population had net wealth of under $5,000 compared to 70 percent of the white population. A test of the reasonableness of the functions may be made by looking at points very near the intercepts and comparing the estimates with a common-sense notion of reality and external data. For instance, it could be agreed that, with rare exceptions, young children, say, under 15, have a net worth of zero. Indeed, it would not strain our credulity to accept a mean net worth of near zero for persons under 18 or 20. At the points of ordinate intercepts, the functions show that 52 percent of the black population had net worth of $100 or less and 16 percent of the white population was similarly situated. Using population estimates of 500,000 blacks and 259,000 whites

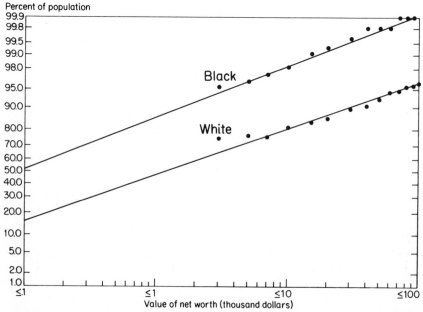

CHART 2: Logarithmic-Normal Distributions of Net Worth of White and Black Populations, Washington, D.C., 1967

in 1967, converts these percents to 260,000 blacks and 33,000 nonblacks with net worth of under $100. In 1970, there were about 225,000 persons under 18 in the District.[21] There were another 36,000 persons not under 18 in poverty families one might include as probably having a net worth under $100. That makes a total of 261,000 persons, and it is not unreasonable to believe that there were another thirty to forty thousand individuals over 18 with net wealth of $100 or less in nonproverty families.

For the city's residents as a group, stocks and bonds were preferred assets. About 2.7 billion dollars of them were held, and they accounted for more than half of the city's personal net worth. Real estate (located in the District) was a weak second choice, accounting for about a fifth of resident's wealth and valued at 1.2 billion dollars. Checking and saving accounts, notes and mortgages, and cash taken together also made up about a fifth of the city's collective personal wealth. District of Columbia residents were in debt .5 billion dollars, an amount equal to about 10 percent of their net worth.

As wealth increases, financial assets—such as stocks and bonds—increase in importance, and real estate decreases in the share it represents of total personal wealth. Stocks and bonds were about 8 percent of the net worth of persons with net assets of $1,000 to $5,000, but 66 percent of the wealth of persons with $100,000 or more. Real estate, which was 63 percent of the lower group's assets, was only 12 percent of the richer group's net worth. In Table 8, asset holdings are shown by size of net worth for persons with net worth of $1,000 or more. The $1,000 net worth cutoff is used because asset composition cannot be satisfactorily estimated below that level with our data. Consequently, the total net worth figure in the table comes to a little less than the 5.5 billion dollar figure noted above.

Portfolios also change with age. Real estate increases as a proportion of net worth up to ages 35 to 40 and then declines. Stocks and bonds are a minor proportion of net worth at younger ages but increase in importance rather steadily with age. (See Table 9.)

Washington is 71 percent black. Following the Supreme Court's decision in 1954, steps were taken to end discrimination in

[21] U.S., Department of Commerce, Bureau of the Census, *U.S. Census of Population: 1970, General Social and Economic Characteristics,* Final Report PC(1)-C10.

TABLE 8   Asset Holdings by Type of Asset and Level of Net Worth for All Persons With Net Worth of $1,000 or More in Washington, D.C., 1967

(thousands of dollars)

Net Worth ($000)		Real Estate	Stocks and Bonds	Notes and Mortgages	Miscellaneous
Total over 1		1,189,305	2,745,300	1,111,969	434,679
1 <	5	63,913	8,265	41,580	35,431
5 <	10	101,770	8,353	46.250	12,684
10 <	15	113,709	11,762	33,665	9,701
15 <	20	59,471	15,145	51,662	7,667
20 <	25	43,900	23,190	52,505	4,116
25 <	30	73,812	20,630	47,279	4,582
30 <	35	55,561	28,899	63,280	4,352
35 <	40	31,764	32,216	31,199	4,303
40 <	45	29,254	41,961	38,859	4,693
45 <	50	26,632	16,237	31,251	2,738
50 <	55	21,083	19,907	26,908	3,099
55 <	60	29,110	20,150	21,060	3,938
60 <	70	60,005	34,698	26,891	11,905
70 <	80	28,915	40,293	39,268	13,833
80 <	90	25,720	22,163	14,885	2,698
90 <	100	18,003	36,989	29,568	6,503
100 <	125	66,407	85,062	51,144	48,383
125 <	150	37,116	109,392	94,054	19,610
150 <	200	118,740	162,931	42,078	48,561
200 <	250	39,496	124,983	27,113	23,741
250 <	500	82,479	557,516	109,891	44,452
500 <	750	21,574	155,402	19,842	35,175
750 < 1,000		11,343	102,728	19,249	56,828
1,000 or more		29,540	1,006,663	152,652	25,746

federal hiring practices. Although there was less than complete compliance by agencies, the process moved rapidly compared to the results in many other large cities. To what extent the improved opportunities have been realized and have benefited blacks is of interest. The classification black includes all persons designated black or Negro on death certificates. All other persons are classified as nonblack.

In Tables 10 and 11, estimates of the mean and total value of assets held by blacks and nonblacks whose net worth was greater

TABLE 8 *(Continued)*

Net Worth ($000)		Life Transfers	Pensions	Powers of Appoint- ment	Gross Assets
Total over 1		181,610	131,323	15,186	5,809,363
1 <	5	60	4,390	30	153,666
5 <	10	1,101	12,795	20	182,973
10 <	15	798	6,086	a	175,720
15 <	20	1,970	8,669	2	144,587
20 <	25	191	9,617	a	133,520
25 <	30	1,345	6,858	a	154,506
30 <	35	524	8,925	748	162,287
35 <	40	183	3,827	a	103,491
40 <	45	1,018	11,456	a	127,241
45 <	50	542	3,623	a	81,025
50 <	55	1,444	3,733	a	76,176
55 <	60	633	1,132	a	76,025
60 <	70	699	592	a	134,790
70 <	80	822	4,854	a	127,984
80 <	90	2,804	7,550	a	75,820
90 <	100	550	1,320	a	92,934
100 <	125	42,292	12,018	2,625	307,931
125 <	150	3,977	3,776	168	268,095
150 <	200	11,283	1,915	520	386,027
200 <	250	8,715	1,710	a	225,758
250 <	500	22,686	11,280	a	828,306
500 <	750	849	3,072	a	235,914
750 < 1,000		22,394	1,183	a	273,724
1,000 or more		54,784	937	11,801	1,280,996

than or equal to $1,000 in 1967 are shown. Nonblacks, whether they were male or female, held a much smaller proportion of their wealth in real estate and a much larger portion in stocks and bonds than blacks (see Table 11). These findings for the District are similar to estimates for the nation made by Terrell using Survey of Economic Opportunity (SEO) data.[22] He found that 67.7 percent of black wealth was held in real estate and 2.3 percent in stocks and bonds. The corresponding figures for the District of Columbia population are 84.9 and 5.2 percent (see Table 12). For the

[22] Henry S. Terrell, "Wealth Accumulation of Black and White Families: The Empirical Evidence," *Journal of Finance* 26 (May 1971):363-77.

TABLE 8 *(Concluded)*

Net Worth ($000)		Debts	Net Worth	Life Insurance[b]	Joint Property Holdings[b]
Total over 1		563,694	5,245,681	627,517	1,167,582
1 <	5	52,181	101,481	76,728	65,473
5 <	10	34,675	148,299	72,203	93,250
10 <	15	47,614	128,105	27,374	97,317
15 <	20	15,290	129,297	22,786	48,354
20 <	25	9,319	124,201	15,023	49,440
25 <	30	4,021	150,485	32,113	88,291
30 <	35	10,201	152,087	29,836	64,457
35 <	40	22,136	81,355	6,419	35,668
40 <	45	6,770	120,471	31,763	33,599
45 <	50	5,085	75,941	5,612	30,597
50 <	55	1,772	74,404	7,268	27,425
55 <	60	2,075	73,949	2,449	35,301
60 <	70	26,274	108,525	19,601	67,583
70 <	80	2,215	125,769	10,318	42,278
80 <	90	920	74,899	5,971	16,448
90 <	100	2,308	90,625	2,876	20,025
100 <	125	20,929	287,002	76,409	68,960
125 <	150	15,405	252,690	7,003	47,892
150 <	200	56,509	329,518	127,714	88,467
200 <	250	11,321	214,437	7,264	39,848
250 <	500	40,015	788,290	26,540	66,147
500 <	750	1,703	234,211	5,322	9,536
750 < 1,000		27,379	246,346	4,128	15,879
1,000 or more		147,557	1,133,418	4,783	15,329

[a] Less than 5 cases.
[b] Life insurance and joint property holdings are shown here as information items. Life insurance is excluded from gross assets and net worth, but jointly owned assets have been included by type in their appropriate category.

nonblack population, the percentages are 18.2 and 34.7 respectively. Black debts represent a greater proportion (28.9 percent) of net worth than do nonblack debts (9.4 percent). The same is true of life insurance. Blacks held life insurance policies which amounted to 26.1 percent of their total net worth, while nonblacks held life insurance equal to only 10.9 percent of their net worth. To a large extent, the difference in portfolio

TABLE 9 Asset Holdings by Type of Asset and Age for All Persons with Net Worth of $1,000 or More in Washington, D.C., 1967

(thousands of dollars)

Age	Real Estate	Stocks and Bonds	Notes and Mortgages	Miscellaneous	Life Transfers	Pensions
All ages	1,189,305	2,745,299	1,111,967	434,671	181,612	131,337
<25	4,921	3,112	9,079	6,436	a	4,392
25 < 30	6,295	2,003	10,748	10,588	a	985
30 < 35	52,038	959	12,197	3,514	a	3,693
35 < 45	192,280	66,436	46,742	78,832	50,078	9,946
45 < 55	273,545	318,119	215,655	57,180	0	34,304
55 < 60	178,987	363,455	112,000	103,315	3,629	39,655
60 < 65	112,763	214,194	116,957	35,531	3,302	16,131
65 < 70	129,817	244,763	132,328	70,354	20,318	14,175
70 < 75	88,890	866,371	258,036	33,303	5,922	5,474
75 < 80	68,249	264,849	68,394	15,304	73,429	993
80 < 85	32,751	136,636	54,962	11,250	6,006	575
85 < 90	31,617	150,206	40,814	4,607	5,309	178
≥90	17,819	114,151	34,032	4,733	13,615	813

TABLE 9 *(Concluded)*

Age	Powers of Appointment	Gross Assets	Debts	Net Worth	Life Insurance[b]	Joint Property Holdings[b]
All ages	15,187	5,809,337	563,699	5,245,638	627,522	1,167,580
<25	a	27,940	2,755	25,186	15,359	510
25 < 30	a	30,619	9,892	20,728	3,921	6,896
30 < 35	a	72,400	12,228	60,172	66,809	52,468
35 < 45	a	444,316	108,165	336,510	201,462	119,013
45 < 55	a	898,802	114,672	784,132	136,515	299,834
55 < 60	a	801,038	76,753	724,287	94,239	172,928
60 < 65	18	458,900	29,126	469,773	41,728	154,751
65 < 70	29	611,783	23,842	587,941	27,549	149,622
70 < 75	749	1,258,743	153,944	1,104,750	20,978	95,977
75 < 80	7,712	498,658	26,372	472,331	11,732	47,614
80 < 85	5,580	247,087	2,267	244,820	4,369	35,402
85 < 90	927	233,657	2,641	231,016	1,810	17,024
≥90	168	185,331	1,028	184,303	1,057	15,531

[a] Less than 5 cases.
[b] Life insurance and joint property are not included in the concept of net worth, but are shown as information items.

TABLE 10 Mean and Total Value of Selected Assets by Sex for All Nonblack Persons With Net Worth of $1,000 or More in Washington, D.C., 1967

(means in dollars, totals in thousands of dollars)

	Male		Female	
Asset	*Mean*	*Total*	*Mean*	*Total*
Real estate	9,099	377,729	11,869	507,164
Stocks and bonds	37,968	1,576,102	26,905	1,149,610
Notes, cash, mortgages	11,864	492,470	12,419	530,635
Miscellaneous	6,354	263,777	2,979	127,308
Pension funds	2,058	85,442	733	31,303
Powers of appointment	5	220	350	14,963
Lifetime transfers	2,697	111,975	1,387	59,255
Gross assets	70,047	2,907,713	56,642	2,420,212
Debts	8,291	344,164	2,614	111,674
Net worth	61,756	2,563,541	54,029	2,308,538
Life Insurance[a]	10,483	435,147	2,224	95,017
Joint property[a]	11,326	470,133	11,695	499,725

NOTE: The estimates are based on the total number of persons with net worth of $1,000 or more, including those with zero holdings of specific assets.

[a] Not included in gross assets or net worth.

composition reflects the different economic status of the two groups.

The estimates reported here are for individuals, not consumer units or families. The marital status of decedents in the sample are known, however, and it is possible to estimate the distribution of wealth by marital status.

The social and legal customs surrounding the process of marriage and its dissolution bear on the distribution of wealth by the manner in which legal rights to assets devolve. In the case of marriage, there is a tendency in custom and in law for spouses to share in each other's wealth, thus reducing the asset level of the richer partner and increasing that of the poorer. Death benefits the surviving partner in every case, except where the cost of the decedent's interment exceeds his net worth, or where his net worth was negative prior to death. Divorce and separation almost always will result in a diminution of both partners' wealth, since settlements presumably are intended to attain in dissolution the

TABLE 11   Mean and Total Value of Selected Assets by Sex for All Black Persons With Net Worth of $1,000 or More in Washington, D.C., 1967

(means in dollars, totals in thousands of dollars)

Asset	Male Mean	Male Total	Female Mean	Female Total
Real estate	8,195	189,301	7,759	115,102
Stocks and bonds	348	8,050	773	11,469
Notes, cash, mortgages	2,149	49,640	2,642	39,187
Miscellaneous	1,470	33,956	649	9,635
Pension funds	416	9,618	334	4,953
Powers of appointment	–	–	–	–
Lifetime transfers	383	8,847	103	1,529
Gross assets	12,962	299,412	12,260	181,877
Debts	3,308	76,405	2,119	31,443
Net worth	9,654	223,009	10,141	150,434
Life insurance[a]	3,796	87,676	653	9,680
Joint property[a]	5,777	133,448	4,330	54,243

NOTE: The estimates are based on the total number of persons with net worth of $1,000 or more, including those with zero holdings of specific assets.

[a] Not included in gross assets or net worth.

economic rights one had in marriage, and the legal costs of separation are positive. Outright desertion may benefit either partner and it is difficult to determine a priori whether on the average the deserter or the deserted benefits (see Tables 13 and 14).

The data for nonblacks supports the contention that outliving one's spouse is the route to increased riches. Widows and widowers had the largest mean net worths of all marital classes. Widowers held, on the average, 11.3 percent more wealth than married men, the next highest marital group, and widows held 63.0 percent more than married women, the next highest marital group for women. The lowest net worth was found for never-married males. Surprisingly, they did less well than never-married females, who, one would suppose, suffered from low wage levels.

Among blacks, the marital-status differences in wealth nearly disappear. Ignoring the "other" category, all of the marital groups except divorced males have means around $10,000. Again the

TABLE 12 Composition of Wealth by Sex for Blacks and Nonblacks With $1,000 or More Net Worth in Washington, D.C., 1967
(percentages of net worth)

Asset	All Racial Groups			Blacks			Nonblacks		
	Total	Male	Female	Total	Male	Female	Total	Male	Female
Real estate	22.7	20.3	25.3	81.5	84.9	76.5	18.2	14.7	22.0
Stocks and bonds	32.6	56.8	5.1	5.2	3.6	7.6	34.7	61.5	5.0
Notes, mortgages, cash and deposits	20.7	19.5	22.1	23.8	22.3	26.2	20.4	19.2	21.8
Miscellaneous	8.3	10.7	5.6	11.7	15.1	6.4	8.0	10.3	5.5
Pension funds	2.5	3.4	1.5	3.9	4.3	3.3	2.4	3.3	1.4
Power of appointment	0.3	a	0.6	a	a	a	0.3	a	0.6
Lifetime transfers	3.5	4.3	2.5	2.8	4.0	1.0	3.5	4.4	2.6
Gross assets	110.7	115.1	105.8	128.9	134.3	120.9	109.4	113.4	104.8
Debts	10.7	15.1	5.8	28.9	34.3	20.9	9.4	13.4	4.8
Net worth	100.0	100.0	100.0	100.0	100.0	100.0	100.0	100.0	100.0
Life insurance[b]	11.9	18.1	4.3	26.1	39.3	6.4	12.0	17.0	4.1
Joint property[b]	14.1	6.5	22.9	52.9	59.8	42.7	19.9	18.3	21.6

[a] Rounds to less than 0.1 percent.
[b] Life insurance and joint property are not included in the concept of net worth, but are shown here as information items.

TABLE 13   Mean and Total Net Worth and Number of Persons by Sex and Marital Status for All Black Persons With Net Worth of $1,000 or More in Washington, D.C., 1967

(mean net worth in dollars, total net worth in thousands of dollars)

Sex and Marital Status	Mean Net Worth	Number of Wealth Holders	Total Net Worth
All individuals	9,845	37,934	374,978
Male	9,654	23,099	222,998
Never married	6,181	2,934	18,135
Married	10,241	19,600	200,723
Widowed	9,480	878	8,323
Divorced	7,331	256	1,877
Other	a	a	a
Female	10,140	14,835	150,427
Never married	10,515	1,670	17,560
Married	10,033	9,276	93,066
Widowed	11,252	3,025	34,037
Divorced	11,349	622	7,059
Other	16,902	242	4,090

[a] Sample size less than 5.

correlation between age and marital status and wealth is reflected in the means for marital status.

To measure the simultaneous impact of all the demographic variables on the level of net worth, a multiple regression was fitted:

Log Net Worth =
      f(Age, Sex, Race, Marital Status, Occupation, Birthplace)

Dummy variables were used for all independent variables. The R^2 was .26 and most dummies are significant. In Table 15, the statistics of the estimation are presented.

It was initially hypothesized that age and net worth would move together up to some postretirement point as savings accrued from income. It was thought that beyond that point, net worth would decline as individuals dissaved. The estimates do not support such a life-cycle hypothesis. The regression coefficients

TABLE 14   Mean and Total Net Worth and Number of Persons by Sex and Marital Status for All Nonblack Persons With Net Worth of $1,000 or More in Washington, D.C., 1967

(mean net worth in dollars, total net worth in thousands of dollars)

Sex and Marital Status	Mean Net Worth	Number of Wealth Holders	Total Net Worth
All individuals	57,836	84,240	4,872,105
Male	61,756	41,511	2,563,553
Never married	19,930	7,635	152,158
Married	72,036	31,359	2,258,977
Widowed	80,203	1,478	118,540
Divorced	32,716	1,029	33,664
Other	a	a	a
Female	54,029	42,728	2,308,551
Never married	35,179	10,945	385,034
Married	53,780	20,939	1,126,099
Widowed	87,641	8,124	711,995
Divorced	31,552	2,678	84,496
Other	22,125	42	929

[a] Sample size less than 5.

increase rather steadily with age; only a slight dip occurs in the range from 60 to 70 years of age.

Being black, as was apparent from the descriptive tabulations, is an important negative factor in wealth holding, lowering the expected value of net worth $3,330.

In conjunction with all other variables, sex is not important nor significant in predicting net worth. Marital status is important, but has mixed significance scores. Widowhood showed up in the tabulated data as being associated with high net worth among whites, but in the multiple regression, where all other factors are at play, it turns out to have minor importance and little significance.

Occupation codes used in the regression are three-digit *Dictionary of Occupational Titles* (DOT) codes for civilian employees and special codes for housewives and military personnel. Although most of the occupation dummies proved significant and impor-

TABLE 15   Statistics From Multiple Regression of Log of Net Worth on Age, Sex, Race, Marital Status, Occupation, and Place of Birth
(log of net worth in thousands of dollars)

Variable	Regression Coefficient	Standard Error	F
Age:			
0 = < 35			
1 = 35 < 40	.277	.146	3.60
2 = 40 < 45	.335	.060	6.42
3 = 45 < 50	.530	.113	21.88
4 = 50 < 55	.538	.109	24.30
5 = 55 < 60	.670	.102	43.24
6 = 60 < 65	.620	.101	37.93
7 = 65 < 70	.640	.100	41.31
8 = 70 < 75	.735	.099	57.92
9 = 75 < 80	.791	.099	63.39
10 = ≥ 80	.839	.098	73.16
Race:			
1 = Nonblack			
2 = Black	−.522	.030	304.66
Sex:			
1 = Male			
2 = Female	.039	.032	1.51
Marital status:			
1 = Never married			
2 = Married	.123	.037	11.12
3 = Widowed	.012	.039	.09
4 = Divorced	−.236	.062	14.46
5 = Other	−.147	.206	.51
Occupation:			
0 = First digit DOT[a]			
1 = First digit DOT[a]	.105	.050	4.48
2 = First digit DOT[a]	−.064	.051	1.56
3 = First digit DOT[a]	−.235	.054	18.48
4 = First digit DOT[a]	−.528	.249	4.50
5 = First digit DOT[a]	−.188	.177	1.12
6 = First digit DOT[a]	−.316	.107	8.74
7 = First digit DOT[a]	−.303	.113	7.12
8 = First digit DOT[a]	−.334	.095	12.44
9 = First digit DOT[a]	−.336	.068	24.15
10 = Housewives	.039	.041	.92

TABLE 15 *(Concluded)*

Variable	Regression Coefficient	Standard Error	F
Age:			
11 = High-rank military	.554	.249	4.92
12 = Middle-rank military	−.898	.607	2.19
13 = Low-rank military	.033	.019	.85
14 = Officer of unspecified rank	.377	.138	7.47
Birthplace:			
1 = Inside U.S.			
2 = Outside U.S.	−.059	.045	1.73
Constant = .62403			
R^2 = .26			
N = 2,585			

[a] U.S., Department of Labor, *Dictionary of Occupational Titles,* 3rd ed. (Washington, D.C., 1965).

tant, it is apparent from work in progress that the DOT coding scheme is not the most satisfactory one for clustering occupations to predict wealth. The created occupation "housewife" was not important nor significant. Military status turned out to be important. Officers of high rank have an expected net worth $3,500 higher than civilian professionals in the highest DOT classification.

DISCUSSION: WHITE WEALTH AND BLACK PEOPLE: THE DISTRIBUTION OF WEALTH IN WASHINGTON, D.C., IN 1967

Vito Natrella

Internal Revenue Service

Washington, D.C. has several distinguishing characteristics. Its population is nearly three-quarters black. The federal government is the largest employer, with large numbers of residents employed in government-related trade and service industries. Very few residents of the District are engaged in manufacturing and virtually none are engaged in agriculture.

These and other factors make Washington an interesting but unique city. Therefore, while the techniques Smith used can be adapted to other large urban centers, the applicability of the results elsewhere is open to question. The main and considerable advantage of Washington was, of course, the ready availability of a very rich data base.

Smith used the estate multiplier technique, which, as he explained, has proven useful in previous work. The paper contains some innovations, resulting, as Smith indicated, from a unique set of data including both estate tax returns and death certificates.

ESTATE MULTIPLIER TECHNIQUE

The only readily available administrative source of information on wealth is the estate tax return. The estate multiplier technique has been applied to federal estate tax returns. In this case, we have a very special group of people. The federal filing requirement for estate tax returns is gross assets of $60,000 or more. We are, therefore, dealing with the wealthiest 4 or 5 percent of the population. If we were to use average mortality rates for the U.S. population to compute the weighting factors, we would obtain lower limit estimates of wealth for the top wealthholders. However, it is reasonable to assume that the mortality rates for the wealthy are more favorable than for the general population. Without going into detail, the mortality rates selected for the

Internal Revenue Service's (IRS) 1962 Personal Wealth report[1] were 11 percent to 31 percent less than the average, depending on age group. These differentials are based on experience for individuals with preferred risk life insurance policies of $5,000 or more. In selecting such mortality rates, we feel that we have succeeded in eliminating the unfavorable mortality rates of the poor, rather than successfully determining the mortality rate of the wealthy.

For our 1969 Personal Wealth[2] estimates, mortality rates were based on the Metropolitan Life Insurance Company's experience for individuals with preferred risk life insurance policies of $25,000 or more. These rates ranged from about 10 percent to 43 percent more favorable than the average 1969 rates. We feel that the "$25,000 or more" rates, which were not available for the 1962 report, are more appropriate. However, estimates for 1969 based on the mortality rates for individuals with preferred risk life insurance policies of $5,000 or more as in the 1962 report, are also presented. Whichever of the two sets of rates is employed, there is the weakness that all those with assets of $60,000 or more are assigned the same mortality rates. We plan to do further research in this field and are considering the possibility of using a sliding scale according to size of estate.

In computing the weights for his District of Columbia estimates, Smith starts with national mortality rates by age, sex, and race. To these mortality rates, two adjustments are made—an adjustment for marital status and an adjustment for social class as measured by occupation. The importance of the marital status adjustment is demonstrated by the fact that two-thirds of the District wealth holders were married, while one-fifth were never married. A social-class adjustment is particularly important in working with federal estate returns because of the high filing threshold. But even in working with District estate returns it is

[1] U.S., Treasury Department, Internal Revenue Service, *Statistics of Income–1962, Personal Wealth Estimated from Estate Tax Returns*, Publication No. 482 (7-67) (Washington, D.C., 1967). This report is available from the Government Printing Office, Washington, D.C. 20402, for $.65.

[2] U.S., Treasury Department, Internal Revenue Service, *Statistics of Income–1969, Personal Wealth Estimated from Estate Tax Returns*, Publication No. 482 (10-73) (Washington, D.C., 1973). This report is available from the Government Printing Office, Washington, D.C. 20402, for $1.50. Some data are presented in the appendix.

important, since only 16 percent of the population held wealth of $1,000 or more.

Using the marital-status adjustment does make a significant improvement. Smith applied 1959–61 differentials to the 1967 mortality rates. Klebba presents marital status mortality rates for 1940, 1950–51, and 1959–61. In reviewing the rates for these periods, it is apparent that there is a significant change in mortality by marital status over time. This being the case, perhaps some adjustment for trend could have been employed in extrapolating to 1967.

In general, I would agree that there is a strong correlation between occupation and social class. However, mortality rates by occupation have probably changed significantly over the years with a tendency toward increased job safety and increased consideration to the long-range health aspects of various jobs. Also, occupational differentials for an urban population may be significantly different from national occupational differentials.

Therefore, I would like to raise the question of the appropriateness of using Moriyama and Guralnick occupational differentials for 1950 to represent social-class differentials in 1967. This procedure relies on the assumption that there were no significant shifts in mortality rate by occupation over the seventeen-year period.

Smith went from the five-class Moriyama-Guralnick differentials presented in Table 6 to the three occupational differentials actually used, shown in Table 7. As the number of groups are reduced, each group becomes less homogeneous, so that with only three groups, lawyers, physicians, and business executives are included with waiters, porters, policemen, and janitors.

ESTIMATES OF DISTRICT OF COLUMBIA WEALTH

I was confronted with some problems concerning internal consistency, since most of the tabulations did not provide frequencies. I also tried to make some rough comparisons with estimates made for the District of Columbia for 1962.

Using information in the text, along with the few frequencies provided and Chart 2, it was possible to approximate frequencies by size of net worth. The chart indicates that 86 percent of the black population had net worth of less than $1,000. Based on these figures, and the 1967 population estimates, 70,000 blacks had net worth of $1,000 or more in 1967, but the number of black wealth holders (Table 13) is esimated to be about 38,000. The chart indicates the total number of wealth holders to be 210,000, while the estimated number from Tables 13 and 14 is 122,000. This problem of inconsistency develops, I believe, because the chart was plotted from the population with net worth of $5,000 or more and extended to the population for which no data were available, whereas the tables show estate multiplier estimates.

COMPARISONS WITH OTHER ESTIMATES

The only other recent estimates of wealth for the District of Columbia are those for 1962 published by the Internal Revenue Service. These estimates cover all top wealth holders with $60,000 or more of gross assets. Unfortunately, similar estimates are not available for 1969, since District residents are included with Maryland residents in the IRS report covering that year.

In order to make Smith's 1967 estimates as comparable as possible with the 1962 estimates, it was necessary to make certain adjustments and assumptions. Net worth of $50,000 or more in Smith's distribution was considered equivalent to gross assets of $60,000 or more, although we recognized that this will overstate the case. An adjustment was made by adding cash surrender value of life insurance to Smith's 1967 estimates of net worth. This was done by deflating face value of life insurance by an interpolated average factor developed by IRS for its own wealth estimates. Another adjustment consisted of excluding all real estate from both estimates. This was done because Smith's estimates did not include real estate located outside the District of Columbia, whereas the IRS estimates include all real estate.

Generally speaking, Smith's 1967 figures did not show the increases from 1962 that one would expect; the number of top wealth holders remained about the same over the five-year period, as did holdings of cash, notes, and mortgages. Holdings of securities showed an 8 percent rise, while total assets other than real estate rose by 6 percent.

In comparison, the Federal Reserve Board shows nationwide increases in individual's holdings of comparable assets in the neighborhood of 50 to 60 percent over the same period. IRS estimates of net worth other than real estate for the District of

Columbia and Maryland combined show it to have more than doubled from 1962 to 1969.

These comparisons point out the possibility that Smith's estimates for 1967 might be low. However, an explanation which appears reasonable could be made on the basis of out-migration to the suburbs of more affluent whites, coupled with in-migration of less affluent blacks. Population figures for the District show a rise of 77,000 for nonwhites and a decline of 71,000 whites over the 1962–67 period.

ALTERNATIVE METHOD FOR DETERMINING WEALTH

In his work, in addition to having the District estate tax return data, Smith also had the death certificates for all decedents for 1967. It seems to me that with this information, Smith can provide an almost independent check on his wealth estimates without making any assumptions as to mortality rates. The only additional information needed is population estimates for 1967 by age, sex, and race. It should be possible to develop these from Census information with little trouble.

For each age, sex, and race group, the weighting factor can be determined by dividing the number of deaths into the population. For those deaths not covered by estate returns, one can, perhaps, assign some reasonable values, by age, up to $1,000. The amounts assigned to these records can be varied in successive tabulations, providing a test of upper and lower limits.

Using this weighting procedure, differences in social class, marital status, and even urban environment are automatically taken into account. The frequencies will match the known population, and it will be possible to compare the asset composition amounts with those computed under the estate multiplier method. In addition, it will provide a measure of the effects of using the marital status and occupational adjustments. It might also be possible with this type of estimate to develop implied differentials in mortality rates due to wealth.

REGRESSION ANALYSIS

In his regression analyses, Smith has made interesting use of dummy variables. The approach appears to be valid in this type of analysis. By and large, Smith's conclusions as to significance of the various variables appear to be supportable by the data provided. However, I might take mild issue as to the standards used for significance. A slightly different conclusion might be reached if a somewhat more rigorous definition of significance were used. If, for instance, the three-standard-error level of significance were used for the regression coefficient confidence limit, it would be found that only four occupation classes out of fourteen appear to be significant. This would indicate results that are more mixed than for marital status. From this analysis, it would appear that only age and race are really significant variables; while to a lesser extent, marital status could also be considered significant.

From his multiple regression, Smith obtained an R^2 of .26, which we agree is significant. The question might be asked: How can the other three-fourths of the variance be explained? I would think that the really significant determinants, which, of course, cannot be measured at this time, would be prior income, inherited wealth, and the propensity to save.

CONCLUSIONS

Smith has made a valuable contribution to the estate multiplier technique. He has shown that marital status can be used to refine the multipliers, and I feel that further work in this field should make use of them. I would, however, be more comfortable if adjustment factors could be based on more recent data, since I feel that there may have been some recent trends in these differentials.

Smith does mention problems which arise when using the occupational classification approach to social-class differentials. In view of this, as well as of the mixed results obtained in terms of significances, I feel that at least at this stage of development, it might be better not to use occupation. Smith has explored the subject thoroughly and has given us a better understanding of what to expect from this approach. However, I feel that further research is needed in order to develop measures of social-class differentials.

In addition to the methodology and technical developments presented by Smith, he has given us some new information on the distribution of wealth with particular emphasis on racial differences.

As regards the paper itself, I think an attempt should be made to clarify the definitions of the occupational differentials, since, as presented by Smith, this is rather difficult to understand. It also appears to me that some improvement in the method of estimating wealth of the under-$5,000 group is needed. In any case, only one set of data should be used, either the extrapolated values or the estate multiplier estimates. Another possibility, and certainly an easier one, would be to exclude the under-$5,000 group at this time.

APPENDIX

TABLE A.1   Number of Top Wealth Holders and Net Worth, by Size of Net Worth, 1962 and 1969

(numbers in thousands, money amounts in billions of dollars)

	Top Wealth holders				Net Worth			
	1962		1969		1962		1969	
Size of Net Worth	Number	Percent of Total	Number	Percent of Total	Amount	Percent of Total	Amount	Percent of Total
Negative net worth	25	0.6	71	0.8	-1.5	-0.2	-3.8	-0.3
0 under $50,000	584	14.1	1,744	19.3	18.0	2.7	48.4	3.5
$50,000 under $70,000	732	17.7	1,475	16.4	45.1	6.7	90.4	6.6
$70,000 under $100,000	991	24.0	2,022	22.4	82.8	12.4	168.6	12.2
$100,000 under $150,000	799	19.3	1,639	18.2	96.6	14.4	198.5	14.4
$150,000 under $300,000	626	15.1	1,298	14.4	128.5	19.2	265.0	19.2
$300,000 under $1,000,000	314	7.6	643	7.1	155.2	23.2	313.7	22.8
$1,000,000 under $5,000,000	56	1.4	111	1.2	100.2	15.0	192.6	14.0
$5,000,000 or more	4	0.1	9	0.1	44.2	6.6	103.5	7.5
Total	4,132	100.0	9,013	100.0	669.3	100.0	1,376.9	100.0

NOTE: All figures are estimates based on estate tax returns samples. Components may not add to totals due to rounding.
SOURCES: U.S., Treasury Department, Internal Revenue Service, *Statistics of Income—1962, Personal Wealth Estimated from Estate Tax Returns* (Washington, D.C., 1967). U.S., Treasury Department, Internal Revenue Service, *Statistics of Income—1969, Personal Wealth Estimated from Estate Tax Returns* (Washington, D.C., 1973).

TABLE A.2   Number of Top Wealth Holders and Net Worth, by Age Group, 1962 and 1969
(numbers in thousands, money amounts in billions of dollars)

Age Group	Top Wealth Holders				Net Worth			
	1962		1969		1962		1969	
	Number	Percent of Total	Number	Percent of Total	Amount	Percent of Total	Amount	Percent of Total
Under 40 years	653	15.8	1,454	16.1	76.3	11.4	129.6	9.4
40 under 50	807	19.5	2,035	22.6	108.8	16.2	272.6	19.8
50 under 55	485	11.7	1,107	12.3	74.6	11.1	162.4	11.8
55 under 60	541	13.1	1,052	11.7	94.6	14.1	168.0	12.2
60 under 65	475	11.5	981	10.9	86.5	12.9	169.2	12.3
65 under 70	430	10.4	819	9.1	80.8	12.0	199.1	14.5
70 under 75	281	6.8	634	7.0	53.2	7.9	126.2	9.2
75 under 80	194	4.7	392	4.3	40.1	6.0	35.0	2.5
80 under 85	110	2.7	221	2.4	23.9	3.6	46.4	3.4
85 or more	68	1.6	146	1.6	17.2	2.6	35.1	2.5
Age unknown	87	2.1	172	1.9	13.1	2.0	33.3	2.4
Total	4,132	100.0	9,013	100.0	669.3	100.0	1,376.9	100.0

NOTE: All figures are estimates based on estate tax returns samples. Components may not add to totals due to rounding.

SOURCES: U.S., Treasury Department, Internal Revenue Service, *Statistics of Income—1962, Personal Wealth Estimated from Estate Tax Returns* (Washington, D.C., 1967). U.S., Treasury Department, Internal Revenue Service, *Statistics of Income—1969, Personal Wealth Estimated from Estate Tax Returns* (Washington, D.C., 1973).

TABLE A.3   Distribution of Assets for All Top Wealth Holders, by Size of Net Worth, 1969

(billions of dollars)

Size of Net Worth	Corporate Stock	Real Estate	Bonds	Cash and Deposits	Notes and Mortgages	Life Insurance	All Other Assets	Total Assets	Debts	Net Worth
Negative net worth	0.8	2.5	0.0	0.4	0.4	0.5	1.3	5.8	9.7	−3.8
0 under $50,000	8.9	48.7	0.8	8.0	1.8	7.4	13.2	88.7	40.2	48.4
$50,000 under $70,000	16.7	47.4	3.1	18.8	4.0	4.1	16.9	111.0	20.5	90.4
$70,000 under $100,000	39.0	71.5	7.8	36.6	7.9	4.6	23.4	190.8	22.2	168.6
$100,000 under $150,000	56.0	76.6	8.6	38.1	9.7	4.6	28.5	222.1	23.6	198.5
$150,000 under $300,000	97.8	83.5	13.0	41.2	14.5	4.9	39.0	293.9	28.9	265.0
$300,000 under $1,000,000	151.4	70.0	22.1	33.7	15.1	3.6	49.3	345.3	31.6	313.7
$1,000,000 under $5,000,000	119.8	22.6	17.2	10.4	5.1	1.1	36.0	212.0	19.3	192.6
$5,000,000 or more	60.9	5.3	12.7	2.5	1.0	0.2	28.5	111.1	7.6	103.5
Total	551.4	428.0	85.4	189.7	59.4	30.9	235.7	1,580.6	203.6	1,376.9

NOTE: All figures are estimates based on estate tax returns samples. Components may not add to totals due to rounding.

SOURCES: U.S., Treasury Department, Internal Revenue Service, *Statistics of Income–1962, Personal Wealth Estimated from Estate Tax Returns* (Washington, D.C., 1967). U.S., Treasury Department, Internal Revenue Service, *Statistics of Income–1969, Personal Wealth Estimated from Estate Tax Returns* (Washington, D.C., 1973).

PART V

THE QUALITY OF INCOME DATA

CHAPTER 12

Measurement of Transfer Income in the Current Population Survey

Dorothy S. Projector
Social Security Administration

and

Judith Bretz
Social Security Administration

(*with the assistance of Mary P. Johnston and Ellen G. Murray*)

The findings of the Current Population Survey (CPS) with regard to total money income and its distribution among consumer units in the United States are widely used in analyses of social and economic well-being. Currently, the CPS provides the basis for analyzing such important problems as the effects on the distribution of income of proposed changes in the income maintenance system. When income aggregates estimated from the CPS or from other cross-section surveys are compared with aggregates from the social accounts, appropriately adjusted, survey totals are usually less than social account totals. The understatement in the survey totals stems from a variety of sources, and, consequently, the implications of the understatement vary with the particular problem being analyzed. For example, the CPS finds less than one-half the property income found in social accounts.

The authors wish to express their gratitude to Lenore E. Bixby, Benjamin Bridges, John J. Carroll, Mollie Orshansky, Alfred M. Skolnik, and Thomas G. Staples of the Office of Research and Statistics, Social Security Administration, for their review and criticism of this paper. Systems support for the paper was expertly provided by Lynn Hollabaugh, assisted by Kenneth Dymond, James Reed, and James Spalding. A technical appendix to accompany this paper is available from the authors.

To the extent that this understatement reflects a failure to enumerate dividend income, it is probably not serious for purposes of estimating the cost of a welfare reform bill or for analyses of the magnitude of the low-income population, because dividend income is concentrated among a relatively few families. On the other hand, the failure of the CPS to find large amounts of wages or of interest income is more of a problem because such income is widely distributed in the population and many families may contribute to the understatement. An understatement of transfer income is important because such income is concentrated among families with small amounts of nontransfer income. If the understatement is attributable largely to low-income families, cost estimates of income maintenance proposals based on the CPS will be affected, as will analyses of the magnitude of the low-income problem.

This paper is addressed to the question of the reliability of data on public transfer payments as reported in the March 1971 CPS. For purposes of this paper, public transfer payments consist of the sum of three items reported in the CPS: (1) Social Security and railroad retirement benefits; (2) public assistance payments; and (3) unemployment and workmen's compensation, government employee pensions, and veteran's payments.

The question is analyzed in two ways. First, the demographic characteristics of the persons and economic units reporting various kinds of public transfer income in the CPS are examined on the basis of the eligibility conditions of the social insurance or welfare program in order to determine whether the presence of a public transfer payment is reasonable. For example, are there many reports of Social Security benefits which cannot be explained by age, disability, and so on? More generally, are public transfer payments and the components thereof being reported by the income and age groups that one would expect, given the characteristics of the programs? Secondly, the number of beneficiaries and the average benefit received under various programs as shown by the CPS are compared with statistics generated by the program.

The first section presents a summary comparison of the CPS income aggregates with 1970 personal income figures from the National Income and Product Accounts, and an overview of the distribution and composition of transfer income received by all families and unrelated individuals, and by units in various income and age groups. Section II deals with Social Security and railroad retirement benefits, the single largest component of public transfer payments.

I. PUBLIC TRANSFER PAYMENTS IN RELATION TO TOTAL INCOME AND AGE

The population represented in the March 1971 CPS data tape which is the basis for this analysis consists of " . . . the civilian noninstitutional population of the United States and approximately 1,164,000 members of the Armed Forces in the United States living off post or with their families on post, but excludes all other members of the Armed Forces."[1] The members of this population belong to 67,305,000 economic units—families and unrelated individuals—distributed by money income and age of head as shown in Table 1.[2] Total money income reported by families and unrelated individuals in the population represented by the CPS data tape amounted to $646.9 billion in 1970.

The income received by persons in 1970, as given by the personal income series of the National Income and Product Accounts, was $806.3 billion. The personal income aggregate exceeds the CPS aggregate for three main reasons: (1) persons, as defined for the income and product accounts, is a broader concept than CPS families and unrelated individuals in that it includes nonprofit institutions, private trust funds, and the like; (2) the personal income concept includes various imputations and pay-

[1] U.S., Commerce Department, Bureau of the Census, *Current Population Reports,* Series P-60, No. 80, "Income in 1970 of Families and Persons in the United States" (Washington, D.C., 1971), page 2.

[2] The March 1971 CPS data tape used for this paper does not incorporate the results of the 1970 Decennial Census with regard to population counts. The Decennial Census count of the civilian resident population as of April 1, 1970, was slightly less than the March 1970 CPS count—201,064,000 and 201,372,000, respectively. However, the Decennial Census found more persons 65 years of age or over—20,067,000—compared with 19,713,000 from the March 1970 CPS. This comparison suggests that the March 1971 CPS figure of 20,093,000 persons 65 years of age or over in the civilian resident population may be too low by 300,000 to 400,000. See U.S., Commerce Department, Bureau of the Census, *Current Population Reports,* Series P-20, No. 212, "Marital Status and Family Status: March 1970;" Series P-20, No. 225, "Marital Status and Living Arrangements: March 1971;" and Series P-25, No. 483, "Preliminary Estimates of the Population of the United States, by Age and Sex: April 1, 1960 to July 1, 1971."

TABLE 1 Families and Unrelated Individuals by Total Money Income in 1970 and Age of Head
(families and unrelated individuals as of March 1971)

Total Money Income	Total	Age of Head					
		Under 25	25-34	35-44	45-54	55-64	65 and over
Total number (thousands)	67,305	5,795	12,447	12,045	12,832	11,202	12,983
1970 income (percent):	100.0	100.0	100.0	100.0	100.0	100.0	100.0
Under $1,000	3.9	9.7	2.4	1.5	2.2	3.8	6.8
$1,000-$1,999	7.4	7.9	2.2	2.1	3.1	6.3	22.2
2,000- 2,999	6.6	9.3	3.1	2.8	2.8	5.8	16.5
3,000- 3,999	6.2	9.8	4.3	3.3	3.7	5.6	11.9
4,000- 4,999	5.8	9.3	4.6	4.0	4.2	5.7	8.8
5,000- 5,999	6.0	9.0	6.0	4.8	4.8	6.2	6.5
6,000- 6,999	6.0	8.0	7.1	5.4	5.3	6.1	4.9
7,000- 7,999	6.1	8.1	8.3	6.1	5.2	6.2	3.8
8,000- 9,999	12.1	12.5	17.2	13.7	11.8	12.0	5.9
10,000-14,999	22.1	14.1	30.2	30.2	26.2	21.3	7.1
15,000-24,999	14.2	1.9	12.8	21.0	23.6	15.8	3.9
25,000 and over	3.7	.2	1.7	5.0	7.0	5.0	1.5

SOURCE: Tabulation prepared by the Social Security Administration Office of Research and Statistics from the March 1971 Current Population Survey.

ments in kind which are not recorded in the CPS; and (3) the population covered by personal income is broader because it includes inmates of institutions and military personnel overseas or living on post in the United States. Personal income adjusted to take these conceptual differences into account amounted to $725.6 billion in 1970—$78.6 billion more than the CPS aggregate (see Table 2). This discrepancy reflects error in both the personal income and the CPS totals, but it is generally accepted that some part of the discrepancy is attributable to understatement in the CPS. Nevertheless, in using the relation between CPS and adjusted personal income as a guide to the reliability of CPS data, it should be borne in mind that the personal income figures are also subject to error.

Comparisons are shown in Table 2 for total income and for components of income. The CPS aggregate was 89 percent of adjusted personal income and the proportions for the various types of income ranged from a high of 96 percent for wages and salaries to a low of 44 percent for property income. With such substantial differences among components, it is tempting to conclude that the data on wages and salaries in the CPS are less subject to error than, say, the data on property income. However, the magnitude of the differences among components may be exaggerated because of classification problems. For example, Social Security/railroad retirement benefits as reported in the CPS were 87 percent of the program totals incorporated in the personal income figure, compared with 76 percent for public assistance. If any substantial amount of public assistance is reported in the CPS as Social Security benefits, this comparison is too favorable to Social Security.

Public transfer income was less than 10 percent of aggregate income, whether CPS or personal income is used as the base, but represented a much larger share of the income of low-income families and of families headed by older persons, according to the CPS. For example, about 18 percent of all families and unrelated individuals received less than $3,000 money income in 1970, more than one-half of which was public transfer income (see Tables 1, 3, and 5). On the other hand, another 18 percent of families and unrelated individuals received $15,000 or more in money income, less than 3 percent of which was a public transfer payment.

Among the 13 million units with head 65 years of age or over, more than one-third of total income was a public transfer. Among

TABLE 2   Aggregate Money Income in 1970: Comparison of March 1971 Current Population Survey Aggregates With Components of Personal Income Adjusted to the CPS Concept

(billions of dollars)

Type of Money Income	Personal Income Adjusted	March 1971 CPS	Personal Income Less CPS	CPS as Percent of Personal Income
Total	725.6	646.9	78.6	89
Wages and salaries	526.8	508.3	18.6	96
Proprietors' income—business and professional	48.9	45.0	3.9	92
Proprietors' income—farm	15.6	7.9	7.7	51
Property income	64.0	28.0	36.0	44
Rent	9.7	a	a	a
Dividends	19.4	a	a	a
Interest	35.0	a	a	a

Public transfer payments	60.7	46.8	13.8	77
Social Security and railroad retirement	30.6	26.5	4.1	87
Public assistance	8.2	6.2	2.0	76
Unemployment and workmen's compensation, government employee and veteran's pensions	21.9	14.2	7.7	65
Unemployment compensation	4.5	2.4	b	b
Workmen's compensation	1.9	.7	b	b
Government employee pensions	9.0	4.3	b	b
Veteran's pensions	6.5	4.5	b	b
Two or more sources or source unidentified in CPS	–	2.2	b	b
Other[c]	9.6	10.9	-1.3	114

SOURCE: See Technical Appendix, tables T-1 through T-3.

[a]Not available from CPS.

[b]The CPS aggregates are not comparable to the personal income figures because of the "two or more sources or sources unidentified" component.

[c]The CPS aggregate of other income is larger than the personal income component, but the two are not comparable because the CPS figure includes interfamily transfers omitted from the personal income figure.

TABLE 3   Composition of 1970 Income: Share Derived From Specified
Source

(percentage distribution of mean amounts)

Group Characteristic	Total	Earnings	Property	Public Transfer	Other
All families and un-related individuals:	100	87	4	7	2
1970 income—					
Under $1,000	100	−32	15	109	8
$1,000- $1,999	100	24	5	68	3
2,000- 2,999	100	34	7	54	5
3,000- 3,999	100	51	7	36	6
4,000- 4,999	100	63	6	26	5
5,000- 5,999	100	74	5	16	4
6,000- 6,999	100	82	5	11	3
7,000- 7,999	100	87	3	8	2
8,000- 9,999	100	90	3	6	2
10,000- 14,999	100	93	3	4	1
15,000- 24,999	100	93	3	3	1
25,000 and over	100	87	10	1	1
Head under 25:	100	94	1	3	1
1970 income—					
Under $1,000	100	77	2	13	9
$1,000- $1,999	100	75	1	19	6
2,000- 2,999	100	76	1	16	6
3,000- 3,999	100	85	1	10	4
4,000- 4,999	100	91	1	5	3
5,000- 5,999	100	94	1	4	2
6,000- 6,999	100	96	a	2	1
7,000- 7,999	100	96	1	2	1
8,000- 9,999	100	98	1	1	1
10,000- 14,999	100	98	1	1	a
15,000 and over	100	92	7	1	a
Head 25-34:	100	95	2	3	1
1970 income—					
$1,000- $1,999	100	58	1	32	9
2,000- 2,999	100	58	1	34	6
3,000- 3,999	100	67	1	26	6
4,000- 4,999	100	81	a	14	3
5,000- 5,999	100	90	a	7	3

TABLE 3 *(Continued)*

Group Characteristic	Total	Earnings	Property	Public Transfer	Other
6,000- 6,999	100	94	1	3	2
7,000- 7,999	100	96	1	3	1
8,000- 9,999	100	97	1	2	1
10,000- 14,999	100	97	1	1	1
15,000- 24,999	100	97	2	1	a
25,000 and over	100	89	10	a	a
Head 35-44:	100	94	2	3	1
1970 income—					
$1,000- $1,999	100	56	1	38	4
2,000- 2,999	100	61	2	32	6
3,000- 3,999	100	72	2	21	5
4,000- 4,999	100	79	2	17	3
5,000- 5,999	100	86	1	10	2
6,000- 6,999	100	91	1	6	2
7,000- 7,999	100	94	1	5	1
8,000- 9,999	100	95	1	3	1
10,000- 14,999	100	96	1	2	1
15,000- 24,999	100	96	2	1	1
25,000 and over	100	93	6	a	a
Head 45-54:	100	92	3	4	1
1970 income—					
$1,000- $1,999	100	48	4	44	4
2,000- 2,999	100	57	3	36	5
3,000- 3,999	100	72	2	22	4
4,000- 4,999	100	80	2	16	1
5,000- 5,999	100	85	2	11	2
6,000- 6,999	100	88	3	8	1
7,000- 7,999	100	92	2	5	1
8,000- 9,999	100	92	2	6	1
10,000- 14,999	100	93	2	4	1
15,000- 24,999	100	94	2	3	a
25,000 and over	100	91	7	2	1
Head 55-64:	100	87	6	6	2
1970 income—					
Under $1,000	100	−106	51	148	8
$1,000- $1,999	100	31	7	58	4
2,000- 2,999	100	42	7	46	5

TABLE 3 *(Concluded)*

Group Characteristic	Total	Earnings	Property	Public Transfer	Other
3,000- 3,999	100	64	7	22	6
4,000- 4,999	100	73	6	17	4
5,000- 5,999	100	78	5	14	4
6,000- 6,999	100	81	5	11	3
7,000- 7,999	100	87	4	7	1
8,000- 9,999	100	88	4	6	2
10,000- 14,999	100	90	4	4	1
15,000- 24,999	100	92	5	3	1
25,000 and over	100	86	11	1	2
Head 65 and over:	100	40	17	36	7
1970 income—					
Under $1,000	100	−16	9	106	2
$1,000- $1,999	100	5	6	86	2
2,000- 2,999	100	9	10	76	5
3,000- 3,999	100	17	14	63	7
4,000- 4,999	100	21	14	55	10
5,000- 5,999	100	30	16	44	11
6,000- 6,999	100	39	18	34	9
7,000- 7,999	100	41	16	33	10
8,000- 9,999	100	52	13	27	9
10,000- 14,999	100	58	17	19	7
15,000- 24,999	100	60	21	12	7
25,000 and over	100	59	31	5	6

NOTES:

Income and age groups with average total money income less than zero are included in the totals but are not shown separately.

Earnings is the sum of three CPS components: wages and salaries; net income from farm self-employment; and net income from nonfarm self-employment.

Property income is the CPS component dividends, interest on savings or bonds, income from estates or trusts, net rental income or royalties.

Public transfer income is the sum of three CPS components: Social Security and railroad retirement; public assistance; and unemployment compensation, government employee pensions, veterans' payments, and workmen's compensation.

Other income is the CPS component private pensions, annuities, alimony, regular contributions from persons not living in the household and other periodic income.

SOURCE: Tabulations prepared by the Social Security Administration Office of Research and Statistics from the March 1971 Current Population Survey.

[a] Less than 0.5 percent.

TABLE 4   Composition of 1970 Income: Percentage of Group Having Income From Specified Source

Group Characteristic	Total	Earnings	Property	Public Transfer	Other
All families and un-related individuals:	99	84	41	38	10
1970 income—					
Under $1,000	81	41	16	41	5
$1,000- $1,999	100	36	25	77	7
2,000- 2,999	100	50	30	72	12
3,000- 3,999	100	69	34	60	16
4,000- 4,999	100	78	34	50	17
5,000- 5,999	100	87	32	42	14
6,000- 6,999	100	92	32	35	11
7,000- 7,999	100	95	34	30	10
8,000- 9,999	100	97	38	29	9
10,000- 14,999	100	98	47	26	7
15,000- 24,999	100	99	61	24	7
25,000 and over	100	98	78	22	9
Head under 25:	97	93	22	19	9
1970 income—					
Under $1,000	71	59	8	9	11
$1,000- $1,999	100	88	16	26	13
2,000- 2,999	100	89	13	26	16
3,000- 3,999	100	96	17	25	14
4,000- 4,999	100	99	18	19	11
5,000- 5,999	100	100	21	19	9
6,000- 6,999	100	100	18	15	7
7,000- 7,999	100	100	27	15	8
8,000- 9,999	100	100	29	18	5
10,000- 14,999	100	100	37	18	5
15,000 and over	100	100	58	17	6
Head 25-34:	99	96	32	20	6
1970 income—					
Under $1,000	68	54	10	18	5
$1,000- $1,999	100	74	8	44	12
2,000- 2,999	100	74	12	48	14
3,000- 3,999	100	81	12	45	11
4,000- 4,999	100	92	11	31	10
5,000- 5,999	100	97	15	25	9
6,000- 6,999	100	99	19	19	7

TABLE 4   *(Continued)*

Group Characteristic	Total	Earnings	Property	Public Transfer	Other
7,000- 7,999	100	100	21	19	6
8,000- 9,999	100	100	31	16	5
10,000- 14,999	100	100	43	16	5
15,000- 24,999	100	100	53	13	4
25,000 and over	100	100	66	12	5
Head 35-44:	100	97	37	21	7
1970 income—					
Under $1,000	72	56	6	21	6
$1,000- $1,999	100	70	8	45	8
2,000- 2,999	100	78	7	43	10
3,000- 3,999	100	88	13	39	11
4,000- 4,999	100	92	12	36	9
5,000- 5,999	100	95	14	28	8
6,000- 6,999	100	98	18	22	8
7,000- 7,999	100	99	26	22	7
8,000- 9,999	100	100	30	18	6
10,000- 14,999	100	100	40	18	5
15,000- 24,999	100	100	57	18	6
25,000 and over	100	100	76	12	5
Head 45-54:	100	96	43	30	6
1970 income—					
Under $1,000	81	57	15	24	4
$1,000- $1,999	100	62	12	53	6
2,000- 2,999	100	76	14	50	9
3,000- 3,999	100	90	18	39	8
4,000- 4,999	100	94	20	35	5
5,000- 5,999	100	97	23	30	8
6,000- 6,999	100	98	28	31	7
7,000- 7,999	100	99	29	27	4
8,000- 9,999	100	100	36	31	5
10,000- 14,999	100	99	46	29	5
15,000- 24,999	100	100	61	26	6
25,000 and over	100	100	76	20	8
Head 55-64:	100	89	49	36	9
1970 income—					
Under $1,000	88	46	23	38	4
$1,000- $1,999	100	48	25	67	7

TABLE 4 *(Concluded)*

Group Characteristic	Total	Earnings	Property	Public Transfer	Other
2,000- 2,999	100	58	29	67	10
3,000- 3,999	100	82	35	44	13
4,000- 4,999	100	90	40	39	10
5,000- 5,999	100	90	38	39	10
6,000- 6,999	100	92	43	35	10
7,000- 7,999	100	98	43	28	9
8,000- 9,999	100	98	51	32	9
10,000- 14,999	100	99	57	28	8
15,000- 24,999	100	99	67	26	6
25,000 and over	100	98	83	21	12
Head 65 and over:	99	41	53	91	20
1970 income—					
Under $1,000	89	16	22	79	4
$1,000- $1,999	100	15	32	97	6
2,000- 2,999	100	25	44	97	13
3,000- 3,999	100	38	59	96	23
4,000- 4,999	100	43	65	94	34
5,000- 5,999	100	56	67	89	35
6,000- 6,999	100	65	68	87	29
7,000- 7,999	100	68	71	85	33
8,000- 9,999	100	76	69	85	33
10,000- 14,999	100	81	76	82	29
15,000- 24,999	100	85	85	75	30
25,000 and over	100	84	89	74	26

SOURCE: Tabulations prepared by the Social Security Administration Office of Research and Statistics from the March 1971 Current Population Survey.

the remaining 54 million units with younger heads, less than 5 percent of income was a public transfer.

Almost four in ten units reported the receipt of some form of public transfer income (see Tables 4 and 6). The frequencies were lowest among high-income units and units headed by young persons. The frequencies were highest—as high as 97 percent— among units headed by older persons at low-income levels.

Social Security was the single most important form of public transfer payment, accounting for more than one-half of the total, using either CPS or adjusted personal income figures as the base

TABLE 5   Composition of 1970 Income: Mean Amount of Income From Specified Source

(dollars)

Group Characteristic	Total	Earnings	Property	Public Transfer	Other
All families and un- related individuals:	9,612	8,338	417	696	162
1970 income—					
Under $1,000	260	−83	39	284	21
$1,000- $1,999	1,508	358	78	1,020	52
2,000- 2,999	2,461	845	160	1,331	125
3,000- 3,999	3,468	1,781	238	1,245	204
4,000- 4,999	4,471	2,824	256	1,161	230
5,000- 5,999	5,445	4,054	261	898	233
6,000- 6,999	6,452	5,275	293	679	204
7,000- 7,999	7,458	6,471	246	578	163
8,000- 9,999	8,920	8,027	227	511	154
10,000- 14,999	12,120	11,213	324	457	126
15,000- 24,999	18,410	17,150	628	467	166
25,000 and over	35,755	31,169	3,612	515	459
Head under 25:	5,940	5,594	64	194	88
1970 income—					
Under $1,000	342	263	6	43	30
$1,000- $1,999	1,442	1,081	10	267	85
2,000- 2,999	2,431	1,861	27	383	159
3,000- 3,999	3,455	2,951	35	329	140
4,000- 4,999	4,458	4,054	27	241	137
5,000- 5,999	5,458	5,122	34	213	89
6,000- 6,999	6,433	6,185	17	136	95
7,000- 7,999	7,449	7,175	55	118	101
8,000- 9,999	8,911	8,690	50	123	49
10,000- 14,999	11,752	11,494	70	145	43
15,000 and over	19,840	18,324	1,341	142	32
Head 25-34:	9,944	9,441	150	260	93
1970 income—					
Under $1,000	−88	−208	15	76	29
$1,000- $1,999	1,484	858	17	482	127
2,000- 2,999	2,467	1,436	37	848	146
3,000- 3,999	3,458	2,303	28	905	222
4,000- 4,999	4,473	3,664	19	646	144

TABLE 5 *(Continued)*

Group Characteristic	Total	Earnings	Property	Public Transfer	Other
5,000- 5,999	5,451	4,929	16	355	152
6,000- 6,999	6,446	6,080	50	206	110
7,000- 7,999	7,468	7,144	42	201	81
8,000- 9,999	8,917	8,647	47	155	69
10,000- 14,999	12,039	11,694	100	179	66
15,000- 24,999	17,769	17,281	277	125	86
25,000 and over	36,557	32,469	3,747	180	161
Head 35-44:	11,912	11,240	228	337	107
1970 income—					
Under $1,000	−58	−263	21	139	45
$1,000- $1,999	1,510	849	16	579	66
2,000- 2,999	2,454	1,491	42	777	143
3,000- 3,999	3,469	2,503	53	729	185
4,000- 4,999	4,468	3,508	70	758	132
5,000- 5,999	5,436	4,680	57	565	135
6,000- 6,999	6,440	5,837	64	410	129
7,000- 7,999	7,474	6,990	48	344	92
8,000- 9,999	8,945	8,511	68	266	100
10,000- 14,999	12,167	11,700	129	254	84
15,000- 24,999	18,312	17,641	285	264	122
25,000 and over	34,279	31,913	2,099	156	111
Head 45-54:	12,586	11,573	387	537	89
1970 income—					
Under $1,000	−125	−345	32	175	12
$1,000- $1,999	1,522	723	67	670	63
2,000- 2,999	2,505	1,421	75	893	115
3,000- 3,999	3,480	2,504	72	771	134
4,000- 4,999	4,482	3,600	88	734	61
5,000- 5,999	5,440	4,627	99	590	124
6,000- 6,999	6,449	5,686	166	506	90
7,000- 7,999	7,444	6,830	155	409	50
8,000- 9,999	8,920	8,177	156	498	90
10,000- 14,999	12,289	11,476	245	505	63
15,000- 24,999	18,715	17,684	437	515	79
25,000 and over	35,286	32,085	2,411	551	239

TABLE 5   *(Concluded)*

Group Characteristic	Total	Earnings	Property	Public Transfer	Other
Head 55-64:	10,334	8,945	602	617	169
1970 income—					
Under $1,000	166	−178	85	245	13
$1,000- $1,999	1,506	470	99	877	60
2,000- 2,999	2,455	1,042	175	1,124	113
3,000- 3,999	3,476	2,235	260	770	210
4,000- 4,999	4,466	3,279	275	738	175
5,000- 5,999	5,420	4,202	287	739	193
6,000- 6,999	6,446	5,229	311	687	219
7,000- 7,999	7,446	6,512	301	521	111
8,000- 9,999	8,923	7,896	360	527	140
10,000- 14,999	12,088	10,895	525	528	141
15,000- 24,999	18,675	17,178	844	513	141
25,000 and over	36,752	31,426	4,147	480	700
Head 65 and over:	5,237	2,090	875	1,894	377
1970 income—					
Under $1,000	560	−93	50	590	14
$1,000- $1,999	1,520	74	97	1,314	35
2,000- 2,999	2,462	224	244	1,878	116
3,000- 3,999	3,469	573	476	2,173	246
4,000- 4,999	4,473	931	626	2,449	467
5,000- 5,999	5,464	1,645	855	2,391	574
6,000- 6,999	6,495	2,511	1,187	2,195	601
7,000- 7,999	7,458	3,079	1,200	2,456	723
8,000- 9,999	8,879	4,580	1,145	2,392	762
10,000- 14,999	12,061	6,969	1,997	2,304	791
15,000- 24,999	18,491	11,171	3,856	2,186	1,278
25,000 and over	38,058	22,369	11,625	1,911	2,153

SOURCE: Tabulations prepared by the Social Security Administration Office of Research and Statistics from the March 1971 Current Population Survey.

(see Tables 2 and 7). The Table 2 comparison indicates that Social Security/railroad retirement income was reported more fully than other components of public transfers.

Almost one in four units reported receipt of a Social Security/ railroad retirement benefit (see Table 6). The proportions were nominal among units headed by younger persons, but rose to 85 percent among units with head aged 65 years or more. At high-income levels, almost seventy in one hundred of the units headed by older persons reported a benefit.

Next in importance in terms of dollar magnitude was government employee pensions, amounting to $9 billion in 1970, according to program data. In the CPS, government employee pensions are reported with unemployment and workmen's compensation and veteran's payments and the interviewer is instructed to indicate by a check on the questionnaire which type(s) of income is covered in the single dollar amount recorded. These indicators are entered in the CPS data tape and were used to identify by type the $14 billion of public transfer, other than Social Security/railroad retirement and public assistance. Two billion of the $14 billion was associated with two or more sources of income or was not identifiable as to type. Government employee pensions amounted to $4.3 billion of the remaining $12 billion which was identified in the CPS. Unless a large share of the unidentified $2 billion is government employee pensions, this type of income seems to be especially poorly reported in the CPS.

Two percent of all families and unrelated individuals reported government employee pensions and the proportion might be as high as 4 percent if most of those with two or more sources, or an unidentified source, received government employee pensions. The proportions were largest—as high as 11 percent—among units headed by older persons with above-average incomes.

The CPS found an aggregate of $6.2 billion in public assistance, compared with a program total of $8.2 billion. Again, using the relation between CPS aggregates and adjusted personal income as a criterion, public assistance is not as well-reported as Social Security/railroad retirement, but is better reported than the other forms of public transfer payments.

Only seven in one hundred units reported receipt of public assistance, with some variation by age—as low as 5 percent to 6 percent for units headed by a younger person, and as high as 11 percent for units headed by persons 65 years or over. With regard to income level, the frequencies decline from about twenty in one hundred among the 18 percent of units with income less than $3,000 to nominal rates at high-income levels, which would be expected in view of the income tests associated with the programs.

Payments to veterans amounted to $6.5 billion according to program data, compared with a CPS total of at least $4.5 billion. Five units in one hundred reported receipt of a veteran's payment

TABLE 6   Composition of Public Transfer Income for 1970: Percentage of Group Having Income From Specified Source

Group Characteristic	Total	Social Security/Railroad Retirement	Public Assistance	Other					
				Total	Unemployment Compensation Only	Workmen's Compensation Only	Government Employee Pensions Only	Veteran's Payments Only	Two or More Sources or Source Unidentified
All families and unrelated individuals: 1970 income—	38	24	7	15	5	1	2	5	2
Under $1,000	41	27	13	3	1	a	a	1	a
$1,000–$1,999	77	60	24	8	1	a	1	5	1
2,000– 2,999	72	55	19	17	3	1	2	9	2
3,000– 3,999	60	43	12	17	5	a	2	7	2
4,000– 4,999	50	35	9	17	6	1	3	6	2
5,000– 5,999	42	27	5	19	7	2	3	5	3
6,000– 6,999	35	21	4	16	6	1	2	4	2
7,000– 7,999	30	16	3	17	8	2	2	4	2
8,000– 9,999	29	14	3	17	7	1	2	4	3
10,000–14,999	26	11	2	17	6	2	2	5	3
15,000–24,999	24	11	1	16	4	1	2	5	3
25,000 and over	22	12	1	12	2	a	3	5	2
Head under 25: 1970 income—	19	2	6	12	6	1	a	4	1
Under $1,000	9	1	7	1	1	a	a	a	a
$1,000–$1,999	26	3	19	5	4	a	a	1	a
2,000– 2,999	26	3	14	12	6	1	a	4	1
3,000– 3,999	25	1	12	14	6	a	a	5	2
4,000– 4,999	19	2	6	12	6	1	a	4	1
5,000– 5,999	19	2	4	16	9	1	a	5	2
6,000– 6,999	15	2	2	13	6	2	a	3	2

1970 income									
…,000- 7,999		1	3	13	8	1	a	2	2
8,000- 9,999	18	1	1	16	8	2	a	5	2
10,000-14,999	18	1	2	15	6	2	1	5	2
15,000 and over	17	a	a	17	2	a	1	14	a
Head 25-34:									
1970 income—	20	2	6	14	7	1	a	3	1
Under $1,000	18	a	12	6	1	1	a	1	2
$1,000-$1,999	44	2	38	4	3	a	a	a	1
2,000- 2,999	48	3	37	10	5	1	a	3	1
3,000- 3,999	45	4	29	16	10	1	a	3	2
4,000- 4,999	31	4	15	15	9	a	a	3	2
5,000- 5,999	25	2	7	19	12	2	a	3	1
6,000- 6,999	19	2	4	15	8	2	a	3	2
7,000- 7,999	19	2	3	17	10	2	a	3	2
8,000- 9,999	16	1	2	14	8	1	a	3	2
10,000-14,999	16	2	1	14	7	2	a	4	1
15,000-24,999	13	3	1	10	4	1	a	3	1
25,000 and over	12	5	2	7	2	a	1	3	1
Head 35-44:									
1970 income—	21	6	5	13	6	1	1	4	2
Under $1,000	21	6	10	6	1	a	a	4	1
$1,000-$1,999	45	6	36	6	2	1	a	1	1
2,000- 2,999	43	9	30	7	4	2	a	2	1
3,000- 3,999	39	9	21	15	8	1	a	4	1
4,000- 4,999	36	9	20	14	7	2	a	4	1
5,000- 5,999	28	10	8	16	9	1	a	3	3
6,000- 6,999	22	5	7	15	7	1	a	4	2
7,000- 7,999	22	6	4	16	9	1	a	4	2
8,000- 9,999	18	5	3	13	6	2	a	3	1
10,000-14,999	18	5	1	14	7	1	1	3	2
15,000-24,999	18	7	1	12	4	1	1	5	2
25,000 and over	12	5	1	7	2	a	1	3	1

TABLE 6 *(Concluded)*

Group Characteristic	Total	Social Security/ Railroad Retirement	Public Assistance	Other Total	Unemployment Compensation Only	Workmen's Compensation Only	Government Employee Pensions Only	Veteran's Payments Only	Two or More Sources or Source Unidentified
Head 45-54: 1970 income—	30	11	5	19	5	1	2	7	3
Under $1,000	24	8	16	4	1	a	a	2	a
$1,000-$1,999	53	18	31	9	1	1	a	6	1
2,000- 2,999	50	22	25	15	4	1	1	8	3
3,000- 3,999	39	16	12	21	9	1	1	8	3
4,000- 4,999	35	17	9	18	6	1	1	8	2
5,000- 5,999	30	15	4	18	5	2	1	6	4
6,000- 6,999	31	14	6	17	6	2	a	5	2
7,000- 7,999	27	10	3	18	7	2	1	5	3
8,000- 9,999	31	12	3	21	7	2	1	7	4
10,000-14,999	29	10	2	21	6	1	2	8	4
15,000-24,999	26	8	1	20	4	1	2	8	4
25,000 and over	20	8	1	14	1	a	3	6	4
Head 55-64: 1970 income—	36	21	6	16	5	1	3	4	3
Under $1,000	38	23	15	3	1	a	1	1	a
$1,000-$1,999	67	37	23	10	1	1	1	5	2

2,000- 2,999	67	47	20	19	4	1	1	9	4
3,000- 3,999	44	32	6	15	7	a	2	4	2
4,000- 4,999	39	24	6	18	7	1	4	4	2
5,000- 5,999	39	26	6	18	6	3	4	4	2
6,000- 6,999	35	23	4	16	6	1	2	4	3
7,000- 7,999	28	17	2	15	6	1	3	4	2
8,000- 9,999	32	16	3	19	7	2	2	4	3
10,000-14,999	28	15	2	17	6	2	3	3	3
15,000-24,999	26	11	1	17	5	1	3	4	3
25,000 and over	21	9	a	13	2	a	5	5	2
Head 65 and over: 1970 income—	91	85	11	17	1	a	5	7	2
Under $1,000	79	64	15	2	a	a	1	1	a
$1,000-$1,999	97	88	23	9	a	a	1	6	1
2,000- 2,999	97	93	15	20	1	a	4	12	2
3,000- 3,999	96	93	7	19	a	a	5	11	2
4,000- 4,999	94	91	6	22	2	a	6	10	3
5,000- 5,999	89	86	3	24	3	1	9	7	3
6,000- 6,999	87	83	3	18	3	a	7	5	3
7,000- 7,999	85	80	2	25	4	1	11	5	4
8,000- 9,999	85	80	3	23	5	a	10	3	5
10,000-14,999	82	77	3	25	4	1	9	6	5
15,000-24,999	75	68	2	20	2	a	11	3	3
25,000 and over	74	69	1	14	3	a	6	3	2

SOURCE: Tabulations prepared by the Social Security Administration Office of Research and Statistics from the March 1971 Current Population Survey.

a Less than 0.5 percent.

TABLE 7   Composition of Public Transfer Income for 1970: Mean Amount of Income From Specified Source

(dollars)

Group Characteristic	Total	Social Security/ Railroad Retirement	Public Assistance	Other Total	Other: Unemployment Compensation Only	Other: Workmen's Compensation Only	Other: Government Employee Pensions Only	Other: Veteran's Payments Only	Other: Two or More Sources or Source Unidentified
All families and unrelated individuals:	696	394	91	210	33	10	62	65	41
1970 income—									
Under $1,000	284	190	75	18	4	a	3	8	3
$1,000–$1,999	1,020	717	235	68	5	3	9	43	8
2,000–2,999	1,331	865	295	170	16	6	33	83	32
3,000–3,999	1,245	804	238	203	37	5	46	90	24
4,000–4,999	1,161	736	206	219	39	9	64	77	30
5,000–5,999	898	541	105	252	52	18	74	67	41
6,000–6,999	679	398	68	213	41	11	56	66	39
7,000–7,999	578	317	39	222	46	15	74	50	38
8,000–9,999	511	256	42	212	44	13	61	55	40
10,000–14,999	457	201	25	232	41	13	61	67	49
15,000–24,999	467	181	10	276	29	10	96	76	64
25,000 and over	515	209	7	299	10	a	148	64	77
Head under 25:	194	17	93	84	30	4	1	37	12
1970 income—									
Under $1,000	43	6	33	4	3	a	a	a	1
$1,000–$1,999	267	27	217	23	17	a	a	6	a
2,000–2,999	383	29	260	94	30	5	a	50	10
3,000–3,999	329	13	226	90	26	a	a	43	20
4,000–4,999	241	24	139	79	30	4	a	32	12
						6	a	48	19

	(1)	(2)	(3)	(4)	(5)	(6)	(7)	(8)	(9)
7,000- 7,999	118	8	25	86	47	11	a	19	8
8,000- 9,999	123	6	7	110	36	5	a	58	11
10,000-14,999	145	13	20	112	38	7	a	46	21
15,000 and over	142	a	a	142	7	a	5	130	a
Head 25-34:									
1970 income—	260	38	109	113	45	11	2	42	13
Under $1,000	76	3	54	19	5	a	a	6	8
$1,000-$1,999	482	18	438	25	15	5	a	1	4
2,000- 2,999	848	52	687	109	35	14	a	38	23
3,000- 3,999	905	81	669	154	83	5	a	50	16
4,000- 4,999	646	109	409	128	74	7	1	31	14
5,000- 5,999	355	27	151	177	87	16	2	53	19
6,000- 6,999	206	25	61	121	49	15	a	47	11
7,000- 7,999	201	36	35	131	53	25	a	37	15
8,000- 9,999	155	17	34	104	45	9	4	31	14
10,000-14,999	179	40	20	120	41	12	2	57	8
15,000-24,999	125	34	7	84	26	3	3	36	16
25,000 and over	180	87	16	77	11	a	31	25	10
Head 35-44:									
1970 income—	337	106	98	133	35	10	17	44	27
Under $1,000	139	38	56	45	19	a	a	25	1
$1,000-$1,999	579	72	462	46	7	7	14	11	7
2,000- 2,999	777	145	555	77	22	7	a	27	21
3,000- 3,999	729	152	418	159	61	19	12	52	15
4,000- 4,999	758	142	496	120	44	25	8	33	11
5,000- 5,999	565	214	204	147	48	13	18	34	34
6,000- 6,999	410	109	116	185	51	5	1	89	39
7,000- 7,999	344	149	58	137	51	6	2	58	20
8,000- 9,999	266	83	63	120	38	17	5	45	16
10,000-14,999	254	82	25	147	40	8	28	33	38
15,000-24,999	264	117	10	138	20	11	19	58	29
25,000 and over	156	73	7	76	11	a	31	21	13

TABLE 7 (Concluded)

Group Characteristic	Total	Social Security/Railroad Retirement	Public Assistance	Other Total	Unemployment Compensation Only	Workmen's Compensation Only	Government Employee Pensions Only	Veteran's Payments Only	Two or More Sources or Source Unidentified
Head 45-54:	537	178	69	289	37	12	61	105	74
1970 income—									
Under $1,000	175	55	94	26	7	2	a	18	a
$1,000-$1,999	670	206	380	84	12	11	3	54	4
2,000- 2,999	893	335	416	142	22	4	9	65	42
3,000- 3,999	771	263	267	241	78	5	15	109	34
4,000- 4,999	734	347	161	226	39	3	30	114	40
5,000- 5,999	590	263	79	248	40	13	44	100	51
6,000- 6,999	506	201	99	206	55	27	8	93	23
7,000- 7,999	409	142	40	227	46	14	34	60	72
8,000- 9,999	498	194	46	257	47	21	42	83	65
10,000-14,999	505	172	28	305	41	15	56	118	76
15,000-24,999	515	126	11	377	31	10	92	136	109
25,000 and over	551	119	8	424	6	a	185	102	131
Head 55-64:	617	291	70	256	40	15	97	54	49
1970 income—									
Under $1,000	245	141	89	15	2	a	8	6	1
$1,000-$1,999	877	549	233	95	10	7	11	44	23

2,000- 2,999	1,124	662	276	186	27	9	23	73	55
3,000- 3,999	770	508	96	166	49	4	45	51	16
4,000- 4,999	738	348	112	278	50	10	111	78	29
5,000- 5,999	739	364	93	282	65	35	82	64	36
6,000- 6,999	687	361	73	253	32	8	93	61	59
7,000- 7,999	521	262	33	225	34	10	98	53	29
8,000- 9,999	527	223	48	255	53	20	73	73	37
10,000-14,999	528	213	18	297	45	23	108	51	70
15,000-24,999	513	150	11	352	48	18	174	35	77
25,000 and over	480	142	3	335	9	a	199	72	55
Head 65 and over:	1,894	1,472	108	315	13	5	158	85	53
1970 income—									
Under $1,000	590	470	100	20	1	a	5	8	5
$1,000-$1,999	1,314	1,063	179	72	1	a	10	54	7
2,000- 2,999	1,878	1,485	178	215	4	5	60	114	33
3,000- 3,999	2,173	1,804	94	276	2	5	98	140	31
4,000- 4,999	2,449	2,025	90	334	19	6	139	121	50
5,000- 5,999	2,391	1,890	47	453	28	19	236	94	76
6,000- 6,999	2,195	1,742	30	423	21	5	241	69	89
7,000- 7,999	2,456	1,758	38	660	43	15	422	78	101
8,000- 9,999	2,392	1,711	38	643	36	a	414	51	143
10,000-14,999	2,304	1,561	52	691	34	16	388	114	140
15,000-24,999	2,186	1,440	17	730	21	1	542	71	95
25,000 and over	1,911	1,347	11	553	22	a	323	35	172

SOURCE: Tabulation prepared by the Social Security Administration Office of Research and Statistics from the March 1971 Current Population Survey.

a Less than $.50.

and the proportion might be as high as 7 percent if most of those with two or more sources, or an unidentified source, received a payment. The proportions were as large as 12 percent among units headed by older persons at rather low income levels—$2,000 to $3,000. The veteran's programs covered in this component include some which are subject to an income test. Thus, a finding that recipients are of more modest income than are recipients of, say, government employee pensions, which are not income tested, should be expected.

Program data show that unemployment compensation amounted to $4.5 billion in 1970, compared with a CPS total of at least $2.4 billion. Five in one hundred units reported receipt of unemployment compensation with little variation by age group among units headed by persons less than 65 years of age. The frequency drops to 1 percent among units headed by older persons.

To sum up, using the CPS–personal-income comparison as a criterion, all forms of public transfer income are understated in the CPS. Social Security and public assistance are more fully reported than other components. For units who report public transfer income, the picture that emerges is one of general consistency or, at least, no glaring inconsistency, with social insurance and welfare program eligibility conditions. Social Security is reported with great frequency among the units headed by older persons; reports of payments under income-tested programs occur to some extent among families with above-average income, but the rates are far higher among families with below-average income.

II. SOCIAL SECURITY AND RAILROAD RETIREMENT PAYMENTS

The analysis of the reliability of Social Security/railroad retirement income was developed as follows. The data record of each person in the CPS sample was examined and assigned a beneficiary code based on rules developed from the eligibility conditions of the Old-Age, Survivors, and Disability Insurance (OASDI) and railroad retirement programs. The results of this coding are presented, and it is shown that most benefit reports can be explained on the basis of an age, disability, or survivor condition. The numbers of beneficiaries thus defined are compared with program totals by sex and age group.

A special economic unit consisting of persons who are inter-dependent under the conditions of the social insurance programs was constructed in order to derive the distribution of benefits in the population. Units were classified as retired worker units, disabled worker units, and so on, to correspond as closely as possible with concepts available from program statistics. Average benefits and distributions of units by size of benefit are presented for the various groups of beneficiary units in comparison with program statistics.

Summary of Methodology for Beneficiary Code

The March 1971 CPS data tape contains a record for each person in the covered population with information on age and sex and on the relation of the person to others in the Census household. For each person 14 years of age or over, the record contains dollar amounts of income received in 1970. Eight types of income were enumerated as follows:

1. wages or salary before deductions;
2. net income from own nonfarm business or professional practice or partnership;
3. net income from own farm;
4. Social Security or railroad retirement;
5. estates, trust or dividends; interest on savings accounts or bonds; net rental income; royalties;
6. welfare payments or other public assistance;
7. unemployment compensation, workmen's compensation, government employee pensions, veteran's payments; and
8. private pensions or annuities, alimony, regular contributions from persons not living in the household, and other.

For persons 14 years of age or over in the civilian population at the time of the interview, the record also contains information about work experience during the year 1970—number of weeks worked and reasons for working less than full year—and about labor-force attachment at time of interview in March 1971.

Based on these data, each person on the CPS data tape was given a code indicating whether or not he was a Social Security/railroad retirement beneficiary in 1970 and classifying him as to type of beneficiary—retired worker, disabled worker, wife of retired worker, and so on. The analysis was facilitated by the development of a special economic unit—the STATS [Simulated Tax and Transfer] unit—and a number of codes.

The STATS unit consists of a head, wife, and dependent children. The unit was formed from the Census family or unrelated individual and may be one of the following types:

1. primary family unit;
2. secondary family unit;
3. subfamily unit;
4. hidden subfamily unit;
5. primary individual unit;
6. secondary individual unit; or
7. individual-from-a-family unit.

Primary and secondary individual STATS units follow the Census definition of unrelated individuals—persons 14 years of age or over not living with any relatives.

The primary family, secondary family, and subfamily units were formed from their Census counterparts and consist of head, wife, never-married children of the head under 18 years of age, never-married children of the head 18 through 21 years of age whose labor-force status indicated that they were students in 1970 and/or early 1971, other never-married relatives of the head under 18 years of age, other never-married relatives of the head 18 through 21 years of age whose labor-force status indicated that they were students in 1970 and/or early 1971, and foster children (secondary individuals less than 14 years of age). For purposes of this analysis, the last five groups are considered dependent children.

Most persons in a Census primary or secondary family who did not meet these criteria became one-person STATS units—individual-from-a-family units. Examples are an own child 22 years of age or over, a grandparent, and so on.

A disability code and a student code were developed for each person on the data tape. The codes were based on work experience during 1970 and on labor-force attachment at time of interview in March 1971. All persons who reported that they worked less than a full year in 1970 because of illness, and that they were not in the labor force or in school in early 1971, were considered disabled for purposes of the analysis. All persons who reported that they worked less than a full year in 1970 because they were attending school and those who reported that their major activity in March 1971 was attending school were classified as students.

Each person in a STATS unit was given a Social Security/railroad retirement recipient code on the basis of such characteristics as age, sex, disability status, marital status, student status, presence of children, and relationship to the person in the unit who reported the Social Security/railroad retirement payment. If no one in the STATS unit reported a payment, all persons in the unit were considered nonbeneficiaries. If one or more persons in the unit reported payments, the unit was considered a beneficiary unit and some, but not necessarily all, of the persons in the unit were counted as beneficiaries. Some persons had characteristics which made them appear eligible for two or more types of benefits. For example, a widow 65 years of age or more could be a retired-worker beneficiary or an aged-widow beneficiary. The codes for such cases indicate all the types of benefits for which the person is eligible. In the example just cited, the woman is coded as retired worker or widow. If no one in the beneficiary unit appeared to be eligible to receive a Social Security benefit—if, for example, the unit contained no person 62 years of age or more, no disabled persons, and so on—the person reporting the payment was counted as a beneficiary and coded "not ascertained" with regard to type of beneficiary. The rules for forming STATS units and for the recipient code are given in the Technical Appendix.

Results of Coding

The results of the beneficiary coding are shown in Tables 8 through 10. Altogether, an estimated 24,007,000 persons were identified as Social Security/railroad retirement beneficiaries. The majority of these—19,086,000—reported Social Security/railroad retirement payments in their own CPS records. Moreover, of those reporting Social Security in their own records, all but a negligible number possessed characteristics which permitted classification by type of beneficiary, such as retired worker, disabled worker, and so on.

Males With Social Security/Railroad Retirement Benefits in Their Records. There were 8,671,000 males 14 years of age or more who reported Social Security/railroad retirement benefits in their own records and virtually all of them were coded as beneficiaries (Table 8). About 7,024,000 were identified as retired-worker beneficiaries because they were 65 years of age or more, or because they were 62 through 64 years of age and their records contained no evidence of disability. Another 544,000 were

TABLE 8 Number of Social Security/Railroad Retirement Individual Beneficiaries by Presence of Benefit Payment in Record: Sex, and Type of Beneficiary, March 1971 Current Population Survey

(thousands)

Type of Beneficiary	All Persons			Social Security/Railroad Retirement in Record			No Social Security/Railroad Retirement in Record		
	Total	Male	Female	Total	Male	Female	Total	Male	Female
Total	201,855	97,477	104,379	19,559	8,671	10,888	182,296	88,806	93,490
Not a beneficiary	177,849	87,549	90,300	473	177	297	177,375	87,372	90,003
No payment in record	177,375	87,372	90,003	—	—	—	177,375	87,372	90,003
Payment in record imputed to children	446	164	282	446	164	282	—	—	—
Payment in record imputed to spouse	27	13	14	27	13	14	—	—	—
Beneficiary	24,007	9,928	14,082	19,086	8,495	10,592	4,919	1,433	3,487
Retired worker	9,360	7,037	2,323	9,345	7,024	2,322	14	13	1
Wife of retired worker with entitled children in her care[a]	124	—	124	29	—	29	95	—	95
Wife of retired worker with no entitled children in her care	3,010	—	3,010	1,183	—	1,183	1,827	—	1,827
Disabled worker	800	548	252	784	544	240	15	4	12
Wife of disabled worker with entitled children in her care[a]	159	—	159	41	—	41	117	—	117
Wife of disabled worker with no entitled children in her care	4	—	4	—	—	—	4	—	4
Widowed mother[b]	444	—	444	444	—	444	—	—	—
Widow	104	—	104	104	—	104	—	—	—

relative of unit head under 18 years of age	105	55	49	43	25	17	62	30	32
Child beneficiary: never-married student child of unit head, 18-21 years of age	600	333	267	297	173	124	303	160	143
Child beneficiary: never-married student relative of unit head, 18-21 years of age	22	6	16	22	6	16	—	—	—
Child beneficiary: never-married head of individual STATS unit, under 18 years of age	4	3	1	4	3	1	—	—	—
Child beneficiary: never-married student head of individual STATS unit, 18-21 years of age	23	20	3	23	20	3	—	—	—
Child beneficiary: other	110	62	48	110	62	48	—	—	—
Retired or disabled worker	286	208	78	286	208	78	—	—	—
Wife of retired or disabled worker with entitled children in her care[a]	17	—	17	4	—	4	13	—	13
Wife of retired or disabled worker with no entitled children in her care	19	—	19	—	—	—	19	—	19
Retired worker or widow	5,350	5,350	5,350	5,350	—	5,350	—	—	—
Retired worker or disabled worker or widow	95	95	95	95	—	95	—	—	—
Disabled worker or widow	42	42	42	42	—	42	—	—	—
Disabled worker or widowed mother	37	37	37	37	—	37	—	—	—
Not ascertained as to type	393	164	229	393	164	229	—	—	—

SOURCE: Tabulation prepared by the Social Security Administration Office of Research and Statistics from the March 1971 Current Population Survey.

a For purposes of this analysis, an entitled child in the wife's or widow's care is a never-married child of the unit head, under 18 years of age.

b A widow under 62 years of age with an entitled child in her care. See footnote a.

TABLE 9   Number of Social Security/Railroad Retirement Individual Female Beneficiaries With Benefit Payment in Record by Marital Status and Type of Beneficiary, March 1971 Current Population Survey

(thousands)

Type of Beneficiary	Total	Married, Spouse Present			Widow	Never Married, Separated, or Divorced
		Head Is Beneficiary		Head Is Not Beneficiary		
		Retired Worker	Other			
Total	10,592	2,301	117	472	6,200	1,499
Retired worker	2,322	996	39	360	—	927
Wife of retired worker with entitled children in her care[a]	29	29	—	—	—	—
Wife of retired worker with no entitled children in her care	1,183	1,183	—	—	—	—
Disabled worker	240	23	7	54	51	106
Wife of disabled worker with entitled children in her care[a]	41	—	41	—	—	—
Wife of disabled worker with no entitled children in her care	—	—	—	—	—	—
Widowed mother[b]	444	—	—	—	444	—
Widow	104	—	—	—	104	—
Child beneficiary: never-married child of unit head under 18 years of age	185	—	—	—	—	185

Child beneficiary: never-married relative of unit head under 18 years of age	17	—	—	—	—	17
Child beneficiary: never-married student child of unit head, 18-21 years of age	124	—	—	—	—	124
Child beneficiary: never-married student relative of unit head, 18-21 years of age	16	—	—	—	—	16
Child beneficiary: never-married head of individual STATS unit under 18 years of age	1	—	—	—	—	1
Child beneficiary: never-married student head of individual STATS unit 18-21 years of age	3	—	—	—	—	3
Child beneficiary: other	48	—	3	13	—	32
Retired or disabled worker	78	38	9	11	—	20
Wife of retired or disabled worker with entitled children in her care[a]	4	—	4	—	—	—
Wife of retired or disabled worker with no entitled children in her care	—	—	—	—	—	—
Retired worker or widow	5,350	—	—	—	5,350	—
Retired worker or disabled worker or widow	95	—	—	—	95	—
Disabled worker or widow	42	—	—	—	42	—
Disabled worker or widowed mother	37	—	—	—	37	—
Not ascertained as to type	229	21	12	49	78	69

SOURCE: Tabulation prepared by the Social Security Administration Office of Research and Statistics from the March 1971 Current Population Survey.

a For purposes of this analysis, an entitled child in the wife's or widow's care is a never-married child of the unit head under 18 years of age. See footnote a.

b A widow under 62 years of age with an entitled child in her care.

TABLE 10   Number of Social Security/Railroad Retirement Beneficiaries 65 Years of Age and Over, by Sex and Type of Beneficiary, March 1971 Current Population Survey

(thousands)

Characteristic	Total	Male	Female
Total	19,119	8,047	11,072
Not a beneficiary	3,082	1,407	1,675
Beneficiary	16,037	6,640	9,397
Retired worker	8,623	6,640	1,982
Wife of retired worker with no entitled children in her care	2,408	–	2,408
Wife of disabled worker with no entitled children in her care	4	–	4
Wife of retired or disabled worker with no entitled children in her care	5	–	5
Retired worker or widow	4,997	–	4,997

SOURCE: Tabulations prepared by the Social Security Administration Office of Research and Statistics from the March 1971 Current Population Survey.

counted as disabled workers on the basis of their age and disability status—that is, they were less than 62 years of age, they worked less than a full year in 1970 because of illness, and were not in the labor force or in school at the time of interview in early 1971. About 555,000 male beneficiaries with payments in their records were coded as child beneficiaries on the basis of their age and disability status—that is, they were 14 through 22 years of age in March 1971 and their records contained no evidence of disability.

Females With Social Security/Railroad Retirement Benefits in Their Records. The majority of the 10,888,000 females 14 years of age or more who reported payments in their own records were 65 years of age or more, or were 62 through 64 years of age with no evidence of disability in their records. About 5,350,000 were coded as widows on the Census marital-status code and were classified as retired worker or widow on the beneficiary code. Another 927,000 were coded "never-married, separated, or divorced" on the Census marital code and were counted as retired workers (see Table 9).

The remainder of these aged female beneficiaries were coded "married, spouse present" and their beneficiary code depended on the beneficiary status of the head as well as on their own age and disability status. If the head was a retired-worker beneficiary and the wife's payment was less than or equal to 50 percent of the head's benefit, she was counted as a wife with no entitled children in her care—an estimated 1,183,000. If the wife's payment was more than 50 percent of the head's benefit, she was counted as a retired worker—an estimated 996,000. In other words, wives whose benefit was larger than that to which a wife is entitled under the Social Security program—at most 50 percent of the head's benefit—were considered retired-worker beneficiaries, and all other wives were classed as wife beneficiaries.[3] If the head was not a retired-worker beneficiary, the wife was classified as a retired worker—about 399,000 cases.

Beneficiaries "Not Ascertained" As to Type. About 393,000 persons with a Social Security/railroad retirement payment in their records were coded "not ascertained" as to type of beneficiary. An estimated 39,000 were persons less than 62 years of age who reported that they did not work during 1970 because they were retired and were not in the labor force or in school in early 1971. These persons may have retired on disability, but they were not coded as disabled workers because the reason that they gave for not working during 1970 was retirement rather than illness. An elaboration of the code to take this case into account was not feasible for this presentation.

The approximately 350,000 remaining in the "not ascertained" group may include some persons who were beneficiaries during 1970, but the basis for the entitlement did not exist in March 1971. For example, if the last entitled child of a widowed mother left the unit before time of interview in early 1971, there is no basis for recognizing that the widow was entitled during 1970 as a widowed mother. Finally, some of the "not ascertained" group may be attributable to the fact that the data tape underlying the analysis incorporates the Census Bureau's allocations for nonresponse.

Beneficiaries With No Social Security/Railroad Retirement in Their Records. An estimated 4,919,000 persons were coded as

---

[3] In a few cases in which own children were present in the unit, the relation between payments of head and wife was not considered a good basis for classifying wives as retired worker or wife beneficiaries, because the child's benefits may have been included in the benefit of the head or of the wife. In these cases, the wife was considered a retired worker.

beneficiaries even though they did not report a Social Security/ railroad retirement benefit in their own records, because they were dependents of the unit head or wife who reported benefits. More than one-half of these were child beneficiaries, and virtually all of the remainder were wives of retired or disabled workers. Women who did not report a benefit were coded as wife beneficiaries when the STATS unit contained head and wife, the head reported a Social Security/railroad retirement payment in his record which was identified as a retired- or disabled-worker benefit, and the wife was of eligible age—62 years or over if there were no children under 18 years of age in the STATS unit and any age if there were such entitled children present.

The majority of the dependent children who were coded as child beneficiaries were the own children of the STATS unit head, and the unit head was identified as a retired or disabled worker or as a widow or a widowed mother. Another large group of dependent children were coded as child beneficiaries as an explanation of the payment received by the head or wife in the STATS unit. It will be recalled that children under 14 years of age do not have income information in their CPS data records. About 446,000 heads or wives reported a Social Security/railroad retirement payment which could not be identified as a retired- or disabled-worker payment, a widowed mother payment, and so on. In these cases, the payment was assumed to be received on behalf of children in the unit—about 1,160,000 children in the aggregate.

Comparison With Program Counts of Beneficiaries

According to program records, more than 26 million persons were receiving OASDI benefits at the end of 1970 and about 1 million were receiving railroad retirement benefits at that time (see Table 11). Taking into account the beneficiaries receiving both Social Security and railroad retirement benefits—about 400,000—there were 26.8 million beneficiaries on either the Social Security or railroad retirement rolls or both in current payment status as of the end of 1970—about 2.8 million more than the CPS found in March 1971. If the results of the 1970 Decennial Census had been incorporated in the March 1971 CPS, this discrepancy would have been smaller (see footnote 2).

Program counts at the close of 1970 are larger than CPS counts because of broader population coverage and because some beneficiaries died in early 1971 before the time of the CPS interview. With respect to population coverage, the CPS does not enumerate persons living outside the fifty states and the District of Columbia, and the data tape which underlies this analysis does not include the institutional population. The number of OASDI beneficiaries living outside the fifty states and the District of Columbia was about 600,000 at the end of 1970 according to program data. In early 1968, the Survey of the Aged found 650,000 Social Security beneficiaries 65 years of age or over who were living in institutions. Social Security data on awards to disabled workers provide a basis for a rough estimate of 260,000 beneficiaries under 65 years of age who were institutionalized. The total number of beneficiaries in institutions at the end of 1970 is estimated at roughly 900,000. With regard to deaths of beneficiaries, the Social Security program estimate is somewhat more than 300,000 in the first quarter of 1971.

Program counts at the end of 1970 are too low as a measure of the CPS concept because some persons were on the rolls early in 1970 but not in December of that year. Social Security terminations data show that there were about 900,000 such persons. About 700,000 would have been identified as child beneficiaries in the CPS. They included 234,000 children who attained age 18 in 1970 and did not convert to student-child beneficiary status, 209,000 who ceased being full-time students, 71,000 who attained age 22, 48,000 children of disabled workers who recovered, 46,000 child beneficiaries who married, and the like. The remaining 200,000 would have been identified as adult beneficiaries under 65 years of age in the CPS. There were 63,000 widowed mothers who lost entitlement because their last entitled child came of age, 41,000 disabled workers who recovered, and so on.

In addition to the 26.2 million Social Security beneficiaries on the rolls in current-payment status at the end of 1970, there were 1.6 million on the rolls whose benefits were being withheld. Most of the cases of withheld benefits involved beneficiaries whose earnings exceeded the amount allowable by the law, and some of them may have been in current-payment status earlier in 1970. The number in current-payment status earlier in 1970 is estimated

TABLE 11   Number of Social Security/Railroad Retirement Beneficiaries, by Age: Reconciliation of Program Data with March 1971 CPS Concept

(millions)

	Total	Children Other Than Disabled Children	Adults, by Age		
			Total	Under 65	65 and Over
On program rolls in current payment status, end of 1970	27.2	3.9	23.3	5.0	18.4
OASDI	26.2	3.9	22.4	4.9	17.5
Railroad retirement	1.0	a	.9	.1	.8
Less: Beneficiaries receiving both OASDI and railroad retirement	.4	a	.4	a	.3
Equals: On OASDI and/or railroad retirement rolls in current payment status, end of 1970	26.8	3.9	22.9	4.9	18.0
Less: OASDI beneficiaries living outside of U.S.	.6	.2	.4	.1	.3
Beneficiaries in institutions[b]	.9	a	.9	.3	.7
Terminations due to death, January-March 1971[c]	.3	a	.3	a	.3

Equals:	25.0	3.7	21.3	4.5	16.7
Plus: Beneficiaries on rolls in 1970, but not in 12/70[d]	.9	.7	.2	.2	a
Beneficiaries in current payment status in 1970, but not 12/70	.2	a	.2	a	.2
One-fourth of OASDI beneficiaries who were 64 years of age in 12/70	—	—	—	-.2	.2
Equals: Program data adjusted to CPS concept	26.1	4.4	21.7	4.5	17.2
March 1971 CPS estimate	24.0	3.8	20.2	4.2	16.0
Excess of program data over CPS	2.1	.6	1.4	.3	1.1
March 1971 CPS as percent of adjusted program total	92	86	93	93	93

SOURCES: 1970 *Annual Statistical Supplement, Social Security Bulletin*, Tables 67, 106, 108, 121, and 123; *Statistical Supplement* to the 1971 *Annual Report of the Railroad Retirement Board*, Tables B-9, B-10, B-20, B-22, B-24, B-26, and B-29; and Tables 8 and 10 of this paper.

a Less than .05.

b Number of beneficiaries 65 years of age or more living in institutions estimated on the basis of data from 1968 Survey of the Aged. See J. Murray, "Living Arrangements of People Aged 65 and Older: Findings from 1968 Survey of the Aged," *Social Security Bulletin*, September 1971, page 10. Beneficiaries less than 65 years of age living in institutions estimated on the basis of Social Security disability applicant statistics for 1966 and 1967.

c Terminations due to death in 1971 is an unpublished Social Security Program estimate.

d Beneficiaries on rolls in 1970, but not in December 1970, based on OASDI terminations data for 1970. Consists of child beneficiaries who came of age, married, or ceased being students; disabled workers who recovered and their dependents; disabled widows who married; widowed mothers who married; widowed mothers and wives of retired or disabled workers whose last entitled child married or attained age 18.

at roughly 200,000 for those 65 years of age and over and is assumed to be negligible for younger beneficiaries.[4]

On balance, the program counts shown in Table 11 exceed the CPS by 2.1 million—8 percent of the adjusted program total. For beneficiaries aged 65 and over, the adjusted program number is 1,100,000 larger than the CPS total of 16 million; and for younger beneficiaries, it is 900,000 larger than the CPS total of 8 million.

The results by age group suggest that reporting for adult beneficiaries may be relatively better than that for child beneficiaries. The CPS count of adult beneficiaries is 93 percent of the adjusted program total compared to 86 percent for child beneficiaries (see Table 11). This result may be attributable in part to CPS procedures, which do not call for income reports from persons under 14 years of age.

Some of the difference between program and CPS counts for the younger adult beneficiaries may arise from an inability to recognize disability by means of the information in the CPS data tape. For example, Table 8 shows that 164,000 men and 282,000 women who were receiving Social Security/railroad retirement payments were considered to be receiving them on behalf of children in the unit, because there was no evidence of disability in the record of the head or wife. If these cases were classified as disabled workers, rather than as child beneficiaries, the program and CPS totals would be in close agreement for young adults, but the discrepancy for the children would be widened.

Comparisons for males and females are shown in Tables 12 and 13 and indicate that more men than women are missing from the

---

[4] At the end of 1968 and of 1970, there were 1 million beneficiaries 65 years of age and over whose benefits were being withheld because of earnings. Information for 1968 shows that about 800,000 had all of their 1968 benefits withheld. See "The Retirement Test Under Social Security," a report on a study called for by the Congress in P.L. 90-248, the Social Security Amendments of 1967 (Washington, D.C.: U.S., Department of Health, Education and Welfare, 1968), Table 1, page 10. Thus, about 200,000 of those whose benefits were being withheld in December 1968 were in current-payment status earlier. It was assumed that the same relation held for 1970.

Similar estimates are not available for younger beneficiaries for 1968. At the end of 1970, there were about 200,000 beneficiaries under 65 years of age whose benefits were being withheld because of the retirement test, and it was assumed that the number of these in current-payment status earlier in the year was negligible.

TABLE 12   Number of Adult Social Security/Railroad Retirement Beneficiaries Under 65 Years of Age, by Sex: Reconciliation of Program Data with March 1971 CPS Concept

(millions)

	Total	Male	Female
On program rolls in current payment status, end of 1970	5.0	1.8	3.1
OASDI	4.9	1.8	3.1
Railroad retirement	.1	a	.1
Less: Beneficiaries receiving both OASDI and railroad retirement	a	a	a
Equals: On OASDI and/or railroad retirement rolls in current payment status, end of 1970	4.9	1.8	3.1
Less: OASDI beneficiaries living outside of U.S.	.1	.1	.1
Beneficiaries in institutions[b]	.3	.2	.1
Terminations due to death, January-March 1971[c]	a	a	a
Equals:	4.5	1.6	3.0
Plus: Beneficiaries on rolls in 1970, but not 12/70[d]	.2	.1	.1
One-fourth of OASDI beneficiaries who were 64 years of age 12/70	-.2	-.1	-.1
Equals: Program data adjusted to CPS concept	4.5	1.5	3.0
March 1971 CPS estimate	4.2	1.3	2.9
Excess of program data over CPS	.3	.2	.1
March 1971 CPS as percent of adjusted program total	93	86	97

NOTES: See Table 11.
SOURCES: 1970 *Annual Statistical Supplement* to the *Social Security Bulletin*, Tables 67, 106, 108, 121, and 123; *Statistical Supplement* to the 1971 *Annual Report of the Railroad Retirement Board*, Tables B-9, B-10, B-15, B-20, B-22, B-24, B-26, and B-29; Tables 8 and 10 of this paper.

TABLE 13   Number of Adult Social Security/Railroad Retirement Beneficiaries 65 Years of Age or More, by Sex: Reconciliation of Program Data With March 1971 CPS Concept

(millions)

	Total	Male	Female
On program rolls in current payment status, end of 1970	18.4	7.6	10.8
OASDI	17.5	7.2	10.3
Railroad retirement	.8	.4	.5
Less: Beneficiaries receiving both OASDI and railroad retirement	.3	.1	.2
Equals: On OASDI and/or railroad retirement rolls in current payment status, end of 1970	18.0	7.4	10.6
Less: OASDI beneficiaries living outside of U.S.	.3	.1	.1
Beneficiaries in institutions[a]	.7	.2	.5
Terminations due to death, January–March 1971[b]	.3	.2	.2
Equals:	16.7	6.9	9.8
Plus: Beneficiaries in current payment status in 1970, but not 12/70	.2	.1	.1
One-fourth of OASDI beneficiaries who were 64 years of age 12/70	.2	.1	.1
Equals: Program data adjusted to CPS concept	17.2	7.1	10.1
March 1971 CPS estimate	16.0	6.6	10.1
Excess of program data over CPS	1.1	.5	.7
March 1971 CPS as percent of adjusted program total	93	93	93

SOURCES: 1970 *Annual Statistical Supplement* to the *Social Security Bulletin*, Tables 67, 106, 108, 121, and 123. *Statistical Supplement* to the 1971 *Annual Report of the Railroad Retirement Board*, Tables B-9, B-10, B-15, B-20, B-22, B-26, and B-29; and Table 10 of this paper.
a Number of beneficiaries 65 years of age or more living in institutions estimated on the basis of data from 1968 Survey of the Aged. See J. Murray, "Living Arrangements of People Aged 65 and Older: Findings from 1968 Survey of the Aged," *Social Security Bulletin*, September 1971, page 10. Beneficiaries less than 65 years of age living in institutions estimated on the basis of Social Security disability applicant statistics for 1966 and 1967.
b Terminations due to death in 1971 is an unpublished Social Security Program estimate.

CPS count in the under 65 age group. Among the older beneficiaries, men and women were equally well reported.

Summary of Methodology for Social Security Unit Coding

The methodology outlined above for deriving STATS units yielded slightly more than 80 million units when it was applied to the March 1971 CPS data tape. Each unit was given a Social Security unit code identifying it as to beneficiary status. The results are shown in Table 14.

The Social Security unit code was based on the beneficiary codes assigned to each person in the STATS unit and on the composition of the STATS unit. For example, a single-person STATS unit coded as a retired worker on the beneficiary code is a retired-worker unit. The codes for head-wife units depend on the relation between the beneficiary codes of head and wife. If the head is a retired worker and the wife is not a beneficiary, the unit is coded as retired worker, or as retired worker and children, if dependent own children are present. If the head is a retired worker

TABLE 14   Number of STATS Units by Type of Social Security/Railroad Retirement Unit, March 1971 Current Population Survey[a]

(thousands)

Type of Unit	Number
Total	80,125
Not a beneficiary unit	63,529
Beneficiary units	16,597
Retired worker	4,040
Male	2,763
Female	1,277
Retired worker and wife	3,005
Retired worker, wife, and children	129
Retired worker and children	74
Two retired workers	980
Two retired workers and children	16
Disabled worker	533
Male	347
Female	186
Disabled worker and wife	4
Disabled worker, wife, and children	159

TABLE 14 *(Concluded)*

Type of Unit	Number
Disabled worker and children	54
Two disabled workers	2
Two disabled workers and children	1
Retired worker (head) and disabled worker (wife)	19
Retired worker, disabled worker, and children	4
Disabled worker (head) and retired worker (wife)	11
Disabled worker, retired worker, and children	b
Retired or disabled worker	155
Male	124
Female	31
Retired or disabled worker and wife	19
Retired or disabled worker, wife, and children	17
Retired or disabled worker and children	9
Two retired or disabled workers	9
Two retired or disabled workers and children	b
Retired or disabled worker (head) and retired worker (wife)	27
Retired or disabled worker, retired worker, and children	1
Retired worker (head) and retired or disabled worker (wife)	36
Retired worker, retired or disabled worker, and children	1
Retired or disabled worker (head) and disabled worker (wife)	1
Retired or disabled worker, disabled worker, and children	b
Disabled worker (head) and retired or disabled worker (wife)	b
Disabled worker, retired or disabled worker, and children	b
Widow	98
Widow and children	5
Widowed mother and children	444
Retired worker or widow	5,335
Retired worker or widow and children	15
Retired worker or disabled worker or widow	95
Retired worker or disabled worker or widow and children	b
Disabled worker or widow	42
Disabled worker or widow and children	b
Disabled worker or widowed mother and children	37
Child beneficiary of deceased worker	831
Not ascertained as to type	387

SOURCE: Tabulation prepared by the Social Security Administration Office of Research and Statistics from the March 1971 Current Population Survey.

[a] An estimated 88,000 STATS units contain second Social Security/railroad retirement beneficiary units, all of which are child beneficiary units. See text.

[b] Less than .5.

and the wife is a wife beneficiary, the unit is coded as retired worker and wife or as retired worker, wife, and children if dependent own children are present. If both head and wife are retired workers, the unit is coded as two retired workers or as two retired workers and children if dependent own children are present; and so on.

About 16.6 million STATS units were classified as Social Security beneficiary units. The single largest group consisted of 5,335,000 STATS units which were headed by women who were coded as retired workers or widows and in which there were no dependent own children present.

In addition to the Social Security beneficiary units shown in Table 14, some STATS units contain a second Social Security unit. The second unit consists of relatives of the head other than wife and own children. There were 88,000 such units receiving Social Security/railroad retirement benefits in March 1971, all of them classified as child beneficiary units.

Comparison With Program Counts of Beneficiary Families

A program beneficiary family consists of all persons whose entitlement to benefits is based on the same earnings record. According to program records, there were 20.1 million family units receiving OASDI and/or railroad retirement benefits at the end of 1970 (see Table 15). About 4.8 million of the program beneficiary families were male retired workers or special age 72[5] families; many of these workers had wives who were receiving benefits on their own records as retired workers. About 9 million of the program family units were widows or female retired workers or special age 72; many of these women were married to male retired workers. About 3 million program families consisted of retired worker and wife, including 370,000 cases of dual entitlement in which the wife had entitlement both as a retired worker and as wife, but her benefit as a wife exceeded her benefit as a retired worker.

The CPS totals shown in Table 15 may be derived from Table 14 by combining various code positions. For example, Table 15 shows 3,800,000 male retired workers and 7,742,000 female

[5] A person (or couple) aged 72 or over with insufficient quarters of coverage to qualify for a retired-worker benefit, either under the full or transitionally insured-status provisions, but eligible for a monthly benefit at age 72 under a 1966 amendment.

TABLE 15   Number of Retired Worker, Survivor, and Disabled Worker Beneficiary Families: Comparison of March 1971 Current Population Survey With Program Data for End of 1970

(thousands)

Family Classification	Total	Program Data, End of 1970				March 1971 CPS
		OASDI[a]			Railroad Retirement Only	
		Total	OASDI Only	OASDI and Railroad Retirement		
Total	20,103	19,637	19,336	299	466	17,792
Retired worker and widow families	17,060	16,641	16,344	297	419	14,792
Male retired workers and special age 72	4,753	4,599	4,519	80	154	3,800
Retired workers	4,688	4,534	4,454	80	154	—
Special age 72	65	65	65	—	—	
Female retired workers, special age 72, and widows	8,908	8,733	8,635	98	175	7,742
Retired workers	5,213	5,213	5,213	b	b	
Special age 72	442	442	442	—	—	
Widows	3,253	3,078	2,980	98	175	
Retired worker and wife and special age 72	2,976	2,886	2,767	119	90	3,005
Retired worker	2,963	2,873	2,754	119	90	
Special age 72	13	13	13	—	—	

Retired worker, wife, and children	205	205	205	—	—	129
Retired worker and children, or widow and children	218	218	218	—	—	116
Retired worker	159	159	159	—	—	—
Widow	59	59	59	—	—	—
Disabled worker and young survivor families	3,041	2,994	2,992	2	49	2,999
Male disabled workers	680	680	680	c	c	520
Female disabled workers and disabled widows	422	420	420	d	2	427
Disabled workers	374	374	374	c	c	
Disabled widows	48	46	46	d	2	
Disabled worker and wife	43	43	43	c	c	23
Disabled worker, wife, and children	240	240	240	—	—	176
Disabled worker and children	158	158	158	—	—	102
Widowed mother	531	523	523	d	8	444
Children	888	851	849	2	37	920
Other[e]	79	79	79	d	d	387

SOURCES: 1970 *Annual Statistical Supplement, Social Security Bulletin*, Table 96; *Statistical Supplement* to the 1970 *Report of the Railroad Retirement Board*, Tables B-22 and B-29; unpublished OASDI data on dual entitlement; and Table 14 of this paper.

a The total number of OASDI beneficiaries is less than that shown in Table 96 of the 1970 *Annual Statistical Supplement, Social Security Bulletin* because of 370,000 cases in which female retired workers were entitled to wife's benefits which exceeded their benefits as retired workers. In these cases of dual entitlement, both the wife and her husband were removed from the counts of retired workers and included in the retired worker and wife unit counts. The number of female retired worker and of retired worker and wife beneficiaries also differ from the Table 96 counts because of 46,000 units in which both head and wife were railroad retirement beneficiaries and the wife but not the head was a Social Security beneficiary; these cases are included with retired workers and wives.

b Included with male retired workers.

c Included with retired workers.

d Less than .5.

e Program total consists of remarried widows (35), parents (28), worker and husband (8), surviving divorced wife (5), and widowers (3); CPS total consists of the cases not ascertained as to type.

retired workers and widows. These totals are obtained from Table 14 as follows:

	Male	Female
	(thousands)	
Retired worker	2,763	1,277
Two retired workers	980	980
Two retired workers and children	–	16
Retired worker (head) and disabled worker (wife)	19	–
Disabled worker (head) and retired worker (wife)	–	11
Retired or disabled worker (head) and retired worker (wife)	–	27
Retired worker (head) and retired or disabled worker (wife)	36	–
Retired or disabled worker, retired worker, and children	–	1
Widow	–	98
Retired worker or widow	–	5,335
Total	3,800	7,742

As this summary shows, a Social Security beneficiary unit may contain two program beneficiary families. For example, there were 980,000 STATS head-wife units with two retired workers (see Table 14). Each of these units contains two program families—a male retired worker and a female retired worker—resulting in 1,960,000 program families. Another example would be two retired workers and children, a category which would be considered as consisting of two program families—a retired worker and children, and a female retired worker. Thus, the total of 116,000 cases of retired worker and children, or widow and children is obtained as follows:

	(thousands)
Retired worker and children	74
Two retired workers and children	16
Retired worker, disabled worker and children	4
Retired worker, retired or disabled worker and children	1
Retired worker or widow and children	15
Widow and children	5
Total	116

The disabled workers group in Table 15 includes those who are coded as retired or disabled workers in Table 14, as well as those coded as disabled workers. For example, Table 15 shows 520,000 male disabled workers and 427,000 women disabled workers or disabled widows for a total of 947,000. These totals may be obtained from Table 14 as follows:

	Male	Female
	(thousands)	
Disabled worker	347	186
Two disabled workers	2	2
Two disabled workers and children	–	1
Retired worker (head) and disabled worker (wife)	–	19
Retired worker, disabled worker and children	–	4
Disabled worker (head) and retired worker (wife)	11	–
Retired or disabled worker	124	31
Two retired or disabled workers	9	9
Retired or disabled worker (head) and retired worker (wife)	27	–
Retired worker (head) and retired or disabled worker (wife)	–	36
Retired worker, retired or disabled worker, and children	–	1
Retired or disabled worker (head) and disabled worker (wife)	1	1
Retired worker or disabled worker or widow	–	95
Disabled worker or widow	–	42
Total	520	427

The total number of beneficiary families thus derived from CPS Social Security beneficiary units was 17,792,000, about 2.3 million less than the program count as of the end of 1970. Reconciliation between program and CPS totals for the population coverage, timing, and other differences discussed above is more difficult for family units than for individual beneficiaries, because data for the reconciliation items are not available on a family basis. Table 16 shows a rough approximation for family units,

TABLE 16   Number of Retired Worker, Survivor, and Disabled Worker Beneficiary Families, by Type: Reconciliation of Program Data With March 1971 CPS Concept

(millions)

Families	Total	Retired Worker and Widow Families	Disabled Worker and Young survivor
On OASDI and/or railroad retirement rolls in current payment status, end of 1970	20.1	17.1	3.0
Less: OASDI beneficiary families living outside of U.S.	.4	.3	.1
Beneficiary families in institutions	.9	.7	.3
Terminations due to death, January-March 1971[a]	.2	.2	b
Equals:	18.6	15.9	2.7
Plus: Beneficiary families on the rolls in 1970, but not 12/70[c]	.7	b	.7

Beneficiary families in current payment status in 1970, but not 12/70	.2	.2	b
One-fourth of disabled worker families in which the disabled worker was 64 years of age in 12/70		b	b
Equals: Program data adjusted to CPS concept	19.5	16.1	3.4
March 1971 CPS estimate	17.8	14.8	3.0
Excess of program data over CPS	1.7	1.3	.4
March 1971 CPS as percent of adjusted program total	91	92	88

SOURCE: See text.

a Of the 300,000 beneficiaries aged 65 or over whose benefits were terminated due to death between January and March 1971 (see Table 11), 200,000 were assumed to be in retired worker or widow units and 100,000 in retired worker and wife units. The terminations due to death in the retired worker and wife units affect the number of beneficiaries but not the number of units. Thus, the number of units whose benefits were terminated due to the deaths of beneficiaries was estimated to be 200,000.

b Less than .05.

c Consists of child beneficiaries who came of age, married, or ceased being students; disabled worker families where the worker recovered; and disabled widows who married.

using data sources cited in Table 11. For retired worker and widow families, the adjusted program total given in Table 16 exceeds the CPS total by about 1.3 million; and for disabled worker and younger survivor families, by about 400,000.

Comparison With Program Data on Average Benefit

The average CPS benefit per beneficiary unit is $1,490, compared with a program figure of $1,661—the December 1970 benefit at an annual rate (see Table 17). The program average may be too low as a measure of payment to the CPS population, because the program average covers beneficiaries living in institutions. Beneficiaries in institutions are primarily one-person units, and their benefits are probably smaller on the average than the benefits of the noninstitutional population. On the other hand, the December benefit at an annual rate is too high as a measure of payment to the CPS population, because the CPS mean covers units which did not receive benefits for the entire year 1970, and because the January 1970 benefit payment incorporated in the CPS mean does not reflect the 15 percent increase of 1970.

The CPS averages are less than program figures for both major groups of beneficiaries—the retired worker and widow group and the disabled worker and young survivor group—but the discrepancy is much smaller for retired workers.

Comparison With Program Data on Size Distributions of Benefits

Distributions of beneficiary families by size of Social Security benefit are given in Tables 18 through 27. Program data represent OASDI beneficiaries as of the end of 1970, including beneficiaries living abroad and in institutions, distributed by their December 1970 OASDI benefit expressed at annual rates. Railroad retirement benefits are excluded from the program data, because information was not available in a form which permitted distributions of the sum of OASDI and railroad retirement benefits.

The CPS distribution of male retired workers and special age 72 beneficiaries by size of benefit received in 1970 is given in Table 18, along with the corresponding OASDI distribution. The CPS distribution shows a larger proportion with small benefits, which one would expect because of the part-of-year cases. The CPS also shows cases with benefits in excess of the OASDI maximum payment. This is attributable in part to the fact that the CPS benefit covers both Social Security and railroad retirement, and the maximum railroad retirement benefit is larger than the maximum Social Security benefit.

The results for female retired workers and widows and for retired workers and wives are similar to those for the male retired workers (see Tables 19 and 20). In other words, the CPS distribution shows higher proportions of very small and very large benefits than the OASDI distributions. The remaining groups for which comparisons are possible are somewhat less amenable to generalization, but in all cases, the CPS shows higher proportions of units with small benefits.

A comparison for all units for which OASDI data were available is given in Table 27. The OASDI distribution of 19.3 million units shows 15 percent receiving monthly benefits of $64 or less—$768 a year or less. The CPS distribution of 17 million units has 19 percent in that range. Both distributions show that 7 percent of units received payments of $2,880 or more.

Economic Status of Missing Beneficiaries

A question posed at the beginning of this paper concerned the relation between understatement of transfer income and the count of the low-income population. Some evidence on this question is provided by a comparison of the average income of the population reporting Social Security benefits with those not reporting benefits. Such a comparison for the aged population is given in Table 28, and Tables 29 and 30 show results for two subgroups of the nonaged population.

In Table 28, STATS units with heads 65 years of age or more are classified into groups, depending on the Social Security/railroad retirement beneficiary status of the head. In about 12.5 million units, the head was coded as a beneficiary and average income of the unit excluding Social Security was $2,161. In the remaining 2.6 million units, the head was not coded as a beneficiary.

An approximation to the retirement test was introduced and shows that 860,000 of the 2.6 million not reporting benefits may have had some or all of their benefits withheld because of the retirement test; their income was high on the average—above $10,000. Some of the remaining units which did not report

TABLE 17   Average Benefit Received by Retired Worker, Survivor, and Disabled Worker Beneficiary Families: Comparison of March 1971 Current Population Survey with Program Data[a]

(dollars)

Family Classification	Program Data–December 1970 Benefit at Annual Rate					March 1971 CPS
	Total	OASDI			Railroad Retirement Only	
		Total	OASDI Only	OASDI and Railroad Retirement		
Total	1,661	1,643	1,617	3,345	2,381	1,490
Retired worker and widow families	1,589	1,566	1,534	3,357	2,500	1,466
Male retired workers and special age 72	1,578	1,541	1,519	2,803	2,675	1,432
Retired workers	1,592	1,555	1,533	2,803	2,675	—
Special age 72	552	552	552	—	—	
Female retired workers, special age 72, and widows	1,219	1,214	1,206	1,932	1,476	1,163
Retired workers	1,244	1,244	1,244	b	b	
Special age 72	522	522	522	—	—	
Widows	1,270	1,258	1,236	1,932	1,476	
Retired worker and wife and special age 72	2,583	2,533	2,430	4,904	4,194	2,248
Retired worker	2,590	2,541	2,438	4,904	4,194	

Special age 72	828	828	828	828	—	—	—
Retired worker, wife, and children	2,754	2,754	2,754	2,754	—	—	2,249
Retired worker and children, or widow and children	2,309	2,309	2,309	2,309	—	—	1,687
Retired worker	2,282	2,282	2,282	2,282	—	—	—
Widow	2,380	2,380	2,380	2,380	—	—	—
Disabled worker and young survivor families	2,062	2,073	2,073	1,603	1,345	1,606
Male disabled workers	1,636	1,636	1,636	c	c	1,431
Female disabled workers and disabled widows	1,318	1,318	1,317	2,040	1,368	1,075
Disabled workers	1,357	1,357	1,357	c	c	
Disabled widows	1,015	997	986	2,040	1,368	
Disabled worker and wife	2,390	2,390	2,390	c	c	1,924
Disabled worker, wife and children	3,244	3,244	3,244	—	—	2,640
Disabled worker and children	2,623	2,623	2,623	—	—	1,950
Widowed mother	3,137	3,158	3,159	2,160	1,740	2,609
Children	1,740	1,761	1,761	1,470	1,257	1,346
Other[d]	1,199	1,198	1,197	1,704	1,500	1,314

SOURCE: See Table 15.

a Average benefit represents the sum of Social Security and railroad retirement for families as shown in Table 15.

b Included with male retired workers.

c Included with retired workers.

d Program total consists of remarried widows (35), parents (28), worker and husband (8), surviving divorced wife (5), and widowers (3); CPS total consists of the not ascertained as to type cases.

TABLE 18   Benefits for Male Retired Workers and Special Age 72 Families: Percentage Distribution by Amount Received in 1970, Old-Age, Survivors, and Disability Insurance, and March 1971 Current Population Survey

Amount Received in 1970[a]	OASDI[b]	March 1971 CPS
Total number (thousands)	4,969	3,800
Total percent	100.0	100.0
Less than $708	{6.8	11.1
$ 708-$ 767		3.7
768	5.3	1.7
769- 839	1.9	3.0
840- 959	4.2	5.6
960-1,079	4.8	6.3
1,080-1,199	6.0	6.0
1,200-1,319	5.8	7.6
1,320-1,439	6.3	5.4
1,440-1,679	13.3	12.9
1,680-1,919	16.9	16.9
1,920-2,159	21.0	12.3
2,160-2,399	6.4	3.0
2,400-2,639	1.0	1.4
2,640-2,879	.4	.8
2,880-3,119	−	1.0
3,120 and over	−	1.3
Average benefit per family	$1,531	$1,432

SOURCES: 1970 *Annual Statistical Supplement, Social Security Bulletin,* Tables 96 and 99; and tabulation prepared by the Social Security Administration Office of Research and Statistics from the March 1971 Current Population Survey.

[a] For OASDI, represents December 1970 benefit at annual rate.

[b] Consists of male retired workers and special age 72 beneficiary families as shown in Table 15 plus 370,000 cases in which the wife of a retired worker had dual entitlement, distributed by the OASDI benefit of the retired worker or special age 72 beneficiary. See footnote *a* to Table 15.

TABLE 19 Benefits for Female Retired Worker, Aged Widow, and Special Age 72 Families: Percentage Distribution by Amount Received in 1970, Old-Age, Survivors, and Disability Insurance, and March 1971 Current Population Survey

Amount Received in 1970[a]	*OASDI*[b]	*March 1971 CPS*
Total number (thousands)	9,148	7,742
Total percent	100.0	100.0
Less than $708	⎰14.6	17.4
$ 708-$ 767	⎱	4.7
768	9.3	2.4
769- 839	3.7	4.6
840- 959	8.7	8.3
960-1,079	8.7	9.0
1,080-1,199	8.7	8.0
1,200-1,319	7.9	9.2
1,320-1,439	7.4	8.0
1,440-1,679	18.6	17.0
1,680-1,919	7.4	5.9
1,920-2,159	3.5	3.1
2,160-2,399	1.2	.9
2,400-2,639	.2	.5
2,640-2,879	.1	.2
2,880 and over	–	.7
Average benefit per family	$1,192	$1,163

SOURCES: 1970 *Annual Statistical Supplement* to the *Social Security Bulletin,* Tables 96, 99, and 100; and tabulation prepared by the Social Security Administration Office of Research and Statistics from the March 1971 Current Population Survey.

[a] For OASDI, represents December 1970 benefit at annual rate.

[b] Consists of female retired workers, special age 72, and widows as shown in Table 15 plus 46,000 cases in which both head and wife were railroad retirement beneficiaries and the wife but not the head was a Social Security beneficiary, distributed by the OASDI benefit of the retired worker, special age 72, or widow beneficiary, and plus 370,000 cases of wives with dual entitlement, distributed by their OASDI benefits as wives. See footnote *a* to Table 15.

TABLE 20   Benefits for Retired Worker and Wife, and Special Age 72 Families: Percentage Distribution by Amount Received in 1970, Old-Age, Survivors, and Disability Insurance, and March 1971 Current Population Survey

Amount Received in 1970[a]	*OASDI*[b]	*March 1971 CPS*
Total number (thousands)	2,470	3,005
Total percent	100.0	100.0
Less than $960	1.0	6.9
$ 960-$1,079	2.6	2.8
1,080- 1,199	6.3	3.1
1,200- 1,319	1.9	3.4
1,320- 1,439	2.4	2.3
1,440- 1,679	6.3	6.2
1,680- 1,919	7.3	9.2
1,920- 2,159	7.4	9.7
2,160- 2,399	7.9	8.6
2,400- 2,639	13.0	12.3
2,640- 2,879	16.0	14.6
2,880- 3,119	16.0	10.6
3,120- 3,359	7.0	3.9
3,360- 3,599	2.6	2.4
3,600- 3,839	1.1	1.3
3,840- 4,079	1.1	.8
4,080 and over	–	2.0
Average benefit per family	$2,379	$2,248

SOURCES: 1970 *Annual Statistical Supplement* to the *Social Security Bulletin,* Tables 96 and 99; and tabluation prepared by the Social Security Administration Office of Research and Statistics from the March 1971 Current Population Survey.

[a] For OASDI, represents December 1970 benefit at annual rate.

[b] Consists of retired worker and wife, and special age 72 beneficiary families as shown in Table 15, less 370,000 cases of dual entitlement and less 46,000 cases in which both head and wife were railroad retirement beneficiaries and the wife but not the head was a Social Security beneficiary.

TABLE 21   Benefits for Male Disabled Worker Families: Percentage Distribution by Amount Received in 1970, Old-Age, Survivors, and Disability Insurance, and March 1971 Current Population Survey

Amount Received in 1970[a]	*OASDI*	*March 1971 CPS*
Total number (thousands)	680	520
Total percent	100.0	100.0
Less than $769	3.3	16.4
$ 769-$ 839	.8	2.9
840- 959	2.5	3.7
960-1,079	3.1	3.6
1,080-1,199	6.8	6.4
1,200-1,319	9.3	7.2
1,320-1,439	9.1	8.6
1,440-1,679	15.1	14.3
1,680-1,919	16.3	11.9
1,920-2,159	25.5	18.1
2,160-2,399	8.0	2.1
2,400-2,639	.2	1.8
2,640-2,879	b	.7
2,880-3,119	b	1.0
3,120 and over	—	1.1
Average benefit per family	$1,636	$1,431

SOURCES: 1970 *Annual Statistical Supplement* to the *Social Security Bulletin,* Table 101; and tabulation prepared by the Social Security Administration Office of Research and Statistics from the March 1971 Current Population Survey.

[a] For OASDI, represents December 1970 benefit at annual rate.

[b] Less than .05 percent.

TABLE 22   Benefits for Female Disabled Worker Families: Percentage Distribution by Amount Received in 1970, Old-Age, Survivors, and Disability Insurance, and March 1971 Current Population Survey

Amount Received in 1970[a]	OASDI	March 1971 CPS
Total number (thousands)	374	427
Total percent	100.0	100.0
Less than $769	8.8	31.3
$ 769-$ 839	2.3	2.8
840- 959	5.8	7.9
960-1,079	5.8	10.4
1,080-1,199	12.7	8.1
1,200-1,319	13.5	8.2
1,320-1,439	12.9	8.9
1,440-1,679	17.2	14.7
1,680-1,919	11.3	5.3
1,920-2,159	8.5	1.0
2,160-2,399	1.2	b
2,400-2,639	b	.6
2,640-2,879	b	b
2,880-3,119	b	b
3,120 and over	—	.7
Average benefit per family	$1,357	$1,075

SOURCES: 1970 *Annual Statistical Supplement* to the *Social Security Bulletin*, Table 101; and tabulation prepared by the Social Security Administration Office of Research and Statistics from the March 1971 Current Population Survey.

[a] For OASDI, represents December 1970 benefit at annual rate.

[b] Less than .05 percent.

TABLE 23   Benefits for Disabled Worker, Wife, and Children Families: Percentage Distribution by Amount Received in 1970, Old-Age, Survivors, and Disability Insurance, and March 1971 Current Population Survey

Amount Received in 1970[a]	OASDI	March 1971 CPS
Total number (thousands)	240	176
Total percent	100.0	100.0
Less than $769	.6	3.9
$ 769-$ 839	b	.7
840- 959	.1	6.1
960-1,079	.1	.6
1,080-1,199	2.7	1.4
1,200-1,319	1.0	.7
1,320-1,439	1.4	3.4
1,440-1,679	3.9	5.4
1,680-1,919	6.1	10.6
1,920-2,159	5.4	4.6
2,160-2,399	5.7	5.7
2,400-2,639	4.7	4.4
2,640-2,879	5.1	6.7
2,880-3,119	6.1	11.2
3,120-3,359	5.8	10.6
3,360-3,599	6.3	2.2
3,600-3,839	6.8	6.6
3,840-4,079	8.9	4.4
4,080-4,319	12.6	6.6
4,320-4,559	6.4	1.5
4,560-4,799	7.2	2.2
4,800 and over	3.3	.7
Average benefit per family	$3,244	$2,640

SOURCES: 1970 *Annual Statistical Supplement* to the *Social Security Bulletin,* Table 101; and tabulation prepared by the Social Security Administration Office of Research and Statistics from the March 1971 Current Population Survey.

[a] For OASDI, represents December 1970 benefit at annual rate.

[b] Less than .05 percent.

TABLE 24 Benefits for Widowed Mother and Children: Percentage Distribution by Amount Received in 1970, Old-Age, Survivors, and Disability Insurance, and March 1971 Current Population Survey

Amount Received in 1970[a]	Total		One Child		Two Children		Three Children		Four or More Children	
	OASDI	CPS	OASDI	CPS	OASDI	CPS	OASDI	CPS	OASDI	CPS
Total number (thousands)	523	444	187	145	155	132	94	98	88	70
Total percent	100.0	100.0	100.0	100.0	100.0	100.0	100.0	100.0	100.0	100.0
Less than $1,200	5.9	13.5	6.4	14.3	5.7	11.1	4.7	11.8	6.2	19.1
$1,200-$1,319	1.5	4.4	1.1	7.1	1.7	5.0	1.7	2.5	1.8	b
1,320-1,439	1.9	2.2	1.9	4.0	1.7	2.0	1.9	b	2.5	1.9
1,440-1,559	1.8	5.0	1.9	9.4	1.9	4.3	1.5	2.9	1.7	b
1,560-1,679	2.0	5.4	1.9	6.3	1.8	3.9	2.1	3.7	2.3	8.8
1,680-1,919	5.5	6.2	7.0	10.1	4.4	7.1	4.1	1.0	5.6	3.4
1,920-2,159	5.3	5.0	8.0	4.5	3.9	7.0	3.6	2.7	3.6	5.6
2,160-2,399	5.0	4.2	7.0	2.7	3.7	7.0	3.8	2.6	4.2	4.1

2,400-2,639	5.7	6.2	10.2	5.6	2.8	6.1	3.5	10.7	3.6	1.6
2,640-2,879	5.8	6.5	10.2	7.6	3.4	3.0	2.7	11.9	3.8	3.1
2,880-3,119	12.0	7.6	25.8	14.6	4.2	6.2	4.0	1.2	4.8	5.0
3,120-3,359	6.8	5.4	12.1	7.7	3.7	4.0	3.4	3.9	4.9	5.6
3,360-3,599	4.8	3.8	5.0	2.3	4.9	5.1	4.7	5.5	4.6	1.8
3,600-3,839	3.1	3.9	.6	1.0	4.5	5.9	4.5	5.7	4.2	3.3
3,840-4,079	3.3	3.9	.2	.9	5.2	3.2	5.0	5.5	4.5	8.8
4,080-4,319	5.7	4.5	.2	1.0	8.8	6.0	9.5	4.3	8.0	9.2
4,320-4,559	7.5	2.4	.1	b	14.4	3.0	10.4	4.1	8.0	5.3
4,560-4,799	9.7	3.9	—	b	14.4	5.0	16.5	9.5	15.0	1.8
4,800 and over	6.6	6.1	—	.9	8.8	5.0	12.1	10.3	10.8	13.3
Average benefit per family	$3,158	$2,609	$2,556	$2,105	$3,493	$2,677	$3,564	$3,056	$3,388	$2,905

SOURCES: 1970 *Annual Statistical Supplement* to the *Social Security Bulletin*, Table 100; and tabulation prepared by the Social Security Administration Office of Research and Statistics from the March 1971 Current Population Survey.
a For OASDI, represents December 1970 benefit at annual rate.
b Less than .05 percent.

TABLE 25 Benefits for Children: Percentage Distribution by Amount Received in 1970, Old-Age, Survivors, and Disability Insurance, and March 1971 Current Population Survey

Amount Received in 1970[a]	*Total*		*One Child*		*Two Children*		*Three Children*		*Four or More Children*	
	OASDI	*CPS*	*OASDI*	*CPS*	*OASDI*	*CPS*	*OASDI*	*CPS*	*OASDI*	*CPS*
Total number (thousands)	851	920	515	578	196	165	82	77	58	101
Total percent	100.0	100.0	100.0	100.0	100.0	100.0	100.0	100.0	100.0	100.0
Less than $708	.9	27.1	1.5	32.8	—	14.0	—	30.2	—	13.0
$ 708- $767		1.5		1.9	—	.8	—	2.2	—	b
768	9.9	1.2	16.4	1.6	—	1.3	—	b	—	b
769- 839	2.4	2.8	4.0	3.8	—	2.5	—	b	—	b
840- 959	6.1	5.0	10.1	5.6	—	4.3	—	5.0	—	2.9
960-1,079	5.8	5.9	9.5	7.1	—	5.5	—	3.5	—	1.3
1,080-1,199	9.0	5.3	7.6	5.5	10.0	1.4	11.3	9.4	15.4	7.7
1,200-1,319	7.9	7.3	11.4	8.2	2.2	8.1	2.5	5.2	3.4	2.4
1,320-1,439	6.4	6.2	8.7	7.4	2.9	5.7	3.0	3.4	2.8	2.3
1,440-1,559	13.6	9.1	20.8	11.5	2.5	8.3	2.8	1.5	2.6	2.8
1,560-1,679	5.5	3.7	7.1	4.2	2.8	2.3	3.1	b	3.7	5.5
1,680-1,919	4.7	4.1	2.4	2.5	8.9	5.7	6.9	6.8	8.0	8.9

1,920-2,159	2.8	1.9	.3	1.4	8.3	2.3	4.7	b	3.6	5.7
2,160-2,399	2.6	2.6	—	1.4	8.0	4.8	4.9	b	3.7	7.4
2,400-2,639	3.1	2.0	—	.7	10.7	4.9	3.4	b	3.8	6.1
2,640-2,879	2.7	1.8	—	.7	9.4	6.4	3.2	b	3.4	1.4
2,880-3,119	5.9	3.6	—	1.8	23.1	8.3	3.9	10.4	3.4	1.2
3,120-3,359	2.4	1.4	—	.7	8.1	4.2	3.5	b	2.9	2.7
3,360-3,599	1.1	.7	—	b	1.9	1.6	3.7	1.9	3.8	2.5
3,600-3,839	.7	1.3	—	.2	.4	4.0	4.0	3.5	3.2	2.7
3,840-4,079	.8	.3	—	—	.4	.7	5.1	1.5	3.5	1.2
4,080-4,319	1.0	.9	—	—	.2	—	5.7	1.6	6.3	6.1
4,320-4,559	1.6	.5	—	—	.1	—	12.0	3.6	6.3	1.4
4,560-4,799	1.8	.7	—	—	—	—	11.6	3.4	10.7	3.8
4,800 and over	1.1	1.4	—	—	—	—	4.8	5.0	9.2	7.8
Not ascertained[c]	—	1.8	—	1.1	—	2.9	—	2.1	—	3.5
Average benefit per family	$1,761	$1,346	$1,184	$1,038	$2,370	$1,702	$3,067	$1,764	$2,947	$2,206

SOURCES: 1970 *Annual Statistical Supplement* to the *Social Security Bulletin*, Table 100; and tabulation prepared by the Social Security Administration Office of Research and Statistics from the March 1971 Current Population Survey.

[a] For OASDI, represents December 1970 benefit at annual rate.

[b] Less than .05 percent.

[c] In cases in which the payment reported by the head or wife was assumed to be received on behalf of children in the family, all children in the unit were considered beneficiaries. However, the entire payment was imputed to own children, if present. Hence there are a few cases in which relative children are considered beneficiaries, but the amount of benefit is not known.

TABLE 26   Benefits for Current Population Survey Units Not Ascertained
As to Benefit Type: Percentage Distribution by Amount
Received in 1970, March 1971 Current Population Survey

Amount Received in 1970	*March 1971 CPS*
Total number (thousands)	<u>387</u>
Total percent March 1971 CPS	<u>100.0</u>
Less than $708	26.6
$ 708-$ 767	3.0
768	.3
769- 839	2.6
840- 959	6.6
960-1,079	5.6
1,080-1,199	2.4
1,200-1,319	7.1
1,320-1,439	4.5
1,440-1,559	8.0
1,560-1,679	5.2
1,680-1,919	5.9
1,920-2,159	7.4
2,160-2,399	1.3
2,400-2,639	4.6
2,640-2,879	3.1
2,880-3,119	2.6
3,120 and over	3.2
Average benefit per family	$1,314

SOURCE: Tabulation prepared by the Social Security Administration Office of
Research and Statistics from the March 1971 Current Population Survey.

benefits may have been subject to the retirement test, but their
earnings were sufficiently low so that they would have received
some benefit had they been beneficiaries; their income of
approximately $2,700 was greater than the income excluding
Social Security of units reporting benefits—about $2,200. If the
missing beneficiaries are contained largely in the second group of
nonreporters, then the suggestion is that the missing aged
beneficiaries are at least as well-off, on the average, as those who
report.

TABLE 27 Benefits for Retired Worker, Disabled Worker, and Survivor Families: Percentage Distribution by Amount Received in 1970, Old-Age, Survivors, and Disability Insurance, and March 1971 Current Population Survey

Amount Received in 1970[a]	OASDI	March 1971 CPS
Total number[b] (thousands)	19,256	17,034
Total percent	100.0	100.0
Less than $708	⎧	13.8
$ 708-$ 767	⎨15.3	3.3
768	⎩	1.7
769- 839	2.5	3.2
840- 959	5.7	6.0
960-1,079	6.2	6.7
1,080-1,199	7.5	6.3
1,200-1,319	6.5	7.4
1,320-1,439	6.3	6.2
1,440-1,679	14.9	13.5
1,680-1,919	10.1	9.1
1,920-2,159	9.5	6.7
2,160-2,399	3.8	2.9
2,400-2,639	2.4	3.1
2,640-2,879	2.5	3.2
2,880-3,119	2.7	2.7
3,120-3,359	1.3	1.2
3,360-3,599	.6	.7
3,600-3,839	.3	.5
3,840-4,079	.4	.3
4,080-4,319	.4	.4
4,320-4,559	.4	.2
4,560-4,799	.4	.2
4,800 and over	.3	.5
Average benefit per family	$1,555	$1,483

SOURCES: 1970 *Annual Statistical Supplement* to the *Social Security Bulletin,* Tables 96, 100, and 101; and tabulations prepared by the Social Security Administration Office of Research and Statistics from the March 1971 Current Population Survey.

[a] For OASDI, represents December 1970 benefit at annual rate.

[b] Consists of the groups shown in Tables 18 through 25.

TABLE 28   Social Security Beneficiary Status and Average Money Income in 1970: STATS Units With Head 65 Years of Age or More, by Social Security/Railroad Retirement Beneficiary Status and Sex of Head

Beneficiary Status and Sex of Head	Number of Units (Thousands)	Average Income of Unit	
		Total	Total, Excluding Social Security
All units	15,109	$ 4,051	$ 2,698
Head is Social Security beneficiary	12,490	3,785	2,161
Head is not Social Security beneficiary	2,619	5,320	5,262
Unit's benefits may have been withheld because of retirement test[a]	860	10,657	10,567
Other units	1,759	2,710	2,668
Head reports public assistance	613	1,297	1,292
Head does not report public assistance	1,146	3,467	3,404
Units with male head	8,047	5,464	3,789
Head is Social Security beneficiary	6,640	4,957	2,950
Head is not Social Security beneficiary	1,407	7,857	7,750
Unit's benefits may have been withheld because of retirement test[a]	696	11,492	11,383
Other units	711	4,301	4,196
Head reports public assistance	169	1,616	1,599
Head does not report public assistance	542	5,140	5,007
Units with female head	7,062	2,442	1,455
Head is Social Security beneficiary	5,850	2,456	1,265
Head is not Social Security beneficiary	1,212	2,376	2,374
Unit's benefits may have been withheld because of retirement test[a]	164	7,125	7,113
Other units	1,048	1,630	1,630
Head reports public assistance	444	1,175	1,175
Head does not report public assistance	604	1,965	1,965

TABLE 29 Social Security Beneficiary Status and Average Money Income in 1970: STATS Units With Disabled Head Under 65 Years of Age, by Social Security/Railroad Retirement Beneficiary Status

Beneficiary Status of Head	Number of Units (Thousands)	Average Income of Unit	
		Total	Total, Excluding Social Security
Total, all units	2,812	$3,233	$2,591
Head is Social Security beneficiary	1,101	3,683	2,059
Head is not Social Security beneficiary	1,711	2,944	2,934
Unit's benefits may have been withheld due to excess earnings[a]	200	8,401	8,386
Other units	1,511	2,221	2,212
Head reports public assistance	635	1,985	1,979
Head does not report public assistance	875	2,392	2,381

SOURCE: Tabulation prepared by the Social Security Administration Office of Research and Statistics from the March 1971 Current Population Survey.

[a] Head with earnings of $3,000 or more.

TABLE 30 Social Security Beneficiary Status and Average Money Income in 1970: STATS Units in Which Head is a Widowed Mother Under 65 Years of Age, by Social Security/Railroad Retirement Beneficiary Status

Beneficiary Status of Head	Number of Units (Thousands)	Average Income of Unit	
		Total	Total, Excluding Social Security
Total, all units	625	$5,345	$3,487
Head is a Social Security beneficiary	444	5,731	3,120
Head is not a Social Security beneficiary	180	4,393	4,393
Unit's benefits may have been withheld due to excess earnings[a]	76	7,178	7,178
Other units	104	2,338	2,338
Head reports public assistance	40	2,708	2,708
Head does not report public assistance	64	2,106	2,106

SOURCE: Tabulation prepared by the Social Security Administration Office of Research and Statistics from the March 1971 Current Population Survey.
[a] Head with earnings of $3,000 or more.

Comparisons for the nonaged population are more tenuous because of the difficulty in specifying groups which might be expected to contain the missing beneficiaries. Two subgroups are specified in Tables 29 and 30—units with a disabled person as head and units with a widowed mother as head. The general result for the units with a disabled head is the same as for the aged population; that is to say, after taking into account the earnings test and excluding Social Security income, the units not reporting Social Security are at least as well-off as those reporting. On the other hand, for units with widowed mothers as head, the reporters have, on the average, higher incomes excluding Social Security than the nonreporters.

Summary of Findings and Conclusion

Following the rules described above, 24 million Social Security/railroad retirement beneficiaries were found in the population covered by the CPS, about 2.1 million less than the program totals adjusted to the CPS concept. Slightly more than one-half the missing beneficiaries were 65 years of age or over, and the remainder were younger. Relatively more young beneficiaries were missing. For most persons identified in the CPS as beneficiaries, the status can be explained on the basis of age, disability, or survivorship.

Comparison of program and CPS data for beneficiary family units is complicated by the fact that the data available to adjust for population coverage and timing differences are approximate. With regard to counts of units, the CPS covers 91 percent of the adjusted program figure. With regard to average benefit, the CPS and program figures are probably in close accord for retired workers and widow units, but the CPS mean for disabled workers and young survivor units may be understated. The combination of missing beneficiaries and probable understatement of the CPS average benefit results in an understatement in aggregate benefit of about $4.1 billion.

CHAPTER 13

The Bureau of Economic Analysis and Current Population Survey Size Distributions: Some Comparisons for 1964

Edward C. Budd
Pennsylvania State University

and

Daniel B. Radner
U.S. Department of Commerce

The annual March income supplement of the Census Bureau's Current Population Survey (CPS) is perhaps the single most important source of information on a historical basis, as regards the distribution of money income by size and by detailed socioeconomic characteristics. Annual data have been published since 1944, although in more limited form for the earlier years. It is therefore important to understand what effect deficiencies and biases in the CPS have on the various types of socioeconomic or size distributions that are obtained from the Survey. In this paper, we attempt to present some measure of the degree of reliability of CPS distributions by comparing them with the recently completed estimates of the distribution of total money income (TMI) and family personal income (FPI) that we have prepared at the Bureau of Economic Analysis (BEA)[1] of the Department of Commerce.

The deficiencies and biases in the CPS referred to above are well-known and need only be mentioned here. Indeed, they tend to be characteristic of all field surveys containing income questions. Respondents make errors in filling out questionnaires or

[1] As of January 1, 1972, the Office of Business Economics (OBE) was redesignated the Bureau of Economic Analysis (BEA) and is referred to by the new name in this paper, even when the references are for earlier years.

449

in answering enumerators' questions and sometimes fail, or refuse, to answer the income questions at all, which results in relatively high income nonresponse rates, at least compared with other questions in the survey. For those who do respond, underreporting of income is a serious problem, averaging perhaps 9 to 15 percent, and much more for certain income types, such as interest and dividends. In addition, the receipt of some income types, particularly property income and certain transfers, is often not reported at all. As a result, the distributions produce estimates of average income which are too low and which fail to capture the precise shape of the income distribution, particularly its upper and lower tails.[2]

In the federal statistics program,[3] there are, of course, sources of information other than the CPS on income distribution. Some of them, such as the Decennial Census and the Consumer Expenditure Survey of the Bureau of Labor Statistics (BLS), suffer from response problems similar to those encountered in the CPS, and in addition are available only once a decade. For a number of reasons, administrative data, such as tax return data tabulated by the Internal Revenue Service (IRS) in its Statistics of Income, are usually unsuitable as size distributions themselves, although they may form an important input into the estimation of such distributions. An alternative series, available annually for about the same period as the CPS, is the Survey of Consumer Finances (SCF), sponsored and published by the Federal Reserve Board until 1959 and by the Survey Research Center of the University of Michigan since, although sample sizes for the Survey have not typically been large enough to permit the kind of detailed tabulations available from the CPS. Differences between the SCF and the CPS will not be examined here.[4]

    [2] See Tables 6 (Steps 1 and 5) and 12 for the extent of underreporting by income type for 1964.

    [3] For a more complete discussion, see T. Paul Schultz, *The Distribution of Personal Income,* prepared for the Subcommittee on Economic Statistics of the Joint Economic Committee, December 1964 (Washington, D.C., 1965), Chapter 3.

    [4] See Selma Goldsmith, "The Relation of Census Income Distribution Statistics to Other Income Data," *An Appraisal of the 1950 Census Income Data,* Studies in Income and Wealth, Volume 23 (Princeton: Princeton University Press for NBER, 1958) pp. 83-91; see also in the same volume, M. G. Sirken, E. Scott Maynes, and J. E. Frechling, "The Survey of Consumer Finances and the Census Quality Check," pp. 127-68, for a study of

The BEA's old income distribution series was perhaps the closest competitor of the CPS for the years for which it was available—1944, 1946, 1947, and annually from 1950 to 1962—and a few words on the differences between the two series may be in order. For one thing, the BEA series used family personal income, derived from BEA's personal income estimates, as the income concept, rather than the Census's total money income. (The reconciliation between personal income, family personal income, and total money income for 1964 presented in Table I should give the reader some notion of the differences in the underlying income concepts, although it is relevant to the new, rather than the old, BEA concept of FPI.) More important was the difference in the underlying methodology. Rather than being based on a field survey, the BEA methods might be described as "synthetic": estimating the distribution from a wide variety of sources, including—besides field surveys such as the CPS—tax returns, other business and governmental administrative records, and the income type aggregates as contained in the National Income Accounts.

It would take us too far afield to give a full account of the old BEA methodology.[5] Suffice it to say that the distributions for nonfarm families, farm operator families, and unattached individuals were estimated separately, with the latter two based on benchmark distributions estimated for 1947. The nonfarm family distribution was estimated from individual tax returns by grouping individual earners into family units on the basis of the IRS-Census matching study for 1949. Non-taxable income types were then added on the basis of information drawn from a number of different sources, and families not in the tax return distribution were added on the basis of information drawn from field surveys, particularly the CPS. Reported incomes were then adjusted to agree with the BEA control totals for each income type.

Two points should be noted. First, because of the estimating

---

differences between survey work conducted by the Bureau of the Census and the Survey Research Center.

[5] Summaries of the old BEA methodology may be found in Selma Goldsmith, "Size Distribution of Personal Income," *Survey of Current Business,* April 1958, pp. 14-19; and Schultz, *Distribution of Personal Income,* pp. 49-56. For the methodology for earlier years, see *Income Distribution in the United States by Size, 1944-1950,* a supplement to the *Survey of Current Business,* 1953.

TABLE 1   Reconciliation Between Personal Income, Family Personal Income, and Total Money Income, 1964

(millions of dollars)

Personal Income		497,462
Less: Income of recipients not in CPS universe		15,571
Decedents	2,793	
Civilians overseas	453	
Military personnel on post and overseas	4,319	
Recipients other than consumer units	8,006	
Plus: Income of recipients in CPS universe, but not in Personal Income		129
Income of migratory workers	129	
Less: Income types excluded from Family Personal Income		16,342
Employer contributions to pension, health, and welfare funds	13,441	
Lump sum payments	2,733	
Auto depreciation reimbursement	168	
Plus: Income types excluded from Personal Income		4,879
Private pension and annuity payments	4,879	
Equals: Family Personal Income		470,557
Less: Imputed income		23,808
Imputed wages	1,788	
Imputed rent on owner-occupied nonfarm dwellings	10,153	
Imputed farm income	1,149	
Imputed interest income	10,718	
Plus: Personal contributions for social insurance		12,328
Equals: Total Money Income (CPS definition)		459,077

method, the old BEA series could not be broken down by type of income or by socioeconomic characteristics of the recipient units, aside from the three component distributions of the series referred to above (nonfarm families, farm operator families, and unattached individuals). The CPS still remained the only source of distributions by detailed demographic or economic characteristic. Second, largely because the BEA estimating procedure started with tax return data, it was impossible to reconcile the estimates with the CPS and to determine precisely the sources of the differences between the two series.

Those differences were quite significant, particularly in the bottom and top brackets of the corresponding distributions. In 1962, for example, the CPS showed over 5 million more families and unrelated individuals below $2,000 than did the BEA estimates; the number estimated by BEA to be above $15,000 was about 2 million more than that shown by the CPS.[6] These discrepancies were the source of some professional discussion and concern. Selma Goldsmith examined them in her paper at a Conference on Income and Wealth over sixteen years ago, and they were the subject of a report prepared by an interagency task force for the Office of Statistical Standards of the Bureau of the Budget in 1964 and of the study prepared by Paul Schultz in 1964 for the Joint Economic Committee.[7]

For the reason already mentioned, these studies were not overly successful in pinpointing the sources of the discrepancies. Too much emphasis, for example, appears to have been placed on differences in the income concept (TMI versus FPI); indeed, the task force report estimated that "nonmoney items account for a little less than one-half of the gap between the OBE and the CPS estimates of the number of families with income under $3,000.[8] Herman Miller was perhaps the first to use methods similar to those employed in this paper to analyze the differences for income year 1959.[9] For each consumer unit, he inflated separately each

[6] Schultz, *Distribution of Personal Income;* Helen H. Lamale, James D. Smith, and Jeanette Fitzwilliams, "Family Income Distribution Statistics Published by Federal Agencies," *The American Statistician* (February 1966): 18-23.

[7] Schultz, *Distribution of Personal Income,* pp. 58-68.

[8] Lamale, Smith, and Fitzwilliams, "Family Income Distribution Statistics," p. 21.

[9] Herman Miller, *Income Distribution in the United States,* a 1960 Census Monograph, (Washington, D.C., 1966), Appendix A, pp. 18-90. Miller's

income type in the CPS by the ratio of the money income control estimated from BEA data to the CPS aggregate, then summed the inflated income types for each observation and retabulated by size, to produce the distributions shown in column (2), as compared with the original CPS distributions in column (1) of Table 2. Imputed income types (wages, interest, rent, other) were then allocated in proportion to the corresponding money income types; for any given income type, the ratio of imputed plus money income to money income alone was used to inflate the amount of money income on each record, a blowup procedure identical to that used for TMI. Miller's results for FPI are shown in column (3), and can be compared with BEA's distribution for 1959 in column (4).

The results are interesting indeed. Miller's CPS blown up to FPI has only 5 percent more consumer units below $2,000 than BEA, and 5 percent fewer units below $4,000! Above $10,000, the number of units exceeds BEA's by 12 percent. Furthermore, nearly all of the change can be accounted for by the under-reporting of money income; the effect on the frequencies in each income bracket of going from the control amount of TMI to FPI is small indeed. This latter finding, incidentally, is consistent with our results for the new BEA series: in going from the original CPS distribution to BEA's distribution of FPI for 1964, only 14 percent of the change in the number of consumer units below $3,250, for example, is accounted for by allocating imputed income and deducting personal contributions for social insurance. The effect of the difference in the income concept on the two size distributions would appear to be minimal.

Some caution, however, should be exercised in interpreting Miller's results. The methods used in adjusting the CPS were relatively crude, and it is often difficult to follow particular steps from the description he gives. For example, Miller's adjusted CPS distribution reflects income in excess of the controls; as a consequence, he has too many high-income units and too few low-income ones. Social Security contributions of employees and imputed rent on owner-occupied dwellings were assigned in proportion to wages and salaries; it is difficult to believe that the distributional effects of these two types fully offset each other.

---

comparisons between the 1960 Census distributions and BEA are not examined here.

TABLE 2 Comparison of Current Population Survey and Bureau of Economic Analysis Estimates of the Size Distribution of Total Money Income (TMI) and Family Personal Income (FPI), Income Year 1959

(millions of units)

Income Class	All Consumer Units				Families				Unrelated Individuals			
		CPS Inflated to:				CPS Inflated to:				CPS Inflated to:		
	Original CPS (1)	TMI Control (2)	FPI (3)	BEA (FPI) (4)	Original CPS (1)	TMI Control (2)	FPI (3)	BEA (FPI) (4)	Original CPS (1)	TMI Control (2)	FPI (3)	BEA (FPI) (4)
Under $2,000	12.1	8.0	7.9	7.5	6.0	3.9	3.9	3.5	6.1	4.1	4.0	4.0
$2,000-$3,999	11.1	10.0	10.0	11.4	8.8	6.8	6.8	7.5	2.3	3.2	3.2	3.9
4,000- 5,999	12.6	12.0	11.9	12.4	11.2	10.2	10.1	10.6	1.4	1.8	1.8	1.8
6,000- 9,999	14.3	16.5	16.5	15.6	13.6	15.5	15.4	14.9	.7	1.0	1.1	.7
10,000-14,999	4.3	9.1	9.4	5.3	4.1	8.6	8.9	5.2	.2	.5	.5	.1
15,000-24,999	1.1			2.3	1.1			2.3	a			a
25,000 or over	.3			.8	.3			.8	a			a
Total	55.8	55.8	55.8	55.3	45.1	45.1	45.1	44.8	10.7	10.7	10.7	10.5
Addendum:												
$10,000 or over	5.7	9.1	9.4	8.4	5.5	8.6	8.9	8.3	.2	.5	.5	.1

SOURCES: Herman F. Miller, *Income Distribution in the United States.* A 1960 Census Monograph (Washington, D.C., 1966), Appendix A, p. 189. T. Paul Schultz, *The Distribution of Personal Income.* Prepared for the Subcommittee on Economic Statistics of the Joint Economic Committee, December 1964 (Washington, D.C., 1965), p. 63.

a Less than 50,000.

(Miller's blowup factor for wage income was 1.0003.) Further, the aggregative character of the income size brackets makes it difficult to determine what is happening at the extremes of the distribution, especially the upper tail. Finally, none of the discussion—a point true of the other authors as well—ran in terms of its effect on the relative distribution (in terms of the Lorenz curve).

The old BEA series was finally discontinued following publication of preliminary estimates for 1963, primarily because the benchmark studies on which it was based had become obsolete. It was simply not possible within the confines of the old methodology to take account of new data sources, particularly those becoming available on computer tape, and new estimating techniques, especially those involving the computer. When the old methodology was developed, the computer revolution had barely begun, and computer cards and tapes were not available outside of the agencies creating them. Therefore, the old methodology relied heavily on published tabulations and cross tabulations, necessitating interpolation within class intervals as items of income were added or deducted.

Consequently, in developing new methods for estimating the BEA series, we had several goals: (1) to use microdata files (computer tape files containing information for individual income recipient units or "records") rather than published tabulations by income size; (2) to preserve the demographic and economic information associated with the individual record so that the new series would be available by a variety of socioeconomic characteristics; (3) to permit a reconciliation with the CPS by starting with the CPS, rather than tax returns, as a base. This last objective necessitated the use of the same recipient unit base: families and unrelated individuals as of the date of the Current Population Survey (in this case, March 1965), rather than the "average" number (and their "average" composition) during the preceding calendar year, as obtains for recipient units in BLS's Consumer Expenditure Survey. Data that would permit such "reconstruction" of family units as they were constituted during the period for which income is measured are simply not available.

Work on the estimates for 1964 has now been completed. Presented here are these results and a comparison of them with the original March 1965 CPS. The next section gives a condensed version of the various steps in the estimation process and the effect of each step on the size distribution of consumer units, as compared with earlier steps and with the original CPS. (Tables showing the distributions separately for families and unrelated individuals at each stage in the estimation process may be found in Appendix A.) Following this, we examine the differences between the CPS and the BEA series by socioeconomic characteristic and the sources of the differences, and show the effect of substituting BEA income estimates for those in the CPS on the composition of the poor.

ESTIMATION OF THE BEA SIZE DISTRIBUTION FOR 1964

In a broad sense, the new estimating procedure can be viewed as using the CPS as a base, then correcting the CPS income types, and adding income types not included in the CPS by the use of other information—primarily information contained in computer tape files. The latter included the 1964 IRS Tax Model of Individual Returns (TM), the 1963 IRS Taxpayer Compliance Measurement Program (TCMP), and the Federal Reserve Board's 1962 Survey of Financial Characteristics of Consumers (SFCC). Use was also made of tabulations from the 1960-61 BLS Consumer Expenditure Survey (CES), the 1966 and 1967 Surveys of Economic Opportunity of the Office of Economic Opportunity (OEO), the Survey of Consumer Finances, and the IRS Statistics of Income for various years, as well as of a few special hand tabulations from the Social Security Administration's three-way link study for 1963.

For the purpose of explanation, it is convenient to split our procedure into seven steps, all of which were performed using the individual observations in the microdata files. After making certain adjustments to the CPS file (Step 1), a record-by-record statistical match was made between the CPS and the TM (Step 2). This step produced corrections of several CPS income types and gave more detailed income-type breakdowns. TM income types were then corrected for audit by use of the TCMP (Step 3). A record-by-record statistical match between the merged CPS-TM file and the SFCC was then executed (Step 4), primarily to add information to the file for use in distributing most types of inputed income. Each money income type was then adjusted to the BEA control aggregate (Step 5), and imputed income types were estimated and added to the files (Step 6). Personal contributions for social insurance were then estimated and deducted (Step 7). The final result was a microdata file containing an estimate of FPI and its components, as well as CPS socioeconomic information, for each observation.

Owing to limited space, it is not possible to furnish a complete account of the procedures used. The following sections are designed to give readers enough familiarity with the various steps so that they will be in some position to judge the quality of the final product.[10]

Step 1: Preliminary Adjustments to the CPS

The first adjustment consisted of inflating the CPS sample weights. Since use was made only of those CPS records which contained income information—three-quarters of the sample in the income year 1964—records in the three-quarters sample were reweighted so that tabulations of the income data would come up to the CPS universe. The reweighting procedure controlled for age, color, sex, family relationship, and farm-nonfarm residence.

The second adjustment required was the allocation of income amounts to nonrespondents to the income questions (NAs). The original Census allocation procedure had assigned to NAs only a total for unearned income, rather than for the four components, or "boxes," separately (Social Security benefits, property income, unemployment compensation and public assistance, and all other money income); and for the earnings allocation had resulted in too many inconsistencies between earnings amounts and work experience for individual records. We, therefore, redid the Census allocation, assigning to NAs (for the particular income types on which they were NA) the income amounts of a respondent

---

[10] In particular, we have omitted a discussion of the techniques used to adjust for the different weighting schemes in the files that were statistically matched in Steps 2 and 4, and in reassembling the file into family units after matching. In addition, the rationale underlying the procedures used at a number of points has not fully been developed. A more complete discussion, particularly of Steps 2, 3, and 4, is given in E. C. Budd, "The Creation of a Microdata File for Estimating the Size Distribution of Income," *The Review of Income and Wealth* (December 1971): 317-33. Step 2 is compared with the methods used in the Brookings match of the SEO and TM files for 1966 in E. C. Budd, "Comments," *Annals of Economic and Social Measurement* 1 (July 1972): 349-54. All the steps are described in more detail in E. C. Budd, D. B. Radner, and J. C. Hinrichs, "Size Distribution of Family Personal Income: Methodology and Estimates for 1964," Bureau of Economic Analysis Staff Paper No. 21, June 1973.

selected at random within approximately 1,500 narrowly specified cells. The latter were defined on the basis of family status, age, color, sex, and work experience last year, producing a matrix considerably more detailed than that used by the Bureau of the Census.

The primary effect of the latter adjustment was to improve the consistency between the socioeconomic characteristics of NAs and the incomes assigned to them. As can be seen by comparing the first two columns in Table 7 and the first two lines in Table 8, Step I had relatively little effect on the size distribution. The effect is most noticeable at the top (where the Bureau of the Census had an inordinate number of high income NAs), with the share of the top 1 percent being reduced by over 4 percent (.26 percentage points). The mean income of consumer units was actually reduced by $33 in this step.

Step 2: CPS-TM Match

The next step involved the establishment of a link between the CPS and the tax return data on a record-by-record basis. Since the option of an exact match—finding the exact returns filed by the individual units in the CPS file—was not open to us, we developed methods for statistically matching the CPS with a tax-return file, using for the latter the IRS's Tax Model, a 95,000 return subsample of the Statistics of Income file. Rather than locating the return the individual in the CPS *actually* filed in real life, the trick was to find among the returns in the TM a return *similar* to the one the person would be expected to have filed, the selection being based on information common to both the CPS and the tax-return data. Unlike the Brookings Match, however, a constraint was imposed that each return be used once and only once, so that the CPS file would represent exactly the tax-return universe after matching.[11]

In contrast to the wealth of socioeconomic information in the CPS, the amount on the tax return is, unfortunately, quite limited. Considerable reliance, therefore, had to be placed on the size and

---

[11] A more precise statement of this constraint would have to take account of the necessity for splitting matched records to allow for the different weighting schemes in the two files to be matched. See Budd, "Creation of a Microdata File," pp. 322-27, and *Annals of Economic and Social Measurement* 1 (July 1972):350-51.

presence of income types in the two files, with wages and salaries, self-employment income, and property income being used as linking variables betweeen the two data sources.

The records in the two files were first separated into six groups, based on the analogy between family status in the CPS and marital status of taxpayer in the TM, and the use of taxpayer exemptions to determine whether the taxpayer (or spouse) was age 65 or over. Since the initial family-status–age groups, as defined in Table 3, were analogous rather than exact, their definitions were modified to increase the comparability of records between the two groups, one consideration being the number of CPS units relative to the number of TM returns in the group, another being the degree of correspondence between the relative distributions of wage and salary income in each group in the two files. To give one example of such modification, separate returns with one taxpayer exemption were distributed among Groups 3, 5, and 6, rather than statistically matching them to convert them to "pseudo-joint" returns to be used in Groups 1 and 2.

The next step was to select the nonfilers, i.e., those who were not to be given a tax return. Since our matching technique required that the (weighted) number of returns and the (weighted) number of CPS units to be assigned a return had to be identical in each of the six groups, the specification of the groups themselves

TABLE 3   Initial Family-Status–Age Groups

CPS Data	TM Data
A. Married couples living together	Joint and separate returns
Group 1: Under age 65	No age exemptions
Group 2: Age 65 or over	One or more age exemptions
B. Other family heads	Head of household, surviving spouse, and single returns with dependent exemption(s)
Group 3: Under age 65	No age exemption
Group 4: Age 65 or over	Age exemption
C. Other persons (i.e., other relatives and unrelated individuals)	Single returns with no dependents
Group 5: Under age 65	No age exemption
Group 6: Age 65 or over	Age exemption

in the preceding step determined the number of nonfilers in each group (i.e., the number in the CPS minus the number of tax returns). The actual procedure was to select those most likely to have filed, with nonfilers being the residual. The likelihood of filing was determined on the basis of the relationship of the CPS income the unit reported to the legal filing requirement, or the advantage to it of filing if not required to do so. Consideration was given to the size of wage income, the existence of property (rent or royalty) loss, the existence and size of self-employment income, and the size of "taxable" income (as nearly as it could be determined from the CPS). Space is lacking to describe the rules used, but it is worth noting that all those who ended up as nonfilers had CPS taxable incomes below IRS filing requirements.

Within each of the six groups, the matching of returns was carried out on the basis of the existence and size of wage and salary income, self-employment income, and property income. A scheme for the determination of cells in which matching took place and the order of matching within the cells is provided in Table 4. Primary importance in linking was given to wage income, since it is more consistently and more accurately reported in both sources than is self-employment income. The units were first ranked by size of wage income and separated into a number of wage rank classes (a total of 151 for all groups), with an equal number of frequencies from the two files in each class, although such frequencies varied from one wage class to the next. The basic idea behind the creation of wage rank classes was that CPS units and TM returns with approximately the same *rank* in the wage distribution should be matched with each other. It should be noted that the upper and lower dollar limits of any class in the two files did not necessarily coincide; indeed, in some classes, the dollar income ranges in the two files did not even overlap. This result is consistent with the fact that wage income is more fully reported on tax returns than in the CPS.

Self-employment income, although given a secondary role in the match, was not put aside entirely; it would have been left out of account in our matching procedure had we matched records simply by their rank in the wage distribution rather than setting up the wage rank classes described above and matching records within those classes, the procedure actually followed. Within each wage rank class, we separated CPS units and TM returns into four subclasses, based on whether the individual record contained only

TABLE 4   Matching Characteristics Used in the CPS-TM Match

Cell Classifications	CPS Data Used	TM Data Used
Family-status—age groups	Family relationship Age	Marital status Age exemptions
Wage classes	Rank in wage distribution	Rank in wage distribution
Self-employment income subclasses	Existence and type of self-employment income	Existence and type of self-employment income
Order for matching within subclass[a]	Size of self-employment income	Size of self-employment income
Size of self-employment income subdivisions[a]	Rank in self-employment income distribution	Rank in self-employment income distribution
Order for matching within subdivision[a]	Size of property income	Size of property income

[a] Only applicable to some records; see text pp. 461 and 463 for explanation.

nonfarm self-employment income (Subclass 1), only farm self-employment (Subclass 2), both self-employment types (Subclass 3), or neither (Subclass 4).[12] About a quarter of the records in the first three subclasses, primarily those in wage rank classes with moderate or large amounts of wage income, were matched by their rank, when ranked from highest to lowest by size of self-employment income.

The remaining three-quarters of the records in wage rank classes with no, or smaller amounts of, wage income were further subdivided into a limited number of additional classes (or "subdivisions") based on size of self-employment income, by a method quite similar to that used in setting up the wage rank classes themselves. This was done to allow some role for the existence and size of property income in the matching of those records with self-employment income but with little or no wage income. Within the above subdivisions of Subclasses 1, 2, and 3, and all of Subclass 4, records were ranked by size of property income from highest to lowest, those with no such income being placed in random order. The records were then matched by their rank.

One result of the matching procedure was that those CPS units reporting property income tended to receive a tax return with a larger property income than the amount they reported in the CPS, and many more reporting "none" in the CPS received a tax return with property income than the opposite case. The percent of filers with TM property income compared with those reporting it in the CPS was significantly increased, particularly for those age 65 and over, as can be seen in Table 5.

From the CPS-TM merged file created by Step 2, we substituted the TM amount of wage and salary income, nonfarm self-employment income, and property income, for those units assigned a tax return ("filers"). The substitution also permitted us to break down the property income total into its components: interest, dividends, and rent. All other income types, and the entire incomes of nonfilers, were left unchanged at their CPS amounts in this step. The effect of these substitutions on the income aggregates is shown in the first two columns of Table 6. This step increased the mean income of the distribution by 8.2

---

[12] This discussion omits the step required to equalize CPS and TM frequencies in each of the four subclasses.

TABLE 5   Percent With Property Income Before and After Matching the CPS With the Tax Model

Group	Number in Group (Thousands)	Percent With Property Income CPS[a]	TM
Married couples:			
(1) Under 65	36,046	32	46
(2) 65 and over	3,368	54	80
Other heads:			
(3) Under 65	3,810	23	28
(4) 65 and over	381	54	87
Other persons:			
(5) Under 65	19,452	18	30
(6) 65 and over	2,145	57	83
All groups:			
Under 65	59,308	27	40
65 and over	5,894	55	81

[a] Exclusive of nonfilers (those not assigned a tax return).

percent. Aggregate money income was raised from the 84 percent implicit in the original CPS to 91 percent of the BEA-TMI control.

The use of TM nonfarm self-employment income did lower the aggregate for that income type by $5.7 billion. Nevertheless, we felt that the tax return distribution, at least after the adjustment for audit in Step 3, better represented the distribution of that type. The same, unfortunately, cannot be said for the TM farm income distribution. The TM aggregate was $2.6 billion, compared with the CPS's $5.8 billion and a money income control of $10.8 billion (Table 12). A major problem with the tax data lies in the reporting of loss incomes: over a third of all Schedule F returns reported a farm loss in 1964, with aggregate losses of $2.1 billion, compared with positive farm income of $4.7 billion. In addition, the number of recipients was significantly lower in the tax return data than in the CPS. It was therefore decided to use the CPS farm income in our estimates.

The effect of Step 2 on the size distribution can be seen in Tables 7 and 8. The number with negative incomes was increased as a result of the larger number of business, partnership, and rent losses in the TM. While the rest of the size distribution was shifted upward, the effect was particularly noticeable in the upper tail

TABLE 6   Income Aggregates, 1964

(billion of dollars)

Income Type	Steps in Estimation Process				
	CPS Reallocated Reweighted (1)	CPS-TM Before Audit (2)	CPS-TM After Audit (3)	Total Money Income (5)	Family Personal Income (7)
Money income					
Wage and salary	297.7	323.9	324.3	324.9	324.9
Nonfarm self-employment	38.5	32.8	37.9	39.3	39.3
Farm self-employment	5.8	5.8	5.8	10.8	0.8
OASDI and railroad retirement	14.7	14.7	14.7	16.1	6.1
Property income	14.9	26.1	27.1	39.4	39.4
Interest		10.8	11.1	18.0	18.0
Dividends		12.6	12.8	14.4	14.4
Rent		2.7	3.2	7.0	7.0
Unemployment compensation and public assistance	4.3	4.3	4.3	6.6	6.6
CPS: all other money income	9.9	9.9	9.9	17.3	17.3
Royalties				0.9	0.9
Estate and trust income				3.7	3.7
Imputed income					23.8
Personal contributions for social insurance					(−) 12.3
Total Income	385.7	417.4	423.9	459.1	470.6

TABLE 7   Size Distributions of Total Income, 1964

(thousands of consumer units)

Size of Total Income	CPS, Census Allocation	Steps in Estimation Process					
		CPS, BEA Allocation (1)	CPS-TM Before Audit (2)	CPS-TM After Audit (3)	Total Money Income (5)	Money and Imputed Income (6)	Family Personal Income (7)
Loss	190	202	288	228	161	135	159
Zero	807	816	827	826	645	266	252
$1-$1,249	5,535	5,562	4,694	4,596	3,570	3,277	3,302
1,250- 3,249	10,936	10,898	10,372	10,185	9,363	8,962	9,320
3,250- 5,749	13,203	13,235	12,682	12,654	12,719	12,454	13,121
5,750- 8,249	12,528	12,581	12,392	12,380	12,499	12,242	12,229
8,250-10,249	6,854	6,822	7,228	7,309	7,653	7,820	7,775
10,250-15,749	7,249	7,229	8,129	8,307	9,140	10,003	9,311
15,750-24,749	1,947	1,898	2,302	2,385	2,824	3,268	3,013
24,750-49,749	502	513	757	788	1,017	1,126	1,076
49,750-98,749	45	56	141	153	206	237	233
98,750 and over	40	24	26	27	39	46	45
Total number	59,836	59,836	59,838	59,838	59,836	59,838	59,836
Mean (dollars)	6,476	6,443	6,974	7,085	7,673	8,071	7,865
Median (dollars)	5,595	5,580	5,940	6,019	6,407	6,682	6,459

TABLE 8 Share of Income for Selected Quantiles of Consumer Units, 1964

(percent)

Steps in Estimation Process:	1-20	21-40	41-60	61-80	81-90	91-95	96-100	100
CPS	3.43	10.35	17.30	24.80	16.56	10.34	17.22	6.05
(1) CPS reallocated	3.41	10.40	17.37	24.85	16.62	10.39	16.96	5.79
(2) CPS-TM	3.29	10.33	17.06	24.24	16.18	10.23	18.67	7.10
(3) CPS-TM after audit	3.47	10.37	16.99	24.12	16.09	10.19	18.77	7.18
(5) Total money income	3.93	10.67	16.70	23.48	15.66	10.01	19.55	7.79
(6) Money and imputed income	4.15	10.71	16.56	23.32	15.58	10.00	19.68	7.84
(7) Family personal income	4.20	10.63	16.44	23.22	15.55	10.00	19.96	8.01
Addendum: CPS inflated to total money income controls	3.72	10.59	16.87	23.98	16.06	10.24	18.54	6.99

where the number over $24,750 was increased by 56 percent.[13] Inequality in the relative distribution increased from Step 1 to Step 2, with the share of the top 1 percent rising by 23 percent (1.3 percentage points) and that of the bottom quintile falling by 3 percent (largely as a result of the increase in losses and the relative fall in the share of nonfilers).

Step 3: Audit Correction

The next step was to correct the TM income types for that part of underreporting on tax returns which would have been eliminated had each return been subject to audit. For this purpose, the sample of about 50,000 tax returns from the 1963 audit study of individual returns (TCMP) was used. This file contained, for each income type, the income amount reported by the taxpayer and the amount as corrected by the auditor. The correction factors were developed separately for eight groups of returns: joint and all other returns; under 65 and 65 or over; short and long form. Each income type was adjusted independently of the others.

In choosing a correction procedure, we had two important goals. The first was to preserve the same relationship between the size distribution of TM income before and after audit adjustment as existed between the before and after audit TCMP size distributions. For example, if the size distributions of a given income type in the TCMP before audit and TM before adjustment were the same, then the TM distribution after adjustment for audit should be identical to the after-audit TCMP distribution. The second was to minimize the distortion produced by the correction procedure in the relationships between CPS socioeconomic characteristics and the various income types. This second goal was important because, like the TM, the TCMP contained very little socioeconomic information.

The chosen procedure consisted of two parts: raising the (nonzero) amounts reported by taxpayers and assigning positive

[13] The size distribution data in Table 7 were tabulated in intervals, the limits of which were defined in terms of 250 and 750 for the last three digits, rather than 000 or 500. This was done so that the mean of any class interval would more nearly approximate its midpoint. Since respondents in the CPS tend to report their incomes rounded off to numbers the last three digits of which are 000 or 500, defining the intervals in terms of the same digits tends to produce a bunching of frequencies at the lower limit of the class interval. This phenomenon does not characterize reporting on tax returns.

amounts of particular income types to some taxpayers who did not report them. Only the first part will be described here. The correction of dividend income may be taken as an example. Returns containing dividend income both before and after audit in the TCMP were first ranked from highest to lowest by size of dividend income as reported by the taxpayer, and the aggregate amount of dividends reported by each percentile of this distribution was determined. Next, the same returns were reranked from highest to lowest by size of dividend income as corrected by the auditors, and the aggregate amount of dividends after audit was computed for each percentile. The ratio of aggregate dividends after audit to dividends before audit, computed separately for each percentile, provided the required correction ratios. Returns with dividend income in the TM were then ranked by size of dividend income from highest to lowest and grouped into percentiles. The appropriate TCMP correction ratios for dividend income were then applied to the dividend income reported by the returns in each percentile group. To minimize the effect of sampling variability for some income groups, the correction ratios were smoothed by combining percentiles into groups containing more than one percentile. The correction of income types which contained some negative amounts was more complex than the technique described above, although the same basic procedure was employed. The effect of the adjustment for the latter types was to change many of the reported losses to positive amounts.

The audit correction resulted in relatively minor changes in the distribution. The mean income was increased by $111 or 1.6 percent; aggregate income was increased from 91 percent to 92.3 percent of the TMI control. Most of the $6.5 billion increase in income was in business and partnership income, although rent experienced a substantial percentage increase. As can be seen from Table 7, the largest effect was on the loss group. In terms of the relative distribution in Table 8, the reduction in the loss group was reflected in a 5.5 percent increase in the share of the bottom quintile, from 3.29 to 3.47 percent.

Looking at Steps 2 and 3 together, as the effect of substituting audited tax returns for CPS reported amounts for wages and salaries, nonfarm self-employment income, and property income of filers, the net effect was to leave the share of the bottom two quintiles of the relative distribution unchanged and to increase the share of the top 5 percent (mostly the top 1 percent) at the expense of the middle group (ranging from the forty-first to the ninety-fifth percentile). The mean dollar income of the top 1 percent was raised by over 36 percent; relative to the mean income of the distribution as a whole, it was raised by 24 percent.

Step 4: SFCC Match

The final merging operation in the methodology was the statistical match of our matched CPS-TM file with the Survey of Financial Characteristics of Consumers, a sample for income year 1962 of 2,557 consumer units stratified by income. The primary purpose of this match was to provide information by which income types not covered in the two basic files could be distributed among consumer units: home ownership and equity in owned home (to allocate imputed rent on owner-occupied dwellings); checking and savings accounts (imputed interest on such accounts); U.S. Savings Bonds (imputed interest on same); interest on state and local bonds; estate and trust income; and life insurance data (imputed interest on life insurance equity).

The characteristics used for matching were those which appeared to be most relevant to home and liquid-asset ownership: dollar income level; type of consumer unit (family or unrelated individual); age (6 age groups); color (white, nonwhite); and major source of earnings, used only for families (wage, farm and nonfarm self-employment, nonworker). Dollar income level rather than relative income position was used in order to account for the rise in real income from 1962 to 1964, since real income appeared to be the relevant variable for home ownership. For major source of earnings, SFCC data indicated that at any given income level, the self-employed had larger asset holdings than wage workers, and that the latter had larger holdings than nonworkers, with the possible exception of the age 65 and over group. Even with this small list of characteristics, some consolidation of cells was required because of the relatively large number of empty cells, partly a consequence of the SFCC sample design. Size of interest income was used as the matching variable within cells, or random order if records had no interest income.

Since no incomes were corrected or assigned in this step, there are no distributional effects to report, and the step is not indicated in Tables 6, 7, and 8.

Step 5: Adjustment of Money Income to BEA Control Totals

After audit adjustment, aggregate money income in our file was still $35.2 billion or 7.7 percent below the TMI control—varying from only .2 percent for wages and salaries to 54 percent for rent. (The discrepancy for each income type can be determined by comparing columns (3) and (5) in Table 6.) For most of the income types, a simple ratio technique was employed to inflate the income type to the control total. For types involving loss incomes, the "reciprocal ratio" technique described in the next section was used. This latter method assumes that losses were overreported in about the same proportion as gains were underreported.

Several exceptions to these ratio techniques should be noted. For rental income, in order to reduce the percent with a loss from the 30 percent shown by tax returns after audit to the approximately 10 percent shown by field surveys such as the SFCC, the CES, and the SEO, a constant dollar amount was added to each record following a reciprocal ratio blowup so that the sum of the two adjustments equaled the difference between the actual and the control amount. For farm income, the reported CPS amounts were inflated by a reciprocal ratio blowup to a money income control net of expenses on imputed farm income; those expenses were then added to each inflated money amount.

Although estate and trust income and state and local bond interest were included by definition in CPS property income, the substitution of TM dividends, rent, and interest for CPS property income for filers excluded, in effect, what little of these two types might have originally been included in the CPS. These two types were therefore drawn from the SFCC part of the merged file and adjusted to control totals by a simple ratio technique. While royalty income by definition was included in CPS "all other money income," it seems unlikely that much of it was actually reported. The royalty income amounts in the TM were used instead, a reciprocal ratio technique being employed to inflate them to the control.

The CPS amounts of unemployment compensation and public assistance (type 6 income) were brought up to control by increasing the number of recipients rather than by inflating reported amounts, since the number reporting receipt of these incomes types was substantially below the estimated control number of recipients. The adjustments were carried out first for unemployment compensation, then for old age assistance, and finally for all other assistance. While space is lacking to describe the methods in detail, the general technique used was to divide the file in turn into cells based on socioeconomic characteristics most relevant to each of the three transfer types, compute the mean amount of type 6 income in that cell for those reporting it, and select at random a unit not reporting that type and assign it the mean amount for the cell from which it was drawn, repeating the process until the control total for that transfer type was met. The probability of selection for any nonreporting unit generally varied from cell to cell, depending on the proportion of units in the particular cell reporting that transfer type.

Since the purpose of Step 5 was to meet the TMI control, it is not surprising that the mean income for the distribution as a whole was increased by $588 or 8.3 percent. As can be seen from Table 7, the size distribution was shifted significantly upward. The number of consumer units below $1,250, for example, was reduced by 1.3 million, or 22 percent; those below $3,250, by 2.1 million, or 13 percent. On the other hand, those with $24,750 or more were increased by .3 million, or over 30 percent. The relative distribution in Table 8 showed substantial increases in the shares of the bottom quintile, from 3.47 to 3.93 percent, a 13 percent increase, and the top 1 percent, from 7.18 percent to 7.79 percent, an increase of 10 percent. The section of the distribution from the forty-first through the ninety-sixth percentiles experienced a decline in its share.[14]

It is useful at this point to summarize the net effect of the steps which adjusted the original CPS money income distribution to the TMI controls (Steps 1 through 5). Mean income was increased by $1,230 per consumer unit, or by 19 percent. All parts of the size distribution were shifted upward. The relative share of the bottom quintile was increased from 3.43 to 3.93 percent or by 15 percent; that of the top 1 percent, from 6.05 to 7.79 percent or by 29 percent. The second quintile and the ninety-seventh through ninety-ninth percentiles also gained, while the share of the forty-first through the ninety-sixth percentiles was reduced.

How would the results have been changed for the relative distribution of all consumer units had we blown up the income

---

[14] More detailed income shares than those found in Table 8 are given in Appendix A.

types in the original CPS to the TMI control by the use of a simple ratio technique, or a reciprocal ratio technique for income types containing negative amounts? This can be seen by comparing the last line in Table 8 with line (5) for TMI. The primary effect would have been to reduce the estimates of the shares of the bottom quintile and the top 1 percent and raise the estimates of shares for the intervening quantiles. The Lorenz curve derived by employing that technique would cut from below the Lorenz curve for our distribution of TMI; it has this property in common with the Lorenz curve for the original CPS distribution.

Step 6: Assignment of Imputed Income

The next step was to distribute imputed income, primarily using information from the SFCC portion of the merged file. Imputed rent on owner-occupied nonfarm dwellings was distributed in proportion to size of equity in owned home at a rate of just under 3 percent, derived by taking the ratio of the BEA nonfarm imputed rent control to the aggregate amount of equity in owned home as contained in the SFCC portion of the file. Imputed interest on checking and savings accounts was assigned in proportion to the amount of such deposits in the SFCC, with the assignment carried out separately for the two types of accounts. Accrued interest on U.S. Savings Bonds was allocated in proportion to holdings of those bonds as given in the SFCC. Imputed interest on equity in life insurance was distributed in proportion to our estimate from the SFCC of the "cash surrender values" of such policies. The latter were derived by computing the ratio of reported cash surrender value to reported face value of nonterm life insurance for six different age groups and applying these ratios to face value of nonterm life insurance for each unit reporting it. This method was preferable to using the cash surrender value actually reported in the individual record, partly because of the greater response error in reporting cash surrender value, and partly because so many units who reported face value were NA on cash surrender value.

Imputed farm income, assigned on the basis of information in the 1960-61 BLS Consumer Expenditure Survey, was allocated to all units with farm residence, even though some of these units did not report the receipt of farm self-employment income. In addition, as noted in the preceding section, operating expenses associated with imputed income were allocated to the money income control as a constant proportion of net imputed income for those units reporting money farm income. The underlying assumption was that farmers deducted all cash expenses in reporting their cash incomes, without bothering to allocate such expenses between cash and imputed income. As indicated by evidence from the CES, the value of food and fuel consumed on farms allocated to individual units varied directly with size of family but was independent of family income. The amount of imputed net rent of farm dwellings assigned to individual units, on the other hand, varied directly with family income but was independent of family size.

Imputed wage income was distributed by size of mean money wages to all workers with less than $5,000 in money wages in six groups for weeks worked, two for work status (full- or part-time), and three for occupational groups (36 cells in all). Farm workers, domestic servants, and several types of commercial and service employees were the occupational groups assigned amounts.

Since imputed income is only 5 percent of TMI, its inclusion did not have a major impact on the distribution. The mean income of consumer units was increased by about $400, and frequencies were shifted upward in the size distribution (columns (5) and (6) of Table 7). The most noticeable effects, at least in terms of the percentage change in frequencies, were on the upper and lower brackets, particularly the loss and no income groups. Similarly, in the relative distribution in Table 8, the share of the bottom quintile was increased by .22 percentage points or 6 percent; that of the top 5 percent by .13 percentage points or less than 1 percent. The shares of the intervening quantiles were reduced by small amounts. These changes can be attributed to the fact that the lower income groups receive most of the imputed farm and wage income, with the major share of imputed nonfarm rent and interest accruing to those with higher incomes. These latter two imputed income types are important to aged units as well, some of whom, at least, are in the bottom part of the distribution.

Step 7: Family Personal Income

The estimation of personal contributions for social insurance was the final step in deriving the distribution of FPI. They were estimated on the basis of statutory contribution rates and information on work experience and earnings contained in the individual records. Contributions of the self-employed were taken virtually without change from the TM. Employee contributions to Old-Age, Survivors, and Disability Insurance (OASDI) were assigned at the legal rate of 3.625 percent up to the $4,800 limit for workers in private jobs likely to have been covered by the program. Since it was impossible to determine, in the case of state and local government workers, which ones were covered by OASDI, their total contributions (i.e., OASDI plus contributions to their particular retirement programs) were assigned in proportion to their wage income, with no upper limit. Contributions to federal civilian retirement programs were allocated to federal employees by taking the legal contribution rate of 6.5 percent of their wage income. Contributions to railroad retirement insurance were assigned to railroad employees on the basis of the rate and the income limit in effect at that time.

Since social insurance contributions were deducted to obtain FPI, frequencies were shifted down income size brackets in going from money plus imputed income (column (6) of Table 7) to FPI (column (7)), the mean income of the distribution being lowered by the mean amount of such contributions ($206 per consumer unit, or 2.6 percent of FPI). The shares of the bottom quintile and the top 5 percent were increased by small amounts—.05 and .38 percentage points respectively—with the shares of intervening quantiles slightly reduced. This effect on the relative distribution is easy to understand, since wage income is a considerably less important income type to the upper and lower tails of the distribution than for the middle groups, and social insurance contributions are associated primarily with wage income. The wage cutoff for OASDI also contributed to this effect. Again, an intersection of the Lorenz curves for money plus imputed income and for FPI is implied, with the latter cutting the former from above.

In summary, our entire adjustment procedure, in going from the original CPS distribution of consumer units by size of money income to BEA's distribution of size of FPI, resulted in a rise in the mean income of consumer units of close to $1,400 or over 21 percent, a substantial upward shift in the size distribution, and significant shifts in the relative distribution in favor of the upper and lower tails at the expense of the middle groups. The mean income of the bottom quintile relative to that of the distribution as a whole, for example, was increased by over 22 percent; the relative mean incomes of the top 5 and the top 1 percent were raised by 16 and 32 percent respectively.

DIFFERENCES BETWEEN CPS AND BEA BY SOCIOECONOMIC CHARACTERISTICS

This section examines differences by socioeconomic characteristic between the BEA and CPS estimates. In the interests of brevity, the comparisons will be restricted to the mean incomes of several subgroups of consumer units, although a complete discussion would have to take account of differences in the shapes of the CPS and BEA relative distributions by socioeconomic characteristic,[15] as well as of a greater number of socioeconomic groups. CPS published means will first be compared with BEA mean amounts of TMI and FPI and the differences will be summarized. Then, the causes of these differences will be examined, along with the implications of various correction techniques. The socioeconomic characteristics (SECs) used as breakdowns will be age, color, sex, residence (farm and nonfarm), and work experience. These are merely examples; others could also have been used. In the case of families, these SECs refer to the head of the family.

Although the reasons for the differences between the CPS and BEA means will be analyzed later in this section, a few general comments about these comparisons may prove useful at the outset. Wage and salary income plays a dominant role in analyzing differences between the BEA and CPS estimates. On the average, the amounts of wage and salary income were increased less than other income types in the process of adjusting from CPS to BEA amounts. Therefore, a socioeconomic group (SEG) which received a large proportion of its income in the form of wages and salaries would have a relatively small differential between its CPS and BEA mean amounts of total money income; on the other hand, one with a large proportion of its income in nonwage income types (e.g., transfer payments) would have a relatively large differential.

---

[15] Mean incomes by socioeconomic characteristics for families and unrelated individuals separately appear in Appendix B, along with size distributions and Lorenz curves of consumer units by socioeconomic characteristics.

The adjustment from TMI to FPI was the net result of additions of imputed income and subtractions of personal contributions for social insurance. Groups relying primarily on earnings have relatively large amounts of personal contributions and, therefore, tend to have small, or even negative, adjustments from TMI to FPI. Groups with large asset holdings receive large amounts of imputed income, and therefore tend to have large differences between TMI and FPI. While these factors represent tendencies and will not be valid in every case, they should be kept in mind when examining the differences summarized below.

The relationship between age and total income was significantly altered by the adjustments from CPS to TMI and FPI. A comparison of mean incomes for each of six age groups shows a definite pattern: after the lowest age group, the differences between CPS and BEA become more pronounced as age increases (Table 9). These differences are dominated by the relatively small correction in wage and salary income referred to above. The increases from CPS to TMI range from 8.9 percent in the 25-34 age group to 36.3 percent in the 65 or over age group. The large correction in the top age group resulted from the relatively minor role played by wage and salary income and the importance of property income, which was significantly underreported in the aggregate in the CPS. The relatively good reporting of OASDI benefits kept the correction for that age group from being even higher.

The differences by age between CPS and FPI are even more pronounced. The increases range from 8.1 percent for the 25-34

TABLE 9 Mean Incomes of Consumer Units, by Age, 1964

Age	CPS	BEA Total Money Income		BEA Family Personal Income	
		Mean	Ratio to CPS	Mean	Ratio to CPS
14-24	$4,280	$4,779	1.117	$4,693	1.096
25-34	6,772	7,372	1.089	7,323	1.081
35-44	7,988	9,108	1.140	9,210	1.153
45-54	8,128	9,380	1.154	9,621	1.184
55-64	6,746	7,929	1.175	8,279	1.227
65 or over	3,980	5,424	1.363	5,843	1.468
All ages	6,569	7,673	1.168	7,865	1.197

age group to 46.8 percent for the 65 or over group. The differences between the FPI and TMI correction ratios result from the fact that the importance of imputed income increases with age, while the importance of personal contributions for social insurance declines. It is interesting to note that for the two age groups under age 35, mean TMI exceeded mean FPI, implying that for these two age groups total personal contributions for social insurance exceeded total imputed income.

The adjustment differences by color are not as striking as those by age. The ratio of nonwhite to white mean income fell from .599 for CPS to .581 for TMI and .571 for FPI (Table 10). The decline from the CPS ratio to the TMI ratio resulted primarily from the greater importance for white units of property income, which had a large correction factor. The decline from the TMI ratio to the FPI ratio primarily reflected the relative concentration of imputed income in white units and the larger role of personal contributions for nonwhites.

The relationship between sex and income was changed significantly. When interpreting these results, however, it should be remembered that the "female" category refers to female unrelated individuals and families headed by females, not all female workers or income recipients. The large correction in transfer payments, and especially in property income, which is an important source of income for female unrelated individuals (many of whom are aged), accounts for the substantial increase in the ratio of female to male income, from .446 in CPS to .509 for TMI and .518 for FPI (Table 10).

The differences by residence are also large. The ratio of the mean of units with farm residence to the mean of units with nonfarm residence rose from .653 for CPS to .849 for TMI and .887 for FPI (Table 10). This large increase was primarily the result of the substantial correction to farm self-employment income, since most, although not all, farm income is received by farm residents. The inclusion of imputed farm income accounted for the increase from the TMI ratio to the FPI ratio.

Work-experience groups also showed differences in adjustment. These differences can be attributed primarily to the relative proportion of total income accounted for by wage and salary income or transfer payments. Units headed by nonworkers, many of whom were retired, had the largest adjustment, 38.9 percent from CPS to TMI and 48.0 percent from CPS to FPI (Table 11).

TABLE 10 Mean Incomes of Consumer Units, by Color, Sex, Residence, and Type of Unit, 1964

		BEA Total Money Income		*BEA Family Personal Income*	
	CPS	*Mean*	*Ratio to CPS*	*Mean*	*Ratio to CPS*
Color:					
White	$6,864	$8,032	1.170	$8,242	1.201
Nonwhite	4,113	4,663	1.134	4,708	1.145
Ratio of nonwhite to white	.599	.581		.571	
Sex:					
Male	$7,417	$8,546	1.152	$8,741	1.179
Female	3,307	4,347	1.314	4,528	1.369
Ratio of female to male	.446	.509		.518	
Residence:					
Nonfarm	$6,707	$7,740	1.154	$7,916	1.180
Farm	4,380	6,570	1.500	7,023	1.603
Ratio of farm to nonfarm	.653	.849		.887	
Type of unit:					
Families	$7,438	$8,631	1.160	$8,838	1.188
Unrelated individuals	3,122	3,874	1.241	4,006	1.283
Ratio of unrelated individuals to families	.420	.449		.453	

TABLE 11   Mean Income of Consumer Units, by Work Experience of Head, 1964

Work Experience of Head	CPS	BEA Total Money Income		BEA Family Personal Income	
		Mean	Ratio to CPS	Mean	Ratio to CPS
Nonworker	$3,270	$4,543	1.389	$4,838	1.480
Full-time, full-year worker	8,280	9,361	1.131	9,532	1.151
Other	4,951	5,952	1.202	6,102	1.232
All units	6,569	7,673	1.168	7,865	1.197

This large correction reflects the importance of transfer payments and property income in the income of that group. Units headed by full-time, full-year workers received an adjustment from CPS to TMI of only 13.1 percent, and from CPS to FPI an adjustment of 15.1 percent.

The reasons for the differences described above must be analyzed in more detail.[16] In particular, there are several possible sources of bias in the CPS—aggregate underreporting, biases in the relative distributions, and biases in the numbers of recipients of specific income types—and they are likely to have differential effects on the mean incomes of SEGs. These three types of bias can occur in any or all specific income types, and the combination of these specific income type biases can produce bias in the size distribution of total income. We will be concerned primarily with correction of the errors in individual income types, making only a brief examination of the effects resulting from combining these types into total income. The three sources of bias and some possible correction techniques will be discussed in turn, followed by a brief examination of their relationship to the BEA estimates.

As noted in an earlier section, using the aggregate amounts in the National Income Accounts (adjusted for definitional differences) as the standard of comparison, the estimates of aggregate income of all seven income types in the CPS are too low. The deficiencies vary according to type of income, ranging from 2

---

[16] The ensuing discussion is restricted to money income and does not cover the effects of differences between TMI and FPI.

percent for nonfarm self-employment income[17] to 66 percent for property income, as shown in Table 12. The effect of aggregate underreporting on the mean total incomes of SEGs can be seen most easily if we assume initially that the number of recipients of each income type in the CPS is correct and that the same correction ratio is applied to each CPS amount of any given income type. It is clear that under these assumptions, the relative distribution of each income type (as measured by the Lorenz curve) would be unchanged after correction for each SEG and for all consumer units taken together.

If it were true that the correction ratios for all income types were identical (say, c), then the ratio of the mean total incomes of any pair of SEGs and the relative distribution of total income would be unchanged after correction for underreporting. In this case, correcting the types individually would be equivalent to correcting total income by c, which obviously would leave the relative positions of SEGs unchanged.

If, however, these correction ratios vary by income type (say c_i for type i), as they do in column (4) of Table 12, then the relative positions of SEGs can be altered by the application of the c_i if the composition of total income by income type in the unadjusted CPS differs among the SEGs. Of course, we know that composition does differ among SEGs, as shown in Table 13 for CPS income. (Table 14 shows the composition of Family Personal Income.) It is clear that SEGs which receive large proportions of their total income in income types which have large correction factors will be better off relative to other SEGs after correction.

The effect of the simple ratio adjustment on the mean total income of various SEGs is shown in columns (2) and (3) of Tables 15, 16, and 17. A comparison of these means with those from the unadjusted CPS and BEA TMI (Tables 9, 10, and 11) shows that the simple ratio adjustment and the BEA TMI means are quite similar, the major exceptions being farm residents and the age groups, especially the 65 and over group. The mean for farm residents produced by the simple ratio adjustment is significantly lower than the BEA TMI estimate because of the special treatment

---

[17] The BEA procedure for allocation of income to nonrespondents produced a nonfarm self-employment income aggregate substantially higher than the estimate derived using the Census procedure. The BEA aggregate was used in Table 12; if the Census aggregate had been used instead, the deficiency would have been roughly 10 percent rather than 2 percent.

TABLE 12   Income Aggregates and Correction Ratios, 1964

(billions of dollars)

Money Income Type	CPS[a] (1)	BEA Money Income Control Totals (2)	CPS as Proportion of BEA (1) ÷ (2) (3)	Simple Correction Ratio (2) ÷ (1) (4)	Reciprocal[b] Ratio (5)
1. Wage and salary	297.7	324.9	.92	1.09	1.09
2. Nonfarm self-employment	38.5	39.4	.98	1.02	{ 1.02, 0.98
3. Farm self-employment	5.8	10.8	.54	1.87	{ 1.75, 0.57
4. OASDI and railroad retirement	14.7	16.1	.91	1.10	1.10
5. Property income (interest, dividends, rent, and royalties)	14.9	43.9	.34	2.96	{ 2.93, 0.34
6. Unemployment compensation and public assistance	4.3	6.6	.65	1.56	1.56
7. All other money income	9.9	17.3	.57	1.75	{ 1.75, 0.57

[a] Using BEA weights and allocation of income to nonrespondents.
[b] See p. 481 for explanation.

TABLE 13   Composition of CPS Total Money Income[a] of Consumer Units, 1964

(percent)

	W&S (1)	*NFSE* (2)	*Farm* (3)	*Prop.* (4)	*UC&PA* (5)	*Other* (6)
Age:						
14-24	93.8	2.2	0.4	0.4	1.3	1.9
25-34	89.0	6.4	1.1	0.9	1.2	1.5
35-44	81.3	12.1	1.6	1.6	0.8	2.6
45-54	81.0	10.8	1.6	3.1	0.8	2.7
55-64	74.4	12.1	1.8	5.8	0.9	5.1
65 or over	36.2	8.7	1.7	14.4	2.6	36.4
Color:						
White	76.7	10.4	1.6	4.0	0.9	6.4
Nonwhite	84.1	3.4	0.4	1.8	4.4	5.9
Sex:						
Male	78.7	10.7	1.6	3.3	0.7	5.0
Female	63.9	3.5	0.8	9.0	4.2	18.5
Residence:						
Farm	49.0	5.3	31.3	5.6	1.1	7.6
Nonfarm	78.3	10.2	0.3	3.8	1.1	6.3
All units	77.2	10.0	1.5	3.9	1.1	6.4

NOTE:
   W&S = Wages and Salaries
   NFSE = Nonfarm Self-Employment Income
   Farm = Farm Self-Employment Income
   Prop. = Property Income
   UC&PA = Unemployment Compensation and Public Assistance
   Other = OASDI, Railroad Retirement, and CPS "all other money income"
[a] Using BEA weights and allocation of income to nonrespondents.

of expenses on imputed farm income in the BEA estimates. The differences by age groups result from one of the sources of error inherent in the simple ratio technique: the fewer the number of income types which are corrected separately, the lower the accuracy of the adjustment. Although Table 12 lists seven income types and correction ratios, because of data problems types (4) and (7) were corrected jointly in the simple ratio estimates shown

TABLE 14 Composition of Bureau of Economic Analysis Family Personal Income of Consumer Units, 1964

(percent)

	W&S (1)	NFSE (2)	Farm (3)	Prop. (4)	UC&PA (5)	Other (6)	Imputed (7)	PCSI[a] (8)
Age:								
14-24	92.8	1.8	0.7	1.6	2.1	2.9	1.8	3.6
25-34	86.1	6.2	1.7	3.0	1.6	2.1	2.5	3.1
35-44	75.8	11.1	2.5	5.1	1.1	3.4	3.9	2.8
45-54	74.2	9.2	2.6	7.1	1.1	3.3	5.3	2.8
55-64	65.3	9.2	2.8	11.6	1.2	5.7	6.8	2.6
65 and over	27.2	5.6	2.1	27.0	2.2	28.7	8.4	1.2
Color:								
White	68.3	8.7	2.4	9.8	1.2	7.1	5.1	2.6
Nonwhite	80.3	2.8	0.7	3.3	5.1	6.8	4.5	3.5
Sex:								
Male	71.3	9.2	2.5	8.2	1.0	5.6	4.9	2.7
Female	52.2	2.5	1.1	18.0	4.1	18.1	6.2	2.2

	W&S	NFSE	Farm	Prop.	UC&PA	Other	Imputed	PCSI
Residence:								
Farm	34.1	4.5	36.7	10.8	1.4	6.0	8.5	2.1
Nonfarm	70.9	8.6	0.4	9.3	1.4	7.2	4.9	2.6
Work experience:								
Nonworker	27.9	1.5	1.2	25.1	4.5	33.7	7.3	1.2
Full-time, full-year worker	76.7	10.1	2.6	6.5	0.4	1.9	4.6	2.8
Other	67.2	5.8	1.9	9.5	3.5	9.5	5.3	2.8
All units	69.0	8.4	2.3	9.3	1.4	7.1	5.1	2.6

NOTE:

W&S = Wages and Salaries
NFSE = Nonfarm Self-Employment Income
Farm = Farm Self-Employment Income
Prop. = Property Income
UC&PA = Unemployment Compensation and Public Assistance
Other = OASDI, Railroad Retirement, and CPS "all other money income"
Imputed = Imputed Income
PCSI = Personal Contributions for Social Insurance

a All figures in this column are to be subtracted from preceding columns. The sum of all rows equals Family Personal Income, Detail does not necessarily add to 100 percent because of rounding.

TABLE 15   Mean Incomes of Consumer Units by Age, 1964

Age	CPS (1)	Simple Ratio Adjustment		Reciprocal Ratio Adjustment	
		Mean (2)	Ratio to CPS (3)	Mean (4)	Ratio to CPS (5)
14-24	$4,280	$4,720	1.103	$4,746	1.109
25-34	6,772	7,368	1.088	7,387	1.091
35-44	7,988	8,904	1.115	8,942	1.119
45-54	8,128	9,314	1.146	9,348	1.150
55-64	6,746	8,074	1.197	8,096	1.200
65 or over	3,980	5,652	1.420	5,470	1.374
All ages	6,569	7,673	1.168	7,673	1.168

in Tables 15, 16, and 17 by using a weighted correction ratio (1.36) applied to the sum of the two income types.[18] This method assumes that the ratio between types (4) and (7) is the same for all SEGs (type (4) is 60 percent of the sum of the two). However, type (4) (OASDI and railroad retirement benefits) is highly concentrated in the 65 and over age group, constituting perhaps 80 percent of the sum of the two for that group. The 80 percent figure implies a weighted correction ratio of 1.23 (rather than 1.36) and results in a mean total income $180 lower than the amount shown in Table 15. The means for the other age groups, with the possible exception of the 55-64 group, would be slightly higher if the two types were corrected independently. This inaccuracy therefore accounts for most of the differences between the simple ratio and BEA TMI estimates of mean incomes by age.

Next, we relaxed the assumption of an unchanged relative distribution and tried a slightly modified form of simple inflation to correct for underreporting. The simple ratio adjustment has the unhappy property of increasing the absolute value of negative as well as positive reported incomes, with a consequent increase in reported losses. While very little is known about the biases in reported negative incomes, especially in the CPS, it seems unlikely that their algebraic value would be overreported, as the simple

[18] This ratio was derived by summing the two BEA amounts ($16.1 billion and $17.3 billion) and dividing that sum by the sum of the two CPS amounts ($14.7 billion and $9.9 billion).

TABLE 16 Mean Incomes of Consumer Units, by Color, Sex, and Residence, 1964

	CPS (1)	Simple Ratio Adjustment		Reciprocal Ratio Adjustment	
		Mean (2)	Ratio to CPS (3)	Mean (4)	Ratio to CPS (5)
Color:					
White	$6,864	$8,029	1.170	$8,030	1.170
Nonwhite	4,113	4,649	1.130	4,651	1.131
Ratio of nonwhite to white	.599	.579		.579	
Sex:					
Male	7,417	8,546	1.152	8,549	1.153
Female	3,307	4,318	1.306	4,319	1.306
Ratio of female to male	.446	.505		.505	
Residence:					
Nonfarm	6,707	7,755	1.156	7,760	1.157
Farm	4,380	6,225	1.421	6,194	1.414
Ratio of farm to nonfarm	.653	.803		.798	
Type of unit:					
Families	7,438	NA	NA	8,598	1.156
Unrelated individuals	3,122	NA	NA	3,990	1.278
Ratio of unrelated individuals to families	.420	NA	NA	.464	

NA = Not available.

TABLE 17   Mean Income of Consumer Units, by Work Experience of Head, 1964

		Simple Ratio Adjustment		Reciprocal Ratio Adjustment	
Work Experience of Head	CPS (1)	Mean (2)	Ratio to CPS (3)	Mean (4)	Ratio to CPS (5)
Nonworker	$3,270	$4,431	1.355	NA	NA
Full-time, full-year worker	8,280	9,319	1.125	NA	NA
Other	4,951	5,873	1.186	NA	NA

NA = Not available.

ratio adjustment would imply. In the modified form (the "reciprocal ratio" adjustment), in the case of income types which could be negative, different correction ratios were applied to positive and negative amounts. For the four (out of the seven) CPS income types containing negative amounts (nonfarm self-employment, farm self-employment, property, and all other money income), the inflated CPS amounts were derived by applying to the negative amounts the reciprocal of the correction factor applied to positive amounts. The following equation was solved to obtain the factor for each income type i:

$$c_i P_i + (1/c_i)(-N_i) = T_i, \qquad (1)$$

where c_i is the correction factor applied to positive amounts, P_i is the CPS aggregate amount of positive income, N_i is the absolute value of the CPS aggregate amount of negative income, and T_i is the BEA control aggregate.[19] It is interesting to note that this method of correction will not leave the Lorenz curve of the income type unchanged if N_i is unequal to zero. If N_i is equal to zero (i.e., type (i) is nonnegative), then equation 1 reduces to the following equation:

$$c_i P_i = T_i, \text{ or } c_i = T_i/P_i, \qquad (2)$$

[19] The specific form of equation 1 is somewhat arbitrary, since very little is known about the relationship between underreporting of positive and negative amounts.

and the Lorenz curve is unchanged after correction.[20] The reciprocal ratio adjustment factors derived using equation 1 are shown in column (5) of Table 12.

Columns (4) and (5) of Tables 15 and 16 show the results of the reciprocal ratio adjustment. These results are not significantly different from those produced by the simple ratio adjustment, with the exception of the 65 and over age group. The upward bias in the simple ratio estimate for that group has already been discussed. Since types (4) and (7) were corrected separately in the reciprocal ratio adjustment, that bias was not present in those estimates. These remarks apply, of course, only to differences between the means; the size and relative distributions would show greater differences.

Changes in the ratios of mean total incomes of SEGs can also be produced by altering the overall relative distributions of individual income types and of total income, although these changes would not be expected to be as large as those produced by inflating to control totals. This point can be illustrated by considering total money income. Assume that there is an initial total money income distribution (CPS) and a more accurate distribution (TM) to which the CPS distribution will be made to conform, and that both distributions contain the same number of recipients and the same aggregate amount of money income. Under these assumptions, any differences between the CPS and TM distributions must be due to differences in the relative distributions.

The correction procedure will transform the CPS distribution into the TM distribution. This transformation can be viewed as the application of a correction factor to the total money income amount for each observation in the CPS. Since the CPS and TM relative distributions differ, it is clear that all observations in the CPS cannot receive the same correction factor. The problem is choosing the correction factor to be applied to each CPS observation, given the constraint that after correction the CPS

[20] The simple ratio correction can be represented by the following equation:

$$c_i^*(P_i - N_i) = T_i, \text{ or } c_i^* = T_i/(P_i - N_i).$$

$(P_i - N_i)$ is merely the CPS aggregate before adjustment and therefore c_i^* is the ratio of the BEA control total to the CPS reported aggregate. It is clear that in this case the Lorenz curve is unchanged.

distribution must be identical to the TM distribution. The choice of these correction factors can affect the ratios between the mean incomes of subgroups (SEGs) of the CPS distribution after correction.

A simple example will clarify the point. Suppose we have a universe consisting of three recipient units, with CPS and TM total money income distributions as shown below:

CPS Unit	CPS Income	TM Income
A	$ 2,000	$ 1,000
B	3,000	3,000
C	5,000	6,000
All units	$10,000	$10,000

If we assume that each of the three CPS units constitutes a different SEG, then it is clear that the ratios of the incomes of the SEGs cannot remain unchanged after the CPS distribution has been transformed into the TM. The problem of correction can be put very simply in the context of this example: Which one of the three TM amounts should be assigned to CPS unit A, which to B, and which to C, given the constraint that each TM amount can be used once and only once?

An exact match between the CPS and TM would give an unequivocal answer to this question, for it would show, for each CPS unit, the TM return that unit actually filed. We would therefore know the TM income amount associated with each of the three CPS units.

If an exact match between the CPS and TM is not available, then assumptions about the relationship between CPS and TM total money income must be made. These assumptions should be consistent with exact match information which exists for data sources similar to the CPS and TM.[21] One possible assumption is a random relation between CPS and TM incomes; this corresponds to drawing TM amounts at random, without replacement. Existing exact match information does not support this hypothesis.

A more reasonable assumption is that the rank in the distribution is the same in the CPS and TM. That is, the highest

[21] The 1950 and 1960 Census-IRS matches and the Social Security Administration's link study are examples of existing exact matches.

CPS unit (C) would be assigned the highest TM amount ($6,000), and so on. Such a "rank ratio" procedure produces different correction ratios for different units, as shown below, although the rank of each unit in the distribution is not altered.

CPS Unit (1)	CPS Income (2)	TM Income (3)	Rank Ratio (3)÷(2) (4)
A	$2,000	$1,000	0.5
B	3,000	3,000	1.0
C	5,000	6,000	1.2

While preserving rank is a reasonable assumption in the absence of any exact match information, the results of exact matches suggest that ranks are changed to some extent. While there tends to be a strong correlation in the ranks, it is substantially less than one.

One way of preserving a correlation of less than one in the ranks is to create subsets of observations in the ranked distribution. This may be called the "modified rank ratio" technique. Assume that we have one hundred observations in both the CPS and TM, ranked by size of total money income. We then create ten rank subsets of ten observations each in each distribution. For example, the top would consist of the ten highest amounts in the CPS and the ten highest amounts in the TM. Then, within each of these subsets, a TM amount would be drawn (without replacement) for each of the ten CPS units. Using this method, rank would be preserved only for the subset as a whole; within the subset the relationship between CPS and TM incomes would be random. It follows that within a given subset, the relationship between SEGs and TM incomes would also be random. Correction ratios can differ among rank subsets, but within any given rank subset, the SEG to which a unit belongs does not affect the size of the TM income assigned to it.

At this point, it may be useful to relate the rank ratio correction to the simple ratio and reciprocal ratio adjustments which were discussed in relation to the adjustment of amounts of aggregate income. This may be done by examining the effects of applying each type of correction to amounts of total income. When applied to such amounts, the simple ratio adjustment leaves the relative distribution and the ratios of mean incomes of all

SEGs unchanged. The reciprocal ratio adjustment, on the other hand, changes the overall relative distribution slightly, although it leaves unchanged the relative distributions of positive and negative amounts taken separately. Using the reciprocal ratio adjustment, the ratios of the means of SEGs will be changed to the extent that the ratio of positive to negative aggregate total income differs among SEGs. In contrast, the rank ratio correction changes the relative distributions of both positive and negative amounts, as well as the relative distribution of all amounts. The ratios of the means of SEGs can be changed even if the ratio of positive to negative total income is identical for all SEGs.

Correcting differences in the numbers of recipients of specific income types can also change the relationship between mean incomes of SEGs. Once again, we will use the CPS and TM as examples to illustrate the point, assuming that the TM number of recipients is more accurate. If the TM contains more recipients (assuming that nonfilers have previously been excluded), then some CPS units which reported zero amounts must be assigned nonzero amounts. The choice of the particular units to receive amounts can affect the relationships among the mean incomes of different SEGs. When possible, the assignments are made on the basis of outside information. If no such information is available, the additional units in the CPS to be assigned amounts could be chosen randomly. Random selection would increase the proportion receiving the income type by a greater percentage for a SEG which had a low proportion initially receiving it than for a group with a high initial proportion. If the same amounts were assigned to units in both groups, then the mean for (all units in) the group with the lower proportion receiving it would rise more than the mean for the group with the higher proportion.

In the cells in the actual CPS-TM match, the TM number of recipients of property income generally exceeded the CPS number. As a result, a substantial number of CPS units reporting zero property income were assigned a TM amount. By assumption, all CPS units with zero property income in a given cell had the same probability of being assigned a nonzero TM amount, regardless of the SEGs to which they belonged. This could lead to changes in the ratios of mean incomes of SEGs through differential increases in the proportions of recipients of property income.

If such effects are not acceptable, an alternative is to constrain the percentage increase in the proportion of recipients to be the same for all relevant SEGs. Thus, if the TM shows 1.5 times the number of recipients shown by the CPS, the number of recipients in each SEG after assignment would be 1.5 times the original number. However, problems arise when the limit of 100 percent of recipients is approached. If the TM were to show 1.5 times the number in the CPS and the initial proportion of recipients in a given SEG were above two-thirds, the percentage after assignment would have to exceed 100 percent for that SEG. If the SEGs are defined in considerable detail, this can be a serious problem.

Correction becomes much more complex when the relationships among different income types are taken into account. One assumption would be to correct each income type independently—an assumption made in the simple ratio and reciprocal ratio methods discussed above. (The rank ratio or modified rank ratio method could also be applied to each income type independently.) At the other extreme, all types could be corrected jointly. One way of doing the latter for types contained in the IRS data would be, for a given CPS unit, to replace the CPS income amounts with amounts from the same tax return for the relevant income types. This, indeed, is what was done in our statistical match between the CPS and TM. Taking all the types from the same tax return will not preserve the rank of the recipient unit in the distribution of each income type, although it does have the advantage of approximating the results of an exact match by retaining a correlation among the ranks. If all types are taken from the same return, the obvious problem is to decide how that return should be chosen. This selection process was described in an earlier section of this paper, and we will merely comment here on the assumptions regarding SEGs.

SEGs played only a minor role in the choice of tax returns in the CPS-TM match. Family status (husband-wife couple, other family head, or other person) and age (under 65, 65 or over) were the only SECs used directly. The assumption was that SEGs made no difference within each of the most narrowly defined linking classifications. In other words, given the group, wage class, subclass, subdivision (if any), and rank of the appropriate income type in its distribution, a unit would have the same expected TM income regardless of the SEG to which it belonged.

Finally, we will relate briefly the major steps in the BEA adjustment procedure to the discussion of correction techniques in this section. All steps, of course, increased the aggregate amount of income. The CPS-TM match combined elements of transformations into more accurate relative distributions with changes in the numbers of recipients. As noted above, joint correction of the income types was used in that step. The audit correction was basically a rank ratio procedure, although some changes in the numbers of recipients were also made. For most income types, adjusting to the BEA money income controls consisted of a reciprocal ratio adjustment, although the technique was modified for rent and farm self-employment income. For unemployment compensation and public assistance, the adjustment was made entirely by increasing the number of recipients, in most cases using the constrained assignment within SEGs described earlier.

To summarize, we have shown in this section that correcting the CPS for underreporting by means of either the simple or reciprocal ratio technique produces mean total money incomes of SEGs very similar to those obtained from the BEA adjustment procedure. We can, therefore, conclude that correcting relative distributions and changing the numbers of recipients of specific income types, both of which were done in the BEA procedure, either offset each other or had very little impact on the mean incomes of SEGs. They did, however, affect the relative distributions of total money income of SEGs.

COMPOSITION OF THE POOR

In this section, we will examine differences in the composition of the poor as estimated from CPS and BEA income data, holding the total number of poor consumer units approximately constant. Because of the rather arbitrary nature of the Social Security Administration (SSA)—or any other—poverty line, it seems more appropriate to emphasize differences in the composition of a given number of poor, produced by moving from the CPS to the BEA distributions, rather than differences in their total numbers.[22] Approximate estimates of changes in composition were obtained

---

[22] Using BEA TMI and the uninflated SSA line, 5.076 million families and 3.919 million unrelated individuals would be classified as poor. Preliminary estimates of changes in the total number of poor units were presented in E. C. Budd and D. B. Radner, "The OBE Size Distribution Series: Methods and Tentative Results for 1964," *American Economic Review, Papers and Proceedings* (May 1969):445-46.

by raising the revised 1964 SSA poverty lines by 19 percent (Table 18)—a figure which represents the percent by which the BEA total money income control exceeds the CPS money income amount—and recomputing the number of poor units on the basis of their BEA money incomes.[23] Simply recomputing the number of units without at the same time adjusting the poverty lines would fail to allow for the fact that the poverty income cutoffs themselves cannot be determined independently of the adequacy of income reporting.

We have confined our calculations to total money income (TMI) rather than using family personal income (FPI), since employing a different income concept would clearly require some recasting of the definition of the poor and the corresponding poverty cutoffs. For example, the poverty lines as defined by the SSA contain a differential between farm and nonfarm residents, reflecting, in part, the receipt of imputed farm income by the former. Since nonmoney farm income is included in family personal income, the

[23] The revised uninflated poverty lines were derived from the U.S. Bureau of the Census, *Current Population Reports,* Series P-23, No. 28, August 12, 1969, "Revision in Poverty Statistics, 1959 to 1968," Table C; and Mollie Orshansky, "Counting the Poor: Another Look at the Poverty Profile," *Social Security Bulletin* 28 (January 1965), Table E.

TABLE 18 Inflated Poverty Lines, 1964

(dollars)

Type of Unit	Nonfarm		Farm	
	Male	*Female*	*Male*	*Female*
1 member				
Under 65	1,990	1,840	1,692	1,564
65 or over	1,785	1,767	1,517	1,502
2 members				
Head under 65	2,492	2,383	2,118	2,026
Head 65 or over	2,232	2,227	1,897	1,893
3 members	2,962	2,836	2,518	2,409
4 members	3,777	3,752	3,210	3,190
5 members	4,446	4,403	3,779	3,743
6 members	4,995	4,971	4,246	4,226
7 or more members	6,153	6,032	5,230	5,127

SSA nonfarm-farm differential would no longer be valid. Similar arguments can be applied to other imputed income types. In studying changes in the composition of the poor, therefore, we believe that it is more meaningful to base the comparisons on money income rather than on family personal income and to confine our adjustment of the SSA lines to the underreporting of money income.

Raising each of the 36 poverty lines by 19 percent and using BEA TMI did not, in fact, leave the number of poor consumer units unchanged. The number declined from 12.2 million, using the SSA lines and CPS incomes, to 11.6 million, using the inflated lines and BEA TMI—a fall of 5.2 percent. Thus, the relative changes in socioeconomic groups must be measured against that overall decline. One way of examining the changes in SEGs is to look at changes in the percentage composition of the total number of poor consumer units. This method is useful for large groups but tends to hide significant changes in groups which constitute only a small percentage of the total poor. Another method is to look at the change in the proportion of the group who are below the poverty line; when using this method, the overall decline of 5.2 percent must be kept in mind and used as a basis of comparison. A third method is to examine the overall decline in terms of the change in the number of units below the line. All three of these techniques will be used here. Table 19 shows the number of consumer units below the poverty line in the two cases for various SEGs.

The most significant change in the four classifications shown in Table 19 occurred in the farm residence group. The number of poor units in that group fell 29.6 percent, from 10.4 percent to 7.7 percent of total poor units. This decline was a direct result of the large difference in total farm money income in the two estimates. Unrelated individuals showed a much sharper decline than families, 10.4 percent as opposed to 1.5 percent. This difference was primarily the result of the large role of unearned income types in the total income of unrelated individuals relative to families. For the same reason, units headed by nonworkers showed a greater decline than those headed by workers—8.3 percent as compared to 2.4 percent. The smallest difference in the categories shown in Table 19 occurred in the white-nonwhite breakdown. Units headed by whites fell 5.6 percent, while those headed by nonwhites fell only 3.9 percent. This was the only one

TABLE 19 Consumer Units Below the Poverty Line,[a] 1964

(thousands)

Group	CPS		BEA TMI			
	Number of Units (1)	Proportion of Total (2)	Number of Units (3)	Proportion of Total (4)	Change in Number of Units (3)–(1) (5)	Percent Change (5)÷(1) (6)
White	9,422	.770	8,894	.767	–528	–5.6
Nonwhite	2,816	.230	2,705	.233	–111	–3.9
Nonworker	5,852	.478	5,368	.463	–484	–8.3
Worker	6,387	.522	6,231	.537	–156	–2.4
Farm	1,269	.104	894	.077	–375	–29.6
Nonfarm	10,969	.896	10,705	.923	–264	–2.4
Families	7,137	.583	7,030	.606	–107	–1.5
Unrelated individuals	5,102	.417	4,569	.394	–533	–10.4
All units	12,238	1.000	11,599	1.000	–639	–5.2

[a] Using inflated poverty lines to compute the BEA numbers of poor units.

TABLE 20 Percent Below the Poverty Line,[a] 1964

Socioeconomic Groups	Families		Unrelated Individuals		Consumer Units	
	CPS	*BEA*	*CPS*	*BEA*	*CPS*	*BEA*
All units	14.9	14.7	42.3	37.9	20.4	19.4
Age:						
14-24	18.6	18.4	39.6	38.7	24.7	24.4
25-34	15.6	16.4	19.1	17.3	15.9	16.5
35-44	13.3	13.5	22.3	20.1	14.2	14.1
45-54	10.3	10.1	32.0	27.2	13.1	12.3
55-64	13.4	12.0	37.1	29.6	19.3	16.4
65 or over	24.0	23.0	59.6	54.9	38.5	36.0
Residence:						
Nonfarm	13.6	14.1	42.0	37.7	19.5	19.0
Farm	34.7	23.7	53.5	44.0	36.7	25.8
Work experience:						
Nonworker	34.8	32.8	69.1	62.0	48.0	44.0
Under 65	40.8	37.8	72.0	61.7	49.1	44.1
65 or over	30.0	28.8	68.1	62.2	47.3	43.9

Full-time, full-year	7.3	7.8	14.8	13.8	8.3	8.5
Other	23.9	22.9	41.0	35.8	28.0	26.0
Family type-color-sex:						
Husband-wife couple	12.1	12.6	NA	NA	NA	NA
White	10.2	10.7				
Nonwhite	33.1	33.8				
Other	33.9	28.8				
White	27.3	22.5	40.2	35.6	36.1	31.5
Male	17.0	12.0	29.1	26.4	26.5	23.4
Female	30.0	25.3	46.5	40.8	40.4	31.2
Nonwhite	58.8	52.7	55.8	52.2	57.1	52.4
Male	32.9	33.4	45.2	42.7	43.2	41.2
Female	62.5	55.4	66.8	62.1	64.3	58.2
Family size:						
2	15.2	14.0	NA	NA	NA	NA
3 or 4	10.4	10.1				
5 or 6	15.9	16.7				
7 or more	36.5	38.3				

NA = Not applicable.

[a]Using inflated poverty lines to compute the BEA numbers of poor units.

TABLE 21 Families and Unrelated Individuals Below the Poverty Line,[a] 1964
(thousands)

| | Families | | | | Unrelated Individuals | | | |
| | CPS | | BEA | | CPS | | BEA | |
Socioeconomic Group	Number of Units	Percentage of Total Poor Units	Number of Units	Percentage of Total Poor Units	Number of Units	Percentage of Total Poor Units	Number of Units	Percentage of Total Poor Units
All units	7,137	100.0	7,030	100.0	5,102	100.0	4,569	100.0
Age:								
14-24	539	7.6	535	7.6	477	9.3	466	10.2
25-34	1,439	20.2	1,514	21.5	198	3.9	180	3.9
35-44	1,484	20.8	1,503	21.4	260	5.1	234	5.1
45-54	1,058	14.8	1,038	14.8	496	9.7	421	9.2
55-64	1,001	14.0	893	12.7	923	18.1	738	16.2
65 or over	1,616	22.6	1,548	22.0	2,748	53.9	2,531	55.4
Residence:								
Nonfarm	6,064	85.0	6,297	89.6	4,906	96.2	4,408	96.5
Farm	1,073	15.0	733	10.4	196	3.8	161	3.5

Work Experience:								
Nonworker	2,622	36.7	2,468	35.1	3,230	63.3	2,900	63.5
Under 65	1,372	19.2	1,269	18.1	873	17.1	748	16.4
65 or over	1,250	17.5	1,199	17.1	2,357	46.2	2,152	47.1
Full-time, full-year	2,263	31.7	2,404	34.2	656	12.9	608	13.3
Other	2,252	31.6	2,158	30.7	1,216	23.8	1,062	23.2
Family type-color-sex:								
Husband-wife couple	5,047	70.7	5,252	74.7	NA	NA	NA	NA
White	3,902	54.7	4,081	58.1				
Nonwhite	1,145	16.0	1,171	16.7				
Other	2,089	29.3	1,779	25.3	NA	NA	NA	NA
White	1,333	18.7	1,101	15.7	4,187	82.1		
Male	174	2.4	123	1.7	1,094	21.4		
Female	1,159	16.2	978	13.9	3,093	60.6		
Nonwhite	756	10.6	678	9.6	915	17.9		
Male	53	0.7	54	0.8	378	7.4		
Female	703	9.9	624	8.9	537	10.5		
Family Size:								
2	2,368	33.2	2,184	31.1	NA	NA	NA	NA
3 or 4	1,995	28.0	1,943	27.6				
5 or 6	1,513	21.2	1,581	22.5				
7 or more	1,261	17.7	1,321	18.8				

NA = Not applicable or not available.
aUsing inflated poverty lines to compute the BEA numbers of poor units.

of the four categories in which the group with a higher proportion of its units classified as poor had a relative increase in the number of poor; nonworkers, farm residents, and unrelated individuals all showed relative declines. However, this change in the white-nonwhite ratio was extremely small and not significantly different from zero, although it can be said that, in contrast to the other three groups mentioned above, there was no decline in the nonwhite share of the total poor. These changes in different groups can, of course, be closely related. For example, since many unrelated individuals are nonworkers, it is not surprising that both groups experienced similar declines.

Changes in the composition of the poor for more detailed socioeconomic breakdowns are presented in Tables 20 and 21. The age distribution of poor families, based on the age of the head, showed a shift away from the older age groups. The work-experience groups for families showed a significant change in the relationships among the groups. The number of poor families headed by a full-time, full-year worker increased slightly, while all other families, including those headed by a nonworker, declined. Roughly the same pattern was observed for unrelated individuals, although for that group the number of full-time, full-year working poor did decline slightly. This shift toward fully employed workers can be explained by the relatively small correction factors applied to wage and salary income, which is, of course, the dominant income source for such workers (and their families). Looking at the family-size breakdown, there was a shift in the number of poor from smaller families (four persons or less) to larger ones (five or more).

The changes by family type, color, and sex are of particular interest. Although the number of poor families as a whole declined by 1.5 percent, the number of families headed by a husband-wife couple rose 4.0 percent. This increase was characteristic of both white families, which rose 4.6 percent, and nonwhite families, which rose 2.3 percent. In contrast, families not headed by a husband-wife couple ("other families") fell 14.9 percent—17.4 percent for whites, and 10.3 percent for nonwhites. This large decline is related to the importance of transfer payments as an income source for those families. The changes in "other families" by color and sex are also worth noting. "Other families" headed by white males fell by 29.6 percent, while those headed by white females fell only 15.7 percent. However, the estimates for white males are subject to a large degree of error due to the small number of poor units involved. The same caution is appropriate when interpreting the change in "other families" headed by nonwhite males, which showed a rise of 1.3 percent. Nonwhite females, a larger group, showed an 11.3 percent fall.

For unrelated individuals, the four color-sex groups all showed declines. Keeping in mind the 10.4 percent decline for all unrelated individuals, whites fell 11.3 percent, with males falling 9.0 percent and females, 12.1 percent. Nonwhites, on the other hand, declined only 6.3 percent, with males falling 5.5 percent and females, 6.9 percent.

These comparisons are perhaps sufficient to show that the composition of the poor—by whatever standards their overall number is determined—is dependent on the pattern of income underreporting in the data source used, as well as on the shapes of the distributions of the various income types themselves. Those whose primary source of income is wages and salaries, for example, evidence a relative rise in numbers; those relying more heavily on such types as farm income, property income, and transfer payments experience a relative decline in the number of poor units.

APPENDIX A

TABLE A.1 Size Distributions of Total Income of Families, 1964

(thousands of families)

Size of Total Income	(1)	(2)	(3)	(4)	(5)	(6)
Loss	165	175	240	188	133	125
Zero	205	206	217	216	129	60
$1-$1,249	1,854	1,879	1,560	1,490	1,015	854
1,250- 3,249	7,317	7,336	6,675	6,508	5,609	5,279
3,250- 5,749	10,812	10,767	10,151	10,100	9,913	10,140
5,750- 8,249	11,366	11,447	11,056	11,037	11,122	10,979
8,250-10,249	6,585	6,555	6,868	6,937	7,167	7,279
10,250-15,749	7,075	7,044	7,902	8,070	8,787	8,886
15,750-24,749	1,855	1,817	2,225	2,304	2,735	2,917
24,750-49,749	470	480	729	760	942	1,001
49,750-98,749	43	54	133	143	192	218
98,750 or over	33	19	23	25	35	41
Total	47,779	47,779	47,779	47,779	47,779	47,779
Mean income (dollars)	7,335	7,303	7,897	8,025	8,631	8,838
Median income (dollars)	6,500	6,500	6,860	6,947	7,306	7,354

NOTE:
Columns: 1. CPS, Census allocation and BEA weights
2. CPS, BEA allocation
3. CPS-TM Match
4. CPS-TM Match, after audit
5. BEA Total Money Income
6. BEA Family Personal Income

TABLE A.2   Size Distributions of Total Income of Unrelated Individuals, 1964

(thousands of unrelated individuals)

Size of Total Income	(1)	(2)	(3)	(4)	(5)	(6)
Loss	25	27	46	37	28	34
Zero	602	610	610	610	517	192
$1-$1,249	3,681	3,681	3,133	3,105	2,555	2,448
1,250- 3,249	3,619	3,563	3,696	3,676	3,754	4,041
3,250- 5,749	2,391	2,468	2,533	2,555	2,806	2,981
5,750- 8,249	1,162	1,134	1,334	1,343	1,378	1,250
8,250-10,249	269	267	361	372	485	496
10,250-15,749	174	185	226	237	353	425
15,750-24,749	92	81	79	81	89	97
24,750-49,749	32	33	27	28	75	74
49,750-98,749	2	2	8	9	14	15
98,750 or over	8	5	3	3	4	4
Total	12,057	12,057	12,057	12,057	12,057	12,057
Mean income (dollars)	3,072	3,035	3,316	3,358	3,874	4,006
Median income (dollars)	1,979	1,980	2,284	2,322	2,635	2,761

NOTE:
Columns: 1. CPS, Census allocation and BEA weights
2. CPS, BEA allocation
3. CPS-TM Match
4. CPS-TM Match, after audit
5. BEA Total Money Income
6. BEA Family Personal Income

TABLE A.3   Income Shares of Families, 1964

(percent of aggregate income)

Percentiles	(1)	(2)	(3)	(4)	(5)	(6)
1- 20	5.13	5.09	4.87	5.09	5.61	5.83
21- 40	12.01	12.04	11.82	11.83	11.96	11.84
41- 60	17.69	17.74	17.39	17.32	16.97	16.73
61- 80	24.01	24.04	23.44	23.30	22.72	22.48
81- 90	15.56	15.63	15.29	15.20	14.88	14.78
91- 95	9.66	9.69	9.61	9.57	9.47	9.51
96-100	15.94	15.77	17.58	17.69	18.39	18.83
100	5.59	5.38	6.63	6.70	7.25	7.47

NOTE:
Columns: 1. CPS, Census allocation and BEA weights
2. CPS, BEA allocation
3. CPS-TM Match
4. CPS-TM Match, after audit
5. BEA Total Money Income
6. BEA Family Personal Income

TABLE A.4   Income Shares of Unrelated Individuals, 1964

(percent of aggregate income)

Percentiles	(1)	(2)	(3)	(4)	(5)	(6)
1- 20	2.45	2.46	2.40	2.53	2.82	3.19
21- 40	7.13	7.22	7.35	7.31	7.45	7.99
41- 60	12.80	13.03	13.87	13.89	13.85	14.00
61- 80	24.46	24.95	24.70	24.65	23.49	22.86
81- 90	18.37	18.54	18.25	18.15	17.10	16.57
91- 95	11.99	12.12	11.67	11.61	11.21	11.23
96-100	22.80	21.68	21.75	21.86	24.08	24.16
100	9.24	8.15	8.87	8.96	11.12	11.14

NOTE:
Columns: 1. CPS, Census allocation and BEA weights
2. CPS, BEA allocation
3. CPS-TM Match
4. CPS-TM Match, after audit
5. BEA Total Money Income
6. BEA Family Personal Income

TABLE A.5 Detailed Income Shares of Consumer Units, 1964

(percent of aggregate income)

Percentiles	(1)	(2)	(3)	(4)	(5)	(6)
1- 5	0.10	0.09	−0.08	0.06	0.21	0.27
6- 10	0.74	0.74	0.74	0.75	0.83	0.90
11- 15	1.08	1.08	1.10	1.11	1.23	1.32
16- 20	1.51	1.50	1.53	1.55	1.66	1.71
21- 25	1.91	1.92	1.95	1.96	2.08	2.12
26- 30	2.36	2.37	2.38	2.39	2.47	2.48
31- 35	2.83	2.83	2.79	2.80	2.87	2.83
36- 40	3.25	3.28	3.21	3.22	3.25	3.20
41- 45	3.71	3.72	3.64	3.63	3.61	3.57
46- 50	4.10	4.12	4.06	4.05	3.99	3.93
51- 55	4.54	4.55	4.47	4.45	4.36	4.28
56- 60	4.95	4.98	4.89	4.86	4.74	4.66
61- 65	5.42	5.43	5.31	5.29	5.16	5.10
66- 70	5.90	5.91	5.77	5.74	5.60	5.54
71- 75	6.41	6.42	6.28	6.25	6.08	6.01
76- 80	7.07	7.09	6.88	6.84	6.64	6.57
81- 85	7.79	7.81	7.59	7.55	7.34	7.29
86- 90	8.77	8.81	8.59	8.54	8.32	8.26
91- 95	10.34	10.39	10.23	10.19	10.01	10.00
96-100	17.22	16.96	18.67	18.77	19.55	19.96
96	2.39	2.39	2.39	2.39	2.37	2.40
97	2.57	2.58	2.60	2.59	2.61	2.64
98	2.87	2.87	2.94	2.95	3.01	3.03
99	3.34	3.33	3.64	3.66	3.77	3.88
100	6.05	5.79	7.10	7.18	7.79	8.01

NOTE:
Columns: 1. CPS, Census allocation and BEA weights
2. CPS, BEA allocation
3. CPS-TM Match
4. CPS-TM Match, after audit
5. BEA Total Money Income
6. BEA Family Personal Income

TABLE A.6   Detailed Income Shares of Families, 1964

(percent of aggregate income)

Percentiles	(1)	(2)	(3)	(4)	(5)	(6)
1- 5	0.36	0.34	0.15	0.31	0.50	0.58
6- 10	1.15	1.14	1.13	1.15	1.27	1.34
11- 15	1.60	1.59	1.58	1.61	1.73	1.77
16- 20	2.02	2.02	2.01	2.02	2.11	2.14
21- 25	2.42	2.42	2.39	2.40	2.49	2.47
26- 30	2.82	2.83	2.78	2.79	2.84	2.81
31- 35	3.22	3.23	3.15	3.15	3.16	3.13
36- 40	3.55	3.56	3.50	3.49	3.47	3.43
41- 45	3.92	3.93	3.85	3.84	3.78	3.72
46- 50	4.23	4.26	4.18	4.16	4.08	4.01
51- 55	4.61	4.61	4.51	4.49	4.39	4.33
56- 60	4.93	4.94	4.85	4.83	4.72	4.67
61- 65	5.32	5.33	5.22	5.19	5.06	5.01
66- 70	5.73	5.73	5.61	5.58	5.45	5.37
71- 75	6.22	6.23	6.05	6.01	5.86	5.79
76- 80	6.74	6.75	6.56	6.52	6.35	6.31
81- 85	7.33	7.36	7.20	7.16	6.99	6.94
86- 90	8.23	8.27	8.09	8.04	7.89	7.84
91- 95	9.66	9.69	9.61	9.57	9.47	9.51
96-100	15.94	15.77	17.58	17.69	18.39	18.83
96	2.21	2.22	2.24	2.24	2.24	2.27
97	2.39	2.40	2.45	2.46	2.48	2.50
98	2.66	2.68	2.80	2.79	2.85	2.89
99	3.09	3.09	3.46	3.50	3.57	3.70
100	5.59	5.38	6.63	6.70	7.25	7.47

NOTE:
Columns: 1. CPS, Census allocation and BEA weights
2. CPS, BEA allocation
3. CPS-TM Match
4. CPS-TM Match, after audit
5. BEA Total Money Income
6. BEA Family Personal Income

TABLE A.7   Detailed Income Shares of Unrelated Individuals, 1964

(percent of aggregate income)

Percentiles	*(1)*	*(2)*	*(3)*	*(4)*	*(5)*	*(6)*
1- 5	−0.13	−0.15	−0.31	−0.20	−0.08	−0.02
6- 10	0.40	0.43	0.46	0.48	0.63	0.74
11- 15	0.94	0.94	0.99	0.99	1.02	1.12
16- 20	1.24	1.24	1.26	1.26	1.25	1.35
21- 25	1.45	1.47	1.48	1.46	1.46	1.57
26- 30	1.66	1.69	1.69	1.69	1.71	1.84
31- 35	1.89	1.90	1.94	1.93	1.96	2.13
36- 40	2.13	2.16	2.24	2.23	2.32	2.45
41- 45	2.46	2.51	2.64	2.64	2.72	2.82
46- 50	2.94	2.99	3.17	3.17	3.16	3.22
51- 55	3.41	3.46	3.74	3.75	3.69	3.71
56- 60	3.99	4.07	4.32	4.33	4.28	4.25
61- 65	4.76	4.88	4.99	5.00	4.89	4.81
66- 70	5.63	5.77	5.75	5.75	5.52	5.38
71- 75	6.57	6.68	6.54	6.52	6.15	5.98
76- 80	7.50	7.62	7.42	7.38	6.93	6.69
81- 85	8.49	8.59	8.49	8.43	7.90	7.65
86- 90	9.88	9.95	9.77	9.72	9.20	8.92
91- 95	11.99	12.12	11.67	11.61	11.21	11.23
96-100	22.80	21.68	21.75	21.86	24.08	24.16
96	2.73	2.76	2.68	2.68	2.63	2.67
97	3.01	3.07	2.92	2.91	2.88	2.91
98	3.41	3.43	3.25	3.26	3.30	3.29
99	4.41	4.27	4.03	4.05	4.15	4.15
100	9.24	8.15	8.87	8.96	11.12	11.14

NOTE:

Columns: 1. CPS, Census allocation and BEA weights
2. CPS, BEA allocation
3. CPS-TM Match
4. CPS-TM Match, after audit
5. BEA Total Money Income
6. BEA Family Personal Income

APPENDIX B

The CPS size distributions and mean amounts in Tables B.7-B.21 are based upon CPS income with BEA allocation of income to nonrespondents. Therefore these means are not consistent with those in Tables B.1-B.6 which incorporate the Census allocation to nonrespondents.

TABLE B.1   Mean Incomes of Families, by Age (1964)

		BEA Total Money Income		BEA Family Personal Income	
Age	CPS	Mean	Ratio to CPS	Mean	Ratio to CPS
14-24	$4,975	$5,575	1.121	$5,467	1.099
25-34	6,987	7,634	1.093	7,590	1.086
35-44	8,323	9,532	1.145	9,650	1.159
45-54	8,760	10,129	1.156	10,396	1.187
55-64	7,866	9,166	1.165	9,573	1.217
65 or over	5,269	6,940	1.317	7,461	1.416
All ages	7,438	8,631	1.160	8,838	1.188

TABLE B.2   Mean Incomes of Unrelated Individuals, by Age (1964)

		BEA Total Money Income		BEA Family Personal Income	
Age	CPS	Mean	Ratio to CPS	Mean	Ratio to CPS
14-24	$2,588	$2,860	1.105	$2,826	1.092
25-34	4,855	5,035	1.037	4,936	1.017
35-44	4,783	5,058	1.057	5,011	1.048
45-54	3,938	4,388	1.114	4,461	1.133
55-64	3,373	4,222	1.252	4,401	1.305
65 or over	2,101	3,218	1.532	3,486	1.659
All ages	3,122	3,874	1.241	4,006	1.283

TABLE B.3 Mean Incomes of Families, by Color, Sex, and Residence (1964)

	CPS	BEA Total Money Income		BEA Family Personal Income	
		Mean	Ratio to CPS	Mean	Ratio to CPS
Color:					
White	$7,732	$8,984	1.162	$9,208	1.191
Nonwhite	4,772	5,438	1.140	5,484	1.149
Ratio, nonwhite to white	.617	.605		.596	
Sex:					
Male	7,776	8,970	1.154	9,178	1.180
Female	4,468	5,721	1.280	5,921	1.325
Ratio, female to male	.575	.638		.645	
Residence:					
Nonfarm	7,634	8,743	1.145	8,932	1.170
Farm	4,670	7,012	1.501	7,491	1.604
Ratio, farm to nonfarm	.612	.802		.839	

TABLE B.4   Mean Incomes of Unrelated Individuals, by Color, Sex, and Residence (1964)

		BEA Total Money Income		BEA Family Personal Income	
	CPS	Mean	Ratio to CPS	Mean	Ratio to CPS
Color:					
White	$3,272	$4,103	1.254	$4,250	1.299
Nonwhite	2,205	2,421	1.098	2,463	1.117
Ratio, nonwhite to white	.674	.590		.580	
Sex:					
Male	4,080	4,595	1.126	4,671	1.145
Female	2,527	3,429	1.357	3,596	1.423
Ratio, female to male	.619	.746		.770	
Residence:					
Nonfarm	3,158	3,906	1.237	4,036	1.278
Farm	1,983	2,838	1.431	3,071	1.549
Ratio, farm to nonfarm	.628	.727		.761	

TABLE B.5 Mean Incomes of Families, by Work Experience of Head (1964)

Work Experience of Head	CPS	BEA Total Money Income		BEA Family Personal Income	
		Mean	Ratio to CPS	Mean	Ratio to CPS
Nonworker	$4,208	$5,639	1.340	$5,983	1.422
Full-time, full-year	8,739	9,933	1.137	10,121	1.158
Other	5,762	6,762	1.174	6,923	1.201
All families	7,438	8,631	1.160	8,838	1.188

TABLE B.6 Mean Incomes of Unrelated Individuals, by Work Experience (1964)

Work Experience of Head	CPS	BEA Total Money Income		BEA Family Personal Income	
		Mean	Ratio to CPS	Mean	Ratio to CPS
Nonworker	$1,760	$2,777	1.578	$2,995	1.702
Full-time, full-year	5,078	5,369	1.057	5,420	1.067
Other	2,355	3,375	1.433	3,494	1.484
All unrelated individuals	3,122	3,874	1.241	4,006	1.283

TABLE B.7   Size Distribution of Total Income of Consumer Units, Age of Head 14-24

A. Number of Units

Size of Total Income	Current Population Survey		Total Money Income		Family Personal Income	
	Number of Units (Thousands)	Percent	Number of Units (Thousands)	Percent	Number of Units (Thousands)	Percent
Loss	3	.07	2	.05	2	.05
Zero	209	5.09	177	4.31	60	1.46
$1-$1,249	442	10.77	295	7.19	397	9.67
1,250- 3,249	895	21.80	830	20.22	843	20.54
3,250- 5,749	1,492	36.35	1,436	34.98	1,511	36.81
5,750- 8,249	721	17.56	900	21.92	847	20.63
8,250-10,249	248	6.04	312	7.60	314	7.65
10,250-15,749	86	2.10	139	3.39	116	2.83
15,750-24,749	5	.12	10	.24	10	.24
24,750-49,749	5	.12	2	.05	2	.05
49,750-98,749	0	.00	2	.05	2	.05
98,750 or over	0	.00	0[a]	.00	0[a]	.00
Total	4,105	100.00	4,105	100.00	4,105	100.00

B. Dollar Totals

Size of Total Income	Current Population Survey		Total Money Income		Family Personal Income	
	Amount of Income (Millions of Dollars)	Percent	Amount of Income (Millions of Dollars)	Percent	Amount of Income (Millions of Dollars)	Percent
Loss	−1	−.01	0[b]	.00	0[b]	.00
Zero	0	.00	0	.00	0	.00
$1-$1,249	271	1.55	200	1.02	201	1.04
1,250- 3,249	2,118	12.14	2,002	10.20	2,009	10.43
3,250- 5,749	6,656	38.15	6,420	32.72	6,695	34.75
5,750- 8,249	4,883	27.98	6,102	31.10	5,740	29.80
8,250-10,249	2,240	12.84	2,839	14.47	2,826	14.67
10,250-15,749	986	5.65	1,655	8.44	1,386	7.19
15,750-24,749	89	.51	178	.91	181	.94
24,750-49,749	210	1.20	85	.43	85	.44
49,750-98,749	0	.00	120	.61	123	.64
98,750 or over	0	.00	19	.10	19	.10
Total	17,449	100.00	19,619	100.00	19,264	100.00
Mean amount (dollars)	4,251		4,779		4,693	

a Less than 500 units but greater than zero.
b Rounds to zero.

TABLE B.8   Size Distribution of Total Income of Consumer Units, Age of Head 25-34

A. Number of Units

Size of Total Income	Current Population Survey		Total Money Income		Family Personal Income	
	Number of Units (Thousands)	Percent	Number of Units (Thousands)	Percent	Number of Units (Thousands)	Percent
Loss	17	.17	10	.10	12	.12
Zero	114	1.11	72	.70	30	.29
$1–$1,249	355	3.45	175	1.70	203	1.97
1,250– 3,249	1,179	11.46	1,009	9.81	1,024	9.95
3,250– 5,749	2,784	27.06	2,485	24.16	2,616	25.43
5,750– 8,249	3,076	29.90	2,977	28.94	2,887	28.06
8,250–10,249	1,557	15.14	1,802	17.52	1,798	17.48
10,250–15,749	1,018	9.90	1,428	13.88	1,387	13.48
15,750–24,749	160	1.56	266	2.59	264	2.57
24,750–49,749	28	.27	54	.52	57	.55
49,750–98,749	0	.00	8	.08	9	.09
98,759 or over	0	.00	1	.01	1	.01
Total	10,287	100.00	10,287	100.00	10,287	100.00

B. Dollar Totals

Size of Total Income	Current Population Survey		Total Money Income		Family Personal Income	
	Amount of Income (Millions of Dollars)	Percent	Amount of Income (Millions of Dollars)	Percent	Amount of Income (Millions of Dollars)	Percent
Loss	−47	−.07	−46	−.06	−43	−.06
Zero	0	.00	0	.00	0	.00
$1–$1,249	282	.42	134	.18	130	.17
1,250– 3,249	2,826	4.18	2,412	3.18	2,455	3.26
3,250– 5,749	12,752	18.86	11,435	15.08	12,011	15.94
5,750– 8,249	21,370	31.61	20,713	27.31	20,027	26.58
8,250–10,249	14,339	21.21	16,556	21.83	16,464	21.85
10,250–15,749	12,358	18.28	17,266	22.77	16,789	22.29
15,750–24,749	2,887	4.27	4,925	6.49	4,915	6.52
24,750–49,749	847	1.25	1,792	2.36	1,885	2.50
49,750–98,749	0	.00	503	.66	550	.73
98,750 or over	0	.00	150	.20	153	.20
Total	67,613	100.00	75,839	100.00	75,335	100.00
Mean amount (dollars)	6,572		7,372		7,323	

TABLE B.9   Size Distribution of Total Income of Consumer Units, Age of Head 35-44

A. Number of Units

Size of Total Income	Current Population Survey		Total Money Income		Family Personal Income	
	Number of Units (Thousands)	Percent	Number of Units (Thousands)	Percent	Number of Units (Thousands)	Percent
Loss	32	.26	26	.21	28	.23
Zero	101	.82	86	.70	68	.55
$1-$1,249	403	3.28	254	2.07	245	1.99
1,250- 3,249	1,227	9.98	954	7.76	935	7.60
3,250- 5,749	2,554	20.77	2,283	18.56	2,354	19.14
5,750- 8,249	3,241	26.35	2,998	24.38	2,923	23.77
8,250-10,249	1,943	15.80	2,016	16.39	2,037	16.56
10,250-15,749	2,141	17.41	2,636	21.43	2,611	21.23
15,750-24,749	524	4.26	697	5.67	737	5.99
24,750-49,749	118	.96	292	2.37	300	2.44
49,750-98,749	11	.09	50	.41	55	.45
98,750 or over	2	.02	6	.05	7	.06
Total	12,299	100.00	12,299	100.00	12,299	100.00

B. Dollar Totals

Size of Total Income	Current Population Survey		Total Money Income		Family Personal Income	
	Amount of Income (Millions of Dollars)	Percent	Amount of Income (Millions of Dollars)	Percent	Amount of Income (Millions of Dollars)	Percent
Loss	−64	−.07	−38	−.03	−34	−.03
Zero	0	.00	0	.00	0	.00
$1-$1,249	285	.30	195	.17	182	.16
1,250- 3,249	2,789	2.89	2,249	2.01	2,190	1.93
3,250- 5,749	11,741	12.17	10,435	9.32	10,753	9.49
5,750- 8,249	22,567	23.40	20,971	18.72	20,399	18.01
8,250-10,249	17,989	18.65	18,575	16.58	18,791	16.59
10,250-15,749	26,483	27.46	32,494	29.01	32,126	28.36
15,750-24,749	9,997	10.36	13,320	11.89	14,150	12.49
24,750-49,749	3,578	3.71	9,377	8.37	9,821	8.67
49,750-98,749	795	.82	3,242	2.89	3,565	3.15
98,750 or over	292	.30	1,195	1.07	1,337	1.18
Total	96,452	100.00	112,015	100.00	113,279	100.00
Mean amount (dollars)	7,842		9,108		9,210	

TABLE B.10   Size Distribution of Total Income of Consumer Units, Age of Head 45-54

	A. Number of Units					
	Current Population Survey		*Total Money Income*		*Family Personal Income*	
Size of Total Income	*Number of Units (Thousands)*	*Percent*	*Number of Units (Thousands)*	*Percent*	*Number of Units (Thousands)*	*Percent*
Loss	56	.47	46	.39	50	.42
Zero	145	1.22	128	1.08	51	.43
$1-$1,249	596	5.02	329	2.77	363	3.06
1,250- 3,249	1,374	11.58	1,183	9.97	1,155	9.74
3,250- 5,749	2,255	19.01	2,077	17.51	2,031	17.12
5,750- 8,249	2,702	22.78	2,446	20.62	2,416	20.37
8,250-10,249	1,618	13.64	1,696	14.30	1,713	14.44
10,250-15,749	2,289	19.30	2,665	22.46	2,714	22.88
15,750-24,749	648	5.46	934	7.87	985	8.30
24,750-49,749	159	1.34	305	2.57	324	2.73
49,750-98,749	11	.09	44	.37	51	.43
98,750 or over	10	.08	9	.08	10	.08
Total	11,863	100.00	11,863	100.00	11,863	100.00

B. Dollar Totals

Size of Total Income	Current Population Survey		Total Money Income		Family Personal Income	
	Amount of Income (Millions of Dollars)	Percent	Amount of Income (Millions of Dollars)	Percent	Amount of Income (Millions of Dollars)	Percent
Loss	−163	−.17	−89	−.08	−83	−.07
Zero	0	.00	0	.00	0	.00
$1-$1,249	475	.50	266	.24	250	.22
1,250- 3,249	3,146	3.32	2,726	2.45	2,682	2.35
3,250- 5,749	10,407	10.97	9,509	8.55	9,305	8.15
5,750- 8,249	18,915	19.94	17,236	15.49	16,942	14.84
8,250-10,249	15,020	15.83	15,643	14.06	15,747	13.80
10,250-15,749	28,433	29.97	33,219	29.85	34,073	29.85
15,750-24,749	12,146	12.80	17,492	15.72	18,489	16.20
24,750-49,749	4,816	5.08	9,959	8.95	10,756	9.42
49,750-98,749	639	.67	2,814	2.53	3,304	2.89
98,750 or over	1,049	1.11	2,495	2.24	2,672	2.34
Total	94,882	100.00	111,270	100.00	114,135	100.00
Mean amount (dollars)	7,998		9,380		9,621	

TABLE B.11   Size Distribution of Total Income of Consumer Units, Age of Head 55-64

A. Number of Units

Size of Total Income	Current Population Survey — Number of Units (Thousands)	Percent	Total Money Income — Number of Units (Thousands)	Percent	Family Personal Income — Number of Units (Thousands)	Percent
Loss	69	.69	61	.61	53	.53
Zero	110	1.11	96	.96	31	.31
$1-$1,249	1,057	10.62	587	5.90	526	5.29
1,250- 3,249	1,824	18.33	1,658	16.66	1,616	16.24
3,250- 5,749	2,186	21.97	2,110	21.21	2,124	21.35
5,750- 8,249	1,928	19.38	1,910	19.20	1,842	18.51
8,250-10,249	1,014	10.19	1,160	11.66	1,215	12.21
10,250-15,749	1,245	12.51	1,525	15.33	1,611	16.19
15,750-24,749	380	3.82	596	5.99	663	6.66
24,750-49,749	107	1.08	184	1.85	195	1.96
49,750-98,749	21	.21	56	.56	65	.65
98,750 or over	10	.10	8	.08	11	.11
Total	9,950	100.00	9,950	100.00	9,950	100.00

B. Dollar Totals

Size of Total Income	Current Population Survey		Total Money Income		Family Personal Income	
	Amount of Income (Millions of Dollars)	Percent	Amount of Income (Millions of Dollars)	Percent	Amount of Income (Millions of Dollars)	Percent
Loss	−211	−.32	−184	−.23	−166	−.20
Zero	0	.00	0	.00	0	.00
$1-$1,249	817	1.24	474	.60	399	.48
1,250- 3,249	4,123	6.27	3,781	4.79	3,700	4.49
3,250- 5,749	9,753	14.83	9,399	11.91	9,375	11.38
5,750- 8,249	13,354	20.31	13,278	16.83	12,754	15.48
8,250-10,249	9,381	14.27	10,689	13.55	11,226	13.63
10,250-15,749	15,589	23.71	18,935	24.00	19,949	24.22
15,750-24,749	7,081	10.77	11,166	14.15	12,564	15.25
24,750-49,749	3,343	5.08	6,184	7.84	6,527	7.92
49,750-98,749	1,385	2.11	3,569	4.52	4,132	5.02
98,750 or over	1,138	1.73	1,606	2.04	1,921	2.33
Total	65,753	100.00	78,897	100.00	82,381	100.00
Mean amount (dollars)	6,608		7,929		8,279	

TABLE B.12   Size Distribution of Total Income of Consumer Units, Age of Head 65 or Over

	A. Number of Units					
	Current Population Survey		Total Money Income		Family Personal Income	
Size of Total Income	Number of Units (Thousands)	Percent	Number of Units (Thousands)	Percent	Number of Units (Thousands)	Percent
Loss	25	.22	15	.13	14	.12
Zero	137	1.21	87	.77	12	.11
$1-$1,249	2,709	23.91	1,930	17.03	1,569	13.85
1,250- 3,249	4,400	38.83	3,728	32.90	3,746	33.06
3,250- 5,749	1,964	17.33	2,328	20.55	2,485	21.93
5,750- 8,249	914	8.07	1,268	11.19	1,313	11.59
8,250-10,249	442	3.90	667	5.89	698	6.16
10,250-15,749	450	3.97	748	6.60	873	7.70
15,750-24,749	181	1.60	321	2.83	354	3.12
24,750-49,749	96	.85	180	1.59	200	1.77
49,750-98,749	12	.11	46	.41	51	.45
98,750 or over	2	.02	14	.12	17	.15
Total	11,331	100.00	11,331	100.00	11,331	100.00

B. Dollar Totals

Size of Total Income	Current Population Survey Amount of Income (Millions of Dollars)	Percent	Total Money Income Amount of Income (Millions of Dollars)	Percent	Family Personal Income Amount of Income (Millions of Dollars)	Percent
Loss	-45	-.10	-82	-.13	-72	-.11
Zero	0	.00	0	.00	0	.00
$1-$1,249	2,314	5.33	1,684	2.74	1,372	2.07
1,250- 3,249	9,208	21.23	7,785	12.67	7,951	12.01
3,250- 5,749	8,523	19.65	10,231	16.65	10,841	16.38
5,750- 8,249	6,270	14.45	8,728	14.20	8,952	13.52
8,250-10,249	4,087	9.42	6,115	9.95	6,429	9.71
10,250-15,749	5,603	12.92	9,313	15.15	10,798	16.31
15,750-24,749	3,341	7.70	6,071	9.88	6,811	10.29
24,750-49,749	3,023	6.97	5,783	9.41	6,493	9.81
49,750-98,749	820	1.89	3,094	5.03	3,567	5.39
98,750 or over	233	.54	2,742	4.46	3,064	4.63
Total	43,376	100.00	61,464	100.00	66,204	100.00
Mean amount (dollars)	3,828		5,424		5,843	

TABLE B.13   Size of Distribution of Total Income of Consumer Units, White

A. Number of Units

Size of Total Income	Current Population Survey		Total Money Income		Family Personal Income	
	Number of Units (Thousands)	Percent	Number of Units (Thousands)	Percent	Number of Units (Thousands)	Percent
Loss	186	.35	152	.28	148	.28
Zero	695	1.30	554	1.04	221	.41
$1-$1,249	4,330	8.10	2,760	5.16	2,573	4.81
1,250- 3,249	8,967	16.78	7,578	14.18	7,458	13.95
3,250- 5,749	11,623	21.75	10,820	20.24	11,174	20.91
5,750- 8,249	11,761	22.00	11,548	21.61	11,295	21.13
8,250-10,249	6,510	12.18	7,285	13.63	7,356	13.76
10,250-15,749	6,949	13.00	8,764	16.40	8,959	16.76
15,750-24,749	1,844	3.45	2,746	5.14	2,933	5.49
24,750-49,749	506	.95	998	1.87	1,056	1.98
49,750-98,749	56	.10	204	.38	230	.43
98,750 or over	22	.04	39	.07	45	.08
Total	53,448	100.00	53,448	100.00	53,448	100.00

B. Dollar Totals

Size of Total Income	Current Population Survey		Total Money Income		Family Personal Income	
	Amount of Income (Millions of Dollars)	Percent	Amount of Income (Millions of Dollars)	Percent	Amount of Income (Millions of Dollars)	Percent
Loss	−504	−.14	−415	−.10	−376	−.09
Zero	0	.00	0	.00	0	.00
$1-$1,249	3,478	.97	2,282	.53	1,955	.44
1,250- 3,249	19,875	5.52	16,932	3.94	16,782	3.81
3,250- 5,749	52,805	14.67	49,113	11.44	50,494	11.46
5,750- 8,249	81,771	22.72	80,497	18.75	78,452	17.81
8,250-10,249	60,210	16.73	67,037	15.61	67,629	15.35
10,250-15,749	86,076	23.91	108,310	25.23	110,895	25.17
15,750-24,749	34,523	9.59	51,700	12.04	55,605	12.62
24,750-49,749	15,556	4.32	32,556	7.58	34,935	7.93
49,750-98,749	3,640	1.01	13,205	3.08	15,096	3.43
98,750 or over	2,502	.70	8,108	1.89	9,061	2.06
Total	359,930	100.00	429,323	100.00	440,526	100.00
Mean amount (dollars)	6,734		8,032		8,242	

TABLE B.14 Size Distribution of Total Income of Consumer Units, Nonwhite

A. Number of Units

Size of Total Income	Current Population Survey		Total Money Income		Family Personal Income	
	Number of Units (Thousands)	Percent	Number of Units (Thousands)	Percent	Number of Units (Thousands)	Percent
Loss	16	.25	9	.14	11	.17
Zero	121	1.89	91	1.42	31	.49
$1-$1,249	1,232	19.29	809	12.66	729	11.41
1,250- 3,249	1,932	30.24	1,784	27.93	1,862	29.15
3,250- 5,749	1,612	25.23	1,899	29.73	1,947	30.48
5,750- 8,249	820	12.84	951	14.89	934	14.62
8,250-10,249	312	4.88	368	5.76	419	6.56
10,250-15,749	280	4.38	376	5.89	352	5.51
15,750-24,749	54	.85	78	1.22	81	1.27
24,750-49,749	7	.11	20	.31	20	.31
49,750-98,749	0	.00	2	.03	2	.03
98,750 or over	2	.03	0[a]	.00	0[a]	.00
Total	6,388	100.00	6,388	100.00	6,388	100.00

B. Dollar Totals

Size of Total Income	Current Population Survey		Total Money Income		Family Personal Income	
	Amount of Income (Millions of Dollars)	Percent	Amount of Income (Millions of Dollars)	Percent	Amount of Income (Millions of Dollars)	Percent
Loss	−30	−.12	−27	−.09	−25	−.08
Zero	0	.00	0	.00	0	.00
$1-$1,249	965	3.77	672	2.26	579	1.93
1,250- 3,249	4,336	16.94	4,024	13.51	4,204	13.98
3,250- 5,749	7,027	27.45	8,315	27.92	8,486	28.22
5,750- 8,249	5,588	21.83	6,533	21.94	6,361	21.15
8,250-10,249	2,846	11.12	3,381	11.35	3,854	12.82
10,250-15,749	3,376	13.19	4,570	15.34	4,227	14.06
15,750-24,749	1,018	3.98	1,453	4.88	1,503	5.00
24,750-49,749	260	1.02	624	2.10	633	2.11
49,750-98,749	0	.00	138	.46	144	.48
98,750 or over	211	.82	100	.34	105	.35
Total	25,596	100.00	29,783	100.00	30,071	100.00
Mean amount (dollars)	4,007		4,663		4,708	

a Less than 500 units but greater than zero.

TABLE B.15 Size Distribution of Total Income of Consumer Units, Male Head

A. Number of Units

Size of Total Income	Current Population Survey Number of Units (Thousands)	Percent	Total Money Income Number of Units (Thousands)	Percent	Family Personal Income Number of Units (Thousands)	Percent
Loss	188	.40	145	.31	146	.31
Zero	227	.48	189	.40	59	.12
$1-$1,249	2,275	4.80	1,331	2.81	1,199	2.53
1,250- 3,249	7,018	14.81	5,751	12.13	5,497	11.60
3,250- 5,749	10,503	22.16	9,583	20.22	9,878	20.84
5,750- 8,249	11,443	24.14	11,005	23.22	10,775	22.74
8,250-10,249	6,469	13.65	7,078	14.93	7,163	15.11
10,250-15,749	6,874	14.50	8,470	17.87	8,588	18.12
15,750-24,749	1,828	3.86	2,671	5.64	2,832	5.98
24,750-49,749	492	1.04	942	1.99	995	2.10
49,750-98,749	56	.12	194	.41	220	.46
98,750 or over	22	.05	36	.08	42	.09
Total	47,393	100.00	47,393	100.00	47,393	100.00

B. Dollar Totals

Size of Total Income	Current Population Survey		Total Money Income		Family Personal Income	
	Amount of Income (Millions of Dollars)	Percent	Amount of Income (Millions of Dollars)	Percent	Amount of Income (Millions of Dollars)	Percent
Loss	−488	−.14	−429	−.11	−391	−.09
Zero	0	.00	0	.00	0	.00
$1–$1,249	1,846	.53	1,082	.27	914	.22
1,250– 3,249	15,973	4.63	13,344	3.29	12,865	3.11
3,250– 5,749	47,797	13.85	43,603	10.77	44,721	10.80
5,750– 8,249	79,571	23.05	76,827	18.97	74,939	18.09
8,250–10,249	59,792	17.32	65,149	16.09	65,869	15.90
10,250–15,749	85,080	24.65	104,634	25.83	106,221	25.64
15,750–24,749	34,259	9.92	50,311	12.42	53,747	12.97
24,750–49,749	15,237	4.41	30,719	7.58	32,860	7.93
49,750–98,749	3,640	1.05	12,553	3.10	14,386	3.47
98,750 or over	2,479	.72	7,223	1.78	8,128	1.96
Total	345,184	100.00	405,014	100.00	414,259	100.00
Mean amount (dollars)	7,283		8,546		8,741	

TABLE B.16   Size Distribution of Total Income of Consumer Units, Female Head

A. Number of Units

Size of Total Income	Current Population Survey		Total Money Income		Family Personal Income	
	Number of Units (Thousands)	Percent	Number of Units (Thousands)	Percent	Number of Units (Thousands)	Percent
Loss	14	.11	16	.13	13	.10
Zero	590	4.74	457	3.67	193	1.55
$1-$1,249	3,287	26.42	2,239	17.99	2,103	16.90
1,250- 3,249	3,880	31.18	3,611	29.02	3,823	30.72
3,250- 5,749	2,733	21.96	3,136	25.20	3,243	26.06
5,750- 8,249	1,138	9.15	1,494	12.01	1,454	11.69
8,250-10,249	353	2.84	576	4.63	612	4.92
10,250-15,749	355	2.85	669	5.38	723	5.81
15,750-24,749	71	.57	153	1.23	181	1.45
24,750-49,749	21	.17	75	.60	81	.65
49,750-98,749	0	.00	12	.10	13	.10
98,750 or over	2	.02	3	.02	3	.02
Total	12,443	100.00	12,443	100.00	12,443	100.00

B. Dollar Totals

Size of Total Income	Current Population Survey		Total Money Income		Family Personal Income	
	Amount of Income (Millions of Dollars)	Percent	Amount of Income (Millions of Dollars)	Percent	Amount of Income (Millions of Dollars)	Percent
Loss	−46	−.11	−13	−.02	−11	−.02
Zero	0	.00	0	.00	0	.00
$1-$1,249	2,597	6.44	1,872	3.46	1,620	2.88
1,250- 3,249	8,238	20.42	7,612	14.07	8,121	14.41
3,250- 5,749	12,035	29.83	13,825	25.56	14,258	25.31
5,750- 8,249	7,789	19.31	10,203	18.86	9,874	17.53
8,250-10,249	3,265	8.09	5,269	9.74	5,614	9.96
10,250-15,749	4,372	10.84	8,247	15.25	8,901	15.80
15,750-24,749	1,282	3.18	2,841	5.25	3,361	5.97
24,750-49,749	579	1.44	2,461	4.55	2,707	4.80
49,750-98,749	0	.00	790	1.46	854	1.52
98,750 or over	233	.58	985	1.82	1,038	1.84
Total	40,342	100.00	54,092	100.00	56,338	100.00
Mean amount (dollars)	3,242		4,347		4,528	

TABLE B.17 Size Distribution of Total Income of Consumer Units, Nonfarm Residence

	Current Population Survey		A. Number of Units Total Money Income		Family Personal Income	
Size of Total Income	Number of Units (Thousands)	Percent	Number of Units (Thousands)	Percent	Number of Units (Thousands)	Percent
Loss	107	.19	98	.17	109	.19
Zero	797	1.41	626	1.11	252	.45
$1-$1,249	4,980	8.83	3,316	5.88	3,094	5.49
1,250- 3,249	9,808	17.40	8,578	15.22	8,589	15.24
3,250- 5,749	12,480	22.14	11,856	21.03	12,251	21.73
5,750- 8,249	12,110	21.48	11,940	21.18	11,629	20.63
8,250-10,249	6,630	11.76	7,345	13.03	7,446	13.21
10,250-15,749	7,045	12.50	8,741	15.51	8,868	15.73
15,750-24,749	1,840	3.26	2,675	4.75	2,854	5.06
24,750-49,749	499	.89	964	1.71	1,018	1.81
49,750-98,749	56	.10	198	.35	221	.39
98,750 or over	24	.04	38	.07	44	.08
Total	56,375	100.00	56,375	100.00	56,375	100.00

B. Dollar Totals

Size of Total Income	Current Population Survey		Total Money Income		Family Personal Income	
	Amount of Income (Millions of Dollars)	Percent	Amount of Income (Millions of Dollars)	Percent	Amount of Income (Millions of Dollars)	Percent
Loss	−308	−.08	−347	−.08	−324	−.07
Zero	0	.00	0	.00	0	.00
$1-$1,249	4,022	1.08	2,765	.63	2,382	.53
1,250- 3,249	21,789	5.88	19,128	4.38	19,256	4.31
3,250- 5,749	56,519	15.24	53,624	12.29	55,136	12.35
5,750- 8,249	84,146	22.69	83,175	19.06	80,670	18.08
8,250-10,249	61,269	16.52	67,611	15.49	68,472	15.34
10,250-15,749	87,194	23.52	107,950	24.74	109,600	24.56
15,750-24,749	34,431	9.29	50,310	11.53	54,033	12.11
24,750-49,749	15,377	4.15	31,454	7.21	33,716	7.55
49,750-98,749	3,640	.98	12,815	2.94	14,528	3.26
98,750 or over	2,713	.73	7,887	1.81	8,824	1.98
Total	370,790	100.00	436,370	100.00	446,293	100.00
Mean amount (dollars)	6,577		7,740		7,916	

TABLE B.18   Size Distribution of Total Income of Consumer Units, Farm Residence

A. Number of Units

Size of Total Income	Current Population Survey		Total Money Income		Family Personal Income	
	Number of Units (Thousands)	Percent	Number of Units (Thousands)	Percent	Number of Units (Thousands)	Percent
Loss	95	2.74	62	1.79	50	1.44
Zero	19	.55	19	.55	0	.00
$1-$1,249	582	16.82	254	7.34	209	6.04
1,250- 3,249	1,090	31.49	785	22.68	730	21.09
3,250- 5,749	756	21.84	863	24.93	870	25.14
5,750- 8,249	471	13.61	560	16.18	600	17.34
8,250-10,249	192	5.55	308	8.90	329	9.51
10,250-15,749	184	5.32	399	11.53	444	12.83
15,750-24,749	59	1.70	149	4.31	159	4.59
24,750-49,749	14	.40	53	1.53	57	1.65
49,750-98,749	0	.00	8	.23	12	.35
98,750 or over	0	.00	1	.03	1	.03
Total	3,461	100.00	3,461	100.00	3,461	100.00

B. Dollar Totals

Size of Total Income	Current Population Survey		Total Money Income		Family Personal Income	
	Amount of Income (Millions of Dollars)	Percent	Amount of Income (Millions of Dollars)	Percent	Amount of Income (Millions of Dollars)	Percent
Loss	−226	−1.53	−95	−.42	−78	−.32
Zero	0	.00	0	.00	0	.00
$1- 1,249	421	2.86	190	.84	152	.63
1,250- 3,249	2,421	16.43	1,828	8.04	1,731	7.12
3,250- 5,749	3,313	22.48	3,804	16.73	3,843	15.81
5,750- 8,249	3,213	21.80	3,855	16.96	4,143	17.05
8,250-10,249	1,787	12.13	2,807	12.35	3,011	12.39
10,250-15,749	2,259	15.33	4,931	21.69	5,521	22.72
15,750-24,749	1,110	7.53	2,843	12.50	3,076	12.66
24,750-49,749	440	2.99	1,726	7.59	1,851	7.62
49,750-98,749	0	.00	527	2.32	713	2.93
98,750 or over	0	.00	321	1.41	342	1.41
Total	14,736	100.00	22,736	100.00	24,304	100.00
Mean amount (dollars)	4,258		6,570		7,023	

TABLE B.19   Size Distribution of Total Income of Consumer Units, Nonworker

			A. Number of Units			
	Current Population Survey		*Total Money Income*		*Family Personal Income*	
Size of Total Income	*Number of Units (Thousands)*	*Percent*	*Number of Units (Thousands)*	*Percent*	*Number of Units (Thousands)*	*Percent*
Loss	14	.11	13	.11	26	.21
Zero	530	4.34	385	3.16	129	1.06
$1-$1,249	3,181	26.07	2,241	18.37	2,066	16.93
1,250- 3,249	4,542	37.22	3,960	32.45	4,045	33.15
3,250- 5,749	2,181	17.87	2,641	21.64	2,774	22.73
5,750- 8,249	885	7.25	1,311	10.74	1,332	10.92
8,250-10,249	395	3.24	622	5.10	673	5.52
10,250-15,749	359	2.94	698	5.72	773	6.34
15,750-24,749	78	.64	203	1.66	245	2.01
24,750-49,749	33	.27	94	.77	101	.83
49,750-98,749	2	.02	27	.22	29	.24
98,750 or over	2	.02	7	.06	9	.07
Total	12,202	100.00	12,202	100.00	12,202	100.00

B. Dollar Totals

Size of Total Income	Current Population Survey		Total Money Income		Family Personal Income	
	Amount of Income (Millions of Dollars)	Percent	Amount of Income (Millions of Dollars)	Percent	Amount of Income (Millions of Dollars)	Percent
Loss	-25	-.06	-85	-.15	-80	-.14
Zero	0	.00	0	.00	0	.00
$1-$1,249	2,642	6.86	1,916	3.46	1,639	2.78
1,250- 3,249	9,507	24.69	8,187	14.77	8,485	14.37
3,250- 5,749	9,439	24.51	11,560	20.85	12,069	20.44
5,750- 8,249	6,062	15.74	8,987	16.21	9,049	15.33
8,250-10,249	3,622	9.41	5,713	10.31	6,188	10.48
10,250-15,749	4,375	11.36	8,677	15.65	9,570	16.21
15,750-24,749	1,480	3.84	3,793	6.84	4,661	7.90
24,750-49,749	1,061	2.76	2,976	5.37	3,296	5.58
49,750-98,749	117	.30	1,840	3.32	2,098	3.55
98,750 or over	233	.61	1,869	3.37	2,061	3.49
Total	38,511	100.00	55,431	100.00	59,035	100.00
Mean amount (dollars)	3,156		4,543		4,838	

TABLE B.20 Size Distribution of Total Income of Consumer Units, Full-Time, Full-Year Worker

A. Number of Units

Size of Total Income	Current Population Survey		Total Money Income		Family Personal Income	
	Number of Units (Thousands)	Percent	Number of Units (Thousands)	Percent	Number of Units (Thousands)	Percent
Loss	152	.43	115	.33	100	.28
Zero	139	.39	132	.37	76	.22
$1-$1,249	835	2.37	462	1.31	423	1.20
1,250- 3,249	2,934	8.32	2,407	6.83	2,311	6.56
3,250- 5,749	7,848	22.27	6,703	19.02	6,922	19.64
5,750- 8,249	9,656	27.40	8,982	25.48	8,690	24.65
8,250-10,249	5,435	15.42	5,861	16.63	5,902	16.74
10,250-15,749	6,107	17.33	7,259	20.59	7,297	20.70
15,750-24,749	1,640	4.65	2,323	6.59	2,455	6.97
24,750-49,749	425	1.21	808	2.29	850	2.41
49,750-98,749	53	.15	164	.47	186	.53
98,750 or over	22	.06	29	.08	34	.10
Total	35,247	100.00	35,247	100.00	35,247	100.00

B. Dollar Totals

Size of Total Income	Current Population Survey		Total Money Income		Family Personal Income	
	Amount of Income (Millions of Dollars)	Percent	Amount of Income (Millions of Dollars)	Percent	Amount of Income (Millions of Dollars)	Percent
Loss	−402	−.14	−221	−.07	−196	−.06
Zero	0	.00	0	.00	0	.00
$1-$1,249	648	.23	353	.11	291	.09
1,250- 3,249	7,077	2.47	5,896	1.79	5,671	1.69
3,250- 5,749	36,207	12.63	30,897	9.36	31,798	9.46
5,750- 8,249	67,236	23.45	62,808	19.04	60,599	18.04
8,250-10,249	50,350	17.56	53,944	16.35	54,282	16.16
10,250-15,749	75,780	26.43	89,810	27.22	90,432	26.92
15,750-24,749	30,687	10.70	43,698	13.24	46,435	13.82
24,750-49,749	13,103	4.57	26,410	8.00	28,130	8.37
49,750-98,749	3,523	1.23	10,588	3.21	12,047	3.59
98,750 or over	2,479	.86	5,762	1.75	6,482	1.93
Total	286,688	100.00	329,946	100.00	335,971	100.00
Mean amount (dollars)	8,134		9,361		9,532	

TABLE B.21   Size Distribution of Total Income of Consumer Units, Other Work Experience

| | A. Number of Units | | | | | |
| | Current Population Survey | | Total Money Income | | Family Personal Income | |
Size of Total Income	Number of Units (Thousands)	Percent	Number of Units (Thousands)	Percent	Number of Units (Thousands)	Percent
Loss	36	.29	33	.27	33	.27
Zero	147	1.19	128	1.03	46	.37
$1-$1,249	1,546	12.48	867	7.00	814	6.57
1,250- 3,249	3,422	27.63	2,995	24.18	2,963	23.92
3,250- 5,749	3,206	25.88	3,375	27.25	3,426	27.66
5,750- 8,249	2,040	16.47	2,206	17.81	2,206	17.81
8,250-10,249	991	8.00	1,170	9.45	1,199	9.68
10,250-15,749	762	6.15	1,182	9.54	1,241	10.02
15,750-24,749	181	1.46	297	2.40	314	2.53
24,750-49,749	56	.45	116	.94	125	1.01
49,750-98,749	0	.00	15	.12	17	.14
98,750 or over	0	.00	3	.02	3	.02
Total	12,387	100.00	12,387	100.00	12,387	100.00

B. Dollar Totals

Size of Total Income	Current Population Survey		Total Money Income		Family Personal Income	
	Amount of Income (Millions of Dollars)	Percent	Amount of Income (Millions of Dollars)	Percent	Amount of Income (Millions of Dollars)	Percent
Loss	−106	−.18	−136	−.18	−125	−.17
Zero	0	.00	0	.00	0	.00
$1–$1,249	1,153	1.91	685	.93	604	.80
1,250– 3,249	7,627	12.64	6,873	9.32	6,830	9.04
3,250– 5,749	14,186	23.52	14,971	20.31	15,113	19.99
5,750– 8,249	14,061	23.31	15,235	20.66	15,164	20.06
8,250–10,249	9,084	15.06	10,761	14.60	11,013	14.57
10,250–15,749	9,297	15.41	14,394	19.52	15,120	20.00
15,750–24,749	3,373	5.59	5,661	7.68	6,014	7.96
24,750–49,749	1,653	2.74	3,794	5.15	4,142	5.48
49,750–98,749	0	.00	914	1.24	1,095	1.45
98,750 or over	0	.00	577	.78	623	.82
Total	60,327	100.00	73,729	100.00	75,591	100.00
Mean amount (dollars)	4,870		5,952		6,102	

Percent of total income

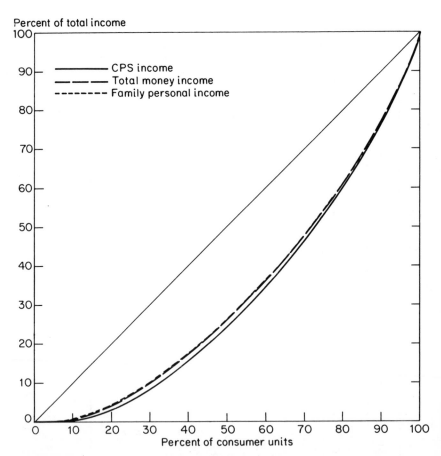

CHART B.1: Lorenz Curve of All Consumer Units: Age of Head 14-24

Percent of total income

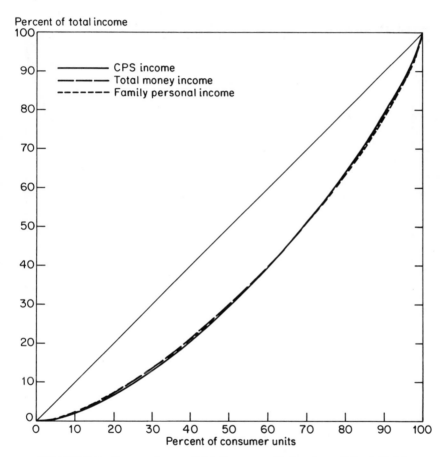

CHART B.2: Lorenz Curve of All Consumer Units: Age of Head 25-34

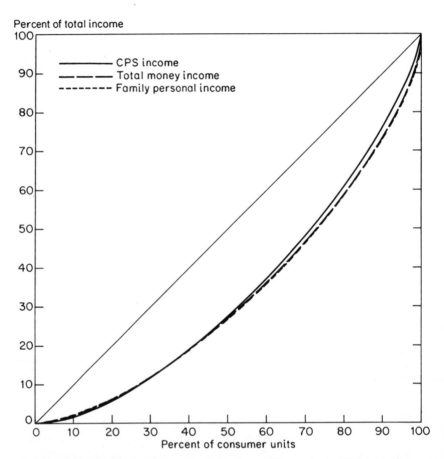

CHART B.3: Lorenz Curve of All Consumer Units: Age of Head 35-44

Percent of total income

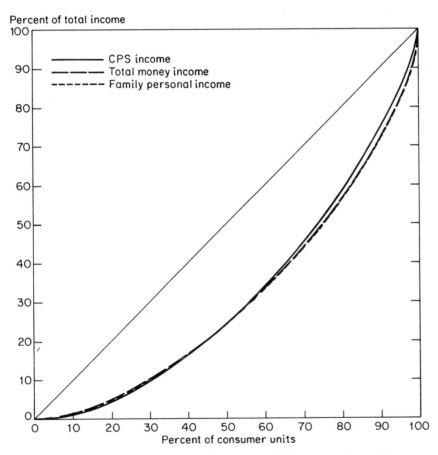

CHART B.4: Lorenz Curve of All Consumer Units: Age of Head 45-54

Percent of total income

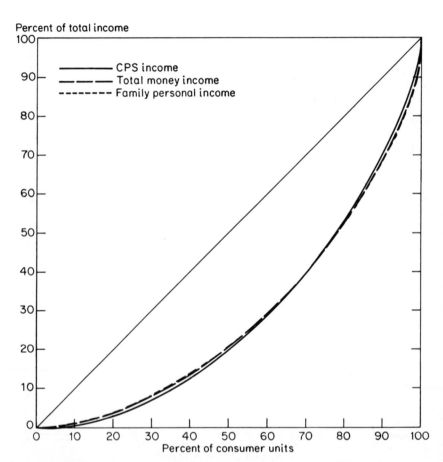

CHART B.5: Lorenz Curve of All Consumer Units: Age of Head 55-64

Percent of total income

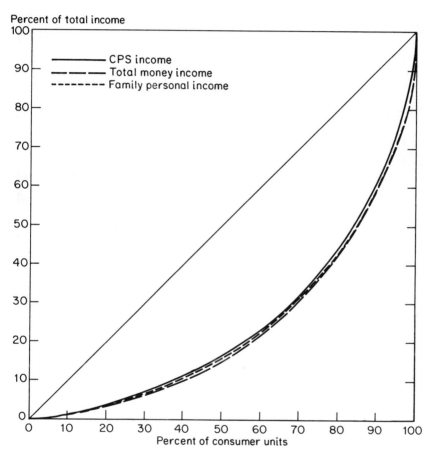

CHART B.6: Lorenz Curve of All Consumer Units: Age of Head 65 or Over

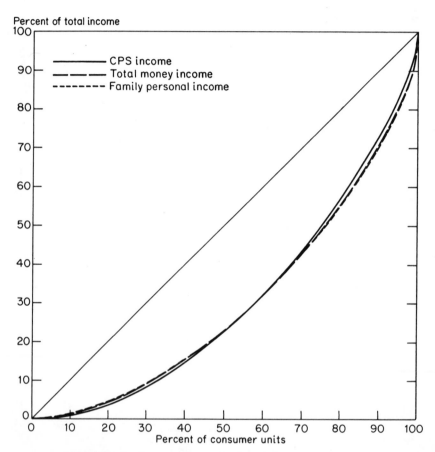

Percent of total income

CPS income
Total money income
Family personal income

Percent of consumer units

CHART B.7: Lorenz Curve of All Consumer Units: White

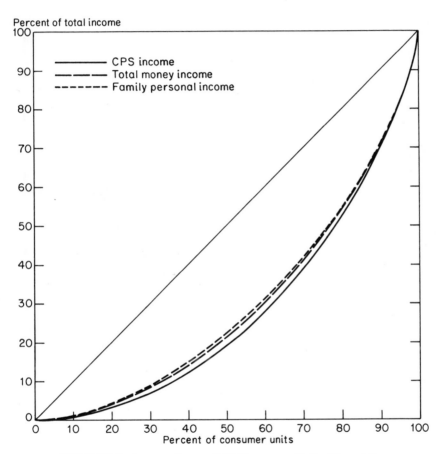

Percent of total income

CPS income
Total money income
Family personal income

Percent of consumer units

CHART B.8: Lorenz Curve of All Consumer Units: Nonwhite

Percent of total income

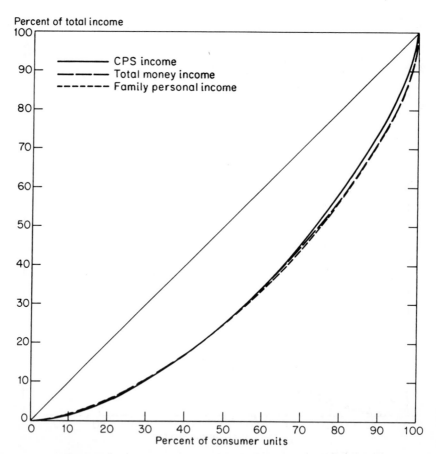

CHART B.9: Lorenz Curve of All Consumer Units: Males Head

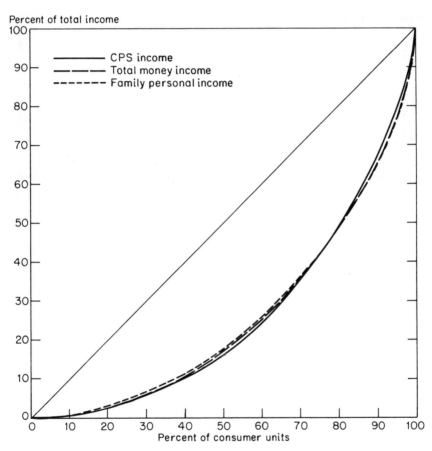

Percent of total income

Percent of consumer units

CHART B.10: Lorenz Curve of All Consumer Units: Female Head

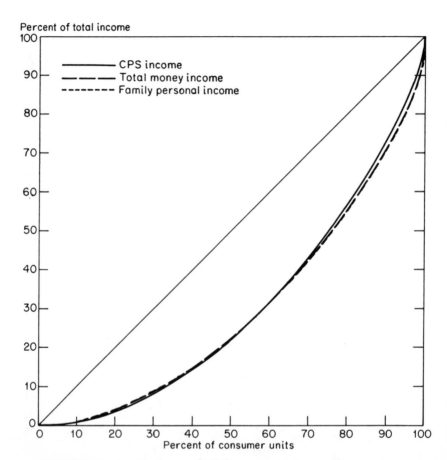

CHART B.11: Lorenz Curve of All Consumer Units: Nonfarm Residence

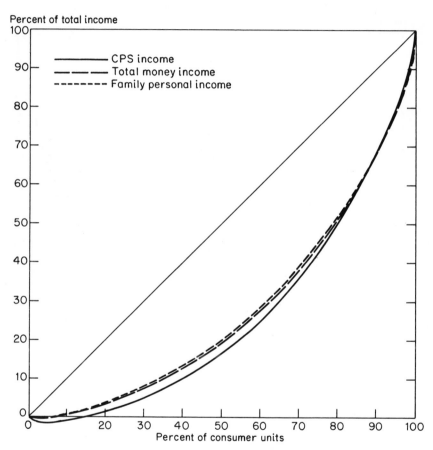

CHART B.12: Lorenz Curve of All Consumer Units: Farm Residence

Percent of total income

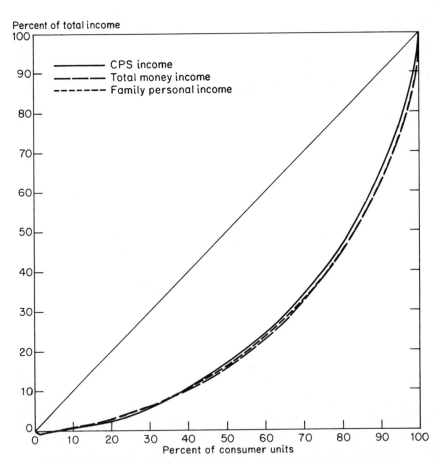

CHART B.13: Lorenz Curve of All Consumer Units: Nonworker

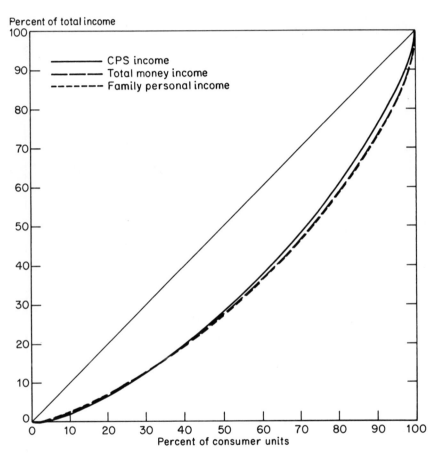

CHART B.14: Lorenz Curve of All Consumer Units: Full-Time, Full-Year Worker

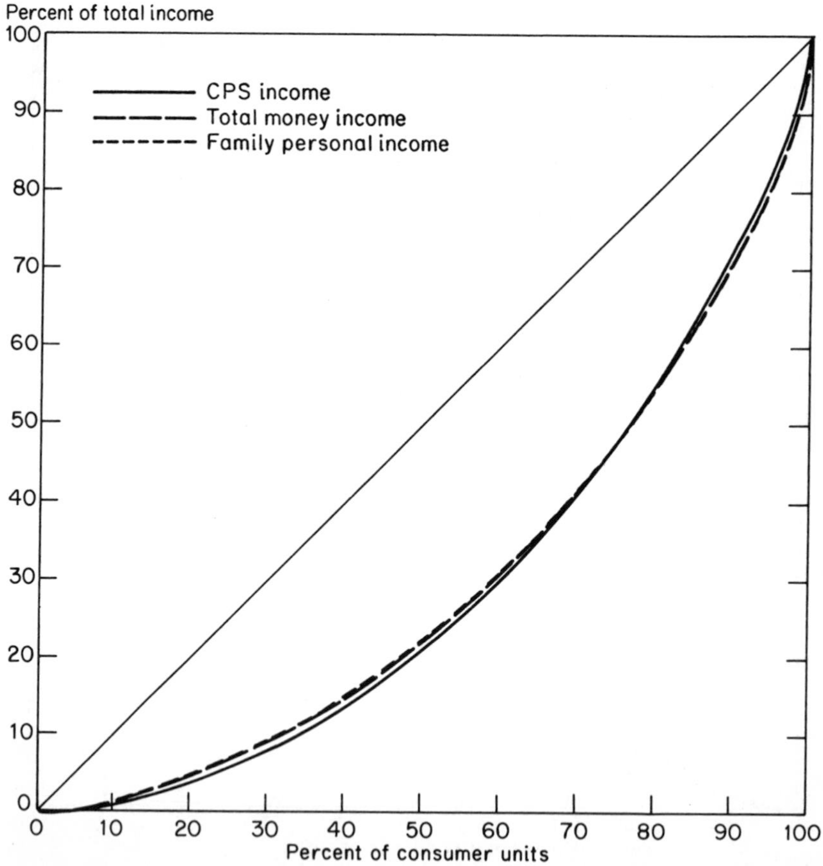

Percent of total income
100
90
80
70
60
50
40
30
20
10
0
CPS income
Total money income
Family personal income
0
10
20
30
40
50
60
70
80
90
100
Percent of consumer units

CHART B.15: Lorenz Curve of All Consumer Units: Other Work Experience

Index of Names and Titles

Aaron, Henry J., 43, 67n

Abel-Smith, Brian, 280n

"The accounting period and the distribution of income" (Hanna), 152n, 215n

"Accrued capital gains, personal income and saving in the United States, 1948-1964" (Bhatia), 124n, 129n

"Adjusted family income: concept and derivation" (Okner), 48n

Aitchison, J., 210n, 303

Alternative approaches to capital gains taxation (David), 48n, 124n, 135n

"The anatomy of income distribution" (Morgan), 159n

Andrews, Frank, 168n, 182, 189n

"Aspects of the dynamics of consumer behavior" (Vandome), 214n, 216n

"Aspects of the dynamics of consumer behavior: income and savings over two years from the 1954 Reinterview Savings Survey" (Vandome), 154n, 159n

Atkinson, A. B., 6-7, 277n, 301, 321-24, 327, 328

Atkinson, Anthony A., 81, 95-96, 99, 114

Bailey, Martin J., 48n

Baker, Elizabeth Lau, 218n

Bauman, Richard, 124n

Benus, Jacob, 5, 121-22, 210n, 225, 227, 228

Bhatia, Kul, 124, 129n

Blinder, A., 301n

Boulding, Kenneth E., 3, 11, 25n, 323n

Boutwell, G. S., 268n

Bowen, William G., 171n

Bowman, Raymond, 2

Brazer, Harvey E., 214n

Bretz, Judith, 7-8, 377

Bristol, R. B., 228

Brittain, John A., 46n, 299

The Brookings Institution, 45n

Brown, J. A. C., 210n, 303

Budd, Edward C., 8, 115, 449, 458n, 459n, 494n

"The burden of direct taxes paid by income classes" (Yaple), 330n

Burr, I. W., 304n

Calvert, Staunton, 331

Campion, H., 277, 288n, 314

"Capital gains and income taxation" (Bailey), 48n

Carter, Charles, 326

"The case for a negative income tax device" (Rolph), 77n

Census of population: 1860 (U.S. Census Bureau), 237n

Census of population: 1970 (U.S. Census Bureau), 351n

Champernowne, D. G., 299, 304

Characteristics of low income population 1970 (U.S. Census Bureau), 80n

"Civil War income tax" (Hill), 268n

Clay, H., 277, 278

Cohen, Wilbur J., 214n

"A cohort analysis of changes in the distribution of wealth" (Lansing and Sonquist), 259n

"Comments" (Budd), 458n

Compendium on the economics of federal subsidy programs (U.S. Congress. Joint Economic Committee), 126n

"Computer graphics as an aid to learning" (Hammond), 18n

"The concentration of personal wealth in America, 1969" (Smith), 329n

"The concentration of personal wealth, 1922-69" (Smith and Franklin), 329n

"The concentration of wealth" (Holmes), 330n

"Constructing a new data base from existing microdata sets: the 1966 MERGE file" (Okner), 47n-48n

Consumer durables and installment debt: a study of American households (Hendricks, Youmans, and Keller), 212n

Consumer response to income increases (Katona and Mueller), 212n

Coughlin, T. A., 333n

"Counting the poor: another look at the poverty profile" (Orshansky), 495n

"The creation of a microdata file for estimating the size distribution of income" (Budd), 458n, 459n

Dales, Sophie R., 38n

Dalton, H., 95

Daniels, G. W., 277, 288n

David, Martin H., 5, 6, 48n, 121, 124, 125n, 135n, 141n, 214n, 225, 227, 228

"Deaths from selected causes by marital status, by age and sex: United States, 1940" (Moriyama), 334n

Democracy in Jonesville (Warner et al.), 241n, 246n

The design of economic accounts (Ruggles and Ruggles), 37n

Dictionary of occupational titles (U.S. Labor Department), 342-44, 361

"Distribution of federal and state income taxes by income classes" (Pechman), 55n

"The distribution of financial assets" (Smith, Franklin, and Wion), 329n

"The distribution of income among taxpayers in the United States, 1863-1935" (Tucker), 268n

"Distribution of income and wealth among individuals" (Stiglitz), 322n

The distribution of personal income (Schultz), 450n, 451n, 453n

"The distribution of tax burden by income group: a case study for 1949" (Musgrave), 3

"Distribution of tax payments by income groups: a case study for 1948" (Musgrave et al.), 47n

"The distribution of wealth" (Lehmann), 330n

The distribution of wealth in Great Britain (Atkinson and Harrison), 277n, 309n

Doane, R. R., 330n

Dunn, Edgar S., Jr., 31

Easterlin, Richard A., 234

"An economic accountant's ledger" (Jaszi), 32n

Economic accounts and their uses (Kendrick), 32n, 37n, 39n

Economic growth and structure (Kuznets), 261n

The economics of labor force participation (Bowen and Finegan), 171n

"Educational differentials in mortality by cause of death, United States, 1960" (Kitagawa and Houser), 335n

Eells, Kenneth, 241n, 246n, 250n, 273n

"Estate multiplier estimates of personal wealth" (French), 330n

"Estimating the wealth of top wealth-holders from estate tax returns" (Smith and Calvert), 331n

"The estimation of the Lorenz Curve and Gini Index" (Gastwirth), 211n

"Evidence on income equality in the United States, 1866-1965" (Soltow), 269n

"Family income distribution statistics published by federal agencies" (Lamale, Smith, and Fitzwilliams), 453n

Fase, M. M. G., 227
Finegan, T. Aldrich, 171n
Fisher, Paul, 31, 41n
Fitzwilliams, Jeannette, 453n
Five thousand American families— patterns of economic progress (Morgan et al.), 213n
Franklin, Stephen D., 329n
Frechling, J. E., 450n
French, Richard, 330n
Friedman, M., 228

Gastwirth, Joseph L., 211n
Gini, Corrado, 155n
Goldsmith, Selma, 234, 450n, 451n, 453
Gould, Peter R., 19n
"Grant economics: a simple introduction" (Boulding, Pfaff, and Horvath), 323n
Grove, David L., 37n
Growth and form (Thomson), 27
Guralnick, Lillian, 335n, 341-42, 367

Hammond, Kenneth R., 18
Hanna, Frank A., 152n, 215n, 228
Harrison, Alan, 277n
Hendricks, Gary, 212n
Hicks, J. R., 321
Hill, J. B., 268n
Hinrichs, J. C., 458n
Historical statistics of the United States from colonial times to the present (U.S. Census Bureau), 262n
A history of interest rates (Homer), 261n
Holmes, G. K., 330n
Holt, Charles C., 130
Homer, Sidney, 261n
Horvath, J., 323n
Houser, Phillip, 335, 340, 341
Huang, D. S., 228
Hunt, Paul S., 241n, 246n

"The imputation of missing income information" (Okner), 58n
"The incidence of taxes and Social Security benefits in 1971," 42n

The income and wealth of top wealth-holders in the United States, 1958 (Smith), 329n
Income and welfare in the United States (Morgan et al.), 214n
Income distribution in the United States (Miller), 453n
Income distribution in the United States by size, 1944-1950, 451n
"Income in 1970 of families and persons in the United States" (U.S. Census Bureau), 379n
"Income instability as a dimension of welfare" (Benus and Morgan), 210n
Income record, 269n
Income tax of residents of Philadelphia and Bucks County, 268n
"An index of the poor and rich of Scotland, 1861-1961" (Soltow), 267n
"Individual income tax erosion by income classes" (Pechman and Okner), 67n
Inland Revenue statistics, 1972, 278n
Institutional investor study report of the Securities and Exchange Commission (House Doc. 94-64), 261n
"The intergenerational transmission of wealth: a simulation experiment" (Smith, Franklin, and Orcutt), 329n

Jaszi, George, 32
Jolly, Richard, 39n

Katona, George, 212n
Keller, Janet, 212n
Kendrick, John W., 32, 37n, 39
King, W. I., 330n
Kitagawa, Evelyn, 335, 340, 341
Klebba, A. Joan, 334, 367
Knibbs, G. H., 333n
Kohen, Andrew I., 5, 121-22, 225-28
Kosobud, R., 228
Kuznets, Simon, 228, 234, 261n, 273, 325n

Lamale, Helen H., 453n

Lampman, Robert J., 3, 31, 44n, 281, 282, 299, 329, 331, 335, 340

Langley, Kathleen M., 7, 277, 283n, 284, 288n, 321

Lansing, John B., 259n

"Legislation, enforcement and the filing of tax returns" (David), 127n

Lehmann, Fritz, 330n

Lerner, Abba P., 78n

Lerner, S., 228

Levin, Robert, 2

"Life-time income profiles" (David), 141n

Lincoln, Abraham, 233

Linkage and retrieval of microeconomic data (David et al.), 125n

"The lock-in effect of the capital gains tax" (Holt and Shelton), 130n

The lognormal distribution (Aitchison and Brown), 210n

Lydall, H. F., 277, 279, 280, 285, 287, 288, 314

McCormick, Cyrus, 233

McGowan, Daniel A., 330n

McGuire, Martin, 43

Mallet, B., 278

"Marital status and family status: March 1970" (U.S. Census Bureau), 379n

"Marital status and living arrangements: March 1971" (U.S. Census Bureau), 379n

Maynes, E. Scott, 128n, 450n

The measurement of personal wealth in Centre County, Pennsylvania (McGowan), 330n

Meeker, Marcia, 241n, 246n, 250n, 273n

Mendershausen, Horst, 329, 331, 335

"Methods used in a current study of social and economic differentials in mortality" (Kitagawa and Houser), 335n

Meyers, J. G., 228

Miller, Herman, 453-56

Miller, Roger F., 5, 6, 124n, 125n, 127n, 228

Mirrlees, J. A., 78n

Modern economic growth (Kuznets), 261n

"Modifications for in-kind transfer entries in the national income accounts" (Stiefel, Smolensky, and Schmundt), 43n

Morgan, James N., 5, 121-22, 159n, 168n, 182, 189n, 210n, 213n, 214n, 218n, 228

Moriyama, I. M., 334, 335n, 341-42, 367

"Mortality among the married" (Shurtleff), 334n

Mortality and miscellaneous statistics, 1860 (U.S. Census Bureau), 237n

"Mortality by occupation and industry among men 20-64 years of age: United States, 1950" (Guralnick), 335n

"Mortality from selected causes by marital status" (Klebba), 334n

Moyer, James T., 145n

Mueller, Eva, 212n

Multiple classification analysis (Andrews, Morgan, and Sonquist), 168n, 182n, 189n

Musgrave, Richard A., 3-4, 47n

Nader, Ralph, 2

"A naive history of individual incomes in Wisconsin, 1947-1959" (David and Miller), 125n, 127n

"The national economic accounts. . ." (Dunn), 31

National wealth and income (U.S. Federal Trade Commission), 330n

Natrella, Vito, 7, 365

Neter, John, 128n

Newbery, David, 99

"The OBE size distribution series: methods and tentative results for 1964" (Budd and Radner), 494n

"Occupational and social class differentials in mortality" (Moriyama and Guralnick), 335n, 341n

Ogden, William, 233

Okner, Benjamin A., 2, 3-4, 45, 46n, 48n, 58n, 66n, 67n, 114, 115, 123

Okun, Arthur, 31

"On mental maps" (Gould), 19n

Ontario Bureau of Industries, *Annual report*, 1887, 263n

"On the appropriateness of the correlation coefficient with a 0, 1 dependent variable" (Neter and Maynes), 128n

"On the measure of concentration with special reference to income and wealth" (Gini), 155n

Orcutt, Guy H., 2, 329n

Orshansky, Mollie, 495n

Pareto, Vilfredo, 328

Parnes, Herbert S., 5, 121-22, 151, 152n

"The pattern of estate wealth" (Mendershausen), 329n, 331n

The payroll tax for Social Security (Brittain), 46n

Pechman, Joseph A., 2, 55, 66n, 67n, 228

Peck, Jon K., 4, 75, 115

Pfaff, M., 323n

Pike, Andrew D., 45n

"Preface to Pygmalion 1912" (Shaw), 323n

"Preliminary estimates of the population of the United States, by age and sex: April 1, 1960 to July 1, 1971" (U.S. Census Bureau), 379n

The pre-retirement years (Parnes et al.), 152n

The present distribution of wealth in the United States (Spohr), 330n

The private wealth of Australia and its growth (Knibbs), 333n

Projector, Dorothy S., 7-8, 259n, 261n, 262n, 263n, 329, 330n, 377

"Public goods and income distribution" (Aaron and McGuire), 43n

Quandt, R. E., 301

Radner, Daniel B., 8, 449, 458n, 494n

"Raising the incomes of the poor" (Tobin), 77n

Rawls, John A., 78n

"Reliability of recall of income" (Withey), 211n

"The relation of Census income distribution statistics to other income data" (Goldsmith), 450n

"The retirement test under Social Security" (U.S. Health, Education and Welfare Department), 416n

Revell, J. R. S., 280, 281, 282n, 283, 284, 287, 288, 292, 293, 309n, 310, 311, 314-17, 322, 324

"Revision in poverty statistics, 1959 to 1968" (U.S. Census Bureau), 495n

Roe, A. R., 309n, 310

Rolph, Earl R., 77n

Ruggles, Nancy, 37

Ruggles, Richard, 2, 37

Sargan, J. D., 300, 302, 304n

Schmundt, M., 43n

Schultz, T. Paul, 210n, 450n, 451n, 453

Searching for structure (Sonquist, Baker, and Morgan), 218n

"Secular trends and cyclical behavior of income distribution in the United States, 1944-1965" (Schultz), 210n

Seers, Dudley, 39n

The share of top wealth-holders in national wealth, 1922-56 (Lampman), 329n, 331n

The share of top wealth-holders in U.S. wealth (Lampman), 340

Shaw, George Bernard, 323

Shea, John R., 5, 121-22, 151

Shelton, John P., 130

Sheshinski, Eytan, 78n

"Shifts in the concentration of income" (Smelker), 159n

Shockley, William B., 12

Shorrocks, A. T., 300

Shurtleff, D., 334

Sims, Christopher A., 115

Sirken, M. G., 450n

"Size distribution of family personal income: methodology and estimates for 1964" (Budd, Radner, and Hinrichs), 458n

"Size distribution of personal income" (Goldsmith), 451n

Skolnik, Alfred M., 38n

Smelker, Mary W., 159n

Smith, Adam, 26

Smith, James D., 1, 6, 7, 287n, 329, 331, 335, 366-71, 453

Smolensky, E., 43n

Snyder, Eleanor M., 210n

"Social and economic differentials in mortality in the United States, 1960" (Kitagawa), 335n, 340n

Social class in America (Warner, Meeker, and Eells), 241n, 246n, 250n, 273n

The social framework (Hicks), 321n

"Social justice as a Holy Grail: the endless quest" (Boulding), 25n

The social life of a modern community (Warner and Hunt), 241n, 246n

"Social reports of the German Federal Republic, 1970-71" (Fisher), 31n, 41n

Social Security: perspectives for reform (Pechman, Aaron, and Taussig), 67n

Social welfare expenditures, 1929-1966 (U.S. Social Security Administration), 38n

"Social welfare expenditures, 1971-72" (Skolnik and Dales), 38n

"Social welfare has no price tag" (Okun), 31n

Soltow, Lee, 6, 7, 233, 267n, 269n

Sonquist, John A., 168n, 182, 189n, 218n, 259n

Spohr, C. B., 330n

Stark, T., 278n

Statistics of income . . . personal wealth (U.S. Internal Revenue Service), 135, 145, 330n, 366n

Steindl, J., 300

Stiefel, L., 43n

Stiglitz, J. E., 301, 322

"Summary of the evidence on national wealth and its increasing diffusion" (Doane), 330n

Survey of changes in family finances (Projector), 261n, 262n

"The survey of consumer finances and the Census quality check" (Sirken, Maynes, and Frechling), 450n

Survey of economic characteristics of consumers (Projector and Weiss), 330n

Survey of financial characteristics of consumers (Projector and Weiss), 259n, 263n

"Survey of readers at IBM" (Grove), 37n

Taussig, Michael K., 67n

The taxpayer's manual (Boutwell), 268n

Tax reform studies and proposals: U.S. Treasury Department (U.S. Ways and Means Committee), 124n

Terrell, Henry S., 353

Thomson, D'Arcy, 27

Tipping, D. G., 277, 279, 280, 286-88, 314

Tobin, James, 71n

"Transfer approaches to distribution policy" (Lampman), 44n

"The treatment of education in national accounting" (Seers and Jolly), 39n

Tucker, Rufus S., 268n

Vandome, Peter, 154n, 159n, 214n, 216n

Warner, W. Lloyd, 234, 241, 245, 246n, 249, 250n, 259, 273, 274

Watts, Harold, 2, 4, 75

"Wealth accumulation of black and white: the empirical evidence" (Terrell), 353n

Wealth and income of the people of the United States (King), 330n

Wealth, an essay on the purposes of economics (Carter), 326n

The wealth of the nation (Revell), 322n, 324n

Weiss, Gertrude S., 259n, 263n, 329, 330n

Whittle, P., 300, 301

Who bears the tax burden (Pechman and Okner), 66n

Wion, Douglas A., 329n

"The Wisconsin assets and incomes studies archive" (Bauman, David, and Miller), 124n

Withey, Stephen B., 211n

Wold, H. O. A., 300, 301

Yaple, Maxine, 330n

Youmans, Kenwood C., 212n

Subject Index

Accounting period variation, 215-24

The Brookings MERGE File, 46-47, 82, 114-17

Capital gains, 121-50; effects of on income, 123; and rate of income growth, 141-44; realization of, and age/sex/wealth category, 126-30, 139, 140-41; recipients and nonrecipients, characteristics of, 144-49; as taxable income, 125; taxation on, and effects, 123-26

Class. *See* Social class

Equality, 11-28; and "disalienation," 26; genetic bases of, 12-13, 27; and income distribution, 20-24; measurement of, 14-24; philosophic ideology of, 11-12, 24-28; and sexual differentiation, 13

Estate duty data, as a measure of personal wealth, 277-318

—alternative method of data use: choice of mortality multipliers, 285; critique of alternative method, 321-28; inclusion of "missing" wealth, 290-99; and wealth distribution functions, 299-306, 327-28

—and national balance sheet totals, 292-99, 324-26; adjusted using balance sheet data, 309-18

—official method of data use: choice of mortality multipliers, 281, 327; comparison of official and alternative methods, 285, 307-9; estate valuation methods, 283-84; and "missing" people, 279-80; and "missing" wealth, 290-91; sampling problems, 281-83, 327

Gini coefficient of inequality, defined, 50n, 51n-52n, 155n

Income: data, quality of (BEA and CPS data compared), 449-503; sources and collection of data, 1-2; and transfer income measurement, 377-447; wealth, social class and, 233-76, 329-63

Income distributions, 20-24; data bases, 46-47; and equality concept, 11-28; and income class, 50-53; and taxation, 45-73; and transfer payment distributions, 61-63, 66-67

—fluctuations in: and capital gains, 121-50; effects of, 123; and taxation, 123-26

—with long and short accounting periods: and capital gains, 121-50; and income stability among age/sex groups, 151-207; variables in the study of, 209-24

—1964 BEA and CPS analyses compared, 449-558; and poverty definitions, 494-503; stages in data preparation, 458-76

—problems with long-run study of, 225-29

Income redistribution plans, 75-117; comparisons of, 110-14; costs of, 76-77, 81; effects of, 86-94; and flat-rate proportional tax, 78, 113; and population groups, 86-94; and poverty threshold, 80, 84, 87-88; "primary" and "final" income concepts, 75-76, 81-84, 87-88; and welfare distribution, 94-110

Income stability; analysis of in two groups: 151-207; by age/color/ social class groupings, 168; by Gini coefficient comparisons, 159-63; by Multiple Classification Analysis, 182-84, 187-90; by Relative Instability Coefficient comparisons, 163-76

—measurement of: 209-24; and accounting period variation, 215-24; and income equality measurement, 210-11; single-year and panel surveys as measurements of, 211-13; unit of analysis and income concept as variables in, 213-15

Inequality. *See* Equality

Poverty: defined, 494-503; threshold, 80, 84, 87-88

Redistributive mechanisms: income redistribution plans, 75-117; taxation, 45-73; transfer payments, 31-44

Social class, wealth and income, relationships between, 233-76, 329-63

Taxation: effects on income, 123-26; and income distribution, 45-73; and transfer payments, 33, 61-63, 66-67. *See also* Estate duty

Transfer income, 377-447; definition of, in the public sector, 378; related to total income and age variables, 379-402; Social Security and railroad pensions as, 402-47

Transfer payments, 31-44; categorized by sector, 34-35; defined, 33, 36-37; education as, 38-39; within family sector, 41-44; and income distribution, 61-63, 66-67, 377-447; relation to GNP, 41; and social accounting, 31-33; types of, 35-37

Wealth generation, theories of, 300-301, 322-24

Wealth/income/social class structure of the U.S.: analysis applied to 1962 data, 259; characteristics of propertyless, 240-43; 1860 data, 233-76; sources of data, 233, 234-35; wealth distribution, 235-40

—class/wealth mobility model, 244-50; applied to age groups, 251-53; applied to deceased, 258-59; applied to nativity groups, 253-58; applied to 1962 population, 259

—income/wealth model, 260-74; and income distributions in the 1860's and 1970, 263-71; requirements of, 260-63; and saving, 271-72; social class and income, 273-74; wealth distribution and income, 272-73

Wealth, personal, distribution of, 235-40

—in Great Britain during the 1960's, 277-319; functions of, 299-306; by log-normal distribution, 302-4; by Pareto distribution, 301-2; by Sech distribution, 304-6

—in selected U.S. cities in 1860, 233-76

—in Washington, D.C., in 1967, 329-63; critique of methodology, 365-74; data source, 332, 345-49; technique of study, 331-32

Wealth, sources and collection of data on, 1-2